PLUNKETT'S HEALTH CARE INDUSTRY ALMANAC 2022

The only comprehensive
guide to the health care industry

Jack W. Plunkett

Published by:
Plunkett Research®, Ltd., Houston, Texas
www.plunkettresearch.com

PLUNKETT'S HEALTH CARE INDUSTRY ALMANAC 2022

Editor and Publisher:
Jack W. Plunkett

Executive Editor and Database Manager:
Martha Burgher Plunkett

Senior Editor and Researchers:
Isaac Snider
Michael Cappelli

Editors, Researchers and Assistants:
Keith Carnes
Blake Lee
Ekaterina Lyubomirova
Annie Paynter
Gina Sprenkel

Information Technology Manager:
Rebeca Tijiboy

Special Thanks to:
American Hospital Association
Organisation for Economic Cooperation and Development (OECD)
The World Bank
U.S. Department of Commerce,
Census Bureau,
International Trade Administration,
National Technical Information Service
U.S. Department of Health and Human Services
Centers for Disease Control,
Centers for Medicare and Medicaid Services,
National Center for Health Statistics,
National Institutes of Health
U.S. Department of Labor
Bureau of Labor Statistics
U.S. National Science Foundation

Plunkett Research®, Ltd.
P. O. Drawer 541737, Houston, Texas 77254 USA
Phone: 713.932.0000   Fax: 713.932.7080
www.plunkettresearch.com

PLUNKETT'S HEALTH CARE INDUSTRY ALMANAC 2022

CONTENTS

Continued on next page

Continued from previous page

Continued on next page

Continued from previous page

INTRODUCTION

PLUNKETT'S HEALTH CARE INDUSTRY ALMANAC is designed to be used as a general source for researchers of all types.

The data and areas of interest covered are intentionally broad, ranging from the costs and effectiveness of the American health care system, to emerging technology, to an in-depth look at the major firms (which we call THE HEALTH CARE 500) within the many industry sectors that make up the health care system.

This reference book is designed to be a general source for researchers. It is especially intended to assist with market research, strategic planning, employment searches, contact or prospect list creation and financial research, and as a data resource for executives and students of all types.

PLUNKETT'S HEALTH CARE INDUSTRY ALMANAC takes a rounded approach for the general reader. This book presents a complete overview of the health care field (see "How To Use This Book"). For example, Medicare and Medicaid growth and expenditures are provided in exacting detail, along with easy-to-use charts and tables on all facets of health care in general: from where health care dollars come from to how they are spent.

THE HEALTH CARE 500 is our unique grouping of the biggest, most successful corporations in all

segments of the health care industry. Tens of thousands of pieces of information, gathered from a wide variety of sources, have been researched and are presented in a unique form that can be easily understood. This section includes thorough indexes to THE HEALTH CARE 500, by geography, industry, sales, brand names, subsidiary names and many other topics. (See Chapter 4.)

Especially helpful is the way in which PLUNKETT'S HEALTH CARE INDUSTRY ALMANAC enables readers who have no business background to readily compare the financial records and growth plans of health care companies and major industry groups. You'll see the mid-term financial record of each firm, along with the impact of earnings, sales and strategic plans on each company's potential to fuel growth, serve new markets and provide investment and employment opportunities.

No other source provides this book's easy-to-understand comparisons of growth, expenditures, technologies, corporations and many other items of great importance to people of all types who may be studying this, one of the largest and most complex industries in the world today.

By scanning the data groups and the unique indexes, you can find the best information to fit your personal research needs. The major companies in health care are profiled and then ranked using several different groups of specific criteria. Which firms are the biggest employers? Which companies earn the most profits? These things and much more are easy to find.

In addition to individual company profiles, an overview of health care markets and trends is provided. This book's job is to help you sort through easy-to-understand summaries of today's trends in a quick and effective manner.

Whatever your purpose for researching the health care field, you'll find this book to be a valuable guide. Nonetheless, as is true with all resources, this volume has limitations that the reader should be aware of:

- Financial data and other corporate information can change quickly. A book of this type can be no more current than the data that was available as of the time of editing. Consequently, the financial picture, management and ownership of the firm(s) you are studying may have changed since the date of this book. For example, this almanac includes the most up-to-date sales figures and profits available to the editors as of late-2021. That means that we have typically used corporate financial data as of the end of 2020.

- Corporate mergers, acquisitions and downsizing are occurring at a very rapid rate. Such events may have created significant change, subsequent to the publishing of this book, within a company you are studying.

- Some of the companies in THE HEALTH CARE 500 are so large in scope and in variety of business endeavors conducted within a parent organization, that we have been unable to completely list all subsidiaries, affiliations, divisions and activities within a firm's corporate structure.

- This volume is intended to be a general guide to a vast industry. That means that researchers should look to this book for an overview and, when conducting in-depth research, should contact the specific corporations or industry associations in question for the very latest changes and data. Where possible, we have listed contact names, toll-free telephone numbers and internet site addresses for the companies, government agencies and industry associations involved so

that the reader may get further details without unnecessary delay.

- Tables of industry data and statistics used in this book include the latest numbers available at the time of printing, generally through the end of 2020. In a few cases, the only complete data available was for earlier years.

- We have used exhaustive efforts to locate and fairly present accurate and complete data. However, when using this book or any other source for business and industry information, the reader should use caution and diligence by conducting further research where it seems appropriate. We wish you success in your endeavors, and we trust that your experience with this book will be both satisfactory and productive.

Jack W. Plunkett
Houston, Texas
October 2021

HOW TO USE THIS BOOK

The two primary sections of this book are devoted first to the health care industry as a whole and then to the "Individual Data Listings" for THE HEALTH CARE 500. If time permits, you should begin your research in the front chapters of this book. Also, you will find lengthy indexes in Chapter 4 and in the back of the book.

THE HEALTH CARE INDUSTRY

Chapter 1: Major Trends Affecting the Health Care Industry. This chapter presents an encapsulated view of the major trends that are creating rapid changes in the health care industry today.

Chapter 2: Health Care Industry Statistics. This chapter presents in-depth statistics on payors, patients, Medicare, Medicaid, hospitals, pharmaceuticals, the Affordable Care Act and more.

Chapter 3: Important Health Care Industry Contacts – Addresses, Telephone Numbers and Internet Sites. This chapter covers contacts for important government agencies, health care organizations and trade groups. Included are numerous important Internet sites.

THE HEALTH CARE 500

Chapter 4: THE HEALTH CARE 500: Who They Are and How They Were Chosen. The companies compared in this book were carefully selected from the health care industry, largely in the United States, although many of the firms are global in nature or are headquartered in other nations. For a complete description, see THE HEALTH CARE 500 indexes in this chapter.

Individual Data Listings:
Look at one of the companies in THE HEALTH CARE 500's Individual Data Listings. You'll find the following information fields:

Company Name:
The company profiles are in alphabetical order by company name. If you don't find the company you are seeking, it may be a subsidiary or division of one of the firms covered in this book. Try looking it up in the Index by Subsidiaries, Brand Names and Selected Affiliations in the back of the book.

Industry Code:
Industry Group Code: An NAIC code used to group companies within like segments.

Types of Business:
A listing of the primary types of business specialties conducted by the firm.

Brands/Divisions/Affiliations:

Major brand names, operating divisions or subsidiaries of the firm, as well as major corporate affiliations—such as another firm that owns a significant portion of the company's stock. A complete Index by Subsidiaries, Brand Names and Selected Affiliations is in the back of the book.

Contacts:

The names and titles up to 27 top officers of the company are listed, including human resources contacts.

Growth Plans/ Special Features:

Listed here are observations regarding the firm's strategy, hiring plans, plans for growth and product development, along with general information regarding a company's business and prospects.

Financial Data:

Revenue (2020 or the latest fiscal year available to the editors, plus up to five previous years): This figure represents consolidated worldwide sales from all operations. These numbers may be estimates.

R&D Expense (2020 or the latest fiscal year available to the editors, plus up to five previous years): This figure represents expenses associated with the research and development of a company's goods or services. These numbers may be estimates.

Operating Income (2020 or the latest fiscal year available to the editors, plus up to five previous years): This figure represents the amount of profit realized from annual operations after deducting operating expenses including costs of goods sold, wages and depreciation. These numbers may be estimates.

Operating Margin % (2020 or the latest fiscal year available to the editors, plus up to five previous years): This figure is a ratio derived by dividing operating income by net revenues. It is a measurement of a firm's pricing strategy and operating efficiency. These numbers may be estimates.

SGA Expense (2020 or the latest fiscal year available to the editors, plus up to five previous years): This figure represents the sum of selling, general and administrative expenses of a company, including costs such as warranty, advertising, interest, personnel, utilities, office space rent, etc. These numbers may be estimates.

Net Income (2020 or the latest fiscal year available to the editors, plus up to five previous years): This figure represents consolidated, after-tax net profit from all operations. These numbers may be estimates.

Operating Cash Flow (2020 or the latest fiscal year available to the editors, plus up to five previous years): This figure is a measure of the amount of cash generated by a firm's normal business operations. It is calculated as net income before depreciation and after income taxes, adjusted for working capital. It is a prime indicator of a company's ability to generate enough cash to pay its bills. These numbers may be estimates.

Capital Expenditure (2020 or the latest fiscal year available to the editors, plus up to five previous years): This figure represents funds used for investment in or improvement of physical assets such as offices, equipment or factories and the purchase or creation of new facilities and/or equipment. These numbers may be estimates.

EBITDA (2020 or the latest fiscal year available to the editors, plus up to five previous years): This figure is an acronym for earnings before interest, taxes, depreciation and amortization. It represents a company's financial performance calculated as revenue minus expenses (excluding taxes, depreciation and interest), and is a prime indicator of profitability. These numbers may be estimates.

Return on Assets % (2020 or the latest fiscal year available to the editors, plus up to five previous years): This figure is an indicator of the profitability of a company relative to its total assets. It is calculated by dividing annual net earnings by total assets. These numbers may be estimates.

Return on Equity % (2020 or the latest fiscal year available to the editors, plus up to five previous years): This figure is a measurement of net income as a percentage of shareholders' equity. It is also called the rate of return on the ownership interest. It is a vital indicator of the quality of a company's operations. These numbers may be estimates.

Debt to Equity (2020 or the latest fiscal year available to the editors, plus up to five previous years): A ratio of the company's long-term debt to its shareholders' equity. This is an indicator of the overall financial leverage of the firm. These numbers may be estimates.

Address:

The firm's full headquarters address, the headquarters telephone, plus toll-free and fax numbers where available. Also provided is the internet address.

Stock Ticker, Exchange: When available, the unique stock market symbol used to identify this firm's common stock for trading and tracking purposes is indicated. Where appropriate, this field may contain "private" or "subsidiary" rather than a ticker symbol. If the firm is a publicly-held company headquartered outside of the U.S., its international ticker and exchange are given.

Total Number of Employees: The approximate total number of employees, worldwide, as of the end of 2020 (or the latest data available to the editors).

Parent Company: If the firm is a subsidiary, its parent company is listed.

Salaries/Bonuses:

(The following descriptions generally apply to U.S. employers only.)

Highest Executive Salary: The highest executive salary paid, typically a 2020 amount (or the latest year available to the editors) and typically paid to the Chief Executive Officer.

Highest Executive Bonus: The apparent bonus, if any, paid to the above person.

Second Highest Executive Salary: The next-highest executive salary paid, typically a 2020 amount (or the latest year available to the editors) and typically paid to the President or Chief Operating Officer.

Second Highest Executive Bonus: The apparent bonus, if any, paid to the above person.

Other Thoughts:

Estimated Female Officers or Directors: It is difficult to obtain this information on an exact basis, and employers generally do not disclose the data in a public way. However, we have indicated what our best efforts reveal to be the apparent number of women who either are in the posts of corporate officers or sit on the board of directors. There is a wide variance from company to company.

Hot Spot for Advancement for Women/Minorities: A "Y" in appropriate fields indicates "Yes." These are firms that appear either to have posted a substantial number of women and/or minorities to high posts or that appear to have a good record of going out of their way to recruit, train, promote and retain women or minorities. (See the Index of Hot Spots For Women and Minorities in the back of the book.) This information may change frequently and can be difficult to obtain and verify. Consequently, the reader should use caution and conduct further investigation where appropriate.

Glossary: A short list of health care industry terms.

Chapter 1

MAJOR TRENDS AND TECHNOLOGIES AFFECTING THE HEALTH CARE INDUSTRY

Major Trends Affecting the Health Care Industry:

1) Introduction to the Health Care Industry
2) The Coronavirus' Effect on the Health Care Industry
3) Continued Rise in Health Care Costs
4) Employers Fight Rapidly Growing Health Care Premiums/Require Employees to Pay a Significant Share of Costs
5) Medicare and Medicaid Spending Continue to Surge/More Baby Boomers Hit 65+ Years of Age
6) U.S. Affordable Care Act (ACA) of 2010 Rewrote the Rules and Increased Coverage, But Costs Continue to Rise
7) Accountable Care Organizations (ACOs) and Hospital Mergers Result from the Affordable Care Act/Many Hospital Chains Grow Dramatically in Market Share
8) Concierge Care/Direct Primary Care Are on the Rise/New Twists on House Calls
9) Insurance Companies Change Strategies Due to Affordable Care Act (ACA) and Rapidly Rising Costs of Care
10) Number of Uninsured Americans Declines But Remains High
11) Health Sharing Ministries Attract Millions of Members
12) Massive R&D Investment Required for Development and Approval of New Blockbuster Drugs/Drug Prices Soar
13) Fast Track Drugs Come to Market in the U.S. with FDA Cooperation
14) Generic Drugs Have Biggest Market Share By Unit Volume, but not by Total Revenues
15) Coupons and Other Marketing Schemes Obscure the Retail Prices of Drugs in the U.S., Which Are Vastly Higher than Prices Paid in Other Nations
16) Biotech and Orphan Drugs Create New Revenues for Drug Firms
17) Quality of Care and Health Care Outcomes Data Are Available Online, Creating a New Level of Transparency

18) Malpractice Suits Are Blamed for Rising Health Care Costs/Tort Reform Is Capping Awards for Damages
19) Obesity Sparks Government, School and Corporate Initiatives/Snack Foods Get Healthier/Taxes on Unhealthy Foods
20) Health Care Goes Offshore, Medical Tourism and Clinical Trials Continue in China, India and Elsewhere
21) Retail Clinics, Urgent Care Centers and Employer Sites Increase Health Care Options/Reduce Costs
22) Health Care Industry Grows Rapidly in China, India and Mexico

The Outlook for Health Care Technology:

23) Health Care Technology Introduction
24) Electronic Health Records (EHR) Digitize Patient Records at an Accelerating Pace
25) Telemedicine and Remote Patient Monitoring Rely on Wireless
26) Stem Cells and 3D Printing—A New Era of Regenerative Medicine Takes Shape
27) Health Care Robotics
28) Patients' Genetic Profiles Plummet in Price as DNA Sequencing Technologies Advance
29) Advances for Cancer Patients in Chemotherapy and Radiation, Including Proton Beams and IMRT
30) Better Imaging, including MRI, PET and 320-Slice CT, Creates Advances in Detection
31) Artificial Intelligence (AI), Deep Learning and Machine Learning Advance into Commercial Applications, Including Health Care and Robotics

1) Introduction to the Health Care Industry

Health Expenditures and Services in the U.S.:

Health care expenditures continue to rise in the U.S. and throughout the world. Total U.S. health care expenditures were estimated to be $4.01 trillion in 2020, and are projected to soar to $6.19 trillion in 2028.

The health care market in the U.S. during 2020 was projected to include massive spending in the major categories of hospital care ($1,316 billion); dental, physician and clinical services ($942.7 billion); and prescription drugs ($493.9 billion), along with nursing home and home health care ($183.2 billion). Registered U.S. hospitals totaled 6,090 properties in 2021, according to an American Hospital Association survey, containing 919,559 beds.

Medicare, the U.S. federal government's health care program for Americans 65 years or older, provided coverage to an estimated 62.6 million seniors during 2020. National expenditures on Medicare for fiscal 2019 were projected to be $796.6 billion, including premiums paid by beneficiaries and health care costs covered by Medicare. By 2030, the number of people covered by Medicare will balloon to about 78 million due to the massive number of Americans who will become of eligible age.

Medicaid is the federal government's health care program for low-income and disabled persons (including qualified children), as well as certain groups of seniors in nursing homes. National expenditures on Medicaid totaled an estimated $672.7 billion in 2020. The majority of that expense was paid for by the federal government. However, the states pick up a significant share of the cost, which is a massive burden on state budgets.

Health spending in the U.S., at about 18% of Gross Domestic Product (GDP) in 2020, is projected to grow steadily. Health care spending in America accounts for a larger share of GDP than in any other country, by a wide margin. Despite the incredible investment America continues to make in health care, 8.6% of people in the U.S. (27.9 million) lacked health care coverage for the entire year of 2020. For some, insurance was unavailable or unaffordable. In other cases, a lack of insurance was due to a personal decision not to pay for it. According to the Kaiser Family Foundation, most uninsured people are in low-income working families, but a large segment of those counted among America's uninsured are non-U.S. citizens, both lawful and illegal residents.

In March 2010, President Obama signed the Patient Protection and Affordable Care Act (ACA), designed to strengthen insurance company regulation and provide medical coverage to millions of uninsured Americans. The act called for sweeping changes. Provisions taking effect within the first six months of signing included coverage for adult children up to age 26 on their parents' policies; making it unlawful for insurers to place lifetime caps on payouts or deny coverage should a policy holder become ill; and new policies are required to pay the full cost of selected preventive care and exempt such care from deductibles. Small businesses with fewer than 25 employees and average annual wages of less than $50,000 became eligible for tax credits to cover up to 35% of staff insurance premiums.

Online health care insurance "exchanges" began enabling consumers to shop for health coverage. A 3.8% unearned income tax is levied on individuals earning more than $200,000 per year and families earning more than $250,000 per year, to fund the programs in the act. As of 2016, employers, with the equivalent of 50 full-time employees, which do not offer health benefits pay a fine per full time staff member if any of the workers receives a tax credit to buy coverage. A similar fine took effect in 2015 for employers with the equivalent of 100 full-time employees. Most businesses with more than 200 employees are required to enroll all staff automatically in health insurance plans. Consumers whose annual incomes do not exceed set amounts may receive federal financial assistance if they purchase their own health insurance.

Enough residents of Colorado signed a petition that "Constitutional Amendment 69" was placed on the ballot for November 2016, which would have provided universal healthcare for all Colorado residents. Although the amendment did not gain approval, largely due to unhappiness with the vast state tax increases that would have been be required, the effort was a clear indication of continued discontent, on the part of some consumers, with current health market conditions.

Health Expenditures Globally and in OECD Developed Nations:

A comprehensive study published by the Organization for Economic Cooperation & Development (OECD) covering more than 30 nations, including the majority of the world's most developed economies (but excluding Brazil, Russia, India or China), found stark contrasts between health costs in the United States and those of other nations. In 2019 (the latest complete data available), the average of a list that includes, for example, the UK, France, Germany, Mexico, Canada, South Korea, Japan, Australia and the U.S., spent 8.8% of GDP (gross domestic product—a measure of a nation's economy) on health care. The highest figures in this study were in America at 17.0% of GDP (which is actually a little low compared to U.S. government estimates), Switzerland at 12.1%, Germany at 11.7%, France at 11.2%, Japan at 11.1%, Sweden at 10.9%, Canada at 10.8% and Norway at 10.5%.

Total health care expenditures around the world are difficult to determine, and the Coronavirus pandemic made 2020 an even more difficult year to forecast. However, $10.0 to $10.5 trillion would be a reasonable estimate for the formal, global health care market for 2020. That would place health care at roughly 12% of global GDP and about $1,400 in health spending per person on average. In the U.S. and other developed nations, the per capita number is much higher. The federal government forecast 2020 spending at $12,118 per capita for 2020. However, the Coronavirus no doubt increased some categories of spending for 2020, such as intensive care in hospitals, while decreasing some types of spending, such as elective surgery. The trend over the near future is for the modest amount now spent on health care in emerging nations to rise dramatically, while OECD nations like America struggle to contain their own mountainous costs. Globally, the total prescription drug market was over $1.25 trillion in 2019 and is expected to reach $1.5 trillion as early as 2023.

Health Care Costs in the U.S.

Particularly in the U.S., continuous increases in the cost of health care, growing at rates far exceeding the rate of inflation in general, have been inflicting financial pain on health consumers and payers of all types. Government agencies are strained by the ever-growing cost of public health care programs such as Medicare, while employers are hit hard by vast increases in the cost of providing coverage to employees and retirees.

Many major employers are utilizing unique new programs in efforts to reduce employee illness, and thereby cut costs. For example, the use of preventive care programs is growing, as is the use of employee education aimed at better managing the effects of diseases such as diabetes. Some very large employers are even hiring in-house physicians and nurses, or contracting with outside providers for on-premises care facilities, to offer primary and preventive care in the workplace.

Patients and insurance companies are also dealing with sticker shock over the nation's prescription drug costs. Other factors edging costs upward include expensive new medical technologies and patients' demands for greater flexibility in choosing doctors and specialists at their own discretion. At the same time, hospitals and health systems write off massive amounts of potential revenues to bad debt, which increases costs for bill-paying patients.

In the wake of the tremendous growth of all aspects of the health care industry from the end of World War II onward, efficiency, competition, price transparency and productivity were, regretfully, largely overlooked. Much of this occurred because employers, plus federal and state governments, pay such a large portion of the health care bill, to the extent that patients were generally not sensitive to health care costs.

As of 2014, according to the National Health Council, 133 million Americans (nearly one-half of all adults) suffered from one or more of the most common chronic diseases, such as cancer, diabetes, heart disease, pulmonary conditions, stroke or hypertension. In addition to the massive cost of health care for these patients, the lost time at work and lost economic output due to these illnesses substantially reduced the nation's GDP. These burdens could be vastly reduced through better consumer health practices and better preventive medicine. For example, obesity, lack of exercise and cigarette smoking are immense contributors to these diseases. The Centers for Disease Control and Prevention reported that medical costs for obesity-related diseases rose as high as $147 billion in 2008, compared to $74 billion in 1998. That number has likely grown to more than $220 billion today.

The American health care industry faces more challenges than ever, due to many significant factors:

- The Coronavirus pandemic created new risks for patients and care givers alike. Significant new safety practices and costs will be standard for years to come—perhaps forever, as we seek to eliminate the spread of the Coronavirus as well as any future viral threats.
- One of the most dramatic results of the Affordable Care act of 2010 has been consolidation within the hospital industry, with mergers creating massive organizations that in many cases have dominant, regional or city-wide market share. A similar effect has been a migration of physicians leaving private practice or small clinics in order to join giant physician practice groups or the staffs of hospitals. Independent physicians are concerned about their ability to meet increased regulatory scrutiny, successfully deploy electronic health records and earn the incomes that they desire. Many older physicians state that they will simply retire earlier than they had planned.
- The U.S. population is aging rapidly. At the same time, the life expectancy of seniors is extending. Senior citizens will place a significant strain on the health care system in coming years. America's millions of surviving Baby Boomers began turning 65 in 2011.
- The future obligations of Medicare and Medicaid are enough to cause vast problems for federal and state budgets for decades to come. The number of seniors covered by Medicare will continue to grow at an exceedingly high rate, from 47.4 million people in 2010 to 82 million in 2030.
- Likewise, costs for Medicaid, which is administered at the state level, have grown so rapidly that they are competing fiercely for budget dollars that might otherwise go to education and other vital state-provided services.
- High, and growing, pharmaceutical costs have created a large backlash among health consumers and payers. Some of the newest cancer drugs cost more than $400,000 to cover one treatment period.
- We are now in what will long be remembered as the beginning of the Biotech Era. Breakthroughs in research for targeted drug therapies are occurring at a rapid pace, and highly advanced, genetically-engineered drugs are available for many diseases.
- Due to rising costs, employers large and small are straining under the financial burden of health care coverage expenses for current employees and retirees.
- Physicians, hospitals, medical device makers and pharmaceutical manufacturers face daunting pressure from litigation and claims regarding malpractice. Lawsuit reform legislation has recently been enacted in many states with very promising results.
- Vast numbers of Americans fail to lead healthy lifestyles that would prevent disease and cut both the amount and the cost of medical care. Obesity-related illnesses are adding an immense amount to the nation's health care costs. Large numbers of people smoke cigarettes and/or do not exercise regularly.

> • The three biggest causes of death in the U.S. are heart disease, cancer and stroke. Nearly one-fourth of America's annual health expenditures go for treatment of these three killers.
> • Only a relatively modest amount of money is spent on preventive medicine and health education. The vast majority of health care funds are spent on the treatment of chronic diseases as well as end-of-life care for dying patients.
>
> *Source: Plunkett Research, Ltd.*

2) The Coronavirus' Effect on the Health Care Industry

The Coronavirus outbreak caused havoc within many parts of the health care sector. Elective surgeries and doctor visits were curtailed, while telemedicine boomed. Shortages of protection gear like face masks and rubber gloves arose. Coronavirus-specific treatment wards and intensive care units sprang up within hospitals, and many were quickly overwhelmed. Health systems could not return to somewhat normal operations until the spread of the Coronavirus peaked, and tens of millions of people were vaccinated.

The pandemic created immense demand for preventative vaccines, and also for treatment therapies for patients suffering from the virus. Billions of dollars are being invested in research. A new drug therapy traditionally takes from 10 to 15 years to research, develop, put through clinical trials and get into the hands of doctors. Historically, new vaccines have also taken as many as 10 years to get to market.

Continuing mutations of the virus, such as the Delta and Lambda variants, will keep Coronavirus research and vaccines at the forefront of the health care industry for an extended period. While the size of the Coronavirus vaccine market is currently hard to estimate, it is likely at least $40 billion for 2021.

With amazing speed, global demand and unprecedented levels of investment resulted in the production of a Coronavirus vaccine in less than 12 months. In the U.S., the Trump administration launched "Operation Warp Speed," making an historic push to bring vaccines and therapies to market quickly, with a goal of having 300 million doses of vaccine ready by January 2021. Billions of federal dollars were made available for research and development at private companies. Manufacturing capabilities had to be boosted at the same time.

Meanwhile, cooperation by and between federal agencies and private companies soared in an effort to remove all unnecessary obstacles to new drug and vaccine development. A number of existing drugs received emergency FDA approval as possible treatments for patients infected with the Coronavirus.

U.S. biotech company Moderna was the first to begin human trials in March 2020, followed by another conducted by Pfizer in partnership with BioNTech SE. Both the Moderna and the Pfizer two-dose vaccines were authorized for emergency use in December 2020 in the U.S. This was followed by the February 2021 authorization of a single-dose vaccine by Janssen Biotech, Inc., a unit of Johnson & Johnson. As of mid-August 2021, 358 million doses of the three vaccines had been given (51.5% of the population was fully vaccinated) according to Our World in Data.

The SII/Covishield vaccine, developed and manufactured by the State Institute of India and SK Bio, received WHO approval in February 2021. AstraZeneca/AZD1222, developed by the University of Oxford, its spin-off firm Vaccitech and AstraZeneca, was approved in February 2021 also. In China, the Sinopharm vaccine was developed by Beijing Bio-Institute of Biological Products Co. Ltd., a subsidiary of China National Biotech Group (CNBG). It was approved by the World Health Organization (WHO) in May 2021. Another Chinese vaccine, Sinovac-Cornavac, developed by Sinovac Biotech Ltd., was approved by WHO in June 2021. On a global basis, 4.8 billion vaccine doses had been given as of August 16, 2021. 1.86 billion, or 23.8% of the world's population, was fully vaccinated according to Our World in Data.

On a global basis, four agencies (The Coalition for Epidemic Preparedness Innovations (CEPI); Gavi, the Vaccine Alliance; the World Health Organization (WHO) and UNICEF) established a joint venture called COVAX in April 2020. The mission of COVAX it to purchase enormous quantities of vaccines from major manufacturers and mete them out to countries around the world. As of mid-2021, COVAX had agreements with manufacturers of 11 vaccines and planned to provide 2 billion doses by early 2022. Funding comes from first world countries as well as private organizations such as the Bill & Melinda Gates Foundation, UNICEF and the World Bank. COVAX was struggling to achieve its goals as of mid-2021, as pandemic numbers surged in India and were once again on the rise in the U.S. and elsewhere, creating supply shortfalls.

With new case numbers on the rise, many researchers were finding that the vaccines were becoming less effective over time. In the U.S., as of August 2021, people 18 years or older are now eligible for a booster dose of the Pfizer or Moderna vaccines beginning at least eight months after their second dose.

3) Continued Rise in Health Care Costs

Total Health Care Spending: Total U.S. health care expenditures were projected to increase to $4.01 trillion in 2020, up from $3.82 trillion in 2019, according to the U.S. Centers for Medicare and Medicaid Services (CMS). Growth in health care costs has been extraordinary. In 1990, national health expenditures were only $696 billion. By 2005, the amount had tripled to $1.98 trillion. For 2028, the CMS projects spending of $6.2 trillion. Health care costs are so enormous that they are crowding out investment in other vital areas such as infrastructure, transportation and scientific research.

Mid-term projections for health care cost growth far exceed those for overall economic growth. Health spending in the U.S., at an estimated 18% of Gross Domestic Product (GDP) in 2020 (compared to only 9% in 1980). Approximately 62.2 million Americans were enrolled in Medicare in 2020 (up from only 34 million in 1990), patients who have reached a stage in life where they require much higher levels of health care than younger people.

Spending by Employers: Employers have been struggling for years to reduce their health coverage costs. Strategies include a steady shift of costs to employees through co-payments and deductibles, wellness programs and the growing use of generic drugs, which cost much less than branded drugs.

In order to find the average cost to employers who provide coverage to their employees, surveys are conducted by several different organizations each year. Results of the studies vary widely depending on methodology. According to a Kaiser Family Foundation survey, during 2020 employees were paying, on average, $5,588, or 29% of the total premium, for their share of the cost of family coverage (in addition to the $15,754 paid on average by the employer, for a combined total cost of $21,342 for a typical family for one year). Annual premiums for coverage of a single worker (without a family) rose 4% in 2020 over the previous year to $7,470, with the worker contributing an average of $1,364.

One way in which employers are attempting to control costs is to implement continuous monitoring and preventive care plans for chronic conditions such as diabetes and heart disease.

The U.S. continues to spend more on health care than any other developed nation, whether measured as total spending, spending per capita or spending as a percentage of GDP. Per capita health expenditures in the U.S. were estimated at $12,118 for 2020, compared to only $4,730 during 2000.

Many cash-strapped Americans have bypassed increasingly expensive private health care plans, choosing not to be insured at all. These individuals and families are also avoiding or putting off health care until absolutely necessary, slowing overall health care spending to some extent. Unfortunately, patients who are not covered by insurance are typically charged much higher rates for care, because insurance providers negotiate the rates that they will pay. For example, a hospital might charge a set price of $1,200 for a CT scan procedure when billing an individual not covered by an insurance contract, but discount the cost to $400 for someone who is covered.

Costs are also rising significantly in cases where private medical practices are being taken over by hospitals. In these cases, Medicare pays more for a number of services performed in hospitals than for the same procedures if performed in doctors' offices.

Insurers are working to lower costs by putting pressure on drug manufacturers. Cancer care is an area that is especially hard hit by costs. Some of the newer cancer drugs cost more than $400,000 per round of treatment.

A RAND Corporation study of hospital practices in mid-2020 found that U.S. hospitals are charging private insurance companies 2.5 times more than they charge to Medicare for the same care. In several U.S. states, private insurers paid three or more times what Medicare paid for inpatient stays of one night or more. In early 2021, a study of only one California hospital disclosed a disparity in charges for a caesarean section birth delivery of between $6,241 on the low end (for Medicaid recipients) and $60,584 on the high end (for women on commercial health insurance who did not have this hospital in their insurer's network). Similar variations by type of coverage were found for other major operations, such as a range form $89,752 for a major, complex-patient heart procedure on Medicare to as much as $425,945 for in-network commercial insurance and $515,697 for out-of-network insured patients.

4) Employers Fight Rapidly Growing Health Care Premiums/Require Employees to Pay a Significant Share of Costs

As employers face continued growth in health care costs, they are shifting more of the burden onto employees. According to the Kaiser Family Foundation, for 2020 (the latest data available) employees were paying, on average, $5,588, or 29% of the total premium, as their share of the cost of covering a typical family (in addition to the $15,754 paid on average by the employer).

The Foundation also reported that 83% of covered workers had a general deductible in 2020, up from only 47% in 2009. The average single deductible was $1,364 in 2020 (compared to $735 in 2008). This means that covered employees are facing a multi-faceted burden: 1) a very expensive personal contribution to the total annual coverage premium, 2) a high deductible that must be met before insurance kicks in, plus 3) costly co-pays (often 20% or more) for most instances of doctor visits, lab or hospital services and pharmacy prescriptions.

Employer-sponsored health plan premiums rose 4% in 2020 and 2019. This adds up to a huge increase in total dollars. Health cost inflation remains much higher than inflation in consumer costs in general.

An initiative in California is the California Public Employees' Retirement System (Calpers), which set a maximum price that Calpers would pay for a number of procedures such as colonoscopies, joint replacements and cataract removal starting in 2011. For example, the maximum for a knee or hip replacement surgery was set at $30,000, with Calpers' members paying 20%, or up to $3,000. Members selecting hospitals that charged more than Calpers' maximum were forced to pay the difference out-of-pocket. As a result, the knee and hip replacement surgery market share for lower-priced hospitals rose by 28%, with higher-priced institutions lowering their prices to stay competitive. Prices for the surgeries fell overall by an average of more than 20%, saving Calpers and its patients $6 million over two years.

This is part of a long-term trend where employers are attempting to force employees to become better, more knowledgeable, and more cost-conscious consumers of health care. It is hoped that consumers who clearly see the costs of health coverage (and are forced to make choices while paying more out of pocket) will take more personal responsibility for their physical condition and habits.

Also, many employers have taken measures to decrease health care benefits for retirees in order to cut costs. Whether by raising retirees' share of premiums, capping the total amount paid or cutting benefits either partially or entirely, employers have been steadily placing more of the financial burden of health care onto their retired employees. These trends will likely continue over the mid-term, with more and more of the cost of elderly health care being pushed onto Medicare.

State and local governments face some of the largest cost problems of all. This is because many cities and other government units provided employees with exceptionally generous health care coverage plans, and in many cases continued this coverage after employees retired.

Employees who practice unhealthy lifestyles cost their employers staggering amounts of money due to health complications. Many employers are taking proactive measures. Examples include employer-sponsored wellness or disease management programs, as well as employers increasing certain employees' share of premiums, co-payments or deductibles. Some firms are penalizing employees who practice poor health behaviors such as smoking. For example, employees who admit to smoking must pay an additional fee per year for health benefits.

Another alternative is called reference-based pricing, in which employees have a choice among hospitals, doctors or procedures. Information regarding pricing and quality of care is available to help employees decide. Should the employee choose a procedure or provider that is more expensive that what is offered under the employer health care plan, he or she may be required to make up the difference. Should the employee go with a less costly option, the employer can offer a health care credit against another procedure. Reference-based pricing encourages employees to learn more about their health benefit options and make cost-effective choices.

Hospital Pricing Transparency Required Online

A Trump administration mandate requiring hospitals to publish list prices for care online took effect in early 2021. The rules require that hospitals must post the following information: gross charges, discounted cash prices, payer-specific negotiated charges and "de-identified" minimum and maximum negotiated rates. A complete file must be filed with the federal CMS office, while up to 300 procedures must be listed on a website available to the general public.

For example, see Methodist Hospitals, Houston, Texas pricing at: https://methodisthospitals.org/insurance-financial-info/methodist-hospitals-price-transparency/

In 2017, dozens of major corporations, including American Express, Marriott, Macy's, IBM and The Coca-Cola Company, formed the Health Transformation Alliance (HTA) to cut health care spending for employees. The alliance created group contracts to purchase prescription drugs through CVS Health Corp. and UnitedHealth Group, Inc., and created specialized physician networks. As of September 2021, HTA had more than 50 corporate members covering more than 7 million employees and their families, and $27 billion in annual spending power. Meanwhile, Haven Health, an alliance between Amazon.com, Inc., Berkshire Hathaway, Inc. and JPMorgan Chase & Co., disbanded in early 2021 due to its inability meet its goal of promoting lower employer costs for health care.

5) Medicare and Medicaid Spending Continue to Surge/More Baby Boomers Hit 65+ Years of Age

The term "Baby Boomer" generally refers to people born from 1946 to 1964. The phrase evolved to include the children of soldiers and war industry workers who were involved in World War II. When those veterans and workers returned to civilian life, they started or added to families in large numbers. As a result, the Baby Boom generation, at one time as large as 78 million, is one of the largest demographic segments in U.S. history.

Medicare: Today, roughly millions of Americans reach traditional retirement age (65) yearly, which is also the age that Medicare coverage kicks in for a typical retiree, subject to meeting eligibility rules. The increased load on Medicare is immense. At the same time, this surging senior population will put a greater strain on virtually all sectors of the health care system. Medicare enrollment in 2021 was estimated by the U.S. Centers for Medicare and Medicaid Services to be 63.3 million, up from 62.2 million in 2020 and up from only 47.4 million in 2010.

Medicare expenditures cover a wide range of patients varying in age and levels of disease, with most spending devoted to the very old and those with a number of chronic conditions. An estimated 25% to 30% of all Medicare spending is for patients in their last year of life. Meanwhile, 21% of Medicare beneficiaries have five or more chronic conditions such as high blood pressure, heart disease or diabetes.

Medicaid: Medicaid was envisioned as a safety net for the poor. Today, while Medicaid covers many of the health needs of low-income households, a vast portion of this program covers nursing home care for seniors and the seriously disabled. In fact, Medicaid pays about 40% of America's total spending on long term care. Medicaid is administered largely at the state level, with major financial support coming from the federal government. The states are straining under costs that have been soaring over the long-term. Total expenditures reached $672.7 billion in 2020, according to the U.S. Centers for Medicare and Medicaid Services (CMS). While most of the money is provided by the federal government, states are required to provide a significant portion.

A serious problem facing both Medicare and Medicaid is fraud. The former head of the CMS and analysts at the RAND Corporation estimated that fraud, along with the costs associated with rules and inspections to fight it, added as much as $98 billion in a recent year to Medicare and Medicaid spending, and $272 billion in costs across the entire U.S. health care system. Numerous cases, including a Miami doctor who fraudulently billed for 1,000 powered wheelchairs, and a New York clinic that wrote fake prescriptions for approximately 5 million painkillers and then sold them on the street for between $30 and $90 each, have come to light under heightened federal screening. In mid-2016, a nationwide sweep led by the Medicare Fraud Strike Force in 36 federal districts, resulted in criminal and civil charges against 301 individuals, including 61 doctors, nurses and other licensed medical professionals, for their alleged participation in health care fraud schemes involving approximately $900 million in false billings. Fortunately, advanced software based on deep-learning and data mining has the potential to spot fraudulent claims on a much faster basis than in the past. Nonetheless, the system will remain very tempting to criminals due to its lack of effective controls and vast total spending.

6) U.S. Affordable Care Act (ACA) of 2010 Rewrote the Rules and Increased Coverage, But Costs Continue to Rise

In March 2010, President Obama signed the Patient Protection and Affordable Care Act (ACA, sometimes referred to as Obamacare). It was designed to force health insurance firms to provide more coverage (and to provide coverage to people regardless of pre-existing health problems), force more individuals and employers to participate in health care insurance and increase the number of people who qualify for Medicaid.

Provisions that took effect within the first six months of signing included coverage for adult children up to age 26 on their parents' policies; making it unlawful for insurers to place lifetime caps on payouts or deny coverage should a policy holder become ill; and new policies being required to pay the full cost of selected preventive care and

exempt that care from deductibles. Small businesses with fewer than 25 employees and average annual wages of less than $50,000 became eligible for tax credits to cover up to 35% of staff insurance premiums.

A 3.8% income tax on investment income was levied on individuals earning more than $200,000 per year and families earning more than $250,000 per year to fund the programs in the act. Also, the government began fining citizens who choose not to carry health insurance. (This penalty was eliminated by the Trump administration.) Employers with more than 50 employees that do not offer health benefits began paying a fine per full time staff member if any of the workers receives a tax credit to buy coverage. Businesses with more than 200 employees are required to enroll all staff automatically in health insurance plans. Self-insurance is an option for large companies and is a common practice. Under self-insurance, employers typically hire large outside health insurance firms to manage their plans.

The act is more than 1,000 pages in length and has far too many provisions to cover succinctly; however, there are a number of additional provisions that are little known. These include allowing insurers to charge smokers as much as 50% more for coverage in new polices; and a 30% break for employees who participate in company wellness programs or meet high health standards. Meanwhile, online health care insurance "exchanges" began enabling consumers to shop for health coverage on a state-by-state basis.

Washington and Colorado passed public health insurance legislation, offering residents state-sponsored health plans to compete with private insurance. Delaware, Massachusetts and New Mexico have adopted similar plans. In Colorado, the plan focuses on the 7% of the population who buy insurance directly rather than rely on employer or government programs such as Medicare or Medicaid. Plan premiums are expected to be from 11% to 17% lower than private plans, and would begin in 2022. The state of Nevada recently adopted a law that requires private insurers to begin bidding on insurance plans with premiums priced 5% less than public plans (meaning those that comply with ACA mandates) by 2026.

7) Accountable Care Organizations (ACOs) and Hospital Mergers Result from the Affordable Care Act/Many Hospital Chains Grow Dramatically in Market Share

An additional change in health care delivery, since the passage of the Affordable Care Act, has been the growth of "accountable care organizations," or ACOs. An ACO is a network of doctors, hospitals and other providers that take a coordinated approach to care for patients. The health care reform act offers financial rewards to ACOs that meet targets for quality of care and cost. The hope is that these networks will be able to eliminate duplicated or unnecessary tests and other procedures while developing more efficient electronic health records on their patients. The goal of the electronic records is to enable all caregivers involved in an individual's care to remain fully informed about that patient's unique needs and medical history.

One of the most dramatic results of the health care reform act to date is consolidation within the hospital industry, with mergers creating massive organizations that in many cases have dominant market share in major markets. Hospital firms have been merging aggressively, while also making investments in outpatient clinics and acquiring physician practices at a rapid pace. This consolidation of care providers under one roof means greater pricing power for ever-larger hospital chains while creating an environment of lessened competition in the marketplace and fewer choices for consumers. The Federal Trade Commission (FTC) has been blocking a few of these hospital mergers over concerns that they stifle price competition, but the FTC's response may have been too little and too late.

Meanwhile, post-ACA, physicians in private practice and smaller groups are concerned about their ability to meet increased regulatory scrutiny, successfully deploy electronic health records and continue earning the incomes that they have enjoyed in the past. As a result, large numbers have signed on as hospital employees, or joined massive, multi-office physician practices.

Doctors are going to find themselves in increasing demand. A study in 2015 by the Association of American Medical Colleges predicted that by 2025, the U.S. will have a shortage of between 46,000 and 90,000 physicians. Doctors' practices will be forced to become more efficient in order to meet growing demand, and as a guard against potential reductions in the fees they are paid by insurers, Medicare and Medicaid. Extremely large practices, based within hospitals or within ACOs, may be able to achieve operating efficiencies unattainable by smaller offices.

Arguments for the Formation of Major Hospital and Physician Groups:

1) Large groups may have access to better, more effective technical support for digital health records.

2) Massive organizations are likely to have greater pricing power, leading to higher fees charged to insurers and higher profits for the groups. They also should have better purchasing power, enabling them to obtain lower costs for supplies and services. At the same time, services and procedures provided by the hospitals, where the physicians are now full-time employees rather than third parties, are typically billed at much higher prices than non-hospital-based services.

3) The ACA provides additional payments to hospitals that meet requirements regarding patient outcomes, such as patient satisfaction and reduction in the amount of re-admission of patients to the hospital for a specific illness. Newly enlarged hospital groups may be able to develop best practices that will meet these goals.

---

8) Concierge Care/Direct Primary Care Are on the Rise/New Twists on House Calls

Some physicians are betting on higher demand for private, on-demand health care for those who can afford it. Some refer to this kind of practice as concierge care. MDVIP, for example, is a national network of primary care physicians who provide personalized care to patients for an additional fee of about $1,800 per year. The plan offers an annual physical exam, personal wellness plan and digital health records available online in addition to a personal doctor web site and secure messaging. Patients are guaranteed same-day or next-day appointments that start on time, as well as after-hours availability by phone or pager.

For 2017, *Concierge Medicine Today* estimated there were as many as 20,000 physicians in the U.S. operating concierge practices. A Merritt Hawkins survey found that 7% to 10% of physicians questioned planned to transition to concierge or cash-only practices. Even in nations where universal health care has been in place for years, such as the UK and Sweden, private health care is extremely popular among those who can afford it.

Health care is taking a page out of the Uber business model in the form of in-person visits on demand. A number of startups are offering health care in the home or office, similar to old fashioned house calls. Treatments run the gamut of minor procedures from flu shots to stitching lacerations to treating strep throat to pregnancy tests. Some firms partner with major insurance companies such as Humana, Anthem and Cigna. California-based Heal sends a doctor in under an hour for a modest flat fee. As of mid-2020, Heal was available in a number of California metropolitan areas, as well as in Atlanta, Washington D.C., New Jersey, New York, Seattle and Spokane. Pager, which is based in New York City, offers a platform to connect patients with nurses and doctors via text, voice and video chat. Other examples include MedZed (with operations in California, Washington, Maryland and New Jersey) and DispatchHealth (available in 18 U.S. states) which was formerly True North Health Navigation.

9) Insurance Companies Change Strategies Due to Affordable Care Act (ACA) and Rapidly Rising Costs of Care

The Patient Protection and Affordable Care Act (ACA) completely changed the rules for health insurance underwriters as well as care providers. Most of these insurance firms are of massive scale. These are among the largest corporations in the U.S., and they have grown to such size by analyzing care providers, patient needs and treatment outcomes in an effort to provide effective coverage while attempting to control costs. Their business requires enormous computer and data mining power, along with legions of claims administrators and utilization managers. It is an extremely complex business, subject to very exacting regulation. Prior to the ACA, such regulation was primarily at the state level, but it now includes extensive federal oversight.

The health reform act placed significant new requirements and restrictions on insurance underwriters, and they, in turn, have altered their relationships with the doctors, clinics and hospitals that serve the patients they insure. For one thing, the act requires insurance firms to provide certain minimums of preventive care. For example, insurers are no longer allowed to charge co-payments for preventive examinations such as mammograms. Firms are required to spend at least 85% of collected premiums on health care for their clients, and no more than 15% on overhead and profit.

Also, the act set up insurance "exchanges" that enable consumers to compare insurance plans and costs, and then purchase the plans that best suit their individual needs. These exchanges are among the most disappointing outcomes of the act. The ACA cannot force Americans to sign up for insurance. It does, however, force insurers to accept new enrollees no matter how sick they may be, and to charge standard rates regardless of whether or not a person is ill.

Health insurers are no longer able to refuse a customer (or charge higher fees) due to pre-existing health conditions. Nonetheless, they may charge higher prices to consumers who smoke or participate in certain other unhealthy activities. Healthy people are far cheaper to insure than sick ones.

A radical shift in the way doctors and hospitals are paid by insurers has begun. Incentives are being paid, by insurers such as Medicare and Blue Cross Blue Shield, to providers that improve outcomes. Improved care and lower costs are measured by closely following patients and coordinating care efforts for best results.

10) Number of Uninsured Americans Declines But Remains High

For 2019, the number of uninsured Americans rose for the first time in a decade to 9.2% (29.6 million), largely driven by lower enrollment in Medicaid. In 2020, the number of uninsured dropped to 8.6% (27.9million). It is worthwhile to note that the official survey of the uninsured attempts to include all people residing in the United States, regardless of whether they are in America legally.

In addition to the number of people with no insurance at all, the number of underinsured Americans remains a massive problem. In many cases, consumers can only afford health plans that have very high deductibles. These deductibles often run from $1,000 to $5,000 yearly, and most types of care must be paid for out of the consumer's pocket before the insurer begins to pay. Many consumers simply do not have sufficient cash on hand to deal with this burden.

The Affordable Care Act was designed to force individuals who are uninsured to purchase coverage or pay a penalty, force larger employers to provide coverage or pay a penalty, greatly increase the number of people who qualify for coverage under Medicaid, provide subsidies for coverage to small employers and provide substantial subsidies to lower income families. Under the Trump administration, penalties for people who do not purchase insurance were eliminated.

11) Health Sharing Ministries Attract Millions of Members

As of mid-2021, about 1.5 million Americans had joined religious health groups known as health sharing ministries according to the Alliance of Health Care Sharing Ministries. These programs are less expensive for members than traditional health insurance and rely on many healthy members with few or no payments to allow substantial payments for those who need expensive treatment. It is basically a cost sharing agreement among members with similar religious beliefs.

The plans are somewhat limited in that they generally do not cover pre-existing conditions or preventive services (e.g. check-ups, mammograms, colonoscopies). Abortions, birth control and addiction treatments are also not typically covered. Examples include Christian Healthcare Ministries in Ohio; Liberty HealthShare (also in Ohio); and Samaritan Ministries International in Illinois.

12) Massive R&D Investment Required for Development and Approval of New Drugs/Drug Prices Soar

Drug spending in the U.S. reached and estimated $358.7 billion in 2020, up from $345.7 billion in 2019 and $344.5 billion in 2018, according to the Centers for Medicare & Medicaid Services (CMS). Prescription drug spending for 2021 is expected to be $375.8 billion. Globally, the total prescription drug market was over $1.25 trillion in 2020, up from $1.2 trillion in 2019, and is expected to reach $1.5 trillion as early as 2023 according to Plunkett Research estimates. In early 2021, major drug companies announced a hike in drug prices by an average of 3.3%. According to one report, Pfizer, Inc. had prices rising by about 5% or less on more than 200 of its medications.

Consumers' voracious need for drugs will continue to soar, thanks in part to the rapidly aging populations of such nations as the U.S., most of Europe and much of Asia, including Japan and China, and also due to the continuing introduction of new drugs. In coming years, taming pharmaceutical costs will be one of the biggest challenges facing the health care system. Prescription drug costs already account for about 10% of all health care expenditures in the U.S. Managed care must be able to determine which promising new drugs can deliver meaningful clinical benefits proportionate to their costs.

Following a brief period in recent years when a number of extremely lucrative "blockbuster" drugs such as the cholesterol therapy Lipitor went off patent and thus opened the door for exploding sales of generic equivalents, several highly effective and extremely expensive new drugs began to hit the market.

Part of the reason that many new drugs command astronomical prices is the total expense and level of risk that drug companies incur in order to develop medicines, including the investment in drugs that fail to be effective or win regulatory approval, and therefore never make it to market, despite massive investments in research and testing.

Massive Investment Required to Get a New Drug Approved by the FDA

In the spring of 2020, three researchers (Olivier Wouters, Martin McKee and Jergen Luyten) published a study that shows the range of investment required to research, develop, test and get a new drug through the approval process and ready to market. Their data was based on 63 new drugs approved by the U.S. FDA, primarily between 2014 and 2018. They estimated a median research and development cost of slightly less than $1 billion per approved drug. The study estimated that it typically took five years on the market after approval and launch for such drugs to generate enough revenues to recover their investments. However, it should be noted that their data were limited mostly to investments by smaller firms. A similar study of cancer drugs (published in 2019 by Kiu Tay-Teo, Andre Ilbawi and Suzanne Hill) found investments per drug to range from $219 million to $2.8 billion, with a median cost of about $800 million.

The Tufts Center for the Study of Drug Development published, in 2019, an estimated average out-of-pocket cost of $1.4 billion per approved new drug. In addition, Tufts estimated additional costs incurred of $1.2 billion per drug when considering the expected investment returns that a company forgoes while a drug is in the non-revenue development phase. Then there is another $312 million in estimated costs of continuing research and development after a new drug is first approved. Tufts estimated that the chances of a new drug candidate moving beyond the clinical development phase to final marketing approval is only 12%.

Extraordinarily high new drug prices are causing backlash, and attempts are being made to limit pharmaceutical costs. With regard to cancer drugs, for example, the American Society of Clinical Oncology suggested a "value framework" in 2015. Points are awarded to drugs based on their effectiveness, possible side effects and costs, not only from the patient's point of view, but also the overall cost of the drug to the health system. Roche's Avastin, for example, received a low 16 out of 130 possible points as a lung cancer treatment, largely because its monthly cost was $11,907.87, compared to $182.09 for using chemotherapy as an alternative.

A growing trend has created a new category for blockbuster drugs based on vanity, convenience or personal choices. Historically, pharmaceutical research was focused primarily on curing life-threatening or severely debilitating illnesses. But a segment of drugs, commonly referred to as "lifestyle" drugs, is transforming the pharmaceutical industry. Lifestyle drugs target a variety of human conditions, ranging from the painful to the inconvenient, including obesity, impotence, memory loss, urinary urgency and depression. Drug companies also continue to develop lifestyle treatments for hair loss and skin wrinkles in an effort to capture their share of the huge anti-aging market aimed at older generations. The use of lifestyle drugs dramatically increases the total annual consumer intake of pharmaceuticals, and creates a great deal of controversy over which drugs should be covered by managed care and which should be paid for by the consumer alone.

Factors leading to high expenditures in the American health care system:

- Millions of members of the Baby Boomers generation (born from 1946 through 1964) are entering their senior years. The lifespan of Americans is increasing, and chronic illnesses are increasing as the population ages.
- Obesity-related illnesses, for patients young and old, are estimated by Plunkett Research to cost as much as $200 billion yearly.
- Fraud, abuse and billing errors in the Medicare and Medicaid system cost an estimated $100 billion yearly. Fraud and billing abuse throughout the rest of the health care system could easily cost another $150 billion+ yearly.
- Malpractice insurance, lawsuits and "defensive" treatment practices intended to limit exposure to lawsuits add billions of dollars to overall health care costs each year.
- Drug prices and total drug expenditures are soaring. Breakthroughs in research and development are creating significant new drug therapies, allowing a wide range of popular, but sometimes extraordinarily expensive, treatments that were not previously available.
- The hospital and clinic industry has merged and consolidated to the extent that major metro markets across the U.S. are often served by only two or three very large health care companies. This limits competition and gives these few companies the ability to command high prices.
- A rapid expansion of government-funded health care, particularly through the Affordable Care Act (ACA), has driven demand and expenses while doing very little to lower costs or prices.
- "Lifestyle" drug use is high, as shown by the popularity of such drugs as Viagra (for the treatment of sexual dysfunction), Propecia (for the treatment of male baldness) and Botox (for the treatment of facial wrinkles). Such drugs are often quite expensive.

Source: Plunkett Research, Ltd.

It is clear that the largest pharma companies, such as Pfizer, invest vast sums in their efforts to develop new drugs, and the number of drugs they finally commercialize as a result is very small. Smaller drug firms that are more focused on a particular type of disease or therapy are likely to spend less, as are firms based in lower-cost nations. Exorbitantly high prices paid in the U.S. foot the bill for much of global drug development, marketing and profits, to the benefit of billions of patients worldwide.

In mid-2018, Amazon acquired online pharmacy PillPack, Inc. for $1 billion, which enabled the launch of Amazon Pharmacy in November 2020. It ships insulin, asthma inhalers and many other common generic or branded drugs, with the exception of most opioids which have a higher risk of theft and fraud. Amazon accepts most health insurance and offers discounts to Prime customers. The new site put the online retail giant in direct competition with CVS Health Corp., Walgreens Boots Alliance, Inc. and Rite Aid Corp., which could possibly result in lower prices for consumers. In March 2020, U.S. mail-order prescriptions were up 21% from 2019, making their share of the prescription drug market 5.8%.

13) Fast Track Drugs Come to Market in the U.S. with FDA Cooperation

Despite exponential advances in biopharmaceutical knowledge and technology, biotech companies enduring the task of getting new drugs to market continue to face long timeframes, daunting costs and immense risks. By one count, of every 1,000 experimental drug compounds in some form of pre-clinical testing, only one makes it to clinical trials. Then, only one in five of those drugs make it to market. Of the drugs that get to market, only one in three bring in enough revenue to recover their costs. Meanwhile, the patent expiration clock is ticking—soon enough, manufacturers of generic alternatives steal market share from the firms that invested all that time and money in the development of the original drug.

Internet Research Tip:
You can review current and historical drug approval reports at the following page at the FDA.
www.fda.gov/Drugs/InformationOnDrugs/default.htm

The FDA regulates biologic products for use in humans. It is a source of a broad variety of data on drugs, including vaccines, blood products, counterfeit drugs, exports, drug shortages, recalls and drug safety.
www.fda.gov/BiologicsBloodVaccines/default.htm

The FDA is attempting to help the drug industry bring the most vital drugs to market in shorter time with programs that include: Fast Track, Priority Review, Breakthrough Therapy Designation and Accelerated Approval. The benefits of Fast Track include scheduled meetings to seek FDA input into development as well as the option of submitting a New Drug Application in sections rather than submitting all components at once. The Fast Track designation is intended for drugs that address an unmet medical need, but is independent of Priority Review, Breakthrough Therapy Designation and Accelerated Approval. Priority drugs are those considered by the FDA to offer improvements over existing drugs or to offer high therapeutic value. The priority program, along with increased budget and staffing at the FDA, is having a positive effect on total approval times for new drugs. Breakthrough therapies show early clinical evidence of very important improvements over currently available drugs.

The FDA quickly approved Novartis' drug Gleevec (a revolutionary and highly effective treatment for patients suffering from chronic myeloid leukemia). After priority review and Fast Track status, it required only two and one-half months in the approval process. This rapid approval, which enabled the drug to promptly begin saving lives, was possible because of two factors aside from the FDA's cooperation. First, Novartis mounted a targeted approach to this niche disease. Its research determined that a specific genetic malfunction causes the disease, and its drug specifically blocks the protein that causes the genetic malfunction. Next, thanks to its use of advanced genetic research techniques, Novartis was so convinced of the effectiveness of this drug that it invested heavily and quickly in its development.

Key Food & Drug Administration (FDA) terms relating to human clinical trials:
Phase I—Small-scale human trials to determine safety. Typically include 20 to 60 patients and are six months to one year in length.
Phase II—Preliminary trials on a drug's safety/efficacy. Typically include 100 to 500 patients and are one and a half to two years in length.
Phase III—Large-scale controlled trials for efficacy/safety; also the last stage before a request for approval for commercial distribution is made to the FDA. Typically include 1,000 to 7,500 patients and are three to five years in length.
Phase IV—Follow-up trials after a drug is released to the public.

Generally, Fast Track approval is reserved for diseases that are life-threatening and have no current therapies, such as rare forms of cancer. However, new policies are setting the stage for accelerated approval of drugs for less deadly but more pervasive conditions such as diabetes and obesity. Approval is also being made easier through the use of genetic testing to determine a drug's efficacy, as well as the practice of drug companies working closely with federal organizations.

In 2020, the FDA approved a record 53 new drugs through Fast Track programs, which was 68% of all new drugs approved for the year. This compares to 41% for 2019. Examples of these approvals include Danyelza for the treatment of high risk neuroblatoma; Margenza, for the treatment of HER2-positive breast cancer; and Zepzelca, which is used to treat adults with small cell lung cancer.

14) Generic Drugs Have Biggest Market Share by Unit Volume, but not by Total Revenues

U.S. patent policy typically grants drug manufacturers the normal 20 years' protection from the date of the original patent (which is most likely filed very early in the research process), plus a period of 14 years after FDA approval. Once the patent on an existing drug expires, competing drug companies may be allowed to market cheaper generic versions which are nearly-identical chemical compounds. (However, the FDA must approve the generic version, which may require several years of effort and a substantial financial investment on the part of the generic manufacturer. Also, the original owner of a drug patent may attempt to extend protection of the drug for many years by continually filing additional patents based on newer formats, delivery methods or uses for a drug. Drug owners that sell in large quantities are willing to go to extensive efforts to try to maintain at least some level of patent protection.)

Generic prescriptions as a percentage of all U.S. pharmaceutical sales rose from 49% by volume in 2000 to 90% in 2018 (but accounted for a significantly lower percentage of total drug expenditures), according to PhRMA. Some drugs sell in such low volume that they aren't taken up by generic manufacturers even though they have gone off-patent.

SPOTLIGHT: Samsung Biologics's Super Plant

Samsung Biologics Co., the drug manufacturing unit of the Samsung Group, is building a $2 billion, 2.56 million square foot manufacturing plant in Incheon, South Korea. Called the Super Plant, will be the world's largest biopharmaceutical manufacturing facility when it opens in 2022. Samsung is capitalizing on the spiraling demand brought about by the Coronavirus, and puts South Korea into competition with China and India in drug ingredient manufacturing.

Retailers including Wal-Mart, Target, Walgreens, Kmart and Publix offer a large number of generic drugs for a flat monthly fee. Wal-Mart offers 90-day supplies of hundreds of generic drugs for $10 each, and 30-day supplies for $4, in an effort to undercut mail-order pharmacy businesses while providing a high-value service to the public that brings more consumers into Wal-Mart drug departments.

Some major drug companies are trying to get in on the generic business by quietly creating their own generic drug subsidiaries. Pfizer, for example, has a division called Greenstone, LLC, which produces generic versions of its blockbuster drugs including Zoloft, an antidepressant that brought in upwards of $2 billion in 2006 sales, at which time its patent expired.

There's a wild card where generic drugs are concerned that has some doctors and patients wary of choosing generics over brand-name drugs. The FDA has a broad definition of bioequivalence, stating that a generic's maximum concentration of active ingredient in the blood must not fall more than 20% below or 25% above that of the brand-name equivalent. The result is a significant potential difference to the original, brand name drug. Also, while the generic must contain the same active ingredient as the original, additional ingredients (called "excipients") can be different and may be of lower quality in a generic. Concern is greatest over generic versions of "narrow therapeutic index drugs" which require precise dosing because even minor variations can cause life threatening complications.

India is the world's largest exporter of generics, fueled by hundreds of manufacturing labs. Major manufacturers include Cipla, Sun Pharmaceutical, Lupin and Dr. Reddy's. About 1 billion prescriptions written by U.S. doctors each year are fulfilled with drugs made in India.

A number of U.S. hospital chains are hoping to get in on the generic drug market. In early 2018, four large hospital companies (with collectively about 300 hospitals) announced plans to work together to create a nonprofit generic drug manufacturing firm. The result, called Civica Rx, delivered its first drug, an antibiotic, in late 2019, enabling greater control of the supply chain for the hospitals, and lower prices for patients.

15) Coupons and Other Marketing Schemes Obscure the Retail Prices of Drugs in the U.S., Which Are Vastly Higher than Prices Paid in Other Nations

Among all the world's nations, the U.S. is in a unique and painfully costly conundrum regarding the retail prices paid for drugs. American universities and corporations discover, test and produce a vast supply of innovative drugs each year. However, while U.S. taxpayers and patients support much of this vital research (through R&D tax credits, cash donations to encourage research and hundreds of billions of dollars in yearly drug purchases), much of the financial benefit (in terms of extremely low drug prices) is passed along to patients everywhere in the world outside of America. Meanwhile patients and payers in the U.S. bear astonishingly high prices, often 10-times the price paid in other nations. Americans spend 44% more on drugs per person than Canadians, the next highest country on the list.

U.S. government regulations do not regulate drug prices (in most other nations they are highly regulated), and they prohibit Medicare from negotiating drug prices. (The Biden administration has stated that it wants to enable Medicare to negotiate drug prices and cap out-of-pocket drug costs for seniors. As of mid-2021, a number of bills had been introduced in this effort, but the end-result remains to be seen). Agents for U.S. health insurers negotiate modest discounts on prices, but final prices remain extremely high and the discounts are not necessarily passed along to patients.

In Germany, pricing rules came into effect in 2010 under which any new drug must prove that it has greater efficacy or more benefits than rival medications in order to be priced at a higher level than the rival. In 2014, Germany went even further, announcing plans to publish the discounts agreed to by drug makers. This transparency might be used by payers outside of Germany to drive down prices in other countries.

Norway, which sets maximum drug prices that can be charged within its borders, uses a QALY gauge which describes a drug's cost per quality-adjusted life year. The same system has been adopted by other government health systems to set thresholds for determining coverage, including the National Institute for Health and Care Excellence (NICE) in Great Britain. Should a drug company refuse to lower prices to what Norway deems acceptable, then Norway refuses to cover the drug at all. A number of drug companies have been willing to cut prices in order to market their products in Norway and other countries with government-controlled health care systems.

While retail prices for many non-generic drugs have become astronomical in America (prices of $300,000+ yearly for new cancer drugs are becoming common), the final pricing has become convoluted and confusing as many drug makers attempt to encourage drug purchases using non-traditional methods such as coupons. The high prices may not only boost drug firms' profits, but also generate larger fees for pharmacy benefits management firms. These are companies that negotiate with drug companies over prices, acting as agents for private health care insurers that are clients. The benefits management companies earn gross fees based on a percentage of the retail drug price, then pass any discount on to the insurance companies after deducting their fees. The higher the retail price, the higher the managers' fees. Patients do not always see benefits from these discounts. For example, a patient who has not yet met his yearly insurance deductible threshold may end up paying a full drug retail price out-of-pocket, while the discount nonetheless gets passed along to the insurer. Another issue is the lists (called formularies) of drugs that are approved by various insurers. In many cases, a doctor will prescribe a drug with recent innovations and advantages, although there may be lower-cost alternatives on the market. The insurer refuses to cover the newer drug, so if the patient desires the drug he must pay full retail out-of-pocket.

Drug makers are attempting to help circumvent high deductibles or high co-pays by offering discount coupons to the patient. The coupons are often available online and in magazines. They are also handed out by doctors in an effort to ease patients' financial pain, even though the doctors may strongly disapprove of the drug makers' pricing and marketing schemes. Such schemes may work well in eliminating the effect of the co-pay for privately insured patients. However, coupons may not be used by patients in any federal or state-funded plan, including Medicare, Medicaid, VA/TriCare, or "if the patient's insurance plan is paying the entire cost of this prescription." In other words, if the money can be pried out of the government or an insurer, then the discount doesn't apply. Worse still, it doesn't work at all for uninsured patients. Total yearly drug expenditures have been soaring. The total cost will get much worse as more and more Baby Boomers hit their senior years. There can be little change without government action.

16) Biotech and Orphan Drugs Create New Revenues for Drug Firms

Many biotech companies have focused on developing drugs for relatively small patient populations. For example, biotech pioneers Genentech and Biogen Idec developed Rituxan for the treatment of non-Hodgkin's lymphoma, an important but relatively small market.

Drugs such as Rituxan are commonly referred to as "orphan drugs," which means that they treat illnesses that no other drug on the market addresses, which are needed by relatively small patient populations. Technically, a drug designated by the FDA with orphan status provides therapeutic benefit for a disease or condition that affects less than 200,000 people in the U.S. These drugs enjoy a unique status due to the Orphan Drug Act of 1983, which gives pharmaceutical companies a seven-year monopoly on the drug without having to file for patent protection, plus a 50% tax credit for research and development costs.

Plunkett Research estimates that combined biotech revenues for publicly held firms headquartered in the U.S. and E.U. were $202 billion during 2020, while the U.S. firms' portion was $135 billion, compared to $189 billion during 2019, with the U.S. firms' portion of $158.9 billion. Orphan drugs, however, receive expedited approval from the FDA, greatly reducing the costs of clinical trials. Long-term profit is also more likely for orphans. While brand-name drugs lose 80% of their market value within one year of patent expiration, biotech and orphan drugs face less generic competition because of the difficulty in developing generic versions once they go off-patent.

The number of new drugs approved by the U.S. FDA in 2020 was 53, of which 31 were orphan drugs. Orphan drugs approved during 2020 included Koselugo, for the treatment of neurofibromatosis in children; Qinlock, for the treatment of advanced gastrointestinal stromal tumors in adults; and Tabrecta, for the treatment of adults with metastatic non-small cell lung cancer.

Commentary: The Challenges Facing the Biopharmaceuticals Industry

- Working with governments to develop methods to safely and effectively speed approval of new drugs. Many observers contend that FDA approval is much too slow and cumbersome.
- Working with the investment community to build confidence and foster patience for the lengthy timeframe required for commercialization of promising new drugs.
- Working with civic, government, religious and academic leaders to deal with ethical questions centered on stem cells, personalized medicine and other new technologies.

- A growing level of consumer and government discontent with soaring drug prices.
- Fostering payer acceptance, diagnostic practices and physician practices that will harness the full potential of genetically targeted, personalized medicine as the base of potentially expensive but highly effective biopharmaceuticals grows.

Source: Plunkett Research, Ltd.

17) Quality of Care and Health Care Outcomes Data Are Available Online, Creating a New Level of Transparency

From the earliest days of the internet, one of the most popular activities online has been searching for information about illness, disease, pharmaceuticals and their side effects, as well as information related to care and diagnosis, such as options for surgery. Now, online activity about health care has risen to a massive level. With rapidly rising health care costs and concerns about the quality of care received for the dollar spent, many patients, employers and insurance providers are using online databases for information regarding doctors and hospitals—call it comparison shopping for health care. For example, there are growing numbers of web sites that track data on hospitals, such as the U.S. Department of Health and Human Services' web site, Hospital Compare (www.medicare.gov/hospitalcompare/search.html). Hospital Compare uses data from Medicare and Medicaid to track performance at thousands of facilities across the U.S. Also, many insurers make hospital data available to members on their web sites.

These databases typically enable an insurer or patient to compare specific hospitals to the national average on statistics such as mortality rates. For example, the Hospital Compare site compares each hospital in Houston, Texas to the Texas state average and to the national average. Data includes many items concerning patient experiences and satisfaction, surgical outcomes, readmission, hospital-related infections, and time spent waiting for care in emergency rooms. Also, average costs for various types of procedures are now available online on web sites that are attempting to earn profits from such services, although the quality of the data may vary.

The Medicare claims database is a digital record of the bills Medicare pays. It is used by federal investigators to sniff out fraud and for analysis by researchers and consultants for cost and utilization studies. Medicare has begun making some data about payments to individual physicians available. The database covers millions of caregivers and beneficiaries, but it is prohibited by law from disclosing patients' names.

<table>
<tr><td>Internet Research Tip:
Top web sites for health care information include:
National Cancer Institute, www.cancer.gov
Centers for Disease Control and Prevention (CDC), www.cdc.gov
FamilyDoctor.org, www.familydoctor.org
Health Finder, www.healthfinder.gov , a service of the U.S. Dept. of Health & Human Services
KidsHealth, kidshealth.org
Mayo Clinic, www.mayoclinic.org
NIH National Institute on Aging, www.nia.nih.gov/health
Medscape, www.medscape.com</td></tr>
</table>

<table>
<tr><td>Internet Research Tip—Checking a Web Site's Accuracy Rating:
When researching health care web sites, look for the seal of approval from the Health on the Net Foundation (www.hon.ch), a nonprofit organization based in Geneva, Switzerland. Founded in 1995 at the behest of international medical experts, the foundation approves medical web sites that meet or exceed its guidelines.</td></tr>
</table>

Elsewhere, corporations in various segments of the health industry may publish interesting cost and outcomes information. For example, health diagnostics and monitoring devices from Abbott, provide an online database giving the exact CPT procedure code and Medicare reimbursement rate for hundreds of procedures such as cholesterol tests at www.codemap.com/alere. The data is sorted geographically as well as by type of care.

Data on individual doctors is becoming available online, at such web sites as www.drscore.com and www.findadoc.com. The quality of the data from such sites may vary, and one should use caution. Nonetheless, the information is intriguing. Findadoc, for example, enables the user to look up doctors by location and specialty, and then view their hospital affiliations, languages spoken and patient ratings for such qualities as bedside manner and wait time.

Quantum Health (www.quantum-health.com), a Columbus, Ohio health care coordinator, offers comparative health care data to its corporate clients, plus a laundry list of services that help employees covered by company insurance navigate the often confusing health care system and get the most out of their health benefits. Quantum Health services include informing patients of what questions they should ask their physicians about their conditions, assistance in finding specialists, advice on medical tests that should or should not be taken and education on disease management and prevention. Quantum reports that its employer clients have enjoyed reduced spending on workers' health care, thanks to reductions in waste and unnecessary care, better results from disease management and a 25% reduction in health benefits-related workload. Two of its most impressive statistics are a 22% reduction in readmissions and a 4% reduction in emergency room usage.

The Affordable Care Act of 2010 (ACA) includes a provision that hospitals and doctors that score poorly on patient surveys can be denied Medicare reimbursement fees. Surveys such as those from Press Ganey, Gallup and National Research Corp., on which patients score health care providers on care experiences (based on patient surveys) including waiting times, pain relief and bedside manner, are becoming powerful arbiters in how patients are treated.

Internet Research Tip:

To compare costs for procedures, try the following site:
www.healthcarebluebook.com

For bill negotiation services, see these sites:
www.medicalcostadvocate.com
www.medliminal.com

To determine whether or not a physician is board certified:
www.abms.org

---

18) Malpractice Suits Are Blamed for Rising Health Care Costs/Tort Reform Is Capping Awards for Damages

Health care costs have long been a hot political topic, and many people have pointed at malpractice lawsuits as a primary cause of rising costs. For years, punitive lawsuits for pain and suffering have levied huge settlements from doctors, hospitals and their insurers. In reaction, premiums for malpractice insurance have burgeoned, growing far faster than the costs for any other type of insurance. Doctors and hospitals, in order to offset malpractice insurance premiums, may raise their own fees and conduct extensive, and often unnecessary, tests in order to protect themselves from legal claims. These factors contribute significantly to the overall cost of health care in the U.S., and a political battle has ensued, particularly between lobbyists for plaintiffs' lawyers and lobbyists for the health care industry.

There is wide disagreement about the causes and actual yearly combined costs of malpractice insurance, litigation, lawsuit awards and defensive medical procedures and tests intended to lessen the likelihood of a malpractice lawsuit loss. A 2013 Jackson Healthcare survey found that 75% of doctors order more tests, medications and procedures than are medically necessary to protect themselves from lawsuits.

Internet Research Tip: Getting Hospital Ratings Online

Patients and concerned family members can now use any of several web sites to check on the quality of hospitals before checking in for treatment. Available data typically includes patient outcomes, fees and whether the latest in technology is available. For patients needing specialized care, this knowledge can be a real windfall. WebMD Health Services, at www.webmdhealthservices.com, (formerly Subimo) gets high marks for its ease of use. It sells subscriptions to major employers and health plans, whose members can then log in.

Other sites include HealthGrades, www.healthgrades.com, Medicare's Hospital Compare at www.medicare.gov/hospitalcompare/search.html and United Healthcare's www.myUHC.com, designed to be used by the millions of patients who are covered by United's health plans.

In addition to adding immense costs to the health care system, malpractice lawsuits have done much to erode the relationship between doctors and their patients. At the same time, fear of malpractice suits can discourage young physicians from pursuing higher-risk specialties, such as obstetrics and emergency room care, rather than fields where they are much less likely to be sued. Relations between doctors and lawyers have also become strained, with many doctors blaming the situation on some lawyers' willingness to take even the most frivolous cases. Malpractice insurance premiums vary widely, according to the type and location of the practice.

Self-interest has caused some physicians to respond. Reports have been published of physicians refusing to treat attorneys, their families or their employees except in cases of emergency. Meanwhile, many would-be patients have learned how hard it can be to get a physician in high-risk fields, such as obstetrics and gynecology, to take a new client.

Many states are tackling the malpractice awards issue through referenda and legislation that limit total damage awards. Texas, after suffering years in which more than 50% of practicing physicians were hit with malpractice suits, passed legislation to limit awards given to plaintiffs for "non-economic" damages, which include pain, inconvenience, suffering and disfigurement. Dozens of states have now limited non-economic damages in medical malpractice cases, generally to amounts between $250,000 and $500,000 dollars. The statutes also generally limit the amount that lawyers can make off such cases via contingency fees, making sure that the plaintiff receives a substantial portion of the reward. Some critics of this move see such laws as contributing to a failure of the justice system. Others feel that a $250,000 to $500,000 award cap is not fair payment for a patient who has been severely disfigured for life.

On the other hand, there may be few limits on the amount of "economic" damages awarded to a patient—that is, loss of earnings due to the inability to function fully at a job or profession. Patients who earn extremely high salaries may seek damages that are proportionately high—even multimillion-dollar amounts. However, attorneys may be discouraged from taking, on contingency, clients who work in low-paying jobs or have very complicated cases.

As in any other legal matter, there are two sides to the story; arguments for and against malpractice award limits abound. California is often named as the poster child for how effective such legislation can be in lowering insurance premiums and health care costs in general.

Texas enjoyed stunning success as a result of its tort reform. Malpractice rates fell with more than 30 malpractice insurance firms competing for business in the state. Texas experienced a resurgence in the numbers of practicing physicians as well since malpractice insurance premiums dropped significantly. The number of malpractice lawsuits in Texas has been cut dramatically.

Meanwhile, the costs and challenges of lawsuits are not limited to physicians. Every sector of the health chain, from equipment makers to hospitals to drug makers, is swamped by lawsuits, and they are forced to pass along the costs of insurance and litigation in the form of higher fees charged to patients. Tort reform is beginning to take hold for these sectors as well. It is worth noting that the 2010 Patient Protection and Affordable Care Act (ACA) did not make any provision for limiting malpractice damages.

Internet Research Tip: Malpractice Awards
The National Practitioner Data Bank, www.npdb.hrsa.gov, is a federal initiative that collects data on malpractice lawsuit awards and license revocations, on a state-by-state basis. It publishes annual reports that provide detailed information.

---

19) Obesity Sparks Government, School and Corporate Initiatives/Snack Foods Get Healthier/Taxes on Unhealthy Foods

Obesity is increasing in countries throughout the world. The problem is acute in the U.S., where obesity is unfortunately very common and has deep links to the high overall cost of health care. Obesity is a much more serious problem than being merely overweight—see the box regarding "Body Mass Index (BMI)" that follows.

According to the World Population Review, approximately 2.1 billion people were obese as of 2021 (about 26% of the global population). More than 2.8 million people die per year from obesity related conditions according to the World Health Organization. The global obesity rate has tripled since 1975.

Numbers from the U.S. CDC (Centers for Disease Control) show that obesity is a massive problem in America, one capable of generating vast annual expenses for treatment of chronic diseases related to obesity. For 2017-2018, the CDC found that 42.4% of all adults over age 20 were obese.

Body Mass Index (BMI) as an indicator of health status based on weight:

Underweight = less than 18.5 BMI
Normal weight = 18.5 to 24.9
Overweight = 25 to 29.9
Obese = 30 or more

To calculate Body Mass Index:
First: divide weight (pounds) by height (inches)
Second: divide the result by height again
Third: multiply the result by 703

Internet Research Tip:
For an easy-to-use, online calculator and a full discussion of BMI, see www.nhlbi.nih.gov/health/educational/lose_wt/BMI/bmicalc.htm
Source: National Institutes of Health, National Heart, Lung and Blood Institute

---

A 2014 report by the McKinsey Global Institute found that the annual global cost for lost productivity and the treatment of conditions such as diabetes, heart disease and certain cancers related to obesity is $2 trillion. An "Obesity Update 2017" published by the OECD estimated that an obese person incurs 25% higher health costs than a person of normal weight in a given year, and that obese people earn up to 18% less than non-obese people.

One of the most critical problems of obesity is the onset of diabetes. The impact of the soaring diabetes problem combined with an accompanying rise in heart disease, cancer, high blood pressure and cholesterol levels may wreak havoc on the global health care system.

The alarming rise in obesity in the U.S. has brought about significant changes in the latest set of dietary guidelines from the U.S. federal government. The 2015 federal dietary guidelines were the result of more than a year's work by an anonymous panel of nutrition experts in the fields of pediatrics, obesity, cardiovascular disease and public health. Panel members remain anonymous to avoid lobbying from food industry groups such as the Soft Drink Association, the Wheat Foods Council, the National Dairy Council and the United Fresh Produce Association. Final results were presented by the U.S. Department of Health and Human Services. Updated guidelines were expected by the end of 2020.

By law, federal dietary guidelines must be revised every five years based on the latest research. The 2015 guidelines recommend eating more fruits and vegetables, filling half of meal plates with them, moving to low-fat and fat-free milk or yogurt, varying proteins and drinking and eating less sodium, saturated fat and added sugars.

Even the USDA's food pyramid, which after going through several permutations in the spring of 2005 and again in 2010, has been abandoned in favor of a plate showing representative portions of vegetables, fruit, grains and protein and a nearby glass representing dairy.

Originally launched in mid-2011, the plate initiative, called MyPlate (www.choosemyplate.gov), was developed by the USDA at a cost of $2.9 million over a three-year period.

The impact of the new guidelines on the food industry is significant. The snack food industry (which tends to make heavily salted snacks) is facing a challenge since the recommended sodium level for about one-half the U.S. population (those who are 51 years of age or older, are African American, or suffer from high blood pressure, diabetes or chronic kidney disease) is only 1,500 milligrams per day.

Wal-Mart has slashed salt, fat and sugar in the grocery products it sells. It completed a five-year plan in 2016 in which sodium would be reduced by 25%, industrially-added trans fats are to be eliminated and added sugars will be reduced by 10% in packaged foods manufactured under its Great Value house brand. The company also announced plans to press major food brands to adopt these standards over the mid-term. Wal-Mart is not alone in these initiatives (ConAgra Foods, for example, reduced sodium in its packaged foods by 20% by 2015), but as America's largest retailer, its focus will have a profound effect on the food industry. Wal-Mart affixes its Great For You icon on foods such as fresh and packaged fruits and vegetables.

In America's massive Affordable Care Act (ACA) passed in 2010, the U.S. federal government set up a requirement that all restaurant chains with 20 or more restaurants post calorie counts for menu and buffet items. The FDA ruled that restaurants with at least 20 locations (and vending machines that have at least 20 units) had to post calorie counts.

Healthy Dining Finder, www.healthydiningfinder.com, a web site that promotes restaurants that offer lower-calorie options, estimates that the number of restaurants it lists on its site has grown dramatically. A number of food companies are promoting products that are lower in calories and fats, and higher in nutrients such as protein, fiber, calcium and certain vitamins. PepsiCo, Inc. packages such food with a distinctive green label. To have the label, foods must contain no more than 35% of their calories from fat, contain one gram or less of saturated fats and no trans fats as well as meet limits for cholesterol, sodium and sugar. Products include Tropicana and Dole juices, Quaker oatmeal, Baked! LAY'S potato chips and Rold Gold pretzels. Nabisco is also promoting healthier 100 Calorie Packs of many of its popular brands such as Chips Ahoy! and Oreo cookies and Ritz and Teddy Grahams crackers.

The Healthy Weight Commitment Foundation (HWCF) is a U.S. effort designed to help reduce obesity, especially childhood obesity. It is a first-of-its-kind coalition that brings together more than 300 retailers, food and beverage manufacturers, restaurants, sporting goods and insurance companies, trade associations and professional sports organizations. The HWCF is helping consumers lead healthier lives by offering healthier nutrition options. The Foundation reported the removal of

6.4 trillion calories from the food marketplace between 2009 and 2019 (400% over its initial goal) and over $1 million in grants and prizes awarded to American schools shown to have the greatest needs.

Along with overeating, sedentary lifestyles are certainly a major contributor to obesity. Vast numbers of people are spending much of their work hours in front of a computer screen, while more and more of their leisure time is spent playing electronic games, watching TV and enjoying digital media—activities that are not burning many calories.

Some countries have national initiatives focused on obesity. Singapore, which requires military service of all adults, has instituted an extended six-week training camp for recruits who are obese in addition to its 10-week basic boot camp. After discharge from the service, most Singaporean men and women remain on reserve status, which requires an annual physical and basic fitness test.

In the UK, Public Health England called for a voluntary reduction of sugar in processed food products such as chocolate, breakfast cereal, yogurt and other foods by 20% between 2015 and 2020. However, a 2020 report found that sugar had been reduced by only 3% in 2019 compared to 2015.

20) Health Care Goes Offshore, Medical Tourism, Clinical Trials Continue in China, India and Elsewhere

Many people might assume that certain professions could never be outsourced, such as the work of health care professionals. This is not entirely true. For example, in a practice called teleradiology, medical technicians and physicians in India and elsewhere are analyzing x-rays and CAT scans performed in the U.S., diagnosing American patients and relaying results back to American hospitals.

Meanwhile, certain less-skilled health care tasks are rapidly moving offshore. Most notably, tens of thousands of jobs in medical record transcription have been moved from the U.S. to offshore centers. Other business process outsourcing (BPO) tasks related to health care include claims processing, human resources and benefits administration, customer relations and supply chain logistics.

Since clinical trials for drugs are exceptionally expensive to conduct, the opportunity to offshore the work and reduce costs is hard for drug firms to resist. However, significant concerns arose regarding the number of deaths of patients in trials. Starting in 2013, India created much tighter regulatory laws for clinical trials. These include requiring trials to be performed in good clinical practice (GCP)-compliant facilities, approval by an ethics committee, registration with regulators and random inspections, all of which come at significant cost.

Meanwhile, medical tourism likely declined significantly due to the Coronavirus, but it is difficult to measure by how much. Analysts vary widely in their estimations of the number of people seeking medical care abroad, and extremely optimistic forecasts have been made that were unreasonable. However, it is clear that high health care costs in the U.S. and other developed nations have in the past contributed to this trade.

A procedure like a hip replacement or a triple bypass can be obtained in nations such as India at as little as 10% to 30% of the cost of the same procedure in the U.S. A heart bypass, for example, may cost only $18,500 in Singapore and $11,000 in Thailand, according to the Thai Public Health Ministry, but could easily cost $60,000 to $100,000 in the U.S. Since many patients in the U.S. are either underinsured or not insured at all, the cost savings sound very appealing. In addition, in nations like Canada and the UK, where medicine is socialized, the wait to get an appointment with and obtain care from a specialist can be months or even years (and some "elective" procedures are not covered by government payment programs). Consequently, such patients are more likely to consider going offshore. Finally, many physicians in India, Thailand, Singapore and elsewhere received their training in the finest clinics and hospitals in the U.S., Canada and the UK. Several of them have returned to their home nations where they are opening clinics specifically for medical tourists. In many offshore clinics that have been adapted to attract foreign patients, surgery and care are of very high quality and outcomes are excellent.

A business sector has opened up that manages medical tourism. For example, MedRetreat (www.medretreat.com), a medical tourism agency based in Odenton, Maryland, partners with hospitals in Argentina, Brazil, Costa Rica, El Salvador, India, Malaysia, Mexico, South Africa, Thailand and Turkey to provide cosmetic, dental and medical procedures to U.S. patients. The company schedules procedures, arranges flights and hotel stays and assigns guides to facilitate the process.

Another medical tourism company, IndUSHealth (www.indushealth.com), is based in North Carolina and outsources medical procedures to hospitals, clinics and physicians in India. IndUSHealth focuses on companies rather than individual patients. Specifically, these are companies that self-insure or pay employees' health care costs directly instead of contracting with an insurance provider.

Agencies like MedRetreat and IndUSHealth generate most of their revenue from commissions for booking hotel rooms and taking approximately 20% of fees on treatments offered by the providers in exchange for referrals. However, there is no regulation of this practice, and lawsuits or severe medical problems that arise as a result of a mishandled procedure could cripple this relatively new industry. Despite these obstacles, medical tourism agencies are betting that low prices and Western-trained practitioners will insure their success. Qunomedical (www.qunomedical.com) is an online startup based in Berlin that allows patients to search from 1,000 doctors in 35 countries for a variety of treatments.

India's famed Dr. Shetty operates a 140-bed acute care hospital in the Cayman Islands, called Health City Cayman Islands, in partnership with the nonprofit health care system Ascension, based in St. Louis, Missouri. Shetty also operates thousands of beds in his respected hospitals in India. Shetty is the world's leader in reducing the cost of high-quality surgery. His Narayana Health firm is a system of dozens of hospitals in India (with plans to expand to Kuala Lumpur and Malaysia) that provide excellent outcomes at very low cost. Open heart surgery, for example, is provided at his Indian facilities for about $2,000. The project in the Caribbean, only a quick flight away from Miami, could have a dramatic effect on health care in the nearby nations of North and South America. Fees for surgery at Health City Cayman Islands run about one-half of fees typically charged in the U.S. The patient experience is excellent, as the hospital is attached to a luxury hotel via a convenient pathway. North America's hospital operators will undoubtedly pay close attention to Shetty's methods, which include high-volume, specialized surgery centers, prompt treatment, and proprietary software called iKare that analyzes real-time clinical data for each patient, and then recommends best protocols for treatment.

21) Retail Clinics, Urgent Care Centers and Employer Sites Increase Health Care Options/Reduce Costs

More and more, the delivery of health care is moving away from the hospital into outpatient clinics and surgery centers. The number of hospitals and hospital beds has been falling while outpatient options have increased. Now, consumers in many U.S. cities can go to the local discount store or drug store for basic health care.

Clinics in Retail Stores: In 2019, CVS Health Corp. and competitor Walgreens Boots Alliance, Inc. each announced plans to remodel hundreds of existing stores to offer consultations and lab tests for patients with chronic diseases such as diabetes, heart disease and hypertension. (The stores will continue to offer prescription drug fulfillment and stock a variety of personal care items, along with foods, beverages and sundries.) An estimated 60% of Americans have at least one chronic condition, according to the U.S. Centers for Disease Control and Prevention (CDC).

CVS planned to have 1,500 health hubs open by the end of 2021, providing medicines, consultations and lab tests. Walgreens is partnering with startup VillageMD to open between 500 and 700 physician-staffed clinics at Walgreens stores through 2025, resulting in Walgreens' having a 30% stake in VillageMD. CVS is calling the new stores "health hubs" while Walgreens is calling them "neighborhood health destinations."

Walmart has begun opening clinics in or nearby its supercenters in the U.S. Doctors and dentists are on site, with services such as primary care office visits, vaccinations, lab tests and dental x-rays at reasonable fees. The firm plans to expand the clinics across its 4,700 U.S. stores.

In late 2018, CVS completed its acquisition of Aetna, affording the drug store chain access to the insurer's customers and making it easy to market these new in-store services. In 2020, Aetna dropped copayments for members who patronize the drug chain's MinuteClinics. Walgreens is using software from Microsoft to manage patient engagement, and it is also working with Alphabet, Inc.'s Verily Life Sciences Unit to develop a system to encourage patients to take their medications as prescribed.

Meanwhile, Amazon spent $1 billion to acquire online pharmacy PillPack, Inc. in 2018, placing it in direct competition in the prescription drug market. The acquisition and its competitive potential may have encouraged CVS and Walgreens to make the changes in their stores and in the way they do business.

The change will also affect the 1,100 MinuteClinics in CVS pharmacies and Target stores, which will also be revamped to cater to chronic illness in addition to giving flu shots and handling simple health issues such as colds and sore throats. Wal-Mart offers a modest number of in-store clinics, typically operated by local hospitals. Wal-Mart is also taking in-store treatment a step further, by providing primary medical care in a few locations. These facilities offer chronic disease management in addition to care for minor health problems. Wal-Mart's huge rural footprint may position the retailer to fill a gap long existent in towns where doctors are hard to find. Another plus is Wal-Mart's low prices.

The in-store clinics offer reasonable costs and great convenience. Also, the setting may seem less intimidating to some consumers than a trip to a medical office center or full-scale clinic building. Visits to these new in-store clinics typically range from about $25 to $75 in cost. Many of the patients will be people with no health insurance coverage—cost will be a major consideration. However, since charges are generally much less than those of traditional doctors' offices, health insurers will also be pleased with these clinics. Procedures provided tend to be basic, such as flu shots, a quick physical required for participation on a sports team, or treatment for a simple infection or a minor illness. However, in-store clinics are adding treatments for more complex illnesses such as asthma and osteoporosis. They tend to be staffed by nurse practitioners. These practitioners have extended educations and special licenses that in many states across the nation allow them to treat minor illnesses and write simple prescriptions. In some states, they must work in conjunction and consultation with MDs, but the MDs need not be present at the time of treatment.

Urgent and Emergency Care Centers: Thousands of urgent care centers, providing a higher level of service than the simple clinics found in retailers, are also growing at a significant rate. These well-equipped clinics are staffed by physicians who can provide emergency care and treat a wide range of conditions, while offering walk-in, no-appointment treatment. Location is a key element, so clinics typically open in high-traffic strip centers close to patients' homes and workplaces. Most are open at least 12 hours a day, including weekends, and many are open 24/7. Total fees are typically much lower than those for a hospital emergency room visit. Some of the clinics are operated as outposts of major hospitals, while others are run by physicians who are owner/operators.

UnitedHealth Group, Inc.'s Optum unit acquired a large network of doctor practices, surgery centers and urgent care clinics in the Los Angeles, California area. The company hopes to expand into additional markets. Meanwhile, Blue Cross & Blue Shield of Texas offers free primary-care visits to its members at its newly opened clinics in the Houston and Dallas, Texas areas.

Workplace Care Centers: CHS Health Services and Take Care Employer Solutions merged and then rebranded the company as Premise Health. The firm offers worksite health and wellness centers, serving corporations including Intel, Goldman Sachs, Continental Airlines and Toyota (in addition to its clinics in drug stores). The clinics provide annual check-ups, flu shots, x-rays and simple blood work and are staffed by two doctors, two pharmacists and a dietician, plus a number of nurses and technicians. Client companies typically expect to lower their overall health care costs by as much as 20%; since more employees are able to utilize preventive care, fewer emergency hospital visits are required and costs per visit to the on-site clinic average out to a very reasonable amount. Productivity is also expected to rise for firms with on-site clinics because employees take fewer sick days. The on-site clinics even offer health coaches to provide lifestyle advice to employees considered at risk for health problems.

Services generally include health screenings and immunizations. Some facilities include fully-equipped gyms to promote wellness and preventive health measures. Another leader in worksite clinics is Marathon Health.

22) Health Care Industry Grows Rapidly in China, India and Mexico

Growing Health Expenditures in China: China is in the process of implementing a broad, national boost to health care availability. Today, about 97% of the people in China are covered by some kind insurance (compared to less than one-third of the population in 2003). However, the health facilities and services available will remain relatively limited for some time, particularly in remote villages and towns. China intends to provide relatively modern health care nationwide. This is an immense undertaking in a nation with little health care infrastructure and few doctors who have been trained to Western standards. While health care coverage has become widespread, the co-pay for care is very high, as much as 50%, which creates a difficult financial burden for many patients.

Health care expenditures in China are expected to rise substantially over the mid-term. China's health care spending was expected to reach about $1 trillion per year by 2020 ($770 per capita), but will remain very low on a per capita basis compared to that in Europe, Japan and the U.S. This will be a dramatic increase from about $300 billion spent in 2009 and $500 billion in 2014.

Over the longer term, China will face a growing elderly portion of its population, even more dramatic than the aging population facing the U.S. China is also challenged by high cigarette smoking rates.

At the same time, new private clinics are attracting wealthy locals in China. Residents who can afford it may sign up for care via a private health program offered by Beijing Universal Medical Assistance, at a fee equal to a few thousand dollars yearly. While the fees are vastly higher than those at the state-run public clinics, these private clinics feature luxury surroundings and prompt, quality service for basic health care needs. Look for the number of larger private hospitals in China to grow. Hospital companies are investing heavily in China and in other countries in Asia, especially Malaysia, Thailand, Vietnam and the Philippines.

In order to provide advanced health care, such as diagnostics and drugs, at extremely low prices suitable to the Indian and rural Chinese markets, a vast amount of innovation and creativity will be required. Much of this innovation will eventually trickle into the developed world, helping to establish new ways to lower health care costs. While initial steps into modern health care in China and India were based on equipment, procedures and technologies from the West, health care delivery in the future will accelerate quickly based on locally developed efficiencies and technologies.

Health Care in India: India, especially, is seeing significant growth in health care initiatives. With its growing middle class clamoring for better and more modern medical care, some health care companies are investing heavily. Indian physicians (many of whom were trained in Western medical schools) are making strides in developing innovative and cost-effective new treatments.

Government spending on health care in India per capita is lower than any other major world economy. Modicare, which is officially called the Prime Minister's People's Healthcare Plan, provides roughly $7,000 in annual hospital coverage for 107 million families, with eligibility determined by the occupation of a family's primary breadwinner. The program pays flat fees for every procedure (unlike the minutely itemized billing in the U.S.). Private hospitals are not required to accept Modicare. Prime Minister Modi allocated just $900 million for the Modicare program for the 2019-2020 fiscal year (health care costs are generally split 60-40 between the national government in Delhi and the Indian states). Modi believes that India's well-regarded private health care providers will be capable of delivering cost effective care to the bulk of the population.

One of the world's most closely watched private doctors is India's Devi Shetty, a surgeon trained in London who has become an extremely successful medical entrepreneur. While he gained fame at one time as Mother Teresa's heart surgeon, he is best known today as a builder of highly cost-effective hospitals. Shetty has been compared, by at least one journalist, to America's Henry Ford. Ford, in one of the most important innovations in industrial history, launched the modern automobile manufacturing industry by creating the assembly line to turn out a high volume of quality cars at affordable cost. Before Ford, the car was just a distant, unaffordable dream for most people, and was assembled slowly, by hand, at great cost. Dr. Shetty, in a vaguely similar vein, employs the economies of scale offered by high volume output to deliver high quality surgery at modest cost at his Narayana Health firm.

At Shetty's massive, 1,000-bed privately-owned hospital in Bangalore (three to six times larger than a typical American hospital), open heart surgery runs about $2,000 or less, and the outcomes are excellent. The hospital is like a surgery factory. Dozens of theaters give this center the capacity to perform up to 70 heart surgeries in one day. The hospital states that about 30% of its heart surgery is done on children.

Adjacent to his Narayana Hrudayalaya Hospital for heart care, he has built a 1,400-bed cancer center and a 300-bed facility for eye care. Another Shetty unit provides a broad range of dental care; yet another runs a stem cell bank to enable mothers to deposit their babies' umbilical cords for potential use in the future for stem cell therapy. Additional surgical specialties at Shetty's hospitals include neurology and orthopedics. He has raised millions of dollars with the goal of building several more medical centers in India, hoping for 30,000 total beds. As of mid-2019, Narayana Hrudayalaya managed or owned a system of 24 hospitals and seven heart centers in India and an international hospital in the Cayman Islands, in addition to a telemedicine practice which links physicians via Skype in facilities in India and in Africa. 2.5 million patients are treated every year.

Shetty's hospital is also a partner in a "micro health insurance" program called Yeshaswini, which covers nearly 3 million farmers at a monthly premium of a few rupees each. The state government of Karnataka contributes an additional five cents per month per person. All told, the program covers surgeries in 400 hospitals across the state. The states of Andhra Pradesh and Tamil Nadu have started similar programs.

Narayana Health's cost efficiency gets a significant boost from Atma, a back-office platform that handles everything from admissions to scheduling the pharmacy operations to payments. All data is stored and analyzed along with outcomes and complications to flag unnecessary costs and plan ways to avoid them in the future.

SPOTLIGHT: Mexico's Health Insurance Program

In 2019, President Obrador signed an executive order replacing the country's Seguro Popular health care program with a new Health Institute for Welfare. The initiative had an initial budget of $4.12 billion from the Fund for Catastrophe Protection Expenses. The Institute took charge of health care on a federal level instead of the state level control under Seguro Popular. Although access to health care is still spotty in rural areas, the country has seen significant improvement in overall health, including the increase in the survival rate for children with leukemia from three in ten to seven in ten.

The Outlook for Health Care Technology

23) Health Care Technology Introduction

In recent years, the health care industry has capitalized on many remarkable advances in medical technology, including breakthroughs in computing, communications, small-incision surgery, drug therapies, diagnostics, advanced radiation and instruments. For example, huge advances are being made in the fields of cardiovascular care, cancer care, diagnostic imaging and testing, organ transplants and minimally invasive surgery.

In the area of drug development, innovative methods, including genome mapping and high-throughput screening, are providing a clearer understanding of the potential of drugs before they are sent into clinical trials. In addition, the FDA has hired legions of employees in recent years to help process applications for new drugs, medical procedures and equipment. Nonetheless, drug development remains a slow, tedious, extremely expensive risk, and very few potential drugs make it through trials and onto the market.

Meanwhile, more emphasis is being placed on the use of computers and advanced telecommunication technology in many phases of hospital operations and patient care, often in conjunction with complex equipment, to diagnose and improve patients' conditions. Investors, well aware of the long term potential growth of the industry, continue to be anxious to fund new health technologies. An extensive use of digitized patient records is slowly becoming a reality.

The first half of the 21st century promises to bring even greater milestones in human health as we begin to reap the benefits of new therapies created through biotechnology and genetic engineering. As our understanding of human biology at the molecular level matures, genetically engineered pharmaceuticals and gene therapies will be developed that target diseases at their molecular origins, thus lessening the need for more costly elements of treatment such as invasive surgery and acute care. If applied during the early stages of disease development, these new biotechnologies will extend and improve the quality of life for the patient. If the disease has already caused the failure or malfunction of vital organs or tissue, it may one day be possible for the patient to receive a fully functioning, engineered replacement, grown from cells harvested from the patient's own tissues.

Gene mapping and proteomics will allow patients to be screened to determine whether they are genetically predisposed to certain diseases. Dramatic breakthroughs are already being made by determining, through personal gene mapping, whether a patient is likely to respond favorably to specific drug therapies for cancer and other diseases. The use of personal genetic profiles in order to avoid adverse reactions to specific drugs will eventually become important as well.

Knowledge obtained from biomedical research will also help to improve the general health of the public by identifying beneficial behavioral changes. Meanwhile, advanced imaging technology, including 320-slice CT scanning (capable of providing incredibly precise, high-resolution scans of the body), will greatly enhance physicians' ability to diagnose patients and lead to earlier intervention and higher rates of cure.

24) Electronic Health Records (EHR) Digitize Patient Data at an Accelerating Pace

There is a strong movement in the United States, the UK, Canada and elsewhere to implement widespread use of electronic health records (EHRs, or sometimes EMRs for electronic medical records). A major goal in this movement is to create Continuity of Care Records (CCRs), which would ensure that a patient's health history could be utilized seamlessly by hospitals, primary care physicians and specialists.

Top EHR platforms in the U.S. include Epic, Cerner, Meditech, CPSI, Allscripts, Medhost and athenahealth. All platforms feature secure log-in where patients can communicate with their care providers, view test results, make payments and schedule appointments. Workers and physicians within clinics and hospitals have instant access to patients' records.

Kaiser Permanente HealthConnect links its hundreds of medical offices and Kaiser hospitals, thousands of physicians and millions of members. Kaiser maintains one of the world's largest non-governmental digital medical data depositories.

Proponents of EHRs estimate that they could significantly reduce medical errors, save lives and cut billions in medical spending a year in shortened hospital stays, reduced nursing time, savings on unnecessary drugs (or drugs that could dangerously react with medications already prescribed for a patient) and the reduction of redundant lab tests and paperwork. Physicians, caregivers and researchers could also benefit enormously by tracking clinical data nationwide and learning which treatments are most effective in any given situation.

The Canadian government developed health information projects including telemedicine, EHR, electronic prescription systems, laboratory information systems and diagnostic imaging systems. This is done via a sophisticated platform called Canada Health Infoway.

Another challenge within healthcare that is being aided through special online tools is filing for insurance claims. There is intense competition in this field. Billions of transactions occur every year. Leading software and solutions providers include PLEXIS, Medvision Solutions, RAM Technologies, DataCare and ClickClaims.

While hospitals and other major health care providers adopted digital methods, concerns about the quality of patient care have been voiced. As a result, caregivers and insurers have combined forces to monitor the changes brought about by the technological boom. The Leapfrog Group, a coalition of companies and private organizations that provides health care benefits, was created to improve, among other things, the flow of patient data and benchmarks for patient outcomes at hospitals. Leapfrog has set exacting standards for the health system to strive for in the creation and utilization of digital data. "Leapfrog compliance" is a catch phrase among hospitals, which are rated on the organization's web site (www.leapfroggroup.org) with regard to compliance issues such as computerized prescription order systems and statistics on staffing and medical procedure success rates.

In addition to Leapfrog, nonprofit HIMMSS formed the Personal Connected Health Alliance (www.pchalliance.org), which includes partners such as AT&T, Eli Lilly & Company, Philips, Samsung, Cisco Systems, Intel and Qualcomm Life. PCHAlliance publishes and promotes standards for data exchange to and from personal health devices called the Continua Design Guidelines.

The use of advanced predictive analytics software for the study of patient care outcomes data will attempt to forecast the best possible treatment for specific diseases and ailments. Patient records are kept in increasingly powerful databases, which can be analyzed to find the history of treatment outcomes. For the first time, payers such as insurance companies have vast amounts of data available to them, including answers to questions such as:

- Which procedures and surgeries bring the best results?
- Which drugs are most cost effective?
- Which physicians and hospitals have the highest and lowest rates of cure (or of untimely deaths of patients)?
- What is the average length of stay required for the treatment and recovery of patients undergoing various surgeries?
- How long should it take for the rehabilitation of a patient with a worker's compensation claim for a specific type of injury?

25) Telemedicine and Remote Patient Monitoring Rely on Wireless

The Coronavirus pandemic spurred exponential growth in telemedicine. At Penn Medicine (the clinical and research arm of the University of Pennsylvania) in Philadelphia, for example, 9,000 health care providers were equipped to meet with patients by video or phone in March 2020. The organization began averaging 5,000

telemedicine visits per day. Meanwhile, Houston Methodist in the Texas Medical Center saw its average telemedicine visits grow from 44 per day before the pandemic to between 2,400 and 2,500 in mid-2020.

Technology to enhance telemedicine is emerging rapidly. TytoCare Ltd. (www.tytocare.com) offers the Tyto Device with an exam camera and thermometer, which also comes with an otoscope adapter for examining ears, a stethoscope adapter for heart and lung sounds and a tongue depressor for the throat, all of which interface with the TytoApp. Another company, binah.ai LTD (www.binah.ai), offers vital signs monitoring using a smartphone camera.

This shift to telemedicine from certain office visits will be permanent to some extent, as long as insurers continue to pay for it. One big question is what price insurers should pay. Should they pay the same rate for a brief telemedicine call as they would for office visits, or reduced rates? Consumers find telemedicine much more convenient than traveling to doctors' offices and sitting through waiting room delays. Doctors often find that they can see more patients per hour. Of course, many types of procedures, tests and exams will still require in-person contact, but a very large portion of medical visits can be conducted simply and quickly via teleconferencing.

The healthcare products business of electronics giant Royal Philips Electronics offers an ICU (intensive care unit) remote monitoring system called eICU. Originally developed by Visicu, Inc., a Baltimore, Maryland medical information technology company that is now part of Phillips, eICU is a combination of software, video and audio feeds and real-time patient vital statistics that hooks patients in ICUs in multiple hospitals to central monitoring facilities manned by ICU specialists. A specialist at the central location mans a standing desk outfitted with a cutting edge graphical dashboard called orb that displays patient data, including real-time video and audio for up to 150 ICU beds at a time. The system ranks patients according to their conditions and flags gravely ill patients in red so that their progress can be more easily monitored. Indications such as changes in blood pressure alert the specialist who then contacts the nurse or physician on duty to treat the patient accordingly. eICU is in use in hundreds of hospitals around the world.

Hospitals that have eICU have experienced significant cost savings since the system cuts the average ICU stay from 4.4 days to 3.6 by lowering the instances of complications such as pneumonia and infections (these conditions generally occur when patients are not closely monitored by ICU specialists). The Leapfrog Group estimates that 54,000 patients per year could be saved if every U.S. ICU were monitored by specialists.

Other remote monitoring systems are allowing patients to be monitored at home or at out-of-the-way care facilities. For example, American Telecare, Inc.'s CareTone Telephonic Stethoscope checks for heart, lung and bowel sounds using a small stethoscope, a phone line and two-way video stations. Cardiocom LLC's Telescale is a telemonitoring device integrated with an electronic scale. The patient steps onto the scale and answers questions using a touch pad about his or her symptoms. The answers and the patient's weight are communicated via two-way messaging to the consulting physician, who is alerted if there is any deterioration in the patient's health. The system also sends alerts back to the patient for follow-up visits or care plan adjustments. Other remote monitoring systems track cardiac patients' vital signs and links them via video chat to a nurse when necessary.

Many of the world's leading technology companies see immense potential in remote home monitoring of elderly and chronically ill patients. One example is the "Health Buddy" from Bosch, which can utilize home monitors for weight, glucose, blood pressure and blood oxygen. Philips, Honeywell and Intel are also developing products. Intel's design includes two-way video between the patient at home and caregivers.

Another slant on telemonitoring is the growing practice of patients connecting with physicians via laptop webcams, video-enabled tablets or smartphones. Rather than an expensive doctor visit, some patients are opting for virtual consultations at much lower costs than office or hospital visits. Insurers including WellPoint, Aetna and United Health are offering virtual visit options in several U.S. states that do not require a face to face meeting before a doctor can prescribe medication. A large number of companies have launched telehealth services, with many of them aimed at saving costs for employee health plans. LiveHealth, for example, is a $49 videoconference platform offered by Anthem Blue Cross. Aetna, through a partnership with Tcladoc, offers its clients $38 remote consultations.

A new player in the wearable sensor arena is Apple's smartwatch which is basically a wearable computer that is part watch, part iPhone, part iPod and much more. With regard to health care, users can download apps to the watch that track readings from external monitors such as those used to measure glucose. DexCom, Inc. offers just such an app to go with its glucose monitor that displays blood sugar data in a simple, easy to read graph. There are now apps and sensors that track other medical data, including electrocardiograms (EKGs), blood oxygen levels and respiratory rates. For example, AliveCor offers KardiaMobile, an FDA-approved clinical grade personal EKG monitor.

Between June 2018 and June 2019, 2,300 patients who were in recovery from cardiac events enrolled in a remote, eight-week rehab program from Kaiser Permanente. The patients wore smart watches to monitor exercise and medication. More than 87% of the patients successfully completed the eight-week program. Hospital readmission rates were fewer than 2% of the participants, an excellent outcome for the program.

Mobile health apps are extremely popular with consumers, and are adding features and capabilities on a continual basis. Examples include MyFitnessPal, which was acquired by Under Armour, and Runkeeper. Apple released the HealthKit and ResearchKit (in addition to its Health tracking and fitness app) that enable physicians search for health apps according to their medical specialty and leverage health resources. Stanford University found that 11,000 people signed up for a cardiovascular study using ResearchKit less than 24 hours after its release.

In the Finnish city of Oulu, a telemonitoring system called Self Care has users who login to their computers to make appointments, refill prescriptions and exchange messages with doctors. People who test blood pressure or blood sugar levels at home can enter the results online for doctors to view. Lab results are posted within hours. Self Care costs the city $390,000 each year, but has saved millions in reducing expensive, face-to-face doctor's visits.

Amazon's Amazon Care telehealth service (amazon.care) is expanding from providing health services to its own Seattle employees to digitally serving employees of companies across the U.S. The program begins with a chatbot which typically leads to a virtual visit with a doctor or nurse practitioner. In Seattle, a full version of the service includes in-person visits from mobile medics within 60 minutes, who perform routine tests, give vaccinations or draw blood samples. Prescriptions can be delivered within two hours. Amazon hoped to provide the full service in the Baltimore and Washington D.C. areas in 2021 and ultimately nationwide.

26) Stem Cells and 3-D Printing—A New Era of Regenerative Medicine Takes Shape

Many firms are conducting product development and research in the areas of skin replacement, vascular tissue replacement and bone grafting or regeneration. Stem cells, as well as transgenic organs harvested from pigs, are under study for use in humans. At its highest and most promising level, regenerative medicine may eventually utilize human stem cells to create virtually any type of replacement organ or tissue.

In one recent, exciting experiment, doctors took stem cells from bone marrow and injected them into the hearts of patients undergoing bypass surgery. The study showed that the bypass patients who received the stem cells were pumping blood 24% better than patients who had not received them.

In another experiment, conducted by Dr. Mark Keating at Harvard, the first evidence was shown that stem cells may be used for regenerating lost limbs and organs. The regenerative abilities of amphibians have long been known, but exactly how they do it, or how it could be applied to mammals, has been little understood. Much of the regenerative challenge lies in differentiation, or the development of stem cells into different types of adult tissue such as muscle and bone. Creatures such as amphibians have the ability to turn their complex cells back into stem cells in order to regenerate lost parts. In the experiment, Dr. Keating made a serum from the regenerating nub (stem cells) of a newt's leg and applied it to adult mouse cells in a petri dish. He observed the mouse cells "de-differentiate," or turn into stem cells. In a later experiment, de-differentiated cells were turned back into muscle, bone and fat. These experiments could be the first steps to true human regeneration. Keating is continuing to make exciting breakthroughs in regenerative research.

The potential of the relatively young science of tissue engineering appears to be unlimited. Transgenics (the use of organs and tissues grown in laboratory animals for transplantation to humans) is considered by many to have great future potential, and improvements in immune system suppression will eventually make it easier for the human body to tolerate foreign tissue instead of rejecting it. There is also increasing theoretical evidence that malfunctioning or defective organs such as livers, bladders and kidneys could be replaced with perfectly functioning "neo-organs" (like spare parts) grown in the laboratory from the patient's own stem cells, with minimal risk of rejection.

The ability of most human tissue to repair itself is a result of the activity of these cells. The potential that cultured stem cells have for transplant medicine and basic developmental biology is enormous.

Diabetics who are forced to cope with daily insulin injection treatments could also benefit from engineered tissues. If they could receive a fully functioning replacement pancreas, diabetics might be able to throw away their hypodermic needles once and for all.

Elsewhere, the harvesting of replacement cartilage, which does not require the growth of new blood vessels, is being used to repair damaged joints and treat urological disorders. Genzyme Corp. won FDA approval for its replacement cartilage product Carticel, the first biologic cell therapy to become licensed. Genzyme's process involves harvesting the patient's own cartilage-forming cells, and, from those cells, re-growing new cartilage in the laboratory. The physician then injects the new cartilage into the damaged area. Full regeneration of the replacement cartilage is expected to take up to 18 months.

Another cartilage therapy has been developed by Vericel Corp. (www.vcel.com). Its matrix-induced autologous chondrocyte implantation (MACI) process was approved by the FDA in 2016. With this process, a small amount of health cartilage is removed from a patient's knee. Cells called chondrocytes are removed from the sample and seeded in a petri dish onto a scaffold made of biodegradable collagen, creating a living mesh which is inserted back into the damaged area of the patient's knee. This procedure is far less invasive than a full knee replacement. Vericel reported that the number of surgeons in the U.S. trained to perform MACI doubled from 2017 to 2018, reaching 900.

The next big thing in tissue replacement is three-dimensional (3D) printers to fabricate a variety of shapes made of living tissue, including tubes suitable for blood vessels, cartilage for use in human joints and patches of skin and muscle. The process takes stem cells harvested from a patient and treats them in the lab to stimulate multiplication, creating cell aggregates. The resulting "bioink" is loaded in cartridges shaped like syringes with extrusion nozzles. Software directs the printer to extrude the bioink in a precise pattern of layers interspersed with hydrogel (a gelatinous water-based substance) used to mold the cells into the desired shape. The printed tissue is then allowed to grow into mature cells suitable for research.

Although in its infancy, one San Diego, California firm called Organovo, Inc. (organovo.com) already produces commercial 3D bioprinters for use in research. In early 2014, Organovo launched its first product, slivers of human liver tissue for use in laboratories to test drug toxicity. Physicians and researchers can find out how a patient's liver will respond to different treatments before going to the expense of clinical trials. As of 2017, the firm was generating kidney tissue, and in 2018 it announced the ability to create functional human liver tissue. In addition to Organovo, industry analysts estimate that 80 teams at research institutions and biotechnology firms are working on the concept. Ultimately, it is hoped that 3D bioprinting will be able to produce viable replacement organs.

Revivicor (www.revivicor.com), a division of United Therapeutics, is working to breed pigs with human genes. Organs from these animals may be transplanted into humans with fewer immune system rejection problems. Researchers at the National Heart, Lung and Blood Institute in Bethesda, Maryland have been testing the specialized pig organs in baboons. Revivicor ultimately plans to breed up to 1,000 pigs per year and ship organs rapidly by helicopter.

Companies to Watch in Replacement Tissues, including 3-D Printing of Tissues:

ViaCord (formerly ViaCell, Inc. before its acquisition by PerkinElmer), in Boston, Massachusetts (www.viacord.com), develops therapies using umbilical cord stems. Also, their ViaCord product enables families to preserve their baby's umbilical cord at the time of birth for possible future use in treating over 40 diseases and genetic disorders.

Cytori Therapeutics, in San Diego, California (www.cytori.com), is focused on the use of adult Adipose-Derived Regenerative Cells (ADRCs). Its goal is to apply these cells as therapies for chronic heart failure, burn care, soft tissue injury and sports medicine.

Allevi (formerly BioBots), in Philadelphia, Pennsylvania (allevi3d.com), offers desktop 3-D bioprinters capable of printing hydrogels such as collagen, hyper-elastic bone and conductive tissues.

Aspect Biosystems Ltd. in Vancouver, British Columbia (www.aspectbiosystems.com) is developing a portfolio of 3-D bio-printed human tissues used in predictive pre-clinical models and implantable tissue therapies.

Materialise NV, in Leuven, Belgium (www.materialise.com) offers 3-D printing technology for many industries including health care, for which it designs implants, surgical guides and other medical devices.

> **Internet Research Tip:**
> For an excellent primer on genetics and basic biotechnology techniques, see:
> **National Center for Biotechnology Information**
> www.ncbi.nlm.nih.gov

27) Health Care Robotics

While robotics are revolutionizing the manufacturing, fulfillment and hospitality industries, the next revolution may well be in health care, in terms of both service robots for tasks like cleaning and deliveries to patients' rooms and highly advanced devices in the form of surgical robots and robotic limbs for patients who have lost arms or legs.

One company on the forefront is Parker Hannifin Corp. which has a long history of motion and control technologies and systems used in construction, factory equipment and aircraft. Its newest venture is the Indego exoskeleton. Weighing in at about 26 pounds, Indego is a set of motorized braces that help paralyzed or otherwise disabled people walk by supporting, moving and bending their legs. Another firm, ReWalk Robotics, has a similar device called the ReWalk Personal 6.0.

Meanwhile, Johns Hopkins University is working on robotic arms that have 26 joints, can lift up to 45 pounds and are controlled by the wearer's mind. In order to communicate with the devices, patients will likely require surgery to remap nerve endings to allow brain signals to reach the prosthetics. For more on the project, see www.jhuapl.edu/prosthetics.

The International Federation of Robotics (IFR) reported that medical service robot sales reached $5.3 billion in 2019 (up 28% from 2018) and forecasted that sales would reach $11.3 billion by 2022. It states that the most important of these devices are used in robot-assisted surgery and other patient therapies.

Robotic surgery has also become common, especially in minimally-invasive procedures. The technology utilizes cameras and mechanical arms wielding surgical instruments controlled by a human surgeon, typically via a small incision. The surgeon uses a console which displays images from the camera in high-definition, magnified, 3-D view. For example, the da Vinci Surgical System (www.davincisurgery.com) is used in a variety of procedures to treat cardiac, colorectal, gynecological, head and neck, thoracic and urological problems.

28) Patients' Genetic Profiles Plummet in Price as DNA Sequencing Technologies Advance

Scientists now believe that nearly all diseases have at least some genetic component. For example, some people have a genetic predisposition for breast cancer or heart disease. The understanding of human genetics is hoped to lead to breakthroughs in therapies for many illnesses. Organizations worldwide are experimenting with personalized drugs that are designed to provide appropriate therapies based on a patient's personal genetic makeup or their lack of specific genes.

The DNA sequencing (genetic testing) of the genes within a patient is the process of determining the order of DNA nucleotides, or bases, in the genome—that is, the entire DNA makeup of the patient. The nucleotides are described on the order of A, C, G and T. The human genome consists of about 3 billion of these genetic letters. Once the genome has been sequenced, much work remains to be done for fully understanding human genetics. Scientists must analyze and translate the strings of A, C, G and T into usable knowledge, which requires sophisticated analytical software.

China's Sichuan University in Chengdu is organizing an ambitious plan to decode the genetic makeup of at least 1 million people. A similar effort in the U.S. is being headed by Regeneron Pharmaceuticals, Inc., and funded by Abbvie, Inc., Alnylam Pharmaceuticals, Inc., AstraZeneca PLC, Biogen, Inc. and Pfizer, Inc. Each company is paying Regeneron $10 million to sequence the genes of 500,000 people. Saudi Arabia, the U.K. and Qatar are also collecting and analyzing data, but on a smaller scale.

DNA sequencing was first achieved in 2001 at a cost of about $100 million per genome (one patient's entire genetic makeup). As of 2019, prices had fallen to between $200 and $1,500, depending upon the extent of the sequence provided. Costs may continue to drop. In addition, some companies offer testing of a small, select group of genes within a patient at very modest prices— typically less than $100. The genome sequencing market is led by Illumina, Inc., a San Diego, California-based company. Competitors include PierianDX (which acquired Tute Genomics in late 2016), Thermo Fisher Scientific, Complete Genomics and BGI, formerly the Beijing Genomics Institute.

The scientific community's improving knowledge of genes and the role they play in disease is leading to several different tracks for improved treatment results. One track is to profile a patient's genetic makeup for a better understanding of a) which drugs a patient may respond to effectively, and b) whether certain defective genes reside in a patient and are causing a patient's disease or illness.

For example, the immunotherapy Keytruda is extremely effective for certain cancer patients who match the required genetic profile. Yet another application of genetic profiling is to study how a patient is able to metabolize medication, which could help significantly when deciding upon proper dosage. Since today's widely used drugs often produce desired results in only about 50% of patients who receive them, the use of specific medications based on a patient's genetic profile could greatly boost treatment results while cutting costs. Each year, by one count, 2.2 million Americans suffer side effects from prescription drugs. Of those, more than 100,000 die, making adverse drug reaction a leading cause of death in the U.S. A Journal of the American Medical Association study states that the annual cost of treating these drug reactions totals $4 billion each year.

Drugs that target the genetic origins of tumors may offer more effective, longer-lasting and far less toxic alternatives to conventional chemotherapy and radiation. In other cases, biotech drugs, used in combination with surgery or chemotherapy, can reduce the chance of a cancer recurrence. One of the most noted drugs that target specific genetic action is Herceptin, a monoclonal antibody that was developed by Genentech. Approved by the FDA in 1998, Herceptin, when used in conjunction with chemotherapy, shows great promise in significantly reducing breast cancer for certain patients who are known to "overexpress" the HER2 protein (that is, there is an excess of HER2-related protein on tumor cell surfaces, or there is an excess of the HER2 gene itself). A simple test is used to determine if this gene is present in the patient. Herceptin, which works by blocking genetic signals, thus preventing the growth of cancerous cells, may show potential in treating other types of cancer, such as ovarian, pancreatic or prostate cancer.

Another genetic test is marketed by Exact Sciences, formerly Genomic Health, (www.exactsciences.com). Its Oncotype DX test provides breast cancer patients with an assessment of the likelihood of the recurrence of their cancer based on the expression of 21 different genes in a tumor. The test enables patients to evaluate the results they may expect from post-operative therapies such as Tamoxifen or chemotherapy. As of mid-2020, more than 1 million patients had been tested worldwide. The firm also offers Cologuard test for colon cancer. Such tests may be standard preventive treatment in coming decades.

The industry has moved onto what is commonly referred to as "Next Generation" sequencing of DNA. That is, highly advanced hardware and software that can determine the DNA of a human sample with extremely rapid output and low cost. This means that scientists worldwide will be able to conduct massive studies of human or other animal genetics at relatively affordable cost compared to the billions of dollars that the first genomic studies required.

A relatively recent entry to the field of biotechnology is epigenetics, a branch of biology focused on gene "silencers," which is used in a technique called "antisense." Scientists involved in epigenetics are studying the function within a gene that regulates whether that gene is operating at full capacity or is toned down to a lower level. The level of operation of a given gene may lead to a higher risk of disease, such as certain types of cancer. Epigenetics may be very effective in combatting abnormal gene expressions that cause cancer. In early 2013, the FDA approved a drug called Kynamro, created by Isis Pharmaceuticals and marketed by Sanofi's Genzyme. Kynamro uses antisense to shut off genes that cause abnormally high blood pressure and heart attacks in young people less than 30 years of age. Today, there are a number of epigenetic drugs on the market including Azacitidine, Decitabine, Vorinostat, Romidepsin and Ruxolitnub.

Pharmacy benefit managers (PBMs) are organizations that provide administrative services in processing and analyzing prescription claims for pharmacy benefit and coverage programs. Some PBMs are selling services that test patients for genetic variations that might indicate which drugs would be more effective for individual patients. Express Scripts (formerly Medco Health Solutions, Inc.) for example, is a PBM and pharmacy mail order business that is selling tests for patients who take drugs such as the blood thinner warfarin and breast cancer treatment Tamoxifen. CVS Caremark partners with Generation Health, Inc. to offer a similar testing service. PBMs are selling their services to employers who are willing to invest in them for improved health outcomes and lower prescription costs. If personally-tailored prescriptions become a widespread reality, billions of dollars each year could be saved as patients take only those drugs which will do them some good and avoid those which could do them harm.

Meanwhile, the American Society of Clinical Oncology (ASCO) was running a Stage II clinical trial in mid-2021 called TAPUR that offers cancer patients a genetic test and then selects drugs that appear to be a good match, even if that drug was developed to treat a different kind of malignancy. In a similar vein, the U.S. National Cancer Institute has a trial named MATCH which sends tumor biopsies to gene-testing laboratories to scan for more than 4,000 possible variants of 143 pertinent genes.

29) Advances for Cancer Patients in Chemotherapy and Radiation, Including Proton Beams and IMRT

Radiation therapy is commonly used in the treatment of cancerous tumors. This technology has been moving toward greater precision in irradiating tumors. Modern x-ray radiation equipment (photon radiation) can focus on and attack tumors while doing less damage to surrounding tissue than previous technologies. State-of-the-art radiation techniques of today involve several different formats. Specific formats have been found to be most effective for specific cancers.

IMRT (Intensity Modulated Radiation Therapy): is a radiation technology that enables the technician to apply narrowly focused radiation directly toward cancerous tumors. IMRT helps to limit the amount of damage to surrounding tissues. The process includes using multiple beams (typically from 7 to 12) aimed at the tumor from various directions. The beams meet at the tumor to administer the desired dosage. Breaking the dose down into multiple beams lessens the level of radiation that healthy tissues are exposed to. The point at which the beams join can be shaped to conform to the exact size, shape and location of the tumor, thus further sparing healthy tissue. Advanced imaging, such as CT, is used to provide precise guidance to the tumor's location.

An important breakthrough in radiation therapy is the ability to provide "respiratory gating," which enables the radiation equipment to accurately track the radiation target while allowing for the natural body motion caused by breathing in and out. This technology was pioneered by Varian.

An enhancement to IMRT is Varian's RapidArc VMAT (Volumetric Modulated Arc Therapy). This technology is able to deliver a radiation dose in a 360-degree rotation that is more targeted in much less time than previous units. Treatments that might take five minutes or more with older technologies can be reduced to two minutes.

Image Guided Radiation Therapy (IGRT): takes advantage of sophisticated imaging technologies in order to best target radiation therapy. Prostate cancer is often treated with IGRT. To treat that disease, tiny metal markers are implanted in the prostate using an outpatient procedure. The IGRT equipment is then able to locate the position of the prostate exactly by determining the location of the markers in real time. Varian is a leading manufacturer of IGRT equipment, as is Accuray, Inc., which makes the TomoTherapy system. The technology is similar to IMRT, but better enables radiation technicians to use ultrasound, CT or X-ray images to line up the radiation beam with the intended target.

Brachytherapy: is a method of internal radiation therapy whereby tiny containers of radioactive material, sometimes referred to as "seeds," are inserted directly in contact with tissue that is afflicted with cancerous tumors. It is a common method of treating prostate cancer and is sometimes used for the treatment of breast, cervical and other cancers.

The latest innovation in this field is called HDR, or high dose rate brachytherapy. In this instance, small radioactive seeds are attached to the end of flexible rods and guided into very specific, imaging-defined locations within the cancerous area. The rods are left in-place for a calculated number of seconds and then removed. This may be repeated a few times over a series of days or weeks. This method exposes the cancer to a very high dose of radiation, and the results have been excellent in many cases. Leaders in this therapy include the UCLA Medical Center, the University of San Francisco Medical Center and Sloan Kettering.

The *Gamma Knife* is a unique type of radiation therapy with tissue-sparing properties. It involves focusing low-dose gamma radiation on a tumor, while exposing only a small amount of healthy, nearby tissue to radiation. It is often used to treat certain brain cancers.

Patient immobilization is an advancing technology. The point is to hold vital parts of the patient as still as possible so that the radiation beam affects only the desired targets. However, since patients must breathe during treatment, some movement of the body is always going to occur, and this can have an effect on radiation of areas such as the lungs. New technologies enable the radiation beam to allow for and synchronize with a patient's breathing rhythm.

PBRT, or Proton Beam Radiation Therapy is the use of a highly advanced technology to deliver external beam radiation therapy (EBRT) to a patient in order to kill cancerous cells and shrink tumors. While traditional radiation therapies rely on photons delivered by X-rays or gamma rays, Proton Beam Radiation Therapy relies on a particle accelerator to create and deliver protons. Protons are high-energy particles that carry a charge. By varying the velocity of the particles at the time that they enter the body, physicists are able to control the exact spot within the body where the radiation is released. The higher the velocity, the deeper within the body the radiation begins to take effect.

With traditional radiation (based on photons rather than protons), there is a significant entry dose of radiation that can be harmful to healthy tissues. Proton beam therapy has virtually no entry dose or exit dose, plus the ability to better focus the radiation on the exact place of the tumor, significantly cutting down on side effects and damage to surrounding tissues.

In the U.S., centers are in place at locations including Loma Linda (California) University Medical Center, which is considered a pioneer in applying this technology; Massachusetts General Hospital in Boston, Massachusetts; The University of Florida Proton Therapy Institute in Jacksonville, Florida; the M.D. Anderson Cancer Center in Houston, Texas; and the ProCure Proton Therapy Center in Oklahoma City, Oklahoma. As of mid-2018, there were 28 centers in the U.S., with another 23 centers under construction or planning. PBRT is in wide use or under planning in dozens of locations outside the U.S. including Japan, Germany and Korea. Recent new sites under planning or construction include Argentina, Australia, Singapore, Saudi Arabia and Thailand.

The Loma Linda, California facility began operations in 1990. It was the only hospital-based proton radiation center in the U.S. until 2003. The center has treated nearly 50 different types of cancers.

PBRT may eventually be in very wide use worldwide. Its tissue sparing nature makes it ideal for eliminating side effects and for treating tumors in challenging locations, such as the eye and brain, while it is an extremely popular way to treat prostate cancer. It may be the best possible way to treat small children who have cancer, in order to spare healthy surrounding tissues near the cancer so that young bodies can continue to grow successfully. And, it has potential for the treatment of non-cancerous conditions such as macular degeneration.

Major obstacles facing the development of new proton beam facilities include the immense investment required, the complexity of the accelerator and other equipment, the need to acquire and train specialized staff, and the need to educate referring physicians about this revolutionary technology and its high success rate. The high costs of proton facilities and proton treatments have caused considerable controversy. Many private insurers in the U.S. are refusing to pay higher rates for PBRT than they pay for more standard means of radiation. Eventually, advances in design and technology may make it easier and less costly to establish proton centers. Today's proton units typically have four treatment rooms.

Newer, smaller and much cheaper proton beam facilities with a single treatment room, and much less adjoining space needed for equipment, are opening, equipped with systems from Mevion Medical Systems, Inc. Its MEVION S250 Proton Therapy System is in use at the S. Lee Kling Center for Proton Therapy at the Siteman Cancer Center at Barnes-Jewish Hospital and Washington University School of Medicine in St. Louis, Missouri. While the older, larger facilities cost between $100 million and $200 million to build, the Mevion system and others like it cost between $25 million and $30 million. Meanwhile, at Loma Linda and elsewhere, highly automated treatment rooms are in use that increase the number of patients that proton centers are able to handle each day, thus amortizing a proton center's capital cost over a much wider base of patients.

Many insurers stopped covering proton beam treatment for prostate cancer treatment. The newer, less expensive facilities may help those firms to reinstate coverage.

For additional information, see The National Association for Proton Therapy, www.proton-therapy.org. Also, see the web site of Loma Linda University Medical Center's proton unit, www.protons.com.

Treating Cancer with Electricity: Another new high-tech tool for treating certain types of cancer is a short burst of electricity directed at the tumor. This process, called electroporation, involves treating the tumor with chemotherapy and then sending short electrical pulses into the tumor with a needle electrode. The electrical pulse allows the tumor to become more porous and thus more susceptible to the chemotherapeutic drugs.

Inovio Biomedical, www.inovio.com, is a leading company in the new field of electroporation therapy. Inovio has clinical trials ongoing for the use of its technology in the treatment of a wide variety of cancers, including breast, head and neck and melanoma.

Radio Frequency Ablation (RFA): RFA is the use of focused radio waves to produce high levels of heat within tumors in order to kill cancer. It is typically applied via needles that have been placed in the tumor, using ultrasound or other imaging techniques to insure correct placement. It is often used in the treatment of cancer of the kidney, and has applications in the treatment of tumors found in the lung, liver, bone, breast and adrenal system.

Carbon Ion Therapy: Already in use in Europe and Asia, carbon ion therapy is a relatively new treatment that promises to have a higher relative effectiveness and linear energy transfer than protons or photons when used to destroy malignant cells. The University of Colorado is working to build a $300 million carbon ion therapy center, the first in the U.S. The technology was pioneered in Japan at the National Institute of Radiological Sciences, and can be utilized in treating human as well as animal cancers.

High-Intensity Focused Ultrasound (HIFU) is an FDA-approved, minimally-invasive procedure typically used for the treatment of prostate cancer. It seeks to destroy malignant cells through the delivery of precisely focused sound waves. Cells are targeted using MRI and

confirmed with traditional ultrasound. The sound waves that are aimed at the prostate tissue rapidly increase tissue temperature, hopefully destroying only the cancerous lesions and protecting the healthy surrounding tissue. HIFU system manufacturers include EDAP TMS, Sonacare Medical, Philips Healthcare, Shenzhen Wikkon and Promedica Bioelectronics. HIFU is also utilized in cosmetic procedures to tighten skin tissue.

Improvements in Chemotherapy: Chemotherapy continues to reduce the need for surgical excision of cancers and enable the treatment of cancers that are considered inoperable. Improvements in chemotherapy continue to reduce the number and severity of side effects and the length of treatment, boosting a shift from inpatient to outpatient care. For example, scientists in the Netherlands at the University of Leiden and the University of Utrecht developed new compounds for platinum-based chemotherapy that could alleviate side effects altogether. Although some cancers show resistance to chemotherapy, researchers have recently discovered a unique gene that causes resistance, so compounds may be added to chemotherapy that will block the gene's ability to resist. In many cases, chemotherapy is combined with radiation, other drugs and/or surgery.

30) Better Imaging, including MRI, PET and 320-Slice CT, Creates Advances in Detection

Today, improved diagnostic imaging, diagnostic catheterization and better monitoring procedures have made earlier detection of many diseases possible and reduced the need for exploratory surgery. Over the long-term, highly advanced new imaging systems, eventually utilizing molecular diagnostics, will enable levels of early intervention undreamed of in the past.

Magnetic resonance imaging (MRI) uses a combination of radio waves and a strong magnetic field to gauge the behavior of hydrogen atoms in water molecules within the body. Improvements in hardware and software have made MRI scans faster and more thorough than before. Ultra-fast MRI has many important clinical applications. Recent studies show that MRI may be the best method for determining the extent of a patient's recovery after a heart attack. Rapid-imaging MRI machines also expedite the diagnosis and treatment of heart conditions and strokes, thus reducing the time and money needed to scan the patient.

However, this technology has been extremely expensive, with equipment costs alone running from $1 million to $2 million. Until recently, very heavy shielding was needed to encapsulate the imaging room, which necessitated special construction of new facilities or very costly reinforcement of older building space. Progress in shielding technology and facility design, combined with more cost-effective mid-field and low-field MRI, has dramatically lowered the cost of most new installations. Some of these lighter, less powerful devices can be used in mobile settings, which makes MRI available in rural areas that could never have justified the expense of permanent installations. Low-field MRI technology has also enabled the development of open-MRI devices, which do not require a patient to be completely surrounded by a tunnel-shaped magnet. Open MRIs reduce patient anxiety and claustrophobia. In addition, the lower intensity of the magnetic field allows technicians, physicians and even family members to be present in the room at the time of the test, if the patient prefers.

Whole-body MRI can be useful for checking the entire skeleton or multiple parts of the body for metastasis of cancer. Although not part of routine patient care in the U.S., many health manufacturers such as Siemens, General Electric and Philips, are making scanners with full-body capability. The technology utilizes a gliding table that moves the patient smoothly enough to keep images clear. Related software takes five to six sets of images and weaves them together for a complete picture. The process generally takes about 20 to 45 minutes, the same amount of time used in traditional MRI.

Magnetoencephalography (MEG) is a newer technology derived from both MRI and electroencephalography (EEG). Like EEG, MEG registers brain patterns, but whereas EEG measures electrical activity in the brain, MEG measures magnetic waves, primarily in the cerebral cortex of the brain. Computer enhancement of the generated data is improving EEG as a diagnostic tool. Recent refinements in EEG technology make it possible to use this device to help diagnose various forms of depression and schizophrenia.

Computed tomography (also known as a CT scan or CAT scan) uses a circular pattern of x-rays to produce high-resolution, cross-sectional images, which can help precisely locate tumors, clots, narrowed arteries and aneurysms. Because CT essentially creates images of distinct slices of the body, it can be referred to as multi-slice or multi-row detector imaging. CT can produce three-dimensional images, which are beneficial in reconstructive surgery. However, CT machines cost between $1.5 million and $2 million or more for 64-slice technology. The advanced electronics enabling 64-slice CT (compared to 8- and 16-slice CT) are an immense breakthrough in the evolution of imaging. For example, 64-slice CT can show a higher level of detail in arteries than angiography, which is the traditional method of looking for arterial blockage and plaque when checking cardiovascular health. In fact, 64-slice CT enables the user to see cross-sections of arteries, including the walls. And, this advanced CT can provide vastly improved images of beating hearts, including the interior. (About 1.5 million U.S. patients undergo angiograms yearly. A CT scan does not bring the risk of arterial puncture associated with angiography's wire-guided probes.) 64-slice CT is extremely useful for early detection of heart disease as a preventive measure, and for guiding surgeons during surgery.

There is some concern about the exposure of patients to radiation during CT scans. In response, General Electric Healthcare developed a device that reduces radiation during cardiac CT scans by up to 70%. The system is called SnapShot Pulse, and it pulses with a patient's heartbeat, automatically turning the X-ray on and off at desired times during the heart rate cycle, which reduces the patient's radiation exposure time.

The latest advance is the 320-slice CT (similar to but more powerful than recently-introduced 256-slice CTs), which has the ability to provide astonishing levels of image resolution. Both 256-slice and 320-slice CTs can scan areas as large as 6.3 inches, wide enough to capture almost all human organs. Each scan takes one second or less, compared to the 64-slice CT which takes up to 10 seconds for a scan of an area of 1.3 inches. In addition, the device measures subtle changes in blood flow or minute blockages forming in blood vessels in the heart and brain. The first 320-slice CT scanner in North America was installed at The Johns Hopkins Hospital in late 2007. There are 320-slice scanners installed around the world, including one in Chennai, India. A second-generation 320-detector row CT scanner requires less time and exposes patients to less radiation. Extremely fast scans will mean that large numbers of patients can be processed daily with one of these expensive machines. The cost of scans may drop proportionately.

As with MRIs, there has recently been some interest in whole-body CT scans. Many independent imaging centers have been offering such scans to the public at reasonable cost. However, there is concern among some physicians that whole-body CTs often lead to a large number of questionable findings, or false positives, and that such scans may be of little value.

Two other imaging machines, single photon emission computed tomography (SPECT) and positron emission tomography (PET), use forms of radioisotope imaging to detect and study conditions such as stroke, epilepsy, schizophrenia and Parkinson's and Alzheimer's diseases. PET is a major research tool for understanding the human brain, and has a substantial indirect impact on medical and surgical practices.

PET offers a unique advantage in that it can offer functional imaging. That is, it can show how an area of the body is functioning and responding. Because it is based on safe, short-lived radioactive substances that are injected into the body, PET enables physicians to see metabolic activity. For example, in addition to imaging of brain activity, PET can be used to determine how cancerous tumors react to certain drugs. The FDA is cooperating with the National Cancer Institute to determine whether PET should be used in clinical trials of new cancer treatments to determine whether tumors are responding to therapies.

Other improvements in x-ray technology include digital subtractive angiography (DSA). DSA involves the use of enhanced x-rays to see blood vessels and arteries, while bones and soft tissues are blotted out of the image. It can clearly image aneurysms and can be used in angioplasty, a procedure that reduces the need for heart bypass surgery. However, as advanced CT becomes more widely accepted, DSA may become irrelevant.

Mammography is another x-ray technology that has been refined over the years. While traditional mammography with film offers sufficient x-ray images of older women's breasts, the film lacks the versatility of gray values that radiologists need to interpret mammograms from younger women. A new digital x-ray sensitive camera produces digital images on a computer screen with a higher dynamic range of gray values. Modern mammography equipment gives detailed and precise images of breast tissue, resulting in high detection levels of very small malignant tumors. The sooner a malignancy is discovered, the better the prognosis is for excision and follow-up treatment success. Advanced mammography techniques reduce the chance for misdiagnoses, the amount of radiation needed to develop the image and the time spent in the exam room.

Another improved imaging technique, sonography, uses ultrasound to create images of internal body tissues and fetuses. Ultrasound is a cheaper alternative to many other imaging techniques, and results are available almost immediately. This scanning technique is recommended for pregnant women, since the sound waves apparently cause no harm to human tissue. Refinements in sonography have led to excellent prenatal images, which can be used to detect even small abnormalities in a fetus. Sonography is also being used in other imaging applications. For example, a recent ultrasound device is capable of displaying a three-dimensional image of organs such as the heart. Ultrasound in real time has even become sensitive enough to show blood flow. Ultrasound units are common in all but the very smallest hospitals.

New ultrasound diagnostic devices are now on the market that are small enough to carry and provide doctors with a comprehensive picture of a patient's major organs and possible problems. These devices, which resemble the handheld scanners used on *Star Trek*, use ultrasonic waves to map out the interior features of a patient and then enhance them to provide an accurate and easy-to-read picture. Not only can doctors spot heart murmurs and breathing abnormalities with a simple inspection, but they can also spot objects like kidney stones and gallstones, or the presence of an abnormal amount of fluid surrounding an organ. The machines could potentially save millions in radiology and other diagnostic bills. In addition, these devices will be carried on ambulances or even on a doctor's person, allowing diagnostics to be performed wherever they are needed. The popular SonoSite M-Turbo is the size of a small laptop computer. A startup called the Butterfly Network (www.butterflynetinc.com) invested $100 million to develop a hand-held ultrasound scanner in which ultrasound emitters are etched directly onto a semiconductor chip. The compact, versatile unit, called Butterfly iQ, costs a few hundred dollars and delivers to create 3-D images in real time. It was introduced in the U.S. in 2018, and received licensing approval in the UK, Europe, Australia and New Zealand in 2019.

Ultrasound may take a giant leap forward with the advent of photoacoustic tomography, which combines sound waves with optics. Pulses of laser light are projected onto tissue which infinitesimally raises the tissue's temperature. The rise in temperature causes the tissue to expand slightly, and in the process emitting sound waves in the ultrasonic range. Sensors on the patient's skin pick up the waves which are analyzed and triangulated by computer. The resulting image may be as detailed as those derived by MRI or CT scans, but use equipment the size of an ultrasound scanner.

Another exciting monitoring technique involves measuring the levels of the chemical creatine in the heart, which indicate the extent of muscle damage caused by a heart attack. Using a combination of MRI and MRS (magnetic resonance spectroscopy), this noninvasive method allows doctors to pinpoint injured heart tissue by measuring depleted levels of creatine in areas of the heart that were difficult to view using older imaging techniques.

Some patients even carry monitoring equipment on or in their bodies for long-term diagnostic purposes relating to biochemical balances, brain and sleep disorders, heart and vascular diseases and metabolic problems. More accurate, easy-to-use equipment has been introduced. For example, Medtronic has released an implantable heart monitoring device the size of three sticks of gum. Released under the company's Reveal brand, the device can detect brief heart stoppages or other abnormalities and report them to a support network.

Light diagnostic devices have also been showing up to diagnose certain forms of cancer. Similar to spectroscopy, which has been used to analyze chemical compositions for decades, these small diagnostic devices detect cancer by finding abnormalities in the body's reaction to light. In one instance, doctors at the University of Texas at Austin found that cervical cancer could be detected using a small ultraviolet light shown on the cervix. Precancerous cells are distinctly more fluorescent than normal cells. A preliminary study showed that the technique was 50% more accurate than a PAP smear and microscope examination, reducing the need to perform further diagnostic biopsies on healthy women. In another instance of light diagnostics, researchers at the University of California, Irvine found that infrared light could assist in finding breast cancer.

SPOTLIGHT: PSMA PET Scans

A breakthrough for prostate cancer patients is the Prostate-Specific Membrane Antigen (PSMA) scan in which patients are injected with a radioactive isotope called Gallium (Ga 68). The isotope quickly finds and clings to malignant cells which "light up" in PET scan images, making cancer detection possible before significant tumors develop. Even more exciting is the possibility in the future to bind radiation to the isotope, thereby killing malignant cells as they are detected. As of mid-2019, PSMA PET scans were in clinical trials in several U.S. locations and in Europe, Asia and Australia.

31) Artificial Intelligence (AI), Deep Learning and Machine Learning Advance into Commercial Applications, Including Health Care and Robotics

While the practical definition and ultimate capabilities of AI are debated, industry has put AI to work and continues to invest very heavily in advanced development. Today, AI has synergies with many highly advanced technologies such as virtual reality, factory automation, robotics, self-driving cars, speech recognition and predictive analytics.

One of the more promising advancements is called "deep learning." Google spent nearly $600 million to acquire UK-based DeepMind, an intensive learning research group. Deep learning is sometimes referred to in conjunction with phrases such as "machine learning" and "neural networking." The main point is that software can be trained by being constantly fed data, queried as to its meaning, and receiving feedback to its responses. It is essentially training a machine to respond correctly to data of a given nature or to data within a given set of circumstances.

The most compelling opportunities for the development and use of artificial intelligence software may be in engineering/research, investment analysis and, especially, health care. Simply put, health care is one of the world's largest and fastest-growing industries, and virtually all of the government and private health initiatives that pay for health care are desperately seeking ways to improve patient care outcomes, cut billing fraud, create operating efficiencies and generally slow the growth of costs overall.

Google and U.S. hospital chain HCA Healthcare, Inc. signed a deal in May 2021 to develop algorithms that will analyze data from digital health care records for 32 million patients. The goal is to improve operating efficiency and promote better medical efficacy. The technology may boost patient monitoring and assist medical personnel in making treatment decisions. Google also signed a similar deal with the Mayo Clinic

IBM created a business unit called Watson Health, based on its advanced "Watson" supercomputing-artificial intelligence hardware/software technology, combined with massive health care database firms that it acquired. In early 2016, IBM announced the acquisition of Truven Health Analytics, Inc. for $2.6 billion, for the Watson Health unit. Nonetheless, technology firms have found that AI faces multiple challenges in analyzing complicated medical conditions in a manner that can improve treatments and outcomes.

By some estimates, the amount of digital health care data doubles every 60 days. One of the first commercial applications of AI to medical equipment to be approved by the FDA was the Acumen Hypotension Prediction Index. This system utilizes machine learning based to alert doctors in real time to the probability that a patient's blood pressure might plummet. It is applicable to patients in life-threatening situations, such as those that doctors are attempting to stabilize after surgery or a trauma. Likewise, AI has tremendous promise for enhancing the ability of ambulance and emergency room personnel to instantly diagnose patient conditions and suggest the best possible treatment—even before the patient arrives at the hospital.

Elsewhere, demand is growing for advanced data tools in factories in order to monitor operations and equipment performance. This will increase efficiency and speed as well as reduce waste. According to some analysts, global manufacturers are expected to increase spending on data management and analytics to $20 billion by 2026, up from approximately $5 billion in 2020.

Chapter 2

HEALTH CARE STATISTICS

Including Medicare & Medicaid

I. Health Care Industry Overview

U.S. Health Care Industry Statistics and Market Size Overview

	Amount	Units	Year	Source
Expenditures				
National Health Care Expenditures	4,014.2	Bil. US$	2020*	CMS
In 2028	6,192.5	Bil. US$	2028*	CMS
National Health Care Expenditures per Capita	12,118	US$	2020*	CMS
National Health Care Expenditures as a Percentage of GDP	18.0	%	2020*	CMS
National Health Care Expenditures by Type:				
Hospital Care	1,316.4	Bil. US$	2020*	CMS
Physician & Clinical Services	794.4	Bil. US$	2020*	CMS
Dental Services	148.3	Bil. US$	2020*	CMS
Nursing Home and Home Health Care	183.2	Bil. US$	2020*	CMS
Prescription Drugs & Medical Products	493.9	Bil. US$	2020*	CMS
Research, Structures & Equipment Investments	190.7	Bil. US$	2020*	CMS
Total Health Care Industry Employment	16.0	Million	Jun-21	BLS
Aging				
U.S. Population Less Than 65 Years of Age	276.5	Million	2020*	WFB
In 2030	282.0	Million	2030*	Census
In 2060	309.8	Million	2060*	Census
U.S. Population Age 65 Years & Older	56.0	Million	2020*	WFB
In 2030	73.1	Million	2030*	Census
In 2060	94.6	Million	2060*	Census
Medicare/Medicaid				
National Health Expenditures from Medicare	796.6	Bil. US$	2019*	CMS
National Health Expenditures from Medicaid	672.7	Bil. US$	2020*	CMS
Medicare Enrollment	62.6	Million	2020*	CMS
Hospital Insurance (HI)	62.2	Million	2020*	CMS
Supplementary Medical Insurance (SMI)	57.3	Million	2020*	CMS
Part D	48.8	Million	2020*	CMS
Medicaid Enrollment	76.7	Million	2020*	CMS
Vital Statistics				
U.S. Fertility Rate	1.84	Children Born/Woman	2020*	WFB
U.S. Birth Rate	12.4	Births/1,000 Pop.	2020*	WFB
U.S. Infant Mortality Rate	5.22	Deaths/1,000 Live Births	2021	WFB
U.S. Life Expectancy at Birth	80.43	Years	2021	WFB
U.S. Death Rate	8.35	Deaths/1,000 Pop.	2021	WFB
Obesity				
Obesity, All Adults 20 & Older[1]	31.7	%	2018	CDC
Diabetes				
Diagnosed Diabetes, Adults 18 & Older	10.5	%	2018	ADA
Diagnosed Diabetes, Adults 65 & Older	26.8	%	2018	ADA
Hospitals				
Number of U.S. Registered[2] Hospitals	6,090		2021	AHA
Staffed Beds in All U.S. Registered[2] Hospitals	919,559		2021	AHA
Uninsured				
Number of People Without Health Insurance for the Entire Year	28.0	Million	2020*	Census
Percent of Population	8.6	%	2020*	Census

* Estimate, where appropriate includes impact of Affordable Care Act but may not include the effect of the Coronavirus..

BLS = U.S. Bureau of Labor Statistics; CMS = U.S. Ctrs. for Medicare & Medicaid Services; WFB = CIA World Fact Book; Census = U.S. Census Bureau; CDC = U.S. Ctrs. for Disease Control & Prevention; ADA = American Diabetes Association; AHA = American Hospital Association.

[1] Age-adjusted using the projected 2000 U.S. population as the standard population and four age groups.

[2] Registered hospitals are those hospitals that meet the AHA's criteria for registration as a hospital facility and include AHA member and nonmember hospitals. For a complete listing of the criteria used for registration, please see www.aha.org.

Source: Plunkett Research, Ltd.

Global Health Statistics, 2014-2020*

Estimated Global Health Care Expenditures	Amount	Units	Year	Source
Total	10.4	Trillion$	2020	PRE
% of GDP	11.8	%	2020	PRE
Per Capita	1,375	US$	2020	PRE

Health Care Expenditures	(As a % of Total GDP)				
	2015	2016	2017	2018	Source
United States	16.84%	17.20%	17.06%	16.90%	TWB
Euro Area	10.20%	10.19%	10.14%	10.10%	TWB
OECD Members	12.38%	12.58%	12.51%	12.50%	TWB
Latin America & Caribbean	7.74%	7.72%	8.02%	7.90%	TWB
Middle East & North Africa	5.60%	5.77%	5.69%	5.80%	TWB
South Asia	3.51%	3.45%	3.46%	3.50%	TWB
Sub-Saharan Africa	5.14%	5.09%	5.12%	5.10%	TWB
East Asia & Pacific	6.49%	6.61%	6.64%	6.70%	TWB
World	**9.54%**	**9.90%**	**10.02%**	**9.90%**	TWB

Health expenditures per capita, PPP	(In Constant 2011 PPP $)				
	2015	2016	2017	2018	Source
United States	9,538.07	9,941.35	10,246.14	10,623.80	TWB
Euro Area	4,171.77	4,333.95	4,545.28	4,699.90	TWB
OECD Members	4,750.89	4,926.53	5,109.36	5,265.70	TWB
Latin America & Caribbean	1,178.24	1,137.68	1,191.21	1,228.20	TWB
Middle East & North Africa	1,105.44	1,336.83	1,328.67	1,336.40	TWB
South Asia	200.59	211.68	229.69	249.00	TWB
Sub-Saharan Africa	198.34	198.77	199.86	205.40	TWB
East Asia & Pacific	916.38	968.42	1,035.71	1,103.80	TWB
World	**1,295.73**	**1,348.88**	**1,408.76**	**1,459.30**	TWB

Life Expectancy at Birth	(In years)					
	1980	1990	2000	2018	2019	Source
United States	78.74	78.74	78.84	78.54	78.80	TWB
Euro Area	81.23	81.51	81.93	82.06	82.00	TWB
OECD Members	79.72	79.90	80.16	81.01	80.20	TWB
Latin America & Caribbean	74.69	74.91	75.13	75.44	75.50	TWB
Middle East & North Africa	72.68	72.88	73.09	74.09	74.30	TWB
South Asia	67.55	67.88	68.18	69.41	69.60	TWB
Sub-Saharan Africa	58.28	58.88	59.44	61.73	61.60	TWB
East Asia & Pacific	74.74	74.92	75.09	76.07	76.30	TWB
World	**71.22**	**71.46**	**71.69**	**72.56**	**72.70**	TWB

Infant Mortality Rate	(Per 1,000 live births)					
	1980	1990	2000	2018	2019	Source
United States	6.00	5.90	5.80	5.60	5.60	TWB
Euro Area	3.31	3.26	3.18	3.02	3.20	TWB
OECD Members	6.69	6.49	6.30	5.81	5.90	TWB
Latin America & Caribbean	16.95	16.36	15.86	14.00	14.00	TWB
Middle East & North Africa	22.00	21.49	21.02	18.30	18.10	TWB
South Asia	45.50	43.70	42.00	34.50	33.10	TWB
Sub-Saharan Africa	60.66	58.63	56.67	52.70	51.70	TWB
East Asia & Pacific	16.37	15.56	14.82	12.50	11.90	TWB
World	**34.70**	**33.60**	**32.40**	**28.90**	**28.20**	TWB

* 2020 estimates may not include the effect of the Coronavirus. Co-operation & Development.
PPP = Purchasing Power Parity, an equalized price for a basket of goods across different markets. OECD = Organisation for Economic
PRE = Plunkett Research Estimates
TWB = The World Bank: World Development Indicators & Global Development Finance, for terms of use see
https://databank.worldbank.org/source/world-development-indicators
Plunkett Research,® Ltd.
www.plunkettresearch.com

Domestic Sales and Sales Abroad, PhRMA Member Companies: 1980–2020

(In Millions of US$)

Year	Domestic Sales	APC	Sales Abroad[1]	APC	Total Sales	APC
2020	307,234.0	1.5%	117,724.0	-6.9%	424,958.0	-1.0%
2019	302,776.4	7.8%	126,394.2	-0.1%	429,170.6	5.4%
2018	280,790.0	24.9%	126,577.1	15.6%	407,367.1	21.8%
2017	224,790.0	3.0%	109,510.6	5.9%	334,399.8	3.9%
2016	218,401.4	7.9%	103,456.8	3.4%	321,858.1	6.4%
2015	202,370.8	13.3%	100,012.5	-6.9%	302,383.3	5.7%
2014	178,645.6	1.6%	107,438.2	0.5%	286,083.9	1.2%
2013	175,759.6	-1.5%	106,880.1	-0.7%	282,639.7	-1.2%
2012	178,437.6	-5.0%	107,677.8	-8.1%	286,115.4	-6.2%
2011	187,870.7	1.7%	117,138.5	9.9%	305,009.2	4.7%
2010	184,660.3	2.0%	106,593.2	12.0%	291,253.5	5.4%
2009	181,116.8	-1.1%	95,162.5	-7.5%	276,279.3	-3.4%
2008	183,167.2	-1.1%	102,842.4	16.6%	286,009.6	4.6%
2007	185,209.2	4.2%	88,213.4	14.8%	273,422.6	7.4%
2006	177,736.3	7.0%	76,870.2	10.0%	254,606.4	7.9%
2005	166,155.5	3.4%	69,881.0	0.1%	236,036.5	2.4%
2004[2]	160,751.0	8.6%	69,806.9	14.6%	230,557.9	10.3%
2003[2]	148,038.6	6.4%	60,914.4	13.4%	208,953.0	8.4%
2002	139,136.4	6.4%	53,697.4	12.1%	192,833.8	8.0%
2001	130,715.9	12.8%	47,886.9	5.9%	178,602.8	10.9%
2000	115,881.8	14.2%	45,199.5	1.6%	161,081.3	10.4%
1999	101,461.8	24.8%	44,496.6	2.7%	145,958.4	17.1%
1998	81,289.2	13.3%	43,320.1	10.8%	124,609.4	12.4%
1997	71,761.9	10.8%	39,086.2	6.1%	110,848.1	9.1%
1996	64,741.4	13.3%	36,838.7	8.7%	101,580.1	11.6%
1995	57,145.5	12.6%	33,893.5	(3)	91,039.0	(3)
1994	50,740.4	4.4%	26,870.7	1.5%	77,611.1	3.4%
1993	48,590.9	1.0%	26,467.3	2.8%	75,058.2	1.7%
1992	48,095.5	8.6%	25,744.2	15.8%	73,839.7	11.0%
1991	44,304.5	15.1%	22,231.1	12.1%	66,535.6	14.1%
1990	38,486.7	17.7%	19,838.3	18.0%	58,325.0	17.8%
1989	32,706.6	14.4%	16,817.9	-4.7%	49,524.5	7.1%
1988	28,582.6	10.4%	17,649.3	17.1%	46,231.9	12.9%
1987	25,879.1	9.4%	15,068.4	15.6%	40,947.5	11.6%
1986	23,658.8	14.1%	13,030.5	19.9%	36,689.3	16.1%
1985	20,742.5	9.0%	10,872.3	4.0%	31,614.8	7.3%
1984	19,026.1	13.2%	10,450.9	0.4%	29,477.0	8.3%
1983	16,805.0	14.0%	10,411.2	-2.4%	27,216.2	7.1%
1982	14,743.9	16.4%	10,667.4	0.1%	25,411.3	9.0%
1981	12,665.0	7.4%	10,658.3	1.4%	23,323.3	4.6%
1980	11,788.6	10.7%	10,515.4	26.9%	22,304.0	17.8%
Average		9.0%		7.1%		8.1%

Notes: Total values may be affected by rounding. APC = Annual Percent Change.

[1]Sales Abroad includes sales generated outside the United States by U.S.-owned PhRMA member companies, and sales generated abroad by the U.S. divisions of foreign-owned PhRMA member companies. Sales generated abroad by the foreign divisions of foreign-owned PhRMA member companies are excluded. Domestic sales, however, includes sales generated within the United States by all PhRMA member companies; [2]Revised in 2007 to reflect updated data; [3]Sales Abroad affected by merger and acquisition activity.

*All Numbers Generated in-house

Source: Pharmaceutical Research and Manufacturers of America (PhRMA), *PhRMA Annual Membership Survey,* 2020

Plunkett Research, Ltd.

www.plunkettresearch.com

Employment in the Health Care Industry, U.S.: 2016-June 2021

(Annual Estimates in Thousands of Employed Workers)

NAICS Code[1]	Industry Sector	2016	2017	2018	2019	2020	Jun-21*
62	Total health care & social assistance	19,103.6	19,573.4	19,943.9	20,412.5	19,512.9	19,993.0
621,2,3	Health care	15,445.3	15,746.2	16,006.8	16,275.2	15,686.2	15,953.7
621	Ambulatory health care services	7,092.4	7,319.1	7,503.0	7,697.2	7,427.0	7,292.6
6211	Offices of physicians	2,530.8	2,587.5	2,618.6	2,672.0	2,590.2	2,697.5
621111	Offices of physicians, except mental health	2,476.5	2,532.0	2,562.7	2,612.7	2,533.6	2,635.9
621112	Offices of mental health physicians	54.5	55.7	56.2	59.3	57.1	61.8
6212	Offices of dentists	924.3	935.1	955.7	969.3	936.8	1,012.0
6213	Offices of other health practitioners	856.6	893.2	930.6	968.7	896.0	977.1
62131	Offices of chiropractors	132.1	136.3	138.7	139.8	143.1	151.5
62132	Offices of optometrists	132.4	134.2	137.0	140.2	131.2	140.2
62133	Offices of mental health practitioners	82.5	91.2	101.6	115.0	124.2	133.3
62134	Offices of specialty therapists	369.0	384.4	406.4	424.0	363.1	408.9
62139	Offices of all other health practitioners	140.9	147.7	147.6	149.8	136.9	147.3
621391	Offices of podiatrists	35.1	34.9	34.6	34.3	32.6	32.7
621399	Offices of miscellaneous health practitioners	105.8	112.7	112.9	115.5	104.2	114.4
6214	Outpatient care centers	855.0	900.9	934.9	963.0	959.4	1,005.4
62142	Outpatient mental health centers	224.7	235.9	242.5	254.0	255.6	271.4
62141,9	Outpatient care centers, except mental health	629.9	664.6	692.0	709.0	704.5	734.8
621491	HMO medical centers	193.8	204.0	210.5	210.8	204.0	210.0
621492	Kidney dialysis centers	122.3	129.9	133.3	130.8	132.3	132.3
621493	Freestanding emergency medical centers	140.9	148.3	152.2	159.3	160.8	175.0
621410,98	Miscellaneous outpatient care centers	172.9	182.3	195.8	208.2	209.8	221.6
6215	Medical & diagnostic laboratories	267.2	266.5	279.6	283.2	276.5	294.1
621511	Medical laboratories	195.3	194.7	204.3	205.2	205.8	222.3
621512	Diagnostic imaging centers	72.3	72.5	75.9	78.1	72.0	72.9
6216	Home health care services	1,366.5	1,429.1	1,474.8	1,527.4	1,467.3	1,502.6
6219	Other ambulatory health care services	292.0	306.8	308.9	313.6	300.8	317.1
62191	Ambulance services	171.7	175.3	173.0	174.0	166.3	175.4
62199	All other ambulatory health care services	119.9	130.9	135.1	139.6	134.7	141.6
621991	Blood & organ banks	68.2	72.6	76.1	76.4	76.4	78.7
621999	Miscellaneous ambulatory health care svcs.	52.0	58.7	59.4	63.2	58.6	62.6

(Continued on next page)

Employment in the Health Care Industry, U.S.: 2016-June 2021 (cont'd)

(Annual Estimates in Thousands of Employed Workers)

NAICS Code[1]	Industry Sector	2016	2017	2018	2019	2020	Jun-21*
622	**Hospitals**	**4,897.5**	**5,023.6**	**5,075.4**	**5,198.7**	**5,105.9**	**5,132.8**
6221	General medical & surgical hospitals	4,499.2	4,615.0	4,673.6	4,779.5	4,678.7	4,713.6
6222	Psychiatric & substance abuse hospitals	137.9	142.4	140.4	148.0	152.1	152.4
6223	Other hospitals	260.5	266.5	261.8	271.2	268.0	274.5
623	**Nursing & residential care facilities**	**3,292.8**	**3,329.3**	**3,351.7**	**3,379.3**	**3,153.3**	**3,015.1**
6231	Nursing care facilities	1,648.3	1,648.9	1,626.2	1,598.4	1,469.7	1,372.4
6232	Residential mental health facilities	606.9	615.3	634.0	647.7	608.6	599.5
62321	Residential intellectual & developmental disability facilities	393.1	394.7	404.2	411.0	375.8	366.2
62322	Residential mental & substance abuse care	213.7	220.9	230.0	236.7	233.3	233.7
6233	Community care facilities for the elderly	875.0	900.1	923.8	967.9	917.9	893.9
623311	Continuing care retirement communities	466.7	478.3	491.9	509.7	476.7	457.0
623212	Assisted living facilities for the elderly	409.4	421.7	431.8	458.1	440.3	436.6
6239	Other residential care facilities	162.6	165.1	167.7	165.3	157.1	149.3
624	**Social assistance**	**3,517.1**	**3,658.3**	**3,827.2**	**4,137.3**	**3,826.7**	**4,039.3**
6241	Individual & family services	2,144.1	2,241.8	2,368.0	2,611.3	2,540.7	2,643.9
62411	Child & youth services	188.1	188.8	197.8	206.1	181.2	194.9
62412	Services for the elderly & disabled	1,557.2	1,637.7	1,738.5	1,965.9	1,946.8	2,008.1
62419	Other individual & family services	399.3	413.6	430.2	439.3	420.4	44.4

[1] For a full description of the NAICS codes used in this table, see www.census.gov/eos/www/naics/.

* Preliminary estimate, seasonally adjusted.

Employment & Earnings in Health Care Practitioner & Technical Occupations, U.S.: May 2020

(Wage & Salary in US$; Latest Year Available)

	Employment[1]	Median Hourly Wage	Mean Hourly Wage	Mean Annual Salary[2]	Mean Wage RSE[3] (%)
Health Diagnosing and Treating Practitioners	**5,611,620**	**40.59**	**50.58**	**105,220**	**0.3%**
Chiropractors	34,760	34.00	40.30	83,830	1.8%
Dentists, General	111,210	78.85	89.57	186,300	1.2%
Oral and Maxillofacial Surgeons	4,120	(5)	112.98	234,990	4.7%
Orthodontists	5,040	(5)	114.42	237,990	5.1%
Dietitians and Nutritionists	66,330	30.33	30.84	64,150	0.4%
Optometrists	36,690	56.76	60.31	125,440	1.2%
Pharmacists	315,470	61.88	60.32	125,460	0.3%
Anesthesiologists	28,590	(5)	130.50	271,440	1.9%
Family and General Practitioners	98,590	99.70	103.06	214,370	1.3%
Internists, General	44,610	96.92	96.85	201,440	2.5%
Obstetricians and Gynecologists	18,900	(5)	114.96	239,120	1.8%
Pediatricians, General	27,550	85.16	88.74	184,570	1.7%
Psychiatrists	25,540	(5)	104.38	217,100	1.8%
Surgeons	37,900	(5)	120.99	251,650	1.8%
Physicians and Surgeons, All Other	375,390	(5)	105.22	219	0.9%
Physician Assistants	125,280	55.48	55.81	116,080	0.5%
Podiatrists	9,710	64.57	72.65	151,110	2.5%
Occupational Therapists	126,610	41.48	42.06	87,480	0.4%
Physical Therapists	220,870	43.75	44.08	91,680	0.3%
Radiation Therapists	17,390	41.76	45.34	94,300	1.2%
Respiratory Therapists	131,890	30.20	31.56	65,640	0.3%
Speech-Language Pathologists	148,450	38.69	40.02	83,420	0.6%
Veterinarians	73,710	47.72	52.09	108,350	1.1%
Registered Nurses	2,986,500	36.22	38.47	80,010	0.4%
Audiologists	13,300	38.95	42.90	89,230	2.2%
Health Technologists and Technicians	2,861,180	21.93	23.55	48,990	0.2%
Clinical Laboratory Technologists and Technicians	326,220	26.05	26.92	55,990	0.4%
Dental Hygienists	194,830	37.06	37.53	78,050	0.6%
Cardiovascular Technologists and Technicians	55,980	28.41	29.30	60,940	0.5%
Diagnostic Medical Sonographers	73,920	36.50	37.40	77,790	0.4%
Nuclear Medicine Technologists	17,510	38.27	39.46	82,080	0.4%
Radiologic Technologists	206,720	35.91	36.52	75,960	0.5%
Emergency Medical Technicians and Paramedics	257,700	17.62	19.41	40,370	0.9%
Pharmacy Technicians	415,310	16.87	17.52	36,450	0.3%
Psychiatric Technicians	85,330	16.84	18.31	38,080	1.1%
Respiratory Therapy Technicians	131,890	30.20	31.56	65,640	0.3%
Surgical Technologists	107,400	23.90	24.77	51,510	0.3%
Veterinary Technologists and Technicians	109,490	17.43	18.20	37,860	0.7%
Licensed Practical and Licensed Vocational Nurses	676,440	23.47	24.08	50,090	0.2%
Medical Records and Health Information Technicians	318,010	21.20	23.21	48,270	0.4%
Opticians, Dispensing	68,180	18.53	19.89	41,380	0.9%
Occupational Health and Safety Specialists	95,960	36.70	37.55	78,110	0.3%
Occupational Health and Safety Technicians	20,950	25.65	27.82	57,870	1.0%

[1] Estimates for detailed occupations do not sum to the totals because the totals include occupations not shown separately. Estimates do not include self-employed workers. [2] Annual wages have been calculated by multiplying the hourly mean wage by a "year-round, full-time" hours figure of 2,080 hours; for those occupations where there is not an hourly mean wage published, the annual wage has been directly calculated from the reported survey data. [3] The relative standard error (RSE) is a measure of the reliability of a survey statistic. The smaller the relative standard error, the more precise the estimate. [4] This wage is equal to or greater than $100.00 per hour.

Source: U.S. Bureau of Labor Statistics
Plunkett Research,® Ltd.
www.plunkettresearch.com

U.S. FDA New Drug (NDA) and Biologic (BLA) Approvals, 2020

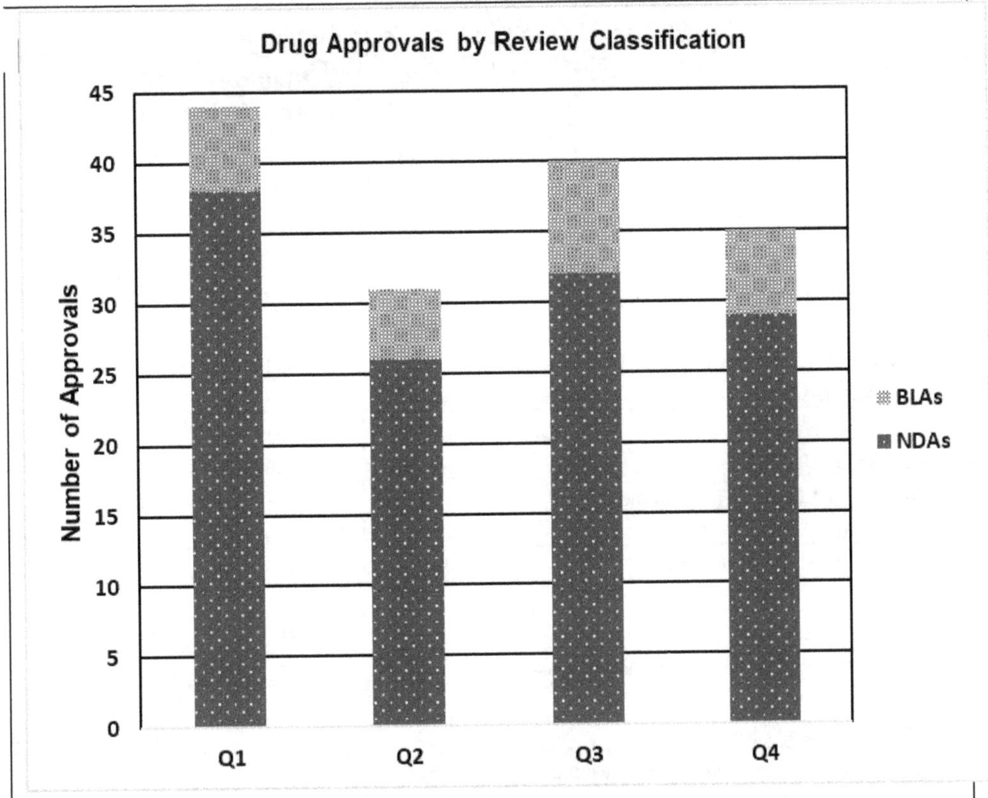

Filed	Q1	Q2	Q3	Q4	Cumulative
NDAs	33	31	29[a]	32	125
BLAs	11	5	8[b]	9	33
Total	44	36	37	41	158
Approved	Q1	Q2	Q3	Q4	Cumulative
NDAs	38	26	32	29	125
BLAs	6	5	8	6	25
Total	44	31	40	35	150

* Data excludes applications that are unacceptable for filing due to nonpayment of user fees, have been withdrawn within 60 days of receipt, or have been refused to file.

a The NDA filed count for quarter 1 decreased by two after the September 30, 2020 report due to the applications being converted to efficacy supplements.

b The BLA filed count for quarter 3 decreased by one after the June 30, 2020 report due to refuse to file action

Source: U.S. Food & Drug Administration (FDA)

Plunkett Research, Ltd.

www.plunkettresearch.com

Federal R&D & R&D Plant Funding for Health and Human Services, U.S.: Fiscal Years 2019-2021

(In Millions of US$; Latest Year Available)

	2019 Actual	2020 Prelim.[1]	2021 Proposed	Change, 2020-21	
				Dollar	Percent
Total	37,094	39,485	36,915	6.4	-6.5
National Cancer Institute	5,989	6,295	5,766	5.1	-8.4
National Institute of Allergy and Infectious Diseases	5,453	5,772	5,356	5.8	-7.2
National Heart, Lung, and Blood Institute	3,348	3,488	3,176	4.2	-9.0
National Institute of General Medical Sciences	3,031	3,496	3,177	15.3	-9.1
National Institute on Aging	2,099	2,189	2,000	4.3	-8.7
National Institute of Diabetes and Digestive and Kidney Diseases	2,202	2,401	2,207	9.0	-8.1
National Institute of Neurological Disorders and Stroke	2,074	2,373	2,181	14.4	-8.1
Office of the Director	1,820	1,991	1,793	9.4	-10.0
National Institute of Mental Health	1,628	1,659	1,893	1.9	14.1
National Institute of Child Health and Human Development	1,457	1,511	1,378	3.7	-8.8
National Institute on Drug Abuse	1,376	1,429	1,402	3.8	-1.8
National Institute of Environmental Health Sciences[1]	831	864	785	4.0	-9.1
National Eye Institute	778	808	733	3.8	-9.3
National Center for Advancing Translational Sciences	778	788	746	1.3	-5.3
National Institute of Arthritis and Musculoskeletal and Skin Diseases	584	606	550	3.8	-9.4
National Human Genome Research Institute	563	591	537	4.9	-9.0
National Institute on Alcohol Abuse and Alcoholism	507	529	481	4.5	-9.1
National Institute on Deafness and Other Communication Disorders	457	474	430	3.8	-9.3
National Institute of Dental and Craniofacial Research	445	462	421	3.7	-8.8
National Library of Medicine	438	455	414	3.8	-9.1
National Institute of Biomedical Imaging and Bioengineering	352	367	334	4.4	-9.1
National Institute on Minority Health and Health Disparities	311	334	303	7.3	-9.1
National Institute of Nursing Research	154	163	149	6.1	-9.1
National Center for Complementary and Integrative Health	142	147	135	3.7	-8.4
John E. Fogarty International Center	60	61	55	2.9	-10.0
National Institute for Research on Safety and Quality[2]	NA	NA	198	NA	NA
National Institute for Occupational Safety and Health[2]	217	230	315	5.8	37.0
National Institute on Disability, Independent Living, and Rehabilitation Research[2]	37,094	39,485	36,915	6.4	-6.5
Buildings and facilities	5,989	6,295	5,766	5.1	-8.4

Notes: Detail may not add to total because of rounding. Percent change is calculated on unrounded data. Institute totals exclude non-R&D components of institute budgets.

[1]Includes funding from Superfund-related transfers and appropriations.

[2]The budget request recommendations consolidating these three agencies within NIH from elsewhere in the Department of Health and Human Services in FY 2021.

Source: EOP, OMB, Analytical Perspectives, Budget of the United States Government, Fiscal Year 2021

Plunkett Research, Ltd.

www.plunkettresearch.com

II. U.S. Health Care Expenditures & Costs

Contents:

The Nation's Health Dollar: 2020***
Where It Came From (Estimated)

($3.72 Trillion Total, Figures in Billions, Latest Year Available)

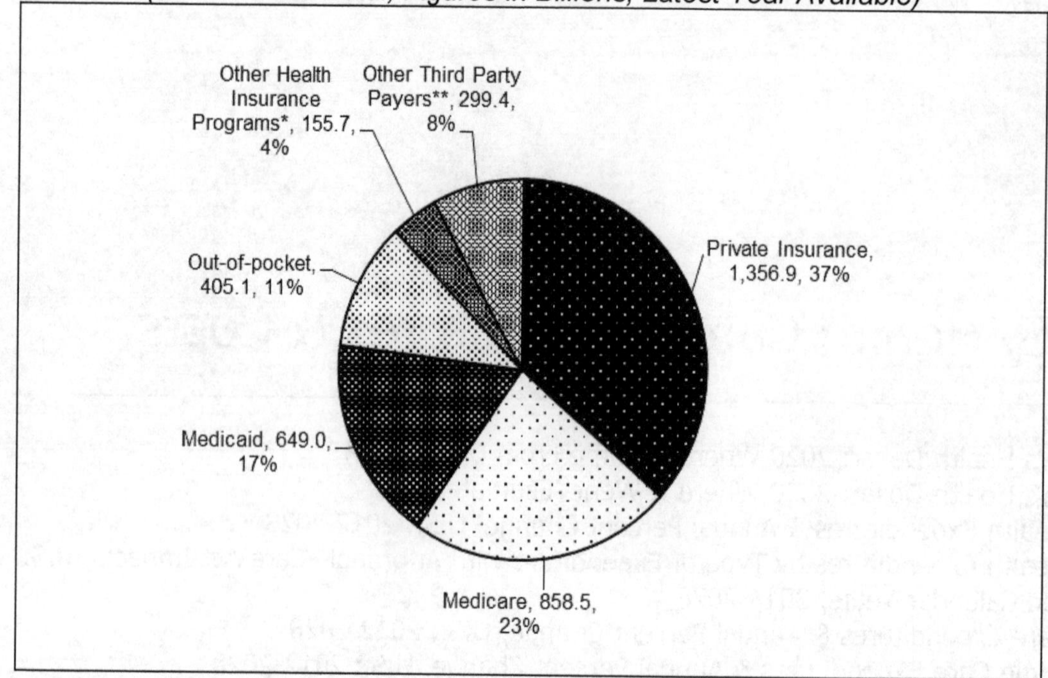

* Includes Children's Health Insurance Program (Titles XIX and XXI), Department of Defense, and Department of Veterans' Affairs. ** Includes worksite health care, other private revenues, Indian Health Service, workers' compensation, general assistance, maternal and child health, vocational rehabilitation, other federal programs, Substance Abuse and Mental Health Services Administration, other state and local programs, and school health. *** May not include the effect of the Coronavirus.

Source: Centers for Medicare & Medicaid Services, Office of the Actuary

Plunkett Research,® Ltd.

www.plunkettresearch.com

The Nation's Health Dollar: 2020*
Where It Went (Estimated)

($4.00 Trillion, Figures in Billions, Latest Year Available)

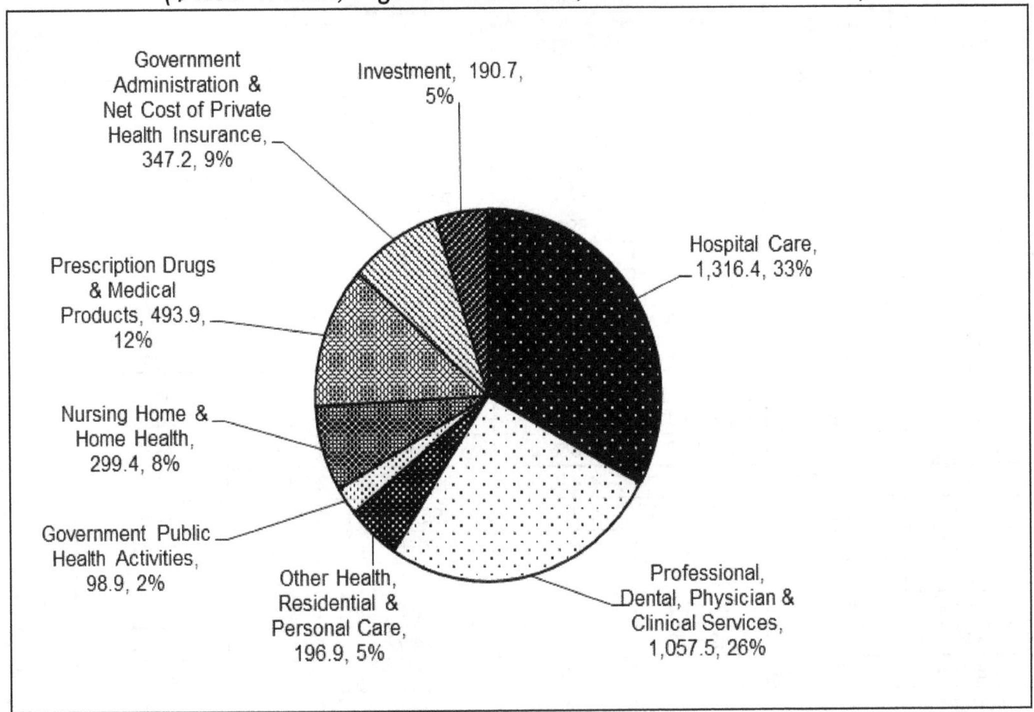

* May not include the effect of the Coronavirus.

Source: Centers for Medicare & Medicaid Services, Office of the Actuary

Plunkett Research,® Ltd.

www.plunkettresearch.com

National Health Expenditures & Annual Percent Change, U.S.: 2012-2028*

(By Source of Funds, Latest Year Available)

Year	Total	Out-of-Pocket Payments	Health Insurance					Other Third Party Payers[2]
			Total	Private Health Insurance	Medicare	Medicaid	Other Health Insurance[1]	
Amount in Billions of US$ (Historical Estimates)								
2012	2,791.1	319.2	2,015.8	922.0	568.5	422.9	102.4	225.5
2013	2,875.0	326.9	2,079.2	939.1	588.9	445.2	105.9	235.9
2014	3,025.4	331.8	2,223.0	994.1	618.5	497.8	112.6	238.8
2015	3,199.6	341.7	2,373.4	1,060.9	648.8	542.6	121.1	244.6
2016	3,347.4	357.2	2,487.5	1,119.9	676.8	565.4	125.4	257.3
2017	3,487.3	365.2	2,592.3	1,175.0	705.1	580.1	132.1	270.1
2018	3,649.4	375.6	2,729.0	1,243.0	750.2	597.4	138.3	276.9
(Projected)								
2019	3,814.6	389.6	2,858.3	1,290.0	800.7	621.0	146.6	288.9
2020	4,014.2	405.1	3,020.2	1,356.9	858.5	649.0	155.7	299.4
2021	4,217.1	421.5	3,182.0	1,410.6	922.6	684.4	164.3	311.3
2022	4,456.0	438.9	3,374.8	1,480.2	996.8	724.5	173.2	324.2
2023	4,706.3	457.7	3,578.2	1,554.7	1,075.6	765.5	182.4	337.6
2024	4,966.1	477.3	3,788.8	1,632.3	1,160.7	804.2	191.7	351.7
2025	5,247.4	497.5	4,018.4	1,713.8	1,250.5	852.6	201.5	366.5
2026	5,549.5	518.6	4,266.0	1,799.1	1,344.7	910.2	212.0	382.1
2027	5,862.9	540.7	4,522.9	1,888.4	1,448.8	962.3	223.4	398.2
2028	6,192.5	563.8	4,793.9	1,981.8	1,559.4	1,017.1	235.7	415.0
Annual Percent Change from Previous Year (Historical Estimates)								
2012	—	—	—	—	—	—	—	—
2013	3.0	2.4	3.1	1.9	3.6	5.3	3.5	4.6
2014	5.2	1.5	6.9	5.9	5.0	11.8	6.3	1.2
2015	5.8	3.0	6.8	6.7	4.9	9.0	7.5	2.4
2016	4.6	4.5	4.8	5.6	4.3	4.2	3.6	5.2
2017	4.2	2.2	4.2	4.9	4.2	2.6	5.3	5.0
2018	4.6	2.8	5.3	5.8	6.4	3.0	4.7	2.5
(Projected)								
2019	4.5	3.7	4.7	3.8	6.7	3.9	6.0	4.3
2020	5.2	4.0	5.7	5.2	7.2	4.5	6.2	3.6
2021	5.1	4.0	5.4	4.0	7.5	5.5	5.5	4.0
2022	5.7	4.2	6.1	4.9	8.0	5.9	5.4	4.1
2023	5.6	4.3	6.0	5.0	7.9	5.7	5.3	4.1
2024	5.5	4.3	5.9	5.0	7.9	5.1	5.1	4.2
2025	5.7	4.2	6.1	5.0	7.7	6.0	5.1	4.2
2026	5.8	4.3	6.2	5.0	7.5	6.8	5.2	4.3
2027	5.6	4.3	6.0	5.0	7.7	5.7	5.4	4.2
2028	5.6	4.3	6.0	4.9	7.6	5.7	5.5	4.2

* May not include the effect of the Coronavirus. [1] Includes Children's Health Insurance Program (Titles XIX and XXI), Department of Defense, and Department of Veterans' Affairs. [2] Includes worksite health care, other private revenues, Indian Health Service, workers' compensation, general assistance, maternal and child health, vocational rehabilitation, other federal programs, Substance Abuse and Mental Health Services Administration, other state and local programs, and school health.

Source: Centers for Medicare & Medicaid Services, Office of the Actuary

Plunkett Research,® Ltd.

www.plunkettresearch.com

National Health Expenditures by Type of Expenditure with Affordable Care Act Impacts, U.S.: Selected Calendar Years, 2014-2028*

(In Billions of US$, Latest Year Available)

Item	2014	2016	2018	2020	2022	2024	2026	2027	2028
National Health Expenditures	3,025.4	3,347.4	3,649.4	4,014.2	4,456.0	4,966.1	5,549.5	5,862.9	6,192.5
Health Consumption Expenditures	2,875.6	3,190.7	3,475.0	3,823.6	4,243.3	4,730.6	5,288.5	5,588.1	5,903.3
Personal Health Care	2,556.0	2,838.3	3,075.5	3,377.5	3,765.5	4,202.1	4,703.0	4,971.8	5,255.5
Hospital Care	978.2	1,089.5	1,191.8	1,316.4	1,475.5	1,653.1	1,862.4	1,971.5	2,088.0
Professional Services	792.5	883.2	965.1	1,057.6	1,172.8	1,302.3	1,448.2	1,526.6	1,608.6
Physician & Clinical Services	595.7	665.6	725.6	794.4	883.5	984.0	1,098.4	1,160.0	1,224.4
Other Professional Services	83.0	92.7	103.9	114.8	127.8	142.2	158.0	166.6	175.5
Dental Services	113.8	124.9	135.6	148.3	161.5	176.1	191.8	200.1	208.7
Other Health, Residential & Personal Care	151.5	173.6	191.6	210.3	235.4	262.2	292.9	309.7	327.1
Home Health Care	84.8	93.0	102.2	116.2	133.4	152.9	175.2	187.8	201.3
Nursing Care Facilities & Continuing Care Retirement Communities	152.4	163.0	168.5	183.2	201.0	220.2	241.1	253.0	266.2
Retail Sales of Medical Prod.	396.6	436.0	456.3	493.9	547.4	611.3	683.3	723.2	764.4
Prescription Drugs	292.4	322.3	335.0	358.7	397.3	445.1	499.2	529.2	560.3
Other Medical Products	104.2	113.6	121.2	135.2	150.1	166.2	184.0	194.0	204.1
Durable Medical Equipment	46.7	51.0	54.9	62.0	69.9	78.4	87.8	93.2	98.4
Other Non-Durable Medical Prod.	57.5	62.7	66.4	73.2	80.2	87.8	96.2	100.8	105.7
Government Administration	42.3	44.9	47.5	52.0	58.4	65.7	74.3	79.2	84.2
Net Cost of Private Health Insurance	195.3	218.8	258.5	295.2	314.0	350.0	389.5	410.8	432.9
Govt. Public Health Activities	82.0	88.7	93.5	98.9	105.4	112.8	121.8	126.2	130.6
Investment	149.8	156.7	174.4	190.7	212.7	235.5	261.0	274.8	289.2
Research[1]	46.0	47.4	52.6	58.6	66.4	73.1	80.6	84.7	89.0
Structures & Equipment	103.7	109.3	121.8	132.0	146.3	162.3	180.4	190.1	200.2

Note: Numbers may not add to totals because of rounding. Figures for 2020-2028 are forecasts.

* May not include the effect of the Coronavirus. [1] Research and development expenditures of drug companies and other manufacturers and providers of medical equipment and supplies are excluded from research expenditures. These research expenditures are implicitly included in the expenditure class in which the product falls, in that they are covered by the payment received for that product.

Source: Centers for Medicare & Medicaid Services, Office of the Actuary

Plunkett Research, ®Ltd.

www.plunkettresearch.com

Hospital Care Expenditures & Annual Percent Change, U.S.: 2012-2028*

(By Source of Funds, Latest Year Available)

Year	Total	Out-of-Pocket Payments	Health Insurance					Other Third Party Payers[2]
			Total	Private Health Insurance	Medicare	Medicaid	Other Health Insurance[1]	
Amount in Billions of US$ (Historical Estimates)								
2012	902.5	31.9	779.9	338.5	237	150	54.4	90.7
2013	937.6	33.9	807.8	349.9	245.0	156.1	56.8	95.9
2014	978.2	32.8	849.4	366.2	252.7	169.8	60.7	95.9
2015	1,034.6	31.2	908.9	400.5	260.5	183.9	63.9	94.5
2016	1,089.5	32.1	959.0	431.0	272.4	189.2	66.4	98.5
2017	1,140.6	34.3	1,000.7	454.1	284.0	192.7	69.7	105.7
2018	1,191.8	34.8	1,046.9	481.1	297.0	196.6	72.2	110.1
(Projected)								
2019	1,253.0	35.7	1,102.8	505.8	315.7	205.3	76.1	114.5
2020	1,316.4	37.1	1,161.1	534.4	337.9	207.7	81.1	118.2
2021	1,392.0	38.7	1,231.0	563.7	365.1	216.2	86.0	122.2
2022	1,475.5	40.4	1,308.7	594.6	394.9	228.1	91.1	126.4
2023	1,563.0	42.3	1,390.0	627.1	426.3	240.2	96.4	130.7
2024	1,653.1	44.1	1,473.7	660.8	459.6	251.7	101.7	135.2
2025	1,752.2	46.1	1,566.0	696.0	494.6	267.9	107.4	140.1
2026	1,862.4	48.1	1,669.2	733.0	532.0	290.8	113.4	145.1
2027	1,971.5	50.3	1,770.9	772.0	572.7	306.2	119.9	150.3
2028	2,088.0	52.4	1,879.9	813.3	617.1	322.5	127.0	155.7
Annual Percent Change from Previous Year (Historical Estimates)								
2012	—	—	—	—	—	—	—	—
2013	3.9	6.2	3.6	3.4	3.4	4.1	4.6	5.7
2014	4.3	-3.0	5.1	4.7	3.1	8.8	6.8	0.0
2015	5.8	-5.0	7.0	9.4	3.1	8.3	5.3	-1.5
2016	5.3	2.8	5.5	7.6	4.6	2.9	3.8	4.2
2017	4.7	6.8	4.3	5.4	4.3	1.9	5.1	7.3
2018	4.5	1.6	4.6	5.9	4.6	2.0	3.5	4.2
(Projected)								
2019	5.1	2.6	5.3	5.1	6.3	4.4	5.4	4.0
2020	5.1	3.8	5.3	5.7	7.1	1.2	6.5	3.2
2021	5.7	4.3	6.0	5.5	8.0	4.1	6.1	3.4
2022	6.0	4.4	6.3	5.5	8.2	5.5	5.9	3.4
2023	5.9	4.6	6.2	5.5	8.0	5.3	5.8	3.4
2024	5.8	4.5	6.0	5.4	7.8	4.7	5.6	3.5
2025	6.0	4.5	6.3	5.3	7.6	6.5	5.6	3.6
2026	6.3	4.4	6.6	5.3	7.5	8.5	5.6	3.6
2027	5.9	4.4	6.1	5.3	7.7	5.3	5.8	3.6
2028	5.9	4.4	6.2	5.3	7.8	5.3	5.9	3.6

* May not include the effect of the Coronavirus. [1] Children's Health Insurance Program (Titles XIX and XXI), Department of Defense, and Department of Veterans' Affairs. [2] Includes worksite health care, other private revenues, Indian Health Service, workers' compensation, general assistance, maternal and child health, vocational rehabilitation, other federal programs, Substance Abuse and Mental Health Services Administration, other state and local programs, and school health.

Source: Centers for Medicare & Medicaid Services, Office of the Actuary

Plunkett Research, ® Ltd.

www.plunkettresearch.com

Nursing Home Care Expenditures & Annual Percent Change, U.S.: 2012-2028

(By Source of Funds, Latest Year Available)

Year	Total	Out-of-Pocket Payments	Health Insurance					Other Third Party Payers[2]
			Total	Private Health Insurance	Medicare	Medicaid	Other Health Insurance[1]	
Amount in Billions of US$ (Historical Estimates)								
2012	147.4	39.2	97.6	11.6	33.9	47.7	4.4	10.5
2013	149.0	39.4	98.9	11.7	34.6	48.1	4.5	10.7
2014	152.4	39.6	101.6	12.2	35.6	49.1	4.7	11.2
2015	158.1	41.5	105.5	14.0	37.1	49.4	5.0	11.1
2016	163.0	44.1	107.3	15.3	37.1	49.8	5.1	11.6
2017	166.2	44.6	109.5	16.6	37.5	50.0	5.4	12.2
2018	168.5	44.8	110.8	17.1	38.1	49.9	5.7	12.9
(Projected)								
2019	175.1	46.8	114.9	18.1	40.1	50.5	6.1	13.5
2020	183.2	48.5	120.6	19.1	42.8	52.2	6.5	14.0
2021	191.8	50.0	127.3	20.0	46.1	54.3	6.9	14.5
2022	201.0	51.4	134.6	21.0	49.8	56.6	7.2	15.0
2023	210.7	52.7	142.4	22.0	53.8	59.1	7.5	15.5
2024	220.2	54.0	150.1	23.1	58.0	61.3	7.7	16.0
2025	230.2	55.1	158.6	24.2	62.5	64.0	8.0	16.5
2026	241.1	56.3	167.7	25.4	67.2	66.9	8.2	17.0
2027	253.0	57.7	177.7	26.7	72.5	69.9	8.5	17.6
2028	266.2	59.4	188.5	28.2	78.4	73.0	8.8	18.3
Annual Percent Change from Previous Year (Historical Estimates)								
2012	—	—	—	—	—	—	—	—
2013	1.1	0.5	1.3	0.8	2.1	0.8	2.3	1.7
2014	2.3	0.3	2.8	4.6	2.9	2.1	5.3	4.3
2015	3.8	4.9	3.8	14.5	4.2	0.7	5.4	-0.5
2016	3.1	6.2	1.8	9.4	0.2	0.9	1.2	4.3
2017	2.0	1.1	2.0	8.4	1.0	0.3	6.3	5.0
2018	1.4	0.6	1.2	2.8	1.6	-0.2	5.4	5.8
(Projected)								
2019	3.9	4.3	3.7	6.0	5.2	1.3	7.4	4.6
2020	4.6	3.8	5.0	5.4	6.8	3.2	7.7	4.0
2021	4.7	3.1	5.5	4.9	7.7	4.0	5.6	3.5
2022	4.8	2.7	5.7	4.8	8.0	4.3	4.1	3.4
2023	4.8	2.7	5.8	5.0	8.1	4.4	3.8	3.5
2024	4.5	2.4	5.4	4.8	7.8	3.8	3.2	3.3
2025	4.5	2.0	5.6	4.6	7.7	4.4	3.3	3.0
2026	4.7	2.2	5.7	5.0	7.6	4.5	3.4	3.2
2027	4.9	2.5	5.9	5.3	7.8	4.6	3.6	3.2
2028	5.2	2.9	6.1	5.6	8.1	4.5	3.7	3.8

[1] Includes Children's Health Insurance Program (Titles XIX and XXI), Department of Defense, and Department of Veterans' Affairs.

[2] Includes worksite health care, other private revenues, Indian Health Service, workers' compensation, general assistance, maternal and child health, vocational rehabilitation, other federal programs, Substance Abuse and Mental Health Services Administration, other state and local programs, and school health.

Source: Centers for Medicare & Medicaid Services, Office of the Actuary

Plunkett Research, ® Ltd. www.plunkettresearch.com

Home Health Care Expenditures & Annual Percent Change, U.S.: 2012-2028*

(By Source of Funds, Latest Year Available)

Year	Total	Out-of-Pocket Payments	Health Insurance					Other Third Party Payers[2]
			Total	Private Health Insurance	Medicare	Medicaid	Other Health Insurance[1]	
Amount in Billions of US$ (Historical Estimates)								
2012	78.3	7.2	68.5	6.9	33.5	27.7	0.4	2.5
2013	81.4	7.8	70.9	8.2	33.6	28.7	0.4	2.6
2014	84.8	8.0	74.2	9.2	34.3	30.3	0.5	2.5
2015	89.2	8.3	78.5	9.7	35.7	32.4	0.7	2.5
2016	93.0	8.5	81.9	10.5	36.9	33.8	0.7	2.5
2017	97.1	9.2	85.3	11.4	38.1	35.0	0.7	2.7
2018	102.2	10.2	89.2	12.2	40.3	35.9	0.8	2.8
(Projected)								
2019	108.9	11.0	94.8	13.4	43.1	37.4	0.9	3.1
2020	116.2	11.8	101.0	14.3	46.3	39.4	1.0	3.4
2021	124.5	12.6	108.3	15.3	50.2	41.7	1.1	3.6
2022	133.4	13.4	116.1	16.5	54.3	44.1	1.2	3.9
2023	143.0	14.4	124.4	17.7	58.7	46.6	1.3	4.2
2024	152.9	15.4	133.0	19.1	63.5	48.9	1.4	4.5
2025	163.7	16.5	142.4	20.5	68.7	51.6	1.5	4.9
2026	175.2	17.7	152.3	22.0	74.1	54.5	1.7	5.2
2027	187.8	18.9	163.3	23.5	80.3	57.7	1.8	5.6
2028	201.3	20.2	175.0	25.2	86.9	60.9	2.0	6.0
Annual Percent Change from Previous Year (Historical Estimates)								
2012	—	—	—	—	—	—	—	—
2013	3.9	7.8	3.6	19.7	0.4	3.3	6.9	3.2
2014	4.2	3.0	4.7	12.0	2.0	5.6	8.9	-5.4
2015	5.3	2.6	5.7	6.0	4.1	6.9	45.9	0.8
2016	4.2	3.0	4.4	7.5	3.5	4.4	5.5	1.6
2017	4.5	7.6	4.1	9.0	3.2	3.6	3.1	5.1
2018	5.2	10.9	4.6	6.9	5.6	2.5	12.1	6.2
(Projected)								
2019	6.6	8.2	6.3	9.4	7.1	4.2	11.0	9.3
2020	6.7	7.3	6.6	7.3	7.4	5.3	9.6	8.0
2021	7.1	6.7	7.2	6.8	8.3	6.0	8.3	7.4
2022	7.2	6.9	7.2	7.5	8.3	5.8	8.6	7.6
2023	7.2	7.2	7.1	7.8	8.2	5.6	8.6	7.8
2024	7.0	7.2	6.9	7.8	8.2	5.0	8.7	7.8
2025	7.1	7.0	7.1	7.4	8.1	5.6	9.0	7.7
2026	7.0	6.9	7.0	7.2	7.9	5.6	9.1	7.6
2027	7.2	7.0	7.2	7.0	8.4	5.7	9.4	7.5
2028	7.2	7.0	7.2	7.0	8.2	5.7	9.5	7.5

* May not include the effect of the Coronavirus. 1 Children's Health Insurance Program (Titles XIX and XXI), Department of Defense, and Department of Veterans' Affairs. [2] Includes worksite health care, other private revenues, Indian Health Service, workers' compensation, general assistance, maternal and child health, vocational rehabilitation, other federal programs, Substance Abuse and Mental Health Services Administration, other state and local programs, and school health.

Source: Centers for Medicare & Medicaid Services, Office of the Actuary

Plunkett Research, ® Ltd.

www.plunkettresearch.com

Prescription Drug Expenditures & Annual Percent Change, U.S.: 2012-2028*

(By Source of Funds, Latest Year Available)

Year	Total	Out-of-Pocket Payments	Health Insurance					Other Third Party Payers[3]
			Total	Private Health Insurance	Medicare	Medicaid	Other Health Insurance[2]	
Amount in Billions of US$ (Historical Estimates)								
2012	253.0	45.5	204.9	106.4	67.5	21.4	9.5	2.5
2013	258.2	44.3	211.5	106.2	74.0	22.1	9.2	2.4
2014	292.4	45.6	244.9	122.6	84.8	27.3	10.2	2.0
2015	317.1	46.3	268.9	134.8	92.4	30.5	11.1	1.9
2016	322.3	47.8	272.7	133.8	96.6	32.0	10.3	1.8
2017	326.8	46.8	278.2	133.2	101.3	32.9	10.8	1.8
2018	335.0	47.1	286.2	134.3	107.2	33.4	11.3	1.8
(Projected)[1]								
2019	345.7	47.5	296.5	135.3	114.6	34.9	11.7	1.8
2020	358.7	48.3	308.6	137.3	122.4	37.0	11.9	1.8
2021	375.8	49.4	324.5	140.9	132.1	39.3	12.2	1.9
2022	397.3	51.3	344.0	146.7	143.2	41.5	12.6	1.9
2023	420.3	53.5	364.8	153.2	154.8	43.9	13.0	2.0
2024	445.1	55.9	387.1	160.7	167.0	46.1	13.3	2.1
2025	470.8	58.5	410.1	168.8	178.9	48.7	13.7	2.2
2026	499.2	61.2	435.7	177.4	192.7	51.5	14.2	2.3
2027	529.2	64.0	462.8	186.4	207.3	54.5	14.6	2.4
2028	560.3	66.8	490.9	195.7	222.6	57.6	15.0	2.5
Annual Percent Change from Previous Year (Historical Estimates)								
2012	—	—	—	—	—	—	—	—
2013	2.1	-2.7	3.2	-0.2	9.7	2.9	-3.4	-6.1
2014	13.3	2.8	15.8	15.4	14.5	23.9	10.9	-16.3
2015	8.4	1.6	9.8	10.0	9.0	11.6	9.3	-3.3
2016	1.7	3.3	1.4	-0.8	4.5	5.0	-7.5	-5.8
2017	1.4	-2.2	2.0	-0.4	4.8	2.7	5.3	-2.1
2018	2.5	0.6	2.9	0.8	5.9	1.4	4.5	-0.8
(Projected)[1]								
2019	3.2	0.8	3.6	0.8	6.9	4.7	2.9	2.1
2020	3.7	1.7	4.1	1.5	6.8	5.8	2.2	2.1
2021	4.8	2.4	5.2	2.6	7.9	6.3	2.4	2.9
2022	5.7	3.9	6.0	4.1	8.4	5.8	3.2	3.4
2023	5.8	4.2	6.0	4.4	8.1	5.6	2.9	4.0
2024	5.9	4.6	6.1	4.9	7.9	5.0	2.9	4.3
2025	5.8	4.6	5.9	5.0	7.1	5.6	3.0	4.7
2026	6.0	4.7	6.2	5.1	7.7	5.7	3.0	4.8
2027	6.0	4.5	6.2	5.1	7.6	5.8	3.0	4.5
2028	5.9	4.4	6.1	5.0	7.3	5.8	3.0	4.5

* May not include the effect of the Coronavirus. [1]Includes Private Health Insurance (Employer Sponsored Insurance and other private insurance, which includes Marketplace plans), Medicare, Medicaid, Children's Health Insurance Program (Titles XIX and XXI), Department of Defense, and Department of Veterans' Affairs. [2] Children's Health Insurance Program (Titles XIX and XXI), Department of Defense, and Department of Veterans' Affairs. [3] Includes worksite health care, other private revenues, Indian Health Service, workers' compensation, general assistance, maternal and child health, vocational rehabilitation, other federal programs, Substance Abuse and Mental Health Services Administration, other state and local programs, and school health.

Source: Centers for Medicare & Medicaid Services, Office of the Actuary

Plunkett Research, ® Ltd.

www.plunkettresearch.com

III. Medicare & Medicaid

Contents:

Medicare Enrollment, 1970-2095

(In Thousands)

Year	HI (Part A)	SMI		Part C	Total[1]
		Part B	Part D		
1970	20,104	19,496	—	—	20,398
1975	24,481	23,744	—	—	24,864
1980	28,002	27,278	—	—	28,433
1985	30,621	29,869	—	1,271	31,081
1990	33,747	32,567	—	2,017	34,251
1995	37,175	35,641	—	3,467	37,594
2000	39,257	37,335	—	6,856	39,688
2005	42,233	39,752	1,841	5,794	42,606
2010	47,365	43,882	34,772	11,693	47,720
2011	48,549	44,917	35,720	12,383	48,896
2012	50,540	46,477	37,448	13,588	50,874
2013	52,169	47,952	39,103	14,843	52,504
2014	53,777	49,413	40,499	16,244	54,115
2015	55,246	50,756	41,804	17,493	55,589
2016	56,729	52,094	43,217	18,392	57,073
2017	58,344	53,446	44,480	19,816	58,683
2018	59,794	54,798	45,778	21,336	60,147
2019	60,857	56,115	47,197	22,942	61,222
2020	62,264	57,311	48,827	24,999	62,642
2021	63,814	58,752	50,268	26,213	64,207
2022	65,485	60,313	51,781	27,207	65,892
2023	67,095	61,824	53,222	28,036	67,516
2024	68,676	63,313	54,609	28,995	69,111
2025	70,303	64,847	55,995	29,862	70,751
2026	71,904	66,362	57,326	30,745	72,367
2027	73,438	67,827	58,606	31,588	73,914
2028	74,916	69,242	59,843	32,391	75,404
2029	76,297	70,570	61,005	33,141	76,797
2030	77,546	71,806	62,073	33,832	78,057
2035	81,926	76,268	65,930	36,136	82,478
2040	84,021	78,451	67,817	37,117	84,592
2045	85,278	79,675	68,876	(2)	85,860
2050	87,177	81,359	70,331	(2)	87,772
2055	89,841	83,774	72,419	(2)	90,449
2060	93,193	86,905	75,125	(2)	93,828
2065	96,479	90,096	77,884	(2)	97,144
2070	99,999	93,481	80,811	(2)	100,700
2075	103,709	97,006	83,858	(2)	104,455
2080	106,073	99,402	85,929	(2)	106,858
2085	107,576	100,953	87,270	(2)	108,400
2090	109,307	102,584	88,679	(2)	110,181
2094	111,951	104,952	90,727	(2)	112,880
2095	109,016	102,211	88,615	(2)	109,722

Note: All data past 2018 are estimated. HI = Hospital Insurance, SMI = Supplementary Medical Insurance.

[1] Number of beneficiaries with HI and/or SMI coverage. [2] Enrollment is not explicitly projected beyond 2040.

Source: The Boards Of Trustees, Federal Hospital Insurance And Federal Supplementary Medical Insurance Trust Funds

Plunkett Research,® Ltd.

www.plunkettresearch.com

Medicaid Enrollment & Expenditures for Medical Assistance Payments & Administration: Selected Years, 1966-2027

(Enrollment in millions of person-year equivalents; Expenditures in billions of dollars)

Fiscal Year	Enrollment	Total Expenditures	Federal Expenditures	State Expenditures
Historical Data:				
1966	4.0	0.9	0.5	0.4
1970	14.0	5.1	2.8	2.3
1975	20.2	13.1	7.3	5.9
1980	19.6	25.2	14.0	11.2
1985	19.8	41.3	22.8	18.4
1990	22.9	72.2	40.9	31.3
1995	33.4	159.5	90.7	68.8
2000	34.5	206.2	117.0	89.2
2005	46.3	315.9	180.4	135.5
2006	46.7	315.1	179.3	135.8
2007	46.4	332.2	189.0	143.2
2008	47.7	351.9	200.2	151.7
2009	50.9	378.6	246.3	132.3
2010	54.5	401.5	269.8	131.7
2011	56.3	427.0	270.5	156.4
2012	58.9	431.0	248.8	182.2
2013*	59.8	456.0	263.0	193.0
2014*	65.1	494.7	299.3	195.4
2015*	69.8	549.1	346.0	203.1
2016*	72.1	577.3	364.5	212.7
2017*	73.4	600.0	370.2	229.9
Projections (Includes impacts of Affordable Care Act):				
2018	73.9	616.1	386.5	229.6
2019	75.1	639.4	399.4	240.0
2020	76.7	672.7	418.7	254.0
2021	77.6	709.2	442.1	267.0
2022	79.3	751.3	467.5	283.3
2023	79.3	798.5	496.6	301.9
2024	80.0	839.6	521.9	317.7
2025	80.7	888.8	552.2	336.6
2026	81.3	952.1	590.6	361.5
2027	82.0	1007.9	624.8	383.0

* Enrollment is estimated for 2013, 2014, 2015, 2016 and 2017.

Source: Centers for Medicare & Medicaid Services, US Department of Health & Human Services.

Plunkett Research,® Ltd.

www.plunkettresearch.com

IV. U.S. Health Insurance Coverage & The Uninsured

Contents:

Number & Percent of Persons of All Ages with and without Health Insurance Coverage, U.S.: 2000-2020

(In Thousands; Latest Year Available)

Year	Total Population	Private Health Insurance	%	Public Health Insurance	%	Total Covered	%	Total Uncovered	%
2000	279,517	205,575	73.5	68,183	24.4	242,932	86.9	36,586	13.1
2001	282,082	204,142	72.4	70,330	24.9	244,059	86.5	38,023	13.5
2002	285,933	204,163	71.4	72,825	25.5	246,157	86.1	39,776	13.9
2003	288,280	201,989	70.1	76,116	26.4	246,332	85.4	41,949	14.6
2004	291,166	203,014	69.7	79,480	27.3	249,414	85.7	41,752	14.3
2005	293,834	203,205	69.2	80,283	27.3	250,799	85.4	43,035	14.6
2006	296,824	203,942	68.7	80,343	27.1	251,610	84.8	45,214	15.2
2007	299,106	203,903	68.2	83,147	27.8	255,018	85.3	44,088	14.7
2008	301,483	202,626	67.2	87,586	29.1	256,702	85.1	44,780	14.9
2009	304,280	196,245	64.5	93,245	30.6	255,295	83.9	48,985	16.1
2010	306,553	196,147	64.0	95,525	31.2	256,603	83.7	49,951	16.3
2011	308,827	197,323	63.9	99,497	32.2	260,214	84.3	48,613	15.7
2012	311,116	198,812	63.9	101,493	32.6	263,165	84.6	47,951	15.4
2013	313,400	201,100	64.2	107,600	34.3	271,400	86.6	42,000	13.4
2014	313,890	208,333	66.4	104,228	33.2	277,220	88.3	36,670	11.7
2015	316,451	213,514	67.5	109,874	34.7	286,693	90.6	29,758	9.4
2016	318,176	215,859	67.8	112,688	35.4	290,872	91.4	27,304	8.6
2017	320,775	216,952	67.6	113,720	35.5	292,756	91.3	28,019	8.7
2018	323,668	217,780	67.3	111,330	34.4	296,206	91.5	27,462	8.5
2019	323,121	217,812	67.4	114,315	35.4	293,482	90.8	29,639	9.2
2020	325,638	216,532	66.5	113,337	34.8	297,680	91.4	27,957	8.6

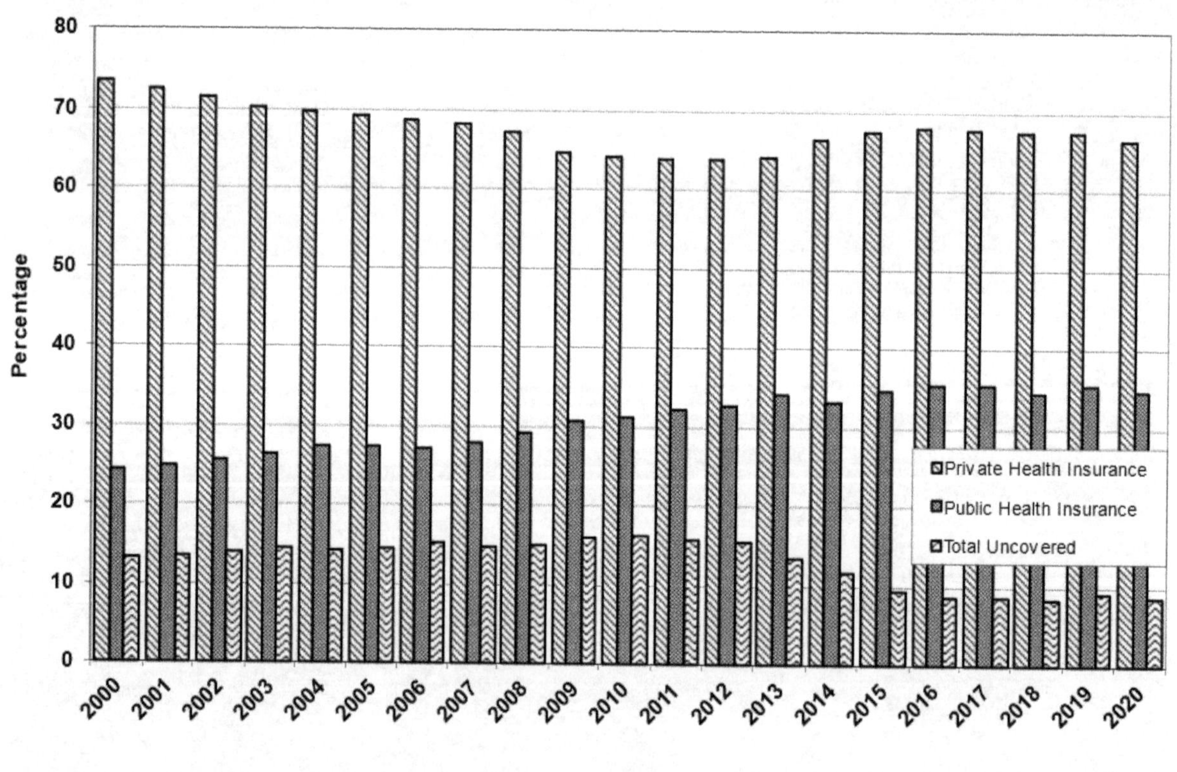

Note: Numbers as of March of the following year. Uncovered persons includes those not covered by private health insurance (such as employment-based or direct purchase) or public health insurance (such as Medicaid, Medicare, or military health care). Individuals are considered to be uninsured if they do not have health insurance coverage for the entire calendar year.

Source: U.S. Census Bureau, Health Insurance Coverage in the United States: 2019

Plunkett Research,® Ltd., www.plunkettresearch.com

Employers' Costs for Total Compensation and Health Insurance, by Selected Characteristics, U.S.: Selected Years, 2017-2021

(Amount per Employee-Hour Worked in US$)

Characteristic	Total Compensation per Employee-Hour Worked					Health Insurance as Percent of Total Compensation				
	2017	2018	2019	2020	2021	2017	2018	2019	2020	2021
	In US$					*In Percent (%)*				
State and local government	48.24	49.40	50.89	52.45	53.68	11.6	11.9	11.6	11.4	11.7
Total private industry	33.11	34.17	34.49	35.34	36.64	7.6	7.5	7.5	7.5	7.7
Census region:										
Northeast	41.19	41.48	39.07	39.76	41.17	7.6	7.6	8.1	7.9	8.1
Midwest	30.51	31.03	31.82	33.73	35.10	8.2	8.4	8.2	8.3	8.8
South	29.84	30.68	31.15	31.00	32.69	7.3	7.1	6.8	6.6	6.7
West	34.35	37.08	38.78	40.20	40.60	7.3	7.3	7.4	7.6	7.7
Union status:										
Union	48.97	47.65	47.27	48.57	50.73	12.5	32.9	13.2	13.2	13.6
Nonunion	31.58	12.90	33.26	34.16	35.46	6.8	6.8	6.8	6.7	7
Establishment employment size:										
1–99 employees	28.16	28.79	28.49	29.18	30.30	6.4	6.3	6.3	6.3	6.5
100 or more	39.05	40.53	41.73	42.66	44.90	8.6	8.6	8.6	8.5	8.8
100–499	32.74	34.76	35.48	36.79	37.68	8.3	8.5	8.2	8.1	8.4
500 or more	48.70	49.16	50.20	50.30	54.43	8.9	8.8	8.9	8.9	9.2

Note: Costs are calculated from March survey data each year.
Total compensation includes wages and salaries, and benefits.

Source: U.S. Department of Labor, Bureau of Labor Statistics, National Compensation Survey, Employer Costs for Employee Compensation, March release

Plunkett Research,® Ltd.

www.plunkettresearch.com

V. U.S. Vital Statistics & Population Indicators

Contents:

Prevalence of Obesity Among Adults, by Age, Sex and Race/Ethnicity: U.S., 2018

(Percent of 20 Years and over Population; Latest Year Available[1])

	Male	Female	Total
Age:			
20-39	27.6	29.4	28.5
40-59	35.4	35.9	35.7
60 and over	32.1	30.1	31.1
Race/Ethnicity[2]:			
Hispanic or Latino	35.2	36.1	--
Not Hispanic or Latino, single race, white	31.3	29.1	--
Not Hispanic or Latino, single race, black	31.7	44.9	--

Note: Obesity is defined as a body mass index of 30 kg/m^2 or more. Data are based on household interviews of a sample of the civilian noninstitutionalized population.

[1]As of 9/15/20, the NHIS has yet to publish a report regarding the prevalence of obesity due to changes in the NHIS survey format. 2018 numbers are still the most up to date numbers.

[2]Estimates are age-adjusted using the projected 2000 U.S. population as the standard population and seven age groups: 20–29, 30–39, 40–49, 50–59, 60–69, 70–79, and 80 and over.

Source: National Center for Health Statistics, *Health, United States, 2018*

Plunkett Research,® Ltd.

www.plunkettresearch.com

Chapter 3

IMPORTANT HEALTH CARE INDUSTRY CONTACTS

Contents:

79)	Privacy Associations
80)	Research & Development, Laboratories
81)	Respiratory
82)	Science & Technology Resources
83)	Seniors Housing
84)	Sexually Transmitted Diseases
85)	Singaporean Government & Agencies - Health Care
86)	Technology Transfer Associations
87)	Textile & Fabric Industry Associations
88)	Trade Associations-General
89)	Trade Associations-Global
90)	U.S. Government Agencies
91)	UK Government Agencies
92)	Urological Disorders
93)	Vitamin & Supplement Industry Associations
94)	Wholesale Distributors Associations

1) Aging

Administration for Community Living (ACL)
One Massachusetts Ave. NW
Washington, DC 20201 US
Phone: 202-619-0724
Fax: 202-357-3555
Toll Free: 800-677-1116
E-mail Address: *aclinfo@acl.hhs.gov*
Web Address: acl.gov
The Administration for Community Living (ACL), combining the efforts of the Administration on Aging (AOA), the Administration on Intellectual and Developmental Disabilities and the Health and Human Services (HHS) Office on Disability, is the federal focal point and advocate agency for the concerns of older persons and people with disabilities across the lifespan. In this role, the ACL works to heighten awareness among other federal agencies, organizations, groups and the public.

Aging with Dignity
3050 Highland Oaks Terr., Ste. 2
Tallahassee, FL 32301-3841 USA
Phone: 850-681-2010
Fax: 850-681-2481
Toll Free: 888-594-7437
E-mail Address:
fivewishes@agingwithdignity.org
Web Address: www.agingwithdignity.org
Aging with Dignity is a nonprofit organization that offers information, advice and legal tools needed to ensure that the wishes of the elderly concerning health and death be respected.

American Society on Aging (ASA)
575 Market St., Ste. 2100
San Francisco, CA 94105-2869 USA
Phone: 415-974-9600
Fax: 415-974-0300
Toll Free: 800-537-9728
E-mail Address:
membership@asaging.org
Web Address: www.asaging.org
The American Society on Aging (ASA) is a nonprofit organization committed to enhancing the knowledge and skills of those working with older adults and their families.

LeadingAge
2519 Connecticut Ave. NW
Washington, DC 20008-1520 USA
Phone: 202-783-2242
Fax: 202-783-2255
Toll Free: 888-508-9441
E-mail Address: info@leadingage.org
Web Address: www.leadingage.org
LeadingAge was formerly the American Association of Home Services for the Aging (AAHSA). The LeadingAge membership community includes over 6,000 not-for-profit organizations in the United States, state partners, businesses, research partners, consumer organizations, foundations and a broad global network of aging services organizations that reach over 30 countries. The work of LeadingAge is focused on advocacy, leadership development, and applied research and promotion of effective services, home health, hospice, community services, senior housing, assisted living residences, continuing care communities, nursing homes, as well as technology solutions, to seniors, children, and others with special needs.

National Association of Area Agencies on Aging (N4A)
1100 New Jersey Ave. SE, Ste. 350
Washington, DC 20003 USA
Phone: 202-872-0888
Fax: 202-872-0057
E-mail Address: info@n4a.org
Web Address: www.n4a.org
The National Association of Area Agencies on Aging (N4A) is the umbrella organization for the 622 area agencies on aging and more than 256 Title VI Native American aging programs in the U.S.

National Council on Aging (NCOA)
251 18th St. S., Ste. 500
Arlington, VA 22202 USA
Phone: 571-527-3900
Web Address: www.ncoa.org
The National Council on Aging (NCOA) is a group of organizations and professionals promoting the dignity, self-determination and well-being of older persons.

2) AIDS/HIV

AIDS United
1101 14th St. NW, Ste. 300
Washington, DC 20005 USA
Phone: 202-408-4848
Fax: 202-408-1818
Web Address: www.aidsunited.org
AIDS United, formed by the 2010 merger of AIDS Action and the National AIDS Fund, is committed to the development, analysis, cultivation, encouragement and implementation of good programs and policies with regard to the HIV/AIDS virus.

CDC National Prevention Information Network (CDCNPIN)
P.O. Box 6003
Rockville, MD 20849-6003 USA
Toll Free: 800-232-4636
E-mail Address: NPIN-info@cdc.gov
Web Address: npin.cdc.gov
The CDC National Prevention Information Network (CDCNPIN) is the U.S. reference, referral and distribution service for information on HIV/AIDS, sexually transmitted diseases and tuberculosis. It is operated by the Centers for Disease Control, a Federal Government agency.

HIV InSite
4150 Clement St., Box 111V
San Francisco, CA 94121 USA
Fax: 415-379-5547
E-mail Address: hivinsite@ucsf.edu
Web Address: hivinsite.ucsf.edu
HIV InSite, which was developed by the Center for HIV Information at the University of California San Francisco, offers comprehensive, up-to-date information on HIV/AIDS treatment, prevention and policy.

HIV/AIDS Treatment Information Service
P.O. Box 4780
Rockville, MD 20849-6303 USA
Fax: 301-315-2818
Toll Free: 800-448-0440
E-mail Address:
contactus@aidsinfo.nih.gov
Web Address: www.aidsinfo.nih.gov
The HIV/AIDS Treatment Information Service is a central resource for federally approved treatment guidelines for HIV and AIDS, HIV treatment and prevention clinical trials and other research information for health care providers and general public.

3) Alzheimer's Disease

Alzheimer's Association
225 N. Michigan Ave., Fl. 17
Chicago, IL 60601 USA
Phone: 312-335-8700
Fax: 866-699-1246
Toll Free: 1-800-272-3900
E-mail Address: info@alz.org
Web Address: www.alz.org
The Alzheimer's Association is the largest national voluntary health organization committed to finding a cure for Alzheimer's and helping those affected by the disease.

Alzheimer's Disease Education and Referral Center (ADEAR)
ADEAR Ctr.
P.O. Box 8250
Silver Spring, MD 20907-8250 USA
Fax: 301-495-3334
Toll Free: 800-438-4380
E-mail Address: adear@nia.nih.gov
Web Address:
www.nia.nih.gov/alzheimers
The Alzheimer's Disease Education and Referral Center (ADEAR) provides information about Alzheimer's disease, its impact on families and health professionals and research into possible causes and cures.

Alzheimer's Foundation of America (AFA)
322 8th Ave., Fl. 16
New York, NY 10001 USA
Fax: 646-638-1546
Toll Free: 866-232-8484
E-mail Address: info@alzfdn.org
Web Address: www.alzfdn.org
From the beginning, AFA's objective has been to unite organizations from coast-to-coast that are dedicated to meeting the educational, social, emotional and practical needs of individuals with Alzheimer's disease and related illnesses, and their caregivers and families. Under AFA's umbrella, these organizations collaborate on education, resources, program design and implementation, fundraising campaigns, and advocacy, all resulting in better care for those affected by the disease.

4) Arthritis

Arthritis Foundation
1355 Peachtree St. NE, Ste. 6
Atlanta, GA 30309 USA
Phone: 404-872-7100
Toll Free: 800-283-7800
Web Address: www.arthritis.org

The Arthritis Foundation is a nonprofit organization providing advocacy, programs, services and research for the treatment of more than 100 types of arthritis and related conditions.

Arthritis National Research Foundation (ANRF)
19200 Von Karman Ave., Ste. 350
Irvine, CA 92612 USA
Phone: 562-437-6808
Toll Free: 800-588-2873
Web Address: www.curearthritis.org
The Arthritis National Research Foundation (ANRF) provides funding for researchers associated with major research institutes, universities and hospitals throughout the country seeking to discover new knowledge for the prevention, treatment and cure of arthritis and related rheumatic diseases.

Arthritis.com
Web Address: www.arthritis.com
Arthritis.com is an online resource for information on chronic joint symptoms. The web site is operated by Pfizer, Inc.

5) Biotechnology & Biological Industry Associations

BIOCOM
10996 Torreyana Rd., Ste. 200
San Diego, CA 92121 USA
Phone: 858-455-0300
E-mail Address: contactus@biocom.org
Web Address: www.biocom.org
BIOCOM is a trade organization which seeks to promote the interests of life science industry through advancements in health, energy and agriculture. Its covers a range of areas, including diagnostic, pharmaceuticals, biotechnology, medical device, bio-renewable energy, agriculture and connected health. With over 700 member companies, service providers and research institutions, the organization offers talent development, networking, public policy initiatives and capital development opportunities.

Biomedical Engineering Society (BMES)
8201 Corporate Dr., Ste. 1125
Landover, MD 20785-2224 USA
Phone: 301-459-1999
Fax: 301-459-2444
Toll Free: 877-871-2637
Web Address: www.bmes.org
The Biomedical Engineering Society (BMES) supports and advances the use of engineering and technology for human health and well being. It promotes the development of professionals in the biomedical engineering and bioengineering industry.

Biotechnology Industry Organization (BIO)
1201 Maryland Ave. SW, Ste. 900
Washington, DC 20024 USA
Phone: 202-962-9200
Fax: 202-488-6301
E-mail Address: info@bio.org
Web Address: www.bio.org
The Biotechnology Industry Organization (BIO) represents members involved in the research and development of health care, agricultural, industrial and environmental biotechnology products. BIO has both small and large member organizations.

California Healthcare Institute (CHI)
250 E. Grand Ave., Ste. 26
La Jolla, CA 92037 USA
Phone: 650-871-3250
E-mail Address: info@califesciences.org
Web Address: http://califesciences.org
California Life Sciences Association (CLSA) was formed in 2015 through the merger between California Health Care Institute and Bay Area Bioscience Association. It works to promote California's life sciences industry in collaboration with government, academia as well as other stakeholders to form public policy and business solutions. CLSA membership includes over 750 biotechnology, pharmaceutical, medical device and diagnostics companies, research universities and institutes, investors and service providers.

International Society for Stem Cell Research (ISSCR)
5215 Old Orchard Rd., Ste. 270
Skokie, IL 60077 USA
Phone: 224-592-5700
Fax: 224-365-0004
E-mail Address: isscr@isscr.org
Web Address: www.isscr.org
The International Society for Stem Cell Research (ISSCR) is an independent, nonprofit organization established to promote the exchange and dissemination of information and ideas relating to stem cells; to encourage the general field of research involving stem cells; and to promote professional and public education in all areas of stem cell research and application.

Society for Biomaterials
1120 Route 73, Ste. 200
Mt. Laurel, NJ 08054 USA
Phone: 856-439-0826
Fax: 856-439-0525
E-mail Address: info@biomaterials.org
Web Address: www.biomaterials.org

The Society for Biomaterials is a professional society that promotes advances in all phases of materials research and development by encouraging cooperative educational programs, clinical applications and professional standards in the biomaterials field.

6) Biotechnology Investing

Burrill & Company
1 Embarcadero Ctr., Ste. 2700
San Francisco, CA 94111 USA
Phone: 415-591-5400
Fax: 415-591-5401
Web Address: www.burrillandco.com
Burrill & Company is a leading private merchant bank concentrated on companies in the life sciences industries: biotechnology, pharmaceuticals, medical technologies, agricultural technologies, animal health and nutraceuticals.

7) Biotechnology Resources

Biospace, Inc.
10506 Justin Dr.
Urbandale, IA 50322 USA
Toll Free: 877-277-7585
E-mail Address: support@biospace.com
Web Address: www.biospace.com
Biospace.com offers information, news and profiles on biotech companies. It also provides an outlet for business and scientific leaders in bioscience to communicate with each other.

Centre for Cellular and Molecular Biology (CCMB)
Habsiguda, Uppal Rd.
Hyderabad, Telangana 500007 India
Phone: 91-40-2716-0222-31
Fax: 91-040-2716-0591
Web Address: www.ccmb.res.in
Centre for Cellular and Molecular Biology (CCMB) is one of the constituent Indian national laboratories of the Council of Scientific and Industrial Research (CSIR), a multidisciplinary research and development organization of the Government of India. CCMB's research is focused on seven areas: Biomedicine and Biotechnology; Genetics, Evolution and Genomics; Cell Biology and Development; Molecular and Structural Biology; Biochemistry and Biophysics; Infectious Diseases; and Computational Biology and Bioinformatics.

Institute for Cellular and Molecular Biology (ICMB)
100 E. 24th St., NHB 4500
Austin, TX 78712 USA
Phone: 512-471-1156
Fax: 512-471-2149
E-mail Address: icmb@austin.utexas.edu
Web Address: www.icmb.utexas.edu
The Institute for Cellular and Molecular Biology (ICMB) web site offers a comprehensive dictionary of biotech terms, plus extensive research data regarding biotechnology. ICMB is located in The Louise and James Robert Moffett Molecular Biology Building at the University of Texas at Austin.

8) Blindness

American Council of the Blind (ACB)
1703 N. Beauregard St., Ste. 420
Arlington, VA 22201-3354 USA
Phone: 202-467-5081
Fax: 703-465-5085
Toll Free: 800-424-8666
E-mail Address: info@acb.org
Web Address: www.acb.org
The American Council of the Blind (ACB) is a leading membership organization for blind and visually impaired people, which strives to increase the independence, opportunity, security and quality of life of such people.

Guide Dog Foundation for the Blind, Inc.
371 E. Jericho Tpke.
Smithtown, NY 11787-2976 USA
Phone: 631-930-9000
Fax: 631-930-9009
Toll Free: 800-548-4337
E-mail Address: info@guidedog.org
Web Address: www.guidedog.org
The Guide Dog Foundation for the Blind, Inc. strives to be the leading resource and provider of premier services to facilitate the independence of people who are blind or visually impaired.

Helen Keller International Organization (HKI)
1 Dag Hammarskjold Plaza, Fl. 2
New York, NY 10017 USA
Phone: 212-532-0544
Toll Free: 877-535-5374
E-mail Address: info@hki.org
Web Address: www.hki.org
The Helen Keller International Organization (HKI) directly addresses the causes of preventable blindness, provides rehabilitation services to blind people and helps reduce micronutrient malnutrition which can cause blindness and death in children.

Learning Ally
20 Roszel Rd.
Princeton, NJ 08540 USA
Phone: 609-750-1830
Toll Free: 800-221-4792
E-mail Address:
custserv@LearningAlly.org
Web Address: www.learningally.org
Learning Ally, formerly Recording for the Blind and Dyslexic (RFB&D), is an educational library serving people who cannot effectively read standard print because of visual impairment, dyslexia or other disabilities.

Lighthouse Guild
250 W 64th St.
New York, NY 10023 USA
Phone: 212-769-6200
Toll Free: 800-284-4422
Web Address: www.lighthouseguild.org
Lighthouse Guild, formed in 2013 by the merger of Jewish Guild Healthcare and Lighthouse International, is a nonprofit vision and healthcare organization. It is dedicated to addressing the needs of blind, visually impaired people, including those with multiple disabilities or chronic medical conditions.

National Eye Institute (NEI)
31 Ctr. Dr., MSC 2510
Bethesda, MD 20892-2510 USA
Phone: 301-496-5248
E-mail Address: 2020@nei.nih.gov
Web Address: www.nei.nih.gov
The National Eye Institute (NEI) conducts and supports research that helps prevent and treat eye diseases and other vision related disorders.

National Federation of the Blind
200 E. Wells St.
Jernigan Place
Baltimore, MD 21230 USA
Phone: 410-659-9314
Fax: 410-685-5653
E-mail Address: nfb@nfb.org
Web Address: www.nfb.org
The National Federation of the Blind website lists information about vision loss as well as resources for visual impaired including products, assistive technology and programs for improving lives for blind people. In addition, the site contains information regarding accessibility web certification and access technology tips.

National Library Service for the Blind and Physically Handicapped (NLS)
1291 Taylor St. NW
Washington, DC 20542 USA
Phone: 202-707-5100
Fax: 202-707-0712
Toll Free: 800-424-8567
E-mail Address: nls@loc.gov
Web Address: www.loc.gov/nls
National Library Service for the Blind and Physically Handicapped (NLS), part of the Library of Congress, administers a

free library program of Braille and audio materials circulated to eligible borrowers in the United States by postage-free mail.

Prevent Blindness America (PBA)
225 W. Wacker Dr., Ste. 400
Chicago, IL 60606 USA
Toll Free: 800-331-2020
E-mail Address:
info@preventblindness.org
Web Address: www.preventblindness.org
Prevent Blindness America (PBA) is a leading volunteer eye health and safety organization dedicated to fighting blindness and saving sight.

VISIONS
500 Greenwich St., Ste. 302
New York, NY 10013-1354 USA
Phone: 212-625-1616
Fax: 212-219-4078
Toll Free: 888-245-8333
E-mail Address: info@visionsvcb.org
Web Address: www.visionsvcb.org
VISIONS is a nonprofit rehabilitation and social service agency that promotes the independence of people who are blind or visually impaired.

9) Blood Bank Industry Associations

American Association of Blood Banks (AABB)
4550 Montgomery Ave., Ste. 700
Bethesda, MD 20814-2749 USA
Phone: 301-907-6977
Fax: 301-907-6895
Web Address: www.aabb.org
The American Association of Blood Banks (AABB) promotes high standards of care for blood banking and transfusion medicine.

10) Burns

American Burn Association (ABA)
311 S. Wacker Dr., Ste. 4150
Chicago, IL 60606 USA
Phone: 312-642-9260
Fax: 312-642-9130
E-mail Address: info@ameriburn.org
Web Address: www.ameriburn.org
The American Burn Association (ABA) dedicates its efforts to the problems of burn injuries and burn victims throughout the U.S., Canada and other countries.

11) Canadian Government Agencies-Health Care

Canadian Institutes of Health Research (CIHR)
160 Elgin St., Fl. 10
Ottawa, ON K1A 0W9 Canada
Phone: 613-941-2672
Fax: 613-954-1800
Toll Free: 888-603-4178
E-mail Address: support@cihr-irsc.gc.ca
Web Address: www.cihr-irsc.gc.ca
The Canadian Institutes of Health Research (CIHR) is the government of Canada's agency for health research. CIHR's mission is to create new scientific knowledge and to catalyze its translation into improved health, more effective health services and products, and a strengthened Canadian health-care system. Composed of 13 Institutes, CIHR provides leadership and support to health researchers and trainees across Canada. The agency provides grants for research in the fields of biomedical, clinical, health systems and environmental health.

Health Canada (Health Portfolio, Canadian Minister of Health)
Health Canada
Address Locator: 0900C2
Ottawa, ON K1A 0K9 Canada
Phone: 613-957-2991
Fax: 613-941-5366
Toll Free: 866-225-0709
E-mail Address: Info@hc-sc.gc.ca
Web Address: www.hc-sc.gc.ca
The Minister of Health is responsible for maintaining and improving the health of Canadians. This objective is supported by the Health Portfolio, which comprises Health Canada, the Public Health Agency of Canada, the Canadian Institutes of Health Research, the Hazardous Materials Information Review Commission, the Patented Medicine Prices Review Board and Assisted Human Reproduction Canada.

Patented Medicine Prices Review Board (PMPRB)
333 Laurier Ave. W, Ste. 1400
Box L40, Standard Life Ctr.
Ottawa, ON K1P 1C1 Canada
Phone: 613-288-9597
Fax: 613-288-9643
Toll Free: 877-861-2350
E-mail Address: PMPRB.Information-Renseignements.CEPMB@pmprb-cepmb.gc.ca
Web Address: www.pmprb-cepmb.gc.ca
The Patented Medicine Prices Review Board (PMPRB) is an independent quasi-judicial body established by Parliament of Canada in 1987 under the Patent Act. Its role includes the regulation of drug prices. It also publishes a wealth of information about the Canadian drug industry and drug development.

12) Cancer

American Cancer Society (ACS)
250 Williams St. NW
Atlanta, GA 30303 USA
Toll Free: 800-227-2345
Web Address: www.cancer.org
The American Cancer Society (ACS) is a nationwide community-based voluntary health organization dedicated to eliminating cancer as a major health problem by preventing the disease, saving lives and diminishing suffering from cancer.

Association of Community Cancer Centers (ACCC)
1801 Research Blvd., Ste. 400
Rockville, MD 20850 USA
Phone: 301-984-9496
Fax: 301-770-1949
Web Address: www.accc-cancer.org
The Association of Community Cancer Centers (ACCC) helps oncology professionals adapt to the complex challenges of program management, cuts in reimbursement, hospital consolidation and mergers, and legislation and regulations that threaten to compromise the delivery of quality cancer care.

LIVESTRONG Foundation
623 W. 38th St., Ste. 300
Austin, TX 78705 USA
Toll Free: 877-236-8820
Web Address: www.livestrong.org
The LIVESTRONG Foundation, formerly the Lance Armstrong Foundation (LAF), provides cancer patients, their families and caregivers with advocacy, education, public health and research programs relating to the treatment of and possible cures for all forms of cancer.

National Association for Proton Therapy (The)
1420 New York Ave. NW, Fl. 5
Washington, DC 20005 USA
Phone: 202-495-3133
Fax: 202-530-0659
E-mail Address: info@proton-therapy.org
Web Address: www.proton-therapy.org
The National Association for Proton Therapy (NAPT) promotes the clinical benefits of proton beam radiation therapy for cancer patients and their families. Founded in 1990, NAPT is an independent, nonprofit, public benefit corporation. It serves as a resource center for cancer patients and their families, physicians and health care providers, academic medical centers, cancer centers, the U.S. Centers for Medicare and Medicaid Services (CMS) and other federal health care agencies, members of

Congress and staff, and the nation's news media.

National Marrow Donor Program (NMDP)
500 N 5th St.
Minneapolis, MN 55401-1206 USA
Phone: 612-627-5800
Toll Free: 800-627-7692
E-mail Address: foundation@nmdp.org
Web Address: bethematch.org
The National Marrow Donor Program (NMDP) is an international leader in the facilitation of marrow and blood stem cell transplantation through non-family donors.

NCI Contact Center
BG 9609 MSC 9760
9609 Medical Ctr. Dr.
Rockville, MD 20850 USA
Toll Free: 800-422-6237
E-mail Address: NCIinfo@nih.gov
Web Address:
http://www.cancer.gov/contact/contact-center
The NCI Contact Center, also known as the Cancer Information Service (CIS) is a national information and education network provided by the National Cancer Institute. It offers updated information on a range of topics, including cancer research and clinical trials, cancer prevention, cancer treatment centers, risk factors, symptoms, treatment, early detection and diagnosis.

OncoLink
3400 Civic Center Blvd., Ste. 2338
Philadelphia, PA 19104 USA
Phone: 215-349-8895
Fax: 215-349-5445
E-mail Address:
hampshire@uphs.upenn.edu
Web Address: www.oncolink.org
OncoLink is the web site maintained by a group of oncology healthcare professionals, which strives to help cancer patients, families, health care professionals and the general public obtain accurate cancer-related information.

Susan G. Komen Breast Cancer Foundation
13770 Noel Rd., Ste. 801889
Dallas, TX 75380 USA
Toll Free: 877-465-6636
E-mail Address: helpline@komen.org
Web Address: ww5.komen.org
The Susan G. Komen Breast Cancer Foundation strives to eradicate breast cancer as a life-threatening disease by advancing research, education, screening and treatment.

13) Careers-Biotech

Chase Group (The)
10975 Grandview Dr., Ste. 100
Overland Park, KS 66210 USA
Phone: 913-663-3100
Fax: 913-663-3131
E-mail Address: chase@chasegroup.com
Web Address: www.chasegroup.com
The Chase Group is an executive search firm specializing in biomedical and pharmaceutical placement.

14) Careers-First Time Jobs/New Grads

CollegeGrad.com, Inc.
950 Tower Ln., Fl. 6
Foster City, CA 94404 USA
E-mail Address: info@quinstreet.com
Web Address: www.collegegrad.com
CollegeGrad.com, Inc. offers in-depth resources for college students and recent grads seeking entry-level jobs.

National Association of Colleges and Employers (NACE)
62 Highland Ave.
Bethlehem, PA 18017-9085 USA
Phone: 610-868-1421
E-mail Address:
customerservice@naceweb.org
Web Address: www.naceweb.org
The National Association of Colleges and Employers (NACE) is a premier U.S. organization representing college placement offices and corporate recruiters who focus on hiring new grads.

15) Careers-General Job Listings

CareerBuilder, Inc.
200 N La Salle Dr., Ste. 1100
Chicago, IL 60601 USA
Phone: 773-527-3600
Fax: 773-353-2452
Toll Free: 800-891-8880
Web Address: www.careerbuilder.com
CareerBuilder, Inc. focuses on the needs of companies and also provides a database of job openings. The site has over 1 million jobs posted by 300,000 employers, and receives an average 23 million unique visitors monthly. The company also operates online career centers for 140 newspapers and 9,000 online partners. Resumes are sent directly to the company, and applicants can set up a special e-mail account for job-seeking purposes. CareerBuilder is primarily a joint venture between three newspaper giants: The McClatchy Company, Gannett Co., Inc. and Tribune Company.

CareerOneStop
Toll Free: 877-872-5627
E-mail Address: info@careeronestop.org
Web Address: www.careeronestop.org
CareerOneStop is operated by the employment commissions of various state agencies. It contains job listings in both the private and government sectors, as well as a wide variety of useful career resources and workforce information. CareerOneStop is sponsored by the U.S. Department of Labor.

LaborMarketInfo (LMI)
Employment Development Dept.
P.O. Box 826880, MIC 57
Sacramento, CA 94280-0001 USA
Phone: 916-262-2162
Fax: 916-262-2352
Web Address:
www.labormarketinfo.edd.ca.gov
LaborMarketInfo (LMI) provides job seekers and employers a wide range of resources, namely the ability to find, access and use labor market information and services. It provides statistics for employment demographics on both a local and regional level, as well as career searching tools for California residents. The web site is sponsored by California's Employment Development Office.

Recruiters Online Network
E-mail Address: rossi.tony@comcast.net
Web Address: www.recruitersonline.com
The Recruiters Online Network provides job postings from thousands of recruiters, Careers Online Magazine, a resume database, as well as other career resources.

USAJOBS
USAJOBS Program Office
1900 E St. NW, Ste. 6500
Washington, DC 20415-0001 USA
Phone: 818-934-6600
Web Address: www.usajobs.gov
USAJOBS, a program of the U.S. Office of Personnel Management, is the official job site for the U.S. Federal Government. It provides a comprehensive list of U.S. government jobs, allowing users to search for employment by location; agency; type of work; or by senior executive positions. It also has special employment sections for individuals with disabilities, veterans and recent college graduates; an information center, offering resume and interview tips and other information; and allows users to create a profile and post a resume.

16) Careers-Health Care

Health Care Source
100 Sylvan Rd., Ste. 100
Woburn, MA 01801 USA
Phone: 781-368-1033
Fax: 800-829-6600
Toll Free: 800-869-5200
E-mail Address:
support@healthcaresource.com
Web Address: www.healthcaresource.com
Health Care Source is a leading provider
of talent management, recruitment and
employment services for healthcare
providers. It offers a comprehensive suite
of solutions, which includes features, such
as applicant tracking and onboarding,
recruitment optimization, reference
checking, behavioral assessments, merit
planning, employee performance and
eLearning courseware among others.

MedicalWorkers.com
Web Address: www.medicalworkers.com
MedicalWorkers.com is an employment
site for medical and health care
professionals.

Medzilla, Inc.
P.O. Box 1710
Marysville, WA 98270 USA
Phone: 360-657-5681
Fax: 425-279-5427
E-mail Address: info@medzilla.com
Web Address: www.medzilla.com
Medzilla, Inc.'s web site offers job
searches, salary surveys, a search agent
and information on employment in the
biotech, pharmaceuticals, healthcare and
science sectors.

Monster Career Advice-Healthcare
133 Boston Post Rd.
Weston, MA 02493 USA
Phone: 978-461-8000
Fax: 978-461-8100
Toll Free: 800-666-7837
Web Address: career-
advice.monster.com/Healthcare/job-
category-3975.aspx
Monster Career Advice-Healthcare, a
service of Monster Worldwide, Inc.,
provides industry-related articles, job
listings, job searches and search agents for
the medical field.

**NationJob Network-Medical and
Health Care Jobs Page**
920 Morgan St., Ste. T
Des Moines, IA 50309 USA
Fax: 515-243-5384
Toll Free: 800-292-7731
E-mail Address:
customerservice@nationjob.com
Web Address:
www.nationjob.com/medical
The NationJob Network-Medical and
Health Care Jobs Page offers information
and listings for health care employment.

Nurse-Recruiter.com
113 Cherry St., Ste. 26760
Seattle, WA 98104 USA
Phone: 1-800-243-3407
Fax: 1-866-608-1781
Toll Free: 877-562-7966
Web Address: www.nurse-recruiter.com
Nurse-Recruiter.com is an online job
portal devoted to bringing health care
employers and the nursing community
together.

PracticeLink
415 2nd Ave.
Hinton, WV 25951 USA
Toll Free: 800-776-8383
E-mail Address:
helpdesk@practicelink.com
Web Address: www.practicelink.com
PracticeLink, one of the largest physician
employment web sites, is a free service
with over 1.7 million page views each
month. There are more than 5,000
hospitals, medical groups, private
practices and health systems, posting over
20,000 physician job opportunities on the
web site.

RPh on the Go USA, Inc.
8430 West Bryn Mawr Ave., Ste. 1150
Chicago, IL 60631 USA
Phone: 847-588-7170
Fax: 904-632-5692
Toll Free: 800-553-7359
Web Address: www.rphonthego.com
RPh on the Go USA, Inc. places
temporary and permanent qualified
professionals in the pharmacy community.
This pharmacy staffing firm offers access
to more than 160,000 pharmacy
professionals and matches the right
pharmacy personnel to help meet clients'
needs.

17) Careers-Job Reference Tools

Vault.com, Inc.
132 W. 31st St., Fl. 16
New York, NY 10001 USA
Fax: 212-366-6117
Toll Free: 800-535-2074
E-mail Address:
customerservice@vault.com
Web Address: www.vault.com
Vault.com, Inc. is a comprehensive career
web site for employers and employees,
with job postings and valuable
information on a wide variety of
industries. Its features and content are
largely geared toward MBA degree
holders.

18) Careers-Science

New Scientist Jobs
25 Bedford St.
London, WC2E 9ES UK
Phone: 617-283-3213
E-mail Address:
nssales@newscientist.com
Web Address: jobs.newscientist.com
New Scientist Jobs is a web site produced
by the publishers of New Scientist
Magazine that connects jobseekers and
employers in the bioscience fields. The
site includes a job search engine and a
free-of-charge e-mail job alert service.

19) Child Development

Human Growth Foundation
997 Glen Cove Ave., Ste. 5
Glen Head, NY 11545 USA
Fax: 516-671-4055
Toll Free: 800-451-6434
E-mail Address: hgf1@hgfound.org
Web Address: www.hgfound.org
The Human Growth Foundation helps
children and adults with disorders related
to growth or growth hormone through
research, education, support and
advocacy.

20) Children-Vital Statistics

**Federal Interagency Forum on Child
and Family Statistics (Childstats)**
E-mail Address: childstats@ed.gov
Web Address: www.childstats.gov
The Forum is a joint effort by 22 U.S.
government agencies. Its signature report,
America's Children: Key National
Indicators of Well-Being, is an annual
indicators report that details the status of
children and families in the United States.
All data are updated annually on the
Forum's website. A more detailed report
alternates every other year with a
condensed version that highlights selected
indicators.

21) Chinese Government Agencies-Science & Technology

**China Ministry of Science and
Technology (MOST)**
15B Fuxing Rd.
Beijing, 100862 China
Web Address: www.most.gov.cn
The China Ministry of Science and
Technology (MOST) is the PRC's official

body for science and technology related activities. It drafts laws, policies and regulations regarding science and technology; oversees budgeting and accounting for funds; and supervises research institutes operating in China, among other duties.

22) Christian Health Coverage Associations

Alliance of Health Care Sharing Ministries
1629 K St. NW, Ste. 300
Washington, DC 20006 USA
Phone: 833-997-4273
Web Address: http://ahcsm.org/
The alliance was established ii 2007 as a 501(c)(6) trade organization to represent the common interests of Christian organizations which are facilitating the sharing of health care needs (financial, emotional, and spiritual) by individuals and families, and their participants. The alliance is comprised of America's three largest health care sharing ministries: Samaritan Ministries, Christian Care Ministry, and Christian Healthcare Ministries.

23) Clinical Trials

Clinical Trials
U.S. National Library of Medicine
8600 Rockville Pike
Bethesda, MD 20894 USA
Phone: 301-594-5983
Toll Free: 888-346-3656
Web Address: www.clinicaltrials.gov
Clinical Trials, a service of the National Library of Medicine (NLM), offers up-to-date information for locating federally and privately supported clinical trials for a wide range of diseases and conditions, both within the U.S. and internationally.

Institute of Clinical Research (ICR)
10 Cedar Ct., Grove Park
White Waltham Rd.
Maidenhead, SL6 3LW UK
Phone: 44-1628-501700
Fax: 44-1628-501709
E-mail Address: info@icr-global.org
Web Address: www.icr-global.org
The Institute of Clinical Research (ICR) is a nonprofit professional organization for clinical researchers in the pharmaceutical industry in the U.K. It has over 3,000 members in 49 countries worldwide, which primarily include professionals involved in the design, management and conduct of human clinical trials.

24) Communications Professional Associations

Health and Science Communications Association (HeSCA)
P.O. Box 31323
Omaha, NE 68132 USA
Phone: 402-915-5373
E-mail Address: hesca@hesca.org
Web Address: hesca.net
The Health and Science Communications Association (HeSCA) is an organization of communications professionals committed to sharing knowledge and resources in the health sciences arena.

Health Industry Business Communications Council (HIBCC)
2525 E. Arizona Biltmore Cir., Ste. 127
Phoenix, AZ 85016 USA
Phone: 602-381-1091
Fax: 602-381-1093
E-mail Address: info@hibcc.org
Web Address: www.hibcc.org
The Health Industry Business Communications Council (HIBCC) seeks to facilitate electronic communications by developing appropriate standards for information exchange among all health care trading partners.

25) Consulting Industry Associations

American Association of Legal Nurse Consultants (AALNC)
330 N. Wabash Ave., Ste. 2000
Chicago, IL 60611 USA
Phone: 312-321-5177
Fax: 312-673-6655
Toll Free: 877-402-2562
E-mail Address: info@aalnc.org
Web Address: www.aalnc.org
The American Association of Legal Nurse Consultants (AALNC) is a nonprofit organization dedicated to the professional enhancement of registered nurses practicing in a consulting capacity in the legal field.

National Society of Certified Healthcare Business Consultants (NSCHBC)
11654 Plaza America Dr., Ste. 199
Reston, VA 20190 USA
Phone: 703-234-4099
Fax: 703-435-4390
E-mail Address: info@nschbc.org
Web Address: www.nschbc.org
The National Society of Certified Healthcare Business Consultants was founded by the membership of the Institute of Certified Healthcare Business Consultants, the National Association of

Healthcare Consultants and the Society of Medical Dental Management Consultants on July 1, 2006. It offers an active platform for sharing best practices, networking and understanding healthcare environment.

26) Corporate Information Resources

Business Journals (The)
120 W. Morehead St., Ste. 400
Charlotte, NC 28202 USA
Toll Free: 866-853-3661
E-mail Address:
gmurchison@bizjournals.com
Web Address: www.bizjournals.com
Bizjournals.com is the online media division of American City Business Journals, the publisher of dozens of leading city business journals nationwide. It provides access to research into the latest news regarding companies both small and large. The organization maintains 42 websites and 64 print publications and sponsors over 700 annual industry events.

Business Wire
101 California St., Fl. 20
San Francisco, CA 94111 USA
Phone: 415-986-4422
Fax: 415-788-5335
Toll Free: 800-227-0845
E-mail Address: info@businesswire.com
Web Address: www.businesswire.com
Business Wire offers news releases, industry- and company-specific news, top headlines, conference calls, IPOs on the Internet, media services and access to tradeshownews.com and BW Connect On-line through its informative and continuously updated web site.

Edgar Online, Inc.
35 W. Wacker Dr.
Chicago, IL 60601 USA
Phone: 301-287-0300
Fax: 301-287-0390
Toll Free: 800-823-5304
Web Address: www.edgar-online.com
Edgar Online, Inc. is a gateway and search tool for viewing corporate documents, such as annual reports on Form 10-K, filed with the U.S. Securities and Exchange Commission.

PR Newswire Association LLC
200 Vesey St., Fl. 19
New York, NY 10281 USA
Fax: 800-793-9313
Toll Free: 800-776-8090
E-mail Address:
mediainquiries@cision.com
Web Address: www.prnewswire.com

PR Newswire Association LLC provides comprehensive communications services for public relations and investor relations professionals, ranging from information distribution and market intelligence to the creation of online multimedia content and investor relations web sites. Users can also view recent corporate press releases from companies across the globe. The Association is owned by United Business Media plc.

Silicon Investor
E-mail Address: si.admin@siliconinvestor.com
Web Address: www.siliconinvestor.com
Silicon Investor is focused on providing information about technology companies. Its web site serves as a financial discussion forum and offers quotes, profiles and charts.

27) Diabetes

American Diabetes Association
2451 Crystal Dr., Ste. 900
Alexandria, VA 22202 USA
Toll Free: 800-342-2383
E-mail Address: askada@diabetes.org
Web Address: www.diabetes.org
The American Diabetes Association is a nonprofit health organization providing diabetes research, information and advocacy. It consists of over 1million volunteers, more than 441,000 members with diabetes, their families and caregivers, over 800 staff members and roughly 16,500 healthcare professionals.

Juvenile Diabetes Research Foundation (JDRF)
200 Vesey St., Fl. 28
New York, NY 10281 USA
Fax: 212-785-9595
Toll Free: 800-533-2873
E-mail Address: info@jdrf.org
Web Address: www.jdrf.org
The Juvenile Diabetes Research Foundation (JDRF) is a major nonprofit, nongovernmental sponsor of type 1 diabetes (T1D) research. JDRF focuses on innovative cure, prevention and treatment of T1D and its complications, which it achieves through funding research, advocating government support of research and new therapies and connecting and engaging the T1D community.

28) Disabling Conditions

Americans with Disabilities Act (ADA)
950 Pennsylvania Ave. NW

Civil Rights Div., Disability Rights Section-NYA
Washington, DC 20530 USA
Phone: 202-307-0663
Fax: 202-307-1197
Toll Free: 800-514-0301
Web Address: www.ada.gov
The Americans with Disabilities Act (ADA) web site provides information and technical assistance on the Americans with Disabilities Act.

Job Accommodation Network (JAN)
P.O. Box 6080
Morgantown, WV 26506-6080 USA
Phone: 304-293-7186
Fax: 304-293-5407
Toll Free: 800-526-7234
E-mail Address: jan@askjan.org
Web Address: askjan.org
The Job Accommodation Network (JAN) is a free consulting service that provides guidance and information about job accommodations, the Americans with Disabilities Act and the employability of people with disabilities.

National Easter Seal Society
141 W Jackson Blvd., Ste. 1400A
Chicago, IL 60604 USA
Phone: 312-726-6200
Fax: 312-726-1494
Toll Free: 800-221-6827
E-mail Address: info@easterseals.com
Web Address: www.easterseals.com
The National Easter Seal Society provides services to children and adults with disabilities and special needs, as well as assistance to their families. It offers education, outreach, advocacy, child development centers, physical rehabilitation and job training for people with disabilities.

29) Diseases, Rare & Other

American Association on Intellectual and Developmental Disabilities (AAIDD)
8403 Colesville Rd., Ste. 900
Silver Spring, MD 20910 USA
Phone: 202-387-1968
Fax: 202-387-2193
E-mail Address: ccarpenter@aaidd.org
Web Address: aaidd.org
The American Association on Intellectual and Developmental Disabilities (AAIDD) promotes progressive policies, sound research, effective practices and universal human rights for people with mental challenges.

American SIDS Institute
528 Raven Way
Naples, FL 34110 USA

Phone: 239-431-5425
Fax: 239-431-5536
Web Address: www.sids.org
The American SIDS Institute is a nonprofit healthcare organization dedicated to the prevention of sudden infant death and the promotion of infant health. It is involved in research and education of both causes and prevention of sudden infant death, as well as offers support for the families affected by it.

Amyotrophic Lateral Sclerosis Association (ALSA)
1300 Wilson Blvd., Ste. 600
Arlington, VA 22209 USA
Phone: 202-407-8580
Fax: 202-464-8869
Toll Free: 800-782-4747
E-mail Address: alsinfo@alsa-national.org
Web Address: www.alsa.org
The Amyotrophic Lateral Sclerosis Association (ALSA) seeks to be the primary resource for Lou Gehrig's Disease by providing information about the disease, products and services, physicians and other information.

Angelman Syndrome Foundation (ASF)
75 Executive Dr., Ste. 327
Aurora, IL 60504 USA
Phone: 630-978-4245
Fax: 630-978-7408
Toll Free: 800-432-6435
Web Address: www.angelman.org
The mission of the Angelman Syndrome Foundation (ASF) is to advance the awareness and treatment of Angelman Syndrome through education, information exchange and research.

Autism Society of America (ASA)
6110 Executive Blvd., Ste. 305
Rockville, MD 20852 USA
Phone: 301-657-0881
Toll Free: 800-328-8476
E-mail Address: info@autism-society.org
Web Address: www.autism-society.org
The Autism Society of America (ASA) seeks to promote lifelong access and opportunity for all individuals affected by autism to be fully participating members of their communities.

Cleft Palate Foundation (CPF)
1504 E. Franklin St., Ste. 102
Chapel Hill, NC 27514-2820 USA
Phone: 919-933-9044
Fax: 919-933-9604
Toll Free: 800-242-5338
E-mail Address: info@cleftline.org
Web Address: www.cleftline.org
The Cleft Palate Foundation (CPF) is a nonprofit organization dedicated to

optimizing the quality of life for individuals affected by facial birth defects. It serves individuals and families affected by cleft lip/palate and other craniofacial conditions through team care, education and personal support.

Cystic Fibrosis Foundation (CFF)
4550 Montgomery Ave., Ste. 1100 N
Bethesda, MD 20814 USA
Phone: 301-951-4422
Fax: 301-951-6378
Toll Free: 800-344-4823
E-mail Address: info@cff.org
Web Address: https://www.cff.org/
The Cystic Fibrosis Foundation (CFF) assures the development of the means to cure and control cystic fibrosis and to improve the quality of life for those affected with the disease.

Dystonia Medical Research Foundation
One E. Wacker Dr., Ste. 2810
Chicago, IL 60601-1905 USA
Phone: 312-755-0198
Fax: 312-803-0138
Toll Free: 800-377-3978
E-mail Address: dystonia@dystonia-foundation.org
Web Address: www.dystonia-foundation.org
The Dystonia Medical Research Foundation seeks to advance research for treatments and ultimately a cure for dystonia, to promote awareness and education of the disease and to support the needs and well-being of affected individuals and families.

Epilepsy Foundation of America
8301 Professional Place W., Ste. 230
Landover, MD 20785-2353 USA
Phone: 301-459-3700
Fax: 301-577-2684
Toll Free: 800-332-1000
E-mail Address: ContactUs@efa.org
Web Address: www.epilepsyfoundation.org
The Epilepsy Foundation of America is the national nonprofit voluntary agency devoted to the wellbeing of people with epilepsy in the U.S. and their families. It is dedicated to prevent, control and cure epilepsy through community services, public education, federal and local advocacy and research into new treatments and therapies.

Hepatitis B Foundation
3805 Old Easton Rd.
Doylestown, PA 18902 USA
Phone: 215-489-4900
Fax: 215-489-4920
E-mail Address: info@hepb.org
Web Address: www.hepb.org

The Hepatitis B Foundation is a national nonprofit organization dedicated to finding a cure and improving the quality of life of those affected by hepatitis B worldwide through research, education and patient advocacy.

Huntington's Disease Society of America, Inc. (HDSA)
505 8th Ave., Ste. 902
New York, NY 10018 USA
Phone: 212-242-1968
Fax: 212-239-3430
Toll Free: 800-345-4372
E-mail Address: hdsainfo@hdsa.org
Web Address: www.hdsa.org
The Huntington's Disease Society of America, Inc. (HDSA) is dedicated to finding a cure for Huntington's disease (HD) while providing support and services for those living with HD and their families.

International Myeloma Foundation (IMF)
12650 Riverside Dr., Ste. 206
North Hollywood, CA 91607 USA
Phone: 818-487-7455
Fax: 818-487-7454
Toll Free: 800-452-2873
E-mail Address: TheIMF@myeloma.org
Web Address: www.myeloma.org
The International Myeloma Foundation (IMF) is a network dedicated to the treatment of myeloma with over 350,000 members in 140 countries.

Lupus Foundation of America
2121 K St. NW, Ste. 200
Washington, DC 20037 USA
Phone: 202-349-1155
Fax: 202-349-1156
Toll Free: 800-558-0121
E-mail Address: info@lupus.org
Web Address: www.lupus.org
The Lupus Foundation of America is a nonprofit voluntary health organization dedicated to improving the diagnosis and treatment of lupus, supporting individuals and families affected by the disease, increasing awareness of lupus among health professionals and the public, and finding the cure.

Muscular Dystrophy Association (MDA)
161 N. Clark, Ste. 3550
Chicago, IL 60601 USA
Toll Free: 800-572-1717
E-mail Address: resourcecenter@mdausa.org
Web Address: www.mda.org
The Muscular Dystrophy Association (MDA) is a voluntary health agency aimed at conquering neuromuscular

diseases that affect more than 1 million Americans.

Myasthenia Gravis Foundation of America (MGFA)
290 Turnpike Rd., Ste. 5-315
Westborough, MA 01581 USA
Fax: 212-297-2159
Toll Free: 800-541-5454
E-mail Address: mgfa2myasthenia.org
Web Address: www.myasthenia.org
The Myasthenia Gravis Foundation of America (MGFA) is a national volunteer health agency dedicated solely to the fight against myasthenia gravis. It consists of a network of chapters, support groups and programs; and works to find cure, improve treatment options and provide information and support to people living with the disease.

National Down Syndrome Congress (NDSC)
30 Mansell Ct., Ste. 108
Roswell, GA 30076 USA
Phone: 770-604-9500
Fax: 770-604-9898
Toll Free: 800-232-6372
E-mail Address: info@ndsccenter.org
Web Address: www.ndsccenter.org
The National Down Syndrome Congress (NDSC) strives to be the national advocacy organization for Down syndrome and to provide support and leadership in all areas of concern related to persons with Down syndrome.

National Multiple Sclerosis Society (NMSS)
101A First Ave., Ste. 6
Waltham, MA 02451 USA
Phone: 212-986-3240
Fax: 781-890-2089
Toll Free: 800-344-4867
E-mail Address: info@nmss.org
Web Address: www.nmss.org
The National Multiple Sclerosis Society (NMSS) and its network of chapters nationwide promote research, educate and advocate on critical issues, as well as organize a wide range of programs for those living with multiple sclerosis.

National Organization for Rare Disorders (NORD)
55 Kenosia Ave.
Danbury, CT 06810 USA
Phone: 203-744-0100
Fax: 203-263-9938
Toll Free: 800-999-6673
Web Address: www.rarediseases.org
The National Organization for Rare Disorders (NORD) is a unique federation of voluntary health organizations dedicated to helping people with rare

diseases and assisting the organizations that serve them.

National Peticulosis Association (NPA)
1005 Boylston St., Ste. 343
Newton, MA 02461 USA
Phone: 617-905-0176
E-mail Address: npa@headlice.org
Web Address: www.headlice.org
The National Peticulosis Association (NPA) is a nonprofit health and education agency dedicated to protecting children from the misuse and abuse of potentially harmful lice and scabies pesticidal treatments.

National Reye's Syndrome Foundation (NRSF)
426 N. Lewis St.
P.O. Box 829
Bryan, OH 43506 USA
Phone: 419-924-9000
Fax: 419-924-9999
Toll Free: 800-233-7393
E-mail Address: nrsf@reyessyndrome.org
Web Address: www.reyessyndrome.org
The National Reye's Syndrome Foundation (NRSF) attempts to generate a concerted, organized lay movement to eradicate Reye's syndrome. It works to raise awareness, educate public, offer support and guidance and conduct research into the cause, management, treatment and prevention of Reye's Syndrome.

Scleroderma Foundation
300 Rosewood Dr., Ste. 105
Danvers, MA 01923 USA
Phone: 978-463-5843
Fax: 978-777-1313
Toll Free: 800-722-4673
E-mail Address: sfinfo@scleroderma.org
Web Address: www.scleroderma.org
The Scleroderma Foundation seeks to help patients and their families cope with scleroderma, as well as raise public awareness and stimulate research.

Sickle Cell Disease Association of America, Inc. (SCDAA)
7240 Parkway Dr., Ste. 5180
Hanover, MD 21076 USA
Phone: 410-528-1555
Fax: 410-528-1495
Toll Free: 800-421-8453
E-mail Address: scdaa@sicklecelldisease.org
Web Address: www.sicklecelldisease.org
The Sickle Cell Disease Association of America (SCDAA) is devoted to the care and cure of individuals with sickle cell disease. The group also organizes conferences and prepares and distributes substantive educational materials about the sickle cell disease problem.

Spina Bifida Association (SBA)
1600 Wilson Blvd., Ste. 800
Arlington, VA 22209 USA
Phone: 202-944-3285
Fax: 202-944-3295
Toll Free: 800-621-3141
E-mail Address: sbaa@sbaa.org
Web Address: www.spinabifidaassociation.org
The Spina Bifida Association is a national voluntary health agency that seeks to promote the prevention of spina bifida and to enhance the lives of all affected. Through its network of chapters, the association is present in over 125 communities across the nation connecting 10,000 people annually.

Tourette Syndrome Association, Inc. (TSA)
42-40 Bell Blvd., Ste. 205
Bayside, NY 11361-2820 USA
Phone: 718-224-2999
Toll Free: 844-480-8738
E-mail Address: support@tourette.org
Web Address: tourette.org
The Tourette Syndrome Association, Inc. (TSA) is a voluntary, nonprofit membership organization that seeks to identify the cause, find the cure for and control the effects of Tourette syndrome.

United Cerebral Palsy (UCP)
1825 K St. NW, Ste. 600
Washington, DC 20006 USA
Phone: 202-776-0406
Toll Free: 800-872-5827
Web Address: www.ucp.org
United Cerebral Palsy (UCP) is a national organization that strives for change and progress for disabled persons within society. It works to advance the independence, productivity and full citizenship of people with disabilities through an affiliate network.

Al-Anon/Alateen
1600 Corporate Landing Pkwy.
Virginia Beach, VA 23454-5617 USA
Phone: 757-563-1600
Fax: 757-563-1655
Toll Free: 888-425-2666
E-mail Address: wso@al-anon.org
Web Address: www.al-anon.alateen.org
Al-Anon/Alateen strives to help families and friends of alcoholics recover from the effects of living with the problem drinking of a relative or friend.

Alcoholics Anonymous (AA)
475 Riverside Dr. at W. 120th St., Fl. 11
NY, NY 10115 USA
Phone: 212-870-3400
Web Address: www.aa.org
Alcoholics Anonymous (AA) is a nonprofit international fellowship dedicated to helping alcoholics in defeating their addictions or drinking problems. Its web site offers many useful resources for those who wish to seek help regarding alcohol addiction and related concerns.

Drug Information Association (DIA)
800 Enterprise Rd., Ste. 200
Horsham, PA 19044-3595 USA
Phone: 215-442-6100
Fax: 215-442-6199
E-mail Address: Americas@DIAglobal.org
Web Address: www.diaglobal.org
The Drug Information Association (DIA) provides a neutral global forum for the exchange and dissemination of information on the discovery, development, evaluation and utilization of medicines and related health care technologies.

National Clearinghouse for Alcohol and Drug Information (NCADI)
P.O. Box 2345
Rockville, MD 20847-2345 USA
Phone: 301-468-2600
Fax: 301-468-6433
Toll Free: 800-729-6686
E-mail Address: info@health.org
Web Address: www.health.org
The National Clearinghouse for Alcohol and Drug Information (NCADI) is the information service of the Center for Substance Abuse Prevention of the Substance Abuse and Mental Health Services Administration in the U.S. Department of Health & Human Services.

Phoenix House Foundation (The)
50 Jay St.
Brooklyn, NY 11201 USA
Phone: 646-505-2080
Fax: 212-595-6365
Toll Free: 888-671-9392
E-mail Address: jinevins@phoenixhouse.org.
Web Address: www.phoenixhouse.org
The Phoenix House Foundation is a drug awareness and rehabilitation group with operations in California, Florida, New England, New York, Maryland, New Hampshire, Massachusetts, Rhode Island, Vermont, Virginia, Texas and Washington D.C. It conducts more than 130 programs including individualized, holistic drug and alcohol addiction treatment.

31) Economic Data & Research

Centre for European Economic Research (The, ZEW)
L 7, 1
Mannheim, 68161 Germany
Phone: 49-621-1235-01
Fax: 49-621-1235-224
E-mail Address: empfang@zew.de
Web Address: www.zew.de/en
Zentrum fur Europaische Wirtschaftsforschung, The Centre for European Economic Research (ZEW), distinguishes itself in the analysis of internationally comparative data in a European context and in the creation of databases that serve as a basis for scientific research. The institute maintains a special library relevant to economic research and provides external parties with selected data for the purpose of scientific research. ZEW also offers public events and seminars concentrating on banking, business and other economic-political topics.

Economic and Social Research Council (ESRC)
Polaris House
North Star Ave.
Swindon, SN2 1UJ UK
Phone: 44-01793 413000
E-mail Address: esrcenquiries@esrc.ac.uk
Web Address: www.esrc.ac.uk
The Economic and Social Research Council (ESRC) funds research and training in social and economic issues. It is an independent organization, established by Royal Charter. Current research areas include the global economy; social diversity; environment and energy; human behavior; and health and well-being.

Eurostat
5 Rue Alphonse Weicker
Joseph Bech Bldg.
Luxembourg, L-2721 Luxembourg
Phone: 352-4301-1
E-mail Address: eurostat-pressoffice@ec.europa.eu
Web Address: ec.europa.eu/eurostat
Eurostat is the European Union's service that publishes a wide variety of comprehensive statistics on European industries, populations, trade, agriculture, technology, environment and other matters.

Federal Statistical Office of Germany
Gustav-Stresemann-Ring 11
Wiesbaden, D-65189 Germany
Phone: 49-611-75-2405
Fax: 49-611-72-4000
Web Address: www.destatis.de
Federal Statistical Office of Germany publishes a wide variety of nation and regional economic data of interest to anyone who is studying Germany, one of the world's leading economies. Data available includes population, consumer prices, labor markets, health care, industries and output.

India Brand Equity Foundation (IBEF)
Fl. 20, Jawahar Vyapar Bhawan
Tolstoy Marg
New Delhi, 110001 India
Phone: 91-11-43845500
Fax: 91-11-23701235
E-mail Address: info.brandindia@ibef.org
Web Address: www.ibef.org
India Brand Equity Foundation (IBEF) is a public-private partnership between the Ministry of Commerce and Industry, the Government of India and the Confederation of Indian Industry. The foundation's primary objective is to build positive economic perceptions of India globally. It aims to effectively present the India business perspective and leverage business partnerships in a globalizing marketplace.

National Bureau of Statistics (China)
57, Yuetan Nanjie, Sanlihe
Xicheng District
Beijing, 100826 China
Fax: 86-10-6878-2000
E-mail Address: info@gj.stats.cn
Web Address: www.stats.gov.cn/english
The National Bureau of Statistics (China) provides statistics and economic data regarding China's economy and society.

Organization for Economic Co-operation and Development (OECD)
2 rue Andre Pascal
Cedex 16
Paris, 75775 France
Phone: 33-1-45-24-82-00
Fax: 33-1-45-24-85-00
E-mail Address: webmaster@oecd.org
Web Address: www.oecd.org
The Organization for Economic Co-operation and Development (OECD) publishes detailed economic, government, population, social and trade statistics on a country-by-country basis for over 30 nations representing the world's largest economies. Sectors covered range from industry, labor, technology and patents, to health care, environment and globalization.

Statistics Bureau, Director-General for Policy Planning (Japan)
19-1 Wakamatsu-cho
Shinjuku-ku
Tokyo, 162-8668 Japan
Phone: 81-3-5273-2020
E-mail Address: toukeisoudan@soumu.go.jp
Web Address: www.stat.go.jp/english
The Statistics Bureau, Director-General for Policy Planning (Japan) and Statistical Research and Training Institute, a part of the Japanese Ministry of Internal Affairs and Communications, plays the central role of producing and disseminating basic official statistics and coordinating statistical work under the Statistics Act and other legislation.

Statistics Canada
150 Tunney's Pasture Driveway
Ottawa, ON K1A 0T6 Canada
Phone: 514-283-8300
Fax: 514-283-9350
Toll Free: 800-263-1136
E-mail Address: STATCAN.infostats-infostats.STATCAN@canada.ca
Web Address: www.statcan.gc.ca
Statistics Canada provides a complete portal to Canadian economic data and statistics. Its conducts Canada's official census every five years, as well as hundreds of surveys covering numerous aspects of Canadian life.

32) Electronic Health Records/Continuity of Care Records

American Health Information Management Association (AHIMA)
233 N. Michigan Ave., Fl. 21
Chicago, IL 60601-5809 USA
Phone: 312-233-1100
Fax: 312-233-1090
Toll Free: 800-335-5535
E-mail Address: info@ahima.org
Web Address: www.ahima.org
The American Health Information Management Association (AHIMA) is a professional association that consists health information management professionals who work throughout the health care industry.

American Medical Informatics Association (AMIA)
4720 Montgomery Ln., Ste. 500
Bethesda, MD 20814 USA
Phone: 301-657-1291
Fax: 301-657-1296
Web Address: www.amia.org
The American Medical Informatics Association (AMIA) is a membership organization of individuals, institutions and corporations dedicated to developing and using information technologies to improve health care.

College of Healthcare Information Management Executives (CHIME)
710 Avis Dr., Ste. 200
Ann Arbor, MI 48108 USA
Phone: 734-665-0000
Fax: 734-665-4922
E-mail Address: staff@cio-chime.org
Web Address: www.cio-chime.org
College of Healthcare Information Management Executives (CHIME) was formed with the dual objective of serving the professional development needs of health care CIOs and advocating the more effective use of information management within health care.

Healthcare Information and Management Systems Society (HIMSS)
33 W Monroe St., Ste. 1700
Chicago, IL 60603-5616 USA
Phone: 312-664-4467
Fax: 312-664-6143
Web Address: www.himss.org
The Healthcare Information and Management Systems Society (HIMSS) provides leadership in the optimal use of technology, information and management systems for the betterment of health care.

National Association of Health Data Organizations (NAHDO)
965 E Center St.
Provo, UT 84606 USA
Phone: 801-532-2299
Fax: 801-532-2228
E-mail Address: info@nahdo.org
Web Address: www.nahdo.org
The National Association of Health Data Organizations (NAHDO) is a nonprofit membership organization dedicated to strengthening the nation's health information system.

---

33) Engineering, Research & Scientific Associations

American Association for the Advancement of Science (AAAS)
1200 New York Ave. NW
Washington, DC 20005 USA
Phone: 202-326-6400
Web Address: www.aaas.org
The American Association for the Advancement of Science (AAAS) is the world's largest scientific society and the publisher of Science magazine. It is an international nonprofit organization dedicated to advancing science around the globe.

American Society for Healthcare Engineering (ASHE)
155 N. Wacker Dr., Ste. 400
Chicago, IL 60606 USA
Phone: 312-422-3800
Fax: 312-422-4571
E-mail Address: ashe@aha.org
Web Address: www.ashe.org
The American Society for Healthcare Engineering (ASHE) is the advocate and resource for continuous improvement in the health care engineering and facilities management professions. It is devoted to professionals who design, build, maintain and operate hospitals and other healthcare facilities.

American Society of Safety Engineers (ASSE)
520 N. Northwest Hwy
Park Ridge, IL 60068 USA
Phone: 847-699-2929
E-mail Address: customerservice@asse.org
Web Address: www.asse.org
The American Society of Safety Engineers (ASSE) is the world's oldest and largest professional safety organization. It manages, supervises and consults on safety, health and environmental issues in industry, insurance, government and education.

Association of the Scientific Medical Societies in Germany (AWMF)
Ubierstr. 20
Dusseldorf, D-40223 Germany
Phone: 49-211-31-28-28
Web Address: www.awmf.org
The Association of the Scientific Medical Societies in Germany (AWMF) represents roughly 173 specialty scientific societies in Germany as well as the medical sciences, research and practices in general.

European Commission Research & Innovation
ORBN 2/65
Brussels, B-1049 Belgium
Phone: 32-2-29-911111
Web Address: ec.europa.eu/research/index.cfm?lg=en
The European Commission Research & Innovation site has over 25,000 pages and links of interest to those in research, through many industries including research, business, teaching. The site offers information in more than 11 languages.

German Association of High-Tech Industries (SPECTARIS)
Werderscher Markt 15
Berlin, 10117 Germany
Phone: 49-30-4140-210
Fax: 49-30-4140-2133
E-mail Address: info@spectaris.de
Web Address: www.spectaris.de
The German Association of High-Tech Industries (SPECTARIS) is the trade association for technology and research in the consumer optics, photonics, biotech, laboratory technology and medical technology sectors.

Institute of Biological Engineering (IBE)
446 E. High St., Ste. 10
Lexington, KY 40507 USA
Phone: 859-977-7450
Fax: 859-271-0607
E-mail Address: info@ibe.org
Web Address: www.ibe.org
The Institute of Biological Engineering (IBE) is a professional organization encouraging inquiry and interest in biological engineering and professional development for its members.

Institute of Electrical and Electronics Engineers (IEEE)
3 Park Ave., Fl. 17
New York, NY 10016-5997 USA
Phone: 212-419-7900
Fax: 212-752-4929
Toll Free: 800-678-4333
E-mail Address: society-info@ieee.org
Web Address: www.ieee.org
The Institute of Electrical and Electronics Engineers (IEEE) is a nonprofit, technical professional association of more than 430,000 individual members in approximately 160 countries. The IEEE sets global technical standards and acts as an authority in technical areas ranging from computer engineering, biomedical technology and telecommunications to electric power, aerospace and consumer electronics.

Institute of Physics and Engineering in Medicine (IPEM)
230 Tadcaster Rd.
Fairmount House
York, YO24 1ES UK
Phone: 44-1904-610-821
Fax: 44-1904-612-279
E-mail Address: office@ipem.ac.uk
Web Address: www.ipem.ac.uk
The Institute of Physics and Engineering in Medicine (IPEM) is an organization of scientists applying physics and engineering in medical and biological applications.

International Union of Microbiological Societies (IUMS)
Web Address: www.iums.org
The International Union of Microbiological Societies (IUMS) works to promote the study of microbiological sciences around the world through its three divisions: Bacteriology & Applied

Microbiology (BAM); Mycology; and Virology. The association is one of the 31 Scientific Unions of the International Council of Science (ICSU).

National Academy of Science (NAS)
500 5th St. NW
Washington, DC 20001 USA
Phone: 202-334-2000
E-mail Address: worldwidefeedback@nas.edu
Web Address: www.nasonline.org
The National Academy of Science (NAS) is a private, nonprofit, self-perpetuating society of scholars engaged in scientific and engineering research. Three organizations comprise the NAS: The National Academy of Engineering, the National Academy of Sciences and the National Academy of Medicine.

National Medical Research Council (NMRC)
1 Maritime Sq.
#09-66, Harbourfront
Centre099253 Singapore
Phone: 65-6325-8130
Fax: 65-6324-3735
E-mail Address: MOH_NMRC@MOH.GOV.SG
Web Address: www.nmrc.gov.sg
National Medical Research Council (NMRC) oversees the development and advancement of medical research in Singapore.

Research in Germany, German Academic Exchange Service (DAAD)
Kennedyallee 50
Bonn, 53175 Germany
Phone: 49-228-882-743
Web Address: www.research-in-germany.de
The Research in Germany portal, German Academic Exchange Service (DAAD), is an information platform and contact point for those looking to find out more about Germany's research landscape and its latest research achievements. The portal is an initiative of the Federal Ministry of Education and Research.

Royal Society (The)
6-9 Carlton House Ter.
London, SW1Y 5AG UK
Phone: 44-20-7451-2500
E-mail Address: science.policy@royalsociety.org
Web Address: royalsociety.org
The Royal Society, originally founded in 1660, is the UK's leading scientific organization and the oldest scientific community in continuous existence. It operates as a national academy of science, supporting scientists, engineers,

technologists and researchers. Its web site contains a wealth of data about the research and development initiatives of its fellows and foreign members.

34) Environmental Industry Associations

Air & Waste Management Association (A&WMA)
436 Seventh Ave., Ste. 2100
Pittsburgh, PA 15219 USA
Phone: 412-232-3444
Fax: 412-232-3450
Toll Free: 800-270-3444
E-mail Address: info@awma.org
Web Address: www.awma.org
The Air & Waste Management Association (A&WMA) is a nonprofit professional organization that provides education and support to more than 5,000 environmental professionals in 65 nations.

35) Fitness Industry Associations

Aerobics and Fitness Association of America (AFAA)
355 E. German Rd., Bldg. 6
Gilbert, AZ 85297 USA
Toll Free: 877-446-2322
E-mail Address: customerservice@afaa.com
Web Address: www.afaa.com
The Aerobics and Fitness Association of America (AFAA) provides certification training for personal trainers, group exercise instructors, kickboxing teachers and others in the fitness instruction field. It also offers workshops and answers questions from the public regarding safe and effective exercise programs and practices.

American Fitness Professionals and Associates (AFPA)
1601 Long Beach Blvd.
P.O. Box 214
Ship Bottom, NJ 08008 USA
Phone: 609-978-7583
Fax: 609-978-7582
Toll Free: 800-494-7782
E-mail Address: afpa@afpafitness.com
Web Address: www.afpafitness.com
American Fitness Professionals and Associates (AFPA) offers health and fitness professionals certification programs, continuing education courses, home correspondence courses and regional conventions.

International Health, Racquet and Sportsclub Association (IHRSA)
70 Fargo St.
Boston, MA 02210 USA

Phone: 617-951-0055
Fax: 617-951-0056
Toll Free: 800-228-4772
E-mail Address: info@ihrsa.org
Web Address: www.ihrsa.org
The International Health, Racquet & Sportsclub Association is the fitness industry's only global trade association. IHRSA represents over 10,000 for profit health and fitness facilities, and over 600 supplier companies in 75 countries.

National Academy of Kinesiology (NAK)
2001 Juniper Dr
Mahomet, IL 61853 USA
Fax: 217-351-1549
E-mail Address: staff@nationalacademyofkinesiology.org
Web Address: www.nationalacademyofkinesiology.org
The National Academy of Kinesiology (NAK), formerly the American Academy of Kinesiology and Physical Education (AAKPE), promotes research of human movement and physical activity. NAK's members transmit knowledge about human movement and physical activity through yearly meetings and publications.

North American Society for the Psychology of Sport and Physical Activity (NASPSPA)
E-mail Address: qalmeida@wlu.ca
Web Address: http://naspspa.com
The North American Society for the Psychology of Sport and Physical Activity (NASPSPA) is an association of scholars from the behavioral sciences and related professions that seeks to advance the scientific study of human behavior in sport and physical activity.

SHAPE America-Society of Health and Physical Educators
P.O. Box 225
Annapolis Junction, MD 20701 USA
Phone: 703-476-3400
Fax: 703-476-9527
Toll Free: 800-213-7193
Web Address: www.shapeamerica.org
SHAPE America-Society of Health and Physical Educators, formerly the American Alliance for Health, Physical Education, Recreation & Dance (AAHPERD) is an organization of professionals who support and assist those involved in physical education, fitness, leisure, dance, health promotion and education. It works with its 50 state affiliates and national partners to support initiatives, including the Presidential Youth Fitness Program and the Jump Rope For Heart/Hoops For Heart programs.

36) Fitness Resources

President's Council on Physical Fitness, Sports and Nutrition (PCPFSN)
200 Independence Ave. SW
Washington, DC 20201 USA
Phone: 240-276-9567
Fax: 240-276-9860
Toll Free: 877-696-6775
E-mail Address: fitness@hhs.gov
Web Address:
www.hhs.gov/fitness/index.html
The President's Council on Physical Fitness, Sports and Nutrition (PCPFSN) offers information about exercise, fitness and nutrition for people of all ages and works to promote active, healthy lifestyles.

YMCA of the USA
101 N. Wacker Dr.
Chicago, IL 60606 USA
Phone: 312-977-0031
Toll Free: 800-872-9622
E-mail Address: fulfillment@ymca.net
Web Address: www.ymca.net
The YMCA of the USA is the largest nonprofit community service organization in America, with over 2,700 YMCA locations in the U.S. These locations offer youth development and sports activities, fitness and other community events.

37) Food Service Industry Associations

Association for Healthcare Foodservices (AHF)
4201 Wilson Blvd., Ste. 110
Arlington, VA 22203 USA
Phone: 703-662-0615
Fax: 703-995-4456
E-mail Address:
sbennett@healthcarefoodservice.org
Web Address:
www.healthcarefoodservice.org
The Association for Healthcare Foodservices (AHF), born out of the merger of the National Society for Healthcare Foodservice Management (HFM) and the American Society for Healthcare Food Service Administrators (ASHFSA), is a society dedicated to professionals and suppliers in the self-operated healthcare foodservice industry.

38) Genetics & Genomics Industry Associations

American College of Medical Genetics and Genomics (ACMG)
7101 Wisconsin Ave., Ste. 1101
Bethesda, MD 20814 USA
Phone: 301-718-9603
Fax: 301-718-9604
E-mail Address: acmg@acmg.net
Web Address: www.acmg.net
The American College of Medical Genetics and Genomics (ACMG) provides education, resources and a voice for the medical genetics profession. The ACMG promotes the development and implementation of methods to diagnose, treat and prevent genetic disease.

39) Headache/Head Injury

American Council for Headache Education (ACHE)
19 Mantua Rd.
Mt. Royal, NJ 08061 USA
Phone: 856-423-0043
Fax: 856-423-0082
E-mail Address: amf@talley.com
Web Address: www.achenet.org
The American Council for Headache Education (ACHE) is a nonprofit patient-health professional partnership dedicated to advancing the treatment and management of headaches and to raising the public awareness of headaches as valid, biologically based illnesses.

Brain Injury Association of America (BIAA)
3057 Nutley St., Ste. 805
Fairfax, VA 22031 USA
Phone: 703-761-0750
Fax: 703-761-0755
Toll Free: 800-444-6443
E-mail Address: info@biausa.org
Web Address: www.biausa.org
The Brain Injury Association of America (BIAA) works to create a better future through brain injury prevention, research, education and advocacy.

National Headache Foundation (NHF)
820 N. Orleans, Ste. 411
Chicago, IL 60610 USA
Phone: 312-274-2650
Fax: 312-640-9049
Toll Free: 888-643-5552
E-mail Address: info@headaches.org
Web Address: www.headaches.org
The National Headache Foundation (NHF) is a nonprofit organization dedicated to educating headache sufferers and health care professionals about headache causes and treatments.

40) Health & Nutrition Associations

Academy of Nutrition and Dietetics
120 S. Riverside Plz., Ste. 2190
Chicago, IL 60606-6995 USA
Phone: 312-899-0040
Toll Free: 800-877-1600
E-mail Address: foundation@eatright.org
Web Address: www.eatright.org
The Academy of Nutrition and Dietetics, formerly known as the American Dietetic Association (ADA) is the world's largest organization of food and nutrition professionals, with nearly 65,000 members. In addition to services for its professional members, this organization's web site offers consumers a respected source for food and nutrition information.

American College of Nutrition (ACN)
211 W Chicago Ave., Ste. 217
Hinsdale, Il 60521 USA
Phone: 727-446-6086
Fax: 727-446-6202
E-mail Address:
office@americancollegeofnutrition.org
Web Address: www.theana.org/educate
The American College of Nutrition exists to promote knowledge and education on a variety of nutrition-related issues. The organization seeks to bring together professionals from diverse disciplines, including the business, education and medical fields.

Food Allergy Research & Education (FARE)
7901 Jones Branch Dr., Ste. 240
McLean, VA 22102 USA
Phone: 703-691-3179
Fax: 703-691-2713
Toll Free: 800-929-4040
E-mail Address: info@foodallergy.org
Web Address: www.foodallergy.org
Food Allergy Research & Education (FARE), formed by the merger of the Food Allergy & Anaphylaxis Network (FAAN) and the Food Allergy Initiative, is a leader in food allergy and anaphylaxis awareness and the issues surrounding these conditions.

National Environmental Health Association (NEHA)
720 S. Colorado Blvd., Ste. 1000-N
Denver, CO 80246-1926 USA
Phone: 303-756-9090
Fax: 303-691-9490
Toll Free: 866-956-2258
E-mail Address: staff@neha.org
Web Address: www.neha.org
The National Environmental Health Association (NEHA) strengthens the foundation of food safety training in the United States by establishing a nationwide network of registered food safety trainers and other environmental health practitioners and by providing effective learning materials to trainers, managers and employees.

41) Health Associations- International

World Health Organization (WHO)
Ave. Appia 20
CH-1211
Geneva, 27 Switzerland
Phone: 41-22-791-2111
Fax: 41-22-791-3111
Web Address: www.who.int
The World Health Organization (WHO), the United Nations' specialized agency for health, works for the attainment by all people of the highest possible level of health. Health is defined in WHO's constitution as a state of complete physical, mental and social well-being and not merely the absence of disease or infirmity. It consists of offices in over 150 countries, with more than 7,000 people in its workforce.

42) Health Care Business & Professional Associations

Academy of Laser Dentistry (ALD)
9900 W. Sample Rd., Ste. 400
Coral Springs, FL 33065 USA
Phone: 954-346-3776
Fax: 954-757-2598
Toll Free: 877-527-3776
Web Address: www.laserdentistry.org
The Academy of Laser Dentistry (ALD) is an international professional membership association of dental practitioners and supporting organizations.

Academy of Medical-Surgical Nurses (AMSN)
200 E. Holly Ave.
Sewell, NJ 08080 USA
Fax: 856-589-7463
Toll Free: 866-877-2676
E-mail Address: amsn@ajj.com
Web Address: www.amsn.org
The Academy of Medical-Surgical Nurses (AMSN) is dedicated to fostering excellence in adult health and in the medical-surgical nursing practice.

Academy of Spinal Cord Injury Nurses
6 Lawrence Sq.
Springfield, IL 62704 USA
Phone: 217-321-2488
Fax: 217-525-1271
E-mail Address: acheatham@firminc.com
Web Address: www.academyscipro.org/
The Academy of Spinal Cord Injury Nurses, formerly the American Association of Spinal Cord Injury Nurses, is a division within the Academy of Spinal Cord Injury Professionals, Inc. and is dedicated to promoting quality care for individuals with spinal cord impairment.

Advanced Medical Technology Association (AdvaMed)
701 Pennsylvania Ave. NW, Ste. 800
Washington, DC 20004-2654 USA
Phone: 202-783-8700
Fax: 202-783-8750
E-mail Address: info@advamed.org
Web Address: www.advamed.org
The Advanced Medical Technology Association (AdvaMed) strives to be the advocate for a legal, regulatory and economic climate that advances global health care by assuring worldwide access to the benefits of medical technology.

AFT Healthcare
555 New Jersey Ave. NW
Washington, DC 20001 USA
Phone: 202-879-4400
Web Address: www.aft.org/healthcare
AFT Healthcare, a division of the American Federation of Teachers, represents its members in the health professions and seeks to enhance the professional norms and ethics of health care workers.

Aging Life Care Association (ALCA), The
3275 W. Ina Rd., Ste. 130
Tucson, AZ 85741-2198 USA
Phone: 520-881-8008
Fax: 520-325-7925
Web Address: www.aginglifecare.org
The Aging Life Care Association (ALCA), formerly the National Association of Professional Geriatric Care Managers (GCM) is a nonprofit, professional organization of practitioners whose goal is the advancement of dignified care for the elderly and their families through education, professional development and highest ethical standards. It has over 2,000 members.

Air and Surface Transport Nurses Association (ASTNA)
13918 E. Mississippi Ave., Ste. 215
Aurora, CO 80012 USA
Phone: 303-344-0457
Fax: 800-937-9890
E-mail Address: astna@astna.org
Web Address: www.astna.org
The Air and Surface Transport Nurses Association (ASTNA) is a nonprofit member organization whose mission is to represent, promote and provide guidance to professional nurses who practice the unique and distinct specialty of transport nursing.

American Academy of Allergy, Asthma & Immunology (AAAAI)
555 E. Wells St., Ste. 1100
Milwaukee, WI 53202-3823 USA

Phone: 414-272-6071
Web Address: www.aaaai.org
The American Academy of Allergy, Asthma & Immunology (AAAAI) offers information and services to allergy and asthma sufferers and their families and friends.

American Academy of Ambulatory Care Nursing (AAACN)
E. Holly Ave., Box 56
Pitman, NJ 08071-0056 USA
Toll Free: 800-262-6877
E-mail Address: aaacn@aacn.org
Web Address: www.aaacn.org
The American Academy of Ambulatory Care Nursing (AAACN) is the association of professional nurses who identify ambulatory care practice as essential to the continuum of high-quality, cost-effective health care.

American Academy of Child and Adolescent Psychiatry (AACAP)
3615 Wisconsin Ave. NW
Washington, DC 20016-3007 USA
Phone: 202-966-7300
Fax: 202-464-0131
E-mail Address: communications@aacap.org
Web Address: www.aacap.org
The American Academy of Child and Adolescent Psychiatry (AACAP) is the leading national professional medical association dedicated to treating and improving the quality of life for children, adolescents and families affected by these disorders.

American Academy of Facial Plastic and Reconstructive Surgery (AAFPRS)
310 S. Henry St.
Alexandria, VA 22314 USA
Phone: 703-299-9291
Fax: 703-299-8898
E-mail Address: info@aafprs.org
Web Address: www.aafprs.org
The American Academy of Facial Plastic and Reconstructive Surgery (AAFPRS) is the world's largest association of facial plastic and reconstructive surgeons. Its membership consists of 2,700 board certified surgeons specializing in surgery of the face, head and neck.

American Academy of Family Physicians (AAFP)
11400 Tomahawk Creek Pkwy.
Leawood, KS 66211-2680 USA
Phone: 913-906-6000
Fax: 913-906-6075
Toll Free: 800-274-2237
E-mail Address: aafp@aafp.org
Web Address: www.aafp.org

The American Academy of Family Physicians (AAFP) is a member association of family doctors, family medicine residents and medical students nationwide.

American Academy of Hospice and Palliative Medicine (AAHPM)
8735 West Higgins Rd., Ste. 300
Chicago, IL 60631 USA
Phone: 847-375-4712
Fax: 847-375-6475
E-mail Address: info@aahpm.org
Web Address: www.aahpm.org
The American Academy of Hospice and Palliative Medicine (AAHPM) is the only organization in the United States for physicians dedicated to the advancement of hospice and palliative medicine.

American Academy of Nursing (AAN)
1000 Vermont Ave., Ste. 910
Washington, DC 20005 USA
Phone: 202-777-1170
E-mail Address: info@aannet.org
Web Address: www.aannet.org
The American Academy of Nursing (AAN) works to enhance nursing profession by advancing health policy and practice and generate, synthesize and disseminate nursing knowledge.

American Academy of Ophthalmology (AAO)
655 Beach St.
San Francisco, CA 94120-7424 USA
Phone: 415-561-8500
Fax: 415-561-8533
Web Address: www.aao.org
The American Academy of Ophthalmology (AAO) is dedicated to advancing the education and interests of ophthalmologists in order to ensure that the public can obtain the best possible eye care.

American Academy of Orthotics and Prosthetics (AAOP)
7910 Woodmont Ave., Ste. 760
Maryland, MD 20814 USA
Phone: 202-380-3663
Fax: 202-380-3447
E-mail Address: info@oandp.org
Web Address: www.oandp.org
The American Academy of Orthotics and Prosthetics (AAOP) promotes high standards of patient care through advocacy, education, collaboration, literature and research.

American Association for Physician Leadership
400 N. Ashley Dr., Ste. 400
Tampa, FL 33602 USA
Phone: 813-287-2000
Fax: 813-287-8993
Toll Free: 800-562-8088
E-mail Address: info@physicianleaders.org
Web Address: www.physicianleaders.org/
The American Association for Physician Leadership, formerly the American College of Physician Executives (ACPE) represents physicians in health care leadership. It offers certification programs, online courses, consulting, physician leadership development programs, as well as career guidance, consulting and mentoring.

American Association of Colleges of Nursing (AACN)
655 K St. NW, Ste. 750
Washington, DC 20001 USA
Phone: 202-463-6930
Fax: 202-785-8320
E-mail Address: info@aacn.nche.edu
Web Address: www.aacn.nche.edu
The American Association of Colleges of Nursing (AACN) is the national voice for U.S. nursing education programs, which works to promote excellence in nursing education, research and practice.

American Association of Critical Care Nurses (AACN)
27071 Aliso Creek Rd.
Aliso Viejo, CA 92656-3399 USA
Phone: 949-362-2000
Fax: 949-362-2020
Toll Free: 800-899-2226
E-mail Address: info@aacn.org
Web Address: www.aacn.org
The American Association of Critical Care Nurses (AACN) is a nonprofit organization which works to promote the interests of 500,000 member nurses caring for acutely and critically ill patients, as well as provides leadership to establish work/care environments that involves respect and healing.

American Association of Immunologists
1451 Rockville Pike, Ste. 650
Rockville, MD 20852 USA
Phone: 301-634-7178
Fax: 301-634-7887
E-mail Address: infoaai@aai.org
Web Address: www.aai.org
The American Association of Immunologists is a nonprofit organization that represents professionals in the immunology field. Its membership consists of professionally trained scientists, who work to advance the knowledge of immunology and its related disciplines, foster the interchange of ideas and information among investigators and address the potential integration of immunologic principles into clinical practice.

American Association of Medical Assistants (AAMA)
20 N. Wacker Dr., Ste. 1575
Chicago, IL 60606 USA
Phone: 312-899-1500
Fax: 312-899-1259
Toll Free: 800-228-2262
Web Address: www.aama-ntl.org
The American Association of Medical Assistants (AAMA) seeks to promote the professional identity and stature of its members and the medical assisting profession through education and credentialing.

American Association of Neuroscience Nurses (AANN)
8735 W. Higgins Rd., Ste. 300
Chicago, IL 60631 USA
Phone: 847-375-4733
Fax: 847-375-6430
Toll Free: 888-557-2266
E-mail Address: info@aann.org
Web Address: www.aann.org
The American Association of Neuroscience Nurses (AANN) is a national organization of registered nurses and other health care professionals that work to improve the care of neuroscience patients and further the interests of health professionals in the neurosciences.

American Association of Nurse Anesthetists (AANA)
222 S. Prospect Ave.
Park Ridge, IL 60068-4001 USA
Phone: 847-692-7050
Fax: 847-692-6968
Toll Free: 855-526-2262
E-mail Address: info@aana.com
Web Address: www.aana.com
The American Association of Nurse Anesthetists (AANA) is a professional member organization that represents 49,000 registered nurse anesthetists nationwide.

American Association of Nurse Practitioners (AANP)
5901 Vega Ave., Ste. 200
Austin, TX 78711 USA
Phone: 512-442-4262
Fax: 512-442-6469
E-mail Address: admin@aanp.org
Web Address: www.aanp.org
The American Association of Nurse Practitioners (AANP), the result of the merger between the American College of Nurse Practitioners (ACNP) and the American Academy of Nurse Practitioners, is focused on advocacy and keeping nurse practitioners current on

legislative, regulatory and clinical practice issues that affect them in the rapidly changing health care arena.

American Association of Occupational Health Nurses (AAOHN)
330 N. Wabash Ave., Ste. 2000
Chicago, IL 60611 USA
Phone: 312-321-5173
Fax: 312-673-6719
Toll Free: 800-241-8014
E-mail Address:
AAOHN@internationalamc.com
Web Address: www.aaohn.org
The American Association of Occupational Health Nurses (AAOHN) seeks to advance the profession of occupational and environmental health nursing as the authority on health, safety, productivity and disability management for worker populations.

American Board of Facial Plastic and Reconstructive Surgery (ABFPRS)
115C S. St. Asaph St.
Alexandria, VA 22314 USA
Phone: 703-549-3223
Fax: 703-549-3357
E-mail Address: lwirth@abfprs.org
Web Address: www.abfprs.org
The American Board of Facial Plastic and Reconstructive Surgery (ABFPRS) is dedicated to improving the quality of facial plastic surgery available to the public by measuring the qualifications of candidate surgeons against rigorous standards.

American Board of Medical Specialties (ABMS)
353 N. Clark St., Ste. 1400
Chicago, IL 60601 USA
Phone: 312-436-2600
Web Address: www.abms.org
The American Board of Medical Specialties (ABMS) is an organization that works with its 24 approved medical specialty boards in the evaluation and certification of physicians.

American Chiropractic Association (ACA)
1701 Clarendon Blvd., Ste. 200
Arlington, VA 22209 USA
Phone: 703-276-8800
Fax: 703-243-2593
E-mail Address:
memberinfo@acatoday.org
Web Address: www.acatoday.org
The American Chiropractic Association (ACA) exists to preserve, protect, improve and promote the chiropractic profession for the benefit of the patients it serves.

American College of Chest Physicians (ACCP)
2595 Patriot Blvd.
Glenview, IL 60026 USA
Phone: 224-521-9800
Fax: 224-521-9801
Toll Free: 800-343-2227
Web Address: www.chestnet.org
The American College of Chest Physicians (ACCP) is the world's largest clinical cardiopulmonary and critical care medical society with 19,000 members in 100 countries. Members include physicians, allied health professionals, and PhDs from the specialties of pulmonology, critical care medicine, thoracic surgery, cardiology, sleep, and other chest-related specialties.

American College of Emergency Physicians (ACEP)
1125 Executive Cir.
Irving, TX 75038-2522 USA
Phone: 972-550-0911
Fax: 972-580-2816
Toll Free: 800-798-1822
E-mail Address: membership@acep.org
Web Address: www.acep.org
The American College of Emergency Physicians (ACEP) exists to support quality emergency medical care and to promote the interests of emergency physicians.

American College of Health Care Administrators (ACHCA)
1101 Connecticut Ave. NW, Ste. 450
Washington, DC 20036 USA
Phone: 800-561-3148
Fax: 800-561-3148
E-mail Address: info@achca.org
Web Address: www.achca.org
The American College of Health Care Administrators (ACHCA) offers educational programming, professional certification and career development opportunities for health care administrators.

American College of Healthcare Executives (ACHE)
300 S. Riverside Plaza, Ste. 1900
Chicago, IL 60606-6698 USA
Phone: 312-424-2800
Fax: 312-424-0023
E-mail Address: contact@ache.org
Web Address: www.ache.org
The American College of Healthcare Executives (ACHE) is an international professional society of health care executives that offers certification and educational programs.

American College of Legal Medicine (ACLM)
9700 W. Bryn Mawr Ave., Ste. 210
Rosemont, IL 60018 USA
Phone: 847-447-1713
Fax: 847-447-1150
E-mail Address: eyeskater1@gmail.com
Web Address: www.aclm.org
The American College of Legal Medicine (ACLM) is an organization for healthcare and legal professionals that works to promote interdisciplinary cooperation and an understanding of issues where law and medicine meet.

American College of Medical Quality (ACMQ)
110 E. Schiller St., Ste. 230
Elmhurst, Il 60126 USA
Phone: 301-718-6516
Fax: 301-656-0989
Web Address: www.acmq.org
The American College of Medical Quality (ACMQ) strives to provide leadership and education for professionals in health care quality management.

American College of Physicians (ACP)
190 N. Independence Mall W.
Philadelphia, PA 19106-1572 USA
Phone: 215-351-2400
Toll Free: 800-523-1546
Web Address: www.acponline.org
The American College of Physicians (ACP) exists to enhance the quality and effectiveness of health care by fostering excellence and professionalism in the practice of medicine. It consists of 143,000 members, including internists, internal medicine specialists, medical students, residents and fellows.

American College of Prosthodontists (ACP)
211 E. Chicago Ave., Ste. 1000
Chicago, IL 60611 USA
Phone: 312-573-1260
Web Address: www.prosthodontics.org/
The American College of Prosthodontists (ACP) is the official sponsoring organization for dentists who specialize in dental implants, dentures, veneers, crowns and teeth whitening.

American College of Rheumatology (ACR)
2200 Lake Blvd. NE
Atlanta, GA 30319 USA
Phone: 404-633-3777
Fax: 404-633-1870
Web Address: www.rheumatology.org
The American College of Rheumatology (ACR) is the professional organization of rheumatologists and associated health professionals dedicated to healing,

preventing disability and curing disorders of the joints, muscles and bones.

American College of Sports Medicine (ACSM)
401 W. Michigan St.
Indianapolis, IN 46202-3233 USA
Phone: 317-637-9200
Fax: 317-634-7817
Web Address: www.acsm.org
The American College of Sports Medicine (ACSM) promotes and integrates research, education and applications of sports medicine and exercise science to maintain and enhance quality of life. ACSM has more than 50,000 members and certified professionals from 90 countries worldwide.

American Correctional Health Services Association (ACHSA)
250 Gatsby Pl.
Alpharetta, GA 30022-6161 USA
Toll Free: 855-825-5559
E-mail Address: admin@achsa.org
Web Address: www.achsa.org
The American Correctional Health Services Association (ACHSA) serves as a forum for communications that address the current issues and needs confronting correctional healthcare. Its members include administrators, nurses, physicians, psychiatrists, nurse practitioners and physician assistants, mental health professionals, medical assistants, administrative personnel and ancillary personnel who work in a correctional setting.

American Dental Association (ADA)
211 E. Chicago Ave.
Chicago, IL 60611-2678 USA
Phone: 312-440-2500
Web Address: www.ada.org
The American Dental Association (ADA) is a nonprofit professional association of dentists committed to enhancing public's oral health with a focus on ethics, science and professional advancement.

American Health Care Association (AHCA)
1201 L St. NW
Washington, DC 20005 USA
Phone: 202-842-4444
Fax: 202-842-3860
E-mail Address: mparkinson@ahca.org
Web Address: www.ahcancal.org
The American Health Care Association (AHCA) is a nonprofit federation of affiliated state health organizations that represent assisted living, nursing facility, developmentally-disabled, and subacute care providers.

American Health Lawyers Association (AHLA)
1099 14th St. NW, Ste. 925
Washington, DC 20005 USA
Phone: 202-833-1100
Fax: 202-833-1105
E-mail Address: msc@healthlawyers.org
Web Address: www.healthlawyers.org
American Health Lawyers Association (AHLA) is an educational organization devoted to legal issues in the health care field. It provides a forum for information exchange and production of quality, non-partisan educational programs, products and services related to health law issues.

American Health Planning Association (AHPA)
3040 Williams Dr., Ste. 200
Fairfax, VA 22031 USA
Phone: 703-573-3101
E-mail Address: info@ahpanet.org
Web Address: www.ahpanet.org
The American Health Planning Association (AHPA) is a nonprofit organization committed to the creation of health policies and systems that assure access for all people to quality care at a reasonable cost.

American Health Quality Association (AHQA)
7918 Jones Branch Dr., Ste. 300
McLean, VA 22102 USA
Phone: 202-331-5790
E-mail Address: info@ahqa.org
Web Address: www.ahqa.org
The American Health Quality Association (AHQA) is a nonprofit national association dedicated to community-based, quality evaluation of health care.

American Holistic Nurses Association (AHNA)
2900 SW Plass Ct.
Topeka, KS 66611-1980 USA
Phone: 785-234-1712
Fax: 785-234-1713
Toll Free: 800-278-2462
E-mail Address: info@ahna.org
Web Address: www.ahna.org
The American Holistic Nurses Association (AHNA) embraces nursing as a lifestyle and a profession by acting as a bridge for nurses between traditional medical philosophy and alternative healing practices.

American Medical Association (AMA)
AMA Plaza
330 N. Wabash Ave.
Chicago, IL 60611 USA
Toll Free: 800-621-8335
Web Address: www.ama-assn.org

The American Medical Association (AMA) is the primary professional society of physicians in the United States, which works to promote sustainable physician practices, smarter medical training and improving professional environment and patient health outcomes. It also provides career support and involvement opportunities for its members.

American Medical Group Association (AMGA)
One Prince St.
Alexandria, VA 22314-3318 USA
Phone: 703-838-0033
Fax: 703-548-1890
E-mail Address: csacdalan@amga.org
Web Address: www.amga.org
The American Medical Group Association (AMGA) represents medical groups by advancing high-quality, cost-effective, patient-centered and physician-directed health care.

American Medical Society for Sports Medicine (AMSSM)
4000 W. 114th St., Ste. 100
Leawood, KS 66211 USA
Phone: 913-327-1415
Fax: 913-327-1491
E-mail Address: kdewitt@amssm.org
Web Address: www.amssm.org
The mission of the American Medical Society for Sports Medicine, Inc. (AMSSM) is to offer a forum that fosters a collegial relationship among dedicated, competent primary care sports medicine physicians as they seek to improve their individual expertise and raise the general level of the sports medicine practice.

American Medical Technologists (AMT)
10700 W. Higgins Rd., Ste. 150
Rosemont, IL 60018 USA
Phone: 847-823-5169
Fax: 847-823-0458
E-mail Address: mail@americanmedtech.org
Web Address: www.americanmedtech.org
American Medical Technologists (AMT) is a nationally and internationally recognized nonprofit certification agency and professional membership association representing allied health professionals. Its members include laboratory health professionals, as well as medical and dental office professionals.

American Medical Women's Association (AMWA)
1100 E. Woodfield Rd., Ste. 350
Schaumberg, IL 60173 USA
Phone: 847-517-2801
Fax: 847-517-7229

Toll Free: 866-564-2483
E-mail Address:
associatedirector@amwa-doc.org
Web Address: www.amwa-doc.org
The American Medical Women's
Association (AMWA) is an organization
of women physicians and medical
students dedicated to serving as the
unique voice for women's health and the
advancement of women in medicine.

**American Nephrology Nurses
Association (ANNA)**
E. Holly Ave., Box 56
Pitman, NJ 08071-0056 USA
Phone: 856-256-2320
Fax: 856-589-7463
Toll Free: 888-600-2662
E-mail Address: anna@annanurse.org
Web Address: www.annanurse.org
The American Nephrology Nurses
Association (ANNA) is a member
organization that seeks to advance the
nephrology nursing practice and
positively influence outcomes for patients
with diseases that require replacement
therapies.

**American Neurological Association
(ANA)**
1120 Route 73, Ste. 200
Mount Laurel, NJ 08054 USA
Phone: 856-380-6892
E-mail Address: info@myana.org
Web Address: https://myana.org
The American Neurological Association
(ANA) is a professional society of
academic neurologists and neuroscientists
devoted to advancing the goals and
science of neurology.

**American Occupational Therapy
Association, Inc. (AOTA)**
6116 Executive Blvd., Ste. 200
North Bethesda, MD 20852-4929 USA
Phone: 301-652-6611
Fax: 301-652-7711
Toll Free: 800-377-8555
Web Address: www.aota.org
The American Occupational Therapy
Association, Inc. (AOTA) advances the
quality, availability, use and support of
occupational therapy through standard-
setting, advocacy, education and research
on behalf of its members and the public.

**American Organization of Nurse
Executives (AONE)**
155 N. Wacker Dr., Ste. 400
Chicago, IL 60606 USA
Phone: 312-422-2800
E-mail Address: aone@aha.org
Web Address: www.aone.org
The American Organization of Nurse
Executives (AONE) is a national

organization focused on advancing
nursing practice and patient care through
leadership, professional development,
advocacy and research.

**American Orthopedic Society for
Sports Medicine (AOSSM)**
9400 W. Higgins Rd., Ste. 300
Rosemont, IL 60018 USA
Phone: 847-292-4900
Fax: 847-292-4905
Toll Free: 877-321-3500
E-mail Address: mary@aossm.org
Web Address: www.sportsmed.org
The American Orthopedic Society for
Sports Medicine (AOSSM) is a trade
association for orthopedic doctors and
sports medicine practitioners. The
AOSSM works to improve the
identification, prevention, treatment and
rehabilitation of sports injuries.

**American Osteopathic Association
(AOA)**
142 E. Ontario St.
Chicago, IL 60611-2864 USA
Phone: 312-202-8000
Fax: 312-202-8200
Toll Free: 800-621-1773
E-mail Address: crc@osteopathic.org
Web Address: www.osteopathic.org
The American Osteopathic Association
(AOA) is organized to advance the
philosophy and practice of osteopathic
medicine by promoting education,
research and the delivery of cost-effective
health care.

**American Pediatric Surgical
Association (APSA)**
111 West Jackson Blvd., Ste. 1412
Chicago, IL 60604 USA
Phone: 847-686-2237
Fax: 847-686-2253
E-mail Address: eapsa@eapsa.org
Web Address: www.eapsa.org
The American Pediatric Surgical
Association (APSA) is a surgical specialty
organization composed of individuals who
have dedicated themselves to the care of
pediatric surgical patients.

**American Psychiatric Association
(APA)**
800 Maine Ave., Ste. 900
Washington, DC 20024 USA
Phone: 703-907-7300
Toll Free: 888-357-7924
Web Address: www.psychiatry.org
The American Psychiatric Association
(APA) seeks to ensure humane care and
effective treatment for all persons with
mental disorders, including intellectual
and developmental disabilities and
substance-related disorders.

**American Public Health Association
(APHA)**
800 I St. NW
Washington, DC 20001-3710 USA
Phone: 202-777-2742
Fax: 202-777-2534
Web Address: www.apha.org
The American Public Health Association
(APHA) is an association of individuals
and organizations working to improve the
public's health and to achieve equity in
health status for all.

**American School Health Association
(ASHA)**
7918 Jones Branch Dr., Ste. 300
McLean, VA 22102 USA
Phone: 703-506-7675
Fax: 703-506-3266
E-mail Address: info@ashaweb.org
Web Address: www.ashaweb.org
The American School Health Association
(ASHA) advocates high-quality school
health instruction, health services and a
healthy school environment.

**American Society for Dermatologic
Surgery, Inc. (ASDS)**
5550 Meadowbrook Dr., Ste. 120
Rolling Meadows, IL 60008 USA
Phone: 847-956-0900
Fax: 847-956-0999
Web Address: www.asds.net
The American Society for Dermatologic
Surgery, Inc. (ASDS) is a member
organization for dermasurgeons, which
seeks to enhance dermatological surgery
and foster the highest standards of patient
care.

**American Society of Addiction
Medicine (ASAM)**
11400 Rockville Pike, Ste. 200
Rockville, MD 20852 USA
Phone: 301-656-3920
Fax: 301-656-3815
E-mail Address: email@asam.org
Web Address: www.asam.org
The American Society of Addiction
Medicine (ASAM) is dedicated to
educating physicians and improving the
treatment of individuals suffering from
alcoholism and other addictions.

**American Society of Clinical Oncology
(ASCO)**
2318 Mill Rd., Ste. 800
Alexandria, VA 22314 USA
Phone: 571-483-1300
Fax: 709-299-0255
E-mail Address:
customerservice@asco.org
Web Address: www.asco.org
The American Society of Clinical
Oncology (ASCO) is a nonprofit

organization, founded in 1964, with overarching goals of improving cancer care and prevention and ensuring that all patients with cancer receive care of the highest quality. Nearly 30,000 oncology practitioners belong to ASCO, representing all oncology disciplines.

American Society of Pain Management Nursing (ASPMN)
4400 College Blvd., Ste. 220
Overland Park, KS 66211 USA
Phone: 913-895-4606
Fax: 913-895-4652
Toll Free: 888-342-7766
Web Address: www.aspmn.org
The American Society of Pain Management Nursing (ASPMN) is an organization of professional nurses dedicated to promoting and providing optimal care of patients with pain.

American Society of Peri-Anesthesia Nurses (ASPAN)
90 Frontage Rd.
Cherry Hill, NJ 08034-1424 USA
Fax: 856-616-9601
Toll Free: 877-737-9696
E-mail Address: aspan@aspan.org
Web Address: www.aspan.org
The American Society of Peri-Anesthesia Nurses (ASPAN) advances perianesthesia nursing practice through education, research and standards. It has over 15,000 members, who specialize in preanesthesia and postanesthesia care, ambulatory surgery and pain management.

American Society of Plastic Surgeons (ASPS)
444 E. Algonquin Rd.
Arlington Heights, IL 60005 USA
Phone: 847-228-9900
E-mail Address:
media@plasticsurgery.org
Web Address: www.plasticsurgery.org
The American Society of Plastic Surgeons (ASPS) seeks to support its members in their efforts to provide the highest-quality patient care and maintain professional and ethical standards through education, research and advocacy of socioeconomic and other professional activities.

American Society of Therapeutic Radiology and Oncology (ASTRO)
251 18th St. S., Fl. 8
Arlington, VA 22202 USA
Phone: 703-502-1550
Fax: 703-502-7852
E-mail Address: info@astro.org
Web Address: www.astro.org
The American Society of Therapeutic Radiology and Oncology (ASTRO) works to advance the practice of radiation

oncology by promoting excellence in patient care, providing opportunities for educational and professional development, promoting research and disseminating research results and representing radiation oncology in a rapidly evolving healthcare environment.

American Telemedicine Association (ATA)
901 N. Glebe Rd., Ste. 850
Arlington, VA 22203 USA
Phone: 703-373-9600
E-mail Address:
info@americantelemed.org
Web Address: www.americantelemed.org
The American Telemedicine Association (ATA) is the leading resource and advocate promoting access to medical care for consumers and health professionals via telecommunications technology.

Association for Applied Sport Psychology (AASP)
8365 Keystone Crossing, Ste. 107
Indianapolis, IN 46240 USA
Phone: 317-205-9225
Fax: 317-205-9481
E-mail Address:
info@appliedsportpsych.org
Web Address: appliedsportpsych.org
The Association for Applied Sport Psychology (AASP) provides information about applied sports psychology to coaches, athletes, students, parents, certified consultants and AASP members.

Association for Dental Sciences of the Republic of China (ADS-ROC)
Hengyang Rd.
Taipei No. 36, 3rd fl.
Taipei City, 10045 Taiwan
Phone: 886-02-2311-6001
Fax: 886-02-2311-6080
E-mail Address: ads.tw@msa.hinet.net
Web Address: www.ads.org.tw
The Association for Dental Sciences of the Republic of China (ADS-ROC) represents the dental industry in the Republic of China.

Association for Healthcare Volunteer Resource Professionals (AHVRP)
155 N. Wacker Dr., Ste. 400
Chicago, IL 60606 USA
Phone: 312-422-3939
Fax: 312-278-0884
Toll Free: 866-488-2379
E-mail Address:
info@theberylinstitute.org
Web Address:
www.theberylinstitute.org/page/Volunteer Professionals

The Association for Healthcare Volunteer Resource Professionals (AHVRP), formerly the American Society of Directors of Volunteer Services, exists to strengthen the profession of volunteer services administration, provide opportunities for professional development and promote volunteerism as a resource in serving the health care needs of the nation.

Association for the Healthcare Environment (AHE)
155 N. Wacker Dr., Ste. 400
Chicago, IL 60606 USA
Phone: 312-422-3860
Fax: 312-422-4578
E-mail Address: ahe@aha.org
Web Address: www.ahe.org
The Association for the Healthcare Environment (AHE), formerly the American Society for Healthcare Environmental Services, is the premier health care association for environmental services, housekeeping and textile professionals.

Association of Camp Nurses (ACN)
19006 Hunt County Ln.
Fisherville, KY 40023 USA
Phone: 502-232-2945
Fax: 844-901-1504
E-mail Address: can@campnurse.org
Web Address: www.acn.org
The Association of Camp Nurses (ACN) promotes and develops the practice of camp nursing for a healthy camp community.

Association of Clinicians for the Underserved (ACU)
1420 Spring Hill Rd., Ste. 600
Tysons Corner, VA 22102 USA
Phone: 844-422-8247
Fax: 703-562-8801
E-mail Address: acu@clinicians.org
Web Address: www.clinicians.org
The Association of Clinicians for the Underserved (ACU) is a nonprofit, interdisciplinary organization whose mission is to improve the health of underserved populations by enhancing the development and support of the health care clinicians serving these populations.

Association of Food and Drug Officials (AFDO)
155 W. Market St., Fl. 3
York, PA 17401 USA
Phone: 717-757-2888
Fax: 717-650-3650
E-mail Address: afdo@afdo.org
Web Address: www.afdo.org
The Association of Food and Drug Officials (AFDO) is a trusted resource for

building consensus and promoting uniformity on public health and consumer protection issues related to the regulation of foods, drugs, devices, cosmetics and consumer products.

Association of Nurses in AIDS Care (ANAC)
11230 Cleveland Ave. NW, Ste. 986
Uniontown, OH 44685 USA
Phone: 330-670-0101
Fax: 330-670-0109
Toll Free: 800-260-6780
E-mail Address: anac@anacnet.org
Web Address: www.nursesinaidscare.org
The Association of Nurses in AIDS Care (ANAC) addresses the specific needs of nurses working in HIV/AIDS. ANAC also publishes a peer-reviewed journal and runs an annual conference on the latest developments in HIV nursing.

Association of periOperative Registered Nurses (AORN), The
2170 S. Parker Rd., Ste. 400
Denver, CO 80231-5711 USA
Phone: 303-755-6300
Fax: 800-847-0045
Toll Free: 800-755-2676
E-mail Address: custsvc@aorn.org
Web Address: www.aorn.org
The Association of periOperative Registered Nurses (AORN) is a nonprofit membership association, which offers nursing education, standards and clinical practice resources to achieve optimal outcomes for patients undergoing operative and other invasive procedures. Its membership includes 41,000 registered nurses, which are engaged in managing, teaching and practicing perioperative nursing.

Association of Rehabilitation Nurses (ARN)
8735 W. Higgins Rd., Ste. 300
Chicago, IL 60631-2738 USA
Toll Free: 800-229-7530
E-mail Address: info@rehabnurse.org
Web Address: www.rehabnurse.org
The Association of Rehabilitation Nurses (ARN) helps nurses stay on top of the skills and knowledge needed to provide quality rehabilitative and restorative care across settings, conditions and age spans.

Association of Women's Health, Obstetric and Neonatal Nurses (AWHONN)
1800 M St. NW, Ste. 7450
Washington, DC 20036 USA
Phone: 202-261-2400
Fax: 202-728-0575
Toll Free: 800-673-8499
E-mail Address: customerservice@awhonn.org
Web Address: www.awhonn.org
The Association of Women's Health, Obstetric and Neonatal Nurses (AWHONN) is nonprofit membership organization, which works to promote the health of women and newborns through advocacy, research, education and provides access to professional and clinical resources to nurses and health care professionals.

British Dental Association
64 Wimpole St.
London, W1G8YS UK
Phone: 44-20-7935-0875
Fax: 44-20-7487-5232
E-mail Address: enquiries@bda.org
Web Address: www.bda.org
The British Dental Association (BDA) is the professional association and trade union for dentists in the United Kingdom. It promotes policies which benefit dental practice and dental care and lobby politicians on issues affecting dentists as business people and clinicians.

British Medical Association
BMA House, Tavistock Sq.
London, WC1H 9JP UK
Phone: 44-20-7387-4499
E-mail Address: info.public@bma.org.uk
Web Address: www.bma.org.uk
The British Medical Association is a trade union, which represents over 170,00 doctors in the U.K. It advocates the interests of its members, including employment issues and work with government for improving healthcare system.

Caregivers Action Network (CAN)
1150 Connecticut Ave. NW, Ste. 501
Washington, DC 20036 USA
Phone: 202-454-3970
E-mail Address: info@caregiveraction.org
Web Address: caregiveraction.org
The Caregivers Action Network (CAN), formerly the National Family Caregivers Association (NFCA), is a grass-roots organization created to educate, support, empower and speak for the millions of Americans who care for loved ones that are chronically ill, aged or disabled.

Case Management Society of America (CMSA)
6301 Ranch Dr.
Little Rock, AR 72223 USA
Phone: 501-225-2229
Fax: 501-221-9068
Toll Free: 800-216-2672
E-mail Address: cmsa@cmsa.org
Web Address: www.cmsa.org

Founded in 1990, the Case Management Society of America (CMSA) has grown to be the leading non-profit association dedicated to the support and development of the profession of case management. It serves more than 9,000 members, 20,000 subscribers, 17,000 social community participants and 75 chapters through educational forums, networking opportunities, legislative advocacy and establishing standards to advance the profession.

Chinese Medical Association (CMA)
42 Dongsi Xidajie
Beijing, 100710 China
Phone: 86-10-8515-8136
Fax: 86-10-8515-8551
E-mail Address: intl@cma.org.cn
Web Address: www.en.cma.org.cn/
The Chinese Medical Association (CMA) is nonprofit association consisting of Chinese medical science and technology professionals representing the medical industry in China. With roughly 500,000 members, it has 85 specialist societies representing all medical fields; and edits and publishes 125 medical and popular science journals.

Chinese-American Medical Society (CAMS)
11 E. Broadway, Ste. 4C
New York, NY 10038 USA
Phone: 212-334-4760
Fax: 646-304-6373
E-mail Address: jlove@camsociety.org
Web Address: www.camsociety.org
The Chinese-American Medical Society (CAMS) exists to promote the scientific association of medical professionals of Chinese descent, advance medical knowledge and scientific research with emphasis on aspects unique to the Chinese and establish scholarships for medical and dental students.

Clinical Immunology Society (CIS)
555 E. Wells St., Ste. 1100
Milwaukee, WI 53202-3823 USA
Phone: 414-224-8095
Fax: 414-272-6070
E-mail Address: info@clinimmsoc.org
Web Address: www.clinimmsoc.org
The Clinical Immunology Society (CIS) is devoted to fostering developments in the science and practice of clinical immunology through education, translational research and novel approaches to therapy.

Contact Lens Manufacturers Association (CLMA)
P.O. Box 29398
Lincoln, NE 68529 USA

Phone: 402-465-4122
Fax: 402-465-4187
Toll Free: 800-344-9060
Web Address: www.clma.net
The Contact Lens Manufacturers
Association (CLMA) seeks to increase
awareness and utilization of custom-
manufactured contact lenses.

**Contact Lens Society of America
(CLSA)**
2025 Woodlane Dr.
St. Paul, MN 55125-2998 USA
Fax: 651-731-0410
Toll Free: 800-296-9776
E-mail Address: clsa@clsa.info
Web Address: www.clsa.info
The Contact Lens Society of America
(CLSA) is a member organization that
strives to educate and share knowledge
among fitters of contact lenses.

Corporate Angel Network, Inc. (CAN)
One Loop Rd.
Westchester County Airport
White Plains, NY 10604-1215 USA
Phone: 914-328-1313
Fax: 914-328-3938
E-mail Address:
info@corpangelnetwork.org
Web Address:
www.corpangelnetwork.org
The Corporate Angel Network (CAN)
exists to ease the emotional stress,
physical discomfort and financial burden
of travel for cancer patients by arranging
free flights to treatment centers, using the
empty seats on corporate aircraft flying on
routine business.

**Cryogenic Society of America, Inc.
(CSA)**
218 Lake St.
Oak Park, IL 60302-2609 USA
Phone: 708-383-6220
Fax: 708-383-9337
E-mail Address:
csa@cryogenicsociety.org
Web Address: www.cryogenicsociety.org
The Cryogenic Society of America, Inc.
(CSA) is a nonprofit organization that
brings together those in all disciplines
concerned with the applications of
cryogenics, which refers to the art and
science of achieving extremely low-
temperatures. With membership spanning
over 47 countries, the organization works
to promote information sharing, increase
awareness and conduct research in low
temperature processes and techniques.

Dental Council of India
Kotla Rd., Temple Ln.
Aiwan-E-Galib Marg
New Delhi, 110 002 India

Phone: 91-11-23238542
E-mail Address: secy-dci@nic.in
Web Address: www.dciindia.org
The Dental Council of India is a statutory
body incorporated to regulate the dental
education and the profession of dentistry
throughout India.

Dental Trade Alliance (DTA)
4350 N. Fairfax Dr.
Ste. 220
Arlington, VA 22203 USA
Phone: 703-379-7755
Fax: 703-931-9429
Web Address:
www.dentaltradealliance.org
The Dental Trade Alliance (DTA)
represents dental manufacturers, dental
dealers and dental laboratories.

Direct Primary Care Coalition
E-mail Address: info@dpcare.org
Web Address: www.dpcare.org
The Direct Primary Care Coalition is an
organization representing primary care
physicians who operate on a business
model whereby patients pay a monthly fee
for unlimited access to their doctors.
Additional enhanced services, such as
preventative care and email access to
doctors, are often added in a
comprehensive package.

Emergency Nurses Association (ENA)
930 E. Woodfield Rd.
Schaumburg, IL 60173 USA
Phone: 847-460-4000
Toll Free: 800-900-9659
E-mail Address: execoffice@ena.org
Web Address: www.ena.org
The Emergency Nurses Association
(ENA) is the specialty nursing association
serving the emergency nursing profession
through research, publications,
professional development and injury
prevention.

**Federation of American Hospitals
(FAH)**
750 9th St. NW, Ste. 600
Washington, DC 20001 USA
Phone: 202-624-1500
Fax: 202-737-6462
E-mail Address: info@fah.org
Web Address: www.fah.org
The Federation of American Hospitals
(FAH) is the national representative of
privately owned and managed community
hospitals and health systems in the U.S.

**German Medical Technology
Association (BVMed)**
Reinhardt Strasse 29b
Berlin, D-10117 Germany
Phone: 49-30-246-255-0

Fax: 49-30-246-255-99
E-mail Address: info@bvmed.de
Web Address: www.bvmed.de
The German Medical Technology
Association (BVMed) represents about
200 manufacturers and service providers
of medical devices.

**Health Industry Distributors
Association (HIDA)**
310 Montgomery St.
Alexandria, VA 22314-1516 USA
Phone: 703-549-4432
Fax: 703-549-6495
E-mail Address: rowan@hida.org
Web Address: www.hida.org
The Health Industry Distributors
Association (HIDA) is the international
trade association representing medical
products distributors.

**Healthcare Financial Management
Association (HFMA)**
3 Westbrook Corp. Ctr., Ste. 600
Westchester, IL 60154 USA
Phone: 708-531-9600
Fax: 708-531-0032
Toll Free: 800-252-4362
E-mail Address: inquiry@hfma.org
Web Address: www.hfma.org
The Healthcare Financial Management
Association (HFMA) is one of the nation's
leading personal membership
organizations for health care financial
management executives and leaders.

**Home Healthcare Nurses Association
(HHNA)**
288 7th St. SE
Washington, DC 20003 USA
Phone: 202-547-7424
Fax: 202-547-3540
Web Address: www.nahc.org/
The Home Healthcare Nurses Association
(HHNA) is a national professional nursing
organization of members involved in
home health care practice, education,
administration and research.

Hong Kong Dental Association (HKDA)
15 Hennessy Rd.
Fl. 8, Duke of Windsor Social Service
Bldg.
Wanchai, Hong Kong Hong Kong
Phone: 852-2528-5327
Fax: 852-2529-0755
E-mail Address: hkda@hkda.org
Web Address: www.hkda.org
The Hong Kong Dental Association
represents the dental profession in Hong
Kong. It works to promote best interests
of dental profession by offering
continuing educational opportunities,
organizing monthly meetings and
workshops for over 1,900 members.

Hong Kong Medical Association
15 Hennessy Rd.
5/F Duke of Windsor Social Service Bldg.
Wanchai, Hong Kong Hong Kong
Phone: 852-2527-8285
Fax: 852-2865-0943
E-mail Address: hkma@hkma.org
Web Address: www.hkma.org
The Hong Kong Medical Association's
objective is to promote the welfare of the
medical profession and the health of the
public of Hong Kong. Its members
include over 8,000 professionals across all
healthcare sectors in Hong Kong.

**Hong Kong Society for Nursing
Education**
P.O. Box 98898
Tsim Sha Tsui Post Office
Kowloon, New Territories Hong Kong
E-mail Address: info@hksne.org.hk
Web Address: www.hksne.org.hk
The Hong Kong Society for Nursing
Education aims to promote the welfare
and protect the interests of the nursing
profession.

**Independent Medical Distributors
Association (IMDA)**
113 Space Park N
Goodlettsville, TN 37072 USA
Phone: 615-859-2337
Fax: 615-859-2997
Toll Free: 866-463-2937
E-mail Address: imda@imda.org
Web Address: www.imda.org
The Independent Medical Distributors
Association (IMDA) is an association of
medical product sales and marketing
organizations. It advances the business
interests of its members by offering
education and networking opportunities.

**Institute for Diversity in Health
Management (IDHM)**
155 N. Wacker, Ste. 400
Chicago, IL 60606 USA
Phone: 312-422-2630
E-mail Address: institute@aha.org
Web Address:
www.diversityconnection.org
The Institute for Diversity in Health
Management (IDHM) is a nonprofit
organization that collaborates with
educators and health services
organizations to expand leadership
opportunities to ethnic minorities in health
services management.

Institute for Health Care Improvement
53 State St., Fl. 19
Boston, MA 02109 USA
Phone: 617-301-4800
Fax: 617-301-4848
Toll Free: 866-787-0831

E-mail Address: info@ihi.org
Web Address: www.ihi.org
The Institute for Healthcare Improvement
(IHI) is a nonprofit organization that
strives for the improvement of health by
advancing the quality and value of
healthcare.

**International Association of Flight and
Critical Care Paramedics (IAFCCP)**
4835 Riveredge Cove
Snellville, GA 30039 USA
Phone: 770-979-6372
Fax: 770-979-6500
Web Address: www.iafccp.org
The International Association of Flight
and Critical Care Paramedics (IAFCCP),
formerly the International Association of
Flight Paramedics (IAFP), provides
education and representation to critical
care paramedics that transport critical care
patients via airborne or ground vehicles.

**International Association of Forensic
Nurses (IAFN)**
6755 Bus. Pkwy., Ste. 303
Elkridge, MD 21075 USA
Phone: 410-626-7805
Fax: 410-626-7804
E-mail Address: info@forensicnurses.org
Web Address: www.forensicnurses.org
The International Association of Forensic
Nurses (IAFN) is an international
professional organization of registered
nurses that develops, promotes and
disseminates information about the
science of forensic nursing.

**International Association of Medical
Equipment Remarketers & Servicers
(IAMERS)**
85 Edgemont Pl.
Teaneck, NJ 07666 USA
Phone: 201-833-1157
Fax: 201-833-2021
E-mail Address: info@iamers.org
Web Address: www.iamers.org
The International Association of Medical
Equipment Remarketers & Servicers
(IAMERS) works to improve the quality
of pre-owned medical equipment, both
domestically and internationally.

International Council of Nurses (ICN)
3 Place Jean Marteau
Geneva, 1201 Switzerland
Phone: 41-22-908-01-00
Fax: 41-22-908-01-01
E-mail Address: icn@icn.ch
Web Address: www.icn.ch
The International Council of Nurses
(ICN) is a federation of national nurses'
associations representing nurses in more
than 130 countries.

**International Nurses Society on
Addiction (IntNSA)**
3416 Primm Ln.
Birmingham, AL 66285-4846 USA
Phone: 205-823-6106
E-mail Address: intnsa@intnsa.org
Web Address: www.intnsa.org
The International Nurses Society on
Addiction (IntNSA) is a global voice for
nurses committed to addressing the
impact of addictions on society. It is
dedicated to advance nursing care for the
prevention and treatment of addictions
through advocacy, education, research and
policy development.

**International Transplant Nurses
Society (ITNS)**
8735 W. Higgins Rd., Ste. 300
Chicago, IL 60631 USA
Phone: 847-375-6340
Fax: 847-375-6341
E-mail Address: info@itns.org
Web Address: www.itns.org
The International Transplant Nurses
Society (ITNS) is a member organization
that promotes transplant clinical nursing
through educational and professional
growth opportunities, interdisciplinary
networking, collaborative activities and
transplant nursing research.

Joint Commission
1 Renaissance Blvd.
Oakbrook Terrace, IL 60181 USA
Phone: 630-792-5100
Fax: 630-792-5005
Toll Free: 800-994-6610
Web Address: www.jointcommission.org
The Joint Commission is an independent,
nonprofit organization, which evaluates
and accredits health care organizations
and programs in the United States.

Medical Council of India
Dwarka Phase 1
Pocket 14, Sector 8
New Delhi, 110 077 India
Phone: 91-11-25367033
Fax: 91-11-25367024
Toll Free: 800-111-1154
E-mail Address: mci@bol.net.in
Web Address: www.mciindia.org
The Medical Council of India establishes
uniform standards of higher qualifications
in medicine and recognition of medical
qualifications in India and abroad.

**Medical Device Manufacturers
Association (MDMA)**
1333 H St., Ste. 400 W.
Washington, DC 20005 USA
Phone: 202-354-7171
Web Address: www.medicaldevices.org

The Medical Device Manufacturers Association (MDMA) is a national trade association that represents independent manufacturers of medical devices, diagnostic products and health care information systems.

Medical Group Management Association (MGMA)

104 Inverness Terrace E.
Englewood, CO 80112-5306 USA
Phone: 303-799-1111
Toll Free: 877-275-6462
E-mail Address: hkohtz@mgma.com
Web Address: www.mgma.com
Medical Group Management Association (MGMA) is one of the nation's principal voices for medical group practice. It represents over 33,000 administrators and executives in 18,000 healthcare organizations in which 385,000 physicians practice.

National Association for Healthcare Quality (NAHQ)

8600 W. Bryn Mawr Ave., Ste. 710 N
Chicago, IL 60631 USA
Phone: 847-375-4720
Fax: 847-375-6320
Toll Free: 800-966-9392
E-mail Address: info@nahq.org
Web Address: www.nahq.org
The National Association for Healthcare Quality (NAHQ) is a member organization for quality and safety healthcare professionals offering education, leadership development opportunities and products to its members.

National Association for Home Care & Hospice (NAHC)

228 Seventh St. SE
Washington, DC 20003 USA
Phone: 202-547-7424
Fax: 202-547-3540
Web Address: www.nahc.org
The National Association for Home Care & Hospice (NAHC) is a nonprofit organization committed to representing the interests of the home care and hospice community.

National Association for the Support of Long-Term Care (NASL)

1444 I St. NW, Ste. 301
Washington, DC 20005 USA
Phone: 202-803-2385
E-mail Address: membership@nasl.org
Web Address: www.nasl.org
The National Association for the Support of Long-Term Care (NASL) provides a task-force-specific committee structure that focuses on payment reform, legislative policy, medical products and

medical services for executives and their associated businesses.

National Association of Clinical Nurse Specialists (NACNS)

11130 Sunrise Valley Dr., Ste. 350
Reston, VA 20191 USA
Phone: 703-436-0092
Fax: 703-435-4390
E-mail Address: info@nacns.org
Web Address: www.nacns.org
The National Association of Clinical Nurse Specialists (NACNS) exists to enhance and promote the contributions of clinical nurse specialists to the health of individuals, families, groups and communities.

National Association of Health Services Executives (NAHSE)

1050 Connecticut Ave. NW, Fl. 5
Washington, DC 20036 USA
Phone: 202-772-1030
Fax: 202-772-1072
Web Address: www.nahse.org
The National Association of Health Services Executives (NAHSE) is a nonprofit association of black health care executives who promote the advancement and development of black health care leaders and elevate the quality of health care services rendered to minority and underserved communities.

National Association of Hispanic Nurses (NAHN)

1500 Sunday Dr., Ste.102
Raleigh, NC 27607 USA
Phone: 919-573-5443
Fax: 919-787-4916
E-mail Address: info@thehispanicnurses.org
Web Address: www.thehispanicnurses.org
The National Association of Hispanic Nurses (NAHN) strives to serve the nursing and health care delivery needs of the Hispanic community and the professional needs of Hispanic nurses.

National Association of Neonatal Nurses (NANN)

8735 W. Higgins Rd., Ste. 300
Chicago, IL 60631 USA
Toll Free: 800-451-3795
E-mail Address: info@nann.org
Web Address: www.nann.org
The National Association of Neonatal Nurses (NANN) represents the community of neonatal nurses that provide evidence-based care to high-risk neonatal patients.

National Association of Orthopedic Nurses (NAON)

330 N. Wabash Ave., Ste. 2000

Chicago, IL 60611 USA
Fax: 312-673-6941
Toll Free: 800-289-6266
E-mail Address: naon@orthonurse.org
Web Address: www.orthonurse.org
The National Association of Orthopedic Nurses (NAON) is a nonprofit organization, which exists to promote education and research related to nursing care of persons with orthopedic conditions, as well as to advance the profession of nursing.

National Association of Pediatric Nurse Practitioners (NAPNAP)

5 Hanover Sq., Ste. 1401
New York, NY 10004 USA
Phone: 917-746-8300
Fax: 212-785-1713
Web Address: www.napnap.org
The National Association of Pediatric Nurse Practitioners (NAPNAP) is the professional organization that advocates for children and provides leadership for pediatric nurse practitioners who deliver primary healthcare in a variety of settings.

National Association of School Nurses (NASN)

1100 Wayne Ave., Ste. 925
Silver Spring, MD 20910 USA
Phone: 240-821-1130
Fax: 301-585-1791
Toll Free: 866-627-6767
E-mail Address: nasn@nasn.org
Web Address: www.nasn.org
The National Association of School Nurses (NASN) improves the health and educational success of children and youth by developing and providing leadership to advance school nursing practice.

National Association of State Mental Health Program Directors (NASMHPD)

66 Canal Ctr. Plz., Ste. 302
Alexandria, VA 22314 USA
Phone: 703-739-9333
Fax: 703-548-9517
Web Address: www.nasmhpd.org
The National Association of State Mental Health Program Directors (NASMHPD) organizes to reflect and advocate for the collective interests of state mental health authorities and their directors at the national level.

National Black Nurses Association (NBNA)

8630 Fenton St., Ste. 330
Silver Spring, MD 20910-3803 USA
Phone: 301-589-3200
Fax: 301-589-3223
E-mail Address: contact@nbna.org
Web Address: www.nbna.org

The National Black Nurses Association (NBNA) is a professional nursing organization representing roughly 150,000 African American nurses from the United States, Canada, Eastern Caribbean and Africa.

National Board of Medical Examiners (NBME)
3750 Market St.
Philadelphia, PA 19104-3102 USA
Phone: 215-590-9500
Web Address: www.nbme.org
The National Board of Medical Examiners (NBME) exists to protect the health of the public through state-of-the-art assessment of health professionals.

National Committee for Quality Assurance (NCQA)
1100 13th St. NW, Ste. 1000
Washington, DC 20005 USA
Phone: 202-955-3500
Fax: 202-955-3599
Toll Free: 888-275-7585
E-mail Address: customersupport@ncqa.org
Web Address: www.ncqa.org
The National Committee for Quality Assurance (NCQA) is a private, nonprofit organization that seeks to drive improvement throughout the health care industry.

National Hospice and Palliative Care Organization (NHPCO)
1731 King St., Ste. 100
Alexandria, VA 22314 USA
Phone: 703-837-1500
Fax: 703-837-1233
Toll Free: 800-646-6460
E-mail Address: nhpco_info@nhpco.org
Web Address: www.nhpco.org
The National Hospice and Palliative Care Organization (NHPCO) is a nonprofit membership organization representing hospice and palliative care programs and professionals in the United States.

National Student Nurses' Association (NSNA)
45 Main St., Ste. 606
Brooklyn, NY 11201 USA
Phone: 718-210-0705
Fax: 718-797-1186
E-mail Address: nsna@nsna.org
Web Address: www.nsna.org
The National Student Nurses' Association (NSNA) is a membership organization representing those in programs preparing students for registered nurse licensure, as well as RNs in BSN completion programs.

Nurse Practitioner Associates for Continuing Education (NPACE)
209 W. Central St., Ste. 228
Natick, MA 01760 USA
Phone: 508-907-6424
Fax: 508-907-6425
E-mail Address: npace@npace.org
Web Address: www.npace.org
Nurse Practitioner Associates for Continuing Education (NPACE) seeks to improve health care in the U.S. by providing continuing education and professional support to nurse practitioners and other clinicians in advanced practice.

Oncology Nursing Society (ONS)
125 Enterprise Dr.
Pittsburgh, PA 15275 USA
Phone: 412-859-6100
Fax: 877-369-5497
Toll Free: 866-257-4667
E-mail Address: help@ons.org
Web Address: www.ons.org
The Oncology Nursing Society (ONS) is a national organization of registered nurses and other health care professionals dedicated to excellence in patient care, teaching, research, administration and education in the field of oncology.

Optometrists & Opticians Board, Singapore
16 College Rd., #01-01
College of Medicine Bldg.
Singapore, 169854 Singapore
Phone: 65-6355-2533
Fax: 65-6258-2134
E-mail Address: OOB@spb.gov.sg
Web Address: https://www.healthprofessionals.gov.sg/oob
The Optometrists & Opticians Board is a professional board established under the Ministry of Health of Singapore which issues guidelines on the standards for the practice of optometry and opticianry.

Regulatory Affairs Professionals Society (RAPS)
5635 Fishers Ln., Ste. 550
Rockville, MD 20852 USA
Phone: 301-770-2920 ext.200
Fax: 301-841-7956
E-mail Address: raps@raps.org
Web Address: www.raps.org
The Regulatory Affairs Professionals Society (RAPS) is an international professional society representing the health care regulatory affairs profession and individual professionals worldwide.

Shanghai Medical Instrument Trade Association (SMITA)
Zhao Jia Bang Rd.
701 No. 2 446 Ln.
Shanghai, 200031 China
Phone: 86-21-61248288
Fax: 86-21-54651421
E-mail Address: smia_sh@yahoo.com.cn
Web Address: www.smianet.com
The Shanghai Medical Instrument Trade Association (SMITA) serves the interests of manufacturers and suppliers of medical radio-diagnostic and radio-therapeutic machines, emergency apparatus, equipment for operating room, medical ultrasonic instrument, medical optical instrument, medical physiologic detecting and diagnostic device, artificial organ, surgical instrument, dental equipment, sanitary material etc.

Singapore Dental Association (SDA)
2985 Jalan Bukit Merah, #02-2D
Singapore, 159457 Singapore
Phone: 65-6258-9252
Fax: 65-6258-8903
Web Address: http://sda.org.sg
The Singapore Dental Association (SDA) is the professional association of dentists dedicated to serving both the public and the profession of dentistry.

Singapore Dental Council
81 Kim Keat Rd.
09-00 NKF Building
Singapore, 328836 Singapore
Phone: 65-6355-2405
Fax: 65-6253-3185
E-mail Address: SDC@spb.gov.sg
Web Address: http://www.healthprofessionals.gov.sg/content/hprof/sdc/en.html
The Singapore Dental Council is the self-regulatory body for the dental professions. Its key objectives are to promote the interests of the dental profession in Singapore.

Singapore Medical Association (SMA)
2985 Jalan Bukit Merah
#02-2C, SMF Building
Singapore, 159457 Singapore
Phone: 65-6223-1264
Fax: 65-6252-9693
E-mail Address: sma@sma.org.sg
Web Address: www.sma.org.sg
Singapore Medical Association (SMA) is the national medical organization representing the majority of medical practitioners in both the public and private sectors. The website contains information and links to medical organizations and hospitals in Singapore.

Society for Social Work Leadership in Health Care (SSWLHC)
295 E. Swedesford Road
Wayne, PA 19087 USA
Phone: 215-599-6134

Toll Free: 866-237-9542
E-mail Address: info@sswlhc.org
Web Address: www.sswlhc.org
The Society for Social Work Leadership
in Health Care (SSWLHC) is dedicated to
promoting the universal availability,
accessibility, coordination and
effectiveness of health care that addresses
the psychosocial components of health
and illness.

Society for Vascular Nursing (SVN)
9400 W. Higgins Rd., Ste. 315
Rosemont, IL 60018 USA
Phone: 414-376-0001
Fax: 414-359-1671
Web Address: www.svnnet.org
The Society for Vascular Nursing (SVN)
is a nonprofit international association
dedicated to the compassionate and
comprehensive care of persons with
vascular disease. The group works to
provide quality education, foster clinical
expertise and support nursing research.

**Society of Critical Care Medicine
(SCCM)**
500 Midway Dr.
Mount Prospect, IL 60056 USA
Phone: 847-827-6888
Fax: 847-439-7226
E-mail Address: support@sccm.org
Web Address: www.sccm.org
The Society of Critical Care Medicine
(SCCM) is a multidisciplinary, multi-
professional organization dedicated to
ensuring excellence and consistency in the
practice of critical care medicine; and to
offer highest quality care for all critically
ill and injured patients.

**Society of Gastroenterology Nurses and
Associates (SGNA)**
330 N. Wabash Ave., Ste. 2000
Chicago, IL 60611-7621 USA
Phone: 312-321-5165
Fax: 312-673-6694
Toll Free: 800-245-7462
E-mail Address: info@sgna.org
Web Address: www.sgna.org
The Society of Gastroenterology Nurses
and Associates (SGNA) is a professional
organization of nurses and associates
dedicated to the safe and effective practice
of gastroenterology and endoscopy
nursing.

**Society of Nuclear Medicine and
Molecular Imaging (SNMI)**
1850 Samuel Morse Dr.
Reston, VA 20190-5316 USA
Phone: 703-708-9000
Fax: 703-708-9015
Web Address: www.snmmi.org

The Society of Nuclear Medicine and
Molecular Imaging (SNMI), formerly The
Society of Nuclear Medicine, is a
nonprofit international scientific and
medical organization founded to promote
the science, technology and practical
application of nuclear medicine. SNMI
works to advance molecular imaging and
therapy.

Society of Pediatric Nurses (SPN)
330 N. Wabash Ave., Ste. 2000
Chicago, IL 60611 USA
Phone: 312-321-5154
Fax: 312-673-6754
E-mail Address: info@pedsnurses.org
Web Address: www.pedsnurses.org
The Society of Pediatric Nurses (SPN)
seeks to promote excellence in nursing
care of children and their families through
support of its members' clinical practice,
education, research and advocacy.

Society of Trauma Nurses (STN)
446 E. High St., Ste. 10
Lexington, KY 40507 USA
Phone: 859-977-7456
Fax: 859-271-0607
E-mail Address: info@traumanurses.org
Web Address: www.traumanurses.org
The Society of Trauma Nurses (STN) is a
membership-based, nonprofit organization
whose members are trauma nurses from
around the world. It is dedicated to ensure
optimal trauma care to all people by
encouraging leadership, mentoring,
interdisciplinary collaboration and
innovation in the delivery of trauma care.

**Society of Urologic Nurses and
Associates (SUNA)**
E. Holly Ave., Box 56
Pitman, NJ 08071-0056 USA
Toll Free: 888-827-7862
E-mail Address: suna@ajj.com
Web Address: www.suna.org
The Society of Urologic Nurses and
Associates (SUNA) is a nonprofit
professional membership organization
committed to excellence in patient care
standards and a continuum of quality care,
clinical practice and research through
education of its members, patients,
families and community. It has over 3,000
urologic healthcare professional members
and publishes a professional, peer-
reviewed bi-monthly journal and a
newsletter.

**Southern Nursing Research Society
(SNRS)**
4400 College Blvd., Ste. 220
Overland Park, KS 66211 USA
Phone: 303-327-7548
Toll Free: 877-314-7677

E-mail Address: info@snrs.org
Web Address: www.snrs.org
The Southern Nursing Research Society
(SNRS) exists to advance nursing
research, promote the utilization of
research finding and facilitate the career
development of nurses as researchers.

Telemedicine Society of India
Sanjay Gandhi Post Graduate Institute of
Medical Sciences
Raebareli Road
Lucknow, 226 014 India
Phone: 91-522-266-8838
Fax: 91-522-266-8839
E-mail Address: contact@tsi.org.in
Web Address: www.tsi.org.in
The Telemedicine Society of India seeks
to promote and encourage development,
advancement and research in the science
of telemedicine and associated fields.

**Urgent Care Association of America
(UCAOA)**
28600 Bella Vista Pkwy., Ste. 2010
Warrenville, IL 60555 USA
Phone: 331-472-3739
Fax: 331-457-5439
Toll Free: 877-698-2262
E-mail Address: info@ucaoa.org
Web Address: www.ucaoa.org
UCAOA represents the many urgent care
centers that provide appropriate and
timely alternatives to the more costly and
inconvenient hospital emergency
departments. True emergencies require
hospital emergency services, but urgent
care centers meet the need for convenient
access for minor injuries and illnesses.

**Visiting Nurse Associations of America
(VNAA)**
2519 Connecticut Ave. NW
Washington, DC 20008 USA
Phone: 202-508-9498
Fax: 571-527-1521
Toll Free: 888-866-8773
E-mail Address: vnaa@vnaa.org
Web Address: www.vnaa.org
Visiting Nurse Associations of America
(VNAA) is the official, national
association of freestanding, nonprofit,
community-based visiting nurse agencies.

**Wound, Ostomy and Continence
Nurses Society (WOCN)**
1120 Rte. 73, Ste. 200
Mt. Laurel, NJ 08054 USA
Fax: 856-439-0525
Toll Free: 888-224-9626
E-mail Address: info@wocn.org
Web Address: www.wocn.org
The Wound, Ostomy and Continence
Nurses Society (WOCN) is a professional,
international nursing society of nurse

professionals who are experts in the care of patients with wound, ostomy and continence problems.

43) Health Care Costs

Kaiser Family Foundation (The Henry J.)

185 Berry St., Ste. 2000
San Francisco, CA 94107 USA
Phone: 650-854-9400
Fax: 650-854-4800
Web Address: www.kff.org
The Henry J. Kaiser Family Foundation publishes an annual study on employers' health care coverage costs and the amount of that coverage that is paid for by employees. The foundation also runs a large healthcare public opinion research program and publishes studies on a continuous basis.

44) Health Care Resources

Directory of Indian Government Websites

Nat'l Portal Secretariat, FL. 3, Nat'l Informatics Ctr.
A-Block, CGO Complex, Lodhi Rd.
New Delhi, 110 003 India
E-mail Address: goidirectory@nic.in
Web Address:
goidirectory.nic.in/sectors_categories.php
?ct=ST016
The Directory of Indian Government Websites is a portal maintained by the National Informatics Centre (NIC) in India. The site lists Indian Government websites at all levels including institutions and organizations relating to the health and medical sector in India.

Health and Medicine Division (HMD), The

500 Fifth St. NW
Washington, DC 20001 USA
Phone: 202-334-2000
E-mail Address: HMD-NASEM@nas.edu
Web Address:
www.nationalacademies.org/hmd/About-HMD.aspx
The Health and Medicine Division (HMD), formerly known as Institute of Medicine (IOM), is a division of the National Academies of Sciences, Engineering, and Medicine (the Academies). HMD's network consists of 3,000 volunteers, who offer their time, knowledge, and expertise, in order to furnish evidence to both government and private sectors to make informed health decisions. Many of the studies that the HMD undertakes begin as specific mandates from Congress; still others are requested by federal agencies and independent organizations

Hong Kong Medical Web

18 Cheung Lee St.
Cheung Tang Ctr., Rm. 504-5
Chai Wan, Hong Kong Hong Kong
Phone: 852-2578-3833
Fax: 852-2578-3929
E-mail Address: hkmw@medcom.com.hk
Web Address: www.medicine.org.hk
The Hong Kong Medical Web is a portal to public health information with links to medical societies and continuing medical education in Hong Kong. The site also has a searchable database of doctors in Hong Kong. The portal is maintained by the Hong Kong Medical Association.

Ministry of Health (MOH) Singapore

16 College Rd.
College of Medicine Bldg.
Singapore, 169854 Singapore
Phone: 65-6325-9220
Toll Free: 800-225-4122
E-mail Address:
MOH_INFO@moh.gov.sg
Web Address: www.moh.gov.sg
Through the Ministry of Health (MOH), the Singapore Government manages the public healthcare system to ensure that good and affordable basic medical services are available to all Singaporeans. The website provides medical information, statistics, publications, news and other links.

Singapore Medical Council (SMC)

16 College Rd.
01-01 College of Medicine Bldg.
Singapore, 169854 Singapore
Phone: 65-6506-2102
Fax: 65-6258-2134
E-mail Address: SMC@spb.gov.sg
Web Address:
www.healthprofessionals.gov.sg/smc
The Singapore Medical Council (SMC), a statutory board under the Ministry of Health, maintains the Register of Medical Practitioners in Singapore, administers the compulsory continuing medical education program and also governs and regulates the professional conduct and ethics of registered medical practitioners.

Singapore Nursing Board (SNB)

81 Kim Keat Rd., #08-00
Singapore, 328836 Singapore
Phone: 65-6478-5413
Fax: 65-6353-3460
E-mail Address: SNB@spb.gov.sg
Web Address:
www.healthprofessionals.gov.sg/snb
The Singapore Nursing Board (SNB) is the regulatory authority for nurses and midwives in Singapore.

TeleMedIndia.com

Web Address: www.telemedindia.org
The TeleMedIndia.com site includes glossary, overview, links, publications and information regarding the telemedicine field which is an upcoming field in health science arising out of the effective fusion of information and communication technologies with medical Science.

45) Health Care-General

MedicAlert Foundation

101 Lander Ave.
Turlock, CA 95380 USA
Toll Free: 800-432-5378
Web Address: www.medicalert.org
The MedicAlert Foundation is a nonprofit service that protects and saves the lives of its members by providing biunique identification and critical personal health information. Products include wrist bands that contain personal health issue information to be read in the event of a health emergency.

46) Health Facts-Global

GlobalHealthReporting.org

185 Berry St., Ste. 2000
San Francisco, CA 94107 USA
Phone: 650-854-9400
Fax: 650-854-4800
Web Address: http://kff.org/global-health-policy/
Globalhealthreporting.org, which is operated by the Kaiser Family Foundation with major support from the Bill & Melinda Gates Foundation, provides coverage of worldwide health care news and reporting on diseases and health programs.

Institute for Health Metrics and Evaluation (IHME)

3980 15th Ave. NE
Seattle, WA 98105 USA
Phone: 206-897-2800
Fax: 206-897-2899
E-mail Address: ihme@healthdata.org
Web Address: www.healthdata.org
The Institute for Health Metrics and Evaluation (IHME) was launched with the goal of providing an unbiased, evidence-based picture of global health trends and determinants to inform the work of a broad range of organizations, policymakers, researchers, and funders. A primary backer is the Bill & Melinda

Gates Foundation. The IHME publishes a wide range of research on health care practices, funding and outcomes.

Kaiser Family Foundation
185 Berry St., Ste. 2000
San Francisco, CA 94107 USA
Phone: 650-854-9400
Fax: 650-854-4800
Web Address: kff.org
KFF (Kaiser Family Foundation) is a non-profit organization focusing on national health issues, as well as the U.S. role in global health policy. KFF develops and runs its own policy analysis, journalism and communications programs, sometimes in partnership with major news organizations.

Organisation for Economic Co-Operation and Development (OECD) - Health Statistics
2 rue Andre Pascal
Paris, 75016 France
Phone: 33-1-4524-8200
Fax: 33-1-4524-8500
Web Address: www.oecd.org
The Organisation for Economic Co-Operation and Development (OECD) offers extensive health statistics on a country-by-country basis. Data ranges from health expenditures per capita to health expenditures as percent of GDP for over 34 nations with the world's largest economies.

---

47) Health Insurance Industry Associations

America's Health Insurance Plans (AHIP)
601 Pennsylvania Ave. NW
S. Bldg., Ste. 500
Washington, DC 20004 USA
Phone: 202-778-3200
Fax: 202-331-7487
E-mail Address: ahip@ahip.org
Web Address: www.ahip.org
America's Health Insurance Plans (AHIP) is a prominent trade association representing the health care insurance community. Its members offer health and supplemental benefits through employer-sponsored coverage, the individual insurance market, and public programs such as Medicare and Medicaid.

American Association of Preferred Provider Organizations (AAPPO)
3774 LaVista Rd., Ste. 101
Tucker, GA 30084 USA
Phone: 502-403-1122
Fax: 502-403-1129
Web Address: www.aappo.org
The American Association of Preferred Provider Organizations (AAPPO) is the leading national association of network-based preferred provider organizations. AAPPO's membership includes payer, network and Workers' Compensation organizations

Blue Cross and Blue Shield Association
225 N. Michigan Ave.
Chicago, IL 60601-7680 USA
Toll Free: 888-630-2583
Web Address: www.bcbs.com
Blue Cross and Blue Shield Association is a nonprofit professional association of health care insurance providers. The 36 local member companies of the Blue Cross and Blue Shield Association provide healthcare coverage for more than nearly 105 million people in the U.S.

International Federation of Health Plans
83 Victoria St.
London, SW1H 0HW UK
Phone: 44-20-3585-5230
Fax: 44-20-3008-6180
E-mail Address: admin@ifhp.com
Web Address: www.ifhp.com
The International Federation of Health Plans was founded in 1968 by a group of health insurance industry leaders, and is now the leading global network of the industry, with 100 member companies in 31 countries. The group publishes a report on comparative prices in several nations for health care procedures.

National Association of Health Underwriters (NAHU)
1212 New York Ave., Ste. 1100
Washington, DC 20005 USA
Phone: 202-552-5060
Fax: 202-747-6820
E-mail Address: info@nahu.org
Web Address: www.nahu.org
The National Association of Health Underwriters (NAHU) is a professional association of licensed health insurance agents, brokers, general agents, consultants and benefit professionals through more than 200 chapters throughout the U.S.

---

48) Hearing & Speech

Alexander Graham Bell Association for the Deaf and Hard of Hearing (AGBELL)
3417 Volta Pl. NW
Washington, DC 20007 USA
Phone: 202-337-5220
Fax: 202-337-8314
E-mail Address: info@agbell.org
Web Address: www.agbell.org/

The Alexander Graham Bell Association for the Deaf and Hard of Hearing (AGBELL) is an international membership organization and resource center on hearing loss and spoken language approaches and related issues.

American Speech-Language-Hearing Association (ASHA)
2200 Research Blvd.
Rockville, MD 20850-3289 USA
Phone: 301-296-5700
Fax: 301-296-8580
Toll Free: 800-638-8255
Web Address: www.asha.org
The American Speech-Language-Hearing Association (ASHA) is the professional, scientific and credentialing association for audiologists, speech-language pathologists and speech, language and hearing scientists.

Bridges
935 Edgehill Ave.
Nashville, TN 37203 USA
Phone: 615-248-8828
Fax: 615-248-4797
Toll Free: 866-385-6524
E-mail Address: info@hearingbridges.org
Web Address: http://bridgesfordeafandhh.org
Bridges, formerly the League for the Deaf and Hard of Hearing and the Ear Foundation, is dedicated to the interests of the hearing impaired. The group funds programs to further medical education on the merits of the early detection of hearing loss.

Hearing Industries Association (HIA)
777 6th St. NW, Ste. 09-114
Washington, DC 20001 USA
Phone: 202-975-0905
Fax: 202-216-9646
E-mail Address: mjones@bostrom.com
Web Address: www.hearing.org
The Hearing Industries Association (HIA) represents and unifies the many aspects of the hearing industry.

National Family Association for Deaf-Blind (NFADB)
P.O. Box 1667
Sands Point, NY 11050 USA
Fax: 516-883-9060
Toll Free: 800-255-0411
E-mail Address: NFADBinfo@gmail.com
Web Address: www.nfadb.org
The National Family Association for Deaf-Blind (NFADB) is the largest nonprofit, volunteer based national network of families focusing on issues surrounding deaf-blindness.

National Institute on Deafness and Other Communication Disorders (NIDCD)
31 Center Dr., MSC 2320
Bethesda, MD 20892-2320 USA
Phone: 301-496-7243
Fax: 301-402-0018
Toll Free: 800-241-1044
E-mail Address: nidcdinfo@nidcd.nih.gov
Web Address: www.nidcd.nih.gov
The National Institute on Deafness and Other Communication Disorders (NIDCD) conducts and supports biomedical and behavioral research and research training in the normal and disordered processes of hearing, balance, smell, taste, voice, speech and language.

49) Heart Disease

American Heart Association (AHA)
7272 Greenville Ave.
Dallas, TX 75231 USA
Phone: 214-570-5978
Toll Free: 800-242-8721
Web Address: www.heart.org
The American Heart Association (AHA) is a national voluntary health agency that seeks to reduce disability and death from cardiovascular diseases and stroke.

50) Hospice Care

Children's Hospice International (CHI)
1800 Diagonal Rd., Ste. 600
Alexandria, VA 22314 USA
Phone: 703-684-0330
E-mail Address: info@chionline.org
Web Address: www.chionline.org
The Children's Hospice International (CHI) is a nonprofit organization founded to promote hospice support through pediatric care facilities, to encourage the inclusion of children in existing and developing hospice and home-care programs and to include the hospice perspectives in all areas of pediatric care, education and the public arena.

Hospice Education Institute
3 Unity Sq.
P.O. Box 98
Machiasport, ME 04655-0098 USA
Phone: 207-255-8800
Fax: 207-255-8008
Toll Free: 800-331-1620
E-mail Address: hospiceall@aol.com
Web Address: www.icpcn.org/members-directory/2169/hospice-education-institute/
The Hospice Education Institute is an independent, not-for-profit organization serving members of the public and health care professions with information and education about the many facets of caring for the dying and the bereaved.

51) Hospital Care

American Hospital Association (AHA)
155 N. Wacker Dr.
Chicago, IL 60606 USA
Phone: 312-422-3000
Fax: 312-422-4796
Toll Free: 800-424-4301
Web Address: www.aha.org
The American Hospital Association (AHA) is a national organization that represents and serves all types of hospitals, health care networks, their patients and communities.

Council of Teaching Hospitals and Health Systems (COTH)
655 K St. NW, Ste. 100
Washington, DC 20001-2399 USA
Phone: 202-828-0400
E-mail Address: lford@aamc.org
Web Address: www.aamc.org/members/coth
The Council of Teaching Hospitals and Health Systems (COTH), part of the Association of American Medical Colleges (AAMC), provides representation and services related to the special needs, concerns and opportunities facing major teaching hospitals in the United States and Canada. The COTH web site offers a listing of member hospitals.

Shriners Hospitals for Children
2900 Rocky Point Dr.
Tampa, FL 33607-1460 USA
Phone: 813-281-0300
Toll Free: 800-237-5055
E-mail Address: shrinepr@shrinenet.org
Web Address: www.shrinershospitalsforchildren.org
Shriners Hospitals for Children is a one-of-a-kind international health care system of 22 hospitals dedicated to improving the lives of children by providing specialty pediatric care, innovative research and outstanding teaching programs. Children up to the age of 18 with orthopedic conditions, burns, spinal cord injuries and cleft lip and palate are eligible for admission and receive all care in a family-centered environment at no charge, regardless of financial need.

52) Human Resources Professionals Associations

American Society for Healthcare Human Resources Administrators (ASHRM)
155 N. Wacker St., Ste. 400
Chicago, IL 60606 USA
Phone: 312-422-3720
Fax: 312-422-4577
E-mail Address: ashrm@aha.org
Web Address: www.ashrm.org
The American Society for Healthcare Human Resources Administrators (ASHRM) is the professional society for healthcare risk management professionals and those responsible for decisions that will promote quality care, maintain a safe environment and preserve human and financial resources in health care organizations.

International Association of Healthcare Central Service Materiel Management (IAHCSMM)
55 W. Wacker Dr., Ste. 501
Chicago, IL 60601 USA
Phone: 312-440-0078
Fax: 312-440-9474
Toll Free: 800-962-8274
E-mail Address: mailbox@iahcsmm.org
Web Address: www.iahcsmm.org
The International Association of Healthcare Central Service Materiel Management (IAHCSMM) exists to provide education, networking, recognition, membership advocacy and professional practices to promote innovative ideas toward the future of the industry.

53) Immunization Resources

CDC National Immunization Program (NIP)
1600 Clifton Rd.
Atlanta, GA 30333 USA
Toll Free: 800-232-4636
Web Address: www.cdc.gov/vaccines/
The CDC National Immunization Program (NIP) offers up-to-date immunization information, including vaccine schedules, side effects, contraindications, recommendations and more.

54) Industry Research/Market Research

Forrester Research
60 Acorn Park Dr.
Cambridge, MA 02140 USA
Phone: 617-613-5730
Toll Free: 866-367-7378

E-mail Address: press@forrester.com
Web Address: www.forrester.com
Forrester Research is a publicly traded company that identifies and analyzes emerging trends in technology and their impact on business. Among the firm's specialties are the financial services, retail, health care, entertainment, automotive and information technology industries.

Gartner, Inc.
56 Top Gallant Rd.
Stamford, CT 06902 USA
Phone: 203-964-0096
E-mail Address: info@gartner.com
Web Address: www.gartner.com
Gartner, Inc. is a publicly traded IT company that provides competitive intelligence and strategic consulting and advisory services to numerous clients worldwide.

MarketResearch.com
6116 Executive Blvd., Ste. 550
Rockville, MD 20852 USA
Phone: 240-747-3093
Fax: 240-747-3004
Toll Free: 800-298-5699
E-mail Address:
customerservice@marketresearch.com
Web Address: www.marketresearch.com
MarketResearch.com is a leading broker for professional market research and industry analysis. Users are able to search the company's database of research publications including data on global industries, companies, products and trends.

Plunkett Research, Ltd.
P.O. Drawer 541737
Houston, TX 77254-1737 USA
Phone: 713-932-0000
Fax: 713-932-7080
E-mail Address:
customersupport@plunkettresearch.com
Web Address: www.plunkettresearch.com
Plunkett Research, Ltd. is a leading provider of market research, industry trends analysis and business statistics. Since 1985, it has served clients worldwide, including corporations, universities, libraries, consultants and government agencies. At the firm's web site, visitors can view product information and pricing and access a large amount of basic market information on industries such as financial services, InfoTech, ecommerce, health care and biotech.

55) Insurance Industry Resources

Center for Risk Management and Insurance Research
35 Broad St.
Georgia State University, 11th Fl.
Atlanta, GA 30303 USA
Phone: 404-413-7471
Fax: 404-413-7516
E-mail Address: rwklein@gsu.edu
Web Address: rmi.robinson.gsu.edu
The Center for Risk Management and Insurance Research in the Robinson College of Business at Georgia State University was established in 1969 through grants and general financial support from the insurance industry through the Educational Foundation, Inc. The Center is established as a leading information source on risk and insurance issues.

56) Internet Usage Statistics

Pew Internet & American Life Project
1615 L St. NW, Ste. 800
Washington, DC 20036 USA
Phone: 202-419-4300
Fax: 202-857-8562
E-mail Address: info@pewinternet.org
Web Address: www.pewinternet.org
The Pew Internet & American Life Project, an initiative of the Pew Research Center, produces reports that explore the impact of the Internet on families, communities, work and home, daily life, education, health care and civic and political life.

57) Learning Disorders

Children and Adults with Attention Deficit Disorder (CHADD)
4227 Forbes Blvd., Ste. 270
Lanham, MD 20706 USA
Phone: 301-306-7070
Fax: 301-306-7090
Toll Free: 800-233-4050
E-mail Address:
customer_service@chadd.org
Web Address: www.chadd.org
Children and Adults with Attention Deficit Disorder (CHADD) is the nation's leading nonprofit membership organization serving individuals with Attention-Deficit/Hyperactivity Disorder (ADHD) through education, advocacy and support. It produces a bi-monthly magazine, Attention, for members and sponsors an annual conference.

58) Libraries-Medical Data

Medical Library Association (MLA)
225 W. Wacker, Ste. 650
Chicago, IL 60601-7246 USA
Phone: 312-419-9094
Fax: 312-419-8950
E-mail Address:
websupport@mail.mlahq.org
Web Address: www.mlanet.org
The Medical Library Association (MLA) is dedicated to improving the quality and leadership of health information professionals in order to foster the art and science of health information services.

National Library of Medicine (NLM)
8600 Rockville Pike
Bethesda, MD 20894 USA
Phone: 301-594-5983
Toll Free: 888-346-3656
Web Address: www.nlm.nih.gov
The National Library of Medicine (NLM) is the world's largest medical library. The web site offers links to several databases of medical research, as well as a variety of online health information.

Weill Cornell Medical Library
1300 York Ave.
New York, NY 10021-4896 USA
Phone: 212-746-6072
Toll Free: 646-962-2570
E-mail Address: email-archives@med.cornell.edu
Web Address: library.weill.cornell.edu/
The Weill Cornell Medical Library houses information on the biomedical sciences, as well as performs data retrieval, management and evaluation.

59) Liver Diseases

American Liver Foundation (ALF)
39 Broadway, Ste. 2700
New York, NY 10006 USA
Phone: 212-668-1000
Fax: 212-483-8179
Toll Free: 800-465-4837
Web Address: www.liverfoundation.org
The American Liver Foundation (ALF) is a national, nonprofit organization dedicated to the prevention, treatment and cure of hepatitis and other liver diseases.

60) Long Term Care, Assisted Living Associations

Argentum
1650 King St., Ste. 602
Alexandria, VA 22314-2747 USA
Phone: 703-894-1805
E-mail Address: editor@argentum.org
Web Address: www.argentum.org

Argentum, formerly the Assisted Living Federation of America (ALFA) represents for-profit and nonprofit providers of assisted living, continuing care retirement communities, independent living and other forms of housing and services.

National Consumer Voice for Quality Long-Term Care
1001 Connecticut Ave. NW, Ste. 632
Washington, DC 20036 USA
Phone: 202-332-2275
Fax: 866-230-9789
E-mail Address: info@theconsumervoice.org
Web Address: www.theconsumervoice.org
The National Consumer Voice for Quality Long-Term Care, formerly the National Citizens' Coalition for Nursing Home Reform (NCCNHR), represents the grassroots membership of concerned advocates of quality long term care nationwide.

61) Managed Care Information

Managed Care On-Line (MCOL)
3430 Tully Rd., Ste. 20, #114
Modesto, CA 95350 USA
Phone: 209-577-4888
Fax: 209-577-3557
E-mail Address: mcare@mcol.com
Web Address: www.mcol.com
MCOL is a leading publisher of health care business information, offering online memberships, newsletters, webinars, training software, resource books, directories, web content, and much more to health care business professionals since 1995.

62) Maternal & Infant Health

Association of Maternal and Child Health Programs (AMCHP)
1825 K St. NW, Ste. 250
Washington, DC 20006 USA
Phone: 202-775-0436
Fax: 202-478-5120
E-mail Address: info@amchp.org
Web Address: www.amchp.org
The Association of Maternal and Child Health Programs (AMCHP) is the national organization representing public health leaders and others working to improve the health and well-being of women, children and youth.

La Leche League International
110 Horizon St., Ste. 210
Raleigh, NC 27651 USA
Phone: 919-459-2167
Fax: 919-459-2075
Toll Free: 877-452-5324
E-mail Address: info@llli.org
Web Address: www.lalecheleague.org
The La Leche League International seeks to help mothers worldwide to breastfeed through mother-to-mother support, encouragement, information and education and to promote a better understanding of breastfeeding.

National Center for Education in Maternal and Child Health (NCEMCH)
3300 Whitehaven St. NW, Ste. 1200A
Washington, DC 20007 USA
Phone: 202-784-9770
Fax: 202-784-9777
E-mail Address: mchlibrary@ncemch.org
Web Address: www.ncemch.org
The National Center for Education in Maternal and Child Health (NCEMCH) provides national leadership to the maternal and child health community to improve the health and well-being of the nation's children and families.

63) MBA Resources

MBA Depot
Web Address: www.mbadepot.com
MBA Depot is an online community and information portal for MBAs, potential MBA program applicants and business professionals.

64) Medical & Health Indexes

Medical World Search
TLC Information Services
P.O. Box 944
Yorktown Heights, NY 10598 USA
Phone: 914-248-6770
Fax: 914-248-6429
E-mail Address: mwsearch@mwsearch.com
Web Address: www.mwsearch.com
Medical World Search is a free medical search engine offered by TLC Information Service that helps patients to understand medical terms and acronyms.

65) Medicare Information

Medicare Rights Center (MRC)
266 W. 37th St., Fl. 3
New York, NY 10018 USA
Phone: 212-869-3850
Fax: 212-869-3532
Toll Free: 800-333-4114
E-mail Address: info@medicarerights.org
Web Address: www.medicarerights.org
The Medicare Rights Center (MRC) is a nonprofit organization that acts as a source for Medicare consumers and professionals. Its web site is a helpful, independent source of Medicare information.

Medicare.gov
P.O. Box 1270
Lawrence, KS 66044 USA
Toll Free: 800-633-4227
Web Address: www.medicare.gov
Medicare.gov is the official U.S. Government web site for people with questions or problems relating to Medicare.

66) Mental Health

International Foundation for Research and Education on Depression (IFRED) (The)
P.O. Box 17598
Baltimore, MD 21297-1598 USA
Fax: 443-782-0739
E-mail Address: info@ifred.org
Web Address: www.ifred.org
The International Foundation for Research and Education on Depression (IFRED) is an organization dedicated to researching causes of depression, to support those dealing with depression, and to combat the stigma associated with depression.

International Society for Mental Health Online (ISMHO)
Phone: 608-618-1774
Web Address: www.ismho.org
The International Society for Mental Health Online (ISMHO) strives to promote the use and development of online communication, information and technology for the mental health community.

Mental Health America
500 Montgomery St., Ste. 820
Alexandria, VA 22314 USA
Phone: 703-684-7722
Fax: 703-684-5968
Toll Free: 800-969-6642
Web Address: www.mentalhealthamerica.net
Mental Health America, formerly the National Mental Health Association (NMHA) is a community-based, nonprofit organization addressing all aspects of mental health, mental wellness and mental illness.

67) Nanotechnology Associations

Alliance for NanoHealth
Phone: 713-441-7350
E-mail Address: jhsakamoto@tmhs.org
Web Address: www.nanohealthalliance.org/index.html

The Alliance for NanoHealth is comprised of eight medical research universities and clinical institutions within the Texas Medical Center, located in Houston. Its purpose is to coordinate efforts to apply advanced research to the use of nanotechnology in health care.

NCI Alliance for Nanotechnology in Cancer
9609 Medical Center Dr.
Bethesda, MD 20892-9725 USA
Phone: 240-760-6600
Fax: 301-451-7440
Toll Free: 800-422-6237
E-mail Address:
ncipressofficers@mail.nig.gov
Web Address: nano.cancer.gov
The NCI Alliance for Nanotechnology in Cancer, a service of the National Cancer Institute, is dedicated to using nanotechnology to advance the prevention, treatment and diagnosis of cancer. It especially seeks to lower the barriers preventing commercial development of advanced oncology therapeutics that use nanotechnology.

68) Neurological Disease

American Parkinson's Disease Association (APDA)
135 Parkinson Ave.
Staten Island, NY 10305 USA
Phone: 718-981-8001
Fax: 718-981-4399
Toll Free: 800-223-2732
E-mail Address: apda@apdaparkinson.org
Web Address:
www.apdaparkinson.org/contact/
The American Parkinson's Disease Association (APDA) seeks to promote a better quality of life for people in the Parkinson's community through a nationwide network of chapters, information and referral centers and support groups. It also funds research and works to enhance patient services and public awareness.

Christopher & Dana Reeve Foundation
636 Morris Tpk., Ste. 3A
Short Hills, NJ 07078 USA
Phone: 973-379-2690
Toll Free: 800-225-0292
Web Address: www.christopherreeve.org
The Christopher & Dana Reeve Foundation is committed to funding research that develops treatments and cures for paralysis caused by spinal cord injury and other central nervous system disorders.

National Rehabilitation Information Center (NARIC)
8400 Corporate Dr., Ste. 500
Landover, MD 20785 USA
Fax: 301-459-4263
Toll Free: 800-346-2742
E-mail Address:
naricinfo@heitechservices.com
Web Address: www.naric.com
The National Rehabilitation Information Center (NARIC) collects and disseminates the results of federally funded research projects.

69) Nutrition & Food Research & Education

Center for Nutrition Policy and Promotion (CNPP)
3101 Park Ctr. Dr., Fl. 10
Alexandria, VA 22302-1594 USA
Phone: 703-305-7600
Fax: 703-305-3300
Web Address: www.fns.usda.gov/cnpp
The Center for Nutrition Policy and Promotion (CNPP) is an arm of the U.S. Department of Agriculture's Food, Nutrition and Consumer Services division. The center develops and promotes science-based dietary guidance and economic information for consumers and professionals in health, education, industry and media.

Center for Science in the Public Interest (CSPI)
1220 L St. NW, Ste. 300
Washington, DC 20009 USA
Phone: 202-332-9110
Fax: 202-265-4954
Toll Free: 866-293-2774
E-mail Address: cspi@cspinet.org
Web Address: www.cspinet.org
The Center for Science in the Public Interest (CSPI) is a nonprofit education and advocacy organization that focuses on improving the safety and nutritional quality of our food supply and on reducing the incidences of alcohol-related injuries.

70) Online Health Data, General

EverydayHealth
345 Hudson St., Fl. 16
New York, NY 10014 USA
Phone: 646-728-9500
Fax: 646-728-9501
E-mail Address:
info@everydayhealth.com
Web Address: www.everydayhealth.com
EverydayHealth.com is a free, comprehensive health and medical information site, specifically designed

with the Family's Chief Medical Officer - women and other caregivers - in mind. EverydayHealth.com offers the best health information, treatment advice and more than 125 online tools.

Health Sciences Library
1959 NE Pacific St.
T334 Health Science Bldg., P.O. Box 357155
Seattle, WA 98195-7155 USA
Phone: 206-543-3390
Web Address: hsl.uw.edu
The Health Sciences Library, based at the University of Washington Health Sciences Center, offers health-related information and articles from the center's HealthBeat publication.

Healthfinder
1101 Wootton Pkwy.
Rockville, MD 20013-113 USA
E-mail Address: healthfinder@nhic.org.
Web Address: www.healthfinder.gov
Healthfinder is a resource for finding government and nonprofit health and human services information on the Internet. It has resources on a range of health topics retrieved from roughly 1,400 government and non-profit organizations.

MedlinePlus
8600 Rockville Pike
Bethesda, MD 20894 USA
Web Address: www.medlineplus.gov/
MedlinePlus offers information from the National Library of Medicine, the world's largest medical library, as well as other governmental and health-related organizations.

Medscape
395 Hudson St., Fl. 3
New York, NY 10014 USA
Phone: 212-301-6700
Web Address: www.medscape.com
Medscape, an online resource for better patient care, provides links to journal articles, health care-related sites and health care information. The site is owned by WebMD.

National Women's Health Information Center (NWHIC)
200 Independence Ave. SW, Room 712E
Washington, DC 20201 USA
Phone: 202-690-7650
Fax: 202-205-2631
Toll Free: 800-994-9662
Web Address: womenshealth.gov
The National Women's Health Information Center (NWHIC) provides a gateway to the vast array of federal and other women's health information resources.

PubMed
8600 Rockville Pike
Bethesda, MD 20894 USA
Toll Free: 888-346-3656
Web Address:
www.pubmed.ncbi.nlm.nih.gov/
PubMed provides access to over 26
million citations dating back to the mid-
1960s from MEDLINE, online books and
life science journals. PubMed includes
links to open access full text articles.

RxList
395 Hudson St., Fl. 3
New York, NY 10014 USA
Phone: 212-624-3700
Web Address: www.rxlist.com
RxList is an online portal, which offers
detailed and current information on
brands and generic drugs. The web site is
owned and operated by WebMD.

WebMD
395 Hudson St., Fl. 3
New York, NY 10014 USA
Phone: 212-624-3700
E-mail Address: newstip@webmd.net
Web Address: www.webmd.com
WebMD serves consumers, physicians,
employers and health plans as a major
provider of health information services
through its broad selection of interrelated
health topics, current medical news and its
own medical search engine.

71) Online Health Information, Reliability & Ethics

Health on the Net Foundation Code of Conduct
C/o HUG-Belle-Idee
Chemin du Petit-Bel-Air 2
Chene-Bourg, 1225 Switzerland
Phone: 41-22-372-62-50
Fax: 41-22-305-57-28
E-mail Address:
honsecretariat@healthonnet.org
Web Address: www.hon.ch/HONcode
The Health on the Net Foundation Code
of Conduct defines a set of rules to help
standardize the reliability of medical and
health information on the Internet.

National Practitioner Data Bank (NPDB)
4094 Majestic Ln., PMB-332
Fairfax, VA 22033 USA
Phone: 703-802-9380
Fax: 703-803-1964
Toll Free: 800-767-6732
E-mail Address: help@npdb.hrsa.gov
Web Address: www.npdb.hrsa.gov
The National Practitioner Data Bank
(NPDB) is an alert or flagging system
intended to facilitate a comprehensive
review of health care practitioners'
professional credentials. It is a joint
operation of several U.S. federal
government agencies, including the
Department of Health and Human
Services, the Health Resources and
Services Administration and the Bureau
of Health Professions. Authorized NPDB
queries and reporters include State
licensing boards, medical malpractice
payers (authorized only to report to the
NPDB), hospitals and other health care
entities, professional societies, and
licensed health care practitioners (self-
query only). Authorized users and
reporters include Federal and State
Government agencies, health plans, and
health care practitioners, providers and
suppliers (self-query only).

72) Organ Donation

Living Bank (The)
4545 Post Oak Place Dr., Ste. 340
Houston, TX 77027 USA
Phone: 713-961-9431
Toll Free: 800-528-2971
E-mail Address: cathleen@livingbank.org
Web Address: www.livingbank.org
The Living Bank is a national organ donor
and transplant education organization that
keeps computerized records of organ
donor data for future retrieval in case of
emergency.

73) Osteoporosis

National Osteoporosis Foundation (NOF)
251 18th St. S., Ste. 630
Arlington, VA 22202 USA
Phone: 202-223-2226
Toll Free: 800-231-4222
E-mail Address: info@nof.org
Web Address: www.nof.org
The National Osteoporosis Foundation
(NOF) is a voluntary health organization
that works to fight osteoporosis and
promote bone health. It also conducts
programs of public and clinician
awareness, education, advocacy and
research.

74) Patent Resources

Patent Docs
E-mail Address: PatentDocs@gmail.com
Web Address:
patentdocs.typepad.com/patent_docs/
Patent Docs is an excellent blog about
patent law and patent news in the fields of
biotechnology and pharmaceuticals.

75) Patients' Rights & Information

Electronic Privacy Information Center (EPIC) - Medical Record Privacy
1519 New Hampshire Ave. NW
Washington, DC 20036 USA
Phone: 202-483-1140
E-mail Address: info@epic.org
Web Address:
www.epic.org/privacy/medical
The Medical Record Privacy section of
the Electronic Privacy Information Center
(EPIC) tracks recent developments in
medical privacy legislation.

FamiliesUSA
1225 New York Ave. NW, Ste. 800
Washington, DC 20005 USA
Phone: 202-628-3030
Fax: 202-347-2417
E-mail Address: info@familiesusa.org
Web Address: www.familiesusa.org
FamiliesUSA is a national nonprofit, non-
partisan organization dedicated to the
achievement of high-quality, affordable
health and long-term care for all
Americans.

Society for Healthcare Consumer Advocacy (SHCA)
155 N. Wacker Dr., Ste. 400
Chicago, IL 60606 USA
Phone: 312-422-3000
Fax: 312-278-0881
Toll Free: 877-243-0027
E-mail Address: hpoe@aha.org
Web Address:
www.hpoe.org/resources/organization-
websites/1105
The Society for Healthcare Consumer
Advocacy (SHCA), a personal
membership group of the American
Hospital Association (AHA) strives to
advance health care consumer advocacy
by supporting professionals that represent
and advocate for consumers throughout
the health care industry.

76) Pharmaceutical Industry Associations (Drug Industry)

Academy of Physicians in Clinical Research (APCR)
1100 E. Woodfield Rd., Ste. 350
Schaumburg, IL 60173 USA
Phone: 904-309-6271
Fax: 904-998-0855
Toll Free: 847-517-7225
E-mail Address: info@apcrnet.org
Web Address: www.apcrnet.org
The Academy of Physicians in Clinical
Research (APCR), formerly the Academy
of Pharmaceutical Physicians and

Investigators (APPI), is an association that arose when the American Academy of Pharmaceutical Physicians and the Association of Clinical Research Professionals merged. It is a nonprofit, membership organization that provides scientific and educational activities on issues concerning pharmaceutical medicine.

Accreditation Council for Pharmacy Education (ACPE)
190 S. LaSalle St., Ste. 2850
Chicago, IL 60603-3499 USA
Phone: 312-664-3575
Fax: 866-228-2631
E-mail Address: info@acpe-accredit.org
Web Address: www.acpe-accredit.org
The Accreditation Council for Pharmacy Education (ACPE) provides accreditation for pharmaceutical programs. It is the national agency for accreditation of professional degree programs as well as providers of continuing pharmacy education.

American Association of Colleges of Pharmacy (AACP)
1400 Crystal Dr., Ste. 300
Arlington, VA 22202 USA
Phone: 703-739-2330
Fax: 703-836-8982
E-mail Address: mail@aacp.org
Web Address: www.aacp.org
The American Association of Colleges of Pharmacy (AACP) is the national organization representing the interests of pharmaceutical education and educators.

American Association of Pharmaceutical Sciences (AAPS)
2107 Wilson Blvd., Ste. 200
Arlington, VA 22201-3042 USA
Phone: 703-243-2800
Fax: 703-243-2800
E-mail Address: aaps@aaps.org
Web Address: www.aaps.org
The American Association of Pharmaceutical Scientists (AAPS) represents scientists in the pharmaceutical field. Members are given access to international forum, scientific programs, ongoing education, opportunities for networking and professional development.

American Pharmacists Association (AphA)
2215 Constitution Ave. NW
Washington, DC 20037 USA
Phone: 202-628-4410
Fax: 202-783-2351
Toll Free: 800-237-2742
E-mail Address: infocenter@aphanet.org
Web Address: www.pharmacist.com

American Pharmaceutical Association (APhA), formerly American Pharmaceutical Association is a national professional society that provides news and information to pharmacists. Its membership includes over 62,000 practicing pharmacists, pharmaceutical scientists, student pharmacists and pharmacy technicians.

American Society for Clinical Pharmacology and Therapeutics (ASCPT)
528 N. Washington St.
Alexandria, VA 22314 USA
Phone: 703-836-6981
E-mail Address: info@ascpt.org
Web Address: www.ascpt.org
The American Society for Clinical Pharmacology and Therapeutics (ASCPT) is a nonprofit organization that is devoted to the discovery, development, regulation and use of safe and effective medications necessary for the prevention and treatment of illness.

American Society for Pharmacology and Experimental Therapeutics (ASPET)
1801 Rockville Pike, Ste. 210
Rockville, MD 20852-1633 USA
Phone: 301-634-7060
Fax: 301-634-7061
Web Address: www.aspet.org
The American Society for Pharmacology and Experimental Therapeutics (ASPET) is a scientific society, with members from academia, industry and the government, conducting research in basic and clinical pharmacology.

Association for Accessible Medicines
601 New Jersey Ave. NW, Ste. 850
Washington, DC 20001 USA
Phone: 202-249-7100
Fax: 202-249-7105
Web Address: www.accessiblemeds.org/
The Association for Accessible Medicines improves access to safe, quality and effective medicine. As manufacturers of 9 out of every 10 prescriptions dispensed in the U.S., members of the Association for Accessible Medicines form an integral, and powerful, part of the health care system.

Association of the British Pharmaceutical Industry (ABPI)
105 Victoria St., Southside, Fl. 7
London, SW1E 6QT UK
Phone: 44-20-7930-3477
Fax: 44-20-7747-1447
Web Address: www.abpi.org.uk
The Association of the British Pharmaceutical Industry (ABPI) is a trade association that provides research and information for the British pharmaceuticals industry.

Canadian Pharmacists Association (CPhA)
1785 Alta Vista Dr.
Ottawa, ON K1G 3Y6 Canada
Phone: 613-523-7877
Fax: 613-523-0445
Toll Free: 800-917-9489
E-mail Address: info@pharmacists.ca
Web Address: www.pharmacists.ca
The Canadian Pharmacists Association (CPhA) is a professional organization providing drug information, pharmacy practice support material, patient information and news about the pharmacy industry.

Chinese Pharmaceutical Association (CPA)
Room 403, Lianri International Mansion, Building 18 Nanlang Jiayuan, Chaoyang District
Beijing, 100022 China
Phone: 0086-10-65660788
Fax: 0086-10-65661656
E-mail Address: int@cpa.org.cn
Web Address: www.cmei.org.cn/
The Chinese Pharmaceutical Association (CPA) is the national organization of pharmaceutical professionals including scientists, legislators and pharmacists serving in the pharmacies, hospitals/clinics and industry.

Indian Drug Manufacturers' Association (IDMA)
102-B, Poonam Chambers, A Wing, FL. 1
Dr. A. B. Rd., Worli
Mumbai, 400 018 India
Phone: 91-22-2494-4624
Fax: 91-22-2495-0723
E-mail Address: admin@idmaindia.com
Web Address: www.idma-assn.org
The Indian Drug Manufacturers' Association (IDMA) is a wholly Indian association mainly promoting the interests of Indian drug manufacturers, as well as protecting the interest of the Indian consumers.

Innovative Medicines Canada
55 Metcalfe St., Ste. 1220
Ottawa, ON K1P 6L5 Canada
Phone: 613-236-0455
E-mail Address: info@imc-mnc.ca
Web Address: innovativemedicines.ca
Innovative Medicines Canada is dedicated to the discovery and development of new medicines and vaccines. Its 50 member companies are guided by strict code of ethical practices ensuring valued

partnership in the Canadian healthcare system.

International Federation of Pharmaceutical Manufacturers & Associations (IFPMA)
Chemin des Mines 9
P.O. Box 195
Geneva 20, 1211 Switzerland
Phone: 41-22-338-32-00
Fax: 41-22-338-32-99
E-mail Address: info@ifpma.org
Web Address: www.ifpma.org
The International Federation of Pharmaceutical Manufacturers & Associations (IFPMA) is a nonprofit organization that represents the world's research-based pharmaceutical and biotech companies.

International Pharmaceutical Excipients Council of the Americas (IPEC-Americas)
3138 N. 10th St., Ste. 500
Arlington, VA 22201 USA
Phone: 571-814-3449
E-mail Address: ipecamer@ipecamericas.org
Web Address: ipecamericas.org
The International Pharmaceutical Excipients Council of the Americas (IPEC-Americas) is a trade organization that promotes standardized approval criteria for drug inert ingredients, or excipients, among different nations. The organization also works to promote safe and useful excipients in the U.S.

International Pharmaceutical Federation (FIP)
Andries Bickerweg 5
The Hague, AE 2517 JP The Netherlands
Phone: 31-70-3021-970
Fax: 31-70-3021-999
E-mail Address: fip@fip.org
Web Address: www.fip.org
The International Pharmaceutical Federation (FIP) is a global federation of national associations representing 3 million pharmacists and pharmaceutical scientists around the world.

International Society for Pharmacoepidemiology (ISPE)
4800 Hampden Ln., Ste. 200
Bethesda, MD 20814-2934 USA
Phone: 301-718-6500
Fax: 301-656-0989
Web Address: www.pharmacoepi.org
The International Society for Pharmacoepidemiology (ISPE) is a nonprofit international organization dedicated to the health of the public by advancing the study of the effects and determinants of pharmacology on epidemic diseases and to help provide risk benefit assessments on drugs with large scale distributions.

International Society of Regulatory Toxicology & Pharmacology (ISRTP)
21517 Fox Field Cir.
Germantown, MD 20876 USA
E-mail Address: admin@isrtp.org
Web Address: www.isrtp.org
The International Society of Regulatory Toxicology & Pharmacology (ISRTP) is an association of professionals that mediates between policy makers and scientists in order to promote sound toxicologic and pharmacologic science as a basis for regulation affecting the environment and human safety and health.

Korean Research-based Pharmaceutical Industry Association (KRPIA)
366 Hangang-daero, Yongsan-gu
Fl. 4
Seoul, 140-821 Korea
Phone: 82-2-456-8553
Fax: 82-2-456-8320
E-mail Address: KRPIA@krpia.or.kr
Web Address: www.krpia.or.kr
The Korean Research-based Pharmaceutical Industry Association (KRPIA) is an association of research-based pharmaceutical companies operating in Korea.

LEEM (French Pharmaceutical Companies Association)
58 Gouvion Blvd.
Saint Cyr, 75017 France
Phone: 33-1-45-03-88-88
Fax: 33-1-45-04-47-71
Web Address: www.leem.org
LEEM (Les Entreprises du Medicament or the French Pharmaceuticals Association) represents the 270 pharmaceutical companies operating in France engaged in the research and/or development of medicines for human use.

National Pharmacy Association
38-42 St. Peter's St.
St. Albans, Mallinson House
Hertfordshire, AL1 3NP UK
Phone: 44-1727-858687
E-mail Address: npa@npa.co.uk
Web Address: www.npa.co.uk
The National Pharmacy Association (NPA), a nonprofit organization was established in 1921 as the trade association of community pharmacy owners in the UK. It works to support, protect and represent the interests of community pharmacies.

Pharmaceutical Research and Manufacturers of America (PhRMA)
950 F St. NW, Ste. 300
Washington, DC 20004 USA
Phone: 202-835-3400
Web Address: www.phrma.org
Pharmaceutical Research and Manufacturers of America (PhRMA) represents the nation's leading research-based pharmaceutical and biotechnology companies.

Pharmaceutical Society of Hong Kong
12 Tak Hing St.
Rm. 1303, Rightful Ctr., Jordan
Hong Kong, Hong Kong Hong Kong
Phone: 852-2376-3090
Fax: 852-2376-3091
E-mail Address: pharmacist@pshk.hk
Web Address: www.pshk.hk
Pharmaceutical Society of Hong Kong is the official representative body of the pharmaceutical industry in Hong Kong.

Pharmaceutical Society of Singapore (PSS)
2985 Jalan Bukit Merah
#02-2B, SMF Building
Singapore, 159457 Singapore
Phone: 65-6259-2313
Fax: 65-6259-2393
E-mail Address: admin@pss.org.sg
Web Address: www.pss.org.sg
The Pharmaceutical Society of Singapore (PSS) is the professional organization representing pharmacists in Singapore. PSS focuses its efforts in two areas: to upgrade pharmacists professionally and public outreach through health education programs. These programs also attract a large number of participants from nearby regions, including Hong Kong, Brunei and Indonesia.

Pharmacy Council of India
NBCC Centre, Fl. 3
Plot No. 2, Community Centre
New Delhi, 110-002 India
Phone: 91-011-61299900
E-mail Address: registrar@pci.nic.in
Web Address: www.pci.nic.in
The Pharmacy Council of India provides regulation of pharmacists under the Pharmacy Act and is a statutory body working under India's Ministry of Health and Family Welfare.

Royal Pharmaceutical Society
66-68 E. Smithfield
London, E1W 1AW UK
Phone: 44-20-7572-2737
Fax: 44-20-7735-7629
E-mail Address: support@rpharms.com
Web Address: www.rpharms.com

The Royal Pharmaceutical Society is the regulatory agency and professional membership organization for pharmacists in England, Wales and Scotland.

Singapore Association of Pharmaceutical Industries (SAPI)
151 Chin Swee Rd.
02-13A/14 Manhattan House
Singapore, 169876 Singapore
Phone: 65-6738-0966
Fax: 65-6738-0977
E-mail Address: admin@sapi.org.sg
Web Address: www.sapi.org.sg
The Singapore Association of Pharmaceutical Industries (SAPI) represents a wide spectrum of pharmaceutical related businesses, namely the trading houses, manufacturers, representative offices and pharmacies in Singapore.

Society of Infectious Diseases Pharmacists (SIDP)
121 W. State St.
Geneva, IL 60134 USA
Phone: 331-248-7888
E-mail Address: sidp@affinity-strategies.com
Web Address: www.sidp.org
The Society of Infectious Diseases Pharmacists (SIDP) is an association of health professionals dedicated to promoting the appropriate use of antimicrobials. It offers members education, advocacy and leadership in all aspects of the treatment of infectious diseases.

77) Pharmaceutical Industry Resources (Drug Industry)

Pharmabiz.com
Flat No. 7, 2nd Floor, 82, Nagin Mahal
Veer Nariman Road, Churchgate,
Mumbai, 400020 India
Phone: 91-022-2204-0015
Fax: 91-022-2204-0038
E-mail Address: editorial@saffronmedia.in
Web Address: www.pharmabiz.com
Pharmabiz.com includes links to most pharmaceutical associations and India's leading industry bodies. The site includes news, company profiles and new drug approvals. It is maintained by Saffron Media Pvt. Ltd.

Tufts Center for the Study of Drug Development
75 Kneeland St., Ste. 1100
Boston, MA 02111 USA
Phone: 617-636-2170
Fax: 617-636-2425
E-mail Address: csdd@tufts.edu

Web Address: csdd.tufts.edu
The Tufts Center for the Study of Drug Development, an affiliate of Tuft's University, provides analyses and commentary on pharmaceutical issues. Its mission is to improve the quality and efficiency of pharmaceutical development, research and utilization. It is famous, among other things, for its analysis of the true total cost of developing and commercializing a new drug. Tuft's Center conducts research in areas of drug development, public policy and regulation and biotechnology.

78) Privacy & Consumer Matters

Federal Trade Commission-Privacy and Security
600 Pennsylvania Ave. NW
Washington, DC 20580 USA
Phone: 202-326-2222
Web Address: business.ftc.gov/privacy-and-security
Federal Trade Commission-Privacy and Security is responsible for many aspects of business-to-consumer and business-to-business trade and regulation.

Privacy International
62 Britton St.
London, EC1M 5UY UK
Phone: 44-20-3422-4321
E-mail Address: info@privacy.org
Web Address: www.privacyinternational.org
Privacy International is a government and business watchdog, alerting individuals to wiretapping and national security activities, medical privacy infringement, police information systems and the use of ID cards, video surveillance and data matching.

TRUSTe
111 Sutter St., Ste. 600
San Francisco, CA 94104 USA
Phone: 415-520-3490
Fax: 415-520-3420
Toll Free: 888-878-7830
E-mail Address: trustarc-info@trustarc.com
Web Address: trustarc.com/consumer-info/privacy-certification-standards/
TRUSTe formed an alliance with all major portal sites to launch the Privacy Partnership campaign, a consumer education program designed to raise the awareness of Internet privacy issues. The organization works to meet the needs of business web sites while protecting user privacy.

79) Privacy Associations

International Association of Privacy Professionals (IAPP)
75 Rochester Ave.
Portsmouth, NH 03801 USA
Phone: 603-427-9200
Fax: 603-427-9249
Toll Free: 800-266-6501
Web Address: www.iapp.org
The International Association of Privacy Professionals (IAPP) is a resource for companies and individuals to learn best practices, advance privacy management issues, and provide education on information privacy. The IAPP aides in providing credentialing programs to privacy information professionals.

80) Research & Development, Laboratories

Battelle Memorial Institute
505 King Ave.
Columbus, OH 43201-2693 USA
Phone: 614-424-6424
Toll Free: 800-201-2011
E-mail Address: solutions@battelle.org
Web Address: www.battelle.org
Battelle Memorial Institute serves commercial and governmental customers in developing new technologies and products. The institute adds technology to systems and processes for manufacturers; pharmaceutical and agrochemical industries; trade associations; and government agencies supporting energy, the environment, health, national security and transportation.

Commonwealth Scientific and Industrial Research Organization (CSRIO)
CSIRO Enquiries
Private Bag 10
Clayton South, Victoria 3169 Australia
Phone: 61-3-9545-2176
Toll Free: 1300-363-400
Web Address: www.csiro.au
The Commonwealth Scientific and Industrial Research Organization (CSRIO) is Australia's national science agency and a leading international research agency. CSRIO performs research in Australia over a broad range of areas including agriculture, minerals and energy, manufacturing, communications, construction, health and the environment.

Computational Neurobiology Laboratory
CNL-S c/o The Salk Institute
10010 N. Torrey Pines Rd.

La Jolla, CA 92037 USA
Phone: 858-453-4100
Fax: 858-587-0417
Web Address: www.cnl.salk.edu
The Computational Neurobiology
Laboratory at The Salk Institute strives to
understand the computational resources of
the brain from the biophysical to the
systems levels.

Fraunhofer-Gesellschaft (FhG) (The)
Fraunhofer-Gesellschaft zur Forderung
der angewandten Forschung e.V.
Postfach 20 07 33
Munich, 80007 Germany
Phone: 49-89-1205-0
Fax: 49-89-1205-7531
Web Address: www.fraunhofer.de
The Fraunhofer-Gesellschaft (FhG)
institute focuses on research in health,
security, energy, communication, the
environment and mobility. FhG includes
over 80 research units in Germany. Over
70% of its projects are derived from
industry contracts.

German Cancer Research Center
Im Neuenheimer Feld 280
Heidelberg, 69120 Germany
Phone: 49-6221-420
Fax: 49-6221-422-995
E-mail Address: kontakt@dkfz.de
Web Address: www.dkfz.de
The German Cancer Research Center
(Deutsches Krebsforschungszentrum,
DKFZ) is the largest biomedical research
institute in Germany and is a member of
the Helmholtz Association of National
Research Centers. More than 2,700 staff
members, including 1,200 scientists, are
investigating the mechanisms of cancer
and are working to identify cancer risk
factors. They provide the foundations for
developing novel approaches in the
prevention, diagnosis and treatment of
cancer. In addition, the staff of the Cancer
Information Service (KID) offers
information about the widespread disease
of cancer for patients, their families and
the general public.

Helmholtz Association
Anna-Louisa-Karsch-Strasse 2
Berlin, 10178 Germany
Phone: 49-30-206329-0
E-mail Address: info@helmholtz.de
Web Address: www.helmholtz.de/en
The Helmholtz Association is a
community of 18 scientific-technical and
biological-medical research centers.
Helmholtz Centers perform top-class
research in strategic programs in several
core fields: energy, earth and
environment, health, key technologies,

structure of matter, aeronautics, space and
transport.

Max Planck Society (MPG)
Hofgartenstr. 8
Munich, 80539 Germany
Phone: 49-89-2108-0
Fax: 49-89-2108-1111
E-mail Address: post@gv.mpg.de
Web Address: www.mpg.de
The Max Planck Society (MPG) currently
maintains 83 institutes, research units and
working groups that are devoted to basic
research in the natural sciences, life
sciences, social sciences, and the
humanities. Max Planck Institutes work
largely in an interdisciplinary setting and
in close cooperation with universities and
research institutes in Germany and
abroad.

**National Research Council Canada
(NRC)**
1200 Montreal Rd., Bldg. M-58
Ottawa, ON K1A 0R6 Canada
Phone: 613-993-9101
Fax: 613-952-9907
Toll Free: 877-672-2672
E-mail Address: info@nrc-cnrc.gc.ca
Web Address: www.nrc-cnrc.gc.ca
National Research Council Canada (NRC)
is comprised of 12 government
organization, research institutes and
programs that carry out multidisciplinary
research. It maintains partnerships with
industries and sectors key to Canada's
economic development.

SRI International
1100 Wilson Blvd., Ste. 2800
Arlington, VA 22209 USA
Phone: 650-859-2000
Web Address: www.sri.com
SRI International is a nonprofit research
organization that offers contract research
services to government agencies, as well
as commercial enterprises and other
private sector institutions. It is organized
around broad divisions including
biosciences, global partnerships,
education, products and solutions
division, advanced technology and
systems and information and computing
sciences division.

81) Respiratory

American Lung Association (ALA)
1301 Pennsylvania Ave. NW, Ste. 800
Washington, DC 20004 USA
Toll Free: 800-548-8252
E-mail Address: info@lung.org
Web Address: www.lung.org
The American Lung Association (ALA) is
dedicated to improving lung health and

fight lung disease in all its forms, with
special emphasis on asthma, tobacco
control and environmental health.

**Asthma and Allergy Foundation of
America (AAFA)**
1235 S. Clark St., Ste. 305
Arlington, VA 22202 USA
Toll Free: 800-727-8462
E-mail Address: info@aafa.org
Web Address: www.aafa.org
The Asthma and Allergy Foundation of
America (AAFA) is dedicated to
improving the quality of life for people
with asthma and allergies through
education, advocacy and research.

**82) Science & Technology
Resources**

Life Science Tennessee
618 Church St., Ste. 210
Nashville, TN 37219 USA
Phone: 615-242-8856
Fax: 615-242-8857
E-mail Address: info@lifesciencetn.org
Web Address: www.lifesciencetn.org
Life Science Tennessee is a statewide,
nonprofit, member organization that
supports the life science industries in
Tennessee through advocacy, partnerships
and alignment with economic and
workforce development.

Technology Review
1 Main St., Fl. 13
Cambridge, MA 02142 USA
Phone: 617-475-8000
Fax: 617-475-8000
Web Address:
www.technologyreview.com
Technology Review, an MIT enterprise,
publishes tech industry news, covers
innovation and writes in-depth articles
about research, development and cutting-
edge technologies.

83) Seniors Housing

**American Seniors Housing Association
(ASHA)**
5225 Wisconsin Ave. NW, Ste. 502
Washington, DC 20015 USA
Phone: 202-237-0900
Fax: 202-237-1616
Web Address: www.seniorshousing.org
The American Seniors Housing
Association (ASHA) was originally
formed as a committee of the National
Multi Housing Council in 1991, and
became an independent non-profit
organization ten years later on January 1,
2001. The group represents building
owners and managers who develop

housing options, services and amenities for seniors.

National Investment Center for the Seniors Housing & Care Industry (NIC)
1 Park Pl., Ste. 450
Annapolis, MD 21401 USA
Phone: 410-267-0504
Fax: 410-268-4620
Web Address: www.nic.org
NIC serves as a resource to lenders, investors, developers/operators, and others interested in meeting the housing and healthcare needs of America's seniors. NIC serves the entire industry as an objective purveyor of information: NIC's research and educational efforts are neither association-driven nor company-oriented. As an impartial observer and unbiased source, NIC has become the primary link between the financial markets and seniors housing developers/operators, connecting each side through relevant research and practical information.

84) Sexually Transmitted Diseases

Herpes Resource Center (HRC)
P.O. Box 13827
Research Triangle Park, NC 27709 USA
Phone: 919-361-8400
Toll Free: 800-783-9877
E-mail Address:
info@ashasexualhealth.org
Web Address:
www.ashasexualhealth.org/stdsstis/herpes
The Herpes Resource Center (HRC), as part of the American Social Health Association, focuses on increasing education, public awareness and support to anyone concerned about herpes.

85) Singaporean Government & Agencies - Health Care

Ministry of Social and Family Development (MSF)
512 Thomson Rd.
MSF Building
Singapore, 298136 Singapore
Phone: 65-6355-5000
Fax: 65-6353-6695
E-mail Address: msf_email@msf.gov.sg
Web Address:
www.msf.gov.sg/Pages/default.aspx
Ministry of Social and Family Development (MSF) develops the social services for Singapore through its policies, community infrastructure, programs and services. Its mission is to

nurture a resilient and caring society that can overcome challenges together.

86) Technology Transfer Associations

Association of University Technology Managers (AUTM)
111 W. Jackson Blvd., Ste. 1412
Chicago, IL 60604 USA
Phone: 847-686-2244
Fax: 847-686-2253
E-mail Address: info@autm.net
Web Address: www.autm.net
The Association of University Technology Managers (AUTM) is a nonprofit professional association whose members belong to over 300 research institutions, universities, teaching hospitals, government agencies and corporations. The association's mission is to advance the field of technology transfer and enhance members' ability to bring academic and nonprofit research to people around the world.

Federal Laboratory Consortium for Technology Transfer
111 W. Jackson Blvd., Ste. 1412
Chicago, IL 60604 USA
Phone: 847-686-2298
E-mail Address: info@federallabs.org
Web Address: www.federallabs.org
In keeping with the aims of the Federal Technology Transfer Act of 1986 and other related legislation, the Federal Laboratory Consortium (FLC) works to facilitate the sharing of research results and technology developments between federal laboratories and the mainstream U.S. economy. FLC affiliates include federal laboratories, large and small businesses, academic and research institutions, state and local governments and various federal agencies. The group has regional support offices and local contacts throughout the U.S.

Licensing Executives Society (USA and Canada), Inc.
11130 Sunrise Valley Dr., Ste. 350
Reston, VA 20191 USA
Phone: 703-234-4058
Fax: 703-435-4390
E-mail Address: info@les.org
Web Address: www.lesusacanada.org
Licensing Executives Society (USA and Canada), Inc., established in 1965, is a professional association composed of about 3,000 members who work in fields related to the development, use, transfer, manufacture and marketing of intellectual property. Members include executives, lawyers, licensing consultants, engineers, academic researchers, scientists and

government officials. The society is part of the larger Licensing Executives Society International, Inc. (same headquarters address), with a worldwide membership of some 12,000 members from approximately 80 countries.

State Science and Technology Institute (SSTI)
5015 Pine Creek Dr.
Westerville, OH 43081 USA
Phone: 614-901-1690
E-mail Address: contactus@ssti.org
Web Address: www.ssti.org
The State Science and Technology Institute (SSTI) is a national nonprofit group that serves as a resource for technology-based economic development. In addition to the information on its web site, the Institute publishes a free weekly digest of news and issues related to technology-based economic development efforts, as well as a members-only publication listing application information, eligibility criteria and submission deadlines for a variety of funding opportunities, federal and otherwise.

87) Textile & Fabric Industry Associations

INDA, Association of the Nonwoven Fabrics Industry
1100 Crescent Gr., Ste. 115
Cary, NC 27518 USA
Phone: 919-459-3700
Fax: 919-459-3701
E-mail Address: info@inda.org
Web Address: www.inda.org
INDA, the Association of the Nonwoven Fabrics Industry, has been representing this sector since 1968. It offers networking events, educational courses, test methods, market data, consultancy and issue advocacy help to its members. Nonwoven textiles are widely used in the health care industry for disposable wipes, drapes, apparel and other items.

88) Trade Associations-General

Associated Chambers of Commerce and Industry of India (ASSOCHAM)
5, Sardar Patel Marg
Chanakyapuri
New Delhi, 110 021 India
Phone: 91-11-4655-0555
Fax: 91-11-2301-7008
E-mail Address: assocham@nic.in
Web Address: www.assocham.org
The Associated Chambers of Commerce and Industry of India (ASSOCHAM) has a membership of more than 300 chambers

and trade associations and serves members from all over India. It works with domestic and international government agencies to advocate for India's industry and trade activities.

BUSINESSEUROPE
168 Ave. de Cortenbergh 168
Brussels, 1000 Belgium
Phone: 32-2-237-65-11
Fax: 32-2-231-14-45
E-mail Address: main@businesseurope.eu
Web Address: www.businesseurope.eu
BUSINESSEUROPE is a major European trade federation that operates in a manner similar to a chamber of commerce. Its members are the central national business federations of the 34 countries throughout Europe from which they come. Companies cannot become direct members of BUSINESSEUROPE, though there is a support group which offers the opportunity for firms to encourage BUSINESSEUROPE objectives in various ways.

United States Council for International Business (USCIB)
1212 Ave. of the Americas
New York, NY 10036 USA
Phone: 212-354-4480
Fax: 212-575-0327
E-mail Address: azhang@uscib.org
Web Address: www.uscib.org
The United States Council for International Business (USCIB) promotes an open system of world trade and investment through its global network. Standard USCIB members include corporations, law firms, consulting firms and industry associations. Limited membership options are available for chambers of commerce and sole legal practitioners.

World Trade Organization (WTO)
Centre William Rappard
Rue de Lausanne 154
Geneva 21, CH-1211 Switzerland
Phone: 41-22-739-51-11
Fax: 41-22-731-42-06
E-mail Address: enquiries@wto.og
Web Address: www.wto.org
The World Trade Organization (WTO) is a global organization dealing with the rules of trade between nations. To become a member, nations must agree to abide by certain guidelines. Membership increases a nation's ability to import and export efficiently.

Agency for Health Care Research and Quality (AHCRQ)
5600 Fishers Ln., Fl. 7
Rockville, MD 20857 USA
Phone: 301-427-1364
Web Address: www.ahrq.gov
The Agency for Health Care Research and Quality (AHCRQ) provides evidence-based information on health care outcomes, quality, cost, use and access. Its research helps people make more informed decisions and improve the quality of health care services.

Bureau of Economic Analysis (BEA)
4600 Silver Hill Rd.
Washington, DC 20233 USA
Phone: 301-278-9004
E-mail Address:
customerservice@bea.gov
Web Address: www.bea.gov
The Bureau of Economic Analysis (BEA), is an agency of the U.S. Department of Commerce, is the nation's economic accountant, preparing estimates that illuminate key national, international and regional aspects of the U.S. economy.

Bureau of Labor Statistics (BLS)
2 Massachusetts Ave. NE
Washington, DC 20212-0001 USA
Phone: 202-691-5200
Fax: 202-691-7890
Toll Free: 800-877-8339
E-mail Address: blsdata_staff@bls.gov
Web Address: stats.bls.gov
The Bureau of Labor Statistics (BLS) is the principal fact-finding agency for the Federal Government in the field of labor economics and statistics. It is an independent national statistical agency that collects, processes, analyzes and disseminates statistical data to the American public, U.S. Congress, other federal agencies, state and local governments, business and labor. The BLS also serves as a statistical resource to the Department of Labor.

Centers for Disease Control and Prevention (CDC)
1600 Clifton Rd.
Atlanta, GA 30333 USA
Toll Free: 800-232-4636
Web Address: www.cdc.gov
The Centers for Disease Control and Prevention (CDC), headquartered in Atlanta, is the federal agency charged with protecting the public health of the nation by providing leadership and direction in the prevention and control of diseases and other preventable conditions

and responding to public health emergencies.

Centers for Medicare and Medicaid Services (CMMS)
7500 Security Blvd.
Baltimore, MD 21244-1850 USA
Phone: 410-786-3000
Toll Free: 877-267-2323
Web Address: www.cms.gov
The Centers for Medicare and Medicaid Services (CMMS) runs the Medicare and Medicaid programs in the U.S., as well as State Children's Health Insurance Program.

Department of Health and Human Services (HHS)
200 Independence Ave. SW
Washington, DC 20201 USA
Phone: 202-619-0257
Toll Free: 877-696-6775
Web Address: www.hhs.gov
The Department of Health and Human Services (HHS) is the principle agency in the United States for safeguarding the health of Americans and for providing necessary health care service programs. Some of the organization's 300 plus programs include Medicare, Medicaid, Head Start, food and drug safety, health information technology and health and social research.

Federal Emergency Management Agency (FEMA)
500 C St. SW
Washington, DC 20472 USA
Phone: 202-646-2500
Toll Free: 800-621-3362
E-mail Address: askia@fema.dhs.gov
Web Address: www.fema.gov
Federal Emergency Management Agency (FEMA) exists to reduce loss of life and property and protect the nation's infrastructure from all types of unexpected hazards. The site has information regarding floods, fires, storms, terrorism and other disaster information including assistance, recovery and preparation.

Health Resources and Services Administration (HRSA)
5600 Fishers Ln.
Rockville, MD 20857 USA
Phone: 301-443-3376
Toll Free: 888-275-4772
Web Address: www.hrsa.gov
Health Resources and Services Administration (HRSA) is an agency within the U.S. Department of Health and Human Services. Its mission is to improve and expand access to quality health care

to low income, uninsured, isolated, vulnerable and special needs populations.

Health.gov
1101 Wootton Pkwy., Ste. 420
Rockville, MD 20852 USA
Phone: 240-453-8280
Fax: 240-453-8282
E-mail Address: odphpinfo@hhs.gov
Web Address: www.health.gov
Health.gov is a portal to the web sites of a number of multi-agency health initiatives and activities of the U.S. Department of Health and Human Services (HHS) and other federal departments and agencies. The web site is coordinated by the Office of Disease Prevention and Health Promotion, Office of the Assistant Secretary for Health, Office of the Secretary, U.S. Department of Health and Human Services

National Cancer Institute (NCI)
9609 Medical Ctr. Dr.
BG 9609 MSC 9760
Bethesda, MD 20892-9760 USA
Toll Free: 800-422-6237
E-mail Address: NCIinfo@nih.gov
Web Address: www.cancer.gov
The National Cancer Institute (NCI) is the Federal Government's principal agency for cancer research and training.

National Center for Chronic Disease Prevention and Health Promotion (NCCDPHP)
600 Clifton Rd.
Atlanta, GA 30329-4027 USA
Toll Free: 800-232-4636
E-mail Address: ccdinfo@cdc.gov
Web Address:
www.cdc.gov/chronicdisease/index.htm
The National Center for Chronic Disease Prevention and Health Promotion (NCCDPHP), a division of the Center for Disease Control (CDC), provides national leadership in areas of health promotion and chronic disease prevention largely through educational initiatives.

National Center for Complementary and Integrative Health (NCCIH)
9000 Rockville Pike
Bethesda, MD 20892 USA
Phone: 301-402-4335
Toll Free: 888-644-6226
E-mail Address: info@nccih.nih.gov
Web Address: nccam.nih.gov
The National Center for Complementary and Integrative Health (NCCIH), part of National Institutes of Health (NIH) is a Federal agency for scientific research on the diverse medical and health care systems, practices, and products that are not generally considered part of conventional medicine.

National Center for Health Statistics (NCHS)
1600 Clifton Rd.
Atlanta, GA 30329 USA
Toll Free: 800-232-4636
E-mail Address: cdcinfo@cdc.gov
Web Address: www.cdc.gov/nchs
The National Center for Health Statistics (NCHS), division of the Center for Disease Control and Prevention (CDC), is the federal government's principal vital and health statistics agency.

National Heart, Lung and Blood Institute (NHLBI)
31 Center Dr.
Bethesda, MD 20892 USA
Phone: 301-592-8573
Fax: 301-592-8563
Toll Free: 877-645-2448
E-mail Address: nhlbiinfo@nhlbi.nih.gov
Web Address: www.nhlbi.nih.gov
The National Heart, Lung, and Blood Institute (NHLBI) provides leadership for a national program in diseases of the heart, blood vessels, lung and blood; blood resources; and sleep disorders.

National Institute of Allergy and Infectious Diseases (NIAID)
5601 Fishers Ln., MSC 9806
Bethesda, MD 20892-9806 USA
Phone: 301-496-5717
Fax: 301-402-3573
Toll Free: 866-284-4107
E-mail Address:
ocpostoffice@niaid.nih.gov
Web Address: www.niaid.nih.gov
The National Institute of Allergy and Infectious Diseases (NIAID) conducts and supports research that strives for understanding, treatment and prevention of the many infectious, immunologic and allergic diseases that threaten people worldwide.

National Institute of Child Health and Human Development (NICHD)
P.O. Box 3006
Rockville, MD 20847 USA
Fax: 1-866-760-5947
Toll Free: 800-370-2943
E-mail Address:
NICHDInformationResourceCenter@mail.nih.gov
Web Address: www.nichd.nih.gov
The National Institute of Child Health and Human Development (NICHD) conducts and supports laboratory, clinical and epidemiological research on the reproductive, neurobiological, developmental and behavioral processes that determine and maintain the health of children, adults, families and populations.

National Institute of Diabetes and Digestive and Kidney Disorders (NIDDK)
9000 Rockville Pike
Bethesda, MD 20892 USA
Phone: 301-496-3583
Toll Free: 800-860-8747
E-mail Address:
healthinfo@niddk.nih.gov
Web Address: www2.niddk.nih.gov
The National Institute of Diabetes and Digestive and Kidney Disorders (NIDDK) conducts and supports basic, translational and clinical research on many of the most serious, chronic diseases and conditions affecting public health.

National Institute of Environmental Health Services (NIEHS)
P.O. Box 12333, Mail Drop K3-16
Research Triangle Park, NC 27709 USA
Phone: 919-541-3345
Fax: 919-541-4395
Web Address: www.niehs.nih.gov
The National Institute of Environmental Health Services (NIEHS) is the segment of the National Institutes of Health that deals with the environmental effects on human health.

National Institute of General Medical Sciences (NIGMS)
45 Center Dr., MSC 6200
Bethesda, MD 20892-6200 USA
Phone: 301-496-7301
E-mail Address: info@nigms.nih.gov
Web Address: www.nigms.nih.gov
The National Institute of General Medical Sciences (NIGMS) supports basic biomedical research that lays the foundation for advances in disease diagnosis, treatment and prevention.

National Institute of Mental Health (NIMH)
6001 Executive Blvd.
Rm. 6200, MSC 9663
Bethesda, MD 20892-9663 USA
Phone: 301-443-4513
Fax: 301-443-4279
Toll Free: 866-615-6464
E-mail Address: nimhinfo@nih.gov
Web Address: www.nimh.nih.gov
The National Institute of Mental Health (NIMII), a part of thc U.S. Department of Health and Human Services, acts as the Federal governments principle biomedical and behavioral research agency. The organization strives to reduce the burden of mental illness and behavioral disorders through research on mind, brain, and behavior.

National Institute of Neurological Disorders and Stroke (NINDS)
6001 Executive Blvd., Ste. 3309
Bethesda, MD 20892-9531 USA
Phone: 301-496-5751
Toll Free: 800-352-9424
Web Address: www.ninds.nih.gov
The National Institute of Neurological Disorders and Stroke (NINDS) works to lead the neuroscience community in seeking knowledge about the brain and nervous system. It supports and performs basic, translational, and clinical neuroscience research; funds and conducts research training and career development programs; and promotes timely dissemination of scientific discoveries and their implications for neurological health to the public, health professionals, researchers, and policy-makers.

National Institute of Nursing Research (NINR)
31 Center Dr., Rm. 5B03
Bethesda, MD 20892-2178 USA
Phone: 301-496-0207
Fax: 301-480-4969
E-mail Address: info@ninr.nih.gov
Web Address: www.ninr.nih.gov
The National Institute of Nursing Research (NINR) supports clinical and basic nursing research to establish a scientific basis for the care of individuals of all ages. From management of patients during illness and recovery to the reduction of risks for disease and disability, NINR promotes healthy lifestyles, quality of life for those with chronic illnesses and care for individuals at the end of life.

National Institute on Aging (NIA)
31 Center Dr., Bldg. 31
MSC 2292, Room 5C27
Bethesda, MD 20892-2292 USA
Phone: 301-496-1752
Fax: 301-496-1072
Toll Free: 800-222-2225
E-mail Address: niaic@nia.nih.gov
Web Address: www.nia.nih.gov
The National Institute on Aging (NIA) is one of the 27 institutes and centers of the National Institutes of Health and leads a broad scientific effort to understand the nature of aging and to extend the healthy, active years of life.

National Institute on Alcohol Abuse and Alcoholism (NIAAA)
9000 Rockville Pike
Bethesda, MD 20892 USA
Phone: 301-443-3860
E-mail Address: niaaaweb-r@exchange.nih.gov
Web Address: www.niaaa.nih.gov
The National Institute on Alcohol Abuse and Alcoholism (NIAAA) provides information on alcohol abuse and the advancement of its treatment. It conducts and supports alcohol-related research, coordinates with other research institutes at state, national and international level and translates and disseminates research findings to health care providers, researchers, public and policymakers.

National Institute on Arthritis and Musculoskeletal and Skin Diseases (NIAMS)
31 Center Dr, Bldg. 21, Room 4C02
MSC 23500
Bethesda, MD 20892-2350 USA
Phone: 301-495-4484
Fax: 301-718-6366
Toll Free: 877-226-4267
E-mail Address: niamsinfo@mail.nih.gov
Web Address: www.niams.nih.gov
The National Institute on Arthritis and Musculoskeletal and Skin Diseases (NIAMS) supports research into the causes, treatment and prevention of arthritis and musculoskeletal and skin diseases, the training of basic and clinical scientists to carry out this research and the dissemination of information on research progress in these diseases.

National Institute on Drug Abuse (NIDA)
6001 Executive Blvd.
Rm. 5213, MSC 9561
Bethesda, MD 20892-9561 USA
Phone: 301-443-1124
Web Address: www.drugabuse.gov
The National Institute on Drug Abuse (NIDA) seeks to lead the nation in bringing the power of science to the advantage of curbing drug abuse and addiction.

National Institutes of Health (NIH)
9000 Rockville Pike
Bethesda, MD 20892 USA
Phone: 301-496-4000
E-mail Address: NIHinfo@od.nih.gov
Web Address: www.nih.gov
The National Institutes of Health (NIH) is the leader of medical and behavioral research in the U.S. and is comprised of 27 institutes and centers ranging from the National Cancer Institute to the National Institute of Mental Health.

National Science Foundation (NSF)
2415 Eisenhower Ave.
Alexandria, VA 22314 USA
Phone: 703-292-5111
Toll Free: 800-877-8339
E-mail Address: info@nsf.gov
Web Address: www.nsf.gov
The National Science Foundation (NSF) is an independent U.S. government agency responsible for promoting science and engineering. The foundation provides colleges and universities with grants and funding for research into numerous scientific fields.

Occupational Safety and Health Administration (OSHA)
200 Constitution Ave. NW
Washington, DC 20210 USA
Toll Free: 800-321-6742
Web Address: www.osha.gov
The Occupational Safety and Health Administration (OSHA), regulates safety within the workplace. It's web site provides information on laws and regulations, safety and health, statistics, compliance assistance and news. OSHA is a unit of the U.S. Department of Labor.

Recalls.gov
E-mail Address: webteam@cpsc.gov
Web Address: www.recalls.gov
Recalls.gov is a one-stop website where six different U.S. government agencies post announcements about governmental recalls in consumer products, motor vehicles, boats, food, medicine, cosmetics and environmental products.

Social Security Administration (SSA)
6401 Security Blvd.
Baltimore, MD 21235 USA
Toll Free: 800-772-1213
Web Address: www.ssa.gov
The Social Security Administration (SSA) offers extensive information on social security and retirement through its web site, Social Security Online.

U.S. Census Bureau
4600 Silver Hill Rd.
Washington, DC 20233-8800 USA
Phone: 301-763-4636
Toll Free: 800-923-8282
E-mail Address: pio@census.gov
Web Address: www.census.gov
The U.S. Census Bureau is the official collector of data about the people and economy of the U.S. Founded in 1790, it provides official social, demographic and economic information. In addition to the Population & Housing Census, which it conducts every 10 years, the U.S. Census Bureau numerous other surveys annually.

U.S. Department of Commerce (DOC)
1401 Constitution Ave. NW
Washington, DC 20230 USA
Phone: 202-482-2000
E-mail Address: TheSec@doc.gov
Web Address: www.commerce.gov

The U.S. Department of Commerce (DOC) regulates trade and provides valuable economic analysis of the economy.

U.S. Department of Labor (DOL)
200 Constitution Ave. NW
Washington, DC 20210 USA
Phone: 202-693-4676
Toll Free: 866-487-2365
Web Address: www.dol.gov
The U.S. Department of Labor (DOL) is the government agency responsible for labor regulations. The Department of Labor's goal is to foster, promote, and develop the welfare of the wage earners, job seekers, and retirees of the United States; improve working conditions; advance opportunities for profitable employment; and assure work-related benefits and rights.

U.S. Environmental Protection Agency (EPA)
1200 Pennsylvania Ave. NW
Ariel Rios Bldg.
Washington, DC 20460 USA
Phone: 202-272-0167
Web Address: www.epa.gov
The U.S. Environmental Protection Agency (EPA) is a government organization that seeks to protect human health and to safeguard the natural environment by developing and enforcing regulations, performing environmental research, sponsoring voluntary programs and offering financial assistance to state environmental programs.

U.S. Food and Drug Administration (FDA)
10903 New Hampshire Ave.
Room 5377, Bldg. 32
Silver Spring, MD 20993 USA
Toll Free: 888-463-6332
Web Address: www.fda.gov
The U.S. Food and Drug Administration (FDA) promotes and protects the public health by helping safe and effective products reach the market in a timely way and by monitoring products for continued safety after they are in use. It regulates both prescription and over-the-counter drugs as well as medical devices and food products.

U.S. Securities and Exchange Commission (SEC)
100 F St. NE
Washington, DC 20549 USA
Phone: 202-942-8088
Fax: 202-772-9295
Toll Free: 800-732-0330
E-mail Address: help@sec.gov
Web Address: www.sec.gov
The U.S. Securities and Exchange Commission (SEC) is a nonpartisan, quasi-judicial regulatory agency responsible for administering federal securities laws. These laws are designed to protect investors in securities markets and ensure that they have access to disclosure of all material information concerning publicly traded securities. Visitors to the web site can access the EDGAR database of corporate financial and business information.

91) UK Government Agencies

National Institute for Health and Clinical Excellence (NICE)
10 Spring Gardens
London, SW1A 2BU UK
Phone: 44-300 323 0140
Fax: 44-300-323-0148
E-mail Address: nice@nice.org.uk
Web Address: www.nice.org.uk
The National Institute for Health and Clinical Excellence (NICE) is the national organization responsible for providing guidance on the promotion of good health and the prevention and treatment of ill health in the UK.

92) Urological Disorders

National Association for Continence (NAFC)
P.O. Box 1019
Charleston, SC 29402 -1019 USA
Phone: 843-377-0900
Toll Free: 800-252-3337
Web Address: www.nafc.org
The National Association for Continence (NAFC) is a national, private, nonprofit organization dedicated to improving the quality of life of people with incontinence. It aims to offer quality continence care through education, collaboration and advocacy.

National Kidney Foundation
30 E. 33rd St.
New York, NY 10016 USA
Phone: 855-653-2273
Fax: 212-689-9261
Toll Free: 800-622-9010
E-mail Address: info@kidney.org
Web Address: www.kidney.org
The National Kidney Foundation seeks to prevent kidney and urinary tract diseases, improve the health and well-being of individuals and families affected by these diseases and increase the availability of all organs for transplantation.

Urology Care Foundation
1000 Corporate Blvd.
Linthicum, MD 21090 USA
Phone: 410-689-3700
Fax: 410-689-3998
Toll Free: 800-828-7866
E-mail Address: info@urologycarefoundation.org
Web Address: www.urologyhealth.org
The Urology Care Foundation, formerly the American Urological Association Foundation (AUAF), seeks the prevention and cure of urologic disease through the expansion of patient education, public awareness, research and advocacy.

93) Vitamin & Supplement Industry Associations

Council for Responsible Nutrition
1828 L St. NW, Ste. 810
Washington, DC 20036-5114 USA
Phone: 202-204-7700
Fax: 202-204-7701
E-mail Address: jblatman@crnusa.org
Web Address: www.crnusa.org
The Council for Responsible Nutrition (CRN), founded in 1973, is a Washington-based trade association representing ingredient suppliers and manufacturers in the dietary supplement industry. CRN members adhere to a strong code of ethics, comply with dosage limits and manufacture dietary supplements to high quality standards under good manufacturing practices. CRN's mission is to improve the environment for member companies to responsibly market dietary supplements by enhancing confidence among media, healthcare professionals, decision makers and consumers.

94) Wholesale Distributors Associations

Global Market Development Center (GMDC)
1275 Lake Plaza Dr.
Colorado Springs, CO 80906-3583 USA
Phone: 719-576-4260
Fax: 719-576-2661
E-mail Address: info@gmdc.org
Web Address: www.gmdc.org
The Global Market Development Center (GMDC) is an international trade association serving the general merchandise, health and beauty care and pharmacy industries.

Chapter 4

THE HEALTH CARE 500:
WHO THEY ARE AND HOW THEY WERE CHOSEN

Includes Indexes by Company Name, Industry & Location,

The companies chosen to be listed in PLUNKETT'S HEALTH CARE INDUSTRY ALMANAC comprise a unique list. THE HEALTH CARE 500 were chosen specifically for their dominance in the many facets of the health care industry in which they operate. Complete information about each firm can be found in the "Individual Profiles," beginning at the end of this chapter. These profiles are in alphabetical order by company name.

THE HEALTH CARE 500 includes leading companies from all parts of the United States as well as many other nations, and from all health care and related industry segments: insurance companies; manufacturers and distributors of health care supplies and products; pharmaceuticals manufacturers; health care providers of all types, including major firms owning clinics, physical rehabilitation centers, hospitals, outpatient surgery centers, nursing homes, home health care offices and other types of health care specialists; specialized service companies that are vital to the health care field, such as medical information management companies; health maintenance organizations and many others.

Simply stated, the list contains the largest, most successful, fastest growing firms in health care and related industries in the world. To be included in our list, the firms had to meet the following criteria:

1) Generally, these are corporations based in the U.S.; however, the headquarters of many firms are located in other nations.
2) Prominence, or a significant presence, in health care and supporting fields. (See the following Industry Codes section for a complete list of types of businesses that are covered).
3) The companies in THE HEALTH CARE 500 do not have to be exclusively in the health care field.
4) Financial data and vital statistics must have been available to the editors of this book, either directly from the company being written about or from outside sources deemed reliable and accurate by the editors. A small number of companies that we would like to have included are not listed because of a lack of sufficient, objective data.

INDEX OF COMPANIES WITHIN INDUSTRY GROUPS

The industry codes shown below are based on the 2012 NAIC code system (NAIC is used by many analysts as a replacement for older SIC codes because NAIC is more specific to today's industry sectors, see www.census.gov/NAICS). Companies are given a primary NAIC code, reflecting the main line of business of each firm.

Industry Group/Company	Industry Code	2020 Sales	2020 Profits
Ambulance Services, Air or Ground			
Air Methods Corporation	621910	1,305,600,000	
Medica Sur SAB de CV	621910		
ModivCare Solutions, LLC	621910	1,000,000,000	
Ambulatory Health Care Services, Other			
Magellan Health Inc	621999	4,577,530,880	382,335,008
Protech Home Medical Corp	621999		
Ambulatory, Outpatient Surgical Clinics, Urgent Care and Emergency Centers			
AMSURG Corporation	621493	3,009,960,000	
LCA-Vision Inc	621493	87,269,379	
Surgery Partners Inc	621493	1,860,099,968	-116,100,000
TLC Laser Eye Centers	621493	230,946,187	
United Surgical Partners International Inc	621493	2,072,000,000	
US NeuroSurgical Holdings Inc	621493	3,173,000	533,000
Blood and Organ Banks			
HemaCare Corporation	621991	33,535,750	
Clinics - General Health			
Concentra Inc	621498	1,501,434,000	
Little Clinic (The)	621498		
MinuteClinic LLC	621498		
Clinics - Outpatient Clinics & Surgery			
Fresenius Medical Care AG & Co KGaA	621400	21,819,793,408	1,422,608,896
Fresenius SE & Co KGaA	621400	44,322,402,304	2,085,573,376
Cloud, Data Processing, Business Process Outsourcing (BPO) and Internet Content Hosting Services			
Global Healthcare Exchange LLC	518210		
Health Catalyst Inc	518210	188,844,992	-115,017,000
Commercial Real Estate Investment and Operations, Including Office Buildings, Shopping Centers, Industrial Properties and Related REITs			
Premier Inc	531120	1,299,591,936	130,364,000
Computer Software, Healthcare & Biotechnology			
Aeon Global Health Corp	511210D		
Allscripts Healthcare Solutions Inc	511210D	1,502,700,032	700,406,976
Cerner Corporation	511210D	5,505,787,904	780,088,000
eClinicalWorks	511210D	615,000,000	
Epic Systems Corporation	511210D	3,300,000,000	
GoodRx Holdings Inc	511210D	550,700,032	-293,623,008
IBM Watson Health	511210D	263,070,281	
Medical Information Technology Inc (MEDITECH)	511210D	502,851,197	74,542,923
NextGen Healthcare Inc	511210D	540,238,976	7,498,000
SHL Telemedicine Ltd	511210D	40,164,000	278,000

Industry Group/Company	Industry Code	2020 Sales	2020 Profits
Welltok Inc	511210D	88,021,500	
Continuing Care Retirement Communities			
Regional Health Properties Inc	623311	17,579,000	-688,000
Dental Equipment and Supplies Manufacturing			
Straumann Holding AG	339114	1,589,612,928	101,765,928
Dentists			
Castle Dental Centers Inc	621210		
Coast Dental Services LLC	621210		
Smile Brands Inc	621210	403,100,775	
Diagnostic Imaging Centers, Including CAT Scan, PET and MRI			
Alliance HealthCare Services Inc	621512	539,673,750	
RadNet Inc	621512	1,071,840,000	-14,840,000
Dialysis Centers			
DaVita Inc	621492	11,550,604,288	773,641,984
Diet and Weight Loss Centers			
Jenny Craig Inc	812191	244,500,000	
Medifast Inc	812191	934,841,984	102,859,000
WW International Inc	812191	1,378,124,032	75,079,000
Disease Management & Utilization Management			
CorVel Corporation	524298A	592,225,024	47,377,000
Tivity Health Inc	524298A	437,713,984	-223,631,008
Document Preparation, Call Centers, Collection Agencies and Other Business Support Services			
HealthTrust Purchasing Group LP	561400		
Intalere Inc	561400		
Vizient Inc	561400		
Equipment Rental and Leasing, Commercial and Industrial Machinery			
InfuSystem Holdings Inc	532490	97,388,000	17,332,000
Factory Automation, Robots (Robotics) Industrial Process, Thermostat, Flow Meter and Environmental Quality Monitoring and Control Manufacturing (incl. Artificial Intelligence, AI)			
Siemens AG	334513	69,811,109,888	4,923,761,152
Health Care Utilization Management			
MultiPlan Inc	524298	937,763,000	-520,564,000
Health Insurance and Medical Insurance Underwriters (Direct Carriers), including Group Health, Supplemental Health and HMOs			
aetnaCVSHealth	524114	75,467,000,000	
AFLAC Incorporated	524114	22,115,999,744	4,777,999,872
Alignment Healthcare LLC	524114	959,222,000	-22,926,000
Amerigroup Corporation	524114	11,210,000,000	
Anthem Inc	524114	121,867,001,856	4,572,000,256
Arkansas Blue Cross and Blue Shield	524114	2,478,000,000	
AvMed Health Plans Inc	524114	1,191,196,125	
AXA Health	524114	2,074,600,000	126,268,000
Blue Care Network of Michigan	524114	4,252,386,000	74,747,000
Blue Cross and Blue Shield Association	524114	698,357,424	

Industry Group/Company	Industry Code	2020 Sales	2020 Profits
Blue Cross and Blue Shield of Florida Inc	524114	10,838,264,063	
Blue Cross and Blue Shield of Louisiana	524114	3,907,083,600	
Blue Cross and Blue Shield of Massachusetts	524114	8,016,835,000	386,710,000
Blue Cross and Blue Shield of Michigan	524114	30,220,000,000	818,000,000
Blue Cross and Blue Shield of Minnesota	524114	13,200,000,000	128,000,000
Blue Cross and Blue Shield of Montana	524114	790,079,062	
Blue Cross and Blue Shield of Nebraska	524114	1,941,245,632	
Blue Cross and Blue Shield of North Carolina	524114	9,900,000,000	260,500,000
Blue Cross and Blue Shield of Oklahoma	524114		
Blue Cross and Blue Shield of Texas	524114		
Blue Cross and Blue Shield of Vermont	524114	479,087,836	13,201,516
Blue Cross and Blue Shield of Wyoming	524114		
Blue Cross Blue Shield of Kansas City (Blue KC)	524114	2,956,147,000	74,788,000
Blue Cross of California	524114		
Blue Cross of Idaho	524114	2,485,977,692	
Blue Shield of California	524114	21,806,000,000	680,000,000
BlueCross BlueShield of Tennessee Inc	524114	8,994,746,250	
British United Provident Association Limited (BUPA)	524114	16,452,900,000	312,276,000
Cambia Health Solutions Inc	524114	9,493,350,000	
Capital BlueCross	524114	4,417,149,713	
CareFirst Inc	524114	10,000,000,000	
Centene Corporation	524114	111,115,001,856	1,808,000,000
Cigna Corporation	524114	160,576,995,328	8,457,999,872
Conviva Care Centers	524114	696,890,250	
Delta Dental Plans Association	524114	33,882,904	
EmblemHealth Inc	524114	10,272,905,526	
Envolve Vision Inc	524114		
EyeMed Vision Care LLC	524114		
First Choice Health Network Inc	524114		
First Health Group Corp	524114		
Harvard Pilgrim Health Care Inc	524114	3,069,000,000	
Health Care Service Corporation (HCSC)	524114	47,300,000,000	
Health Net Inc	524114	21,057,198,750	
HealthNow New York Inc	524114	2,996,000,000	
Highmark Health	524114	18,000,000,000	450,000,000
Horizon Healthcare Services Inc	524114	14,124,000,000	
Humana Inc	524114	77,155,000,320	3,367,000,064
Lifetime Healthcare Companies (The)	524114	6,000,000,000	
Lumeris Inc	524114	714,833,437	
Medical Mutual of Ohio	524114	3,414,982,173	
Molina Healthcare Inc	524114	19,423,000,576	673,000,000
Premera Blue Cross	524114	4,657,650,165	
SafeGuard Health Enterprises Inc	524114		
Tufts Associated Health Plans Inc	524114	8,700,000,000	32,800,000
UnitedHealth Group Inc	524114	255,638,994,944	15,402,999,808
UnitedHealthcare Community & State	524114	46,487,000,000	
Vision Service Plan	524114		
WellCare Health Plans Inc	524114	36,644,650,000	

Industry Group/Company	Industry Code	2020 Sales	2020 Profits
Home Health Care Services			
Addus HomeCare Corporation	621610	764,774,976	33,133,000
Amedisys Inc	621610	2,071,518,976	183,608,000
American HomePatient Inc	621610	382,318,621	
Aveanna Healthcare LLC	621610	1,495,105,000	-57,050,000
Chemed Corporation	621610	2,079,582,976	319,465,984
Civitas Solutions Inc	621610	1,683,273,403	
Elara Caring	621610		
Envision Healthcare Corporation	621610	8,478,750,000	
Kindred at Home	621610	2,552,100,000	
LHC Group Inc	621610	2,063,203,968	111,596,000
New York Health Care Inc	621610		
Home Health Equipment Rental			
Apria Healthcare Group LLC	532291	1,108,717,000	46,139,000
Hospitals, General Medical and Surgical			
AdventHealth	622110	10,230,000,000	
Advocate Aurora Health	622110	13,132,189,000	608,125,000
AHMC Healthcare Inc	622110	1,272,240,000	
Allina Health	622110	4,469,220,860	
Ardent Health Services LLC	622110	4,400,000,000	
Ascension	622110	25,261,514,000	-1,039,856,000
Avera Health	622110	295,600,192	28,871,571
Banner Health	622110	10,400,000,000	586,700,000
Baylor Scott & White Health	622110	1,158,505,975	-136,407,231
BJC HealthCare	622110	5,500,000,000	
Bon Secours Mercy Health System Inc	622110	3,426,000,000	
Cancer Treatment Centers of America Inc (CTCA)	622110	5,151,431,250	
CHRISTUS Health	622110	5,728,344,000	128,698,000
Cleveland Clinic Foundation (The)	622110	10,627,906,000	1,325,244,000
CommonSpirit Health	622110	29,580,000,000	-550,000,000
Community Health Systems Inc	622110	11,788,999,680	511,000,000
Detroit Medical Center (DMC)	622110		
Dynacq Healthcare Inc	622110	6,541,496	
Fairview Health Services	622110	5,626,287,960	
HCA Healthcare Inc	622110	51,533,000,704	3,753,999,872
Healthscope Limited	622110	1,724,723,296	
Henry Ford Health System	622110	6,500,000,000	225,600,000
Houston Methodist	622110	3,859,500,000	
Indiana University Health	622110	6,810,000,000	656,000,000
Intermountain Healthcare	622110	7,700,000,000	378,000,000
Iowa Health System (dba UnityPoint Health)	622110	4,612,051,000	275,755,000
Johns Hopkins Medicine	622110	8,304,900,000	
Kaiser Permanente	622110	88,700,000,000	6,400,000,000
KPC Healthcare Inc	622110	356,107,500	
Life Healthcare Group Holdings Ltd	622110	1,845,284,224	-6,760,082
LifePoint Health Inc	622110	7,153,500,000	
Magee Rehabilitation Hospital	622110	63,715,771	-9,591,082
Main Line Health System	622110	1,650,000,000	-67,600,000
Mass General Brigham Incorporated	622110	13,020,000,000	

Industry Group/Company	Industry Code	2020 Sales	2020 Profits
Mayo Clinic	622110	13,910,000,000	1,971,000,000
Mediclinic International plc	622110	4,364,630,016	-453,026,816
MedStar Health	622110	5,788,600,000	136,400,000
Memorial Hermann Healthcare System	622110	5,747,742,387	
Mercy	622110	5,000,000,000	
Mercy Health	622110	6,512,499,304	
Narayana Hrudayalaya Ltd	622110	300,848,000	9,003,930
National Healthcare Group Pte Ltd	622110	1,911,820,995	
National University Health System (NUHS)	622110		
Netcare Limited	622110	1,369,679,872	32,419,316
New York City Health and Hospitals Corporation	622110	9,053,438,000	423,504,000
NewYork-Presbyterian Healthcare System	622110	5,490,390,000	
OhioHealth Corporation	622110	5,100,000,000	
Prime Healthcare Services Inc	622110	3,992,612,912	
Providence	622110	25,675,000,000	740,000,000
Ramsay Health Care Limited	622110	9,254,960,128	220,267,568
Rhon Klinikum AG	622110	1,924,830,000	3,025,170
Sanford Health	622110	5,917,528,150	
Sentara Healthcare	622110	5,957,709,587	693,174,966
Spectrum Health	622110	8,300,000,000	714,100,000
SSM Health	622110	8,253,201,000	286,038,000
Steward Health Care System LLC	622110	5,413,904,000	-395,670,000
Surgical Care Affiliates Inc	622110	1,923,750,000	
Sutter Health Inc	622110	13,220,000,000	200,000,000
Tenet Healthcare Corporation	622110	17,639,999,488	399,000,000
Texas Health Resources	622110	4,900,000,000	
Thomas Jefferson University Hospitals Inc	622110		
Trinity Health	622110	18,833,027,000	-34,546,000
UnityPoint Health	622110	4,612,051,000	181,665,000
Universal Health Services Inc	622110	11,558,896,640	943,953,024
UPMC	622110	16,487,763,608	87,594,040
USMD Health System	622110	360,658,068	
Hospitals, Psychiatric and Substance Abuse			
Acadia Healthcare Company Inc	622210	2,089,928,960	-672,131,968
Hospitals, Specialty			
CareRx Corporation	622310	134,390,592	-15,131,328
Hanger Inc	622310	1,001,150,016	38,192,000
MD Anderson Cancer Center	622310	5,005,869,368	1,161,429,710
Medical Facilities Corporation	622310	363,854,016	8,813,000
Memorial Sloan Kettering Cancer Center	622310	5,407,196,000	-417,172,000
St Jude Children's Research Hospital	622310	2,210,506,498	504,534,171
Insurance Agencies, Risk Management Consultants and Insurance Brokers			
Sidecar Health Inc	524210		
Insurance Claims Administration and Services			
athenahealth Inc	524292	1,465,750,000	
Change Healthcare Inc	524292	196,792,000	-947,596,992
HMS	524292		
UnitedHealthcare National Accounts	524292		

Industry Group/Company	Industry Code	2020 Sales	2020 Profits
Internet Search Engines, Online Publishing, Sharing, Gig and Consumer Services, Online Radio, TV and Entertainment Sites and Social Media			
Everyday Health Inc	519130	259,000,000	
Healthgrades Operating Company Inc	519130	100,000,000	
Ping An Healthcare and Technology Company Limited	519130	1,076,055,424	-148,647,952
So-Young International Inc	519130	202,953,920	910,088
WebMD Health Corp	519130	852,906,949	
Laboratory Instruments and Lab Equipment Manufacturing			
Bruker Corporation	334516	1,987,500,032	157,800,000
Mettler-Toledo International Inc	334516	3,085,177,088	602,739,008
Medical Diagnostics, Reagents, Assays and Test Kits Manufacturing			
Adaptive Biotechnologies Corporation	325413	98,382,000	-146,227,008
Bio-Rad Laboratories Inc	325413	2,545,626,112	3,806,266,880
Bio-Techne Corporation	325413	738,691,008	229,296,000
Caris Life Sciences	325413		
Foundation Medicine Inc	325413		
GenMark Diagnostics Inc	325413	100,000,000	
Hologic Inc	325413	3,776,399,872	1,115,200,000
Immucor Inc	325413	475,714,091	
Interpace Biosciences Inc	325413		
Livongo Health Inc	325413		
Meridian Bioscience Inc	325413	253,667,008	46,186,000
PerkinElmer Inc	325413	3,782,745,088	727,886,976
Quidel Corporation	325413	1,661,667,968	810,286,976
Twist Bioscience Corporation	325413	90,100,000	-139,931,008
Medical Equipment and Supplies Manufacturing			
3M Company	339100	32,184,000,512	5,384,000,000
Abiomed Inc	339100	840,883,008	203,008,992
Advanced Bionics LLC	339100	266,200,000	
Align Technology Inc	339100	2,471,941,120	1,775,888,000
AngioDynamics Inc	339100	264,156,992	-166,787,008
Ansell Limited	339100	1,821,471,744	179,133,408
Arthrex Inc	339100	2,877,050,000	
Atrion Corporation	339100	147,591,008	32,115,000
Auris Health Inc	339100	17,073,100	
Avanos Medical Inc	339100	714,800,000	-27,200,000
Avinger Inc	339100	8,761,000	-19,006,000
Bausch & Lomb Incorporated	339100	4,408,000,000	1,159,000,000
Baxter International Inc	339100	11,672,999,936	1,102,000,000
Becton Dickinson and Company	339100	17,116,999,680	874,000,000
BioTelemetry Inc	339100		
Boston Scientific Corporation	339100	9,912,999,936	-82,000,000
CIVCO Medical Instruments Co Ltd	339100	4,224,000,000	
ClearPoint Neuro Inc	339100		
Coloplast AS	339100	3,047,168,512	689,655,168
CONMED Corporation	339100		

Industry Group/Company	Industry Code	2020 Sales	2020 Profits
ConvaTec Inc	339100		
Cooper Companies Inc (The)	339100	2,430,899,968	238,400,000
Cordis Corporation	339100	996,715,125	
CryoLife Inc	339100	253,227,008	-16,682,000
Dentsply Sirona Inc	339100	3,342,000,128	-83,000,000
DePuy Synthes Inc	339100	10,587,500,000	
DexCom Inc	339100	1,926,700,032	493,600,000
DJO Global Inc	339100	1,377,530,000	
Draegerwerk AG & Co KGaA	339100	4,161,709,568	305,638,528
EDAP TMS SA	339100	50,901,672	-2,081,908
Edwards Lifesciences Corporation	339100	4,386,299,904	823,400,000
Electromed Inc	339100	32,470,688	4,161,439
Elekta AB	339100	1,766,306,944	131,133,264
Endologix LLC	339100		
EssilorLuxottica SA	339100	17,629,020,160	103,851,040
Ethicon Inc	339100	6,820,000,000	
Exactech Inc	339100	265,000,000	
Fielmann AG	339100	1,745,837,440	142,224,608
GE Healthcare	339100	18,009,000,000	3,060,000,000
Gerresheimer AG	339100	1,733,440,128	108,199,344
Getinge Industrier AB	339100	3,607,253,504	391,827,168
Globus Medical Inc	339100	789,041,984	102,285,000
Haemonetics Corporation	339100	988,478,976	76,526,000
Hill-Rom Holdings Inc	339100	2,880,999,936	223,000,000
ICU Medical Inc	339100	1,271,004,032	86,870,000
Integra LifeSciences Holdings Corporation	339100	1,371,868,032	133,892,000
Intersect ENT Inc	339100	80,554,000	-72,319,000
Intuitive Surgical Inc	339100	4,358,400,000	1,060,600,000
Invacare Corporation	339100	850,689,024	-28,280,000
Keystone Dental Inc	339100	32,725,000	
Lakeland Industries Inc	339100	107,809,000	3,281,000
Lumenis Ltd	339100	261,333,843	
Medical Action Industries Inc	339100	355,253,250	
Medline Industries Inc	339100		
Medtronic MiniMed Inc	339100	2,368,000,000	
Medtronic Vascular Inc	339100	10,468,000,000	
Merit Medical Systems Inc	339100	963,875,008	-9,843,000
Mindray Medical International Limited	339100	3,221,260,000	1,139,600,000
Misonix Inc	339100	62,483,652	-17,418,374
Molnlycke Health Care AB	339100	2,202,240,000	
MSA Safety Inc	339100	1,348,222,976	120,101,000
Natus Medical Incorporated	339100	415,684,000	-16,613,000
Nordion (Canada) Inc	339100	114,745,000	66,803,000
NuVasive Inc	339100	1,050,582,016	-37,153,000
Olympus Corporation	339100	7,282,758,144	471,902,336
Opto Circuits (India) Ltd	339100	24,716,500	-183,364,000
Orthofix International NV	339100	406,561,984	2,517,000
Safilo Group SpA	339100	953,350,080	-84,766,888

Industry Group/Company	Industry Code	2020 Sales	2020 Profits
Shandong Weigao Group Medical Polymer Co Ltd	339100	1,778,057,728	318,168,384
Smiths Group plc	339100	3,607,225,856	375,162,816
Span America Medical Systems Inc	339100	87,781,149	
STAAR Surgical Company	339100	163,460,000	5,913,000
STERIS plc	339100	3,030,895,104	407,604,992
Stryker Corporation	339100	14,350,999,552	1,599,000,064
Sunrise Medical GmbH	339100	558,851,000	
Symmetry Surgical Inc	339100	109,511,325	
Teleflex Incorporated	339100	2,537,156,096	335,324,000
Terumo Corporation	339100	5,743,719,424	778,232,448
Utah Medical Products Inc	339100	42,178,000	10,798,000
Wright Medical Group NV	339100		
Zimmer Biomet Holdings Inc	339100	7,024,500,224	-138,900,000
Zoll Medical Corporation	339100	1,484,654,062	
Medical Imaging and Electromedical (Medical Devices) Equipment, including MRI, Ultrasound, Pacemakers, EKG and CAT			
Accuray Incorporated	334510	382,928,000	3,827,000
Analogic Corporation	334510	557,674,135	-68,049,346
Avantor Inc	334510	6,393,600,000	116,600,000
Axonics Modulation Technologies Inc	334510	111,535,000	-54,915,000
Beckman Coulter Inc	334510	6,232,950,000	
Biosensors International Group Ltd	334510		
Cochlear Limited	334510	1,024,244,224	-184,823,104
Coherent Inc	334510	1,228,999,040	-414,139,008
Cynosure Inc	334510	500,000,000	
Danaher Corporation	334510	22,283,999,232	3,646,000,128
Demant AS	334510	2,377,560,320	184,203,824
Fujifilm Healthcare Americas Corporation	334510	232,508,981	
IDEXX Laboratories Inc	334510	2,706,654,976	581,776,000
Intarcia Therapeutics Inc	334510		
IRIDEX Corporation	334510	36,347,000	-6,329,000
Masimo Corporation	334510	1,143,744,000	240,302,000
Medtronic plc	334510	28,913,000,448	4,789,000,192
Novanta Inc	334510	590,622,976	44,521,000
Optos plc	334510	117,700,000	21,700,000
Philips Healthcare	334510	24,021,030,000	
Precision Optics Corporation	334510	9,923,355	-1,426,150
Predictive Oncology Inc	334510	1,252,272	-25,884,396
ResMed Inc	334510	2,957,012,992	621,673,984
Semler Scientific Inc	334510	38,603,000	14,007,000
ShockWave Medical Inc	334510	67,789,000	-65,699,000
Siemens Healthineers AG	334510	18,000,000,000	
Silk Road Medical Inc	334510	75,227,000	-47,365,000
Sonova Holding AG	334510	3,251,912,192	538,696,512
Starkey Hearing Technologies	334510	883,200,000	
Tandem Diabetes Care Inc	334510	498,830,016	-34,382,000
TransEnterix Inc	334510		
TransMedics Group Inc	334510	25,639,000	-28,748,000

Industry Group/Company	Industry Code	2020 Sales	2020 Profits
Vapotherm Inc	334510	125,733,000	-51,502,000
Varian Medical Systems Inc	334510		
Medical Laboratories			
AmeriPath Inc	621511	1,078,440,000	
Bio-Reference Laboratories Inc	621511	940,123,800	
iKang Healthcare Group Inc	621511	562,522,201	
Laboratory Corporation of America Holdings	621511	13,978,500,096	1,556,099,968
Quest Diagnostics Incorporated	621511	9,436,999,680	1,431,000,064
Sonic Healthcare Limited	621511	5,260,501,504	409,316,832
Medical, Dental and Hospital Equipment and Supplies (Medical Devices) Wholesale Distribution			
Amplifon SpA	423450	1,900,526,592	123,404,360
Carl Zeiss Meditec AG	423450	1,631,624,576	149,527,168
Fisher & Paykel Healthcare Limited	423450	923,637,184	208,387,728
Henry Schein Inc	423450	10,119,141,376	403,793,984
Owens & Minor Inc	423450	8,480,177,152	29,871,000
Patterson Companies Inc	423450	5,490,011,136	-588,446,016
Sartorius Stedim Biotech SA	423450	2,333,692,928	437,211,648
Thermo Fisher Scientific Inc	423450	32,217,999,360	6,375,000,064
Nursing Care Facilities (Skilled Nursing Facilities)			
Diversicare Healthcare Services Inc	623110	475,718,016	5,159,000
Ensign Group Inc (The)	623110	2,402,596,096	170,478,000
Extendicare Inc	623110	959,725,760	44,899,328
Genesis Healthcare Inc	623110		
Kindred Healthcare LLC	623110	6,186,936,910	
National HealthCare Corporation	623110	980,712,000	41,871,000
ORPEA ACT	623110	4,792,288,256	195,540,512
ProMedica Senior Care	623110	3,441,850,000	
Offices of Optometrists			
Capital Vision Services LP (MyEyeDr)	621320		
EyeCare Partners LLC	621320		
Offices of Physical, Occupational and Speech Therapists, and Audiologists			
HearUSA Inc	621340		
US Physical Therapy Inc	621340	422,968,992	35,194,000
Offices of Physicians			
Apollo Medical Holdings Inc	621100	682,225,984	37,866,000
Pharmaceuticals and Druggists' Merchandise Distributors			
Alfresa Holdings Corporation	424210	24,645,914,624	367,813,472
AmerisourceBergen Corporation	424210	189,893,918,720	-3,408,716,032
BioMerieux SA	424210	3,747,922,944	494,086,592
Cardinal Health Inc	424210	152,921,997,312	-3,696,000,000
Ebos Group Limited	424210	6,805,011,456	126,168,704
McKesson Corporation	424210	231,051,001,856	900,000,000
Medipal Holdings Corporation	424210	29,710,778,368	346,761,920
Profarma Distribuidora de Produtos Farmaceuticos SA	424210	1,218,160,000	146,805,000
Sigma Healthcare Limited	424210	2,181,480,000	-7,710,540
Sinopharm Group Co Ltd	424210	71,530,496,000	1,126,408,960

Industry Group/Company	Industry Code	2020 Sales	2020 Profits
Suzuken Co Ltd	424210	20,216,197,120	257,669,456
Toho Holdings Co Ltd	424210	12,350,297,400	146,411,307
Pharmaceuticals, Biopharmaceuticals, Generics and Drug Manufacturing			
3SBio Inc	325412	856,052,000	118,137,000
Abbott Laboratories	325412	34,608,001,024	4,495,000,064
AEterna Zentaris Inc	325412	3,652,000	-5,118,000
Akero Therapeutics Inc	325412	0	-79,207,000
Alcon Inc	325412	6,832,999,936	-531,000,000
Alector Inc	325412	21,098,000	-190,228,000
Allergan Aesthetics, an AbbVie Company	325412	16,732,456,000	
Amgen Inc	325412	25,423,998,976	7,264,000,000
Applied Therapeutics Inc	325412	0	-93,961,000
Astellas Pharma Inc	325412	11,880,604,672	1,784,689,536
AstraZeneca plc	325412		
Atreca Inc	325412	0	-86,335,000
Bausch Health Companies Inc	325412	8,026,999,808	-560,000,000
Bayer AG	325412	50,581,565,440	-12,822,548,480
Bayer Corporation	325412	17,627,800,000	
Bayer HealthCare Pharmaceuticals Inc	325412	4,734,880,000	
Biogen Inc	325412	13,444,599,808	4,000,600,064
Bristol-Myers Squibb Company	325412	42,517,999,616	-9,015,000,064
China Resources Pharmaceutical Group Limited	325412	25,851,600,000	686,718,000
Cipla Limited	325412	2,309,538,048	212,273,680
Cumberland Pharmaceuticals Inc	325412	37,441,136	-3,339,408
Eli Lilly and Company	325412	24,539,799,552	6,193,699,840
Endo International plc	325412	2,903,074,048	183,944,000
Equillium Inc	325412	0	-29,813,000
Eton Pharmaceuticals Inc	325412	39,000	-27,970,000
Galderma SA	325412	300,000,000	
Genentech Inc	325412	21,840,000,000	
Gilead Sciences Inc	325412	24,689,000,448	123,000,000
GlaxoSmithKline Pharmaceuticals Ltd	325412		
GlaxoSmithKline plc	325412	48,274,251,776	8,138,910,208
Guardion Health Sciences Inc	325412	1,889,844	-8,571,657
HOOKIPA Pharma Inc	325412	19,584,000	-44,082,000
Hoth Therapeutics Inc	325412	0	-7,197,816
Incyte Corporation	325412	2,666,702,080	-295,696,992
Jiangsu Hengrui Medicine Co Ltd	325412	4,249,070,000	966,553,000
Johnson & Johnson	325412	82,584,002,560	14,714,000,384
Karuna Therapeutics Inc	325412	0	-68,554,000
Lupin Limited	325412		
Medicure Inc	325412	9,619,687	-5,671,555
Merck & Co Inc	325412	47,993,999,360	7,066,999,808
Merck Serono SA	325412	8,180,550,000	
Morphic Holding Inc	325412	44,945,000	-44,999,000
Mylan NV	325412		
NextCure Inc	325412	22,378,000	-36,603,000
Novartis AG	325412	49,898,000,384	8,072,000,000

Industry Group/Company	Industry Code	2020 Sales	2020 Profits
Novo Nordisk AS	325412	20,859,891,712	6,924,157,952
Osmotica Pharmaceuticals plc	325412	177,884,000	-79,589,000
Par Pharmaceutical Companies Inc	325412	4,540,205,250	
Pfizer Inc	325412	41,907,998,720	9,616,000,000
Regeneron Pharmaceuticals Inc	325412	8,497,099,776	3,513,200,128
Roche Holding AG	325412	65,021,517,824	15,936,809,984
Sanofi Genzyme	325412	13,443,100,000	
Sanofi SA	325412	45,656,584,192	15,044,962,304
Simcere Pharmaceutical Group Ltd	325412	690,757,000	101,772,000
Sun Pharmaceutical Industries Ltd	325412		
Suven Life Sciences Limited	325412	3,781,510	-12,522,800
Synthorx Inc	325412	0	
Takeda Oncology	325412	3,904,160,000	
Takeda Pharmaceutical Company Limited	325412	30,058,434,560	404,053,248
Teva Pharmaceutical Industries Limited	325412	16,657,999,872	-3,990,000,128
Trevi Therapeutics Inc	325412	0	-32,758,000
Turning Point Therapeutics Inc	325412	25,000,000	-157,292,000
Yuhan Corporation	325412	1,488,210,000	174,927,000
Pharmacies and Drug Stores			
Accredo Health Group Inc	446110		
CVS Health Corporation	446110	268,706,004,992	7,178,999,808
Jean Coutu Group (PJC) Inc (The)	446110	2,667,628,213	
Omnicare Inc	446110	8,091,798,750	
PharMerica Corporation	446110	2,500,911,000	
Rite Aid Corporation	446110	21,928,392,704	-452,174,016
Walgreens Boots Alliance Inc	446110	139,537,006,592	456,000,000
Photographic and Photocopying Equipment Manufacturing			
Agfa-Gevaert NV	333316		
Physicians (except Mental Health Specialists)			
American Well Corporation (Amwell)	621111	245,264,992	-224,432,000
HealthTronics Inc	621111	220,000,000	
MEDNAX Inc	621111	1,733,950,976	-796,488,000
Oak Street Health Inc	621111		
Team Health Holdings Inc	621111	4,222,200,000	
Teladoc Health Inc	621111	1,093,961,984	-485,136,000
US Oncology Inc	621111		
Professional Training, Management Development and Corporate Employee Training			
HealthStream Inc	611430	244,826,000	14,091,000
Residential Intellectual and Developmental Disability Facilities			
BrightSpring Health Services	623210	2,099,500,000	
Residential Mental Health and Substance Abuse Facilities			
AAC Holdings Inc	623220		
Ontrak Inc	623220		

Industry Group/Company	Industry Code	2020 Sales	2020 Profits
Scientific Research and Development (R&D) in Life Sciences, Medical Devices, Biotechnology and Pharmaceuticals (Drugs)			
IQVIA Holdings Inc	541711	11,358,999,552	279,000,000
Personalis Inc	541711	78,648,000	-41,280,000
PPD Inc	541711	4,681,474,048	153,691,008
Security Systems Services (except Locksmiths)			
SECOM Co Ltd	561621	9,681,624,064	813,568,000
Semiconductor and Solar Cell Manufacturing, Including Chips, Memory, LEDs, Transistors and Integrated Circuits, Artificial Intelligence (AI), & Internet of Things (IoT)			
Hoya Corporation	334413	5,319,701,504	1,044,870,528
Surgical Appliance and Supplies (Medical Devices) Manufacturing			
SI-BONE Inc	339113	73,387,000	-43,697,000
Smith & Nephew plc	339113	4,560,000,000	448,000,000
Temporary Staffing, Help and Employment Agencies			
Allied Healthcare International Inc	561320	483,787,500	
AMN Healthcare Services Inc	561320	2,393,713,920	70,665,000
Vaccines, Skin Replacement Products and Biologicals Manufacturing			
Allogene Therapeutics Inc	325414	0	-250,220,992
Axcella Health Inc	325414	0	-56,527,000
CSL Behring LLC	325414	7,853,700,000	
CSL Limited	325414	10,272,234,496	2,373,207,040
Gamida Cell Ltd	325414	0	-72,704,000
Grifols SA	325414	6,524,335,616	755,725,248
Harpoon Therapeutics Inc	325414	17,444,000	-49,908,000
Kaleido Biosciences Inc	325414	975,000	-81,620,000
LogicBio Therapeutics Inc	325414	3,454,000	-32,621,000
MiMedx Group Inc	325414		
Orchard Therapeutics plc	325414	2,595,000	-151,979,008
Organogenesis Inc	325414		
Prevail Therapeutics Inc	325414		
Shanghai RAAS Blood Products Co Ltd	325414	227,170,000	145,659,000
TCR2 Therapeutics Inc	325414	0	-67,124,000
Veterinary Services			
VCA Inc	541940	3,213,000,000	

ALPHABETICAL INDEX

Ethicon Inc
Eton Pharmaceuticals Inc
Everyday Health Inc
Exactech Inc
Extendicare Inc
EyeCare Partners LLC
EyeMed Vision Care LLC
Fairview Health Services
Fielmann AG
First Choice Health Network Inc
First Health Group Corp
Fisher & Paykel Healthcare Limited
Foundation Medicine Inc
Fresenius Medical Care AG & Co KGaA
Fresenius SE & Co KGaA
Fujifilm Healthcare Americas Corporation
Galderma SA
Gamida Cell Ltd
GE Healthcare
Genentech Inc
Genesis Healthcare Inc
GenMark Diagnostics Inc
Gerresheimer AG
Getinge Industrier AB
Gilead Sciences Inc
GlaxoSmithKline Pharmaceuticals Ltd
GlaxoSmithKline plc
Global Healthcare Exchange LLC
Globus Medical Inc
GoodRx Holdings Inc
Grifols SA
Guardion Health Sciences Inc
Haemonetics Corporation
Hanger Inc
Harpoon Therapeutics Inc
Harvard Pilgrim Health Care Inc
HCA Healthcare Inc
Health Care Service Corporation (HCSC)
Health Catalyst Inc
Health Net Inc
Healthgrades Operating Company Inc
HealthNow New York Inc
Healthscope Limited
HealthStream Inc
HealthTronics Inc
HealthTrust Purchasing Group LP
HearUSA Inc
HemaCare Corporation
Henry Ford Health System
Henry Schein Inc
Highmark Health
Hill-Rom Holdings Inc
HMS
Hologic Inc
HOOKIPA Pharma Inc
Horizon Healthcare Services Inc
IIoth Therapeutics Inc
Houston Methodist
Hoya Corporation
Humana Inc
IBM Watson Health
ICU Medical Inc
IDEXX Laboratories Inc
iKang Healthcare Group Inc
Immucor Inc

Incyte Corporation
Indiana University Health
InfuSystem Holdings Inc
Intalere Inc
Intarcia Therapeutics Inc
Integra LifeSciences Holdings Corporation
Intermountain Healthcare
Interpace Biosciences Inc
Intersect ENT Inc
Intuitive Surgical Inc
Invacare Corporation
Iowa Health System (dba UnityPoint
Health)
IQVIA Holdings Inc
IRIDEX Corporation
Jean Coutu Group (PJC) Inc (The)
Jenny Craig Inc
Jiangsu Hengrui Medicine Co Ltd
Johns Hopkins Medicine
Johnson & Johnson
Kaiser Permanente
Kaleido Biosciences Inc
Karuna Therapeutics Inc
Keystone Dental Inc
Kindred at Home
Kindred Healthcare LLC
KPC Healthcare Inc
Laboratory Corporation of America
Holdings
Lakeland Industries Inc
LCA-Vision Inc
LHC Group Inc
Life Healthcare Group Holdings Ltd
LifePoint Health Inc
Lifetime Healthcare Companies (The)
Little Clinic (The)
Livongo Health Inc
LogicBio Therapeutics Inc
Lumenis Ltd
Lumeris Inc
Lupin Limited
Magee Rehabilitation Hospital
Magellan Health Inc
Main Line Health System
Masimo Corporation
Mass General Brigham Incorporated
Mayo Clinic
McKesson Corporation
MD Anderson Cancer Center
Medica Sur SAB de CV
Medical Action Industries Inc
Medical Facilities Corporation
Medical Information Technology Inc
(MEDITECH)
Medical Mutual of Ohio
Mediclinic International plc
Medicure Inc
Medifast Inc
Medipal Holdings Corporation
Medline Industries Inc
MEDNAX Inc
MedStar Health
Medtronic MiniMed Inc
Medtronic plc
Medtronic Vascular Inc

Memorial Hermann Healthcare System
Memorial Sloan Kettering Cancer Center
Merck & Co Inc
Merck Serono SA
Mercy
Mercy Health
Meridian Bioscience Inc
Merit Medical Systems Inc
Mettler-Toledo International Inc
MiMedx Group Inc
Mindray Medical International Limited
MinuteClinic LLC
Misonix Inc
ModivCare Solutions, LLC
Molina Healthcare Inc
Molnlycke Health Care AB
Morphic Holding Inc
MSA Safety Inc
MultiPlan Inc
Mylan NV
Narayana Hrudayalaya Ltd
National HealthCare Corporation
National Healthcare Group Pte Ltd
National University Health System
(NUHS)
Natus Medical Incorporated
Netcare Limited
New York City Health and Hospitals
Corporation
New York Health Care Inc
NewYork-Presbyterian Healthcare System
NextCure Inc
NextGen Healthcare Inc
Nordion (Canada) Inc
Novanta Inc
Novartis AG
Novo Nordisk AS
NuVasive Inc
Oak Street Health Inc
OhioHealth Corporation
Olympus Corporation
Omnicare Inc
Ontrak Inc
Opto Circuits (India) Ltd
Optos plc
Orchard Therapeutics plc
Organogenesis Inc
ORPEA ACT
Orthofix International NV
Osmotica Pharmaceuticals plc
Owens & Minor Inc
Par Pharmaceutical Companies Inc
Patterson Companies Inc
PerkinElmer Inc
Personalis Inc
Pfizer Inc
PharMerica Corporation
Philips Healthcare
Ping An Healthcare and Technology
Company Limited
PPD Inc
Precision Optics Corporation
Predictive Oncology Inc
Premera Blue Cross
Premier Inc

INDEX OF U.S. HEADQUARTERS LOCATION BY STATE

To help you locate members of the firms geographically, the city and state of the headquarters of each company are in the following index.

ALABAMA

ARIZONA

ARKANSAS

CALIFORNIA

Health Net Inc; Woodland Hills
HemaCare Corporation; Northridge
ICU Medical Inc; San Clemente
Intersect ENT Inc; Menlo Park
Intuitive Surgical Inc; Sunnyvale
IRIDEX Corporation; Mountain View
Jenny Craig Inc; Carlsbad
Kaiser Permanente; Oakland
KPC Healthcare Inc; Santa Ana
Livongo Health Inc; Mountain View
Masimo Corporation; Irvine
Medtronic MiniMed Inc; Northridge
Medtronic Vascular Inc; Santa Rosa
Molina Healthcare Inc; Long Beach
Natus Medical Incorporated; Pleasanton
NextGen Healthcare Inc; Irvine
NuVasive Inc; San Diego
Ontrak Inc; Santa Monica
Personalis Inc; Menlo Park
Prime Healthcare Services Inc; Ontario
Quidel Corporation; San Diego
RadNet Inc; Los Angeles
ResMed Inc; San Diego
SafeGuard Health Enterprises Inc; Aliso
Viejo
Semler Scientific Inc; San Jose
ShockWave Medical Inc; Santa Clara
SI-BONE Inc; Santa Clara
Sidecar Health Inc; El Segundo
Silk Road Medical Inc; Sunnyvale
Smile Brands Inc; Irvine
STAAR Surgical Company; Lake Forest
Sutter Health Inc; Sacramento
Synthorx Inc; La Jolla
Tandem Diabetes Care Inc; San Diego
Turning Point Therapeutics Inc; San Diego
Twist Bioscience Corporation; San
Francisco
Varian Medical Systems Inc; Palo Alto
VCA Inc; Los Angeles
Vision Service Plan; Rancho Cordova

COLORADO

Air Methods Corporation; Greenwood
Village
DaVita Inc; Denver
Global Healthcare Exchange LLC;
Louisville
Healthgrades Operating Company Inc;
Denver
Welltok Inc; Denver

CONNECTICUT

aetnaCVSHealth; Hartford
Cigna Corporation; Bloomfield
Trevi Therapeutics Inc; New Haven
UnitedHealthcare National Accounts;
Hartford

DELAWARE

Incyte Corporation; Wilmington

FLORIDA

AdventHealth; Altamonte Springs
AmeriPath Inc; Orlando
Arthrex Inc; Naples
AvMed Health Plans Inc; Miami
Blue Cross and Blue Shield of Florida Inc;
Jacksonville
Cancer Treatment Centers of America Inc
(CTCA); Boca Raton
Coast Dental Services LLC; Tampa
Conviva Care Centers; Boca Raton
Exactech Inc; Gainesville
HearUSA Inc; Palm Beach Gardens
MEDNAX Inc; Sunrise
WellCare Health Plans Inc; Tampa

GEORGIA

Aeon Global Health Corp; Gainesville
AFLAC Incorporated; Columbus
Avanos Medical Inc; Alpharetta
Aveanna Healthcare LLC; Atlanta
CryoLife Inc; Kennesaw
Immucor Inc; Norcross
Kindred at Home; Atlanta
MiMedx Group Inc; Marietta
ModivCare Solutions, LLC; Atlanta
Regional Health Properties Inc; Suwanee

IDAHO

Blue Cross of Idaho; Meridian

ILLINOIS

Abbott Laboratories; Abbott Park
Advocate Aurora Health; Downers Grove
Allscripts Healthcare Solutions Inc;
Chicago
Baxter International Inc; Deerfield
Blue Cross and Blue Shield Association;
Chicago
CommonSpirit Health; Chicago
Delta Dental Plans Association; Oak Brook
Eton Pharmaceuticals Inc; Deer Park
First Health Group Corp; Downers Grove
GE Healthcare; Chicago
Health Care Service Corporation (HCSC);
Chicago
Hill-Rom Holdings Inc; Chicago
IBM Watson Health; Chicago
Medline Industries Inc; Northfield
Oak Street Health Inc; Chicago
Surgical Care Affiliates Inc; Deerfield
Walgreens Boots Alliance Inc; Deerfield

INDIANA

Anthem Inc; Indianapolis
Apria Healthcare Group LLC; Indianapolis
Eli Lilly and Company; Indianapolis
Indiana University Health; Indianapolis
Zimmer Biomet Holdings Inc; Warsaw

IOWA

CIVCO Medical Instruments Co Ltd;
Coralville
Iowa Health System (dba UnityPoint
Health); West Des Moines
UnityPoint Health; West Des Moines

KENTUCKY

BrightSpring Health Services; Louisville
Humana Inc; Louisville
Kindred Healthcare LLC; Louisville
PharMerica Corporation; Louisville
Protech Home Medical Corp; Wilder

LOUISIANA

Amedisys Inc; Baton Rouge
Blue Cross and Blue Shield of Louisiana;
Baton Rouge
LHC Group Inc; Lafayette

MAINE

IDEXX Laboratories Inc; Westbrook

MARYLAND

CareFirst Inc; Baltimore
Johns Hopkins Medicine; Baltimore
Medifast Inc; Baltimore
MedStar Health; Columbia
NextCure Inc; Beltsville
US NeuroSurgical Holdings Inc; Rockville

MASSACHUSETTS

Abiomed Inc; Danvers
American Well Corporation (Amwell);
Boston
Analogic Corporation; Peabody
athenahealth Inc; Watertown
Axcella Health Inc; Cambridge
Biogen Inc; Cambridge
Blue Cross and Blue Shield of
Massachusetts; Boston
Boston Scientific Corporation;
Marlborough
Bruker Corporation; Billerica
Civitas Solutions Inc; Boston
Cynosure Inc; Westford
DePuy Synthes Inc; Raynham
eClinicalWorks; Westborough
Foundation Medicine Inc; Cambridge
Fujifilm Healthcare Americas Corporation;
Lexington
Haemonetics Corporation; Boston
Harvard Pilgrim Health Care Inc;
Wellesley
Hologic Inc; Marlborough
Intarcia Therapeutics Inc; Boston
Kaleido Biosciences Inc; Lexington
Karuna Therapeutics Inc; Boston
Keystone Dental Inc; Burlington
LogicBio Therapeutics Inc; Lexington
Mass General Brigham Incorporated;
Boston
Medical Information Technology Inc
(MEDITECH); Westwood
Morphic Holding Inc; Waltham
Novanta Inc; Bedford

Organogenesis Inc; Canton
PerkinElmer Inc; Waltham
Philips Healthcare; Cambridge
Precision Optics Corporation; Gardner
Sanofi Genzyme; Cambridge
Steward Health Care System LLC; Boston
Takeda Oncology; Cambridge
TCR2 Therapeutics Inc; Cambridge
Thermo Fisher Scientific Inc; Waltham
TransMedics Group Inc; Andover
Tufts Associated Health Plans Inc;
Watertown
Zoll Medical Corporation; Chelmsford

MICHIGAN

Blue Care Network of Michigan;
Southfield
Blue Cross and Blue Shield of Michigan;
Detroit
Detroit Medical Center (DMC); Detroit
Henry Ford Health System; Detroit
InfuSystem Holdings Inc; Rochester Hills
Spectrum Health; Grand Rapids
Stryker Corporation; Kalamazoo
Trinity Health; Livonia

MINNESOTA

3M Company; St. Paul
Allina Health; Minneapolis
Bio-Techne Corporation; Minneapolis
Blue Cross and Blue Shield of Minnesota;
Eagan
Electromed Inc; New Prague
Fairview Health Services; Minneapolis
Mayo Clinic; Rochester
Patterson Companies Inc; St. Paul
Predictive Oncology Inc; Eagan
Starkey Hearing Technologies; Eden
Prairie
UnitedHealth Group Inc; Minnetonka

MISSOURI

Ascension; St. Louis
BJC HealthCare; St. Louis
Blue Cross Blue Shield of Kansas City
(Blue KC); Kansas City
Centene Corporation; St. Louis
Cerner Corporation; North Kansas City
EyeCare Partners LLC; Ballwin
Intalere Inc; St. Louis
Lumeris Inc; Maryland Heights
SSM Health; St. Louis

MONTANA

Blue Cross and Blue Shield of Montana;
Helena

NEBRASKA

Blue Cross and Blue Shield of Nebraska;
Omaha

NEW HAMPSHIRE

Vapotherm Inc; Exeter

NEW JERSEY

Bausch & Lomb Incorporated; Bridgewater
Bayer Corporation; Whippany
Bayer HealthCare Pharmaceuticals Inc;
Whippany
Becton Dickinson and Company; Franklin
Lakes
Bio-Reference Laboratories Inc; Elmwood
Park
ConvaTec Inc; Bridgewater
Ethicon Inc; Raritan
Horizon Healthcare Services Inc; Newark
Integra LifeSciences Holdings Corporation;
Princeton
Interpace Biosciences Inc; Parsippany
Johnson & Johnson; New Brunswick
Merck & Co Inc; Kenilworth
Osmotica Pharmaceuticals plc; Bridgewater
Quest Diagnostics Incorporated; Secaucus

NEW YORK

AngioDynamics Inc; Latham
Applied Therapeutics Inc; New York
Bristol-Myers Squibb Company; New York
CONMED Corporation; Utica
EmblemHealth Inc; New York
Everyday Health Inc; New York
HealthNow New York Inc; Buffalo
Henry Schein Inc; Melville
HOOKIPA Pharma Inc; New York
Hoth Therapeutics Inc; New York
Lifetime Healthcare Companies (The);
Rochester
Memorial Sloan Kettering Cancer Center;
New York
Misonix Inc; Farmingdale
MultiPlan Inc; New York
New York City Health and Hospitals
Corporation; New York
New York Health Care Inc; Valley Stream
NewYork-Presbyterian Healthcare System;
New York
Par Pharmaceutical Companies Inc;
Chestnut Ridge
Pfizer Inc; New York
Prevail Therapeutics Inc; New York
Regeneron Pharmaceuticals Inc; Tarrytown
Teladoc Health Inc; Purchase
WebMD Health Corp; New York
WW International Inc; New York

NORTH CAROLINA

Blue Cross and Blue Shield of North
Carolina; Durham
Dentsply Sirona Inc; Charlotte
Envolve Vision Inc; Rocky Mount
IQVIA Holdings Inc; Durham
Laboratory Corporation of America
Holdings; Burlington
PPD Inc; Wilmington

Premier Inc; Charlotte
TransEnterix Inc; Morrisville

OHIO

Bon Secours Mercy Health System Inc;
Cincinnati
Cardinal Health Inc; Dublin
Chemed Corporation; Cincinnati
Cleveland Clinic Foundation (The);
Cleveland
EyeMed Vision Care LLC; Mason
Invacare Corporation; Elyria
LCA-Vision Inc; Cincinnati
Medical Mutual of Ohio; Cleveland
Mercy Health; Cincinnati
Meridian Bioscience Inc; Cincinnati
Mettler-Toledo International Inc;
Columbus
OhioHealth Corporation; Columbus
Omnicare Inc; Cincinnati
ProMedica Senior Care; Toledo

OKLAHOMA

Blue Cross and Blue Shield of Oklahoma;
Tulsa
Mercy; Tishomingo

OREGON

Cambia Health Solutions Inc; Portland

PENNSYLVANIA

AmerisourceBergen Corporation;
Conshohocken
Avantor Inc; Radnor
BioTelemetry Inc; Malvera
Capital BlueCross; Harrisburg
CSL Behring LLC; King of Prussia
Genesis Healthcare Inc; Kennett Square
Globus Medical Inc; Audubon
Highmark Health; Pittsburgh
Magee Rehabilitation Hospital;
Philadelphia
Main Line Health System; Bryn Mawr
MSA Safety Inc; Pittsburgh
Rite Aid Corporation; Camp Hill
Teleflex Incorporated; Wayne
Thomas Jefferson University Hospitals Inc;
Philadelphia
Universal Health Services Inc; King Of
Prussia
UPMC; Pittsburgh

RHODE ISLAND

CVS Health Corporation; Woonsocket
MinuteClinic LLC; Woonsocket

SOUTH CAROLINA

AEterna Zentaris Inc; Summerville
Span America Medical Systems Inc;
Greenville

SOUTH DAKOTA

Avera Health; Sioux Falls
Sanford Health; Sioux Falls

TENNESSEE

AAC Holdings Inc; Brentwood
Acadia Healthcare Company Inc; Franklin
Accredo Health Group Inc; Memphis
American HomePatient Inc; Brentwood
AMSURG Corporation; Nashville
Ardent Health Services LLC; Nashville
BlueCross BlueShield of Tennessee Inc;
Chattanooga
Change Healthcare Inc; Nashville
Community Health Systems Inc; Franklin
Cumberland Pharmaceuticals Inc;
Nashville
Diversicare Healthcare Services Inc;
Brentwood
Envision Healthcare Corporation; Nashville
HCA Healthcare Inc; Nashville
HealthStream Inc; Nashville
HealthTrust Purchasing Group LP;
Nashville
LifePoint Health Inc; Brentwood
Little Clinic (The); Nashville
National HealthCare Corporation;
Murfreesboro
St Jude Children's Research Hospital;
Memphis
Surgery Partners Inc; Brentwood
Symmetry Surgical Inc; Antioch
Team Health Holdings Inc; Knoxville
Tivity Health Inc; Franklin

TEXAS

Addus HomeCare Corporation; Frisco
AMN Healthcare Services Inc; Dallas
Atrion Corporation; Allen
Baylor Scott & White Health; Dallas
Blue Cross and Blue Shield of Texas;
Richardson
Caris Life Sciences; Irving
Castle Dental Centers Inc; Houston
CHRISTUS Health; Irving
Concentra Inc; Addison
CorVel Corporation; Fort Worth
DJO Global Inc; Dallas
Dynacq Healthcare Inc; Pasadena
Elara Caring; Dallas
Guardion Health Sciences Inc; Houston
Hanger Inc; Austin
HealthTronics Inc; Austin
HMS; Irving
Houston Methodist; Houston
McKesson Corporation; Irving
MD Anderson Cancer Center; Houston
Memorial Hermann Healthcare System;
Houston
Tenet Healthcare Corporation; Dallas
Texas Health Resources; Arlington
United Surgical Partners International Inc;
Dallas
US Oncology Inc; The Woodlands

US Physical Therapy Inc; Houston
USMD Health System; Irving
Vizient Inc; Irving

UTAH

Health Catalyst Inc; South Jordan
Intermountain Healthcare; Salt Lake City
Merit Medical Systems Inc; South Jordan
Utah Medical Products Inc; Midvale

VIRGINIA

Amerigroup Corporation; Virginia Beach
Capital Vision Services LP (MyEyeDr);
Vienna
Medical Action Industries Inc;
Mechanicsville
Owens & Minor Inc; Mechanicsville
Sentara Healthcare; Norfolk
UnitedHealthcare Community & State;
Vienna

VERMONT

Blue Cross and Blue Shield of Vermont;
Berlin

WASHINGTON

Adaptive Biotechnologies Corporation;
Seattle
Danaher Corporation; Washington
First Choice Health Network Inc; Seattle
Premera Blue Cross; Mountlake Terrace
Providence; Renton

WISCONSIN

Epic Systems Corporation; Verona

WYOMING

Blue Cross and Blue Shield of Wyoming;
Cheyenne

INDEX OF NON-U.S. HEADQUARTERS LOCATION BY COUNTRY

AUSTRALIA

Ansell Limited; Richmond
Cochlear Limited; Lane Cove
CSL Limited; Parkville
Ebos Group Limited; Docklands
Healthscope Limited; Melbourne
Ramsay Health Care Limited; Sydney
Sigma Healthcare Limited; Rowville
Sonic Healthcare Limited; Sydney

BELGIUM

Agfa-Gevaert NV; Mortsel

BRAZIL

Profarma Distribuidora de Produtos
Farmaceuticos SA; Rio de Janeiro

CANADA

Bausch Health Companies Inc; Laval
CareRx Corporation; Toronto
Extendicare Inc; Markham
Jean Coutu Group (PJC) Inc (The);
Varennes
Medical Facilities Corporation; Toronto
Medicure Inc; Winnipeg
Nordion (Canada) Inc; Ottawa
TLC Laser Eye Centers; Mississauga

CHINA

3SBio Inc; Shenyang
iKang Healthcare Group Inc; Chaoyang
District, Beijing
Jiangsu Hengrui Medicine Co Ltd;
Lianyungang
Mindray Medical International Limited;
Shenzhen
Ping An Healthcare and Technology
Company Limited; Shanghai
Shandong Weigao Group Medical Polymer
Co Ltd; Weihai
Shanghai RAAS Blood Products Co Ltd;
Shanghai
Simcere Pharmaceutical Group Ltd;
Nanjing
Sinopharm Group Co Ltd; Shanghai
So-Young International Inc; Chaoyang
Distr., Beijing

DENMARK

Coloplast AS; Humlebaek
Demant AS; Smorum
Novo Nordisk AS; Bagsværd

FRANCE

BioMerieux SA; Lyon
EDAP TMS SA; Vaulx-en-Velin

EssilorLuxottica SA; Paris
ORPEA ACT; Puteaux Cedex
Sanofi SA; Paris

GERMANY
Bayer AG; Leverkusen
Carl Zeiss Meditec AG; Jena
Draegerwerk AG & Co KGaA; Lubeck
Fielmann AG; Hamburg
Fresenius Medical Care AG & Co KGaA;
Bad Homburg
Fresenius SE & Co KGaA; Bad Homburg
v.d.H
Gerresheimer AG; Duesseldorf
Merck Serono SA; Darmstadt
Rhon Klinikum AG; Bad Neustadt/Saale
Sartorius Stedim Biotech SA; Goettingen
Siemens AG; Munich
Siemens Healthineers AG; Erlangen
Sunrise Medical GmbH; Malsch

HONG KONG
China Resources Pharmaceutical Group
Limited; Hong Kong

INDIA
Cipla Limited; Mumbai
GlaxoSmithKline Pharmaceuticals Ltd;
Mumbai
Lupin Limited; Mumbai
Narayana Hrudayalaya Ltd; Bengaluru
Opto Circuits (India) Ltd; Bengaluru,
Kamataka
Sun Pharmaceutical Industries Ltd;
Mumbai
Suven Life Sciences Limited; Banjara
Hills, Hyderabad

IRELAND
Endo International plc; Ballsbridge
Medtronic plc; Dublin
STERIS plc; Dublin

ISRAEL
Gamida Cell Ltd; Jerusalem
Lumenis Ltd; Yokneam
SHL Telemedicine Ltd; Tel Aviv
Teva Pharmaceutical Industries Limited;
Petach Tikva

ITALY
Amplifon SpA; Milano
Orthofix International NV; Bussolengo
Verona
Safilo Group SpA; Padova

JAPAN
Alfresa Holdings Corporation; Tokyo
Astellas Pharma Inc; Tokyo
Hoya Corporation; Tokyo
Medipal Holdings Corporation; Tokyo
Olympus Corporation; Tokyo

SECOM Co Ltd; Tokyo
Suzuken Co Ltd; Nagoya
Takeda Pharmaceutical Company Limited;
Osaka
Terumo Corporation; Tokyo
Toho Holdings Co Ltd; Tokyo

KOREA
Yuhan Corporation; Seoul

MEXICO
Medica Sur SAB de CV; Mexico DF

NEW ZEALAND
Fisher & Paykel Healthcare Limited;
Auckland

SINGAPORE
Biosensors International Group Ltd;
Singapore
National Healthcare Group Pte Ltd;
Singapore
National University Health System
(NUHS); Singapore

SOUTH AFRICA
Life Healthcare Group Holdings Ltd;
Johannesburg
Netcare Limited; Sandown

SPAIN
Grifols SA; Barcelona

SWEDEN
Elekta AB; Stockholm
Getinge Industrier AB; Gothenburg
Molnlycke Health Care AB; Gothenburg

SWITZERLAND
Alcon Inc; Geneva
Galderma SA; La Tour-de-Peilz
Novartis AG; Basel
Roche Holding AG; Basel
Sonova Holding AG; Stafa
Straumann Holding AG; Basel

THAILAND

THE NETHERLANDS
Wright Medical Group NV; Amsterdam

UNITED KINGDOM
Allied Healthcare International Inc;
Stafford
AstraZeneca plc; London
AXA Health; Turnbridge Wells
British United Provident Association
Limited (BUPA); London
GlaxoSmithKline plc; Middlesex
Mediclinic International plc; London

Mylan NV; Hatfield
Optos plc; Dunfermline
Orchard Therapeutics plc; London
Smith & Nephew plc; Watford,
Herfordshire
Smiths Group plc; London

Individual Profiles
On Each Of
THE HEALTH CARE 500

3M Company

NAIC Code: 339100

www.3m.com

TYPES OF BUSINESS:

Health Care Products
Specialty Materials & Textiles
Industrial Products
Safety, Security & Protection Products
Display & Graphics Products
Consumer & Office Products
Electronics & Communications Products
Fuel Cell Technology

BRANDS/DIVISIONS/AFFILIATES:

3M Purification Inc
Thinsulate
Scotch
Command
Filtrete

CONTACTS: *Note: Officers with more than one job title may be intentionally listed here more than once.*

Michael Roman, CEO
Jon Lindekugel, Sr. VP, Divisional
Theresa Reinseth, Chief Accounting Officer
John Banovetz, Chief Technology Officer
Joaquin Delgado, Executive VP, Divisional
Julie Bushman, Executive VP, Divisional
Michael Vale, Executive VP, Divisional
Mojdeh Poul, Executive VP, Divisional
Ashish Khandpur, Executive VP, Divisional
Paul Keel, Executive VP, Divisional
James Bauman, Executive VP, Divisional
Ivan Fong, General Counsel
Inge Thulin, President
Eric Hammes, Senior VP, Divisional
Kristen Ludgate, Senior VP, Divisional
Denise Rutherford, Senior VP, Divisional

GROWTH PLANS/SPECIAL FEATURES:

3M Company is involved in the research, manufacturing and marketing of a variety of products. Its operations are organized in five segments: industrial, safety and graphics, electronics and energy, healthcare and consumer. The industrial segment serves the automotive, electronics, appliance, paper, printing, food, beverage and construction markets. Its major industrial products include Thinsulate acoustic insulation and 3M paint finishing and detail products. Also, 3M Purification, Inc. provides a line of filtration products. The safety and graphics segment serves a range of markets, with major product offerings including personal protection, traffic safety, border and civil security solutions, commercial graphics sheeting, architectural surface and lighting solutions, cleaning products and roofing granules for asphalt shingles. The electronics and energy segment serves customers with telecommunications networks, electrical products, power generation and distribution and infrastructure protection. Major products include LCD computers and televisions, hand-held mobile devices, notebook PCs and automotive displays. The healthcare segment serves medical clinics, hospitals, pharmaceuticals, dental and orthodontic practitioners, health information systems and food manufacturing and testing. Products include medical and surgical supplies, skin health, and infection prevention. The consumer segment serves markets such as consumer retail, office retail, home improvement and building maintenance. Major products include the Scotch tape, Command adhesive and Filtrete filtration family lines of products. 3M has more than 100,000 patents worldwide. During 2020, 3M company sold substantially all of its drug delivery business to an affiliate of Altaris Capital Partners, LLC, for approximately $650 million.

3M offers its employees medical and dental insurance, tuition reimbursement, flexible spending accounts, disability coverage, a 401(k), adoption assistance and more.

FINANCIAL DATA: *Note: Data for latest year may not have been available at press time.*

In U.S. $	2020	2019	2018	2017	2016	2015
Revenue	32,184,000,000	32,136,000,000	32,765,000,000	31,657,000,000	30,109,000,000	30,274,000,000
R&D Expense	1,878,000,000	1,911,000,000	1,821,000,000	1,850,000,000	1,735,000,000	1,763,000,000
Operating Income	6,822,000,000	6,128,000,000	6,733,000,000	7,234,000,000	7,223,000,000	6,946,000,000
Operating Margin %		.19%	.20%	.23%	.24%	.23%
SGA Expense	6,879,000,000	6,961,000,000	7,529,000,000	6,572,000,000	6,111,000,000	6,182,000,000
Net Income	5,384,000,000	4,570,000,000	5,349,000,000	4,858,000,000	5,050,000,000	4,833,000,000
Operating Cash Flow	8,113,000,000	7,070,000,000	6,439,000,000	6,240,000,000	6,662,000,000	6,420,000,000
Capital Expenditure	1,501,000,000	1,699,000,000	1,577,000,000	1,373,000,000	1,420,000,000	1,461,000,000
EBITDA	9,151,000,000	7,753,000,000	8,838,000,000	9,414,000,000	8,726,000,000	8,407,000,000
Return on Assets %		.11%	.14%	.14%	.15%	.15%
Return on Equity %		.46%	.50%	.44%	.46%	.39%
Debt to Equity		1.812	1.377	1.051	1.041	0.752

CONTACT INFORMATION:

Phone: 651 733-1110   Fax: 651 733-9973
Toll-Free: 800-364-3577
Address: 3M Center, St. Paul, MN 55144 United States

STOCK TICKER/OTHER:

Stock Ticker: MMM   Exchange: NYS
Employees: 95,000   Fiscal Year Ends: 12/31
Parent Company:

SALARIES/BONUSES:

Top Exec. Salary: $ Bonus: $
Second Exec. Salary: $ Bonus: $

OTHER THOUGHTS:

Estimated Female Officers or Directors: 7
Hot Spot for Advancement for Women/Minorities: Y

3SBio Inc

www.3sbio.com

NAIC Code: 325412

TYPES OF BUSINESS:

Biopharmaceutical Manufacturing & Design
Biopharmaceutical Production
Biopharmaceutical Development
Oncology
Autoimmune
Nephrology
Dermatology
Metabolism

BRANDS/DIVISIONS/AFFILIATES:

TPIAO
Cipterbin
Yisaipu
SEPO
EPIAO
Xenopax
Mandi
BYETTA

CONTACTS: Note: Officers with more than one job title may be intentionally listed here more than once.

Jing Lou, CEO
Dongmei Su, VP-R&D
Ke Li, Corp. Sec.

GROWTH PLANS/SPECIAL FEATURES:

3SBio, Inc. is a biotechnology company that researches, develops, manufactures and markets biopharmaceutical products, primarily in China. The company's products are divided into five groups: oncology, autoimmunity, nephrology, dermatology and metabolism. Oncology is comprised of four products, including: TPIAO, for the treatment of certain types of thrombocytopenia, a deficiency of platelets; Cipterbin (inetetamab-injection), an anti-HER2 monoclonal antibody for breast cancer; Intefen, for lymphatic or hematopoietic malignancies and viral infections, hepatitis B, chronic hepatitis C and condyloma acuminate; and Inleusin, for renal cell carcinoma, melanoma, thoracic fluid build-up caused by cancer and tuberculosis. Autoimmunity has one product, Yisaipu, a recombinant human type 2 tumor necrosis factor receptor, for the treatment of moderate to severe rheumatoid arthritis and for the treatment of moderate to severe plaque psoriasis in adults aged 18 and above. Nephrology offers four products, including: SEPO, for anemia associated with chronic kidney disease and more; EPIAO, for anemia caused by chronic kidney disease, chemotherapy and more; SPARIN, for prophylaxis and treatment of deep vein thrombosis, and prevention of clotting during hemodialysis; and Xenopax, for the prevention of acute rejection after renal transplantation. Dermatology offers one product, Mandi (minoxidil), for male-pattern alopecia and alopecia areata, a non-prescription drug for hair loss. Last, metabolism offers BYETTA (exenatide injection), to improve the glycemic control in patients with type 2 diabetes. 3SBio's manufacturing bases are located in Shenyang, Shanghai, Shenzhen and Hangzhou, China, as well as in Italy Como.

FINANCIAL DATA: Note: Data for latest year may not have been available at press time.

In U.S. $	2020	2019	2018	2017	2016	2015
Revenue	856,052,000	701,198,000	666,436,000	585,649,216	438,694,080	262,393,504
R&D Expense						
Operating Income						
Operating Margin %						
SGA Expense						
Net Income	118,137,000	194,941,000	185,695,000	146,695,472	111,750,192	82,535,600
Operating Cash Flow						
Capital Expenditure						
EBITDA						
Return on Assets %						
Return on Equity %						
Debt to Equity						

CONTACT INFORMATION:

Phone: 86 2425811820   Fax:
Toll-Free:
Address: Shenyang Development Zone, No. 3 A1, Rd. 10, Shenyang, Liaoning 110027 China

STOCK TICKER/OTHER:

Stock Ticker: 1530
Employees: 6,323
Parent Company: Decade Sunshine Limited

Exchange: Hong Kong
Fiscal Year Ends: 12/31

SALARIES/BONUSES:

Top Exec. Salary: $ Bonus: $
Second Exec. Salary: $ Bonus: $

OTHER THOUGHTS:

Estimated Female Officers or Directors: 1
Hot Spot for Advancement for Women/Minorities: Y

AAC Holdings Inc

NAIC Code: 623220

americanaddictioncenters.org

TYPES OF BUSINESS:
Substance Abuse Facilities
Substance Abuse Treatment

BRANDS/DIVISIONS/AFFILIATES:
American Addiction Centers

CONTACTS: *Note: Officers with more than one job title may be intentionally listed here more than once.*
Andrew W. McWilliams, CEO
Andrew McWilliams, CFO
Kathryn Phillips, General Counsel
Michael Blackburn, Senior VP, Divisional
Bowen Diehl, Chmn.

GROWTH PLANS/SPECIAL FEATURES:
AAC Holdings, Inc. provides inpatient and outpatient substance use treatment services for individuals with drug addiction, alcohol addiction and co-occurring mental/behavioral health issues. AAC stands for American Addiction Centers, at which perform clinical diagnostic laboratory services and provide physician services to its clients. AAC has rehab facilities nationwide, with programs in California, Florida, Massachusetts, Mississippi, Nevada, New Jersey, Rhode Island and Texas. Treatment includes intervention, rehab, detox and recovery processes, as well as medication-assisted therapies, family therapy, animal-assisted therapy, music therapy, among others. In addition, through AAC's websites Rehabs.com and Recovery.org, the firm serves families and individuals struggling with addiction and seeking treatment options through comprehensive online directories of treatment providers, treatment provider reviews, forums and professional communities. AAC also provides online marketing solutions to other treatment providers such as enhanced facility profiles, audience targeting, lead generation and tools for digital reputation management. In December 2020, AAC Holdings emerged from bankruptcy protection and ceased from public trading.

FINANCIAL DATA: *Note: Data for latest year may not have been available at press time.*

In U.S. $	2020	2019	2018	2017	2016	2015
Revenue		309,072,343	295,763,008	317,640,992	279,769,984	212,260,992
R&D Expense						
Operating Income						
Operating Margin %						
SGA Expense						
Net Income		-57,621,880	-59,404,000	-20,579,000	-589,000	11,174,000
Operating Cash Flow						
Capital Expenditure						
EBITDA						
Return on Assets %						
Return on Equity %						
Debt to Equity						

CONTACT INFORMATION:
Phone: 615 732-1231   Fax:
Toll-Free:
Address: 200 Powell Pl., Brentwood, TN 37027 United States

STOCK TICKER/OTHER:
Stock Ticker: Private
Employees: 3
Parent Company:

Exchange: NYS
Fiscal Year Ends: 12/31

SALARIES/BONUSES:
Top Exec. Salary: $ Bonus: $
Second Exec. Salary: $ Bonus: $

OTHER THOUGHTS:
Estimated Female Officers or Directors:
Hot Spot for Advancement for Women/Minorities:

Abbott Laboratories

www.abbott.com

NAIC Code: 325412

TYPES OF BUSINESS:

Nutritional Products Manufacturing
Immunoassays
Diagnostics
Consumer Health Products
Medical & Surgical Devices
Generic Pharmaceutical Products
LASIK Devices

BRANDS/DIVISIONS/AFFILIATES:

BinaxNOW

CONTACTS: *Note: Officers with more than one job title may be intentionally listed here more than once.*

Miles White, CEO
Jaime Contreras, Sr. VP, Divisional
Brian Yoor, CFO
Robert Funck, Chief Accounting Officer
Robert Ford, COO
Andrew Lane, Executive VP, Divisional
Stephen Fussell, Executive VP, Divisional
John Capek, Executive VP, Divisional
Brian Blaser, Executive VP, Divisional
Daniel Salvadori, Executive VP, Divisional
Hubert Allen, Executive VP
Roger Bird, Senior VP, Divisional
Jared Watkin, Senior VP, Divisional
Sharon Bracken, Senior VP, Divisional
Sammy Karam, Senior VP, Divisional

GROWTH PLANS/SPECIAL FEATURES:

Abbott Laboratories develops, manufactures and sells healthcare products and technologies in over 150 countries. The firm operates in four product segments: established pharmaceuticals, diagnostic, nutritional and medical devices. Established pharmaceuticals include a line of branded generic pharmaceuticals manufactured worldwide and marketed and sold outside the U.S. in emerging markets. These products are primarily sold directly to wholesalers, distributors, government agencies, healthcare facilities, pharmacies and independent retailers. This segment's principal therapeutic offerings include gastroenterology, women's health, cardiovascular, metabolic, pain, central nervous system, respiratory and vaccination products. The diagnostics segment includes systems and tests manufactured, marketed and sold worldwide to blood banks, hospitals, commercial laboratories, clinics, physicians' offices, government agencies, alternate care testing sites and plasma protein therapeutic companies from Abbot-owned distribution centers, public warehouses and third-party distributors. This segment's products include core laboratory systems in the areas of immunoassay, clinical chemistry, hematology and transfusions; molecular diagnostics systems; point of care systems; rapid diagnostic systems; and informatics and automation solutions for use in laboratories. The nutritional segment offers a line of pediatric and adult nutritional products manufactured, marketed and sold worldwide. This segment's products include various forms of prepared infant formula and follow-on formula; adult and other pediatric nutritional products; and nutritional products used in enteral feeding in healthcare institutions. The medical devices segment products include broad line of rhythm management, electrophysiology, heart failure, vascular and structural heart devices for the treatment of cardiovascular diseases, and diabetes care products for people with diabetes, as well as neuromodulation devices for the management of chronic pain and movement disorders. During 2020, due to the COVID-19 pandemic, the FDA issued Emergency Use Authorizations for Abbott diagnostic tests. In April 2021, Abbott began shipping its BinaxNOW COVID-19 Ag Self Test to retailers in the U.S.

Abbott offers its employees comprehensive benefits.

FINANCIAL DATA: *Note: Data for latest year may not have been available at press time.*

In U.S. $	2020	2019	2018	2017	2016	2015
Revenue	34,608,000,000	31,904,000,000	30,578,000,000	27,390,000,000	20,853,000,000	20,405,000,000
R&D Expense	2,420,000,000	2,440,000,000	2,300,000,000	2,235,000,000	1,422,000,000	1,405,000,000
Operating Income	5,357,000,000	4,532,000,000	3,650,000,000	1,726,000,000	3,185,000,000	2,867,000,000
Operating Margin %		.14%	.12%	.06%	.15%	.14%
SGA Expense	9,696,000,000	9,765,000,000	9,744,000,000	9,117,000,000	6,672,000,000	6,785,000,000
Net Income	4,495,000,000	3,687,000,000	2,368,000,000	477,000,000	1,400,000,000	4,423,000,000
Operating Cash Flow	7,901,000,000	6,136,000,000	6,300,000,000	5,570,000,000	3,203,000,000	2,966,000,000
Capital Expenditure	2,177,000,000	1,638,000,000	1,394,000,000	1,135,000,000	1,121,000,000	1,110,000,000
EBITDA	8,841,000,000	7,761,000,000	6,977,000,000	6,156,000,000	3,197,000,000	4,818,000,000
Return on Assets %		.05%	.03%	.01%	.03%	.11%
Return on Equity %		.12%	.08%	.02%	.07%	.21%
Debt to Equity		0.56	0.634	0.881	1.007	0.277

CONTACT INFORMATION:

Phone: 847 937-6100　　Fax: 847 937-1511
Toll-Free:
Address: 100 Abbott Park Rd., Abbott Park, IL 60064-6400 United States

STOCK TICKER/OTHER:

Stock Ticker: ABT　　Exchange: NYS
Employees: 107,000　　Fiscal Year Ends: 12/31
Parent Company:

SALARIES/BONUSES:

Top Exec. Salary: $　　Bonus: $
Second Exec. Salary: $　　Bonus: $

OTHER THOUGHTS:

Estimated Female Officers or Directors: 5
Hot Spot for Advancement for Women/Minorities: Y

Sales, profits and employees may be estimates. Financial information, benefits and other data can change quickly and may vary from those stated here.

Abiomed Inc

www.abiomed.com

NAIC Code: 339100

TYPES OF BUSINESS:

Equipment-Cardiac Assistance
Heart Replacement Technology
Mechanical Circulatory Support Devices
Manufacturing

BRANDS/DIVISIONS/AFFILIATES:

Impella

CONTACTS: *Note: Officers with more than one job title may be intentionally listed here more than once.*

Michael Minogue, CEO
Todd Trapp, CFO
Ian McLeod, Controller
David Weber, COO
Michael Howley, General Manager, Divisional
Andrew Greenfield, Other Executive Officer

GROWTH PLANS/SPECIAL FEATURES:

Abiomed, Inc. is a global provider of mechanical circulatory support devices, offering a continuum of care in heart support and recovery. The company manufactures temporary mechanical circulatory support devices to assist heart patients. Abiomed's product portfolio consists of the Impella family of heart pumps, which includes the Impella 2.5, Impella CP, Impella 5.0, Impella LD, Impella 5.5 and Impella RP devices. The Impella 2.5 device is a percutaneous micro heart pump with an integrated motor and sensors. The device is designed primarily for use by interventional cardiologists to support patients in the cath lab who may require assistance to maintain circulation. The Impella CP device provides blood flow of approximately one liter more per minute than the Impella 2.5 device and is primarily used by either interventional cardiologists to support patients in the cath lab or by cardiac surgeons in the heart surgery suite. The Impella 5.0 and Impella LD devices are percutaneous micro heart pumps with integrated motors and sensors for use primarily in the heart surgery suite. The Impella 5.5 device is a minimally-invasive heart pump with peak flows up to six liters per minute. The Impella RP is a percutaneous catheter-based axial flow pump that is designed to allow greater than four liters of blood flow per minute and is intended to provide the flow and pressure needed to compensate for right side heart failure. In addition, the Impella SmartAssist platform includes optical sensor technology for improved pump positioning and the use of algorithms that enable native heart assessment during the weaning process. Impella Connect is a cloud-based technology that enables remote viewing of the Automated Impella Controller for physicians and hospital staff from anywhere with internet connectivity.

Abiomed offers its employees comprehensive benefits.

FINANCIAL DATA: *Note: Data for latest year may not have been available at press time.*

In U.S. $	2020	2019	2018	2017	2016	2015
Revenue	840,883,000	769,432,000	593,749,000	445,304,000	329,543,000	
R&D Expense	98,759,000	93,503,000	75,297,000	66,386,000	49,759,000	
Operating Income	249,219,000	224,812,000	157,137,000	90,138,000	65,104,000	
Operating Margin %	.30%	.29%	.26%	.20%	.20%	
SGA Expense	341,600,000	321,550,000	262,734,000	218,153,000	164,261,000	
Net Income	203,009,000	259,016,000	112,170,000	52,116,000	38,147,000	
Operating Cash Flow	314,920,000	252,197,000	192,546,000	115,116,000	76,795,000	
Capital Expenditure	44,006,000	44,004,000	55,863,000	50,415,000	15,624,000	
EBITDA	269,649,000	238,933,000	168,142,000	96,340,000	68,381,000	
Return on Assets %	.18%	.28%	.17%	.11%	.10%	
Return on Equity %	.20%	.32%	.20%	.13%	.12%	
Debt to Equity				0.034		

CONTACT INFORMATION:

Phone: 978 646-1400   Fax: 978 777-8411
Toll-Free:
Address: 22 Cherry Hill Dr., Danvers, MA 01923 United States

STOCK TICKER/OTHER:

Stock Ticker: ABMD   Exchange: NAS
Employees: 1,725   Fiscal Year Ends: 03/31
Parent Company:

SALARIES/BONUSES:

Top Exec. Salary: $ Bonus: $
Second Exec. Salary: $ Bonus: $

OTHER THOUGHTS:

Estimated Female Officers or Directors: 1
Hot Spot for Advancement for Women/Minorities:

Acadia Healthcare Company Inc

www.acadiahealthcare.com

NAIC Code: 622210

TYPES OF BUSINESS:

Psychiatric and Substance Abuse Hospitals
Residential Treatment Facilities
Behavioral Health Care Centers

BRANDS/DIVISIONS/AFFILIATES:

CONTACTS: *Note: Officers with more than one job title may be intentionally listed here more than once.*

Debra Osteen, CEO
David Duckworth, CFO
Reeve Waud, Chairman of the Board
Ronald Fincher, COO
Christopher Howard, Executive VP

GROWTH PLANS/SPECIAL FEATURES:

Acadia Healthcare Company, Inc. provides inpatient behavioral healthcare services via 299 facilities with more than 10,100 licensed beds in 40 U.S. states and in Puerto Rico. Acadia provides psychiatric and chemical dependency services in a variety of settings, including psychiatric hospitals, residential treatment centers, outpatient clinics and therapeutic school-based programs. Treatment specializes in helping children, teenagers and adults suffering from mental health disorders and/or alcohol and drug addiction. Acadia operates through four types of facilities: acute inpatient psychiatric facilities, residential treatment centers, outpatient community-based services and specialty. Acute inpatient psychiatric facilities help stabilize patients that are either a threat to themselves or to others, and have 24-hour observation, daily intervention and residential treatment centers. Residential treatment centers treat patients with behavioral disorders in a non-hospital setting, and balance therapy activities with social, academic and other activities. Certain residential treatment centers provide group home and therapeutic foster care programs. Outpatient community-based services are usually divided between children and adolescents (7-18 years of age) and young children (three months to six years old). Community-based programs provide therapeutic treatment to minors who have clinically-defined emotional, psychiatric or chemical dependency disorders while enabling the youth to remain at home and within their community. Specialty treatment facilities include residential recovery facilities, eating disorder facilities and comprehensive treatment centers (CTCs) for addictive disorders, co-occurring mental disorders and detoxification. Acadia's U.K. operations work under the Partnerships in Care (PiC) name. During 2021, Acadia Healthcare formed a joint venture with Bronson Healthcare, which will build a new 96-bed facility in Battle Creek, Michigan, expected to open in early 2023. That same year, Acadia sold its U.K. facilities.

FINANCIAL DATA: *Note: Data for latest year may not have been available at press time.*

In U.S. $	2020	2019	2018	2017	2016	2015
Revenue	2,089,929,000	3,107,462,000	3,012,442,000	2,836,316,000	2,810,914,000	1,794,492,000
R&D Expense						
Operating Income	332,787,000	404,532,000	412,743,000	437,882,000	445,142,000	320,810,000
Operating Margin %		.13%	.14%	.15%	.16%	.18%
SGA Expense	157,851,000	323,212,000	307,707,000	272,998,000	258,834,000	148,991,000
Net Income	-672,132,000	108,923,000	-175,750,000	199,835,000	6,143,000	112,554,000
Operating Cash Flow	658,807,000	332,904,000	414,080,000	399,577,000	361,478,000	240,403,000
Capital Expenditure	216,615,000	284,682,000	341,462,000	274,177,000	307,472,000	276,047,000
EBITDA	437,158,000	487,126,000	175,288,000	555,815,000	349,383,000	335,045,000
Return on Assets %		.02%	- .03%	.03%	.00%	.03%
Return on Equity %		.05%	- .07%	.08%	.00%	.09%
Debt to Equity		1.44	1.354	1.246	1.501	1.304

CONTACT INFORMATION:

Phone: 615 861-6000   Fax: 615 261-9685
Toll-Free:
Address: 6100 Tower Circle, Ste. 1000, Franklin, TN 37067 United States

STOCK TICKER/OTHER:

Stock Ticker: ACHC
Employees: 42,200
Parent Company:

Exchange: NAS
Fiscal Year Ends: 12/31

SALARIES/BONUSES:

Top Exec. Salary: $ Bonus: $
Second Exec. Salary: $ Bonus: $

OTHER THOUGHTS:

Estimated Female Officers or Directors:
Hot Spot for Advancement for Women/Minorities:

Accredo Health Group Inc

www.accredo.com

NAIC Code: 446110

TYPES OF BUSINESS:

Drug Distribution-Specialty Pharmacy
Reimbursement Assistance Services
Pharmacy Services
Therapeutic Resource Centers

BRANDS/DIVISIONS/AFFILIATES:

Cigna
Express Scripts Inc

CONTACTS: *Note: Officers with more than one job title may be intentionally listed here more than once.*

Tim Wentworth, CEO
Michael A. James, Sr. VP-Oper.

GROWTH PLANS/SPECIAL FEATURES:

Accredo Health Group, Inc., a wholly-owned subsidiary of Express Scripts, Inc., provides specialty pharmacy and related services to treat certain chronic diseases. Through its therapeutic resource centers (TRCs), the company works with patients in a single disease state offering tailored and individualized counseling and education. Patients have access to: specialty-trained pharmacists on the phone; specialty-trained infusion nurses that meet patients face-to-face in their homes; nutrition support for oncology; therapy management programs to protect patient health and safety; coordination of care between the medical benefit, pharmacy benefit and physicians; and safe, prompt delivery of medications, including training on administration of the medication. Specialized pharmacy care is provided for patients with chronic illnesses such as cancer, growth hormone deficiency, hemophilia and other bleeding disorders, hepatitis C, HIV/AIDS, infertility, multiple sclerosis, psoriasis, pulmonary arterial hypertension/fibrosis/arthritis and respiratory syncytial virus (RSV). Additionally, Accredo provides services including the collection of medication use and patient compliance information; patient education and monitoring; reimbursement expertise; and overnight, temperature-controlled drug delivery. Accredo offers comprehensive clinical and reimbursement services for healthcare professionals; and collaborates with pharmaceutical and biotech companies to provide high-touch services to patients based on their needs and therapy. Parent Express Scripts itself operates as a subsidiary of American worldwide health services organization, Cigna.

Accredo employees receive comprehensive health benefits, 401(k) and company perks.

FINANCIAL DATA: *Note: Data for latest year may not have been available at press time.*

In U.S. $	2020	2019	2018	2017	2016	2015
Revenue						
R&D Expense						
Operating Income						
Operating Margin %						
SGA Expense						
Net Income						
Operating Cash Flow						
Capital Expenditure						
EBITDA						
Return on Assets %						
Return on Equity %						
Debt to Equity						

CONTACT INFORMATION:

Phone: 901-385-3688   Fax: 901-385-3689
Toll-Free: 877-222-7336
Address: 1640 Century Center Pkwy., Memphis, TN 38134 United States

STOCK TICKER/OTHER:

Stock Ticker: Subsidiary
Employees: 5,000
Parent Company: Cigna

Exchange:
Fiscal Year Ends: 12/31

SALARIES/BONUSES:

Top Exec. Salary: $ Bonus: $
Second Exec. Salary: $ Bonus: $

OTHER THOUGHTS:

Estimated Female Officers or Directors: 1
Hot Spot for Advancement for Women/Minorities:

Accuray Incorporated

www.accuray.com

NAIC Code: 334510

TYPES OF BUSINESS:

Surgical and Medical Instrument Manufacturing
Oncology Radiation Services
Oncology Solutions
Manufacturing

BRANDS/DIVISIONS/AFFILIATES:

CyberKnife
TomoTherapy
Radixact
Onrad
ClearRT

CONTACTS: *Note: Officers with more than one job title may be intentionally listed here more than once.*

Joshua Levine, CEO
Shigeyuki Hamamatsu, CFO
Louis Lavigne, Chairman of the Board
Andy Kirkpatrick, COO
Lionel Hadjadjeba, Other Executive Officer

GROWTH PLANS/SPECIAL FEATURES:

Accuray Incorporated is a radiation oncology company that develops, manufactures, sells and supports precise, innovative treatment solutions. The firm's innovative technologies, the CyberKnife and TomoTherapy systems, including the Radixact system, Accuray's next-generation TomoTherapy platform, are designed to deliver advanced treatments, including stereotactic radiosurgery (SRS), stereotactic body radiation therapy (SBRT), intensity modulated radiation therapy (IMRT), image guided radiation therapy (IGRT) and adaptive radiation therapy. The CyberKnife systems, the TomoTherapy systems and the Radixact systems have complementary clinical applications. CyberKnife systems are fully robotic systems that deliver SRS and SBRT, and are used to treat multiple types of cancer and tumors throughout the body. They automatically track, detect and correct for tumor and patient movement in real-time during the procedure. TomoTherapy systems, including Rradixact, encompass a radiation therapy platform specifically designed for image-guided intensity-modulated radiation therapy (IG-IMRT). The TomoTherapy system provides continuous delivery of radiation from 360 degrees around the patient, or delivery from clinician-specified direct beam angles, enabling physicians to deliver dose distributions which precisely conform to the shape of the patient's tumor while minimizing dose to normal, healthy tissue, resulting in fewer side effects for patients. In China, Accuray also offers a lower-priced direct delivery system called Onrad. Accuray provides site planning and installation of its treatment products, as well as training, technology updates and service support. During 2021, Accuray announced that it received Shonin approval and CE Mark certification for its ClearRT helical fan-beam kVCT imaging technology for its Radixact System, offering enhanced imaging capabilities.

Accuray offers its employees comprehensive benefits and compensation.

FINANCIAL DATA: *Note: Data for latest year may not have been available at press time.*

In U.S. $	2020	2019	2018	2017	2016	2015
Revenue	382,928,000	418,785,000	404,897,000	383,414,000	398,800,000	
R&D Expense	49,784,000	56,493,000	57,251,000	49,921,000	56,652,000	
Operating Income	12,539,000	583,000	-3,797,000	-9,823,000	-4,873,000	
Operating Margin %		.00%	-.01%	-.03%	-.01%	
SGA Expense	87,398,000	105,575,000	108,241,000	101,243,000	106,934,000	
Net Income	3,827,000	-16,430,000	-23,899,000	-29,579,000	-25,504,000	
Operating Cash Flow	-1,469,000	-29,641,000	18,331,000	-380,000	33,538,000	
Capital Expenditure	3,728,000	4,311,000	6,609,000	5,364,000	8,066,000	
EBITDA	31,311,000	11,231,000	1,670,000	6,804,000	12,588,000	
Return on Assets %		-.04%	-.06%	-.07%	-.05%	
Return on Equity %		-.33%	-.50%	-.56%	-.38%	
Debt to Equity		3.205	2.695	1.108	2.858	

CONTACT INFORMATION:

Phone: 408 716-4600   Fax: 408 716-4601
Toll-Free:
Address: 1310 Chesapeake Terrace, Sunnyvale, CA 94089 United States

STOCK TICKER/OTHER:

Stock Ticker: ARAY   Exchange: NAS
Employees: 932   Fiscal Year Ends: 06/30
Parent Company:

SALARIES/BONUSES:

Top Exec. Salary: $ Bonus: $
Second Exec. Salary: $ Bonus: $

OTHER THOUGHTS:

Estimated Female Officers or Directors: 3
Hot Spot for Advancement for Women/Minorities: Y

Sales, profits and employees may be estimates. Financial information, benefits and other data can change quickly and may vary from those stated here.

Adaptive Biotechnologies Corporation

www.adaptivebiotech.com

NAIC Code: 325413

TYPES OF BUSINESS:

In-Vitro Diagnostic Substance Manufacturing
Immune System Assay
Cell Sequencing
Cell Monitoring

BRANDS/DIVISIONS/AFFILIATES:

immunoSEQ
clonoSEQ

CONTACTS: Note: Officers with more than one job title may be intentionally listed here more than once.

Chad Robins, CEO
Julie Rubinstein, Pres.
Chad Cohen, CFO
Nancy Hill, Sr. VP-Operations
Francis Lo, Chief People Officer
Sean Nolan, CTO
Harlan Robins, Chief Scientific Officer

GROWTH PLANS/SPECIAL FEATURES:

Adaptive Biotechnologies Corporation is a commercial-stage biotechnology company focused on harnessing the inherent biology of the adaptive immune system to transform the diagnosis and treatment of disease. The company's proprietary immune medicine platform reveals and translates the massive genetics of the adaptive immune system with scale, precision and speed to develop products in life sciences research, clinical diagnostics and drug discovery. Adaptive Biotech's products and services are grouped into three categories: life sciences research, clinical diagnostics and drug discovery. The life sciences research category encompasses immunoSEQ, which reveals the breadth and depth of the immune system with accurate, quantitative immunosequencing. This sequencing information about the individual's immune system reveals: answers in relation to disease, how the individual is responding to a therapy and any new prognostic and diagnostic biomarkers that arise. immunoSEQ unmasks the identity of millions of T- and B-cell receptors in a single sample using bias-controlled multiplex polymerase chain reaction (PCR) amplification, high-throughput sequencing and bioinformatics. The clinical diagnostics category encompasses clonoSEQ, a U.S. Food and Drug Administration (FDA)-cleared assay for the detection and monitoring of measurable residual disease (MRD) in bone marrow samples from patients with myeloma and B-cell acute lymphoblastic leukemia (ALL). clonoSEQ is also available for use in other lymphoid cancers as a laboratory developed test. Moreover, this division's T-cell receptor screening capabilities have the potential to guide the design and development of next-generation vaccines by characterizing the immunogenicity of hundreds of antigens at a time. This platform could also be used to then monitor early signs of antigen-specific T-cell responses. Based in Seattle, Washington, Adaptive has offices in San Francisco and New York City.

FINANCIAL DATA: Note: Data for latest year may not have been available at press time.

In U.S. $	2020	2019	2018	2017	2016	2015
Revenue	98,382,000	85,071,000	55,663,000	38,448,000		
R&D Expense	116,072,000	70,705,000	39,157,000	31,995,000		
Operating Income	-152,817,000	-78,391,000	-49,756,000	-43,635,000		
Operating Margin %		- .92%	- .89%	-1.13%		
SGA Expense	110,894,000	68,785,000	44,895,000	32,714,000		
Net Income	-146,227,000	-68,606,000	-46,447,000	-42,831,000		
Operating Cash Flow	-149,683,000	205,404,000	-32,259,000	-34,858,000		
Capital Expenditure	18,803,000	11,200,000	6,318,000	2,506,000		
EBITDA	-144,345,000	-70,600,000	-43,756,000	-37,839,000		
Return on Assets %		- .11%	- .13%	- .12%		
Return on Equity %		- .44%				
Debt to Equity		0.064				

CONTACT INFORMATION:

Phone: 206 659-0067   Fax: 206 659-0667
Toll-Free:
Address: 1551 Eastlake Ave. East, Ste. 200, Seattle, WA 98102 United States

STOCK TICKER/OTHER:

Stock Ticker: ADPT   Exchange: NAS
Employees: 453   Fiscal Year Ends: 12/31
Parent Company:

SALARIES/BONUSES:

Top Exec. Salary: $ Bonus: $
Second Exec. Salary: $ Bonus: $

OTHER THOUGHTS:

Estimated Female Officers or Directors:
Hot Spot for Advancement for Women/Minorities:

Addus HomeCare Corporation

www.addus.com

NAIC Code: 621610

TYPES OF BUSINESS:

Home Health Care Services
Home Care Services
Hospice Services
Home Health Services

BRANDS/DIVISIONS/AFFILIATES:

Addus HealthCare Inc

CONTACTS: *Note: Officers with more than one job title may be intentionally listed here more than once.*

Brian Poff, CFO
James Zoccoli, Chief Information Officer
Sean Gaffney, Chief Legal Officer
W. Bickham, COO
Steven Geringer, Director
R. Allison, Director
Darby Anderson, Executive VP
Laurie Manning, Executive VP

GROWTH PLANS/SPECIAL FEATURES:

Addus HomeCare Corporation is the holding company for home care services provider Addus HealthCare, Inc. Addus HealthCare operates in three segments: personal care, hospice and home health. The company's services are principally provided in-home under agreements with federal, state and local government agencies, managed care organizations, commercial insurers and private individuals. Addus HealthCare's consumers are predominantly dual eligible, meaning they are eligible to receive both Medicare and Medicaid benefits. Addus HealthCare provides personal care services to the elderly and other infirm adults who require long-term care and assistance with activities of daily living. Services include assistance with bathing, grooming, oral care, feeding, dressing, medication reminders, meal planning, housekeeping and transportation. The hospice segment offers hospice care such as physical, emotional and spiritual care for people who are terminally ill as well as related services for their families. Hospice services include palliative nursing care, social work, spiritual counseling, homemaker services and bereavement counseling. Generally, patients receiving hospice services have a life expectancy of six months or less. The home health segment provides services that are primarily medical in nature to individuals who may require assistance during an illness or after hospitalization, and include skilled nursing and physical, occupational and speech therapy. Home health services are generally provided on a short-term, intermittent or episodic basis to individuals recovering from an illness or injury. The firm serves approximately 56,000 consumers in 22 states through 207 locations (as of June 30, 2021). During 2021, Addus agreed to acquire Armada Skilled Home Health of New Mexico, LLC, Armada Hospice of New Mexico, LLC and Armada Hospice of Santa Fe, LLC for approximately $29 million in cash.

FINANCIAL DATA: *Note: Data for latest year may not have been available at press time.*

In U.S. $	2020	2019	2018	2017	2016	2015
Revenue	764,775,000	648,791,000	518,119,000	425,715,000	400,688,000	336,815,000
R&D Expense						
Operating Income	44,507,000	34,752,000	24,337,000	23,772,000	15,235,000	16,154,000
Operating Margin %			.05%	.06%	.04%	.05%
SGA Expense	169,679,000	133,569,000	105,025,000	76,902,000	84,213,000	70,452,000
Net Income	33,133,000	25,237,000	17,503,000	13,608,000	12,024,000	11,623,000
Operating Cash Flow	109,411,000	12,019,000	33,203,000	52,771,000	-743,000	4,106,000
Capital Expenditure	6,831,000	4,621,000	5,349,000	3,616,000	1,712,000	2,359,000
EBITDA	57,182,000	46,849,000	35,533,000	33,185,000	24,900,000	20,788,000
Return on Assets %			.06%	.05%	.06%	.06%
Return on Equity %			.08%	.08%	.08%	.09%
Debt to Equity			0.063	0.228	0.141	0.013

CONTACT INFORMATION:

Phone: 469-535-8200   Fax:
Toll-Free:
Address: 6303 Cowboys Way, Ste. 600, Frisco, TX 75034 United States

STOCK TICKER/OTHER:

Stock Ticker: ADUS   Exchange: NAS
Employees: 35,139   Fiscal Year Ends: 12/31
Parent Company:

SALARIES/BONUSES:

Top Exec. Salary: $ Bonus: $
Second Exec. Salary: $ Bonus: $

OTHER THOUGHTS:

Estimated Female Officers or Directors:
Hot Spot for Advancement for Women/Minorities:

Sales, profits and employees may be estimates. Financial information, benefits and other data can change quickly and may vary from those stated here.

Advanced Bionics LLC

www.advancedbionics.com

NAIC Code: 339100

TYPES OF BUSINESS:

Medical Equipment-Manufacturing
Bionic Hearing Devices
Cochlear Implant Technology

BRANDS/DIVISIONS/AFFILIATES:

Sonova Holding AG
HiResolution Bionic Ear System
HiRes 3D
Naida CI
AutoSense
T-Mic
Kinder Clip
Phonal ComPilot

CONTACTS: Note: Officers with more than one job title may be intentionally listed here more than once.

Victoria E. Carr-Brendel, Pres.
Hansjurg Emch, VP-Medical
Mark Downing, Dir.-Product Mgmt. & Surgical Support

GROWTH PLANS/SPECIAL FEATURES:

Advanced Bionics LLC, a subsidiary of hearing aid manufacturer Sonova Holding AG, develops and markets bionic technologies used in implantable neurostimulation devices such as cochlear implants for the restoration of hearing in severely hearing-impaired and deaf individuals. Unlike traditional hearing aids, cochlear implants bypass the inner ear to send sounds as electric pulses directly to the brain. The hearing systems consist of implanted receivers and external sound processors. Products in the company's HiResolution Bionic Ear System includes the HiRes 3D cochlear implant, designed to provide hearing that closely resembles how a normal ear hears; the Naida CI sound processor worn over the ear and equipped with microphones and digital technology for understanding speech; and the AutoSense operating system, which automatically senses the sound and setting the CI wearer is in and makes adjustments instantly. Products are offered for adults and children. Advanced Bionics partners with fellow nanotech company Phonak for the development, manufacture and distribution of the Naida CI processors. In addition to the implant systems, Advanced Bionics produces various accessories for users, including: T-Mic microphones; the Kinder Clip, which allows the hearing aid device to be worn on a shirt collar; the Phonal ComPilot, which links the unit to Bluetooth devices, mobile phones, computers, media players, TVs and other devices; the Roger digital wireless microphone and receiver that picks up the voice of the speaker while reducing background noise; and Skinit device covers.

FINANCIAL DATA: Note: Data for latest year may not have been available at press time.

In U.S. $	2020	2019	2018	2017	2016	2015
Revenue	266,200,000	242,000,000	230,000,000	210,000,000	200,000,000	188,802,915
R&D Expense						
Operating Income						
Operating Margin %						
SGA Expense						
Net Income						
Operating Cash Flow						
Capital Expenditure						
EBITDA						
Return on Assets %						
Return on Equity %						
Debt to Equity						

CONTACT INFORMATION:

Phone: 661-362-1400   Fax: 661-362-1500
Toll-Free: 877-829-0026
Address: 28515 Westinghouse Pl., Valencia, CA 91355 United States

STOCK TICKER/OTHER:

Stock Ticker: Subsidiary
Employees: 724
Parent Company: Sonova Holding AG

Exchange:
Fiscal Year Ends: 12/31

SALARIES/BONUSES:

Top Exec. Salary: $ Bonus: $
Second Exec. Salary: $ Bonus: $

OTHER THOUGHTS:

Estimated Female Officers or Directors:
Hot Spot for Advancement for Women/Minorities:

AdventHealth

www.adventhealth.com

NAIC Code: 622110

TYPES OF BUSINESS:

General Medical and Surgical Hospitals
Nursing Homes
Home Health Care Services

BRANDS/DIVISIONS/AFFILIATES:

Seventh-day Adventist Church

CONTACTS: *Note: Officers with more than one job title may be intentionally listed here more than once.*

Terry Shaw, CEO
Paul Rathbun, CFO
Olesea Azevedo, Chief Human Resources Officer
Brent G. Snyder, CIO
Robert R. Henderschedt, Sr. VP-Admin.
Jeffrey S. Bromme, Chief Legal Officer
Sandra K. Johnson, VP-Bus. Dev., Risk Mgmt. & Compliance
Womack H. Rucker, Jr., VP-Corp. Rel.
Lewis Seifert, Sr. VP-Finance
Amanda Brady, Chief Acct. Officer
Amy L. Zbaraschuk, VP-Finance
T.L. Trimble, VP-Legal Svcs.
Ted Hamilton, VP-Medical Mission
Carlene Jamerson, Sr. VP
Ron Smith, Chmn.
John Brownlow, Sr. VP-Managed Care
Celeste M. West, VP-Supply Chain Mgmt.

GROWTH PLANS/SPECIAL FEATURES:

AdventHealth is sponsored by the Seventh-day Adventist Church and is one of the largest nonprofit Protestant healthcare organizations in the U.S. The firm operates nearly 50 hospitals and hundreds of care sites in diverse markets throughout nine states. The company serves millions of patients annually through its more than 80,000 caregivers. Adventist Health's services span bariatric/weight care, behavioral health, cancer, children's care, diabetes, digestive, emergency/urgent, heart/vascular, home care, hospice care, imaging services, lab services, men's health, mother and baby care, neurology/neurosurgical care, orthopedic, pain, primary care, senior care, skilled nursing, sleep care, spine, sports medicine, rehab, surgical care, transplant care, wellness care, women's health and wound care. The firm is guided by its Christian mission, combining disease treatment, preventative medicine, education and advocacy of a wholesome lifestyle. Hospitals within the health group provide a wide range of free or reduced-price services in their communities, including free medical vans and community clinics, free screening and education programs, debt forgiveness, abuse shelters and programs for the homeless and jobless.

FINANCIAL DATA: *Note: Data for latest year may not have been available at press time.*

In U.S. $	2020	2019	2018	2017	2016	2015
Revenue	10,230,000,000	11,000,000,000	10,000,000,000	9,699,947,345	9,651,689,000	9,116,187,000
R&D Expense						
Operating Income						
Operating Margin %						
SGA Expense						
Net Income				229,800,000	89,559,000	-131,403,000
Operating Cash Flow						
Capital Expenditure						
EBITDA						
Return on Assets %						
Return on Equity %						
Debt to Equity						

CONTACT INFORMATION:

Phone: 407-357-1000   Fax:
Toll-Free:
Address: 900 Hope Way, Altamonte Springs, FL 32714 United States

STOCK TICKER/OTHER:

Stock Ticker: Nonprofit   Exchange:
Employees: 80,000   Fiscal Year Ends: 12/31
Parent Company:

SALARIES/BONUSES:

Top Exec. Salary: $ Bonus: $
Second Exec. Salary: $ Bonus: $

OTHER THOUGHTS:

Estimated Female Officers or Directors: 6
Hot Spot for Advancement for Women/Minorities: Y

Advocate Aurora Health
NAIC Code: 622110

www.advocateaurorahealth.org

TYPES OF BUSINESS:
General Medical and Surgical Hospitals
Clinics & Outpatient Centers
Home Health Care
Physician Groups

BRANDS/DIVISIONS/AFFILIATES:
Advocate Health Care
Aurora Health Care

GROWTH PLANS/SPECIAL FEATURES:
Advocate Aurora Health is a nonprofit healthcare provider serving nearly 3 million patients annually in Illinois and Wisconsin. The firm is a national leader in clinical innovation, health outcomes, consumer experience and value-based care, serving from more than 500 sites of care. Advocate Aurora is engaged in hundreds of clinical trials and research studies and is nationally recognized for its expertise in cardiology, neurosciences, oncology and pediatrics. Advocate Health Care is a faith-based health system serving Illinois, with nearly 400 sites of care and 12 hospitals, including two children's hospitals. Aurora Health Care serves eastern Wisconsin and northern Illinois, operating through 15 hospitals and more than 150 clinics and 70 pharmacies.

CONTACTS:
Note: Officers with more than one job title may be intentionally listed here more than once.
Jim Skogsbergh, CEO
Bill Santulli, COO
Dominic Nakis, CFO
Kevin Brady, Chief Human Resources Officer
Lee Sacks, Chief Medical Officer
Bobbie Byrne, CIO
Gail D. Hasbrouck, General Counsel
Scott Powder, Sr. VP-Strategic Planning & Growth
Dominic Nakis, Treasurer
Lee Sacks, CEO-Advocate Physician Partners
James R. Dan, Pres., Advocate Medical Group
Kathie Bender Schwich, Sr. VP-Mission & Spiritual Care

FINANCIAL DATA:
Note: Data for latest year may not have been available at press time.

In U.S. $	2020	2019	2018	2017	2016	2015
Revenue	13,132,189,000	12,805,423,000	9,213,406,000	6,233,413,000	5,587,420,000	5,329,562,000
R&D Expense						
Operating Income						
Operating Margin %						
SGA Expense						
Net Income	608,125,000	1,546,697,000	38,416,000	811,343,000	597,604,000	78,605,000
Operating Cash Flow						
Capital Expenditure						
EBITDA						
Return on Assets %						
Return on Equity %						
Debt to Equity						

CONTACT INFORMATION:
Phone: 630-572-9393   Fax:
Toll-Free:
Address: 3075 Highland Pkwy., Ste. 600, Downers Grove, IL 60515 United States

STOCK TICKER/OTHER:
Stock Ticker: Nonprofit   Exchange:
Employees: 75,000   Fiscal Year Ends: 12/31
Parent Company:

SALARIES/BONUSES:
Top Exec. Salary: $ Bonus: $
Second Exec. Salary: $ Bonus: $

OTHER THOUGHTS:
Estimated Female Officers or Directors: 3
Hot Spot for Advancement for Women/Minorities: Y

Sales, profits and employees may be estimates. Financial information, benefits and other data can change quickly and may vary from those stated here.

Aeon Global Health Corp

aeonglobalhealth.com

NAIC Code: 511210D

TYPES OF BUSINESS:

Computer Software, Healthcare & Biotechnology
Clinical Services
Medical Tests
Software
Records Management Software
Revenue Cycle Software

BRANDS/DIVISIONS/AFFILIATES:

CONTACTS: *Note: Officers with more than one job title may be intentionally listed here more than once.*

Hanif Roshan, CEO
Peter Hellwig, CFO

GROWTH PLANS/SPECIAL FEATURES:

Aeon Global Health Corp. and its subsidiaries provide clinical services to healthcare professionals. These services include, but are not limited to: medical tests used for monitoring both therapeutic drugs as well as drugs of abuse; the ability of an individual to metabolize or potentially have an adverse reaction to a number of drugs and other compounds; and the potential risk of an individual to develop certain cancers based on their genetic makeup. Aeon also provides web-based revenue cycle management applications and telehealth products and services, which enable health care clinical testing organizations to increase revenues, improve productivity, reduce costs, coordinate patient care, enhance related administrative and clinical workflows, and comply with regulatory requirements. The web-based services interface seamlessly with billing, information and records management systems. Primary client groups serviced by Aeon include physicians, clinics, medical centers, hospitals, accountable care organizations, rehab centers, intensive outpatient care centers and employer health programs. The company's services are paid through a mix of reimbursement from Medicare, Medicaid and private health insurance carriers, along with direct-paying clientele.

FINANCIAL DATA: *Note: Data for latest year may not have been available at press time.*

In U.S. $	2020	2019	2018	2017	2016	2015
Revenue		12,932,310	16,301,140	20,198,770	34,576,920	24,445,340
R&D Expense					21,950	
Operating Income		-2,950,074	-780,536	-5,379,298	5,796,621	10,393,960
Operating Margin %		- .23%	- .05%	- .27%	.17%	.43%
SGA Expense		10,400,760	12,477,020	14,575,710	20,731,530	8,976,359
Net Income		-7,975,387	-8,000,377	-32,073,510	5,265,028	9,237,112
Operating Cash Flow		40,748	-888,585	536,971	7,921,749	9,129,946
Capital Expenditure		10,510	20,037	22,103	1,730,664	547,913
EBITDA		-2,012,973	-960,492	1,832,826	6,968,134	10,123,540
Return on Assets %		-1.12%	- .60%	- .95%	.18%	1.15%
Return on Equity %			-1.99%	-1.36%	.23%	1.75%
Debt to Equity						

CONTACT INFORMATION:

Phone: Fax:
Toll-Free: 888-661-0226
Address: 2225 Centennial Dr., Gainesville, GA 30504 United States

STOCK TICKER/OTHER:

Stock Ticker: AGHC Exchange: PINX
Employees: 52 Fiscal Year Ends: 06/30
Parent Company:

SALARIES/BONUSES:

Top Exec. Salary: $ Bonus: $
Second Exec. Salary: $ Bonus: $

OTHER THOUGHTS:

Estimated Female Officers or Directors:
Hot Spot for Advancement for Women/Minorities:

AEterna Zentaris Inc

www.aezsinc.com

NAIC Code: 325412

TYPES OF BUSINESS:

Drug Development
Biopharmaceutical Development
Biopharmaceutical Licensing

BRANDS/DIVISIONS/AFFILIATES:

Macimorelin

CONTACTS: Note: Officers with more than one job title may be intentionally listed here more than once.

Leslie Auld, CFO
Nicola Ammer, Chief Medical Officer
Carolyn Egbert, Director
Michael Ward, President
Brian Garrison, Senior VP, Divisional
Gunther Grau, Vice President, Divisional
Eckhard Guenther, Vice President, Divisional
Michael Teifel, Vice President, Divisional

GROWTH PLANS/SPECIAL FEATURES:

AEterna Zentaris, Inc. is a Canadian specialty biopharmaceutical company focused on serving the unmet medical needs of patients with rare endocrine diseases through acquisition, development and licensing orphan products. The firm's current macimorelin product is an oral growth hormone secretagogue (GHS) receptor agonist used to test for Adult Growth Hormone Deficiency, a rare endocrine disorder. AGHD may occur in an adult subject who has a history of childhood onset GHD or may occur during adulthood as an acquired condition. GHS are potent regulators of lipid, sugar and protein metabolism that directly stimulate growth hormone secretion from the pituitary gland without the involvement of Growth Hormone-Releasing Hormone or somatostatin. Macimorelin stimulates the secretion of GH from the pituitary gland into the circulatory system. Stimulated GH levels are measured in only four blood samples over ninety minutes after oral administration of macimorelin (no intravenous infusions or intramuscular injections involved). Novo Nordisk A/S is licensed to carry out the development, manufacturing, registration and commercialization of macimorelin in the U.S. and Canada; Consilient Health has commercial rights in Europe; MegaPharm has commercial rights in Israel; and AEterna Zentaris has commercial rights in the rest of the world. AEterna continues to explore licensing opportunities worldwide.

FINANCIAL DATA: Note: Data for latest year may not have been available at press time.

In U.S. $	2020	2019	2018	2017	2016	2015
Revenue	3,652,000	532,000	26,881,000	923,000	911,000	545,000
R&D Expense	1,506,000	1,837,000	2,932,000	10,704,000	16,495,000	17,234,000
Operating Income	-6,064,000	-9,544,000	9,842,000	-23,074,000	-29,476,000	-34,884,000
Operating Margin %		-17.94%	.37%	-25.00%	-32.36%	-64.01%
SGA Expense	5,893,000	7,829,000	12,003,000	13,293,000	13,892,000	18,195,000
Net Income	-5,118,000	-6,042,000	4,187,000	-16,796,000	-24,959,000	-50,143,000
Operating Cash Flow	-4,129,000	-10,725,000	6,825,000	-22,913,000	-29,010,000	-33,844,000
Capital Expenditure			9,000	4,000	66,000	26,000
EBITDA	-5,832,000	-5,322,000	9,900,000	-22,980,000	-29,196,000	-34,543,000
Return on Assets %		-.27%	.18%	-.62%	-.60%	-1.01%
Return on Equity %				-9.80%	-1.79%	-2.78%
Debt to Equity						

CONTACT INFORMATION:

Phone: 843-900-3223   Fax:
Toll-Free:
Address: 315 Sigma Dr., Summerville, SC 29486 United States

SALARIES/BONUSES:

Top Exec. Salary: $ Bonus: $
Second Exec. Salary: $ Bonus: $

STOCK TICKER/OTHER:

Stock Ticker: AEZS   Exchange: NAS
Employees: 11   Fiscal Year Ends: 12/31
Parent Company:

OTHER THOUGHTS:

Estimated Female Officers or Directors:
Hot Spot for Advancement for Women/Minorities:

aetnaCVSHealth

www.aetnacvshealth.com

NAIC Code: 524114

TYPES OF BUSINESS:

Insurance-Medical & Health
Health Care Benefits
Dental Benefits
Medicare Plans
Life Insurance

BRANDS/DIVISIONS/AFFILIATES:

CVS Health Corporation
CVS Health
CVS Pharmacy Inc
MinuteClinic LLC
Aetna Inc
Aetna Life Insurance Company
Aetna Health Inc

CONTACTS: *Note: Officers with more than one job title may be intentionally listed here more than once.*

Daniel Finke, Pres.
Shawn Guertin, CFO
Francis Soistman, Executive VP, Divisional
Margaret McCarthy, Executive VP, Divisional
Richard Jelinek, Executive VP, Divisional
Thomas Sabatino, Executive VP

GROWTH PLANS/SPECIAL FEATURES:

AetnaCVSHealth represents the health care benefits segment of CVS Health Corporation, offering solutions to employers and government businesses, serving more than 34 million members. Aetna Inc, CVS Health, CVS Pharmacy Inc. and MinuteClinic LLC are part of the CVS Health family of companies. Aetna is the brand name for products and services provided by Aetna Life Insurance Company and its affiliates. Health plans are offered or underwritten or administered by Coventry Health Plan of Florida Inc., Aetna Health Inc. (Georgia), Aetna Health of Utah Inc., Aetna Health Inc. (Pennsylvania), or Aetna Health Inc. (Texas). Health benefits and health insurance plans contain exclusive exclusions and limitations. Affordable Care Act (ACA) plans cover essential benefits such as hospitalization, preventive care and mental health services. some plans offer extras such as dental and vision. Open enrollment for ACA begins November 1 and closes January 15. Aetna offers a Medicare plan with hospital, medical, prescription coverage and other benefits, as well as individual and family plans.

FINANCIAL DATA: *Note: Data for latest year may not have been available at press time.*

In U.S. $	2020	2019	2018	2017	2016	2015
Revenue	75,467,000,000	69,604,000,000	61,500,000,000	60,535,001,088	63,154,999,296	60,336,500,736
R&D Expense						
Operating Income						
Operating Margin %						
SGA Expense						
Net Income		4,400,000,000	4,000,000,000	1,904,000,000	2,271,000,004	2,390,200,064
Operating Cash Flow						
Capital Expenditure						
EBITDA						
Return on Assets %						
Return on Equity %						
Debt to Equity						

CONTACT INFORMATION:

Phone: 860 273-0123   Fax:
Toll-Free: 800-872-3862
Address: 151 Farmington Ave., Hartford, CT 06156 United States

SALARIES/BONUSES:

Top Exec. Salary: $ Bonus: $
Second Exec. Salary: $ Bonus: $

STOCK TICKER/OTHER:

Stock Ticker: Subsidiary
Employees: 49,500
Parent Company: CVS Health Corporation

Exchange:
Fiscal Year Ends: 12/31

OTHER THOUGHTS:

Estimated Female Officers or Directors: 8
Hot Spot for Advancement for Women/Minorities: Y

AFLAC Incorporated

www.aflac.com

NAIC Code: 524114

TYPES OF BUSINESS:

Insurance-Supplemental & Specialty Health
Life Insurance
Cancer Insurance
Long-Term Care Insurance
Accident & Disability Insurance
Vision Plans
Dental Plans

BRANDS/DIVISIONS/AFFILIATES:

Aflac Life Insurance Japan Ltd
One Day Pay
American Family Life Assurance Company
Continental American Insurance Company
Aflac Group Insurance/AGI
Tier One Insurance Company

CONTACTS: Note: Officers with more than one job title may be intentionally listed here more than once.

Daniel Amos, CEO
James Daniels, CFO, Divisional
June Howard, Chief Accounting Officer
Masatoshi Koide, COO, Divisional
Eric Kirsch, Executive VP, Subsidiary
Frederick Crawford, Executive VP
Audrey Tillman, Executive VP
Koji Ariyoshi, Executive VP
Richard Williams, Executive VP
Albert Riggieri, Other Corporate Officer
Teresa White, President, Divisional
Charles Lake, President, Subsidiary
Max Broden, Senior VP

GROWTH PLANS/SPECIAL FEATURES:

AFLAC Incorporated provides supplemental insurance to more than 50 million people through its subsidiaries in Japan and the U.S. In short, the firm pays cash when policyholders get sick or injured. Aflac Life Insurance Japan Ltd. is the leading provider of medical and cancer insurance in Japan, where it insures one in four households. Through its One Day Pay initiative in the U.S. (for eligible claims), AFLAC can process, approve and electronically send funds to claimants for quick access to cash in one business day. AFLAC helps protect its customers from asset loss, income loss and supplemental medical expenses. In the U.S., AFLAC is a leader in voluntary insurance sales at the work site, including short-term disability, life insurance, accident insurance, cancer coverage, critical illness coverage, hospital intensive care, hospital indemnity, dental care and vision care. U.S. subsidiaries are collectively referred to as Aflac U.S., and include American Family Life Assurance Company of Columbus, Continental American Insurance Company (branded as Aflac Group Insurance/AGI), American Family Life Assurance Company of New York and Tier One Insurance Company. Aflac Japan's revenues accounted for 82% of the company's total revenues at June 30, 2021, with Aflac U.S. accounting for the remainder.

FINANCIAL DATA: Note: Data for latest year may not have been available at press time.

In U.S. $	2020	2019	2018	2017	2016	2015
Revenue	22,116,000,000	22,223,000,000	21,689,000,000	21,600,000,000	22,380,000,000	20,845,000,000
R&D Expense						
Operating Income						
Operating Margin %						
SGA Expense						
Net Income	4,778,000,000	3,304,000,000	2,920,000,000	4,604,000,000	2,659,000,000	2,533,000,000
Operating Cash Flow	5,958,000,000	5,455,000,000	6,014,000,000	6,128,000,000	5,987,000,000	6,776,000,000
Capital Expenditure						
EBITDA						
Return on Assets %		.02%	.02%	.03%	.02%	.02%
Return on Equity %		.13%	.12%	.20%	.14%	.14%
Debt to Equity		0.227	0.246	0.215	0.262	0.283

CONTACT INFORMATION:

Phone: 706 323-3431 Fax:
Toll-Free: 800-235-2667
Address: 1932 Wynnton Rd., Columbus, GA 31999 United States

STOCK TICKER/OTHER:

Stock Ticker: AFL
Employees: 11,729
Parent Company:

Exchange: NYS
Fiscal Year Ends: 12/31

SALARIES/BONUSES:

Top Exec. Salary: $ Bonus: $
Second Exec. Salary: $ Bonus: $

OTHER THOUGHTS:

Estimated Female Officers or Directors: 8
Hot Spot for Advancement for Women/Minorities: Y

Agfa-Gevaert NV

www.agfa.com

NAIC Code: 333316

TYPES OF BUSINESS:

Imaging Equipment
Commercial Printing Equipment & Products
Image Publishing Software
Consumer Photographic Products
Medical Imaging Systems
X-Ray Films
Inkjet Printers
Network Collaboration Software

BRANDS/DIVISIONS/AFFILIATES:

ORBIS

CONTACTS: *Note: Officers with more than one job title may be intentionally listed here more than once.*

Pascal Juery, CEO
Dirk De Man, CFO
Luc Thijs, Pres., Agfa HealthCare
Luc Delagaye, Pres., Agfa Materials
Stefaan Vanhooren, Pres., Agfa Graphics
Frank Aranzana, Chmn.

GROWTH PLANS/SPECIAL FEATURES:

Agfa-Gevaert NV is a leading imaging equipment company that develops, produces and markets analog and digital systems as well as information technology (IT) solutions primarily for the printing and healthcare sectors. Agfa has four main divisions: offset solutions, digital print and chemicals, radiology solutions, and healthcare IT. The offset solutions segment serves the printing industry, including commercial, newspaper and packaging printers worldwide. Solutions range from computer-to-plate systems with digital offset plates over color management and workflow optimization software to pressroom chemicals. The digital print and chemicals segment supplies sign and display printing companies with a range of inkjet printers and inks, as well as workflow software, cutting machines and inkjet media. This division develops high-performance inkjet inks and fluids for various industrial inkjet printing systems and applications, which enable manufacturers to integrate print into their existing production processes. The radiology solutions segment supplies radiology departments of hospitals with traditional X-ray film, hardcopy film and printers, digital radiography equipment and image processing software. Last, the healthcare IT segment offers an enterprise imaging platform that creates an imaging record for every patient, making it accessible throughout the hospital, the care organization, and all care facilities included within a regional network. This division offers its hospital information system/clinical information system ORBIS, which connects medical departments and administrative departments of hospitals into one virtual network, with access to all relevant patient information as well as billing, planning of appointments and examinations and financial reporting. This division is also engaged in the integrated care market, offering solutions that support collaboration across care organizations and medical disciplines, and enables hospitals to actively engage with its stakeholders in the expanded care process, including physicians, informal care-givers and patients.

FINANCIAL DATA: *Note: Data for latest year may not have been available at press time.*

In U.S. $	2020	2019	2018	2017	2016	2015
Revenue	2,088,017,000	2,735,559,000	2,745,333,000	2,984,801,000	3,099,648,000	3,232,822,000
R&D Expense	116,068,800	179,601,200	172,270,500	175,935,900	172,270,500	175,935,900
Operating Income	32,987,980	131,951,900	85,524,380	189,375,400	238,246,500	218,698,100
Operating Margin %			.04%	.07%	.08%	.07%
SGA Expense	448,392,200	580,344,100	602,336,100	616,997,400	624,328,000	637,767,600
Net Income	748,949,200	-64,754,180	-29,322,650	45,205,750	85,524,380	75,750,170
Operating Cash Flow		150,278,600	-53,758,190	47,649,300	173,492,300	182,044,800
Capital Expenditure		46,427,520	48,871,080	56,201,740	53,758,190	45,205,750
EBITDA	17,104,880	135,617,200	146,613,200	228,472,300	278,565,200	232,137,600
Return on Assets %			-.01%	.02%	.03%	.03%
Return on Equity %			-.09%	.15%	.32%	.39%
Debt to Equity			0.869	0.171	0.344	0.601

CONTACT INFORMATION:

Phone: 32 34442111   Fax: 32 34447094
Toll-Free:
Address: Septestraat 27, Mortsel, B-2640 Belgium

STOCK TICKER/OTHER:

Stock Ticker: AFGVY   Exchange: PINX
Employees: 10,018   Fiscal Year Ends: 12/31
Parent Company:

SALARIES/BONUSES:

Top Exec. Salary: $ Bonus: $
Second Exec. Salary: $ Bonus: $

OTHER THOUGHTS:

Estimated Female Officers or Directors:
Hot Spot for Advancement for Women/Minorities:

AHMC Healthcare Inc

www.ahmchealth.com

NAIC Code: 622110

TYPES OF BUSINESS:

General Medical and Surgical Hospitals
Hospitals
Acute Care

BRANDS/DIVISIONS/AFFILIATES:

Alhambra Hospital Medical Center
Anaheim Regional Medical Center
Garfield Medical Center
Monterey Park Hospital
Parkview Community Hospital Medical Center
San Gabriel Valley Medical Center
Seton Medical Center
Whittier Hospital Medical Center

CONTACTS: *Note: Officers with more than one job title may be intentionally listed here more than once.*

Philip Cohen, COO

GROWTH PLANS/SPECIAL FEATURES:

AHMC Healthcare, Inc. operates comprehensive acute care hospitals that provide healthcare services in the Greater San Gabriel Valley area. AHMC stands for Alhambra Hospital Medical Center. The firm owns and operates the following hospitals: Anaheim Regional Medical Center, Garfield Medical Center, Greater El Monte Community Hospital, Monterey Park Hospital, Parkview Community Hospital Medical Center, San Gabriel Valley Medical Center, Seton Medical Center, Seton Medical Center Coastside and Whittier Hospital Medical Center. AHMC hospitals offer advanced diagnostic tools such as the MRI GE Signa HDxt1.5TMR system and the Toshiba Aquilon 128-slice CT scanner, and some are designated STEMI-receiving centers, designated stroke-receiving centers and designated baby-friendly hospitals.

AHMC offers its employees medical, dental and vision coverage; 401(k) matching; flexible spending accounts, tuition reimbursement; and a wellness program.

FINANCIAL DATA: *Note: Data for latest year may not have been available at press time.*

In U.S. $	2020	2019	2018	2017	2016	2015
Revenue	1,272,240,000	1,368,000,000	1,355,000,000	1,302,000,000	1,240,000,000	1,215,000,000
R&D Expense						
Operating Income						
Operating Margin %						
SGA Expense						
Net Income						
Operating Cash Flow						
Capital Expenditure						
EBITDA						
Return on Assets %						
Return on Equity %						
Debt to Equity						

CONTACT INFORMATION:

Phone: 626-457-7400   Fax: 626-457-7455
Toll-Free:
Address: 500 E. Main St., Alhambra, CA 91801 United States

STOCK TICKER/OTHER:

Stock Ticker: Private   Exchange:
Employees: 7,000   Fiscal Year Ends:
Parent Company:

SALARIES/BONUSES:

Top Exec. Salary: $ Bonus: $
Second Exec. Salary: $ Bonus: $

OTHER THOUGHTS:

Estimated Female Officers or Directors:
Hot Spot for Advancement for Women/Minorities:

Air Methods Corporation

www.airmethods.com

NAIC Code: 621910

TYPES OF BUSINESS:

Air Emergency Medical Transport Service
Helicopter Medical Services
Aviation Maintenance
Helicopter Fleet
Fixed-Wing Aircraft
Aircraft Equipment
Land Vehicle Equipment
Helicopter Tours

BRANDS/DIVISIONS/AFFILIATES:

American Services LLC
ASP AMC Intermediate Holdings Inc
United Rotorcraft
Blue Hawaiian Helicopters

CONTACTS: Note: Officers with more than one job title may be intentionally listed here more than once.

JaeLynn Williams, CEO
Leo Morrissette, Exec. VP-Oper.
David Portugal, CFO
Dallan Huff, Sr. VP-Mktg. & Communications
Trevor Thompson, Sr. VP-Sales
David Doerr, Executive VP, Divisional
Crystal Gordon, General Counsel
Michael Allen, President, Divisional
Jamie Cutter, Sr. VP-IT

GROWTH PLANS/SPECIAL FEATURES:

Air Methods Corporation offers air medical services, delivering life-saving care to more than 70,000 people each year. The firm's workforce encompasses pilots, clinicians, mechanics, air communications specialists, support teams and more. Air Methods works 24/7 to maintain equipment and supplies, coordinate logistics and provide tools and expertise. More than 20% of its team members are U.S. veterans, active duty or in the reserves. The company is a preferred partner for hospitals and one of the largest community-based providers of air medical services. Air Methods has a comprehensive aviation, clinical and maintenance training routine, including continuous curriculum of learning and simulation-based training. The company has more than 300 bases of operations serving 48 states, and also operates eight maintenance centers and a national communications center. United Rotorcraft, a division of Air Methods, specializes in the design and manufacture of aeromedical and aerospace technology. United Rotorcraft provides aircraft and land vehicle equipment and systems to meet customer's mission requirements, including equipment and systems for emergency medical services, firefighting, search and rescue missions, and airborne law enforcement missions. Air Methods' fleet of owned, leased or maintained aircraft features more than 450 helicopters and fixed-wing aircraft. In addition, Blue Hawaiian Helicopters is a tour company in Hawaii, in business since 1985. Air Methods operates as a wholly-owned subsidiary of ASP AMC Intermediate Holdings, Inc., itself an indirect wholly-owned subsidiary of owned American Services, LLC.

FINANCIAL DATA: Note: Data for latest year may not have been available at press time.

In U.S. $	2020	2019	2018	2017	2016	2015
Revenue	1,305,600,000	1,360,000,000	1,250,000,000	1,200,000,000	1,170,455,040	1,085,686,016
R&D Expense						
Operating Income						
Operating Margin %						
SGA Expense						
Net Income						
Operating Cash Flow						
Capital Expenditure						
EBITDA						
Return on Assets %						
Return on Equity %						
Debt to Equity						

CONTACT INFORMATION:

Phone: 303-792-7400   Fax:
Toll-Free:
Address: 5500 S. Quebec St., Ste. 300, Greenwood Village, CO 80111 United States

STOCK TICKER/OTHER:

Stock Ticker: Private
Employees: 5,000
Parent Company: American Securities LLC

Exchange:
Fiscal Year Ends: 12/31

SALARIES/BONUSES:

Top Exec. Salary: $ Bonus: $
Second Exec. Salary: $ Bonus: $

OTHER THOUGHTS:

Estimated Female Officers or Directors: 5
Hot Spot for Advancement for Women/Minorities: Y

Sales, profits and employees may be estimates. Financial information, benefits and other data can change quickly and may vary from those stated here.

Akero Therapeutics Inc

NAIC Code: 325412

www.akerotx.com

TYPES OF BUSINESS:

Pharmaceutical Preparation Manufacturing
Drug Development
Metabolic Balance Restoration

BRANDS/DIVISIONS/AFFILIATES:

Akero Securities Corporation
Efruxifermin

CONTACTS: *Note: Officers with more than one job title may be intentionally listed here more than once.*

Andrew Cheng, CEO
William White, CFO
Mark Iwicki, Chairman of the Board
Timothy Rolph, Chief Scientific Officer
Jonathan Young, Co-Founder
Kitty Yale, Other Executive Officer
Arindam Bose, Vice President, Divisional

GROWTH PLANS/SPECIAL FEATURES:

Akero Therapeutics, Inc., together with its wholly-owned subsidiary Akero Securities Corporation, is a cardio-metabolic non-alcoholic steatohepatitis (NASH) company developing medicines designed to restore metabolic balance and improve the overall health of patients with NASH. NASH is a severe form of nonalcoholic fatty liver disease characterized by inflammation and fibrosis in the liver that can progress to cirrhosis, liver failure, cancer and death. Akero's lead product candidate is efruxifermin (EFX), an analog of fibroblast growth factor 21 (FGF21). By delivering sustained signaling through FGF21's receptors, EFX has the potential to address NASH by reducing liver fat, inflammation and fibrosis. Results from Akero's Phase 2a BALANCED study showed EFX's potential to be a foundational HASH monotherapy, and results of exploratory endpoints were reported after 16 weeks of treatment, that 48% of all EFX patients achieved at least a one stage improvement in fibrosis without worsening of NASH, and that 28% of all EFX patients achieved at least a two-stage improvement in fibrosis stage. Therefore, Akero continues to develop EFX. In early-2021, Akero announced that its first patient had been randomized for dosing in its Phase 2b clinical study of EFX for patients with F2/F3 NASH, referred to as the HARMONY study.

FINANCIAL DATA: *Note: Data for latest year may not have been available at press time.*

In U.S. $	2020	2019	2018	2017	2016	2015
Revenue						
R&D Expense	64,916,000	37,046,000	11,882,000			
Operating Income	-80,154,000	-45,651,000	-13,778,000			
Operating Margin %						
SGA Expense	15,238,000	8,605,000	1,896,000			
Net Income	-79,207,000	-43,755,000	-81,714,000			
Operating Cash Flow	-70,804,000	-35,627,000	-4,625,000			
Capital Expenditure	148,000		5,000,000			
EBITDA	-80,137,000	-45,651,000	-13,778,000			
Return on Assets %		- .41%	- .50%			
Return on Equity %		-1.11%				
Debt to Equity						

CONTACT INFORMATION:

Phone: 650 487-6488   Fax:
Toll-Free:
Address: 601 Gateway Blvd., Ste. 350, South San Francisco, CA 94080 United States

STOCK TICKER/OTHER:

Stock Ticker: AKRO   Exchange: NAS
Employees: 22   Fiscal Year Ends: 12/31
Parent Company:

SALARIES/BONUSES:

Top Exec. Salary: $ Bonus: $
Second Exec. Salary: $ Bonus: $

OTHER THOUGHTS:

Estimated Female Officers or Directors:
Hot Spot for Advancement for Women/Minorities:

Alcon Inc

www.alcon.com

NAIC Code: 325412

TYPES OF BUSINESS:

Eye Care Products
Ophthalmic Products & Equipment
Contact Lens Care Products
Surgical Instruments

BRANDS/DIVISIONS/AFFILIATES:

CONTACTS: *Note: Officers with more than one job title may be intentionally listed here more than once.*

David Endicott, CEO
Tim Stonesifer, CFO
Sabri Markabi, Chief Medical Officer
Ed McGough, Sr. VP-Global Mfg.
Christina Ackerman, General Counsel
Bettina Maunz, Head-Comm.
Robert Karsunky, Sr. VP-Finance
Sergio Duplan, Pres., Latin America & Caribbean
Stuart Raetzman, Pres., Europe, Middle East & Africa
Robert Warner, Pres., U.S. & Canada
Roy Acosta, Pres., Asia
Sue Whitfill, Head-Global Quality

GROWTH PLANS/SPECIAL FEATURES:

Alcon, Inc. is a leading eye care products company that has been in business for more than 70 years. The firm researches, develops, manufactures, sells and distributes a full suite of eye care products within two key businesses: surgical and vision care. The surgical division offers a complete line of ophthalmic surgical products, including technologies and devices for cataract, retinal, glaucoma and refractive surgery as well as advanced technology intraocular lenses to treat cataracts and refractive errors (presbyopia and astigmatism). This segment also provides advanced viscoelastics, surgical solutions, surgical packs and other disposable products for cataract vitreoretinal surgery. The vision care division manufactures contact lenses and lens care products. These include daily disposable, monthly replacement and color-enhancing contact lenses for comfortable and convenient vision correction options. Lens care products include: multipurpose and hydrogen-peroxide based solutions to clean, rinse and disinfect contact lenses; rewetting drops to provide added comfort throughout the day; and daily protein remover that removes protein deposits from lenses.

FINANCIAL DATA: *Note: Data for latest year may not have been available at press time.*

In U.S. $	2020	2019	2018	2017	2016	2015
Revenue	6,833,000,000	7,508,000,000	7,276,000,000	6,792,000,000	6,596,000,000	
R&D Expense	673,000,000	656,000,000	587,000,000	584,000,000	499,000,000	
Operating Income	-427,000,000	159,000,000	-196,000,000	24,000,000	86,000,000	
Operating Margin %		-.02%	-.03%	-.01%	.00%	
SGA Expense	2,694,000,000	2,847,000,000	2,801,000,000	2,596,000,000	2,526,000,000	
Net Income	-531,000,000	-656,000,000	-315,000,000	256,000,000	-170,000,000	
Operating Cash Flow	823,000,000	920,000,000	1,140,000,000	1,218,000,000	1,245,000,000	
Capital Expenditure	567,000,000	676,000,000	712,000,000	496,000,000	506,000,000	
EBITDA	1,115,000,000	1,206,000,000	1,353,000,000	1,205,000,000	1,207,000,000	
Return on Assets %		-.02%	-.01%	.01%		
Return on Equity %		-.03%	-.01%	.01%		
Debt to Equity		0.181	0.094	0.004		

CONTACT INFORMATION:

Phone: 4158 911 2000   Fax: 4158 911 3222
Toll-Free:
Address: Chemin de Blandonnet 8, Geneva, 1214 Switzerland

SALARIES/BONUSES:

Top Exec. Salary: $ Bonus: $
Second Exec. Salary: $ Bonus: $

STOCK TICKER/OTHER:

Stock Ticker: ALC   Exchange: NYS
Employees: 22,142   Fiscal Year Ends: 12/31
Parent Company:

OTHER THOUGHTS:

Estimated Female Officers or Directors: 3
Hot Spot for Advancement for Women/Minorities: Y

Alector Inc

NAIC Code: 325412

www.alector.com

TYPES OF BUSINESS:

Pharmaceutical Preparation Manufacturing
Drug Discovery
Drug Development
Clinical Testing

BRANDS/DIVISIONS/AFFILIATES:

Discovery Platform
AL001
AL002
AL003
AL101

CONTACTS: *Note: Officers with more than one job title may be intentionally listed here more than once.*

Arnon Rosenthal, CEO
Calvin Yu, CFO
Tillman Gerngross, Chairman of the Board
Robert Paul, Chief Medical Officer
Robert King, Other Executive Officer
Sabah Oney, Other Executive Officer

GROWTH PLANS/SPECIAL FEATURES:

Alector, Inc. is a clinical stage biotechnology company engaged in immuno-neurology therapies for the treatment of neurodegenerative diseases. Immuno-neurology targets immune dysfunction as a root cause of multiple pathologies that are drivers of degenerative brain disorders. Alector is developing therapies designed to simultaneously counteract these pathologies by restoring healthy immune function to the brain. Its Discovery Platform enables the firm to advance a broad portfolio of product candidates, and therefore as a result, Alector has identified over 120 immune system targets since 2013, progressing over 10 programs into pre-clinical research. The company also advanced four product candidates into clinical development: AL001, AL002, AL003 and AL101. AL001 modulates progranulin (PGRN), a regulator of immune activity in the brain with genetic links to multiple neurodegenerative disorders, including frontotemporal dementia (FTD), Alzheimer's disease and Parkinson's disease. AL002 and AL003 focus on modulating check-point receptors on the brain's immune cells, with AL002 targeting triggering receptor expressed on myeloid cells 2 and AL003 targeting sialic acid binding Ig-like lectin 3. AL002 and AL003 are aimed at treating Alzheimer's disease patients. AL101 is a second product candidate for Alector's PGRN program, for patients suffering from more prevalent neurodegenerative diseases including Alzheimer's disease and Parkinson's disease, in addition to FTD. In September 2021, Alector announced that the first participant had been dosed in a Phase 2 clinical study evaluating the safety, tolerability, pharmacokinetics and pharmacodynamics of AL001 in people with amyotrophic lateral sclerosis (ALS).

FINANCIAL DATA: *Note: Data for latest year may not have been available at press time.*

In U.S. $	2020	2019	2018	2017	2016	2015
Revenue	21,098,000	21,219,000	27,677,000	3,735,000	416,000	
R&D Expense	156,869,000	100,528,000	73,031,000	29,911,000	13,674,000	
Operating Income	-195,174,000	-114,404,000	-57,288,000	-32,679,000	-15,132,000	
Operating Margin %		-5.39%	-2.07%	-8.75%	-36.38%	
SGA Expense	59,403,000	35,095,000	11,934,000	6,503,000	1,874,000	
Net Income	-190,228,000	-105,385,000	-52,248,000	-32,480,000	-15,110,000	
Operating Cash Flow	-166,734,000	-99,308,000	127,464,000	-17,771,000	-12,993,000	
Capital Expenditure	5,032,000	15,265,000	1,884,000	801,000	2,250,000	
EBITDA	-187,909,000	-108,830,000	-56,269,000	-31,999,000	-14,931,000	
Return on Assets %		- .29%	- .19%	- .22%	- .28%	
Return on Equity %		-2.17%				
Debt to Equity		0.213				

CONTACT INFORMATION:

Phone: 415 231-5660   Fax:
Toll-Free:
Address: 131 Oyster Point Blvd., Ste. 600, South San Francisco, CA 94080 United States

STOCK TICKER/OTHER:

Stock Ticker: ALEC
Employees: 171
Parent Company:

Exchange: NAS
Fiscal Year Ends: 12/31

SALARIES/BONUSES:

Top Exec. Salary: $ Bonus: $
Second Exec. Salary: $ Bonus: $

OTHER THOUGHTS:

Estimated Female Officers or Directors:
Hot Spot for Advancement for Women/Minorities:

Alfresa Holdings Corporation

www.alfresa.com

NAIC Code: 424210

TYPES OF BUSINESS:

Drugs and Druggists' Sundries Merchant Wholesalers
Pharmaceuticals
Diagnostic Reagents
Medical Devices
Manufacturing
Wholesale
Marketing

BRANDS/DIVISIONS/AFFILIATES:

Alfresa Corporation
Alfresa Healthcare Corporation
Alfresa Pharma Corporation
Alfresa System Corporation
Apollo Medical Holdings Inc

CONTACTS: *Note: Officers with more than one job title may be intentionally listed here more than once.*

Ryuji Arakawa, Pres.
Taizo Kubo, Chmn.

GROWTH PLANS/SPECIAL FEATURES:

Alfresa Holdings Corporation, through its subsidiaries, engage in the wholesale, manufacture, marketing and import/export of pharmaceuticals, diagnostic reagents, medical devices and related equipment. Alfresa divides its business into four groups: ethical pharmaceuticals wholesaling, self-medication products wholesaling, manufacturing and medical-related business. The ethical pharmaceuticals wholesaling business group delivers a wide range of products, including diagnostic reagents and medical devices and related equipment. It accomplishes this by distributing the products from its nationwide distribution centers to hospitals, clinics and dispensing pharmacies. The self-medication products wholesaling business group delivers over-the-counter drugs, health foods, supplements and other products to drug stores and pharmacies. The manufacturing business group manufactures and markets high-quality active pharmaceutical ingredients (APIs), pharmaceuticals, diagnostic reagents and medical devices that meet stringent requirements. This division also researches, develops, manufactures and markets distinctive, unique products and undertake contract manufacturing of pharmaceuticals. Last, the medical-related business group engages in expanding business within the healthcare industry primarily to meet the medical needs of Alfresa's dispensing pharmacy and medical-related businesses. Just a few of Aflresa Holdings' many subsidiaries include: Alfresa Corporation, Aflresa Healthcare Corporation, Alfresa Pharma Corporation, Alfresa System Corporation and Apollo Medical Holdings, Inc.

FINANCIAL DATA: *Note: Data for latest year may not have been available at press time.*

In U.S. $	2020	2019	2018	2017	2016	2015
Revenue	24,645,910,000	24,115,960,000	23,772,530,000	23,306,690,000	23,529,910,000	
R&D Expense						
Operating Income	435,151,100	408,893,800	381,366,900	303,480,600	413,624,600	
Operating Margin %	.02%	.02%	.02%	.01%	.02%	
SGA Expense						
Net Income	367,813,500	380,837,200	325,034,500	282,145,900	319,426,800	
Operating Cash Flow	308,951,300	428,155,200	434,502,700	313,645,700	345,556,400	
Capital Expenditure	187,920,700	124,839,000	112,957,000	124,281,900	130,081,400	
EBITDA	649,429,700	658,370,900	568,301,200	509,667,300	594,239,000	
Return on Assets %	.03%	.03%	.03%	.02%	.03%	
Return on Equity %	.09%	.10%	.09%	.08%	.10%	
Debt to Equity	0.01	0.01	0.01	0.012	0.013	

CONTACT INFORMATION:

Phone: 81 352195100   Fax: 81 352195102
Toll-Free:
Address: 1-1-3 Otemachi, Tokyo, 100-0004 Japan

STOCK TICKER/OTHER:

Stock Ticker: ALFRY
Employees: 14,718
Parent Company:

Exchange: GREY
Fiscal Year Ends:

SALARIES/BONUSES:

Top Exec. Salary: $ Bonus: $
Second Exec. Salary: $ Bonus: $

OTHER THOUGHTS:

Estimated Female Officers or Directors:
Hot Spot for Advancement for Women/Minorities:

Align Technology Inc

NAIC Code: 339100

www.aligntech.com

TYPES OF BUSINESS:

Orthodontic Equipment
Dental Alignment Products
Oral Scanners
Digital Services
Dentistry
Orthodontics
Dental Records Storage
Product Manufacturing

BRANDS/DIVISIONS/AFFILIATES:

Invisalign
ClinCheck
Vivera Retainers
Invisalign Comprehensive Package
Mandibular Advancement
iTero
OrthoCAD
exocad Global Holdings GmbH

CONTACTS: Note: Officers with more than one job title may be intentionally listed here more than once.

Joseph Hogan, CEO
John Morici, CFO
Charles Larkin, Chairman of the Board
Roger George, Chief Legal Officer
Raphael Pascaud, Chief Marketing Officer
Vamsi Pudipeddi, Chief Marketing Officer
Zelko Relic, Chief Technology Officer
Yuval Shaked, Managing Director, Divisional
Jennifer Olson, Managing Director, Divisional
Julie Tay, Managing Director, Geographical
Simon Beard, Managing Director, Geographical
Stuart Hockridge, Senior VP, Divisional
Sreelakshmi Kolli, Senior VP, Divisional
Emory Wright, Senior VP, Divisional

GROWTH PLANS/SPECIAL FEATURES:

Align Technology, Inc. (ATI) designs, manufactures and markets a system of clear aligner therapy, intra-oral scanners and CAD/CAM (computer-aided design and computer-aided manufacturing) digital services used in dentistry, orthodontics and dental records storage. The company operates in two segments: clear aligner and scanners and services. Clear aligner produces Invisalign for the treatment of malocclusion (misalignment of the teeth). Invisalign is series of doctor prescribed, custom manufactured, clear plastic removable orthodontic aligners. Customized systems are designed in conjunction with the ClinCheck software program, which works off an original mold of the patient's mouth and makes incremental adjustments that eventually lead to total alignment. Upon completion of the treatment, the patient may be prescribed a single clear retainer product or one of the company's Vivera Retainers. Invisalign Comprehensive Package replaces, yet includes, the features of both Invisalign Full and Invisalign Teen treatments, but also encompasses the Mandibular Advancement feature, which is used for a wide range of malocclusion and orthodontic needs. Scanners and CAD/CAM services utilize intra-oral scanning to create a 3D image of a patient's teeth using a handheld intra-oral scanner inside the mouth, as opposed to the traditional methods of taking a mold or physical impression. The company's iTero scanner is used by dental professionals and/or labs for restorative and orthodontic digital procedures as well as Invisalign digital impression submission. It stands as the only intra-oral scanner system in the market based on parallel confocal imaging, which can capture 100,000 points of laser light in perfect focus. These images are used in the OrthoCAD program, which aid in the fabrication of veneers, inlays, onlays, crowns, bridges and implant abutment; Invisalign digital impressions; and digital records storage.

FINANCIAL DATA: Note: Data for latest year may not have been available at press time.

In U.S. $	2020	2019	2018	2017	2016	2015
Revenue	2,471,941,000	2,406,796,000	1,966,492,000	1,473,413,000	1,079,874,000	845,486,000
R&D Expense	175,307,000	157,361,000	128,899,000	97,559,000	75,720,000	61,237,000
Operating Income	387,171,000	514,483,000	466,564,000	353,611,000	248,921,000	188,634,000
Operating Margin %		.21%	.24%	.24%	.23%	.22%
SGA Expense	1,200,757,000	1,072,053,000	852,404,000	665,777,000	490,653,000	390,239,000
Net Income	1,775,888,000	442,776,000	400,235,000	231,418,000	189,682,000	144,020,000
Operating Cash Flow	662,174,000	747,270,000	554,681,000	438,539,000	247,654,000	237,997,000
Capital Expenditure	154,916,000	149,707,000	223,312,000	195,695,000	70,576,000	53,451,000
EBITDA	480,709,000	593,473,000	521,291,000	391,350,000	272,923,000	206,638,000
Return on Assets %		.19%	.21%	.15%	.15%	.13%
Return on Equity %		.34%	.33%	.22%	.21%	.18%
Debt to Equity		0.032				

CONTACT INFORMATION:

Phone: 602-742-2000   Fax:
Toll-Free:
Address: 410 N. Scottsdale Rd., Ste. 1300, Tempe, AZ 85281 United States

STOCK TICKER/OTHER:

Stock Ticker: ALGN
Employees: 18,070
Parent Company:

Exchange: NAS
Fiscal Year Ends: 12/31

SALARIES/BONUSES:

Top Exec. Salary: $ Bonus: $
Second Exec. Salary: $ Bonus: $

OTHER THOUGHTS:

Estimated Female Officers or Directors: 2
Hot Spot for Advancement for Women/Minorities:

Alignment Healthcare LLC

www.alignmenthealthcare.com

NAIC Code: 524114

TYPES OF BUSINESS:

Medicare Plans
Population Health Management Solutions
End-to-End Care Program
Health Evaluation
Diabetes Management
Post-Hospitalization Care
Wound Care
Technologies

BRANDS/DIVISIONS/AFFILIATES:

Alignment Health Services
Alignment Health Plan

CONTACTS: Note: Officers with more than one job title may be intentionally listed here more than once.

John Kao, CEO

GROWTH PLANS/SPECIAL FEATURES:

Alignment Healthcare, LLC and its subsidiaries provide population health management to medical partners in California and North Carolina, USA. Based in Orange, California, Alignment Healthcare focuses on improving the health and wellness of seniors. The firm offers healthcare partners a continuous end-to-end care program, including clinical care coordination, risk management capabilities and IT enablement. The company's offerings include health evaluation, diabetes management, post hospitalization care and wound care services; and a command center solution that allows its clinical care teams to access and stratify large quantities of real time and historical patient data. Management capabilities include risk contracting, revenue optimization, catastrophic case management, care management, Rx management, claims adjustment and much more. Alignment Healthcare operates a Medicare Advantage prescription drug plan organization that provides care and service to its Medicare Advantage members in select areas. Alignment Health Services is a business unit that offers the company's proprietary technology to third parties, allowing partner companies to access Alignment's clinical model and population health technology while taking on financial risk themselves. Alignment Health Plan offers health plan options.

FINANCIAL DATA: Note: Data for latest year may not have been available at press time.

In U.S. $	2020	2019	2018	2017	2016	2015
Revenue	959,222,000	756,961,000				
R&D Expense						
Operating Income	-5,263,000	-29,484,000				
Operating Margin %						
SGA Expense	156,398,000	110,134,000				
Net Income	-22,926,000	-44,732,000				
Operating Cash Flow	7,561,000	9,208,000				
Capital Expenditure	15,708,000	10,245,000				
EBITDA	9,466,000	-13,252,000				
Return on Assets %						
Return on Equity %						
Debt to Equity						

CONTACT INFORMATION:

Phone: 844-310-2247   Fax: 844-320-2247
Toll-Free:
Address: 1100 W. Town and Country Rd., Ste. 1600, Orange, CA 92868 United States

STOCK TICKER/OTHER:

Stock Ticker: ALHC
Employees: 775
Parent Company:

Exchange: NAS
Fiscal Year Ends: 12/31

SALARIES/BONUSES:

Top Exec. Salary: $ Bonus: $
Second Exec. Salary: $ Bonus: $

OTHER THOUGHTS:

Estimated Female Officers or Directors:
Hot Spot for Advancement for Women/Minorities:

Sales, profits and employees may be estimates. Financial information, benefits and other data can change quickly and may vary from those stated here.

Allergan Aesthetics, an AbbVie Company

www.allergan.com

NAIC Code: 325412

TYPES OF BUSINESS:

Pharmaceutical Development
Aesthetics Products
Dermatological Products
Facial Injectables
Body Contouring
Skin Care
Research and Development

BRANDS/DIVISIONS/AFFILIATES:

AbbVie Inc
BOTOX
JUVEDERM
KYBELLA
CoolSculpting
Natrelle
KELLER FUNNEL 2
Allergian plc

CONTACTS: Note: Officers with more than one job title may be intentionally listed here more than once.

Carrie Storm, Pres.
William Meury, Executive VP, Divisional
Charles Mayr, Other Executive Officer
Patrick Eagan, Other Executive Officer
Karen Ling, Other Executive Officer
Robert Bailey, Other Executive Officer

GROWTH PLANS/SPECIAL FEATURES:

Allergan Aesthetics, an AbbVie Company (formerly Allergan plc), develops, manufactures and markets products and technologies that drive the advancement of aesthetic medicine. The firm's portfolio includes facial injectables, body contouring, plastics, skin care and more. Allergan Aesthetics' research and development team focuses on the innovation of science-based aesthetic products. The company's brands include BOTOX cosmetics, JUVEDERM fillers, KYBELLA injections, CoolSculpting, CoolTone, Natrelle, KELLER FUNNEL 2, REVOLVD, Skin Medica, and LATISSE. During 2020, Allergan was acquired by AbbVie, Inc. Allergan Aesthetics' regenerative medicines portfolio offers plastic and general surgery customers with dermal matrix products under the AlloDerm (regenerative tissue) and Strattice (reconstructive tissue) brand names.

FINANCIAL DATA: Note: Data for latest year may not have been available at press time.

In U.S. $	2020	2019	2018	2017	2016	2015
Revenue	16,732,456,000	16,088,900,000	15,787,400,192	15,940,700,160	14,570,600,448	15,070,999,552
R&D Expense						
Operating Income						
Operating Margin %						
SGA Expense						
Net Income		-5,271,000,000	-5,096,399,872	-4,125,499,904	14,973,400,064	3,915,200,000
Operating Cash Flow						
Capital Expenditure						
EBITDA						
Return on Assets %						
Return on Equity %						
Debt to Equity						

CONTACT INFORMATION:

Phone: 714-246-4500   Fax:
Toll-Free:
Address: 2525 Dupont Dr., Irvine, CA 92612 United States

STOCK TICKER/OTHER:

Stock Ticker: Subsidiary
Employees: 17,400
Parent Company: AbbVie Inc

Exchange:
Fiscal Year Ends: 12/31

SALARIES/BONUSES:

Top Exec. Salary: $ Bonus: $
Second Exec. Salary: $ Bonus: $

OTHER THOUGHTS:

Estimated Female Officers or Directors: 2
Hot Spot for Advancement for Women/Minorities: Y

Alliance HealthCare Services Inc **www.alliancehealthcareservices-us.com**

NAIC Code: 621512

TYPES OF BUSINESS:

Diagnostic Imaging Centers
Diagnostic Imaging Support Services
MRI Imaging
PET Imaging
CT Imaging
Radiation Therapy

BRANDS/DIVISIONS/AFFILIATES:

Akumin Inc
Alliance HealthCare Radiology
Alliance Oncology LLC
Alliance HealthCare Interventional Partners LLC

CONTACTS: *Note: Officers with more than one job title may be intentionally listed here more than once.*

Riadh Zine, Co-CEO
Rhonda A. Longmore-Grund, Co-CEO
Laurie Miller, Executive VP, Divisional
Richard Jones, President, Divisional
Gregory Spurlock, President, Divisional
Steven Siwek, President, Divisional
Larry Buckelew, Vice Chairman of the Board

GROWTH PLANS/SPECIAL FEATURES:

Alliance HealthCare Services, Inc. provides outsourced health care services to hospitals and providers. The company also operates freestanding outpatient radiology, oncology and interventional clinics, as well as ambulatory surgical centers (ASCs) that are not owned by hospitals or providers. Mobile imaging services is provided, as well as various modalities of fixed site locations. The radiology segment offers operations management solutions, including patient scheduling, prior authorization services, physician sales and marketing support, and certified clinical staffing. Diagnostic radiology services are delivered through Alliance HealthCare Radiology; and radiation oncology services through Alliance Oncology, LLC. Alliance Oncology partners directly with hospitals, physicians and other healthcare providers to offer the latest oncology technologies to them. Interventional and pain management services are provided at ambulatory surgical centers and pain management centers through Alliance HealthCare Interventional Partners, LLC. This division specializes in combatting opioid use. Headquartered in California, Alliance HealthCare operates diagnostic radiology, radiation therapy and interventional systems, including fixed-site radiology locations, cancer care centers and pain management/interventional procedures clinics. The firm provides clinical services for hospitals and healthcare partners throughout the U.S. In September 2021, Alliance HealthCare Services was acquired by Akumin, Inc. for approximately $820 million.

Alliance HealthCare offers its employees health coverage, life and disability insurance, tax-deferred savings plan, education assistance and more.

FINANCIAL DATA: *Note: Data for latest year may not have been available at press time.*

In U.S. $	2020	2019	2018	2017	2016	2015
Revenue	539,673,750	606,375,000	577,500,000	550,000,000	505,548,992	473,054,016
R&D Expense						
Operating Income						
Operating Margin %						
SGA Expense						
Net Income						
Operating Cash Flow						
Capital Expenditure						
EBITDA						
Return on Assets %						
Return on Equity %						
Debt to Equity						

CONTACT INFORMATION:

Phone: Fax:
Toll-Free: 800-544-3215
Address: 18201 Von Karman Ave., Ste. 600, Irvine, CA 92612 United States

STOCK TICKER/OTHER:

Stock Ticker: Subsidiary
Employees: 2,750
Parent Company: Akumin Inc

Exchange:
Fiscal Year Ends: 12/31

SALARIES/BONUSES:

Top Exec. Salary: $ Bonus: $
Second Exec. Salary: $ Bonus: $

OTHER THOUGHTS:

Estimated Female Officers or Directors: 1
Hot Spot for Advancement for Women/Minorities:

Sales, profits and employees may be estimates. Financial information, benefits and other data can change quickly and may vary from those stated here.

Allied Healthcare International Inc

www.alliedhealthcare.com

NAIC Code: 561320

TYPES OF BUSINESS:

Temporary Staffing
Home Health Care
Nursing & Para-Professional Services
Home Medical Equipment & Oxygen
Respiration Therapy
Medical Staffing

BRANDS/DIVISIONS/AFFILIATES:

Castlerock Recruitment Group Ltd

CONTACTS: Note: Officers with more than one job title may be intentionally listed here more than once.

Narinder Singh, CEO

GROWTH PLANS/SPECIAL FEATURES:

Allied Healthcare International, Inc. provides flexible healthcare staffing throughout the U.K. market, England, Scotland and Wales. Allied Healthcare outsources nurses, nurse aides and home health aides to hospitals, nursing homes, care homes, private companies, prisons, police stations, armed services hospitals and private homes on a per diem basis. A large portion of the company's revenues come from U.K. government entities, primarily local social-services departments and National Health Service (NHS) hospitals. Homecare for individuals includes traditional homecare, dementia care, care for those with learning disabilities, end-of-life care, as well as related children and family services. Live-in care is provided for those who need full-time support and 24-hour care to continue living in their own home. Live-in care can be a short-term solution during recovery periods, or a long-term option. Re-ablement care helps patients learn new skills or re-learn existing ones, whether the patient is recovering from an operation or illness, or lives with physical difficulties. Allied Healthcare's nurses are experienced in a wide-range of specialties to serve public and private hospitals, clinics and healthcare professionals. Allied Healthcare is owned by Castlerock Recruitment Group Ltd., a U.K.-based specialist healthcare recruitment agency.

FINANCIAL DATA: Note: Data for latest year may not have been available at press time.

In U.S. $	2020	2019	2018	2017	2016	2015
Revenue	483,787,500	509,250,000	485,000,000	462,000,000	440,000,000	430,000,000
R&D Expense						
Operating Income						
Operating Margin %						
SGA Expense						
Net Income						
Operating Cash Flow						
Capital Expenditure						
EBITDA						
Return on Assets %						
Return on Equity %						
Debt to Equity						

CONTACT INFORMATION:

Phone: Fax:
Toll-Free: 800-542-1078
Address: Cavendish House, Lakhpur Court, Staffordshire Tech, Stafford, ST18 0FX United Kingdom

STOCK TICKER/OTHER:

Stock Ticker: Subsidiary
Employees: 8,000
Parent Company: Castlerock Recruitement Group Ltd
Exchange:
Fiscal Year Ends: 12/31

SALARIES/BONUSES:

Top Exec. Salary: $ Bonus: $
Second Exec. Salary: $ Bonus: $

OTHER THOUGHTS:

Estimated Female Officers or Directors:
Hot Spot for Advancement for Women/Minorities: Y

Allina Health

www.allinahealth.org

NAIC Code: 622110

TYPES OF BUSINESS:

General Medical and Surgical Hospitals
Clinics
Medical Equipment Rental
Emergency Medical Transportation Services
Hospice Care
Pharmacies
Rehabilitation Services

BRANDS/DIVISIONS/AFFILIATES:

Abbott Northwestern Hospital
Buffalo Hospital
Cambridge Medical Center
New Ulm Medical Center
Phillips Eye Institute
River Falls Area Hospital
Courage Kenny Rehabilitation Institute

CONTACTS: *Note: Officers with more than one job title may be intentionally listed here more than once.*

Lisa Shannon, Pres.
Ric Magnuson, CFO
Jeff Shoemate, CMO
Christine Webster Moore, Chief Human Resources Officer
Penny Ann Wheeler, Chief Clinical Officer
Jonathan Shoemaker, CIO
Duncan P. Gallagher, Exec. VP-Admin.
Elizabeth Truesdell Smith, General Counsel
Robert Wieland, Exec. VP-Clinic & Community Div.
Thomas O'Connor, VP
Ben Bache-Wiig, VP
Sara Criger, VP

GROWTH PLANS/SPECIAL FEATURES:

Allina Health is a nonprofit network of hospitals, clinics and other healthcare services located throughout Minnesota and western Wisconsin. The company's operations encompass 11 hospitals, more than 90 clinics (primary care, urgent care, every day care and hospital-based clinics), 52 rehabilitation locations, 15 retail pharmacies, two ambulatory care centers and specialty medical services. The firm's hospitals include Abbott Northwestern Hospital, Buffalo Hospital, Cambridge Medical Center, New Ulm Medical Center, Phillips Eye Institute and River Falls Area Hospital. Phillips Eye Institute is one of the largest specialty hospitals in the U.S. dedicated to eye diseases and disorders. The Courage Kenny Rehabilitation Institute treats patients for conditions such as stroke and back pain as well as sports-related, spinal cord and brain injuries. Specialty medical services by Allina Health include hospice care, oxygen and home medical equipment and emergency medical transportation.

Employee benefits include medical and dental coverage, wellness programs, an employee assistance program, a retirement savings account, a health savings account, life and AD&D insurance, short- and long-term disability, tuition reimbursement, adoption ass

FINANCIAL DATA: *Note: Data for latest year may not have been available at press time.*

In U.S. $	2020	2019	2018	2017	2016	2015
Revenue	4,469,220,860	4,655,438,396	4,563,320,184	4,279,104,311	4,103,552,249	3,937,422,813
R&D Expense						
Operating Income						
Operating Margin %						
SGA Expense						
Net Income		116,522,712	167,923,797	173,116,225	30,812,991	199,411,489
Operating Cash Flow						
Capital Expenditure						
EBITDA						
Return on Assets %						
Return on Equity %						
Debt to Equity						

CONTACT INFORMATION:

Phone: 612-262-9000   Fax:
Toll-Free: 800-859-5077
Address: 2925 Chicago Ave., Minneapolis, MN 55407 United States

STOCK TICKER/OTHER:

Stock Ticker: Nonprofit   Exchange:
Employees: 29,382   Fiscal Year Ends: 12/31
Parent Company:

SALARIES/BONUSES:

Top Exec. Salary: $ Bonus: $
Second Exec. Salary: $ Bonus: $

OTHER THOUGHTS:

Estimated Female Officers or Directors: 8
Hot Spot for Advancement for Women/Minorities: Y

Allogene Therapeutics Inc

www.allogene.com

NAIC Code: 325414

TYPES OF BUSINESS:

Biological Product (except Diagnostic) Manufacturing
Drug Development
Clinical Testing
Cancer Therapies
Cell Therapy Manufacturing

BRANDS/DIVISIONS/AFFILIATES:

UCART19
ALLO-501
ALLO-715
ALLO-501A
ALLO-715
ALLO-316
ALLO-605

CONTACTS: Note: Officers with more than one job title may be intentionally listed here more than once.

David Chang, CEO
Eric Schmidt, CFO
Arie Belldegrun, Chairman of the Board
Alison Moore, Chief Technology Officer

GROWTH PLANS/SPECIAL FEATURES:

Allogene Therapeutics, Inc. is a clinical stage immuno-oncology company engaged in the development and commercialization of genetically-engineered allogeneic T cell therapies for the treatment of cancer. The firm is developing a pipeline of off-the-shelf T cell product candidates designed to target and kill cancer cells. Allogene's T cells are allogenic, meaning they are derived from healthy donors for intended use in any patient, rather than from an individual patient for that patient's use, as in the case of autologous T cells. In collaboration with Servier, Allogene is developing UCART19 and ALLO-501, chimeric antigen receptor (CAR) T cell product candidates targeting CD19 (a B-lymphocyte antigen). Phase 1 clinical trials of UCART19 included: two trials in patients with relapsed/refractory B-cell precursor acute lymphoblastic leukemia (ALL), one for adult patients and one for pediatric patients. Other pipeline product candidates include those in Phase 1 studies for the treatment of relapsed/refractory non-Hodgkin lymphoma (NHL), relapsed/refractory multiple myeloma (MM) and renal cell carcinoma include ALLO-715, ALLO-501A, ALLO-715, ALLO-316 and ALLO-605. Allogene uses TALEN gene-editing technology (by Cellectis SA). The company also leases a facility in Newark, California where it manufactures cell therapies. During 2021, Allogene announced that it was granted U.S. Food and Drug Administration (FDA) Orphan Drug Designation for ALLO-715 for the treatment of MM; and was granted FDA Fast Track Designation for ALLO-605 for the treatment of relapsed/refractory MM.

FINANCIAL DATA: Note: Data for latest year may not have been available at press time.

In U.S. $	2020	2019	2018	2017	2016	2015
Revenue						
R&D Expense	192,987,000	144,535,000	151,860,000			
Operating Income	-258,243,000	-202,008,000	-192,842,000			
Operating Margin %						
SGA Expense	65,256,000	57,473,000	40,982,000			
Net Income	-250,221,000	-184,594,000	-211,505,000			
Operating Cash Flow	-115,093,000	-137,350,000	-44,653,000			
Capital Expenditure	65,958,000	50,791,000	3,234,000			
EBITDA	-242,635,000	-179,898,000	-206,764,000			
Return on Assets %		- .25%	- .55%			
Return on Equity %		- .28%	- .60%			
Debt to Equity		0.082	0.049			

CONTACT INFORMATION:

Phone: 650 457-2700   Fax:
Toll-Free:
Address: 210 East Grand Ave., South San Francisco, CA 94080 United States

STOCK TICKER/OTHER:

Stock Ticker: ALLO
Employees: 265
Parent Company:

Exchange: NAS
Fiscal Year Ends: 12/31

SALARIES/BONUSES:

Top Exec. Salary: $ Bonus: $
Second Exec. Salary: $ Bonus: $

OTHER THOUGHTS:

Estimated Female Officers or Directors:
Hot Spot for Advancement for Women/Minorities:

Allscripts Healthcare Solutions Inc

www.allscripts.com

NAIC Code: 511210D

TYPES OF BUSINESS:

Computer Software, Healthcare & Biotechnology
Interactive Education Services
Clinical Software
Electronic Records Systems
Care Management Software

BRANDS/DIVISIONS/AFFILIATES:

Sunrise
Paragon
Allscripts TouchWorks EHR
Allscripts Professional EHR
Veradigm
FollowMyHealth
Allscripts CareInMotion
2bPrecise

CONTACTS: *Note: Officers with more than one job title may be intentionally listed here more than once.*

Paul Black, CEO
Dennis Olis, CFO
Brian Farley, Chief Administrative Officer
Michael Klayko, Director
Lisa Khorey, Executive VP
Richard Poulton, President

GROWTH PLANS/SPECIAL FEATURES:

Allscripts Healthcare Solutions, Inc. provides clinical software, connectivity and information solutions for physicians and healthcare providers. The firm provides software solutions to physicians, hospitals, governments, health systems, health plans, life-sciences companies, retail clinics, retail pharmacies, pharmacy benefit managers, insurance companies, employer wellness clinics, post-acute organizations, consumers and lab companies. The company's electronic health records (EHR) solutions are built on an open platform with advanced clinical decision support via analysis and insights. EHR brands include Sunrise, Paragon, Allscripts TouchWorks EHR and Allscripts Professional EHR. Payer and life sciences solutions include the Veradigm brand of integrated data systems and services, which combine data-driven clinical insights with actionable tools for clinical workflow, research, analytics and media. Consumer solutions include the FollowMyHealth platform, for patient engagement via telehealth and remote patient monitoring. Financial management solutions support revenue cycle, claims management, budgeting and analytic functions for healthcare organizations. These tools can help change clinician behavior to improve patient flow, increase quality, advance outcomes, optimize referral networks, decrease leakage and reduce costs. Population health management solutions includes Allscripts CareInMotion, a community-connected population health management platform that delivers care coordination, connectivity, data aggregation and analytics. 2bPrecise is a precision medicine solution for enabling a personalized approach regarding diagnostic, therapeutic and preventive interventions. Allscripts offers customizable professional and managed service offerings, from hosting, consulting, optimization and managed IT services to revenue cycle services. Allscripts' facilities are primarily located in the U.S., but the company also maintains facilities in Canada, India, Israel and the U.K.

Allscripts offers its employees medical, dental and vision insurance; flex spending accounts; 401(k); adoption assistance; and education assistance.

FINANCIAL DATA: *Note: Data for latest year may not have been available at press time.*

In U.S. $	2020	2019	2018	2017	2016	2015
Revenue	1,502,700,000	1,771,677,000	1,749,962,000	1,806,342,000	1,549,899,000	1,386,393,000
R&D Expense	206,061,000	254,509,000	268,409,000	220,219,000	187,906,000	184,791,000
Operating Income	-55,911,000	12,081,000	-21,420,000	41,917,000	64,421,000	33,427,000
Operating Margin %		.01%	-.01%	.02%	.04%	.02%
SGA Expense	389,941,000	419,774,000	450,967,000	486,271,000	392,865,000	339,175,000
Net Income	700,407,000	-182,178,000	363,740,000	-196,459,000	-25,652,000	-2,226,000
Operating Cash Flow	-106,715,000	46,254,000	67,891,000	279,415,000	269,004,000	211,579,000
Capital Expenditure	105,018,000	130,436,000	144,617,000	185,271,000	137,982,000	67,586,000
EBITDA	97,782,000	66,296,000	256,398,000	96,398,000	220,523,000	191,544,000
Return on Assets %		-.06%	.10%	-.05%	-.01%	.00%
Return on Equity %		-.13%	.27%	-.17%	-.02%	.00%
Debt to Equity		0.503	0.418	1.373	1.059	0.435

CONTACT INFORMATION:

Phone: 866 358-6869   Fax:
Toll-Free: 800-654-0889
Address: 222 Merchandise Mart Plz., Ste. 2024, Chicago, IL 60654
United States

STOCK TICKER/OTHER:

Stock Ticker: MDRX
Employees: 8,400
Parent Company:

Exchange: NAS
Fiscal Year Ends: 12/31

SALARIES/BONUSES:

Top Exec. Salary: $ Bonus: $
Second Exec. Salary: $ Bonus: $

OTHER THOUGHTS:

Estimated Female Officers or Directors: 2
Hot Spot for Advancement for Women/Minorities: Y

Sales, profits and employees may be estimates. Financial information, benefits and other data can change quickly and may vary from those stated here.

Amedisys Inc

NAIC Code: 621610

www.amedisys.com

TYPES OF BUSINESS:

Home Health Care Services
Home Health Care
Hospice Care
Personal Assistance Care

BRANDS/DIVISIONS/AFFILIATES:

CONTACTS: *Note: Officers with more than one job title may be intentionally listed here more than once.*

Donald Washburn, Chairman of the Board
Scott Ginn, Chief Accounting Officer
Michael North, Chief Information Officer
Christopher Gerard, COO
Paul Kusserow, Director
David Kemmerly, General Counsel
David Pearce, Other Executive Officer
Sharon Brunecz, Other Executive Officer

GROWTH PLANS/SPECIAL FEATURES:

Amedisys, Inc. is a healthcare services company focused on providing care in the home. The firm serves patients across 39 U.S. states through three business segments: home health, hospice and personal care. The home health segment provides care to a variety of patients: those recovering from surgery or illness, those living with chronic diseases, and to those who want to prevent being re-admitted in a hospital. This division includes more than 320 care centers located in 34 U.S. states and the District of Columbia. Within these care centers, Amedisys deploys skilled nurses, rehabilitation therapists and social workers. The hospice segment provides comfort and support for those dealing with a terminal illness. It is a benevolent form of care that promotes dignity and affirms quality of life for the patient, family members and other loved ones. Those eligible for hospice care include individuals with heart disease, pulmonary disease, Alzheimer's, HIV/AIDS or cancer, if they have a life expectancy of six months or less. Amedisys operates 180 Medicare-certified hospice care centers throughout the country. Last, the personal care segment provides assistance with the essential activities of daily living, enabling patients to maintain a sense of independence.

FINANCIAL DATA: *Note: Data for latest year may not have been available at press time.*

In U.S. $	2020	2019	2018	2017	2016	2015
Revenue	2,071,519,000	1,955,633,000	1,662,578,000	1,533,680,000	1,437,454,000	1,280,541,000
R&D Expense						
Operating Income	223,420,000	178,942,000	155,148,000	108,559,000	61,772,000	68,102,000
Operating Margin %		.09%	.09%	.07%	.04%	.05%
SGA Expense	668,300,000	607,926,000	501,306,000	482,213,000	503,430,000	452,435,000
Net Income	183,608,000	126,833,000	119,346,000	30,301,000	37,261,000	-3,021,000
Operating Cash Flow	288,952,000	202,000,000	223,483,000	105,731,000	62,259,000	107,785,000
Capital Expenditure	5,332,000	7,888,000	6,558,000	10,707,000	15,717,000	21,429,000
EBITDA	289,799,000	239,258,000	179,619,000	102,955,000	86,408,000	30,511,000
Return on Assets %		.13%	.16%	.04%	.05%	.00%
Return on Equity %		.23%	.24%	.06%	.09%	-.01%
Debt to Equity		0.45	0.012	0.152	0.191	0.232

CONTACT INFORMATION:

Phone: 225 292-2031   Fax:
Toll-Free: 800-467-2662
Address: 3854 American Way, Ste. A, Baton Rouge, LA 70816 United States

STOCK TICKER/OTHER:

Stock Ticker: AMED
Employees: 21,000
Parent Company:

Exchange: NAS
Fiscal Year Ends: 12/31

SALARIES/BONUSES:

Top Exec. Salary: $ Bonus: $
Second Exec. Salary: $ Bonus: $

OTHER THOUGHTS:

Estimated Female Officers or Directors: 3
Hot Spot for Advancement for Women/Minorities: Y

American HomePatient Inc

www.ahom.com

NAIC Code: 621610

TYPES OF BUSINESS:

Home Health Care Services
Respiratory Therapy Services
Infusion Therapy Services
Equipment Leasing
Home Health Supplies
Enteral Nutrition Products and Services

BRANDS/DIVISIONS/AFFILIATES:

Linde Group (The)
Lincare Holdings Inc

CONTACTS: *Note: Officers with more than one job title may be intentionally listed here more than once.*

Mark Lamp, CEO
Mark L. Lamp, Pres.

GROWTH PLANS/SPECIAL FEATURES:

American HomePatient, Inc. provides home healthcare services and products consisting primarily of respiratory and infusion therapies and the rental and sale of home medical equipment and home healthcare supplies. The firm provides products and services to over 250 centers. These products and services are paid for primarily by Medicare, Medicaid and other third-party payers. American HomePatient provides a wide variety of home respiratory services primarily to patients with severe and chronic pulmonary diseases. The firm's respiratory services consist of oxygen systems to assist in breathing, including oxygen concentrators, liquid oxygen systems and high-pressure oxygen cylinders; nebulizers and related inhalation drugs; respiratory assist devices for patients with obstructive sleep apnea; home ventilators; non-invasive positive-pressure ventilation masks; and home respiratory evaluations and related diagnostic equipment. Its home infusion therapy services include pumps and related supplies, infusion pharmacy services and infusion therapies and treatments. Its home medical equipment operations consist principally of the rental and sale of wheelchairs, walking aids, lift chairs, hospital beds and rehabilitation equipment. American HomePatient is owned by Lincare Holdings, Inc., which itself is a subsidiary of industrial gas and engineering company, The Linde Group.

FINANCIAL DATA: *Note: Data for latest year may not have been available at press time.*

In U.S. $	2020	2019	2018	2017	2016	2015
Revenue	382,318,621	347,562,383	331,011,794	315,249,328	300,237,455	292,000,000
R&D Expense						
Operating Income						
Operating Margin %						
SGA Expense						
Net Income						
Operating Cash Flow						
Capital Expenditure						
EBITDA						
Return on Assets %						
Return on Equity %						
Debt to Equity						

CONTACT INFORMATION:

Phone: 615-221-8884   Fax:
Toll-Free: 800-890-7271
Address: 5200 Maryland Way, Ste. 400, Brentwood, TN 37027 United States

STOCK TICKER/OTHER:

Stock Ticker: Subsidiary
Employees: 2,177
Parent Company: Linde Group (The)

Exchange:
Fiscal Year Ends: 12/31

SALARIES/BONUSES:

Top Exec. Salary: $ Bonus: $
Second Exec. Salary: $ Bonus: $

OTHER THOUGHTS:

Estimated Female Officers or Directors:
Hot Spot for Advancement for Women/Minorities:

American Well Corporation (Amwell)

business.amwell.com

NAIC Code: 621111

TYPES OF BUSINESS:

Telemedical Clinic
Telehealth

BRANDS/DIVISIONS/AFFILIATES:

Amwell

CONTACTS: *Note: Officers with more than one job title may be intentionally listed here more than once.*

Ido Schoenberg, CEO
Roy Schoenberg, Pres.
Keith Anderson, CFO
Mary Modahl, CMO
Amber Howe, Chief People Officer
Jason Medeiros, CIO
Ido Schoenberg, Chmn.

GROWTH PLANS/SPECIAL FEATURES:

American Well Corporation operates as Amwell and is a telehealth company offering digital delivery of care. The firm connects and enables providers, insurers and innovators with patients to deliver greater access to affordable, quality care. Amwell offers clients core technology and services for developing and distributing telehealth programs that meet their strategic, operational and social objectives under their own brands. Its scalable technology embeds with the clients' existing offerings and clinical workflows, spanning the continuum of care and enabling care delivery across a wide range of clinical, retail, school and home settings. As of June 30, 2020, Amwell powered the digital care programs of 55 health plans, which support over 36,000 employers and collectively represent more than 80 million covered lives, as well as 150 of the U.S.'s largest health systems, encompassing 200+ hospitals. Since its 2006 inception, Amwell has powered over 5.6 million telehealth visits for clients, including more than 2.9 million in the six months ending June 30, 2020. In September 2020, Amwell announced a partnership with Tyto Care, an all-in-one modular device and examination platform for artificial intelligence (AI)-powered, on-demand, remote medical exams. Together the companies will introduce exclusive integrations, workflows and tools to enhance the ability for providers using the Amwell platform to examine and diagnose patients virtually. In addition, Amwell will become a reseller of Tyto Care's integrated devices.

FINANCIAL DATA: *Note: Data for latest year may not have been available at press time.*

In U.S. $	2020	2019	2018	2017	2016	2015
Revenue	245,265,000	148,857,000	113,955,000			
R&D Expense	84,412,000	53,941,000	36,273,000			
Operating Income	-227,431,000	-94,704,000	-55,106,000			
Operating Margin %						
SGA Expense	221,341,000	101,883,000	68,846,000			
Net Income	-224,432,000	-87,190,000	-52,674,000			
Operating Cash Flow	-112,464,000	-81,892,000	-74,006,000			
Capital Expenditure	3,318,000	1,338,000	1,911,000			
EBITDA	-217,278,000	-86,943,000	-49,776,000			
Return on Assets %						
Return on Equity %						
Debt to Equity						

CONTACT INFORMATION:

Phone: 617 205-3500 Fax:
Toll-Free:
Address: 75 State St., 26/Fl, Boston, MA 02109 United States

SALARIES/BONUSES:

Top Exec. Salary: $ Bonus: $
Second Exec. Salary: $ Bonus: $

STOCK TICKER/OTHER:

Stock Ticker: AMWL Exchange: NYS
Employees: 812 Fiscal Year Ends:
Parent Company:

OTHER THOUGHTS:

Estimated Female Officers or Directors:
Hot Spot for Advancement for Women/Minorities:

Amerigroup Corporation

www.amerigroup.com

NAIC Code: 524114

TYPES OF BUSINESS:

Managed Health Care
State-Sponsored Health Benefits

BRANDS/DIVISIONS/AFFILIATES:

Anthem Inc

GROWTH PLANS/SPECIAL FEATURES:

Amerigroup Corporation is the state-sponsored program services division of health benefits company Anthem, Inc. These programs include Medicaid, Family Care and the Children's Health Insurance Program (CHIP), across all states. Amerigroup also offers Medicare plans throughout the U.S. The firm reduces costs for families and state governments by combining social and behavioral health services to help members obtain health care. Amerigroup's provider networks consist of: hospitals; and physicians, including primary care physicians, specialists and ancillary providers. The company connects members to the services and supports they need for physical health, mental health and substance abuse. It addresses members' psychosocial needs and goals for housing, education/employment, transportation and meaningful participation in the community. Amerigroup works with individuals with intellectual and developmental disabilities, children and youth in foster care, individuals with mental health and substance abuse needs, individuals who need long-term services and support, and children with special needs.

CONTACTS: Note: Officers with more than one job title may be intentionally listed here more than once.

Felicia F. Norwood, Exec. VP-Anthem
Richard C. Zoretic, Exec. VP
Mary T. McCluskey, Exec. VP
Jack Young, VP
Ken Aversa, Sr. VP-Customer Svc. Oper., Medicaid, WellPoint
Georgia Dodds Foley, Chief Compliance Officer, Medicaid, WellPoint
John E. Little, Interim Sr. VP-Gov't Affairs, WellPoint
Aileen McCormick, CEO-Western Region, Medicaid, WellPoint

FINANCIAL DATA: Note: Data for latest year may not have been available at press time.

In U.S. $	2020	2019	2018	2017	2016	2015
Revenue	11,210,000,000	11,800,000,000	11,500,000,000	11,000,000,000	10,500,000,000	10,000,000,000
R&D Expense						
Operating Income						
Operating Margin %						
SGA Expense						
Net Income						
Operating Cash Flow						
Capital Expenditure						
EBITDA						
Return on Assets %						
Return on Equity %						
Debt to Equity						

CONTACT INFORMATION:

Phone: 757 490-6900   Fax:
Toll-Free: 800-600-4441
Address: 4425 Corporation Ln., Virginia Beach, VA 23462 United States

STOCK TICKER/OTHER:

Stock Ticker: Subsidiary
Employees: 8,000
Parent Company: Anthem Inc

Exchange:
Fiscal Year Ends: 12/31

SALARIES/BONUSES:

Top Exec. Salary: $ Bonus: $
Second Exec. Salary: $ Bonus: $

OTHER THOUGHTS:

Estimated Female Officers or Directors: 3
Hot Spot for Advancement for Women/Minorities: Y

AmeriPath Inc

NAIC Code: 621511

www.ameripath.com

TYPES OF BUSINESS:

Anatomic Pathology Practice Management
Cancer Diagnostic Services
Staffing Services
Operations Management
Health Care Information Services

BRANDS/DIVISIONS/AFFILIATES:

Quest Diagnostics Inc

CONTACTS: Note: Officers with more than one job title may be intentionally listed here more than once.

Joan Miller, Pres.
Stephen H. Rusckowski, Chmn.-Quest Diagnostics

GROWTH PLANS/SPECIAL FEATURES:

AmeriPath, Inc., owned by Quest Diagnostics, Inc., provides medical diagnostic services and other related services. The company's specialized team of board-certified pathologists have broad expertise in: breast pathology, cytology, fine needle aspiration, gastrointestinal pathology, genitourinary pathology, gynecological pathology, hematopathology and surgical pathology. AmeriPath's wide range of pathology, molecular and clinical testing includes immunohistochemistry (IHC), histology, special stains, tissue consultation, technical and professional component (TC/PC), flow cytometry, cytogenetics and molecular. Personalized services include direct access to AmeriPath's pathology team for case consultation and specimen discussion, comprehensive IHC, molecular testing on complex cases and fast turnaround time (24-48 hours for most tissue and cytology evaluations). AmeriPath is contracted with most major health plans in the U.S

AmeriPath offers comprehensive benefits and a variety of employee assistance programs.

FINANCIAL DATA: Note: Data for latest year may not have been available at press time.

In U.S. $	2020	2019	2018	2017	2016	2015
Revenue	1,078,440,000	946,000,000	940,000,000	922,000,000	900,000,000	875,000,000
R&D Expense						
Operating Income						
Operating Margin %						
SGA Expense						
Net Income						
Operating Cash Flow						
Capital Expenditure						
EBITDA						
Return on Assets %						
Return on Equity %						
Debt to Equity						

CONTACT INFORMATION:

Phone: Fax:
Toll-Free: 800-395-7284
Address: 8150 Chancellor Dr., Ste. 110, Orlando, FL 32809 United States

STOCK TICKER/OTHER:

Stock Ticker: Subsidiary
Employees: 450
Parent Company: Quest Diagnostics Inc

Exchange:
Fiscal Year Ends: 12/31

SALARIES/BONUSES:

Top Exec. Salary: $ Bonus: $
Second Exec. Salary: $ Bonus: $

OTHER THOUGHTS:

Estimated Female Officers or Directors: 1
Hot Spot for Advancement for Women/Minorities:

AmerisourceBergen Corporation

www.amerisourcebergen.com

NAIC Code: 424210

TYPES OF BUSINESS:

Drug Distribution
Pharmacy Management & Consulting Services
Packaging Solutions
Information Technology
Healthcare Equipment

BRANDS/DIVISIONS/AFFILIATES:

AmerisourceBergen Consulting Services
MWI
World Courier

CONTACTS: *Note: Officers with more than one job title may be intentionally listed here more than once.*

Steven Collis, CEO
Lazarus Krikorian, Chief Accounting Officer
Gina Clark, Chief Administrative Officer
Kathy Gaddes, Chief Compliance Officer
Dale Danilewitz, Chief Information Officer
John Chou, Chief Legal Officer
James Cleary, Executive VP
Robert Mauch, Executive VP

GROWTH PLANS/SPECIAL FEATURES:

AmerisourceBergen Corporation is one of the largest wholesale distributors of pharmaceutical products and services to a wide variety of health care providers and pharmacies. The firm offers brand name and generic pharmaceuticals, supplies and equipment and serves the U.S., Canada and selected global markets. The company's operations are divided into two segments: pharmaceutical distribution services (PDS) and other. PDS provides drug distributes a comprehensive offering of brand-name, specialty brand-name and generic pharmaceuticals, over-the-counter healthcare products, home healthcare supplies and equipment, outsourced compounded sterile preparations and related services to a wide variety of healthcare providers, including acute care hospitals and health systems, independent and chain retail pharmacies, mail order pharmacies, medical clinics, long-term care and alternate site pharmacies and other customers. Through a number of operating businesses, the PDS reportable segment provides pharmaceutical distribution (including plasma and other blood products, injectible pharmaceuticals, vaccines and other specialty pharmaceutical products) and additional services to physicians who specialize in a variety of disease states, especially oncology, and to other healthcare providers, including hospitals and dialysis clinics. Additionally, the PDS provides data analytics, outcomes research and additional services for biotechnology and pharmaceutical manufacturers. The other segment oversees: AmerisourceBergen Consulting Services (ABCS), which provides commercialization support services such as reimbursement support programs, outcomes research, contract field staffing, patient assistance and copay assistance programs; MWI, a leading animal health distribution company in the U.S. and in the U.K.; and World Courier, which is a global specialty transportation and logistics provider for the biopharmaceutical industry serving more than 50 countries. During 2021, AmerisourceBergen acquired the majority of Walgreens Boots Alliance, Inc.'s healthcare businesses for $6.275 billion in cash.

Employee benefits include comprehensive health benefits, 401(k), employee stock purchase program, life and disability insurance, adoption assistance and more.

FINANCIAL DATA: *Note: Data for latest year may not have been available at press time.*

In U.S. $	2020	2019	2018	2017	2016	2015
Revenue	189,893,900,000	179,589,100,000	167,939,600,000	153,143,800,000	146,849,700,000	135,961,800,000
R&D Expense						
Operating Income	2,033,605,000	2,012,397,000	1,686,889,000	2,019,669,000	1,816,634,000	1,367,988,000
Operating Margin %		.01%	.01%	.01%	.01%	.01%
SGA Expense	2,767,217,000	2,663,508,000	2,460,301,000	2,128,730,000	2,091,237,000	1,918,045,000
Net Income	-3,408,716,000	855,365,000	1,658,405,000	364,484,000	1,427,929,000	-134,887,000
Operating Cash Flow	2,207,040,000	2,344,023,000	1,411,388,000	1,504,138,000	3,178,497,000	3,920,379,000
Capital Expenditure	369,677,000	310,222,000	336,411,000	466,397,000	464,616,000	231,585,000
EBITDA	-4,727,296,000	1,660,092,000	1,877,172,000	1,499,260,000	1,927,425,000	625,735,000
Return on Assets %		.02%	.05%	.01%	.05%	- .01%
Return on Equity %		.29%	.66%	.17%	1.03%	- .10%
Debt to Equity		1.401	1.418	1.661	1.688	5.514

CONTACT INFORMATION:

Phone: 610 727-7000   Fax: 610 647-0141
Toll Free: 800-829-3132
Address: 1 West First Ave., Conshohocken, PA 19428-1800 United States

STOCK TICKER/OTHER:

Stock Ticker: ABC
Employees: 22,000
Parent Company:

Exchange: NYS
Fiscal Year Ends: 09/30

SALARIES/BONUSES:

Top Exec. Salary: $ Bonus: $
Second Exec. Salary: $ Bonus: $

OTHER THOUGHTS:

Estimated Female Officers or Directors: 7
Hot Spot for Advancement for Women/Minorities: Y

Sales, profits and employees may be estimates. Financial information, benefits and other data can change quickly and may vary from those stated here.

Amgen Inc

NAIC Code: 325412

www.amgen.com

TYPES OF BUSINESS:

Drugs-Diversified
Oncology Drugs
Nephrology Drugs
Inflammation Drugs
Neurology Drugs

BRANDS/DIVISIONS/AFFILIATES:

ENBREL
Prolia
Neulasta
Otezla
XGEVA
Aranesp
KYPROLIS
Repatha

CONTACTS: *Note: Officers with more than one job title may be intentionally listed here more than once.*

Robert Bradway, CEO
David Meline, CFO
Murdo Gordon, Executive VP, Divisional
David Reese, Executive VP, Divisional
Esteban Santos, Executive VP, Divisional
Cynthia Patton, Other Executive Officer
Lori Johnston, Senior VP, Divisional
David Piacquad, Senior VP, Divisional
Jonathan Graham, Senior VP

GROWTH PLANS/SPECIAL FEATURES:

Amgen, Inc. is a global biotechnology medicines company that discovers, develops, manufactures and markets human therapeutics based on cellular and molecular biology. Amgen's current pipeline products in Phase 3 include, but are not limited to: EVENITY, a humanized monoclonal antibody that inhibits the action of sclerostin for male osteoporosis; KYPROLIS, a proteasome inhibitor for multiple myeloma; Omecamtiv Mecarbil, a small molecule activator of cardiac myosin for the treatment of chronic heart failure; and Tezepelumab, a human monoclonal antibody that inhibits the action of thymic stromal lymphopoietin for severe asthma and atopic dermatitis. During 2020, Amgen's largest marketed product was ENBREL (21%), which is used in indications for the treatment of adult patients with types of rheumatoid arthritis and psoriasis. Prolia is second (11%) and approved for different indications, patient populations, doses and frequencies of administration, but primarily used for the treatment of post-menopausal women with osteoporosis at high risk of fracture. Other leading products include Neulasta, Otezla, XGEVA, Aranesp, KYPROLIS, and Repatha. A substantial majority of Amgen's U.S. product sales is made to three pharmaceutical product wholesaler distributors, including AmerisourceBergen, McKesson and Cardinal Health. In May 2021, the FDA accepted Amgen's supplemental new drug application for Otezla (apremilast) for adults with mild-to-moderate plaque psoriasis.

Amgen offers its employees health, disability and life insurance; paid time off; home and auto insurance; tuition reimbursement; childcare services; telecommuting options; and recreation/fitness classes.

FINANCIAL DATA: *Note: Data for latest year may not have been available at press time.*

In U.S. $	2020	2019	2018	2017	2016	2015
Revenue	25,424,000,000	23,362,000,000	23,747,000,000	22,849,000,000	22,991,000,000	21,662,000,000
R&D Expense	4,207,000,000	4,116,000,000	3,737,000,000	3,562,000,000	3,840,000,000	4,070,000,000
Operating Income	9,139,000,000	9,674,000,000	10,263,000,000	9,973,000,000	9,794,000,000	8,470,000,000
Operating Margin %		.41%	.43%	.44%	.43%	.39%
SGA Expense	5,730,000,000	5,150,000,000	5,332,000,000	4,870,000,000	5,062,000,000	4,846,000,000
Net Income	7,264,000,000	7,842,000,000	8,394,000,000	1,979,000,000	7,722,000,000	6,939,000,000
Operating Cash Flow	10,497,000,000	9,150,000,000	11,296,000,000	11,177,000,000	10,354,000,000	9,077,000,000
Capital Expenditure	608,000,000	618,000,000	738,000,000	664,000,000	837,000,000	649,000,000
EBITDA	12,996,000,000	12,633,000,000	12,883,000,000	12,856,000,000	12,528,000,000	11,181,000,000
Return on Assets %		.12%	.11%	.03%	.10%	.10%
Return on Equity %		.71%	.44%	.07%	.27%	.26%
Debt to Equity		2.786	2.361	1.355	1.011	1.044

CONTACT INFORMATION:

Phone: 805 447-1000   Fax: 805 447-1010
Toll-Free: 800-772-6436
Address: 1 Amgen Center Dr., Thousand Oaks, CA 91320 United States

STOCK TICKER/OTHER:

Stock Ticker: AMGN
Employees: 19,200
Parent Company:

Exchange: NAS
Fiscal Year Ends: 12/31

SALARIES/BONUSES:

Top Exec. Salary: $ Bonus: $
Second Exec. Salary: $ Bonus: $

OTHER THOUGHTS:

Estimated Female Officers or Directors: 4
Hot Spot for Advancement for Women/Minorities: Y

AMN Healthcare Services Inc

www.amnhealthcare.com

NAIC Code: 561320

TYPES OF BUSINESS:

Temporary Medical Staffing
Employment Placement Agencies
Recruiting and Placement
Vendor Management

BRANDS/DIVISIONS/AFFILIATES:

American Mobile
Nursefinders
NursesRx
HealthSource Global Staffing
Med Travelers
Onward Healthcare
AMN Revenue Cycle Solutions
Stratus Video

CONTACTS: *Note: Officers with more than one job title may be intentionally listed here more than once.*

Susan Salka, CEO
Brian Scott, CFO
Denise Jackson, Chief Legal Officer
Douglas Wheat, Director
Ralph Henderson, President, Divisional

GROWTH PLANS/SPECIAL FEATURES:

AMN Healthcare Services, Inc. is a healthcare staffing company in the U.S. As a nationwide provider of travel nurse and allied staffing services, locum tenens (temporary physician staffing) and physician permanent placement services, the firm recruits physicians, nurses and allied healthcare professionals nationally and internationally, and places them on assignments of variable lengths and in permanent positions at acute-care hospitals, physician practice groups and other healthcare settings. AMN Healthcare also offers a managed services program in which it manages clinical vendors for clients, as well as recruitment process outsourcing services, where it provides recruitment for permanent clinical positions. The company's hospital and healthcare facility clients utilize its temporary staffing services to cost-effectively manage both short and long-term shortages in their staff due to a variety of circumstances such as a lack of qualified, specialized local healthcare professionals, attrition, leave schedules, new unit openings, and to identify candidates for permanent positions. The firm's staffing services are marketed to healthcare professionals, as well as to hospitals, physician practice groups and other healthcare centers. AMN Healthcare uses distinct brands to market its differentiated services throughout the healthcare staffing spectrum. These brands include, but are not limited to, American Mobile, Nursefinders, NurseChoice, NursesRx, HealthSource Global Staffing, Med Travelers, Club Staffing, Onward Healthcare, B.E. Smith, O'Grady Peyton International, Staff Care, Locum Leaders, Merritt Hawkins and AMN Revenue Cycle Solutions.

FINANCIAL DATA: *Note: Data for latest year may not have been available at press time.*

In U.S. $	2020	2019	2018	2017	2016	2015
Revenue	2,393,714,000	2,222,107,000	2,136,074,000	1,988,454,000	1,902,225,000	1,463,065,000
R&D Expense						
Operating Income	149,265,000	176,915,000	202,828,000	212,440,000	191,632,000	128,879,000
Operating Margin %		.08%	.09%	.11%	.10%	.09%
SGA Expense	549,747,000	508,030,000	452,318,000	399,700,000	398,472,000	319,531,000
Net Income	70,665,000	113,988,000	141,741,000	132,558,000	105,838,000	81,891,000
Operating Cash Flow	256,826,000	224,862,000	226,993,000	115,262,000	131,851,000	56,313,000
Capital Expenditure	39,102,000	36,458,000	36,386,000	26,529,000	21,956,000	27,010,000
EBITDA	243,452,000	235,435,000	244,065,000	244,719,000	221,252,000	149,832,000
Return on Assets %		.07%	.10%	.11%	.10%	.10%
Return on Equity %		.17%	.24%	.26%	.27%	.27%
Debt to Equity		0.961	0.69	0.569	0.799	0.52

CONTACT INFORMATION:

Phone: 866 871-8519   Fax:
Toll-Free:
Address: 8840 Cypress Waters Blvd., Dallas, TX 75019 United States

STOCK TICKER/OTHER:

Stock Ticker: AMN
Employees: 3,000
Parent Company:

Exchange: NYS
Fiscal Year Ends: 12/31

SALARIES/BONUSES:

Top Exec. Salary: $ Bonus: $
Second Exec. Salary: $ Bonus: $

OTHER THOUGHTS:

Estimated Female Officers or Directors:
Hot Spot for Advancement for Women/Minorities:

Amplifon SpA

NAIC Code: 423450

corporate.amplifon.com

TYPES OF BUSINESS:

Medical, Dental, and Hospital Equipment and Supplies Merchant
Wholesalers
Hearing Systems
Hearing Retail Points of Sale

BRANDS/DIVISIONS/AFFILIATES:

Ampli-Easy
Ampli-Mini
Ampli-Connect
Amplifon
Ampli-Energy

CONTACTS: *Note: Officers with more than one job title may be intentionally listed here more than once.*

Enrico Vita, CEO
Alberto Baroli, Chief Innovation & Dev. Officer
Paul Mirabelle, Regional Market Dir.-Asia Pacific
Heinz Ruch, Regional Market Dir.-North America
Susan Carol Holland, Chmn.
Gilbert Ferraroli, Regional Market Dir.-Europe
Enrico Bortesi, Chief Supply Chain & Purchasing Officer

GROWTH PLANS/SPECIAL FEATURES:

Amplifon SpA is an Italian company that distributes, fits and personalizes hearing systems to the needs of clients with hearing impairment. The firm has operations in 26 countries through approximately 11,400 points of sale (consisting of direct and indirect channels), and a network of about 9,100 hearing care professionals. Amplifon's products use state-of-the-art receiver-in-canal (RIC) technology, including the incorporation of Bluetooth technology to integrate users' hearing aids with the environment around them. The Ampli-Easy product family is easy to use for everyday life. Ampli-Mini devices are discreet and nearly invisible. Ampli-Connect connects directly to televisions, smartphones and sound systems, and automatically recognize the environment and the microphones point toward the direction of the sound. Ampli-Connect devices also connect to the Amplifon app via Bluetooth. Ampli-Energy devices can be recharged using a charger and have up to 30 hours of battery life. The Amplifon App allows users to manage their device functions in real-time directly from their smartphones, and offers the ability to book an appointment with hearing care specialists. The majority of Amplifon's annual revenues are primarily derived from the Europe/Middle East/Africa market (such as Italy, Spain, France, Germany, Netherlands, Switzerland, Belgium, Luxembourg, Portugal, United Kingdom, Ireland, Hungary, Poland, Israel, Egypt and Andora), a minority percentage from the Americas (such as the U.S., Canada, Argentina, Chile, Ecuador, Panama, Colombia and Mexico), and the remainder from Asia-Pacific (such as Australia, New Zealand, India and China). In mid-2021, Amplifon agreed to acquire Bay Audio Pty Limited, a private independent Australian hearing care retailer that operates a network of over 100 points of sale across the east coast.

FINANCIAL DATA: *Note: Data for latest year may not have been available at press time.*

In U.S. $	2020	2019	2018	2017	2016	2015
Revenue	1,900,527,000	2,116,195,000	1,664,346,000	1,546,762,000	1,384,392,000	1,263,289,000
R&D Expense						
Operating Income	210,134,700	218,315,700	188,338,100	184,248,800	164,209,300	141,586,800
Operating Margin %		.10%	.11%	.12%	.12%	.11%
SGA Expense						
Net Income	123,404,400	132,765,600	122,718,900	122,883,900	77,729,450	57,185,270
Operating Cash Flow	478,284,100	390,195,300	221,014,600	206,416,800	175,555,900	154,067,300
Capital Expenditure	74,326,800	111,319,800	95,263,170	88,176,860	76,378,170	58,768,690
EBITDA	453,076,400	451,548,000	274,260,800	258,228,700	226,179,000	202,331,200
Return on Assets %		.04%	.05%	.07%	.05%	.04%
Return on Equity %		.17%	.17%	.18%	.12%	.10%
Debt to Equity		1.574	1.467	0.211	0.716	0.789

CONTACT INFORMATION:

Phone: 39 2574721   Fax: 39 257300033
Toll-Free:
Address: Via Ripamonti, 133, Milano, 20141 Italy

STOCK TICKER/OTHER:

Stock Ticker: AMFPY   Exchange: GREY
Employees: 11,265   Fiscal Year Ends: 12/31
Parent Company:

SALARIES/BONUSES:

Top Exec. Salary: $ Bonus: $
Second Exec. Salary: $ Bonus: $

OTHER THOUGHTS:

Estimated Female Officers or Directors: 3
Hot Spot for Advancement for Women/Minorities: Y

AMSURG Corporation

www.amsurg.com

NAIC Code: 621493

TYPES OF BUSINESS:

Practice-Based Ambulatory Surgery Centers
Physician Services
Surgical Centers
Ambulatory Services

BRANDS/DIVISIONS/AFFILIATES:

Envision Healthcare Corporation

CONTACTS: *Note: Officers with more than one job title may be intentionally listed here more than once.*

Jeff Snodgrass, Pres.
Steven Geringer, Chairman of the Board
Sarah Belmont, CFO
Sandy Clingan Smith, VP-Mktg.
Roxane Plant, VP-Human Resources
Phillip Clendenin, Executive VP, Divisional
Robert Coward, Other Executive Officer
Christopher Holden, President
Kevin Eastridge, Senior VP, Divisional

GROWTH PLANS/SPECIAL FEATURES:

AMSURG Corporation, a subsidiary of Envision Healthcare Corporation, is a leading physician-centric surgical center and physician services firm. The company operates in two business segments: ambulatory services and physician services. Ambulatory services acquire, develop and operate ambulatory surgery centers (ASCs) in partnerships with physicians. This segment operates more than 250 ASCs and one surgical hospital in 34 states, in partnership with approximately 2,000 physicians. The typical size of a single-specialty ASC is 3,000 to 6,000 square feet; and the size of a multi-specialty ASC is approximately 8,000 to 12,000 square feet. Each center has two or three operating/procedure rooms with areas for reception, preparation, recovery and administration. Each surgery center is specifically tailored to meet the needs of physician partners. The physician services segment provides outsourced physician services in multiple specialties to hospitals, ASCs and other healthcare facilities, primarily in the areas of anesthesiology, radiology, children's services and emergency medicine.

AMSURG offers its employees comprehensive health benefits, life and disability insurance, a 401(k) and a variety of employee assistance programs.

FINANCIAL DATA: *Note: Data for latest year may not have been available at press time.*

In U.S. $	2020	2019	2018	2017	2016	2015
Revenue	3,009,960,000	3,240,000,000	3,200,000,000	3,000,000,000	2,800,000,000	2,566,884,096
R&D Expense						
Operating Income						
Operating Margin %						
SGA Expense						
Net Income						
Operating Cash Flow						
Capital Expenditure						
EBITDA						
Return on Assets %						
Return on Equity %						
Debt to Equity						

CONTACT INFORMATION:

Phone: 615 665-1283   Fax: 615 665-0755
Toll-Free: 800-945-2301
Address: 1A Burton Hills Blvd., Nashville, TN 37215 United States

STOCK TICKER/OTHER:

Stock Ticker: Subsidiary
Employees: 10,500
Parent Company: Envision Healthcare Corporation
Exchange:
Fiscal Year Ends: 12/31

SALARIES/BONUSES:

Top Exec. Salary: $ Bonus: $
Second Exec. Salary: $ Bonus: $

OTHER THOUGHTS:

Estimated Female Officers or Directors: 2
Hot Spot for Advancement for Women/Minorities: Y

Analogic Corporation

www.analogic.com

NAIC Code: 334510

TYPES OF BUSINESS:

Equipment-Medical Image Processing
Signal Processing Equipment
Patient Monitoring Equipment
Computed Tomography Imaging Systems
Explosive Detection Security Systems
Power Technologies
Amplifier Technologies
Motion Control Motors

BRANDS/DIVISIONS/AFFILIATES:

Altaris Capital Partners LLC
eXaminer
ConneCT
Copley Controls Corporation

CONTACTS: *Note: Officers with more than one job title may be intentionally listed here more than once.*

Tom Ripp, CEO
Bernard Bailey, Chairman of the Board
Will Rousmaniere, CFO
Steve Urchuk, CTO
Fred Parks, Director
John Fry, General Counsel
Mervat Faltas, General Manager, Divisional
Brooks West, General Manager, Divisional

GROWTH PLANS/SPECIAL FEATURES:

Analogic Corporation provides leading-edge healthcare and security technology solutions to advance the practice of medicine. The company's advanced imaging and real-time guidance technologies are used for disease diagnosis and treatment as well as for automated threat detection. Analogic develops and manufactures its products. The firm's medical imaging technology solutions are applied to a wide range of diagnostic imaging modalities, including computed tomography (CT), magnetic resonance imaging (MRI) and digital mammography. Analogic develops state-of-the-art automatic explosives detection systems (EDSs) for checked and checkpoint baggage applications. The EDSs generate 3D continuous-flow volumetric images of the entire contents of a bag or parcel. This division's eXaminer family of EDSs are used in major airports worldwide, and include: eXaminer SX, for small to mid-sized airports; eXaminer 3DX, for medium to large airports; and eXaminer XLB, for large airports. ConneCT is a checkpoint security system for airports that handle large passenger volumes. It can detect emerging security threats. Analogic's power technologies division is a global provider of subsystems and solutions that monitor, deliver, analyze, power and control motion in high precision complex automated manufacturing processes. Its amplifier technology solves demanding system needs that require precisions amplification. Last, its precision motion controls for servo motors and stepper motors provide accuracy from high-speed applications to delicate actions including semiconductor processing, life sciences, automated automobile assembly, test and measurement, and high-performance mil-aero products. Precision motion controls are manufactured by wholly-owned Copley Controls Corporation. Analogic itself is privately-owned by Altaris Capital Partners, LLC.

Analogic offers comprehensive benefits, a 401(k) and a wellness program.

FINANCIAL DATA: *Note: Data for latest year may not have been available at press time.*

In U.S. $	2020	2019	2018	2017	2016	2015
Revenue	557,674,135	536,225,130	510,690,600	486,372,000	508,848,000	540,291,008
R&D Expense						
Operating Income						
Operating Margin %						
SGA Expense						
Net Income	-68,049,346	-70,153,965	-77,948,850	-74,237,000	12,127,000	33,481,000
Operating Cash Flow						
Capital Expenditure						
EBITDA						
Return on Assets %						
Return on Equity %						
Debt to Equity						

CONTACT INFORMATION:

Phone: 978 326-4000   Fax: 978 977-6811
Toll-Free:
Address: 8 Centennial Dr., Peabody, MA 01960 United States

STOCK TICKER/OTHER:

Stock Ticker: Private   Exchange:
Employees: 1,510   Fiscal Year Ends: 07/31
Parent Company: Altaris Capital Partners LLC

SALARIES/BONUSES:

Top Exec. Salary: $ Bonus: $
Second Exec. Salary: $ Bonus: $

OTHER THOUGHTS:

Estimated Female Officers or Directors: 3
Hot Spot for Advancement for Women/Minorities: Y

AngioDynamics Inc

www.angiodynamics.com

NAIC Code: 339100

TYPES OF BUSINESS:

Medical Device Manufacturing
Catheters
Ablation Products
Medical Devices
Surgical Devices
Diagnostic Devices

BRANDS/DIVISIONS/AFFILIATES:

NanoKnife System
AngioVac
Soft-Vu
VenaCure EVLT
BioFlo
Xcela
PASV
Auryon Atherectomy System

CONTACTS: *Note: Officers with more than one job title may be intentionally listed here more than once.*

Michael Greiner, CFO
Howard Donnelly, Director
Stephen Trowbridge, General Counsel
Chad Campbell, General Manager, Divisional
Robert Simpson, General Manager, Divisional
Brent Boucher, General Manager, Divisional
James Clemmer, President
Warren Nighan, Senior VP, Divisional
Kim Seabury, Senior VP, Divisional
Heather Daniels-Cariveau, Senior VP, Divisional
Benjamin Davis, Senior VP, Divisional
David Helsel, Senior VP, Divisional

GROWTH PLANS/SPECIAL FEATURES:

AngioDynamics, Inc. designs, manufactures and sells a wide range of medical, surgical and diagnostic devices used by professional healthcare providers for the treatment of peripheral vascular disease, vascular access and for use in oncology and surgical settings. These devices are generally used in minimally-invasive, image-guided procedures. AngioDynamics' products fall within three global units: oncology/surgery, endovascular therapies, and vascular access. All of the company's products have been cleared for sale in the U.S. by the Food and Drug Administration (FDA), and international regulatory clearances vary by product and jurisdiction. The oncology/surgery products unit offers a range of comprehensive ablation technologies, including thermal tissue ablation systems (microwave energy and radiofrequency energy), surgical resection and the NanoKnife System. The NanoKnife ablation systems utilizes low energy direct current electrical pulses to permanently open pores in target cell membranes. The treated tissue is then removed by the body's natural processes in a matter of weeks, mimicking natural cell death. The endovascular therapies unit offers products that support the medical areas of venous insufficiency, thrombus management, atherectomy and peripheral products. Brands within this division include AngioVac, Auryon Atherectomy System, Soft-Vu, Accu-Vu, AngiOptic, Mariner, Nit-Vu, Exodus, Micro Access and VenaCure EVLT (endovenous laser treatment). Last, the vascular access unit offers a broad range of peripherally-inserted central catheters, midline catheters, implantable ports, dialysis catheters and related accessories and supplies. Brands within this division include BioFlo, Xcela, PASV, SmartPort and DuraMax. AngioDynamics owns two primary manufacturing properties that provide manufacturing, service, engineering, research, warehouse and distribution services. During 2021, AngioDynamics announced that it received FDA approval for its PRESERVE study to evaluate the use of the NanoKnife System as a focal therapy option for prostate cancer patients, and assess its safety and effectiveness when used to ablate prostate tissue in intermediate-risk patients.

FINANCIAL DATA: *Note: Data for latest year may not have been available at press time.*

In U.S. $	2020	2019	2018	2017	2016	2015
Revenue	264,157,000	270,634,000	344,285,000	349,643,000	353,890,000	
R&D Expense	29,682,000	28,258,000	25,459,000	25,269,000	25,053,000	
Operating Income	-14,037,000	-1,045,000	26,240,000	25,216,000	14,557,000	
Operating Margin %		.02%	.08%	.12%	.04%	
SGA Expense	116,506,000	111,731,000	108,541,000	110,225,000	114,326,000	
Net Income	-166,787,000	-11,146,000	16,335,000	5,008,000	-43,590,000	
Operating Cash Flow	-14,554,000	37,440,000	41,287,000	55,745,000	45,216,000	
Capital Expenditure	7,585,000	3,118,000	3,656,000	3,001,000	5,594,000	
EBITDA	-143,423,000	16,277,000	33,690,000	37,497,000	28,258,000	
Return on Assets %		-.01%	.02%	.01%	-.06%	
Return on Equity %		-.02%	.03%	.01%	-.08%	
Debt to Equity		0.202	0.16	0.177	0.207	

CONTACT INFORMATION:

Phone: 518 795-1400   Fax: 518 795 1401
Toll-Free: 800-772-6446
Address: 14 Plaza Dr., Latham, NY 12110 United States

STOCK TICKER/OTHER:

Stock Ticker: ANGO   Exchange: NAS
Employees: 1,250   Fiscal Year Ends: 05/31
Parent Company:

SALARIES/BONUSES:

Top Exec. Salary: $ Bonus: $
Second Exec. Salary: $ Bonus: $

OTHER THOUGHTS:

Estimated Female Officers or Directors: 2
Hot Spot for Advancement for Women/Minorities:

Ansell Limited

NAIC Code: 339100

www.ansell.com

TYPES OF BUSINESS:

Protective Wear Manufacture
Latex Gloves
Condoms

BRANDS/DIVISIONS/AFFILIATES:

AlphaTec
HyFlex
ActivArmr
MicroFlex
TouchNTuff
GAMMEX
Sandel
Primus

CONTACTS: *Note: Officers with more than one job title may be intentionally listed here more than once.*

Neil Salmon, CEO
Zubair Javeed, CFO
Amanda Manzoni, Chief Human Resources Officer
Deanna Johnston, CIO
William Reilly, General Counsel
Steve Genzer, Sr. VP-Oper.
Craig Cameron, Sec.
Scott Corriveau, Pres.
Thomas Draskovics, Pres.
Peter Carroll, Pres.
John A. Bevan, Chmn.
Peter Dobbelsteijn, Sr. VP

GROWTH PLANS/SPECIAL FEATURES:

Ansell Limited is an Australian advanced solutions provider specializing in the manufacture of rubber latex products. The company serves global customers and operates through three business units: industrial, healthcare and life sciences. The industrial business unit manufactures and markets high-performance hand and body protection solutions for a wide range of industrial applications. This division's products protect workers in almost every industry, including automotive, chemical, first responders, food processing, machinery/equipment, metal fabrication and oil and gas. Primary brands within this business unit include AlphaTec, HyFlex, ActivArmr, MicroFlex and TouchNTuff. The healthcare business unit manufactures and markets surgical, exam and specialty gloves, as well as related safety devices for hospitals, surgical centers, dental practices, general health care, animal health and first responders. Primary brands within this business unit include GAMMEX, MicroFlex, TouchNTuff, Sandel, Encore and Micro-Touch. The life sciences business unit manufactures gloves, protective clothing, goggles, face masks and related accessories for the production, manufacturing, controlled/critical environment, laboratory/research and cleanroom industries. Brands within the life sciences division include BioClean, MicroFlex and TouchNTuff. Corporate offices and manufacturing facilities are located across Asia Pacific, the Americas, Europe, the Middle East and Africa. In mid-2021, Ansell announced the opening of its first plant in Russia. Earlier that year, Ansell acquired the Primus brand and related assets that constitute the life science business of Primus Gloves and Sanrea Healthcare Products.

FINANCIAL DATA: *Note: Data for latest year may not have been available at press time.*

In U.S. $	2020	2019	2018	2017	2016	2015
Revenue	1,821,472,000	1,660,067,000	1,572,947,000	1,387,270,000	1,633,474,000	1,663,523,000
R&D Expense						
Operating Income	204,869,000	182,286,200	161,855,800	134,134,700	206,365,300	204,970,000
Operating Margin %		.14%	.13%	.13%	.15%	.14%
SGA Expense	466,175,700	422,159,700	411,343,800	366,776,300	425,401,200	463,129,000
Net Income	179,133,400	123,702,100	511,329,100	149,072,200	165,237,600	189,599,800
Operating Cash Flow						
Capital Expenditure	73,230,700	53,084,730	47,956,250	51,423,680	70,185,360	85,133,120
EBITDA	294,943,600	225,144,500	220,981,200	228,402,500	289,555,300	289,101,700
Return on Assets %		.05%	.20%	.06%	.07%	.09%
Return on Equity %		.08%	.36%	.12%	.14%	.18%
Debt to Equity		0.376	0.36	0.592	0.612	0.637

CONTACT INFORMATION:

Phone: 61 3 9270 7229   Fax: 61 3 9270 7300
Toll-Free:
Address: 678 Victoria St., Richmond, VIC 3121 Australia

STOCK TICKER/OTHER:

Stock Ticker: ANSLF
Employees: 13,513
Parent Company:

Exchange: PINX
Fiscal Year Ends: 06/30

SALARIES/BONUSES:

Top Exec. Salary: $ Bonus: $
Second Exec. Salary: $ Bonus: $

OTHER THOUGHTS:

Estimated Female Officers or Directors: 2
Hot Spot for Advancement for Women/Minorities:

Anthem Inc

www.antheminc.com

NAIC Code: 524114

TYPES OF BUSINESS:

Health Insurance
Health Maintenance Organizations (HMOs)
Point-of-Service Plans
Dental and Vision Plans
Plan Management (ASO) for Self-Insured Organizations
Prescription Plans
Wellness Programs
Medicare Administrative Services

BRANDS/DIVISIONS/AFFILIATES:

Blue Cross and Blue Shield Association
Aim Specialty Health
CareMore
Freedom Health
HealthSun
Optimum HealthCare
IngenioRx
myNEXUS Inc

CONTACTS: *Note: Officers with more than one job title may be intentionally listed here more than once.*

Gail Boudreaux, CEO
John Gallina, CFO
Elizabeth Tallett, Chairman of the Board
Ronald Penczek, Chief Accounting Officer
Gloria McCarthy, Chief Administrative Officer
Thomas Zielinski, Executive VP
Leah Stark, Executive VP
Felicia Norwood, Executive VP
Prakash Patel, Executive VP
Peter Haytaian, Executive VP

GROWTH PLANS/SPECIAL FEATURES:

Anthem, Inc. is a health benefits company, serving more than 43 million medical members through its affiliated health plans (as of mid-2021). Through its affiliated companies, Anthem services more than 116 million people. The firm is an independent licensee of the Blue Cross and Blue Shield Association, an association of independent health benefit plans, and also serves customers throughout the country under the Aim Specialty Health, America's 1st Choice, Amerigroup, Aspire Health, CareMore, Freedom Health, HealthLink, HealthSun, Optimum HealthCare, Simply Healthcare and UniCare brands. Anthem also provides pharmacy benefits management services through its IngenioRx subsidiary. Anthem is licensed to conduct insurance operations in all 50 U.S. states and the District of Columbia through its subsidiaries. Anthem offers a broad spectrum of network-based managed care plans to large group, small group, individual, Medicaid and Medicare markets. Managed care plans include preferred provider organizations (PPOs), health maintenance organizations (HMOs), point-of-service (POS) plans, traditional indemnity plans and other hybrid plans. The firm also offers hospital only and limited benefit products, as well as an array of managed care services to self-funded customers, including claims processing, stop loss insurance, actuarial services, provider network access, medical cost management, disease management, wellness programs and other administrative services. Anthem provides specialty and other insurance products and services such as dental, vision, life and disability benefits, radiology benefit management and analytics-driven personal healthcare. The firm provides services to the federal government in connection with the Federal Employee Program (FEP). During 2021, Anthem acquired myNEXUS, Inc. a home-based nursing management company for payors; and acquired MMM Holdings, LLC and its Medicare Advantage plan MMM Healthcare LLC, as well as affiliated companies and Medicaid plan.

Anthem offers comprehensive health benefits, retirement plans and a variety of employee assistance programs.

FINANCIAL DATA: *Note: Data for latest year may not have been available at press time.*

In U.S. $	2020	2019	2018	2017	2016	2015
Revenue	121,867,000,000	104,213,000,000	92,105,000,000	90,039,400,000	84,863,000,000	79,156,500,000
R&D Expense						
Operating Income						
Operating Margin %						
SGA Expense	17,450,000,000	13,364,000,000	14,020,000,000	12,649,600,000	12,557,900,000	12,534,800,000
Net Income	4,572,000,000	4,807,000,000	3,750,000,000	3,842,800,000	2,469,800,000	2,560,000,000
Operating Cash Flow	10,688,000,000	6,061,000,000	3,827,000,000	4,184,800,000	3,204,500,000	4,116,000,000
Capital Expenditure	1,021,000,000	1,077,000,000	1,208,000,000	799,500,000	583,600,000	638,200,000
EBITDA						
Return on Assets %		.06%	.05%	.06%	.04%	.04%
Return on Equity %		.16%	.14%	.15%	.10%	.11%
Debt to Equity		0.561	0.603	0.656	0.572	0.665

CONTACT INFORMATION:

Phone: 317 488-6000   Fax:
Toll-Free: 800-331-1476
Address: 220 Virginia Ave., Indianapolis, IN 46204 United States

STOCK TICKER/OTHER:

Stock Ticker: ANTM   Exchange: NYS
Employees: 70,600   Fiscal Year Ends: 12/31
Parent Company:

SALARIES/BONUSES:

Top Exec. Salary: $ Bonus: $
Second Exec. Salary: $ Bonus: $

OTHER THOUGHTS:

Estimated Female Officers or Directors: 1
Hot Spot for Advancement for Women/Minorities: Y

Apollo Medical Holdings Inc

www.apollomed.net

NAIC Code: 621100

TYPES OF BUSINESS:

Physician Group Management
Population Health Management
Medical Management
Care Coordination Services

BRANDS/DIVISIONS/AFFILIATES:

Network Medical Management
Apollo Medical Management Inc
APA ACO Inc

CONTACTS: *Note: Officers with more than one job title may be intentionally listed here more than once.*

Thomas Lam, CEO
Eric Chin, CFO
Kenneth Sim, Chairman of the Board
Adrian Vazquez, Chief Medical Officer
Albert Young, Chief Medical Officer
Hing Ang, COO

GROWTH PLANS/SPECIAL FEATURES:

Apollo Medical Holdings, Inc. (ApolloMed) is an integrated population health management company. The firm coordinates care and provides medical management for over 1.1 million patients in California, the majority of whom are covered by private or public insurance provided through Medicare, Medicaid and health maintenance organizations (HMOs), and a small portion of non-insured patients. ApolloMed provides care coordination services to each major constituent of the healthcare delivery system, including patients, families, primary care physicians, specialists, acute care hospitals, alternative sites of inpatient care, physician groups and health plans. The company's physician network consists of primary care physicians, specialist physicians and hospitalists. ApolloMed subsidiaries include Network Medical Management (NMM), Apollo Medical Management Inc. (AMM) and APA ACO Inc. NMM and AMM operate as a management service organization (MSO), providing management services to physician practice corporations under long-term management and/or administrative services agreements, pursuant to which the MSO manages certain non-medical services for the physician groups and have exclusive authority over all non-medical decision making related to ongoing business operations. APA ACO is a next-generation accountable care organization for the Centers for Medicare & Medicaid Services (CMS), a program that allows provider groups to assume higher levels of financial risk and potentially achieve higher reward from participating in this new attribution-based risk sharing model. In addition, ApolloMed's commercial accountable care organizations (ACOs) and exclusive provider organizations (EPOs) manage nearly 60,000 members' medical lives. An ACO is a group of providers that join together to coordinate care for patients and are accountable for the quality, cost and overall care of their aligned beneficiaries. An EPO is a health plan that delivers care under risk-bearing and capitated arrangements with employers. Members must use their local network of providers for care. In mid-2021, ApolloMed agreed to acquire 80% of Access Primary Care Medical Group.

FINANCIAL DATA: *Note: Data for latest year may not have been available at press time.*

In U.S. $	2020	2019	2018	2017	2016	2015
Revenue	682,226,000	555,409,300	514,681,700	57,427,700	44,048,740	
R&D Expense						
Operating Income	80,503,000	34,413,990	92,231,020	-10,536,950	-7,266,129	
Operating Margin %		.06%	.18%	- .18%	- .16%	
SGA Expense	49,116,000	41,482,380	43,353,790	18,583,370	16,962,690	
Net Income	37,866,000	14,116,550	10,835,000	-8,969,816	-9,344,044	
Operating Cash Flow	46,163,000	13,673,380	25,496,040	-8,139,078	-1,839,125	
Capital Expenditure	1,164,000	1,041,670	1,170,064	297,561	262,108	
EBITDA	206,276,000	49,326,480	102,490,800	-8,000,763	-7,350,734	
Return on Assets %		.02%	.02%	- .45%	- .54%	
Return on Equity %		.08%	.06%			
Debt to Equity		1.274	0.075			

CONTACT INFORMATION:

Phone: 626-282-0288 Fax:
Toll-Free:
Address: 1668 S. Garfield Ave., Fl. 2, Alhambra, CA 91801 United States

STOCK TICKER/OTHER:

Stock Ticker: AMEH
Employees: 555
Parent Company:

Exchange: NAS
Fiscal Year Ends: 01/31

SALARIES/BONUSES:

Top Exec. Salary: $ Bonus: $
Second Exec. Salary: $ Bonus: $

OTHER THOUGHTS:

Estimated Female Officers or Directors:
Hot Spot for Advancement for Women/Minorities:

Applied Therapeutics Inc
www.appliedtherapeutics.com

NAIC Code: 325412

TYPES OF BUSINESS:

Pharmaceutical Preparation Manufacturing
Biopharmaceuticals
Clinical-Stage Development

BRANDS/DIVISIONS/AFFILIATES:

AT-007
AT-001
AT-003
AT-104

CONTACTS: *Note: Officers with more than one job title may be intentionally listed here more than once.*

Shoshana Shendelman, CEO
Mark Vignola, CFO
Riccardo Perfetti, Chief Medical Officer

GROWTH PLANS/SPECIAL FEATURES:

Applied Therapeutics, Inc. is a clinical-stage biopharmaceutical company developing a pipeline of novel product candidates against validated molecular targets in indications of high unmet medical need, particularly cardiovascular disease, galactosemia and diabetic complications. Applied's lead product candidate, AT-007, is a novel central nervous system (CNS) penetrant AR inhibitor being developed for the treatment of galactosemia, a rare pediatric metabolic disease that affects how the body processes a simple sugar called galactose, and for which there is no known cure or approved treatment available. High levels of galactose circulating in the blood and tissues of galactosemia patients enable AR to convert galactose to a toxic metabolite, galactitol, which results in long-term complication ranging from CNS dysfunction to cataracts. AT-007 has received both Orphan Drug and Pediatric Rare Disease designations, as well as Fast Track Designation (mid-2021) from the U.S. Food and Drug Administration (FDA) for the treatment of galactosemia. Other product candidates include: AT-001, a novel AR inhibitor in various stages of studies for the treatment of diabetic cardiomyopathy, diabetic peripheral neuropathy and acute myocardial infarction; AT-003, in pre-clinical stage for the treatment of diabetic retinopathy; and AT-104, in pre-clinical stage for the treatment of peripheral T-cell lymphoma, cutaneous T-cell lymphoma and T-cell acute lymphoblastic leukemia.

FINANCIAL DATA: *Note: Data for latest year may not have been available at press time.*

In U.S. $	2020	2019	2018	2017	2016	2015
Revenue						
R&D Expense	61,788,000	32,350,000	11,471,000	3,703,000		
Operating Income	-94,466,000	-45,582,000	-13,518,000	-4,285,000		
Operating Margin %						
SGA Expense	32,678,000	13,232,000	2,047,000	582,000		
Net Income	-93,961,000	-45,513,000	-16,521,000	-4,282,000		
Operating Cash Flow	-78,209,000	-36,307,000	-11,182,000	-3,195,000		
Capital Expenditure						
EBITDA	-94,086,000	-45,559,000	-13,518,000	-4,285,000		
Return on Assets %		-1.33%	-1.40%	-1.30%		
Return on Equity %		-1.88%	-2.79%			
Debt to Equity		0.052				

CONTACT INFORMATION:

Phone: 212 220-9226   Fax:
Toll-Free:
Address: 545 Fifth Ave., Ste. 1400, New York, NY 10017 United States

STOCK TICKER/OTHER:

Stock Ticker: APLT
Employees: 24
Parent Company:

Exchange: NAS
Fiscal Year Ends: 12/31

SALARIES/BONUSES:

Top Exec. Salary: $ Bonus: $
Second Exec. Salary: $ Bonus: $

OTHER THOUGHTS:

Estimated Female Officers or Directors:
Hot Spot for Advancement for Women/Minorities:

Apria Healthcare Group LLC

NAIC Code: 532291

www.apria.com

TYPES OF BUSINESS:

Home Medical Equipment Rentals
In-Home Infusion Therapy Equipment Rentals
In-Home Respiratory Therapy Equipment Rentals
Oxygen Therapy
Sleep Therapy
Negative Pressure Wound Therapy
Ecommerce

BRANDS/DIVISIONS/AFFILIATES:

Apria Inc
ApriaDirect.com

CONTACTS: Note: Officers with more than one job title may be intentionally listed here more than once.

Daniel J. Starck, CEO
Debra L. Morris, CFO
Celina M. Scally, Chief Human Resources Officer
Mark E. Litkovitz, CIO
Robert S. Holcombe, General Counsel
Cameron Thompson, Exec. VP-Oper.
Lisa M. Getson, Exec. VP-Gov't Rel. & Corp. Compliance
Peter A. Reynolds, Chief Acct. Officer
Nichola Denney, Exec. VP-Revenue Mgmt.
Daniel E. Greenleaf, Pres., Coram Specialty Infusion Svcs.
Bradley R. Kreick, Exec. VP-Payor & Provider Arrangements
John G. Figueroa, Chmn.

GROWTH PLANS/SPECIAL FEATURES:

Apria Healthcare Group, LLC is a leading provider of integrated home healthcare services and equipment, operating in more than 290 service locations across 48 U.S. states. The firm is contracted with most insurance companies to provide a range of therapies and services, including home oxygen therapy, respiratory services, sleep therapy, supply refills, non-invasive ventilation therapy and negative pressure wound therapy. Apria helps transition patients from hospital to home and then partners with patients to provide support and care throughout the therapy process. ApriaDirect.com is an online retail site where customers can purchase a wide range of home medical products, such as CPAP machines, masks, tubing, filters, humidifiers, comfort products, cleaning supplies, home oxygen accessories, breast pumps, mobility products, hospital bed accessories, diagnostic testing equipment, bath/safety products, personal care products and more. In early-2021, Apria Healthcare Group reorganized into an LLC operating as an indirect wholly-owned subsidiary of Apria, Inc.

Apria offers its employees medical plans, dental plans, a vision plan, 401(k), life and disability coverage and a variety of employee assistance plans and programs.

FINANCIAL DATA: Note: Data for latest year may not have been available at press time.

In U.S. $	2020	2019	2018	2017	2016	2015
Revenue	1,108,717,000	1,088,875,000	1,110,883,000	1,073,810,000		
R&D Expense						
Operating Income	71,148,000	27,415,000	20,397,000	26,151,000		
Operating Margin %						
SGA Expense	709,299,000	720,746,000	698,681,000	672,442,000		
Net Income	46,139,000	15,622,000	13,127,000	96,951,000		
Operating Cash Flow	196,713,000	161,850,000	159,578,000	155,345,000		
Capital Expenditure	109,097,000	114,485,000	122,123,000	126,408,000		
EBITDA	186,876,000	140,436,000	146,283,000	145,934,000		
Return on Assets %						
Return on Equity %						
Debt to Equity						

CONTACT INFORMATION:

Phone: Fax:
Toll-Free: 800-990-9799
Address: 7353 Company Dr., Indianapolis, IN 46237 United States

STOCK TICKER/OTHER:

Stock Ticker: APR   Exchange: NAS
Employees: 6,500   Fiscal Year Ends: 12/31
Parent Company: Apria Inc

SALARIES/BONUSES:

Top Exec. Salary: $ Bonus: $
Second Exec. Salary: $ Bonus: $

OTHER THOUGHTS:

Estimated Female Officers or Directors: 4
Hot Spot for Advancement for Women/Minorities: Y

Ardent Health Services LLC

www.ardenthealth.com

NAIC Code: 622110

TYPES OF BUSINESS:

General Medical and Surgical Hospitals
Health Systems
Hospitals
Clinics
Health Care

BRANDS/DIVISIONS/AFFILIATES:

BSA Health System
Hilcrest Healthcare System
Lovelace Health System
BSA Hospital
Quail Creek Surgical Hospital
Lovelace Medical Center
St Joseph's Healthcare System
Roswell Regional Hospital

CONTACTS: *Note: Officers with more than one job title may be intentionally listed here more than once.*

Marty Bonick, Pres.
Terika Richardson, COO
Alfred Lumsdaine, CFO
Tyra Palmer, CMO
Carolyn Schneider, Chief Human Resources Officer
James J. Mayercik, VP-IT

GROWTH PLANS/SPECIAL FEATURES:

Ardent Health Services, LLC is the parent of several subsidiaries which operate in the health care field. Since 2001, the company has invested more than $1.5 billion in the industry. As of mid-2021, Ardent owned and operated three health systems with 30 hospitals and 180 clinics in the U.S. states of Oklahoma, Texas, New Jersey, New Mexico, Idaho and Kansas, comprising nearly 4,280 licensed beds and 130 managed beds. The three health systems include: BSA Health System, Hillcrest Healthcare System and Lovelace Health System. BSA Health System is located in Amarillo, Texas, and consists of: the BSA Hospital, the Harrington Cancer Center and the Quail Creek Surgical Hospital. Hillcrest Healthcare System is located in Oklahoma and consists of: Hillcrest Medical Center, the system's flagship facility in downtown Tulsa; other Hillcrest hospitals throughout the state; investments such as in the Spine and Orthopedic Institute, the Tulsa Spine & Special Hospital, the Oklahoma Heart Institute and the Bailey Medical Center. Last, the Lovelace Health System is located in New Mexico, and consists of: the St. Joseph's Healthcare System; the Northeast Heights Medical Center; West Mesa Medical Center; the Lovelace Medical Center; and the Roswell Regional Hospital. Other hospitals and health systems within Ardent's group include: Hackensack Meridian Health, Heart Hospital of New Mexico, Physicians Surgical Hospitals, Seton Medical Center Harker Heights, The University of Kansas Health System, UT Health, among others.

Ardent offers its employees medical, dental, vision and pharmaceutical benefits; a health savings account, flexible spending account and a retirement account; and life insurance and pet insurance.

FINANCIAL DATA: *Note: Data for latest year may not have been available at press time.*

In U.S. $	2020	2019	2018	2017	2016	2015
Revenue	4,400,000,000	4,369,986,750	4,161,875,000	3,002,076,000	2,105,216,000	2,029,372,000
R&D Expense						
Operating Income						
Operating Margin %						
SGA Expense						
Net Income			-103,325,000	774,000	36,352,000	-19,127,000
Operating Cash Flow						
Capital Expenditure						
EBITDA						
Return on Assets %						
Return on Equity %						
Debt to Equity						

CONTACT INFORMATION:

Phone: 615-296-3000   Fax:
Toll-Free:
Address: 1 Burton Hills Blvd., Ste. 250, Nashville, TN 37215 United States

STOCK TICKER/OTHER:

Stock Ticker: Subsidiary
Employees: 26,000
Parent Company: Ventas Inc

Exchange:
Fiscal Year Ends: 12/31

SALARIES/BONUSES:

Top Exec. Salary: $ Bonus: $
Second Exec. Salary: $ Bonus: $

OTHER THOUGHTS:

Estimated Female Officers or Directors:
Hot Spot for Advancement for Women/Minorities:

Arkansas Blue Cross and Blue Shield

www.arkbluecross.com

NAIC Code: 524114

TYPES OF BUSINESS:

Insurance-Medical & Health, HMOs & PPOs
Mutual Insurance
Health Insurance
Employer Group Insurance
Individual Insurance
Federal Employee Insurance

BRANDS/DIVISIONS/AFFILIATES:

CONTACTS: *Note: Officers with more than one job title may be intentionally listed here more than once.*

Curtis Barnett, CEO
Gray Dillard, COO
Scott Winter, CFO
Alison Melson, VP-Corp. Mktg.
Odell Nickelberry, VP-Human Resources
Robert Griffin, Chief Medical Officer
Brett Trelfa, CIO
Karen Raley, VP-Prod. Dev.
Lee Douglass, Chief Legal Officer
David Bridges, Exec. VP-Internal Oper.
Calvin Kellogg, Exec. VP
Karen Raley, VP-Comm.
Steve Abell, VP-Strategic Svcs.
Jim Bailey, Sr. VP-National Bus. & Inter-Plan Rel.
Ron DeBerry, Sr. VP-Statewide Bus.
Bob Heard, VP-IT Infrastructure

GROWTH PLANS/SPECIAL FEATURES:

Arkansas Blue Cross and Blue Shield (ABCBS) is a nonprofit mutual insurance company providing comprehensive health insurance and related services to members throughout Arkansas. The company offers insurance for individuals and families, including medical, dental and vision plans for Arkansas residents under age 65 and their families who are not on Medicare. ABCBS also provides Medicare health and prescription drug plans for Medicare-eligible Arkansas residents. For employer groups, the firm offers health and dental plans for companies of all sizes. Other options include just dental insurance, or dental and vision plans for individuals and/or businesses, as well as customizable short- and long-term health plans for people living and traveling abroad. In addition, ABCBS offers a federal employee program that includes dental, vision, pharmacy, maternity-related depression, substance abuse treatment and other benefits, as well as hearing aids and speech-generating devices.

Employee benefits include an onsite gym, employee health clinic, wellness incentives and tuition reimbursement.

FINANCIAL DATA: *Note: Data for latest year may not have been available at press time.*

In U.S. $	2020	2019	2018	2017	2016	2015
Revenue	2,478,000,000	2,360,000,000	2,480,000,000	2,520,000,000	1,600,000,000	1,500,000,000
R&D Expense						
Operating Income						
Operating Margin %						
SGA Expense						
Net Income						
Operating Cash Flow						
Capital Expenditure						
EBITDA						
Return on Assets %						
Return on Equity %						
Debt to Equity						

CONTACT INFORMATION:

Phone: 501-378-2000   Fax: 501-378-3258
Toll-Free: 800-238-8379
Address: 601 S. Gaines St., Little Rock, AR 72201 United States

STOCK TICKER/OTHER:

Stock Ticker: Nonprofit   Exchange:
Employees: 3,200   Fiscal Year Ends: 12/31
Parent Company:

SALARIES/BONUSES:

Top Exec. Salary: $ Bonus: $
Second Exec. Salary: $ Bonus: $

OTHER THOUGHTS:

Estimated Female Officers or Directors: 7
Hot Spot for Advancement for Women/Minorities: Y

Arthrex Inc

www.arthrex.com

NAIC Code: 339100

TYPES OF BUSINESS:

Surgical Appliance and Supplies Manufacturing
Medical Devices
Manufacturing
Orthopedic Surgical Devices
Product Development

BRANDS/DIVISIONS/AFFILIATES:

Arthrex Manufacturing Inc
Arthrex California Inc
Arthrex GmbH
Arthrex Adria doo
Arthrex Austria GesmbH
Arthrex do Brazil
Arthrex Denmark AS
Arthrex Singapore Pte Ltd

CONTACTS: *Note: Officers with more than one job title may be intentionally listed here more than once.*

Reinhold D. Schmieding, Pres.
Karen Gallen, Dir.-Eng. (Distal Extremities)
John Schmieding, VP-Legal Counsel
Lisa Gardiner, Mgr.-Comm.
Andy Stewart, VP-North America
Randy Hacker, Dir.-Eng. (Pump & RF)
Peter Dreyfuss, Dir.-Eng.(Shoulder & Elbow)
Ken Adams, Dir.-Eng. (Powered Resection)
Alex Seifert, VP-Iberoamerica, Africa, Middle East & AsiaPacific
Peter Russano, Dir.-Supply Chain

GROWTH PLANS/SPECIAL FEATURES:

Arthrex, Inc. is a private medical device company specializing in the manufacturing of orthopedic surgical supplies. Over the course of its history, the firm has developed thousands of innovative products and procedures that have helped to advance minimally invasive orthopedics. Arthrex divides its products and procedures into eight specialized groups: shoulder, knee, elbow, hand/wrist, foot/ankle, hip, orthobiologics, and imaging and resection. The shoulder, knee, hand, wrist, foot, ankle and hip groups contain products and procedures specifically developed to treat those anatomical regions. Procedures in these groups include acromioclavicular reconstruction, distal bicep repair, ACL (anterior cruciate ligament) reconstruction, carpal tunnel release, ankle arthritis and labral reconstruction. The orthobiologics group contains products and procedures that are used in tissue, bone and soft tissue grafting and cartilage repair. The imaging and resection group encompasses the firm's endoscopes, camera systems, pumps, punches and arthroscopic instrument sets. The firm is headquartered in Florida, but has regional head offices in Germany and Singapore, as well as subsidiaries and distribution centers throughout the eastern and western hemispheres. Arthrex's many subsidiaries include, but are not limited to: Arthrex Manufacturing, Inc.; Arthrex California, Inc.; Arthrex GmbH; Arthrex Adria d.o.o.; Arthrex Austria GesmbH; Arthrex do Brazil; Arthrex Denmark AS; Arthrex France; Arthrex Italia SRL; Arthrex Japan GK; Arthrex Ltd.; and Arthrex Singapore Pte. Ltd.

Arthrex Inc provides for its employees medical and dental insurance, catered lunches, short- and long-term disability, an annual performance/profit sharing bonus and a 401(k) with company match.

FINANCIAL DATA: *Note: Data for latest year may not have been available at press time.*

In U.S. $	2020	2019	2018	2017	2016	2015
Revenue	2,877,050,000	2,615,500,000	2,200,000,000	2,000,000,000	1,800,000,000	1,600,000,000
R&D Expense						
Operating Income						
Operating Margin %						
SGA Expense						
Net Income						
Operating Cash Flow						
Capital Expenditure						
EBITDA						
Return on Assets %						
Return on Equity %						
Debt to Equity						

CONTACT INFORMATION:

Phone: 239-643-5553   Fax: 239-598-5534
Toll-Free: 800-933-7001
Address: 1370 Creekside Blvd., Naples, FL 34108-1945 United States

STOCK TICKER/OTHER:

Stock Ticker: Private
Employees: 3,188
Parent Company:

Exchange:
Fiscal Year Ends:

SALARIES/BONUSES:

Top Exec. Salary: $ Bonus: $
Second Exec. Salary: $ Bonus: $

OTHER THOUGHTS:

Estimated Female Officers or Directors: 4
Hot Spot for Advancement for Women/Minorities: Y

Ascension

NAIC Code: 622110

healthcare.ascension.org

TYPES OF BUSINESS:

General Medical and Surgical Hospitals
Acute Care Hospitals
Rehabilitation Hospitals
Psychiatric Hospitals
Pharmacy Management
Pharmacy Collaboration Hub

BRANDS/DIVISIONS/AFFILIATES:

Ascension At Home
Ascension Care Management
Ascension Global Mission
Ascension Investment Management LLC
Ascension Leader Institute
Ascension Living
Ascension Technologies
Ascension Ventures

CONTACTS: *Note: Officers with more than one job title may be intentionally listed here more than once.*

Joseph R. Impicciche, CEO
Craig Cordola, COO
Elizabeth Foshage, CFO
Nick Ragone, CMO
Herbert J. Vallier, Chief Human Resources Officer
Ziad Haydar, Chief Medical Officer
Eduardo Conrado, Chief Strategy & Innovation Officer
Christine Kocot McCoy, General Counsel
Patricia A. Maryland, Pres., Health Care Oper.
Eric S. Engler, Sr. VP-Strategic Planning & Dev.
Jon Glaudemans, Chief Advocacy & Communications Officer
Ann Espoito, Sr. VP
Bonnie Phipps, CEO., St. Agnes HealthCare
Susan L. Davis, New York
Scott Caldwell, Chief Supply Chain Officer

GROWTH PLANS/SPECIAL FEATURES:

Ascension is a faith-based, nonprofit healthcare organization in the U.S. Its headquarters are in St. Louis, Missouri, and the network is comprised of 139 hospitals in 19 states and the District of Columbia. Ascension has more than 2,600 sites of care and more than 40 senior care facilities. Ascension's medical group has a clinical care model that utilizes a care team that supports its providers and patients via seamless care delivery, transitions of care, disease management and case management. Services offered at Ascension's sites of care include behavioral health, counseling, support groups, child development, early childhood education, dental care, health education, wellness, exercise, disease management programs, legal and social services, (rent and utility assistance, and food pantries) and senior services. Ascension At Home helps support patients as they transition from acute care facilities to their homes. Ascension Care Management is a population health engagement company that offers a range of customizable healthcare services to three primary groups: providers, members and payers. Ascension Global Mission supports international efforts that improve the health and well-being of poor and vulnerable populations in developing countries. Ascension Investment Management, LLC manages investment portfolios for Ascension. Ascension Leader Institute provides continued education and training. Ascension Living provides holistic, person-centered care and support to meet the physical, mental and spiritual needs of seniors. Ascension Risk Services manages commercial and self-insured risk management functions. Ascension Technologies is a healthcare information technology services organization, leveraging technology to create collaborative solutions for everyday health decisions. Ascension Ventures is a venture fund focused on the medical device, healthcare technology and healthcare services sectors. In mid-2021, Ascension announced the opening of an Austin, Texas-based pharmacy services center, Ascension Rx, to serve as a specialty pharmacy, distribution center and patient engagement hub for Ascension Rx sites erected throughout the country.

Employee benefits offered.

FINANCIAL DATA: *Note: Data for latest year may not have been available at press time.*

In U.S. $	2020	2019	2018	2017	2016	2015
Revenue	25,261,514,000	25,322,807,000	23,158,956,000	22,713,753,000	21,900,000,000	20,538,803,000
R&D Expense						
Operating Income						
Operating Margin %						
SGA Expense						
Net Income	-1,039,856,000	1,226,615,000	2,374,986,000	1,861,183,000	477,700,000	562,596,000
Operating Cash Flow						
Capital Expenditure						
EBITDA						
Return on Assets %						
Return on Equity %						
Debt to Equity						

CONTACT INFORMATION:

Phone: 314-733-8000   Fax: 314-733-8013
Toll-Free:
Address: 101 S. Hanley Rd., Ste. 450, St. Louis, MO 63105 United States

STOCK TICKER/OTHER:

Stock Ticker: Nonprofit
Employees: 160,000
Parent Company:

Exchange:
Fiscal Year Ends: 06/30

SALARIES/BONUSES:

Top Exec. Salary: $ Bonus: $
Second Exec. Salary: $ Bonus: $

OTHER THOUGHTS:

Estimated Female Officers or Directors: 9
Hot Spot for Advancement for Women/Minorities: Y

Sales, profits and employees may be estimates. Financial information, benefits and other data can change quickly and may vary from those stated here.

Astellas Pharma Inc

www.astellas.com

NAIC Code: 325412

TYPES OF BUSINESS:

Drugs, Manufacturing
Biologics
Technology
Disease Prevention
Diagnostic Solutions
Data and Analytics
Product Pipeline

BRANDS/DIVISIONS/AFFILIATES:

CONTACTS: *Note: Officers with more than one job title may be intentionally listed here more than once.*

Kenjl Yasukawa, CEO
Yoshiro Miyokawa, Exec. VP
Shinichi Tsukamoto, Sr. Corp. Exec. Officer
Masao Yoshida, Sr. Corp. Exec. Officer
Masaru Imahori, Sr. Corp. Exec. VP

GROWTH PLANS/SPECIAL FEATURES:

Astellas Pharma, Inc. is one of the largest pharmaceutical manufacturers in Japan. The company's focus is on the combination of three components, namely biology, modality/technology and disease. Astellas' Rx+ business integrates innovative medical technology with cutting-edge technology in various fields, to contribute to the patient's medical care journey, including diagnostic, preventive, therapeutic and prognostic care. This division is actively developing new businesses in the spheres of chronic disease progression prevention, motor function support and replacement, digital neuroscience, patients without effective medicines, patient outcome maximization via precise diagnosis and surgery, and sensory function support and replacement. Last, Astellas' data, informatics and analytics division collaborates with partners to create and enhance ideas, molecules and therapy across its operations. This division helps to elevate the company's entire value chain and business by optimizing operational efficiencies, by enhancing decision making, and by enhancing the value of existing and pipeline products. In May 2021, Astellas Pharma announced that the European Commission approved its XTANDI (enzalutamide) oral therapy for the treatment of three distinct types of advanced prostate cancer, including men with metastatic hormone-sensitive prostate cancer.

FINANCIAL DATA: *Note: Data for latest year may not have been available at press time.*

In U.S. $	2020	2019	2018	2017	2016	2015
Revenue	11,880,600,000	11,930,880,000	11,875,790,000	11,979,440,000	12,536,930,000	
R&D Expense	2,047,857,000	1,905,894,000	2,016,394,000	1,900,843,000	2,061,000,000	
Operating Income	2,243,541,000	2,242,509,000	1,969,788,000	2,399,195,000	2,285,342,000	
Operating Margin %	.19%	.19%	.17%	.20%	.18%	
SGA Expense	4,560,063,000	4,477,574,000	4,368,590,000	4,299,609,000	4,569,781,000	
Net Income	1,784,690,000	2,029,947,000	1,504,014,000	1,997,397,000	1,768,944,000	
Operating Cash Flow	2,027,509,000	2,362,069,000	2,855,105,000	2,151,845,000	2,865,361,000	
Capital Expenditure	711,351,400	476,085,200	367,923,100	444,302,400	1,078,763,000	
EBITDA	2,874,613,000	2,865,270,000	2,600,696,000	3,174,048,000	3,037,500,000	
Return on Assets %	.09%	.12%	.09%	.12%	.11%	
Return on Equity %	.15%	.18%	.13%	.17%	.15%	
Debt to Equity						

CONTACT INFORMATION:

Phone: 81-3-3244-3000   Fax:
Toll-Free:
Address: 2-5-1, Nihonbashi-Honcho, Tokyo, 103-8411 Japan

STOCK TICKER/OTHER:

Stock Ticker: ALPMF
Employees: 16,243
Parent Company:

Exchange: PINX
Fiscal Year Ends: 03/31

SALARIES/BONUSES:

Top Exec. Salary: $ Bonus: $
Second Exec. Salary: $ Bonus: $

OTHER THOUGHTS:

Estimated Female Officers or Directors:
Hot Spot for Advancement for Women/Minorities:

AstraZeneca plc

www.astrazeneca.com

NAIC Code: 325412

TYPES OF BUSINESS:

Drugs-Diversified
Pharmaceutical Research & Development

BRANDS/DIVISIONS/AFFILIATES:

Atacand
Crestor
Lokelma
Arimidex
Faslodex
Accolate
Bricanyl
Symbicort pMDI

CONTACTS: *Note: Officers with more than one job title may be intentionally listed here more than once.*

Pascal Soriot, CEO
Marc Dunoyer, CFO
Jeff Pott, Exec. VP-Human Resources
Briggs Morrison, Chief Medical Officer
Pam Cheng, Exec. VP-IT & Operations
Jeff Pott, General Counsel
David Smith, Exec. VP-Global Oper.
Katarina Ageborg, Chief Compliance Officer
Menelas (Mene) Pangalos, Exec. VP-Innovative Medicines & Early Dev.
Bahija Jallal, Exec. VP-MedImmune
Briggs Morrison, Exec. VP-Global Medicines Dev.
Leif Johansson, Chmn.
Mark Mallon, Exec. VP-Intl

GROWTH PLANS/SPECIAL FEATURES:

AstraZeneca plc is a global biopharmaceutical business focused on the discovery, development and commercialism of prescription medicines in oncology and biopharmaceuticals. The firm's products are utilized for the treatment or prevention of diseases in the cardiovascular, renal, metabolism, oncology, respiratory and immunology categories, among others. AstraZeneca's cardiovascular, renal and metabolism (CVRM) division aims to protect people from the consequences of heart failure, cardiovascular, metabolic and renal diseases. Medicines within this division include, but are not limited to, Atacand, Crestor, Lokelma, Seloken, XIGDUO XR and Brilinta. It has more than 25 therapies and therapy combinations in its early-to-late stage pipeline. The oncology division aims to provide cures for cancers of all types and forms by discovering, developing and delivering treatments. Key disease areas within this division include lung, breast, ovarian, haematology, prostate, bladder, liver, pancreatic and cervical cancer. A few of AstraZeneca's oncology medicines include Arimidex, Faslodex, Lynparza and Calquence, as well as several pipeline therapies in Phase 1 to Phase 3 and lifecycle management projects. The respiratory and immunology category aims to transform the treatment of asthma and chronic obstructive pulmonary disease (COPD), as well as chronic lung diseases via altered immune systems. This division's medicines include Accolate, Bricanyl Turbuhaler, Fasenra, Rhinocort and Symbicort pMDI, as well as several pipeline therapies in Phase 1-3 and lifecycle management projects. Other disease areas of AstraZeneca include infection, vaccines, neuroscience and eosinophilic immune dysfunction. The firm developed a COVID-19 vaccine in partnership with the University of Oxford.

FINANCIAL DATA: *Note: Data for latest year may not have been available at press time.*

In U.S. $	2020	2019	2018	2017	2016	2015
Revenue	26,617,000,000	24,384,000,000	22,090,000,000	22,465,000,000	23,002,000,000	24,708,000,000
R&D Expense	6,213,000,000	6,059,000,000	5,932,000,000	5,757,000,000	5,890,000,000	5,997,000,000
Operating Income	3,694,000,000	3,000,000,000	1,510,000,000	2,292,000,000	3,572,000,000	3,132,000,000
Operating Margin %						
SGA Expense	11,896,000,000	10,723,000,000	10,362,000,000	10,303,000,000	9,739,000,000	11,451,000,000
Net Income	3,196,000,000	1,335,000,000	2,155,000,000	3,001,000,000	3,499,000,000	2,825,000,000
Operating Cash Flow	4,799,000,000	2,969,000,000	2,618,000,000	3,578,000,000	4,145,000,000	3,324,000,000
Capital Expenditure	2,606,000,000	2,460,000,000	1,371,000,000	1,620,000,000	2,314,000,000	2,788,000,000
EBITDA	8,337,000,000	6,712,000,000	7,112,000,000	5,976,000,000	7,276,000,000	6,960,000,000
Return on Assets %						
Return on Equity %						
Debt to Equity						

CONTACT INFORMATION:

Phone: 44 2037495000   Fax: 44 1223352858
Toll-Free:
Address: 15 Stanhope Gate, London, W1K 1LN United Kingdom

STOCK TICKER/OTHER:

Stock Ticker: AZN   Exchange: NAS
Employees: 70,600   Fiscal Year Ends: 12/31
Parent Company:

SALARIES/BONUSES:

Top Exec. Salary: $ Bonus: $
Second Exec. Salary: $ Bonus: $

OTHER THOUGHTS:

Estimated Female Officers or Directors: 3
Hot Spot for Advancement for Women/Minorities: Y

athenahealth Inc

www.athenahealth.com

NAIC Code: 524292

TYPES OF BUSINESS:

Outsourced Health Reimbursement Services
Patient Information Management
Billing & Collection Services for Health Care Providers
Automated Messaging
Telehealth Solutions

BRANDS/DIVISIONS/AFFILIATES:

Veritas Capital
Evergreen Coast Capital
Virence Health Technologies

GROWTH PLANS/SPECIAL FEATURES:

athenahealth, Inc. is a provider of network-enabled services and mobile applications for medical groups and health systems. Services and solutions provided by the company include electronic health records, medical billing, patient engagement, care coordination, enterprise revenue cycle, telehealth, mobile capabilities and advisory services. athenahealth primarily serves obstetrics/gynecology groups, orthopedic groups, federally-qualified health centers (FQHCs), health plans, member-centric organizations, startups and ancillary service providers. The company offers an embedded telehealth solution, ranging from scheduling to billing, for both clinicians and patients. athenahealth is privately-held by Veritas Capital and Evergreen Coast Capital. The firm is combined with Veritas' Virence Health Technologies, but operates under the athenahealth brand.

athenahealth offers comprehensive benefits to its employees.

CONTACTS: *Note: Officers with more than one job title may be intentionally listed here more than once.*

Bob Segert, CEO
Karl Salnoske, Sr. VP-Oper. & Cloud Engineering
Jeffrey Immelt, Chairman of the Board
Luis Borgen, CFO
William J. Conway, Chief Sales Officer
Fran Lawler, Chief Human Resources Officer
Paul Brient, Chief Product Officer
Stephen Kahane, Other Corporate Officer
Kyle Armbrester, Other Executive Officer
Jonathan Porter, Other Executive Officer
Simon Mouyal, CMO

FINANCIAL DATA: *Note: Data for latest year may not have been available at press time.*

In U.S. $	2020	2019	2018	2017	2016	2015
Revenue	1,465,750,000	1,430,000,000	1,300,000,000	1,220,300,032	1,082,899,968	924,728,000
R&D Expense						
Operating Income						
Operating Margin %						
SGA Expense						
Net Income		55,245,240	54,162,000	53,100,000	21,000,000	14,027,000
Operating Cash Flow						
Capital Expenditure						
EBITDA						
Return on Assets %						
Return on Equity %						
Debt to Equity						

CONTACT INFORMATION:

Phone: 617 402-1000   Fax: 617 402-1099
Toll-Free: 800-981-5084
Address: 311 Arsenal St., Watertown, MA 02472 United States

STOCK TICKER/OTHER:

Stock Ticker: Private
Employees: 5,305
Parent Company: Veritas Capital

Exchange:
Fiscal Year Ends: 12/31

SALARIES/BONUSES:

Top Exec. Salary: $ Bonus: $
Second Exec. Salary: $ Bonus: $

OTHER THOUGHTS:

Estimated Female Officers or Directors: 1
Hot Spot for Advancement for Women/Minorities:

Atreca Inc

NAIC Code: 325412

www.atreca.com

TYPES OF BUSINESS:

Pharmaceutical Preparation Manufacturing
Biopharmaceuticals
Drug Discovery
Clinical Testing
Antibody Immunotherapeutics
Oncology

BRANDS/DIVISIONS/AFFILIATES:

ATRC-101
APN-122597

CONTACTS: *Note: Officers with more than one job title may be intentionally listed here more than once.*

John Orwin, CEO
Herbert Cross, CFO
Brian Atwood, Chairman of the Board
Norman Greenberg, Chief Scientific Officer
Tito Serafini, Chief Strategy Officer
Guy Cavet, Chief Technology Officer
Lawrence Steinman, Director
William Robinson, Director

GROWTH PLANS/SPECIAL FEATURES:

Atreca, Inc. is a biopharmaceutical company utilizing its proprietary platform to discover and develop novel antibody-based immunotherapeutics to treat various types of solid tumors. Atreca's lead product candidate is ATRC-101, a monoclonal antibody with a novel mechanism of action and target derived from an antibody identified using its discovery platform. The firm's immunotherapy goal is to drive an attack by a patient's own immune system against tumor tissue in order to destroy a tissue that the patient does not want. ATRC-101 is in a Phase 1 study (as of mid-2021) to target the novel ribonucleoprotein (RNP) complex, binding to target reconstituted in vitro using a single recombinant protein, polyadenylate-binding protein 1, and in vitro transcribed poly(A) RNA (ribonucleic acid). Another oncology pipeline candidate is APN-122597, which is in pre-clinical development to target ephrin type-A receptor A2 (EphA2), a protein in humans that is encoded by the EPHA2 gene. In addition, Atreca and Xencor Inc. have a 3-year strategic collaboration to discover, develop and commercialize novel T-cell-engaging bispecific antibodies as potential therapeutics in oncology.

FINANCIAL DATA: *Note: Data for latest year may not have been available at press time.*

In U.S. $	2020	2019	2018	2017	2016	2015
Revenue						
R&D Expense	62,045,000	54,726,000	32,513,000	24,873,000		
Operating Income	-88,879,000	-72,571,000	-39,573,000	-29,435,000		
Operating Margin %						
SGA Expense	26,834,000	17,845,000	7,060,000	4,562,000		
Net Income	-86,335,000	-67,484,000	-37,940,000	-27,527,000		
Operating Cash Flow	-66,671,000	-58,538,000	-34,700,000	-25,096,000		
Capital Expenditure	5,026,000	3,447,000	1,764,000	1,377,000		
EBITDA	-83,953,000	-65,780,000	-36,523,000	-26,305,000		
Return on Assets %		-.43%	-.48%	-.76%		
Return on Equity %		-.44%	-1.26%			
Debt to Equity		0.00	0.001			

CONTACT INFORMATION:

Phone: 650 595-2595   Fax: 650 453-2410
Toll-Free:
Address: 835 Industrial Rd., Ste. 400, San Carlos, CA 94070 United States

STOCK TICKER/OTHER:

Stock Ticker: BCEL   Exchange: NAS
Employees: 113   Fiscal Year Ends: 12/31
Parent Company:

SALARIES/BONUSES:

Top Exec. Salary: $ Bonus: $
Second Exec. Salary: $ Bonus: $

OTHER THOUGHTS:

Estimated Female Officers or Directors:
Hot Spot for Advancement for Women/Minorities:

Atrion Corporation

www.atrioncorp.com

NAIC Code: 339100

TYPES OF BUSINESS:

Equipment-Ophthalmic, Diagnostic & Cardiovascular
Fluid Delivery Devices
Medical Device Components
Contract Manufacturing
Product Development

BRANDS/DIVISIONS/AFFILIATES:

CONTACTS: *Note: Officers with more than one job title may be intentionally listed here more than once.*

David Battat, CEO
Jeffery Strickland, CFO
Emile Battat, Chairman of the Board

GROWTH PLANS/SPECIAL FEATURES:

Atrion Corporation develops and manufactures products primarily for medical applications. The company's medical products are used in a number of fields, including fluid delivery, cardiovascular and ophthalmic applications. Atrion's fluid delivery products accounted for 51% of net revenues in 2020, and include a wide variety of proprietary valves designed to precisely fill, hold and release controlled amounts of fluids or gasses on-demand for use in various intubation, intravenous, catheter and other applications in fields such as anesthesia and oncology. The firm's cardiovascular products (33%) include the MPS2 myocardial protection system, a proprietary technology that is used in open-heart surgery, delivering essential fluids and medications to the heart. The system also mixes critical drugs and controls temperature, pressure and other variables. This division also develops and manufactures other cardiovascular products such as: surgery vacuum relief valves; silicone vessel loops for retracting and occluding vessels in minimally-invasive surgical procedures; inflation devices for balloon catheter dilation, stent deployment and fluid dispensing; and products used in heart bypass surgery to make a precision opening in the heart for attachment of the bypass vessels. Atrion's ophthalmic division (3%) manufactures specialized medical devices that disinfect contact lenses, as well as a proprietary line of balloon catheters used in the treatment of nasolacrimal duct obstruction in children and adults. Other medical and non-medical products (13%) include instruments and associated disposables used to measure the activated clotting time of blood, needle and scalpel blade containment products, inflation systems and valves used in marine and aviation safety products, inflatable survival components, and one-way and two-way pressure relief valves. Atrion's manufacturing facilities are located in Florida, Alabama and Texas.

Atrion offers its employees medical, dental, prescription, life and short-and long-term disability; paid vacation; and retirement plans.

FINANCIAL DATA: *Note: Data for latest year may not have been available at press time.*

In U.S. $	2020	2019	2018	2017	2016	2015
Revenue	147,591,000	155,066,000	152,448,000	146,595,000	143,487,000	145,733,000
R&D Expense	5,645,000	5,038,000	5,513,000	5,799,000	6,574,000	6,346,000
Operating Income	35,668,000	40,529,000	41,707,000	41,274,000	39,126,000	42,510,000
Operating Margin %		.26%	.27%	.28%	.27%	.29%
SGA Expense	24,850,000	25,121,000	24,558,000	23,681,000	21,930,000	22,125,000
Net Income	32,115,000	36,761,000	34,255,000	36,593,000	27,581,000	28,925,000
Operating Cash Flow	39,220,000	42,465,000	43,236,000	47,037,000	37,403,000	40,427,000
Capital Expenditure	21,886,000	20,446,000	17,507,000	9,677,000	10,639,000	9,323,000
EBITDA	47,320,000	51,382,000	50,830,000	49,951,000	48,079,000	51,333,000
Return on Assets %		.15%	.16%	.19%	.16%	.17%
Return on Equity %		.16%	.17%	.21%	.18%	.20%
Debt to Equity						

CONTACT INFORMATION:

Phone: 972 390-9800   Fax:
Toll-Free:
Address: 1 Allentown Pkwy., Allen, TX 75002 United States

STOCK TICKER/OTHER:

Stock Ticker: ATRI   Exchange: NAS
Employees: 636   Fiscal Year Ends: 12/31
Parent Company:

SALARIES/BONUSES:

Top Exec. Salary: $ Bonus: $
Second Exec. Salary: $ Bonus: $

OTHER THOUGHTS:

Estimated Female Officers or Directors:
Hot Spot for Advancement for Women/Minorities:

Auris Health Inc

www.aurishealth.com

NAIC Code: 339100

TYPES OF BUSINESS:

Surgical Equipment-Robotics
Medical Robotics
Micro-Instrumentation
Endoscopes
Data Science

BRANDS/DIVISIONS/AFFILIATES:

Johnson & Johnson
Monarch Platform

CONTACTS: *Note: Officers with more than one job title may be intentionally listed here more than once.*

Frederic Moll, Chief Development Officer
Christopher Lowe, CFO
Michael Eagle, Director
Robert Cathcart, Senior VP, Divisional
Brian Sheahan, Vice President, Divisional

GROWTH PLANS/SPECIAL FEATURES:

Auris Health, Inc., part of Johnson & Johnson's medical devices unit, creates platforms that enhance physician capabilities and evolve minimally-invasive techniques. The company engages in transforming medical intervention by integrating robotics, micro-instrumentation, endoscope design, sensing and data science into a single platform called the Monarch Platform. This platform enables physicians to accurately access small and hard-to-reach peripheral nodules for diagnosing and targeting treatment for a multitude of diseases, including lung cancer. The Monarch Platform demonstrated efficacy to successfully reach nodules and biopsy tissue, reporting success in 52 of 54 procedures (96.3%) in late-2019. The platform integrates a variety of technologies designed to empower physicians with greater reach, uninterrupted vision and precise control. It maintains vision throughout the procedure, including the biopsy. All of Auris' technology is driven by a patient-specific approach for maintaining the integrity of the human body.

Auris offers employees comprehensive health, dental, vision and pet insurance; and 401k options.

FINANCIAL DATA: *Note: Data for latest year may not have been available at press time.*

In U.S. $	2020	2019	2018	2017	2016	2015
Revenue	17,073,100	15,521,000	15,435,000	14,700,000	14,000,000	16,068,000
R&D Expense						
Operating Income						
Operating Margin %						
SGA Expense						
Net Income						
Operating Cash Flow						
Capital Expenditure						
EBITDA						
Return on Assets %						
Return on Equity %						
Debt to Equity						

CONTACT INFORMATION:

Phone: 650-610-0750   Fax:
Toll-Free:
Address: 150 Shoreline Dr., Redwood City, CA 94065 United States

STOCK TICKER/OTHER:

Stock Ticker: Private
Employees: 169
Parent Company: Johnson & Johnson

Exchange:
Fiscal Year Ends:

SALARIES/BONUSES:

Top Exec. Salary: $ Bonus: $
Second Exec. Salary: $ Bonus: $

OTHER THOUGHTS:

Estimated Female Officers or Directors: 3
Hot Spot for Advancement for Women/Minorities: Y

Avanos Medical Inc

avanos.com

NAIC Code: 339100

TYPES OF BUSINESS:

Medical Equipment and Supplies Manufacturing
Surgical Products
Infection Prevention
Pain Management
Respiratory Products
Product Manufacturing
Product Development
Digestive Health

BRANDS/DIVISIONS/AFFILIATES:

On-Q
Game Ready
Coolief
AMBIT
Mic-Key
Cortrak
NeoMed
Endoclear

CONTACTS: Note: Officers with more than one job title may be intentionally listed here more than once.

Joseph Woody, CEO
Warren Machan, CFO
Ronald Dollens, Chairman of the Board
Renato Negro, Chief Accounting Officer
John Wesley, General Counsel
John Tushar, President, Divisional
Arjun Sarker, Senior VP, Divisional

GROWTH PLANS/SPECIAL FEATURES:

Avanos Medical, Inc. is a medical technology company that develops, manufactures and markets solutions in more than 90 countries worldwide. The firm's innovative product offerings are focused on respiratory and digestive health, as well as surgical and interventional pain management. Respiratory and digestive health products include closed airway suction systems and enteral feeding tubes. Pain management products include the On-Q surgical pain pumps, Game Ready cold and compression therapy systems, Coolief interventional pain therapy, and AMBIT surgical pain pumps. Enteral feeding products include the Mic-Key enteral feeding tubes, Cortrak patient feeding solutions, and NeoMed neonatal and pediatric feeding solutions. Respiratory health products such as closed airway suction systems and other airway management devices are marketed under the Ballard, Microcuff and Endoclear brands. Avanos owns or leases facilities located throughout the world that handle manufacturing production, assembly, research, quality assurance testing, distribution and packaging of its products. The firm's principal medical device production facilities are located in Mexico, the U.S., France and Tunisia.

FINANCIAL DATA: Note: Data for latest year may not have been available at press time.

In U.S. $	2020	2019	2018	2017	2016	2015
Revenue	714,800,000	697,600,000	652,300,000	611,600,000	1,592,300,000	1,574,400,000
R&D Expense	34,900,000	37,700,000	41,800,000	38,200,000	41,100,000	32,300,000
Operating Income	-46,100,000	-55,700,000	500,000	-43,100,000	87,400,000	96,300,000
Operating Margin %		- .08%	.00%	- .07%	.05%	.06%
SGA Expense	332,600,000	399,100,000	340,400,000	321,700,000	411,100,000	308,500,000
Net Income	-27,200,000	-45,900,000	57,500,000	79,300,000	39,800,000	-426,300,000
Operating Cash Flow	-2,500,000	-74,500,000	-145,600,000	144,200,000	188,800,000	97,600,000
Capital Expenditure	20,200,000	50,600,000	49,100,000	43,200,000	29,100,000	70,400,000
EBITDA	-2,000,000	-12,100,000	41,800,000	18,900,000	153,200,000	-312,000,000
Return on Assets %		- .03%	.03%	.04%	.02%	- .19%
Return on Equity %		- .04%	.05%	.07%	.04%	- .33%
Debt to Equity		0.246	0.191	0.445	0.525	0.548

CONTACT INFORMATION:

Phone: 678 425-9273   Fax:
Toll-Free:
Address: 5405 Windward Parkway, Ste. 100, Alpharetta, GA 30004 United States

STOCK TICKER/OTHER:

Stock Ticker: AVNS
Employees: 12,000
Parent Company:

Exchange: NYS
Fiscal Year Ends: 02/28

SALARIES/BONUSES:

Top Exec. Salary: $ Bonus: $
Second Exec. Salary: $ Bonus: $

OTHER THOUGHTS:

Estimated Female Officers or Directors:
Hot Spot for Advancement for Women/Minorities:

Avantor Inc

NAIC Code: 334510

www.avantorsciences.com/site

TYPES OF BUSINESS:

Electromedical and Electrotherapeutic Apparatus Manufacturing
Medical Materials
Clinical Trial Kits
Process Chemicals
Lab Products
Product Manufacturing
Filtration Systems
Equipment Services

BRANDS/DIVISIONS/AFFILIATES:

NuSil
JT Baker
VWR
Macron Fine Chemicals
Puritan Products
BeneSphera
RANKEM
POCH

CONTACTS: *Note: Officers with more than one job title may be intentionally listed here more than once.*

Michael Stubblefield, CEO
Thomas Szlosek, CFO
Rajiv Gupta, Chairman of the Board
Steven Eck, Chief Accounting Officer
Michael Wondrasch, Chief Information Officer
Ashish Kulkarni, Chief Technology Officer
Bjorn Hofman, COO
James Bramwell, Executive VP, Divisional
Gerard Brophy, Executive VP, Divisional
Christophe Couturier, Executive VP, Divisional
Devashish Ohri, Executive VP, Geographical
Frederic Vanderhaegen, Executive VP, Geographical
Corey Walker, Executive VP, Geographical
Justin Miller, Executive VP
Eric McAllister, Executive VP
Michael DePetris, Other Executive Officer

GROWTH PLANS/SPECIAL FEATURES:

Avantor, Inc. is a global manufacturer and distributor of products and services to customers in the biopharmaceutical, healthcare, education, government, advanced technologies and applied materials industries. The company has more than 200 manufacturing, distribution and sales centers in over 30 countries. This network includes seven innovation centers, where it conducts both proprietary and customer-specific development activities, 13 cGMP manufacturing facilities supporting its material technology platforms, and 19 ISO-certified distribution facilities. Avantor's offerings are categorized into three groups: materials and consumables, equipment and instrumentation, and services and specialty procurement. The materials and consumables group includes ultra-high purity process chemicals and reagents, lab products and supplies, materials used for medical implants, customized excipients, single-use assemblies, silicone materials, process chromatography resins and columns, analytical sample prep kits and education/microbiology/clinical trial kits. The equipment and instrumentation group includes filtration systems, virus inactivation systems, incubators, analytical instruments, evaporators, ultra-low-temperature freezers, biological safety cabinets and critical environment supplies. Last, the services and specialty procurement group includes lab and production services, equipment services, procurement and sourcing services, clinical services, and product and process development services. Avantor has solutions supporting COVID-19, helping life science companies to detect, research and fast-track treatments for the coronavirus disease and related conditions. Brands of the company include NuSil, J.T.Baker, VWR, Macron Fine Chemicals, Puritan Products, BeneSphera, RANKEM and POCH. In September 2021, Avantor agreed to acquire the Masterflex bioprocessing business and related assets of Antylia Scientific per an all-cash transaction valued at $2.9 billion.

FINANCIAL DATA: *Note: Data for latest year may not have been available at press time.*

In U.S. $	2020	2019	2018	2017	2016	2015
Revenue	6,393,600,000	6,040,300,000	5,864,300,000	1,247,400,000	691,300,000	
R&D Expense						
Operating Income	706,800,000	551,800,000	413,500,000	-210,400,000	9,900,000	
Operating Margin %		.09%	.07%	- .17%	.01%	
SGA Expense	1,373,700,000	1,368,900,000	1,406,300,000	643,200,000	309,800,000	
Net Income	116,600,000	37,800,000	-86,900,000	-112,700,000	-42,400,000	
Operating Cash Flow	929,800,000	354,000,000	200,500,000	-167,500,000	72,900,000	
Capital Expenditure	61,600,000	51,600,000	37,700,000	25,200,000	29,900,000	
EBITDA	765,300,000	879,500,000	814,600,000	-160,100,000	70,000,000	
Return on Assets %		- .03%	- .01%	- .04%		
Return on Equity %						
Debt to Equity		3.444				

CONTACT INFORMATION:

Phone: 610 386-1700   Fax: 610 573-2650
Toll-Free:
Address: 100 Matsonford Rd., Ste. 200, Radnor Corp. Cntr., Bldg. 1, Radnor, PA 19087 United States

STOCK TICKER/OTHER:

Stock Ticker: AVTR   Exchange: NYS
Employees: 12,400   Fiscal Year Ends: 12/31
Parent Company:

SALARIES/BONUSES:

Top Exec. Salary: $ Bonus: $
Second Exec. Salary: $ Bonus: $

OTHER THOUGHTS:

Estimated Female Officers or Directors:
Hot Spot for Advancement for Women/Minorities:

Aveanna Healthcare LLC

www.aveanna.com

NAIC Code: 621610

TYPES OF BUSINESS:

Pediatric Health Care & Related Services
Case Management Services
Private Duty Nursing
Prescribed Pediatric Extended Care

BRANDS/DIVISIONS/AFFILIATES:

Aveanna Healthcare LLC
PSA Healthcare

GROWTH PLANS/SPECIAL FEATURES:

Aveanna Healthcare, LLC is a leading provider of pediatric home care, with locations in more than 20 U.S. states. The company offers pediatric skilled nursing, pediatric therapy, autism services, enteral nutrition, therapy and adult services. Other services include private duty nursing, respite care, pediatric day health care, personal care, physical therapy, occupational therapy, speech language therapy, a variety of medical solutions, hourly adult skilled nursing, companionship, habilitation services, home health, workplace wellness and other support services. Aveanna's website offers resources for families, as well as for continuing education.

CONTACTS: Note: Officers with more than one job title may be intentionally listed here more than once.

Tony Strange, CEO
Jeff Shaner, COO
Jim McCurry, Pres.
Dave Afshar, CFO
Debbie Lewis, VP-Oper. Dev.
Rod Windley, Chmn.

FINANCIAL DATA: Note: Data for latest year may not have been available at press time.

In U.S. $	2020	2019	2018	2017	2016	2015
Revenue	1,495,105,000	1,384,065,000	1,253,673,000			
R&D Expense						
Operating Income	81,804,000	61,615,000	54,610,000			
Operating Margin %						
SGA Expense	354,774,000	340,997,000	321,843,000			
Net Income	-57,050,000	-76,516,000	-47,146,000			
Operating Cash Flow	116,618,000	-8,714,000	21,596,000			
Capital Expenditure	15,237,000	16,637,000	19,579,000			
EBITDA	61,473,000	44,279,000	37,821,000			
Return on Assets %						
Return on Equity %						
Debt to Equity						

CONTACT INFORMATION:

Phone: 770-441-1580   Fax:
Toll-Free:
Address: 400 Interstate North Parkway, SE, Ste. 1600, Atlanta, GA 30339 United States

STOCK TICKER/OTHER:

Stock Ticker: AVAH
Employees: 4,200
Parent Company:

Exchange: NAS
Fiscal Year Ends: 12/31

SALARIES/BONUSES:

Top Exec. Salary: $ Bonus: $
Second Exec. Salary: $ Bonus: $

OTHER THOUGHTS:

Estimated Female Officers or Directors: 3
Hot Spot for Advancement for Women/Minorities: Y

Avera Health

NAIC Code: 622110

www.avera.org

TYPES OF BUSINESS:

General Medical and Surgical Hospitals
Nursing Homes
HMO
Health Insurance Consultation

BRANDS/DIVISIONS/AFFILIATES:

Careflight
Avera Addiction Care Center

CONTACTS: *Note: Officers with more than one job title may be intentionally listed here more than once.*

Bob Sutton, CEO
Julie Lautt, CFO
Kendra Calhoun, Sr. VP-Mktg., Communications & PR
Kim Jensen, Chief Human Resources Officer
Bruk Kammerman, CIO

GROWTH PLANS/SPECIAL FEATURES:

Avera Health was created by, and is currently sponsored through, an agreement between the Benedictine Sisters of Yankton, South Dakota and the Presentation Sisters of Aberdeen, South Dakota. The faith-based partnership is comprised of 35 hospitals, 215 primary and specialty care clinics, 40 senior living facilities, as well as home care, hospice, sports/wellness facilities and home medical equipment outlets via more than 300 locations throughout central and eastern South Dakota and areas of four surrounding states. Within these regions, Avera Health serves a population of nearly 1 million throughout 72,000 square miles and 86 counties. Avera's Careflight program encompasses helicopters for serving rural residents and improving response times across the region. The Avera Addiction Care Center is located on Avera's Louise Health Campus in Sioux Falls, and offers programs based on a range of approaches. The care center features a residential building with more than 30 private rooms and a main building with space for day treatment, group dining and a meditation room. In mid-2021, Avera Health sold its telemedicine services, Avera eCare, to Aquiline Capital Partners, which formed it as a subsidiary named Avel eCare.

FINANCIAL DATA: *Note: Data for latest year may not have been available at press time.*

In U.S. $	2020	2019	2018	2017	2016	2015
Revenue	295,600,192	273,884,389	225,457,103	218,893,740	191,441,200	169,384,234
R&D Expense						
Operating Income						
Operating Margin %						
SGA Expense						
Net Income	28,871,571	3,050,714	-9,440,695	23,177,939	20,048,913	19,283,729
Operating Cash Flow						
Capital Expenditure						
EBITDA						
Return on Assets %						
Return on Equity %						
Debt to Equity						

CONTACT INFORMATION:

Phone: 605-322-4700   Fax: 605-322-4799
Toll-Free:
Address: 3900 W. Avera Dr., Sioux Falls, SD 57108 United States

STOCK TICKER/OTHER:

Stock Ticker: Nonprofit   Exchange:
Employees: 19,700   Fiscal Year Ends: 06/30
Parent Company:

SALARIES/BONUSES:

Top Exec. Salary: $ Bonus: $
Second Exec. Salary: $ Bonus: $

OTHER THOUGHTS:

Estimated Female Officers or Directors:
Hot Spot for Advancement for Women/Minorities:

Avinger Inc

www.avinger.com

NAIC Code: 339100

TYPES OF BUSINESS:

Catheters Manufacturing
Medical Device Development
Medical Device Manufacture
Image-Guided Systems
Cather-Based Systems

BRANDS/DIVISIONS/AFFILIATES:

Lumivascular
Lightbox
Wildcat
Kittycat
Ocelot
TigerEye
Pantheris

CONTACTS: *Note: Officers with more than one job title may be intentionally listed here more than once.*

Jeffrey Soinski, CEO
Mark Weinswig, CFO
James Cullen, Chairman of the Board
Himanshu Patel, Chief Technology Officer

GROWTH PLANS/SPECIAL FEATURES:

Avinger, Inc. is a commercial-stage medical device company that designs, manufactures and sells image-guided, catheter-based systems that are used by physicians to treat patients with peripheral artery disease (PAD). The firm manufactures and sells a suite of products in the U.S. and select European markets based on its Lumivascular platform, the only intravascular image-guided system available in those markets. Avinger's Lumivascular platform combines interventional devices with optical coherence tomography (OCT) a high resolution, light-based, radiation-free intravascular imaging technology. The platform provides physicians with real-time OCT images from the inside of an artery. Avinger's current products include: its Lightbox imaging console; its Wildcat, Kittycat and the Ocelot family of catheters, which are designed to allow physicians to penetrate a total blockage in an artery, known as a chronic total occlusion (CTO); its TigerEye next-generation CTO crossing system utilizing Avinger's proprietary image-guided technology platform; and Pantheris, its image-guided atherectomy device, designed to allow physicians to precisely remove arterial plaque in PAD patients. In May 2021, Avinger announced the issuance and allowance of seven U.S. patents to date. That August, the company announced the submission of a 501(k) application to the U.S. Food and Drug Administration for its new Lightbox 3 imaging console, offering a compact size, next-generation laser system and streamlined workflow capabilities.

FINANCIAL DATA: *Note: Data for latest year may not have been available at press time.*

In U.S. $	2020	2019	2018	2017	2016	2015
Revenue	8,761,000	9,131,000	7,915,000	9,934,000	19,214,000	10,713,000
R&D Expense	5,695,000	5,692,000	6,009,000	11,319,000	15,536,000	15,694,000
Operating Income	-17,404,000	-19,359,000	22,067,000	-39,507,000	-50,717,000	-40,690,000
Operating Margin %		-2.12%	-2.79%	-3.98%	-2.64%	-3.80%
SGA Expense	14,327,000	16,534,000	17,442,000	25,120,000	39,950,000	29,231,000
Net Income	-19,006,000	-19,450,000	-27,558,000	-48,732,000	-56,128,000	-47,344,000
Operating Cash Flow	-14,835,000	-17,264,000	-18,466,000	-34,476,000	-53,069,000	-40,883,000
Capital Expenditure		88,000	32,000	45,000	971,000	577,000
EBITDA	-16,417,000	-17,080,000	-20,585,000	-40,957,000	-49,098,000	-40,877,000
Return on Assets %		-.97%	-1.84%	-1.42%	-1.04%	-1.26%
Return on Equity %		-2.82%			-5.66%	
Debt to Equity		0.60				1.897

CONTACT INFORMATION:

Phone: 650 241-7900   Fax: 800 229-2696
Toll-Free:
Address: 400 Chesapeake Dr., Redwood City, CA 94063 United States

STOCK TICKER/OTHER:

Stock Ticker: AVGR   Exchange: NAS
Employees: 75   Fiscal Year Ends: 12/31
Parent Company:

SALARIES/BONUSES:

Top Exec. Salary: $ Bonus: $
Second Exec. Salary: $ Bonus: $

OTHER THOUGHTS:

Estimated Female Officers or Directors:
Hot Spot for Advancement for Women/Minorities:

AvMed Health Plans Inc

NAIC Code: 524114

www.avmed.org

TYPES OF BUSINESS:

Insurance-Medical & Health, HMOs & PPOs
Health Maintenance Organization Provider
Health Education Services
Disease Management
Point-of-Service Health Plans
Self-Funded Health Plans

BRANDS/DIVISIONS/AFFILIATES:

SantaFe Healthcare Inc
Nurse On-Call

CONTACTS: Note: Officers with more than one job title may be intentionally listed here more than once.

James M. Repp, Pres.
Randall L. Stuart, CFO
Ashley Allen, CMO
Christine Shipley, Chief People Officer
Ann O. Wehr, Sr. VP
Eric Johnson, CIO
Steven M. Ziegler, General Counsel
Susan Knapp Pinnas, Sr. VP-Provider & Service Oper.
Michael P. Gallagher, CEO
Kay Ayers, Sr. VP-Member Svcs.
Brad Bentley, Sr. VP-Underwriting, Actuarial & Regulatory Affair

GROWTH PLANS/SPECIAL FEATURES:

AvMed Health Plans, Inc. is a statewide nonprofit company and one of Florida's leading HMO (health maintenance organization) providers, serving approximately 230,000 members with a network of over 35,000 physicians, specialists and hospitals. AvMed is owned by SantaFe HealthCare, Inc. The firm's policies include employer group HMO, Medicare HMO, point-of-service (POS) and self-funded plans. AvMed offers a variety of affordable coverage solutions for businesses of all sizes in most major metropolitan areas of the state. In addition, the company offers health promotion opportunities, smoking cessation programs and a number of onsite health-related seminars. For members with chronic conditions, AvMed offers care management programs that focus on education and individualized attention. These offerings include asthma, diabetes care, high-risk obstetrics, neonatal management, congestive heart failure, chronic obstructive pulmonary disease, oncology care, wound care, catastrophic cases, end-stage renal disease and organ/bone marrow transplant. Such programs aim to help patients navigate the health care systems to actively manage their health. In addition, the firm provides Nurse On-Call, a free, 24-hour phone service staffed by Florida-based registered nurses who help members make informed health care decisions. Beyond standard care options, AvMed offers a range of alternative health and wellness programs in fields such as massage therapy, acupuncture, nutrition, relaxation/meditation training, Yoga, Tai Chi, biofeedback, holistic medicine, Chinese herbal medicine, homeopathy, fitness and spa services.

AvMed offers its employees health and wellness benefits, retirement and savings options, career-building opportunities and more.

FINANCIAL DATA: Note: Data for latest year may not have been available at press time.

In U.S. $	2020	2019	2018	2017	2016	2015
Revenue	1,191,196,125	1,134,472,500	1,080,450,000	1,029,000,000	1,035,029,269	889,662,514
R&D Expense						
Operating Income						
Operating Margin %						
SGA Expense						
Net Income						
Operating Cash Flow						
Capital Expenditure						
EBITDA						
Return on Assets %						
Return on Equity %						
Debt to Equity						

CONTACT INFORMATION:

Phone: 305-671-5437 Fax: 305-671-4782
Toll-Free: 800-882-8633
Address: 9400 S. Dadeland Blvd., Ste. 120, Miami, FL 33156 United States

STOCK TICKER/OTHER:

Stock Ticker: Subsidiary
Employees: 765
Parent Company: SantaFe HealthCare Inc

Exchange:
Fiscal Year Ends: 12/31

SALARIES/BONUSES:

Top Exec. Salary: $ Bonus: $
Second Exec. Salary: $ Bonus: $

OTHER THOUGHTS:

Estimated Female Officers or Directors: 3
Hot Spot for Advancement for Women/Minorities: Y

AXA Health
www.axahealth.co.uk

NAIC Code: 524114

TYPES OF BUSINESS:
Insurance-Medical & Health, HMOs & PPOs
Health Information Services
Dental & Travel Insurance
Employee Assistance

BRANDS/DIVISIONS/AFFILIATES:
AXA Group
Ask the Expert

CONTACTS: *Note: Officers with more than one job title may be intentionally listed here more than once.*
Tracey Garrad, CEO
Anna Matty, COO
Richard Turner, Dir.-Strategy
Nicola Bell, Financial Dir.
Nick Groom, Dir.-Distribution

GROWTH PLANS/SPECIAL FEATURES:
AXA Health, a subsidiary of the AXA Group, is one of the U.K.'s largest private managed healthcare companies, providing service through a network of hospitals and scanning centers. The firm divides its coverage options into three divisions: personal, business and health and wellbeing. Through its personal division, AXA Health provides private health coverage to individuals and families in the U.K. Products in this division include private medical insurance; a cancer cash cover program that offers tax-free cash payment on first diagnosis of cancer and other benefits; child healthcare insurance; dental insurance; and international health cover for individuals living or working abroad on short-or long-term basis. The company's business division includes small to medium business healthcare; corporate health cover for over 225 employees; dental plans; health cash plans; travel cover; and a business health center which offers professional counseling, employee health engagement and stress management. The division also offers occupational health insurance services, including a fixed-cost package of occupational health and safety services, on-call expert support, executive care health assessment for key employees, safety services that manage the risk of work-related accidents or illnesses, a free health information service, a tailored package of health and fitness services for employees, an independent referral review service for patients with long-term health problems, attendance management and pre-employment medical clearance services. AXA Health's health and wellbeing division includes centers that provide information about medical conditions and illnesses. Its online channel, Ask the Expert, comprises nurses, pharmacists and midwives on hand. Topics or concerns can be related to aging, allergies, cancer, dental health, diabetes, diet/nutrition, fitness/exercise, healthy living, heart, mental health, musculoskeletal, pregnancy and childcare.

FINANCIAL DATA: *Note: Data for latest year may not have been available at press time.*

In U.S. $	2020	2019	2018	2017	2016	2015
Revenue	2,074,600,000	2,039,540,000	1,931,960,000	1,983,350,000	1,710,170,000	1,883,490,000
R&D Expense						
Operating Income						
Operating Margin %						
SGA Expense						
Net Income	126,268,000	132,472,000	159,897,000	106,176,000	92,139,000	87,459,200
Operating Cash Flow						
Capital Expenditure						
EBITDA						
Return on Assets %						
Return on Equity %						
Debt to Equity						

CONTACT INFORMATION:
Phone: 44-0189-251-2345   Fax: 44-0189-251-5143
Toll-Free:
Address: Phillips House, Crescent Rd., Turnbridge Wells, Kent TN1 2PL United Kingdom

STOCK TICKER/OTHER:
Stock Ticker: Subsidiary
Employees:
Parent Company: AXA SA

Exchange:
Fiscal Year Ends: 12/31

SALARIES/BONUSES:
Top Exec. Salary: $ Bonus: $
Second Exec. Salary: $ Bonus: $

OTHER THOUGHTS:
Estimated Female Officers or Directors: 1
Hot Spot for Advancement for Women/Minorities:

Axcella Health Inc

www.axcellahealth.com

NAIC Code: 325414

TYPES OF BUSINESS:

Biological Product (except Diagnostic) Manufacturing
Biotechnology
Novel Multifactorial Interventions
Clinical Development
Clinical Testing

BRANDS/DIVISIONS/AFFILIATES:

AXA
AxcellaDB
AXA1665
AXA1125

CONTACTS: Note: Officers with more than one job title may be intentionally listed here more than once.

William Hinshaw, CEO
Thomas Leggett, CFO
David Epstein, Chairman of the Board
Manu Chakravarthy, Chief Medical Officer
Tony Tramontin, Chief Scientific Officer
Paul Fehlner, Other Executive Officer
Stephen Mitchener, Other Executive Officer

GROWTH PLANS/SPECIAL FEATURES:

Axcella Health, Inc. is a biotechnology company engaged in the research and development of novel multifactorial interventions to support health and address dysregulated metabolism for consumers and patients with limited options. Endogenous metabolic modulators (EMMs) are a broad family of molecules that fundamentally impact and regulate human metabolism. Axcella believes its approach to EMMs has the potential to bring about a transformation in health and medicine. The firm's human-focused development platform enables it to design and test proprietary AXA candidates that simultaneously target multiple biologies and metabolic pathways by integrating: advanced analytics of metabolism regulation and dysregulation; correlative reasoning algorithms to interrogate data in its proprietary database, AxcellaDB; proprietary human primary cell systems to directly test the multiple biologies that drive any particular disease or metabolic dysregulation; predictive combinational drug metabolism and pharmacokinetics analytics to inform dose exposure relationships; and the EMM safety database. The data and learnings generated from the AXA candidate design process further informs the design pathway, which therefore increases the AXA development platform's efficiency. Axcella's platform has produced a pipeline of AXA candidates with programs in liver, muscle blood, with current candidates (mid-2021) including AXA1665 for the reduction in risk of recurrent overt hepatic encephalopathy (OHE), and AXA1125 for non-alcoholic steatohepatitis (NASH). Axcella conducts non-IND (investigational new drug), Institutional Review Board--approved clinical studies to evaluate the safety and tolerability of its AXA candidates in human subjects, or effects on the normal structure or function of the body.

FINANCIAL DATA: Note: Data for latest year may not have been available at press time.

In U.S. $	2020	2019	2018	2017	2016	2015
Revenue						
R&D Expense	37,039,000	41,658,000	25,486,000	22,916,000		
Operating Income	-53,836,000	-57,439,000	-33,896,000	-28,921,000		
Operating Margin %						
SGA Expense	16,797,000	15,781,000	8,410,000	6,005,000		
Net Income	-56,527,000	-59,037,000	-36,069,000	-30,940,000		
Operating Cash Flow	-49,771,000	-50,962,000	-30,712,000	-26,861,000		
Capital Expenditure	239,000	136,000	659,000	1,090,000		
EBITDA	-53,101,000	-54,980,000	-32,825,000	-27,532,000		
Return on Assets %		-.67%	-.55%	-.63%		
Return on Equity %		-1.09%				
Debt to Equity		0.413	0.505			

CONTACT INFORMATION:

Phone: 857 320-2200   Fax: 617 441-6243
Toll-Free:
Address: 840 Memorial Dr., Cambridge, MA 02139 United States

STOCK TICKER/OTHER:

Stock Ticker: AXLA   Exchange: NAS
Employees: 59   Fiscal Year Ends: 12/31
Parent Company:

SALARIES/BONUSES:

Top Exec. Salary: $ Bonus: $
Second Exec. Salary: $ Bonus: $

OTHER THOUGHTS:

Estimated Female Officers or Directors:
Hot Spot for Advancement for Women/Minorities:

Axonics Modulation Technologies Inc

www.axonics.com

NAIC Code: 334510

TYPES OF BUSINESS:

Electromedical and Electrotherapeutic Apparatus Manufacturing
Implantable Neurostimulation Systems
Product Development
Product Manufacturing
Urinary Incontinence Solution

BRANDS/DIVISIONS/AFFILIATES:

RELAX-OAB
ARTISAN-SNM
Bulkamid

CONTACTS: *Note: Officers with more than one job title may be intentionally listed here more than once.*

Raymond Cohen, CEO
Danny Dearen, CFO
Raphael Wisniewski, Chairman of the Board
Karen Noblett, Chief Medical Officer
Guangqiang Jiang, Chief Technology Officer
Rinda Sama, COO
Michael Williamson, General Counsel
Prabodh Mathur, Other Executive Officer
Alfred Ford, Other Executive Officer

GROWTH PLANS/SPECIAL FEATURES:

Axonics Modulation Technologies, Inc. is a medical technology company that has developed and is commercializing innovative and minimally-invasive implantable neurostimulation systems. The firm's rechargeable sacral neuromodulation (r-SNM) system delivers mild electrical pulses to the targeted sacral nerve in order to restore normal communication to and from the brain to reduce the symptoms of urinary and fecal dysfunction. SNM therapy is primarily used to treat patients with overactive bladder (OAB), urinary urgency incontinence (UUI) and urinary urgency frequency (UUF), fecal incontinence (FI) and urinary retention (UR). r-SNM is designed to last approximately 15 years, and is market-approved in Europe, Canada and Australia. Axonics is also developing a growing body of clinical evidence that demonstrates the safety, effectiveness and benefits of its r-SNM system, including two clinical studies: a European study, RELAX-OAB; and a U.S. study, ARTISAN-SNM. RELAX-OAB's study evaluated patients in Europe that suffered from OAB subtypes UUI and/or UUF, and all showed at least a 50% reduction in the number of average leaks or voids per day or a reduction to less than eight voids per day. The study has completed one-year follow-ups and completed two-year follow-ups with no reports of serious device-related adverse events. ARTISAN-SNM's study completed the enrollment and implantation of patients with UUI, who were evaluated in the U.S. and in Europe. The study's primary endpoint defined that patients had at least a 50% reduction in the number of UUI episodes per day on a three-day bladder diary at six months post-implant. No serious device-related events have been reported. In addition, Axonics also markets Bulkamid, a urethral bulking agent to treat female stress urinary incontinence. During 2021, Axonics announced European CE Mark approval for its implantable sacral neurostimulator and wireless patient remote control technology.

FINANCIAL DATA: *Note: Data for latest year may not have been available at press time.*

In U.S. $	2020	2019	2018	2017	2016	2015
Revenue	111,535,000	13,820,000	707,000	128,118		
R&D Expense	29,170,000	20,181,000	19,402,000	12,332,050	12,510,280	
Operating Income	-53,760,000	-80,599,000	-32,137,000	-18,175,220	-17,484,430	
Operating Margin %		-5.83%	-45.46%	-141.86%		
SGA Expense	91,681,000	67,748,000	13,086,000	5,852,456	4,973,351	
Net Income	-54,915,000	-79,935,000	-32,483,000	-18,060,860	-17,400,700	
Operating Cash Flow	-83,742,000	-83,454,000	-31,370,000	-18,173,880	-17,335,260	
Capital Expenditure	2,938,000	1,339,000	1,228,000	1,039,037	292,115	
EBITDA	-51,299,000	-76,434,000	-30,193,000	-17,335,460	-16,775,590	
Return on Assets %		-.41%	-.32%	-.90%	-1.60%	
Return on Equity %		-.49%	-.85%			
Debt to Equity		0.135	0.159			

CONTACT INFORMATION:

Phone: 949 396-6322   Fax: 949 396-6321
Toll-Free:
Address: 26 Technology Dr., Irvine, CA 92618 United States

STOCK TICKER/OTHER:

Stock Ticker: AXNX   Exchange: NAS
Employees: 416   Fiscal Year Ends: 12/31
Parent Company:

SALARIES/BONUSES:

Top Exec. Salary: $ Bonus: $
Second Exec. Salary: $ Bonus: $

OTHER THOUGHTS:

Estimated Female Officers or Directors:
Hot Spot for Advancement for Women/Minorities:

Sales, profits and employees may be estimates. Financial information, benefits and other data can change quickly and may vary from those stated here.

Banner Health

www.bannerhealth.com

NAIC Code: 622110

TYPES OF BUSINESS:

General Medical and Surgical Hospitals
Long-Term Care Centers
Home Care Services
Home Medical Equipment Services
Family Clinics
Nursing Registry
Medical Research

BRANDS/DIVISIONS/AFFILIATES:

Banner Alzheimers Foundation
Banner Concussion Center
Banner Heart Hospital
Banner MD Anderson Cancer Center
Banner Childrens
Western States Burn Center
Banner-University Medicine

CONTACTS: *Note: Officers with more than one job title may be intentionally listed here more than once.*

Peter S. Fine, CEO/Pres.
Becky Kuhn, COO
Dennis Laraway, CFO
Alexandra Morehouse, CMO
Naomi Cramer, Chief Human Resources Officer
John Hensing, Chief Medical Officer
Deanna Wise, CIO
Ron Bunnell, Chief Admin. Officer
David Bixby, General Counsel
Jim Ferando, Pres., Western Region
Rebecca Kuhn, Pres., Arizona East Region
Kathy Bollinger, Pres., Arizona West Region
Andy Kramer, CEO/Pres., Banner Health Foundation
Quentin P. Smith, Jr., Chmn.

GROWTH PLANS/SPECIAL FEATURES:

Banner Health, based in Phoenix, Arizona, is one of the nation's largest nonprofit health care systems. The company operates 30 acute-care hospitals, including three academic medical centers, as well as other related health entities and services in six states, including Arizona, California, Colorado, Nebraska, Nevada and Wyoming. Banner Health currently serves more than 1 million members within its provider network system. Comprehensive services, physician services, hospice and home care is offered, and specialized services are offered at the Banner Alzheimer's institute, Banner Concussion Center, Banner Heart Hospital, Banner MD Anderson Cancer Center, Banner Children's, and Western States Burn Center. Banner Health also offers services such as telehealth urgent care, virtual waiting rooms for in-person physician care, imaging, surgery centers and maternity care. Telehealth offers access to the patient's providers in a safe environment and comprehensive care from the patient's home. They can talk to doctors via computer/smartphone video or other audio/video device. With a Banner Health account, individuals can view their lab results, request medical records, schedule appointments, message a doctor's office and access important documents. Banner Medical Group places health centers and clinics throughout the communities served by Banner Health. Banner-University Medicine is a partnership with the University of Arizona Health Network in Tucson, Arizona, and engages in medicine research, teaching and patient care across three academic medical centers: Banner-University Medical Center Tucson, Banner-University Medical Center Phoenix and Banner-University Medical Center South.

Banner Health offers its employees health and retirement benefits, learning and development opportunities and more.

FINANCIAL DATA: *Note: Data for latest year may not have been available at press time.*

In U.S. $	2020	2019	2018	2017	2016	2015
Revenue	10,400,000,000	9,426,648,000	8,519,779,000	7,835,266,000	7,633,205,000	6,971,132,000
R&D Expense						
Operating Income						
Operating Margin %						
SGA Expense						
Net Income	586,700,000	73,932,600	70,412,000	735,116,000	551,992,949	444,821,035
Operating Cash Flow						
Capital Expenditure						
EBITDA						
Return on Assets %						
Return on Equity %						
Debt to Equity						

CONTACT INFORMATION:

Phone: 602-495-4000   Fax:
Toll-Free:
Address: 2901 N. Central Ave., Ste. 160, Phoenix, AZ 85012 United States

STOCK TICKER/OTHER:

Stock Ticker: Nonprofit   Exchange:
Employees: 50,000   Fiscal Year Ends: 12/31
Parent Company:

SALARIES/BONUSES:

Top Exec. Salary: $ Bonus: $
Second Exec. Salary: $ Bonus: $

OTHER THOUGHTS:

Estimated Female Officers or Directors: 3
Hot Spot for Advancement for Women/Minorities: Y

Bausch & Lomb Incorporated

www.bausch.com

NAIC Code: 339100

TYPES OF BUSINESS:

Supplies-Eye Care
Contact Lens Products
Ophthalmic Pharmaceuticals
Surgical Products

BRANDS/DIVISIONS/AFFILIATES:

Bausch Health Companies Inc
Biotrue
Bausch + Lomb
PureVision
ReNu
Alaway
Alrex
PreserVision

CONTACTS: *Note: Officers with more than one job title may be intentionally listed here more than once.*

Robert Bertolini, Pres.
John R. Barr, Pres., Surgical Bus.
Mariano Garcia-Valino, Corp. VP
Sheila A. Hopkins, Pres., Vision Care Bus.
Rodney William Unsworth, Pres., Asia Pacific
Joseph C. Papa, Chmn.

GROWTH PLANS/SPECIAL FEATURES:

Bausch & Lomb Incorporated (B&L), owned by Bausch Health Companies, Inc., is a world leader in the development, marketing and manufacturing of eye care products. The firm's products are marketed in more than 100 countries, and include contact lenses, contact lens care, dry eye products, allergy/redness relief, Rx pharmaceutical, eye vitamins, surgical products and vision accessories. B&L's contact lenses are for people who are nearsighted, farsighted, have astigmatism or presbyopia; they are soft hydrophilic discs that float on the cornea of the eye. Brands include Biotrue, Bausch + Lomb, Optima, PureVision, SofLens and Boston Multivision GP. Lens care products include Biotrue eye solution, PeroxiClear cleaning solution, ReNu solution and drops and Boston One Step cleaner and drops as well as Sensitive Eyes solutions. Dry eye product brands include Soothe eye drops, THERA PEARL Eye mask, Advanced Eye Relief and Muro 128 solutions. Allergy and redness relief product brands include Alaway, Opcon and Advanced. Rx pharmaceutical product brands include Alrex, Lotemax, Miochol-E, Visudyne, Zirgan, Bepreve, Istalol, Timoptic, Besivance, Prolensa, Vyzulta, and Lacrisert, among others. Eye washing products are marketed under the Advanced brand. Eye vitamins are marketed under the PreserVision and Ocuvite brands. Surgical product brands include enVista, Crystalens, Trulign, Akreos and SofPort. Last, vision accessories include magnifiers, cleaning kits, eyewear cleaning products and lens cases, all under the Bausch + Lomb name. In April 2021, B&L announced that the U.S. Food and Drug Administration approved ClearVisc dispersive ophthalmic viscosurgical device (OVD) for use in ophthalmic surgery.

B&L offers its employees medical and dental coverage, a 401(k) account plan, a vacation buy/sell program, flexible spending accounts and education reimbursement.

FINANCIAL DATA: *Note: Data for latest year may not have been available at press time.*

In U.S. $	2020	2019	2018	2017	2016	2015
Revenue	4,408,000,000	4,739,000,000	4,664,000,000	4,795,000,000	4,857,000,000	4,603,000,000
R&D Expense						
Operating Income						
Operating Margin %						
SGA Expense						
Net Income	1,159,000,000	1,332,000,000	1,330,000,000	1,412,000,000	1,456,000,000	
Operating Cash Flow						
Capital Expenditure						
EBITDA						
Return on Assets %						
Return on Equity %						
Debt to Equity						

CONTACT INFORMATION:

Phone: 585-338-6000   Fax: 585-338-6896
Toll-Free: 800-553-5340
Address: 400 Somerset Corporate Blvd, Bridgewater, NJ 08807 United States

STOCK TICKER/OTHER:

Stock Ticker: Subsidiary   Exchange:
Employees: 12,500   Fiscal Year Ends: 12/31
Parent Company: Bausch Health Companies Inc

SALARIES/BONUSES:

Top Exec. Salary: $ Bonus: $
Second Exec. Salary: $ Bonus: $

OTHER THOUGHTS:

Estimated Female Officers or Directors: 1
Hot Spot for Advancement for Women/Minorities: Y

Bausch Health Companies Inc

www.bauschhealth.com

NAIC Code: 325412

TYPES OF BUSINESS:

Prescription & Non-Prescription Pharmaceuticals
Specialty Pharmaceuticals
Medical Devices
Development
Manufacture

BRANDS/DIVISIONS/AFFILIATES:

Bausch + Lomb
Salix
Solta

CONTACTS: *Note: Officers with more than one job title may be intentionally listed here more than once.*

Joseph Papa, CEO
Paul Herendeen, CFO
Sam Eldessouky, Chief Accounting Officer
Thomas Appio, Co-President
Joseph Gordon, Co-President
Christina Ackermann, Executive VP
William Humphries, President, Divisional
Mark McKenna, President, Subsidiary

GROWTH PLANS/SPECIAL FEATURES:

Bausch Health Companies, Inc. is a specialty pharmaceutical and medical device company that develops, manufactures and markets its products globally. The firm operates through five business segments: Bausch + Lomb, Salix, international Rx, ortho dermatologics, and diversified products. The Bausch + Lomb segment consists of global sales of Bausch + Lomb vision care, consumer, surgical and ophthalmology prescription products. The Salix segment consists of sales in the U.S. of gastrointestinal products. The international Rx segment consists of sales outside the U.S. and Puerto Rico of branded pharmaceutical products, branded generic pharmaceutical products and over-the-counter (OTC) products, with the exception of Bausch + Lomb products and Solta medical aesthetic devices. The ortho dermatologics segment consists of sales in the U.S. of dermatological products, and global sales of Solta medical aesthetic devices. The diversified products segment consists of sales in the U.S. of pharmaceutical products in the areas of neurology and certain other therapeutic classes, as well as generic products and dentistry products. In August 2021, Bausch Health Companies sold its equity interest in Amoun Pharmaceutical Company S.A.E. to Abu Dhabi-based ADQ.entistry products.

FINANCIAL DATA: *Note: Data for latest year may not have been available at press time.*

In U.S. $	2020	2019	2018	2017	2016	2015
Revenue	8,027,000,000	8,601,000,000	8,380,000,000	8,724,000,000	9,674,000,000	10,446,500,000
R&D Expense	452,000,000	471,000,000	414,000,000	366,000,000	455,000,000	334,400,000
Operating Income	1,314,000,000	1,329,000,000	498,000,000	538,000,000	1,125,000,000	2,409,300,000
Operating Margin %		.15%	.06%	.06%	.11%	.21%
SGA Expense	2,367,000,000	2,554,000,000	2,473,000,000	2,582,000,000	2,810,000,000	2,699,800,000
Net Income	-560,000,000	-1,788,000,000	-4,148,000,000	2,404,000,000	-2,409,000,000	-291,700,000
Operating Cash Flow	1,111,000,000	1,501,000,000	1,501,000,000	2,290,000,000	2,087,000,000	2,200,400,000
Capital Expenditure	309,000,000	278,000,000	235,000,000	336,000,000	291,000,000	303,300,000
EBITDA	2,425,000,000	1,850,000,000	350,000,000	2,957,000,000	2,267,000,000	4,035,400,000
Return on Assets %		-.05%	-.12%	.06%	-.05%	-.01%
Return on Equity %		-.94%	-.97%	.53%	-.53%	-.05%
Debt to Equity		23.199	8.81	4.314	9.469	5.12

CONTACT INFORMATION:

Phone: 514 744-6792   Fax: 514 744-6272
Toll-Free: 800-361-1448
Address: 2150 St. Elzear Blvd. W., Laval, QC H7L 4A8 Canada

STOCK TICKER/OTHER:

Stock Ticker: BHC
Employees: 21,700
Parent Company:

Exchange: NYS
Fiscal Year Ends: 12/31

SALARIES/BONUSES:

Top Exec. Salary: $ Bonus: $
Second Exec. Salary: $ Bonus: $

OTHER THOUGHTS:

Estimated Female Officers or Directors: 3
Hot Spot for Advancement for Women/Minorities: Y

Baxter International Inc

www.baxter.com

NAIC Code: 339100

TYPES OF BUSINESS:

Medical Equipment Manufacturing
Supplies-Intravenous & Renal Dialysis Systems
Medication Delivery Products & IV Fluids
Biopharmaceutical Products
Plasma Collection & Processing
Vaccines
Software
Contract Research

BRANDS/DIVISIONS/AFFILIATES:

Cheetah Medical inc
Seprafilm

CONTACTS: *Note: Officers with more than one job title may be intentionally listed here more than once.*

Jose Almeida, CEO
James Saccaro, CFO
Brian Stevens, Chief Accounting Officer
Sean Martin, General Counsel
Andrew Frye, President, Geographical
Giuseppe Accogli, President, Geographical
Cristiano Franzi, President, Geographical
Scott Pleau, Senior VP, Divisional
Jeanne Mason, Senior VP, Divisional

GROWTH PLANS/SPECIAL FEATURES:

Baxter International, Inc., through its subsidiaries, provides a broad portfolio of essential healthcare products. These offerings include: acute and chronic dialysis therapies; sterile intravenous (IV) solutions; infusion systems and devices; parenteral nutrition therapies; inhaled anesthetics; generic injectable pharmaceuticals; and surgical hemostat and sealant products. In addition, Baxter's renal portfolio addresses the needs of patients with kidney failure or kidney disease. This portfolio includes innovative technologies and therapies for peritoneal dialysis, in-center and home hemodialysis, continuous renal replacement therapy, multi-organ extracorporeal support therapy, and additional dialysis services. Baxter's scientists are currently pursuing a range of next-generation monitors, dialyzers, devices, dialysis solutions and connectivity technology for home patients. Baxter manufactures its products in several countries, and sells them in more than 100 countries worldwide. The majority of the firm's revenues (approximately 60%) are generated outside the U.S., with an international presence including operations in Europe (Eastern and Central Europe), the Middle East, Africa, Asia-Pacific, Latin America and Canada. Each of these regions provide a wide range of essential healthcare products across the company's entire portfolio. Baxter maintains manufacturing facilities worldwide. During 2020, Baxter International acquired Cheetah Medical, Inc., a provider of non-invasive hemodynamic monitoring technologies; and acquired Sanofi's Seprafilm adhesion barrier product line, complementing Baxter's hemostat and sealant portfolio used in surgery procedures.

FINANCIAL DATA: *Note: Data for latest year may not have been available at press time.*

In U.S. $	2020	2019	2018	2017	2016	2015
Revenue	11,673,000,000	11,362,000,000	11,127,000,000	10,561,000,000	10,163,000,000	9,968,000,000
R&D Expense	521,000,000	595,000,000	655,000,000	617,000,000	647,000,000	603,000,000
Operating Income	1,551,000,000	876,000,000	1,647,000,000	1,258,000,000	724,000,000	449,000,000
Operating Margin %		.08%	.15%	.12%	.07%	.05%
SGA Expense	2,515,000,000	3,290,000,000	2,569,000,000	2,587,000,000	2,739,000,000	3,094,000,000
Net Income	1,102,000,000	1,001,000,000	1,624,000,000	717,000,000	4,965,000,000	968,000,000
Operating Cash Flow	1,868,000,000	2,104,000,000	2,096,000,000	1,837,000,000	1,654,000,000	1,647,000,000
Capital Expenditure	709,000,000	696,000,000	681,000,000	634,000,000	719,000,000	911,000,000
EBITDA	2,268,000,000	1,870,000,000	2,571,000,000	2,063,000,000	5,843,000,000	1,333,000,000
Return on Assets %		.06%	.10%	.04%	.27%	.04%
Return on Equity %		.13%	.19%	.08%	.58%	.11%
Debt to Equity		0.675	0.446	0.385	0.335	0.445

CONTACT INFORMATION:

Phone: 847 948-2000   Fax: 847 948-2964
Toll-Free: 800-422-9837
Address: 1 Baxter Pkwy., Deerfield, IL 60015 United States

STOCK TICKER/OTHER:

Stock Ticker: BAX
Employees: 50,000
Parent Company:

Exchange: NYS
Fiscal Year Ends: 12/31

SALARIES/BONUSES:

Top Exec. Salary: $ Bonus: $
Second Exec. Salary: $ Bonus: $

OTHER THOUGHTS:

Estimated Female Officers or Directors: 6
Hot Spot for Advancement for Women/Minorities: Y

Sales, profits and employees may be estimates. Financial information, benefits and other data can change quickly and may vary from those stated here.

Bayer AG

www.bayer.com

NAIC Code: 325412

TYPES OF BUSINESS:

Chemicals Manufacturing
Pharmaceuticals
Animal Health Products
Health Care Products
Crop Science
Plant Biotechnology
Over-the-Counter Drugs
Personal Care Products

BRANDS/DIVISIONS/AFFILIATES:

Capital Group International Inc
Aspirin
Aleve
Bepanthen
Canesten
Talcid
Elevit
Claritin

CONTACTS: *Note: Officers with more than one job title may be intentionally listed here more than once.*

Wolfgang Nickl, CFO
Werner Baumann, Chmn.

GROWTH PLANS/SPECIAL FEATURES:

Bayer AG is a German life science company with core competencies in the areas of healthcare and agriculture. With the company's innovative products, Bayer contributes to finding solutions to some of the major challenges confronting these sectors. It seeks to improve quality of life by preventing, alleviating and treating diseases; and the firm helps to provide a reliable supply of high-quality food, feed and plant-based raw materials. Bayer develops new molecules for use in innovative products. Its research and development activities are based on the biochemical processes in living organisms. The company groups its business into three divisions. The pharmaceuticals division focuses on prescription products, especially for cardiology and women's healthcare, and on specialty therapeutics in the areas of oncology, hematology and ophthalmology. Products include Xarelto, Eylea, Stivarga, Xofigo and Adempas. This division also includes a radiology unit, which markets contrast-enhanced diagnostic imaging equipment together with contrast agents. The consumer health division markets non-prescription products in dermatology, dietary supplement, analgesic, gastrointestinal, allergy, cold and flu, foot care, sun protection and cardiovascular risk prevention categories. These products include globally known brands such as Claritin, Aspirin, Aleve, Bepanthen, Canesten, Talcid and Elevit. The crop science division comprises businesses in seeds, crop protection and non-agricultural pest control. This segment also focuses on animal health and offers products and services for the prevention and treatment of diseases in companion and farm animals.

FINANCIAL DATA: *Note: Data for latest year may not have been available at press time.*

In U.S. $	2020	2019	2018	2017	2016	2015
Revenue	50,581,570,000	53,202,280,000	48,365,260,000	42,780,520,000	57,141,290,000	56,597,590,000
R&D Expense	8,706,383,000	6,526,733,000	6,409,442,000	5,502,883,000	5,700,811,000	5,230,427,000
Operating Income	-872,348,700	5,537,093,000	394,634,000	7,465,057,000	8,959,290,000	8,311,749,000
Operating Margin %		.10%	.01%	.17%	.16%	.15%
SGA Expense	19,465,350,000	19,748,800,000	18,911,890,000	16,056,590,000	17,996,780,000	17,673,010,000
Net Income	-12,822,550,000	4,998,289,000	2,070,912,000	8,962,956,000	5,535,871,000	5,021,503,000
Operating Cash Flow	5,990,372,000	10,027,120,000	9,672,808,000	9,937,934,000	11,104,730,000	8,418,043,000
Capital Expenditure	2,954,257,000	3,237,709,000	3,168,068,000	2,890,724,000	3,149,741,000	3,075,213,000
EBITDA	-2,926,156,000	12,331,390,000	12,565,980,000	9,906,168,000	12,960,610,000	11,749,830,000
Return on Assets %		.03%	.02%	.09%	.06%	.06%
Return on Equity %		.09%	.04%	.22%	.17%	.19%
Debt to Equity		0.78	0.82	0.33	0.507	0.673

CONTACT INFORMATION:

Phone: 49 214301   Fax: 49 2143066328
Toll-Free: 800-269-2377
Address: Kaiser-Wilhelm-Allee 1, Leverkusen, 51368 Germany

STOCK TICKER/OTHER:

Stock Ticker: BAYZF   Exchange: PINX
Employees: 99,538   Fiscal Year Ends: 12/31
Parent Company:

SALARIES/BONUSES:

Top Exec. Salary: $ Bonus: $
Second Exec. Salary: $ Bonus: $

OTHER THOUGHTS:

Estimated Female Officers or Directors: 1
Hot Spot for Advancement for Women/Minorities:

Bayer Corporation

www.bayer.us

NAIC Code: 325412

TYPES OF BUSINESS:

Chemicals Manufacturing
Animal Health Products
Over-the-Counter Drugs
Diagnostic Products
Coatings, Adhesives & Sealants
Polyurethanes & Plastics
Herbicides, Fungicides & Insecticides

BRANDS/DIVISIONS/AFFILIATES:

Capital Group International Inc
Bayer AG
Elmiron
Aleve
Bayer
Alka-Seltzer Plus
Bactine
One-A-Day

CONTACTS: *Note: Officers with more than one job title may be intentionally listed here more than once.*

Patrick Lockwood-Taylor, Pres.
Kelly S. Gast, CFO
Lisa Massa, Head of Human Resources-US
Lars Benecke, General Counsel
Stefan Scholz, VP-Corp. Auditing
Philip Blake, Head-Bayer Representative, U.S.
Mark Torsten Minuth, VP-Mergers & Acquisitions
Tracy Spagnol, VP

GROWTH PLANS/SPECIAL FEATURES:

Bayer Corporation., the U.S. subsidiary of chemical and pharmaceutical giant Bayer AG, operates through three divisions: pharmaceuticals, consumer health and crop science. The pharmaceuticals division consists of women's healthcare, oncology, hemophilia, multiple sclerosis (MS), cardiovascular, pulmonary hypertension and radiology. Products within this division include Elmiron, Angeliq and Refludan. The consumer health unit manufactures analgesics (Aleve and Bayer), cold and cough treatments (Alka-Seltzer and Aleve Cold & Sinus), digestive relief products (Phillips' Milk of Magnesia), topical skin preparations (Domeboro and Bactine) and vitamins (One-A-Day and Flintstones). The crop science manufactures crop protection, environmental science and bioscience products, such as herbicides, fungicides and insecticides.

The company offers its employees life, disability, medical, dental and vision coverage; prescription drug reimbursement; a 401(k); and adoption assistance.

FINANCIAL DATA: *Note: Data for latest year may not have been available at press time.*

In U.S. $	2020	2019	2018	2017	2016	2015
Revenue	17,627,800,000	6,850,000,000	6,800,000,000	6,350,000,000	6,300,000,000	6,150,000,000
R&D Expense						
Operating Income						
Operating Margin %						
SGA Expense						
Net Income						
Operating Cash Flow						
Capital Expenditure						
EBITDA						
Return on Assets %						
Return on Equity %						
Debt to Equity						

CONTACT INFORMATION:

Phone: 862-404-3000   Fax: 781-356-0165
Toll-Free:
Address: 100 Bayer Blvd., Whippany, NJ 07981-0915 United States

STOCK TICKER/OTHER:

Stock Ticker: Subsidiary
Employees: 19,111
Parent Company: Bayer AG

Exchange:
Fiscal Year Ends: 12/31

SALARIES/BONUSES:

Top Exec. Salary: $ Bonus: $
Second Exec. Salary: $ Bonus: $

OTHER THOUGHTS:

Estimated Female Officers or Directors: 1
Hot Spot for Advancement for Women/Minorities:

Bayer HealthCare Pharmaceuticals Inc

www.pharma.bayer.com

NAIC Code: 325412

TYPES OF BUSINESS:

Pharmaceuticals Discovery, Development & Manufacturing
Cardiovascular Treatments
Kidney Disease Treatments
Cancer Treatments
Hemophilia Treatments
Eye Condition Treatments
Womens Health Therapies
Pulmonary Hypertension Treatment

BRANDS/DIVISIONS/AFFILIATES:

Bayer AG

CONTACTS: *Note: Officers with more than one job title may be intentionally listed here more than once.*

Stefan Oelrich, Mngr.-Pharmaceuticals
Michael Devoy, Head-Medical Affairs & Pharmacovigilance
Oliver Renner, Head-Global Corp. Comm.
Werner Baumann, Chmn.

GROWTH PLANS/SPECIAL FEATURES:

Bayer HealthCare Pharmaceuticals, Inc. is the pharmaceutical division and subsidiary of Bayer AG. The firm utilizes advanced technologies, collaboration and pipeline development for the manufacture and marketing of its prescription drugs and therapeutic products. Bayer Healthcare Pharmaceuticals engages in five main disease groups: cardiovascular and kidney diseases, cancer, hemophilia, eye conditions, and women's healthcare. Cardiovascular disease is a group of disorders of the heart and blood vessels, and a leading cause of death; chronic kidney disease is characterized by a gradual loss of kidney function and is associated with an increased risk of cardiovascular disease and end-stage renal disease. Cancer requires an individual approach because there are so many types of cancer, symptoms and treatment options. Bayer works to find new ways of treating cancer so that patients do not have to undergo invasive treatments. Hemophilia is a rare bleeding disorder where one of the clotting factors is missing or deficient that affects the blood's ability to clot normally. Bayer has numerous compounds in various stages of development for this disorder. The firm's eye conditions division addresses retinal disease, both preventable and yet to be addressed, with a focus on eye conditions such as diabetic macular edema and age-related macular degeneration. Women's healthcare addresses menstrual cycles, birth control, pregnancy, menopause, endometriosis/myomas, uterine fibroids and acne therapy. In addition, Bayer is engaged in developing treatment for pulmonary hypertension, a disorder in which blood vessels in the lungs become very narrow and hamper oxygen uptake. The company has discovered a new way to widen the blood vessels, to lower blood pressure in the lungs and to relieve the heart.

FINANCIAL DATA: *Note: Data for latest year may not have been available at press time.*

In U.S. $	2020	2019	2018	2017	2016	2015
Revenue	4,734,880,000	4,524,240,000	4,535,130,000	5,065,760,000	4,418,630,000	4,301,330,000
R&D Expense						
Operating Income						
Operating Margin %						
SGA Expense						
Net Income						
Operating Cash Flow						
Capital Expenditure						
EBITDA						
Return on Assets %						
Return on Equity %						
Debt to Equity						

CONTACT INFORMATION:

Phone: 862-404-3000 Fax:
Toll-Free:
Address: 100 Bayer Blvd., Whippany, NJ 07981 United States

STOCK TICKER/OTHER:

Stock Ticker: Subsidiary
Employees: 39,000
Parent Company: Bayer AG
Exchange:
Fiscal Year Ends: 12/31

SALARIES/BONUSES:

Top Exec. Salary: $ Bonus: $
Second Exec. Salary: $ Bonus: $

OTHER THOUGHTS:

Estimated Female Officers or Directors:
Hot Spot for Advancement for Women/Minorities:

Baylor Scott & White Health

www.bswhealth.com

NAIC Code: 622110

TYPES OF BUSINESS:

General Medical and Surgical Hospitals
Long-Term Care
Retirement & Nursing Homes
Retail Pharmacies
Rehabilitation Services

BRANDS/DIVISIONS/AFFILIATES:

Baylor Health Care System
Scott & White Healthcare
MyBSWHealth
FollowMyHealth

CONTACTS: *Note: Officers with more than one job title may be intentionally listed here more than once.*

Pete McCanna, CEO
Jennifer Mitzner, CFO
Nikki Moll, Sr. VP-Mktg. & Communications
Nakesha Lopez, Chief Human Resources Officer
Matthew Chambers, CIO
Alejandro Arroliga, Chief Medical Officer

GROWTH PLANS/SPECIAL FEATURES:

Baylor Scott & White Health is a non-profit healthcare system in Texas, and created through the 2013 combination of Baylor Health Care System and Scott & White Healthcare. Today, Baylor Scott & White includes 52 hospitals, more than 800 patient care sites and over 7,300 active physicians. The firm provides full-range, inpatient, outpatient, rehabilitation and emergency medical services, serving more than 7.5 million patients each year. Specialties include allergy, anesthesiology, back and neck care, behavioral and psychological health, breast imaging, cancer care, dentistry, diabetes, ear/nose/throat, genetics, heart/vascular, hospice, infectious diseases, kidney disease, lung care, men's health, neuroscience, pediatric care, pharmacy, rheumatology, sleep disorders, surgical services, transplants, urology, weight loss surgery and more. Appointments can be made by phone and online, and patient registration and billing can also be completed online. MyBSWHealth and FollowMyHealth enable patients to access their personal health records, set or change appointments, view test results and communicate with providers from any computer, tablet or smartphone device. Insurance products are available including a variety of health plans as well as dental and life insurance.

FINANCIAL DATA: *Note: Data for latest year may not have been available at press time.*

In U.S. $	2020	2019	2018	2017	2016	2015
Revenue	1,158,505,975	982,475,378	960,710,546	946,738,753	938,248,557	877,345,140
R&D Expense						
Operating Income						
Operating Margin %						
SGA Expense						
Net Income	-136,407,231	-17,194,766	-23,838,306	-16,448,684	7,205,412	-17,805,755
Operating Cash Flow						
Capital Expenditure						
EBITDA						
Return on Assets %						
Return on Equity %						
Debt to Equity						

CONTACT INFORMATION:

Phone: 254-724-2111   Fax:
Toll-Free: 844-279-3627
Address: 301 N. Washington Ave., Dallas, TX 75246 United States

STOCK TICKER/OTHER:

Stock Ticker: Nonprofit
Employees: 49,000
Parent Company:

Exchange:
Fiscal Year Ends: 06/30

SALARIES/BONUSES:

Top Exec. Salary: $ Bonus: $
Second Exec. Salary: $ Bonus: $

OTHER THOUGHTS:

Estimated Female Officers or Directors:
Hot Spot for Advancement for Women/Minorities:

Sales, profits and employees may be estimates. Financial information, benefits and other data can change quickly and may vary from those stated here.

Beckman Coulter Inc

www.beckmancoulter.com

NAIC Code: 334510

TYPES OF BUSINESS:

Electromedical and Electrotherapeutic Apparatus Manufacturing
Chemistry Systems
Genetic Analysis/Nucleic Acid Testing
Biomedical Research Supplies
Immunoassay Systems
Cellular Systems
Discovery & Automation Systems

BRANDS/DIVISIONS/AFFILIATES:

Danaher Corporation
Access SARS-CoV-2 IgM

CONTACTS: *Note: Officers with more than one job title may be intentionally listed here more than once.*

Julie Sawyer-Montgomery, Pres.
Marianne Ovesen, Sr. VP-Global Oper.
Chris Hagen, VP-Global Mktg.
Mickey Blanks, Sr. VP-Human Resources & Communications
Pedro Diaz, Dir.-Research
John Blackwood, Sr. VP-Product Mgmt.
Jeff Linton, Sr. VP
Ken Hyek, Dir.-Service Oper.
Allan Harris, Sr. VP-Strategy & Bus. Dev.
Jerry Battenberg, VP-Finance
Clair O'Donovan, Sr. VP-Quality & Regulatory Affairs
Jennifer Honeycutt, Pres., Life Sciences
Richard Creager, Sr. VP
Michael K. Samoszuk, VP
Brian Burnett, Sr. VP-Global Oper.

GROWTH PLANS/SPECIAL FEATURES:

Beckman Coulter, Inc., a wholly-owned subsidiary of Danaher Corporation, designs, develops, manufactures and markets clinical diagnostic products and laboratory solutions. The company's products and solutions are used in clinical settings worldwide to deliver test result. Disciplines of the firm encompass automation, blood banking, clinical chemistry, clinical centrifugation, clinical information management tools, hematology, immunoassay, microbiology, protein chemistry and urinalysis. Diagnostic solutions include sepsis diagnosis and management, early sepsis indicator, cardiovascular disease, reproductive health, anemia, drug monitoring & detection and life sciences. Beckman's Access SARS-CoV-2 Immunoglobulin M (IgM) assay is an antibody test that demonstrated 99.9% specificity against 1,400 negative samples and 98.3% sensitivity at 15-30 days post-symptom onset. Access SARS-CoV-2 IgG II received U.S. Emergency Use Authorization from the U.S. Food and Drug Administration in 2021, which measures a patient's level of antibodies in response to a previous SARS-CoV-2 infection and provides a qualitative and numerical result of antibodies in arbitrary units. Headquartered in California, the firm has additional centers in Minnesota and Florida.

Beckman offers its employees medical, dental and vision coverage; a wellness program; a 401(k) and company retirement plan; life insurance; disability income protection; credit union membership; and employee discounts.

FINANCIAL DATA: *Note: Data for latest year may not have been available at press time.*

In U.S. $	2020	2019	2018	2017	2016	2015
Revenue	6,232,950,000	6,561,000,000	6,257,000,000	5,839,000,000	5,050,000,000	5,000,000,000
R&D Expense						
Operating Income						
Operating Margin %						
SGA Expense						
Net Income						
Operating Cash Flow						
Capital Expenditure						
EBITDA						
Return on Assets %						
Return on Equity %						
Debt to Equity						

CONTACT INFORMATION:

Phone: 714-993-5321 Fax: 800-232-3828
Toll-Free: 800-526-3821
Address: 250 S. Kraemer Blvd., Brea, CA 92821 United States

STOCK TICKER/OTHER:

Stock Ticker: Subsidiary
Employees: 11,000
Parent Company: Danaher Corporation
Exchange:
Fiscal Year Ends: 12/31

SALARIES/BONUSES:

Top Exec. Salary: $ Bonus: $
Second Exec. Salary: $ Bonus: $

OTHER THOUGHTS:

Estimated Female Officers or Directors: 5
Hot Spot for Advancement for Women/Minorities: Y

Becton Dickinson and Company

www.bd.com

NAIC Code: 339100

TYPES OF BUSINESS:

Medical Equipment-Injection/Infusion
Drug Delivery Systems
Infusion Therapy Products
Diabetes Care Products
Surgical Products
Microbiology Products
Diagnostic Products
Consulting Services

BRANDS/DIVISIONS/AFFILIATES:

BD Medical
BD Life Sciences
BD Interventional
V Muller

CONTACTS: Note: Officers with more than one job title may be intentionally listed here more than once.

Vincent Forlenza, CEO
Roland Goette, Executive VP
Christopher Reidy, CFO
Charles Bodner, Chief Accounting Officer
James Borzi, Executive VP, Divisional
Betty Larson, Executive VP, Divisional
Samrat Khichi, Executive VP
Alberto Mas, Executive VP
Patrick Kaltenbach, Executive VP
Simon Campion, Executive VP
James Lim, Executive VP
Thomas Polen, President
Gary DeFazio, Secretary

GROWTH PLANS/SPECIAL FEATURES:

Becton, Dickinson and Company (BD) is a global medical technology company engaged in the development, manufacture and sale of medical supplies, devices, laboratory equipment and diagnostic products. These offerings are primarily used by healthcare institutions, life science researchers, clinical laboratories, the pharmaceutical industry and the general public. The company operates in three worldwide business segments: BD Medical, BD Life Sciences and BD Interventional. BD Medical's principal product lines include a broad range of medication delivery solutions, medication management solutions, diabetes care solutions and pharmaceutical systems. BD Life Sciences offers products for safe collection and transport of diagnostics specimens, and instruments and reagent systems to detect infectious diseases, healthcare-associated infections and cancers. This division produces research and clinical tools that facilitate the study of cells, and the components of cells, to gain a better understanding of normal and disease processes. This information is used to aid the discovery and development of new drugs and vaccines, among other purposes. Last, the BD Interventional segment provides vascular, urology, oncology and surgical specialty products intended to be used once and then discarded or are either temporarily or permanently implanted. V. Muller-trademarked surgical laparoscopic instrumentation products are an exception to these temporary offerings. Manufacturing operations outside the U.S. include Bosnia/Herzegovina, Brazil, Canada, China, Dominican Republic, France, Germany, Hungary, India, Ireland, Israel, Italy, Japan, Malaysia, Mexico, Netherlands, Singapore, Spain and the U.K. Products are marketed and distributed in the U.S. and internationally through distribution channels, and directly to end users by BD and independent sales representatives. In late-2020, BD acquired the medical business assets of Cubex LLC, expanding its automated dispensing portfolio; and announced plans to invest $1.2 billion in pre-fillable syringe manufacturing capacity over the next four years.

BD offers its employees comprehensive benefits.

FINANCIAL DATA: Note: Data for latest year may not have been available at press time.

In U.S. $	2020	2019	2018	2017	2016	2015
Revenue	17,117,000,000	17,290,000,000	15,983,000,000	12,093,000,000	12,483,000,000	10,282,000,000
R&D Expense	1,096,000,000	1,062,000,000	1,006,000,000	774,000,000	828,000,000	632,000,000
Operating Income	1,800,000,000	2,238,000,000	2,241,000,000	1,833,000,000	2,158,000,000	1,500,000,000
Operating Margin %		.13%	.14%	.15%	.17%	.15%
SGA Expense	4,318,000,000	4,334,000,000	4,015,000,000	2,925,000,000	3,005,000,000	2,563,000,000
Net Income	874,000,000	1,233,000,000	311,000,000	1,100,000,000	976,000,000	695,000,000
Operating Cash Flow	3,539,000,000	3,328,000,000	2,865,000,000	2,550,000,000	2,559,000,000	1,729,000,000
Capital Expenditure	810,000,000	957,000,000	895,000,000	727,000,000	718,000,000	633,000,000
EBITDA	3,667,000,000	4,068,000,000	3,857,000,000	2,585,000,000	2,576,000,000	2,001,000,000
Return on Assets %		.02%	.00%	.03%	.04%	.04%
Return on Equity %		.05%	.01%	.10%	.13%	.11%
Debt to Equity		0.858	0.90	1.442	1.382	1.587

CONTACT INFORMATION:

Phone: 201 847-6800 Fax:
Toll-Free: 800-284-6845
Address: 1 Becton Dr., Franklin Lakes, NJ 07417 United States

STOCK TICKER/OTHER:

Stock Ticker: BDX
Employees: 72,000
Parent Company:

Exchange: NYS
Fiscal Year Ends: 09/30

SALARIES/BONUSES:

Top Exec. Salary: $ Bonus: $
Second Exec. Salary: $ Bonus: $

OTHER THOUGHTS:

Estimated Female Officers or Directors: 6
Hot Spot for Advancement for Women/Minorities: Y

Sales, profits and employees may be estimates. Financial information, benefits and other data can change quickly and may vary from those stated here.

Biogen Inc

NAIC Code: 325412

www.biogen.com

TYPES OF BUSINESS:

Drugs-Immunology, Neurology & Oncology
Autoimmune & Inflammatory Disease Treatments
Drugs-Multiple Sclerosis
Drugs-Cancer

BRANDS/DIVISIONS/AFFILIATES:

TECFIDERA
AVONEX
PLEGRIDY
SPINRAZA
FUMADERM
RITUXAN
GAZYVA
OCREVUS

CONTACTS: *Note: Officers with more than one job title may be intentionally listed here more than once.*

Michel Vounatsos, CEO
Jeffrey Capello, CFO
Gregory Covino, Chief Accounting Officer
Alfred Sandrock, Chief Medical Officer
Stelios Papadopoulos, Director
Michael Ehlers, Executive VP, Divisional
Paul McKenzie, Executive VP, Divisional
Kenneth Dipietro, Executive VP, Divisional
Adriana Karaboutis, Executive VP, Divisional
Chirfi Guindo, Executive VP
Ginger Gregory, Executive VP
Susan Alexander, Executive VP

GROWTH PLANS/SPECIAL FEATURES:

Biogen, Inc. is a biotechnology company focused on discovering, developing, manufacturing and marketing therapies for people living with serious neurological and neurodegenerative diseases. The company's core growth areas in relation to these diseases include multiple sclerosis (MS), neuroimmunology, Alzheimer's disease, dementia, movement disorders, and neuromuscular disorders such as spinal muscular atrophy (SMA) and amyotrophic lateral sclerosis (ALS). Biogen announced plans to invest in emerging growth areas such as pain, ophthalmology, neuropsychiatry and acute neurology, as well as discovering potential treatments for rare and genetic disorders. The firm also manufactures and commercializes biosimilars of advanced biologics. Biogen's marketed products include: TECFIDERA, AVONEX, PLEGRIDY, TYSABRI, VUMERITY and FAMPRYA for the treatment of MS; SPINRAZA for the treatment of SMA; and FUMADERM for the treatment of severe plaque psoriasis. In addition, the company has certain business and financial rights with respect to: RITUXAN and RITUXAN HYCELA for the treatment of non-Hodgkin's lymphoma and chronic lymphocytic leukemia (CLL) and other conditions; GAZYVA for the treatment of CLL and follicular lymphoma; OCREVUS for the treatment of primary progressive MS and relapsing MS; and other potential anti-CD20 therapies under a collaboration agreement with Genentech, Inc., which is wholly-owned by Roche Group. In order to support its future growth and drug development pipeline, Biogen announced plans to expand its large molecule production capacity by building a large-scale biologics manufacturing facility in Solothurn, Switzerland, which was expected to be partially operational by mid-2021.

Biogen offers its employees medical, dental and vision insurance; tuition reimbursement; flexible spending accounts; and an employee assistance program.

FINANCIAL DATA: *Note: Data for latest year may not have been available at press time.*

In U.S. $	2020	2019	2018	2017	2016	2015
Revenue	13,444,600,000	14,377,900,000	13,452,900,000	12,273,900,000	11,448,800,000	10,763,800,000
R&D Expense	3,990,900,000	2,280,600,000	2,597,200,000	2,253,600,000	1,973,300,000	2,012,800,000
Operating Income	4,446,300,000	7,035,700,000	6,000,800,000	5,527,800,000	5,653,100,000	5,014,900,000
Operating Margin %		.49%	.45%	.45%	.49%	.47%
SGA Expense	2,504,500,000	2,374,700,000	2,106,300,000	1,935,500,000	1,947,900,000	2,113,100,000
Net Income	4,000,600,000	5,888,500,000	4,430,700,000	2,539,100,000	3,702,800,000	3,547,000,000
Operating Cash Flow	4,229,800,000	7,078,600,000	6,187,700,000	4,551,000,000	4,522,400,000	3,716,100,000
Capital Expenditure	551,800,000	669,500,000	886,100,000	1,962,800,000	727,700,000	643,000,000
EBITDA	5,734,800,000	7,993,900,000	7,116,800,000	6,460,600,000	5,875,700,000	5,463,200,000
Return on Assets %		.22%	.18%	.11%	.17%	.21%
Return on Equity %		.45%	.35%	.21%	.34%	.35%
Debt to Equity		0.365	0.455	0.471	0.536	0.696

CONTACT INFORMATION:

Phone: 617-679-2000   Fax: 619 679-2617
Toll-Free:
Address: 225 Binney St., Cambridge, MA 02142 United States

STOCK TICKER/OTHER:

Stock Ticker: BIIB
Employees: 7,400
Parent Company:

Exchange: NAS
Fiscal Year Ends: 12/31

SALARIES/BONUSES:

Top Exec. Salary: $ Bonus: $
Second Exec. Salary: $ Bonus: $

OTHER THOUGHTS:

Estimated Female Officers or Directors: 4
Hot Spot for Advancement for Women/Minorities: Y

BioMerieux SA

www.biomerieux.com

NAIC Code: 424210

TYPES OF BUSINESS:

Diagnostic Reagents Merchant Wholesalers
Biotechnology
Diagnostic Solutions
Reagents
Diagnostic Instruments
Software

BRANDS/DIVISIONS/AFFILIATES:

AIR IDEAL
BACT/ALERT
BIOBALL
CONNECT-UP
CULTURE MEDIA
DILUMAT
eGENE-UP
ENDOEXT

CONTACTS: *Note: Officers with more than one job title may be intentionally listed here more than once.*

Alexandre Merieux, CEO
Pierre Boulud, COO
Guillaume Bouhours, CFO
Valerie Leylde, Exec. VP-Human Resources & Communications
Mark Miller, Chief Medical Officer
Stefan Willemsen, Corp. VP-Legal
Stefan Willemsen, Corp. VP-Bus. Dev.
Michel Baguenault, Corp. VP-Comm.
Thierry Bernard, Corp. VP-Investor Rel.
Marc Mackowiak, CEO-bioMerieux, Inc.
Nicolas Cartier, Corp. VP-Industrial Microbiology Unit
Francois Lacoste, Corp. VP-Immunoassay Unity & Quality
Alain Pluquet, Corp. VP-Innovation & Systems Unit
Thierry Bernard, Exec. VP-Greater China

GROWTH PLANS/SPECIAL FEATURES:

BioMerieux SA is a French multi-national biotechnology company founded in 1963. The company provides diagnostic solutions, reagents, instruments, services and software that determine the source of disease and contamination in order to improve patient health and ensure consumer safety. BioMerieux is present in 44 countries and serves more than 160 countries through its distributors. The firm has 15 production sites and 17 research and development sites. BioMerieux primary focuses are: clinical diagnostics, which accounts for 85% of annual sales; and industrial microbiology (15%). Clinical diagnostic products by specialty include immunoassay, microbiology, molecular diagnostics, performance management and lab automation. Diagnostic products by pathology include COVID-19, bacterial infections, bone and mineral metabolism, cancer, cardiology, central nervous system infections, congenital/perinatal infections, emergency/critical care, hormones/fertility, fungal infections, gastro-intestinal infections, hepatitis, HIV, immune-compromised/transplant infections, perinatal infections/pregnancy, resistance detection, respiratory tract infections, sepsis, sexually-transmitted diseases, thrombosis/coagulation, thyroid diseases, tuberculosis, tumor diseases, urinary tract infections, and more. The industrial microbiology division offers testing systems to improve public health and safety for industries such food, healthcare and pharmaceuticals. It develops solutions that cater to each client's requirements for consistent product quality and safety. Industrial microbiology products and solutions include: AIR IDEAL air testing system, API microbial identification system, BACT/ALERT culture media bottles, BACT/ALERT 3D rapid microbial detection system, BACT/ALERT VIRTUO platelet testing solution, BIOBALL standardized strains, BIOFIRE mycoplasma nucleic acid amplification detection system, CONNECT-UP lab data management solution, CULTURE MEDIA solutions, DILUMAT gravimetric diluter system, eGENE-UP lysis and RNA/DNA purification system, ENDOEXT endotoxin detection solution, among many others. During 2021, BioMerieux launched EPSIEQ SARS-CoV-2, a cloud-based software application to support microbiology labs in identification and reporting from raw sequencing data related to SARS-CoV-2 variants.

FINANCIAL DATA: *Note: Data for latest year may not have been available at press time.*

In U.S. $	2020	2019	2018	2017	2016	2015
Revenue	3,747,923,000	3,218,283,000	2,915,771,000	2,795,670,000	2,569,641,000	2,400,303,000
R&D Expense	487,244,600	457,311,100	399,398,900	371,908,900	332,201,200	291,882,500
Operating Income	666,357,200	424,811,800	398,543,600	409,050,900	363,845,200	317,662,000
Operating Margin %		.13%	.13%	.14%	.13%	.12%
SGA Expense	964,348,500	916,088,400	788,657,100	737,831,200	695,802,000	646,564,400
Net Income	494,086,600	333,300,800	313,508,000	290,905,100	218,820,300	135,006,400
Operating Cash Flow	712,051,600	498,362,800	472,705,500	436,785,300	410,028,400	378,750,800
Capital Expenditure	339,043,100	332,934,200	277,099,000	224,196,100	284,674,000	254,374,000
EBITDA	929,650,000	682,851,100	605,879,200	548,211,300	512,291,100	383,760,100
Return on Assets %		.08%	.08%	.08%	.06%	.04%
Return on Equity %		.13%	.14%	.14%	.12%	.08%
Debt to Equity		0.07	0.232	0.225	0.226	0.207

CONTACT INFORMATION:

Phone: 33 478872000   Fax: 33 478872090
Toll-Free:
Address: Marcy l'Etoile, Lyon, 69280 France

STOCK TICKER/OTHER:

Stock Ticker: BMXXY   Exchange: GREY
Employees: 11,029   Fiscal Year Ends: 12/31
Parent Company:

SALARIES/BONUSES:

Top Exec. Salary: $ Bonus: $
Second Exec. Salary: $ Bonus: $

OTHER THOUGHTS:

Estimated Female Officers or Directors: 2
Hot Spot for Advancement for Women/Minorities:

Sales, profits and employees may be estimates. Financial information, benefits and other data can change quickly and may vary from those stated here.

Bio-Rad Laboratories Inc

NAIC Code: 325413

www.bio-rad.com

TYPES OF BUSINESS:

Clinical Diagnostics Products
Diagnostics Products
Manufacture
Distribution
Reagents
Laboratory Instruments
Diagnostics Tests
Biological Materials

BRANDS/DIVISIONS/AFFILIATES:

CONTACTS: *Note: Officers with more than one job title may be intentionally listed here more than once.*

Norman Schwartz, CEO
Ilan Daskal, CFO
James Stark, Chief Accounting Officer
Andrew Last, COO
Michael Crowley, Executive VP, Divisional
Timothy Ernst, Executive VP
Giovanni Magni, Executive VP
Annette Tumolo, Executive VP
John Hertia, Executive VP
Ronald Hutton, Executive VP

GROWTH PLANS/SPECIAL FEATURES:

Bio-Rad Laboratories, Inc. is a multinational manufacturer and distributor of its own life science research and clinical diagnostics products. Bio-Rad supplies the life science research, healthcare, analytical chemistry and other markets with a range of products and systems used to separate complex chemical and biological materials and to identify, analyze and purify their components. The firm has direct distribution channels in over 36 countries outside the U.S. via subsidiaries whose focus is sales, customer service and product distribution. Bio-Rad operates its business through two segments: life science and clinical diagnostics, which generated 49% and 51% of net sales in 2020. The life science segment develops, manufactures and markets approximately 6,000 reagents, apparatus and laboratory instruments. Many of these products are used in research techniques, biopharmaceutical production processes and food testing regimes. The clinical diagnostics segment designs, manufactures, sells and supports test systems, informatics systems, test kits and specialized quality controls that serve clinical laboratories in the global diagnostics market. These products currently address specific niches within the in vitro diagnostics (IVD) test market. This division supplies more than 3,000 different products that cover 300+ clinical diagnostic tests to the IVD test market. Bio-Rad utilizes a wide variety of chemicals, biological materials, electronic components, machined metal parts, optical parts, computing and peripheral devices, most of which are available from numerous sources. Bio-Rad owns over 2,200 U.S. and international patents and numerous trademarks.

FINANCIAL DATA: *Note: Data for latest year may not have been available at press time.*

In U.S. $	2020	2019	2018	2017	2016	2015
Revenue	2,545,626,000	2,311,659,000	2,289,415,000	2,160,153,000	2,068,172,000	2,019,441,000
R&D Expense	226,598,000	202,710,000	199,196,000	250,301,000	205,864,000	192,972,000
Operating Income	410,957,000	229,661,000	189,172,000	128,156,000	115,499,000	166,708,000
Operating Margin %		.10%	.08%	.06%	.06%	.08%
SGA Expense	800,267,000	824,625,000	834,783,000	808,942,000	816,724,000	761,990,000
Net Income	3,806,267,000	1,758,675,000	365,614,000	122,249,000	28,125,000	113,093,000
Operating Cash Flow	575,328,000	457,897,000	285,494,000	103,885,000	216,433,000	186,210,000
Capital Expenditure	98,920,000	98,532,000	129,828,000	115,127,000	141,571,000	113,372,000
EBITDA	5,067,599,000	2,418,697,000	674,721,000	268,419,000	206,402,000	299,339,000
Return on Assets %		.26%	.07%	.03%	.01%	.03%
Return on Equity %		.36%	.11%	.04%	.01%	.05%
Debt to Equity		0.033	0.109	0.148	0.168	0.175

CONTACT INFORMATION:

Phone: 510 724-7000   Fax: 510 741-5817
Toll-Free: 800-424-6723
Address: 1000 Alfred Nobel Dr., Hercules, CA 94547 United States

STOCK TICKER/OTHER:

Stock Ticker: BIO   Exchange: NYS
Employees: 8,120   Fiscal Year Ends: 12/31
Parent Company:

SALARIES/BONUSES:

Top Exec. Salary: $ Bonus: $
Second Exec. Salary: $ Bonus: $

OTHER THOUGHTS:

Estimated Female Officers or Directors: 3
Hot Spot for Advancement for Women/Minorities: Y

Bio-Reference Laboratories Inc   www.bioreference.com

NAIC Code: 621511

TYPES OF BUSINESS:

Medical Laboratories & Testing
Diagnostic Solutions
Clinical Laboratories
Genetics
Genomics
Specimen Collection Services

BRANDS/DIVISIONS/AFFILIATES:

OPKO Health Inc
GeneDX
GenPath Oncology
GenPath Urology
GenPath Womens Health
my-labology
Scarlet Health

CONTACTS: *Note: Officers with more than one job title may be intentionally listed here more than once.*

Geoff Monk, Pres.
Craig Allen, COO
Kevin Feeley, CFO
Natalie Cummins, CCO
Greg Cahill, VP-Human Resources
David Evans, CIO
Marc Grodman, Founder
Jon R. Cohen, Chmn.

GROWTH PLANS/SPECIAL FEATURES:

Bio-Reference Laboratories, Inc., a subsidiary of OPKO Health, Inc., offers innovative diagnostic solutions tailored to the specific needs of healthcare providers, consumers and organizations. Bio-Reference focuses on genetics, oncology, urology and women's health, and is in-network with leading health plans in the U.S., serving approximately 19 million patients annually. The company operates a network of 10 laboratory locations, comprising a medical staff of more than 300 doctors, genetic counselors and other professional clinical and scientific personnel. Bio-Reference solutions meet the needs of employers, government agencies, education systems, hospitals, health systems, correctional institutions, sports leagues, travel and leisure industries, and retail markets. The firm also provides custom solutions for COVID-19, including point-of-care testing and large-scale screening programs. Other testings include allergies, chronic fatigue, chronic hepatitis, diabetes, gastric distress, heart disease, hematologic cancers, hereditary cancers, prostate cancer, seasonal influenza, sexual health, solid tumors, tuberculosis and Zika virus. Bio-Reference brands and subsidiaries include: GeneDx, Inc., a global leader in genomics; GenPath Oncology, a specialist in cancer diagnostics; GenPath Urology, offering comprehensive tests and services to help diagnose and manage a variety of urologic conditions; GenPath Women's Health, a one-source laboratory solution for all testing and service needs for women at every stage of their lives; my-labology, a consumer-initiated testing service that streamlines the path from test requests to results by making testing accessible to all; and Scarlet Health, an in-home, fully integrated digital platform that provides access to on-demand specimen collection services. During 2021, Bio-Reference acquired the U.S. Ariosa laboratory prenatal testing business from Roche.

FINANCIAL DATA: *Note: Data for latest year may not have been available at press time.*

In U.S. $	2020	2019	2018	2017	2016	2015
Revenue	940,123,800	921,690,000	970,200,000	924,000,000	880,000,000	865,640,000
R&D Expense						
Operating Income						
Operating Margin %						
SGA Expense						
Net Income						
Operating Cash Flow						
Capital Expenditure						
EBITDA						
Return on Assets %						
Return on Equity %						
Debt to Equity						

CONTACT INFORMATION:

Phone: 201 791-2600   Fax:
Toll-Free: 800-229-5227
Address: 481 Edward H. Ross Dr., Elmwood Park, NJ 07407 United States

STOCK TICKER/OTHER:

Stock Ticker: Subsidiary
Employees: 4,660
Parent Company: OPKO Health Inc

Exchange:
Fiscal Year Ends: 10/31

SALARIES/BONUSES:

Top Exec. Salary: $ Bonus: $
Second Exec. Salary: $ Bonus: $

OTHER THOUGHTS:

Estimated Female Officers or Directors: 3
Hot Spot for Advancement for Women/Minorities: Y

Biosensors International Group Ltd

www.biosensors.com

NAIC Code: 334510

TYPES OF BUSINESS:

Electromedical and Electrotherapeutic Apparatus Manufacturing
Medical Devices
Product Development
Product Manufacturing
Stents
Catheters

BRANDS/DIVISIONS/AFFILIATES:

Blue Sail Medical Co Ltd
BioFreedom
BioMatrix
Chroma
BioStream
Powerline
RISE NC
BioPath

CONTACTS: *Note: Officers with more than one job title may be intentionally listed here more than once.*

Jeffrey B. jump, Pres., Cardiovascular Bus. Unit.
Wen Jing Liu, Chmn.-Corp.

GROWTH PLANS/SPECIAL FEATURES:

Biosensors International Group Ltd. is an international group of companies which develop, manufacture and market innovative medical devices for interventional cardiology and endovascular procedures. The cardiovascular division focuses on the development, manufacture and commercialization of drug-eluting stents, drug-coated stents and bare metal stents, as well as angioplasty catheters for the treatment of coronary artery disease (balloon dilatation catheters and drug eluting balloons). Branded products within this segment include BioFreedom, BioMatrix, Chroma, BioStream, Powerline and RISE NC. The endovascular division offers interventional devices to treat peripheral arterial disease, and also offers stenting and ballooning solutions for superficial femoral artery and below-the-knee interventions. Branded products in this segment includes BioStream and BioPath. Biosensors developed its own proprietary technology in Biolimus A9, a limus drug designed specifically for coronary stent applications. The firm is a subsidiary of Blue Sail Medical Co., Ltd., a global manufacturer and marketer of health protection gloves. Biosensors is headquartered in Singapore, its European headquarters are in Morges, Switzerland, and the company's network of direct sales and distributors operate throughout the world.

FINANCIAL DATA: *Note: Data for latest year may not have been available at press time.*

In U.S. $	2020	2019	2018	2017	2016	2015
Revenue						
R&D Expense						
Operating Income						
Operating Margin %						
SGA Expense						
Net Income						
Operating Cash Flow						
Capital Expenditure						
EBITDA						
Return on Assets %						
Return on Equity %						
Debt to Equity						

CONTACT INFORMATION:

Phone: 65 6213-5777   Fax: 65 6213-5737
Toll-Free:
Address: 36, Jalan Tukang, Singapore, 619266 Singapore

STOCK TICKER/OTHER:

Stock Ticker: Subsidiary   Exchange:
Employees: Fiscal Year Ends: 03/31
Parent Company: Blue Sail Medical Co Ltd

SALARIES/BONUSES:

Top Exec. Salary: $ Bonus: $
Second Exec. Salary: $ Bonus: $

OTHER THOUGHTS:

Estimated Female Officers or Directors:
Hot Spot for Advancement for Women/Minorities:

Bio-Techne Corporation

www.techne-corp.com

NAIC Code: 325413

TYPES OF BUSINESS:

Biotechnology Products
Reagents, Antibodies & Assay Kits
Hematology Products
Genomics
Diagnostics

BRANDS/DIVISIONS/AFFILIATES:

R&D Systems
Novus Biologicals
Tocris
ProteinSimple
BiosPacific
Advanced Cell Diagnostics Inc
Exosome Diagnostics
Boston Biochem Inc

CONTACTS: *Note: Officers with more than one job title may be intentionally listed here more than once.*

Charles Kummeth, CEO
James Hippel, CFO
Robert Baumgartner, Chairman of the Board
David Eansor, President, Divisional
Kim Kelderman, President, Divisional
Brenda Furlow, Senior VP

GROWTH PLANS/SPECIAL FEATURES:

Bio-Techne Corporation and its subsidiaries develop, manufacture and sell biotechnology reagents and instruments for research and clinical diagnostic markets worldwide. The firm operates through two segments: protein sciences and diagnostics and genomics. The protein segment develops and manufactures high-quality purified proteins and reagent solutions, most notably cytokines and growth factors, antibodies, immunoassays, biologically active small molecule compounds, tissue culture reagents and T-Cell activation technologies. This division also includes protein analysis solutions that offer researchers options for automated western blot and multiplexed ELISA workflow (antibody coating, protein capture, detection, streptavidin-enzyme conjugate, addition of substrate and analysis). The genomics and diagnostics segment develops and manufactures diagnostic products, including U.S. Food and Drug Administration (FDA)-regulated controls, calibrators, blood gas and clinical chemistry controls and other reagents for original equipment manufacturer (OEM) and clinical customers, as well as a portfolio of clinical molecular diagnostic oncology assays, including the ExoDx Prostate (IntelliScore) test for prostate cancer diagnosis. This division also manufactures and sells advanced tissue-based in-situ hybridization assays (ISH) for research and clinical use. Brands of Bio-Techne include R&D Systems, Novus Biologicals, Tocris, ProteinSimple, BiosPacific, Advanced Cell Diagnostics Inc., Exosome Diagnostics, R&D Systems Hematology, RNA Medical, and Boston Biochem Inc. In August 2020, Bio-Techne announced that it released a new SARS-CoV-1/2 spike RBD LlaMABody recombinant antibody, which binds to the SARS-CoV-2 spike receptor binding domain (RBD) and blocks the virus from binding to its host receptor, ACE-2, inhibiting viral infection. In April 2021, the firm completed its acquisition of Asuragen, Inc., a leader in the development, manufacturing and commercialization of genetic carrier screening and oncology testing kits.

FINANCIAL DATA: *Note: Data for latest year may not have been available at press time.*

In U.S. $	2020	2019	2018	2017	2016	2015
Revenue	738,691,000	714,006,000	642,993,000	563,003,000	499,023,000	452,246,000
R&D Expense	65,192,000	62,413,000	55,329,000	53,514,000	45,187,000	40,853,000
Operating Income	148,847,000	147,104,000	134,375,000	144,555,000	150,593,000	147,023,000
Operating Margin %		.21%	.21%	.26%	.30%	.33%
SGA Expense	240,882,000	236,867,000	240,636,000	153,326,000	140,879,000	119,401,000
Net Income	229,296,000	96,072,000	126,150,000	76,086,000	104,476,000	107,735,000
Operating Cash Flow	205,217,000	181,619,000	170,367,000	143,448,000	143,870,000	139,359,000
Capital Expenditure	51,744,000	25,411,000	20,934,000	15,179,000	16,898,000	19,905,000
EBITDA	378,411,000	211,891,000	200,603,000	179,358,000	191,993,000	192,932,000
Return on Assets %		.06%	.08%	.06%	.10%	.11%
Return on Equity %		.09%	.12%	.08%	.12%	.13%
Debt to Equity		0.423	0.314	0.362	0.104	0.086

CONTACT INFORMATION:

Phone: 612 379-2956   Fax: 612 656-4400
Toll-Free: 800 343 7475
Address: 614 McKinley Place NE, Minneapolis, MN 55413 United States

STOCK TICKER/OTHER:

Stock Ticker: TECH   Exchange: NAS
Employees: 2,300   Fiscal Year Ends: 06/30
Parent Company:

SALARIES/BONUSES:

Top Exec. Salary: $ Bonus: $
Second Exec. Salary: $ Bonus: $

OTHER THOUGHTS:

Estimated Female Officers or Directors:
Hot Spot for Advancement for Women/Minorities:

Sales, profits and employees may be estimates. Financial information, benefits and other data can change quickly and may vary from those stated here.

BioTelemetry Inc

NAIC Code: 339100

www.gobio.com

TYPES OF BUSINESS:

Mobile Cardiac Monitoring Equipment
Cardiac Monitoring
Mobile-Blood Glucose Monitoring
Medical Imaging
Product Manufacture
Research and Development
Clinical Trials

BRANDS/DIVISIONS/AFFILIATES:

Koninklijke Philips NV
MCOT
ePatch
Geneva

CONTACTS: *Note: Officers with more than one job title may be intentionally listed here more than once.*

Heather Getz, Exec. VP
Peter Ferola, General Counsel
Fred Broadway, President, Divisional
Daniel Wisniewski, Senior VP, Divisional

GROWTH PLANS/SPECIAL FEATURES:

BioTelemetry, Inc. provides cardiac and mobile-blood glucose monitoring, centralized medical imaging and original equipment manufacturing products and services for the health care and clinical research sectors. The company's heart monitoring division offers a data platform that integrates data from almost any remote cardiac monitoring device, providing analysis and support to streamline practice workflow. Approximately 1.2 million patients are monitored annually. This division has four logistics distribution centers and five clinical analysis monitoring centers located in the U.S. Brands include MCOT, ePatch and Geneva. BioTelemetry's clinical research division has provided centralized cardiac monitoring and medical imaging analysis in more than 2,000 clinical trials, spanning 70 countries, and comprising all major therapeutic areas. It has 350 clinical trials actively under management, including Phases 1-4 (as of mid-2021). This division provides comprehensive imaging services for clinical trials including oncology, cardiovascular, musculoskeletal, neurologic and imaging for metabolic diseases; and services include electrocardiogram (ECG), blood pressure and Holter monitoring as well as echocardiogram (ECHO) and mutigated acquisition scan (MUGA) studies for clinical trials. In early-2021, BioTelemetry was acquired by Koninklijke Philips NV (Royal Philips) and ceased from being publicly traded. The firm operates as a subsidiary of Royal Philips.

FINANCIAL DATA: *Note: Data for latest year may not have been available at press time.*

In U.S. $	2020	2019	2018	2017	2016	2015
Revenue		439,107,008	399,472,000	286,776,000	208,332,000	178,512,992
R&D Expense						
Operating Income						
Operating Margin %						
SGA Expense						
Net Income		29,844,000	42,820,000	-15,956,000	53,437,000	7,428,000
Operating Cash Flow						
Capital Expenditure						
EBITDA						
Return on Assets %						
Return on Equity %						
Debt to Equity						

CONTACT INFORMATION:

Phone: 610 729-7000   Fax: 610 828-8048
Toll-Free: 888-312-2328
Address: 1000 Cedar Hollow Rd., Ste. 102, Malvera, PA 19355 United States

STOCK TICKER/OTHER:

Stock Ticker: Subsidiary
Employees: 1,700
Parent Company: Koninklijke Philips NV

Exchange: NAS
Fiscal Year Ends: 12/31

SALARIES/BONUSES:

Top Exec. Salary: $ Bonus: $
Second Exec. Salary: $ Bonus: $

OTHER THOUGHTS:

Estimated Female Officers or Directors: 3
Hot Spot for Advancement for Women/Minorities: Y

BJC HealthCare

www.bjc.org

NAIC Code: 622110

TYPES OF BUSINESS:

General Medical and Surgical Hospitals
Home Health Services
Physical Rehab Center
Physician Groups
Long-Term Health Care
Occupational Health Services
Hospice Services
Teaching Hospitals

BRANDS/DIVISIONS/AFFILIATES:

Barnes-Jewish Hospital
St Louis Childrens Hospital
BJC Home Care Services
BarnesCare
BJC Community Health Services
BJC Employee Assistance Program
BJC Hospice

CONTACTS: Note: Officers with more than one job title may be intentionally listed here more than once.

Richard J. Liekweg, CEO
Nick Barto, CFO
June McAllister Fowler, Sr. VP-Mktg. & Communications
Jackie Tischler, Chief People Officer
Jerry Fox, CIO
Michael A. DeHaven, General Counsel
Robert W. Cannon, Group Pres., Strategic Planning
June McAllister Fowler, VP-Corp. & Public Comm.
Larry Tracy, Pres., Barnes-Jewish St. Peters Hospital
JoAnn M. Shaw, Chief Learning Officer
Richard J. Liekweg, VP
Lee F. Fetter, Group Pres., Clinical Quality
Robert W. Cannon, Group Pres., Supply Chain Oper.

GROWTH PLANS/SPECIAL FEATURES:

BJC HealthCare is a nonprofit healthcare organization primarily serving the areas of St. Louis, Missouri, mid-Missouri and southern Illinois. The firm operates 15 hospitals as well as long-term care facilities, physician offices and rehabilitation and imaging centers. BJC (Barnes-Jewish/Christian) has over 4,700 physicians and approximately 3,025 staffed beds. Two of the company's hospitals, Barnes-Jewish Hospital and St. Louis Children's Hospital, are ranked highly among America's elite medical centers and teaching hospitals. Both are affiliated with Washington University in St. Louis' School of Medicine. The company's services include inpatient and outpatient care, primary care, community health, workplace health, home health, mental health, rehabilitation, long-term care and hospice. BJC Home Care Services offers patients in Missouri and Illinois a wide range of in-home services, including skilled nursing, adult and pediatric supportive care, rehabilitation therapy, respiratory care, infusion therapy and hospice services. Through BarnesCare, an occupational medicine service, BJC provides occupational health services to the St. Louis metropolitan business community. The company provides a variety of preventive and early detection services for employers and community members through its BJC Community Health Services program, which includes screenings, wellness coaching and other services. The BJC Employee Assistance Program assists in the identification and resolution of health, behavioral and productivity problems. BJC Hospice provides support for terminally ill adults and children, and their families.

FINANCIAL DATA: Note: Data for latest year may not have been available at press time.

In U.S. $	2020	2019	2018	2017	2016	2015
Revenue	5,500,000,000	5,380,000,000	5,300,000,000	5,000,000,000	4,800,000,000	4,300,000,000
R&D Expense						
Operating Income						
Operating Margin %						
SGA Expense						
Net Income						
Operating Cash Flow						
Capital Expenditure						
EBITDA						
Return on Assets %						
Return on Equity %						
Debt to Equity						

CONTACT INFORMATION:

Phone: 314-286-2000   Fax: 314-286-2060
Toll-Free:
Address: 4901 Forest Park Ave., St. Louis, MO 63108 United States

STOCK TICKER/OTHER:

Stock Ticker: Nonprofit
Employees: 30,647
Parent Company:

Exchange:
Fiscal Year Ends: 12/31

SALARIES/BONUSES:

Top Exec. Salary: $ Bonus: $
Second Exec. Salary: $ Bonus: $

OTHER THOUGHTS:

Estimated Female Officers or Directors: 5
Hot Spot for Advancement for Women/Minorities: Y

Blue Care Network of Michigan
www.bcbsm.com/index/about-us/our-company/about-bcn.html

NAIC Code: 524114

TYPES OF BUSINESS:
Insurance-Medical & Health, HMOs & PPOs
Health Maintenance Organization
Technology Support Services
Online Health Resources & Information
Health Insurance Plans

BRANDS/DIVISIONS/AFFILIATES:
Blue Cross and Blue Shield of Michigan
BlueHealthConnection
OneBlue
Blue Cross Preferred HMO
MyBlue Medigap
BCN 65
Blue Elect Self-Referral Option
Healthy Blue Living

CONTACTS: *Note: Officers with more than one job title may be intentionally listed here more than once.*
Kathryn G. Levine, CEO
David Nelson, Sr. VP
Carla Chambers, VP-Health & Medical Affairs
William H. Black, Chmn.

GROWTH PLANS/SPECIAL FEATURES:
Blue Care Network of Michigan (BCN), a subsidiary of Blue Cross and Blue Shield of Michigan (BCBSM), is one of the largest health maintenance organization (HMO) networks in the state, with more than 840,000 members. The company works together with BCBSM by sharing resources to identify and fight fraud, protect member privacy and support common technology infrastructures. BCN offers its members traditional indemnity and Medicare as well as supplementary management and care services. BCN works closely with its physician network and provides services and technology tools to support its partners. The company's network is one of the largest in the state, including nearly 6,300 primary care physicians, over 26,400 specialists and 132 Michigan hospitals. Its BlueHealthConnection service, in collaboration with BCBSM, combines diverse programs to assist members with chronic or complex illnesses. The company's products include coverage options for individuals and groups as well as extended coverage after having left a group. Its individual coverage options consist of the following programs: Blue Cross Preferred HMO and Blue Cross Select HMO, which offers a broad choice of physicians and hospitals to users; BCN Advantage for the individual, which replaces Medicare coverage with comprehensive HMO coverage; MyBlue Medigap, which provides additional coverage for individuals enrolled in Medicare; and BCN 65, which works with Medicare to cover more healthcare costs. The company's group coverage options include the BCN HMO; the Blue Elect Self-Referral Option for employer groups of two or more in size; Healthy Blue Living, which has decreased co-payment and deductibles for members who live a healthy lifestyle; the Self-funded Option, which lets the employer assume the claims cost risk; BCN Advantage for groups; and BCN 65 for groups.

FINANCIAL DATA: *Note: Data for latest year may not have been available at press time.*

In U.S. $	2020	2019	2018	2017	2016	2015
Revenue	4,252,386,000	4,094,482,000	4,239,171,000	3,580,930,000	3,399,338,000	3,252,461,000
R&D Expense						
Operating Income						
Operating Margin %						
SGA Expense						
Net Income	74,747,000	132,355,000	250,612,000	242,457,000	93,756,000	18,045,000
Operating Cash Flow						
Capital Expenditure						
EBITDA						
Return on Assets %						
Return on Equity %						
Debt to Equity						

CONTACT INFORMATION:
Phone: 248-799-6400   Fax: 248-799-6979
Toll-Free: 800-662-6667
Address: 20500 Civic Center Dr., Southfield, MI 48076 United States

STOCK TICKER/OTHER:
Stock Ticker: Subsidiary
Employees: 8,100
Parent Company: Blue Cross and Blue Shield of Michigan
Exchange:
Fiscal Year Ends: 12/31

SALARIES/BONUSES:
Top Exec. Salary: $ Bonus: $
Second Exec. Salary: $ Bonus: $

OTHER THOUGHTS:
Estimated Female Officers or Directors: 2
Hot Spot for Advancement for Women/Minorities: Y

Blue Cross and Blue Shield Association

www.bcbs.com

NAIC Code: 524114

TYPES OF BUSINESS:

Insurance-Medical & Health, HMOs & PPOs
Health Insurance Operations
Healthcare Companies

BRANDS/DIVISIONS/AFFILIATES:

Blue Cross and Blue Shield
BCBS Federal Employee Program
BlueCard
BCBSA National Labor Office

CONTACTS: *Note: Officers with more than one job title may be intentionally listed here more than once.*

Kim A. Keck, CEO
Maureen Sullivan, Chief Strategy & Innovation Officer
Robert Kolodgy, CFO
Kari Hedges, Sr. VP-Commercial Markets & Enterprise Data Solutions
Kelly Williams, Chief Human Resources Officer
Trent Haywood, Chief Medical Officer
Lachlan Tidmarsh, CIO
William J. Colbourne, Sr. VP-Admin. Svcs.
Roger G. Wilson, General Counsel
Doug Porter, Sr. VP-Oper.
Maureen E. Sullivan, Chief Strategy Officer
Paul Gerrard, VP-Strategic Comm.
William A. Breskin, VP-Gov't Programs
Jennifer Vachon, Chief of Staff
Cynthia Rolfe, VP-Consumer Brand Strategy
Shirley S. Lady, VP-Informatics & Data Oper.
Jennifer Vachon, Exec. VP

GROWTH PLANS/SPECIAL FEATURES:

Blue Cross and Blue Shield Association (BCBSA) oversees a national federation of 35 independent and locally operated Blue Cross and Blue Shield (BCBS) companies across the U.S. Together these health insurance and care providers constitute the BCBS System, the oldest and largest group of healthcare companies in the country. The Association owns and manages the Blue Cross and Blue Shield trademarks and names in more than 170 countries; and grants licenses to independent companies to use the trademark's and names. Throughout the U.S., nearly all hospitals and physicians contract with BCBSA plans. BCBSA National Labor Office works with organized labor to cover working Americans with health coverage that insures one in three Americans. BCBSA serves more than 17 million unionized workers, retirees and their families. The BCBS Federal Employee Program is among the largest privately underwritten health insurance contracts in the world, covering roughly 5.6 million people. The firm's BlueCard program electronically links independent Blue Plans through a single electronic network for claims processing and reimbursement, allowing employees of corporations nationwide to participate and allowing individuals with local plans to file claims while traveling outside their region. The BlueCard worldwide program provides members with access to coverage when traveling or living abroad. BCBSA has two office locations, its headquarters in Chicago and another office in Washington DC.

BCBSA offers its employees comprehensive health benefits, retirement plans, life and disability coverage and a variety of employee assistance plans and programs.

FINANCIAL DATA: *Note: Data for latest year may not have been available at press time.*

In U.S. $	2020	2019	2018	2017	2016	2015
Revenue	698,357,424	652,670,490	621,590,943	591,991,374	536,103,105	504,178,349
R&D Expense						
Operating Income						
Operating Margin %						
SGA Expense						
Net Income		-1,333,805	-1,375,057	-1,432,352	1,173,776	-5,511,767
Operating Cash Flow						
Capital Expenditure						
EBITDA						
Return on Assets %						
Return on Equity %						
Debt to Equity						

CONTACT INFORMATION:

Phone: 312-297-6000   Fax: 312-297-6609
Toll-Free:
Address: 225 N. Michigan Ave., Chicago, IL 60601 United States

STOCK TICKER/OTHER:

Stock Ticker: Nonprofit
Employees: 5,000
Parent Company:

Exchange:
Fiscal Year Ends: 12/31

SALARIES/BONUSES:

Top Exec. Salary: $ Bonus: $
Second Exec. Salary: $ Bonus: $

OTHER THOUGHTS:

Estimated Female Officers or Directors: 9
Hot Spot for Advancement for Women/Minorities: Y

Blue Cross and Blue Shield of Florida Inc
www.floridablue.com
NAIC Code: 524114

TYPES OF BUSINESS:
Insurance-Medical & Health, HMOs & PPOs
Life Insurance
Dental Insurance
Medicare & Medicaid Services
Staffing
Administrative Services
Information Technology Services

BRANDS/DIVISIONS/AFFILIATES:
GuideWell Mutual Holding Corporation
Florida Blue
Onlife Health
Health Options Inc
Florida Combined Life Insurance Company Inc

CONTACTS: *Note: Officers with more than one job title may be intentionally listed here more than once.*
Patrick J. Geraghty, CEO
Jonathan B. Gavras, Chief Medical Officer
R. Chris Doerr, Chief Admin. Officer
Charlie Joseph, General Counsel
Joyce Kramzer, Sr. VP-Bus. Oper.
Craig Thomas, Chief Strategy & Mktg. Officer
Sharon Wamble-King, Sr. VP-Enterprise Comm.
R. Chris Doerr, Exec. VP-Finance
Camille Harrison, Chief Customer Experience Officer
Elizabeth Strombom, Sr. VP-Gov't Markets

GROWTH PLANS/SPECIAL FEATURES:
Blue Cross and Blue Shield of Florida, Inc. is a nonprofit mutual health insurance company providing comprehensive health insurance and related services to a membership of more than 4 million. The company does business as Florida Blue, offering PPO (preferred provider organization) and HMO (health maintenance organization) group healthcare plans for both small and large companies. For individuals under 65 years of age, offerings include PPOs; and individuals over 65 have several plans to choose from, involving a combination of Medicare supplements, HMOs and other services. Florida Blue also provides multiple options for pharmacy coverage, dental coverage, life insurance, accidental death and dismemberment, disability, long-term care and workers' compensation. The company's website provides health-related resources and information, as well as support services to help members make educated healthcare choices. The site also offers members access to detailed information about hospitals, such as success rates in medical procedures, complication and infection rates and technological capabilities. Florida Blue's Onlife Health well-being engagement platform serves its Medicare, Individual Under 65, commercial and employee group populations. Independent licensees of the Blue Cross and Blue Shield Association include Health Options, Inc., which offers HMO coverage; and Florida Combined Life Insurance Company, Inc., which offers dental, life and disability coverage. Florida Blue itself operates as a subsidiary of GuideWell Mutual Holding Corporation.

BCBSF offers its employees comprehensive health coverage, flexible spending accounts, an employee assistance program, a 401(k) plan and tuition reimbursement, among other benefits.

FINANCIAL DATA: *Note: Data for latest year may not have been available at press time.*

In U.S. $	2020	2019	2018	2017	2016	2015
Revenue	10,838,264,063	10,129,218,750	9,646,875,000	9,187,500,000	8,750,000,000	8,100,000,000
R&D Expense						
Operating Income						
Operating Margin %						
SGA Expense						
Net Income						
Operating Cash Flow						
Capital Expenditure						
EBITDA						
Return on Assets %						
Return on Equity %						
Debt to Equity						

CONTACT INFORMATION:
Phone: 904-791-6111   Fax:
Toll-Free: 800-352-2583
Address: 4800 Deerwood Campus Pkwy., Jacksonville, FL 32246 United States

STOCK TICKER/OTHER:
Stock Ticker: Nonprofit   Exchange:
Employees: 7,600   Fiscal Year Ends: 12/31
Parent Company: GuideWell Mutual Holding Corporation

SALARIES/BONUSES:
Top Exec. Salary: $ Bonus: $
Second Exec. Salary: $ Bonus: $

OTHER THOUGHTS:
Estimated Female Officers or Directors: 8
Hot Spot for Advancement for Women/Minorities: Y

Blue Cross and Blue Shield of Louisiana

www.bcbsla.com

NAIC Code: 524114

TYPES OF BUSINESS:

Insurance-Medical & Health, HMOs & PPOs
Life Insurance
Health Insurance Plans
Senior Insurance Plans
Group Insurance Plans

BRANDS/DIVISIONS/AFFILIATES:

HMO Louisiana Inc
Southern National Life Insurance Company Inc

CONTACTS: *Note: Officers with more than one job title may be intentionally listed here more than once.*

I. Steven Udvarhelyi, CEO
Michele Calandro, General Counsel
John Maginnis, VP-Corp. Comm.
Adam Short, VP-Finance
Brian Small, Chief Actuary
Dawn Cantrell, VP-Network Admin.
Sabrina Heltz, Sr. VP-Health Care System, Quality
Allison Young, Sr. VP-Benefits Admin.

GROWTH PLANS/SPECIAL FEATURES:

Blue Cross and Blue Shield of Louisiana (BCBS LA) and its subsidiaries, HMO Louisiana, Inc. and Southern National Life Insurance Company, Inc. provide insurance and related services to 1.8 million members in Louisiana. BCBS LA offers various coverage health plans, including HMO (health maintenance organization), PPO (preferred provider organization), POS (point-of-service), senior plans and group plans. The firm also offers health saving accounts (HSAs), which typically have lower premiums, and contributions are tax free (federal and Louisiana state) and lower tax liability. Other insurance products include dental, Medicare, travel, cancer and VIP. VIP stands for variable income plan, which is an addition to regular healthcare coverage and pays the member dollars per day for any covered hospital stay. BCBS LA is a tax-paying nonprofit insurer with offices in Alexandria, Baton Rouge, Houma, Lafayette, Lake Charles, Monroe, New Orleans and Shreveport. The firm is an independent licensee of the Blue Cross and Blue Shield Association, and a private mutual company owned by its policyholders.

BCBS LA offers its employees comprehensive health benefits, retirement options, life and disability coverage and a variety of employee assistance plans and programs.

FINANCIAL DATA: *Note: Data for latest year may not have been available at press time.*

In U.S. $	2020	2019	2018	2017	2016	2015
Revenue	3,907,083,600	3,651,480,000	3,651,480,000	3,477,600,000	3,312,000,000	3,250,000,000
R&D Expense						
Operating Income						
Operating Margin %						
SGA Expense						
Net Income						
Operating Cash Flow						
Capital Expenditure						
EBITDA						
Return on Assets %						
Return on Equity %						
Debt to Equity						

CONTACT INFORMATION:

Phone: 225-295-3307   Fax: 225-295-2054
Toll-Free: 800-599-2583
Address: 5525 Reitz Ave., Baton Rouge, LA 70809 United States

STOCK TICKER/OTHER:

Stock Ticker: Private
Employees: 2,500
Parent Company:

Exchange:
Fiscal Year Ends: 12/31

SALARIES/BONUSES:

Top Exec. Salary: $ Bonus: $
Second Exec. Salary: $ Bonus: $

OTHER THOUGHTS:

Estimated Female Officers or Directors: 19
Hot Spot for Advancement for Women/Minorities: Y

Blue Cross and Blue Shield of Massachusetts   www.bcbsma.com

NAIC Code: 524114

TYPES OF BUSINESS:

Insurance-Medical & Health, HMOs & PPOs
Indemnity Insurance
Insurance
Medicare Extension Programs
Healthcare Services
Dental Plans
Behavioral Health Services

BRANDS/DIVISIONS/AFFILIATES:

Associated Hospital Service Corporation

CONTACTS: Note: Officers with more than one job title may be intentionally listed here more than once.

Andrew Dreyfus, CEO
Andrew Dreyfus, Pres.
John A. Fallon, Chief Physician Exec.
Stephanie Lovell, General Counsel
Sarah Iselin, Chief Strategy Officer
Jay McQuaide, Sr. VP-Corp. Comm.

GROWTH PLANS/SPECIAL FEATURES:

Blue Cross and Blue Shield of Massachusetts (BCBSMA) is an independent, nonprofit healthcare company that provides health services and insurance in Massachusetts. The firm began as the Associated Hospital Service Corporation of Massachusetts in 1937 and is now one of New England's largest health plan providers, including primary care providers, specialists, hospitals, dentists, ancillary providers and behavioral health providers. BCBSMA has approximately 2.8 million members, including health maintenance organization (HMO) members, preferred provider organization (PPO) members and senior products/Medicare members. Approximately 24,000 businesses across the state are customers of BCBSMA, as well as 79% of the state's cities and towns, and approximately 112,500 federal employees. BCBMA also offers affordable mental health services to its members, including telehealth sessions.

BCBSMA offers its employees medical, dental and vision coverage; life and disability insurance; a 529 college savings plan; 401(k) and pension plans; work/life benefits; flexible spending accounts; and tuition reimbursement.

FINANCIAL DATA: Note: Data for latest year may not have been available at press time.

In U.S. $	2020	2019	2018	2017	2016	2015
Revenue	8,016,835,000	8,360,126,000	7,880,433,750	7,505,175,000	7,111,253,000	6,797,415,000
R&D Expense						
Operating Income						
Operating Margin %						
SGA Expense						
Net Income	386,710,000	214,917,000	-6,712,400	-6,920,000	78,091,000	15,058,000
Operating Cash Flow						
Capital Expenditure						
EBITDA						
Return on Assets %						
Return on Equity %						
Debt to Equity						

CONTACT INFORMATION:

Phone: 617-246-5000   Fax: 617-246-4832
Toll-Free: 800-262-2583
Address: 101 Huntington Ave., Ste 1300, Boston, MA 02199-7611
United States

STOCK TICKER/OTHER:

Stock Ticker: Nonprofit   Exchange:
Employees: 3,700   Fiscal Year Ends: 12/31
Parent Company:

SALARIES/BONUSES:

Top Exec. Salary: $ Bonus: $
Second Exec. Salary: $ Bonus: $

OTHER THOUGHTS:

Estimated Female Officers or Directors: 6
Hot Spot for Advancement for Women/Minorities: Y

# Blue Cross and Blue Shield of Michigan					www.bcbsm.com

NAIC Code: 524114

TYPES OF BUSINESS:

Insurance-Medical & Health, HMOs & PPOs
Workers Compensation
Dental & Vision Insurance
Health Care Management Services
Prescription Drug Plans

BRANDS/DIVISIONS/AFFILIATES:

Advantasure
Blue Care Network of Michigan
Blue Cross Blue Shield of Michigan Foundation
AF Group
LifeSecure Insurance Company
Dearborn National Life Insurance
Assurity Life Insurance Company
LifeSecure Insurance Company

CONTACTS: *Note: Officers with more than one job title may be intentionally listed here more than once.*

Daniel J. Loepp, CEO/Pres.
Darrell E. Middleton, COO
Mark R. Bartlett, CFO
Thomas L. Simmer, Chief Medical Officer
William M Fandrich, CIO
Lynda M. Rossi, Chief of Staff
Tricia A. Keith, Corp. Sec.
Darrell E. Middleton, Exec. VP-Oper. & Bus. Performance
David A. Share, Sr. VP-Value Partnerships
Lynda M. Rossi, Sr. VP-Public Affairs
Carolynn Walton, Treas.
Elizabeth R. Haar, CEO/Pres., Accident Fund Holdings, Inc.
Darrell E. Middleton, Sr. VP-Bus. Performance
Mark R. Bartlett, Pres., Emerging Markets
Elizabeth R. Haar, Sr. VP-Subsidiary Oper.
Gregory A. Sudderth, Chmn.

GROWTH PLANS/SPECIAL FEATURES:

Blue Cross and Blue Shield of Michigan (BCBSM) is a nonprofit organization providing healthcare plans. It is one of the nation's top Blue Cross Blue Shield health insurance associations, serving nearly 4.5 million in state members and 1.6 million more in other states. The firm offers individual and family health plans, dental and vision plans, Medicare and Medicaid coverage, group plans, specialty benefits and international plans. Plans include traditional, preferred provider organization (PPO), health maintenance organization (HMO), wellness-based plans, and plans with health spending accounts. BCBSM's network in Michigan comprises 152 hospitals and more than 33,000 doctors. Subsidiaries of the firm include Advantasure, Blue Care Network of Michigan, Blue Cross Blue Shield of Michigan Foundation, AF Group and LifeSecure Insurance Company. Specialty benefits are provided through Dearborn National Life Insurance, Assurity Life Insurance Company and LifeSecure Insurance Company. Member service locations are in Detroit, Flint, Grand Rapids, Holland, Lansing, Marquette, Portage, Southfield and Traverse City.

BCBSM offers employees medical, dental and vision plans; 401(k) matching; long- and short-term disability; and tuition reimbursement.

FINANCIAL DATA: *Note: Data for latest year may not have been available at press time.*

In U.S. $	2020	2019	2018	2017	2016	2015
Revenue	30,220,000,000	29,420,000,000	29,330,000,000	26,945,000,000	25,902,000,000	24,222,000,000
R&D Expense						
Operating Income						
Operating Margin %						
SGA Expense						
Net Income	818,000,000	528,200,000	556,000,000	1,191,000,000	122,000,000	-68,000,000
Operating Cash Flow						
Capital Expenditure						
EBITDA						
Return on Assets %						
Return on Equity %						
Debt to Equity						

CONTACT INFORMATION:

Phone: 313-225-9000			Fax: 313-225-6764
Toll-Free:
Address: 600 E. Lafayette Blvd., Detroit, MI 48226 United States

STOCK TICKER/OTHER:

Stock Ticker: Nonprofit							Exchange:
Employees: 8,100								Fiscal Year Ends: 04/01
Parent Company:

SALARIES/BONUSES:

Top Exec. Salary: $			Bonus: $
Second Exec. Salary: $			Bonus: $

OTHER THOUGHTS:

Estimated Female Officers or Directors: 6
Hot Spot for Advancement for Women/Minorities: Y

Sales, profits and employees may be estimates. Financial information, benefits and other data can change quickly and may vary from those stated here.

Blue Cross and Blue Shield of Minnesota
www.bluecrossmn.com

NAIC Code: 524114

TYPES OF BUSINESS:
Insurance-Medical & Health, HMOs & PPOs
Managed Care
Insurance-Life
Investment Management
Pharmacy Benefit Management
Behavioral Health Services
Workers' Compensation

BRANDS/DIVISIONS/AFFILIATES:
Aware Integrated Inc
Blue Cross Blue Shield Association
Blue Cross and Blue Shield of Minnesota Foundation

CONTACTS: Note: Officers with more than one job title may be intentionally listed here more than once.
Kathleen A. Blatz, Interim CEO
Tina Holmes, Chief of Staff
Scott Lynch, Chief Legal Officer
James Egan, Sr. VP-Corp. Oper.
Rochelle Myers, VP-Strategic Planning & Portfolio Mgmt.
Patricia Riley, Chief Gov't Officer
Garrett Black, Sr. VP-Health Mgmt.

GROWTH PLANS/SPECIAL FEATURES:
Blue Cross and Blue Shield of Minnesota (BCBSM), a subsidiary of Aware Integrated, Inc., offers health insurance plans and related programs to its members in Minnesota. BCBSM is a nonprofit independent licensee of the Blue Cross and Blue Shield Association, and offers medical, dental, life, indemnity and short-term insurance. Insurance plans include health maintenance organizations (HMOs), preferred provider organizations (PPOs) and Medicare supplemental. The firm has a short-term coverage plan for people who are out of work, between jobs and recently out of school. BCBSM's plans range from a high-deductible health plan with a financial account, health management services and an online member service center to tailored plans for young adults, which omit family and childbirth labor coverage, resulting in lower monthly rates. The Blue Cross and Blue Shield of Minnesota Foundation is a leading grant-making foundation in Minnesota, focused on early childhood development, housing, social connectedness and the environment. The company offers wellness information on its website focused on addressing general health, stress management, behavioral choices and nutrition. In addition, supportive care services from Livio Health is available to members throughout the entire state of Minnesota. Livio Health provides supportive medical care for people with serious illness via in-home, phone and video visits.

BCBSM offers its employees medical, dental and life insurance; flexible spending accounts; disability protection; a 401(k) company match; seniority tiered paid time off; flexible work schedule; and wellness programs.

FINANCIAL DATA: Note: Data for latest year may not have been available at press time.

In U.S. $	2020	2019	2018	2017	2016	2015
Revenue	13,200,000,000	13,300,000,000	13,100,000,000	12,477,401,000	12,090,953,000	10,692,369,000
R&D Expense						
Operating Income						
Operating Margin %						
SGA Expense						
Net Income	128,000,000	-55,000,000	-60,522,180	-62,394,000	-322,400,000	-153,549,000
Operating Cash Flow						
Capital Expenditure						
EBITDA						
Return on Assets %						
Return on Equity %						
Debt to Equity						

CONTACT INFORMATION:
Phone: 615-662-8000 Fax:
Toll-Free: 800-382-2000
Address: 3535 Blue Cross Rd., Eagan, MN 55122 United States

STOCK TICKER/OTHER:
Stock Ticker: Subsidiary Exchange:
Employees: 3,500 Fiscal Year Ends: 12/31
Parent Company: Aware Integrated Inc

SALARIES/BONUSES:
Top Exec. Salary: $ Bonus: $
Second Exec. Salary: $ Bonus: $

OTHER THOUGHTS:
Estimated Female Officers or Directors: 7
Hot Spot for Advancement for Women/Minorities: Y

Sales, profits and employees may be estimates. Financial information, benefits and other data can change quickly and may vary from those stated here.

Blue Cross and Blue Shield of Montana

www.bcbsmt.com

NAIC Code: 524114

TYPES OF BUSINESS:

Insurance-Medical & Health, HMOs & PPOs
Healthcare Coverage
Travel Medical Coverage
Expatriate Coverage
Employee Benefit Programs

BRANDS/DIVISIONS/AFFILIATES:

Health Care Service Corporation
Blue Cross and Blue Shield Association

CONTACTS: *Note: Officers with more than one job title may be intentionally listed here more than once.*

Collette Hanson, CEO
Michael Frank, Pres.
Monica Berner, Chief Medical Officer
Mary Belcher, General Counsel
Deb Thompson, Sr. Dir.-Corp. Affairs & Compliance Officer
Jim Spencer, Chief Actuary

GROWTH PLANS/SPECIAL FEATURES:

Blue Cross and Blue Shield of Montana (BCBS MT), a division of Health Care Service Corporation, provides approximately 300,000 members with a full spectrum of healthcare coverage. Plans and products include individual and family health insurance, student health insurance, travel medical and expatriate, among other types of special enrollment plans. BCBS MT has three levels of health care plans: bronze, members pay 40% out of pocket costs; silver, members pay 30%; and gold, members pay 20%. Medicare and Medicaid plans are also provided, as well as Healthy Montana Kids, which offers a free or low-cost health insurance plan to eligible Montana children up to age 19. Benefits are offered to Montana University system's employee benefits program, Choices (for faculty and staff). BCBS MT is an independent licensee of the Blue Cross and Blue Shield Association.

BCBSMT offers its employees health coverage, flexible spending accounts, life and disability insurance, tuition reimbursement, an employee assistance program, a defined contribution retirement plan and a 401(k) savings plan, among other benefits.

FINANCIAL DATA: *Note: Data for latest year may not have been available at press time.*

In U.S. $	2020	2019	2018	2017	2016	2015
Revenue	790,079,062	752,456,250	716,625,000	682,500,000	650,000,000	632,000,000
R&D Expense						
Operating Income						
Operating Margin %						
SGA Expense						
Net Income						
Operating Cash Flow						
Capital Expenditure						
EBITDA						
Return on Assets %						
Return on Equity %						
Debt to Equity						

CONTACT INFORMATION:

Phone: 406-437-5000   Fax:
Toll-Free: 800-447-7828
Address: 3645 Alice St., PO Box 7982, Helena, MT 59604-7982 United States

STOCK TICKER/OTHER:

Stock Ticker: Subsidiary   Exchange:
Employees: 440   Fiscal Year Ends: 12/31
Parent Company: Health Care Service Corporation

SALARIES/BONUSES:

Top Exec. Salary: $ Bonus: $
Second Exec. Salary: $ Bonus: $

OTHER THOUGHTS:

Estimated Female Officers or Directors: 5
Hot Spot for Advancement for Women/Minorities: Y

Blue Cross and Blue Shield of Nebraska

www.nebraskablue.com

NAIC Code: 524114

TYPES OF BUSINESS:

Insurance-Medical & Health, HMOs & PPOs
Health Insurance
Group Plans
Individual Plans
Family Plans
Medication Management
Benefits Management

BRANDS/DIVISIONS/AFFILIATES:

Blue Cross and Blue Shield Association

GROWTH PLANS/SPECIAL FEATURES:

Blue Cross and Blue Shield of Nebraska (BCBS NE) provides health insurance and related services to Nebraskans. BCBS NE's plans include group health plans, individual and family plans, and Medicare plans. Group health plans for businesses include small groups (2-50 employees), mid-sized groups (51-150 employees) and large groups (151 or more). The firm offers member support regarding finding the right doctor, managing medications, managing benefits and more. BCBS NE is an independent licensee of the Blue Cross and Blue Shield Association.

BCBS NE offers its employees a health, vision and dental plan; flexible spending accounts; a 401(k) plan; tuition reimbursement; access to a free wellness center; and a smoke-free campus.

CONTACTS:
Note: Officers with more than one job title may be intentionally listed here more than once.

Steven H. Grandfield, CEO
Susan Courtney, Exec. VP-Oper.
Chad Werner, CFO
Malorie Maddox, Chief Communications, Mktg & Strategy. Officer
Joni Wheeler, Exec. VP-Talent
Rama Kolli, CIO
Lee Handke, Sr. VP-Prod. & Providers
Sarah A. Waldman, Sr. VP-Admin.
Russell Collins, General Counsel
Jennifer Richardson, Sr. VP-Oper.
Brian Pickering, Sr. VP-Comm. & Mktg.
Jerry Byers, Sr. VP-Finance
Dan Alm, Chief Underwriting Officer
Dave Anderson, VP-Finance
Dan Archuleta, VP-Member Svcs.
David Filipi, VP-Quality Advancement
Gretchen Twohig, Chief Compliance Officer

FINANCIAL DATA:
Note: Data for latest year may not have been available at press time.

In U.S. $	2020	2019	2018	2017	2016	2015
Revenue	1,941,245,632	1,848,805,364	1,760,767,014	1,676,920,966	1,744,144,657	1,648,177,433
R&D Expense						
Operating Income						
Operating Margin %						
SGA Expense						
Net Income		44,558,409	45,936,505	46,873,985	-21,564,221	-31,513,777
Operating Cash Flow						
Capital Expenditure						
EBITDA						
Return on Assets %						
Return on Equity %						
Debt to Equity						

CONTACT INFORMATION:

Phone: 402-982-7000   Fax: 402-392-4153
Toll-Free: 800-422-2763
Address: 1919 Aksarben Dr., Omaha, NE 68180 United States

STOCK TICKER/OTHER:

Stock Ticker: Nonprofit
Employees:
Parent Company: GoodLife Partners Inc
Exchange:
Fiscal Year Ends: 12/31

SALARIES/BONUSES:

Top Exec. Salary: $ Bonus: $
Second Exec. Salary: $ Bonus: $

OTHER THOUGHTS:

Estimated Female Officers or Directors: 5
Hot Spot for Advancement for Women/Minorities: Y

Sales, profits and employees may be estimates. Financial information, benefits and other data can change quickly and may vary from those stated here.

Blue Cross and Blue Shield of North Carolina   www.bcbsnc.com

NAIC Code: 524114

TYPES OF BUSINESS:

Insurance-Medical & Health, HMOs & PPOs
Insurance
Individual Plans
Family Plans
Employer Plans

BRANDS/DIVISIONS/AFFILIATES:

Blue Cross and Blue Shield Association
BlueCard
Blue Cross NC Foundation

CONTACTS: *Note: Officers with more than one job title may be intentionally listed here more than once.*

Tunde Sotunde, CEO
Von Nguyen, Chief Medical Officer
Mitch Perry, CFO
Gerald Petkau, Sr. VP-Commercial Markets
Fara Palumbo, Chief People Officer
Don W. Bradley, Chief Medical Officer
Jo Abernathy, CIO
N. King Prather, General Counsel
Maureen K. O'Connor, Chief Strategy Officer
Don W. Bradley, Sr. VP-Health Care

GROWTH PLANS/SPECIAL FEATURES:

Blue Cross and Blue Shield of North Carolina (BCBS NC) is a fully taxed nonprofit insurance provider, with major operations centers in Durham, Fayetteville and Winston-Salem. BCBS NC is an independent licensee of the Blue Cross and Blue Shield Association, and serves more than 3.8 million customers, including individuals, families and businesses. BCBS NC also offers Medicare plans. The Blue Cross NC preferred provider organization (PPO) network of providers includes nearly all of the state's medical doctors and general acute-care hospitals. Outside the state, members have BlueCard coverage with doctors and hospitals in all 50 states. The Blue Cross NC Foundation is an independent foundation that focuses on healthcare, healthy living and nonprofit leadership.

BCBS NC offers employees fitness programs and services, paid time off and ten paid holidays throughout the year, onsite cafeterias and child care, an onsite BCBSNC credit union, continuing education opportunities with Blue University and a matching 401(k)

FINANCIAL DATA: *Note: Data for latest year may not have been available at press time.*

In U.S. $	2020	2019	2018	2017	2016	2015
Revenue	9,900,000,000	9,940,000,000	9,900,000,000	9,400,000,000	7,880,000,000	8,200,000,000
R&D Expense						
Operating Income						
Operating Margin %						
SGA Expense						
Net Income	260,500,000	492,000,000	684,600,000	734,000,000	185,000,000	500,000
Operating Cash Flow						
Capital Expenditure						
EBITDA						
Return on Assets %						
Return on Equity %						
Debt to Equity						

CONTACT INFORMATION:

Phone: 919-489-7431   Fax: 919-765-7818
Toll-Free:
Address: 4615 University Dr., Durham, NC 27707 United States

STOCK TICKER/OTHER:

Stock Ticker: Nonprofit   Exchange:
Employees: 4,700   Fiscal Year Ends: 12/31
Parent Company:

SALARIES/BONUSES:

Top Exec. Salary: $ Bonus: $
Second Exec. Salary: $ Bonus: $

OTHER THOUGHTS:

Estimated Female Officers or Directors:
Hot Spot for Advancement for Women/Minorities: Y

Blue Cross and Blue Shield of Oklahoma
NAIC Code: 524114

www.bcbsok.com

TYPES OF BUSINESS:
Insurance-Medical & Health, HMOs & PPOs
Managed Care
Life Insurance
Property & Casualty Insurance
Prescription & Dental Insurance

BRANDS/DIVISIONS/AFFILIATES:
Health Care Service Corporation
Blue Cross and Blue Shield Association
Oklahoma Caring Foundation

CONTACTS: *Note: Officers with more than one job title may be intentionally listed here more than once.*
Joseph R. Cunningham, Pres.
Nicole Amend, Chief of Staff
Ashley Hudgeons, Media Contact

GROWTH PLANS/SPECIAL FEATURES:
Blue Cross and Blue Shield of Oklahoma (BCBS OK), a subsidiary of Health Care Service Corporation, is one of the oldest private health insurers in Oklahoma and provides benefits plans for over 700,000 customers across the state. BCBS OK offers individual and family healthcare plans, group plans, Medicare plans, student health plans, and travel medical and expatriate plans. Group options include preferred provider organization (PPO), health maintenance organization (HMO) or self-funded employer plans. Another group option is the consumer-directed health plans (CDHPs), which pairs a high deductible PPO plan with a tax-advantaged account. The Oklahoma Caring Foundation, administered by the firm as an in-kind donation, provides vaccinations, education and basic healthcare access to children in Oklahoma. The foundation is funded by community contributions.

BCBS OK offers health and wellness benefits, retirement plans and a variety of employee assistance programs.

FINANCIAL DATA: *Note: Data for latest year may not have been available at press time.*

In U.S. $	2020	2019	2018	2017	2016	2015
Revenue						
R&D Expense						
Operating Income						
Operating Margin %						
SGA Expense						
Net Income						
Operating Cash Flow						
Capital Expenditure						
EBITDA						
Return on Assets %						
Return on Equity %						
Debt to Equity						

CONTACT INFORMATION:
Phone: 918-560-3500   Fax: 918-560-3060
Toll-Free: 800-942-5837
Address: 1400 S. Boston, Tulsa, OK 74102 United States

STOCK TICKER/OTHER:
Stock Ticker: Subsidiary   Exchange:
Employees: 1,000   Fiscal Year Ends: 12/31
Parent Company: Health Care Service Corporation

SALARIES/BONUSES:
Top Exec. Salary: $ Bonus: $
Second Exec. Salary: $ Bonus: $

OTHER THOUGHTS:
Estimated Female Officers or Directors: 2
Hot Spot for Advancement for Women/Minorities:

Blue Cross and Blue Shield of Texas

www.bcbstx.com

NAIC Code: 524114

TYPES OF BUSINESS:

Insurance-Medical & Health, HMOs & PPOs
Health Insurance
Health Maintenance Organization
Individual Plans
Family Plans
Travel Medical Plans
Expatriate Plans

BRANDS/DIVISIONS/AFFILIATES:

Health Care Service Corporation
Blue Cross and Blue Shield Association

CONTACTS: Note: Officers with more than one job title may be intentionally listed here more than once.

James Springfield, Pres.
Darrell Beckett, Sr. VP-Mktg.&Sales
Paul B. Handel, Chief Medical Officer
Mark Chassay, Chief Medical Officer

GROWTH PLANS/SPECIAL FEATURES:

Blue Cross and Blue Shield of Texas (BCBS TX), a division of Health Care Service Corporation, is a nonprofit insurer providing members with health maintenance organization (HMO) networks. The firm emphasizes preventive medicine through education outreach programs in order to control operating costs. BCBS TX offers health care plans for individuals and families, Medicare plans and Medicaid plans (including STAR and CHIP), as well as student health plans, supplemental health plans, travel medical and expatriate plans. BCBS TX works with nearly 80,000 physicians and healthcare practitioners, and 500 hospitals to serve 6 million members in all 254 counties. The company's website offers the ability to compare plans and to obtain resources. BCBS TX is an independent licensee of the Blue Cross and Blue Shield Association. BCBS TX is headquartered in Richardson, with regional offices in Houston, Austin and Lubbock, and customer service facilities in Abilene, Marshall, Richardson, San Angelo, Waco and Wichita Falls.

BCBS TX offers its employees comprehensive health benefits, retirement options, life and disability insurance and a variety of employee assistance plans and programs.

FINANCIAL DATA: Note: Data for latest year may not have been available at press time.

In U.S. $	2020	2019	2018	2017	2016	2015
Revenue						
R&D Expense						
Operating Income						
Operating Margin %						
SGA Expense						
Net Income						
Operating Cash Flow						
Capital Expenditure						
EBITDA						
Return on Assets %						
Return on Equity %						
Debt to Equity						

CONTACT INFORMATION:

Phone: 972-766-6900   Fax:
Toll-Free: 800-451-0287
Address: 1001 E. Lookout Dr., Richardson, TX 75082 United States

STOCK TICKER/OTHER:

Stock Ticker: Subsidiary   Exchange:
Employees: 7,800   Fiscal Year Ends: 12/31
Parent Company: Health Care Service Corporation

SALARIES/BONUSES:

Top Exec. Salary: $ Bonus: $
Second Exec. Salary: $ Bonus: $

OTHER THOUGHTS:

Estimated Female Officers or Directors:
Hot Spot for Advancement for Women/Minorities:

Blue Cross and Blue Shield of Vermont

NAIC Code: 524114

www.bcbsvt.com

TYPES OF BUSINESS:

Insurance-Medical & Health, HMOs & PPOs
Health Insurance
Dental Insurance
Vision Insurance
Health Maintenance Organization
Point of Sale
Telemedicine

BRANDS/DIVISIONS/AFFILIATES:

Blue Cross and Blue Shield Association

CONTACTS: *Note: Officers with more than one job title may be intentionally listed here more than once.*

Don George, CEO
Dawn Schneiderman, COO
Ruth Greene, CFO
Joshua Plavin, Chief Medical Officer
Robert Wheeler, Chief Medical Dir.
David Yoo, CIO
Chris Gannon, Chief Admin. Officer
Chris Gannon, General Counsel
Doug Warren, VP-Oper.
Catherine Hamilton, VP-Corp. Planning
Kevin Goddard, VP-External Affairs & Sales
Chris Gannon, Treas.
Charles Smith, Chmn.

GROWTH PLANS/SPECIAL FEATURES:

Blue Cross and Blue Shield of Vermont (BCBS VT), a nonprofit organization, is one of the largest health insurance providers in Vermont. In addition to offering Medicare supplement, vision and dental plans, BCBS VT offers preferred provider organization (PPO), health maintenance organization (HMO), point-of-sale (POS) and high deductible (PPO, HMO and out of state) plans. Exchange coverage options include individual and family plans, coverage for an employee who works for a small business and small group employer (1-100 employees) plans. Non-exchange coverage options are provided for large groups (101 or more employees) and Medicare-eligible persons. BCBS VT has a partnership with American Well which enables members 24/7/365 access to doctors via telemedicine. Telemedicine provides online video consultation access with a provider via a computer, or an app on a smartphone or tablet. BCBS VT operates under a license with the Blue Cross and Blue Shield Association.

Employee benefits include medical, vision and dental coverage; a worksite wellness program; a 401(k) and company pension plan; life insurance; short- and long-term disability; and tuition reimbursement.

FINANCIAL DATA: *Note: Data for latest year may not have been available at press time.*

In U.S. $	2020	2019	2018	2017	2016	2015
Revenue	479,087,836	537,658,660	517,449,153	578,276,649	547,330,815	539,866,593
R&D Expense						
Operating Income						
Operating Margin %						
SGA Expense						
Net Income	13,201,516	13,403,091	-6,670,376	7,582,497	-9,714,555	12,220,330
Operating Cash Flow						
Capital Expenditure						
EBITDA						
Return on Assets %						
Return on Equity %						
Debt to Equity						

CONTACT INFORMATION:

Phone: 802-223-6131   Fax: 802-223-4229
Toll-Free: 800-247-2583
Address: 445 Industrial Ln., Berlin, VT 05602 United States

STOCK TICKER/OTHER:

Stock Ticker: Nonprofit
Employees: 400
Parent Company:

Exchange:
Fiscal Year Ends: 12/31

SALARIES/BONUSES:

Top Exec. Salary: $ Bonus: $
Second Exec. Salary: $ Bonus: $

OTHER THOUGHTS:

Estimated Female Officers or Directors: 7
Hot Spot for Advancement for Women/Minorities: Y

Blue Cross and Blue Shield of Wyoming
www.bcbswy.com

NAIC Code: 524114

TYPES OF BUSINESS:

Insurance-Medical & Health, HMOs & PPOs
Life Insurance
Health Insurance
Dental Insurance
Individual Plans
Group Plans
Employer Plans
Family Plans

BRANDS/DIVISIONS/AFFILIATES:

BlueChoice Business
Caring Foundation of Wyoming

CONTACTS: *Note: Officers with more than one job title may be intentionally listed here more than once.*

Diane Gore, CEO
Renee Dilly, VP-Internal Oper.
Lois Huff, CFO
Lee Shannon, VP-Sales
Michael Wells, CIO
Tom Lockhart, Vice Chmn.

GROWTH PLANS/SPECIAL FEATURES:

Blue Cross Blue Shield of Wyoming (BCBSWY) is a nonprofit insurance company and a Blue Cross Blue Shield Association member serving more than 100,000 members at 10 locations across Wyoming. The firm provides medical, vision and dental insurance to groups, employers, individuals and families, as well as Medicare supplemental coverage, group life insurance, cancer and critical illness coverage, flexible benefits administration, worksite benefits and a prescription drug program. The firm's BlueChoice Business program is a comprehensive health insurance plan, providing benefits to small-, medium- and large-sized companies. BlueChoice Business provides a wide range of administrative services for both partially and fully self-funded plans. Some of the benefits include a choice of prescription drug coverage, life and disability insurance, dental and vision coverage, flexible spending accounts, accidental death insurance and short- and long-term disability. BCBSWY covers all administrative costs for the Caring Foundation of Wyoming, Inc., which provides basic healthcare services to uninsured children, meets the healthcare needs of uninsured women and aids in the prevention of domestic violence. The company is also the carrier for the Wyoming Department of Health's Kid Care CHIP program, which offers health insurance coverage for uninsured children from lower-income families.

BCBSWY offers its employees an extended illness time bank, a wellness program, health insurance, life insurance, flexible spending accounts, long-term disability, paid time off and educational assistance, among other benefits.

FINANCIAL DATA: *Note: Data for latest year may not have been available at press time.*

In U.S. $	2020	2019	2018	2017	2016	2015
Revenue						
R&D Expense						
Operating Income						
Operating Margin %						
SGA Expense						
Net Income						
Operating Cash Flow						
Capital Expenditure						
EBITDA						
Return on Assets %						
Return on Equity %						
Debt to Equity						

CONTACT INFORMATION:

Phone: 307-634-1393   Fax: 307-634-5742
Toll-Free: 800-442-2376
Address: 4000 House Ave., Cheyenne, WY 82001 United States

STOCK TICKER/OTHER:

Stock Ticker: Nonprofit
Employees: 200
Parent Company:

Exchange:
Fiscal Year Ends: 12/31

SALARIES/BONUSES:

Top Exec. Salary: $ Bonus: $
Second Exec. Salary: $ Bonus: $

OTHER THOUGHTS:

Estimated Female Officers or Directors: 1
Hot Spot for Advancement for Women/Minorities: Y

Blue Cross Blue Shield of Kansas City (Blue KC) www.bluekc.com

NAIC Code: 524114

TYPES OF BUSINESS:

Insurance-Medical & Health, HMOs & PPOs
Health Insurance
Individual Plans
Family Plans
Group Plans
Short-term Security Plans
Dental Insurance
Long-term Care Insurance

BRANDS/DIVISIONS/AFFILIATES:

Blue Cross and Blue Shield Association

GROWTH PLANS/SPECIAL FEATURES:

Blue Cross Blue Shield of Kansas City (Blue KC) is an independent licensee of the Blue Cross and Blue Shield Association and a nonprofit health insurance provider with more than 1 million members. Blue KC serves people in more than 30 counties of greater Kansas City and northwestern Missouri, as well as Johnson and Wyandotte counties in Kansas. The company offers individual and family health insurance plans as well as small group and large group options, Medicare and other choices, such as a short-term security plan for individuals and families who are temporarily without health insurance. Blue KC offers dental insurance, travel insurance and long-term care insurance.

CONTACTS: Note: Officers with more than one job title may be intentionally listed here more than once.

Erin Stucky, CEO
Ron Rowe, COO
Henri Cournand, CFO
Jenny Housley, CMO
Mark Garrett, Chief Human Resources Officer
Christopher Henchey, Exec.-IT & Transformation
Gret Sweat, Chief Medical Officer

FINANCIAL DATA: Note: Data for latest year may not have been available at press time.

In U.S. $	2020	2019	2018	2017	2016	2015
Revenue	2,956,147,000	2,948,568,000	2,848,446,000	3,044,207,000	2,869,020,000	2,649,500,000
R&D Expense						
Operating Income						
Operating Margin %						
SGA Expense						
Net Income	74,788,000	96,483,000	9,875,000	108,863,000	63,361,000	40,737,000
Operating Cash Flow						
Capital Expenditure						
EBITDA						
Return on Assets %						
Return on Equity %						
Debt to Equity						

CONTACT INFORMATION:

Phone: 816-395-3558   Fax:
Toll-Free: 888-989-8842
Address: 2301 Main St., Kansas City, MO 64108 United States

STOCK TICKER/OTHER:

Stock Ticker: Nonprofit   Exchange:
Employees: 1,596   Fiscal Year Ends: 12/31
Parent Company:

SALARIES/BONUSES:

Top Exec. Salary: $ Bonus: $
Second Exec. Salary: $ Bonus: $

OTHER THOUGHTS:

Estimated Female Officers or Directors:
Hot Spot for Advancement for Women/Minorities:

Blue Cross of California

www.anthem.com/ca

NAIC Code: 524114

TYPES OF BUSINESS:

Insurance-Medical & Health, HMOs & PPOs
Point of Service Plans
Indemnity Plans
Health Insurance
Health Care Services

BRANDS/DIVISIONS/AFFILIATES:

Anthem Inc
Anthem Blue Cross
Anthem Blue Cross Life and Health Insurance

CONTACTS: Note: Officers with more than one job title may be intentionally listed here more than once.

Paul Markovich, Pres.
Kevin Hayden, Pres. State Sponsored Bus. Div.
Michael C. Higgins, Sr. VP-Large Group Div.

GROWTH PLANS/SPECIAL FEATURES:

Blue Cross of California does business as Anthem Blue Cross and is a provider of health insurance and related care services to members in California. The company is a subsidiary of Anthem, Inc.; so, together with affiliate Anthem Blue Cross Life and Health Insurance, the company provides health maintenance organizations (HMOs), preferred provider organizations (PPOs), traditional indemnity plans and point-of-service (POS) plans as well as Medicare and Medicaid. Anthem Blue Cross offers group plans for businesses of every size, including a variety of group medical, pharmacy, dental, vision, life and disability plans. Medicare supplemental plans and Medicare risk plans are provided for seniors, including Medicare Advantage and Medicare Part D coverage.

Through parent company Anthem Inc., Blue Cross of California offers its employees tuition assistance, flexible spending account, medical/dental/vision coverage, a 401(k) plan, an employee stock purchase plan, life insurance and long-term disability.

FINANCIAL DATA: Note: Data for latest year may not have been available at press time.

In U.S. $	2020	2019	2018	2017	2016	2015
Revenue						
R&D Expense						
Operating Income						
Operating Margin %						
SGA Expense						
Net Income						
Operating Cash Flow						
Capital Expenditure						
EBITDA						
Return on Assets %						
Return on Equity %						
Debt to Equity						

CONTACT INFORMATION:

Phone: 805-557-6655   Fax: 805-557-6872
Toll-Free: 800-393-6130
Address: P.O. Box 272540, Chico, CA 95927-2540 United States

STOCK TICKER/OTHER:

Stock Ticker: Subsidiary
Employees: 5,000
Parent Company: Anthem Inc

Exchange:
Fiscal Year Ends: 12/31

SALARIES/BONUSES:

Top Exec. Salary: $ Bonus: $
Second Exec. Salary: $ Bonus: $

OTHER THOUGHTS:

Estimated Female Officers or Directors: 2
Hot Spot for Advancement for Women/Minorities: Y

Blue Cross of Idaho

NAIC Code: 524114

www.bcidaho.com

TYPES OF BUSINESS:

Insurance-Medical & Health, HMOs & PPOs
Dental & Vision Insurance
Life Insurance
Health Savings Accounts

BRANDS/DIVISIONS/AFFILIATES:

Blue Cross and Blue Shield Association

GROWTH PLANS/SPECIAL FEATURES:

Blue Cross of Idaho (BCI) is a nonprofit health insurer serving Idaho residents. BCI offers plans for individuals, families and employers, and also offers Medicare and Medicaid plans, and short- and long-term travel insurance. Hospitals, medical offices, urgent care centers and dental offices can be located on the company's website, as well as cost comparison information. Customers can enroll in value-added services through the BCI's discount programs, which offer discounted rates for fitness club memberships, hearing and vision services, natural medicine and orthodontia rate reductions. BCI is an independent licensee of the Blue Cross and Blue Shield Association.

BCI offers comprehensive health benefits, retirement plans and a variety of employee assistance programs.

CONTACTS: *Note: Officers with more than one job title may be intentionally listed here more than once.*

Charlene Maher, CEO
Valerie A. Reardon, COO
Steve Tobiason, General Counsel
Laurie Heyer, Sr. VP-Oper.
Debra M. Henry, Sr. VP-Organizational Dev.
Rex Warwick, VP-Sales
David J. Hutchins, VP-Actuarial Svcs. & Underwriting
Drew S. Forney, VP-Benefits Mgmt. & Member Svcs.
Jeanie Phillips, VP-Medicare & Medicaid Programs
Jo Anne Stringfield, Chmn.

FINANCIAL DATA: *Note: Data for latest year may not have been available at press time.*

In U.S. $	2020	2019	2018	2017	2016	2015
Revenue	2,485,977,692	2,367,597,802	2,254,855,050	2,147,481,000	2,090,508,000	1,985,982,600
R&D Expense						
Operating Income						
Operating Margin %						
SGA Expense						
Net Income		83,060,334	81,431,700	79,835,000	11,019,000	
Operating Cash Flow						
Capital Expenditure						
EBITDA						
Return on Assets %						
Return on Equity %						
Debt to Equity						

CONTACT INFORMATION:

Phone: 208-345-4550   Fax: 208-331-7311
Toll-Free: 800-274-4018
Address: 3000 E. Pine Ave., Meridian, ID 83642 United States

STOCK TICKER/OTHER:

Stock Ticker: Nonprofit
Employees: 995
Parent Company:

Exchange:
Fiscal Year Ends: 12/31

SALARIES/BONUSES:

Top Exec. Salary: $ Bonus: $
Second Exec. Salary: $ Bonus: $

OTHER THOUGHTS:

Estimated Female Officers or Directors: 9
Hot Spot for Advancement for Women/Minorities: Y

Blue Shield of California   www.blueshieldca.com

NAIC Code: 524114

TYPES OF BUSINESS:

Insurance-Medical & Health, HMOs & PPOs
Managed Care
Life Insurance
Dental Insurance
Health Insurance
Health Maintenance Organization

BRANDS/DIVISIONS/AFFILIATES:

Blue Cross and Blue Shield Association
Blue Shield of California Life & Health Insurance
Blue Shield of California Foundation

CONTACTS: *Note: Officers with more than one job title may be intentionally listed here more than once.*

Paul S. Markovich, CEO
Sarah Iselin, COO
Sandra Clarke, CFO
Jeffrey Robertson, Sr. VP-Mktg. & Consumer Growth
Mary O'Hara, Exec. VP-People
Marcus Thygeson, Chief Health Officer
Lisa Davis, CIO
Seth A. Jacobs, General Counsel
Steve Shivinsky, VP-Corp. Comm.
Tom Brophy, VP-Finance & Treas. Svcs.
Ed Cymerys, Chief Actuary
Juan Davila, Exec. VP-Health Care Quality & Affordability
Rob Geyer, Sr. VP-Customer Quality
Kirsten Gorsuch, Sr. VP-External Affairs
Kristina Leslie, Chmn.

GROWTH PLANS/SPECIAL FEATURES:

Blue Shield of California (BSC) is a nonprofit mutual benefit corporation and a member of the Blue Cross Blue Shield Association, serving approximately 4.5 million members. The firm offers insurance plans including health maintenance organizations (HMOs) and preferred provider organizations (PPOs), as well as dental and Medicare supplemental through its offices in California. BSC works with HMO physicians and specialists, PPO physicians and specialists, HMO hospitals and PPO hospitals. The company also offers executive medical reimbursement, life and vision insurance and short-term health plans through Blue Shield of California Life & Health Insurance Company (Blue Shield Life). The Blue Shield of California Foundation provides charitable contributions and conducts research and supports programs with an emphasis on domestic violence prevention and medical technology assessments. BSC also offers plans for self-employed California workers not covered by employer-sponsored health plans, as well as low cost PPO plans for individuals. The company offers an enhanced small group dental benefit for pregnant women to reduce risks of periodontal disease and pregnancy gingivitis and is expanding dental coverage options with four new dental PPO plans for small groups.

BSC offers its employees medical, dental and vision coverage; life insurance; disability insurance; tuition reimbursement; flexible spending accounts; discounts on entertainment and chiropractic and massage therapy; income protection benefits; a 401(k) sa

FINANCIAL DATA: *Note: Data for latest year may not have been available at press time.*

In U.S. $	2020	2019	2018	2017	2016	2015
Revenue	21,806,000,000	21,086,000,000	20,632,000,000	17,684,000,000	17,598,000,000	14,836,000,000
R&D Expense						
Operating Income						
Operating Margin %						
SGA Expense						
Net Income	680,000,000	573,000,000	413,000,000	296,000,000	67,000,000	115,000,000
Operating Cash Flow						
Capital Expenditure						
EBITDA						
Return on Assets %						
Return on Equity %						
Debt to Equity						

CONTACT INFORMATION:

Phone: 510-607-2000   Fax:
Toll-Free:
Address: 601 12th St., Oakland, CA 94607 United States

STOCK TICKER/OTHER:

Stock Ticker: Nonprofit   Exchange:
Employees: 7,500   Fiscal Year Ends: 12/31
Parent Company:

SALARIES/BONUSES:

Top Exec. Salary: $ Bonus: $
Second Exec. Salary: $ Bonus: $

OTHER THOUGHTS:

Estimated Female Officers or Directors: 14
Hot Spot for Advancement for Women/Minorities: Y

Sales, profits and employees may be estimates. Financial information, benefits and other data can change quickly and may vary from those stated here.

BlueCross BlueShield of Tennessee Inc

www.bcbst.com

NAIC Code: 524114

TYPES OF BUSINESS:

Insurance-Medical & Health, HMOs & PPOs
Health & Disease Management
Health Benefits
Dental Plans
Vision Plans

BRANDS/DIVISIONS/AFFILIATES:

Blue Cross and Blue Shield Association

CONTACTS: Note: Officers with more than one job title may be intentionally listed here more than once.

J.D. Hickey, CEO
Scott Pierce, COO
John Giblin, CFO
Dalya Qualls, Chief Communications Officer
Roy Vaughn, Chief Human Resources Officer
Inga Himelright, Chief Medical Officer
Kelly Paulk, VP-Product Strategy & Individual Mkts.
Bob Worthington, Chief Strategy Officer
Roy Vaughn, VP-Corp. Comm.
Steven Coulter, Pres., Gov't Bus. & Emerging Markets
Sherri Zink, VP-Medical Informatics
Andrea D. Willis, Chief Medical Officer

GROWTH PLANS/SPECIAL FEATURES:

BlueCross BlueShield of Tennessee, Inc. (BCBST) is a leading health benefits company in the state of Tennessee. As part of the nationwide Blue Cross and Blue Shield Association, it offers customers the full range of Blue Cross and Blue Shield insurance products. BCBST serves over 3.5 million members and provides benefits to more than 11,000 employer groups. Plans include individual health plans, group plans, dental plans, vision plans and Medicare coverage. The firm's website offers links to locate doctors, hospitals and pharmacies; price a drug; read about claims and coverage; getting fit and living healthy; food and nutrition; health conditions; and pregnancy/birthing.

BCBST offers comprehensive health benefits, retirement plans and a variety of employee assistance programs.

FINANCIAL DATA: Note: Data for latest year may not have been available at press time.

In U.S. $	2020	2019	2018	2017	2016	2015
Revenue	8,994,746,250	8,566,425,000	8,158,500,000	7,770,000,000	7,400,000,000	7,273,097,000
R&D Expense						
Operating Income						
Operating Margin %						
SGA Expense						
Net Income		453,004,300	439,810,000	427,000,000	118,000,000	6,028,000
Operating Cash Flow						
Capital Expenditure						
EBITDA						
Return on Assets %						
Return on Equity %						
Debt to Equity						

CONTACT INFORMATION:

Phone: 423-755-5600   Fax:
Toll-Free: 800-565-9140
Address: 1 Cameron Hill Cir., Chattanooga, TN 37402 United States

STOCK TICKER/OTHER:

Stock Ticker: Nonprofit   Exchange:
Employees: 6,500   Fiscal Year Ends: 12/31
Parent Company:

SALARIES/BONUSES:

Top Exec. Salary: $ Bonus: $
Second Exec. Salary: $ Bonus: $

OTHER THOUGHTS:

Estimated Female Officers or Directors: 3
Hot Spot for Advancement for Women/Minorities: Y

Bon Secours Mercy Health System Inc

bsmhealth.org

NAIC Code: 622110

TYPES OF BUSINESS:

General Medical and Surgical Hospitals
Health Care
Hospitals
Points of Care

BRANDS/DIVISIONS/AFFILIATES:

Lirio LLC
Trilliant Health

CONTACTS: *Note: Officers with more than one job title may be intentionally listed here more than once.*

John M. Starcher, Jr., CEO
Brian Smith, COO
Deborah Bloomfield, CFO
Sandra Mackey, CMO
Joe Gage, Chief Human Resources Officer
Jason Siegert, Chief Transformation Officer
Peter J. Bernard, CEO-Bon Secours Virginia Health System
Terence O'Brien, CEO-Bon Secours Charity Health System
Michael K. Kerner, CEO-Bon Secours Hampton Roads Heath System
Kevin Halter, CEO-Bon Secours Kentucky Health System
Katherine W. Vestal, Chmn.

GROWTH PLANS/SPECIAL FEATURES:

Bon Secours Mercy Health System, Inc. is a Catholic-based healthcare system with locations in seven U.S. states as well as in Ireland. In total, Bon Secours Mercy Health comprises 50 hospitals, more than 1,200 points of care and 60,000 associates across the states of Florida, Kentucky, Maryland, New York, Ohio, South Carolina and Virginia. Founding sisters and sponsors of the group include the Sisters of Bon Secours, Sisters of Mercy, Sisters of the Humility of Mary, Sisters of Charity of Montreal and the Franciscan Sisters of the poor. In 2018, Bon Secours Health System and Mercy Health combined, becoming a leading Catholic health care ministry. Bon Secours Mercy provides service to all who need care and help, especially the poor, underserved and dying. In addition, Bon Secours and Lirio LLC has a strategic partnership by a direct investment from Bon Secours Mercy Health in Lirio's innovative behavior change artificial intelligence (AI) platform. This strategy enables Bon Secours Mercy Health to leverage technology to continuously learn from its patients, families and community members and make informed decisions. During 2021, Bon Secours Mercy announced an investment in Trilliant Health, a health care analytics company that helps providers develop strategies for increasing market share growth and predicting consumer preferences to improve patient experience. The investment will help Trilliant to accelerate the development of its predictive analytics platform.

FINANCIAL DATA: *Note: Data for latest year may not have been available at press time.*

In U.S. $	2020	2019	2018	2017	2016	2015
Revenue	3,426,000,000	3,315,000,000	3,255,000,000	3,100,000,000	3,300,000,000	3,500,000,000
R&D Expense						
Operating Income						
Operating Margin %						
SGA Expense						
Net Income						
Operating Cash Flow						
Capital Expenditure						
EBITDA						
Return on Assets %						
Return on Equity %						
Debt to Equity						

CONTACT INFORMATION:

Phone: 513-952-5000   Fax:
Toll-Free:
Address: 1701 Mercy Health Pl., Cincinnati, OH 45237 United States

STOCK TICKER/OTHER:

Stock Ticker: Nonprofit   Exchange:
Employees: 60,000   Fiscal Year Ends: 08/31
Parent Company:

SALARIES/BONUSES:

Top Exec. Salary: $ Bonus: $
Second Exec. Salary: $ Bonus: $

OTHER THOUGHTS:

Estimated Female Officers or Directors: 1
Hot Spot for Advancement for Women/Minorities: Y

Boston Scientific Corporation

NAIC Code: 339100

www.bostonscientific.com

TYPES OF BUSINESS:

Supplies-Surgery
Interventional Medical Products
Catheters
Guide wires
Stents
Oncology Research

BRANDS/DIVISIONS/AFFILIATES:

CONTACTS: *Note: Officers with more than one job title may be intentionally listed here more than once.*

Michael Mahoney, CEO
Eric Thepaut, Pres., Geographical
Daniel Brennan, CFO
Jodi Eddy, Chief Information Officer
Ian Meredith, Chief Medical Officer
Edward Mackey, Executive VP, Divisional
Joseph Fitzgerald, Executive VP
David Pierce, Executive VP
Kevin Ballinger, Executive VP
Desiree Ralls-Morrison, General Counsel
Jonathan Monson, Other Corporate Officer
Arthur Butcher, President, Divisional
Jeffrey Mirviss, President, Divisional
Maulik Nanavaty, President, Divisional
Warren Wang, President, Geographical
John Sorenson, Senior VP, Divisional
Wendy Carruthers, Senior VP, Divisional

GROWTH PLANS/SPECIAL FEATURES:

Boston Scientific Corporation is a global developer, manufacturer and marketer of medical devices used in a broad range of interventional medical specialties. The firm comprises seven core businesses organized into three segments: cardiovascular, rhythm management and MedSurg. The cardiovascular segment has two units: the interventional cardiology unit develops and manufactures technologies for diagnosing and treating coronary artery disease and other cardiovascular disorders, including structural heart conditions; and the peripheral interventions unit develops and manufactures products to diagnose and treat peripheral arterial diseases, including a broad line of medical devices used in percutaneous transluminal angioplasty (PTA) and peripheral vascular diseases, as well as products to diagnose, treat and ease various forms of cancer. The rhythm management segment has three units: the cardiac rhythm management unit develops and manufactures a variety of implantable devices that monitor the heart and deliver electricity to treat cardiac abnormalities; the electrophysiology unit develops and manufactures less-invasive medical technologies used in the diagnosis and treatment of rate and rhythm disorders of the heart, including a broad portfolio of therapeutic and diagnostic catheters and a variety of equipment used in the electrophysiology lab; and the neuromodulation unit develops and manufactures devices to treat various neurological movement disorders and manage chronic pain. Last, the MedSurg segment has three units: the endoscopy unit develops and manufactures devices to diagnose and treat a range of gastrointestinal and pulmonary conditions with innovative, less-invasive technologies; the urology and pelvic health unit develops and manufactures devices to treat various urological and pelvic conditions for both male and female anatomies; and the neuromodulation unit develops and manufactures devices to treat various neurological movement disorders and manage chronic pain. In early 2021, Boston Scientific agreed to acquire Preventice Solutions Inc. and Lumenis Ltd.

The firm offers its employees comprehensive health benefits and assistance programs.

FINANCIAL DATA: *Note: Data for latest year may not have been available at press time.*

In U.S. $	2020	2019	2018	2017	2016	2015
Revenue	9,913,000,000	10,735,000,000	9,823,000,000	9,048,001,000	8,386,000,000	7,477,000,000
R&D Expense	1,143,000,000	1,174,000,000	1,113,000,000	997,000,000	920,000,000	876,000,000
Operating Income	684,000,000	1,740,000,000	1,659,000,000	1,531,000,000	1,319,000,000	990,000,000
Operating Margin %		.16%	.17%	.17%	.16%	.13%
SGA Expense	3,787,000,000	3,941,000,000	3,569,000,000	3,294,000,000	3,099,000,000	2,873,000,000
Net Income	-82,000,000	4,700,000,000	1,671,000,000	104,000,000	347,000,000	-239,000,000
Operating Cash Flow	1,508,000,000	1,836,000,000	310,000,000	1,426,000,000	972,000,000	600,000,000
Capital Expenditure	376,000,000	461,000,000	316,000,000	319,000,000	376,000,000	247,000,000
EBITDA	1,405,000,000	2,171,000,000	2,557,000,000	2,006,000,000	1,225,000,000	403,000,000
Return on Assets %		.18%	.08%	.01%	.02%	-.01%
Return on Equity %		.42%	.21%	.02%	.05%	-.04%
Debt to Equity		0.639	0.55	0.544	0.805	0.898

CONTACT INFORMATION:

Phone: 508 683-4000   Fax: 508 647-2200
Toll-Free: 888-272-1001
Address: 300 Boston Scientific Way, Marlborough, MA 01752-1234 United States

STOCK TICKER/OTHER:

Stock Ticker: BSX
Employees: 36,000
Parent Company:

Exchange: NYS
Fiscal Year Ends: 12/31

SALARIES/BONUSES:

Top Exec. Salary: $ Bonus: $
Second Exec. Salary: $ Bonus: $

OTHER THOUGHTS:

Estimated Female Officers or Directors: 5
Hot Spot for Advancement for Women/Minorities: Y

Sales, profits and employees may be estimates. Financial information, benefits and other data can change quickly and may vary from those stated here.

BrightSpring Health Services   www.brightspringhealth.com

NAIC Code: 623210

TYPES OF BUSINESS:

Residential Intellectual and Developmental Disability Facilities
Job Corps Training Services
Employment Training Services
Home Care Services

BRANDS/DIVISIONS/AFFILIATES:

ResCare Community Living
Brightway Community Living
All Ways Caring HomeCare
Equus Workforce Solutions
Pharmacy Alternatives
StepStone Family & Youth Services
Rest Assured Telecare

CONTACTS: *Note: Officers with more than one job title may be intentionally listed here more than once.*

Jon Rousseau, CEO
Steven S. Reed, Chief Legal Officer
Nel Taylor, Chief Comm. Officer
Michael Hough, Exec. VP-Workforce Svcs.

GROWTH PLANS/SPECIAL FEATURES:

BrightSpring Health Services, formerly ResCare, Inc., is a diversified health and human services provider in the U.S. The company operates in six segments. The residential services segment operates through ResCare Community Living, which offers support services to adults and youths with intellectual, cognitive and other developmental disabilities in community home settings. In Oklahoma this segment operates as Brightway Community Living.The homecare services segment operates through All Ways Caring HomeCare, which primarily offers periodic in-home care services to the elderly and persons with disabilities. Its services include medication preparation and adherence monitoring, managing daily schedules, grocery shopping, providing/arranging transportation, ambulatory assistance, housework, laundry and managing communications such as phone, mail, email, etc. The workforce services segment operates through Equus Workforce Solutions, with more than 350 locations nationwide, which offer job training and placement programs to assist welfare recipients and disadvantaged job seekers in finding employment and improving their careers prospects. The pharmacy services segment operates through Pharmacy Alternatives, a national pharmacy focused on serving individuals with cognitive, intellectual and developmental disabilities. This division fills prescriptions and offers pharmacist consulting and clinical support, and stays abreast with regulatory compliance, policies and procedures. The youth services segment connects children and youth who need homes to foster families through StepStone Family & Youth Services, which offers training for foster parents, training for young adults, youth residential services, respite care, counseling and more. Last, Rest Assured Telecare is a proprietary platform offering a full suite of home 24/7 monitoring services and solutions, including real-time telecommunication interactions to avoid adverse events, improve health outcomes and lower health costs. BrightSpring serves nearly 60,000 people daily in 42 states, Canada and Puerto Rico.

FINANCIAL DATA: *Note: Data for latest year may not have been available at press time.*

In U.S. $	2020	2019	2018	2017	2016	2015
Revenue	2,099,500,000	2,210,000,000	2,000,000,000	1,875,000,000	1,825,000,000	1,800,000,000
R&D Expense						
Operating Income						
Operating Margin %						
SGA Expense						
Net Income						
Operating Cash Flow						
Capital Expenditure						
EBITDA						
Return on Assets %						
Return on Equity %						
Debt to Equity						

CONTACT INFORMATION:

Phone: 502-394-2100   Fax: 502-394-2206
Toll-Free: 800-866-0860
Address: 805 N. Whittington Pkwy., Louisville, KY 40222 United States

STOCK TICKER/OTHER:

Stock Ticker: Private   Exchange:
Employees: 60,000   Fiscal Year Ends: 12/31
Parent Company:

SALARIES/BONUSES:

Top Exec. Salary: $ Bonus: $
Second Exec. Salary: $ Bonus: $

OTHER THOUGHTS:

Estimated Female Officers or Directors: 1
Hot Spot for Advancement for Women/Minorities: Y

Bristol-Myers Squibb Company

www.bms.com

NAIC Code: 325412

TYPES OF BUSINESS:

Drugs-Diversified
Biopharmaceuticals
Manufacturing
Distribution
Marketing

BRANDS/DIVISIONS/AFFILIATES:

MyoKardia Inc

CONTACTS: *Note: Officers with more than one job title may be intentionally listed here more than once.*

Giovanni Caforio, CEO
Charles Bancroft, CFO
Adam Dubow, Chief Compliance Officer
Paul von Autenried, Chief Information Officer
Thomas Lynch, Chief Scientific Officer
Christopher Boerner, Executive VP
Sandra Leung, General Counsel
Ann Judge, Other Executive Officer
Louis Schmukler, President, Divisional
John Elicker, Senior VP, Divisional
Paul Biondi, Senior VP, Divisional
Karen Santiago, Senior VP

GROWTH PLANS/SPECIAL FEATURES:

Bristol-Myers Squibb Company (BMS) discovers, develops, licenses, manufactures, markets, distributes and sells biopharmaceutical products on a global basis. BMS focuses on discovering, developing and delivering transformational medicines for patients facing serious diseases such as cancer, as well as immunology, cardiovascular and fibrosis. The company's products are sold worldwide, primarily to wholesalers, distributors, specialty pharmacies, and to a lesser extent, directly to retailers, hospitals, clinics and government agencies. BMS manufactures its products in the U.S. and Puerto Rico, with most revenues coming from products in hematology, oncology, cardiovascular and immunology therapeutic classes. More than 60% of annual revenues is derived from the U.S., 23% from Europe and the remainder from the rest of the world. In late-2020, BMS acquired MyoKardia, Inc., a clinical-stage biopharmaceutical company, for $13.1 billion in cash.

BMS offers its employees medical and dental insurance; pension and 401(k) plans; short- and long-term disability coverage; travel accident insurance; an employee assistance plan; and adoption assistance.

FINANCIAL DATA: *Note: Data for latest year may not have been available at press time.*

In U.S. $	2020	2019	2018	2017	2016	2015
Revenue	42,518,000,000	26,145,000,000	22,561,000,000	20,776,000,000	19,427,000,000	16,560,000,000
R&D Expense	11,143,000,000	6,148,000,000	6,345,000,000	6,411,000,000	4,940,000,000	5,920,000,000
Operating Income	1,647,000,000	5,612,000,000	4,987,000,000	3,157,000,000	4,430,000,000	1,612,000,000
Operating Margin %		.23%	.23%	.17%	.23%	.10%
SGA Expense	7,661,000,000	4,871,000,000	4,551,000,000	4,849,000,000	5,002,000,000	5,001,000,000
Net Income	-9,015,000,000	3,439,000,000	4,920,000,000	1,007,000,000	4,457,000,000	1,565,000,000
Operating Cash Flow	14,052,000,000	8,067,000,000	5,940,000,000	5,275,000,000	2,850,000,000	1,832,000,000
Capital Expenditure	753,000,000	836,000,000	951,000,000	1,055,000,000	1,215,000,000	820,000,000
EBITDA	4,929,000,000	7,377,000,000	6,788,000,000	6,116,000,000	6,464,000,000	2,637,000,000
Return on Assets %		.04%	.14%	.03%	.14%	.05%
Return on Equity %		.10%	.38%	.07%	.29%	.11%
Debt to Equity		0.854	0.402	0.594	0.353	0.459

CONTACT INFORMATION:

Phone: 212 546-4000   Fax: 212 546-4020
Toll-Free:
Address: 430 E. 29th St., 14/Fl, New York, NY 10016 United States

STOCK TICKER/OTHER:

Stock Ticker: BMY   Exchange: NYS
Employees: 30,000   Fiscal Year Ends: 12/31
Parent Company:

SALARIES/BONUSES:

Top Exec. Salary: $ Bonus: $
Second Exec. Salary: $ Bonus: $

OTHER THOUGHTS:

Estimated Female Officers or Directors: 4
Hot Spot for Advancement for Women/Minorities: Y

British United Provident Association Limited (BUPA)

www.bupa.co.uk

NAIC Code: 524114

TYPES OF BUSINESS:

Insurance-Medical & Health, HMOs & PPOs
Life & Disability Insurance
Long-Term Health Care
Hospitals, Clinics & Health Screening Centers
Travel Insurance
Child Care Services
Cosmetic Surgery

BRANDS/DIVISIONS/AFFILIATES:

Bupa Health Insurance
Bupa Centres
Bupa Dental Centres
Bupa Cromwell Hospital
Bupa Arabia

CONTACTS: Note: Officers with more than one job title may be intentionally listed here more than once.

Inaki Ereno, CEO
James Lenton, CFO
Nigel Sullivan, Chief People Officer
Paul Zollinger-Read, Chief Medical Officer
Mark Glenn, Chief Transformation Officer
Theresa Heggie, Chief Strategy & Mktg. Dir.
Steve John, Corp. Affairs Dir.
Alison Platt, Managing Dir.-Int'l Dev. Markets
Robert Lang, Managing Dir.-Int'l Private Medical Insurance
Dean Holden, Managing Dir.-Australia & New Zealand
Inaki Ereno, Managing Dir.-Spain & Latin America
Paula Franklin, Chief Medical Officer

GROWTH PLANS/SPECIAL FEATURES:

British United Provident Association (Bupa) is a leading international healthcare company that provides service to customers in in the U.K. and other countries. Bupa is one of the largest private health insurance companies in the U.K., both for individuals and corporations. Bupa Health Insurance provides medical insurance in the U.K., while Bupa International provides international health insurance, offering access to hospitals and clinics worldwide. The company has care homes throughout the U.K., including long-term nursing, residential care, short-term respite care and specialist dementia care. Insurance is not required to stay in these care homes. Bupa Centres are located throughout the U.K., offering a range of health services such as physiotherapy and cosmetic treatment, or even guidance when physically training for a big event, recovering from an illness or desiring a checkup. Bupa Dental Centres offer a range of preventive and specialist treatments, including general dentistry, dental examinations, hygiene treatment and cosmetic dentistry. Bupa Cromwell Hospital is a London hospital that provides patients with access to over 400 consultants, up-to-date technology and equipment. For businesses, Bupa offers healthcare and insurance solutions for those with two to more than 250 employees. Solutions include health insurance, business mental health, dental plans, travel plans, cash plans, flu vaccinations, employee assistance programs, health assessments and private general practitioner and nurse services. The company also offers a range of products for intermediaries to offer their clients, whether looking for a health insurance product on behalf of an individual, for a company startup or a corporate client considering to offer health and wellbeing options for their employees. For health care professionals, Bupa's facilities, products, solutions and services are also available to them and their patients. Pay-as-you-go treatments are available to all.

FINANCIAL DATA: Note: Data for latest year may not have been available at press time.

In U.S. $	2020	2019	2018	2017	2016	2015
Revenue	16,452,900,000	16,153,700,000	15,049,400,000	16,459,300,000	14,345,049,146	12,817,392,334
R&D Expense						
Operating Income						
Operating Margin %						
SGA Expense						
Net Income	312,276,000	-276,749,000	395,936,000	655,539,000	504,432,802	362,936,011
Operating Cash Flow						
Capital Expenditure						
EBITDA						
Return on Assets %						
Return on Equity %						
Debt to Equity						

CONTACT INFORMATION:

Phone: 44-20-7656-2000   Fax: 44-20-7656-2700
Toll-Free:
Address: 1 Angel Court, London, EC2R 7HJ United Kingdom

STOCK TICKER/OTHER:

Stock Ticker: Private
Employees: 84,000
Parent Company:

Exchange:
Fiscal Year Ends: 12/31

SALARIES/BONUSES:

Top Exec. Salary: $ Bonus: $
Second Exec. Salary: $ Bonus: $

OTHER THOUGHTS:

Estimated Female Officers or Directors: 5
Hot Spot for Advancement for Women/Minorities: Y

Bruker Corporation

NAIC Code: 334516

www.bruker.com

TYPES OF BUSINESS:

Scientific Equipment Manufacturing
Scientific Instrument Development
Manufacturing
Analytic Solutions
Diagnostic Solutions
Magnetic Resonance Imaging
Spectrometry Solutions
X-ray Instruments

BRANDS/DIVISIONS/AFFILIATES:

Bruker BioSpin Group
Bruker CALID Group
Bruker Scientific Instruments Nano Group
Bruker Energy & Supercon Technologies

CONTACTS: *Note: Officers with more than one job title may be intentionally listed here more than once.*

Burkhard Prause, CEO, Subsidiary
Frank Laukien, CEO
Gerald Herman, CFO
Mark Munch, Executive VP
Juergen Srega, President, Divisional
Falko Busse, President, Subsidiary

GROWTH PLANS/SPECIAL FEATURES:

Bruker Corporation develops, manufactures and distributes high-performance scientific instruments and analytical and diagnostic solutions that enable customers to explore life and materials at microscopic, molecular and cellular levels. The company operates through four segments: Bruker BioSpin Group, Bruker CALID Group, Bruker Scientific Instruments (BSI) Nano Group and Bruker Energy & Supercon Technologies (BEST). Bruker BioSpin designs, manufactures and distributes enabling life science tools based on magnetic resonance technology, with customers including academic and government research, pharmaceutical and biotechnology companies, nonprofit laboratories, chemical companies, food and beverage companies, clinical companies and industrial companies. Bruker CALID designs, manufactures and distributes life science mass spectrometry and ion mobility spectrometry solutions, analytical and process analysis instruments and solutions based in infrared and Raman molecular spectroscopy technologies and radiological/nuclear detectors for chemical, biological, radiological, nuclear and explosive detection. BSI Nano designs, manufactures and distributes advanced X-ray instruments; atomic force instrumentation; advanced fluorescence optical microscopy instruments; analytical tools for electron microscopes and X-ray metrology; defect-detection equipment for semiconductor process control; handheld, portable and mobile X-ray fluorescence spectrometry instruments; spark optical emissions spectroscopy systems; chip cytometry products and services for targeted spatial proteomics, multi-omic services, and products and services for special genomics research. Last, BEST develops and manufactures superconducting and non-superconducting materials and devices for use in healthcare, renewable energy, energy infrastructure and big science research. This segment focuses on metallic low temperature superconductors for use in magnetic resonance imaging, nuclear magnetic resonance, fusion energy research and other applications.

FINANCIAL DATA: *Note: Data for latest year may not have been available at press time.*

In U.S. $	2020	2019	2018	2017	2016	2015
Revenue	1,987,500,000	2,072,600,000	1,895,600,000	1,765,900,000	1,611,300,000	1,623,800,000
R&D Expense	198,000,000	187,700,000	173,400,000	162,700,000	149,000,000	145,700,000
Operating Income	261,500,000	299,100,000	268,700,000	230,000,000	196,800,000	151,200,000
Operating Margin %		.15%	.14%	.13%	.12%	.09%
SGA Expense	477,800,000	504,800,000	453,100,000	416,100,000	390,500,000	402,800,000
Net Income	157,800,000	197,200,000	179,700,000	78,600,000	153,600,000	101,600,000
Operating Cash Flow	332,200,000	213,400,000	239,700,000	154,400,000	130,800,000	229,200,000
Capital Expenditure	97,200,000	73,000,000	49,200,000	43,700,000	37,100,000	34,200,000
EBITDA	320,600,000	372,000,000	322,200,000	277,100,000	245,100,000	194,300,000
Return on Assets %		.08%	.09%	.04%	.09%	.06%
Return on Equity %		.22%	.22%	.11%	.22%	.14%
Debt to Equity		0.948	0.36	0.573	0.571	0.366

CONTACT INFORMATION:

Phone: 978 663-3660   Fax: 978 663-2471
Toll-Free:
Address: 40 Manning Rd., Billerica, MA 01821 United States

STOCK TICKER/OTHER:

Stock Ticker: BRKR
Employees: 7,400
Parent Company:

Exchange: NAS
Fiscal Year Ends: 12/31

SALARIES/BONUSES:

Top Exec. Salary: $ Bonus: $
Second Exec. Salary: $ Bonus: $

OTHER THOUGHTS:

Estimated Female Officers or Directors: 1
Hot Spot for Advancement for Women/Minorities:

Sales, profits and employees may be estimates. Financial information, benefits and other data can change quickly and may vary from those stated here.

Cambia Health Solutions Inc

www.cambiahealth.com

NAIC Code: 524114

TYPES OF BUSINESS:

Insurance-Medical & Health, HMOs & PPOs
Health Solutions
Healthcare Plans
Healthcare Financial Tools
Healthcare Management Software
Medication Information Platform

BRANDS/DIVISIONS/AFFILIATES:

Regional Health Plans
Asuris Northwest Health
BridgeSpan Health
Healthcare Management Administrators
Journi
LifeMap
MedSavvy
BeyondWell

CONTACTS: *Note: Officers with more than one job title may be intentionally listed here more than once.*

Jared L. Short, CEO
Vince Price, CFO
Gail Baker, Sr. VP-Strategic Communications
Elizabeth Cole, Chief Human Resources Officer
Richard Popiel, Exec. VP-Health Care Svcs.
Laurent Rotival, CIO
Scott Power, Sr. VP-Health Insurance Operations
Jonathan Hensley, Pres., Regence BlueShield of Washington
Jared L. Short, Pres., Health Insurance Svcs.
Scott Kreiling, Pres., Regence BlueShield of Idaho
Jennifer Danielson, Pres., Regence BlueCross BlueShield of Utah
Marion Couch, Chief Medical Officer

GROWTH PLANS/SPECIAL FEATURES:

Cambia Health Solutions, Inc. is a nonprofit health solutions company comprised of businesses engaged in the health industry. Cambia's health plans consist of provider networks and partner organizations across Oregon, Washington, Idaho and Utah. They include: Regional Health Plans, serving more than 3.2 million members in Oregon, Washington, Idaho and Utah; Asuris Northwest Health, serving more than 71,000 residents in Washington; BridgeSpan Health, offering medical coverage, members-only discounts, access to health coaches and a 24/7 nurse line; and Healthcare Management Administrators, a leading administrator of health plans serving employers who choose to self-fund their health care. Cambia platforms, solutions and subsidiaries include: Journi, offering real-time access to address health care questions, financial tools, and 24/7 access to Care Guides who manage, coordinate and help support health management; LifeMap, a provider of ancillary benefits plans offering financial protection; MedSavvy, which provides online transparency tools and reviews to find the most effective medication at the lowest cost; and BeyondWell, offering personalized programs that connect to the support, apps and gadgets for living a healthy life.

Cambia offers comprehensive benefits, retirement plans and employee assistance programs.

FINANCIAL DATA: *Note: Data for latest year may not have been available at press time.*

In U.S. $	2020	2019	2018	2017	2016	2015
Revenue	9,493,350,000	9,993,000,000	9,975,000,000	9,500,000,000	9,000,000,000	8,800,000,000
R&D Expense						
Operating Income						
Operating Margin %						
SGA Expense						
Net Income						
Operating Cash Flow						
Capital Expenditure						
EBITDA						
Return on Assets %						
Return on Equity %						
Debt to Equity						

CONTACT INFORMATION:

Phone: 503-225-5221   Fax: 503-225-5274
Toll-Free: 800-452-7278
Address: 100 SW Market St., Portland, OR 97201 United States

STOCK TICKER/OTHER:

Stock Ticker: Nonprofit
Employees: 5,000
Parent Company:

Exchange:
Fiscal Year Ends: 12/31

SALARIES/BONUSES:

Top Exec. Salary: $ Bonus: $
Second Exec. Salary: $ Bonus: $

OTHER THOUGHTS:

Estimated Female Officers or Directors: 1
Hot Spot for Advancement for Women/Minorities: Y

Sales, profits and employees may be estimates. Financial information, benefits and other data can change quickly and may vary from those stated here.

Cancer Treatment Centers of America Inc (CTCA)

www.cancercenter.com

NAIC Code: 622110

TYPES OF BUSINESS:

General Medical and Surgical Hospitals
Cancer Treatment
Cancer Diagnosis
Oncology Rehabilitation
Pain Management
Nutritional Support
Hospitals
Outpatient Care Centers

BRANDS/DIVISIONS/AFFILIATES:

CONTACTS: *Note: Officers with more than one job title may be intentionally listed here more than once.*

Pat A. Basu, CEO
Pete Govorchin, COO
Douglas A. Costa, CFO
Ken Chaplin, CMO
Zane A. Zumbahlen, Chief Human Resources Officer
Jennifer Greenman, CIO
Richard J. Stephenson, Chmn.

GROWTH PLANS/SPECIAL FEATURES:

Cancer Treatment Centers of America (CTCA) is a comprehensive cancer care network with three hospitals, as well as outpatient care centers and other locations. CTCA's hospitals are located in Atlanta, Chicago and Phoenix, and outpatient care centers are located in Illinois and Arizona. Founded in 1988 on a personalized, patient-centered approach to cancer care, CTCA tailors a combination of cancer treatments to meet the needs of each patient. The network treats all stages of cancer, including breast cancer, colorectal cancer, lung cancer, prostate cancer, melanoma, leukemia and dozens more. Treatment options include bloodless medicines, chemotherapy, clinical trial programs, precision medicine, radiation therapy, surgery and cryosurgery, among other options. Diagnosis services include related procedures, diagnostic imaging, laboratory tests, genetic tests and genomic tests. In addition, integrative care services span nutritional support, oncology rehabilitation, pain management, spiritual support, behavioral health support and naturopathic support.

FINANCIAL DATA: *Note: Data for latest year may not have been available at press time.*

In U.S. $	2020	2019	2018	2017	2016	2015
Revenue	5,151,431,250	5,788,125,000	5,512,500,000	5,250,000,000	5,000,000,000	4,415,000,000
R&D Expense						
Operating Income						
Operating Margin %						
SGA Expense						
Net Income						
Operating Cash Flow						
Capital Expenditure						
EBITDA						
Return on Assets %						
Return on Equity %						
Debt to Equity						

CONTACT INFORMATION:

Phone: 561-923-3149   Fax:
Toll-Free:
Address: 5900 Broken Sound Pkwy. NW, Boca Raton, FL 33487 United States

STOCK TICKER/OTHER:

Stock Ticker: Private   Exchange:
Employees: Fiscal Year Ends:
Parent Company:

SALARIES/BONUSES:

Top Exec. Salary: $ Bonus: $
Second Exec. Salary: $ Bonus: $

OTHER THOUGHTS:

Estimated Female Officers or Directors:
Hot Spot for Advancement for Women/Minorities:

Sales, profits and employees may be estimates. Financial information, benefits and other data can change quickly and may vary from those stated here.

Capital BlueCross

www.capbluecross.com

NAIC Code: 524114

TYPES OF BUSINESS:

Insurance-Medical & Health, HMOs & PPOs
Health Insurance
Pharmacy Benefits
Dental Plans
Vision Plans
Pet Health
Travel Coverage
Hearing Discounts

BRANDS/DIVISIONS/AFFILIATES:

Capital Advantage Insurance Company
Capital Advantage Assurance Company
Keystone Health Plan Central

CONTACTS: *Note: Officers with more than one job title may be intentionally listed here more than once.*

Todd A. Shamash, CEO
Glenn Heisey, COO
David B. Skerpon, Sr. VP-Enterprise Mktg.
Jodi Woleslagle, Sr. VP-Human Resources
Scott Frank, CIO
Brian L. Sullivan, General Counsel
Aji M. Abraham, VP-Bus. Dev.
David B. Skerpon, VP-Retail Strategies & Brand Mgmt.
William B. Reineberg, Chief Internal Auditor
Anne Baum, VP-Lehigh Valley
Sherry E. Baskin, Corp. Sec.
Jennifer Chambers, Chief Medical Officer
Glenn Heisey, Sr. VP-Strategy & Network
Jennifer Chambers, Chief Medical Officer
Tracy Onorofsky, Sr. VP-Commercial Group Sales

GROWTH PLANS/SPECIAL FEATURES:

Capital BlueCross provides health insurance and related services to members throughout 21 counties in central Pennsylvania and the Lehigh Valley. The company offers a comprehensive range of products for groups and individuals, including a choice of several preferred provider organizations (PPOs) and dental, vision and pharmacy benefit programs. The firm also offers the Children's Health Insurance Program (CHIP), a low-cost or free health insurance program for uninsured children and adolescents who do not qualify for medical assistance through the Department of Public Welfare and who meet certain guidelines with respect to family size and income. Wholly-owned subsidiaries Capital Advantage Insurance Company and Capital Advantage Assurance Company offer comprehensive health coverage alone or in combination with Capital BlueCross. Wholly-owned Keystone Health Plan Central administers Capital BlueCross' family health plans under the brand KHP Central. Other offerings include pet heath, trip protection (for when plans change) and travel coverage (while traveling) as well as hearing discounts.

Capital BlueCross offers its employees comprehensive health benefits, retirement options, life and disability coverage, and a variety of employee assistance plans and programs.

FINANCIAL DATA: *Note: Data for latest year may not have been available at press time.*

In U.S. $	2020	2019	2018	2017	2016	2015
Revenue	4,417,149,713	4,206,809,250	4,006,485,000	3,815,700,000	3,634,000,000	3,530,000,000
R&D Expense						
Operating Income						
Operating Margin %						
SGA Expense						
Net Income						
Operating Cash Flow						
Capital Expenditure						
EBITDA						
Return on Assets %						
Return on Equity %						
Debt to Equity						

CONTACT INFORMATION:

Phone: 717-541-7000   Fax: 717-541-6915
Toll-Free: 800-962-2242
Address: 2500 Elmerton Ave., Harrisburg, PA 17177 United States

SALARIES/BONUSES:

Top Exec. Salary: $ Bonus: $
Second Exec. Salary: $ Bonus: $

STOCK TICKER/OTHER:

Stock Ticker: Nonprofit
Employees: 1,850
Parent Company:

Exchange:
Fiscal Year Ends: 12/31

OTHER THOUGHTS:

Estimated Female Officers or Directors: 11
Hot Spot for Advancement for Women/Minorities: Y

Capital Vision Services LP (MyEyeDr)   www.capitalvisionservices.com

NAIC Code: 621320

TYPES OF BUSINESS:

Offices of Optometrists
Optometry Services
Eye Care Services
Prescription Glasses
Contact Lenses
Financial Processing Solutions
Optometry Information Technology
Claims Processing Solutions

BRANDS/DIVISIONS/AFFILIATES:

Goldman Sachs Group Inc (The)
MyEyeDr

GROWTH PLANS/SPECIAL FEATURES:

Capital Vision Services LP manages independently-owned optometry practices throughout the U.S., which operate under the trade name MyEyeDr. These more than 600 MyEyeDr. practices offer full scope optometry and personalized optical services. Patients receive personalized and essential eyecare services, a selection of prescription eyeglasses and sunglasses, and standard and specialty contact lenses. Capital Vision Services directly benefits the individual practices with broad operational and administrative support regarding financial, marketing, human resources, IT, purchasing, credentialing and claims processing. Capital Vision Services operates as a subsidiary of The Goldman Sachs Group, Inc.

CONTACTS: Note: Officers with more than one job title may be intentionally listed here more than once.

Sue Downes, CEO

FINANCIAL DATA: Note: Data for latest year may not have been available at press time.

In U.S. $	2020	2019	2018	2017	2016	2015
Revenue						
R&D Expense						
Operating Income						
Operating Margin %						
SGA Expense						
Net Income						
Operating Cash Flow						
Capital Expenditure						
EBITDA						
Return on Assets %						
Return on Equity %						
Debt to Equity						

CONTACT INFORMATION:

Phone: 703-847-8899   Fax:
Toll-Free:
Address: 1950 Old Gallows Rd., Vienna, VA 22182 United States

STOCK TICKER/OTHER:

Stock Ticker: Subsidiary   Exchange:
Employees: Fiscal Year Ends:
Parent Company: Goldman Sachs Group Inc (The)

SALARIES/BONUSES:

Top Exec. Salary: $ Bonus: $
Second Exec. Salary: $ Bonus: $

OTHER THOUGHTS:

Estimated Female Officers or Directors:
Hot Spot for Advancement for Women/Minorities:

Cardinal Health Inc

www.cardinalhealth.com

NAIC Code: 424210

TYPES OF BUSINESS:

Healthcare Products & Services
Pharmaceutical Distribution
Pharmacy Operations
Medication Management Solutions
Medical Product Manufacturing
Surgical Products

BRANDS/DIVISIONS/AFFILIATES:

Cardinal.com

CONTACTS: *Note: Officers with more than one job title may be intentionally listed here more than once.*

Jon Giacomin, CEO, Divisional
Michael Kaufmann, CEO
Jorge Gomez, CFO
Gregory Kenny, Chairman of the Board
Stuart Laws, Chief Accounting Officer
Michele Holcomb, Executive VP, Divisional
Pamela Kimmet, Other Executive Officer

GROWTH PLANS/SPECIAL FEATURES:

Cardinal Health, Inc. is a provider of products and services that improve the safety and productivity of health care. The company operates in two segments: pharmaceuticals and medical products. The pharmaceutical segment distributes a broad line of branded and generic pharmaceutical products, specialty pharmaceutical, over-the-counter health care products and consumer products. It is also a full-service wholesale distributor to retail customers, hospitals and alternate care providers located throughout the U.S. In addition, this segment operates nuclear pharmacies and cyclotron facilities, provides pharmacy operations, medication therapy management and patient outcomes services to hospitals and other healthcare providers. The segment offers a broad range of support services including computerized order entry provided through Cardinal.com; generic sourcing programs; product movement, inventory and management reports; and consultation on store operations and merchandising. Through its medical products segment manufactures and sources Cardinal Health branded general and specialty medical, surgical and laboratory products and devices. These include: exam and surgical gloves; needle, syringe and sharps disposal; compression; incontinence; nutritional delivery; wound care; single-use surgical drapes, gowns and apparel; fluid suction and collection systems; urology; operating room supply; and electrode product lines. Branded products are sold directly through third-party distributors in the U.S., Canada, Europe, Asia and other markets. During 2021, Cardinal Health sold its Cordis business to Hellman & Friedman for approximately $1 billion.

Cardinal Health offers its employees medical, dental, vision short/long-term disability and life insurance; a 401(k); and various employee assistance programs.

FINANCIAL DATA: *Note: Data for latest year may not have been available at press time.*

In U.S. $	2020	2019	2018	2017	2016	2015
Revenue	152,922,000,000	145,534,000,000	136,809,000,000	129,976,000,000	121,546,000,000	
R&D Expense						
Operating Income	1,772,000,000	1,733,000,000	1,878,000,000	2,242,000,000	2,436,000,000	
Operating Margin %		.01%	.01%	.02%	.02%	
SGA Expense	4,572,000,000	4,480,000,000	4,596,000,000	3,775,000,000	3,648,000,000	
Net Income	-3,696,000,000	1,363,000,000	256,000,000	1,288,000,000	1,427,000,000	
Operating Cash Flow	1,960,000,000	2,722,000,000	2,768,000,000	1,184,000,000	2,971,000,000	
Capital Expenditure	375,000,000	328,000,000	384,000,000	387,000,000	465,000,000	
EBITDA	-2,621,000,000	3,045,000,000	1,133,000,000	2,842,000,000	3,095,000,000	
Return on Assets %		.03%	.01%	.03%	.04%	
Return on Equity %		.22%	.04%	.19%	.22%	
Debt to Equity		1.198	1.322	1.332	0.756	

CONTACT INFORMATION:

Phone: 614 757-5000   Fax:
Toll-Free: 800-234-8701
Address: 7000 Cardinal Pl., Dublin, OH 43017 United States

STOCK TICKER/OTHER:

Stock Ticker: CAH
Employees: 48,000
Parent Company:

Exchange: NYS
Fiscal Year Ends: 06/30

SALARIES/BONUSES:

Top Exec. Salary: $ Bonus: $
Second Exec. Salary: $ Bonus: $

OTHER THOUGHTS:

Estimated Female Officers or Directors: 8
Hot Spot for Advancement for Women/Minorities: Y

CareFirst Inc

NAIC Code: 524114

www.carefirst.com

TYPES OF BUSINESS:

Insurance-Medical & Health, HMOs & PPOs
Healthcare Insurance Provider
Hospitalization Services
Medical Services
Insurance Claims Processing

BRANDS/DIVISIONS/AFFILIATES:

Group Hospitalization and Medical Services Inc
CareFirst of Maryland Inc
CareFirst BlueCross BlueShield
Service Benefit Plan Administrative Services Corp
Federal Employee Program Operations Center
Capital Area Services Company LLC

CONTACTS: *Note: Officers with more than one job title may be intentionally listed here more than once.*

Brian D. Pieninck, CEO
Jon Shematek, Chief Medical Officer
John A. Picciotto, General Counsel
Kenny W. Kan, Chief Actuary
Kevin O'Neill, Sr. VP-Strategic Managed Care Initiatives
Fred. Plumb, Sr. VP-Federal Employee Program
Gwendolyn D. Skillern, Gen. Auditor
Stephen L. Waechter, Chmn.

GROWTH PLANS/SPECIAL FEATURES:

CareFirst, Inc. is one of the largest healthcare insurers in the Mid-Atlantic, serving 3.5 million members. CareFirst is the nonprofit parent company of Group Hospitalization and Medical Services, Inc. (GHMSI) and CareFirst of Maryland, Inc., which collectively do business as CareFirst BlueCross BlueShield. GHMSI's subsidiary Service Benefit Plan Administrative Services Corporation operates the Federal Employee Program (FEP) Operations Center, serving approximately 631,000 FEP members. The company also operates West Virginia-based subsidiary Capital Area Services Company, LLC (CASCI), which annually processes millions of claims from federal government subscribers and dependents as part of FEP. CareFirst offers individual as well as corporate customer health plans such as individual and family medical plans, Medigap plans, prescription drug plans, dental plans and vision plans. More than 80% of healthcare providers in the firm's operating region participate in one or more of its provider networks. CareFirst has corporate office locations and licensed affiliates throughout Maryland, Washington, D.C. and northern Virginia; and maintains regional offices in Annapolis, Frederick, Cumberland, Hagerstown, Easton and Salisbury, Maryland.

CareFirst offers its employees medical, dental, vision and prescription drug coverage; a 401(k) plan; paid holidays; college savings plans; short- and long-term disability; tuition reimbursement; paid time off; and flexible spending accounts.

FINANCIAL DATA: *Note: Data for latest year may not have been available at press time.*

In U.S. $	2020	2019	2018	2017	2016	2015
Revenue	10,000,000,000	9,870,000,000	9,400,000,000	8,800,000,000	8,800,000,000	8,600,000,000
R&D Expense						
Operating Income						
Operating Margin %						
SGA Expense						
Net Income		131,955,000	138,900,000	240,600,000	9,400,000	38,600,000
Operating Cash Flow						
Capital Expenditure						
EBITDA						
Return on Assets %						
Return on Equity %						
Debt to Equity						

CONTACT INFORMATION:

Phone: 410-581-3000 Fax:
Toll-Free:
Address: 1501 South Clinton St., Baltimore, MD 21224 United States

STOCK TICKER/OTHER:

Stock Ticker: Nonprofit Exchange:
Employees: 8,000 Fiscal Year Ends: 12/31
Parent Company:

SALARIES/BONUSES:

Top Exec. Salary: $ Bonus: $
Second Exec. Salary: $ Bonus: $

OTHER THOUGHTS:

Estimated Female Officers or Directors: 18
Hot Spot for Advancement for Women/Minorities: Y

CareRx Corporation

carerx.ca

NAIC Code: 622310

TYPES OF BUSINESS:

Specialty (except Psychiatric and Substance Abuse) Hospitals
Pharmacy Services
Resident Health Care
Medication Packaging Solutions
Medication Monitoring Services

BRANDS/DIVISIONS/AFFILIATES:

Karie
SmartMeds Pharmacy Inc

CONTACTS: *Note: Officers with more than one job title may be intentionally listed here more than once.*

David Murphy, CEO
Jeff May, COO
Andrew Mok, CFO
Nina Freier, Chief Human Resources Officer
Paul Rakowski, General Counsel
Ryan Stempfle, General Manager, Geographical
Nina Freier, Other Executive Officer

GROWTH PLANS/SPECIAL FEATURES:

CareRx Corporation provides pharmacy services and solutions to home health operators and residents in four Canadian provinces. CareRx takes an active role in resident health, care team education and medication system quality and efficiency. CareRx offers round-the-clock access to a clinical pharmacist who works directly with the healthcare team, and offers a range of medication packaging options. CareRx pharmacists are integrated into the customer's care team, continuously monitoring medication safety and resident outcomes, and stays abreast with regulatory compliance and medication safety. The company performs benchmarking and trend analysis of medication use and incidents to create action plans for continuous quality improvement, better health outcomes and care improvement. Since each home is unique, CareRx provides guidance and education tailored to individual health conditions and working environments. CareRx offers computerized physician order entry solutions, which minimize paperwork and optimize prescription safety and efficiency. Online pharmacy training is also provided, and home administrators and management have access to reports and auditing to measure quality and performance of their medication management program. Karie is a medication dispenser device that automatically provides notifications to caregivers if a dose is missed and delivers medication with the touch of a button. During 2021, CareRx acquired SmartMeds Pharmacy Inc., a specialty pharmacy serving over 2,400 residents in long-term care, assisted living and other institutional settings in Ontario; acquired a portion of the Rexall Pharmacy Group's long-term care pharmacy services business, adding about 4,200 residents serviced in Canada; and acquired the long-term care pharmacy division of Medical Pharmacies Group Limited.

CareRx offers its employees critical illness insurance, employee and family assistance programs and paid time off.

FINANCIAL DATA: *Note: Data for latest year may not have been available at press time.*

In U.S. $	2020	2019	2018	2017	2016	2015
Revenue	134,390,600	103,261,200	102,528,800	140,000,800	138,671,800	134,577,000
R&D Expense						
Operating Income	-997,597	-1,745,795	-5,436,242	5,886,155	1,591,681	-5,079,957
Operating Margin %		- .02%	- .05%	.04%	.01%	- .04%
SGA Expense	17,131,490	15,799,160	16,940,090	37,007,210	21,225,450	22,184,110
Net Income	-15,131,330	-24,282,870	-25,762,700	1,529,539	-16,303,750	38,182,950
Operating Cash Flow	189,742	5,265,557	5,461,927	13,317,590	1,408,567	24,398,870
Capital Expenditure	1,619,853	2,899,163	3,687,132	6,338,554	2,438,479	4,245,588
EBITDA	-4,489,187	-6,249,897	-17,137,290	14,436,160	2,703,621	16,875,470
Return on Assets %		- .28%	- .23%	.01%	- .07%	.13%
Return on Equity %			-5.25%	.17%	-2.33%	
Debt to Equity				0.007	23.914	15.065

CONTACT INFORMATION:

Phone: 416-927-8400   Fax: 416-927-8405
Toll-Free: 800-265-9197
Address: 20 Eglinton Ave. W., Ste. 2100, Toronto, ON M4R 1K8 Canada

STOCK TICKER/OTHER:

Stock Ticker: CHHHF
Employees: 922
Parent Company:

Exchange: PINX
Fiscal Year Ends: 12/31

SALARIES/BONUSES:

Top Exec. Salary: $ Bonus: $
Second Exec. Salary: $ Bonus: $

OTHER THOUGHTS:

Estimated Female Officers or Directors: 3
Hot Spot for Advancement for Women/Minorities: Y

Caris Life Sciences

www.carislifesciences.com

NAIC Code: 325413

TYPES OF BUSINESS:

In-Vitro Diagnostic Substance Manufacturing
Molecular Science Innovation
Artificial Intelligence
Precision Medicine Development
Molecular Profiling
Cancer Treatments
Exome Sequencing
Transcriptome Sequencing

BRANDS/DIVISIONS/AFFILIATES:

MI Exome
MI Transcriptome

CONTACTS: *Note: Officers with more than one job title may be intentionally listed here more than once.*

David D. Halbert, CEO
W. Michael Korn, Chief Medical Officer
Luke Power, Chief Accounting Officer
Michael Sullivan, Chief Commercial Officer
Michael Halbert, Sr. VP-Human Resources
Jim Abraham, Chief Data Officer
David D. Halbert, Chmn.

GROWTH PLANS/SPECIAL FEATURES:

Caris Life Sciences is an innovator in molecular science and artificial intelligence (AI),with a focus on offering precision medicine. The company's suite of molecular profiling offerings assess deoxyribonucleic acid (DNA), ribonucleic acid (RNA) and proteins to reveal a molecular blueprint that helps physicians and cancer patients make more precise and personalized treatment decisions. Caris' MI Exome whole exome sequencing (with 22,000 DNA genes) and MI Transcriptome whole transcriptome sequencing (with 22,000 RNA genes), along with cancer-related pathogens, bacteria, viruses and fungi analysis run on every patient profiles. Exome is the part of the genome that consists of exons, and transcriptome is the total of all the messenger RNA molecules expressed from the genes of an organism. Caris is also advancing precision medicine with its AI platform, which combines molecular intelligence with proprietary AI analytics engine, DEAN, to analyze the whole exome, whole transcriptome and complete cancer proteome. Proteome is the entire complement of proteins that is or can be expressed by a cell, tissue or organism at a certain time. Caris' information, in combination with clinical outcomes on patients, provides molecular solutions for patients, physicians, payers and biopharmaceutical organizations. Headquartered in Texas, Caris has offices throughout the U.S., Europe and Asia and other international markets.

Caris offers its employees health benefits, 401(k) and savings plans.

FINANCIAL DATA: *Note: Data for latest year may not have been available at press time.*

In U.S. $	2020	2019	2018	2017	2016	2015
Revenue						
R&D Expense						
Operating Income						
Operating Margin %						
SGA Expense						
Net Income						
Operating Cash Flow						
Capital Expenditure						
EBITDA						
Return on Assets %						
Return on Equity %						
Debt to Equity						

CONTACT INFORMATION:

Phone:
Fax: 214 294-55690
Toll-Free: 855 771-8946
Address: 750 W. John Carpenter Freeway, Ste. 800, Irving, TX 75039 United States

SALARIES/BONUSES:

Top Exec. Salary: $
Bonus: $
Second Exec. Salary: $
Bonus: $

STOCK TICKER/OTHER:

Stock Ticker: Private
Employees:
Parent Company:
Exchange:
Fiscal Year Ends:

OTHER THOUGHTS:

Estimated Female Officers or Directors:
Hot Spot for Advancement for Women/Minorities:

Carl Zeiss Meditec AG

www.meditec.zeiss.com

NAIC Code: 423450

TYPES OF BUSINESS:

Medical, Dental, and Hospital Equipment and Supplies Merchant
Wholesalers
Medical Technology
Diagnostic Treatment Solutions
Microsurgery Solutions
Imaging Technology

BRANDS/DIVISIONS/AFFILIATES:

Carl Zeiss AG
CIRRUS HD-OCT
VISULAS green

CONTACTS: *Note: Officers with more than one job title may be intentionally listed here more than once.*

Ludwin Monz, CEO
Justus Felix Wehmer, CFO
Christian Muller, Manager-Legal & Taxes
Christian Muller, Manager-Investor Relations
Michael Kaschke, Chmn.

GROWTH PLANS/SPECIAL FEATURES:

Carl Zeiss Meditec AG is a German supplier of medical technology. The firm offers complete diagnostic and treatment solutions for ophthalmic diseases; and in the field of microsurgery, provides innovative visualization solutions, especially in the dental treatment and gynecology fields. For example, Meditec's U.S. FDA-cleared CIRRUS HD-OCT (optical coherence tomography) posterior ocular imaging technology enables clinical researchers to open new frontiers of discovery in diseases affecting the retina through images of the epithelium; and the VISULAS green, is a photocoagulator that supports easy, efficient and highly-focused surgical treatments for retinal diseases and glaucoma. Meditec's medical disciplines include ophthalmology, neurosurgery, plastic and reconstructive surgery, spine surgery, surgery of the ear/nose/throat, dentistry, gynecology and oncology. The firm is majority-owned by Carl Zeiss AG, and has subsidiaries, production sites and office locations worldwide, including the U.S., Europe, Asia and the Middle East.

FINANCIAL DATA: *Note: Data for latest year may not have been available at press time.*

In U.S. $	2020	2019	2018	2017	2016	2015
Revenue	1,631,625,000	1,782,965,000	1,564,925,000	1,453,787,000	1,329,739,000	1,270,723,000
R&D Expense	267,329,700	211,748,600	195,029,800	178,125,300	150,774,600	136,786,500
Operating Income	216,928,900	323,354,300	240,848,900	210,513,400	188,559,300	159,553,100
Operating Margin %		.18%	.15%	.14%	.14%	.13%
SGA Expense	426,596,900	481,273,800	432,076,500	412,529,300	368,742,000	363,032,700
Net Income	149,527,200	195,106,200	154,509,600	164,261,800	120,137,300	76,113,040
Operating Cash Flow	218,120,200	268,343,800	228,725,200	46,100,090	136,558,000	69,328,510
Capital Expenditure	54,962,860	57,070,420	42,464,080	47,676,180	34,108,350	20,492,860
EBITDA	326,251,100	349,963,400	260,387,600	263,277,100	202,548,600	151,084,900
Return on Assets %		.09%	.08%	.09%	.08%	.06%
Return on Equity %		.12%	.10%	.13%	.13%	.08%
Debt to Equity		0.109	0.006	0.003	0.01	0.013

CONTACT INFORMATION:

Phone: 49-3641220-0   Fax: 49-3641220-112
Toll-Free:
Address: Goschwitzer Strasse 51-52, Jena, TH 07745 Germany

STOCK TICKER/OTHER:

Stock Ticker: CZMWY   Exchange: PINX
Employees: 3,290   Fiscal Year Ends: 09/30
Parent Company: Carl Zeiss AG

SALARIES/BONUSES:

Top Exec. Salary: $ Bonus: $
Second Exec. Salary: $ Bonus: $

OTHER THOUGHTS:

Estimated Female Officers or Directors:
Hot Spot for Advancement for Women/Minorities:

Castle Dental Centers Inc

www.castledental.com

NAIC Code: 621210

TYPES OF BUSINESS:

Dental Practice Management
Dental Services
Orthodontic Services
Dental Centers
Multi-Specialty Dental Care
Operations Management Software
Payment Solutions

BRANDS/DIVISIONS/AFFILIATES:

Smile Brands Group Inc

CONTACTS: *Note: Officers with more than one job title may be intentionally listed here more than once.*

Steve Bilt, CEO-Smile Brands
Roy D. Smith, Chief Oper. Officer
Steven C. Bilt, CEO

GROWTH PLANS/SPECIAL FEATURES:

Castle Dental Centers, Inc. develops, manages and operates integrated dental networks through contracts with general, orthodontic and multi-specialty dental practices in the U.S. The company operates dental centers in Arkansas, Arizona, California, Colorado, Florida, Indiana, Maryland, Ohio, Oregon, Pennsylvania, Tennessee, Texas, Utah, Virginia and Washington. The typical Castle Dental Center provides general dentistry, preventive care, cosmetic dental care, as well as a full range of dental specialties, including orthodontics, pedodontics, periodontics, endodontics, oral surgery and implantology. Bringing together multi-specialty dental services within a single practice allows Castle Dental Centers to operate more efficiently, use facilities more completely and share dental specialists among multiple locations. Its operating model also incorporates quality assurance and quality control programs, such as peer review and continuing education. Castle Dental Centers establishes regional dental care networks in order to centralize its advertising, billing and collections, payroll and accounting systems. The firm offers a discount program for patients without insurance, and provides communication access to deaf, hard-of-hearing and communication-disabled patients. Castle Dental is a wholly-owned subsidiary of Smile Brands Group, Inc.

FINANCIAL DATA: *Note: Data for latest year may not have been available at press time.*

In U.S. $	2020	2019	2018	2017	2016	2015
Revenue						
R&D Expense						
Operating Income						
Operating Margin %						
SGA Expense						
Net Income						
Operating Cash Flow						
Capital Expenditure						
EBITDA						
Return on Assets %						
Return on Equity %						
Debt to Equity						

CONTACT INFORMATION:

Phone: 281-999-9999 Fax:
Toll-Free: 800-867-6453
Address: 3701 Kirby Dr., Ste. 550, Houston, TX 77098 United States

SALARIES/BONUSES:

Top Exec. Salary: $ Bonus: $
Second Exec. Salary: $ Bonus: $

STOCK TICKER/OTHER:

Stock Ticker: Subsidiary Exchange:
Employees: 1,025 Fiscal Year Ends: 12/31
Parent Company: Smile Brands Group Inc

OTHER THOUGHTS:

Estimated Female Officers or Directors: 1
Hot Spot for Advancement for Women/Minorities:

Centene Corporation

www.centene.com

NAIC Code: 524114

TYPES OF BUSINESS:

Insurance-Medical & Health, HMOs & PPOs
Medicaid Managed Care
Specialty Services
Behavioral Health
Disease Management
Managed Vision
Nurse Triage
Pharmacy Benefit Management

BRANDS/DIVISIONS/AFFILIATES:

CONTACTS: *Note: Officers with more than one job title may be intentionally listed here more than once.*

Michael Neidorff, CEO
Jeffrey Schwaneke, CFO
Mark Brooks, Chief Information Officer
Jesse Hunter, Chief Strategy Officer
Christopher Bowers, Executive VP, Divisional
Brandy Burkhalter, Executive VP, Divisional
Keith Williamson, Executive VP
Christopher Isaak, Senior VP

GROWTH PLANS/SPECIAL FEATURES:

Centene Corporation is a multi-line healthcare plan firm operating in two segments: managed care and specialty services. In the managed care segment, the company provides programs and services to people receiving benefits from foster care, Medicaid, the State Children's Health Insurance Program (CHIP), Medicare special needs plans, supplemental security income (SSI), dual eligible individuals (Duals), long term care (LTC) and federally-facilitated and state-based Marketplaces. This segment accounted for 95% of total annual revenue. Centene's specialty services segment (5%) provides healthcare services to state programs, correctional facilities, healthcare organizations, and to the firm's own subsidiaries. The firm's locally-based staff assists members in accessing care, coordinating referrals to related health and social services and addressing member concerns and questions. Centene's health plans generally provide the following services: primary and specialty physician care, in- and out-patient hospital care, prenatal care, laboratory and x-ray services, home-based primary care, transportation assistance, vision care, dental care, telehealth services, immunizations, prescriptions and limited over-the-counter drugs, specialty pharmacy, provision of durable medical equipment, behavioral health and substance abuse services, 24-hour nurse advice line, therapies, social work services and care coordination. The company also provides a comprehensive set of education and outreach programs to inform and assist members to access healthcare services. During 2021, Centene agreed to acquire Magellan Health Inc., an American for-profit managed health care company. The transaction was expected to close by year's end.

Centene offers its employees comprehensive health benefits, retirement options, life and disability coverage and a variety of employee assistance plans and programs.

FINANCIAL DATA: *Note: Data for latest year may not have been available at press time.*

In U.S. $	2020	2019	2018	2017	2016	2015
Revenue	111,115,000,000	74,639,000,000	60,116,000,000	48,382,000,000	40,607,000,000	22,760,000,000
R&D Expense						
Operating Income	3,154,000,000	2,052,000,000	1,458,000,000	1,199,000,000	1,260,000,000	705,000,000
Operating Margin %		.03%	.02%	.02%	.03%	.03%
SGA Expense	11,343,000,000	6,533,000,000	6,752,000,000	4,446,000,000	4,137,000,000	2,041,000,000
Net Income	1,808,000,000	1,321,000,000	900,000,000	828,000,000	562,000,000	355,000,000
Operating Cash Flow	5,503,000,000	1,483,000,000	1,234,000,000	1,489,000,000	1,851,000,000	658,000,000
Capital Expenditure	869,000,000	730,000,000	675,000,000	422,000,000	306,000,000	150,000,000
EBITDA	4,760,000,000	2,837,000,000	2,206,000,000	1,750,000,000	1,652,000,000	851,000,000
Return on Assets %		.04%	.03%	.04%	.04%	.05%
Return on Equity %		.11%	.10%	.13%	.14%	.18%
Debt to Equity		1.087	0.609	0.685	0.789	0.564

CONTACT INFORMATION:

Phone: 314 725-4477   Fax: 314 725-5180
Toll-Free:
Address: 7700 Forsyth Blvd., St. Louis, MO 63105 United States

STOCK TICKER/OTHER:

Stock Ticker: CNC
Employees: 56,600
Parent Company:

Exchange: NYS
Fiscal Year Ends: 12/31

SALARIES/BONUSES:

Top Exec. Salary: $ Bonus: $
Second Exec. Salary: $ Bonus: $

OTHER THOUGHTS:

Estimated Female Officers or Directors: 4
Hot Spot for Advancement for Women/Minorities: Y

Cerner Corporation

www.cerner.com

NAIC Code: 511210D

TYPES OF BUSINESS:

Computer Software, Healthcare & Biotechnology
Medical Information Systems
Application Hosting
Integrated Delivery Networks
Access Management
Consulting Services
Safety & Risk Management

BRANDS/DIVISIONS/AFFILIATES:

Cerner Millennium
HealtheIntent
Cerner Health Services Inc
CernerWorks
Kantar Health

CONTACTS: *Note: Officers with more than one job title may be intentionally listed here more than once.*

Marc Naughton, CFO
David Shafer, Chairman of the Board
Michael Battaglioli, Chief Accounting Officer
Michael Nill, COO
Donald Trigg, Executive VP, Divisional
Jeffrey Townsend, Executive VP
John Peterzalek, Executive VP
Randy Sims, Executive VP
Julia Wilson, Other Executive Officer

GROWTH PLANS/SPECIAL FEATURES:

Cerner Corporation designs, develops, installs and supports information technology and content applications for health care organizations, consumers and physicians. Cerner's applications are designed to help eliminate error, variance and waste in the care process as well as provide appropriate health information and knowledge to care givers, clinicians and consumers, and appropriate management information to healthcare administrations. Cerner solutions are offered on the unified Cerner Millennium architecture and on the HealtheIntent cloud-based platform. Cerner Millennium combines clinical, financial and management information systems and provides secure access to an individual's electronic medical record at the point of care and organizes and proactively delivers information to meet the specific needs of the physician, nurse, laboratory technician, pharmacist or other care provider, front- and back-office professionals as well as consumers. HealtheIntent offers EHR-agnostic (electronic health record) solutions based on sophisticated, statistical algorithms to help providers predict and improve outcomes, control costs, improve quality and manage the health of their patients. Cerner also offers a broad range of services including implementation and training, remote hosting, operational management services, revenue cycle services, support and maintenance, healthcare data analysis, clinical process optimization, transaction processing, employer health centers, employee wellness programs and third-party administrator (TPA) services for employer-based health plans. Cerner Health Services, Inc. offers a portfolio of enterprise-level clinical and financial healthcare information technology solutions, as well as departmental, connectivity, population health and care coordination solutions globally. CernerWorks is the company's remote-hosting business. These facilities include hospitals; physician practices; ambulatory facilities such as laboratories, ambulatory centers, cardiac facilities, radiology clinics and surgery centers; home health facilities; and retail pharmacies. During 2021, Cerner acquired Kantar Health, a division of Kantar Group. Kantar Health was combined with Cerner's data and technology and is expected to accelerate innovation in life sciences research and improve patient outcomes worldwide.

FINANCIAL DATA: *Note: Data for latest year may not have been available at press time.*

In U.S. $	2020	2019	2018	2017	2016	2015
Revenue	5,505,788,000	5,692,598,000	5,366,325,000	5,142,272,000	4,796,473,000	4,425,267,000
R&D Expense	749,007,000	737,136,000	683,663,000	605,046,000	551,418,000	539,799,000
Operating Income	694,044,000	600,669,000	774,785,000	960,471,000	911,013,000	781,136,000
Operating Margin %		.11%	.14%	.19%	.19%	.18%
SGA Expense	3,074,201,000	3,195,935,000	2,883,165,000	2,632,088,000	2,464,380,000	2,262,024,000
Net Income	780,088,000	529,454,000	630,059,000	866,978,000	636,484,000	539,362,000
Operating Cash Flow	1,436,705,000	1,313,099,000	1,454,009,000	1,307,675,000	1,155,612,000	947,526,000
Capital Expenditure	617,501,000	780,976,000	757,440,000	665,877,000	771,595,000	648,220,000
EBITDA	1,717,976,000	1,356,947,000	1,451,429,000	1,555,864,000	1,427,149,000	1,245,425,000
Return on Assets %		.08%	.10%	.14%	.11%	.11%
Return on Equity %		.11%	.13%	.20%	.16%	.15%
Debt to Equity		0.241	0.089	0.108	0.137	0.146

CONTACT INFORMATION:

Phone: 816 221-1024 Fax:
Toll-Free:
Address: 2800 Rock Creek Pkwy., North Kansas City, MO 64117 United States

STOCK TICKER/OTHER:

Stock Ticker: CERN
Employees: 27,400
Parent Company:

Exchange: NAS
Fiscal Year Ends: 12/31

SALARIES/BONUSES:

Top Exec. Salary: $ Bonus: $
Second Exec. Salary: $ Bonus: $

OTHER THOUGHTS:

Estimated Female Officers or Directors: 13
Hot Spot for Advancement for Women/Minorities: Y

Sales, profits and employees may be estimates. Financial information, benefits and other data can change quickly and may vary from those stated here.

Change Healthcare Inc

www.changehealthcare.com

NAIC Code: 524292

TYPES OF BUSINESS:

Healthcare Business & Administration Management
Healthcare Information Technology
Healthcare Analytics
Healthcare Data
Healthcare Payments Solutions
Patient Engagement
Collaborative Communication
Cost Transparency

BRANDS/DIVISIONS/AFFILIATES:

Change Healthcare Platform

CONTACTS: *Note: Officers with more than one job title may be intentionally listed here more than once.*

Neil de Crescenzo, CEO
August Calhoun, Exec. VP-Oper. & Sales
Fredrik Eliasson, CFO
W. Thomas McEnery, CMO
Linda Whitley-Taylor, Chief People Officer
Alex Choy, CIO
Miriam Paramore, Exec. VP-Prod. Mgmt. & Strategy
Gregory T. Stevens, General Counsel
Frank Manzella, Sr. VP-Corp. Dev.
Kevin Mahoney, Exec. VP-Pharmacy Svcs.
Gary D. Stuart, Exec. VP-Payer Svcs.
Sajid Khan, Exec. VP-Ambulatory Svcs.
T. Ulrich Brechbuhl, Exec. VP-Revenue Cycle Solutions

GROWTH PLANS/SPECIAL FEATURES:

Change Healthcare, Inc. is a healthcare information technology company, primarily serving healthcare payers, providers, pharmacies, partners and developers. The firm's Change Healthcare Platform provides analytics, data, connection and data transfer between providers, payers and consumers to help improve workflows, increase administrative and financial efficiencies, and improve clinical decisions. Change Healthcare's payments and revenue cycle division seeks to optimize financial performance through its products and solutions across revenue cycle management, payment accuracy, consumer payments, communications, medical networks, clinical decision support, healthcare data/analytics, dental networks, provider network optimization and provide payment management. Its clinical and imaging division seeks to transform operational effectiveness and care through its products and solutions across clinical decision support, clinical networks, enterprise imaging solutions, medical record retrieval, clinical reviews, healthcare data and analytics, value-based care, risk adjustment, pharmacy solutions and consulting services. Its patient and member engagement division seeks to enhance the healthcare experience through its products and solutions across patient engagement, member engagement, consumer payments, communications, cost transparency, eligibility and enrollment, healthcare data and analytics, risk adjustment, pharmacy solutions and consulting services. In April 2021, Change Healthcare announced stockholder approval to combine/merge with OptumInsight, which is part of UnitedHealth Group. OptumInsight provides data, analytics, research, consulting, technology and managed services solutions to hospitals, physicians, health plans, government systems, employers and more.

FINANCIAL DATA: *Note: Data for latest year may not have been available at press time.*

In U.S. $	2020	2019	2018	2017	2016	2015
Revenue	196,792,000					
R&D Expense	11,559,000					
Operating Income	-134,197,000	-1,159,000	-180,000			
Operating Margin %	-.68%					
SGA Expense	39,893,000	1,159,000	180,000			
Net Income	-947,597,000	-52,012,000	60,955,000			
Operating Cash Flow	-153,928,000	3,408,000				
Capital Expenditure	13,002,000					
EBITDA	-1,043,361,000	-1,159,000	-180,000			
Return on Assets %	-.17%	-.04%	.04%			
Return on Equity %	-.43%	-.05%	.05%			
Debt to Equity	1.434					

CONTACT INFORMATION:

Phone: 615-932-3000   Fax:
Toll-Free:
Address: 424 Church St., Ste. 1400, Nashville, TN 37219 United States

STOCK TICKER/OTHER:

Stock Ticker: CHNG   Exchange: NAS
Employees: 15,000   Fiscal Year Ends: 03/31
Parent Company:

SALARIES/BONUSES:

Top Exec. Salary: $ Bonus: $
Second Exec. Salary: $ Bonus: $

OTHER THOUGHTS:

Estimated Female Officers or Directors: 1
Hot Spot for Advancement for Women/Minorities:

Chemed Corporation

www.chemed.com

NAIC Code: 621610

TYPES OF BUSINESS:

Home Health Care Services
Hospice Care
Plumbing Services
Pressure Washer Jetting
Leak Detection Services
Pipe Inspections
Pipe Repair

BRANDS/DIVISIONS/AFFILIATES:

VITAS Healthcare Corporation
Roto-Rooter Corporation

CONTACTS: *Note: Officers with more than one job title may be intentionally listed here more than once.*

Nicholas Westfall, CEO, Subsidiary
Kevin McNamara, CEO
David Williams, CFO
George Walsh, Chairman of the Board
Michael Witzeman, Chief Accounting Officer
Thomas Hutton, Director
Spencer Lee, Executive VP
Naomi Dallob, Secretary

GROWTH PLANS/SPECIAL FEATURES:

Chemed Corporation, through its wholly-owned subsidiaries VITAS Healthcare Corporation and Roto-Rooter Corporation, offers hospice care and plumbing services, respectively. VITAS is one of the largest national providers of hospice care and end-of-life services. Its team members include registered nurses, licensed practical nurses, home health aides, physicians, social workers, chaplains and other caregiving professionals. VITAS provides hospice care services in the patient's home, including music therapy and pet visits. Additionally, the firm manages inpatient hospice units, providing service in hospitals, nursing homes and assisted living communities/residential care facilities. Approximately 95% of VITAS' service revenues consist of payments from Medicare and Medicaid. Roto-Rooter supports the maintenance needs of residential and commercial markets by providing services such as plumbing, drain cleaning, high-pressure water jetting, underground leak and line detection, video camera pipe inspections, grease trap and liquid waste pumping, backflow protection, emergency services, automated drain care programs and pipe repair and replacement. One of the largest businesses of its type in North America, Roto-Rooter operates hundreds of company-owned and franchises throughout the U.S. Concerning revenues, Roto-Rooter's largest share is generated by plumbing repair and maintenance, followed by sewer and drain cleaning, HVAC (heating, ventilation and air conditioning) repair and other products and services.

FINANCIAL DATA: *Note: Data for latest year may not have been available at press time.*

In U.S. $	2020	2019	2018	2017	2016	2015
Revenue	2,079,583,000	1,938,555,000	1,782,648,000	1,666,724,000	1,576,881,000	1,543,388,000
R&D Expense						
Operating Income	394,810,000	266,512,000	244,932,000	203,915,000	178,749,000	184,458,000
Operating Margin %		.14%	.14%	.12%	.11%	.12%
SGA Expense	330,218,000	305,712,000	270,209,000	276,652,000	243,572,000	237,821,000
Net Income	319,466,000	219,923,000	205,544,000	98,177,000	108,743,000	110,274,000
Operating Cash Flow	489,289,000	301,249,000	287,138,000	162,495,000	135,393,000	171,500,000
Capital Expenditure	58,831,000	53,022,000	52,872,000	64,300,000	39,772,000	44,135,000
EBITDA	454,928,000	311,349,000	283,453,000	156,814,000	215,407,000	217,270,000
Return on Assets %		.20%	.22%	.11%	.13%	.13%
Return on Equity %		.33%	.36%	.18%	.21%	.23%
Debt to Equity		0.243	0.151	0.169	0.191	0.163

CONTACT INFORMATION:

Phone: 513 762-6900   Fax: 513 762-6919
Toll-Free:
Address: 255 E. 5th St., Ste. 2600, Cincinnati, OH 45202 United States

STOCK TICKER/OTHER:

Stock Ticker: CHE   Exchange: NYS
Employees: 15,544   Fiscal Year Ends: 12/31
Parent Company:

SALARIES/BONUSES:

Top Exec. Salary: $ Bonus: $
Second Exec. Salary: $ Bonus: $

OTHER THOUGHTS:

Estimated Female Officers or Directors: 3
Hot Spot for Advancement for Women/Minorities: Y

China Resources Pharmaceutical Group Limited

www.crpharm.com/en
NAIC Code: 325412

TYPES OF BUSINESS:

Pharmaceutical Preparation Manufacturing
Pharmaceutical Manufacture
Pharmaceutical Distribution
Nutraceutical Products
Logistics Centers
Retail Pharmacy
Direct-to-Patient Pharmacies
Consultancy Services

BRANDS/DIVISIONS/AFFILIATES:

China Resources Pharmaceutical Commercial Group
China Resources Double-Crane Pharmaceutical Co Ltd
Dong-E-E-Jiao Pharmaceutical Co Ltd
China Resources Care Co Ltd
CR Sanjiu
CR Double-Crane
CR Liangzhong
Levonorgestrel Tablets

CONTACTS: *Note: Officers with more than one job title may be intentionally listed here more than once.*

Yuewei Han, CEO

GROWTH PLANS/SPECIAL FEATURES:

China Resources Pharmaceutical Group Limited (CR Pharma) is an integrated pharmaceutical company in China, specializing in the manufacture, distribution and retail of medicines and nutraceutical products. CR Pharma engages in the research and development of pharmaceuticals, including chemical drugs, traditional Chinese medicines, biological drugs and supplements. These cover a wide range of treatment fields, such as the cardiovascular system, digestive tract, metabolism, large-volume intravenous infusion, pediatrics, the respiratory system and more. CR Pharma owns a number of brands, including CR Sanjiu, Dong-E-E-Jiao, CR Double-Crane, CR Jiangzhong, and Levonorgestrel Tablets. The company operates a distribution network comprised of logistics centers covering 28 Chinese provinces, municipalities and autonomous regions. The firm directly distributes products to Chinese hospitals and other medical institutions. CR Pharma's retail pharmacy network consists of more than 860 self-operated pharmacies and over 190 direct-to-patient pharmacies. The company's integrated strategy distributes prescription drugs and offers value-added services, such as online prescription dispensing, door-to-door delivery, medical consultation and health management services. CR Pharma has many subsidiaries, including China Resources Pharmaceutical Commercial Group Co. Ltd., China Resources Double-Crane Pharmaceutical Co. Ltd., Dong-E-E-Jiao Pharmaceutical Co. Ltd. and China Resources Care Co. Ltd.

FINANCIAL DATA: *Note: Data for latest year may not have been available at press time.*

In U.S. $	2020	2019	2018	2017	2016	2015
Revenue	25,851,600,000	26,253,500,000	24,221,000,000	22,075,000,000	20,206,800,000	18,910,400,000
R&D Expense						
Operating Income						
Operating Margin %						
SGA Expense						
Net Income	686,718,000	654,623,000	974,643,000	878,616,000	769,562,000	784,732,000
Operating Cash Flow						
Capital Expenditure						
EBITDA						
Return on Assets %						
Return on Equity %						
Debt to Equity						

CONTACT INFORMATION:

Phone: 852-2593-8991   Fax: 852-259-38992
Toll-Free:
Address: 26 Harbour Rd., China Resources Bldg., Fl. 41, Wanc, Hong Kong, 4101-05 Hong Kong

STOCK TICKER/OTHER:

Stock Ticker: 3320
Employees: 64,000
Parent Company: China Resources Company Limited

Exchange: Hong Kong
Fiscal Year Ends: 12/31

SALARIES/BONUSES:

Top Exec. Salary: $ Bonus: $
Second Exec. Salary: $ Bonus: $

OTHER THOUGHTS:

Estimated Female Officers or Directors:
Hot Spot for Advancement for Women/Minorities:

CHRISTUS Health

www.christushealth.org

NAIC Code: 622110

TYPES OF BUSINESS:

General Medical and Surgical Hospitals
Long-Term & Hospice Care
Behavioral Health
Orthopedic Medicine
Online Health Information

BRANDS/DIVISIONS/AFFILIATES:

Sisters of Charity of the Incarnate Word
Sisters of the Holy Family of Nazareth

CONTACTS: *Note: Officers with more than one job title may be intentionally listed here more than once.*

Ernie Sadau, CEO
John Gillean, Sr. VP-Physician Integration Svcs.

GROWTH PLANS/SPECIAL FEATURES:

CHRISTUS Health is a faith-based, not-for-profit health care organization sponsored by the charities Sisters of Charity of the Incarnate Word in Houston and San Antonio and the Sisters of the Holy Family of Nazareth. Today, CHRISTUS is one of the top Catholic health systems in the U.S. as ranked by size, comprised of more than 600 centers, including long-term care facilities, community hospitals, walk-in clinics and health ministries. The organization has over 15,000 physicians providing individualized care. CHRISTUS operates in Texas, Arkansas, Iowa, Louisiana, Georgia and New Mexico, USA, as well as in Mexico, Chile and Colombia. Some of the services provided by CHRISTUS's facilities include hospice, long-term and assisted care, emergency and outpatient treatment, surgical, cardiology, emergency, rehabilitation, orthopedics and women's and children's health. The group's website provides a support and resource site for physicians, information on healthy recipes, health news and information and a section on miracles and success stories connected with the organization. The group also operates an advocacy program on both the state and federal levels in the healthcare field with the hope of providing its patients with a healthcare system that can better serve them. Community outreach, especially focusing on the underserved, is a priority for CHRISTUS.

CHRISTUS offers employees health, dental, life, long-term care and AD&D insurance; a flexible spending account and other benefits.

FINANCIAL DATA: *Note: Data for latest year may not have been available at press time.*

In U.S. $	2020	2019	2018	2017	2016	2015
Revenue	5,728,344,000	5,561,344,000	5,374,625,000	4,922,429,000	4,212,413,000	3,599,712,000
R&D Expense						
Operating Income						
Operating Margin %						
SGA Expense						
Net Income	128,698,000	126,445,000	142,009,000	141,369,000	220,630,000	13,269,000
Operating Cash Flow						
Capital Expenditure						
EBITDA						
Return on Assets %						
Return on Equity %						
Debt to Equity						

CONTACT INFORMATION:

Phone: 469-282-2000 Fax:
Toll-Free:
Address: 919 Hidden Ridge, Irving, TX 75038 United States

STOCK TICKER/OTHER:

Stock Ticker: Nonprofit Exchange:
Employees: 45,000 Fiscal Year Ends: 06/30
Parent Company:

SALARIES/BONUSES:

Top Exec. Salary: $ Bonus: $
Second Exec. Salary: $ Bonus: $

OTHER THOUGHTS:

Estimated Female Officers or Directors: 5
Hot Spot for Advancement for Women/Minorities: Y

Cigna Corporation

www.cigna.com

NAIC Code: 524114

TYPES OF BUSINESS:

Insurance-Medical & Health, HMOs & PPOs
Indemnity Insurance
Investment Management Services
Group Life, Accident & Disability

BRANDS/DIVISIONS/AFFILIATES:

Evernorth
Cigna

CONTACTS: *Note: Officers with more than one job title may be intentionally listed here more than once.*

David Cordani, CEO
Michael Triplett, Pres., Divisional
Eric Palmer, CFO
Isaiah Harris, Chairman of the Board
Mary Agoglia Hoeltzel, Chief Accounting Officer
Mark Boxer, Chief Information Officer
Lisa Bacus, Chief Marketing Officer
John Murabito, Executive VP, Divisional
Alan Muney, Executive VP
Nicole Jones, Executive VP
Steven Miller, Executive VP
Jason Sadler, President, Divisional
Brian Evanko, President, Divisional
Timothy Wentworth, President, Divisional
Matthew Manders, President, Divisional

GROWTH PLANS/SPECIAL FEATURES:

Cigna Corporation is a global health services organization. The firm offers a differentiated set of pharmacy, medical, behavioral, dental and supplemental products and services, primarily through two brands: Cigna and Evernorth. Cigna operates in three main segments: Evernorth, U.S. Medical and International Markets. Evernorth brings together coordinated and point solution health services including pharmacy solutions, benefits management solutions, care solutions and intelligence solutions, and specialized to deliver custom and flexible solutions that meet the needs of clients and customers. U.S. Medical includes Cigna's U.S. Commercial and U.S. Government businesses that provide comprehensive medical and coordinated solutions. U.S. Commercial products and services include medical, pharmacy, behavioral health, dental, vision, health advocacy programs and other products and services for insured and self-insured customers. U.S. Government solutions include Medicare Advantage, Medicare Supplement, and Medicare Part D plans for seniors, Medicaid plans, and individual health insurance plans both on and off the public exchanges. Cigna's International Markets segment has operations in over 30 countries or jurisdictions providing a full range of comprehensive medical and supplemental health, life and accident benefits to individuals and employers. Products and services include comprehensive health coverage, hospitalization, dental, critical illness, personal accident, term life, medical cost containment and variable universal life. In December 2020, New York Life Insurance Company completed its $6.3 billion acquisition of Cigna's group life, accident, and disability insurance business. In April 2021, Molina Healthcare, Inc. agreed to acquired Cigna's Texas Medicaid and Medicare-Medicaid Plan contracts and certain operating assets for approximately $60 million.

FINANCIAL DATA: *Note: Data for latest year may not have been available at press time.*

In U.S. $	2020	2019	2018	2017	2016	2015
Revenue	160,577,000,000	153,743,000,000	48,569,000,000	41,616,000,000	39,668,000,000	37,876,000,000
R&D Expense						
Operating Income						
Operating Margin %						
SGA Expense	14,072,000,000	14,053,000,000	11,934,000,000			
Net Income	8,458,000,000	5,104,000,000	2,637,000,000	2,237,000,000	1,867,000,000	2,094,000,000
Operating Cash Flow	10,350,000,000	9,485,000,000	3,770,000,000	4,086,000,000	4,026,000,000	2,717,000,000
Capital Expenditure	1,094,000,000	1,050,000,000	528,000,000	471,000,000	461,000,000	510,000,000
EBITDA						
Return on Assets %		.03%	.02%	.04%	.03%	.04%
Return on Equity %		.12%	.10%	.16%	.14%	.18%
Debt to Equity		0.703	0.963	0.379	0.347	0.417

CONTACT INFORMATION:

Phone: 860 226-6000   Fax: 215 761-3596
Toll-Free: 800-997-1654
Address: 900 Cottage Grove Rd., Bloomfield, CT 06002 United States

STOCK TICKER/OTHER:

Stock Ticker: CI
Employees: 73,700
Parent Company:

Exchange: NYS
Fiscal Year Ends: 12/31

SALARIES/BONUSES:

Top Exec. Salary: $ Bonus: $
Second Exec. Salary: $ Bonus: $

OTHER THOUGHTS:

Estimated Female Officers or Directors: 4
Hot Spot for Advancement for Women/Minorities: Y

Cipla Limited

NAIC Code: 325412

www.cipla.com

TYPES OF BUSINESS:

Pharmaceuticals Manufacturing
Generic Medicine
Specialty Medicine
Consumer Health

BRANDS/DIVISIONS/AFFILIATES:

Cipla Technologies LLC
Cipla Health Limited
Nicotex
ActivKids ImmunoBoosters
Kidzania
Cofsils
UnoBiotics

CONTACTS: *Note: Officers with more than one job title may be intentionally listed here more than once.*

Umang Vohra, CEO
Kedar Upadhye, CFO
Raju Mistry, Chief People Officer
Geena Malhotra, CTO
S. Radhakrishnan, Whole-Time Dir.
Y.K. Hamied, Chmn.

GROWTH PLANS/SPECIAL FEATURES:

Cipla Limited, founded in 1935, is a leading Indian pharmaceutical company, selling more than 1,500 products in various therapeutic categories in 50+ dosage forms. The company's products are grouped into three categories: generics and branded generics, specialty and consumer health. The generics and branded generics business in India consists of more over 4,000 partners covering the entire country. The specialty category offers innovative and specialty medicines, with focus areas including respiratory, central nervous system (CNS) and critical care. This division includes Cipla Technologies LLC, based in San Diego, California, which participates and operates as a biotech and innovation hub in the U.S. The consumer health category operates through subsidiary Cipla Health Limited, which focuses on driving innovation and simplifying healthcare by creating solutions that address unmet consumer needs. This division includes: Nictoex, Cipla Health's flagship smoking cessation brand; ActivKids ImmunoBoosters, a nutritional supplement for kids; Kidzania, an edutainment asset active in Mumbai and Delhi, used for generating aided trials; Cofsils cough drops and herbal throat lozenges; and UnoBiotics, a probiotic brand serving the lactobacillus rhamnosus GG (digestion and bowel) market. Therapy focus areas of Cipla include HIV/AIDS, oncology, respiratory and others. Cipla's active pharmaceutical ingredient (API) division encompasses state-of-the-art research facilities at three locations in India, for its API process development, with teams working on synthetic, organic chemistry, process engineering and analytical development. During 2020, Cipla received regulatory approval for the launch of Ciplenza (favipiravir 200mg) in India to treat mild to moderate COVID-19; and received U.S. FDA approval for the generic version of Shire's Firazyr (Icatibant injectable pre-filled syringe 30mg/3mL) for the treatment of acute attacks of hereditary angioedema in adults 18 years of age and older.

FINANCIAL DATA: *Note: Data for latest year may not have been available at press time.*

In U.S. $	2020	2019	2018	2017	2016	2015
Revenue	2,309,538,000	2,217,496,000	2,056,157,000	1,949,308,000	1,875,425,000	
R&D Expense	48,661,040	48,982,220	36,874,620	38,469,560	30,017,160	
Operating Income	289,687,700	279,338,400	258,760,500	225,594,700	270,684,200	
Operating Margin %		.12%	.12%	.12%	.14%	
SGA Expense	241,654,000	216,479,300	184,658,600	165,910,400	126,869,800	
Net Income	212,273,700	209,690,500	193,607,800	138,136,000	206,701,000	
Operating Cash Flow	421,172,200	232,124,100	200,776,900	327,001,600	246,224,700	
Capital Expenditure	137,260,300	72,354,670	112,032,100	155,923,400	147,812,800	
EBITDA	486,179,400	489,907,300	425,711,400	361,372,600	359,385,100	
Return on Assets %		.07%	.06%	.05%	.08%	
Return on Equity %		.10%	.11%	.08%	.13%	
Debt to Equity		0.255	0.257	0.291	0.019	

CONTACT INFORMATION:

Phone: 91 2223082891   Fax: 91 2223070013
Toll-Free:
Address: Cipla House, Peninsula Bus. Park, Ganpatrao Kadam, Mumbai, 400 013 India

STOCK TICKER/OTHER:

Stock Ticker: CPLFY   Exchange: GREY
Employees: 21,645   Fiscal Year Ends: 03/31
Parent Company:

SALARIES/BONUSES:

Top Exec. Salary: $ Bonus: $
Second Exec. Salary: $ Bonus: $

OTHER THOUGHTS:

Estimated Female Officers or Directors:
Hot Spot for Advancement for Women/Minorities:

CIVCO Medical Instruments Co Ltd

www.civco.com

NAIC Code: 339100

TYPES OF BUSINESS:

Diagnostic & Therapeutic Medical Equipment
Ultrasound Products
Minimally Invasive Surgical Products
Medical Monitors
Needle & Biopsy Instruments
Disinfectants
Medical Printers & Print Supplies
Custom Design Services

BRANDS/DIVISIONS/AFFILIATES:

Roper Technologies Inc
CIVCO Medical Solutions

CONTACTS: Note: Officers with more than one job title may be intentionally listed here more than once.

Robin Therme, Pres.
Lisa Jonshon, VP-Finance
Kevin Cleary, VP-Global Commercialization
Mike Marshall, VP-Prod. Dev.
David S. Schultz, VP-Oper.
Lisa Johnson, Corp. Controller
Nat Geissel, Sr. VP
Robin Therme, Sr. VP
Michael McVey, VP
Hap Peterson, VP-North American Sales, Radiation Oncology

GROWTH PLANS/SPECIAL FEATURES:

CIVCO Medical Instruments Co., Ltd., which does business as CIVCO Medical Solutions, designs, manufactures and markets specialty products for the medical industry. The company's specialties include radiology, anesthesia, pain medicine, cardiology, point-of-care ultrasound, central sterile processing, women's health, men's health and infection control. CIVCO's products include ultrasound probe covers, probe cleaning and disinfection, ultrasound needle guides, fusion technology, tracking technology, transperineal prostate solutions and related accessories such as ECG electrodes, acoustic standoff pads, lubricating gels, ultrasound gels, bands and probe clips, probe grips, hydrogel pads, trunk cables and lead wires. CIVCO partners with original equipment manufacturers (OEMs) to offer innovative products that help improve clinical outcome. The company has clinical connections and customers in 85 countries worldwide. CIVCO operates as a wholly-owned subsidiary of Roper Technologies, Inc.

CIVCO offers medical, dental, vision and prescription coverage; life and AD&D insurance; flexible spending account; short-and long-term disability; and an employee assistance program.

FINANCIAL DATA: Note: Data for latest year may not have been available at press time.

In U.S. $	2020	2019	2018	2017	2016	2015
Revenue	4,224,000,000	3,840,000,000	3,780,000,000	3,600,000,000		
R&D Expense						
Operating Income						
Operating Margin %						
SGA Expense						
Net Income						
Operating Cash Flow						
Capital Expenditure						
EBITDA						
Return on Assets %						
Return on Equity %						
Debt to Equity						

CONTACT INFORMATION:

Phone: 319-656-4447   Fax: 319-656-4451
Toll-Free: 800-445-6741
Address: 2301 Jones Blvd., Coralville, IA 52241 United States

STOCK TICKER/OTHER:

Stock Ticker: Subsidiary
Employees:
Parent Company: Roper Technologies Inc

Exchange:
Fiscal Year Ends:

SALARIES/BONUSES:

Top Exec. Salary: $ Bonus: $
Second Exec. Salary: $ Bonus: $

OTHER THOUGHTS:

Estimated Female Officers or Directors: 3
Hot Spot for Advancement for Women/Minorities: Y

Sales, profits and employees may be estimates. Financial information, benefits and other data can change quickly and may vary from those stated here.

Civitas Solutions Inc

NAIC Code: 621610

civitas-solutions.com

TYPES OF BUSINESS:

Home Health Care Services

BRANDS/DIVISIONS/AFFILIATES:

Centerbridge Partners LP
Vistria Group LP (The)
Sevita
Mentors
MENTOR Network (The)

CONTACTS: *Note: Officers with more than one job title may be intentionally listed here more than once.*

William McKinney, CEO
Brett Cohen, COO
Peter Gladitsch, CFO
Samantha Dwinell, Chief People Officer
Mark Lantzy, CIO
Gina Martin, General Counsel
Gerald Morrissey, Other Executive Officer

GROWTH PLANS/SPECIAL FEATURES:

Civitas Solutions, Inc. is a provider of home- and community-based health and human services to must-serve individuals with intellectual, developmental, physical or behavioral disabilities and other special needs. The company's clinicians and caregivers develop customized service plans, delivered in non-institutional settings, designed to address a broad range of often life-long conditions and to enable them to thrive in less restrictive settings. Civitas markets its services nationally as Sevita. This network of local health and human services providers are located in 36 U.S. states, offering services to adults and children, as well as their families. Cevitas' services include youth and families at risk, youth and adults with intellectual and developmental disabilities, youth and adults with brain and spinal cord injuries, and elders in need of support. For at risk individuals, Cevitas offers family preservation services designed to keep families together and foster care when it is not possible for a biological family to remain intact. It also offers a range of specialized school-based and non-residential programs for young people. Residential and non-residential services for individuals with intellectual and developmental disabilities include living in caring homes of their choosing with individuals called Mentors, or a range of community-based residences. Those with brain and spinal cord injury, and those with medically-intensive conditions, Cevitas offers options designed to empower individuals to live as independently as possible. Sevita also provides adult day health programs for elders and other individuals with complex medical and rehabilitative needs. Civitas Solutions is a joint venture between Centerbridge Partners LP and The Vistria Group LP. In September 2021, the firm announced that The MENTOR Network was being rebranded as Sevita.

FINANCIAL DATA: *Note: Data for latest year may not have been available at press time.*

In U.S. $	2020	2019	2018	2017	2016	2015
Revenue	1,683,273,403	1,650,268,043	1,602,201,984	1,474,509,952	1,407,586,944	1,366,946,048
R&D Expense						
Operating Income						
Operating Margin %						
SGA Expense						
Net Income			14,886,000	6,331,000	9,187,000	3,072,000
Operating Cash Flow						
Capital Expenditure						
EBITDA						
Return on Assets %						
Return on Equity %						
Debt to Equity						

CONTACT INFORMATION:

Phone: 617 790-4800   Fax:
Toll-Free:
Address: 313 Congress St.. 6/Fl, Boston, MA 02210 United States

STOCK TICKER/OTHER:

Stock Ticker: Joint Venture
Employees: 22,300
Parent Company: Centerbridge Partners LP
Exchange:
Fiscal Year Ends: 09/30

SALARIES/BONUSES:

Top Exec. Salary: $ Bonus: $
Second Exec. Salary: $ Bonus: $

OTHER THOUGHTS:

Estimated Female Officers or Directors:
Hot Spot for Advancement for Women/Minorities:

ClearPoint Neuro Inc

www.clearpointneuro.com

NAIC Code: 339100

TYPES OF BUSINESS:

Medical Device Manufacturing
MRI-Guided Surgical Equipment

BRANDS/DIVISIONS/AFFILIATES:

MRI Interventions Inc
ClearPoint
ClearTrace
SmartFrame

CONTACTS: Note: Officers with more than one job title may be intentionally listed here more than once.

Harold Hurwitz, CFO
Kimble Jenkins, Chairman of the Board
Peter Piferi, COO
Francis Grillo, President
Oscar Thomas, Secretary
Robert Korn, Vice President, Divisional
Wendelin Maners, Vice President, Divisional

GROWTH PLANS/SPECIAL FEATURES:

ClearPoint Neuro, Inc., formerly MRI Interventions, Inc., is a medical device company that develops and commercializes platforms for performing minimally invasive surgical procedures in the brain and heart. The procedures are performed under direct, intra-procedural magnetic resonance imaging (MRI) guidance. ClearPoint Neuro's ClearPoint system is in commercial use in the U.S. and is used to perform minimally invasive surgical procedures in the brain. The system is used in procedures such as biopsies and the insertion of catheters and electrodes and is intended to be used with both 1.5T (tesla) and 3T MRI scanners. ClearPoint includes disposables such as the company's SmartFrame trajectory device; and software, which guides the physician in surgical planning, device alignment, navigation to the target and procedure monitoring. The ClearTrace system is still in development and will be used to perform minimally invasive surgical procedures in the heart. ClearTrace is similar to traditional catheter-based cardiac interventions performed in a fluoroscopy suite (Cath Lab or EP Lab), but with two distinctions. First, ClearTrace will provide a continuous, high resolution, four-dimensional imaging environment (the fourth being time), which will include detailed visualization of cardiac tissue, along with the cardiac catheters used to deliver the therapy. Second, the system will eliminate all radiation exposure for both the patient and the physician from the X-ray utilized in current procedures. ClearPoint and ClearTrace are designed to work in a hospital's existing MRI suite. In February 2020, MRi Interventions changed its name to ClearPoint Neuro to better the firm's expanded strategic focus as the medical device extension of its biologics and drug delivery partners.

FINANCIAL DATA: Note: Data for latest year may not have been available at press time.

In U.S. $	2020	2019	2018	2017	2016	2015
Revenue	12,829,000	11,216,940	7,353,266	7,379,525	5,749,454	4,594,192
R&D Expense	4,686,000	2,922,279	2,310,139	2,813,733	2,628,179	1,957,332
Operating Income	-6,220,000	-4,593,678	-5,247,768	-6,335,837	-7,488,738	-7,721,525
Operating Margin %		-.41%	-.71%	-.86%	-1.30%	-1.68%
SGA Expense	10,654,000	9,055,452	7,857,826	8,002,821	7,967,250	8,370,749
Net Income	-6,782,000	-5,539,790	-6,163,469	-7,167,353	-8,069,895	-8,449,246
Operating Cash Flow	-7,807,000	-2,849,515	-4,630,592	-5,992,511	-5,820,043	-8,637,734
Capital Expenditure	482,000	160,190	63,490	26,752	101,002	76,883
EBITDA	-4,788,000	-4,334,064	-5,073,647	-6,219,383	-6,854,123	-6,974,957
Return on Assets %		-.56%	-.57%	-.67%	-.92%	-.72%
Return on Equity %		-1.82%	-1.68%	-2.83%		
Debt to Equity		0.512	2.304	0.501		

CONTACT INFORMATION:

Phone: 949-900-6833   Fax: 949-900-6834
Toll-Free:
Address: 5 Musick, Irvine, CA 92618 United States

STOCK TICKER/OTHER:

Stock Ticker: CLPT
Employees: 33
Parent Company:

Exchange: NAS
Fiscal Year Ends: 12/31

SALARIES/BONUSES:

Top Exec. Salary: $ Bonus: $
Second Exec. Salary: $ Bonus: $

OTHER THOUGHTS:

Estimated Female Officers or Directors: 1
Hot Spot for Advancement for Women/Minorities:

Cleveland Clinic Foundation (The)

NAIC Code: 622110

www.clevelandclinic.org

TYPES OF BUSINESS:
General Medical and Surgical Hospitals

BRANDS/DIVISIONS/AFFILIATES:

CONTACTS: *Note: Officers with more than one job title may be intentionally listed here more than once.*

Tomislav Mihaljevic, CEO
Robert Wyllie, Chief Medical Oper. Officer
Cindy Hundorfean, Chief Admin. Officer-Clinical Svcs.
David W. Rowan, Chief Legal Officer
Michael Harrington, Chief Acct. Officer
Kristen D.W. Morris, Chief Gov't. & Community Rel. Officer
Linda McHugh, Exec. Admin.-CEO & Board of Governors
K. Kelly Hancock, Interim Exec. Chief Nursing Officer
Ann Huston, Chief Strategy Officer

GROWTH PLANS/SPECIAL FEATURES:

The Cleveland Clinic Foundation is a nonprofit corporation in Ohio that combines medical care with education and research. It is noted for very advanced surgical techniques and advanced care. Founded in 1921, Cleveland Clinic cares for millions of patients annually, with nearly 10 million outpatient visits at its locations throughout the world. The firm's health system includes 18 hospitals, more than 220 outpatient locations and over 6,025 beds. The Cleveland Clinic runs a 170-acre campus in Cleveland, as well as affiliated hospitals and family health centers in Ohio, Florida and Nevada. Outside the U.S., the firm operates the Cleveland Clinic Abu Dhabi hospital and an outpatient sports medicine clinic in Toronto. In 2020-21, Cleveland Clinic was ranked as second overall hospital in the U.S. by the U.S. News & World Report, with high-rankings in the fields of cardiology, heart surgery, urology, gastroenterology, nephrology, rheumatology, orthopedic surgery, pulmonology, lung surgery, cancer, diabetes, endocrinology, otolaryngology, geriatrics, gynecology, neurology, ophthalmology and psychiatry. In September 2021, the nonprofit announced the opening of its London hospital and the ground breaking at the future site of Cleveland Clinic Mentor Hospital, set to open in early 2023 in Ohio.

The Cleveland Clinic offers its employees comprehensive health benefits, savings and retirement options and career development resources.

FINANCIAL DATA: *Note: Data for latest year may not have been available at press time.*

In U.S. $	2020	2019	2018	2017	2016	2015
Revenue	10,627,906,000	10,559,521,000	8,900,000,000	8,400,000,000	8,037,207,000	7,156,972,000
R&D Expense						
Operating Income						
Operating Margin %						
SGA Expense						
Net Income	1,325,244,000	2,025,222,000	266,000,000	328,000,000	139,352,000	480,224,000
Operating Cash Flow						
Capital Expenditure						
EBITDA						
Return on Assets %						
Return on Equity %						
Debt to Equity						

CONTACT INFORMATION:
Phone: 216-444-2200 Fax:
Toll-Free: 800-223-2273
Address: 9500 Euclid Ave., Cleveland, OH 44195 United States

STOCK TICKER/OTHER:
Stock Ticker: Nonprofit Exchange:
Employees: 60,000 Fiscal Year Ends: 12/31
Parent Company:

SALARIES/BONUSES:
Top Exec. Salary: $ Bonus: $
Second Exec. Salary: $ Bonus: $

OTHER THOUGHTS:
Estimated Female Officers or Directors: 22
Hot Spot for Advancement for Women/Minorities: Y

Coast Dental Services LLC

www.coastdental.com

NAIC Code: 621210

TYPES OF BUSINESS:

Dental Practice Management

BRANDS/DIVISIONS/AFFILIATES:

Coast Dental & Orthodontics
SmilePlus

CONTACTS: *Note: Officers with more than one job title may be intentionally listed here more than once.*

Derek Diasti, CEO
Adam Diasti, Pres.

GROWTH PLANS/SPECIAL FEATURES:

Coast Dental Services, LLC is a dental provider, operating over 100 affiliated practices operating under the Coast Dental & Orthodontics brand name. These locations are primarily in Florida, but also in Georgia, Nevada and Texas. Patient services include: first visit comprehensive oral examination and X-rays to look for signs of tooth decay, bone loss, oral cancer and periodontal (gum) disease; dental cleanings, dental procedures; orthodontics; specialty services; and emergency services. The practices provide preventive dentistry, cosmetic procedures, crowns, bridges, implants, restorations, dentures, partials, laser, tooth extraction, fillings, inlays/onlays, tooth bonding, porcelain veneers, teeth whitening and more. Coast Dental accepts more than 200 dental insurance plans and files insurance claims for its customers. The firm offers financing to qualified applicants, as well as SmilePlus for uninsured patients.

Employees working at least 25 hours per week are eligible for group health insurance, disability and life insurance, a 401(k) plan and other employee assistance options.

FINANCIAL DATA: *Note: Data for latest year may not have been available at press time.*

In U.S. $	2020	2019	2018	2017	2016	2015
Revenue						
R&D Expense						
Operating Income						
Operating Margin %						
SGA Expense						
Net Income						
Operating Cash Flow						
Capital Expenditure						
EBITDA						
Return on Assets %						
Return on Equity %						
Debt to Equity						

CONTACT INFORMATION:

Phone: 813-288-1999   Fax: 813-289-4500
Toll-Free:
Address: 5706 Benjamin Center Dr., Ste. 103, Tampa, FL 33634 United States

STOCK TICKER/OTHER:

Stock Ticker: Private
Employees: 677
Parent Company:

Exchange:
Fiscal Year Ends: 12/31

SALARIES/BONUSES:

Top Exec. Salary: $ Bonus: $
Second Exec. Salary: $ Bonus: $

OTHER THOUGHTS:

Estimated Female Officers or Directors: 2
Hot Spot for Advancement for Women/Minorities: Y

Sales, profits and employees may be estimates. Financial information, benefits and other data can change quickly and may vary from those stated here.

Cochlear Limited

NAIC Code: 334510

www.cochlear.com

TYPES OF BUSINESS:

Audiological Equipment, Electromedical, Manufacturing
Auditory Devices & Hearing Aids
Cochlear Implants

BRANDS/DIVISIONS/AFFILIATES:

Cochlear Nucleus
Cochlear Osia
Cochlear Baha

CONTACTS: *Note: Officers with more than one job title may be intentionally listed here more than once.*

Dig Howitt, CEO
Stuart Sayers, CFO
Dean Phizacklea, Sr. VP-Global Mktg.
Jennifer Hornery, Sr. VP-People & Culture
Jim Patrick, Sr. VP
David Hackshall, CIO
Jan Janssen, Sr. VP-Design & Dev.
Dig Howitt, Sr. VP-Mfg.
Neville Mitchell, Corp. Sec.
Bronwyn Evans, Sr. VP-Quality & Regulatory
Mark Salmon, Pres., Asia Pacific Region
Chris Smith, Pres., Americas Region
Alison Deans, Chmn.
Richard Brook, Pres., European Region
Dig Howitt, Sr. VP-Logistics

GROWTH PLANS/SPECIAL FEATURES:

Cochlear Limited is an Australian developer of multi-channel hearing aid implant devices. The company's products use electrical stimulation to allow deaf or hard-of-hearing users to clearly hear sound. Its current (as of 2021) products include the Cochlear Nucleus system and sound processor, the Cochlear Osia System and sound processor, and the Cochlear Baha system, sound processors and implants. The processors play a critical role in helping the user to hear with their cochlear implant, and designed to help hear more clearly. Cochlear's implants are designed to last a lifetime with performance and preservation of structures in mind. The firm's broad range of implants and electrodes allow surgeons to choose which is best for the type of hearing loss, cochlea anatomy, among other reasons. The implants are designed for future advances in sound processor technology without the need for additional surgeries. Accessories by Cochlear include wireless accessories, water-safe accessories and options for keeping the processor secure during certain types of activities. The company's manufacturing operations are primarily located in Australia and Sweden, while research operations are conducted in collaboration with more than 100 research partners in 20 countries.

FINANCIAL DATA: *Note: Data for latest year may not have been available at press time.*

In U.S. $	2020	2019	2018	2017	2016	2015
Revenue	1,024,244,000	1,106,534,000	1,057,672,000	972,464,200	876,844,900	717,909,400
R&D Expense	143,561,700	143,018,800	130,066,400	117,834,600	111,013,300	99,263,890
Operating Income	153,915,800	238,106,100	237,485,700	217,103,200	166,718,500	133,190,500
Operating Margin %		.24%	.25%	.25%	.22%	.22%
SGA Expense	437,277,600	423,239,400	383,451,700	335,366,700	314,406,300	248,456,400
Net Income	-184,823,100	214,605,800	190,640,000	173,434,300	146,525,200	113,112,000
Operating Cash Flow						
Capital Expenditure	101,214,500	88,882,620	38,546,820	47,945,420	29,126,510	22,047,700
EBITDA	-179,743,000	317,449,000	297,206,100	269,561,000	230,011,300	183,783,800
Return on Assets %		.22%	.21%	.21%	.21%	.18%
Return on Equity %		.41%	.43%	.45%	.47%	.43%
Debt to Equity		0.246	0.236	0.247	0.422	0.125

CONTACT INFORMATION:

Phone: 61 294286555
Fax: 61 294286539
Toll-Free:
Address: 1 University Ave., Macquarie University, Lane Cove, NSW 2109 Australia

STOCK TICKER/OTHER:

Stock Ticker: CHEOF
Employees: 4,000
Parent Company:

Exchange: PINX
Fiscal Year Ends: 06/30

SALARIES/BONUSES:

Top Exec. Salary: $
Bonus: $
Second Exec. Salary: $
Bonus: $

OTHER THOUGHTS:

Estimated Female Officers or Directors: 1
Hot Spot for Advancement for Women/Minorities:

Coherent Inc
www.coherent.com

NAIC Code: 334510

TYPES OF BUSINESS:
Equipment-Lasers & Laser Systems
Precision Optics
Laser Accessories

BRANDS/DIVISIONS/AFFILIATES:

CONTACTS: *Note: Officers with more than one job title may be intentionally listed here more than once.*

John Ambroseo, CEO
Kevin Palatnik, CFO
Garry Rogerson, Chairman of the Board
Paul Sechrist, Executive VP, Divisional
Bret DiMarco, Executive VP
Thomas Merk, Executive VP
Mark Sobey, Executive VP

GROWTH PLANS/SPECIAL FEATURES:

Coherent, Inc. is a world-leading photonic manufacturer and innovator. The firm is headquartered in California, USA, with offices throughout the globe. Coherent's products are grouped into five categories: lasers, sub-systems, machines and systems, components and laser measurement. Laser products serve the materials processing, scientific research, life sciences, instrumentation and defense markets, and include CO and CO_2, CW solid state, diode, excimer, fiber and ion lasers, as well as laser diode modules, marking lasers, nanosecond lasers, scientific ultrafast lasers and ultrashort pulse lasers. Sub-systems provide materials processing solutions, beam delivery and electronics control, and used for cutting, drilling, marking, engraving, surface structuring, ablating, cleaning, scribing and welding. The machines and systems category provides turnkey materials processing systems for cutting, welding, microstructuring and marking, and include additive manufacturing systems, cutting systems, excimer ultraviolet (UV) systems, marking systems, multi-purpose systems, specialty systems and welding systems. The components category offers advanced optical fiber assemblies, beam delivery components, laser diodes, specialty optical fibers, THz-Raman instrumentation, Tinsley custom optics, volume holographic grafting filters and wavelength stabilized diode components. Last, the laser measurement category manufactures laser output measurement instruments for the lab and for industrial process control. Laser measurement products include laser energy sensors, laser power sensors, laser power and energy meters, beam diagnostics and related accessories and support. Applications that utilize Coherent's products and solutions include life sciences, medical, scientific, materials processing, industrial, microelectronics, solar cell manufacturing, military/defense laser technology, graphics arts and display, and original equipment manufacturer (OEM) components. In March 2021, the firm agreed to be acquired by I-VI Incorporated, an engineered materials and optoelectronic components company. The transaction is expected to close bY the end of 2021.

Coherent offers its employees comprehensive health benefits, retirement options, life and disability insurance and a variety of employee assistance plans and programs.

FINANCIAL DATA: *Note: Data for latest year may not have been available at press time.*

In U.S. $	2020	2019	2018	2017	2016	2015
Revenue	1,228,999,000	1,430,640,000	1,902,573,000	1,723,311,000	857,385,000	802,460,000
R&D Expense	115,578,000	117,353,000	132,586,000	119,166,000	81,801,000	81,455,000
Operating Income	20,845,000	83,095,000	393,783,000	322,995,000	127,614,000	101,448,000
Operating Margin %		.06%	.21%	.19%	.15%	.13%
SGA Expense	270,464,000	272,257,000	293,632,000	292,084,000	169,138,000	149,829,000
Net Income	-414,139,000	53,825,000	247,358,000	207,122,000	87,502,000	76,409,000
Operating Cash Flow	206,907,000	181,401,000	236,111,000	384,116,000	105,299,000	124,458,000
Capital Expenditure	64,919,000	83,283,000	90,757,000	63,774,000	49,327,000	22,163,000
EBITDA	-332,820,000	195,555,000	500,783,000	440,662,000	158,597,000	132,675,000
Return on Assets %		.02%	.11%	.12%	.08%	.08%
Return on Equity %		.04%	.20%	.20%	.10%	.09%
Debt to Equity		0.305	0.32	0.506		

CONTACT INFORMATION:
Phone: 408 764-4000   Fax: 408 764-4800
Toll-Free: 800-527-3786
Address: 5100 Patrick Henry Dr., Santa Clara, CA 95054 United States

STOCK TICKER/OTHER:
Stock Ticker: COHR
Employees. 4,875
Parent Company:

Exchange: NAS
Fiscal Year Ends: 09/30

SALARIES/BONUSES:
Top Exec. Salary: $ Bonus: $
Second Exec. Salary: $ Bonus: $

OTHER THOUGHTS:
Estimated Female Officers or Directors: 2
Hot Spot for Advancement for Women/Minorities:

Sales, profits and employees may be estimates. Financial information, benefits and other data can change quickly and may vary from those stated here.

Coloplast AS

NAIC Code: 339100

www.coloplast.com

TYPES OF BUSINESS:

Ostomy Supplies

BRANDS/DIVISIONS/AFFILIATES:

SenSura
Brava
Conveen Active
SpeediCath
Peristeen
Biatain
Coloplast
Vortek

CONTACTS: *Note: Officers with more than one job title may be intentionally listed here more than once.*

Kristian Villumsen, CEO
Allan Rasmussen, Exec. VP-Global Oper.
Anders Lonning-Skovgaard, CFO
Camilla G. Mohl, Sr. VP-People & Culture
Oliver Johansen, Sr. VP-Global R&D
Peter Volkers, Sr. VP-Corp. Legal
Anders Monrad Rendtorff, Sr. VP-People & Communications
Lars Einar Hansen, Sr. VP-Corp. Finance
Claus Bjerre, Sr. VP-Sales, North America, Japan & Australia
Jesper Kalenberg, VP-Corp. Procurement
Kristian Villumsen, Sr. VP-Emerging Markets
Nicolas Nemery, Sr. VP-Global Mktg.
Lars Rasmussen, Chmn.
Allan Rasmussen, Sr. VP-Global Oper.

GROWTH PLANS/SPECIAL FEATURES:

Coloplast A/S is a Denmark-based medical device manufacturer that designs products for ostomy care, continence, wound care, skin care and urology care. The company's ostomy segment offers appliances for people with stomas under the brand name SenSura and Brava. Stomas are a result of surgery to correct an intestinal dysfunction resulting from disease, accident or birth defects, where a part of the intestine is surgically redirected through the abdominal wall. Due to the sensitivity of stomas, ostomy bags must be manufactured with extreme care and quality. Coloplast's continence segment sells intermittent catheters, urine bags, urisheaths and anal irrigation systems, which are marketed under the Conveen Active, SpeediCath and Peristeen brands. The wound care segment offers Biatain, a bandage dressing line that provides mobility and function to people with injuries and also have been shown to kill mature biofilms and prevent them from forming. This division's Comfeel Plus dressing product encompasses hydrocolloid, providing moist wound healing and protection for wounds and skin at risk. Coloplast's skin care division offers products such as cleansers, moisturizers, skin protectants, antifungals, hand cleansers and odor control solutions through brands such as Coloplast, Isagel, InterDry and Hex-On. Last, the urology care segment develops, produces and markets products for surgical treatment of urological and gynecological disorders such as urinary stone disease, benign prostate hyperplasia, voiding dysfunctions, erectile dysfunction and urinary incontinence (male and female). Products within this division include prostatic catheters, bladder evacuators, post-operative bags, stone extractors, ureteral stents, access sheaths, guidewires, balloon dilators, irrigation lines, slings, meshes and penile/malleable implants. Brands within this segment include Dormia, N.Stone, Vortek, Orchestra, In-Ka, Restorelle, Virtue, Titan Touch, Genesis and more. In November 2020, Coloplast acquired Nine Continents Medical, Inc., a developer of solutions for over-active bladders, for $145 million.

FINANCIAL DATA: *Note: Data for latest year may not have been available at press time.*

In U.S. $	2020	2019	2018	2017	2016	2015
Revenue	3,047,169,000	2,947,754,000	2,702,916,000	2,551,576,000	2,412,397,000	2,285,541,000
R&D Expense	116,339,300	113,710,100	105,165,400	94,320,250	83,639,380	72,629,880
Operating Income	961,935,100	912,967,400	836,558,100	825,548,700	796,299,500	745,195,700
Operating Margin %		.31%	.31%	.32%	.33%	.33%
SGA Expense	998,907,300	979,846,000	883,061,000	820,619,000	770,994,000	749,632,300
Net Income	689,655,200	636,415,200	631,814,200	623,926,800	516,460,900	147,724,600
Operating Cash Flow	782,003,600	715,946,600	716,603,800	534,207,600	497,564,000	548,339,100
Capital Expenditure	152,982,800	104,508,200	109,930,700	112,559,900	106,644,300	101,386,000
EBITDA	1,042,945,000	934,164,900	927,756,400	915,760,900	758,998,600	285,096,900
Return on Assets %		.32%	.32%	.33%	.29%	.08%
Return on Equity %		.58%	.62%	.69%	.64%	.16%
Debt to Equity		0.019	0.014	0.016		

CONTACT INFORMATION:

Phone: 45 49111111 Fax:
Toll-Free:
Address: Holtedam 1-3, Humlebaek, 3050 Denmark

STOCK TICKER/OTHER:

Stock Ticker: CLPBF Exchange: PINX
Employees: 12,500 Fiscal Year Ends: 09/30
Parent Company:

SALARIES/BONUSES:

Top Exec. Salary: $ Bonus: $
Second Exec. Salary: $ Bonus: $

OTHER THOUGHTS:

Estimated Female Officers or Directors:
Hot Spot for Advancement for Women/Minorities:

CommonSpirit Health

commonspirit.org

NAIC Code: 622110

TYPES OF BUSINESS:

BRANDS/DIVISIONS/AFFILIATES:

Catholic Health Initiatives
Dignity Health
Precision Medicine Alliance LLC

CONTACTS: *Note: Officers with more than one job title may be intentionally listed here more than once.*

Lloyd H. Dean, CEO
Marvin O'Quinn, Pres.
Daniel Morissette, CFO
Darryl Robinson, Chief People Officer
Suja Chandrasekaran, CIO

GROWTH PLANS/SPECIAL FEATURES:

CommonSpirit Health was formed by the 2019 merger between Catholic Health Initiatives and Dignity Health, and is a leading nonprofit Catholic health system in the U.S. Thousands of physicians, advanced practice clinicians, nurses and staff operate through CommonSpirit's network of hospitals and other care centers covering 21 states. The health system also has a survivor/advocate-led program for training caregivers on how to identify and respond to actively-trafficked victims; provides home-based health care in regards to hospice, medication therapies and other care in the home environment; utilizes virtual- and artificial intelligence (AI)-scribing technologies so that physicians can spend more time with patients and less time on administrative work; provides physicians with a data-rich technology platform to help them deliver cancer treatment based on individual genetic profiles through subsidiary Precision Medicine Alliance, LLC; and uses digital technology so that patients can self-manage their conditions, such as asthma-management and heart monitoring. In 2020, CommonSpirit Health announced the opening of its Reference Lab, increasing the country's COVID-19 test capacity by up to 70,000 tests per week.

FINANCIAL DATA: *Note: Data for latest year may not have been available at press time.*

In U.S. $	2020	2019	2018	2017	2016	2015
Revenue	29,580,000,000	29,000,000,000				
R&D Expense						
Operating Income						
Operating Margin %						
SGA Expense						
Net Income	-550,000,000	-222,000,000				
Operating Cash Flow						
Capital Expenditure						
EBITDA						
Return on Assets %						
Return on Equity %						
Debt to Equity						

CONTACT INFORMATION:

Phone: 312-741-7000   Fax:
Toll-Free:
Address: 444 W. Lake St., Ste. 2500, Chicago, IL 60606-0097 United States

STOCK TICKER/OTHER:

Stock Ticker: Nonprofit
Employees:
Parent Company:

Exchange:
Fiscal Year Ends: 06/30

SALARIES/BONUSES:

Top Exec. Salary: $ Bonus: $
Second Exec. Salary: $ Bonus: $

OTHER THOUGHTS:

Estimated Female Officers or Directors:
Hot Spot for Advancement for Women/Minorities:

Community Health Systems Inc

NAIC Code: 622110

www.chs.net

TYPES OF BUSINESS:

General Medical and Surgical Hospitals
Surgical & Emergency Services
Acute Care Services
Internal Medicine
Obstetrics
Emergency Room Services
Diagnostic Services
Ambulatory Surgery Centers

BRANDS/DIVISIONS/AFFILIATES:

GROWTH PLANS/SPECIAL FEATURES:

Community Health Systems, Inc. operates general acute care hospitals and outpatient facilities throughout the U.S. As of June 2021, the company owned, leased or operated 84 hospitals in 16 states. Community Health Systems provides healthcare for local residents, offering a wide range of diagnostic, medical and surgical services in inpatient and outpatient settings. In 2020, the firm divested itself of 13 hospitals. Through June 2021, Community Health Systems had divested itself of 5 hospitals.

The company offers employees medical, dental and vision insurance; flexible spending accounts; life and disability insurance; and a 401(k) savings plan.

CONTACTS: *Note: Officers with more than one job title may be intentionally listed here more than once.*

Benjamin Fordham, Assistant Secretary
Wayne Smith, CEO
Kevin Hammons, Chief Accounting Officer
Lynn Simon, Chief Medical Officer
Tim Hingtgen, COO
Thomas Aaron, Executive VP
Beryl Ramsey, President, Divisional
P. Smith, President, Divisional

FINANCIAL DATA: *Note: Data for latest year may not have been available at press time.*

In U.S. $	2020	2019	2018	2017	2016	2015
Revenue	11,789,000,000	13,210,000,000	14,155,000,000	15,353,000,000	18,438,000,000	19,437,000,000
R&D Expense						
Operating Income	1,174,000,000	881,000,000	887,000,000	214,000,000	1,075,000,000	1,409,000,000
Operating Margin %		.07%	.06%	.01%	.06%	.07%
SGA Expense	327,000,000	321,000,000	337,000,000	394,000,000	450,000,000	457,000,000
Net Income	511,000,000	-675,000,000	-788,000,000	-2,459,000,000	-1,721,000,000	158,000,000
Operating Cash Flow	2,178,000,000	385,000,000	274,000,000	773,000,000	1,137,000,000	921,000,000
Capital Expenditure	441,000,000	451,000,000	553,000,000	570,000,000	867,000,000	1,010,000,000
EBITDA	2,014,000,000	1,222,000,000	968,000,000	-1,030,000,000	347,000,000	2,558,000,000
Return on Assets %		-.04%	-.05%	-.12%	-.07%	.01%
Return on Equity %				-5.80%	-.61%	.04%
Debt to Equity					9.157	4.186

CONTACT INFORMATION:

Phone: 615 465-7000   Fax: 615 645-7001
Toll-Free:
Address: 4000 Meridian Blvd., Franklin, TN 37067 United States

STOCK TICKER/OTHER:

Stock Ticker: CYH
Employees: 80,000
Parent Company:

Exchange: NYS
Fiscal Year Ends: 12/31

SALARIES/BONUSES:

Top Exec. Salary: $ Bonus: $
Second Exec. Salary: $ Bonus: $

OTHER THOUGHTS:

Estimated Female Officers or Directors: 18
Hot Spot for Advancement for Women/Minorities: Y

Concentra Inc

www.concentra.com

NAIC Code: 621498

TYPES OF BUSINESS:

Health Clinics
Workplace Injury Treatment & Management
Group Health & Automobile Claims Management
Claims Cost Control
Case Management
Medical Advisory Services
Workplace-Based Clinics

BRANDS/DIVISIONS/AFFILIATES:

CONTACTS: *Note: Officers with more than one job title may be intentionally listed here more than once.*

Keith Newton, CEO
Su Zan Nelson, CFO
Jon Conser, Sr. VP-Sales
Dani Kendall, VP-Human Resources
W. Tom Fogarty, Chief Medical Officer
Jim Talalai, CIO
William R. Lewis, Sr. VP-Medical Oper.
Daryl Risinger, Sr. VP-Service & Dev. Management
Gregory M. Gilbert, Sr. VP-Reimbursement
Kate Blackmon, VP-Primary Care Oper. & Integration
Keith Newton, Chmn.

GROWTH PLANS/SPECIAL FEATURES:

Concentra, Inc. is a national healthcare company that operates over 520 medical centers in 42 states and Washington, D.C. The firm also serves patients at more than 130 onsite workplace clinics that it establishes at employer sites as well as programs in which it travels to its customers. Concentra divides its business into four segments: occupational health, physical therapy services, physical exams, and tests & screenings. The firm's occupational health segment offers a vast array of services such as mobile medical services, drug testing and screening, specialist care, clinical and forensic services, medical advisory services, health risk assessments, biometric screenings, vaccinations, health coaching and medical compliance administration. The physical therapy services segment offers specialized treatments with a focus on early intervention for trauma, repetitive stress, chronic and orthopedic injuries. The physical exams segment provides Department of Transportation (DOT) physicals, pre-placement physicals, respirator fit tests, fit for duty exams and HazMat and Hazwoper tests. The tests & screenings segment provides drug testing, preventive screenings, DOT drug testing, surveillance screenings and pulmonary function testing. Onsite centers are tailored specifically for employers and can provide a variety of services, including occupational health, injury care, urgent care, preventive care, physical therapy and wellness.

FINANCIAL DATA: *Note: Data for latest year may not have been available at press time.*

In U.S. $	2020	2019	2018	2017	2016	2015
Revenue	1,501,434,000	1,628,817,000	1,557,673,000	1,034,035,000	1,000,624,000	1,000,000,000
R&D Expense						
Operating Income						
Operating Margin %						
SGA Expense						
Net Income						
Operating Cash Flow						
Capital Expenditure						
EBITDA						
Return on Assets %						
Return on Equity %						
Debt to Equity						

CONTACT INFORMATION:

Phone: 972-364-8211   Fax:
Toll-Free: 800-232-3550
Address: 5080 Spectrum Dr., Ste. 1200 W., Addison, TX 75001 United States

STOCK TICKER/OTHER:

Stock Ticker: Subsidiary
Employees: 11,700
Parent Company: Select Medical Holdings Corporation

Exchange:
Fiscal Year Ends: 12/31

SALARIES/BONUSES:

Top Exec. Salary: $ Bonus: $
Second Exec. Salary: $ Bonus: $

OTHER THOUGHTS:

Estimated Female Officers or Directors: 3
Hot Spot for Advancement for Women/Minorities: Y

CONMED Corporation

www.conmed.com

NAIC Code: 339100

TYPES OF BUSINESS:

Equipment-Surgical & Medical Procedure
Patient Care Products
Sports Medicine Equipment
Arthroscopic surgery devices

BRANDS/DIVISIONS/AFFILIATES:

Hall
CONMED Linvatec
Concept
Shutt
AirSeal
VCARE

CONTACTS: *Note: Officers with more than one job title may be intentionally listed here more than once.*

Sarah Oliker, Assistant General Counsel
Todd Garner, CFO
Terence Berge, Controller
Curt Hartman, Director
Mark Tryniski, Director
Heather Cohen, Executive VP, Divisional
Peter Shagory, Executive VP, Divisional
Wilfredo Ruiz-Caban, Executive VP, Divisional
Daniel Jonas, Executive VP, Divisional
Nathan Folkert, General Manager, Divisional
Stanley Peters, General Manager, Divisional
John Kennedy, General Manager, Divisional
Patrick Beyer, President, Divisional
Johonna Pelletier, Vice President, Divisional

GROWTH PLANS/SPECIAL FEATURES:

CONMED Corporation is a medical technology company focused on surgical devices and equipment for minimally-invasive procedures. The company's products are used by surgeons and physicians in a variety of specialties, including orthopedics, general surgery, gynecology, neurosurgery and gastroenterology. Orthopedic surgery products derived 43% of CONMED's 2020 net sales, and general surgery products derived 57%. Orthopedic surgery products include sports medicine, powered surgical instruments, sports biologics and tissue. These products are marketed under a number of brands, including Hall, CONMED Linvatec, Concept and Shutt. The general surgery division offers a large range of products in the areas of advanced surgical, endoscopic technologies and critical care. Advanced surgical products include the AirSeal clinical insufflation system, which encompasses valve-less access ports. Electrosurgical offerings consist of monopolar and bipolar generators, beam coagulation generators, handpieces, smoke management systems and other accessories. Endomechanical products include tissue retrieval bags, trocars, suction irrigation devices, graspers, scissors and dissectors. CONMED's uterine manipulator, VCARE, is used for laparoscopic hysterectomies and other gynecologic laparoscopic procedures. The firm's endoscopic technologies include a comprehensive line of minimally-invasive diagnostic and therapeutic products used in conjunction with procedures which utilize flexible endoscopy. These include mucosal management devices, forceps, scope management accessories, bronchoscopy devices, dilation, stricture management devices, hemostasis, biliary devices and polypectomy. Critical care products include ECG electrodes and accessories, cardiac defibrillation and pacing pads and a line of suction instruments and tubing. CONMED's products are sold in more than 100 foreign countries, and sales are coordinated through local country dealers.

FINANCIAL DATA: *Note: Data for latest year may not have been available at press time.*

In U.S. $	2020	2019	2018	2017	2016	2015
Revenue		955,097,000	859,633,984	796,392,000	763,520,000	719,168,000
R&D Expense						
Operating Income						
Operating Margin %						
SGA Expense						
Net Income		42,896,700	40,854,000	55,487,000	14,664,000	30,498,000
Operating Cash Flow						
Capital Expenditure						
EBITDA						
Return on Assets %						
Return on Equity %						
Debt to Equity						

CONTACT INFORMATION:

Phone: 315 797-8375   Fax: 315 797-0321
Toll-Free:
Address: 525 French Rd., Utica, NY 13502 United States

STOCK TICKER/OTHER:

Stock Ticker: CNMD   Exchange: NAS
Employees: 3,300   Fiscal Year Ends: 12/31
Parent Company:

SALARIES/BONUSES:

Top Exec. Salary: $ Bonus: $
Second Exec. Salary: $ Bonus: $

OTHER THOUGHTS:

Estimated Female Officers or Directors: 2
Hot Spot for Advancement for Women/Minorities:

ConvaTec Inc

www.convatec.com

NAIC Code: 339100

TYPES OF BUSINESS:

Wound Care Products
Skin Care Products
Ostomy Products

BRANDS/DIVISIONS/AFFILIATES:

ConvaTec Group PLC
AQUACEL
Hydrofiber
Flexi-Seal
UnoMeter
AbViser
GentleCath

CONTACTS: Note: Officers with more than one job title may be intentionally listed here more than once.

Karim Bitar, CEO
Frank Schulkes, CFO
Natalia Kozmina, Exec. VP-Human Resources
Divakar Ramakrishnan, CTO
Robbie Heginbotham, Sr. VP-Oper.
Jorgen B. Hansen, Sr. VP-Bus. Dev.
Robert McKee, Sr. VP-Comm.
John Lindskog, Pres., Global Infusion Devices & Asia Pacific
Todd Brown, CEO-180 Medical
Mark Valentine, Pres., Americas
Paul Moraviec, Pres., EMEA

GROWTH PLANS/SPECIAL FEATURES:

ConvaTec, Inc. is a U.S.-based global medical products and technologies company. The firm focuses on therapies for the management of chronic conditions, with leading positions in advanced wound care, ostomy care, continence and critical care, and infusion devices. ConvaTec's products provide a range of clinical and economic benefits including infection prevention, protection of at-risk skin, improved patient outcomes and reduced total cost of care. The U.S. FDA cleared AQUACEL Ag Advantage is an enhanced Hydrofiber dressing with silver and strengthening fiber features, which absorbs and retains excess exudate to maintain a moist wound environment to support the healing process. AQUACEL and Hydrofiber are trademarks of ConvaTec, Inc. The company's ostomy care franchise specializes in devices, accessories and services for individuals with a stoma (a surgically-created opening where bodily waste is discharged) commonly resulting from colorectal cancer, inflammatory bowel disease, bladder cancer, obesity and other causes. Its continence and critical care franchise distributes disposable, intermittent (single-use) urological catheters directly to patients in the U.S. This division also distributes the Flexi-Seal line of fecal management systems, the UnoMeter urine meter, the AbViser intra-abdominal pressure measurement device and the GentleCath intermittent catheters. The infusion devices franchise specializes in providing disposable infusion sets to manufacturers of insulin pumps for diabetes and similar pumps used in continuous infusion treatments for other conditions. ConvaTec operates as a subsidiary of U.K.-based ConvaTec Group PLC.

FINANCIAL DATA: Note: Data for latest year may not have been available at press time.

In U.S. $	2020	2019	2018	2017	2016	2015
Revenue						
R&D Expense						
Operating Income						
Operating Margin %						
SGA Expense						
Net Income						
Operating Cash Flow						
Capital Expenditure						
EBITDA						
Return on Assets %						
Return on Equity %						
Debt to Equity						

CONTACT INFORMATION:

Phone: 908-904-2500   Fax: 908-904-2780
Toll-Free: 800-422-8811
Address: CenterPoint II, 1160 Route 22 East, Ste. 201, Bridgewater, NJ 08807 United States

STOCK TICKER/OTHER:

Stock Ticker: Subsidiary
Employees: 9,550
Parent Company: ConvaTec Group PLC

Exchange:
Fiscal Year Ends: 12/31

SALARIES/BONUSES:

Top Exec. Salary: $ Bonus: $
Second Exec. Salary: $ Bonus: $

OTHER THOUGHTS:

Estimated Female Officers or Directors: 1
Hot Spot for Advancement for Women/Minorities:

Conviva Care Centers

www.convivacarecenters.com

NAIC Code: 524114

TYPES OF BUSINESS:

Provider Service Network
Health Centers

BRANDS/DIVISIONS/AFFILIATES:

Humana Inc

GROWTH PLANS/SPECIAL FEATURES:

Conviva Care Centers is a physician-led delivery organization, consisting of more than 90 health center locations throughout Florida and Texas. The centers are comprised of a multi-disciplinary team of over 300 primary care physicians and 800+ affiliated specialists that provide a wide range of vital healthcare services. These centers include senior care activity centers and 24/7 on-call physicians. Services offered by Conviva Care Centers include wound care, flu and pneumonia vaccines, electrocardiogram (EKG) tests, physical examinations, minor procedures, sutures, suture removal, diabetic education, ear lavage, lab drawling stations, nebulizer treatments and transportation. Conviva Care Centers operates as a subsidiary of Humana, Inc.

CONTACTS: *Note: Officers with more than one job title may be intentionally listed here more than once.*

Kevin Meriwether, Pres.
Maria A. Xirau, Sr. VP-Medical Oper.-South Florida
Richard Bell, Medical Dir.-Central Florida
Barry Stone, Associate Medical Dir.-South & Coastal Florida
Gerald Leichman, Associate Medical Dir.-South Florida
Kevin McAdams, Sr. VP-Oper.-Central & Coastal Florida

FINANCIAL DATA: *Note: Data for latest year may not have been available at press time.*

In U.S. $	2020	2019	2018	2017	2016	2015
Revenue	696,890,250	810,337,500	771,750,000	735,000,000	700,000,000	670,000,000
R&D Expense						
Operating Income						
Operating Margin %						
SGA Expense						
Net Income						
Operating Cash Flow						
Capital Expenditure						
EBITDA						
Return on Assets %						
Return on Equity %						
Debt to Equity						

CONTACT INFORMATION:

Phone: 561-241-0025   Fax: 561-241-3883
Toll-Free:
Address: 2900 North Military Trail, Ste. 201, Boca Raton, FL 33431 United States

STOCK TICKER/OTHER:

Stock Ticker: Subsidiary   Exchange:
Employees: 1,140   Fiscal Year Ends: 12/31
Parent Company: Humana Inc

SALARIES/BONUSES:

Top Exec. Salary: $ Bonus: $
Second Exec. Salary: $ Bonus: $

OTHER THOUGHTS:

Estimated Female Officers or Directors: 3
Hot Spot for Advancement for Women/Minorities: Y

Sales, profits and employees may be estimates. Financial information, benefits and other data can change quickly and may vary from those stated here.

Cooper Companies Inc (The)

www.coopercos.com

NAIC Code: 339100

TYPES OF BUSINESS:

Medical Devices
Contact Lenses
Gynecological Instruments
Diagnostic Products

BRANDS/DIVISIONS/AFFILIATES:

CooperVision
CooperSurgical
Proclear
Phosphorylcholine (PC) Technology
obp Medical Corporation
MiSight

CONTACTS: *Note: Officers with more than one job title may be intentionally listed here more than once.*

Albert White, CEO
A. Bender, Chairman of the Board
Agostino Ricupati, Chief Accounting Officer
Holly Sheffield, Chief Strategy Officer
Daniel McBride, COO
Allan Rubenstein, Director
Randal Golden, General Counsel
Robert Auerbach, President, Subsidiary
Brian Andrews, Senior VP

GROWTH PLANS/SPECIAL FEATURES:

The Cooper Companies, Inc. develops, manufactures and markets healthcare products, primarily medical devices. The company operates through two business units: CooperVision and CooperSurgical. CooperVision develops, manufactures and markets a broad range of contact lenses, including disposable spherical and specialty contact lenses. It is a leading manufacturer of toric and multifocal lenses, which correct astigmatism; multifocal lenses for presbyopia, the blurring of vision due to advancing age; and spherical lenses, including hydrogel lenses, which correct the most common near- and far-sighted visual defects. CooperVision offers single-use, two-week, monthly and quarterly disposable sphere and toric lenses as well as custom toric lenses to correct a high degree of astigmatism. CooperVision's Proclear line of spherical, toric and multifocal lenses are manufactured with omafilcon, a material that incorporates its proprietary Phosphorylcholine (PC) Technology to enhance tissue-device compatibility. CooperVision's products are primarily manufactured at its facilities in the U.S., the U.K., Hungary, Costa Rico and Puerto Rico. It distributes its products out of its facilities in the U.S., the U.K., Belgium and various smaller international distribution facilities. CooperSurgical develops, manufactures and markets medical devices, diagnostic products and surgical instruments and accessories used primarily by gynecologists and obstetricians. This unit manufactures and distributes its products at its facilities in Connecticut, Texas and New York, USA, as well as in Denmark, Costa Rica and the U.K. In 2021, Cooper Companies announced the creation of a 50/50 joint venture with EssilorLuxottica for the acquisition of SightGlass Vision, a life sciences company focused on developing innovative spectacle lenses to reduce the progression of myopia in children; the acquisition of obp Medical Corporation, a medical device company; and the approval of MiSight one day contact lenses by the Chinese National Medical Products Administration for use within China.

FINANCIAL DATA: *Note: Data for latest year may not have been available at press time.*

In U.S. $	2020	2019	2018	2017	2016	2015
Revenue	2,430,900,000	2,653,400,000	2,532,800,000	2,139,000,000	1,966,814,000	1,797,060,000
R&D Expense	93,300,000	86,700,000	84,800,000	69,200,000	65,411,000	69,589,000
Operating Income	311,800,000	528,100,000	427,500,000	429,100,000	324,080,000	236,671,000
Operating Margin %		.20%	.17%	.20%	.16%	.13%
SGA Expense	992,500,000	996,200,000	973,300,000	799,100,000	722,798,000	712,543,000
Net Income	238,400,000	466,700,000	139,900,000	372,900,000	273,917,000	203,523,000
Operating Cash Flow	486,600,000	713,200,000	668,900,000	593,600,000	509,637,000	390,970,000
Capital Expenditure	310,400,000	292,100,000	193,600,000	127,200,000	152,640,000	243,023,000
EBITDA	590,400,000	826,200,000	689,700,000	615,800,000	520,097,000	424,991,000
Return on Assets %		.08%	.03%	.08%	.06%	.05%
Return on Equity %		.13%	.04%	.13%	.10%	.08%
Debt to Equity		0.348	0.60	0.362	0.41	0.415

CONTACT INFORMATION:

Phone: 925 460-3600   Fax: 949 597-0662
Toll-Free:
Address: 6140 Stoneridge Mall Rd., Ste. 590, Pleasanton, CA 94588
United States

STOCK TICKER/OTHER:

Stock Ticker: COO
Employees: 12,000
Parent Company:

Exchange: NYS
Fiscal Year Ends: 10/31

SALARIES/BONUSES:

Top Exec. Salary: $ Bonus: $
Second Exec. Salary: $ Bonus: $

OTHER THOUGHTS:

Estimated Female Officers or Directors: 2
Hot Spot for Advancement for Women/Minorities: Y

Cordis Corporation

NAIC Code: 339100

www.cordis.com

TYPES OF BUSINESS:

Vascular Treatment Products
Guidewires & Balloons
Stents & Catheters

BRANDS/DIVISIONS/AFFILIATES:

Hellman & Friedman LLC
AVANTI
EMERALD
INFINITI
EXOSEAL
AQUATRACK
ELITECROSS
FRONTRUNNER

CONTACTS: *Note: Officers with more than one job title may be intentionally listed here more than once.*

Shar Matin, CEO
Campbell Rogers, Chief Scientific Officer
Charles McDowell, VP-Corp. Rel.
Barbara G. Ramseyer, VP-Regulatory Affairs & Quality Assurance
Paul I. Chang, VP-Worldwide Clinical Research & Oper.

GROWTH PLANS/SPECIAL FEATURES:

Cordis Corporation develops and manufactures interventional vascular technology. Its business and products are divided into two segments: cardiology and endovascular. The cardiology segment develops and manufactures products to treat patients who suffer from cardiovascular disease. These products include sheaths, diagnostic guidewires, diagnostic catheters, steerable guidewires and PTCA balloons. Brands within this segment include AVANTI, EMERALD, INFINITI, EXOSEAL and MYNX. The endovascular segment produces sheaths, access accessories, diagnostic guidewires, crossing devices, diagnostic catheters, steerable guidewires, guiding catheters, PTA balloons, specialty balloons, self-expanding stents, self-expanding and balloon expandable biliary stents, balloon expandable stents, vena cava filters and vascular closure devices. Brands within this segment include AVANTI, EMERALD, AQUATRACK, TEMPO AQUA, ELITECROSS, OUTBACK, MYNXGRIP and FRONTRUNNER. Cordis' range of self-expanding and balloon expandable biliary stents include flex biliary stents, transhepatic biliary stents and carotid stents. In August 2021, Cardinal Health announced the completion of the sale of Cordis to Hellman & Friedman LLC for approximately $1 billion. Cordis now operates as a wholly-owned subsidiary of Hellman & Friedman.

FINANCIAL DATA: *Note: Data for latest year may not have been available at press time.*

In U.S. $	2020	2019	2018	2017	2016	2015
Revenue	996,715,125	949,252,500	904,050,000	861,000,000	820,000,000	800,000,000
R&D Expense						
Operating Income						
Operating Margin %						
SGA Expense						
Net Income						
Operating Cash Flow						
Capital Expenditure						
EBITDA						
Return on Assets %						
Return on Equity %						
Debt to Equity						

CONTACT INFORMATION:

Phone: 408-273-3700 Fax:
Toll-Free: 800-447-7585
Address: 5452 Betsy Ross Dr., Santa Clara, CA 95054 United States

SALARIES/BONUSES:

Top Exec. Salary: $ Bonus: $
Second Exec. Salary: $ Bonus: $

STOCK TICKER/OTHER:

Stock Ticker: Subsidiary Exchange:
Employees: 5,000 Fiscal Year Ends: 12/31
Parent Company: Hellman & Friedman LLC

OTHER THOUGHTS:

Estimated Female Officers or Directors: 1
Hot Spot for Advancement for Women/Minorities:

CorVel Corporation

www.corvel.com

NAIC Code: 524298A

TYPES OF BUSINESS:

Utilization Management and Claims Administration
Managed Care Services
Preferred Provider Networks
Payment Processing
Workers' Compensation Services
Claims Cost Control Services

BRANDS/DIVISIONS/AFFILIATES:

24/7 Nurse Triage

CONTACTS: *Note: Officers with more than one job title may be intentionally listed here more than once.*

Michael Combs, CEO
Brandon O'Brien, CFO
V. Clemons, Chairman of the Board
Jennifer Yoss, Chief Accounting Officer
Maxim Shishin, Chief Information Officer
Diane Blaha, Chief Marketing Officer
Michael Saverien, Executive VP, Divisional
Richard Schweppe, Vice President, Divisional

GROWTH PLANS/SPECIAL FEATURES:

CorVel Corporation is an independent nationwide provider of medical cost containment and managed care services, designed to manage the medical costs of workers' compensation and other liability claims management, primarily for coverage under group health and auto insurance policies. The company offers services in two categories: network solutions and patient management. Its network solution services provide savings and management solutions for employee medical bills; services include preferred provider organization (PPO) management, medical bill re-pricing, provider reimbursement, pharmacy services, true line item review, professional nurse review, Medicare services, directed care services, clearinghouse services and automated adjudication. Through its patient management solution category, the firm administers claims to its managed care customers. Claims administration services include automated first notice of loss, three-point contact within 24 hours, prompt claims investigations, claim history data and litigation management. This segment also offers case management; a 24/7 Nurse Triage system, where injured workers can speak with a registered nurse with expertise in occupational injuries; and utilization review services, which address disability management and recovery, vocational rehabilitation services, utilization management, life care planning, liability claims management and auto claims management. CorVel's services are sold as a bundled solution, as a standalone service and as additional services for existing customers. The firm offers its services to insurers, third-party administrators, self-administered employers, government agencies, municipalities and state funds to help them manage the medical costs and monitor the quality of care associated with health care claims.

FINANCIAL DATA: *Note: Data for latest year may not have been available at press time.*

In U.S. $	2020	2019	2018	2017	2016	2015
Revenue	592,225,000	595,740,000	558,350,000	518,686,000	503,584,000	
R&D Expense						
Operating Income	60,711,000	61,513,000	47,903,000	47,549,000	46,060,000	
Operating Margin %	.10%	.10%	.09%	.09%	.09%	
SGA Expense	65,210,000	63,296,000	59,350,000	57,243,000	58,484,000	
Net Income	47,377,000	46,703,000	35,695,000	29,479,000	28,525,000	
Operating Cash Flow	80,826,000	78,639,000	62,152,000	52,052,000	51,311,000	
Capital Expenditure	32,360,000	15,274,000	27,689,000	31,041,000	16,756,000	
EBITDA	83,227,000	84,497,000	69,678,000	68,497,000	66,012,000	
Return on Assets %	.13%	.16%	.14%	.13%	.13%	
Return on Equity %	.25%	.26%	.23%	.22%	.22%	
Debt to Equity	0.449					

CONTACT INFORMATION:

Phone: 817-390-1416   Fax:
Toll-Free:
Address: 5128 Apache Plume Rd., Ste. 400, Fort Worth, TX 76109 United States

STOCK TICKER/OTHER:

Stock Ticker: CRVL
Employees: 3,681
Parent Company:

Exchange: NAS
Fiscal Year Ends: 03/31

SALARIES/BONUSES:

Top Exec. Salary: $ Bonus: $
Second Exec. Salary: $ Bonus: $

OTHER THOUGHTS:

Estimated Female Officers or Directors: 3
Hot Spot for Advancement for Women/Minorities: Y

CryoLife Inc

www.cryolife.com

NAIC Code: 339100

TYPES OF BUSINESS:

Surgical Implants Manufacturing
Surgical Adhesives
Heart Valves
Medical Implants
Biomedical Research

BRANDS/DIVISIONS/AFFILIATES:

JOTECH GmbH
On-X Life Technologies Holdings Inc
BioGlue
BioForm
CardioGenesis
PhotoFix
SynerGraft

CONTACTS: Note: Officers with more than one job title may be intentionally listed here more than once.

Amy Horton, Chief Accounting Officer
Jean Holloway, Chief Compliance Officer
David Lee, Executive VP
Thomas Bogenschutz, General Manager, Subsidiary
James Mackin, President
Michael Simpson, Senior VP, Divisional
John Davis, Senior VP, Divisional
Scott Capps, Vice President, Divisional

GROWTH PLANS/SPECIAL FEATURES:

CryoLife, Inc. manufactures, processes and distributes medical devices, as well as implantable human tissues for use in cardiac and vascular surgeries. The company's surgical sealants and hemostats include BioGlue surgical adhesive and BioFoam surgical matrix. CryoLife distributes these products internationally for Starch Medical, Inc. The firm's CardioGenesis cardiac laser therapy product line is used for the treatment of coronary artery disease in patients with severe angina. CryoLife also distributes PhotoFix, a bovine pericardial patch stabilized using a dye-mediated photo-fixation process that requires no glutaraldehyde. The cardiac and vascular human tissues distributed by the company include the CryoValve SG pulmonary heart valve and the CryoPatch SG pulmonary cardiac patch tissue, both of which are processed using CryoLife's proprietary SynerGraft decellularization technology. Other products include On-X prosthetic heart valves; Chord-X mitral chordal replacement products; cardiac and vascular allografts; and CarbonAid, a carbon dioxide diffuser that reduces air embolism during open heart surgery. Primary operating subsidiaries include: JOTEC GmbH, a Germany-based endovascular and surgical products firm; On-X Life Technologies Holdings, Inc., a Texas-based mechanical heart valve company; CryoLife Europa Ltda., a provider of marketing and distribution support services in Europe, the Middle East and Africa; CryoLife France SAS, which provides direct sales operations in France; CryoLife Canada, Inc., which provides direct sales operations in Canada; and CryoLife Asia Pacific Pte. Ltd., which provides sales and marketing support for the Asia Pacific region. CyroLife itself is headquartered in Georgia, U.S., and markets and sells its products in approximately 95 countries worldwide. During 2021, CryoLife sold its PerClot product line to a subsidiary of Baxter International, Inc.

CyroLife offers its employees medical, prescription and dental coverage; life insurance; long-term disability; paid vacation; a 401(k) plan; an employee stock purchase plan; and tuition reimbursement.

FINANCIAL DATA: Note: Data for latest year may not have been available at press time.

In U.S. $	2020	2019	2018	2017	2016	2015
Revenue	253,227,000	276,222,000	262,841,000	189,702,000	180,380,000	145,898,000
R&D Expense	24,207,000	22,960,000	23,098,000	19,461,000	13,446,000	10,436,000
Operating Income	2,441,000	17,042,000	9,312,000	7,970,000	13,905,000	5,354,000
Operating Margin %		.06%	.04%	.04%	.08%	.04%
SGA Expense	141,136,000	143,011,000	140,574,000	101,211,000	91,548,000	74,929,000
Net Income	-16,682,000	1,720,000	-2,840,000	3,704,000	10,778,000	4,005,000
Operating Cash Flow	12,369,000	15,827,000	9,881,000	10,803,000	19,719,000	11,442,000
Capital Expenditure	7,328,000	8,072,000	5,786,000	7,041,000	7,424,000	4,103,000
EBITDA	20,236,000	34,847,000	27,492,000	18,187,000	29,839,000	11,217,000
Return on Assets %		.00%	.00%	.01%	.04%	.02%
Return on Equity %		.01%	-.01%	.01%	.06%	.03%
Debt to Equity		0.833	0.806	0.812	0.321	

CONTACT INFORMATION:

Phone: 770 419-3355 Fax: 770 426-0031
Toll-Free: 800-438-8285
Address: 1655 Roberts Blvd. NW, Kennesaw, GA 30144 United States

STOCK TICKER/OTHER:

Stock Ticker: CRY Exchange: NYS
Employees: 1,200 Fiscal Year Ends: 12/31
Parent Company:

SALARIES/BONUSES:

Top Exec. Salary: $ Bonus: $
Second Exec. Salary: $ Bonus: $

OTHER THOUGHTS:

Estimated Female Officers or Directors: 3
Hot Spot for Advancement for Women/Minorities: Y

CSL Behring LLC

www.cslbehring.com

NAIC Code: 325414

TYPES OF BUSINESS:

Plasma Products
Coagulants
Anticoagulants
Immunoglobulins
Surgical Wound Healers
Plasma Expanders
Plasma Collection

BRANDS/DIVISIONS/AFFILIATES:

CSL Limited
CSL Plasma
BERINERT

CONTACTS: *Note: Officers with more than one job title may be intentionally listed here more than once.*

Paul Perreault, CEO
Paul McKenzie, COO
Joy Linton, CFO
Bill Campbell, CCO
Elizabeth Walker, Chief Human Resources Officer
Andrew Cuthbertson, Chief Scientific Officer
Mark Hill, Chief Digital Information Officer
Mary Sontrop, Exec. VP-Manufacturing
Greg Boss, General Counsel
Ingolf Sieper, Exec. VP-Commercial Oper.
Mary Sontrop, Exec. VP-Planning
Dennis Jackman, Sr. VP-Public Affairs
Bill Mezzanotte, Chief Medical Officer
Karen Etchberger, Exec. VP-Quality & Bus. Svcs.

GROWTH PLANS/SPECIAL FEATURES:

CSL Behring, LLC, a subsidiary of CSL Limited, is a biotechnology company that specializes in the manufacture of plasma-based products. The company researches, develops, manufactures and markets biotherapies used to treat serious and rare conditions. Users of the firm's therapies rely on them for quality of life and even for life itself. Conditions treated include coagulation (bleeding) disorders such as hemophilia and von Willebrand disease, immune deficiencies and genetic emphysema (inherited respiratory disease). Biotherapies are also used in critical care settings to treat shock, sepsis and severe burns; to prevent hemolytic disease in the newborn resulting from Rh factor incompatibilities; during cardiac surgery; and for wound healing. Therapeutic areas include immunology, hematology, respiratory, cardiovascular, metabolic and transplant. CSL Behring operates a world-leading plasma collection network, CSL Plasma, with more than 300 collection centers across China, Europe and North America. Manufacturing locations are in Switzerland, Germany, Australia, the U.S. and China. During 2021, the U.S. Food and Drug Administration approved BERINERT (C1 esterase inhibitor, human-intravenous) administration kit indicated for the treatment of acute abdominal, facial or laryngeal attacks of hereditary angioedema (HAE) in adult and pediatric patients.

FINANCIAL DATA: *Note: Data for latest year may not have been available at press time.*

In U.S. $	2020	2019	2018	2017	2016	2015
Revenue	7,853,700,000	7,168,350,000	6,827,000,000	6,023,000,000	5,383,900,000	5,049,000,000
R&D Expense						
Operating Income						
Operating Margin %						
SGA Expense						
Net Income						
Operating Cash Flow						
Capital Expenditure						
EBITDA						
Return on Assets %						
Return on Equity %						
Debt to Equity						

CONTACT INFORMATION:

Phone: 610-878-4000   Fax: 610-878-4009
Toll-Free:
Address: 1020 First Ave., King of Prussia, PA 19406 United States

SALARIES/BONUSES:

Top Exec. Salary: $ Bonus: $
Second Exec. Salary: $ Bonus: $

STOCK TICKER/OTHER:

Stock Ticker: Subsidiary   Exchange:
Employees: 14,000   Fiscal Year Ends: 06/30
Parent Company: CSL Limited

OTHER THOUGHTS:

Estimated Female Officers or Directors: 8
Hot Spot for Advancement for Women/Minorities: Y

CSL Limited

NAIC Code: 325414

www.csl.com

TYPES OF BUSINESS:

Human Blood-Plasma Collection
Plasma Products
Immunohematology Products
Vaccines
Pharmaceutical Marketing
Antivenom
Drugs-Cancer

BRANDS/DIVISIONS/AFFILIATES:

CSL Behring
CSL Plasma
Seqirus

CONTACTS: *Note: Officers with more than one job title may be intentionally listed here more than once.*

Paul Perreault, CEO
Paul McKenzie, COO
Joy Linton, CFO
Bill Campbell, CCO
Megan Clark, Chief Human Resources Officer
Andrew Cuthbertson, Chief Scientific Officer
Mark Hill, Chief Digital Information Officer
Mary Sontrop, Exec. VP-Mfg. & Planning
Greg Boss, General Counsel
Ingolf Sieper, Exec. VP-Commercial Oper.
Karen Etchberger, Exec. VP-Quality & Bus. Svcs.
Brian McNamee, Chmn.

GROWTH PLANS/SPECIAL FEATURES:

CSL Limited develops, manufactures and markets pharmaceutical products of biological origin in more than 35 countries worldwide. The company focuses on rare and serious diseases and vaccines. Within the rare and serious diseases division, CSL's innovations are used around the world to treat immunodeficiencies, bleeding disorders, hereditary angioedema, Alpha-1 antitrypsin deficiency and neurological disorders. This division's CSL Behring subsidiary manufactures and markets safe and effective products and is engaged in researching and developing innovative biotherapies. CSL Plasma, a division within CSL Behring, is one of the world's largest and most efficient plasma collection networks, with centers in the U.S. and Europe, as well as production facilities in the U.S., Germany, Switzerland and Australia. Within the vaccine division, joint venture Seqirus (with Novartis), is a leading influenza company with corporate offices in the U.K., and manufacturing plants in the U.S., the U.K., Germany and Australia. Seqirus is a transcontinental partner in pandemic preparedness and a major contributor to the prevention and control of influenza globally. CSL's current product pipeline (May 2021) includes seven research/pre-clinical products, 24 clinical development products and eight registration/post-launch products. These products include immunoglobulins, specialty products, breakthrough medicines, vaccines, inactivated polio vaccines, hemophilia products and transplant products. In May 2021, CSL announced the closing of its global commercialization and license agreement with uniQure for etranacogene dezaparvovec (AMT-061), a novel gene therapy for the treatment of hemophilia B. Per the agreement, uniQure will complete the AMT-061 trial and scale up manufacture for initial commercial supply.

CSL Limited offers its employees flexible work arrangements, an employee share plan, tuition reimbursement and technology training.

FINANCIAL DATA: *Note: Data for latest year may not have been available at press time.*

In U.S. $	2020	2019	2018	2017	2016	2015
Revenue	10,272,230,000	9,424,284,000	8,011,386,000	6,677,266,000	6,137,471,000	5,519,729,000
R&D Expense	1,040,486,000	921,176,400	741,601,400	651,295,400	637,478,600	467,881,700
Operating Income	2,535,635,000	2,325,533,000	1,854,215,000	1,312,583,000	1,050,417,000	1,438,835,000
Operating Margin %		.29%	.27%	.22%	.21%	
SGA Expense	1,792,463,000	1,596,499,000	1,373,610,000	1,192,780,000	1,068,903,000	794,600,000
Net Income	2,373,207,000	2,124,863,000	1,825,391,000	1,349,826,000	1,290,328,000	1,394,443,000
Operating Cash Flow						
Capital Expenditure	1,545,529,000	1,420,901,000	1,041,606,000	867,749,200	590,831,200	417,889,500
EBITDA	3,548,015,000	3,204,073,000	2,836,224,000	1,959,235,000	1,919,083,000	1,976,792,000
Return on Assets %		.17%	.18%	.16%	.18%	
Return on Equity %		.42%	.49%	.46%	.48%	
Debt to Equity		0.808	1.02	1.218	1.20	

CONTACT INFORMATION:

Phone: 61-3-9389-1911   Fax: 61-3-9389-1434
Toll-Free:
Address: 45 Poplar Rd., Parkville, VIC 3052 Australia

STOCK TICKER/OTHER:

Stock Ticker: CMXHF   Exchange: PINX
Employees: 27,009   Fiscal Year Ends: 06/30
Parent Company:

SALARIES/BONUSES:

Top Exec. Salary: $ Bonus: $
Second Exec. Salary: $ Bonus: $

OTHER THOUGHTS:

Estimated Female Officers or Directors: 4
Hot Spot for Advancement for Women/Minorities: Y

Cumberland Pharmaceuticals Inc

www.cumberlandpharma.com

NAIC Code: 325412

TYPES OF BUSINESS:

Prescription Drugs Manufacturing
Pharmaceuticals
Late-Stage Development
Drug Commercialization

BRANDS/DIVISIONS/AFFILIATES:

Acetadote
Caldolor
Kristalose
Omeclamox-Pak
Vaprisol
Vibativ
RediTrex
Ifetroban

CONTACTS: *Note: Officers with more than one job title may be intentionally listed here more than once.*

A. Kazimi, CEO
Michael Bonner, CFO
James Herman, Chief Compliance Officer
Martin Cearnal, Director
Leo Pavliv, Executive VP, Divisional

GROWTH PLANS/SPECIAL FEATURES:

Cumberland Pharmaceuticals, Inc. is a specialty pharmaceutical company that focuses on hospital acute care and gastroenterology. The firm primarily concentrates on the acquisition, development and commercialization of late-stage and FDA-approved branded prescription drugs. Cumberland has seven actively marketed products: Acetadote, Caldolor, Kristalose, Omeclamox-Pak, Vaprisol, Vibativ and RediTrex. Acetadote (acetylcysteine) is an injection for the treatment of acetaminophen poisoning. Caldolor (ibuprofen) is an injection for the treatment of pain and fever. Kristalose (lactulose) is an oral solution, a prescription laxative, for the treatment of chronic and acute constipation. Omeclamox-Pak (omeprazole, clarithromycin and amoxicillin) is for the treatment of Helicobacter pylori infection and related duodenal ulcer disease. Vaprisol (conivaptan) is an injection for raising serum sodium levels in hospitalized patients with euvolemic and hypervolemic hyponatremia. Vibativ (telavancin) is an injection for the treatment of certain serious bacterial infections including hospital-acquired and ventilator-associated bacterial pneumonia, as well as complicated skin and skin structure infections. RediTrex (methotrexate) is an injection for the treatment of active rheumatoid, juvenile idiopathic and severe psoriatic arthritis, as well as disabling psoriasis. Cumberland also has Phase 2 clinical programs evaluating its ifetroban product candidates in patients with cardiomyopathy associated with Duchenne Muscular Dystrophy, Systemic Sclerosis and Aspirin-Exacerbated Respiratory Disease; and completed Phase 2 clinical programs with ifetroban in patients with Hepatorenal Syndrome (HRS) and patients with portal hypertension.

FINANCIAL DATA: *Note: Data for latest year may not have been available at press time.*

In U.S. $	2020	2019	2018	2017	2016	2015
Revenue	37,441,140	47,533,640	40,741,760	41,150,130	33,025,560	33,519,050
R&D Expense	5,773,825	6,478,592	7,320,797	3,901,365	3,190,700	3,847,651
Operating Income	-6,381,595	-3,623,005	-7,390,772	-4,081,348	-1,433,131	1,111,610
Operating Margin %		-.08%	-.18%	-.10%	-.04%	.03%
SGA Expense	24,961,760	31,791,470	30,664,180	31,523,310	23,115,290	21,602,360
Net Income	-3,339,408	-3,537,759	-6,963,068	-7,978,633	-944,683	731,351
Operating Cash Flow	5,415,061	3,056,356	3,112,737	-557,714	569,478	5,876,865
Capital Expenditure	2,113,927	1,019,146	4,275,055	1,489,070	2,131,098	2,699,430
EBITDA	-1,557,685	1,024,534	-3,843,585	-1,134,269	1,168,438	3,567,602
Return on Assets %		-.03%	-.07%	-.09%	-.01%	.01%
Return on Equity %		-.07%	-.12%	-.12%	-.01%	.01%
Debt to Equity		0.402	0.358	0.153	0.056	0.022

CONTACT INFORMATION:

Phone: 615 255-0068   Fax: 615 255-0094
Toll-Free: 877-484-2700
Address: 2525 West End Ave., Ste. 950, Nashville, TN 37203 United States

STOCK TICKER/OTHER:

Stock Ticker: CPIX
Employees: 94
Parent Company:

Exchange: NAS
Fiscal Year Ends: 12/31

SALARIES/BONUSES:

Top Exec. Salary: $ Bonus: $
Second Exec. Salary: $ Bonus: $

OTHER THOUGHTS:

Estimated Female Officers or Directors: 4
Hot Spot for Advancement for Women/Minorities: Y

CVS Health Corporation

cvshealth.com

NAIC Code: 446110

TYPES OF BUSINESS:

Drug Stores
Pharmacy Benefits Management
Online Pharmacy Services
Healthcare Services
Health Benefits
Pharmacy Retail
Clinic Retail

BRANDS/DIVISIONS/AFFILIATES:

MinuteClinic
Omnicare
SilverScript Insurance Company
CVS Pharmacy
Aetna Inc

CONTACTS: *Note: Officers with more than one job title may be intentionally listed here more than once.*

Karen Lynch, CEO
Thomas Moriarty, Executive VP
Eva Boratto, CFO
David Dorman, Chairman of the Board
James Clark, Chief Accounting Officer
Troyen Brennan, Chief Medical Officer
Joshua Flum, Executive VP, Divisional
Alan Lotvin, Executive VP, Divisional
Karen Lynch, Executive VP, Divisional
Jonathan Roberts, Executive VP
Derica Rice, Executive VP
Kevin Hourican, Executive VP
Lisa Bisaccia, Other Executive Officer

GROWTH PLANS/SPECIAL FEATURES:

CVS Health Corporation is a leading provider of prescription and related healthcare services in the U.S. It operates in four segments: corporate, retail/LTC, pharmacy services and health care benefits. The corporate segment provides management and administrative services to support the company's overall operations. The retail/LTC (long-term care) segment operated more than 9,900 retail locations, over 1,100 MinuteClinic locations as well as online retail pharmacy websites, LTC pharmacies and onsite pharmacies. LTC pharmacy services are through the Omnicare business. Omnicare provides pharmacy consulting, including monthly patient drug therapy evaluations, to assist in compliance with state and federal regulations and provide proprietary clinical and health management programs. It also provides pharmaceutical case management services for retirees, employees and dependents who have drug benefits under corporate-sponsored health care programs. The pharmacy services segment provides a full range of pharmacy benefit management services, including mail order pharmacy services, plan design and administration, formulary management, claims processing and health management programs. Through subsidiary SilverScript Insurance Company, the division is a national provider of drug benefits to eligible beneficiaries under Medicare Part D. The segment operates a national network of approximately 66,000 retail pharmacies, consisting of approximately 40,000 chain pharmacies (which includes CVS Pharmacy locations) and 26,000 independent pharmacies, in the U.S., including Puerto Rico, the District of Columbia, Guam and the U.S. Virgin Islands. The health care benefits segment is one of the nation's leading diversified health care benefits providers, serving an estimated 34 million people. The segment offers a range of traditional, voluntary and consumer-directed health insurance products and related services.

Employee benefits include medical, dental, vision and prescription coverage; 401(k), stock and savings plans; short- and long-term disability; and a variety of employee assistance plans and programs.

FINANCIAL DATA: *Note: Data for latest year may not have been available at press time.*

In U.S. $	2020	2019	2018	2017	2016	2015
Revenue	268,706,000,000	256,776,000,000	194,579,000,000	184,765,000,000	177,526,000,000	153,290,000,000
R&D Expense						
Operating Income	13,911,000,000	11,987,000,000	10,170,000,000	9,517,000,000	10,338,000,000	9,454,000,000
Operating Margin %		.05%	.05%	.05%	.06%	.06%
SGA Expense						
Net Income	7,179,000,000	6,634,000,000	-594,000,000	6,622,000,000	5,317,000,000	5,237,000,000
Operating Cash Flow	15,865,000,000	12,848,000,000	8,865,000,000	8,007,000,000	10,069,000,000	8,412,000,000
Capital Expenditure	2,437,000,000	2,457,000,000	2,037,000,000	1,918,000,000	2,224,000,000	2,367,000,000
EBITDA	17,118,000,000	16,403,000,000	6,743,000,000	11,809,000,000	12,190,000,000	11,567,000,000
Return on Assets %		.03%	.00%	.07%	.06%	.06%
Return on Equity %		.11%	-.01%	.18%	.14%	.14%
Debt to Equity		1.309	1.227	0.588	0.695	0.706

CONTACT INFORMATION:

Phone: 401 765-1500   Fax: 401 762-2137
Toll-Free: 888-746-7287
Address: 1 CVS Dr., Woonsocket, RI 02895 United States

STOCK TICKER/OTHER:

Stock Ticker: CVS   Exchange: NYS
Employees: 202,000   Fiscal Year Ends: 12/31
Parent Company:

SALARIES/BONUSES:

Top Exec. Salary: $ Bonus: $
Second Exec. Salary: $ Bonus: $

OTHER THOUGHTS:

Estimated Female Officers or Directors: 4
Hot Spot for Advancement for Women/Minorities: Y

Cynosure Inc

www.cynosure.com

NAIC Code: 334510

TYPES OF BUSINESS:

Electromedical and Electrotherapeutic Apparatus Manufacturing
Aesthetic Products
Medical Treatment Products
Product Development
Product Manufacture
Marketing

BRANDS/DIVISIONS/AFFILIATES:

Clayton Dubilier & Rice LLC
PicoSure
Icon
Pelleve
Vectus
Apogee+
ReveLite SI
TempSure

CONTACTS: *Note: Officers with more than one job title may be intentionally listed here more than once.*

Todd Tillemans, CEO
Renika Sehgal, CFO
Katie Cheng, CMO
Kellie Teal-Guess, Chief Human Resources Officer
Pamela Baxter, CIO
Douglas Delaney, Other Executive Officer
Peter Anastos, Senior VP
Sandi Peterson, Chmn.

GROWTH PLANS/SPECIAL FEATURES:

Cynosure, Inc. develops, manufactures and markets light-based aesthetic and medical treatment systems used by physicians and other practitioners to perform non- and minimally-invasive procedures. Treatments include hair removal, skin revitalization, vascular lesions and scar reduction, as well as tattoo removal, and addressing cellulite and wrinkles. Products include: the PicoSure, a high-powered laser that provides fast treatment for removing benign epidermal and dermal pigmented lesions such as freckles, acquired dermal melanocytosis and multi-colored tattoos; the Icon vascular workstation, which treats all types of vascular lesions, including facial and leg telangiectasias, spider veins, hemangiomas, and rosacea; the Pelleve radio-frequency system, for the treatment of wrinkles head-to-toe; and the Vectus laser system, for high-volume hair removal. Other product lines by the firm include Apogee+, Cellulaze, Cynergy, Elite, Icon, MedLite C6, MonaLisa Touch, Nitronox, Potenza, PrecisionTx, Radiolase, RevLite SI, SculpSure, Smartlipo Triplex, Smartskin+, Surgitron and TempSure. Cynosure is owned by private equity firm Clayton, Dubilier & Rice LLC.

FINANCIAL DATA: *Note: Data for latest year may not have been available at press time.*

In U.S. $	2020	2019	2018	2017	2016	2015
Revenue	500,000,000	501,867,482	477,969,030	455,208,600	433,532,000	339,462,016
R&D Expense						
Operating Income						
Operating Margin %						
SGA Expense						
Net Income						
Operating Cash Flow						
Capital Expenditure						
EBITDA						
Return on Assets %						
Return on Equity %						
Debt to Equity						

CONTACT INFORMATION:

Phone: 978 256-4200   Fax:
Toll-Free:
Address: 5 Carlisle Rd., Westford, MA 01886 United States

STOCK TICKER/OTHER:

Stock Ticker: Private   Exchange:
Employees: 825   Fiscal Year Ends: 12/31
Parent Company: Clayton Dubilier & Rice LLC

SALARIES/BONUSES:

Top Exec. Salary: $ Bonus: $
Second Exec. Salary: $ Bonus: $

OTHER THOUGHTS:

Estimated Female Officers or Directors:
Hot Spot for Advancement for Women/Minorities:

Danaher Corporation

www.danaher.com

NAIC Code: 334510

TYPES OF BUSINESS:

Medical Diagnostic Equipment
Life Science Research Tools
Diagnostic Instruments
Software
Environmental Analytic Instruments
Water Measure Systems
Water Detection Solutions
Biotechnology

BRANDS/DIVISIONS/AFFILIATES:

Aldevron LLC

CONTACTS: Note: Officers with more than one job title may be intentionally listed here more than once.

Thomas Joyce, CEO
Matthew McGrew, CFO
Steven Rales, Chairman of the Board
Robert Lutz, Chief Accounting Officer
Brian Ellis, Chief Compliance Officer
Mitchell Rales, Co-Founder
Rainer Blair, Executive VP
Daniel Comas, Executive VP
William Daniel II, Executive VP
Joakim Weidemanis, Executive VP
Angela Lalor, Senior VP, Divisional
Daniel Raskas, Senior VP, Divisional
William King, Senior VP, Divisional

GROWTH PLANS/SPECIAL FEATURES:

Danaher Corporation designs, manufactures and markets professional, medical, industrial and commercial products and services. The company operates through three segments: life sciences, diagnostics, and environmental & applied solutions. The life sciences segment offers a range of research tools that scientists use to study genes, proteins, metabolites and cells in an effort to understand the cause of disease and identify new therapies and test new drugs and vaccines. The diagnostics segment offers analytical instruments, reagents, consumables, software and services that hospitals, physicians' offices, reference laboratories and other critical care settings use to diagnose disease and make treatment decisions. Last, the environmental & applied solutions segment offers products and services that help protect resources and keep global food and water supplies safe. This division's products include a wide range of analytical instruments, software and related equipment that detect and measure water; ultraviolet disinfection systems; and industrial water treatment solutions. Danaher's manufacturing locations and worldwide presence include North America, Europe, Asia, Australia and Latin America. In August 2021, Danaher acquired Aldevron LLC, which manufactures high-quality plasmid DNA, mRNA and proteins, serving biotechnology and pharmaceutical customers across research, clinical and commercial applications. Aldevron operates as a standalone company, but its business is also included in the life sciences segment.

FINANCIAL DATA: Note: Data for latest year may not have been available at press time.

In U.S. $	2020	2019	2018	2017	2016	2015
Revenue	22,284,000,000	17,911,100,000	19,893,000,000	18,329,700,000	16,882,400,000	20,563,100,000
R&D Expense	1,348,000,000	1,126,000,000	1,231,200,000	1,128,800,000	975,100,000	1,239,100,000
Operating Income	4,231,000,000	3,269,400,000	3,403,800,000	3,021,200,000	2,750,900,000	3,469,100,000
Operating Margin %		.18%	.17%	.16%	.16%	.17%
SGA Expense	6,896,000,000	5,588,300,000	6,472,100,000	6,042,500,000	5,608,600,000	6,054,300,000
Net Income	3,646,000,000	3,008,200,000	2,650,900,000	2,492,100,000	2,553,700,000	3,357,400,000
Operating Cash Flow	6,208,000,000	3,951,600,000	4,022,000,000	3,477,800,000	3,521,800,000	3,801,800,000
Capital Expenditure	791,000,000	635,500,000	655,700,000	619,600,000	589,600,000	633,000,000
EBITDA	6,545,000,000	4,603,400,000	4,757,900,000	4,339,800,000	3,923,800,000	4,538,100,000
Return on Assets %		.05%	.06%	.05%	.05%	.08%
Return on Equity %		.11%	.10%	.10%	.11%	.14%
Debt to Equity		0.773	0.343	0.392	0.421	0.508

CONTACT INFORMATION:

Phone: 202 828-0850   Fax: 202 828-0860
Toll-Free:
Address: 2200 Pennsylvania Ave. NW, Ste. 800W, Washington, WA 20037-1701 United States

STOCK TICKER/OTHER:

Stock Ticker: DHR
Employees: 69,000
Parent Company:

Exchange: NYS
Fiscal Year Ends: 12/31

SALARIES/BONUSES:

Top Exec. Salary: $ Bonus: $
Second Exec. Salary: $ Bonus: $

OTHER THOUGHTS:

Estimated Female Officers or Directors: 2
Hot Spot for Advancement for Women/Minorities: Y

DaVita Inc

www.davita.com

NAIC Code: 621492

TYPES OF BUSINESS:

Renal Care Services
Dialysis Services
Laboratory Services
Administrative Services
Integrated Kidney Care
Physician Services
Clinical Research

BRANDS/DIVISIONS/AFFILIATES:

CONTACTS: *Note: Officers with more than one job title may be intentionally listed here more than once.*

Javier Rodriguez, CEO
Joel Ackerman, CFO
Kent Thiry, Chairman of the Board
James Hilger, Chief Accounting Officer
James Hearty, Chief Compliance Officer
Kathleen Waters, Chief Legal Officer
Leanne Zumwalt, Vice President, Divisional

GROWTH PLANS/SPECIAL FEATURES:

DaVita, Inc. is a leading provider of dialysis services for patients suffering from chronic kidney failure, also known as end stage renal disease (ESRD). The company operates through a network of outpatient dialysis centers located in the U.S. and 10 countries outside the U.S., serving more than 200,000 patients. Loss of kidney function is normally irreversible, and typically caused by Type I and Type II diabetes, hypertension, polycycstic kidney disease, long-term autoimmune attack on the kidneys and prolonged urinary tract obstruction. End stage renal disease or end stage kidney disease (ESRD or ESKD) is the stage of advanced kidney impairment that requires continued dialysis treatments or a kidney transplant to sustain life. Dialysis is the removal of toxins, fluids and salt from the blood of patients by artificial means. DaVita's U.S. dialysis and related lab services business treats patients with chronic kidney failure and ESRD in the U.S. Internationally, DaVita provides dialysis and administrative services to approximately 320 outpatient dialysis centers located in 10 countries outside the U.S., serving approximately 36,200 patients. DaVita also provides ancillary services, consisting primarily of integrated kidney care, physician services, ESCO joint ventures and clinical research programs.

DaVita offers its employees health benefits, 401(k), employee stock purchase plan, career development opportunities and a variety of employee assistance plans and programs.

FINANCIAL DATA: *Note: Data for latest year may not have been available at press time.*

In U.S. $	2020	2019	2018	2017	2016	2015
Revenue	11,550,600,000	11,388,480,000	11,404,850,000	10,876,630,000	14,745,110,000	13,781,840,000
R&D Expense						
Operating Income	1,683,972,000	1,755,530,000	1,490,149,000	1,619,725,000	1,773,742,000	1,362,604,000
Operating Margin %		.15%	.13%	.15%	.12%	.10%
SGA Expense	1,247,584,000	1,103,312,000	1,135,454,000	1,064,026,000	1,592,698,000	1,452,135,000
Net Income	773,642,000	810,981,000	159,394,000	663,618,000	879,874,000	269,732,000
Operating Cash Flow	1,979,028,000	2,072,355,000	1,771,640,000	1,907,449,000	1,963,444,000	1,557,200,000
Capital Expenditure	674,541,000	766,546,000	987,138,000	905,250,000	829,095,000	707,998,000
EBITDA	2,252,808,000	2,254,415,000	2,126,948,000	2,607,905,000	2,623,529,000	1,769,540,000
Return on Assets %		.04%	.01%	.04%	.05%	.01%
Return on Equity %		.28%	.04%	.14%	.18%	.05%
Debt to Equity		5.016	2.207	1.953	1.925	1.848

CONTACT INFORMATION:

Phone: 303 405-2100   Fax: 310 792-8928
Toll-Free:
Address: 2000 16th St., Denver, CO 80202 United States

STOCK TICKER/OTHER:

Stock Ticker: DVA
Employees: 67,000
Parent Company:

Exchange: NYS
Fiscal Year Ends: 12/31

SALARIES/BONUSES:

Top Exec. Salary: $ Bonus: $
Second Exec. Salary: $ Bonus: $

OTHER THOUGHTS:

Estimated Female Officers or Directors: 3
Hot Spot for Advancement for Women/Minorities: Y

Delta Dental Plans Association

www.deltadental.com

NAIC Code: 524114

TYPES OF BUSINESS:

Dental Insurance & Dental Care
Dental PPO & HMO

BRANDS/DIVISIONS/AFFILIATES:

Delta Dental Premier
Delta Dental PPO
Delta Dental PPO Plus Premier
DeltaCare USA
DeltaCare
DeltaUSA

CONTACTS: Note: Officers with more than one job title may be intentionally listed here more than once.

James W. Hutchison, CEO
Stefany Currier, Dir.-Admin

GROWTH PLANS/SPECIAL FEATURES:

Delta Dental Plans Association, a nonprofit organization, is one of the largest dental benefits systems and dental service corporations in the U.S. The firm offers dental insurance coverage in all 50 states, Puerto Rico and other U.S. territories to individuals and employers. Delta Dental Plans is comprised of 39 independent Dental Delta companies. For Delta Dental customers who have a Delta Dental PPO (preferred provider organization), a Delta Dental Premier or a Delta Dental PPO Plus Premier plan, can choose any dentist they want, but are offered additional advantages if they choose a dentist within Delta Dental's own network. Those with a DeltaCare USA HMO (health maintenance organization) plan select a primary care dentist from the DeltaCare network and may have a pay a co-payment. Delta Dental Patient Direct is a dental service discount plan, choosing a dentist from a panel who charge discounted fees for their services. The company's website offers a cost estimation link for information on the price range for particular dental care needs. It will display what the member's plan covers as well as out-of-pocket costs; but the estimate is just an estimate and does not guarantee the exact overall fees for the procedures. DeltaVision is a vision plan that offers pre-negotiated discounts on eye exams, glasses, contact lenses and laser vision correction. DeltaVision is available separately or in combination with Delta's dental insurance.

FINANCIAL DATA: Note: Data for latest year may not have been available at press time.

In U.S. $	2020	2019	2018	2017	2016	2015
Revenue	33,882,904	32,269,433	28,810,629	27,438,694	23,349,500	20,561,327
R&D Expense						
Operating Income						
Operating Margin %						
SGA Expense						
Net Income		-24,776	1,770,124	340,236	1,703,457	-648,878
Operating Cash Flow						
Capital Expenditure						
EBITDA						
Return on Assets %						
Return on Equity %						
Debt to Equity						

CONTACT INFORMATION:

Phone: 630-574-6001   Fax: 630-574-6999
Toll-Free:
Address: 1515 W. 22nd St., Ste. 450, Oak Brook, IL 60523 United States

STOCK TICKER/OTHER:

Stock Ticker: Nonprofit
Employees: 3,200
Parent Company:

Exchange:
Fiscal Year Ends: 12/31

SALARIES/BONUSES:

Top Exec. Salary: $ Bonus: $
Second Exec. Salary: $ Bonus: $

OTHER THOUGHTS:

Estimated Female Officers or Directors: 2
Hot Spot for Advancement for Women/Minorities:

Demant AS

www.demant.com

NAIC Code: 334510

TYPES OF BUSINESS:

Human Hearing Assistance Technology
Hearing Aids
Cochlear Implants
Diagnostic Instruments
Product Development
Product Manufacture
Audio Solutions

BRANDS/DIVISIONS/AFFILIATES:

William Demant Invest AS
Oticon
Bernafon
Sonic
Maico
Interacoustics
Amplivox
EPOS

CONTACTS: *Note: Officers with more than one job title may be intentionally listed here more than once.*

Soren Nielsen, CEO
Rene Schneider, CFO
Niels B. Christiansen, Chmn.

GROWTH PLANS/SPECIAL FEATURES:

Demant A/S is a Danish holding company that oversees the operations of several subsidiaries engaged in the development and manufacturing of hearing devices, hearing implants and diagnostic instruments which are sold in more than 130 countries. The hearing devices division includes the Oticon, Bernafon, Sonic and Audika brands of devices. Oticon is a leading manufacturer of hearing care solutions such as hearing aids and fitting systems; Bernafon develops quality hearing systems via Swiss engineering and technology; Sonic is a U.S.-based manufacturer of hearing instruments renowned for superior sound processing, noise reduction, directional capabilities and award-winning design; and Audika is a French retailer of hearing aids, with more than 450 dispensing centers in the country. In addition, Demant is an exclusive hearing aid brand licensee of Philips, offering Philips HearLink hearing aids and related hearing solutions. The hearing implants division is comprised of Oticon Medical, which develops bone-anchored hearing systems and implant solutions such as cochlear implants that help overcome severe to total bilateral (second degree) hearing loss. The diagnostic instruments division includes the Maico, Interacoustics, Amplivox, Grason-Stadler, MedRx and Sennheiser brands which develop, manufacture and distribute audiometers for hearing measurement, as well as other instruments used by audiologists and ear-nose-and-throat specialists. In addition, subsidiary EPOS manufactures and sells high-end audio solutions designed for enterprises and gamers, with its products marketed under the EPOS brand. Demant is wholly-owned by William Demant Invest A/S.

FINANCIAL DATA: *Note: Data for latest year may not have been available at press time.*

In U.S. $	2020	2019	2018	2017	2016	2015
Revenue	2,377,560,000	2,455,941,000	2,290,142,000	2,167,230,000	1,972,180,000	1,752,483,000
R&D Expense	207,208,800	184,039,500	165,799,900	151,011,000	137,865,300	125,376,900
Operating Income	168,429,000	334,064,600	394,041,800	375,473,400	305,801,300	300,707,400
Operating Margin %		.14%	.17%	.17%	.16%	.17%
SGA Expense	1,299,286,000	1,359,263,000	1,212,196,000	1,120,998,000	1,040,152,000	871,229,900
Net Income	184,203,800	240,237,300	299,557,200	288,219,000	239,744,300	235,964,900
Operating Cash Flow	430,685,300	353,125,800	276,552,200	307,608,900	275,894,900	261,599,000
Capital Expenditure	111,902,600	125,869,900	101,550,400	71,972,590	77,395,180	72,465,560
EBITDA	410,966,800	498,385,600	478,502,700	443,666,700	378,595,600	357,233,900
Return on Assets %		.07%	.11%	.11%	.10%	.11%
Return on Equity %		.20%	.25%	.24%	.22%	.24%
Debt to Equity		0.531	0.311	0.311	0.282	0.32

CONTACT INFORMATION:

Phone: 45 39177300   Fax: 45 39278900
Toll-Free:
Address: Kongebakken 9, Smorum, 2765 Denmark

STOCK TICKER/OTHER:

Stock Ticker: WILYY   Exchange: PINX
Employees: 16,591   Fiscal Year Ends: 12/31
Parent Company: William Demant Invest AS

SALARIES/BONUSES:

Top Exec. Salary: $ Bonus: $
Second Exec. Salary: $ Bonus: $

OTHER THOUGHTS:

Estimated Female Officers or Directors: 1
Hot Spot for Advancement for Women/Minorities:

Dentsply Sirona Inc

www.dentsplysirona.com/en-us

NAIC Code: 339100

TYPES OF BUSINESS:

Dental Device Manufacturing
Dental Products
Product Manufacture
Dental Product Technologies
Consumable Medical Devices
Imaging Equipment
Dental Implants
Orthodontic Appliances

BRANDS/DIVISIONS/AFFILIATES:

CONTACTS: Note: Officers with more than one job title may be intentionally listed here more than once.

Nick Alexos, CFO
Donald Casey, Director
Eric Brandt, Director
Keith Ebling, Executive VP
Walter Petersohn, Other Executive Officer
Daniel Key, Other Executive Officer
Maureen MacInnis, Other Executive Officer
Markus Boehringer, Senior VP, Divisional
William Newell, Senior VP, Divisional
Henning Mueller, Vice President, Divisional

GROWTH PLANS/SPECIAL FEATURES:

Dentsply Sirona, Inc. is a world-leading manufacturer of professional dental products and technologies. With a 135-year history (since 1886) of innovation and service to the dental industry and to patients worldwide, the firm's products and solutions include dental and oral health products as well as other consumable medical devices under a strong portfolio of renowned brands. Dentsply's products provide innovative, high-quality and effective solutions for the purpose of advancing patient care and for delivering better, safer and faster dentistry. The company's primary products consist of: dental technology and equipment, including imaging equipment, computer aided design and machining (CAD/CAM) systems, dental implants, scanning equipment, treatment software, orthodontic appliances and a variety of dental restoration products; dental consumables, including endodontic (root canal) instruments and materials, dental anesthetics, prophylaxis paste, dental sealants, impression materials, restorative materials, tooth whiteners, topical fluoride, dental handpieces, intraoral curing light systems, dental diagnostic systems and ultrasonic scalers and polishers; and healthcare consumables, including urology catheters, surgical products, medical drills and other non-medical products. Dentsply Sirona's global headquarters are based in Charlotte, North Carolina. Approximately two-thirds of the company's sales are derived from regions outside the U.S.

FINANCIAL DATA: Note: Data for latest year may not have been available at press time.

In U.S. $	2020	2019	2018	2017	2016	2015
Revenue	3,342,000,000	4,029,200,000	3,986,300,000	3,993,400,000	3,745,300,000	2,674,300,000
R&D Expense						
Operating Income	222,000,000	441,600,000	348,700,000	513,800,000	477,900,000	439,900,000
Operating Margin %		.11%	.09%	.13%	.13%	.16%
SGA Expense	1,435,000,000	1,723,500,000	1,719,100,000	1,674,700,000	1,523,000,000	1,077,300,000
Net Income	-83,000,000	262,900,000	-1,011,000,000	-1,550,000,000	429,900,000	251,200,000
Operating Cash Flow	635,000,000	632,800,000	499,800,000	601,900,000	563,400,000	497,400,000
Capital Expenditure	87,000,000	122,900,000	188,000,000	151,000,000	126,100,000	72,000,000
EBITDA	322,000,000	697,600,000	-590,300,000	-1,248,800,000	748,500,000	508,500,000
Return on Assets %		.03%	-.11%	-.14%	.05%	.06%
Return on Equity %		.05%	-.17%	-.21%	.08%	.11%
Debt to Equity		0.305	0.306	0.244	0.186	0.488

CONTACT INFORMATION:

Phone: 844-546-3722   Fax:
Toll-Free: 800-877-0020
Address: 13320 Ballantyne Corporate Pl., Charlotte, NC 28277-3607 United States

STOCK TICKER/OTHER:

Stock Ticker: XRAY
Employees: 15,000
Parent Company:

Exchange: NAS
Fiscal Year Ends: 09/30

SALARIES/BONUSES:

Top Exec. Salary: $ Bonus: $
Second Exec. Salary: $ Bonus: $

OTHER THOUGHTS:

Estimated Female Officers or Directors: 1
Hot Spot for Advancement for Women/Minorities:

DePuy Synthes Inc

www.depuy.com

NAIC Code: 339100

TYPES OF BUSINESS:

Orthopedic Devices
Fixative Products
Orthopedic Systems
Orthopedic Devices
Product Manufacturing
Digital Surgery
Robotics
Hip Replacement

BRANDS/DIVISIONS/AFFILIATES:

Johnson & Johnson
VELYS
ATTUNE
ANTERIOR ADVANTAGE
TFN-ADVANCED
SYMPHONY
ON MY WAY
Patients & Caregiver Resource Center

CONTACTS: *Note: Officers with more than one job title may be intentionally listed here more than once.*

David Baker, Pres.
Steven L. Artusi, Sec.
Robert E. Morel, Pres., Depuy Ace Medical Company
Max Reinhardt, Pres., Depuy Synthes Spine

GROWTH PLANS/SPECIAL FEATURES:

DePuy Synthes, Inc., a subsidiary of Johnson & Johnson, designs, manufactures and distributes orthopedic systems and devices. The firm's products and solutions are utilized in fields such as joint reconstruction, trauma, craniomaxillofacial, spinal surgery and sports medicine. Featured innovations by DePuy Synthes include: VELYS digital surgery, ATTUNE knee system, ANTERIOR ADVANTAGE hip replacement, TFN-ADVANCED proximal femoral nailing system, SYMPHONY occipito-cervico-thoracic system, and TRUESPAN meniscal repair system, among many others. The company's ON MY WAY platform is a personalized digital patient program designed to help motivate, educate and support those considering joint replacement. The Patients & Caregiver Resource Center provides information on conditions, treatment options and the ability to find a local physician. During 2021, DePuy Synthes announced that it was further advancing its VELYS digital surgery platform using digital technology, robotics and data insights to improve patient care.

DePuy Synthes offers its employees medical, dental, vision, life, disability, accident, auto and home insurance; and flexible spending accounts.

FINANCIAL DATA: *Note: Data for latest year may not have been available at press time.*

In U.S. $	2020	2019	2018	2017	2016	2015
Revenue	10,587,500,000	9,625,000,000	9,555,000,000	9,100,000,000	9,003,500,000	9,320,000,000
R&D Expense						
Operating Income						
Operating Margin %						
SGA Expense						
Net Income						
Operating Cash Flow						
Capital Expenditure						
EBITDA						
Return on Assets %						
Return on Equity %						
Debt to Equity						

CONTACT INFORMATION:

Phone: Fax:
Toll-Free: 800-227-6633
Address: 325 Paramount Dr., Raynham, MA 02767 United States

STOCK TICKER/OTHER:

Stock Ticker: Subsidiary   Exchange:
Employees: 18,000   Fiscal Year Ends: 12/31
Parent Company: Johnson & Johnson

SALARIES/BONUSES:

Top Exec. Salary: $ Bonus: $
Second Exec. Salary: $ Bonus: $

OTHER THOUGHTS:

Estimated Female Officers or Directors:
Hot Spot for Advancement for Women/Minorities:

Detroit Medical Center (DMC)

NAIC Code: 622110

www.dmc.org

TYPES OF BUSINESS:

General Medical and Surgical Hospitals
Childrens Hospital
Emergency Care
Cancer Care
Women's Health
Orthopedic Services
Teaching Facilities
Ophthalmic Services

BRANDS/DIVISIONS/AFFILIATES:

Tenet Healthcare Corporation
Childrens Hospital of Michigan
DMC Detroit Receiving Hospital
DMC Harper University Hospital
DMC Huron Valley-Sinai Hospital
DMC Hutzel Women's Hospital
DMC Sinai-Grace Hospital
DMC Heart Hospital

CONTACTS: *Note: Officers with more than one job title may be intentionally listed here more than once.*

Rudolph P. Valentini, Chief Medical Officer
Joseph Mullany, Co-Pres.
Brittany Lavis, CFO
Gennie Snow, Chief Strategy Officer
Quadiru Kent, Chief Human Resources Officer
Suzanne R. White, Chief Medical Officer
Brian Taylor, Dir.-Communications & Media Relations
Conrad L. Mallett, Jr., Chief Admin. Officer
Shawn Levitt, Chief Nursing Officer
Sheri Underwood, Chief Nursing Officer

GROWTH PLANS/SPECIAL FEATURES:

Detroit Medical Center (DMC), part of Tenet Healthcare Corporation, is a healthcare provider in southeast Michigan. DMC comprises 10 hospitals, as well as ambulatory surgery centers, emergency centers, imaging centers, off-campus emergency departments and micro-hospitals, urgent care centers, surgery centers and rehabilitation/physical therapy centers. Some of DMC's hospitals are as follows. The Children's Hospital of Michigan is an international leader in pediatric neurology, neonatal and prenatal care, cardiology, rehabilitation and pediatric critical care. DMC Detroit Receiving Hospital trains almost 50% of Michigan's emergency physicians in the southeast; and provides back and spine, brain and neurology, diagnostics, digestive disorder, DMC, elderly care, emergency, same-day surgery and urology services. DMC Behavioral Health-Ardmore Clinic offers multidisciplinary evaluation and diagnosis, individual and family therapy, occupational therapy groups, medication management and case management services. DMC Harper University Hospital is a teaching institution offering neurological, hypertension and heart failure treatments as well as vascular and organ transplants. DMC Huron Valley-Sinai Hospital covers every stage of life from birthing to senior services and includes surgical suites and cardiac services. DMC Hutzel Women's Hospital's offerings include high-risk obstetrics, infertility treatment, reproductive genetics and gynecology. DMC Sinai-Grace Hospital's general medical services include family medicine, heart and cancer care, emergency medicine, obstetrics and gynecology. DMC Heart Hospital is Michigan's first and only heart hospital and provides immediate care to patients suffering from all forms of heart disease and vascular disease. The Rehabilitation Institute of Michigan (RIM) is one of the nation's largest hospitals that specializes in rehabilitation medicine and research. RIM provides spinal cord injury, brain injury, stroke, complex trauma and orthopedics and catastrophic injury care. It also serves sports injury patients.

FINANCIAL DATA: *Note: Data for latest year may not have been available at press time.*

In U.S. $	2020	2019	2018	2017	2016	2015
Revenue						
R&D Expense						
Operating Income						
Operating Margin %						
SGA Expense						
Net Income						
Operating Cash Flow						
Capital Expenditure						
EBITDA						
Return on Assets %						
Return on Equity %						
Debt to Equity						

CONTACT INFORMATION:

Phone: 313-745-5111		Fax: 313-578-3225
Toll-Free: 888-362-2500
Address: 3990 John R. St., Detroit, MI 48201 United States

STOCK TICKER/OTHER:

Stock Ticker: Subsidiary			Exchange:
Employees: 10,700			Fiscal Year Ends: 12/31
Parent Company: Tenet Healthcare Corporation

SALARIES/BONUSES:

Top Exec. Salary: $		Bonus: $
Second Exec. Salary: $		Bonus: $

OTHER THOUGHTS:

Estimated Female Officers or Directors: 3
Hot Spot for Advancement for Women/Minorities: Y

DexCom Inc

www.dexcom.com

NAIC Code: 339100

TYPES OF BUSINESS:

Surgical and Medical Instrument Manufacturing
Continuous Glucose Monitoring Systems
Manufacturing
Product Design

BRANDS/DIVISIONS/AFFILIATES:

DexCom G6
DexCom CLARITY
DexCom Follow App

CONTACTS: *Note: Officers with more than one job title may be intentionally listed here more than once.*

Quentin Blackford, CFO
Kevin Sayer, Director
Steven Pacelli, Executive VP, Divisional
Donald Abbey, Executive VP, Divisional
Andrew Balo, Executive VP, Divisional
Richard Doubleday, Executive VP
Patrick Murphy, General Counsel
Jeffrey Moy, Senior VP, Divisional
Jake Leach, Senior VP, Divisional
Heather Ace, Senior VP, Divisional

GROWTH PLANS/SPECIAL FEATURES:

DexCom, Inc. is a medical device company primarily focused on the design, development and commercialization of continuous glucose monitoring (CGM). These CGM systems are used by people with diabetes and by healthcare providers. DexCom's 6th generation of CGM systems, DexCom G6, sends glucose readings to the receiver's compatible smart device every five minutes with no fingersticks necessary. With the built-in Share functionality, the DexCom G6 can keep loved ones and caregivers informed about the glucose levels as well. DexCom CLARITY is a diabetes data reporting and management online platform that enables connected CGM users to view their data in easy-to-read graphs, view trends, statistics and day-by-day data, and even mail them to their healthcare professional from the DexCom CLARITY webpage. DexCom mobile and watch apps displays real-time glucose readings along with other features for diabetes management. The DexCom Follow App is for friends and family, enabling them to follow a user's glucose levels. DexCom manufactures its products at its headquarters in San Diego, California, which includes more than 31,000 square feet of laboratory space and approximately 28,000 square feet of controlled environment rooms. DexCom has a second manufacturing facility in Mesa, Arizona, and commenced construction of a new facility in Malaysia in 2020.

FINANCIAL DATA: *Note: Data for latest year may not have been available at press time.*

In U.S. $	2020	2019	2018	2017	2016	2015
Revenue	1,928,700,000	1,476,000,000	1,031,600,000	718,500,000	573,300,000	402,000,000
R&D Expense	359,900,000	273,500,000	417,400,000	185,400,000	156,100,000	137,500,000
Operating Income	299,500,000	142,300,000	-186,300,000	-42,500,000	-63,900,000	-57,100,000
Operating Margin %		.10%	-.18%	-.06%	-.11%	-.14%
SGA Expense	620,700,000	515,700,000	432,800,000	349,200,000	286,200,000	198,000,000
Net Income	493,600,000	101,100,000	-127,100,000	-50,200,000	-65,600,000	-57,600,000
Operating Cash Flow	475,600,000	314,500,000	123,200,000	92,000,000	56,200,000	49,000,000
Capital Expenditure	199,000,000	180,000,000	67,100,000	66,000,000	55,700,000	33,300,000
EBITDA	376,800,000	213,200,000	-74,700,000	-19,700,000	-49,200,000	-46,300,000
Return on Assets %		.05%	-.09%	-.08%	-.19%	-.24%
Return on Equity %		.13%	-.23%	-.14%	-.26%	-.32%
Debt to Equity		1.299	1.534	0.797		

CONTACT INFORMATION:

Phone: 855 200-0200   Fax: 858 200-0201
Toll-Free:
Address: 6340 Sequence Dr., San Diego, CA 92121 United States

STOCK TICKER/OTHER:

Stock Ticker: DXCM   Exchange: NAS
Employees: 6,400   Fiscal Year Ends: 12/31
Parent Company:

SALARIES/BONUSES:

Top Exec. Salary: $ Bonus: $
Second Exec. Salary: $ Bonus: $

OTHER THOUGHTS:

Estimated Female Officers or Directors:
Hot Spot for Advancement for Women/Minorities:

Diversicare Healthcare Services Inc

www.dvcr.com

NAIC Code: 623110

TYPES OF BUSINESS:

Nursing Care Facilities
Assisted Living Facilities
Post-Acute Care Services
Skilled Nursing Facilities

BRANDS/DIVISIONS/AFFILIATES:

CONTACTS: *Note: Officers with more than one job title may be intentionally listed here more than once.*

James McKnight, CEO
Kerry Massey, CFO
Angie Mulder, Sr. VP-Chief Compliance Officer
Alix Coulter Cross, Sr. VP-Human Resources
April Marbury, CIO
Chad McCurdy, Director

GROWTH PLANS/SPECIAL FEATURES:

Diversicare Healthcare Services, Inc. provides post-acute care services to skilled nursing facilities, patients and residents in eight U.S. states, primarily in the southeast, midwest and southwest regions. The firm serves aging, infirmed or disabled individuals who require extensive assistance and intensive care. These services include skilled nursing, comprehensive rehabilitation, memory care and other specialty care offerings. As of mid-2021, Diversicare's operations consisted of 61 nursing centers, with 7,250 licensed skilled nursing beds. The company owns 15 and leases 46 of its nursing centers, which range in size from 50 to 320 licensed nursing beds, which does not include 397 licensed assisted living beds. The centers are located in Alabama, Indiana, Kansas, Mississippi, Missouri, Ohio, Tennessee and Texas.

FINANCIAL DATA: *Note: Data for latest year may not have been available at press time.*

In U.S. $	2020	2019	2018	2017	2016	2015
Revenue	475,718,000	475,020,000	563,462,000	574,794,000	426,063,000	387,595,000
R&D Expense						
Operating Income	11,201,000	-2,967,000	-85,000	6,707,000	2,748,000	7,431,000
Operating Margin %		-.01%	.00%	.01%	.01%	.02%
SGA Expense	90,002,000	87,995,000	101,660,000	99,063,000	72,091,000	61,605,000
Net Income	5,159,000	-36,063,000	-7,396,000	-4,827,000	-1,811,000	1,624,000
Operating Cash Flow	46,816,000	5,332,000	5,651,000	12,060,000	-5,618,000	3,277,000
Capital Expenditure	5,596,000	4,980,000	8,578,000	18,480,000	13,572,000	15,546,000
EBITDA	44,018,000	25,226,000	9,750,000	19,215,000	10,320,000	15,294,000
Return on Assets %		-.12%	-.05%	-.03%	-.01%	.01%
Return on Equity %			-2.81%	-.54%	-.15%	.13%
Debt to Equity				11.545	6.317	4.09

CONTACT INFORMATION:

Phone: 615-771-7575   Fax:
Toll-Free:
Address: 1621 Galleria Blvd., Brentwood, TN 37027 United States

STOCK TICKER/OTHER:

Stock Ticker: DVCR   Exchange: PINX
Employees: 4,800   Fiscal Year Ends: 12/31
Parent Company:

SALARIES/BONUSES:

Top Exec. Salary: $ Bonus: $
Second Exec. Salary: $ Bonus: $

OTHER THOUGHTS:

Estimated Female Officers or Directors: 2
Hot Spot for Advancement for Women/Minorities:

DJO Global Inc

www.djoglobal.com

NAIC Code: 339100

TYPES OF BUSINESS:

Clinical Orthopedic Rehabilitation Products & Devices
Electrotherapy Products
Rehabilitation Products

BRANDS/DIVISIONS/AFFILIATES:

Colfax Corporation
Aircast
DJO Surgical
DonJoy
CMF
Dr Comfort
Compex
EMPOWR

CONTACTS: *Note: Officers with more than one job title may be intentionally listed here more than once.*

Brady R. Shirley, CEO
Ben Berry, CFO
James Keller, Sr. VP-Human Resources
Donald M. Roberts, General Counsel
Gerry McDonnell, Exec. VP-Global Oper.
Matt Simmons, Sr. VP-Bus. Dev.
Matt Simmons, Sr. VP-Investor Rel.
Vickie L. Capps, Treas.
Stephen Murphy, Exec. VP-Sales & Mktg., Int'l Commercial Bus.

GROWTH PLANS/SPECIAL FEATURES:

DJO Global, Inc. designs, manufactures, markets and distributes orthopedic devices, sports medicine equipment and other related products for the orthopedic industry worldwide. The firm's products are used to treat patients with musculoskeletal conditions resulting from degenerative diseases, deformities and acute injuries. DJO Global is the largest non-surgical orthopedic rehabilitation device company in the U.S. The company's products are used by orthopedic specialists, spine surgeons, primary care physicians, pain management specialists, physical therapists, podiatrists, chiropractors, athletic trainers and other healthcare professionals. In addition, many of DJO Global's non-surgical medical devices and accessories are used by athletes and patients for injury prevention and at-home physical therapy treatment. Products include walking braces, ankle braces, knee braces, wrist braces, custom braces, spine braces, treatment tables, therapy systems, cold therapy, bone growth stimulation, orthotics, compression solutions, shoes, muscle stimulators and more. Brands of DJO include Aircast, DJO Surgical, Chattanooga, DonJoy, CMF (combined magnetic field), Dr. Comfort, Compex, EMPOWR and Procare, among others. DJO has approximately 12 facilities worldwide, and over 1,000 medical devices. DJO Global operates as a subsidiary of Colfax Corporation, a diversified technology company. During 2021, DJO Global acquired MedShape, Inc., an orthopedic medical device company that provides innovative surgical solutions for foot and ankle surgeons using its patented super-elastic nickel titanium (NiTiNOL) shape memory alloy and shape memory polymer technologies.

DJO offers its employees medical, dental, vision, home, life, AD&D, auto, pet and disability insurance; a 401(k); spending and savings accounts; and legal services, among other benefits.

FINANCIAL DATA: *Note: Data for latest year may not have been available at press time.*

In U.S. $	2020	2019	2018	2017	2016	2015
Revenue	1,377,530,000	1,252,300,000	1,249,500,000	1,190,000,000	1,155,288,000	1,113,627,000
R&D Expense						
Operating Income						
Operating Margin %						
SGA Expense						
Net Income				-35,900,000	-286,303,000	-340,927,000
Operating Cash Flow						
Capital Expenditure						
EBITDA						
Return on Assets %						
Return on Equity %						
Debt to Equity						

CONTACT INFORMATION:

Phone: Fax:
Toll-Free: 800-321-9549
Address: 2900 Lake Vista Dr., Ste. 200, Dallas, TX 75067 United States

STOCK TICKER/OTHER:

Stock Ticker: Subsidiary   Exchange:
Employees: 5,000   Fiscal Year Ends: 12/31
Parent Company: Colfax Corporation

SALARIES/BONUSES:

Top Exec. Salary: $ Bonus: $
Second Exec. Salary: $ Bonus: $

OTHER THOUGHTS:

Estimated Female Officers or Directors: 2
Hot Spot for Advancement for Women/Minorities:

Draegerwerk AG & Co KGaA

www.draeger.com/en_corp/Home

NAIC Code: 339100

TYPES OF BUSINESS:

Surgical and Medical Instrument Manufacturing
Clinical Software and IT Solutions
Fire Detectors
Gas Detectors
Medical Gas Management Systems
Ventilation Systems
Patient Monitoring Systems

BRANDS/DIVISIONS/AFFILIATES:

Drager Babylog
Carina
Oxylog
Infinity
Innovian
STIMIT AG

CONTACTS: *Note: Officers with more than one job title may be intentionally listed here more than once.*

Gert-Hartwig Lescow, CFO
Herbert Fehrecke, Head-R&D
Gert-Hartwig Lescow, Head-Finance
Anton Schrofner, Head-Production & Logistics
Stefan Drager, Chmn.
Herbert Fehrecke, Head-Purchasing

GROWTH PLANS/SPECIAL FEATURES:

Draegerwerk AG & Co KGaA is an international enterprise active in the fields of medical and safety technology. The firm's products include fire and gas detectors; medical gas management systems; ventilation systems for pediatric, adult and neonatal care; anesthesia workstations; warming therapy and neonatal care systems; jaundice management; patient monitoring systems; accessories and consumables such as expiration valves, breathing masks and peep valves; maintenance and training services; clinical IT and software solutions; and architectural systems and lights. Some of the firm's ventilation family of brands include Drager Babylog, Carina and Oxylog. Patient monitoring systems include the Infinity brand line. Clinical software and solutions consist of Innovian Anesthesia and the Infinity suite. The enterprise is represented in over 190 countries, with sales and service subsidiaries in over 50 countries. The firm's development and production facilities are based in Germany, Chile, China, Czech Republic, India, Norway, South Africa, Sweden, the U.K. and the U.S. During 2021, Draegerwerk acquired the majority share of STIMIT AG, a Swiss medical technology startup that will further expand Draegerwerk's expertise in the field of lung-protective ventilation.

Draegerwerk offers its employees a work/life balance schedule, retirement plans and an employee assistance program. Other benefits vary by region.

FINANCIAL DATA: *Note: Data for latest year may not have been available at press time.*

In U.S. $	2020	2019	2018	2017	2016	2015
Revenue	4,161,710,000	3,397,547,000	3,170,523,000	3,142,723,000	3,083,567,000	3,187,518,000
R&D Expense	353,820,500	322,191,100	308,096,700	286,719,300	267,596,000	282,349,000
Operating Income	502,964,000	100,965,200	78,290,250	186,956,300	188,587,400	97,727,500
Operating Margin %		.03%	.02%	.06%	.06%	.03%
SGA Expense	1,108,255,000	1,027,936,000	966,534,300	933,440,000	931,115,000	1,052,170,000
Net Income	305,638,500	40,746,260	41,974,150	120,308,400	100,284,700	40,319,860
Operating Cash Flow	561,993,000	200,884,600	4,997,068	175,124,600	238,639,900	48,701,250
Capital Expenditure	140,431,000	78,670,220	75,415,410	86,410,180	97,448,930	139,757,800
EBITDA	488,011,900	85,088,220	80,741,130	192,318,700	171,168,500	81,617,140
Return on Assets %		.01%	.01%	.03%	.03%	.01%
Return on Equity %		.02%	.02%	.07%	.06%	.04%
Debt to Equity		0.186	0.123	0.137	0.197	0.155

CONTACT INFORMATION:

Phone: 49 4518820   Fax: 49 4518822080
Toll-Free:
Address: Moislinger Allee 53-55, Lubeck, 23558 Germany

STOCK TICKER/OTHER:

Stock Ticker: DRWKF   Exchange: GREY
Employees: 15,657   Fiscal Year Ends: 12/31
Parent Company:

SALARIES/BONUSES:

Top Exec. Salary: $ Bonus: $
Second Exec. Salary: $ Bonus: $

OTHER THOUGHTS:

Estimated Female Officers or Directors:
Hot Spot for Advancement for Women/Minorities:

Dynacq Healthcare Inc

www.dynacq.com

NAIC Code: 622110

TYPES OF BUSINESS:

Acute Care Hospital
Outpatient Surgery Facilities
Freestanding Ambulatory Surgical and Emergency Centers
Fertility Treatments
Orthopedic Surgery
Bariatric Surgery

BRANDS/DIVISIONS/AFFILIATES:

GROWTH PLANS/SPECIAL FEATURES:

Dynacq Healthcare, Inc. developed and manages a specialty surgical hospital and ambulatory surgery center in Pasadena, Texas. The facility specializes in orthopedics, neurosurgery and general surgery. Surgeons are able to reserve large blocks of time in adjoining operating rooms to perform consecutive procedures without disruptions likened to those within general hospitals, such as emergencies. Surgeons have access to adjacent operating rooms in close proximity to intensive care and diagnostic units.

CONTACTS: *Note: Officers with more than one job title may be intentionally listed here more than once.*

Eric K. Chan, CEO
Hemant Khemka, CFO
Ringo Cheng, Dir.-IT
Eric K. Chan, Chmn.

FINANCIAL DATA: *Note: Data for latest year may not have been available at press time.*

In U.S. $	2020	2019	2018	2017	2016	2015
Revenue	6,541,496	7,695,878	7,329,408	7,715,167	7,347,778	6,997,884
R&D Expense						
Operating Income						
Operating Margin %						
SGA Expense						
Net Income						
Operating Cash Flow						
Capital Expenditure						
EBITDA						
Return on Assets %						
Return on Equity %						
Debt to Equity						

CONTACT INFORMATION:

Phone: 713 378-2000   Fax: 713 944-0201
Toll-Free:
Address: 4301 Vista Rd., Pasadena, TX 77504 United States

STOCK TICKER/OTHER:

Stock Ticker: Private   Exchange:
Employees: 126   Fiscal Year Ends: 08/31
Parent Company:

SALARIES/BONUSES:

Top Exec. Salary: $ Bonus: $
Second Exec. Salary: $ Bonus: $

OTHER THOUGHTS:

Estimated Female Officers or Directors:
Hot Spot for Advancement for Women/Minorities:

Ebos Group Limited

NAIC Code: 424210

www.ebos.co.nz

TYPES OF BUSINESS:

Drugs and Druggists' Sundries Merchant Wholesalers
Healthcare Products
Medical Products
Pharmaceuticals
Pet Care Products

BRANDS/DIVISIONS/AFFILIATES:

Symbion
Endeavor Consumer Health
TerryWhite Chemmart
EBOS Healthcare
LMT
OneLink
Masterpet
Lyppard

CONTACTS: *Note: Officers with more than one job title may be intentionally listed here more than once.*

John Cullity, CEO
Leonard Hansen, CFO
Andrea Bell, CIO

GROWTH PLANS/SPECIAL FEATURES:

Ebos Group Limited is a diversified Australian marketer, wholesaler and distributor of healthcare, medical and pharmaceutical products. The firm also markets and distributes animal care products. Ebos' business is divided into four categories: community pharmacy, institutional healthcare, contract logistics and animal care. The community pharmacy business delivers pharmaceutical, over-the-counter medicines and related consumer products to pharmacies across Australia and New Zealand. Product brands include Symbion, Endeavor Consumer Health, ProPharma, DoseAid, Minfos, Red Seal, Ventura Health, TerryWhite Chemmart, Pharmacy Choice, healthSAVE, Pharmacy Wholesalers Russells, Intellipharm and Good Price Pharmacy Warehouse. The institutional healthcare business supplies a range of products and services to public and private hospitals, doctors' surgeries and aged care facilities. Product brands include EBOS Healthcare, LMT, Onelink, Symbion Hospital Services, Clinect, Zest and HPS. The contract logistics business offers services to pharmaceutical manufacturers, medical device suppliers and consumer healthcare companies. These services primarily include warehousing, distribution and logistics support, but also includes specialized logistics services for the clinical research industry. Last, animal care business provides sales, marketing, wholesale and distribution support to pet retailers, veterinarians and grocery stores. It also holds a retail presence in New Zealand. Animal care brands include Masterpet, Lyppard, Animates, Vitapet and Black Hawk.

FINANCIAL DATA: *Note: Data for latest year may not have been available at press time.*

In U.S. $	2020	2019	2018	2017	2016	2015
Revenue	6,805,011,000	5,259,268,000	5,519,401,000	5,531,272,000	5,150,909,000	4,401,370,000
R&D Expense						
Operating Income	205,067,800	173,127,900	172,228,500	159,564,200	148,329,600	125,546,200
Operating Margin %		.03%	.03%	.03%	.03%	.03%
SGA Expense	252,191,500	259,386,800	259,211,700	214,401,500	191,449,100	172,095,100
Net Income	126,168,700	104,496,900	108,483,500	96,357,380	92,114,920	76,842,340
Operating Cash Flow						
Capital Expenditure	18,137,560	21,602,100	45,945,400	10,641,340	8,069,313	11,199,840
EBITDA	253,753,500	191,491,900	198,859,100	171,545,200	165,359,600	144,336,600
Return on Assets %		.04%	.05%	.04%	.04%	.04%
Return on Equity %		.12%	.13%	.12%	.12%	.10%
Debt to Equity		0.293	0.397	0.39	0.24	0.26

CONTACT INFORMATION:

Phone: 613-9918-5555   Fax: 613-9918-5599
Toll-Free:
Address: Level 7, 737 Bourke St., Docklands, VIC 3008 Australia

STOCK TICKER/OTHER:

Stock Ticker: EBOSY   Exchange: GREY
Employees: 3,700   Fiscal Year Ends: 06/30
Parent Company:

SALARIES/BONUSES:

Top Exec. Salary: $ Bonus: $
Second Exec. Salary: $ Bonus: $

OTHER THOUGHTS:

Estimated Female Officers or Directors:
Hot Spot for Advancement for Women/Minorities:

eClinicalWorks

www.eClinicalWorks.com

NAIC Code: 511210D

TYPES OF BUSINESS:

Computer Software, Healthcare & Biotechnology
Electronic Prescription Filing
Patient Flow Management
Claims Submission & Management Software
Business Optimization Software

BRANDS/DIVISIONS/AFFILIATES:

healow TeleVisits

CONTACTS: *Note: Officers with more than one job title may be intentionally listed here more than once.*

Girish Kumar Navani, CEO

GROWTH PLANS/SPECIAL FEATURES:

eClinicalWorks is a private company operating in the ambulatory clinical systems market. The company primarily provides electronic health record (EHR) and practice management tools for its clients, including physicians; large and small health systems; large and medium medical group practices, including federally qualified health centers and community health centers; and small, solo provider practices. The firm's customer base consists of more than 130,000 physicians and over 850,000 medical professionals in all 50 states and 24 countries. eClinicalWorks' EHR cloud solution provides patient flow management, patient record access, registry reporting, electronic prescription request, referring physician communication and clinical data transfers, all while keeping the data private. When used with the firm's patient management system, the solution enables clients to: review patient history, current medications, allergies and diagnostic tests; streamline medical billing management; check patient insurance eligibility; electronically submit and manage claims; and perform clinical and financial analyses through its patient engagement and enterprise business optimizing tools. Healow TeleVisits delivers an in-office experience via online devices, and offer pre-op consultations, post-op checkups and routine-based encounters. TeleVisits are secure and fully integrated into EHR and patient records. eClincialWorks's population health solution covers the population health across all functional accountable care organization (ACO) categories; and the revenue cycle management console assists in processing claims, financial analytics, reimbursement evaluation and six levels of clearinghouse integrations. The company's cloud platform keeps private data private, and each client's database cannot be affected by another practice's upgrades.

eClinicalWorks offers its employees health, dental, vision, life and disability insurance; flexible spending accounts; and a 401(k) plan.

FINANCIAL DATA: *Note: Data for latest year may not have been available at press time.*

In U.S. $	2020	2019	2018	2017	2016	2015
Revenue	615,000,000	600,000,000	490,000,000	462,000,000	440,000,000	358,000,000
R&D Expense						
Operating Income						
Operating Margin %						
SGA Expense						
Net Income						
Operating Cash Flow						
Capital Expenditure						
EBITDA						
Return on Assets %						
Return on Equity %						
Debt to Equity						

CONTACT INFORMATION:

Phone: 508-836-2700   Fax: 508-836-4466
Toll-Free: 866-888-6929
Address: 2 Technology Dr., Westborough, MA 01581 United States

STOCK TICKER/OTHER:

Stock Ticker: Private
Employees: 5,000
Parent Company:

Exchange:
Fiscal Year Ends: 12/31

SALARIES/BONUSES:

Top Exec. Salary: $ Bonus: $
Second Exec. Salary: $ Bonus: $

OTHER THOUGHTS:

Estimated Female Officers or Directors:
Hot Spot for Advancement for Women/Minorities:

EDAP TMS SA

www.edap-tms.com

NAIC Code: 339100

TYPES OF BUSINESS:

Ultrasound Equipment
High Intensity Focused Ultrasound Equipment
Prostate Cancer Treatment Technology

BRANDS/DIVISIONS/AFFILIATES:

Ablatherm
Ablatherm Fusion
Focal One
EXACTVU
Sonolith i-move
Sonolith i-sys
Laserlith i-dust
Endo-UP

CONTACTS: *Note: Officers with more than one job title may be intentionally listed here more than once.*

Marc Oczachowski, CEO
Francois Dietsch, CFO

GROWTH PLANS/SPECIAL FEATURES:

EDAP TMS SA is a French holding company that through its subsidiaries develops, manufactures, markets and distributes minimally-invasive medical devices for urology using ultrasound technology. The firm's operations are grouped into two divisions: high-intensity focused ultrasound (HIFU) and urology devices and services (UDS). The HIFU division produces devices for the minimally-invasive removal of certain types of localized tumors using HIFU technology. This technology uses a high-intensity ultrasound beam generated by transducers to produce heat. The process allows the surgeon to destroy an area of diseased tissue without damaging surrounding tissue and organs, thereby eliminating the need for incisions, transfusions and general anesthesia and associated complications. The HIFU division markets four devices: the Ablatherm, the Ablatherm Fusion, EXACTVU and the Focal One. Ablatherm and Ablatherm Fusion treat organ-defined prostate cancer; EXACTVU is a micro-ultrasound system for targeted biopsies for prostate cancer; and Focal One is a fully robotic device for localizing and destroying the targeted cancer cells and nothing else. The UDS division produces medical devices for the diagnosis and treatment of urological disorders, primarily urinary stones, but other clinical indications as well. These devices are known as lithotripters, which treat urinary stones via extracorporeal shockwave lithotripsy (ESWL) technology. The shockwaves can be focused at urinary stones within the human body to fragment the stones, and thereby enabling their natural elimination and preventing the need for incisions, transfusions, general anesthesia and associated complications. The UDS division manufactures two models of lithotripters: the Sonolith i-move and the Sonolith i-sys. In addition, Laserlith i-dust assures a more stable position of the calculi/stone and therefore eliminates the need for basket extraction, reducing the total procedure duration; and Endo-UP is an endourology multi-modality platform designed for the management of urinary stones.

FINANCIAL DATA: *Note: Data for latest year may not have been available at press time.*

In U.S. $	2020	2019	2018	2017	2016	2015
Revenue	50,901,670	54,871,220	47,871,660	43,673,640	43,508,700	39,405,970
R&D Expense	5,493,109	4,554,785	4,994,624	4,741,717	4,725,834	3,286,580
Operating Income	328,658	2,687,909	-1,606,637	-2,476,542	477,715	595,005
Operating Margin %		.05%	- .03%	- .06%	.01%	.02%
SGA Expense	16,633,270	18,417,070	17,280,810	15,826,900	14,847,030	12,960,610
Net Income	-2,081,908	1,847,327	-412,961	-832,030	4,694,067	-2,036,702
Operating Cash Flow	2,415,453	4,642,753	213,811	-3,737,416	1,367,168	1,634,738
Capital Expenditure	2,410,566	1,772,798	2,283,501	2,531,522	1,620,076	794,155
EBITDA	1,252,321	5,174,226	2,127,114	1,617,633	6,751,540	194,263
Return on Assets %		.03%	- .01%	- .01%	.09%	- .05%
Return on Equity %		.06%	- .01%	- .03%	.20%	- .11%
Debt to Equity		0.122	0.088	0.054	0.029	0.061

CONTACT INFORMATION:

Phone: 33 472153150   Fax: 33 472153150
Toll-Free: 800-541-8414
Address: 4/6 rue du Dauphine, Vaulx-en-Velin, 69120 France

STOCK TICKER/OTHER:

Stock Ticker: EDAP
Employees: 223
Parent Company:

Exchange: NAS
Fiscal Year Ends: 12/31

SALARIES/BONUSES:

Top Exec. Salary: $ Bonus: $
Second Exec. Salary: $ Bonus: $

OTHER THOUGHTS:

Estimated Female Officers or Directors:
Hot Spot for Advancement for Women/Minorities:

Edwards Lifesciences Corporation

www.edwards.com

NAIC Code: 339100

TYPES OF BUSINESS:

Supplies-Cardiovascular Disease Related
Cardiac Surgery Products
Critical Care Products
Vascular Products
Heart Valve Implants
Software

BRANDS/DIVISIONS/AFFILIATES:

Carpentier-Edwards PERIMOUNT
Edwards Intuity
Edwards SAPIEN
PASCAL
Cardioband
PERIMOUNT Magna Ease
INSPIRIS RESILIA

CONTACTS: *Note: Officers with more than one job title may be intentionally listed here more than once.*

Michael Mussallem, CEO
Scott Ullem, CFO
Donald Bobo, Vice President
Larry Wood, Vice President, Divisional
Catherine Szyman, Vice President, Divisional
Daveen Chopra, Vice President, Divisional
Jean-Luc Lemercier, Vice President, Geographical
Huimin Wang, Vice President, Geographical

GROWTH PLANS/SPECIAL FEATURES:

Edwards Lifesciences Corporation designs products for cardiovascular diseases, such as heart valve disease, coronary artery disease, peripheral vascular disease (PVD) and congestive heart failure. The firm operates in four main areas: surgical structural heart (16% of 2020 net sales), transcatheter aortic valve replacement (65%), transcatheter mitral and tricuspid therapies, and critical care (9%). Surgical structural heart products include the Carpentier-Edwards PERIMOUNT line of pericardial heart valves made from biologically inert porcine tissue, often on a wire-form stent; and valve repair therapies, such as the Edwards Intuity valve system, a minimally-invasive aortic system designed to enable a faster procedure and a smaller incision. Transcatheter aortic valve replacement technologies are designed for the non-surgical replacement of heart valves. Its main products are the Edwards SAPIEN, Edwards Sapien XT, Edwards Sapien 3 and Edwards Sapien 3 Ultra transcatheter aortic heart valves and delivery systems used to treat heart valve disease using catheter-based approaches for patients deemed at high risk for traditional open-heart surgery. The transcatheter mitral and tricuspid therapies division is making investments in the development of transcatheter heart valve repair and replacement technologies designed to treat mitral and tricuspid valve diseases. Many of these technologies are in early development and clinical phases, but the PASCAL transcatheter valve repair system and the Cardioband systems are commercially available in Europe. Surgical structural heart products include annuloplasty rings, cardiac cannula devices and the Carpentier-Edwards PERIMOUNT pericardial valve platform, including the line of PERIMOUNT Magna Ease valves for aortic and mitral surgical valve replacement. This division's INSPIRIS RESILIA aortic valve is built on the PERMOUNT platform and offers RESILIA tissue and VFit technology. In mid-2021, Edwards announced that its Acumen Hypotension Prediction Index software with the Acumen IQ finger cuff received U.S. Food and Drug Administration clearance.

Edwards offers comprehensive benefits and retirement plans.

FINANCIAL DATA: *Note: Data for latest year may not have been available at press time.*

In U.S. $	2020	2019	2018	2017	2016	2015
Revenue	4,386,300,000	4,348,000,000	3,722,800,000	3,435,300,000	2,963,700,000	2,493,700,000
R&D Expense	760,700,000	752,700,000	622,200,000	552,600,000	477,800,000	383,100,000
Operating Income	1,316,600,000	1,238,700,000	1,072,700,000	1,022,700,000	783,800,000	642,700,000
Operating Margin %		.28%	.29%	.30%	.26%	.26%
SGA Expense	1,228,400,000	1,242,200,000	1,088,500,000	984,700,000	904,700,000	850,700,000
Net Income	823,400,000	1,046,900,000	722,200,000	583,600,000	569,500,000	494,900,000
Operating Cash Flow	1,054,300,000	1,179,400,000	926,800,000	1,000,700,000	704,400,000	549,700,000
Capital Expenditure	407,300,000	278,400,000	241,700,000	175,500,000	217,400,000	106,500,000
EBITDA	1,039,700,000	1,276,500,000	868,700,000	1,140,000,000	828,300,000	705,400,000
Return on Assets %		.18%	.13%	.11%	.13%	.13%
Return on Equity %		.29%	.24%	.21%	.22%	.21%
Debt to Equity		0.157	0.189	0.148	0.314	0.24

CONTACT INFORMATION:

Phone: 949 250-2500   Fax: 949 250-2525
Toll-Free: 800-424-3278
Address: 1 Edwards Way, Irvine, CA 92614 United States

SALARIES/BONUSES:

Top Exec. Salary: $ Bonus: $
Second Exec. Salary: $ Bonus: $

STOCK TICKER/OTHER:

Stock Ticker: EW
Employees: 14,900
Parent Company:

Exchange: NYS
Fiscal Year Ends: 12/31

OTHER THOUGHTS:

Estimated Female Officers or Directors: 3
Hot Spot for Advancement for Women/Minorities: Y

Sales, profits and employees may be estimates. Financial information, benefits and other data can change quickly and may vary from those stated here.

Elara Caring

www.elara.com

NAIC Code: 621610

TYPES OF BUSINESS:

Home Health Care Services
Disease Management Services
Physical, Occupational & Speech Therapies
Staffing Services
Medical Social Services
Mental Health Services

BRANDS/DIVISIONS/AFFILIATES:

Blue Wolf Capital Partners LLC
Kelso & Company
National Home Health Care Corp
Great Lakes Home Health Services Inc
Jordan Health Services

CONTACTS: Note: Officers with more than one job title may be intentionally listed here more than once.

Scott Powers, CEO
Ian Gordon, Pres.-Oper.
Steven Fialkow, Pres.
Bruce Jarvie, CFO
Jeff Bonham, Pres.-Markets
Patricia Bradford, Chief Human Resources Officer
Kyle Seiter, CIO
Steven Fialkow, Corp. Sec.
R. Scott Gasset, Chief Bus. Dev. & Strategic Officer
Robert P. Heller, VP-Finance
Joseph Jasser, Chief Medical Officer

GROWTH PLANS/SPECIAL FEATURES:

Elara Caring, a product of the merger of National Home Health Care Corp.; Great Lakes Home Health Services, Inc.; and Jordan Health Services, is a provider of home health care services. The company is comprised of 35,000 caregivers serving over 60,000 patients and their families daily, in 225 locations across 16 states. Elara Caring provides home health care services including nursing, physical therapy, occupational therapy, speech therapy, medical social work and home health aide; hospice care services including physician services, nursing care, Chaplain, spiritual counseling, bereavement support and dietary counseling; behavioral health services supporting a wide-range of behavioral health conditions, with focus on assessment, education & action plans that promote recovery; and personal care services where a team personal care nurses, certified home health aides and attendants provide in-home assistance for qualified individuals with focus on help with activities of daily living, home safety and personal care. Elara Caring is owned by the private equity firms Blue Wolf Capital Partners, LLC and Kelso & Company.

FINANCIAL DATA: Note: Data for latest year may not have been available at press time.

In U.S. $	2020	2019	2018	2017	2016	2015
Revenue						
R&D Expense						
Operating Income						
Operating Margin %						
SGA Expense						
Net Income						
Operating Cash Flow						
Capital Expenditure						
EBITDA						
Return on Assets %						
Return on Equity %						
Debt to Equity						

CONTACT INFORMATION:

Phone: Fax:
Toll-Free: 800-286-6300
Address: 3010 Lyndon B. Johnson Fwy., Ste. 1100, Dallas, TX 75234 United States

STOCK TICKER/OTHER:

Stock Ticker: Private   Exchange:
Employees: 35,000   Fiscal Year Ends: 07/31
Parent Company: Blue Wolf Capital Partners LLC

SALARIES/BONUSES:

Top Exec. Salary: $ Bonus: $
Second Exec. Salary: $ Bonus: $

OTHER THOUGHTS:

Estimated Female Officers or Directors:
Hot Spot for Advancement for Women/Minorities:

Electromed Inc

NAIC Code: 339100

www.smartvest.com

TYPES OF BUSINESS:

Medical Device Manufacturing
Medical Devices
Product Development
Product Manufacture
Airway Clearance Therapy

BRANDS/DIVISIONS/AFFILIATES:

SmartVest Airway Clearance System
SmartVest Connect
SmartVest Wrap

CONTACTS: *Note: Officers with more than one job title may be intentionally listed here more than once.*

Kathleen Skarvan, CEO
Jeremy Brock, CFO
Stephen Craney, Chairman of the Board

GROWTH PLANS/SPECIAL FEATURES:

Electromed, Inc. is a medical device company that develops, manufactures, markets and sells products that provide airway clearance therapy to patients with compromised pulmonary functioning. Its principal product is the SmartVest Airway Clearance System. The SmartVest System generates high frequency chest wall oscillation (HFCWO), a technique for airway clearance therapy, also known as High Frequency Chest Compression. The vest, which is FDA approved to treat the condition of excess lung secretions, is worn over the torso and repeatedly compresses and releases the chest at frequencies from 5 to 20 cycles per second. Each compression (or oscillation) produces pulsations within the lungs that shear secretions from the surfaces of the airways and propels them toward the mouth where they can be removed by normal coughing. Consequently, it may be prescribed to patients suffering from cystic fibrosis, chronic obstructive pulmonary disease (COPD), muscular dystrophy, post-surgical airway complications and a variety of other diseases and conditions associated with impaired lung and airway capacity. By clearing airways, patients are able to rid their lungs of retained secretions and are therefore less likely to develop lung infections such as pneumonia. The SmartVest System is a doctor-prescribed therapy and, depending on the circumstances of the patient, its cost to an individual is generally reimbursable by Medicare, Medicaid and private insurance, or a combination of the three. Therapy can be tracked via SmartVest Connect wireless technology, providing collaboration between patient and healthcare professionals in treatment decisions. Additionally, Electromed markets the SmartVest Wrap, which functions in the same manner as the full system, but lacks a vest outer shell, making it more suitable for patients recovering from surgery and short-term illnesses.

FINANCIAL DATA: *Note: Data for latest year may not have been available at press time.*

In U.S. $	2020	2019	2018	2017	2016	2015
Revenue	32,470,690	31,299,750	28,697,620	25,861,140	22,992,000	19,408,380
R&D Expense	1,049,612	583,311	251,443	596,876	380,392	315,647
Operating Income	5,118,691	2,818,511	3,008,525	3,569,339	3,109,308	1,310,196
Operating Margin %		.09%	.10%	.14%	.14%	.07%
SGA Expense	19,944,850	20,446,120	19,596,050	16,402,210	14,386,560	11,974,380
Net Income	4,161,439	1,969,218	1,902,396	2,229,472	2,212,502	1,092,486
Operating Cash Flow	4,196,448	2,589,874	2,442,200	1,191,121	2,166,903	2,781,214
Capital Expenditure	977,196	1,388,388	571,777	687,148	579,521	624,507
EBITDA	5,856,921	3,743,738	3,798,552	4,341,510	3,848,010	2,048,739
Return on Assets %		.07%	.08%	.10%	.12%	.07%
Return on Equity %		.08%	.09%	.13%	.15%	.08%
Debt to Equity				0.058	0.071	0.086

CONTACT INFORMATION:

Phone: 952 758-9299   Fax:
Toll-Free: 800-462-1045
Address: 500 Sixth Ave. NW, New Prague, MN 56071 United States

SALARIES/BONUSES:

Top Exec. Salary: $ Bonus: $
Second Exec. Salary: $ Bonus: $

STOCK TICKER/OTHER:

Stock Ticker: ELMD   Exchange: ASE
Employees: 120   Fiscal Year Ends: 06/30
Parent Company:

OTHER THOUGHTS:

Estimated Female Officers or Directors: 1
Hot Spot for Advancement for Women/Minorities: Y

Sales, profits and employees may be estimates. Financial information, benefits and other data can change quickly and may vary from those stated here.

Elekta AB

NAIC Code: 339100

www.elekta.com

TYPES OF BUSINESS:

Radiation Technology
Radiosurgery Equipment
Medical Software
Medical Technology Development
Magnetic Resonance Products
Radiation Therapy Products
Particle Therapy

BRANDS/DIVISIONS/AFFILIATES:

Leksell Gamma Knife Icon
Versa HD
MOSAIQ
elekta Neuromag TRIUX
XiO

CONTACTS: *Note: Officers with more than one job title may be intentionally listed here more than once.*

Gustaf Salford, CEO
Asa Hedin, Exec. VP-Neuroscience
Michelle Joiner, Dir.-Global Public Rel.
Johan Andersson Melbi, Dir.-Investor Rel.
Gilbert Wai, Exec. VP-Asia Pacific
Ian Alexander, Exec. VP-Latin America & EMEA
Bill Yaeger, Exec. VP-Oncology
John Lapre, Exec. VP-Brachytherapy
James P. Hoey, Exec. VP-North America

GROWTH PLANS/SPECIAL FEATURES:

Elekta AB is a global developer of medical technology for oncology and the management of brain disorders. Products are divided into seven categories: radiotherapy, stereotactic radiosurgery, oncology informatics, brachytherapy, neurosurgery, particle therapy and MR/RT. Radiotherapy products include treatment delivery systems and solutions such as imaging, motion management, quality assurance solutions, beam shaping and patient positioning. Stereotactic radiosurgery (also referred to as Gamma Knife surgery) products include: the Leksell Gamma Knife Icon device, which limits radiation dose to healthy tissue and allows for precise treatment target areas during brain surgery; Leksell Gamma Knife Perfexion, for extreme accuracy during cranial radiosurgery; and Versa HD, an advanced linear accelerator capable of delivering dose conformance for an expanded range of targets. Oncology informatics include: the MOSAIQ Oncology line, which provides access to clinical and patient information; tools for sharing, analyzing and applying information; and treatment management for planning, delivery and assessment. Brachytherapy products include treatment delivery systems and solutions for precise, targeted treatment of various cancers such as prostate, breast, skin and surface, rectum and gynecological anatomy. Brachytherapy is suited as a single modality or in combination with other treatments such as external beam radiation. Neurosurgery diagnostic solutions include magnetoencephalography (MEG), a neuroimaging technique for mapping brain activity via magnetic signals. This division's Elekta Neuromag TRIUX addresses key MEG requirements critical for mapping studies. Particle therapy products include integrated software, services and treatment tools for building a proton therapy practice. This includes the MOSAIQ oncology information system, for care management; the XiO treatment planning software, with automated tools and dose calculation algorithms; patient positioning, immobilization and motion management tools; and support services. Last, MR/RT (magnetic resonance/radiation therapy) products enable clinicians to see and track difficult-to-visualize soft-tissue anatomies. Thousands of hospitals worldwide rely on Elekta technology.

FINANCIAL DATA: *Note: Data for latest year may not have been available at press time.*

In U.S. $	2020	2019	2018	2017	2016	2015
Revenue	1,766,307,000	1,639,771,000	1,370,972,000	1,294,881,000	1,357,423,000	
R&D Expense	200,450,000	192,586,800	132,464,000	123,149,100	128,834,800	
Operating Income	236,499,600	214,845,600	181,094,500	159,198,700	143,472,400	
Operating Margin %	.13%	.13%	.13%	.12%	.11%	
SGA Expense	306,905,100	282,468,800	260,814,900	253,193,600	285,735,000	
Net Income	131,133,300	144,924,000	132,947,800	15,121,460	16,573,120	
Operating Cash Flow	122,665,200	196,095,000	290,815,800	220,047,400	141,536,800	
Capital Expenditure	92,180,390	79,720,310	103,309,800	93,632,050	94,720,800	
EBITDA	356,019,600	324,083,000	267,589,300	145,649,900	128,592,900	
Return on Assets %	.04%	.05%	.05%	.01%	.01%	
Return on Equity %	.14%	.15%	.15%	.02%	.02%	
Debt to Equity	1.004	0.457	0.548	0.778	0.479	

CONTACT INFORMATION:

Phone: 46 858725400 Fax: 46 858725500
Toll-Free:
Address: Kungstensgatan 18, Stockholm, 113 57 Sweden

STOCK TICKER/OTHER:

Stock Ticker: EKTAY
Employees: 4,265
Parent Company:

Exchange: PINX
Fiscal Year Ends: 04/30

SALARIES/BONUSES:

Top Exec. Salary: $ Bonus: $
Second Exec. Salary: $ Bonus: $

OTHER THOUGHTS:

Estimated Female Officers or Directors: 4
Hot Spot for Advancement for Women/Minorities: Y

Sales, profits and employees may be estimates. Financial information, benefits and other data can change quickly and may vary from those stated here.

Eli Lilly and Company

www.lilly.com

NAIC Code: 325412

TYPES OF BUSINESS:

Pharmaceuticals Discovery & Development
Pharmaceuticals
Drug Development
Drug Discovery
Drug Production

BRANDS/DIVISIONS/AFFILIATES:

Humalog
Trulicity
Forteo
Cymbalta
Zyprexa
Alimta
Olumiant
Promoter Technologies

CONTACTS: *Note: Officers with more than one job title may be intentionally listed here more than once.*

Jeffrey Simmons, CEO, Subsidiary
Anne White, Pres., Divisional
David Ricks, CEO
Joshua Smiley, CFO
Donald Zakrowski, Chief Accounting Officer
Melissa Barnes, Chief Compliance Officer
Aarti Shah, Chief Information Officer
Daniel Skovronsky, Chief Scientific Officer
Michael Harrington, General Counsel
Alfonso Zulueta, President, Divisional
Enrique Conterno, President, Divisional
Myles ONeill, President, Divisional
Leigh Pusey, Senior VP, Divisional
Johna Norton, Senior VP, Divisional
Stephen Fry, Senior VP, Divisional

GROWTH PLANS/SPECIAL FEATURES:

Eli Lilly and Company discovers, develops, manufactures and markets human pharmaceutical products. Human pharmaceutical products are grouped into five divisions: endocrinology, neuroscience, oncology, immunology and other. Endocrinology products include: Humalog, Humulin, Baqsimi, Basaglar, Trajenta, Jardiance and Trulicity, for the treatment of diabetes; and Forteo, for osteoporosis in women. Neuroscience products include: Cymbalta, for major depressive disorder; Zyprexa, for schizophrenia; Strattera, for attention-deficit hyperactivity disorder; Emgality, for migraine prevention; and Reyvow, for acute treatment of migraine. Oncology products include: Alimta, for non-small cell lung cancer; Erbitux, for colorectal cancers; Cyramza, for advanced or metastatic gastric cancer; and Verzenio, for advanced/metastatic breast cancer. Immunology products include: Olumiant, for adults with moderately-to-severe active rheumatoid arthritis; and Taltz, for moderate-to-severe plaque psoriasis and active psoriatic arthritis. The other division consists of Cialis, a product for the treatment of erectile dysfunction and benign prostatic hyperplasia. In July 2021, Eli Lilly acquired Promoter Technologies, a private biotech company whose proprietary peptide- and protein-engineering platform is used to identify and synthesize molecules that can sense glucose or other endogenous modulators of protein activity. That same month, Eli Lilly announced a multi-year, exclusive collaboration with Kumquat Biosciences to discover, develop and commercialize potential novel small molecules that stimulate tumor-specific immune responses.

FINANCIAL DATA: *Note: Data for latest year may not have been available at press time.*

In U.S. $	2020	2019	2018	2017	2016	2015
Revenue	24,539,800,000	22,319,500,000	24,555,700,000	22,871,300,000	21,222,100,000	19,958,700,000
R&D Expense	6,085,700,000	5,595,000,000	5,307,100,000	5,281,800,000	5,243,900,000	4,796,400,000
Operating Income	6,849,600,000	5,789,500,000	6,186,800,000	4,417,500,000	3,871,300,000	3,592,100,000
Operating Margin %		.25%	.17%	.14%	.18%	.15%
SGA Expense	6,121,200,000	6,213,800,000	6,631,800,000	7,101,800,000	6,452,000,000	6,533,000,000
Net Income	6,193,700,000	8,318,400,000	3,232,000,000	-204,100,000	2,737,600,000	2,408,400,000
Operating Cash Flow	6,499,600,000	4,836,600,000	5,524,500,000	5,615,600,000	4,851,000,000	2,772,800,000
Capital Expenditure	2,029,100,000	1,353,500,000	3,018,200,000	2,163,600,000	1,092,000,000	1,626,200,000
EBITDA	8,913,400,000	6,899,100,000	5,676,800,000	3,989,700,000	5,055,800,000	4,378,900,000
Return on Assets %		.20%	.07%	.00%	.07%	.07%
Return on Equity %		1.34%	.30%	- .02%	.19%	.16%
Debt to Equity		5.487	1.184	0.858	0.597	0.547

CONTACT INFORMATION:

Phone: 317 276-2000   Fax:
Toll-Free:
Address: Lilly Corporate Center, Indianapolis, IN 46285 United States

STOCK TICKER/OTHER:

Stock Ticker: LLY
Employees: 33,625
Parent Company:

Exchange: NYS
Fiscal Year Ends: 12/31

SALARIES/BONUSES:

Top Exec. Salary: $ Bonus: $
Second Exec. Salary: $ Bonus: $

OTHER THOUGHTS:

Estimated Female Officers or Directors: 8
Hot Spot for Advancement for Women/Minorities: Y

EmblemHealth Inc

NAIC Code: 524114

www.emblemhealth.com

TYPES OF BUSINESS:

Insurance-Medical & Health, HMOs & PPOs
Health Insurance
Medicare
Medicaid
Enhanced Care Plus
Child Health Plus

BRANDS/DIVISIONS/AFFILIATES:

AdvantageCare
ConnectiCare
WellSpark

CONTACTS: Note: Officers with more than one job title may be intentionally listed here more than once.

Karen. M. Ignagni, CEO
Jennifer Truscott, Chief of Operations
Healther Tamborino, CFO
Debra Lightner, Chief Compliance Officer
Donna Hughes, Chief Human Resources Officer
William A. Gillespie, Chief Medical Officer
Thomas MacMillan, CIO
William Mastro, Corp. Sec.
Anne R. Cooke, Sr. VP-Corp. Oper.
Michael Palmateer, Sr. VP-Finance
Shawn M. Fitzgibbon, Sr. VP-Network Mgmt.
George Babitsch, Sr. VP-Underwriting & Account Management
David S. Abernethy, Sr. VP-Gov't Rel.
Jeffrey D. Chansler, Sr. VP
Richard Dal Col, Chief Medical Officer

GROWTH PLANS/SPECIAL FEATURES:

EmblemHealth, Inc. is a nonprofit health insurer, offering a range of commercial and government-sponsored health plans for large and small groups, individuals and families. The company primarily serves the state of New York, but also participates in state exchanges established within New Jersey and Connecticut. EmblemHealth's healthcare plans include Medicare Advantage options with low monthly premiums; the firm is one of the largest Medicare providers in the New York area. Other options include: health and wellness and pharmacy plans for large groups with more than 100 full-time eligible employees, including labor unions and higher education institutions; health and wellness and pharmacy plans for small groups, with less than 100 full-time eligible employees; standard and non-standard plans, catastrophic options and an essential plan that includes dental and vision options for individuals and families; and Medicaid, Enhanced Care Plus (HARP) and Child Health Plus government-sponsored plans. EmblemHealth offers supplements to its traditional health insurance options with a range of programs and discounts for alternative medical practices such as acupuncture, massage therapy and nutritional counseling; mental health services and chemical dependency treatments; pharmacy services; dental plans; and women's wellness programs. EmblemHealth family of companies include AdvantageCare, practicing primary and specialty care; ConnectiCare, a leading health plan in Connecticut; and WellSpark, offering well-being solutions for companies and their employees.

EmblemHealth offers its employees helth insurance, tuition reimbursement, professional development programs, 401(k), income protection and employee assistance programs.

FINANCIAL DATA: Note: Data for latest year may not have been available at press time.

In U.S. $	2020	2019	2018	2017	2016	2015
Revenue	10,272,905,526	9,600,846,286	9,143,663,130	8,708,250,600	8,293,572,000	8,163,969,000
R&D Expense						
Operating Income						
Operating Margin %						
SGA Expense						
Net Income						
Operating Cash Flow						
Capital Expenditure						
EBITDA						
Return on Assets %						
Return on Equity %						
Debt to Equity						

CONTACT INFORMATION:

Phone: 646-447-5000   Fax:
Toll-Free:
Address: 55 Water St., New York, NY 10041 United States

STOCK TICKER/OTHER:

Stock Ticker: Private
Employees: 4,700
Parent Company:

Exchange:
Fiscal Year Ends: 12/31

SALARIES/BONUSES:

Top Exec. Salary: $ Bonus: $
Second Exec. Salary: $ Bonus: $

OTHER THOUGHTS:

Estimated Female Officers or Directors: 5
Hot Spot for Advancement for Women/Minorities: Y

Sales, profits and employees may be estimates. Financial information, benefits and other data can change quickly and may vary from those stated here.

Endo International plc

www.endo.com

NAIC Code: 325412

TYPES OF BUSINESS:

Drugs-Pain Management
Specialty Pharmaceuticals
Branded Pharmaceuticals
Sterile Injectables
Generic Pharmaceuticals

BRANDS/DIVISIONS/AFFILIATES:

XIAFLEX
NASCOBAL
PERCOCET
LIDODERM
VASOSTRICT
APLISOL
Paladin Labs Inc

CONTACTS: *Note: Officers with more than one job title may be intentionally listed here more than once.*

Blaise Coleman, CEO
Daniel Rudio, Controller
Mark Bradley, Exec. VP
Domenico Ciarico, Exec. VP-Global Communications
Tracy Basso, Chief Human Resources Officer
Ruth Thrope, Sr. VP-IT
Roger Kimmel, Director
Rajiv De Silva, Director
Susan Hall, Executive VP
Caroline Manogue, Executive VP
Camille Farhat, President, Divisional
Brian Lortie, President, Divisional

GROWTH PLANS/SPECIAL FEATURES:

Endo International plc is a specialty pharmaceutical company. The company operates through four business segments, including branded pharmaceuticals, sterile injectables, generic pharmaceuticals and international pharmaceuticals. The branded pharmaceuticals segment invests in product candidates that have inherent scientific, regulatory, legal and technical complexities and market such products under brand names that are trademarked. For products Endo develops in the U.S. market, after the completion of required clinical trials and testing, this segment seeks approvals from required regulatory bodies. Branded specialty pharmaceutical products include, but not limited to: XIAFLEX, a non-surgical treatment for adults with abnormal building of collagen in specific areas of the body; and NASCOBAL, a nasal spray used as a supplement to treat vitamin B12 deficiency. Established branded pharmaceutical products include, but not limited to: PERCOCET, an opioid analgesic approved for the treatment of moderate-to-severe pain; and LIDODERM, a topical patch containing lidocaine approved for the relief of pain associated with post-herpetic neuralgia. The sterile injectables segment comprises more than 30 product families, and include: VASOSTRICT, indicated to increase blood pressure in adults with vasodilatory shock; and APLISOL, a sterile aqueous solution of a purified protein derivative for intradermal administration as an aid in the diagnosis of tuberculosis. The generic pharmaceuticals segment includes a portfolio of about 135 product families including solid oral extended-release, solid oral immediate-release, liquids, semi-solids, patches, powders, ophthalmics and sprays, and includes products that treat and manage a wide range of medical conditions. Last, the international pharmaceuticals segment includes a variety of specialty pharmaceutical products sold outside the U.S., primarily in Canada via subsidiary Paladin Labs, Inc. The key products in this segment serve various therapeutic areas, including attention deficit hyperactivity disorder, pain, women's health, oncology and transplantation.

Endo offers its employees comprehensive health and retirement benefits, employee assistance programs and more.

FINANCIAL DATA: *Note: Data for latest year may not have been available at press time.*

In U.S. $	2020	2019	2018	2017	2016	2015
Revenue	2,903,074,000	2,914,364,000	2,947,078,000	3,468,858,000	4,010,274,000	3,268,718,000
R&D Expense	158,902,000	130,732,000	185,826,000	172,067,000	183,372,000	102,197,000
Operating Income	603,155,000	581,874,000	483,533,000	438,387,000	421,201,000	349,566,000
Operating Margin %		.20%	.16%	.13%	.11%	.11%
SGA Expense	698,506,000	632,420,000	646,037,000	629,874,000	770,728,000	741,304,000
Net Income	183,944,000	-422,636,000	-1,031,469,000	-2,035,433,000	-3,347,066,000	-1,495,042,000
Operating Cash Flow	397,392,000	98,052,000	267,270,000	553,985,000	524,439,000	62,026,000
Capital Expenditure	721,475,000	63,854,000	86,398,000	125,654,000	158,062,000	125,742,000
EBITDA	1,029,398,000	826,638,000	319,725,000	-4,545,000	-2,484,151,000	-426,207,000
Return on Assets %		- .04%	- .09%	- .16%	- .20%	- .10%
Return on Equity %				-1.28%	- .77%	- .36%
Debt to Equity				16.998	3.014	1.383

CONTACT INFORMATION:

Phone: 353 12682000   Fax: 877-329-3636
Toll-Free: 800-462-3636
Address: Fl. 1, Minerva House, Simmonscourt Rd., Ballsbridge, Dublin 4 Ireland

STOCK TICKER/OTHER:

Stock Ticker: ENDP
Employees: 3,397
Parent Company:

Exchange: NAS
Fiscal Year Ends: 12/31

SALARIES/BONUSES:

Top Exec. Salary: $ Bonus: $
Second Exec. Salary: $ Bonus: $

OTHER THOUGHTS:

Estimated Female Officers or Directors: 3
Hot Spot for Advancement for Women/Minorities: Y

Sales, profits and employees may be estimates. Financial information, benefits and other data can change quickly and may vary from those stated here.

Endologix LLC

NAIC Code: 339100

www.endologix.com

TYPES OF BUSINESS:

Surgical and Medical Instrument Manufacturing
Medical Devices
Product Development
Product Manufacture
Endovascular System
Seal Technology
Stent Graft System

BRANDS/DIVISIONS/AFFILIATES:

AFX Endovascular AAA System
ActiveSeal
ALTO
CustomSeal
Deerfield Partners

CONTACTS: Note: Officers with more than one job title may be intentionally listed here more than once.

Richard Mott, CEO
David Saul, COO
Cindy Pinto, CFO
Robert Ricker, VP-Mktg.
Christopher Leach, VP-Sales
Matt Thompson, Chief Medical Officer
Daniel Lemaitre, Director
Jeremy Hayden, General Counsel
Richard Mott, Chmn.

GROWTH PLANS/SPECIAL FEATURES:

Endologix, LLC is a global medical device company that provides innovative therapies for the interventional treatment of vascular disease. The California-based firm has a therapeutic portfolio designed to treat diseases which currently have clinically relevant unmet needs, treating a wide spectrum of vascular disease through abdominal aortic aneurysms (AAA) to lower limb peripheral vascular disease. AAA occurs when a portion of the abdominal aorta bulges into an aneurysm due to a weakening of the vessel wall, which may result in life threatening internal bleeding upon rupture. Endologix engages in product design, manufacture and training, backed by clinical evidence. The company's primary products include AFX and ALTO. The AFX Endovascular AAA System integrates anatomical fixation with an advanced delivery system and graft material technology to treat a variety of anatomies, and encompasses a distinct advantage of separating seal and fixation. Its ActiveSeal extends the effective seal zone beyond the neck for broader anatomical applicability. The AFX bifurcated unibody endograft allows for natural blood flow and preserves the native bifurcation. ALTO is an abdominal stent graft system with a unique sealing technology that provides durable outcomes and personalized repair for a wide range of AAA patients. It ensures a precise seal in the healthiest tissue closest to renal arteries, treats anatomies such as hostile, large, reverse taper and conical necks, and replaces the need for adjunct or custom-made devices. Endologix's CustomSeal technology conforms to the vessel's wall and does not exert chronic radial force. During 2020, Endologix Inc. was acquired out of bankruptcy by Deerfield Partners, and became a privately-owned Limited Liability Corporation (LLC).

FINANCIAL DATA: Note: Data for latest year may not have been available at press time.

In U.S. $	2020	2019	2018	2017	2016	2015
Revenue		143,370,000	156,472,992	181,156,992	192,924,992	153,612,000
R&D Expense						
Operating Income						
Operating Margin %						
SGA Expense						
Net Income		-64,757,000	-79,714,000	-66,400,000	-154,676,992	-50,424,000
Operating Cash Flow						
Capital Expenditure						
EBITDA						
Return on Assets %						
Return on Equity %						
Debt to Equity						

CONTACT INFORMATION:

Phone: 949 595-7200   Fax: 949 457-9561
Toll-Free:
Address: 2 Musick, Irvine, CA 92618 United States

STOCK TICKER/OTHER:

Stock Ticker: Private   Exchange: NAS
Employees: 782   Fiscal Year Ends: 12/31
Parent Company: Deerfield Partners

SALARIES/BONUSES:

Top Exec. Salary: $ Bonus: $
Second Exec. Salary: $ Bonus: $

OTHER THOUGHTS:

Estimated Female Officers or Directors:
Hot Spot for Advancement for Women/Minorities:

Ensign Group Inc (The)

www.ensigngroup.net

NAIC Code: 623110

TYPES OF BUSINESS:

Nursing Care Facilities
Skilled Nursing
Assisted Living
In-House Therapy
Health Care Services
Senior Care
Real Estate

BRANDS/DIVISIONS/AFFILIATES:

GROWTH PLANS/SPECIAL FEATURES:

Ensign Group, Inc., through its subsidiaries, provides health care services across the post-acute care continuum. As of October 2021, Ensign operated 245 facilities and other ancillary operations located in Arizona, California, Colorado, Idaho, Iowa, Kansas, Nebraska, Nevada, South Carolina, Texas, Utah, Washington and Wisconsin. These subsidiaries have a collective capacity of approximately 25,000 operational skilled nursing beds and more than 2,200 senior living units. Ensign services include in-house therapy, skilled nursing, independent senior living and assisted senior living. In addition, Ensign owns an additional 95 real estate properties, including operations the company manages, senior living operations leased to The Pennant Group, Inc. and a service center location.

CONTACTS: *Note: Officers with more than one job title may be intentionally listed here more than once.*

Christopher Christensen, CEO
Suzanne Snapper, CFO
Roy Christensen, Chairman of the Board
Barry Port, COO, Subsidiary
Chad Keetch, Executive VP
Beverly Wittekind, General Counsel
Spencer Burton, President, Geographical

FINANCIAL DATA: *Note: Data for latest year may not have been available at press time.*

In U.S. $	2020	2019	2018	2017	2016	2015
Revenue	2,402,596,000	2,036,524,000	2,040,659,000	1,849,317,000	1,654,864,000	1,341,826,000
R&D Expense						
Operating Income	223,155,000	129,180,000	126,824,000	94,606,000	80,622,000	93,082,000
Operating Margin %		.06%	.06%	.05%	.05%	.07%
SGA Expense	129,743,000	110,873,000	100,307,000	80,617,000	69,165,000	64,163,000
Net Income	170,478,000	110,534,000	92,364,000	40,475,000	49,990,000	55,432,000
Operating Cash Flow	373,351,000	192,223,000	210,302,000	72,952,000	73,888,000	33,369,000
Capital Expenditure	50,326,000	71,541,000	54,948,000	57,166,000	65,699,000	60,018,000
EBITDA	281,539,000	182,883,000	177,895,000	127,366,000	131,636,000	122,038,000
Return on Assets %		.06%	.08%	.04%	.06%	.09%
Return on Equity %		.18%	.17%	.09%	.11%	.16%
Debt to Equity		1.986	0.395	0.615	0.604	0.232

CONTACT INFORMATION:

Phone: 949-487-9500   Fax:
Toll-Free:
Address: 29222 Rancho Viejo Rd., Ste. 127, San Juan Capistrano, CA 92675 United States

STOCK TICKER/OTHER:

Stock Ticker: ENSG
Employees: 24,400
Parent Company:

Exchange: NAS
Fiscal Year Ends: 12/31

SALARIES/BONUSES:

Top Exec. Salary: $ Bonus: $
Second Exec. Salary: $ Bonus: $

OTHER THOUGHTS:

Estimated Female Officers or Directors: 3
Hot Spot for Advancement for Women/Minorities: Y

Sales, profits and employees may be estimates. Financial information, benefits and other data can change quickly and may vary from those stated here.

Envision Healthcare Corporation

NAIC Code: 621610

www.evhc.net

TYPES OF BUSINESS:

Home Health Care Services
Physician Services
Surgery Services
Home Health Services
Hospice Services
Surgery Centers
Surgical Hospital
Ambulatory Services

BRANDS/DIVISIONS/AFFILIATES:

KKR & Co Inc
Envision Physician Services
Evolution Health
AMSURG

CONTACTS: *Note: Officers with more than one job title may be intentionally listed here more than once.*

Jim Rechtin, CEO
William Sanger, Chairman of the Board
Henry Howe, CFO
April Zepeda, Sr. VP-Communication
Beth Sweetman, Chief People Officer
Megan Barney, CIO
Karey Witty, Executive VP
Phillip Clendenin, Executive VP
Brian Jackson, Executive VP
Craig Wilson, General Counsel
Patrick Solomon, Other Executive Officer
Christopher Holden, President
Kenneth Zongor, Senior VP
Chan Chuang, Chief Medical Officer

GROWTH PLANS/SPECIAL FEATURES:

Envision Healthcare Corporation, privately-owned by KKR & Co. Inc, is a physician-led organization operating through three primary business units: Envision Physician Services, Evolution Health and AMSURG. The company delivers its services to clinical departments in healthcare facilities throughout the U.S. and the District of Columbia. The Envision Physician Services business unit provides tailored physician services to hospital and health systems, including anesthesia, emergency medicine, hospital medicine, radiology and surgical services, as well as women's and children's services. The Evolution Health business unit provides home health, hospice and home infusion services, which are patient-centered solutions. Evolution Health focuses on hiring compassionate, highly-experienced clinicians to deliver outcomes that will reduce re-hospitalizations and increase patient satisfaction. This division provides comprehensive traditional home health services reimbursed by Medicare, Medicaid and commercial payers or can provide custom solutions to health plans, hospital partners and other care models. Last, AMSURG owns and operates more than 250 surgery centers and one surgical hospital across 34 U.S. states and the District of Columbia. The company's medical specialties range from gastroenterology to ophthalmology and orthopedics. AMSURG is a leader in the ambulatory surgery center quality movement, and therefore provides an approach that combines technology, data analytics, patient engagement and quality reporting for optimal outcomes for patients.

FINANCIAL DATA: *Note: Data for latest year may not have been available at press time.*

In U.S. $	2020	2019	2018	2017	2016	2015
Revenue	8,478,750,000	8,925,000,000	8,500,000,000	7,819,299,840	3,696,000,000	2,566,884,096
R&D Expense						
Operating Income						
Operating Margin %						
SGA Expense						
Net Income		-214,525,200	-221,160,000	-228,000,000	-18,600,000	162,947,008
Operating Cash Flow						
Capital Expenditure						
EBITDA						
Return on Assets %						
Return on Equity %						
Debt to Equity						

CONTACT INFORMATION:

Phone: 615-665-1283   Fax:
Toll-Free:
Address: 1A Burton Hills Blvd., Nashville, TN 37215 United States

SALARIES/BONUSES:

Top Exec. Salary: $ Bonus: $
Second Exec. Salary: $ Bonus: $

STOCK TICKER/OTHER:

Stock Ticker: Subsidiary   Exchange:
Employees: 48,000   Fiscal Year Ends: 12/31
Parent Company: KKR & Co Inc

OTHER THOUGHTS:

Estimated Female Officers or Directors:
Hot Spot for Advancement for Women/Minorities:

Envolve Vision Inc

visionbenefits.envolvehealth.com

NAIC Code: 524114

TYPES OF BUSINESS:

Managed Vision Care Plans
Eye Health Centers

BRANDS/DIVISIONS/AFFILIATES:

Centene Corporation
Envolve Benefit Options Inc

GROWTH PLANS/SPECIAL FEATURES:

Envolve Vision, Inc. provides managed vision care plans. The company collaborates with national and local managed care organizations, providers and benefit managers to design and administer eye care programs. Envolve administers various vision benefits directly for health plans, employer groups, unions and associations. The firm offers a wide range of benefit options that cover routine eye exams, eyeglasses (lenses and frames), contacts and prescription sunglasses. Envolve's offerings include discounts on routine eye exams and optical hardware, discounts on laser surgery in select markets, complete coverage of routine exams with choice of hardware allowances and full medical surgical eye care carve outs. In addition, the firm also offers an online health manager where providers can submit and research claims, verify member benefits and enter and view authorizations. Envolve Vision is a subsidiary of Envolve Benefit Options, Inc., which itself is a subsidiary of Centene Corporation.

CONTACTS: *Note: Officers with more than one job title may be intentionally listed here more than once.*

Michael F. Neidorff, CEO
David Lavely, Pres.
Mark Ruchman, Nat'l Dir.-Medical
Tara Price, VP-Oper.
Annie Mayo, VP-Bus. Dev.
George Verrastro, Sr. VP-Finance
Tara Price, Sr. VP-Quality Mgmt.
Larry Keeley, Sr. VP-Regulatory Affairs & Account Svcs.
Connie Cook, Sr. Bus. Analyst
Shaheen Chaudhry, VP-Member & Provider Svcs.

FINANCIAL DATA: *Note: Data for latest year may not have been available at press time.*

In U.S. $	2020	2019	2018	2017	2016	2015
Revenue						
R&D Expense						
Operating Income						
Operating Margin %						
SGA Expense						
Net Income						
Operating Cash Flow						
Capital Expenditure						
EBITDA						
Return on Assets %						
Return on Equity %						
Debt to Equity						

CONTACT INFORMATION:

Phone: Fax:
Toll-Free: 800-334-3937
Address: 1151 Falls Rd., Ste. 2000, Rocky Mount, NC 27804 United States

STOCK TICKER/OTHER:

Stock Ticker: Subsidiary   Exchange:
Employees: Fiscal Year Ends: 12/31
Parent Company: Centene Corporation

SALARIES/BONUSES:

Top Exec. Salary: $ Bonus: $
Second Exec. Salary: $ Bonus: $

OTHER THOUGHTS:

Estimated Female Officers or Directors: 1
Hot Spot for Advancement for Women/Minorities: Y

Epic Systems Corporation

www.epic.com

NAIC Code: 511210D

TYPES OF BUSINESS:

Computer Software, Healthcare & Biotechnology
Information Networks
Support Services
Software
Clinical Software
Health Records Management

BRANDS/DIVISIONS/AFFILIATES:

Epicenter
EpicCare
Lucy
Community Library Exchange

CONTACTS: *Note: Officers with more than one job title may be intentionally listed here more than once.*

Judy Faulkner, CEO
Carl Dvorak, Exec. VP

GROWTH PLANS/SPECIAL FEATURES:

Epic Systems Corporation is a developer of health industry clinical, access and revenue software for mid-and large-sized medical groups, hospitals, academic facilities, children's organizations, multi-hospital systems and integrated health care organizations. All Epic software applications are designed to share a single database, called Epicenter, so that each viewer can access available patient data through a single interface from anywhere in the organization. The firm's clinical software products include integrated inpatient and ambulatory systems under the EpicCare brand as well as health information management tools and specialty information systems. The firm's interoperability service, Lucy, personal health record that allows patients to organize and access their medical history independently of any one facility. Other products offer access services, including scheduling, inpatient and ambulatory registration, call management and nurse triage; revenue cycle services, such as hospital and professional billing; health plan and managed care administration systems; clinical and financial data repositories; enterprise reporting; patient medical record access systems; and connectivity tools, including voice recognition, interfacing and patient monitoring devices. In conjunction with its software applications, the company provides extensive client services, including training, process engineering, tailoring of applications to the client's situation and access to network specialists who plan and implement client systems. In addition, Epic hosts Community Library Exchange, an online collection of application tools and pre-made content that allows clients to share report and registration templates, custom forms, enterprise report formats and documentation shortcuts. Epic is headquartered in Wisconsin, USA, with international offices in the Netherlands, Australia, Denmark, Norway, United Arab Emirates, the U.K., Saudi Arabia, Finland and Singapore.

FINANCIAL DATA: *Note: Data for latest year may not have been available at press time.*

In U.S. $	2020	2019	2018	2017	2016	2015
Revenue	3,300,000,000	3,200,000,000	2,890,000,000	2,740,000,000	2,550,000,000	2,015,000,000
R&D Expense						
Operating Income						
Operating Margin %						
SGA Expense						
Net Income						
Operating Cash Flow						
Capital Expenditure						
EBITDA						
Return on Assets %						
Return on Equity %						
Debt to Equity						

CONTACT INFORMATION:

Phone: 608-271-9000   Fax: 608-271-7237
Toll-Free:
Address: 1979 Milky Way, Verona, WI 53593 United States

STOCK TICKER/OTHER:

Stock Ticker: Private   Exchange:
Employees: 10,000   Fiscal Year Ends: 12/31
Parent Company:

SALARIES/BONUSES:

Top Exec. Salary: $ Bonus: $
Second Exec. Salary: $ Bonus: $

OTHER THOUGHTS:

Estimated Female Officers or Directors: 1
Hot Spot for Advancement for Women/Minorities:

Sales, profits and employees may be estimates. Financial information, benefits and other data can change quickly and may vary from those stated here.

Equillium Inc

www.equilliumbio.com

NAIC Code: 325412

TYPES OF BUSINESS:

Pharmaceutical Preparation Manufacturing
Biotechnology
Immunology Treatments
Clinical Trials
Drug Development

BRANDS/DIVISIONS/AFFILIATES:

Itolizumab (EQ001)

CONTACTS: *Note: Officers with more than one job title may be intentionally listed here more than once.*

Daniel Bradbury, CEO
Jason Keyes, CFO
Krishna Polu, Chief Medical Officer
Stephen Connelly, Chief Scientific Officer
Bruce Steel, Co-Founder

GROWTH PLANS/SPECIAL FEATURES:

Equillium, Inc. is a biotechnology company leveraging deep understanding of immunobiology to develop products to treat severe autoimmune and inflammatory disorders with high unmet medical need. The firm's initial product candidate, itolizumab (EQ001), is a clinical-stage, first-in-class monoclonal antibody that selectively targets the novel immune checkpoint receptor CD6. CD6 plays a central role in the modulation of effector T cell (Teff cell), activity and trafficking. Activated Teff cells drive a number of immuno-inflammatory diseases across therapeutic areas including transplant science, systemic autoimmunity, pulmonary, neurologic, gastrointestinal, renal, vascular, ophthalmic and dermatologic disorders. As a result, Equillium believes Itolizumab may have broad therapeutic utility in treating a large and diverse set of severe immuno-inflammatory diseases. The company is currently studying Itolizumab in a number of clinical trials in diseases where immune-inflammation plays a role, including graft-versus-host disease, uncontrolled moderate to severe asthma, and SLE/lupus nephritis. In mid-2021, Equillium announced plans to initiate a Phase 3 study of Itolizumab in first-line treatment of acute graft-versus-host disease following an end-of-phase meeting with the U.S. Food and Drug Administration. The Phase 3 study was scheduled to be initiated in the 4th quarter of 2021.

Equillium offers its employees comprehensive health benefits, retirement and financial benefits, life and disability insurance and a variety of employee assistance programs.

FINANCIAL DATA: *Note: Data for latest year may not have been available at press time.*

In U.S. $	2020	2019	2018	2017	2016	2015
Revenue						
R&D Expense	19,384,000	17,640,000	4,943,149			
Operating Income	-29,548,000	-26,727,000	-8,615,587			
Operating Margin %						
SGA Expense	10,164,000	9,087,000	3,672,438			
Net Income	-29,813,000	-25,600,000	-13,250,480			
Operating Cash Flow	-24,624,000	-22,949,000	-7,526,250			
Capital Expenditure	202,000	74,000	34,858			
EBITDA	-28,669,000	-25,298,000	-10,686,860			
Return on Assets %		-.42%	-.36%			
Return on Equity %		-.48%	-.42%			
Debt to Equity		0.231				

CONTACT INFORMATION:

Phone: 858 412-5302   Fax:
Toll-Free:
Address: 2223 Avenida De La Playa, Ste. 105, La Jolla, CA 92037 United States

STOCK TICKER/OTHER:

Stock Ticker: EQ
Employees: 31
Parent Company:

Exchange: NAS
Fiscal Year Ends: 12/31

SALARIES/BONUSES:

Top Exec. Salary: $ Bonus: $
Second Exec. Salary: $ Bonus: $

OTHER THOUGHTS:

Estimated Female Officers or Directors:
Hot Spot for Advancement for Women/Minorities:

EssilorLuxottica SA

NAIC Code: 339100

www.essilor.com

TYPES OF BUSINESS:

Supplies-Ophthalmic Products
Corrective Lenses
Lens Treatments
Ophthalmic Instruments
Technical Consulting
Retail

BRANDS/DIVISIONS/AFFILIATES:

CONTACTS: Note: Officers with more than one job title may be intentionally listed here more than once.

Francesco Milleri, CEO
Jean-Luc Schuppiser, Corp. Sr. VP-R&D
Patrick Poncin, Corp. Sr. VP-Global Eng.
Kevin Rupp, Exec. VP-Admin., Essilor Of America
Carol Xueref, Corp. Sr. VP-Legal Affairs & Dev.
Claude Brignon, Corp. Sr. VP-Worldwide Oper.
Kate Philipps, VP-Corp. Comm.
Veronique Gillet, Sr. VP-Investor Rel.
Kevin Rupp, Exec. VP-Finance, Essilor Of America
Eric Bernard, Pres., Essilor China
Norbert Gorny, Pres., Satisloh
Jean Carrier-Guillomet, Pres., Essilor of America
Eric Leonard, Pres., European Region
Tadeu Alves, Pres., Latin America

GROWTH PLANS/SPECIAL FEATURES:

EssilorLuxottica SA develops innovative eyecare and eyewear solutions for consumers. The firm invents new ways to reach the 2.7 billion people who suffer from uncorrected poor vision and the 7.7 billion people who do not protect their eyes from harmful rays. It has more than 11,000 patents. EssilorLuxottica's vertically integrated business focuses on two areas: lens technologies and eyewear. The lens technology division creates lens brands, and partners with leading companies such as Nikon to distribute specific technologies that enable each consumer's needs to be fully addressed. Lens brands include Crizal, Essilor, Eyezen, Kodak Lens, Oakley, Optifog, Ray-Ban, Transitions, Varilux and Xperio. This division's designing equipment and solutions are used by opticians, optometrists and ophthalmologists worldwide. These include lens surfacing and coating equipment, instruments for refraction, diagnostic equipment, imaging equipment, measurement equipment and tools, edging and mounting tools as well as related support services. The eyewear division engages in continuous investments in research and development, new technologies, equipment, materials, processes and more. Eyewear brands offered by the firm include Alaim Mikli, Armani Exchange, Arnette, Bolon, Brooks Brothers, Burberry, Bvlgari, Chanel, Coach, Costa, Dolce & Gabbana, Foster Grant, Luxottica, Persol, Prada, Steroflex, Tory Burch, Valentino and many more. EssilorLuxottica's retail network consists of approximately 9,000 retail stores that offer vision care and vision wear products. Eyewear products are also provided through EssilorLuxottica's ecommerce and managed vision channels. In early-2021, EssilorLuxottica agreed to acquire GrandVision NV; and agreed to acquire U.S.-based lab network Walman.

FINANCIAL DATA: Note: Data for latest year may not have been available at press time.

In U.S. $	2020	2019	2018	2017	2016	2015
Revenue	17,629,020,000	21,247,920,000	13,195,190,000	9,151,109,000	8,692,943,000	8,205,454,000
R&D Expense	664,646,700	669,533,800	232,137,600	265,125,600	261,460,300	261,460,300
Operating Income	564;460,900	2,263,953,000	1,666,504,000	1,385,495,000	1,557,766,000	1,502,786,000
Operating Margin %		.10%	.13%	.15%	.18%	.18%
SGA Expense	8,962,956,000	10,078,440,000	6,262,829,000	2,254,178,000	2,138,110,000	2,050,142,000
Net Income	103,851,000	1,315,854,000	1,328,072,000	963,982,000	993,304,600	924,885,200
Operating Cash Flow	3,607,907,000	4,030,642,000	2,298,162,000	1,506,451,000	1,458,802,000	1,458,802,000
Capital Expenditure	794,155,000	1,103,265,000	867,461,600	376,307,300	359,202,400	399,521,100
EBITDA	3,164,402,000	4,674,519,000	2,597,498,000	1,990,275,000	1,949,956,000	1,920,633,000
Return on Assets %		.02%	.04%	.06%	.06%	.07%
Return on Equity %		.03%	.06%	.12%	.13%	.14%
Debt to Equity		0.244	0.079	0.257	0.204	0.334

CONTACT INFORMATION:

Phone: 33-1-49-77-42-16   Fax: 33-1-49-77-44-20
Toll-Free:
Address: 147 rue de Paris,, Paris, 75008 France

STOCK TICKER/OTHER:

Stock Ticker: ESLOF
Employees: 68,972
Parent Company:

Exchange: PINX
Fiscal Year Ends: 12/31

SALARIES/BONUSES:

Top Exec. Salary: $ Bonus: $
Second Exec. Salary: $ Bonus: $

OTHER THOUGHTS:

Estimated Female Officers or Directors: 5
Hot Spot for Advancement for Women/Minorities: Y

Ethicon Inc

NAIC Code: 339100

www.ethicon.com

TYPES OF BUSINESS:

Medical Equipment & Supplies
Sutures, Surgical Mesh, Needles & Skin Adhesives
Wound Management Products
Burn & Skin Care Products
Women's Health Surgical Products
Cardiovascular Surgery Products

BRANDS/DIVISIONS/AFFILIATES:

Johnson & Johnson
SURGICEL
STRATAFIX
DERMABOND PRINEO
PROLENE
PDS
NEUWAVE
MEGADYNE

CONTACTS: *Note: Officers with more than one job title may be intentionally listed here more than once.*

Alex Gorsky, CEO-Johnson & Johnson
Jeffrey Hammond, Group Dir.-Medical Affairs

GROWTH PLANS/SPECIAL FEATURES:

Ethicon, Inc., a Johnson & Johnson subsidiary, develops and markets medical devices, products and solutions for surgical procedures to healthcare professionals worldwide. Ethicon's bio-surgical products include hemostatic solutions (used during surgery to control blood loss) such as the SURGICEL family of absorbable hemostats, including SURGICEL ORIGINAL, SURGICEL FIBRILLAR, SURGICEL NU-KNIT and SURGICEL SNoW, which can be cut to size for use in endoscopic procedures. The STRATAFIX brand of symmetric barbed sutures provides strong, secure closure for high-tension areas such as fascia. STRATAFIX Symmetric PDS offers knotless tissue control. Other branded products include the DERMABOND PRINEO skin closure system, the coated VICRYL plus antibacterial suture, the PROLENE polypropylene suture with Hemo-Seal Technology, the PDS plus anti-bacterial (polydioxanone) suture, the NEUWAVE soft tissue microwave ablation system, and the MEGADYNE line of smoke evacuators which minimize exposure to surgical smoke for both open and laparoscopic procedures.

FINANCIAL DATA: *Note: Data for latest year may not have been available at press time.*

In U.S. $	2020	2019	2018	2017	2016	2015
Revenue	6,820,000,000	6,200,000,000	6,090,000,000	5,800,000,000	5,600,000,000	5,500,000,000
R&D Expense						
Operating Income						
Operating Margin %						
SGA Expense						
Net Income						
Operating Cash Flow						
Capital Expenditure						
EBITDA						
Return on Assets %						
Return on Equity %						
Debt to Equity						

CONTACT INFORMATION:

Phone: 908-808-6306   Fax: 908-927-7230
Toll-Free:
Address: 1000 U.S. Highway 202 S., Raritan, NJ 08869 United States

STOCK TICKER/OTHER:

Stock Ticker: Subsidiary
Employees: 8,500
Parent Company: Johnson & Johnson

Exchange:
Fiscal Year Ends: 12/31

SALARIES/BONUSES:

Top Exec. Salary: $ Bonus: $
Second Exec. Salary: $ Bonus: $

OTHER THOUGHTS:

Estimated Female Officers or Directors: 2
Hot Spot for Advancement for Women/Minorities:

Eton Pharmaceuticals Inc

www.etonpharma.com

NAIC Code: 325412

TYPES OF BUSINESS:

Pharmaceutical Preparation Manufacturing
Drug Development
Pharmaceuticals
Drug Commercialization

BRANDS/DIVISIONS/AFFILIATES:

Biorphen
EM-100
Alaway
Alkindi Sprinkle
Zonisamide
Topiramate
Lamotrigine
ZENEO

CONTACTS: *Note: Officers with more than one job title may be intentionally listed here more than once.*

W. Troutman, CFO
Norbert Riedel, Director
Sean Brynjelsen, President

GROWTH PLANS/SPECIAL FEATURES:

Eton Pharmaceuticals, Inc. is a specialty pharmaceutical company focused on developing, acquiring and commercializing innovative pharmaceutical products. The company has a diversified portfolio of pharmaceutical products, primarily focused on the two categories of hospital injectable products and pediatric retail prescription products. Eton's Biorphen (phenylephrine) product was approved by the U.S. Food and Drug Administration (FDA) in 2019 as a ready-to-use injection for the treatment of clinically important hypotension resulting primarily from vasodilation in the setting of anesthesia. Eton's EM-100 product was sold to Bausch Health and become FDA-approved in September 2020. Bausch Health renamed EM-100 as Alaway in January 2021, and Eton receives royalties from the sale of the product. Eton also owns the licensing rights to FDA-approved Alkindi Sprinkle. In early-2021, Eton sold three pediatric neurology products that were under development to Azurity Pharmaceuticals, and anticipates additional revenues from Azurity based on various product-related milestones, including the commercial launch for the products which are currently (mid-2021) under review with the FDA. Other royalty products include: Zonisamide (marketing partner Bausch Health), a liquid formulation under FDA review for the treatment of partial seizures in patients with epilepsy; Topiramate (Azurity), a liquid under FDA review for three indications including monotherapy treatment of partial-onset or primary general tonic-clonic seizures, adjunctive therapy for partial-onset seizures and as a preventive treatment of migraine; Lamotrigine (Azurity), a liquid under FDA review for the treatment of partial on-set seizures, primary generalized tonic-clonic seizures, and seizures of Lennox-Gastaut syndrome; Cysteine, an hydrochloric injection product candidate with a submitted Abbreviated New Drug Application to the FDA; and Ephedrine, a ready-to-use injection medication and stimulant for patients in hospital settings. In mid-2021, Eton acquired the U.S. and Canadian rights to ZENEO hydrocortisone auto-injector, which is under development as a rescue treatment for adrenal crisis.

Eton offers comprehensive employee benefits.

FINANCIAL DATA: *Note: Data for latest year may not have been available at press time.*

In U.S. $	2020	2019	2018	2017	2016	2015
Revenue	39,000	959,000				
R&D Expense	14,104,000	11,555,000	5,627,000			
Operating Income	-27,111,000	-18,601,000	-10,321,000			
Operating Margin %		-19.40%				
SGA Expense	12,760,000	7,552,000	4,694,000			
Net Income	-27,970,000	-18,320,000	-12,740,000			
Operating Cash Flow	-22,346,000	-18,026,000	-8,145,000			
Capital Expenditure	50,000	1,846,000	236,000			
EBITDA	-26,460,000	-18,154,000	-10,258,000			
Return on Assets %		-.81%	-1.78%			
Return on Equity %		-.99%	-3.83%			
Debt to Equity		0.432				

CONTACT INFORMATION:

Phone: 847 787-7361 Fax:
Toll-Free:
Address: 21925 West Field Pkwy, Ste. 235, Deer Park, IL 60010-7278 United States

STOCK TICKER/OTHER:

Stock Ticker: ETON Exchange: NAS
Employees: 16 Fiscal Year Ends: 12/31
Parent Company:

SALARIES/BONUSES:

Top Exec. Salary: $ Bonus: $
Second Exec. Salary: $ Bonus: $

OTHER THOUGHTS:

Estimated Female Officers or Directors:
Hot Spot for Advancement for Women/Minorities:

Sales, profits and employees may be estimates. Financial information, benefits and other data can change quickly and may vary from those stated here.

Everyday Health Inc

www.everydayhealth.com

NAIC Code: 519130

TYPES OF BUSINESS:

Online Health Information Services
Health Care Digital Platform
Communications
Marketing
Data Analytics
Health Care Information

BRANDS/DIVISIONS/AFFILIATES:

j2 Global Inc

CONTACTS: *Note: Officers with more than one job title may be intentionally listed here more than once.*

Arefa Cassoobhoy, VP-Chief Medical Editor
Patrice Harris, Medical Editor in Chief
Brian Cooper, CFO
Scott Wolf, Executive VP
Jed Savage, Executive VP
Alan Shapiro, General Counsel

GROWTH PLANS/SPECIAL FEATURES:

Everyday Health, Inc. operates a digital marketing and communications platform for health care marketers primarily in the U.S. The platform combines digital content from leading health brands with data and analytics technology to present updated, informed content for users. The content can be accessed by Everyday Health's consumers and professionals anytime, anywhere, across multiple channels, including the web, mobile devices, video and social media. The multi-brand, multi-channel content experience helps with decision making, and allows companies to engage with consumers and healthcare professionals. Its portfolio of properties consists of websites, mobile applications and social media destinations. Consumers use Everyday Health's tools to manage health and wellness needs such as weight loss, exercise, healthy pregnancy, nutrition and medical conditions. The company also provides health care professionals with news, tools and information needed to keep in touch with current industry, legislative and regulatory developments in major medical specialties. More than 700,000 practicing U.S. physicians can be reached, ranging across numerous specialty areas. Everyday Health's website offers links and access to free newsletters, a symptom checker, drug finder, calorie counter, meal planner and recipes. Everyday Health operates as a wholly-owned subsidiary of j2 Global, Inc., an American technology company based in California.

FINANCIAL DATA: *Note: Data for latest year may not have been available at press time.*

In U.S. $	2020	2019	2018	2017	2016	2015
Revenue	259,000,000	280,000,000	279,300,000	266,000,000	250,000,000	231,991,008
R&D Expense						
Operating Income						
Operating Margin %						
SGA Expense						
Net Income						
Operating Cash Flow						
Capital Expenditure						
EBITDA						
Return on Assets %						
Return on Equity %						
Debt to Equity						

CONTACT INFORMATION:

Phone: 646-728-9500   Fax: 646-728-9501
Toll-Free:
Address: 345 Hudson St., Fl. 16, New York, NY 10014 United States

STOCK TICKER/OTHER:

Stock Ticker: Subsidiary   Exchange:
Employees: 560   Fiscal Year Ends:
Parent Company: j2 Global Inc

SALARIES/BONUSES:

Top Exec. Salary: $ Bonus: $
Second Exec. Salary: $ Bonus: $

OTHER THOUGHTS:

Estimated Female Officers or Directors: 4
Hot Spot for Advancement for Women/Minorities: Y

Exactech Inc

NAIC Code: 339100

www.exac.com

TYPES OF BUSINESS:

Equipment-Joint Replacement
Orthopedic Implant Devices
Surgical Instruments
Biologic Products
Bone Fusion Materials

BRANDS/DIVISIONS/AFFILIATES:

TPG Capital
Newton

CONTACTS: *Note: Officers with more than one job title may be intentionally listed here more than once.*

Darin Johnson, CEO
Kerem Bolukbasi, CFO
Gary Miller, Executive VP, Divisional
Betty Petty, Founder
Donna Edwards, General Counsel
Bruce Thompson, General Manager, Divisional
Jeffrey R. Binder, Chmn.

GROWTH PLANS/SPECIAL FEATURES:

Exactech, Inc. develops, manufactures, distributes and sells orthopedic implant devices, surgical instrumentation and biologic services to hospitals and physicians in the U.S. and in more than 35 international markets across Europe, Latin America, Asia and the Pacific. The company's innovative bone and joint restoration products help surgeons make patients more mobile. Exactech's devices and systems are used for hip, knee, ankle and shoulder restoration and replacements, and other products are used to strengthen, line and stabilize bone structures. Products include stems, systems, prosthesis, liners, spacers, bone cement, cartilage processors, autologous platelet concentrating systems, collagen wraps and grafting material. Exactech manufactures many of its orthopedic devices at its Gainesville, Florida facility. Exactech is privately owned by TPG Capital. In mid-2021, Exactech announced the first surgeries using Newton, an innovative soft tissue management technology that combines ligament balancing and real-time guidance, offering a personalized intraoperative solution designed to improve total knee surgery outcomes.

Exactech offers employees comprehensive health benefits, life insurance, paid time off and retirement benefits.

FINANCIAL DATA: *Note: Data for latest year may not have been available at press time.*

In U.S. $	2020	2019	2018	2017	2016	2015
Revenue	265,000,000	287,752,500	274,050,000	261,000,000	257,572,992	241,838,000
R&D Expense						
Operating Income						
Operating Margin %						
SGA Expense						
Net Income						
Operating Cash Flow						
Capital Expenditure						
EBITDA						
Return on Assets %						
Return on Equity %						
Debt to Equity						

CONTACT INFORMATION:

Phone: 352 377-1140   Fax: 352 378-2617
Toll-Free: 800-266-7883
Address: 2320 NW 66th Ct., Gainesville, FL 32653 United States

STOCK TICKER/OTHER:

Stock Ticker: Private   Exchange:
Employees: 770   Fiscal Year Ends: 12/31
Parent Company: TPG Capital

SALARIES/BONUSES:

Top Exec. Salary: $ Bonus: $
Second Exec. Salary: $ Bonus: $

OTHER THOUGHTS:

Estimated Female Officers or Directors: 3
Hot Spot for Advancement for Women/Minorities: Y

Extendicare Inc

www.extendicare.com

NAIC Code: 623110

TYPES OF BUSINESS:

Long-Term Care
Assisted Living Facilities
Sub-Acute Care
Rehabilitative Services

BRANDS/DIVISIONS/AFFILIATES:

ParaMed Home Health Care
Silver Group Purchasing
Nutritional Support System
Extendicare Assist

CONTACTS: *Note: Officers with more than one job title may be intentionally listed here more than once.*

Michael Guerriere, CEO
Michael Guerriere, CEO
David Bacon, CFO
Alan Torrie, Chairman of the Board
Brandon Parent, General Counsel
Christopher Dennis, President, Subsidiary
Jillian Fountain, Vice President, Divisional
Matthew Morgan, Chief Medical Officer

GROWTH PLANS/SPECIAL FEATURES:

Extendicare, Inc. is a leading provider of long-term care and related services in Canada. Through its subsidiaries, the firm owns and manages 111 senior care centers. The company's long-term care provides long-stay services, short-stay services and complex continuing care for patients with complex health issues. This division includes a chronic care unit and 96 long-term care homes providing support to approximately 13,000 residents across Ontario, Manitoba, Alberta and Saskatchewan. The retirement living segment provides services such as daily personal care, medication reminders, housekeeping, meals and planned social opportunities. Through ParaMed Home Health Care, the firm delivers care directly to the clients and families living within ParaMed communities. These services include in-home personal care, and homemaking and nursing services such as wound and palliative care. ParaMed's workplace health and wellness division meets the health and wellness needs of companies and their employees. These services include health and wellness clinics, mask fit test clinics, immunization clinics, seminars, education, consultation and customized health/wellness programs targeted to the needs of specific workplaces. Through Silver Group Purchasing, Extendicare provides cost saving measures concerning brand product standards and specifications, as well as menu development, nutritional analysis and costing through its Nutritional Support System. Subsidiary Extendicare Assist provides management and consulting services, including customized solutions.

Extendicare offers its employees opportunities for advancement within the organization, training and professional development programs, and benefits.

FINANCIAL DATA: *Note: Data for latest year may not have been available at press time.*

In U.S. $	2020	2019	2018	2017	2016	2015
Revenue	959,725,800	937,898,700	928,003,200	909,214,500	878,911,300	811,673,700
R&D Expense						
Operating Income	78,169,690	42,688,710	48,859,060	54,577,020	49,337,140	47,615,380
Operating Margin %		.05%	.05%	.06%	.06%	.06%
SGA Expense	40,565,910	35,080,780	32,932,310	31,672,050	32,366,390	35,761,870
Net Income	44,899,330	23,721,930	26,297,120	1,766,509	29,374,430	192,292,700
Operating Cash Flow	100,476,400	37,443,040	32,706,110	39,075,320	-232,828	43,746,790
Capital Expenditure	27,425,640	27,493,580	41,965,360	34,084,840	32,179,140	29,395,970
EBITDA	104,518,200	76,691,520	62,286,020	84,534,760	81,391,170	78,764,600
Return on Assets %		.03%	.03%	.00%	.04%	.16%
Return on Equity %		.24%	.25%	.01%	.20%	2.74%
Debt to Equity		3.661	3.606	3.694	2.568	2.49

CONTACT INFORMATION:

Phone: 905-470-4000   Fax: 905-470-4003
Toll-Free:
Address: 3000 Steeles Ave. E, Ste. 103, Markham, ON L3R 4T9 Canada

STOCK TICKER/OTHER:

Stock Ticker: EXETF   Exchange: PINX
Employees: 23,000   Fiscal Year Ends: 12/31
Parent Company:

SALARIES/BONUSES:

Top Exec. Salary: $ Bonus: $
Second Exec. Salary: $ Bonus: $

OTHER THOUGHTS:

Estimated Female Officers or Directors: 7
Hot Spot for Advancement for Women/Minorities: Y

Sales, profits and employees may be estimates. Financial information, benefits and other data can change quickly and may vary from those stated here.

EyeCare Partners LLC

www.eyecare-partners.com

NAIC Code: 621320

TYPES OF BUSINESS:

Offices of Optometrists
Optometry
Ophthalmology
Eyecare Business Solutions

BRANDS/DIVISIONS/AFFILIATES:

Partners Group

CONTACTS: *Note: Officers with more than one job title may be intentionally listed here more than once.*

David A. Clark, CEO
Atul Kavthekar, CFO
Mike Koehler, Chief Human Resources Officer
Supantha Banerjee, CIO

GROWTH PLANS/SPECIAL FEATURES:

EyeCare Partners, LLC comprises a network of more than 550 medical optometry and ophthalmology practices. These medical eyecare businesses provide services from locations in nearly 20 U.S. states. EyeCare manages all aspects of business operations, including revenue cycle, purchasing, marketing, human resources, recruiting, training, information technology (IT), and other office support functions. Network practices include, but are not limited to, Clarkson Eyecare, Nationwide Vision, eyecarecenter, The Eye Doctors, EyeCare Associates, Ophthalmology Consultants, St. Charles Surgery Center, Bennett & Bloom Eye Centers, McPeak Vision Partners, Grene Vision Group, Reynolds & Anliker, Physicians Surgery Center, Tukel Eye Center, EyesFirst Vision Center, and Tuscaloosa Opththalmology. EyeCare Partners is backed by the global investment firm, Partners Group, with EyeCare Partners' management team and physician partners together owning a majority interest.

FINANCIAL DATA: *Note: Data for latest year may not have been available at press time.*

In U.S. $	2020	2019	2018	2017	2016	2015
Revenue						
R&D Expense						
Operating Income						
Operating Margin %						
SGA Expense						
Net Income						
Operating Cash Flow						
Capital Expenditure						
EBITDA						
Return on Assets %						
Return on Equity %						
Debt to Equity						

CONTACT INFORMATION:

Phone: 636 227-2600 Fax:
Toll-Free:
Address: 15933 Clayton Rd., Ste. 210, Ballwin, MO 63011 United States

STOCK TICKER/OTHER:

Stock Ticker: Private Exchange:
Employees: Fiscal Year Ends:
Parent Company: Partners Group

SALARIES/BONUSES:

Top Exec. Salary: $ Bonus: $
Second Exec. Salary: $ Bonus: $

OTHER THOUGHTS:

Estimated Female Officers or Directors:
Hot Spot for Advancement for Women/Minorities:

EyeMed Vision Care LLC

eyemed.com/en-us

NAIC Code: 524114

TYPES OF BUSINESS:

Vision Plans
Vision Care Insurance Plans
Insurance Administration
Employer-Sponsored Benefits

BRANDS/DIVISIONS/AFFILIATES:

Luxottica Group SpA
OneSight

CONTACTS: *Note: Officers with more than one job title may be intentionally listed here more than once.*

Lukas Ruecker, Pres.
John Lahr, Dir.-Medical
Troy Hall, Associate VP-Mktg. & Strategic Planning
Maury Williams, Dir.-Comm.

GROWTH PLANS/SPECIAL FEATURES:

EyeMed Vision Care, LLC administers vision care plans for more than 60 million members in large-, medium- and small-sized companies and government entities and through insurance companies in the U.S. The company's members are enrolled through employer-sponsored benefits sold directly by EyeMed or bundled with benefits offered in partnership with many of the leading healthcare organizations in the U.S. EyeMed offers a network with vision care and eyewear services from well-known optical retailers such as LensCrafters, Pearle Vision and Target Optical. The company's member website offers self-service tools that are available any day or night, and can be accessed via desktop or smartphone. Benefit information can be retrieved from the web site, with access to view/print ID cards, explanation of benefits, locate a provider, check claim status and schedule appointments options. In addition, EyeMed is a sponsor of OneSight, which offers onsite vision care services such as comprehensive eye exams and new prescription eyewear to underserved communities throughout the nation. EyeMed is a wholly-owned subsidiary of Italian eyewear designer Luxottica Group SpA.

FINANCIAL DATA: *Note: Data for latest year may not have been available at press time.*

In U.S. $	2020	2019	2018	2017	2016	2015
Revenue						
R&D Expense						
Operating Income						
Operating Margin %						
SGA Expense						
Net Income						
Operating Cash Flow						
Capital Expenditure						
EBITDA						
Return on Assets %						
Return on Equity %						
Debt to Equity						

CONTACT INFORMATION:

Phone: 513-765-6000   Fax: 513-765-6388
Toll-Free: 800-521-3605
Address: 4000 Luxottica Pl., Mason, OH 45040 United States

STOCK TICKER/OTHER:

Stock Ticker: Subsidiary
Employees:
Parent Company: Luxottica Group SpA

Exchange:
Fiscal Year Ends: 12/31

SALARIES/BONUSES:

Top Exec. Salary: $ Bonus: $
Second Exec. Salary: $ Bonus: $

OTHER THOUGHTS:

Estimated Female Officers or Directors: 1
Hot Spot for Advancement for Women/Minorities:

Fairview Health Services

NAIC Code: 622110

www.fairview.org

TYPES OF BUSINESS:

General Medical and Surgical Hospitals
Specialty Clinics
Home Care
Hospice Services
Children's Services
Cancer Care
Senior Care
Academic Teaching Hospital

BRANDS/DIVISIONS/AFFILIATES:

www.fairview.org

CONTACTS: *Note: Officers with more than one job title may be intentionally listed here more than once.*

James Hereford, CEO
Laura Reed, COO
Hayes Batson, CFO
Scott Weber, CMO
Mary Nease, Chief People Officer
Brent Asplin, Chief Clinical Officer
Sameer Badlani, Chief Digital Officer
Mark Hansberry, VP-Strategic Planning
Mark Hansberry, VP-Comm.
Brent Asplin, Pres., Fairview Medical Group
Daniel K. Anderson, Pres., Fairview Community Hospitals
Bob Beacher, Pres., Fairview Pharmacy Services
Richard Howard, Pres., Fairview Foundation
Rich Ostlund, Chmn.
Mark Thomas, Pres., Senior Services

GROWTH PLANS/SPECIAL FEATURES:

Fairview Health Services is a nonprofit health care system with numerous primary care and specialty clinics across Minnesota. The company's network is comprised of more than 5,000 system providers, 90+ senior housing locations, 40+ primary-care clinics, 36 pharmacy locations and 10 hospitals and medical centers. Fairview's services and specialties include family medicine, obstetrics, gynecology, urgent care, pharmacy, pediatrics, orthopedics, sports medicine, weight loss, caregiver assurance, acupuncture, aquatic therapy, audiology, bone marrow transplant, cancer care, counseling, dermatology, ear/nose/throat, home infusion, imaging, kidney care, laboratory/diagnostic, neonatal intensive care, pain management and many more. For employers, Fairview offers a portfolio of services that include: an employee assistance program; a single-day, comprehensive annual physical and wellness consultation performed at the University of Minnesota Health Clinics and Surgery Center; an online clinic available 24/7 for the treatment of routine health conditions such as cold, flu, allergies, ear infections, pink eye and more; a customized onsite clinic solution that offers convenient access to high-quality care for employees and dependents; and sleep health. Fairview's website, www.fairview.org, offers patients the capability to pay their related health bills, obtain a prescription refill, pre-register for a hospital visit, obtain personal medical records and request for an appointment. Ebenezer is a part of Fairview's health services and is focused on serving senior adults. For medical professionals, Fairview offers continuing medical education and credentialing services.

Fairview offers employees life, disability, health and dental insurance; various employee assistance programs; and 403(b) and other retirement options.

FINANCIAL DATA: *Note: Data for latest year may not have been available at press time.*

In U.S. $	2020	2019	2018	2017	2016	2015
Revenue	5,626,287,960	6,049,772,000	5,712,332,000	5,210,371,000	4,363,540,000	3,867,550,000
R&D Expense						
Operating Income						
Operating Margin %						
SGA Expense						
Net Income		13,392,000	11,090,000	451,928,000	213,786,000	64,908,000
Operating Cash Flow						
Capital Expenditure						
EBITDA						
Return on Assets %						
Return on Equity %						
Debt to Equity						

CONTACT INFORMATION:

Phone: 612-672-7272   Fax: 612-672-7186
Toll-Free: 800-824-1953
Address: 2450 Riverside Ave., Minneapolis, MN 55454 United States

STOCK TICKER/OTHER:

Stock Ticker: Nonprofit
Employees: 36,000
Parent Company:

Exchange:
Fiscal Year Ends: 12/31

SALARIES/BONUSES:

Top Exec. Salary: $ Bonus: $
Second Exec. Salary: $ Bonus: $

OTHER THOUGHTS:

Estimated Female Officers or Directors: 9
Hot Spot for Advancement for Women/Minorities: Y

Fielmann AG

www.fielmann.de

NAIC Code: 339100

TYPES OF BUSINESS:

Ophthalmic Goods Manufacturing
Optical Product Design
Optical Product Manufacture
Eye Glasses
Eye Contact Lenses
Retail Sites
Ecommerce Sites
Sunglasses

BRANDS/DIVISIONS/AFFILIATES:

Korva SE

GROWTH PLANS/SPECIAL FEATURES:

Fielmann AG is engaged in the design, manufacture, retail and trade of optical products. The company is 71%-owned by the Fielmann family's holding company, Korva SE. Operations are conducted in Germany, Switzerland, Austria, Luxembourg, the Netherlands, Italy and Poland. Fielmann is a market leader in eyewear sales, operating more than 870 retail optical stores as well as eCommerce sites, and selling 7.26 million pairs of glasses in 2020 alone. Products include spectacles, contact lenses and other optical products. Its spectacles include bifocal and varifocal optical glasses, sunglasses, prescription sunglasses, computer glasses and contact lenses. To customers, the company offers free eye exams as well as online eye tests. For current and future employees, Fielmann provides optician training in Germany. Moreover, in several stores, Fielmann also sells hearing aids and related accessories.

CONTACTS: *Note: Officers with more than one job title may be intentionally listed here more than once.*

Marc Fielmann, CEO
Georg Alexander Zeiss, CFO
Bastian Koerber, Dir.-Sales
Gunter Schmid, Head-Material Mgmt. & Production

FINANCIAL DATA: *Note: Data for latest year may not have been available at press time.*

In U.S. $	2020	2019	2018	2017	2016	2015
Revenue	1,745,837,000	1,858,011,000	1,744,696,000	1,693,351,000	1,633,735,000	1,588,241,000
R&D Expense						
Operating Income	219,858,800	310,507,300	305,348,900	310,710,100	293,307,100	293,605,200
Operating Margin %		.17%	.18%	.18%	.18%	.18%
SGA Expense	194,255,200	200,742,800				
Net Income	142,224,600	210,393,700	206,344,700	204,802,800	203,191,300	202,243,200
Operating Cash Flow	340,229,500	368,076,100	251,245,000	350,822,200	267,761,000	196,269,900
Capital Expenditure	110,045,400	122,419,600	92,856,270	80,877,970	59,491,980	64,037,000
EBITDA	412,453,600	471,913,800	362,776,100	357,410,100	346,087,800	342,291,800
Return on Assets %		.15%	.18%	.18%	.18%	.19%
Return on Equity %		.24%	.24%	.24%	.25%	.26%
Debt to Equity		0.411	0.001	0.002	0.002	0.001

CONTACT INFORMATION:

Phone: 49 4027076-0   Fax: 49 4027076-150
Toll-Free:
Address: Weidestrasse 118a, Hamburg, 22083 Germany

STOCK TICKER/OTHER:

Stock Ticker: FLMNY
Employees: 21,853
Parent Company: Korva SE

Exchange: GREY
Fiscal Year Ends: 12/31

SALARIES/BONUSES:

Top Exec. Salary: $ Bonus: $
Second Exec. Salary: $ Bonus: $

OTHER THOUGHTS:

Estimated Female Officers or Directors:
Hot Spot for Advancement for Women/Minorities:

First Choice Health Network Inc

www.fchn.com

NAIC Code: 524114

TYPES OF BUSINESS:

Insurance-Medical & Health, HMOs & PPOs
Employer Benefits
Health Benefits Administration
Preferred Provider Organization Access
Employee Assistance Programs
Medical Management Solutions
Physicians Assistance Programs

BRANDS/DIVISIONS/AFFILIATES:

CONTACTS: *Note: Officers with more than one job title may be intentionally listed here more than once.*

Jaja Okigwe, CEO
Jacqueline Brainard, VP-Oper.
Anisha Sood, CFO
Curtis Taylor, CMO
Kevin Conefrey, VP-Human Resources
Dan Brown, CTO
John Robinson, Chief Medical Officer

GROWTH PLANS/SPECIAL FEATURES:

First Choice Health Network, Inc. is a Seattle-based, provider-owned healthcare organization with operations primarily in Washington, Oregon and Montana, and a growing presence in Alaska, Idaho, Wyoming and other states. The firm serves employers of all sizes and across industries with health benefits administration services, offering access to clinically-integrated networks and a traditional preferred provider organization (PPO). Other services include an employee assistance program (EAP) that addresses mental health and work-life support, health plan administration, a physician assistance program, as well as medical management solutions. Combined, First Choice Health's network offers over 120,000 directly contracted and credentialed providers and approximately 370 hospitals used by a variety of insurance companies, third-party administrators and plan sponsors. In December 2020, First Choice Health announced it was entering 2021 with a direct-to-employer focus.

First Choice offers its employees medical, dental and vision insurance; short-and long-term disability; flexible spending accounts; a 401(k) with company match; profit sharing; tuition reimbursement; an employee assistance program; and free public transpo

FINANCIAL DATA: *Note: Data for latest year may not have been available at press time.*

In U.S. $	2020	2019	2018	2017	2016	2015
Revenue						
R&D Expense						
Operating Income						
Operating Margin %						
SGA Expense						
Net Income						
Operating Cash Flow						
Capital Expenditure						
EBITDA						
Return on Assets %						
Return on Equity %						
Debt to Equity						

CONTACT INFORMATION:

Phone: 206-292-8255   Fax: 206-667-8062
Toll-Free: 800-467-5281
Address: 600 University St., Ste. 1400, Seattle, WA 98101-3129 United States

STOCK TICKER/OTHER:

Stock Ticker: Private   Exchange:
Employees: 156   Fiscal Year Ends:
Parent Company:

SALARIES/BONUSES:

Top Exec. Salary: $ Bonus: $
Second Exec. Salary: $ Bonus: $

OTHER THOUGHTS:

Estimated Female Officers or Directors: 2
Hot Spot for Advancement for Women/Minorities:

Sales, profits and employees may be estimates. Financial information, benefits and other data can change quickly and may vary from those stated here.

First Health Group Corp

providerlocator.firsthealth.com/home/index

NAIC Code: 524114

TYPES OF BUSINESS:

Insurance-Medical & Health, PPOs
Health Benefits Provider
Preferred Provider Organization Services
Regional Provider Networks
Business Administration Solutions

BRANDS/DIVISIONS/AFFILIATES:

Aetna Inc
First Health
Cofinity

GROWTH PLANS/SPECIAL FEATURES:

First Health Group Corp., an indirect wholly-owned subsidiary of Aetna, Inc., provides health benefits to a wide range of healthcare payers, including third-party administrators, carriers, employers, Taft-Hartley trusts and government entities. The firm offers its products through two brands: First Health, comprising a national preferred provider organization (PPO) network; and Cofinity, comprising a regional network that offers budge-friendly plans. Together, these brands have: a national network with urban, suburban and rural access; regional networks in Michigan and Colorado; a range of solutions for out-of-network claims; networks for dental and transplant services; and easy-to-use implementation and administration solutions.

First Health Group offers its employees medical, dental, vision, life, AD&D and short/long-term disability insurance; 401(k); and various employee assistance programs.

CONTACTS: *Note: Officers with more than one job title may be intentionally listed here more than once.*

Paul Lavin, CEO
Kara Dornig, VP-Bus. Dev.
Susan Korth, VP-Account Mgmt.
John Bryan, Dir.-Sales
Darlene Colyer, Dir.-Oper. Support

FINANCIAL DATA: *Note: Data for latest year may not have been available at press time.*

In U.S. $	2020	2019	2018	2017	2016	2015
Revenue						
R&D Expense						
Operating Income						
Operating Margin %						
SGA Expense						
Net Income						
Operating Cash Flow						
Capital Expenditure						
EBITDA						
Return on Assets %						
Return on Equity %						
Debt to Equity						

CONTACT INFORMATION:

Phone: 630-737-7900   Fax:
Toll-Free:
Address: 3200 Highland Ave., Downers Grove, IL 60515 United States

STOCK TICKER/OTHER:

Stock Ticker: Subsidiary   Exchange:
Employees: Fiscal Year Ends: 12/31
Parent Company: Aetna Inc

SALARIES/BONUSES:

Top Exec. Salary: $ Bonus: $
Second Exec. Salary: $ Bonus: $

OTHER THOUGHTS:

Estimated Female Officers or Directors: 4
Hot Spot for Advancement for Women/Minorities: Y

Fisher & Paykel Healthcare Limited

www.fphcare.com

NAIC Code: 423450

TYPES OF BUSINESS:

Medical, Dental, and Hospital Equipment and Supplies Merchant Wholesalers
Humidification Products
Product Development
Product Manufacture

BRANDS/DIVISIONS/AFFILIATES:

Evora Full

CONTACTS: Note: Officers with more than one job title may be intentionally listed here more than once.

Lewis Gradon, CEO
Nicholas Fourie, VP-IT & ICT
Lyndal York, CFO
Paul Shearer, Sr. VP-Sales & Mktg.
Nicola Talbort, VP-Human Resources
Andrew Somervell, VP-IT & Products
Lewis Gradon, Sr. VP-Products & Technology
Anthony Barclay, Company Secretary
Paul Adreassi, VP-Quality & Regulatory
Scott St. John, Chmn.

GROWTH PLANS/SPECIAL FEATURES:

Fisher & Paykel Healthcare Limited designs, manufactures and markets heated humidification products and systems for respiratory care, acute care, surgery and treatment of obstructive sleep apnea. Exporting to over 120 countries, Fisher & Paykel's head office is located in New Zealand, with manufacturing operations located in New Zealand and Mexico. 99% of revenue is derived overseas. The firm's major clients include hospitals, home health care providers, distributors and manufacturers of medical devices. Products are divided into two major groups: respiratory and acute care and obstructive sleep apnea. Respiratory and acute care offers products for the treatment of respiratory conditions by ventilation or oxygen therapy. These products include humidifiers, single-use and reusable chambers and breathing circuits, infant resuscitators, infant warmers; and accessories. This division also offers special humidification systems for the surgical room, which conditions dry carbon dioxide gas to normal physiological level of temperature and humidity. Obstructive sleep apnea offers a range of products utilizing continuous positive airway pressure therapy (CPAP). The group primarily sells a range of CPAP devices, masks and humidifiers. In October 2021, Fisher & Paykel announced the launch of Evora Full, a compact full-face mask for sleep apnea. Its compact seal floats under the nose to provide patients with a clear line of sight, while stability wings keep the seal stable.

FINANCIAL DATA: Note: Data for latest year may not have been available at press time.

In U.S. $	2020	2019	2018	2017	2016	2015
Revenue	923,637,200	777,627,800	699,582,200	630,680,100	593,678,000	
R&D Expense	85,951,780	72,823,280	68,688,890	62,379,230	53,158,090	
Operating Income	282,154,000	209,838,400	180,244,900	152,474,800	151,655,900	
Operating Margin %	.31%	.27%	.26%	.24%	.26%	
SGA Expense	245,162,000	237,763,700	210,998,900	195,339,800	175,732,600	
Net Income	208,387,700	151,739,300	137,958,000	122,691,300	104,030,700	
Operating Cash Flow						
Capital Expenditure	123,814,100	96,686,690	71,590,220	45,677,750	47,697,800	
EBITDA	271,564,100	214,625,600	196,927,500	175,504,800	153,177,700	
Return on Assets %	.22%	.19%	.20%	.21%	.20%	
Return on Equity %	.30%	.25%	.27%	.28%	.28%	
Debt to Equity	0.045	0.076	0.069	0.06	0.086	

CONTACT INFORMATION:

Phone: 649 574 0100   Fax: 649 574 0158
Toll-Free:
Address: 15 Maurice Paykel Pl., Auckland, 2013 New Zealand

STOCK TICKER/OTHER:

Stock Ticker: FSPKF   Exchange: PINX
Employees: 4,751   Fiscal Year Ends: 03/31
Parent Company:

SALARIES/BONUSES:

Top Exec. Salary: $ Bonus: $
Second Exec. Salary: $ Bonus: $

OTHER THOUGHTS:

Estimated Female Officers or Directors: 2
Hot Spot for Advancement for Women/Minorities:

Foundation Medicine Inc

www.foundationmedicine.com

NAIC Code: 325413

TYPES OF BUSINESS:

In-Vitro Diagnostic Substance Manufacturing
Genomic Profiling Products
Molecular Insights
Cancer Therapies
Drug Development
Diagnostic Products

BRANDS/DIVISIONS/AFFILIATES:

FoundationOne

CONTACTS: *Note: Officers with more than one job title may be intentionally listed here more than once.*

Brian Alexander, CEO
Konstantin Fiedler, COO
Rita Kale, CFO
Andrew Suchoff, Chief People Officer

GROWTH PLANS/SPECIAL FEATURES:

Foundation Medicine, Inc. comprises a portfolio of comprehensive genomic profiling products that help physicians make informed decisions in the area of cancer care. Through innovation in molecular insights, the company works with partners to deliver breakthrough innovations that improve outcomes for individuals with cancer. Foundation Medicine's approach offers test results and insights that can help doctors match patients to more treatment options and help accelerate the development of new therapies. As of October 2021, Foundation Medicine comprised more than 500,000 patient sample profiles, over 65 biopharmaceutical partners and 500+ peer-reviewed publications. The firm's FoundationOne liquid companion diagnostic (CDx) has been approved by the U.S. Food and Drug Administration (FDA) as a blood-based CGP companion diagnostic for Tabrecta (capmatinib), approved of both CGP tissue- and blood-based tests in identifying advanced non-small cell lung cancer in patients with mutations that lead to METex14 skipping mutations. The OneFoundation CDx tissue-based test has been FDA-approved as a companion diagnostic to detect various solid tumor (NTRK1/2/3) fusions for Vitrakvi (larotrectinib). It analyzes 324 genes. Foundation Medicine helps accelerate clinical trials via design, planning and enrollment, offering a portfolio of assay platforms based on FoundationOne CDx and FoundationOne Liquid CDx. Commercialization services are also provided, spanning CDx development acceleration, development mitigation, regulatory services, commercial risk and commercial adoption. In mid-2021, Foundation Medicine announced that it received U.S. Food and Drug Administration approval for FoundationOne CDx to be used as a companion diagnostic for ALUNBRIG (brigatinib), an FDA-approved treatment for adult patients with anaplastic lymphoma kinase (ALK)-positive metastatic non-small cell lung cancer.

FINANCIAL DATA: *Note: Data for latest year may not have been available at press time.*

In U.S. $	2020	2019	2018	2017	2016	2015
Revenue						
R&D Expense						
Operating Income						
Operating Margin %						
SGA Expense						
Net Income						
Operating Cash Flow						
Capital Expenditure						
EBITDA						
Return on Assets %						
Return on Equity %						
Debt to Equity						

CONTACT INFORMATION:

Phone: 617 418-2200   Fax: 617 418-2290
Toll-Free:
Address: 150 Second St., Cambridge, MA 02141 United States

STOCK TICKER/OTHER:

Stock Ticker: Private   Exchange:
Employees: Fiscal Year Ends:
Parent Company:

SALARIES/BONUSES:

Top Exec. Salary: $ Bonus: $
Second Exec. Salary: $ Bonus: $

OTHER THOUGHTS:

Estimated Female Officers or Directors:
Hot Spot for Advancement for Women/Minorities:

Sales, profits and employees may be estimates. Financial information, benefits and other data can change quickly and may vary from those stated here.

Fresenius Medical Care AG & Co KGaA www.freseniusmedicalcare.com

NAIC Code: 621400

TYPES OF BUSINESS:

Dialysis Products & Services
Health Care Product Development
Health Care Product Manufacturing
Dialysis Products
Non-Dialysis Products
Specialty Services
Ambulatory Surgery Center Services
Transplant Medicine

BRANDS/DIVISIONS/AFFILIATES:

CONTACTS: Note: Officers with more than one job title may be intentionally listed here more than once.

Rice Powell, CEO
Helen Giza, CFO
Olaf Schermeier, CEO-Global R&D
Kent Wanzek, CEO-Global Mfg. Oper.
Rainer Runte, Dir.-Law, Compliance & Intellectual Property
Emanuele Gatti, Global Chief Strategist
Ronald Kuerbitz, CEO-North America
Emanuele Gatti, CEO-Latin America & EMEA
Roberto Fuste, CEO-Asia Pacific

GROWTH PLANS/SPECIAL FEATURES:

Fresenius Medical Care AG & Co. KGaA is a provider of health care products and services. The company operates in four geographical segments: North America, EMEA (Europe, Middle East and Africa), Asia-Pacific and Latin America. Fresenius develops, manufactures and distributes a variety of health care products, which includes dialysis and non-dialysis products. Dialysis products include hemodialysis machines, peritoneal cyclers, dialyzers, peritoneal solutions, hemodialysis concentrates, solutions and granulates, bloodlines, renal pharmaceuticals and systems for water treatment. Non-dialysis products include acute cardiopulmonary and apheresis products. Fresenius supplies dialysis clinics that it owns, operates or manages with a broad range of products and also sells dialysis products to other dialysis service providers. Fresenius owns more than 4,000 clinics in its four geographical regions, which provides treatment for approximately 344,000 dialysis patients every year. Other health services offered includes, but are not limited to, pharmacy, vascular, cardiovascular and endovascular specialty services, as well as ambulatory surgery center services, physician nephrology and cardiology services, urgent care services and ambulant treatment services. In September 2021, Fresenius announced that it created a position of Head of Transplantation Medicine, placing U.S. citizen Dr. Benjamin Hippen to fill the role of leading the company's worldwide efforts in expanding access to and understanding of transplant medicine.

Fresenius offers its employees a health plan, subsidized childcare, risk insurance, a pension plan and profit-sharing programs.

FINANCIAL DATA: Note: Data for latest year may not have been available at press time.

In U.S. $	2020	2019	2018	2017	2016	2015
Revenue	21,819,790,000	21,352,450,000	20,216,590,000	21,727,560,000	20,807,220,000	18,704,420,000
R&D Expense	236,748,600	205,292,700	163,247,700	159,691,100	188,620,600	156,789,000
Operating Income	2,662,389,000	2,647,702,000	2,633,478,000	2,804,271,000	2,988,644,000	2,565,000,000
Operating Margin %		.12%	.13%	.13%	.14%	.14%
SGA Expense	3,866,385,000	3,739,532,000	3,501,221,000	4,371,245,000	3,537,029,000	3,235,842,000
Net Income	1,422,609,000	1,465,667,000	2,421,469,000	1,563,615,000	1,444,321,000	1,150,416,000
Operating Cash Flow	5,171,973,000	3,136,241,000	2,519,195,000	2,677,904,000	2,485,932,000	2,190,373,000
Capital Expenditure	1,285,289,000	1,374,244,000	1,291,756,000	1,153,919,000	1,196,557,000	1,064,924,000
EBITDA	5,048,709,000	4,794,662,000	4,777,214,000	3,837,864,000	4,019,662,000	3,532,036,000
Return on Assets %		.04%	.08%	.05%	.05%	.04%
Return on Equity %		.10%	.18%	.13%	.12%	.11%
Debt to Equity		0.88	0.429	0.59	0.666	0.794

CONTACT INFORMATION:

Phone: 49 6172 6082522   Fax: 49 61726082488
Toll-Free:
Address: Else-Kroener-Strasse 1, Bad Homburg, HE 61352 Germany

STOCK TICKER/OTHER:

Stock Ticker: FMS   Exchange: NYS
Employees: 125,364   Fiscal Year Ends: 12/31
Parent Company:

SALARIES/BONUSES:

Top Exec. Salary: $ Bonus: $
Second Exec. Salary: $ Bonus: $

OTHER THOUGHTS:

Estimated Female Officers or Directors:
Hot Spot for Advancement for Women/Minorities:

Fresenius SE & Co KGaA

www.fresenius.com

NAIC Code: 621400

TYPES OF BUSINESS:

Dialysis Clinics
Dialysis Products & Services
Nutrition, Infusion Therapy & Transfusion Products
Hospital Management & Engineering
Management & Consulting Services
Pharmaceutical Plant Engineering
Information Technology Services

BRANDS/DIVISIONS/AFFILIATES:

Fresenius Medical Care
Fresenius Kabi
Fresenius Helios
Fresenius Vamed
Quironsalud

CONTACTS: *Note: Officers with more than one job title may be intentionally listed here more than once.*

Ulf M. Schneider, Pres.
Rachel Empey, CFO
Jurgen Gotz, Chief Legal & Compliance Officer
Mats Henriksson, CEO-Fresenius Kabi
Francesco De Meo, CEO-Fresenius Helios
Rice Powell, CEO-Fresenius Medical Care
Ernst Wastler, CEO-Fresenius Vamed
Stephan Sturm, Chmn.

GROWTH PLANS/SPECIAL FEATURES:

Fresenius SE & Co. KGaA is an international healthcare group offering products and services primarily for dialysis, with operations in approximately 100 countries. The company is comprised of four business segments: Fresenius Medical Care (FMC), Fresenius Kabi, Fresenius Helios and Fresenius Vamed. FMC is a leading manufacturer of chronic kidney failure products, such as hemodialysis machines, dialyzers and related disposable products as well as renal pharmaceuticals to support patients with chronic kidney failure. It owns and operates approximately 4,000 dialysis clinics in Asia-Pacific, Latin America, North America, and EMEA (Europe, Middle East and Africa). Fresenius Kabi provides parenteral nutrition products that supply nutrients to patients while bypassing the gastro-intestinal tract; enteral nutrition products that artificially feed a patient via the intestinal tract; infusion therapy products, blood replacement and rinsing solutions as well as carrier solutions for drugs; transfusion technology products; and ambulatory care outpatient services. Helios is one of Germany's largest private hospital managers. Fresenius Helios is Europe's leading private hospital operator, with Fresenius Helios owning and operating 89 hospitals in Germany (seven of which are maximum care facilities), 130 medical care centers and six prevention centers; and subsidiary Quironsalud operating 53 hospitals, 70 outpatient centers and approximately 300 occupational risk centers. Fresenius Vamed operates in the project and management business of healthcare facilities worldwide. These include hospitals and healthcare centers as well as spas and wellness centers. Fresenius Vamed has completed more than 960 projects in 95 countries since its founding in 1982.

FINANCIAL DATA: *Note: Data for latest year may not have been available at press time.*

In U.S. $	2020	2019	2018	2017	2016	2015
Revenue	44,322,400,000	43,261,900,000	40,966,180,000	41,401,130,000	35,532,940,000	33,752,810,000
R&D Expense	917,554,500	788,046,100	822,255,900	681,751,600	610,888,500	566,904,500
Operating Income	5,319,617,000	5,622,618,000	5,427,133,000	5,606,735,000	5,286,629,000	4,734,386,000
Operating Margin %		.13%	.13%	.14%	.15%	.14%
SGA Expense	6,634,249,000	6,604,926,000	5,953,719,000	6,767,422,000	5,254,863,000	4,582,885,000
Net Income	2,085,573,000	2,300,606,000	2,476,542,000	2,216,303,000	1,946,291,000	1,659,173,000
Operating Cash Flow	8,001,418,000	5,208,435,000	4,571,890,000	4,810,136,000	4,366,631,000	4,064,852,000
Capital Expenditure	2,939,596,000	3,004,350,000	3,932,900,000	9,911,054,000	1,989,053,000	1,819,226,000
EBITDA	8,788,241,000	8,851,774,000	8,596,423,000	7,603,118,000	6,837,064,000	6,408,220,000
Return on Assets %		.03%	.04%	.04%	.04%	.03%
Return on Equity %		.12%	.14%	.14%	.14%	.13%
Debt to Equity		1.296	0.911	1.182	1.027	1.244

CONTACT INFORMATION:

Phone: 49 61726080   Fax: 49 61726082294
Toll-Free:
Address: Else-Kroener-Strasse 1, Bad Homburg v.d.H, 61352 Germany

STOCK TICKER/OTHER:

Stock Ticker: FSNUY
Employees: 311,269
Parent Company:

Exchange: PINX
Fiscal Year Ends: 12/31

SALARIES/BONUSES:

Top Exec. Salary: $ Bonus: $
Second Exec. Salary: $ Bonus: $

OTHER THOUGHTS:

Estimated Female Officers or Directors:
Hot Spot for Advancement for Women/Minorities:

Fujifilm Healthcare Americas Corporation

hca.fujifilm.com

NAIC Code: 334510

TYPES OF BUSINESS:

Marketing-Medical Imaging Systems
Healthcare Diagnostic Solutions
Medical Imaging Solutions
Product Development
Data Access Technology
Artificial Intelligence
Product Manufacture

BRANDS/DIVISIONS/AFFILIATES:

Fujifilm Holdings Corporation
Synapse Enterprise Imaging
REiLI
Hitachi Healthcare Americas Corporation

CONTACTS: Note: Officers with more than one job title may be intentionally listed here more than once.

Donald Broomfield, Pres.
Richard Katz, General Counsel
Richard Kurz, Controller
Sheldon Schaffer, VP
Douglas Thistlethwaite, Mgr.-Regulatory Affairs
James Confer, VP-Service
Kenji Sukeno, Chmn.-Corp.

GROWTH PLANS/SPECIAL FEATURES:

Fujifilm Healthcare Americas Corporation (formerly Hitachi Healthcare Americas Corporation) is an innovator in diagnostic and enterprise imaging solutions. The company's products are designed to meet the needs of healthcare across prevention, diagnosis and treatment. Fujifilm's medical imaging portfolio includes solutions for digital radiography, mammography, computed tomography, magnetic resonance imaging, ultrasound, endoscopy and endosurgery. Its Synapse Enterprise Imaging portfolio provides healthcare professionals with the imaging and data access needed to deliver a complete patient record. REiLI combines Fujifilm's image processing with artificial intelligence (AI) innovations. The firm's in-vitro diagnostic portfolio provides molecular-based immunoassay technology for liver surveillance, clinical diagnostic chemicals for laboratories and diagnostic chemicals of original equipment manufacturer (OEM) white labeling products. Fujifilm Healthcare is a subsidiary of Fujifilm Holdings Corporation. In mid-2021, following the acquisition of Hitachi Ltd.'s diagnostic imaging business by Fujifilm Corporation, Hitachi Healthcare America Corporation was renamed as Fujifilm Healthcare Americas Corporation.

FINANCIAL DATA: Note: Data for latest year may not have been available at press time.

In U.S. $	2020	2019	2018	2017	2016	2015
Revenue	232,508,981	225,736,875	214,987,500	204,750,000	195,000,000	190,000,000
R&D Expense						
Operating Income						
Operating Margin %						
SGA Expense						
Net Income						
Operating Cash Flow						
Capital Expenditure						
EBITDA						
Return on Assets %						
Return on Equity %						
Debt to Equity						

CONTACT INFORMATION:

Phone: 330-425-1313   Fax: 330-425-1410
Toll-Free: 800-800-3106
Address: 81 Hartwell Ave., Ste. 300, Lexington, MA 02421 United States

SALARIES/BONUSES:

Top Exec. Salary: $ Bonus: $
Second Exec. Salary: $ Bonus: $

STOCK TICKER/OTHER:

Stock Ticker: Subsidiary   Exchange:
Employees: 400   Fiscal Year Ends: 03/31
Parent Company: Fujifilm Holdings Corporation

OTHER THOUGHTS:

Estimated Female Officers or Directors:
Hot Spot for Advancement for Women/Minorities:

Galderma SA

www.galderma.com

NAIC Code: 325412

TYPES OF BUSINESS:

Dermatological Pharmaceuticals
Dermatological Product Research & Development

BRANDS/DIVISIONS/AFFILIATES:

Akleif
Epiduo
Differin
Soolantra
Proactiv
Cetaphil
Benzac
Loceryl

CONTACTS: *Note: Officers with more than one job title may be intentionally listed here more than once.*

Flemming Ornskov, CEO
Cecile Dussart, VP-Oper.
Humberto C. Antunes, Pres.
Thomas Dittrich, CFO

GROWTH PLANS/SPECIAL FEATURES:

Galderma SA is a global dermatology company that operates in 40 countries, is present in approximately 100 countries, and is based in Switzerland. The firm engages in research and development for skin solutions, with innovation areas including acne, rosacea, psoriasis, atopic dermatitis, skin aging, sun protection and skin cancer. Galderma has an extensive product portfolio of prescription medicines, aesthetics solutions and consumer care products, and also partners with health care practitioners to meet skin health needs. Prescription and aesthetics brands include Akleif, Epiduo, Differin, Soolantra, Mirvaso, Oracea, Metvix, Restylane, Azzalure, Dysport and Sculptra. Consumer solutions brands include Proactiv, Cetaphil, Benzac and Loceryl. Galderma operates four manufacturing sites. In June 2021, Galderma announced the signing of two exclusive five-year license agreements with Sol-Gel Technologies Ltd. for the commercialization of EPSOLAY and TWYNEO in the U.S. EPSOLAY (benzoyl peroxide, 5% cream) is under investigation for the treatment of inflammatory lesions of rosacea in adults; and TWYNEO (benzoyl peroxide, 3%, and tretinoin, 0.1%, cream) is under investigation for the treatment of acne vulgaris.

FINANCIAL DATA: *Note: Data for latest year may not have been available at press time.*

In U.S. $	2020	2019	2018	2017	2016	2015
Revenue	300,000,000	288,332,000	248,062,500	236,250,000	225,000,000	215,000,000
R&D Expense						
Operating Income						
Operating Margin %						
SGA Expense						
Net Income						
Operating Cash Flow						
Capital Expenditure						
EBITDA						
Return on Assets %						
Return on Equity %						
Debt to Equity						

CONTACT INFORMATION:

Phone: 41-21-642-78-00   Fax: 41-21-642-78-01
Toll-Free:
Address: Rue d'Entre-deux-Villes 10, La Tour-de-Peilz, 1814 Switzerland

STOCK TICKER/OTHER:

Stock Ticker: Joint Venture
Employees: 4,600
Parent Company:

Exchange:
Fiscal Year Ends:

SALARIES/BONUSES:

Top Exec. Salary: $ Bonus: $
Second Exec. Salary: $ Bonus: $

OTHER THOUGHTS:

Estimated Female Officers or Directors: 1
Hot Spot for Advancement for Women/Minorities:

Sales, profits and employees may be estimates. Financial information, benefits and other data can change quickly and may vary from those stated here.

Gamida Cell Ltd

www.gamida-cell.com

NAIC Code: 325414

TYPES OF BUSINESS:

Biological Product (except Diagnostic) Manufacturing
Biopharmaceuticals
Cell Therapy Development
Clinical Trials

BRANDS/DIVISIONS/AFFILIATES:

Omidubicel

CONTACTS: *Note: Officers with more than one job title may be intentionally listed here more than once.*

Julian Adams, CEO

GROWTH PLANS/SPECIAL FEATURES:

Gamida Cell Ltd. is a clinical-stage biopharmaceutical company that develops advanced cell therapies with the potential to cure cancer and rare, serious hematologic diseases. Since cell therapies are limited by the availability of donor cells, matching a donor to the patient and the decline in donor cell functionality when expanding the cells to achieve a therapeutic dose, Gamida has leveraged its nicotinamide-based (NAM) cell expansion technology to develop a pipeline of products designed to address the limitations of cell therapies. The firm's proprietary technology allows for the proliferation of donor cells while maintaining the cells' functional therapeutic characteristics, which, if approved, will provide a treatment alternative for patients. Gamida's most advanced product candidate is its Phase 3 clinical study evaluating the safety and efficacy of Omidubicel, an investigational advanced cell therapy for patients in need of bone marrow transplant as well as other hematologic malignancies. Omidubicel is also in a Phase 1 study for the treatment of severe aplastic anemia. Other product candidates include GDA-201 for the treatment of non-Hodgkin lymphoma, GDA-301 for the treatment of solid tumors, GDA-401 for the treatment of solid tumors, GDA-501 for the treatment of solid tumors, and GDA-601 for the treatment of multiple myeloma. Headquartered in Israel, Gamida Cell has a U.S. office in Boston, Massachusetts.

FINANCIAL DATA: *Note: Data for latest year may not have been available at press time.*

In U.S. $	2020	2019	2018	2017	2016	2015
Revenue						
R&D Expense	40,071,000	31,462,000	22,045,000	15,018,000	19,095,000	
Operating Income	-62,300,000	-48,245,000	-33,644,000	-19,490,000	-23,709,000	
Operating Margin %						
SGA Expense	19,785,000	11,168,000	11,599,000	4,472,000	4,614,000	
Net Income	-72,704,000	-34,351,000	-52,931,000	-19,011,000	-22,671,000	
Operating Cash Flow	-48,627,000	-37,930,000	-26,426,000	-17,760,000	-12,590,000	
Capital Expenditure	11,804,000	3,055,000	1,645,000	402,000	284,000	
EBITDA	-69,600,000	-31,520,000	-33,375,000	-19,328,000	-23,585,000	
Return on Assets %		- .51%	- .96%	- .59%	-1.18%	
Return on Equity %		-1.15%	-2.22%	-1.12%	-2.07%	
Debt to Equity		0.117				

CONTACT INFORMATION:

Phone: 972 26595666   Fax: 972 26595616
Toll-Free:
Address: 5 Nahum Heftsadie St., Jerusalem, 95484 Israel

STOCK TICKER/OTHER:

Stock Ticker: GMDA   Exchange: NAS
Employees: 112   Fiscal Year Ends: 12/31
Parent Company:

SALARIES/BONUSES:

Top Exec. Salary: $ Bonus: $
Second Exec. Salary: $ Bonus: $

OTHER THOUGHTS:

Estimated Female Officers or Directors:
Hot Spot for Advancement for Women/Minorities:

GE Healthcare

www.gehealthcare.com

NAIC Code: 339100

TYPES OF BUSINESS:

Medical Imaging & Information Technology
Magnetic Resonance Imaging Systems
Patient Monitoring Systems
Clinical Information Systems
Nuclear Medicine
Surgery & Vascular Imaging
X-Ray & Ultrasound Bone Densitometers
Clinical & Business Services

BRANDS/DIVISIONS/AFFILIATES:

General Electric Company (GE)
Zionexa

CONTACTS: *Note: Officers with more than one job title may be intentionally listed here more than once.*

Kieran Murphy, CEO
Michael Harsh, CTO
Keith Newman, General Counsel
Markus Ewert, Exec. VP-Bus. Dev.
Jeff DeMarrais, Chief Comm. Officer
Dee Miller, Chief Quality Officer
Rachel Duan, CEO
Tom Gentile, CEO-Health Care Systems
Terri Bresenham, CEO
Brian Masterson, VP-Supply Chain

GROWTH PLANS/SPECIAL FEATURES:

GE Healthcare is a division of General Electric Company and a leading medical technology and life sciences company. The firm offers medical products such as imaging and ultrasound systems and devices, anesthesia delivery systems, diagnostic electrocardiogram (ECG) equipment, maternal infant care equipment, patient monitoring systems and ventilators, as well as related refurbished equipment. Other products and services by GE Healthcare include pharmaceutical imaging agents, healthcare information technology (IT) solutions, performance intelligence and analytic software, radiology IT, command centers, consulting, clinical network solutions, site planning, financial solutions and more. GE Healthcare specializes in breast health, labor and delivery, outpatient solutions, electrophysiology, federal health solutions, intensive care unit solutions, hybrid operating room, neurology, oncology, orthopedics, stroke and rural health. In May 2021, GE Healthcare acquired Zionexa, an innovator of in-vivo oncology and neurology biomarkers that help enable more personalized healthcare.

FINANCIAL DATA: *Note: Data for latest year may not have been available at press time.*

In U.S. $	2020	2019	2018	2017	2016	2015
Revenue	18,009,000,000	19,942,000,000	19,784,000,000	19,017,000,000	18,291,000,000	17,639,000,000
R&D Expense						
Operating Income						
Operating Margin %						
SGA Expense						
Net Income	3,060,000,000	3,896,000,000	3,698,000,000	3,448,000,000	3,161,000,000	2,882,000,000
Operating Cash Flow						
Capital Expenditure						
EBITDA						
Return on Assets %						
Return on Equity %						
Debt to Equity						

CONTACT INFORMATION:

Phone: 312-243-0787   Fax:
Toll-Free:
Address: 1053 W. Grand Ave., Chicago, IL 60642 United States

STOCK TICKER/OTHER:

Stock Ticker: Subsidiary   Exchange:
Employees: 47,000   Fiscal Year Ends: 12/31
Parent Company: General Electric Company (GE)

SALARIES/BONUSES:

Top Exec. Salary: $ Bonus: $
Second Exec. Salary: $ Bonus: $

OTHER THOUGHTS:

Estimated Female Officers or Directors: 4
Hot Spot for Advancement for Women/Minorities: Y

Genentech Inc

www.gene.com

NAIC Code: 325412

TYPES OF BUSINESS:

Drug Development & Manufacturing
Genetically Engineered Drugs
Biotechnology

BRANDS/DIVISIONS/AFFILIATES:

Roche Holding AG
www.gene.com
Tecentriq

CONTACTS: *Note: Officers with more than one job title may be intentionally listed here more than once.*

Alexander Hardy, CEO
Ed Harrington, CFO
Cynthia Burks, Sr. VP-Human Resources
Richard H. Scheller, Exec. VP-Research
Frederick C. Kentz, Sec.
Timothy Moore, Head-Pharmaceutical Technical Operation Biologics
Severin Schwan, Chmn.

GROWTH PLANS/SPECIAL FEATURES:

Genentech, Inc., a wholly owned subsidiary of Roche Holding AG, is a biotechnology company that discovers, develops, manufactures and commercializes medicines to treat patients with serious or life-threatening medical conditions. The firm makes medicines by splicing genes into fast-growing bacteria that then produce therapeutic proteins and combat diseases on a molecular level. Genentech uses cutting-edge technologies such as computer visualization of molecules, micro arrays and sensitive assaying techniques to develop, manufacture and market pharmaceuticals for unmet medical needs. For patients, the company's website (www.gene.com) provides access for viewing medicine information, investigational medicines, finding open clinical trials and information on diseases in general. Genentech's range of programs and services help make sure that price is not a barrier for patients. For medical professionals, the website offers information on the medicines that are on the market by Genentech, as well as what is on the current pipeline, compliance, product security and various types of medical resources. There were over 40 medicines on the market by the company, and 54 molecules in the pipeline. These medicines and molecules are in various phases in relation to oncology, metabolism, immunology, infectious disease, neuroscience, ophthalmology or other conditions. Approximately half of Genentech's marketed and pipeline products are derived from collaborations with companies and institutions worldwide; therefore, the firm is open to having partners.

Genentech provides employees benefits including a 401(k); disability, life, AD&D, medical, dental and vision coverage; flexible spending accounts; and paid vacations.

FINANCIAL DATA: *Note: Data for latest year may not have been available at press time.*

In U.S. $	2020	2019	2018	2017	2016	2015
Revenue	21,840,000,000	21,000,000,000	20,000,000,000	19,000,000,000	18,000,000,000	17,000,000,000
R&D Expense						
Operating Income						
Operating Margin %						
SGA Expense						
Net Income						
Operating Cash Flow						
Capital Expenditure						
EBITDA						
Return on Assets %						
Return on Equity %						
Debt to Equity						

CONTACT INFORMATION:

Phone: 650-225-1000   Fax: 650-225-6000
Toll-Free: 800-626-3553
Address: 1 DNA Way, South San Francisco, CA 94080-4990 United States

STOCK TICKER/OTHER:

Stock Ticker: Subsidiary
Employees: 13,500
Parent Company: Roche Holding AG

Exchange:
Fiscal Year Ends: 12/31

SALARIES/BONUSES:

Top Exec. Salary: $ Bonus: $
Second Exec. Salary: $ Bonus: $

OTHER THOUGHTS:

Estimated Female Officers or Directors: 1
Hot Spot for Advancement for Women/Minorities: Y

Genesis Healthcare Inc   www.genesishcc.com

NAIC Code: 623110

TYPES OF BUSINESS:

Nursing Care Facilities
Assisted Living Communities
Rehabilitation Services
Skilled Nursing Centers

BRANDS/DIVISIONS/AFFILIATES:

ReGen Healthcare LLC

GROWTH PLANS/SPECIAL FEATURES:

Genesis Healthcare, Inc. owns and operates nearly 250 skilled nursing centers and assisted/senior living communities in 23 U.S. states (as of September 2021). Genesis offers rehabilitation therapy, memory support, long-term care and assisted/senior living services, as well as cardiac management, on-site dialysis care, independent living services, mental health and recovery services, neuro-rehabilitation, pulmonary rehabilitation, short-stay care, transitional care, VA-contracted care, ventilator care and more. During 2021, Genesis Healthcare ceased from public trading after receiving an investment that gave New York private-equity firm ReGen Healthcare LLC control of the company.

CONTACTS: *Note: Officers with more than one job title may be intentionally listed here more than once.*

Harry Wilson, CEO
George Hager, CEO
Robert Fish, Director
JoAnne Reifsnyder, Executive VP, Divisional

FINANCIAL DATA: *Note: Data for latest year may not have been available at press time.*

In U.S. $	2020	2019	2018	2017	2016	2015
Revenue		4,565,834,240	4,976,650,240	5,373,740,032	5,732,429,824	5,619,224,064
R&D Expense						
Operating Income						
Operating Margin %						
SGA Expense						
Net Income		14,619,000	-235,231,008	-578,982,016	-64,013,000	-426,195,008
Operating Cash Flow						
Capital Expenditure						
EBITDA						
Return on Assets %						
Return on Equity %						
Debt to Equity						

CONTACT INFORMATION:

Phone: 610-444-6350   Fax: 610-925-4000
Toll-Free:
Address: 101 E. State St., Kennett Square, PA 19348 United States

STOCK TICKER/OTHER:

Stock Ticker: Private   Exchange: NYS
Employees: 55,000   Fiscal Year Ends:
Parent Company:

SALARIES/BONUSES:

Top Exec. Salary: $ Bonus: $
Second Exec. Salary: $ Bonus: $

OTHER THOUGHTS:

Estimated Female Officers or Directors: 2
Hot Spot for Advancement for Women/Minorities:

GenMark Diagnostics Inc

www.genmarkdx.com

NAIC Code: 325413

TYPES OF BUSINESS:

Diagnostic Instruments
Multiplex Molecular Diagnostics
Molecular Detection Technology

BRANDS/DIVISIONS/AFFILIATES:

Roche Holding AG
eSensor
ePlex
ePlex: The True Sample-to-Answer

GROWTH PLANS/SPECIAL FEATURES:

GenMark Diagnostics, Inc. is a leading provider of multiplex molecular diagnostic solutions designed to enhance patient care, improve key quality metrics and reduce the total cost-of-care. Utilizing GenMark's proprietary eSensor detection technology, the company's eSensor XT-8 and ePlex systems are designed to support a broad range of molecular diagnostic sample-to-answer tests with compact workstations and self-contained, disposable test cartridges. GenMark's ePlex: The True Sample-to-Answer Solution is designed to optimize laboratory efficiency and address a broad range of infectious disease testing needs, including respiratory, bloodstream and gastrointestinal infections. In April 2021, Roche Holding AG acquired GenMark, which became a wholly-owned subsidiary and ceased from public trading on the NASDAQ stock market.

CONTACTS:
Note: Officers with more than one job title may be intentionally listed here more than once.

Scott Mendel, CEO
Abe Chohan, Sr. VP-Oper.
James Fox, Chairman of the Board
Johnny Ek, CFO
Hollis Winkler, VP-Human Resources
Hany Massarany, Director
Eric Stier, General Counsel
James McNally, Senior VP, Divisional
Brian Mitchell, Senior VP, Divisional
Michael Gleeson, Senior VP, Divisional

FINANCIAL DATA:
Note: Data for latest year may not have been available at press time.

In U.S. $	2020	2019	2018	2017	2016	2015
Revenue	100,000,000	88,021,000	70,759,000	52,519,000	49,274,000	39,411,000
R&D Expense						
Operating Income						
Operating Margin %						
SGA Expense						
Net Income		-47,350,000	-50,500,000	-61,850,000	-50,601,000	-42,197,000
Operating Cash Flow						
Capital Expenditure						
EBITDA						
Return on Assets %						
Return on Equity %						
Debt to Equity						

CONTACT INFORMATION:

Phone: 760 448-4300   Fax: 760 448-4301
Toll-Free: 800-373-6767
Address: 5964 La Place Ct., Carlsbad, CA 92008 United States

STOCK TICKER/OTHER:

Stock Ticker: Subsidiary   Exchange: NAS
Employees: 437   Fiscal Year Ends: 12/31
Parent Company: Roche Holding AG

SALARIES/BONUSES:

Top Exec. Salary: $ Bonus: $
Second Exec. Salary: $ Bonus: $

OTHER THOUGHTS:

Estimated Female Officers or Directors: 2
Hot Spot for Advancement for Women/Minorities:

Gerresheimer AG

www.gerresheimer.com/en/home.html

NAIC Code: 339100

TYPES OF BUSINESS:

Surgical and Medical Instrument Manufacturing
Packaging Manufacturer
Plastic Packaging
Glass Packaging
Advanced Technologies
Drug Delivery Systems
Containers & Jars

BRANDS/DIVISIONS/AFFILIATES:

Sensile Medical AG

CONTACTS: *Note: Officers with more than one job title may be intentionally listed here more than once.*

Dietmar Siemssen, CEO
Bernd Metzner, CFO
Andreas Schutte, Head-Plastics Systems Div.
Stefan Grote, Head-Tubular Glass Div.

GROWTH PLANS/SPECIAL FEATURES:

Gerresheimer AG is a German manufacturer of specialty products made of glass and plastic for the global pharmacy and healthcare industry. The company has manufacturing plants in Europe, North America, South America and Asia. Gerresheimer operates through three business divisions: plastics and devices, packaging glass and advanced technologies. The plastics and devices division includes complex, customer-specific products for the simple and safe administration of medicines, such as insulin pens, inhalers and pre-fillable syringes. This division also produces diagnostics and medical technology products such as lancets and test systems, as well as pharmaceutical plastic containers for liquid and solid medicines with closure and safety systems. The packaging glass division produces glass primary packaging for medicines and cosmetics, such as pharma jars, ampoules, injection vials, cartridges, perfume flacons and cream jars, as well as special glass containers for the food and beverage industry. Last, the advanced technologies division develops and manufactures intelligent drug delivery systems. Swiss tech company Sensile Medical AG forms the basis of this division, where Gerresheimer offers pharmaceutical and biotech companies drug delivery systems with state-of-the-art digital and electronic capabilities. Its portfolio comprises patented micro pumps, which are used to self-administer medication for Parkinson's, heart failure or other purposes. The technologies division is currently developing a platform for smart inhalation measurement systems. More than 80% of annual sales are derived from the pharmaceutical and healthcare industries, 12% from the cosmetics industry and 7% from the food and beverage and related supplements industries.

FINANCIAL DATA: *Note: Data for latest year may not have been available at press time.*

In U.S. $	2020	2019	2018	2017	2016	2015
Revenue	1,733,440,000	1,701,025,000	1,671,061,000	1,647,267,000	1,680,505,000	1,682,670,000
R&D Expense	9,353,924	4,387,401	3,566,367	4,285,994	3,864,481	2,256,622
Operating Income	219,835,600	39,850,700	190,377,300	214,327,800	219,715,800	185,270,300
Operating Margin %		.00%	.11%	.13%	.13%	.11%
SGA Expense	284,079,000	285,034,500	316,935,000	312,248,300	312,010,100	320,119,000
Net Income	108,199,300	98,696,370	157,566,500	123,261,400	148,614,500	127,329,900
Operating Cash Flow	271,471,500	235,710,100	211,944,100	267,768,300	211,962,400	248,968,800
Capital Expenditure	212,719,900	201,045,800	139,971,600	142,360,200	135,276,400	153,698,300
EBITDA	368,257,000	479,932,300	334,771,800	373,004,800	374,698,200	375,008,500
Return on Assets %		.03%	.05%	.04%	.05%	.05%
Return on Equity %		.09%	.16%	.14%	.18%	.18%
Debt to Equity		0.539	0.861	0.905	1.025	1.183

CONTACT INFORMATION:

Phone: 49 0211618100   Fax: 49 02116181295
Toll-Free:
Address: Klaus-Bungert-Strasse 4, Duesseldorf, NW 40468 Germany

STOCK TICKER/OTHER:

Stock Ticker: GRRMY   Exchange: GREY
Employees: 9,880   Fiscal Year Ends: 12/31
Parent Company:

SALARIES/BONUSES:

Top Exec. Salary: $ Bonus: $
Second Exec. Salary: $ Bonus: $

OTHER THOUGHTS:

Estimated Female Officers or Directors: 3
Hot Spot for Advancement for Women/Minorities: Y

Sales, profits and employees may be estimates. Financial information, benefits and other data can change quickly and may vary from those stated here.

Getinge Industrier AB

www.getinge.com/int

NAIC Code: 339100

TYPES OF BUSINESS:

Medical Equipment Manufacturing
Healthcare Operating Rooms
Intensive Care Units
Emergency Rooms
Laboratories
Hybrid Healthcare Rooms
Recovery Rooms
Sterile Services

BRANDS/DIVISIONS/AFFILIATES:

CONTACTS: Note: Officers with more than one job title may be intentionally listed here more than once.

Mattias Perjos, CEO
Lars Sandstrom, CFO
Carsten Blecker, CCO
Magnus Lundback, Exec. VP-Human Resources
Heinz Jacqui, Exec. VP-Medical Systems
Anders Grahn, Exec. VP-Infection Control
Alex Myers, Exec. VP-Extended Care
Johan Malmqvist, Chmn.

GROWTH PLANS/SPECIAL FEATURES:

Getinge Industrier AB was founded in 1904 in Sweden, and provides products and solutions to health care and life science organizations. For hospital departments, Getinge offers complete settings for operating rooms, intensive care units, emergency rooms, catheter labs, flexible endoscope reprocessing, hybrid operating rooms, recovery rooms and central sterile services departments, when it comes to integrated solutions and patient outcomes. The firm offers acute care therapies for clinical professionals practicing in a hospital setting, as well as sterilization and hygiene solutions for practices of all sizes-whether a single clinician studio or a multi-unit clinic. Acute care solutions include beating heart surgery, dialysis access, endoscopic vessel harvesting, hernia repair, mechanical ventilation, on-pump surgery, peripheral stenting and more. Getinge's life science solutions include a comprehensive line of equipment, technical expertise and consultative services to meet both common and highly-specialized process needs for contamination prevention in biopharmaceutical production, biomedical research, medical device manufacturing and laboratory applications. Besides hospitals and acute care facilities, the company also serves clinics and dental facilities. Getinge builds workplaces with the ability to keep up with current demands while also adapting to future growth. The company's integrated workflow solutions include patient flow management, operating room integration and sterile supply management. Getinge operates in more nearly 40 countries, and sells its products in over 125 countries. Production is conducted at facilities in France, China, Germany, Poland, Sweden, Turkey, Netherlands, the U.K. and the U.S.

FINANCIAL DATA: Note: Data for latest year may not have been available at press time.

In U.S. $	2020	2019	2018	2017	2016	2015
Revenue	3,607,254,000	3,212,886,000	2,924,126,000	2,721,257,000	3,599,632,000	3,657,578,000
R&D Expense	124,963,700	92,180,390	83,591,410	71,857,150	81,171,980	72,341,040
Operating Income	600,140,300	326,139,600	-34,355,950	272,912,000	438,038,300	413,602,000
Operating Margin %		.10%	- .01%	.10%	.12%	.11%
SGA Expense	1,062,494,000	1,071,083,000	1,003,097,000	923,013,600	1,162,417,000	1,198,224,000
Net Income	391,827,200	147,827,300	-116,979,600	166,457,000	143,714,300	168,150,600
Operating Cash Flow	870,874,900	463,563,300	302,792,000	334,244,600	444,086,900	418,319,900
Capital Expenditure	126,415,400	147,585,400	166,940,900	201,175,900	172,384,600	211,458,400
EBITDA	871,358,700	550,058,000	193,796,600	490,419,000	274,242,700	328,559,000
Return on Assets %		.03%	- .02%	.03%	.02%	.03%
Return on Equity %		.06%	- .05%	.07%	.06%	.07%
Debt to Equity		0.345	0.384	0.256	0.776	0.834

CONTACT INFORMATION:

Phone: 46 103350000   Fax: 46 103355640
Toll-Free:
Address: Theres Svenssons gata 7, Gothenburg, 402 72 Sweden

STOCK TICKER/OTHER:

Stock Ticker: GNGBF   Exchange: PINX
Employees: 10,818   Fiscal Year Ends: 12/31
Parent Company:

SALARIES/BONUSES:

Top Exec. Salary: $ Bonus: $
Second Exec. Salary: $ Bonus: $

OTHER THOUGHTS:

Estimated Female Officers or Directors: 2
Hot Spot for Advancement for Women/Minorities:

Gilead Sciences Inc

www.gilead.com

NAIC Code: 325412

TYPES OF BUSINESS:

Viral & Bacterial Infections Drugs
Biopharmaceuticals
Drug Development
Drug Commercialization

BRANDS/DIVISIONS/AFFILIATES:

MYR GmbH
Hepcludex

CONTACTS: *Note: Officers with more than one job title may be intentionally listed here more than once.*

Daniel O'Day, CEO
Robin Washington, CFO
Brett Pletcher, Chief Compliance Officer
John McHutchison, Chief Scientific Officer
Laura Hamill, Executive VP, Divisional
Gregg Alton, Other Executive Officer

GROWTH PLANS/SPECIAL FEATURES:

Gilead Sciences, Inc. is a biopharmaceutical company that discovers, develops and commercializes innovative medicines to prevent and treat life-threatening diseases. The firm's primary areas of focus include human immunodeficiency virus (HIV), acquired immunodeficiency syndrome (AIDS), COVID-19, liver diseases, hematology/oncology/cell therapy, and other. In HIV/AIDS, Gilead offers eight treatments, namely Biktarvy, Genvoya, Descovy, Odefsey, Truvada, Complera/Eviplera, Stribild and Atripla, all of which are oral formulations. In COVID-19, Gilead offers Veklury (remdesivir), an injection for intravenous use. In liver diseases, the firm offers five treatments, including Epclusa, Harvoni, Vosevi, Vemlidy and Viread, each of which are oral formulations. In hematology/oncology/cell therapy, Gilead offers four treatments, including Yescarta, Tecartus, Trodelvy and Zydelig, with the first three being intravenous and Zydelig being an oral formulation. Other medicines include: Letairis, an oral formulation for the treatment of pulmonary arterial hypertension (PAH); Ranexa, an oral formulation for the treatment of chronic angina; and AmBisome, a proprietary liposomal formulation for the treatment of serious invasive fungal infections. In early-2021, Gilead acquired MYR GmbH, which encompasses Hepcludex for the treatment of chronic hepatitis delta virus in adults with compensated liver disease; and Gilead announced that the U.S. Food and Drug Administration accelerated approval for Trodelvy for the treatment of metastatic urothelial cancer.

Gilead offers its employees comprehensive benefits.

FINANCIAL DATA: *Note: Data for latest year may not have been available at press time.*

In U.S. $	2020	2019	2018	2017	2016	2015
Revenue	24,689,000,000	22,449,000,000	22,127,000,000	26,107,000,000	30,390,000,000	32,639,000,000
R&D Expense	5,039,000,000	9,106,000,000	5,018,000,000	3,734,000,000	5,098,000,000	3,014,000,000
Operating Income	9,927,000,000	4,287,000,000	8,200,000,000	14,124,000,000	17,633,000,000	22,193,000,000
Operating Margin %		.19%	.37%	.54%	.58%	.68%
SGA Expense	5,151,000,000	4,381,000,000	4,056,000,000	3,878,000,000	3,398,000,000	3,426,000,000
Net Income	123,000,000	5,386,000,000	5,455,000,000	4,628,000,000	13,501,000,000	18,108,000,000
Operating Cash Flow	8,168,000,000	9,144,001,000	8,400,000,000	11,898,000,000	16,669,000,000	20,329,000,000
Capital Expenditure	650,000,000	825,000,000	924,000,000	590,000,000	748,000,000	747,000,000
EBITDA	4,133,000,000	7,559,000,000	10,305,000,000	15,933,000,000	19,219,000,000	23,445,000,000
Return on Assets %		.09%	.08%	.07%	.25%	.42%
Return on Equity %		.25%	.26%	.24%	.72%	1.07%
Debt to Equity		0.981	1.149	1.506	1.395	1.144

CONTACT INFORMATION:

Phone: 650 574-3000   Fax: 650 578-9264
Toll-Free: 800-445-3235
Address: 333 Lakeside Dr., Foster City, CA 94404 United States

STOCK TICKER/OTHER:

Stock Ticker: GILD   Exchange: NAS
Employees: 11,800   Fiscal Year Ends: 12/31
Parent Company:

SALARIES/BONUSES:

Top Exec. Salary: $ Bonus: $
Second Exec. Salary: $ Bonus: $

OTHER THOUGHTS:

Estimated Female Officers or Directors: 4
Hot Spot for Advancement for Women/Minorities: Y

GlaxoSmithKline Pharmaceuticals Ltd

www.gsk-india.com

NAIC Code: 325412

TYPES OF BUSINESS:

Pharmaceuticals, Manufacturing & Distribution
Pharmaceuticals
Vaccines
Prescription Medicines
Drug Development
Research and Development

BRANDS/DIVISIONS/AFFILIATES:

GlaxoSmithKline plc

CONTACTS: *Note: Officers with more than one job title may be intentionally listed here more than once.*

Sridhar Venkatesh, Managing Dir.
Puja Thakur, CFO
Ransom D'Souza, VP-Communications
Chinmay Sharma, Exec. VP-Human Resources
S. Joglekar, Exec. VP-Medical & Clinical Research
Abhinav Kashyap, Dir.-Pharma Technology
Kaizad Hazari, Head-Legal & Corp. Affairs, South Asia
S. Khanna, VP-Finance
M.B. Kapadia, Sr. Exec. Dir.
R. Krishnaswamy, Dir.-Tech
H. M. Buch, Exec. VP-Pharmaceuticals
R. Bartaria, VP-Pharmaceuticals
R.S. Karnad, Chmn.

GROWTH PLANS/SPECIAL FEATURES:

GlaxoSmithKline Pharmaceuticals Ltd. (GSK India), a subsidiary of GlaxoSmithKline plc, is a leading Indian pharmaceutical company. The firm operates two business segments: pharmaceuticals and vaccines. The pharmaceuticals segment has served the health care needs of India for nearly 100 years (since 1924), and offers a wide range of prescription medicines across therapy areas such as immune-inflammation, respiratory, dermatology, nutrition, gastrointestinal and rare diseases. This division's leading pharmaceutical brands include Augmentin, Calpol, Ceftum (Zinnat) and Betnovate. The vaccines segment has a broad portfolio and innovative pipeline of vaccines to protect people of all ages, including critical diseases such as pneumococcal disease, meningitis, hepatitis, rotavirus, whooping cough, smallpox and influenza. Leading vaccine brands include Synflorix, Infanrix hexa, Havrix, boostrix and Menveo. Headquartered in Mumbai, GSK India has regional and sales hubs across India. The company has two global research and development center is based in India.

FINANCIAL DATA: *Note: Data for latest year may not have been available at press time.*

In U.S. $	2020	2019	2018	2017	2016	2015
Revenue		434,834,568	414,128,160	418,433,440	398,559,104	476,486,464
R&D Expense						
Operating Income						
Operating Margin %						
SGA Expense						
Net Income		53,111,683	50,582,556	48,575,872	54,346,776	68,709,176
Operating Cash Flow						
Capital Expenditure						
EBITDA						
Return on Assets %						
Return on Equity %						
Debt to Equity						

CONTACT INFORMATION:

Phone: 91-22-2495-9595   Fax: 91-22-2494-9494
Toll-Free:
Address: Dr. Annie Besant Rd., Worli, Mumbai, 400 030 India

STOCK TICKER/OTHER:

Stock Ticker: 500660
Employees: 4,620
Parent Company: GlaxoSmithKline plc

Exchange: Bombay
Fiscal Year Ends: 12/31

SALARIES/BONUSES:

Top Exec. Salary: $ Bonus: $
Second Exec. Salary: $ Bonus: $

OTHER THOUGHTS:

Estimated Female Officers or Directors: 2
Hot Spot for Advancement for Women/Minorities:

GlaxoSmithKline plc

www.gsk.com

NAIC Code: 325412

TYPES OF BUSINESS:

Prescription Medications
Pharmaceuticals
Vaccines
Consumer Healthcare
Drug Development
Commercialization

BRANDS/DIVISIONS/AFFILIATES:

CONTACTS: *Note: Officers with more than one job title may be intentionally listed here more than once.*

Emma Walmsley, CEO
Ian Mackay, CFO
Diana Conrad, Sr. VP-Human Resources
Moncef Slaoui, Chmn.-Global R&D & Vaccines
Karenann Terrell, CTO
Roger Connor, Pres., Global Mfg. & Supply
Dan Troy, General Counsel
David Redfern, Chief Strategy Officer
Phil Thomson, Sr. VP-Global Comm.
Simon Bicknell, Sr. VP-Governance, Ethics & Assurance
Deirdre Connelly, Pres., North American Pharmaceuticals
Bill Louv, Sr. VP-Core Bus. Svcs.
Emma Walmsley, Pres., Consumer Health Care Worldwide
Philip Hampton, Chmn.
Abbas Hassain, Pres., Europe, Japan & EMAP
Roger Connor, Pres., Global Mfg. & Supply

GROWTH PLANS/SPECIAL FEATURES:

GlaxoSmithKline plc (GSK) is a leading science-led global healthcare company. The firm has three global businesses that research, develop and manufacture innovative pharmaceutical medicines, vaccines and consumer healthcare products. GSK's pharmaceuticals business has a broad portfolio of innovative and established medicines in respiratory, human immunodeficiency virus (HIV), immune-inflammation and oncology. This division strengthens its research and development pipeline through a focus on immunology, human genetics and advanced technologies to deliver transformational new medicines for patients. The vaccines business delivers vaccines that help protect people at all stages of life. Its R&D focuses on developing vaccines against infectious diseases that combine high medical need and market potential. Last, the consumer healthcare business combines science and consumer insights to create innovative healthcare brands for oral health, pain relief, cold, flu, allergy, digestive health, vitamins, minerals and supplements. GSK and Pfizer combined their consumer healthcare businesses into a new consumer healthcare joint venture in 2019, and announced plans to separate the JV through a demerger process within three years' time (through 2022). The demerger would present a pathway for GSK to create a new global pharmaceuticals/vaccines company and a new consumer healthcare company.

FINANCIAL DATA: *Note: Data for latest year may not have been available at press time.*

In U.S. $	2020	2019	2018	2017	2016	2015
Revenue	48,274,250,000	47,785,830,000	43,633,560,000	42,734,580,000	39,482,700,000	33,868,000,000
R&D Expense	7,217,283,000	6,466,958,000	5,511,354,000	6,336,713,000	5,136,191,000	5,039,923,000
Operating Income	8,811,372,000	8,907,639,000	10,000,570,000	8,580,611,000	8,531,061,000	3,720,483,000
Operating Margin %		.19%	.23%	.20%	.22%	.11%
SGA Expense	16,218,360,000	16,141,910,000	14,036,750,000	13,692,730,000	13,259,530,000	13,069,820,000
Net Income	8,138,910,000	6,575,968,000	5,129,113,000	2,168,866,000	1,291,126,000	11,923,100,000
Operating Cash Flow	11,950,000,000	11,353,980,000	11,921,680,000	9,793,874,000	9,197,860,000	3,636,956,000
Capital Expenditure	3,169,772,000	3,062,178,000	2,542,613,000	3,117,391,000	3,329,747,000	2,691,262,000
EBITDA	14,404,840,000	13,364,290,000	10,514,470,000	8,753,327,000	6,271,590,000	18,249,900,000
Return on Assets %		.07%	.06%	.03%	.02%	.18%
Return on Equity %		.59%	1.69%	2.90%	.29%	1.80%
Debt to Equity		2.068	4.649		13.044	2.996

CONTACT INFORMATION:

Phone: 44 20-8047-5000   Fax: 44 20-8047-7807
Toll-Free: 888-825-5249
Address: 980 Great W. Rd., Brentford, Middlesex, TW8 9GS United Kingdom

STOCK TICKER/OTHER:

Stock Ticker: GSK
Employees: 99,437
Parent Company:

Exchange: NYS
Fiscal Year Ends: 12/31

SALARIES/BONUSES:

Top Exec. Salary: $ Bonus: $
Second Exec. Salary: $ Bonus: $

OTHER THOUGHTS:

Estimated Female Officers or Directors: 8
Hot Spot for Advancement for Women/Minorities: Y

Global Healthcare Exchange LLC

NAIC Code: 518210

www.ghx.com

TYPES OF BUSINESS:

Healthcare Supply Chain Management
Cloud-Based Healthcare Solutions
Healthcare Consulting Solutions
Technologies
Automated Supply Chain Solutions
Contract Management Solutions
Data Management
Payment Automation Solutions

BRANDS/DIVISIONS/AFFILIATES:

Temasek Holdings PL
Warburg Pincus LLC

CONTACTS: Note: Officers with more than one job title may be intentionally listed here more than once.

Bruce Johnson, CEO
Rob Gillespie, CFO
Laura Dunbar, Sr. VP-Global Mktg.
Alexis Kearns, Sr. VP-Global Human Resources
Sloane Stricker, Sr. VP
Christopher McManus, General Counsel
Paul Feicht, VP-Customer Oper.
Tina Vatanka Murphy, Sr. VP-Global Markets

GROWTH PLANS/SPECIAL FEATURES:

Global Healthcare Exchange LLC (GHX) improves health care efficacy through automation, cost reductions and improved decision making. The firm was founded by various top medical products manufacturers such as Johnson & Johnson, GE Healthcare, Abbott Laboratories, Baxter International Inc. and Medtronic Inc. At present, GHX operates its business electronically through more than 4,100 healthcare providers and 600 manufacturer divisions in North America, and another 1,500 provider organizations and 350 suppliers in Europe. GHX delivers a cloud-based technology and healthcare consulting services. Its products and services help automate and eliminated manual supply chain processes. For healthcare providers, solutions include purchasing automation, contract and price management, item master management, requisition and workflow control, invoice and payment automation, supply chain optimization, implantable device supply chain and credentialing. For healthcare suppliers, solutions include sales data analytics, eCommerce, master data management, pricing alignment, order-to-case optimization, implantable device supply chain, UDI (unique device identification) data distribution and invoice and payment automation. GHX is headquartered in Colorado, USA, with offices in Nebraska and Georgia, as well as internationally in Canada and five European countries. Temasek Holdings PL holds a majority stake in GHX, with Warburg Pincus, LLC holding a minority position. During 2021, GHX announced a minority investment from Warburg Pincus to help GHX in the areas of Cloud ERP, advanced automation, predictive analytics and value-based care. As part of the transaction, minority investor Thoma Bravo exited its investment and Temasek remains the majority equity holder.

GHX offers its employees health benefits, 401(k), savings/spending accounts, life and disability insurance and an employee assistance program.

FINANCIAL DATA: Note: Data for latest year may not have been available at press time.

In U.S. $	2020	2019	2018	2017	2016	2015
Revenue						
R&D Expense						
Operating Income						
Operating Margin %						
SGA Expense						
Net Income						
Operating Cash Flow						
Capital Expenditure						
EBITDA						
Return on Assets %						
Return on Equity %						
Debt to Equity						

CONTACT INFORMATION:

Phone: 720-887-7000   Fax: 720-887-7200
Toll-Free: 800-968-7449
Address: 1315 W. Century Dr., Ste. 100, Louisville, CO 80027 United States

STOCK TICKER/OTHER:

Stock Ticker: Private
Employees: 800
Parent Company: Temasek Holdings PL

Exchange:
Fiscal Year Ends: 12/31

SALARIES/BONUSES:

Top Exec. Salary: $ Bonus: $
Second Exec. Salary: $ Bonus: $

OTHER THOUGHTS:

Estimated Female Officers or Directors: 1
Hot Spot for Advancement for Women/Minorities: Y

Sales, profits and employees may be estimates. Financial information, benefits and other data can change quickly and may vary from those stated here.

Globus Medical Inc

www.globusmedical.com

NAIC Code: 339100

TYPES OF BUSINESS:

Surgical and Medical Instrument Manufacturing
Surgical Implants and Fixation Systems
Surgical Technologies
Orthopedic Trauma Systems
Robotics

BRANDS/DIVISIONS/AFFILIATES:

ExcelsiusGPS
Surgimap
Excelsius3D

CONTACTS: *Note: Officers with more than one job title may be intentionally listed here more than once.*

David Demski, CEO
Daniel Scavilla, CFO
David Paul, Chairman of the Board
Steven Payne, Chief Accounting Officer

GROWTH PLANS/SPECIAL FEATURES:

Globus Medical, Inc. is a medical device company that develops and commercializes healthcare solutions for patients with musculoskeletal disorders. The firm delivers service to hospitals, ambulatory surgery centers and physicians to advance patient care and improve efficiency. Its sales operations serve customers in more than 50 countries worldwide. With over 200 products on the market, Globus Medical offers products in two major categories: musculoskeletal solutions and enabling technologies. Musculoskeletal solutions primarily consist of implantable devices, biologics, accessories and unique surgical instruments used in a range of spinal, orthopedic and neurosurgical procedures. Products include fusion implants, plating systems, intervertebral spacers, corpectomy devices, fracture plates, compression screws, intramediullary nails and external fixations, as well as regenerative biologic products such as bone void fillers and allograft struts. Enabling technologies are advanced computer-assisted intelligent systems designed to enhance a surgeon's capabilities and streamline surgical procedures to be safer, less invasive, more accurate and more reproducible, to ultimately improve patient care and reduce radiation exposure for all involved. Globus Medical's current enabling technologies are comprised of imaging, navigation and robotic assisted surgery solutions. Its ExcelsiusGPS platform is a robotic guidance and navigation system that supports minimally-invasive and open procedures by improving visualization of patient anatomy using patient images and by guiding instruments and implants to the specified trajectory using a robotic arm, to ultimately enhance the surgeon's decision-making process. Surgimap is a pre-planning software used for surgical planning in real-time. During 2021, Globus Medical announced FDA 510(k) clearance for Excelsius3D, an intelligent intraoperative 3-in-1 imaging system. That same year, Globus Medical announced the first surgery had been performed with its ExcelsiusGPS cranial solution for robot-assisted deep brain stimulation, which is commercially available in the U.S.

Globus offers employees comprehensive health coverage, a 401(k) and various incentives.

FINANCIAL DATA: *Note: Data for latest year may not have been available at press time.*

In U.S. $	2020	2019	2018	2017	2016	2015
Revenue	789,042,000	785,368,000	712,969,000	635,977,000	563,994,000	544,753,000
R&D Expense	84,519,000	60,073,000	55,496,000	43,679,000	44,532,000	36,982,000
Operating Income	115,472,000	176,754,000	176,884,000	166,119,000	159,123,000	160,954,000
Operating Margin %		.22%	.24%	.26%	.28%	.32%
SGA Expense	354,757,000	354,757,000	311,591,000	267,817,000	222,156,000	214,014,000
Net Income	102,285,000	155,210,000	156,474,000	107,348,000	104,341,000	112,784,000
Operating Cash Flow	198,793,000	171,975,000	181,643,000	159,535,000	171,893,000	121,957,000
Capital Expenditure	63,658,000	70,750,000	59,697,000	51,303,000	40,909,000	50,760,000
EBITDA	178,346,000	225,274,000	216,957,000	205,387,000	192,993,000	195,585,000
Return on Assets %		.11%	.13%	.11%	.12%	.15%
Return on Equity %		.12%	.15%	.12%	.13%	.17%
Debt to Equity						

CONTACT INFORMATION:

Phone: 610 930-1800   Fax:
Toll-Free:
Address: 2560 General Armistead Ave., Audubon, PA 19403 United States

STOCK TICKER/OTHER:

Stock Ticker: GMED
Employees: 2,000
Parent Company:

Exchange: NYS
Fiscal Year Ends: 12/31

SALARIES/BONUSES:

Top Exec. Salary: $ Bonus: $
Second Exec. Salary: $ Bonus: $

OTHER THOUGHTS:

Estimated Female Officers or Directors:
Hot Spot for Advancement for Women/Minorities:

Sales, profits and employees may be estimates. Financial information, benefits and other data can change quickly and may vary from those stated here.

GoodRx Holdings Inc

www.goodrx.com

NAIC Code: 511210D

TYPES OF BUSINESS:

Computer Software: Healthcare & Biotechnology
Prescription Savings
Telehealth
Prescription Price Comparison
Software Platform

BRANDS/DIVISIONS/AFFILIATES:

GoodRx Care LLC
RxSaver Inc
HealthiNation Inc

CONTACTS: Note: Officers with more than one job title may be intentionally listed here more than once.

Doug Hirsch, Co-CEO
Trevor Bezdek, Co-CEO
Karsten Voermann, CFO

GROWTH PLANS/SPECIAL FEATURES:

GoodRx Holdings, Inc. and its subsidiaries offer information and tools to help consumers compare prices and save on their prescription drug purchases. The company operates a price comparison platform that provides consumers with curated, geographically relevant prescription pricing, and provides access to negotiated prices through GoodRx codes that can be used to save money on prescriptions across the U.S. The services are free to consumers and GoodRx primarily earns revenue from its core business from pharmacy benefit managers that manage formularies and prescription transactions including establishing pricing between consumers and pharmacies. The firm also offers other healthcare products and serves, including subscriptions, pharma manufacturer solutions and telehealth services. Wholly-owned GoodRx Care, LLC provides management and other services to professional service corporation, which are owned by medical professionals in accordance with certain state laws that restrict the corporate practice of medicine and require medical practitioners to own such entities. During 2021, GoodRx acquired RxSaver, Inc., which operates a price comparison platform; and acquired HealthiNation, Inc., a provider of engaging and informative health video content across all main categories of healthy living.

GoodRx offers its employees comprehensive health benefits, 401(k) and company perks.

FINANCIAL DATA: Note: Data for latest year may not have been available at press time.

In U.S. $	2020	2019	2018	2017	2016	2015
Revenue	550,700,000	388,224,000	249,522,000			
R&D Expense	61,816,000	29,300,000	43,894,000			
Operating Income	-275,719,000	139,676,000	77,251,000			
Operating Margin %						
SGA Expense	716,586,000	191,659,000	112,536,000			
Net Income	-293,623,000	66,048,000	43,793,000			
Operating Cash Flow	131,341,000	83,286,000	45,253,000			
Capital Expenditure	35,824,000	5,749,000	3,458,000			
EBITDA	-257,107,000	146,120,000	84,347,000			
Return on Assets %						
Return on Equity %						
Debt to Equity						

CONTACT INFORMATION:

Phone: 855-268-2822   Fax:
Toll-Free:
Address: 2701 Olympic Blvd., Santa Monica, CA 90404 United States

STOCK TICKER/OTHER:

Stock Ticker: GDRX   Exchange: NAS
Employees: 475   Fiscal Year Ends:
Parent Company:

SALARIES/BONUSES:

Top Exec. Salary: $ Bonus: $
Second Exec. Salary: $ Bonus: $

OTHER THOUGHTS:

Estimated Female Officers or Directors:
Hot Spot for Advancement for Women/Minorities:

Grifols SA

www.grifols.com

NAIC Code: 325414

TYPES OF BUSINESS:

Biotherapeutics Research, Development & Manufacturing
Plasma Derivatives
Diagnostics Products
Plasma Collection Centers
Product Development
Product Manufacture

BRANDS/DIVISIONS/AFFILIATES:

Grifols UK Ltd
Grifols Italia SpA
Biomat USA Inc
Australia Pty Ltd
Diagnostics AG
Grifols Therapeutics Inc
Haema AG
Biotest Pharma Corp

CONTACTS: *Note: Officers with more than one job title may be intentionally listed here more than once.*

Victor Grifols Roura, Pres.
Gregory Gene Rich, Pres., U.S. Oper.
Albert Grifols Roura, VP
Victor Grifols Roura, Chmn.

GROWTH PLANS/SPECIAL FEATURES:

Grifols SA produces and sells plasma derivative products, with activities that include sourcing raw material, manufacturing various plasma derivative products and selling and distributing final products to healthcare providers. The company has more than 310 operating plasma collection centers located across the U.S. and Germany. Grifols planned to reach approximately 21 million liters fractionation capacity by 2022, and 435 plasma collection centers globally by 2025. The firm also researches, develops, manufactures and markets in vitro diagnostics products, including analytical instruments, reagents, software and associated products for use in clinical and blood bank laboratories and hospital products. Grifols operates through four primary business segments, consisting of: bioscience, which includes all activities with products derived from human plasma for therapeutic use; hospital, which includes all non-biological pharmaceutical products and medical supplies manufactured by subsidiaries earmarked for hospital pharmacy, and also includes the marketing of supplementary products not manufactured by the Grifols group; diagnostic, which includes the marketing of diagnostic testing equipment, reagents and other equipment manufactured by Grifols and other companies; and bio supplies, which groups together all transactions related to biological products for non-therapeutic use, as well as third-party plasma sales. Just a few of the company's subsidiaries include: Grifols UK Ltd., Grifols Italia SpA, Biomat USA Inc., Australia Pty Ltd., Diagnostics AG, Grifols Therapeutics Inc., Haema AG, and Biotest Pharma Corp. In September 2021, Grifols agreed to acquire the existing share capital of Tiancheng (Germany) Pharmaceutical Holdings, which is the owner of 90% of Biotest ordinary shares and 1% of Biotest preferred shares. Upon completion of the transaction, Grifols will indirectly own approximately 89.88% of Biotest's voting rights and 44.94% of total share capital.

FINANCIAL DATA: *Note: Data for latest year may not have been available at press time.*

In U.S. $	2020	2019	2018	2017	2016	2015
Revenue	6,524,336,000	6,229,463,000	5,481,776,000	5,275,722,000	4,947,989,000	4,807,158,000
R&D Expense	359,466,300	337,232,400	294,034,000	352,262,700	241,443,900	273,913,800
Operating Income	1,191,639,000	1,371,314,000	1,214,598,000	1,225,861,000	1,147,747,000	1,185,576,000
Operating Margin %		.22%	.22%	.23%	.23%	.25%
SGA Expense	1,204,203,000	1,151,917,000	995,473,300	1,051,153,000	947,202,100	899,759,300
Net Income	755,725,200	763,789,000	728,963,500	809,671,600	666,425,600	650,162,500
Operating Cash Flow	1,356,583,000	695,109,200	900,972,500	1,028,426,000	675,982,300	907,509,100
Capital Expenditure	442,967,500	503,744,700	375,967,600	394,601,000	357,601,900	692,772,000
EBITDA	1,738,690,000	1,764,171,000	1,501,091,000	1,418,171,000	1,397,010,000	1,349,596,000
Return on Assets %		.04%	.05%	.06%	.06%	.06%
Return on Equity %		.14%	.15%	.18%	.16%	.18%
Debt to Equity		1.407	1.425	1.62	1.258	1.387

CONTACT INFORMATION:

Phone: 34 935710165   Fax: 34 935710267
Toll-Free:
Address: Avinguda de la Generalitat, 152-158 Parc de Negoc, Barcelona, 08174 Spain

STOCK TICKER/OTHER:

Stock Ticker: GRFS   Exchange: NAS
Employees: 23,655   Fiscal Year Ends: 12/31
Parent Company:

SALARIES/BONUSES:

Top Exec. Salary: $ Bonus: $
Second Exec. Salary: $ Bonus: $

OTHER THOUGHTS:

Estimated Female Officers or Directors:
Hot Spot for Advancement for Women/Minorities:

Sales, profits and employees may be estimates. Financial information, benefits and other data can change quickly and may vary from those stated here.

Guardion Health Sciences Inc

www.guardionhealth.com

NAIC Code: 325412

TYPES OF BUSINESS:

Pharmaceutical Preparation Manufacturing
Clinical Nutrition Products
Diagnostics Products
Medical Foods
Supplements
Medical Devices
Eye Tests

BRANDS/DIVISIONS/AFFILIATES:

Viactiv
Lumega-Z
GlaucoCetin
VectorVision
MapcatSF
Activ Nutritional LLC

CONTACTS: Note: Officers with more than one job title may be intentionally listed here more than once.

Michael Favish, CEO
John Townsend, Chief Accounting Officer
David Evans, Director
Vincent Roth, General Counsel

GROWTH PLANS/SPECIAL FEATURES:

Guardion Health Sciences, Inc. is a clinical nutrition and diagnostics company that distributes clinically-supported nutrition, medical foods, supplements and medical devices. The company's portfolio of products and devices are designed to support healthcare professionals and providers, and their patients and consumers. Branded products of Guardion Health include: Viactiv, which provides bone strengthening and immune support nutrients that support bodies of every age from teens through post-menopause; Lumega-Z, a lipid-based, micronized eye health formula used for restoring the macular pigment by an average of 30% in three-six months' time; GlaucoCetin, which supports the mitochondrial function of optic nerve cells through the use of neuroprotective ingredients, and can reduce oxidative stress and increase blood flow for eye support and ocular health; VectorVision, which provides vision tests such as contrast sensitivity, glare testing and early treatment diabetic retinopathy study (ETDRS) acuity testing; and MapcatSF, which is a test for measuring the macular pigment optical density by determining the amount of blue light radiation being absorbed through the eye. In mid-2021, Guardion acquired Activ Nutritional LLC from Adare Pharmaceuticals, Inc., which manufactures the Viactiv line of chewable mineral supplements for bone health and other applications.

FINANCIAL DATA: Note: Data for latest year may not have been available at press time.

In U.S. $	2020	2019	2018	2017	2016	2015
Revenue	1,889,844	902,937	942,153	437,349	141,029	112,811
R&D Expense	160,978	194,311	231,847	259,463	64,026	401,909
Operating Income	-8,502,283	-8,933,417	-6,143,721	-5,281,442	-3,695,954	-6,130,133
Operating Margin %		-9.89%	-6.52%	-12.08%	-26.21%	-54.34%
SGA Expense	8,284,514	9,300,728	6,455,848	5,283,858	3,697,255	5,790,963
Net Income	-8,571,657	-10,878,310	-7,767,407	-5,305,169	-5,748,397	-8,841,296
Operating Cash Flow	-8,013,929	-6,030,004	-4,173,831	-3,403,696	-1,653,574	-1,139,758
Capital Expenditure	40,733	171,076	310,243	37,280	3,354	2,162
EBITDA	-8,344,786	-9,994,157	-7,469,446	-5,162,621	-4,583,711	-8,034,607
Return on Assets %		-1.31%	-1.41%	-1.63%	-25.77%	-35.97%
Return on Equity %		-1.43%	-1.54%	-1.91%		
Debt to Equity		0.036				

CONTACT INFORMATION:

Phone: Fax:
Toll-Free: 800-873-5141
Address: 2925 Richmond Ave., Ste. 1200, Houston, TX 77098 United States

STOCK TICKER/OTHER:

Stock Ticker: GHSI Exchange: NAS
Employees: 13 Fiscal Year Ends: 12/31
Parent Company:

SALARIES/BONUSES:

Top Exec. Salary: $ Bonus: $
Second Exec. Salary: $ Bonus: $

OTHER THOUGHTS:

Estimated Female Officers or Directors:
Hot Spot for Advancement for Women/Minorities:

Haemonetics Corporation

www.haemonetics.com

NAIC Code: 339100

TYPES OF BUSINESS:

Equipment-Blood-Recovery Systems
Surgical Blood Salvage Equipment
Blood Component Therapy Equipment
Automated Blood Collection Equipment

BRANDS/DIVISIONS/AFFILIATES:

PCS
NexSys
NexLynk
MCS
SafeTrace Tx
Hemasphere
Donor Doc
Cardiva Medical Inc

CONTACTS: *Note: Officers with more than one job title may be intentionally listed here more than once.*

Christopher Simon, CEO
William Burke, CFO
Richard Meelia, Chairman of the Board
Dan Goldstein, Chief Accounting Officer
Mirsaid Seyed-Bolorforosh, Chief Technology Officer
Michelle Basil, Executive VP
Jacqueline Scanlan, Senior VP, Divisional
Josep Llorens, Senior VP, Divisional

GROWTH PLANS/SPECIAL FEATURES:

Haemonetics Corporation manufactures and provides a suite of innovative hematology products and solutions. The firm divides its product lines into three categories: plasma, blood center and hospital. The plasma business offers automated plasma collection and donor management software systems that improve the plasma centers' yield, efficiency, quality, safety and overall plasma donor experience. Plasma products include automated collection devices, related disposables and software, and this segment's portfolio of products and services are designed to support multiple facets of plasma collector operations. Brands within this division include PCS, NexSys and NexLynk. The blood center business offers a range of solutions that improve donor collections centers ability for acquiring blood, filtering blood and separating blood components. These products and technologies help donor collection centers optimize blood collection capabilities and donor processing management. This division also offers software solutions that help blood collection centers with blood drive planning, donor recruitment and retention, blood collection, component manufacturing and distribution. Brands within this segment include MCS, SafeTrace Tx, El-Dorado Donor, Hemasphere, Donor Doc and eDonor. Last, the hospital business offers three product lines: hemostasis management, cell salvage and transfusion management, all of which help decision makers in hospitals optimize blood acquisition, storage and usage in critical settings. Hemostasis management encompasses a portfolio of diagnostic systems that enable clinicians to holistically assess the coagulation of a patient at the point of care or laboratory setting. Cell salvage devices are designed to transfuse back a patient's own blood during or after surgery, and includes the Cell Saver Elite autologous blood recovery system and transfusion management software solutions. In September 2021, Haemonetics Corporation announced that its VASCADE MVP venous vascular closure system received FDA approval for same-day discharge following atrial fibrillation ablation. This is a result of Haemonetics' acquisition of Cardiva Medical, Inc.

FINANCIAL DATA: *Note: Data for latest year may not have been available at press time.*

In U.S. $	2020	2019	2018	2017	2016	2015
Revenue	988,479,000	967,579,000	903,923,000	886,116,000	908,832,000	
R&D Expense	30,883,000	35,714,000	39,228,000	37,556,000	44,965,000	
Operating Income	153,950,000	83,545,000	56,157,000	39,212,000	43,726,000	
Operating Margin %	.16%	.09%	.06%	.04%	.05%	
SGA Expense	299,680,000	298,277,000	316,523,000	301,726,000	317,223,000	
Net Income	76,526,000	55,019,000	45,572,000	-26,268,000	-55,579,000	
Operating Cash Flow	158,217,000	159,281,000	220,350,000	159,738,000	121,865,000	
Capital Expenditure	48,758,000	118,961,000	74,799,000	76,135,000	102,405,000	
EBITDA	213,640,000	192,963,000	153,404,000	128,945,000	45,969,000	
Return on Assets %	.06%	.04%	.04%	- .02%	- .04%	
Return on Equity %	.12%	.08%	.06%	- .04%	- .07%	
Debt to Equity	0.609	0.483	0.079	0.343	0.505	

CONTACT INFORMATION:

Phone: 781 848-7100   Fax: 781 356-3558
Toll-Free: 800-225-5242
Address: 125 Summer St., Boston, MA 02110 United States

STOCK TICKER/OTHER:

Stock Ticker: HAE
Employees: 2,708
Parent Company:

Exchange: NYS
Fiscal Year Ends: 02/28

SALARIES/BONUSES:

Top Exec. Salary: $ Bonus: $
Second Exec. Salary: $ Bonus: $

OTHER THOUGHTS:

Estimated Female Officers or Directors: 2
Hot Spot for Advancement for Women/Minorities: Y

Hanger Inc

www.hanger.com

NAIC Code: 622310

TYPES OF BUSINESS:

Orthotic & Prosthetic Patient Care Centers
Orthotic & Prosthetic Devices & Components Distribution

BRANDS/DIVISIONS/AFFILIATES:

Hanger Clinic

CONTACTS: *Note: Officers with more than one job title may be intentionally listed here more than once.*

Vinit Asar, CEO
Gabrielle Adams, Chief Accounting Officer
Mitchell Dobson, Chief Compliance Officer
Scott Ranson, Chief Information Officer
Samuel Liang, COO, Subsidiary
Christopher Begley, Director
Thomas Kiraly, Executive VP
Thomas Hartman, General Counsel
Keri Jolly, Other Executive Officer
James Campbell, Other Executive Officer
Jay Wendt, President, Divisional

GROWTH PLANS/SPECIAL FEATURES:

Hanger, Inc. provides services and products that enhance human physical capabilities via orthotic and prosthetic (O&P) devices and components. Hanger is built on the legacy of James Edward Hanger, the first amputee of the American Civil War. The company operates through two segments: patient care and products and services. The patient care segment is comprised of Hanger Clinic, which designs, fabricates and delivers custom O&P devices through more than 720 patient care clinics and 112 satellite locations in 46 U.S. states and the District of Columbia (as of June 30, 2021). This division also provides payor network contracting services to other O&P providers. The products and services segment includes Hanger's distribution and rehabilitative solutions businesses. It coordinates the procurement and distribution of a broad catalog of O&P parts, componentry and devices to independent O&P providers nationwide. These products are delivered from distribution facilities located in Nevada, Georgia, Illinois, Pennsylvania and Texas. The products and services segment also comprises the firm's rehabilitative solutions business, which develops specialized rehabilitation technologies and provides evidence-based clinical programs for post-acute rehabilitation to patients at approximately 3,900 skilled nursing and post-acute providers throughout the U.S.

Employees are offered medical, dental, vision, prescription and life insurance; a 401(k); disability coverage; and flexible spending accounts.

FINANCIAL DATA: *Note: Data for latest year may not have been available at press time.*

In U.S. $	2020	2019	2018	2017	2016	2015
Revenue	1,001,150,000	1,098,046,000	1,048,760,000	1,040,769,000	1,042,054,000	1,067,172,000
R&D Expense						
Operating Income	71,907,000	65,428,000	59,830,000	35,049,000	14,078,000	36,205,000
Operating Margin %		.06%	.06%	.03%	.01%	.03%
SGA Expense	479,132,000	503,979,000	490,556,000	507,407,000	511,994,000	507,502,000
Net Income	38,192,000	27,525,000	-858,000	-104,671,000	-106,471,000	-327,091,000
Operating Cash Flow	155,567,000	58,846,000	78,527,000	30,105,000	68,808,000	59,514,000
Capital Expenditure	28,092,000	33,105,000	28,819,000	22,355,000	23,624,000	32,252,000
EBITDA	106,122,000	100,662,000	78,401,000	19,573,000	-33,230,000	-310,496,000
Return on Assets %		.04%	.00%	-.15%	-.12%	-.29%
Return on Equity %				-5.60%	-.92%	-1.01%
Debt to Equity		60.873			6.752	3.244

CONTACT INFORMATION:

Phone: 512 777-3800   Fax: 301 986-0702
Toll-Free:
Address: 10910 Domain Dr., Ste. 300, Austin, TX 78758 United States

STOCK TICKER/OTHER:

Stock Ticker: HNGR   Exchange: NYS
Employees: 4,800   Fiscal Year Ends: 12/31
Parent Company:

SALARIES/BONUSES:

Top Exec. Salary: $ Bonus: $
Second Exec. Salary: $ Bonus: $

OTHER THOUGHTS:

Estimated Female Officers or Directors: 3
Hot Spot for Advancement for Women/Minorities: Y

Harpoon Therapeutics Inc

www.harpoontx.com

NAIC Code: 325414

TYPES OF BUSINESS:

Biological Product (except Diagnostic) Manufacturing
Clinical Stage Immunotherapy
T-Cell Drug Development
T-Cell Engagers

BRANDS/DIVISIONS/AFFILIATES:

Tri-specific T cell Activating Construct (TriTAC)
HPN424
HPN536
HPN217
HPN328

GROWTH PLANS/SPECIAL FEATURES:

Harpoon Therapeutics, Inc. is a clinical-stage immunotherapy company developing a novel class of T cell engagers that utilizes the body's immune system to treat patients suffering from cancer and other diseases. T cell engagers are engineered proteins that direct a patient's own T cells to kill target cells that express specific proteins, or antigens, carried by the target cells. Using its proprietary Tri-specific T cell Activating Construct (TriTAC) platform, Harpoon is developing a pipeline of novel T cell engagers (TriTACs), with a focus on solid tumors and hematologic malignancies. Harpoon has created four TriTAC product candidates. HPN424 is in a Phase 1 clinical trial for the treatment of prostate cancer (mCRPC); HPN536 is in Phase 1 clinical trial for the treatment of ovarian cancer and other solid tumors; HPN217 is in Phase 1 clinical trial for the treatment of multiple myeloma; and HPN328 is in Phase 1 clinical trial for the treatment of small cell lung cancer.

CONTACTS:

Note: Officers with more than one job title may be intentionally listed here more than once.

Gerald McMahon, CEO
Georgia Erbez, CFO
Luke Evnin, Chairman of the Board
Natalie Sacks, Chief Medical Officer
Holger Wesche, Chief Scientific Officer
Patrick Baeuerle, Co-Founder

FINANCIAL DATA:

Note: Data for latest year may not have been available at press time.

In U.S. $	2020	2019	2018	2017	2016	2015
Revenue	17,444,000	5,777,000	4,750,000	708,000		
R&D Expense	52,565,000	41,592,000	26,368,000	13,622,000	7,778,000	
Operating Income	-51,331,000	-58,206,000	-27,724,000	-16,528,000	-11,147,000	
Operating Margin %		-10.08%	-5.84%	-23.34%		
SGA Expense	16,210,000	22,391,000	8,106,000	3,614,000	3,369,000	
Net Income	-49,908,000	-55,572,000	-27,366,000	-16,830,000	-11,406,000	
Operating Cash Flow	-8,616,000	-2,891,000	-27,126,000	1,714,000	-10,794,000	
Capital Expenditure	683,000	3,516,000	663,000	2,275,000	553,000	
EBITDA	-49,249,000	-54,672,000	-26,722,000	-16,179,000	-10,947,000	
Return on Assets %		-.40%	-.41%	-.84%	-1.36%	
Return on Equity %		-2.73%				
Debt to Equity		0.146				

CONTACT INFORMATION:

Phone: 650 443-7400 Fax:
Toll-Free:
Address: 131 Oyster Point Blvd., Ste. 300, South San Francisco, CA 94080 United States

STOCK TICKER/OTHER:

Stock Ticker: HARP Exchange: NAS
Employees: 78 Fiscal Year Ends: 12/31
Parent Company:

SALARIES/BONUSES:

Top Exec. Salary: $ Bonus: $
Second Exec. Salary: $ Bonus: $

OTHER THOUGHTS:

Estimated Female Officers or Directors:
Hot Spot for Advancement for Women/Minorities:

Harvard Pilgrim Health Care Inc

www.harvardpilgrim.org

NAIC Code: 524114

TYPES OF BUSINESS:

Insurance-Medical & Health, HMOs & PPOs
Health Benefits
Medicare Plans

BRANDS/DIVISIONS/AFFILIATES:

Point32Health Inc
Health Plans Inc
MedWatch
Trestletree
Harvard Pilgrim Health Care Foundation (The)
Department of Population Medicine (DPM)

CONTACTS: *Note: Officers with more than one job title may be intentionally listed here more than once.*

Michael Sherman, Chief Medical Officer
Pranav Mehta, Sr. VP-Prod. Dev.
Maura Lapping, Dir.-Admin.
William J. Graham, VP-Policy & Gov't Affairs
Beth Roberts, VP-Regional Markets
Bill Breidenbach, CEO-Health Plans, Inc.
Rick Weisblatt, Sr. VP-Provider Network
Joyce Murphy, Chmn.

GROWTH PLANS/SPECIAL FEATURES:

Harvard Pilgrim Health Care, Inc. consists of a family of companies that provide health benefit plans, programs and services to customers in New England and beyond. Plans are offered to individuals and families, including Medicare plans. Help and guidance is offered by the company, and its online platform offers tips for choosing the right plan. Health Plans, Inc. (HPI) is a leading third-party administrator of self-funded plans, and also delivers customized solutions to employers throughout the U.S. MedWatch is an HPI affiliate and a population health management company delivering a wide range of services, from biometric screening and chronic disease management to care management and utilization review. Trestletree is an HPI affiliate and provides behavior-focused coaching to support individuals, families, workplaces, physician practices and communities. The Harvard Pilgrim Health Care Foundation provides tools, training and leadership to help communities to be healthy, with a focus on increasing access to fresh affordable food to low- and moderate-income families in the region; providing grant contributions and community service; and addressing health disparities that affect diverse populations. Last, The Harvard Pilgrim Health Care Institute's Department of Population Medicine (DPM) is a medical school department that collaborates with Harvard Pilgrim and Harvard Medical School, with a focus on innovative teaching and research to address health care issues. In early-2021, Harvard Pilgrim Health Care announced that it combined with Tufts Health Plan, each of which operate as brands and entities under new parent Point32Health, Inc.

FINANCIAL DATA: *Note: Data for latest year may not have been available at press time.*

In U.S. $	2020	2019	2018	2017	2016	2015
Revenue	3,069,000,000	3,300,000,000	3,200,000,000	3,000,000,000	3,100,000,000	2,733,898,000
R&D Expense						
Operating Income						
Operating Margin %						
SGA Expense						
Net Income		82,503,000	80,100,000	-8,700,000	-48,500,000	-54,774,000
Operating Cash Flow						
Capital Expenditure						
EBITDA						
Return on Assets %						
Return on Equity %						
Debt to Equity						

CONTACT INFORMATION:

Phone: 617-509-1000   Fax:
Toll-Free: 888-888-4742
Address: 93 Worcester St., Wellesley, MA 02481 United States

STOCK TICKER/OTHER:

Stock Ticker: Nonprofit   Exchange:
Employees: 28,000   Fiscal Year Ends: 12/31
Parent Company: Point32Health Inc

SALARIES/BONUSES:

Top Exec. Salary: $ Bonus: $
Second Exec. Salary: $ Bonus: $

OTHER THOUGHTS:

Estimated Female Officers or Directors: 8
Hot Spot for Advancement for Women/Minorities: Y

HCA Healthcare Inc

www.hcahealthcare.com

NAIC Code: 622110

TYPES OF BUSINESS:

General Medical and Surgical Hospitals
Hospital
Surgery
Emergency Care
Clinics
Diagnostics
Rehabilitation
Psychiatric

BRANDS/DIVISIONS/AFFILIATES:

CONTACTS: *Note: Officers with more than one job title may be intentionally listed here more than once.*

Samuel Hazen, CEO
Victor Campbell, Senior VP, Divisional
William Rutherford, CFO
Thomas Frist, Chairman of the Board
Kathleen Whalen, Chief Compliance Officer
Martin Paslick, Chief Information Officer
Jonathan Perlin, Chief Medical Officer
Robert Waterman, General Counsel
John Steele, Other Executive Officer
Joseph Sowell, Other Executive Officer
Jane Englebright, Other Executive Officer
Michael Cuffe, President, Divisional
A. Moore, President, Divisional
Jon Foster, President, Geographical
Charles Hall, President, Geographical
Kathryn Torres, Senior VP, Divisional
Sandra Morgan, Senior VP, Divisional
Phillip Billington, Senior VP, Divisional

GROWTH PLANS/SPECIAL FEATURES:

HCA Healthcare, Inc. owns and operates 187 hospitals and approximately 2,000 sites of care, including surgery centers, freestanding emergency rooms, urgent care centers and physician clinics in 20 U.S. states and the U.K. The company's acute care hospitals provide a full range of services, including internal medicine, general surgery, cardiology, oncology, neurosurgery, orthopedics and obstetrics, as well as diagnostic and emergency services. Outpatient and ancillary health care services are provided by HCA's general, acute care hospitals, freestanding surgery centers, freestanding emergency care facilities, urgent care facilities, walk-in clinics, diagnostic centers and rehabilitation facilities. Its psychiatric hospitals provide a full range of mental health care services through inpatient, partial hospitalization and outpatient settings. In September 2021, HCA Healthcare agreed to acquire five Steward Health Care hospitals in Utah, which would become part of HCA Healthcare's mountain division, which includes hospitals in Utah, Idaho and Alaska.

FINANCIAL DATA: *Note: Data for latest year may not have been available at press time.*

In U.S. $	2020	2019	2018	2017	2016	2015
Revenue	51,533,000,000	51,336,000,000	46,677,000,000	43,614,000,000	41,490,000,000	39,678,000,000
R&D Expense						
Operating Income	7,262,000,000	7,218,000,000	6,642,000,000	6,057,000,000	6,198,000,000	5,965,000,000
Operating Margin %		.14%	.14%	.14%	.15%	.15%
SGA Expense	23,874,000,000	23,560,000,000	21,425,000,000	20,059,000,000	18,897,000,000	18,115,000,000
Net Income	3,754,000,000	3,505,000,000	3,787,000,000	2,216,000,000	2,890,000,000	2,129,000,000
Operating Cash Flow	9,232,000,000	7,602,000,000	6,761,000,000	5,426,000,000	5,653,000,000	4,734,000,000
Capital Expenditure	2,835,000,000	4,158,000,000	3,573,000,000	3,015,000,000	2,760,000,000	2,375,000,000
EBITDA	9,735,000,000	9,664,000,000	9,368,001,000	8,202,000,000	8,483,000,000	7,526,000,000
Return on Assets %		.08%	.10%	.06%	.09%	.07%
Return on Equity %						
Debt to Equity						

CONTACT INFORMATION:

Phone: 615 344-9551   Fax: 615 320-2266
Toll-Free:
Address: 1 Park Plaza, Nashville, TN 37203 United States

STOCK TICKER/OTHER:

Stock Ticker: HCA
Employees: 280,000
Parent Company:

Exchange: NYS
Fiscal Year Ends: 12/31

SALARIES/BONUSES:

Top Exec. Salary: $ Bonus: $
Second Exec. Salary: $ Bonus: $

OTHER THOUGHTS:

Estimated Female Officers or Directors: 2
Hot Spot for Advancement for Women/Minorities:

Sales, profits and employees may be estimates. Financial information, benefits and other data can change quickly and may vary from those stated here.

Health Care Service Corporation (HCSC)

NAIC Code: 524114

www.hcsc.com

TYPES OF BUSINESS:

Insurance-Medical & Health, HMOs & PPOs
Traditional Indemnity Plans
Medicare Supplemental Health
Life Insurance
Dental & Vision Insurance
Electronic Claims & Information Network
Workers' Compensation
Retirement Services

BRANDS/DIVISIONS/AFFILIATES:

Blue Cross and Blue Shield
Dental Network of America Inc
Availity LLC
Medicision Inc

CONTACTS: Note: Officers with more than one job title may be intentionally listed here more than once.

Maurice Smith, CEO
Opella Ernest, COO
James Walsh, CFO
James Gibbs, Chief Human Resources Officer
Stephen Ondra, Chief Medical Officer
John Cannon, Chief Admin. Officer
Deborah Dorman-Rodriguez, Corp. Sec.
Martin G. Foster, Pres., Plan Oper.
Paula A. Steiner, Chief Strategy Officer
Ross Blackstone, Contact-Media
Ted Haynes, Pres., Oklahoma Div.
Kurt Shipley, Pres., New Mexico Div.
Karen M. Atwood, Pres., Illinois Div.
Bert E. Marshall, Pres., Texas Div.

GROWTH PLANS/SPECIAL FEATURES:

Health Care Service Corporation (HCSC) is a customer-owned health insurer which operates through its Blue Cross and Blue Shield divisions in Illinois, Montana, New Mexico, Oklahoma and Texas. HCSC is a legal reserve company, meaning that it maintains policy reserves according to the standards established by the insurance laws of the various states it serves. The firm provides preferred provider organizations (PPOs), health maintenance organizations (HMOs), point of service (POS), traditional indemnity and Medicare supplemental health plans to nearly 17 million members. The company also has several subsidiaries that offer a variety of health and life insurance products and related services to employers and individuals. Through its non-Blue Cross and Blue Shield subsidiaries, HCSC offers prescription drug plans, Medicare supplemental insurance, dental and vision coverage, life and disability insurance, workers' compensation, retirement services and medical financial services. One such subsidiary, Dental Network of America, Inc., functions as a third-party administrator for all company dental programs and is registered in every state except Florida. It also offers a dental discount card program. Availity, LLC, a partially-owned subsidiary, operates a health care clearinghouse and provides internet-based health information services. Medicision, Inc. is an integrated health solutions company that partners with other organizations to manage more than 50 million members in commercial, Medicare Advantage and various Medicaid programs.

Employee benefits include: medical, short/long-term disability, AD&D and life insurance; 401(k) and pension plans; and various employee assistance programs.

FINANCIAL DATA: Note: Data for latest year may not have been available at press time.

In U.S. $	2020	2019	2018	2017	2016	2015
Revenue	47,300,000,000	38,600,000,000	35,900,000,000	36,800,000,000	33,000,000,000	35,000,000,000
R&D Expense						
Operating Income						
Operating Margin %						
SGA Expense						
Net Income						
Operating Cash Flow						
Capital Expenditure						
EBITDA						
Return on Assets %						
Return on Equity %						
Debt to Equity						

CONTACT INFORMATION:

Phone: 312-653-6000   Fax: 312-819-1220
Toll-Free: 800-654-7385
Address: 300 E. Randolph St., Chicago, IL 60601 United States

STOCK TICKER/OTHER:

Stock Ticker: Mutual Company
Employees: 24,000
Parent Company:

Exchange:
Fiscal Year Ends: 12/31

SALARIES/BONUSES:

Top Exec. Salary: $ Bonus: $
Second Exec. Salary: $ Bonus: $

OTHER THOUGHTS:

Estimated Female Officers or Directors: 6
Hot Spot for Advancement for Women/Minorities: Y

Health Catalyst Inc

www.healthcatalyst.com

NAIC Code: 518210

TYPES OF BUSINESS:

Data Processing, Hosting, and Related Services
Healthcare Data Technology
Healthcare Analytics Technology
Software
Cloud

BRANDS/DIVISIONS/AFFILIATES:

CONTACTS: *Note: Officers with more than one job title may be intentionally listed here more than once.*

Dan Burton, CEO
Brent Dover, Pres.
Patrick Nelli, CFO
LInda Llewelyn, Chief People Officer
Dale Sanders, Pres.-Technology
Paul Horstmeier, COO

GROWTH PLANS/SPECIAL FEATURES:

Health Catalyst, Inc. is a leading provider of data and analytics technology and services to healthcare organizations. The firm's solution comprises a cloud-based data platform, analytics software and professional services expertise. Its customers are primarily healthcare providers who use the solution to manage their data, drive analytical insights to operate their organizations, and produce measurable clinical, financial and operational improvements. Solutions within this platform include accountable care, analytics adoption, care management, dashboard, data operating system, executive decision support, healthcare analytics and benchmarking, healthcare mergers/acquisitions/partnerships, late-binding data warehouse, life sciences, machine learning, Medicare Access and CHIP Reauthorization Act (MACRA), patient safety, payer solutions, population health foundations, population health management, predictive analytics, rapid response analytics, text analytical and more. In mid-2021, Health Catalyst agreed to acquire Twistle, Inc., an Albuquerque, New Mexico-based healthcare patient engagement software-as-a-service technology company that automates patient-centered, HIPAA-compliant communication between care teams and patients.

FINANCIAL DATA: *Note: Data for latest year may not have been available at press time.*

In U.S. $	2020	2019	2018	2017	2016	2015
Revenue	188,845,000	154,941,000	112,574,000	73,081,000		
R&D Expense	53,517,000	46,252,000	38,592,000	28,470,000		
Operating Income	-96,125,000	-54,865,000	-60,095,000	-45,540,000		
Operating Margin %		- .35%	- .53%	- .62%		
SGA Expense	114,651,000	78,997,000	66,813,000	40,617,000		
Net Income	-115,017,000	-60,096,000	-61,984,000	-47,035,000		
Operating Cash Flow	-26,148,000	-32,184,000	-40,296,000	-36,829,000		
Capital Expenditure	10,465,000	4,334,000	2,503,000	3,344,000		
EBITDA	-83,770,000	-44,481,000	-52,120,000	-39,648,000		
Return on Assets %		-1.17%	- .56%	- .53%		
Return on Equity %						
Debt to Equity		0.248				

CONTACT INFORMATION:

Phone: 801-708-6800   Fax:
Toll-Free:
Address: 10897 S. River Front Pkwy. #300, South Jordan, UT 84095
United States

STOCK TICKER/OTHER:

Stock Ticker: HCAT
Employees: 1,000
Parent Company:

Exchange: NAS
Fiscal Year Ends:

SALARIES/BONUSES:

Top Exec. Salary: $ Bonus: $
Second Exec. Salary: $ Bonus: $

OTHER THOUGHTS:

Estimated Female Officers or Directors:
Hot Spot for Advancement for Women/Minorities:

Health Net Inc

www.healthnet.com

NAIC Code: 524114

TYPES OF BUSINESS:

Insurance-Medical & Health, HMOs & PPOs
Utilization Management
Health Care Services Management
Administrative Services
Health Insurance Underwriting
Life Insurance Underwriting

BRANDS/DIVISIONS/AFFILIATES:

Centene Corporation
Health Net LLC
Health Net of California Inc
Health Net Life Insurance Company
Health Net Community Solutions Inc

GROWTH PLANS/SPECIAL FEATURES:

Health Net, Inc. operates a network of 85,000 network providers that serve healthcare benefits to more than 3 million Californians. The firm provides health plans for individuals, families, employers, people with Medicare and those with Medical. Health Net also offers access to behavioral health services, substance abuse prevention programs, managed healthcare services for prescription drugs and employee assistance programs. These health plans and services are offered through Health Net, LLC and its subsidiaries: Health Net of California, Inc.; Health Net Life Insurance Company; and Health Net Community Solutions, Inc. Health Net, Inc. itself is a subsidiary of Centene Corporation.

CONTACTS:
Note: Officers with more than one job title may be intentionally listed here more than once.

Brian Ternan, CEO
Roger Greaves, Chairman of the Board
Scott Law, Other Corporate Officer
Andy Ortiz, Other Executive Officer
Steven Tough, President, Divisional
Steven Sell, President, Divisional
Karin Mayhew, Senior VP, Divisional
Kathleen Waters, Senior VP

FINANCIAL DATA:
Note: Data for latest year may not have been available at press time.

In U.S. $	2020	2019	2018	2017	2016	2015
Revenue	21,057,198,750	19,679,625,000	18,742,500,000	17,850,000,000	17,000,000,000	16,243,587,072
R&D Expense						
Operating Income						
Operating Margin %						
SGA Expense						
Net Income						
Operating Cash Flow						
Capital Expenditure						
EBITDA						
Return on Assets %						
Return on Equity %						
Debt to Equity						

CONTACT INFORMATION:

Phone: 818 676-6000   Fax: 818 676-6000
Toll-Free: 800-291-6911
Address: 21281 Burbank Blvd., Woodland Hills, CA 91367 United States

STOCK TICKER/OTHER:

Stock Ticker: Subsidiary   Exchange:
Employees: 3,295   Fiscal Year Ends: 12/31
Parent Company: Centene Corporation

SALARIES/BONUSES:

Top Exec. Salary: $ Bonus: $
Second Exec. Salary: $ Bonus: $

OTHER THOUGHTS:

Estimated Female Officers or Directors: 8
Hot Spot for Advancement for Women/Minorities: Y

Healthgrades Operating Company Inc

www.healthgrades.com

NAIC Code: 519130

TYPES OF BUSINESS:

Online Health Information
Health Providers Ratings Data
Consulting Services
Marketing Assistance Services

BRANDS/DIVISIONS/AFFILIATES:

Vestar Capital Partners

CONTACTS: *Note: Officers with more than one job title may be intentionally listed here more than once.*

Rob Draughon, CEO
James Hallick, Exec. VP-R&D
James Hallick, Exec. VP-Prod. Dev.
Rob Draughon, Chief Admin. Officer
Erick J. Hallick, Exec. VP-Bus. Oper.
Joel Liffmann, Exec. VP-Corp. Dev.
Andrea Pearson, Exec. VP-Internet Prod. Strategy & Oper.
Kurt Blasena, Chief Revenue Officer
Brad Graner, Pres., inHealth Div.
Evan Marks, Exec. VP-Informatics & Strategy
M. John Neal, Exec. VP-Corp. Strategy & Dev.

GROWTH PLANS/SPECIAL FEATURES:

Healthgrades Operating Company, Inc. is a customer relationship management provider that connects consumers and healthcare providers. The firm helps millions of consumers each month find and schedule appointments with their provider of choice. Healthgrades' scheduling solutions and advanced analytics applications help health system clients (including more than 1,500 hospitals throughout the U.S.) to cultivate patient relationships, improve patient access and build customer loyalty. Healthgrades helps patients find the right doctor or the right hospital, and offers hospital quality information as well as doctor reviews, diagnosis information and more. For providers and hospitals, Healthgrades' online platform includes a free profile for promoting their practice, group or facility. Healthgrades' website provides answers and information about various health concerns such as bipolarism, diabetes treatment, heart failure, overactive bladder, stage 3 lung cancer and more. Trending videos are also retrievable, and currently include the topics of breast cancer, depression, diabetes and psoriasis. Healthgrades is headquartered in Denver, with offices in Atlanta, Birmingham, Madison and Raleigh. The company is owned by Vestar Central Partners.

Healthgrades offers its employees comprehensive benefits, tuition assistance and more.

FINANCIAL DATA: *Note: Data for latest year may not have been available at press time.*

In U.S. $	2020	2019	2018	2017	2016	2015
Revenue	100,000,000	93,767,625	89,302,500	85,050,000	81,000,000	80,000,000
R&D Expense						
Operating Income						
Operating Margin %						
SGA Expense						
Net Income						
Operating Cash Flow						
Capital Expenditure						
EBITDA						
Return on Assets %						
Return on Equity %						
Debt to Equity						

CONTACT INFORMATION:

Phone: 303-716-0041   Fax: 303-716-1298
Toll-Free:
Address: 1801 California St., Denver, CO 80202 United States

STOCK TICKER/OTHER:

Stock Ticker: Private
Employees: 800
Parent Company: Vestar Capital Partners

Exchange:
Fiscal Year Ends: 12/31

SALARIES/BONUSES:

Top Exec. Salary: $ Bonus: $
Second Exec. Salary: $ Bonus: $

OTHER THOUGHTS:

Estimated Female Officers or Directors: 2
Hot Spot for Advancement for Women/Minorities: Y

HealthNow New York Inc

www.healthnowny.com

NAIC Code: 524114

TYPES OF BUSINESS:

Insurance-Medical & Health, HMOs & PPOs
Health Benefits Provider
Health Care Technologies

BRANDS/DIVISIONS/AFFILIATES:

HealthNow Systems Inc
BlueCross BlueShield of Western New York
Highmark Inc
Highmark Blue Cross Blue Shield of Western New Yor
Highmark Blue Shield of Northeastern New York

CONTACTS: *Note: Officers with more than one job title may be intentionally listed here more than once.*

David W. Anderson, CEO
Cheryl A. Howe, Exec. VP
Linda Kramer, Dir.-Bus. Intelligence & Enterprise Architecture
Karen Merkel-Liberatore, Sr. Dir.-Public Rel. & Comm.

GROWTH PLANS/SPECIAL FEATURES:

HealthNow New York, Inc. provides diversified health benefits. The company offers its innovative products, services and technologies to individuals, families, employers and organizations to help improve the availability, quality and cost of health care. Coverage for members includes $0 co-pay on select services; discounts at health facilities; and online tools for personal health management. Products and services include a personal health concierge to advocate for members, worksite wellness programs, health promotion services, behavioral health services, disease and care management services, pharmacy benefit management, as well as a nationally-recognized physician and hospital quality incentive plan. Subsidiary BlueCross BlueShield of Western New York offers commercial health plans, Medicare Advantage plans, individual and family plans, dental plans, vision plans, Medicaid and Child Health Plus benefits. HealthNow New York itself is a subsidiary of HealthNow Systems, Inc. During 2021, HealthNow New York announced that its affiliation with Highmark, Inc. became effective, and would serve members in western and northeaster New York. In the coming months, the newly affiliated organization would be rebranded as Highmark Blue Cross Blue Shield of Western New York and Highmark Blue Shield of Northeastern New York.

Healthnow New York provides its employees comprehensive benefits, life and disability insurance, 401(k) and a variety of employee assistance plans and programs.

FINANCIAL DATA: *Note: Data for latest year may not have been available at press time.*

In U.S. $	2020	2019	2018	2017	2016	2015
Revenue	2,996,000,000	2,800,000,000	2,600,000,000	2,415,000,000	2,300,000,000	2,250,000,000
R&D Expense						
Operating Income						
Operating Margin %						
SGA Expense						
Net Income		55,000,000	47,000,000		4,200,000	350,000,000
Operating Cash Flow						
Capital Expenditure						
EBITDA						
Return on Assets %						
Return on Equity %						
Debt to Equity						

CONTACT INFORMATION:

Phone: 716-887-9380   Fax: 716-887-8981
Toll-Free:
Address: 257 West Genesee St., Buffalo, NY 14202 United States

STOCK TICKER/OTHER:

Stock Ticker: Private   Exchange:
Employees: 1,350   Fiscal Year Ends: 12/31
Parent Company: HealthNow Systems Inc

SALARIES/BONUSES:

Top Exec. Salary: $ Bonus: $
Second Exec. Salary: $ Bonus: $

OTHER THOUGHTS:

Estimated Female Officers or Directors:
Hot Spot for Advancement for Women/Minorities: Y

Healthscope Limited

www.healthscope.com.au

NAIC Code: 622110

TYPES OF BUSINESS:

General Medical and Surgical Hospitals
Health Care Services
Hospitals
Maternity
Surgical
Rehabilitation
Emergency

BRANDS/DIVISIONS/AFFILIATES:

Brookfield Asset Management Inc
Brookfield Business Partners LP

GROWTH PLANS/SPECIAL FEATURES:

Healthscope Limited is a private healthcare provider in Australia with 42 hospitals, serving every state and territory. Included in the 42 hospitals are three managed on behalf of Adelaide Community Healthcare Alliance Group in South Australia. Services offered include maternity, medical, surgical, mental health, rehabilitation and emergency. Healthscope operates as a subsidiary of Brookfield Business Partners LP, itself a subsidiary of Brookfield Asset Management, Inc.

CONTACTS: *Note: Officers with more than one job title may be intentionally listed here more than once.*

Steven Rubic, CEO
Arthur Yannakou, COO
Ellen Lambridis, CFO
Jenny Patton, Chief Commercial Officer
Katherine MacHutchison, Group Exec.-Human Resources
Victoria Atkinson, Chief Medical Officer
Len Chersky, Chmn.

FINANCIAL DATA: *Note: Data for latest year may not have been available at press time.*

In U.S. $	2020	2019	2018	2017	2016	2015
Revenue	1,724,723,296	1,674,488,637	1,627,297,024	1,590,330,624	1,566,652,416	1,480,242,304
R&D Expense						
Operating Income						
Operating Margin %						
SGA Expense						
Net Income			63,189,140	78,385,632	128,003,952	99,553,288
Operating Cash Flow						
Capital Expenditure						
EBITDA						
Return on Assets %						
Return on Equity %						
Debt to Equity						

CONTACT INFORMATION:

Phone: 61 399267500   Fax: 61 399267599
Toll-Free:
Address: Level 1, 312 St. Kilda Rd., Melbourne, VIC 3004 Australia

STOCK TICKER/OTHER:

Stock Ticker: Subsidiary   Exchange:
Employees: 19,000   Fiscal Year Ends: 06/30
Parent Company: Brookfield Asset Management Inc

SALARIES/BONUSES:

Top Exec. Salary: $ Bonus: $
Second Exec. Salary: $ Bonus: $

OTHER THOUGHTS:

Estimated Female Officers or Directors:
Hot Spot for Advancement for Women/Minorities:

Sales, profits and employees may be estimates. Financial information, benefits and other data can change quickly and may vary from those stated here.

HealthStream Inc

www.healthstream.com

NAIC Code: 611430

TYPES OF BUSINESS:

Educational & Training Content
Internet-based Educational Programs
Workforce Management
Credentialing
Online Training
Online Learning

BRANDS/DIVISIONS/AFFILIATES:

hStream
VerityStream
EchoCredentialing
MSOW
EchoOneApp
CredentialMyDoc
EchoAccess
ComplyALIGN

CONTACTS: *Note: Officers with more than one job title may be intentionally listed here more than once.*

Scott Roberts, CFO
Jeffrey Cunningham, Chief Technology Officer
J. Pearson, COO
Robert Frist, Founder
Michael Collier, General Counsel
Trisha Coady, General Manager, Divisional
Michael Sousa, President, Subsidiary
Michael McQuigg, Senior VP, Divisional

GROWTH PLANS/SPECIAL FEATURES:

HealthStream, Inc. provides workforce and provider solutions for healthcare organizations, and is organized through these two business segments. The workforce solutions segment is comprised of Software-as-a-Service (SaaS) and Platform-as-a-Service (PaaS), subscription-based products, used by healthcare organizations to meet a broad range of their clinical development, talent management, training, certification, competency assessment, performance appraisal and additional needs. This division has numerous content libraries, allowing subscription customers access to a wide array of courseware as well as online training and support. The firm's hStream technology powers activity in the HealthStream ecosystem, with approximately 4.52 million subscribers. Other applications are offered on the hStream platform, each serving a unique function for hospitals and health systems, including applications for learning, performance appraisal, compensation management, succession planning, competency management, disclosure management and more. The provider solutions segment offers the VerityStream marketplace, which delivers enterprise-class solutions to transform the healthcare provider experience for healthcare organizations and providers. VerityStream serves hospitals and outpatient facilities, including ambulatory surgery centers, urgent care facilities, clinics, medical groups and other healthcare organizations. Other products in the provider solutions division include: EchoCredentialing and MSOW, which are platforms that manage medical staff credentialing and privilege processes for hospitals; EchoOneApp, a provider of enrollment platform for medical groups: CredentialMyDoc, a SaaS solution for credential providers; and EchoAccess, an enterprise-class platform to support hospital call centers with physical referral and provider directories functionalities. HealthStream markets its products and services through direct sales teams based in Nashville, Tennessee (corporate headquarters), as well as in additional offices in New York, Tennessee, California, Illinois and Colorado. In early-2021, HealthStream acquired ComplyALIGN, a Chicago-based healthcare technology company.

FINANCIAL DATA: *Note: Data for latest year may not have been available at press time.*

In U.S. $	2020	2019	2018	2017	2016	2015
Revenue	244,826,000	254,112,000	231,616,000	247,662,000	225,974,000	209,002,000
R&D Expense	32,305,000	29,109,000	25,735,000	27,899,000	28,897,000	24,214,000
Operating Income	15,818,000	14,720,000	15,491,000	9,800,000	5,567,000	13,557,000
Operating Margin %		.06%	.07%	.04%	.02%	.06%
SGA Expense	77,182,000	78,524,000	70,145,000	77,680,000	72,669,000	64,848,000
Net Income	14,091,000	15,770,000	32,217,000	10,004,000	3,755,000	8,621,000
Operating Cash Flow	35,874,000	65,657,000	43,246,000	46,712,000	24,234,000	34,917,000
Capital Expenditure	18,803,000	36,510,000	18,450,000	17,873,000	14,806,000	15,359,000
EBITDA	46,007,000	42,589,000	39,722,000	36,083,000	27,774,000	30,554,000
Return on Assets %		.03%	.08%	.02%	.01%	.03%
Return on Equity %		.05%	.10%	.03%	.01%	.04%
Debt to Equity		0.091				

CONTACT INFORMATION:

Phone: 615 301-3100   Fax: 615 301-3200
Toll-Free: 800-521-0574
Address: 500 11th Ave. N., Ste. 1000, Nashville, TN 37203 United States

STOCK TICKER/OTHER:

Stock Ticker: HSTM   Exchange: NAS
Employees: 1,069   Fiscal Year Ends: 12/31
Parent Company:

SALARIES/BONUSES:

Top Exec. Salary: $ Bonus: $
Second Exec. Salary: $ Bonus: $

OTHER THOUGHTS:

Estimated Female Officers or Directors:
Hot Spot for Advancement for Women/Minorities:

HealthTronics Inc

www.healthtronics.com

NAIC Code: 621111

TYPES OF BUSINESS:

Urologists' offices
Prostate Cancer Treatment
Urologic Staffing

BRANDS/DIVISIONS/AFFILIATES:

HT Intermediate Company LLC
Navigo
EDAP Ablatherm
Sonablate
AMICA

CONTACTS: Note: Officers with more than one job title may be intentionally listed here more than once.

Bill Linder, CEO
Richard A. Rusk, CFO
Jose Martinez, VP-Human Resources
Argil J. Wheelock, Chief Medical Advisor
Scott Eden, VP-Mfg. Oper.
Clint B. Davis, General Counsel
Richard A. Rusk, Treas.
Cornelius J. Merlini, Sr. VP
Joanna K. Napp, Compliance Officer
Russell Newman, VP

GROWTH PLANS/SPECIAL FEATURES:

HealthTronics, Inc. is a health care service provider and medical device manufacturer. The firm offers a broad array of minimally invasive, mobile medical therapies for clinical applications. Healthcare facilities throughout the U.S. have access to HealthTronics' solutions, which include lithotripsy solutions, cryoablation solutions and laser treatment solutions as well as other related products. The company offers more than 100 lithotripsy units, with the ability to serve remote and rural communities as well as contract facilities. Cryoablation systems consist of a compact, easy-to-operate console and associated accessories that include cryoprobes to deliver cold temperatures to the therapeutic tissue and temperature probes to monitor temperatures in the surrounding tissue. Cryoablation systems are intended for use in open, minimally invasive or endoscopic procedures in the areas of general surgery, urology, gynecology, oncology, neurology, dermatology, ear/nose/throat, proctology, pulmonary surgery and thoracic surgery. The systems are designed to freeze/ablate tissue by the application of extreme cold temperatures including prostate and kidney tissue, liver metastases, tumors, skin lesions and warts. Lasers offered by HealthTronics provide a minimally invasive treatment option for a variety of conditions, including urology, aesthetics, ENT, gynecology, neurology, orthopedics, podiatry and vascular surgery. Additional products by the firm include the Navigo magnetic resonance imaging (MRI)/ultrasound fusion system, the EDAP Ablatherm high-intensity fusion ultrasound (HIFU) system, the Sonablate HIFU system, and the AMICA line of microwave ablation systems. HealthTronics is owned by HT Intermediate Company, LLC.

FINANCIAL DATA: Note: Data for latest year may not have been available at press time.

In U.S. $	2020	2019	2018	2017	2016	2015
Revenue	220,000,000	231,000,000	220,000,000	210,000,000	200,000,000	230,000,000
R&D Expense						
Operating Income						
Operating Margin %						
SGA Expense						
Net Income						
Operating Cash Flow						
Capital Expenditure						
EBITDA						
Return on Assets %						
Return on Equity %						
Debt to Equity						

CONTACT INFORMATION:

Phone: 512-328-2892   Fax: 512-328-8303
Toll-Free: 888-252-6575
Address: 9825 Spectrum Dr., Bldg. 3, Austin, TX 78717 United States

STOCK TICKER/OTHER:

Stock Ticker: Subsidiary
Employees: 600
Parent Company: HT Intermediate Company LLC

Exchange:
Fiscal Year Ends: 12/31

SALARIES/BONUSES:

Top Exec. Salary: $ Bonus: $
Second Exec. Salary: $ Bonus: $

OTHER THOUGHTS:

Estimated Female Officers or Directors: 2
Hot Spot for Advancement for Women/Minorities:

HealthTrust Purchasing Group LP

healthtrustpg.com

NAIC Code: 561400

TYPES OF BUSINESS:

Group Buying Programs for Medical Supplies
Group Purchasing Organization (GPO)

BRANDS/DIVISIONS/AFFILIATES:

HCA Healthcare Inc
CoreTrust
EasiBuy

CONTACTS: *Note: Officers with more than one job title may be intentionally listed here more than once.*

Ed Jones, CEO
Michael Berryhill, COO
John Paul, CFO
Michael Seestedt, Co-CIO
Laura DeMotte, Group VP-Human Resources
Kent Petty, Co-CIO
John Young, Chief Medical Officer

GROWTH PLANS/SPECIAL FEATURES:

HealthTrust Purchasing Group LP provides consulting, managed and/or outsourcing services to health care providers. More than 1,600 hospitals and health systems, and over 43,000 other member locations such as ambulatory surgery centers, physician practices, long-term care and alternate care sites have partnered with HealthTrust to strengthen performance and clinical excellence through its total spend management advisory solutions. HealthTrust specializes in optimizing operations across the healthcare continuum via sourcing, value analysis, spend analytics, collections, payments and healthcare IT. The company's supply chain solutions provide significant savings on products and supplies through its group purchasing capabilities. CoreTrust is the company's group purchasing organization for non-healthcare organizations, primarily large corporations and private equity firms. Members are also offered the flexibility to customize contracts for preferred health care items when demand is high within local markets. The firm's physician advisory program consists of a group of more than 150 physician advisors nationwide that combine HealthTrust's clinical research and data capabilities to: present reviews, study and analyze drug- and device-utilization trends, and identify ways to drive value for partners and members across physician-preferred product categories. For the health care workforce, HealthTrust offers labor management solutions that improve patient care and employee satisfaction, enhance operational performance and save money. Workforce management solutions include staffing, recruiting, credentialing and advisory services. HealthTrust Purchasing Group operates as a subsidiary of HCA Healthcare, Inc. In mid-2021, HealthTrust and affiliate CoreTrust acquired EasiBuy, a full-service reverse-auction technology company specializing in cooperative sourcing for government agencies.

HealthTrust offers its employees medical, dental, vision, life and disability insurance; 401(k); and various employee assistance programs.

FINANCIAL DATA: *Note: Data for latest year may not have been available at press time.*

In U.S. $	2020	2019	2018	2017	2016	2015
Revenue						
R&D Expense						
Operating Income						
Operating Margin %						
SGA Expense						
Net Income						
Operating Cash Flow						
Capital Expenditure						
EBITDA						
Return on Assets %						
Return on Equity %						
Debt to Equity						

CONTACT INFORMATION:

Phone: 615-344-3000   Fax:
Toll-Free:
Address: 1100 Dr. Martin L. King Jr. Blvd, Ste. 1100, Nashville, TN 37203 United States

STOCK TICKER/OTHER:

Stock Ticker: Subsidiary   Exchange:
Employees: Fiscal Year Ends:
Parent Company: HCA Healthcare Inc

SALARIES/BONUSES:

Top Exec. Salary: $ Bonus: $
Second Exec. Salary: $ Bonus: $

OTHER THOUGHTS:

Estimated Female Officers or Directors:
Hot Spot for Advancement for Women/Minorities:

Sales, profits and employees may be estimates. Financial information, benefits and other data can change quickly and may vary from those stated here.

HearUSA Inc

www.hearusa.com

NAIC Code: 621340

TYPES OF BUSINESS:

Hearing Care Centers
Hearing Benefits Management
Hearing Aids
Hearing Care Devices

BRANDS/DIVISIONS/AFFILIATES:

Siemens Hearing Instruments Inc
Audiology Distribution LLC
HearUSA Hearing Care Network
Total Care Program

CONTACTS: *Note: Officers with more than one job title may be intentionally listed here more than once.*

Craig Cameron, CEO
Jill Botkin, VP-Oper.
Tino Schweighoefer, CFO
Nancy Werner, VP-Human Resources
Scott Davis, CEO-Siemens Hearing Instruments, Inc

GROWTH PLANS/SPECIAL FEATURES:

HearUSA, Inc. owns and manages a network of HearUSA hearing care centers that provide a full range of audiological products and services for the hearing impaired. HearUSA is a wholly-owned subsidiary of Audiology Distribution, LLC, which is itself a wholly-owned subsidiary of Siemens Hearing Instruments, Inc. The company serves customers through more than 250 company-owned hearing centers throughout the U.S. HearUSA also sponsors the HearUSA Hearing Care Network, consisting of approximately 4,000 credentialed audiologist providers that participate in selected hearing benefit programs contracted by the company with employer groups, health insurers and benefit sponsors in 49 states. Through the network, the company can pursue national hearing care contracts and offer managed hearing benefits in areas outside its center markets. HearUSA services over 400 benefit programs for hearing care with various health maintenance organizations (HMOs), preferred provider organizations (PPOs), insurers, benefit administrators and healthcare providers. Each HearUSA center is staffed by a licensed audiologist or hearing instrument specialist, and most are located in shopping or medical centers. The centers offer a complete range of high-quality hearing aids, with emphasis on the latest digital technology along with assessment and evaluation of hearing. In addition, HearUSA offers other products related to hearing care, such as telephone and television amplifiers, telecaptioners and decoders, pocket talkers, specially adapted telephones, alarm clocks, doorbells and fire alarms. It also offers online information about hearing loss, hearing aids, assistive listening devices and the services offered by hearing healthcare professionals. The company's Total Care Program includes a hearing assessment, explanation of results, assistance in selecting products and technologies, hearing aid fitting and adjustments, measurable improvement outcomes and ongoing support.

HearUSA offers its employees medical benefits, a 401(k) plan, access to rehabilitation programs and continuing education programs.

FINANCIAL DATA: *Note: Data for latest year may not have been available at press time.*

In U.S. $	2020	2019	2018	2017	2016	2015
Revenue						
R&D Expense						
Operating Income						
Operating Margin %						
SGA Expense						
Net Income						
Operating Cash Flow						
Capital Expenditure						
EBITDA						
Return on Assets %						
Return on Equity %						
Debt to Equity						

CONTACT INFORMATION:

Phone: 561-478-8770   Fax: 888-888-0009
Toll-Free: 800-323-3277
Address: 11400 N. Jog Rd., Palm Beach Gardens, FL 33418 United States

STOCK TICKER/OTHER:

Stock Ticker: Subsidiary   Exchange:
Employees: 850   Fiscal Year Ends: 12/31
Parent Company: Siemens Hearing Instruments Inc

SALARIES/BONUSES:

Top Exec. Salary: $ Bonus: $
Second Exec. Salary: $ Bonus: $

OTHER THOUGHTS:

Estimated Female Officers or Directors: 1
Hot Spot for Advancement for Women/Minorities:

Sales, profits and employees may be estimates. Financial information, benefits and other data can change quickly and may vary from those stated here.

HemaCare Corporation

NAIC Code: 621991

www.hemacare.com

TYPES OF BUSINESS:

Blood and Organ Banks
Blood Products
Stem-Cell Collection
Therapeutics
Temporary Equipment & Staffing

BRANDS/DIVISIONS/AFFILIATES:

Charles River Laboratories International Inc

GROWTH PLANS/SPECIAL FEATURES:

HemaCare Corporation is a global leader in the customization of human-derived biological products and services for biomedical research, drug discovery, process development and cell and gene therapy starting material. The company's network of U.S. Food and Drug Administration (FDA)-registered, GMP/GTP-compliant collection centers ensure fresh donor material is available to customers and for use within HemaCare's isolation laboratory. GMP and GTP stands for good manufacturing practices and good tissue practices. Human biological material including peripheral blood, bone marrow and cord blood is isolated into various primary cell types for fresh and frozen distribution. Services offered by HemaCare include donor recruitment, tissue collection, cell isolation and processing, packaging, shipping and consulting. HemaCare Corporation operates as a subsidiary of Charles River Laboratories International, Inc.

CONTACTS: Note: Officers with more than one job title may be intentionally listed here more than once.

Peter van der Wal, CEO
Lisa Bacerra, CFO

FINANCIAL DATA: Note: Data for latest year may not have been available at press time.

In U.S. $	2020	2019	2018	2017	2016	2015
Revenue	33,535,750	31,637,500	28,500,000	20,212,000	13,876,000	9,702,000
R&D Expense						
Operating Income						
Operating Margin %						
SGA Expense						
Net Income		4,590,000	4,500,000	4,432,000	781,000	3,236,000
Operating Cash Flow						
Capital Expenditure						
EBITDA						
Return on Assets %						
Return on Equity %						
Debt to Equity						

CONTACT INFORMATION:

Phone: 877-397-3087   Fax: 818-647-0232
Toll-Free:
Address: 8500 Balboa Blvd., Ste. 130, Northridge, CA 91325 United States

STOCK TICKER/OTHER:

Stock Ticker: Subsidiary   Exchange:
Employees: 120   Fiscal Year Ends: 12/31
Parent Company: Charles River Laboratories International Inc

SALARIES/BONUSES:

Top Exec. Salary: $ Bonus: $
Second Exec. Salary: $ Bonus: $

OTHER THOUGHTS:

Estimated Female Officers or Directors: 2
Hot Spot for Advancement for Women/Minorities: Y

Henry Ford Health System

www.henryford.com

NAIC Code: 622110

TYPES OF BUSINESS:

General Medical and Surgical Hospitals
Nursing Homes
Home Health Care
Medical Equipment
Insurance
Psychiatric Services
Research & Education
Osteopathy

BRANDS/DIVISIONS/AFFILIATES:

Henry Ford Hospital
Henry Ford Wyandotte Hospital
Henry Ford Macomb Hospital in Clinton Township
Henry Ford West Bloomfield Hospital
Henty Ford Allegiance Health

CONTACTS: Note: Officers with more than one job title may be intentionally listed here more than once.

Wright L. Lassiter III, Pres.
Robert G. Riney, COO
Robin Damschroder, CFO
Healther Geisler, CMO
Nina Ramsey, Chief Human Resources Officer
John Popovich, Chief Medical Officer
Carladenise Edwards, Chief Strategy Officer
James M. Connelly, Exec. VP-Admin.
David Lee, General Counsel
William Schramm, Sr. VP-Strategic Bus. Dev.
Rose Glenn, Sr. VP-Comm.
James M. Connelly, Exec. VP-Finance
Edie Eisenmann, VP
Susan S. Hawkins, Sr. VP-Performance Excellence
Barbara Rossman, Pres.
Veronica Hall, Chief Nursing Officer

GROWTH PLANS/SPECIAL FEATURES:

Henry Ford Health System is a not-for-profit collection of hospitals and other healthcare facilities in southeastern Michigan. Hospitals include: Henry Ford Hospital, which provides bariatric surgery, cancer care and cancer surgery, heart and vascular care, neuroscience care, organ transplantation, orthopedic surgery, urology care, dialysis, nursing care at home, hospice and eye care; Henry Ford Wyandotte Hospital, which provides bariatric surgery, heart and vascular care, neurosurgery, orthopedics, radiology, robotic surgery, women's healthcare, dialysis, eye care and home care services; Henry Ford Macomb Hospital in Clinton Township, which provides bariatric surgery, cancer care, heart and vascular care, joint replacement services, stroke care, weight management, women's healthcare, business health, dialysis, at-home care services, eye care, radiology, spine care and wound care; Henry Ford West Bloomfield Hospital, which provides cancer care, emergency room services, heart and vascular care, neurology and neurosurgery services, orthopedic surgery, stroke services, urology care, women's healthcare services, dialysis, at-home care services, eye care and pharmacy services; and Henry Ford Allegiance Health, providing cancer care, hearth and vascular care, prevention care, surgery, family and internal medicine, orthopedics and joint replacement, spine/stroke/neurology care and women and children care. Henry Ford Health System is one of the largest group practices in the U.S., with more than 1,200 physicians and researchers in 40 specialties.

Henry Ford Health offers its employees comprehensive health benefits, disability coverage, retirement and pension programs, and a variety of employee assistance plans and programs.

FINANCIAL DATA: Note: Data for latest year may not have been available at press time.

In U.S. $	2020	2019	2018	2017	2016	2015
Revenue	6,500,000,000	6,330,000,000	5,800,000,000	6,000,000,000	5,700,000,000	5,100,000,000
R&D Expense						
Operating Income						
Operating Margin %						
SGA Expense						
Net Income	225,600,000	138,800,000	142,000,000	146,500,000	95,100,000	112,000,000
Operating Cash Flow						
Capital Expenditure						
EBITDA						
Return on Assets %						
Return on Equity %						
Debt to Equity						

CONTACT INFORMATION:

Phone: Fax:
Toll-Free: 800-436-7936
Address: 1 Ford Pl., Detroit, MI 48202 United States

STOCK TICKER/OTHER:

Stock Ticker: Nonprofit   Exchange:
Employees: 30,000   Fiscal Year Ends: 12/31
Parent Company:

SALARIES/BONUSES:

Top Exec. Salary: $ Bonus: $
Second Exec. Salary: $ Bonus: $

OTHER THOUGHTS:

Estimated Female Officers or Directors: 10
Hot Spot for Advancement for Women/Minorities: Y

Henry Schein Inc

NAIC Code: 423450

www.henryschein.com

TYPES OF BUSINESS:

Health Care Products Distribution
Dental Supplies Distribution
Veterinary Products Distribution
Electronic Catalogs
Technology Solutions
Dental Management Software
Financial Services

BRANDS/DIVISIONS/AFFILIATES:

Henry Schein
Prism Medical Products LLC
eAssist Dental Solutions

CONTACTS: *Note: Officers with more than one job title may be intentionally listed here more than once.*

Jonathan Koch, CEO, Divisional
Brad Connett, Pres., Divisional
James Harding, CEO, Subsidiary
Stanley Bergman, CEO
Steven Paladino, CFO
Gerald Benjamin, Chief Administrative Officer
Mark Mlotek, Chief Strategy Officer
Christopher Pendergast, Chief Technology Officer
James Breslawski, Director
Walter Siegel, General Counsel
Michael Ettinger, Other Executive Officer
Lorelei McGlynn, Other Executive Officer
Michael Racioppi, Other Executive Officer
David Brous, President, Divisional
James Mullins, Senior VP, Divisional

GROWTH PLANS/SPECIAL FEATURES:

Henry Schein, Inc. is a global provider of health care products and services, primarily to office-based dental and medical practitioners. The company serves more than 1 million customers worldwide, including dental practitioners and laboratories and physician practices, as well as government, institutional health care clinics and other alternate care clinics. Henry Schein operates throughout the U.S. and in more than 30 other countries. The firm offers a comprehensive selection of products and services and value-added solutions for operating efficient practices and delivering quality care. Henry Schein operates through a centralized and automated distribution network with a selection of more than 120,000 branded products and Henry Schein private brand products in stock, as well as more than 180,000 additional products available as special order items. The company also offers innovative technology solutions, including practice management software, ecommerce solutions and a range of financial services. During 2021, Henry Schein acquired a majority interest in Prism Medical Products, LLC, a provider of specialty home medical supplies with a core competency in advanced wound care products; and acquired a 70% ownership position in eAssist Dental Solutions, the developer of a virtual dental billing outsourcing service.

Henry Schein offers its employees medical, dental, vision, life, AD&D and disability insurance; flexible spending accounts; 401(k); college savings plan; tuition assistance; and paid time off.

FINANCIAL DATA: *Note: Data for latest year may not have been available at press time.*

In U.S. $	2020	2019	2018	2017	2016	2015
Revenue	10,119,140,000	9,985,803,000	13,201,990,000	12,461,540,000	11,571,670,000	10,629,720,000
R&D Expense						
Operating Income	567,396,000	732,966,000	893,208,000	859,369,000	817,465,000	768,903,000
Operating Margin %		.07%	.07%	.07%	.07%	.07%
SGA Expense	2,246,947,000	2,357,920,000	2,701,876,000	2,539,734,000	2,416,504,000	2,243,356,000
Net Income	403,794,000	694,734,000	535,881,000	406,299,000	506,778,000	479,058,000
Operating Cash Flow	598,910,000	654,087,000	684,706,000	545,515,000	615,461,000	586,841,000
Capital Expenditure	48,829,000	76,219,000	90,637,000	81,501,000	70,179,000	71,684,000
EBITDA	726,810,000	916,041,000	981,694,000	1,069,574,000	957,508,000	905,893,000
Return on Assets %		.09%	.07%	.06%	.08%	.08%
Return on Equity %		.23%	.19%	.14%	.18%	.17%
Debt to Equity		0.267	0.339	0.323	0.256	0.161

CONTACT INFORMATION:

Phone: 631 843-5500   Fax: 631 843-5665
Toll-Free:
Address: 135 Duryea Rd., Melville, NY 11747 United States

STOCK TICKER/OTHER:

Stock Ticker: HSIC
Employees: 19,000
Parent Company:

Exchange: NAS
Fiscal Year Ends: 12/31

SALARIES/BONUSES:

Top Exec. Salary: $ Bonus: $
Second Exec. Salary: $ Bonus: $

OTHER THOUGHTS:

Estimated Female Officers or Directors: 6
Hot Spot for Advancement for Women/Minorities: Y

Highmark Health

www.highmarkhealth.org/hmk/index.shtml

NAIC Code: 524114

TYPES OF BUSINESS:

Insurance-Medical & Health, HMOs & PPOs
Health Care Networks
Dental Care
Vision Care
Home Health
Eyeglasses Manufacturing
Eye Care Product Distribution

BRANDS/DIVISIONS/AFFILIATES:

Highmark Inc
Allegheny Health Network
HM Health Solutions
HM Insurance Group LLC
United Concordia Companies Inc
Davis Vision
Visionworks
HVHC Inc

CONTACTS: *Note: Officers with more than one job title may be intentionally listed here more than once.*

David L. Holmberg, Pres.
Karen L. Hanlon, COO
Saurabh Tripathi, CFO
Cindy Donohoe, CMO
Larry Kleinman, Chief Human Resources Officer
Michael J. Bennett, Chief Transformation Officer & Strategy
Nanette DeTurk, Chief Admin. Officer
Thomas L. VanKirk, Chief Legal Officer
Jayanth Godla, Chief Strategy Officer
Nanette DeTurk, Treas.
David L. Holmberg, Pres., Diversified Services
John W. Paul, Pres., Integrated Delivery Network
Joseph C. Guyaux, Chmn.

GROWTH PLANS/SPECIAL FEATURES:

Highmark Health and its subsidiaries and affiliates comprise a national, nonprofit health and wellness organization that serves individual consumers and businesses in all 50 states and the District of Columbia. The organization includes businesses in health insurance, health care delivery, post-acute care management solutions, dental solutions and eye care services and solutions. Highmark Health is the parent of: Highmark, Inc. (Health Plan), a health insurance organization and an independent licensee of the Blue Cross Blue Shield Association, offers health plans that cover the insurance needs of members in Pennsylvania, Delaware and West Virginia; Allegheny Health Network, a tax-exempt charitable organization that operates a health care delivery network of hospitals located in Pennsylvania and New York, as well as ambulatory surgery centers, an employed physician organization, home- and community-based health services, wellness pavilions and a research institute; HM Health Solutions, which delivers business solutions to health plan payers to administer business efficiently and effectively; HM Insurance Group, LLC, which provides insurance products for employers and health care entities throughout the U.S., protecting them from the financial risks associated with catastrophic health care costs; United Concordia Companies, Inc., provides dental solutions and is licensed in all 50 U.S. states, the District of Columbia and Puerto Rico; Davis Vision, a provider of comprehensive, managed vision care with a network of 47,000 points of care throughout the U.S.; Visionworks, a provider of eye care services in the U.S., with more than 650 optical retail stores in 40 states and the District of Columbia; and HVHC, Inc., which manufactures and distributes eye lenses and eye wear products. In September 2021, Highmark acquired Gateway Health Plan, Inc., an affiliated Medicaid managed care health insurer.

FINANCIAL DATA: *Note: Data for latest year may not have been available at press time.*

In U.S. $	2020	2019	2018	2017	2016	2015
Revenue	18,000,000,000	18,098,000,000	18,776,000,000	18,261,000,000	18,233,000,000	18,231,900,000
R&D Expense						
Operating Income						
Operating Margin %						
SGA Expense						
Net Income	450,000,000	843,000,000	570,000,000	1,063,000,000	58,500,000	-84,700,000
Operating Cash Flow						
Capital Expenditure						
EBITDA						
Return on Assets %						
Return on Equity %						
Debt to Equity						

CONTACT INFORMATION:

Phone: 412-544-7000   Fax:
Toll-Free:
Address: 120 Fifth Ave., Pittsburgh, PA 15222-3099 United States

STOCK TICKER/OTHER:

Stock Ticker: Nonprofit   Exchange:
Employees: 35,000   Fiscal Year Ends: 12/31
Parent Company:

SALARIES/BONUSES:

Top Exec. Salary: $ Bonus: $
Second Exec. Salary: $ Bonus: $

OTHER THOUGHTS:

Estimated Female Officers or Directors: 5
Hot Spot for Advancement for Women/Minorities: Y

Hill-Rom Holdings Inc

www.hillrom.com

NAIC Code: 339100

TYPES OF BUSINESS:

Equipment-Hospital Beds & Related Products
Specialized Therapy Products
Rentals

BRANDS/DIVISIONS/AFFILIATES:

Hillrom

CONTACTS: *Note: Officers with more than one job title may be intentionally listed here more than once.*

John Groetelaars, CEO
Barbara Bodem, CFO
William Dempsey, Chairman of the Board
Richard Wagner, Chief Accounting Officer
Deborah Rasin, Chief Legal Officer
Kenneth Meyers, Other Executive Officer
Francisco Vega, President, Divisional
Paul Johnson, President, Divisional
Andreas Frank, President, Divisional
Carlos Alonso-Marum, President, Subsidiary
Mary Ladone, Senior VP, Divisional
Jason Richardson, Treasurer

GROWTH PLANS/SPECIAL FEATURES:

Hill-Rom Holdings, Inc. (branded as Hillrom) is a global medical technology company. Hillrom partners with healthcare providers in more than 100 countries, with a focus on patient care solutions that improve clinical and economic outcomes. The firm operates through three segments: patient support systems, front line care and surgical solutions. The patient support systems segment globally provides Hillrom's medical surgery and specialty bed systems and surfaces, safe patient handling equipment and mobility solutions, as well as the company's care communications platform that delivers software and information technologies to improve care and deliver insight to caregivers and patients. The front line care segment globally provides patient monitoring and diagnostic technologies, including a diversified portfolio of physical assessment tools that help diagnose, treat and manage a wide variety of illnesses and diseases, including respiratory and a portfolio of vision care health devices. The surgical solutions segment globally provides products that improve safety and efficiency in the surgical space, including tables, lights, pendants, precision positioning devices and other accessories. In September 2021, Hill-Rom agreed to be acquired by Baxter International, Inc., a global medical products company. Hillrom will bring its complementary product portfolio and innovation pipeline that will enable Baxter to provide a broader array of medical products and services. The combination is also expected to accelerate the companies' expansion into digital and connected care solutions. The transaction was expected to close in early-2022.

FINANCIAL DATA: *Note: Data for latest year may not have been available at press time.*

In U.S. $	2020	2019	2018	2017	2016	2015
Revenue	2,881,000,000	2,907,300,000	2,848,000,000	2,743,700,000	2,655,200,000	1,988,200,000
R&D Expense	136,500,000	139,500,000	135,600,000	133,700,000	133,500,000	91,800,000
Operating Income	409,200,000	344,500,000	367,100,000	310,800,000	270,200,000	124,300,000
Operating Margin %		.12%	.13%	.11%	.10%	.06%
SGA Expense	820,400,000	941,000,000	891,500,000	876,100,000	853,300,000	664,200,000
Net Income	223,000,000	152,200,000	252,400,000	133,600,000	124,100,000	47,700,000
Operating Cash Flow	481,700,000	401,400,000	395,200,000	311,100,000	281,200,000	213,800,000
Capital Expenditure	105,900,000	90,500,000	89,500,000	97,500,000	83,300,000	121,300,000
EBITDA	524,000,000	493,000,000	488,700,000	482,700,000	437,700,000	201,700,000
Return on Assets %		.03%	.06%	.03%	.03%	.02%
Return on Equity %		.10%	.17%	.10%	.10%	.05%
Debt to Equity		1.133	1.108	1.561	1.58	1.897

CONTACT INFORMATION:

Phone: 3120819-7200   Fax:
Toll-Free:
Address: 130 E. Randolph St., Ste. 1000, Chicago, IL 60601 United States

STOCK TICKER/OTHER:

Stock Ticker: HRC
Employees: 10,000
Parent Company:

Exchange: NYS
Fiscal Year Ends: 09/30

SALARIES/BONUSES:

Top Exec. Salary: $ Bonus: $
Second Exec. Salary: $ Bonus: $

OTHER THOUGHTS:

Estimated Female Officers or Directors: 1
Hot Spot for Advancement for Women/Minorities: Y

HMS

www.hms.com

NAIC Code: 524292

TYPES OF BUSINESS:

Health Care Benefit Management
Healthcare Technology
Analytics Solutions
Population Health Management
Payment Solutions
Advisory Services

BRANDS/DIVISIONS/AFFILIATES:

Veritas Capital Fund Management LLC
Gainwell Technologies Company
HMS Holdings Corp

CONTACTS: *Note: Officers with more than one job title may be intentionally listed here more than once.*

Paul Saleh, CEO-Gainwell
Jeffrey Sherman, CFO
Maria Perrin, Chief Marketing Officer
Douglas Williams, COO
Emmet OGara, President, Divisional
Greg Aunan, Senior VP

GROWTH PLANS/SPECIAL FEATURES:

HMS, a Gainwell Technologies Company, provides healthcare technology and analytics solutions for payers, providers and members. The company's solutions include the coordination of benefits, payment integrity, population health management and advisory services. HMS' website also offers resources on these solutions as well as on topics such as behavioral health, COVID-19, flu season, opioid use and others. Headquartered in Irving, Texas, HMS has locations in several U.S. states, including Alaska, Alabama, Arizona, California, Colorado, Connecticut, Georgia, Idaho, Kansas, Massachusetts, Missouri, Nevada, New Jersey, New York, North Carolina and Ohio. During 2021, HMS Holdings Corp. was acquired by Gainwell Technologies, a portfolio company of Veritas Capital Fund Management LLC.

HMS offers its employees comprehensive benefits, retirement and savings options, short/long-term disability coverage and more.

FINANCIAL DATA: *Note: Data for latest year may not have been available at press time.*

In U.S. $	2020	2019	2018	2017	2016	2015
Revenue		626,395,008	598,289,984	521,212,000	489,720,000	474,216,000
R&D Expense						
Operating Income						
Operating Margin %						
SGA Expense						
Net Income		87,224,000	54,989,000	40,054,000	37,636,000	24,527,000
Operating Cash Flow						
Capital Expenditure						
EBITDA						
Return on Assets %						
Return on Equity %						
Debt to Equity						

CONTACT INFORMATION:

Phone: 214-453-3000   Fax:
Toll-Free:
Address: 5615 High Point Dr., Irving, TX 75038 United States

STOCK TICKER/OTHER:

Stock Ticker: Private   Exchange: NAS
Employees: 2,315   Fiscal Year Ends: 12/31
Parent Company: Veritas Capital Fund Management LLC

SALARIES/BONUSES:

Top Exec. Salary: $ Bonus: $
Second Exec. Salary: $ Bonus: $

OTHER THOUGHTS:

Estimated Female Officers or Directors: 8
Hot Spot for Advancement for Women/Minorities: Y

Hologic Inc

www.hologic.com

NAIC Code: 325413

TYPES OF BUSINESS:

Medical Diagnostic & Imaging Equipment
Mammography Systems
X-Ray Bone Densitometers
Radiography Systems
Biopsy Systems
Imaging Systems
Diagnostics

BRANDS/DIVISIONS/AFFILIATES:

Aquilex
Definity
Fluent
MyoSure
NovaSure
Omni
Novodiag
Mobidiag Oy

CONTACTS: *Note: Officers with more than one job title may be intentionally listed here more than once.*

Stephen Macmillan, CEO
Karleen Oberton, CFO
Benjamin Cohn, Chief Accounting Officer
John Griffin, General Counsel
Peter Valenti, President, Divisional
Thomas West, President, Divisional
Allison Bebo, Senior VP, Divisional

GROWTH PLANS/SPECIAL FEATURES:

Hologic, Inc. develops, manufactures and supplies diagnostic products, medical imaging systems and surgical products primarily serving women's healthcare. Products are grouped into four categories, including: breast, skeletal, diagnostic and gynecology (GYN) surgical. Breast health solutions enable early detection, diagnosis and treatment, with products and solutions spanning screening devices, diagnostic systems, biopsy systems, breast surgery radiography systems and targeted radiation therapy. Skeletal solutions help physicians make informed diagnosis and treatment decisions, with products consisting of imaging systems. Diagnostic products include innovative technology for cytology, molecular and perinatal testing, with products covering vaginal health, virology, cervical health, assays, perinatal tests and others. GYN surgical solutions include a suite of minimally invasive treatment options for women facing gynecologic conditions that affect their comfort, health and wellbeing. GYN surgical products include the Aquilex fluid management system, the Definity cervical dilator, the Fluent fluid management system, the MyoSure tissue removal suite, the NovaSure endometrial ablation system, the Omni hysteroscope and the Omni Lok cervical seal. In October 2021, Hologic announced its European launch of the Novodiag system, a fully automated molecular diagnostic solution for on-demand testing of infectious diseases and antimicrobial resistance. The launch follows Hologic's acquisition of Mobidiag Oy in June 2021.

Hologic offers its employees comprehensive benefits and retirement plans.

FINANCIAL DATA: *Note: Data for latest year may not have been available at press time.*

In U.S. $	2020	2019	2018	2017	2016	2015
Revenue	3,776,400,000	3,367,300,000	3,217,900,000	3,058,800,000	2,832,700,000	2,705,000,000
R&D Expense	222,500,000	232,200,000	218,700,000	232,800,000	232,100,000	214,900,000
Operating Income	1,124,700,000	-10,500,000	508,000,000	483,800,000	559,100,000	483,600,000
Operating Margin %		.00%	.16%	.16%	.20%	.18%
SGA Expense	840,600,000	897,200,000	910,700,000	841,900,000	682,400,000	624,000,000
Net Income	1,115,200,000	-203,600,000	-111,300,000	755,500,000	330,800,000	131,600,000
Operating Cash Flow	896,600,000	649,500,000	732,900,000	8,300,000	787,200,000	786,100,000
Capital Expenditure	156,400,000	113,600,000	105,600,000	107,600,000	98,500,000	89,400,000
EBITDA	1,494,400,000	346,200,000	210,400,000	1,832,900,000	1,036,000,000	874,100,000
Return on Assets %		-.03%	-.01%	.10%	.04%	.02%
Return on Equity %		-.09%	-.04%	.31%	.16%	.06%
Debt to Equity		1.325	1.122	0.788	1.423	1.562

CONTACT INFORMATION:

Phone: 508-263-2900   Fax:
Toll-Free:
Address: 250 Campus Dr., Marlborough, MA 01752 United States

STOCK TICKER/OTHER:

Stock Ticker: HOLX   Exchange: NAS
Employees: 6,478   Fiscal Year Ends: 09/30
Parent Company:

SALARIES/BONUSES:

Top Exec. Salary: $ Bonus: $
Second Exec. Salary: $ Bonus: $

OTHER THOUGHTS:

Estimated Female Officers or Directors: 4
Hot Spot for Advancement for Women/Minorities: Y

HOOKIPA Pharma Inc

www.hookipapharma.com

NAIC Code: 325412

TYPES OF BUSINESS:

Pharmaceutical Preparation Manufacturing
Biophamraceuticals
Clinical Trials
Drug Development
Immuno Therapeutics
Infectious Disease Therapies
Cancer Therapies

BRANDS/DIVISIONS/AFFILIATES:

CONTACTS: *Note: Officers with more than one job title may be intentionally listed here more than once.*

Jorn Aldag, CEO
Reinhard Kandera, CFO
Jan van de Winkel, Chairman of the Board
Igor Matushansky, Chief Medical Officer
Daniel Pinschewer, Chief Scientific Officer
Anders Lilja, Senior VP, Divisional
Klaus Orlinger, Senior VP, Divisional

GROWTH PLANS/SPECIAL FEATURES:

HOOKIPA Pharma, Inc. is a clinical-stage biopharmaceutical company developing a new class of immunotherapeutics targeting infectious diseases and cancers based on its proprietary arenavirus platform, which is designed to reprogram the body's immune system. HOOKIPA's technology is capable of reprogramming the immune response. Its science is based on a novel and highly-differentiated delivery platform based on arenaviruses. HOOKIPA's scientists can engineer these viruses and aim to deliver disease-specific proteins (antigens) to the immune system. The immune system detects the antigens and builds defenses to target them, killing any cell that expresses them and by inactivating infectious intruders. As of mid-2021, HOOKIPA was developing the following product candidates for multiple cancers and infectious diseases, with HB 200 and 300s referring to cancers and HB 101 referring to infectious diseases. HB-200 is in Phase 1 development, HB-201 is scheduled to begin Phase 2 in Q1 2022, HB-201/HB-202 to begin Phase 2 in Q1 2022, HB-300 is in pre-clinical stage, and HB-101 is in Phase 2 development. There are also pre-clinical developments for the treatment of Hepatitis B and HIV, both of which are in collaboration and licensing agreements with Gilead Sciences, Inc.

FINANCIAL DATA: *Note: Data for latest year may not have been available at press time.*

In U.S. $	2020	2019	2018	2017	2016	2015
Revenue	19,584,000	11,942,000	7,629,000			
R&D Expense	54,787,000	46,312,000	21,965,000	9,772,000		
Operating Income	-46,768,000	-44,348,000	-15,568,000	-12,088,000		
Operating Margin %		-3.71%	-2.04%			
SGA Expense	18,082,000	16,715,000	6,844,000	4,385,000		
Net Income	-44,082,000	-43,037,000	-16,237,000	-12,723,000		
Operating Cash Flow	-39,339,000	-41,731,000	-14,998,000	-11,913,000		
Capital Expenditure	2,371,000	1,999,000	2,150,000	1,297,000		
EBITDA	-39,146,000	-40,717,000	-14,795,000	-11,715,000		
Return on Assets %		- .41%	- .23%	- .17%		
Return on Equity %		- .53%	-18.63%			
Debt to Equity		0.075	0.099			

CONTACT INFORMATION:

Phone: 431 890-6360   Fax:
Toll-Free:
Address: 350 Fifth Ave., Fl. 72, Ste. 7240, New York, NY 10118 United States

STOCK TICKER/OTHER:

Stock Ticker: HOOK
Employees: 136
Parent Company:

Exchange: NAS
Fiscal Year Ends: 12/31

SALARIES/BONUSES:

Top Exec. Salary: $ Bonus: $
Second Exec. Salary: $ Bonus: $

OTHER THOUGHTS:

Estimated Female Officers or Directors:
Hot Spot for Advancement for Women/Minorities:

Sales, profits and employees may be estimates. Financial information, benefits and other data can change quickly and may vary from those stated here.

Horizon Healthcare Services Inc

www.horizon-bcbsnj.com

NAIC Code: 524114

TYPES OF BUSINESS:

Insurance-Medical & Health, HMOs & PPOs
Workers' Compensation
Utilization Management
Insurance-Dental
Insurance-Behavioral Health
Insurance-Casualty
Insurance-Life

BRANDS/DIVISIONS/AFFILIATES:

Horizon Blue Cross Blue Shield of New Jersey
Horizon BCBSNJ Dental
Horizon Casualty Services
Horizon NJ Health

GROWTH PLANS/SPECIAL FEATURES:

Horizon Healthcare Services, Inc. is a health care insurance provider that does business as Horizon Blue Cross Blue Shield of New Jersey (HBCBSNJ), The firm serves members throughout the state and is a not-for-profit health service corporation. HBCBSNJ provides a wide array of medical, dental, vision and prescription insurance products and services. Its family of companies include: Horizon BCBSNJ Dental, providing oral health; Horizon Casualty Services, providing administrative services to the workers' compensation and personal injury protection business sectors; and Horizon NJ Health, providing healthcare management to publicly-insured individuals in the Medicaid and NJ FamilyCare programs.

CONTACTS:
Note: Officers with more than one job title may be intentionally listed here more than once.

Gary D. St. Hilaire, CEO
Mark L. Barnard, VP-Operations
Douglas R. Simpson, CFO
David R. Huber, Sr. VP-Admin.
Linda Willet, General Counsel
Mark Bernard, Sr. VP
Christopher M. Lepre, Sr. VP-Market Bus. Units
Kevin P. Conlin, Exec. VP-Health Care Mgmt.

FINANCIAL DATA:
Note: Data for latest year may not have been available at press time.

In U.S. $	2020	2019	2018	2017	2016	2015
Revenue	14,124,000,000	13,200,000,000	13,000,000,000	12,661,596,150	12,058,663,000	11,331,172,000
R&D Expense						
Operating Income						
Operating Margin %						
SGA Expense						
Net Income						
Operating Cash Flow						
Capital Expenditure						
EBITDA						
Return on Assets %						
Return on Equity %						
Debt to Equity						

CONTACT INFORMATION:

Phone: 973-466-4000   Fax: 973-466-4317
Toll-Free: 800-224-4426
Address: 3 Penn Plz. E., Newark, NJ 07105 United States

STOCK TICKER/OTHER:

Stock Ticker: Nonprofit   Exchange:
Employees: 5,500   Fiscal Year Ends: 12/31
Parent Company:

SALARIES/BONUSES:

Top Exec. Salary: $ Bonus: $
Second Exec. Salary: $ Bonus: $

OTHER THOUGHTS:

Estimated Female Officers or Directors: 2
Hot Spot for Advancement for Women/Minorities: Y

Hoth Therapeutics Inc

www.hoththerapeutics.com

NAIC Code: 325412

TYPES OF BUSINESS:

Pharmaceutical Preparation Manufacturing
Dermatological Preparations Manufacturing
Biopharmaceuticals
Drug Therapy Development
Clinical Trials

BRANDS/DIVISIONS/AFFILIATES:

BioLexa

CONTACTS: *Note: Officers with more than one job title may be intentionally listed here more than once.*

Robb Knie, CEO
David Briones, CFO
Jane Behrmann, Vice President, Divisional

GROWTH PLANS/SPECIAL FEATURES:

Hoth Therapeutics, Inc. is a clinical-stage biopharmaceutical company focused on developing new generation therapies for dermatological disorders. The firm's pipeline is for patients suffering from conditions such as atopic dermatitis (eczema), chromic wounds, psoriasis, asthma and acne. Hoth's primary asset is a sublicense agreement with Chelexa Biosciences, Inc., in which Chelexa has granted Hoth an exclusive sublicense to make, use, have made, import, offer for sale, and sell products based on or involving the use of: topical compositions comprising a zinc chelator and gentamicin; and zinc chelators to inhibit biofilm formulation (the BioLexa platform). In addition, Chelexa granted Hoth the right to issue exclusive and non-exclusive sublicenses (with the right to further sublicense to third parties) to make, use, have made, import, offer for sale, and sell products based upon the BioLexa platform. The license enables Hoth to develop the platform for any indications in humans. The company's initial focus is on the treatment of eczema through the application of a topical cream, with the intention to develop a second topical cream to reduce post-procedure infections, accelerate healing and improve clinical outcomes for patients undergoing aesthetic dermatology procedures. Hoth also intends to conduct a pilot study on the efficacy of BioLexa to accelerate diabetic wound healing. BioLexa combines a U.S. Food and Drug Administration (FDA)-approved zinc chelator with one or more approved antibiotics in a topical dosage form to address unchecked eczema flare-ups by preventing the formation of infectious biofilms and the resulting clogging of sweat ducts which trigger symptoms. In September 2021, Hoth announced completed safety results in Cohort 1 of its first in human clinical trial of BioLexa to treat eczema. That same month, Hoth submitted to the Human Research Ethics Committee overseeing the BioLexa trial to obtain official approval to initiate patient Cohort 2 with mild-to-moderate eczema.

FINANCIAL DATA: *Note: Data for latest year may not have been available at press time.*

In U.S. $	2020	2019	2018	2017	2016	2015
Revenue						
R&D Expense	2,888,925	2,120,120	1,015,967			
Operating Income	-7,301,974	-7,714,997	-2,495,525			
Operating Margin %						
SGA Expense	3,958,842	5,056,300	1,220,848			
Net Income	-7,197,816	-7,704,636	-2,495,525			
Operating Cash Flow	-6,133,198	-4,947,215	-2,102,626			
Capital Expenditure	167,457	95,000				
EBITDA	-7,300,931	-7,713,772	-2,494,301			
Return on Assets %		-4.61%	-2.87%			
Return on Equity %		-6.04%	-3.73%			
Debt to Equity						

CONTACT INFORMATION:

Phone: 646 756-2997   Fax:
Toll-Free:
Address: 1 Rockefeller Plaza, Ste. 1039, New York, NY 10020 United States

STOCK TICKER/OTHER:

Stock Ticker: HOTH
Employees: 5
Parent Company:

Exchange: NAS
Fiscal Year Ends: 12/31

SALARIES/BONUSES:

Top Exec. Salary: $ Bonus: $
Second Exec. Salary: $ Bonus: $

OTHER THOUGHTS:

Estimated Female Officers or Directors:
Hot Spot for Advancement for Women/Minorities:

Houston Methodist

www.houstonmethodist.org

NAIC Code: 622110

TYPES OF BUSINESS:

General Medical and Surgical Hospitals
Hospitals
Academic Medical Centers
Emergency Care
Imaging Center
Breast Care Center
Outpatient Center
Technologies

BRANDS/DIVISIONS/AFFILIATES:

Houston Methodist Hospital
Houston Methodist Emergency Care
Houston Methodist Imaging
Houston Methodist Breast Care
Houston Methodist Outpatient Center
Houston Methodist Academic Institute
Houston Methodist Institute for Technology
Houston Methodist Hospital Foundation

CONTACTS: Note: Officers with more than one job title may be intentionally listed here more than once.

Marc L. Boom, CEO
Gregory Nelson, Sec.
Carlton Caucum, Treas.
Joseph Walter III, Assistant Treas.
Robert K. Moses, Jr., Assistant Sec.
Gregory V. Nelson, Chmn.

GROWTH PLANS/SPECIAL FEATURES:

Houston Methodist comprises an academic medical center in the Texas Medical Center and six community hospitals serving the greater Houston area. Houston Methodist Hospital is the system's flagship, with other available centers including Houston Methodist Emergency Care Centers, the Houston Methodist Imaging Center, the Houston Methodist Breast Care Center and the Houston Methodist Outpatient Center. These centers offer care in areas of cancer, digestive disorders, heart and vascular disease, neurology, neurosurgery, orthopedics, sports medicine and transplant. Houston Methodist Academic Institute comprises physician-scientists who work in a collaborative environment on more than 800 clinical trials. The Houston Methodist Institute for Technology, Innovation and Education is a 35,000-square-foot surgical training center and virtual hospital that provides ongoing physician education and surgical training in the latest techniques and technologies. Houston Methodist Hospital Foundation accepts all gifts on Houston Methodist's behalf and can assist with choosing an area to apply donations. Houston Methodist Community Benefits provides financial and medical assistance across the group's hospitals. Houston Methodist Specialty Physician Group consist of doctors employed by Houston Methodist who offer academic and research services to support teaching, continued education and collaboration. Houston Methodist Primary Care Group has locations throughout Houston and provides patient care for the entire family.

FINANCIAL DATA: Note: Data for latest year may not have been available at press time.

In U.S. $	2020	2019	2018	2017	2016	2015
Revenue	3,859,500,000	4,150,000,000	4,000,000,000	3,045,000,000	2,900,000,000	2,800,000,000
R&D Expense						
Operating Income						
Operating Margin %						
SGA Expense						
Net Income						
Operating Cash Flow						
Capital Expenditure						
EBITDA						
Return on Assets %						
Return on Equity %						
Debt to Equity						

CONTACT INFORMATION:

Phone: 713-790-3311   Fax:
Toll-Free:
Address: 6565 Fannin St., Houston, TX 77030 United States

STOCK TICKER/OTHER:

Stock Ticker: Nonprofit   Exchange:
Employees: 25,543   Fiscal Year Ends: 12/31
Parent Company:

SALARIES/BONUSES:

Top Exec. Salary: $ Bonus: $
Second Exec. Salary: $ Bonus: $

OTHER THOUGHTS:

Estimated Female Officers or Directors: 5
Hot Spot for Advancement for Women/Minorities: Y

Hoya Corporation

www.hoya.co.jp

NAIC Code: 334413

TYPES OF BUSINESS:

Semiconductor Manufacturing Equipment
Glass Semiconductor Components
Medical Equipment
Eyeglass Lenses
Optical Glass
Bio-Compatible Bone Replacement
Laser & UV Light Sources
Nanoimprint Technology

BRANDS/DIVISIONS/AFFILIATES:

ViXion Inc

CONTACTS: *Note: Officers with more than one job title may be intentionally listed here more than once.*

Hiroshi Suzuki, CEO
Ryo Hirooka, CFO
Eiichiro Ikeda, CTO
Mitsudo Urano, Chmn.

GROWTH PLANS/SPECIAL FEATURES:

HOYA Corporation, established in 1941, primarily manufactures innovative high-tech and healthcare products. HOYA operates through two segments: healthcare and information technology. The healthcare segment manufactures products such as eyeglass lenses; medical related products such as intraocular lenses for cataract surgery, medical endoscopes, surgical equipment, laser equipment and artificial bones and implants; and the operation of HOYA's contact lens retail stores. Information technology focuses on electronics products for the semiconductor industry; LCD panels, glass disks for hard disk drives (HDDs); and optical lenses for digital cameras and smart phones. Health care and medical products and solutions generate approximately 62% of annual revenues, and information technology in regards to imaging and electronic products and equipment generates more than 35%. HOYA comprises over 160 offices and subsidiaries worldwide. During 2021, HOYA announced plans to spin off its electronic eyeglass business for the visually impaired into a separate company, with the new entity being named as ViXion, Inc.

FINANCIAL DATA: *Note: Data for latest year may not have been available at press time.*

In U.S. $	2020	2019	2018	2017	2016	2015
Revenue	5,319,702,000	5,227,348,000	4,942,535,000	4,472,697,000	4,705,187,000	
R&D Expense						
Operating Income	2,768,278,000	2,846,091,000	2,577,151,000	2,286,146,000	2,324,587,000	
Operating Margin %	.46%	.48%	.46%	.45%	.44%	
SGA Expense	111,550,500	116,162,700	119,505,400	117,925,400	119,432,300	
Net Income	1,044,871,000	1,115,167,000	908,679,200	792,196,800	850,967,700	
Operating Cash Flow	1,492,022,000	1,338,789,000	1,237,513,000	983,277,600	1,204,543,000	
Capital Expenditure	412,601,800	243,595,500	164,156,600	196,615,300	166,074,500	
EBITDA	1,666,162,000	1,565,981,000	1,404,017,000	1,294,165,000	1,402,820,000	
Return on Assets %	.15%	.17%	.15%	.13%	.14%	
Return on Equity %	.18%	.21%	.19%	.17%	.17%	
Debt to Equity	0.022	0.001	0.001	0.001	0.072	

CONTACT INFORMATION:

Phone: 81339521151   Fax: 81339520726
Toll-Free:
Address: Fl. 20, Nittochi Nishishinjuku Bldg, 6-10-1 Nishi-S, Tokyo, 160-8347 Japan

STOCK TICKER/OTHER:

Stock Ticker: HOCPF
Employees: 37,412
Parent Company:

Exchange: PINX
Fiscal Year Ends: 03/31

SALARIES/BONUSES:

Top Exec. Salary: $ Bonus: $
Second Exec. Salary: $ Bonus: $

OTHER THOUGHTS:

Estimated Female Officers or Directors:
Hot Spot for Advancement for Women/Minorities:

Humana Inc

NAIC Code: 524114

www.humana.com

TYPES OF BUSINESS:

Insurance-Medical & Health, HMOs & PPOs
Insurance-Dental
Employee Benefit Plans
Insurance-Group Life
Wellness Programs
Health Benefits
Home Health
Hospice Services

BRANDS/DIVISIONS/AFFILIATES:

Kindred at Home

CONTACTS: Note: Officers with more than one job title may be intentionally listed here more than once.

Bruce Broussard, CEO
Alan Wheatley, Pres., Divisional
Brian Kane, CFO
Kurt Hilzinger, Chairman of the Board
Cynthia Zipperle, Chief Accounting Officer
Brian LeClaire, Chief Information Officer
Joseph Ventura, Chief Legal Officer
Roy Beveridge, Chief Medical Officer
Samir Deshpande, Chief Risk Officer
Vishal Agrawal, Chief Strategy Officer
Christopher Hunter, Other Corporate Officer
Jody Bilney, Other Executive Officer
Timothy Huval, Other Executive Officer
Elizabeth Bierbower, President, Divisional
William Fleming, President, Divisional

GROWTH PLANS/SPECIAL FEATURES:

Humana, Inc. is a leading health benefits company in the U.S., serving millions of medical benefit plan and specialty products members in the U.S. and Puerto Rico. The firm operates in three segments: retail, group and specialty and healthcare services. The retail segment consists of Medicare and commercial fully-insured medical and specialty health insurance benefits, including dental, vision and other supplemental health and financial protection products, marketed directly to individuals. The group and specialty segment consist of employer group commercial fully-insured medical and specialty health insurance benefits marketed to individuals and employer groups, including dental, vision, and other supplemental health and voluntary insurance benefits, as well as administrative services only (ASO) products marketed to employer groups. Humana provides health benefits and related services to companies ranging from fewer than 10 to over 10,000 employees. The healthcare services segment includes services offered to health plan members as well as to third parties that promote health and wellness, including provider services, pharmacies, integrated wellness and home care services. Other businesses consist of military services, Medicaid and closed-block long-term care businesses as well as the firm's contract with the Centers for Medicare and Medicaid Services to administer the Limited Income Newly Eligible Transition program, known as LI-NET. Many of its products are offered through HMOs (health maintenance organizations), private fee-for-service (PFFS) and preferred provider organizations (PPOs). During 2021, Humana fully acquired Kindred at Home, a leading home health and hospice provider in the U.S.

Humana offers its employees comprehensive health benefits, 401(k), life insurance, tuition assistance, career development and a variety of employee assistance plan/programs and company perks.

FINANCIAL DATA: Note: Data for latest year may not have been available at press time.

In U.S. $	2020	2019	2018	2017	2016	2015
Revenue	77,155,000,000	64,888,000,000	56,912,000,000	53,767,000,000	54,379,000,000	54,289,000,000
R&D Expense						
Operating Income						
Operating Margin %						
SGA Expense	10,052,000,000	7,381,000,000	7,525,000,000	6,567,000,000	7,277,000,000	7,318,000,000
Net Income	3,367,000,000	2,707,000,000	1,683,000,000	2,448,000,000	614,000,000	1,276,000,000
Operating Cash Flow	5,639,000,000	5,284,000,000	2,173,000,000	4,051,000,000	1,936,000,000	868,000,000
Capital Expenditure	964,000,000	736,000,000	612,000,000	526,000,000	527,000,000	523,000,000
EBITDA						
Return on Assets %		.10%	.06%	.09%	.02%	.05%
Return on Equity %		.24%	.17%	.24%	.06%	.13%
Debt to Equity		0.413	0.431	0.485	0.355	0.369

CONTACT INFORMATION:

Phone: 502 580-1000   Fax: 502 580-1441
Toll-Free:
Address: 500 W. Main St., Louisville, KY 40202 United States

STOCK TICKER/OTHER:

Stock Ticker: HUM
Employees: 47,200
Parent Company:

Exchange: NYS
Fiscal Year Ends: 12/31

SALARIES/BONUSES:

Top Exec. Salary: $ Bonus: $
Second Exec. Salary: $ Bonus: $

OTHER THOUGHTS:

Estimated Female Officers or Directors: 3
Hot Spot for Advancement for Women/Minorities: Y

Sales, profits and employees may be estimates. Financial information, benefits and other data can change quickly and may vary from those stated here.

IBM Watson Health

www.ibm.com/watson-health

NAIC Code: 511210D

TYPES OF BUSINESS:

Computer Software, Healthcare & Biotechnology
Custom-Designed Medical Products
Engineering Services
Healthcare Solutions
Health Data
Analytics
Health Plan Solutions
Health Imaging Products

BRANDS/DIVISIONS/AFFILIATES:

International Business Machines Corporation
IBM iConnect
Merge PACS
Study Advance
Watson Oncology Clinical Trial Matching
Watson for Genomics
IBM Micromedex
IBM Phytel

CONTACTS: *Note: Officers with more than one job title may be intentionally listed here more than once.*

Paul Roma, Global Gen. Mngr.
Steven Tolle, Other Executive Officer
Kurt Hammond, Other Executive Officer
Antonia Wells, Other Executive Officer

GROWTH PLANS/SPECIAL FEATURES:

IBM Watson Health is a provider of innovative solutions to improve the healthcare experience for patients, providers and payers. Employer solutions include benefits mentoring, health data and analytics, return-to-workplace advisory and more. Health plan solutions help with making decisions about plan options, offers access to data and reports, and embeds analytic content to see if health goals are being met (individually and corporately). Government solutions help drive change through person-centric health and human services, including insights and analytic data, social program management and care management. Imaging solutions help to advance healthcare via innovative artificial intelligence (AI), enterprise imaging and interoperability. Imaging products include: IBM iConnect Enterprise Archive, for storing DICOM and non-DICOM images from disparate PACS, specialties and sites; IBM iConnect Access, which aggregates all access and exchange of DICOM and non-DICOM clinical data with collaboration; and Merge PACS, which simplifies clinical workflows and enables IT organizations to scale their delivery of care. Life sciences products help development customers move toward clinical trial efficiency through IBM Watson Health's: Study Advance, a data insight and collaboration platform for improving efficiency; Clinical Development, a cloud estimated date of confinement (EDC) that supports studies with integrated medical coding, ePRO and more; and MarketScan Research Databases, offering patient-centric data that reflect treatment patterns and the full cost of care. Oncology solutions enable customers to focus on delivery patient-centric cancer care at scale, with products including: Watson Oncology Clinical Trial Matching, for identifying more patients for trials in less time; and Watson for Genomics, which provides comprehensive content to enable molecular pathology laboratories to scale precision oncology programs. Last, provider solutions offer evidence-based insights at the point of care, engage patients and optimize performance, with products including IBM Micromedex and IBM Phytel.

IBM offers employees comprehensive health benefits and a 401(k) retirement plan.

FINANCIAL DATA: *Note: Data for latest year may not have been available at press time.*

In U.S. $	2020	2019	2018	2017	2016	2015
Revenue	263,070,281	250,543,125	248,062,500	236,250,000	225,000,000	215,000,000
R&D Expense						
Operating Income						
Operating Margin %						
SGA Expense						
Net Income						
Operating Cash Flow						
Capital Expenditure						
EBITDA						
Return on Assets %						
Return on Equity %						
Debt to Equity						

CONTACT INFORMATION:

Phone: 312 565-6868   Fax: 312 565-6870
Toll-Free: 877-446-3743
Address: 71 S. Wacker Dr., Fl. 20, Chicago, IL 60606 United States

STOCK TICKER/OTHER:

Stock Ticker: Subsidiary   Exchange:
Employees: 800   Fiscal Year Ends: 12/31
Parent Company: International Business Machines Corporation

SALARIES/BONUSES:

Top Exec. Salary: $ Bonus: $
Second Exec. Salary: $ Bonus: $

OTHER THOUGHTS:

Estimated Female Officers or Directors: 2
Hot Spot for Advancement for Women/Minorities: Y

ICU Medical Inc

www.icumed.com

NAIC Code: 339100

TYPES OF BUSINESS:

Equipment-Intravenous Connection Devices
Pharmacy Intravenous Compounding Systems
Infusion Systems
Product Manufacturing

BRANDS/DIVISIONS/AFFILIATES:

Plum 360
LifeCare PCA
ICU Medical MedNet
Cogent
CardioFlo
TDQ
TriOx
SafeSet

CONTACTS: *Note: Officers with more than one job title may be intentionally listed here more than once.*

Vivek Jain, CEO
Scott Lamb, CFO
Kevin McGrody, Chief Accounting Officer
Christian Voigtlander, COO
Virginia Sanzone, General Counsel
Alison Burcar, Vice President, Divisional

GROWTH PLANS/SPECIAL FEATURES:

ICU Medical, Inc. is a pure-play infusion company and a manufacturer of automated pharmacy intravenous (IV) compounding systems. The company's products are categorized into four main lines: infusion consumables, infusion systems, IV solutions and critical care. Infusion consumables include: infusion therapy sets, used in hospitals and ambulatory clinics, which consist of a tube running from a bottle or plastic bag containing a solution to a catheter inserted in a patient's vein, that may or may not be used with an IV pump; and closed system transfer devices and hazardous drug compounding systems, which are used to prepare and deliver hazardous IV medications such as those used in chemotherapy, which, if released, can have harmful effects to the healthcare worker and environment. Infusion systems include a wide range of infusion pumps, IV sets and related software, with brands including Plum 360, LifeCare PCA, and ICU Medical MedNet. The company's wide range of IV solutions are grouped into two categories: IV therapy and diluents, including sodium chloride, dextrose, balanced electrolyte solutions, lactated ringer's, ringer's, mannitol, sodium chloride/dextrose and sterile water; and irrigation, including sodium chloride irrigation, sterile water irrigation, physiologic solutions, ringer's irrigation, acetic acid irrigation, glycine irrigation, sorbitol-mannitol irrigation, flexible containers and pour bottle options. Last, ICU Medical's critical care products help clinicians get accurate real-time access to patients' hemodynamic and cardiac status through its extensive portfolio of monitoring systems and advanced sensors and catheters, with brands including Cogent, CardioFlo, TDQ, TriOx, Transpac and SafeSet. ICU Medical operates four primary manufacturing facilities and four main service centers globally. In September 2021, ICU Medical agreed to acquire the Smiths Medical division of Smiths Group plc. The Smiths Medical business includes syringe and ambulatory infusion devices, vascular access and vital care products. The transaction was expected to close by mid-2022.

FINANCIAL DATA: *Note: Data for latest year may not have been available at press time.*

In U.S. $	2020	2019	2018	2017	2016	2015
Revenue	1,271,004,000	1,266,208,000	1,400,040,000	1,292,613,000	379,372,000	341,668,000
R&D Expense	42,948,000	48,611,000	52,867,000	51,253,000	12,955,000	15,714,000
Operating Income	135,571,000	140,534,000	189,015,000	70,889,000	99,017,000	81,867,000
Operating Margin %		.12%	.14%	.05%	.26%	.24%
SGA Expense	283,953,000	276,982,000	328,146,000	303,953,000	89,426,000	83,216,000
Net Income	86,870,000	101,035,000	28,793,000	68,644,000	63,084,000	44,985,000
Operating Cash Flow	222,752,000	101,918,000	160,215,000	154,423,000	89,941,000	54,865,000
Capital Expenditure	100,390,000	106,040,000	100,779,000	79,682,000	24,553,000	13,935,000
EBITDA	194,094,000	200,466,000	97,818,000	119,899,000	118,067,000	99,940,000
Return on Assets %		.06%	.02%	.06%	.09%	.08%
Return on Equity %		.08%	.02%	.07%	.10%	.08%
Debt to Equity		0.021				

CONTACT INFORMATION:

Phone: 949 366-2183   Fax:
Toll-Free: 800-824-7890
Address: 951 Calle Amanecer, San Clemente, CA 92673 United States

STOCK TICKER/OTHER:

Stock Ticker: ICUI
Employees: 7,900
Parent Company:

Exchange: NAS
Fiscal Year Ends: 12/31

SALARIES/BONUSES:

Top Exec. Salary: $ Bonus: $
Second Exec. Salary: $ Bonus: $

OTHER THOUGHTS:

Estimated Female Officers or Directors: 1
Hot Spot for Advancement for Women/Minorities:

Sales, profits and employees may be estimates. Financial information, benefits and other data can change quickly and may vary from those stated here.

IDEXX Laboratories Inc

www.idexx.com

NAIC Code: 334510

TYPES OF BUSINESS:

Veterinary Laboratory Testing Equipment
Point-of-Care Diagnostic Products
Veterinary Pharmaceuticals
Information Management Software
Food & Water Testing Products
Laboratory Testing Services
Consulting

BRANDS/DIVISIONS/AFFILIATES:

IDEXX VetLab
VetLyte
VetStat
Catalyst Dx
SNAP Beta-Lactam
Colilert
Pseudalert
Legiolert

CONTACTS: *Note: Officers with more than one job title may be intentionally listed here more than once.*

Jonathan Ayers, CEO
Brian Mckeon, CFO
Jay Mazelsky, Executive VP
Sharon Underberg, General Counsel
Giovani Twigge, Other Executive Officer
Kathy Turner, Vice President
Michael Lane, Vice President

GROWTH PLANS/SPECIAL FEATURES:

IDEXX Laboratories, Inc. develops, manufactures and distributes products and provides services for the veterinary and the food and water testing markets. The company operates in three business segments: companion animal group, which provides diagnostic and information technology-based products and services for the veterinary markets; livestock, poultry and dairy, which provides diagnostic products and services for animal health, and to ensure the quality and safety of milk and food; and water quality products. IDEXX markets an integrated and flexible suite of in-house laboratory analyzers for use in veterinary practices, which is referred to as the IDEXX VetLab suite. The suite includes in-clinic chemistry, hematology, immunoassay, urinalysis and coagulation analyzers such as the VetTest, VetLyte, VetStat, LaserCyte Dx, Catalyst One, Catalyst Dx, Coag Dx and ProCyte Dx; and the hand-held IDEXX SNAPshot Dx rapid assay test kits which provide quick, accurate and convenient point-of-care diagnostic test results. Catalyst SDMA allows customers to use the Catalyst One and Catalyst Dx to screen for symmetrical dimethyl arginine (SDMA), a biomarker that detects kidney disease. In addition, the company provides assay kits, software and instrumentation for accurate assessment of infectious disease in production animals, such as cattle, swine and poultry. IDEXX's principal product for use in testing for antibiotic residue in milk is the SNAP Beta-Lactam test, which detects penicillin, amoxicillin, ampicillin, ceftiofur and cephapirin residues. SNAPduo Beta-Tetra ST detects certain tetracycline antibiotic residues in addition to those detected by the Beta-Lactam test kits. Last, water quality products include Colilert, Colilert-18 and Colisure tests, which simultaneously detect total coliforms and E. coli in water; Enterolert products detect the presence of enterococci in waters; Pseudalert detects pseudomonas in waters; Filta-Max products detect cryptosporidium and giardia in water; Legiolert detects legionella pneumophila in water; and Quanti-Tray products measure microbial contamination in water. In mid-2021, IDEXX acquired ezyVet.

FINANCIAL DATA: *Note: Data for latest year may not have been available at press time.*

In U.S. $	2020	2019	2018	2017	2016	2015
Revenue	2,706,655,000	2,406,908,000	2,213,242,000	1,969,058,000	1,775,423,000	1,601,892,000
R&D Expense	141,249,000	133,193,000	117,863,000	109,182,000	101,122,000	99,681,000
Operating Income	694,524,000	552,846,000	491,335,000	413,028,000	350,239,000	308,124,000
Operating Margin %		.23%	.22%	.21%	.20%	.19%
SGA Expense	735,267,000	679,510,000	632,344,000	575,172,000	524,075,000	482,465,000
Net Income	581,776,000	427,720,000	377,031,000	263,144,000	222,045,000	192,078,000
Operating Cash Flow	648,063,000	459,158,000	400,084,000	373,276,000	334,571,000	216,364,000
Capital Expenditure	107,876,000	155,224,000	122,936,000	76,704,000	64,787,000	82,921,000
EBITDA	791,108,000	641,284,000	575,664,000	501,422,000	432,113,000	371,336,000
Return on Assets %		.25%	.23%	.16%	.15%	.13%
Return on Equity %		5.09%				11.50%
Debt to Equity		4.318				

CONTACT INFORMATION:

Phone: 207 556-0300　　Fax: 207 856-0346
Toll-Free: 800-548-6733
Address: 1 Idexx Dr., Westbrook, ME 04092 United States

STOCK TICKER/OTHER:

Stock Ticker: IDXX
Employees: 9,300
Parent Company:

Exchange: NAS
Fiscal Year Ends: 12/31

SALARIES/BONUSES:

Top Exec. Salary: $　　Bonus: $
Second Exec. Salary: $　　Bonus: $

OTHER THOUGHTS:

Estimated Female Officers or Directors: 2
Hot Spot for Advancement for Women/Minorities: Y

Sales, profits and employees may be estimates. Financial information, benefits and other data can change quickly and may vary from those stated here.

iKang Healthcare Group Inc

www.ikanggroup.com

NAIC Code: 621511

TYPES OF BUSINESS:

Medical Services
Medical Examinations
Health Screening
Dental Services

BRANDS/DIVISIONS/AFFILIATES:

CONTACTS: *Note: Officers with more than one job title may be intentionally listed here more than once.*

Lee Ligang Zhang, CEO

GROWTH PLANS/SPECIAL FEATURES:

iKang Healthcare Group, Inc. provides comprehensive and high-quality preventive healthcare solutions to individuals throughout China. The company's services include a wide range of medical examinations, disease screening, dental services and more. iKang's nationwide network is comprised of self-owned medical centers, covering most affluent cities in the country. iKang also contracts with third-party service provider facilities, including independent medical examination centers and hospitals across all of China's provinces, creating a nationwide network that allows the firm to serve customers in markets in which it does not own medical centers. The company's medical examinations typically include internal, gynecology, ophthalmology, ear/nose/throat, dental, lab testing, electrocardiogram, ultrasound and X-ray examination services and solutions. Disease screening focuses on cancer screening, cardiovascular disease screening, certain chronic disease screening and functional medicine testing. Dental care includes oral health services, pediatric dentistry, cosmetic dentistry, orthodontics and dental implants. Outpatient services include acupuncture, Chinese medicine, gynecology, internal medicine, obstetrics, ophthalmology, pediatrics, urology and minor surgery. On-site healthcare management is provided by the firm, as well as clinics at certain locations in which iKang assigns small medical teams to provide scheduling services or operate primary care clinics on the customer's premises. iKang's self-owned medical centers and third-party network provides vaccination services to corporate employees and families, coving both children and adults. Exclusive private health care services is offered to elites in China, including health risk assessment, disease screening, diagnosis, doctor referral and second opinions.

FINANCIAL DATA: *Note: Data for latest year may not have been available at press time.*

In U.S. $	2020	2019	2018	2017	2016	2015
Revenue	562,522,201	592,128,633	563,932,032	435,712,992	370,812,000	290,780,992
R&D Expense						
Operating Income						
Operating Margin %						
SGA Expense						
Net Income		-18,174,450	-17,309,000	-11,251,000	18,325,000	27,113,000
Operating Cash Flow						
Capital Expenditure						
EBITDA						
Return on Assets %						
Return on Equity %						
Debt to Equity						

CONTACT INFORMATION:

Phone: 86 10-5320-6688   Fax: 86 10-5320-6689
Toll-Free:
Address: Fl. 6, Tower B, No. 92 (A) Jianguo Rd., Chaoyang District, Beijing, 100022 China

STOCK TICKER/OTHER:

Stock Ticker: Private   Exchange:
Employees: 15,918   Fiscal Year Ends: 12/31
Parent Company:

SALARIES/BONUSES:

Top Exec. Salary: $ Bonus: $
Second Exec. Salary: $ Bonus: $

OTHER THOUGHTS:

Estimated Female Officers or Directors:
Hot Spot for Advancement for Women/Minorities:

Immucor Inc

NAIC Code: 325413

www.immucor.com

TYPES OF BUSINESS:

Diagnostic Products
Automated Blood Bank Instruments
Blood Reagents

BRANDS/DIVISIONS/AFFILIATES:

TPG Capital
PreciseType
Echo Lumena
NEO Iris

CONTACTS: *Note: Officers with more than one job title may be intentionally listed here more than once.*

Avi Pelossof, CEO
Dominique Petitgenet, COO

GROWTH PLANS/SPECIAL FEATURES:

Immucor, Inc., owned by firm TPG Capital, provides transfusion and transplantation diagnostic products worldwide. The firm matches donors with patients in need of blood or an organ, and offers healthcare organizations solutions regarding innovation and productivity. Immucor operates through three segments: transfusion diagnostics, transplant diagnostics and hemostasis. The transfusion diagnostics segment develops, manufactures and sells a complete line of serology-based reagents and instruments used by hospitals, reference labs and donor centers to perform pre-transfusion typing and screening of blood The firm's PreciseType HEA test is an FDA-approved in-vitro diagnostic for molecular typing of red blood cell antigens. Transfusion products include: Capture technology for serology-based antibody screening and identification; Echo Lumena, an instrument designed for small-to-medium volume laboratories; NEO Iris, an instrument for high-volume laboratories; reagents; platelets; and molecular assays. The transplant diagnostics segment develops, manufactures and sells assays to perform pre-transplant typing and screening and post-transplant monitoring. This division's portfolio of molecular and antibody-based assays use ELISA and xMAP technology to evaluate human leukocyte antigens (HLA) compatibility between donors and recipients, and are sold to HLA labs worldwide. The hemostasis segment offers a line of products that provide information to help determine an individual's risk of excessive bleeding or thrombosis. Based in the U.S., Immucor has offices throughout the world, including Canada, Belgium, France, Germany, Italy, Spain, Portugal, the U.K., Japan and India.

FINANCIAL DATA: *Note: Data for latest year may not have been available at press time.*

In U.S. $	2020	2019	2018	2017	2016	2015
Revenue	475,714,091	461,858,341	439,865,087	418,919,130	379,972,000	389,300,000
R&D Expense						
Operating Income						
Operating Margin %						
SGA Expense						
Net Income						
Operating Cash Flow						
Capital Expenditure						
EBITDA						
Return on Assets %						
Return on Equity %						
Debt to Equity						

CONTACT INFORMATION:

Phone: 770-441-2051   Fax: 770-441-3807
Toll-Free: 800-829-2553
Address: 3130 Gateway Dr., Norcross, GA 30091-5625 United States

STOCK TICKER/OTHER:

Stock Ticker: Private   Exchange:
Employees: 1,125   Fiscal Year Ends: 05/31
Parent Company: TPG Capital

SALARIES/BONUSES:

Top Exec. Salary: $ Bonus: $
Second Exec. Salary: $ Bonus: $

OTHER THOUGHTS:

Estimated Female Officers or Directors:
Hot Spot for Advancement for Women/Minorities:

Incyte Corporation

www.incyte.com

NAIC Code: 325412

TYPES OF BUSINESS:

Drug Discovery & Development
Drug Development
Drug Research
Drug Discovery
Biopharmaceuticals

BRANDS/DIVISIONS/AFFILIATES:

JAKAFI
ICLUSIG
Pemazyre
Monjuvi

CONTACTS: *Note: Officers with more than one job title may be intentionally listed here more than once.*

Herve Hoppenot, CEO
Christiana Stamoulis, CFO
Paul Trower, Chief Accounting Officer
Dashyant Dhanak, Chief Scientific Officer
Paula Swain, Executive VP, Divisional
Vijay Iyengar, Executive VP, Divisional
Steven Stein, Executive VP
Maria Pasquale, Executive VP
Barry Flannelly, Executive VP
Wenqing Yao, Executive VP

GROWTH PLANS/SPECIAL FEATURES:

Incyte Corporation is a biopharmaceutical company focused on the discovery, development and commercialization of proprietary therapeutics. The firm's four marketed indications include JAKAFI (ruxolitinib), ICLUSIG (ponatinib), Pemazyre (pemigatinib) and Monjuvi (tafasitamab-cxix). JAKAIF is Incyte's first product to be approved for sale in the U.S. for the treatment of patients with intermediate or high-risk myelofibrosis, as well as for patients with polycythemia vera who have had an inadequate response to first-line therapies such as hydroxyurea. Myelofibrosis and polycythemia vera are both rare blood cancers. ICLUSIG is a kinase inhibitor which primarily targets BCR-ABL, an abnormal tyrosine kinase that is expressed in chronic myeloid leukemia (CML) and Philadelphia-chromosome positive acute lymphoblastic leukemia (Ph+ALL). ICLUSIG is a kinase inhibitor. The primary target for ICLUSIG is BCR-ABL, an abnormal tyrosine kinase expressed in chronic myeloid leukemia (CML) and Philadelphia-chromosome positive acute lymphoblastic leukemia. In the European Union, ICLUSIG is approved for the treatment of adult patients with CML and Ph+ ALL and in late phases and/or are resistant or intolerant to other treatments. Pemigatinib is a potent and selective inhibitor of the fibroblast growth factor receptor (FGFR) isoforms 1, 2 and 3. The U.S. Food and Drug Administration (FDA) approved pemigatinib as PEMAZYRE for the treatment of adults with previously treated, unresectable locally advanced or metastatic cholangiocarcinoma with an FGFR2 fusion or other rearrangement as detected by an FDA-approved test. Monjuvi is co-commercialized with MorphoSys AG and is FDA-approved in combination with lenalidomide for the treatment of adult patients with relapsed or refractory diffuse large B-cell lymphoma. Incyte and MorphoSys have a collaboration and license agreement to further develop and commercialize MorphoSys' proprietary anti-CD19 antibody tafasitamab (MOR208) globally. Tafasitamab is an Fc-engineered antibody against CD19 currently in clinical development for the treatment of B cell malignancies.

Incyte offers comprehensive benefits and retirement plans.

FINANCIAL DATA: *Note: Data for latest year may not have been available at press time.*

In U.S. $	2020	2019	2018	2017	2016	2015
Revenue	2,666,702,000	2,158,759,000	1,881,883,000	1,536,216,000	1,105,719,000	753,751,000
R&D Expense	2,215,942,000	1,154,111,000	1,197,957,000	1,326,361,000	581,861,000	479,514,000
Operating Income	-240,241,000	421,737,000	155,419,000	-236,051,000	162,407,000	50,651,000
Operating Margin %		.20%	.08%	-.15%	.15%	.07%
SGA Expense	516,900,000	468,711,000	434,407,000	366,406,000	303,251,000	196,614,000
Net Income	-295,697,000	446,906,000	109,493,000	-313,142,000	104,222,000	6,531,000
Operating Cash Flow	-124,599,000	710,656,000	336,227,000	-92,988,000	304,756,000	86,536,000
Capital Expenditure	187,379,000	78,064,000	73,483,000	111,021,000	120,277,000	26,003,000
EBITDA	-178,237,000	543,179,000	171,859,000	-253,212,000	204,574,000	53,159,000
Return on Assets %		.15%	.04%	-.16%	.08%	.01%
Return on Equity %		.20%	.06%	-.31%	.35%	.15%
Debt to Equity		0.012	0.009	0.01	1.553	3.622

CONTACT INFORMATION:

Phone: 302 498-6700   Fax: 302 425-2750
Toll-Free: 855-446-2983
Address: 1801 Augustine Cut-Off, Wilmington, DE 19803 United States

STOCK TICKER/OTHER:

Stock Ticker: INCY
Employees: 1,773
Parent Company:

Exchange: NAS
Fiscal Year Ends: 12/31

SALARIES/BONUSES:

Top Exec. Salary: $ Bonus: $
Second Exec. Salary: $ Bonus: $

OTHER THOUGHTS:

Estimated Female Officers or Directors: 2
Hot Spot for Advancement for Women/Minorities: Y

Sales, profits and employees may be estimates. Financial information, benefits and other data can change quickly and may vary from those stated here.

Indiana University Health

www.iuhealth.org

NAIC Code: 622110

TYPES OF BUSINESS:

General Medical and Surgical Hospitals
Childrens Services
Medical Research
Hospitals
Preeminent Health Care Services
Cancer Care
Cardiovascular Care
Orthopedic Care

BRANDS/DIVISIONS/AFFILIATES:

IU Health Cancer
IU Health Cardiovascular
IU Health Neuroscience
IU Health Orthopedics
Riley Hospital for Children
IU Health Transplant
Video Visits

CONTACTS: *Note: Officers with more than one job title may be intentionally listed here more than once.*

Dennis Murphy, CEO
John C. Kohne, Chief Medical Officer
Linda Q. Everett, Chief Nurse Exec.

GROWTH PLANS/SPECIAL FEATURES:

Indiana University Health (IU Health) is a leading network of physicians in the state of Indiana. IU Health partners with Indiana University School of Medicine, and is comprised of hospitals, physicians and allied services dedicated to providing preeminent care throughout Indiana and beyond. Its care services for children and adults include the areas of: cancer, via its IU Health Cancer centers; cardiovascular, via IU Health Cardiovascular, which treats some of the most complex cases; neuroscience, via IU Health Neuroscience, providing a range of neurological and neurosurgical services; orthopedics, via IU Health Orthopedics, which is Indiana's only nationally-ranked orthopedics program, providing comprehensive joint, spine, bone and muscle care; pediatrics, via Riley Hospital for Children, providing routine care as well as complex care; and transplant, via IU Health Transplant, providing organ transplant such as kidney, lung and liver. In total, the firm's hospitals have approximately 2,700 beds and 118,000 patient admissions annually. IU Health also offers access to health care through its telemedicine program, Video Visits, in which patients connect via live video with a highly-skilled IU Health or IU Health affiliated physician to diagnose low-intensity complaints such as bronchitis, flu, pink eye or similar ailments. Most visits take less than 20 minutes, including registration and wait times, and the program is available via tablet, smartphone or computer.

FINANCIAL DATA: *Note: Data for latest year may not have been available at press time.*

In U.S. $	2020	2019	2018	2017	2016	2015
Revenue	6,810,000,000	6,749,234,100	6,427,842,000	6,341,094,000	6,233,578,000	6,100,815,000
R&D Expense						
Operating Income						
Operating Margin %						
SGA Expense						
Net Income	656,000,000	678,304,000	611,100,000	989,249,000	260,095,000	612,676,000
Operating Cash Flow						
Capital Expenditure						
EBITDA						
Return on Assets %						
Return on Equity %						
Debt to Equity						

CONTACT INFORMATION:

Phone: 317-962-2000   Fax: 317-962-4533
Toll-Free:
Address: 340 West 10th St., Ste. 4100, Indianapolis, IN 46202 United States

STOCK TICKER/OTHER:

Stock Ticker: Nonprofit
Employees: 33,000
Parent Company:

Exchange:
Fiscal Year Ends: 12/31

SALARIES/BONUSES:

Top Exec. Salary: $ Bonus: $
Second Exec. Salary: $ Bonus: $

OTHER THOUGHTS:

Estimated Female Officers or Directors: 4
Hot Spot for Advancement for Women/Minorities: Y

InfuSystem Holdings Inc

www.infusystem.com

NAIC Code: 532490

TYPES OF BUSINESS:

Infusion Pump Rental
Medical Equipment Rental
Health Care Services
Integrated Therapy Services
Pain Management Solutions
Negative Pressure Wound Therapy
IT-based Services

BRANDS/DIVISIONS/AFFILIATES:

InfuSystem Holdings USA Inc
InfuSystem Inc
First Biomedical Inc
IFC LLC
OB Healthcare Corporation

CONTACTS: *Note: Officers with more than one job title may be intentionally listed here more than once.*

Richard Dilorio, CEO
Greg Schulte, CFO
Scott Shuda, Chairman of the Board
Carrie Lachance, COO
Gregg Lehman, Director
Thomas Ruiz, Senior VP, Divisional

GROWTH PLANS/SPECIAL FEATURES:

InfuSystem Holdings, Inc. is a national health care services provider that facilitates outpatient care for durable medical equipment manufacturers and health care providers. The firm offers its products and services to hospitals, oncology practices, ambulatory surgery centers and other alternate site health care providers. InfuSystem's services are provided under a two-platform model: integrated therapy services (ITS), which offers last-mile solutions for clinic-to-home healthcare where the continuing treatment involves complex durable medical equipment and services; and durable medical equipment services (DME services), which supports the ITS platform by renting/selling new and pre-owned pole-mounted and ambulatory infusion pumps, selling treatment-related consumables, and providing biomedical recertification/maintenance/repair services for oncology practices as well as other alternate site settings. Additional focus areas within the ITS segment include: pain management, providing ambulatory pumps, products and services for pain management in the area of post-surgical continuous peripheral nerve block; negative pressure wound therapy; information technology-based services; and acquisitions of smaller, regional health care service providers. Subsidiaries of the company include InfuSystem Holdings USA, Inc.; InfuSystem, Inc.; First Biomedical, Inc.; and IFC, LLC. During 2021, InfuSystem Holdings acquired the operating assets of OB Healthcare Corporation, a Texas-based biomedical services company. The transaction expands InfuSystem's DME services platform in acute care.

FINANCIAL DATA: *Note: Data for latest year may not have been available at press time.*

In U.S. $	2020	2019	2018	2017	2016	2015
Revenue	97,388,000	81,115,000	67,138,000	71,077,000	70,497,000	72,125,000
R&D Expense						
Operating Income	8,827,000	4,227,000	1,185,000	-2,819,000	974,000	8,864,000
Operating Margin %		.05%	.02%	-.04%	.01%	.12%
SGA Expense	44,856,000	38,253,000	33,184,000	34,979,000	34,286,000	34,202,000
Net Income	17,332,000	1,361,000	-1,095,000	-20,707,000	-222,000	3,743,000
Operating Cash Flow	20,280,000	13,875,000	11,391,000	7,583,000	7,909,000	7,054,000
Capital Expenditure	16,914,000	22,595,000	8,303,000	3,595,000	8,795,000	10,245,000
EBITDA	22,823,000	15,770,000	11,686,000	8,598,000	11,724,000	15,521,000
Return on Assets %		.02%	-.02%	-.25%	.00%	.04%
Return on Equity %		.06%	-.04%	-.51%	.00%	.08%
Debt to Equity		1.564	1.411	0.82	0.575	0.583

CONTACT INFORMATION:

Phone: 248 291-1210 Fax:
Toll-Free:
Address: 3851 W. Hamlin Rd., Rochester Hills, MI 48309 United States

STOCK TICKER/OTHER:

Stock Ticker: INFU
Employees: 292
Parent Company:

Exchange: ASE
Fiscal Year Ends: 12/31

SALARIES/BONUSES:

Top Exec. Salary: $ Bonus: $
Second Exec. Salary: $ Bonus: $

OTHER THOUGHTS:

Estimated Female Officers or Directors:
Hot Spot for Advancement for Women/Minorities:

Intalere Inc

www.intalere.com

NAIC Code: 561400

TYPES OF BUSINESS:

Group Buying Programs for Medical Supplies
Health Care Consultation Services and Solutions
Healthcare Provider Insurance
Pharmacy Solutions

BRANDS/DIVISIONS/AFFILIATES:

Vizient Inc
Intalere Choice
Intalere Insurance Services
Health Industry Technology Trust

CONTACTS: Note: Officers with more than one job title may be intentionally listed here more than once.

Todd Larkin, COO
Steve Schoch, CFO
Steve Kiewiet, Chief Commercial Officer

GROWTH PLANS/SPECIAL FEATURES:

Intalere, Inc. is a group purchasing organization (GPO) that connects healthcare organizations with manufacturers, distributors and vendors and negotiating discounts on their behalf. The company offers solutions designed for improved financial, operational and clinical health via three subsidiaries: Intalere Choice, Intalere Insurance Services, and Health Industry Technology Trust (HITT). Intalere Choice identifies actionable opportunities for contract savings and product standardization within health care facilities, from assessment and strategic expense reduction to on-site contract utilization management and operational benchmarking. Intalere Choice's expertise in supply chain management strategies help to maximize operating margins. Intalere Insurance Services offers benefit and risk cost containment strategies that provide long-term insurance solutions for health care providers. It partners with Gallagher and Myron Steves, healthcare industry insurance leaders, to help solve the challenges of operating a sustainable health care organization while meeting the needs of employees and the community. Insurance solutions by Gallagher include ancillary, risk management, health, pharmacy, human resources, consulting, health care analytics and retirement planning; and insurance solutions by Myron Steves focus on catastrophic occurrences. HITT improves operational performance and reduces financial, product, regulatory and safety risk by empowering the supply chain to more efficiently leverage data to perform analytics. Intalere operates as a subsidiary of Vizient, Inc.

FINANCIAL DATA: Note: Data for latest year may not have been available at press time.

In U.S. $	2020	2019	2018	2017	2016	2015
Revenue						
R&D Expense						
Operating Income						
Operating Margin %						
SGA Expense						
Net Income						
Operating Cash Flow						
Capital Expenditure						
EBITDA						
Return on Assets %						
Return on Equity %						
Debt to Equity						

CONTACT INFORMATION:

Phone: Fax:
Toll-Free: 877-711-5700
Address: Two CityPlace Dr., Ste. 400, St. Louis, MO 63141 United States

STOCK TICKER/OTHER:

Stock Ticker: Subsidiary Exchange:
Employees: Fiscal Year Ends:
Parent Company: Vizient Inc

SALARIES/BONUSES:

Top Exec. Salary: $ Bonus: $
Second Exec. Salary: $ Bonus: $

OTHER THOUGHTS:

Estimated Female Officers or Directors:
Hot Spot for Advancement for Women/Minorities:

Intarcia Therapeutics Inc

www.intarcia.com

NAIC Code: 334510

TYPES OF BUSINESS:

Electromedical and Electrotherapeutic Apparatus Manufacturing
Biopharmaceuticals
Therapy Development
Drug Delivery System
Product Development

BRANDS/DIVISIONS/AFFILIATES:

Medici Drug Delivery System
ITCA 650
ITCA 1061

CONTACTS: *Note: Officers with more than one job title may be intentionally listed here more than once.*

Kurt Graves, CEO
Fred Fiedorek, Chief Medical Officer
Thomas Alessi, VP-Dev. & Manufacturing
Andrew Young, Chief Scientific Officer
Anders Vinther, Global Head-Technical Oper.
Kurt Graves, Chmn.

GROWTH PLANS/SPECIAL FEATURES:

Intarcia Therapeutics, Inc. is a biopharmaceutical company that develops innovative therapies which merge medicine with technology and have the potential to transform therapeutic categories, which is called the Medici Drug Delivery System. Intarcia focuses on serious diseases that are prevalent and poorly controlled. The firm's goal is to provide a new level of freedom for patients with type 2 diabetes (T2D). Intarcia's lead product, ITCA 650 (continuous subcutaneous delivery of exenatide), is an advanced clinical drug for the treatment of T2D. This platform technology system comprises a small, matchstick-sized osmotic pump placed sub-dermally (just beneath the skin) to deliver a slow and consistent flow of medication. Each device contains an appropriate volume of drug product to treat a patient for a predetermined extended duration of time. The device can be sub-dermally placed in various locations in the abdomen in as little as five minutes by a physician or physician's assistant. A file for ITCA 650 has been submitted to the U.S. Food and Drug Administration as a GLP-1 receptor agonist (RA) exenatide-twice yearly program for the treatment of T2D. ITCA 1061 (amylin RA) is in pre-clinical phase for the treatment of type 1 diabetes (T1D). In addition, Intarcia and the Bill & Melinda Gates Foundation are collaborating to prevent the spread of HIV in Sub-Saharan Africa and other areas where the HIV epidemic is most severe. The collaboration focuses on combining the Medici Drug Delivery System with preventive medicine capable of significantly lowering the epidemic rate of new infections in these areas.

FINANCIAL DATA: *Note: Data for latest year may not have been available at press time.*

In U.S. $	2020	2019	2018	2017	2016	2015
Revenue						
R&D Expense						
Operating Income						
Operating Margin %						
SGA Expense						
Net Income						
Operating Cash Flow						
Capital Expenditure						
EBITDA						
Return on Assets %						
Return on Equity %						
Debt to Equity						

CONTACT INFORMATION:

Phone: 617-936-2500   Fax:
Toll-Free:
Address: One Marina Park Dr., Fl. 13, Boston, MA 02210 United States

STOCK TICKER/OTHER:

Stock Ticker: Private   Exchange:
Employees: Fiscal Year Ends:
Parent Company:

SALARIES/BONUSES:

Top Exec. Salary: $ Bonus: $
Second Exec. Salary: $ Bonus: $

OTHER THOUGHTS:

Estimated Female Officers or Directors:
Hot Spot for Advancement for Women/Minorities:

Integra LifeSciences Holdings Corporation www.integralife.com

NAIC Code: 339100

TYPES OF BUSINESS:

Medical Equipment Manufacturing
Implants & Biomaterials
Absorbable Medical Products
Tissue Regeneration Technology
Neurosurgery Products
Skin Replacement Products

BRANDS/DIVISIONS/AFFILIATES:

AccuDrain
Capture
DigiFuse
Integra
Redmond
SurgiMend
Uni-CP
zRIP

CONTACTS: *Note: Officers with more than one job title may be intentionally listed here more than once.*

Peter Arduini, CEO
Glenn Coleman, CFO
Stuart Essig, Chairman of the Board
Eric Schwartz, General Counsel
Lisa Evoli, Other Executive Officer
Robert Davis, President, Divisional
Daniel Reuvers, President, Divisional
John Mooradian, Vice President, Divisional
Judith OGrady, Vice President, Divisional
Joseph Vinhais, Vice President, Divisional
Kenneth Burhop, Vice President
Jeffrey Mosebrook, Vice President

GROWTH PLANS/SPECIAL FEATURES:

Integra LifeSciences Holdings Corporation develops, manufactures and markets surgical implants and medical instruments primarily for use in neurosurgery, orthopedics and general surgery. The company operates through two business segments: Codman specialty surgical solutions and orthopedics & tissue technologies. Codman specialty surgical solutions offers global, market-leading technologies, brands and instrumentation. The product portfolio represents a continuum of care from pre-operative, to the neurosurgery operating room, to the neuro-critical care unit and post care for both adult and pediatric patients suffering from brain tumors, brain injury, cerebrospinal fluid pressure complications and other neurological conditions. The orthopedics & tissue technologies segment offers differentiated soft tissue repair and tissue regeneration products, as well as small bone fixation and joint replacement solutions. This division sells regenerative technology products that can be used to provide treatment for acute and chronic wounds, as well as for surgical tissue repair, including hernia repair, peripheral nerve repair and tendon repair. For extremity bone and joint reconstruction procedures, Integra sells hardware products such as bone and joint fixation and replacement devices, implants and instruments that provide orthopedic reconstruction of bone. A few of the many trademarks of the company include AccuDrain, Capture, DigiFuse, Integra, Movement, Redmond, SafeGuard, SurgiMend, TruArch, Uni-CP and zRIP. In July 2021, Integra LifeSciences announced positive clinical outcomes for its PriMatrix dermal repair scaffold for the management of hard-to-heal diabetic foot ulcers.

Integra offers its employees health, retirement and savings benefits, and paid time off.

FINANCIAL DATA: *Note: Data for latest year may not have been available at press time.*

In U.S. $	2020	2019	2018	2017	2016	2015
Revenue	1,371,868,000	1,517,557,000	1,472,441,000	1,188,236,000	992,075,000	882,734,000
R&D Expense	77,381,000	79,573,000	78,041,000	63,455,000	58,155,000	50,895,000
Operating Income	151,370,000	158,676,000	110,998,000	44,804,000	115,340,000	79,587,000
Operating Margin %		.10%	.08%	.04%	.12%	.09%
SGA Expense	594,526,000	687,599,000	690,746,000	624,096,000	455,629,000	415,757,000
Net Income	133,892,000	50,201,000	60,801,000	64,743,000	74,564,000	-3,519,000
Operating Cash Flow	203,832,000	231,433,000	199,683,000	114,544,000	116,405,000	94,483,000
Capital Expenditure	63,890,000	134,532,000	77,741,000	43,503,000	47,328,000	33,413,000
EBITDA	281,132,000	223,523,000	232,816,000	135,349,000	188,874,000	143,051,000
Return on Assets %		.02%	.02%	.03%	.04%	.00%
Return on Equity %		.04%	.05%	.07%	.09%	.00%
Debt to Equity		0.989	0.968	1.851	0.792	0.932

CONTACT INFORMATION:

Phone: 609-275-0500 Fax:
Toll-Free:
Address: 100 Campus Rd., Princeton, NJ 08540 United States

STOCK TICKER/OTHER:

Stock Ticker: IART Exchange: NAS
Employees: 4,000 Fiscal Year Ends: 12/31
Parent Company:

SALARIES/BONUSES:

Top Exec. Salary: $ Bonus: $
Second Exec. Salary: $ Bonus: $

OTHER THOUGHTS:

Estimated Female Officers or Directors: 4
Hot Spot for Advancement for Women/Minorities: Y

Sales, profits and employees may be estimates. Financial information, benefits and other data can change quickly and may vary from those stated here.

Intermountain Healthcare

www.intermountainhealthcare.org

NAIC Code: 622110

TYPES OF BUSINESS:

General Medical and Surgical Hospitals
Surgical Centers
Emergency Air Transport
Pharmacies
Counseling Services
Rehabilitation Centers
Home Care
Health Insurance

BRANDS/DIVISIONS/AFFILIATES:

Life Flight
Intermountain Home Care
Intermountain Medical Group
InstaCare
KidsCare
WorkMed
Intermountain Medical Center Campus
LiVe

CONTACTS: Note: Officers with more than one job title may be intentionally listed here more than once.

A. Marc Harrison, CEO
Robert W. Allen, COO
Bert Zimmerli, CFO
Heather Brace, Chief People Officer
Greg Poulsen, Chief Strategy Officer

GROWTH PLANS/SPECIAL FEATURES:

Intermountain Healthcare is a nonprofit healthcare provider, operating 24 hospitals, approximately 160 clinics and telehealth services across a six-state region, primarily in Utah, southern Idaho and southern Nevada. Intermountain Healthcare runs Life Flight, an emergency air transport system; a collection of pharmacies; and counseling, dialysis and rehabilitation centers. Additionally, the company runs a variety of subsidiaries for additional patient assistance. Intermountain Home Care offers adult and pediatric skilled home nursing, rehabilitation therapies and certified Home Health Aide services. Intermountain Medical Group offers services through a multi-specialty network of approximately 2,400 physicians and advanced practice clinicians, with clinics such as InstaCare and KidsCare, ExpressCare clinics located in grocery stores and WorkMed clinics. SelectHealth, more than 850,000 members, supplies medical, prescription and dental insurance to corporate and individual clients. The Intermountain Medical Center Campus, in addition to a central laboratory, physician offices and medical education and research facilities, includes five specialized hospitals: a heart and lung hospital, a women's and newborn hospital, a cancer treatment hospital, an ambulatory and outpatient diagnostics hospital and a critical care and trauma hospital. IHC also maintains a child obesity public service program, LiVe, to encourage youth fitness. In October 2021, Intermountain Healthcare agreed to acquire a minority stake in Northpointe Surgery Center, located in Tooele County, Utah.

Intermountain Healthcare offers its employees comprehensive health benefits, retirement options, disability coverage and a range of employee assistance plans and programs.

FINANCIAL DATA: Note: Data for latest year may not have been available at press time.

In U.S. $	2020	2019	2018	2017	2016	2015
Revenue	7,700,000,000	7,000,000,000	7,724,200,000	6,940,000,000	6,954,100,000	6,109,200,000
R&D Expense						
Operating Income						
Operating Margin %						
SGA Expense						
Net Income	378,000,000	4,000,000	598,500,000	655,100,000	495,400,000	279,100,000
Operating Cash Flow						
Capital Expenditure						
EBITDA						
Return on Assets %						
Return on Equity %						
Debt to Equity						

CONTACT INFORMATION:

Phone: 801-442-3443   Fax: 801-442-3327
Toll-Free: 800-888-3134
Address: 36 S. State St., Salt Lake City, UT 84111 United States

STOCK TICKER/OTHER:

Stock Ticker: Nonprofit
Employees: 41,000
Parent Company:

Exchange:
Fiscal Year Ends: 12/31

SALARIES/BONUSES:

Top Exec. Salary: $ Bonus: $
Second Exec. Salary: $ Bonus: $

OTHER THOUGHTS:

Estimated Female Officers or Directors: 3
Hot Spot for Advancement for Women/Minorities: Y

Interpace Biosciences Inc

www.interpace.com

NAIC Code: 325413

TYPES OF BUSINESS:

Molecular Diagnostic Tests
Specialized Therapeutic Services
Diagnosis
Prognostic Services
Pharmaceutical Services
Biomarkers
Cytogenetics
High Plex Resolution Tools

BRANDS/DIVISIONS/AFFILIATES:

PancraGEN
ThyGenNEXT
ThyraMIR
RespriDX
BarreGEN

GROWTH PLANS/SPECIAL FEATURES:

Interpace Biosciences, Inc. offers specialized therapeutic services, from early diagnosis and prognostic planning to targeted therapeutic applications and pharma services. The firm provides molecular diagnostics, bioinformatics and pathology services for evaluation of risk of cancer; and provides pharmacogenomics testing, genotyping, biorepository and other specialized services to the pharmaceutical and biotech industries. Interpace advances personalized medicine by partnering with pharmaceutical, academic and technology leaders to integrate pharmacogenomics into their drug development and clinical trial programs. The company's solutions span biomarkers, anatomic path/flow/cytogenetics, integrated biorepository, bioformatics and high plex special resolution tools. Its product lines include PancraGEN, ThyGeNEXT, ThyraMIR, RespriDX and BarreGEN.

CONTACTS: Note: Officers with more than one job title may be intentionally listed here more than once.

Jack Stover, CEO
Bill Finger, COO
Thomas Freeburg, Chief Accounting Officer
Fred Knechtel, CFO
Michael McCartney, CCO
Stephen Sullivan, Director

FINANCIAL DATA: Note: Data for latest year may not have been available at press time.

In U.S. $	2020	2019	2018	2017	2016	2015
Revenue		24,079,000	21,896,000	15,897,000	13,085,000	9,432,000
R&D Expense						
Operating Income						
Operating Margin %						
SGA Expense						
Net Income		-26,727,000	-12,189,000	-12,216,000	-8,332,000	-11,356,000
Operating Cash Flow						
Capital Expenditure						
EBITDA						
Return on Assets %						
Return on Equity %						
Debt to Equity						

CONTACT INFORMATION:

Phone: 862 207-7800   Fax:
Toll-Free: 800-242-7494
Address: 300 Interpace Pkwy., Morris Corp. Ctr. 1, Bldg. C, Parsippany, NJ 07054 United States

STOCK TICKER/OTHER:

Stock Ticker: IDXG   Exchange: OTC
Employees: 178   Fiscal Year Ends: 12/31
Parent Company:

SALARIES/BONUSES:

Top Exec. Salary: $ Bonus: $
Second Exec. Salary: $ Bonus: $

OTHER THOUGHTS:

Estimated Female Officers or Directors: 4
Hot Spot for Advancement for Women/Minorities: Y

Intersect ENT Inc

www.intersectent.com

NAIC Code: 339100

TYPES OF BUSINESS:

Surgical and Medical Instrument Manufacturing
Commercial Stage Drug Devices
Implant Technology

BRANDS/DIVISIONS/AFFILIATES:

PROPEL
PROPEL mini
PROPEL Contour
SINUVA
fiagon AG Medical Technologies
VenSure

CONTACTS: *Note: Officers with more than one job title may be intentionally listed here more than once.*

Thomas A. West, CEO
Jeryl Hilleman, CFO
Kieran Gallahue, Chairman of the Board
Susan Stimson, Chief Strategy Officer
Christine Kowalski, COO
David Lehman, General Counsel
Robert Binney, Other Corporate Officer
Gwen Carscadden, Other Executive Officer

GROWTH PLANS/SPECIAL FEATURES:

Intersect ENT, Inc. is a commercial stage drug-device company focusing on patients with ear, nose and throat (ENT) conditions. The firm has developed a drug releasing bioabsorbable implant technology that enables targeted and sustained release of therapeutic agents. FDA approved products of Intersect ENT include PROPEL, PROPEL mini and PROPEL Contour. PROPEL and PROPEL mini are inserted by a physician into the ethmoid sinuses following sinus surgery. The self-expanding implants are designed to conform to and hold open the surgically enlarged sinus, while gradually releasing an anti-inflammatory steroid over a period of approximately 30 days, before being fully absorbed into the body. PROPEL Contour is a steroid releasing implant designed to fit the ostia, or openings, of the dependent sinuses following enlargement of the sinuses. When used with balloon openings, PROPEL Contour provides a less invasive procedure performed in the physician's office for patients with primary chronic sinusitis who have not had sinus surgery. SINUVA (mometasone furoate) is a steroid releasing implant designed to provide a cost-effective, less invasive solution for patients that have had ethmoid sinus surgery yet suffer from recurrent sinus obstruction due to polyps. The SINUVA implant is designed to be placed in the ethmoid sinus in a procedure conducted in the physician's office as an alternative to other treatment options such as further medical therapy or revision surgery. In late-2020, Intersect completed its acquisition of Fiagon AG Medical Technologies, which offers electromagnetic surgical navigation solutions and an expansive ENT product portfolio, including the U.S. FDA-cleared VenSure sinus dilation balloon. In August 2021, Intersect ENT agreed to merge with Medtronic, Inc., a wholly-owned subsidiary of Medtronic plc.

FINANCIAL DATA: *Note: Data for latest year may not have been available at press time.*

In U.S. $	2020	2019	2018	2017	2016	2015
Revenue	80,554,000	109,142,000	108,472,000	96,301,000	78,708,000	61,593,000
R&D Expense	19,350,000	24,283,000	19,262,000	18,360,000	18,890,000	16,608,000
Operating Income	-67,652,000	-45,394,000	-25,006,000	-17,603,000	-26,111,000	-26,940,000
Operating Margin %		-.42%	-.23%	-.18%	-.33%	-.44%
SGA Expense	98,550,000	108,480,000	91,603,000	80,045,000	72,926,000	59,637,000
Net Income	-72,319,000	-42,994,000	-22,922,000	-16,363,000	-25,222,000	-26,634,000
Operating Cash Flow	-35,694,000	-27,251,000	-13,840,000	-8,041,000	-20,059,000	-20,087,000
Capital Expenditure	873,000	3,727,000	2,116,000	2,281,000	2,069,000	1,524,000
EBITDA	-67,142,000	-41,493,000	-23,122,000	-16,139,000	-24,945,000	-26,114,000
Return on Assets %		-.30%	-.17%	-.12%	-.18%	-.26%
Return on Equity %		-.36%	-.19%	-.14%	-.21%	-.29%
Debt to Equity		0.092				

CONTACT INFORMATION:

Phone: 650 641-2100 Fax:
Toll-Free:
Address: 1555 Adams Dr., Menlo Park, CA 94025 United States

STOCK TICKER/OTHER:

Stock Ticker: XENT Exchange: NAS
Employees: 406 Fiscal Year Ends: 12/31
Parent Company:

SALARIES/BONUSES:

Top Exec. Salary: $ Bonus: $
Second Exec. Salary: $ Bonus: $

OTHER THOUGHTS:

Estimated Female Officers or Directors:
Hot Spot for Advancement for Women/Minorities:

Intuitive Surgical Inc

www.intuitivesurgical.com

NAIC Code: 339100

TYPES OF BUSINESS:

Endoscopic Surgery Products
Operative Surgical Robots
Product Manufacturing
Surgical Product Components

BRANDS/DIVISIONS/AFFILIATES:

da Vinci Surgical System
da Vinci Skills Simulator
Firefly
EndoWrist

CONTACTS: *Note: Officers with more than one job title may be intentionally listed here more than once.*

Gary Guthart, CEO
Marshall Mohr, CFO
Lonnie Smith, Chairman of the Board
Reiter Andersen, Chief Compliance Officer
Myriam Curet, Chief Medical Officer
Salvatore Brogna, Executive VP
David Rosa, Executive VP

GROWTH PLANS/SPECIAL FEATURES:

Intuitive Surgical, Inc. is a global technology leader in minimally invasive care and a manufacturer of robotic-assisted surgery. The firm's operative surgical robotics include the da Vinci Surgical System, which consists of a surgeon's console, a patient-side cart, a high-performance vision system and Intuitive's proprietary wristed instruments. The system provides the surgeon with the control, range of motion, fine tissue manipulation capability and 3D visualization characteristics of open surgery, but utilizes the small ports of minimally invasive surgery (MIS). The da Vinci Surgical System controls Intuitive's endoscopic instruments. Surgeons operate while seated at a console viewing a 3D high definition (HD) vision system, which enhances visualization of tissue planes and critical anatomy and has a digital zoom feature, allowing surgeons to magnify the surgical field of view without adjusting endoscope position. The system also includes a motorized patient cart. The da Vinci Skills Simulator provides a way for users to practice their skills and gain familiarity with the surgeon console controls. Firefly fluorescence imaging is a standard feature of da Vinci surgical systems, with a specialized camera head, endoscope and laser-based illuminator. Related instruments and accessories are also available. Moreover, Intuitive manufactures a variety of EndoWrist instruments; each incorporates a wrist joint with tips customized for various surgical procedures. In early-2020, Intuitive acquired Orpheus Medical, which provides hospitals with information technology connectivity, as well as expertise in processing and archiving surgical video. Orpheus operates as a wholly-owned subsidiary of Intuitive.

Intuitive offers comprehensive benefits, retirement plans and a variety of employee assistance programs.

FINANCIAL DATA: *Note: Data for latest year may not have been available at press time.*

In U.S. $	2020	2019	2018	2017	2016	2015
Revenue	4,358,400,000	4,478,500,000	3,724,200,000	3,128,900,000	2,704,400,000	2,384,400,000
R&D Expense	595,100,000	557,300,000	418,100,000	328,600,000	239,600,000	197,400,000
Operating Income	1,049,800,000	1,374,500,000	1,199,400,000	1,054,600,000	945,200,000	740,000,000
Operating Margin %	.31%	.32%	.34%	.35%	.31%	
SGA Expense	1,216,300,000	1,178,400,000	986,600,000	810,900,000	705,300,000	640,500,000
Net Income	1,060,600,000	1,379,300,000	1,127,900,000	660,000,000	735,900,000	588,800,000
Operating Cash Flow	1,484,800,000	1,598,200,000	1,169,600,000	1,143,900,000	1,042,900,000	771,900,000
Capital Expenditure	341,500,000	425,600,000	187,400,000	190,700,000	53,900,000	81,000,000
EBITDA	1,326,000,000	1,577,500,000	1,322,200,000	1,153,700,000	1,037,300,000	829,500,000
Return on Assets %	.16%	.17%	.11%	.13%	.13%	
Return on Equity %	.18%	.20%	.13%	.15%	.15%	
Debt to Equity						

CONTACT INFORMATION:

Phone: 408 523-2100   Fax: 408 523-1390
Toll-Free: 888-868-4647
Address: 1020 Kifer Rd., Sunnyvale, CA 94086 United States

STOCK TICKER/OTHER:

Stock Ticker: ISRG
Employees: 8,081
Parent Company:

Exchange: NAS
Fiscal Year Ends: 12/31

SALARIES/BONUSES:

Top Exec. Salary: $ Bonus: $
Second Exec. Salary: $ Bonus: $

OTHER THOUGHTS:

Estimated Female Officers or Directors: 3
Hot Spot for Advancement for Women/Minorities: Y

Sales, profits and employees may be estimates. Financial information, benefits and other data can change quickly and may vary from those stated here.

Invacare Corporation

www.invacare.com

NAIC Code: 339100

TYPES OF BUSINESS:

Supplies-Wheelchairs
Home Health Care Equipment
Home Respiratory Products
Medical Supplies
Wheel Chairs

BRANDS/DIVISIONS/AFFILIATES:

Invacare AVIVA STORM RX

CONTACTS: *Note: Officers with more than one job title may be intentionally listed here more than once.*

Matthew Monaghan, CEO
Kathleen Leneghan, CFO
Ralf Ledda, General Manager, Geographical
Darcie Karol, Senior VP, Divisional
Anthony LaPlaca, Senior VP

GROWTH PLANS/SPECIAL FEATURES:

Invacare Corporation is a leading manufacturer and distributor in markets for medical equipment used in non-acute care settings. The firm's products help people to move, breathe, rest and perform essential hygiene. Invacare also provides clinically-complex medical device solutions for congenital (cerebral palsy, muscular dystrophy, spina bifida), acquired (stroke, spinal cord injury, traumatic brain injury, post-acute recovery, pressure ulcers) and degenerative (ALS, multiple sclerosis, chronic obstructive pulmonary disease, elderly, bariatric) ailments. Product categories include beds, furnishings, powered mobility, manual mobility, patient transfer equipment, respiratory equipment, respiratory therapy systems, bath/shower safety products (seats and grab bars), pressure cushions, wound-care products, back products and more. The company sells its products primarily to home medical equipment providers with retail and ecommerce channels, residential care operators, distributors and government health services in North America, Europe and Asia-Pacific. During 2021, Invacare introduced the Invacare AVIVA STORM RX, a next-generation rear wheel drive power wheelchair.

FINANCIAL DATA: *Note: Data for latest year may not have been available at press time.*

In U.S. $	2020	2019	2018	2017	2016	2015
Revenue	850,689,000	927,964,000	972,347,000	966,497,000	1,047,474,000	1,142,338,000
R&D Expense						
Operating Income	8,895,000	2,006,000	-14,230,000	-27,565,000	-20,154,000	-7,023,000
Operating Margin %		.00%	-.01%	-.03%	-.02%	-.01%
SGA Expense	236,357,000	260,061,000	281,906,000	296,816,000	303,781,000	319,847,000
Net Income	-28,280,000	-53,327,000	-43,922,000	-76,541,000	-42,856,000	-26,190,000
Operating Cash Flow	21,917,000	2,743,000	-46,423,000	-25,774,000	-56,613,000	-5,378,000
Capital Expenditure	22,304,000	10,874,000	9,823,000	14,569,000	10,151,000	7,522,000
EBITDA	25,328,000	9,541,000	9,790,000	-28,712,000	953,000	10,601,000
Return on Assets %		-.06%	-.05%	-.08%	-.05%	-.03%
Return on Equity %		-.16%	-.11%	-.18%	-.10%	-.05%
Debt to Equity		0.836	0.717	0.822	0.419	0.097

CONTACT INFORMATION:

Phone: 440 329-6000　　　Fax: 440 366-9008
Toll-Free: 800-333-6900
Address: 1 Invacare Way, Elyria, OH 44035 United States

STOCK TICKER/OTHER:

Stock Ticker: IVC　　　　　　　　Exchange: NYS
Employees: 3,400　　　　　　　　Fiscal Year Ends: 12/31
Parent Company:

SALARIES/BONUSES:

Top Exec. Salary: $　　　　Bonus: $
Second Exec. Salary: $　　　Bonus: $

OTHER THOUGHTS:

Estimated Female Officers or Directors: 3
Hot Spot for Advancement for Women/Minorities: Y

Iowa Health System (dba UnityPoint Health)

www.unitypoint.org/about.aspx

NAIC Code: 622110

TYPES OF BUSINESS:

General Medical and Surgical Hospitals
Health Care System
Clinics
Hospitals
Home Health Services
Hospice Services
Telehealth Services
Pharmacy Services

BRANDS/DIVISIONS/AFFILIATES:

UnityPoint at Home
UnityPoint at Home Specialty Pharmacy
UnityPoint Health Colleges
UnityPoint Health at Work
Telehealth

CONTACTS: *Note: Officers with more than one job title may be intentionally listed here more than once.*

Denny Drake, General Counsel
Kevin Vermeer, Chief Strategy Officer
Kara Dunham, VP-Finance
Alan S. Kaplan, Chief Clinical Officer
Matthew Kirschner, Treas.
Sabra Rosener, VP-Gov't Rel.
Aric Sharp, VP-Accountable Care Organization
Brad Brody, Chmn.
Katie Marchik, VP-Supply Chain Mgmt.

GROWTH PLANS/SPECIAL FEATURES:

Iowa Health System does business as UnityPoint Health, and is a health system that encompasses clinics and hospitals, and provides home health, hospice, telehealth and specialty pharmacy services, among others. The organization's network spans Iowa, Illinois and Wisconsin. UnityPoint clinics offer Ob/Gyn, pediatric, internal medicine, family medicine, home medical and primary care services. UnityPoint Health's more than 20 hospitals (under various names) offer the latest in advanced medical technology. In coordination with UnityPoint Clinics, UnityPoint at Home provides patients with resources and care necessary for wellness at home. Hospice care is a coordinated care approach between a medical director, physician, nurse and others, with services including pain and symptom management, spiritual care, home care, inpatient care, respite care, family conferences and bereavement support. Telehealth is a secure video access that allows for consultation with a physician or provider off-site. UnityPoint at Home Specialty Pharmacy offers a range of specialty prescriptions to treat complex or chronic conditions. In addition, UnityPoint Health Colleges offer a wide variety of entry-level nursing and allied health programs designed for individuals who wish to continue their career in healthcare. These colleges include: Allen College in Waterloo, Iowa; Methodist College in Peoria, Illinois; St. Luke's College in Sioux City, Iowa; and Trinity College of Nursing & Health Sciences in Quad Cities, Iowa. Community mental health centers are affiliated with UnityPoint Health, and are located in Cedar Rapids, Des Moines, Fort Dodge, Peoria, Quad cities and Waterloo. UnityPoint Health at Work addresses employee health, including physical and mental as well as managing chronic conditions, in an effort to lower employee illness and injury.

FINANCIAL DATA: *Note: Data for latest year may not have been available at press time.*

In U.S. $	2020	2019	2018	2017	2016	2015
Revenue	4,612,051,000	4,558,446,000	4,411,461,000	4,157,199,000	3,866,776,000	
R&D Expense						
Operating Income						
Operating Margin %						
SGA Expense						
Net Income	275,755,000	380,998,000	-9,427,000	233,231,000	144,771,000	
Operating Cash Flow						
Capital Expenditure						
EBITDA						
Return on Assets %						
Return on Equity %						
Debt to Equity						

CONTACT INFORMATION:

Phone: 515-241-6161   Fax:
Toll-Free:
Address: 1776 W. Lakes Pkwy., Ste. 400, West Des Moines, IA 50266 United States

STOCK TICKER/OTHER:

Stock Ticker: Nonprofit
Employees: 28,100
Parent Company:

Exchange:
Fiscal Year Ends: 12/31

SALARIES/BONUSES:

Top Exec. Salary: $ Bonus: $
Second Exec. Salary: $ Bonus: $

OTHER THOUGHTS:

Estimated Female Officers or Directors: 5
Hot Spot for Advancement for Women/Minorities: Y

IQVIA Holdings Inc

www.iqvia.com

NAIC Code: 541711

TYPES OF BUSINESS:

Contract Research
Pharmaceutical, Biotech & Medical Device Research
Consulting & Training Services
Sales & Marketing Services

BRANDS/DIVISIONS/AFFILIATES:

IQVIA CORE
Q2 Solutions

CONTACTS: *Note: Officers with more than one job title may be intentionally listed here more than once.*

Michael Mcdonnell, CFO
Ari Bousbib, Chairman of the Board
Emmanuel Korakis, Chief Accounting Officer
Eric Sherbet, Executive VP
W. Staub, President, Divisional
Kevin Knightly, President, Divisional

GROWTH PLANS/SPECIAL FEATURES:

IQVIA Holdings, Inc. provides advanced analytics, technology solutions and contract research services to the life sciences industry. The firm applies human data science, leveraging analytics and data science to the scope of human science, to enable companies to reimagine and develop new approaches to clinical development and commercialization, speed innovation and accelerate improvements in healthcare outcomes. Its IQVIA CORE platform delivers actionable insights at the intersection of large-scale analytics, transformative technology and extensive domain expertise as well as execution capabilities to help biotech, medical device and pharmaceutical companies, medical researchers, government agencies, payers and other healthcare stakeholders better understand diseases, human behaviors and scientific advances, for the purpose of finding cures. Capabilities of the company include healthcare-specific global IT infrastructure, analytics-driven clinical development, artificial intelligence, machine learning, human data science, decentralized trials, proprietary clinical and commercial applications and more. IQVIA'a product portfolio spans research and development, pre-launch, launch and in-market. The company conducts operations in more than 100 countries worldwide. In April 2021, IQVIA acquired the 40% minority share of Q2 Solutions from Quest Diagnostics, resulting in 100% ownership by IQVIA. Q2 Solutions is a global clinical laboratory services organization that provides comprehensive testing, project management, supply chain, biorepository and biospecimen and consent tracking solutions for clinical trials.

FINANCIAL DATA: *Note: Data for latest year may not have been available at press time.*

In U.S. $	2020	2019	2018	2017	2016	2015
Revenue	11,359,000,000	11,088,000,000	10,412,000,000	9,739,000,000	6,878,000,000	5,737,619,000
R&D Expense						
Operating Income	783,000,000	852,000,000	809,000,000	822,000,000	828,000,000	679,848,000
Operating Margin %		.08%	.08%	.08%	.12%	.12%
SGA Expense	1,789,000,000	1,734,000,000	1,716,000,000	1,605,000,000	1,011,000,000	920,985,000
Net Income	279,000,000	191,000,000	259,000,000	1,309,000,000	115,000,000	387,205,000
Operating Cash Flow	1,959,000,000	1,417,000,000	1,254,000,000	970,000,000	860,000,000	475,691,000
Capital Expenditure	616,000,000	582,000,000	459,000,000	369,000,000	164,000,000	78,391,000
EBITDA	2,076,000,000	2,001,000,000	1,883,000,000	1,688,000,000	912,000,000	768,529,000
Return on Assets %		.01%	.01%	.06%	.01%	.11%
Return on Equity %		.03%	.03%	.16%	.03%	
Debt to Equity		1.989	1.625	1.248	0.823	

CONTACT INFORMATION:

Phone: 919-998-2000　　　　Fax:
Toll-Free: 866-267-4479
Address: 4820 Emperor Blvd., Durham, NC 27703 United States

STOCK TICKER/OTHER:

Stock Ticker: IQV　　　　　　　　　Exchange: NYS
Employees: 67,000　　　　　　　　Fiscal Year Ends: 12/31
Parent Company:

SALARIES/BONUSES:

Top Exec. Salary: $　　　　Bonus: $
Second Exec. Salary: $　　　Bonus: $

OTHER THOUGHTS:

Estimated Female Officers or Directors: 3
Hot Spot for Advancement for Women/Minorities: Y

IRIDEX Corporation

www.iridex.com

NAIC Code: 334510

TYPES OF BUSINESS:

Equipment-Laser Systems
Ophthalmological & Dermatological Laser Systems
Medical Technologies
Product Development
Product Commercialization

BRANDS/DIVISIONS/AFFILIATES:

MicroPulse
Cyclo G6
IQ
OcuLight
TxCell
G-Probe
EndoProbe

CONTACTS: *Note: Officers with more than one job title may be intentionally listed here more than once.*

David Bruce, CEO
William Moore, Chairman of the Board
Romeo Dizon, Chief Accounting Officer

GROWTH PLANS/SPECIAL FEATURES:

IRIDEX Corporation is an ophthalmic medical technology company that develops and commercializes breakthrough products and procedures used to treat sight-threatening eye conditions, including glaucoma and retinal diseases. Some of the firm's laser products are powered by its proprietary MicroPulse technology, a method that delivers laser energy through a mode that chops the continuous wave laser beam into short, microsecond-long laser pulses. IRIDEX's products generally consist of laser consoles, delivery devices and consumable instrumentation such as laser probes. Laser consoles include the following product lines: glaucoma, which includes the Cyclo G6 laser systems; medical retina, which includes the IQ 532 and IQ 577 laser photocoagulation systems used for the treatment of diabetic macular edema and other retinal diseases; and surgical retina, which includes the OcuLight TX, OcuLight SL, OcuLight SLx, OcuLight GL and OcuLight GLx laser photocoagulation systems. Delivery devices are typically used with IRIDEX's IQ and OcuLight laser systems, and include: the TxCell scanning laser delivery system, which allows the physician to perform multi-spot pattern scanning for efficient delivery of the MicroPulse laser; slit lamp adapters, which allow the physician to utilize a standard slit lamp in both diagnosis and treatment procedures; and laser indirect ophthalmoscope, which is designed to be worn on the physician's head and to be used in procedures to treat peripheral retinal disorders, particularly in infants or adults requiring treatment in the supine position. Single-use laser probes include the following product lines: MicroPulse P3 and G-Probe for glaucoma procedures; and EndoProbe, for surgical retina/vitrectomy procedures. IRIDEX develops, manufactures, markets, sells and services its medical laser systems and associated instrumentation.

FINANCIAL DATA: *Note: Data for latest year may not have been available at press time.*

In U.S. $	2020	2019	2018	2017	2016	2015
Revenue	36,347,000	43,447,000	42,600,000	41,593,000	46,158,000	41,757,000
R&D Expense	3,282,000	3,682,000	4,006,000	5,730,000	5,365,000	5,214,000
Operating Income	-6,583,000	-8,974,000	-12,868,000	-13,028,000	-2,445,000	288,000
Operating Margin %		-.21%	-.30%	-.31%	-.05%	.01%
SGA Expense	18,859,000	23,231,000	26,333,000	22,801,000	17,919,000	14,451,000
Net Income	-6,329,000	-8,813,000	-12,813,000	-12,867,000	-11,713,000	474,000
Operating Cash Flow	-3,237,000	-7,913,000	-10,025,000	-3,565,000	-144,000	-593,000
Capital Expenditure	97,000	128,000	440,000	575,000	1,062,000	875,000
EBITDA	-6,079,000	-8,286,000	-12,059,000	-12,170,000	-1,797,000	810,000
Return on Assets %		-.23%	-.31%	-.29%	-.26%	.01%
Return on Equity %		-.33%	-.42%	-.37%	-.32%	.01%
Debt to Equity		0.079				

CONTACT INFORMATION:

Phone: 650 940-4700   Fax: 650 940-4710
Toll-Free: 800-388-4747
Address: 1212 Terra Bella Ave., Mountain View, CA 94043-1824 United States

STOCK TICKER/OTHER:

Stock Ticker: IRIX
Employees: 128
Parent Company:

Exchange: NAS
Fiscal Year Ends: 12/31

SALARIES/BONUSES:

Top Exec. Salary: $ Bonus: $
Second Exec. Salary: $ Bonus: $

OTHER THOUGHTS:

Estimated Female Officers or Directors:
Hot Spot for Advancement for Women/Minorities:

Sales, profits and employees may be estimates. Financial information, benefits and other data can change quickly and may vary from those stated here.

Jean Coutu Group (PJC) Inc (The)

www.jeancoutu.com

NAIC Code: 446110

TYPES OF BUSINESS:

Drug Stores
Pharmaceuticals
Warehousing
Distribution

BRANDS/DIVISIONS/AFFILIATES:

Metro Inc
PJC Jean Coutu
PJC Sante
PJC Sante Beaute

GROWTH PLANS/SPECIAL FEATURES:

The Jean Coutu Group (PJC), Inc. is a leading Canadian distributor and retailer of pharmaceuticals and over-the-counter drugs. The company, a wholly-owned subsidiary of Metro, Inc., oversees Metro's pharmaceutical operations and provides its approximately 415 franchise stores with a range of professional and technical support services. Jean Coutu Group also supplies, warehouses and delivers pharmaceuticals, pharmaceutical products and consumer goods. Stores and/or distribution centers are located in Quebec, New Brunswick and Ontario, with retail banners including PJC jean Coutu, PJC Sante and PJC Sante Beaute.

CONTACTS: Note: Officers with more than one job title may be intentionally listed here more than once.

Alain Champagne, Pres.
Jean Coutu, Chairman of the Board
Nicolle Forget, Director
Alain Lafortune, Executive VP, Divisional
Andre Belzile, Executive VP, Divisional
Normand Messier, Executive VP, Divisional
Richard Mayrand, Executive VP, Divisional
Jean-Michel Coutu, Executive VP, Divisional
Marcel Raymond, President, Subsidiary
Brigite Dufour, Secretary
Louis Coutu, Vice President, Divisional
Jean Coutu, Chmn.
Marie-Chantal Lamothe, Vice President, Divisional
Daniel Cote, Vice President, Divisional

FINANCIAL DATA: Note: Data for latest year may not have been available at press time.

In U.S. $	2020	2019	2018	2017	2016	2015
Revenue	2,667,628,213	2,356,600,000	2,478,632,486	2,360,602,368	2,263,020,032	2,230,360,576
R&D Expense						
Operating Income						
Operating Margin %						
SGA Expense						
Net Income			166,052,308	158,145,056	169,401,504	173,523,584
Operating Cash Flow						
Capital Expenditure						
EBITDA						
Return on Assets %						
Return on Equity %						
Debt to Equity						

CONTACT INFORMATION:

Phone: 450 646-9760　　Fax:
Toll-Free:
Address: 245, Jean Coutu St., Varennes, QC J3X 0E1 Canada

STOCK TICKER/OTHER:

Stock Ticker: Subsidiary
Employees: 1,074
Parent Company: Metro Inc

Exchange:
Fiscal Year Ends: 03/31

SALARIES/BONUSES:

Top Exec. Salary: $　　Bonus: $
Second Exec. Salary: $　　Bonus: $

OTHER THOUGHTS:

Estimated Female Officers or Directors: 13
Hot Spot for Advancement for Women/Minorities: Y

Jenny Craig Inc
www.jennycraig.com

NAIC Code: 812191

TYPES OF BUSINESS:
Weight Management Programs
Packaged Food
Video Production
Franchising
Online Sales & Services

BRANDS/DIVISIONS/AFFILIATES:
HIG Capital

CONTACTS: *Note: Officers with more than one job title may be intentionally listed here more than once.*
David Pastrana, CEO
Erin Parashkevov, VP-Human Resources
Yash Muralidharan, VP-IT
Kim Matthews, General Counsel
Andy Henton, VP-Oper.
Corrinne Peritano, VP-North America Bus.

GROWTH PLANS/SPECIAL FEATURES:
Jenny Craig, Inc. is a weight management, diet and nutrition company. The firm has approximately 600 company-owned and franchised locations in the U.S., Canada, Australia, New Zealand and Puerto Rico, with consultants worldwide. Jenny Craig offers clients personalized diet programs with the help of one-on-one consultations with weight loss counselors. Weight loss is achieved via personalized diet plans, which include Jenny's Cuisine food products and fresh foods prepared using Jenny Craig recipes; exercise plans; and counseling and support available online, by phone or in person at Jenny Craig centers. In a given week, around 75,000 unique customers follow a Jenny Craig program. The firm provides options for clients with significant weight loss goals as well as for clients who wish to track daily calorie intake and expenditure. Both options can be conducted either from home, supplemented by weekly phone consultations, or in-center, with regular visits to Jenny Craig locations. Once a weight goal is achieved, the firm offers weight maintenance programs with consultations and menu planning. Information is available for members on personal weight tracking, lifestyle planning and selected recipes through the company's online service. The website also features 100 popular food products such as Jenny's Cuisine breakfast, lunch, dinner and snack items as well as sauces, dressings, cookbooks and exercise videos. In addition, the company produces and markets DVDs, journals, CDs and workout accessories. Jenny Craig is owned by H.I.G. Capital, a global private equity investment firm.

The company offers comprehensive benefits, retirement plans and employee assistance programs.

FINANCIAL DATA: *Note: Data for latest year may not have been available at press time.*

In U.S. $	2020	2019	2018	2017	2016	2015
Revenue	244,500,000	326,000,000	315,000,000	300,000,000	298,000,000	300,000,000
R&D Expense						
Operating Income						
Operating Margin %						
SGA Expense						
Net Income						
Operating Cash Flow						
Capital Expenditure						
EBITDA						
Return on Assets %						
Return on Equity %						
Debt to Equity						

CONTACT INFORMATION:
Phone: 760-696-4000   Fax: 760-696-4009
Toll-Free: 800-597-5366
Address: 5770 Fleet St., Carlsbad, CA 92008 United States

STOCK TICKER/OTHER:
Stock Ticker: Private
Employees: 3,510
Parent Company: HIG Capital

Exchange:
Fiscal Year Ends: 12/31

SALARIES/BONUSES:
Top Exec. Salary: $ Bonus: $
Second Exec. Salary: $ Bonus: $

OTHER THOUGHTS:
Estimated Female Officers or Directors: 3
Hot Spot for Advancement for Women/Minorities: Y

Sales, profits and employees may be estimates. Financial information, benefits and other data can change quickly and may vary from those stated here.

Jiangsu Hengrui Medicine Co Ltd

NAIC Code: 325412

www.hrs.com.cn

TYPES OF BUSINESS:

Pharmaceutical Preparation Manufacturing
Pharmaceuticals
Raw Materials

BRANDS/DIVISIONS/AFFILIATES:

GROWTH PLANS/SPECIAL FEATURES:

Jiangsu Hengrui Medicine Co., Ltd. develops, manufactures and markets a variety of pharmaceutical medicines, raw materials and related packaging materials. The company's products include anti-neoplastic drugs, angiomyocardiac drugs, drugs for surgery, pain management medicines, antibiotics, specialty infusions, contrast agents, aluminum foil and other related products. Hengrui Medicine distributes its medicines both domestically and overseas. The firm's pharmaceutical business engages in the research, development, production and marketing of medicines. Hengrui Medicine has applied for nearly 900 domestic invention patents, with 201 granted in China and 286 granted in Europe, the U.S., Japan and other countries. The firm owns eight manufacturing facilities for small and large molecules and medical devices. Hengrui Medicine has research and development centers located in China and the U.S. Its in-house sales and marketing team services over 15,000 hospitals in China, covering nearly all the major hospitals and medical centers in the country.

CONTACTS: *Note: Officers with more than one job title may be intentionally listed here more than once.*

Yunshu Zhou, Pres.

FINANCIAL DATA: *Note: Data for latest year may not have been available at press time.*

In U.S. $	2020	2019	2018	2017	2016	2015
Revenue	4,249,070,000	2,658,957,000	2,532,340,000	2,124,320,000	1,596,280,000	1,475,460,000
R&D Expense						
Operating Income						
Operating Margin %						
SGA Expense						
Net Income	966,553,000	619,967,250	590,445,000	505,169,000	378,457,000	345,510,000
Operating Cash Flow						
Capital Expenditure						
EBITDA						
Return on Assets %						
Return on Equity %						
Debt to Equity						

CONTACT INFORMATION:

Phone: 86-518-8122-0983 Fax:
Toll-Free:
Address: 38 Huanghe Rd., Eco & Tech Dev. Park, Lianyungang, Jiangsu 222000 China

STOCK TICKER/OTHER:

Stock Ticker: 600276
Employees: 28,903
Parent Company:

Exchange: Shanghai
Fiscal Year Ends: 12/31

SALARIES/BONUSES:

Top Exec. Salary: $ Bonus: $
Second Exec. Salary: $ Bonus: $

OTHER THOUGHTS:

Estimated Female Officers or Directors:
Hot Spot for Advancement for Women/Minorities:

Johns Hopkins Medicine

www.hopkinsmedicine.org

NAIC Code: 622110

TYPES OF BUSINESS:

General Medical and Surgical Hospitals
Medical Research
Medical School
Home Care Services
Physician Network Management

BRANDS/DIVISIONS/AFFILIATES:

Johns Hopkins University School of Medicine
Johns Hopkins Hospital
Johns Hopkins Health System
Johns Hopkins Bayview Medical Center
Johns Hopkins Medicine International

CONTACTS: *Note: Officers with more than one job title may be intentionally listed here more than once.*

Paul B. Rothman, CEO
Ronald J. Daniels, Pres., The Johns Hopkins University
Joanne E. Pollak, Sr. VP
Judy A. Reitz, Exec. VP
Ronald R. Peterson, Exec. VP

GROWTH PLANS/SPECIAL FEATURES:

Johns Hopkins Medicine is a nonprofit organization that includes Johns Hopkins University School of Medicine, the Johns Hopkins Hospital and the Johns Hopkins Health System. Johns Hopkins Medicine operates six academic and community hospitals, four suburban healthcare and surgery centers and more than 40 primary and specialty care outpatient sites. The university has a multitude of academic departments ranging from anesthesiology to urology. The Johns Hopkins Hospital is a partner with the University medical school and faculty, with a training school for nurses and comprises more than 30 state-of-the-art operating rooms (neurosurgery/general surgery, pediatric, cardiac and obstetric), private inpatient rooms for adults, private inpatient rooms for children, and emergency departments for adults and children. The Johns Hopkins Health System provides comprehensive healthcare services, operating clinics and hospitals in and around Baltimore. Johns Hopkins Bayview Medical Center, in eastern Baltimore, is a teaching hospital housing a neonatal intensive care unit, sleep disorders center, area-wide trauma center, a regional burn center and a nationally regarded geriatrics center. The organization also maintains a home care group that provides visits by nurses, physical and occupational therapists, home health aides and social workers; a network of physicians providing community-based healthcare; several facilities at which faculty physicians practice; and programs to assist patients and families from foreign countries or other U.S. cities with physician appointments, lodging, transportation, interpreter services, financial arrangements, daycare centers and sightseeing. Johns Hopkins Medicine International offers hospital management, healthcare consulting and clinical education services through alliances and affiliations in North America, Latin America, Europe, the Middle East and Asia.

FINANCIAL DATA: *Note: Data for latest year may not have been available at press time.*

In U.S. $	2020	2019	2018	2017	2016	2015
Revenue	8,304,900,000	8,930,000,000	8,820,000,000	8,400,000,000	8,000,000,000	7,700,000,000
R&D Expense						
Operating Income						
Operating Margin %						
SGA Expense						
Net Income						
Operating Cash Flow						
Capital Expenditure						
EBITDA						
Return on Assets %						
Return on Equity %						
Debt to Equity						

CONTACT INFORMATION:

Phone: 410-955-5000   Fax: 410-955-4452
Toll-Free:
Address: 1800 Orleans St, Baltimore, MD 21287 United States

STOCK TICKER/OTHER:

Stock Ticker: Nonprofit   Exchange:
Employees: 41,000   Fiscal Year Ends: 06/30
Parent Company:

SALARIES/BONUSES:

Top Exec. Salary: $ Bonus: $
Second Exec. Salary: $ Bonus: $

OTHER THOUGHTS:

Estimated Female Officers or Directors: 18
Hot Spot for Advancement for Women/Minorities: Y

Johnson & Johnson

NAIC Code: 325412

www.jnj.com

TYPES OF BUSINESS:

Personal Health Care & Hygiene Products
Sterilization Products
Surgical Products
Pharmaceuticals
Skin Care Products
Baby Care Products
Contact Lenses
Medical Equipment

BRANDS/DIVISIONS/AFFILIATES:

Motrin
Band-Aid
Listerine
Tylenol
Neosporin
Risperdal Consta
Remicade
Momenta Pharmaceuticals Inc

CONTACTS: *Note: Officers with more than one job title may be intentionally listed here more than once.*

Alex Gorsky, CEO
Joaquin Duato, Vice Chairman
Joseph Wolk, CFO
Jorge Mesquita, Chairman of the Board, Divisional
Ronald Kapusta, Chief Accounting Officer
Paulus Stoffels, Chief Scientific Officer
Thibaut Mongon, Executive VP, Divisional
Ashley McEvoy, Executive VP, Divisional
Jennifer Taubert, Executive VP, Divisional
Michael Sneed, Executive VP, Divisional
Kathy Wengel, Executive VP
Peter Fasolo, Executive VP
Michael Ullmann, General Counsel

GROWTH PLANS/SPECIAL FEATURES:

Johnson & Johnson, founded in 1886, is one of the world's most comprehensive and well-known researchers, developers and manufacturers of healthcare products. Johnson & Johnson's worldwide operations are divided into three segments: consumer, pharmaceuticals and medical devices. The company's principal consumer goods are personal care and hygiene products, including baby care, skin care, oral care, wound care and women's healthcare products as well as nutritional and over-the-counter pharmaceutical products. Major consumer brands include Motrin, Band-Aid, Listerine, Tylenol, Neosporin, Aveeno and Pepcid AC. The pharmaceutical segment covers a wide spectrum of health fields, including anti-infective, antipsychotic, contraceptive, dermatology, gastrointestinal, hematology, immunology, neurology, oncology, pain management and virology. Among its pharmaceutical products are Risperdal Consta, an antipsychotic used to treat schizophrenia, and Remicade for the treatment of immune mediated inflammatory diseases. In the medical devices segment, Johnson & Johnson makes a number of products including orthopedic joint reconstruction devices, surgical care, glucose monitoring devices, diagnostic products and disposable contact lenses. The firm owns more than 260 companies in virtually all countries of the world, and is headquartered in New Brunswick, New Jersey. In October 2020, Johnson & Johnson completed its acquisition of Momenta Pharmaceuticals, Inc., a company that discovers and develops novel therapies for immune-mediated diseases, for $6.5 billion. The firm developed a one-dose vaccine for COVID-19 which began administration in 2021.

FINANCIAL DATA: *Note: Data for latest year may not have been available at press time.*

In U.S. $	2020	2019	2018	2017	2016	2015
Revenue	82,584,000,000	82,059,000,000	81,581,000,000	76,450,000,000	71,890,000,000	70,074,000,000
R&D Expense	12,159,000,000	11,355,000,000	10,775,000,000	10,554,000,000	9,095,000,000	9,046,000,000
Operating Income	19,914,000,000	20,970,000,000	21,175,000,000	19,122,000,000	21,165,000,000	18,289,000,000
Operating Margin %		.24%	.25%	.24%	.29%	.26%
SGA Expense	22,084,000,000	22,178,000,000	22,540,000,000	21,420,000,000	19,945,000,000	21,203,000,000
Net Income	14,714,000,000	15,119,000,000	15,297,000,000	1,300,000,000	16,540,000,000	15,409,000,000
Operating Cash Flow	23,536,000,000	23,416,000,000	22,201,000,000	21,056,000,000	18,767,000,000	19,279,000,000
Capital Expenditure	3,347,000,000	3,498,000,000	3,670,000,000	3,279,000,000	3,226,000,000	3,463,000,000
EBITDA	23,929,000,000	24,655,000,000	25,933,000,000	24,249,000,000	24,283,000,000	23,494,000,000
Return on Assets %		.10%	.10%	.01%	.12%	.12%
Return on Equity %		.25%	.26%	.02%	.23%	.22%
Debt to Equity		0.445	0.463	0.51	0.319	0.181

CONTACT INFORMATION:

Phone: 732 524-0400   Fax: 732 214-0332
Toll-Free:
Address: 1 Johnson & Johnson Plaza, New Brunswick, NJ 08933 United States

STOCK TICKER/OTHER:

Stock Ticker: JNJ
Employees: 134,500
Parent Company:

Exchange: NYS
Fiscal Year Ends: 12/31

SALARIES/BONUSES:

Top Exec. Salary: $ Bonus: $
Second Exec. Salary: $ Bonus: $

OTHER THOUGHTS:

Estimated Female Officers or Directors: 4
Hot Spot for Advancement for Women/Minorities: Y

Sales, profits and employees may be estimates. Financial information, benefits and other data can change quickly and may vary from those stated here.

Kaiser Permanente

www.kaiserpermanente.org

NAIC Code: 622110

TYPES OF BUSINESS:

General Medical and Surgical Hospitals
Telemedicine
Outpatient Facilities
HMO
Medical School
Integrated Health Care System
Physician Networks
Clinical Record Management

BRANDS/DIVISIONS/AFFILIATES:

Kaiser Foundation Health Plan Inc
Kaiser Foundation Hospitals
Permanente Medical Groups
Kaiser Permanente Center for Health Research
KP HealthConnect
Kaiser Permanente Bernard J Tyson School of Med

CONTACTS: *Note: Officers with more than one job title may be intentionally listed here more than once.*

Gregory A. Adams, CEO
Janet A. Liang, COO
Kathy Lancaster, CFO
Catherine Hernandez, CCO
Christian Meisner, Sr. VP-Chief Human Resources Officer
Raymond J. Baxter, Sr. VP-Community Benefit, Research & Health Policy
Diane Comer, Interim CIO
Mark S. Zemelman, General Counsel
Arthur M. Southam, Exec. VP-Health Plan Oper.
Chris Grant, Sr. VP-Corp. Dev. & Care Delivery Strategy
Diane Gage Lofgren, Sr. VP
Cynthia Powers Overmyer, Sr. VP-Internal Audit Svcs.
Daniel P. Garcia, Chief Compliance Officer
Anthony Barrueta, Sr. VP-Gov't Rel.
Amy Compton-Phillips, Associate Exec. Dir.-Quality, Permanente
Gregory A. Adams, Chmn.

GROWTH PLANS/SPECIAL FEATURES:

Kaiser Permanente is a nonprofit company dedicated to providing integrated health care coverage. The firm operates in California, Colorado, Georgia, Hawaii, Maryland, Washington D.C., Oregon, Virginia and Washington. It serves 12.4 million members, most of which are in California. Kaiser has three main operating divisions: Kaiser Foundation Health Plan, Inc., which contracts with individuals and groups to provide medical coverage; Kaiser Foundation Hospitals and their subsidiaries, operating community hospitals and outpatient facilities in several states; and Permanente Medical Groups, the company's network of physicians providing healthcare to its members. As of mid-2020, the company's assets consist of 39 medical centers, including hospitals and outpatient facilities; 715 medical offices; and more than 23,270 physicians. Kaiser Permanente is one of the largest health plans serving the Medicare program. Kaiser Foundation Hospitals also fund medical- and health-related research. The Kaiser Permanente Center for Health Research, founded in 1964, is a single research center that spans two regions of Kaiser Permanente: Northwest and Hawaii. The center pursues a vigorous agenda of public health research within large, diverse populations, and specializes in the disciplines of biostatistics, clinical research support services, data resources, evidence-based practices and qualitative research. In addition, the company's KP HealthConnect platform integrates clinical records with appointments, registration and billing, thereby significantly improving care delivery and patient satisfaction. In mid-2020, Kaiser inaugurated its first class of medical students at the new Kaiser Permanente Bernard J. Tyson School of Medicine, located in Pasadena, California. The school will offer conventional medical education as well as ground-breaking integrated health care to prepare future physicians to become collaborative and transformative in the health care sector.

Kaiser offers its employees comprehensive health benefits, retirement options, life and disability insurance and a variety of employee assistance plans and programs.

FINANCIAL DATA: *Note: Data for latest year may not have been available at press time.*

In U.S. $	2020	2019	2018	2017	2016	2015
Revenue	88,700,000,000	84,500,000,000	79,700,000,000	72,700,000,000	64,600,000,000	60,700,000,000
R&D Expense						
Operating Income						
Operating Margin %						
SGA Expense						
Net Income	6,400,000,000	7,400,000,000	2,500,000,000	3,800,000,000	3,100,000,000	1,900,000,000
Operating Cash Flow						
Capital Expenditure						
EBITDA						
Return on Assets %						
Return on Equity %						
Debt to Equity						

CONTACT INFORMATION:

Phone: 510-271-5910 Fax:
Toll-Free:
Address: 1 Kaiser Plaza, 19/Fl, Oakland, CA 94612 United States

STOCK TICKER/OTHER:

Stock Ticker: Nonprofit
Employees: 217,000
Parent Company:

Exchange:
Fiscal Year Ends: 12/31

SALARIES/BONUSES:

Top Exec. Salary: $ Bonus: $
Second Exec. Salary: $ Bonus: $

OTHER THOUGHTS:

Estimated Female Officers or Directors: 9
Hot Spot for Advancement for Women/Minorities: Y

Sales, profits and employees may be estimates. Financial information, benefits and other data can change quickly and may vary from those stated here.

Kaleido Biosciences Inc

kaleido.com

NAIC Code: 325414

TYPES OF BUSINESS:

Biological Product (except Diagnostic) Manufacturing

BRANDS/DIVISIONS/AFFILIATES:

Cadena Bio Inc
Kaleido Biosciences Securities Corporation

CONTACTS: *Note: Officers with more than one job title may be intentionally listed here more than once.*

Alison Lawton, CEO
Joshua Brumm, COO
Stephen Sofen, Sr. VP-IT

GROWTH PLANS/SPECIAL FEATURES:

Kaleido Biosciences, Inc. is a clinical-stage healthcare company with a chemistry-driven approach to leveraging the microbiome organ to treat disease and improve human health. This approach focuses on developing novel microbiome metabolic therapies (MMTs) to drive functional outputs of the microbiome organ. Kaleido Biosciences has built a human-centric proprietary product platform for discovery and development to enable the rapid advancement of a broad portfolio of novel product candidates/MMTs. This approach has the potential to be faster and more cost-efficient than traditional discovery and development. Using its product platform, the company has created a library of more than 1,500 MMT candidates, all designed to modulate the metabolic output and profile of the microbiome by driving the function and distribution of the organ's existing microbes. Kaleido Biosciences' MMTs are orally administered, selectively metabolized in the gut and have limited systemic exposure. They are also related to a class generally recognized as safe. The firm's pipeline of MMT candidates span a variety of diseases and conditions with significant unmet need, including programs that have advanced into non-investigational new drug human clinical studies. These programs target urea cycle disorders, hepatic encephalopathy, COVID-19, inflammatory bowel disease and infections caused by multi-drug resistant bacteria, among others. Wholly-owned subsidiaries of the firm include Cadena Bio, Inc. and Kaleido Biosciences Securities Corporation. In September 2020, Kaleido announced that its first patient had been dosed in its clinical study evaluating MMT candidate KB295 for the treatment of mild-to-moderate ulcerative colitis.

FINANCIAL DATA: *Note: Data for latest year may not have been available at press time.*

In U.S. $	2020	2019	2018	2017	2016	2015
Revenue	975,000					
R&D Expense	55,967,000	64,232,000	42,062,000	20,992,000	7,863,000	
Operating Income	-78,874,000	-86,660,000	-60,683,000	-27,030,000	-9,436,000	
Operating Margin %						
SGA Expense	23,882,000	22,428,000	18,621,000	6,038,000	1,573,000	
Net Income	-81,620,000	-86,331,000	-61,744,000	-27,559,000	-9,685,000	
Operating Cash Flow	-61,518,000	-75,796,000	-46,316,000	-22,495,000	-9,350,000	
Capital Expenditure	4,024,000	3,586,000	3,002,000	1,406,000	195,000	
EBITDA	-76,995,000	-84,036,000	-59,947,000	-26,808,000	-9,445,000	
Return on Assets %		-1.03%	-1.05%	-1.54%	-1.94%	
Return on Equity %		-1.61%	-8.38%			
Debt to Equity		0.417	0.255			

CONTACT INFORMATION:

Phone: 617-674-9000   Fax:
Toll-Free:
Address: 65 Hayden Ave., Lexington, MA 02421 United States

STOCK TICKER/OTHER:

Stock Ticker: KLDO   Exchange: NAS
Employees: 82   Fiscal Year Ends: 12/31
Parent Company:

SALARIES/BONUSES:

Top Exec. Salary: $ Bonus: $
Second Exec. Salary: $ Bonus: $

OTHER THOUGHTS:

Estimated Female Officers or Directors:
Hot Spot for Advancement for Women/Minorities:

Karuna Therapeutics Inc

www.karunatx.com

NAIC Code: 325412

TYPES OF BUSINESS:
Pharmaceutical Preparation Manufacturing

BRANDS/DIVISIONS/AFFILIATES:
KarXT

CONTACTS: *Note: Officers with more than one job title may be intentionally listed here more than once.*
Steve Paul, CEO
Andrew Miller, COO
Troy A. Ignelzi, CFO
Steve Paul, Chmn.

GROWTH PLANS/SPECIAL FEATURES:
Karuna Therapeutics, Inc. is engaged in developing novel therapies to address disabling neuropsychiatric conditions characterized by significant unmet medical need. These conditions include schizophrenia, Alzheimer's disease and pain. KarXT is the company's lead product candidate and relies on a novel mechanism of action supported by four clinical trials. KarXT combines: xanomeline, a muscarinic receptor agonist that preferentially stimulates M1 and M4 muscarinic receptors; and trospium, an approved muscarinic receptor antagonist that does not measurably cross the blood-brain barrier, confining its effects to peripheral tissues. Therefore, KarXT stands for Karuna, Xanomeline and Trospium. The four trials utilizing KarXT include: a completed (2020) Phase 2 trial for the treatment of psychosis in people suffering with schizophrenia; a Phase 2 trial for adjunctive treatment of psychosis; a Phase 1 trial for the treatment of negative and cognitive symptoms regarding schizophrenia; and a Phase 1 trial for the treatment of psychosis in patients with dementia-related diseases. A Phase 1b initiation was occurring during 2020, utilizing KarXT as a muscarinic-targeted drug candidate. In mid-2020, Karuna announced a multi-year drug discovery and development agreement with PGI Drug Discovery, LLC, to identify potential novel drug candidates for the treatment of severe neuropsychiatric disorders. Karuna also announced positive outcome of end-of-Phase 2 meeting with the U.S. Food and Drug Administration for KarXT for the treatment of acute psychosis in patients with schizophrenia.

FINANCIAL DATA: *Note: Data for latest year may not have been available at press time.*

In U.S. $	2020	2019	2018	2017	2016	2015
Revenue						
R&D Expense	43,408,000	24,536,000	11,536,000	3,616,000		
Operating Income	-71,816,000	-45,405,000	-14,510,000	-4,806,000		
Operating Margin %						
SGA Expense	28,408,000	20,869,000	2,974,000	1,190,000		
Net Income	-68,554,000	-43,957,000	-17,512,000	-6,032,000		
Operating Cash Flow	-69,856,000	-30,923,000	-15,377,000	-4,027,000		
Capital Expenditure	419,000	115,000	132,000	13,000		
EBITDA	-68,366,000	-42,954,000	-14,923,000	-4,860,000		
Return on Assets %		-.18%	-.37%	-2.83%		
Return on Equity %		-.18%	-.45%			
Debt to Equity		0.00	0.001			

CONTACT INFORMATION:
Phone: 857 449-2244   Fax:
Toll-Free:
Address: 33 Arch St., Ste. 3110, Boston, MA 2110 United States

STOCK TICKER/OTHER:
Stock Ticker: KRTX
Employees: 63
Parent Company:

Exchange: NAS
Fiscal Year Ends: 12/31

SALARIES/BONUSES:
Top Exec. Salary: $ Bonus: $
Second Exec. Salary: $ Bonus: $

OTHER THOUGHTS:
Estimated Female Officers or Directors:
Hot Spot for Advancement for Women/Minorities:

Sales, profits and employees may be estimates. Financial information, benefits and other data can change quickly and may vary from those stated here.

Keystone Dental Inc

www.keystonedental.com

NAIC Code: 339100

TYPES OF BUSINESS:

Dental Device Manufacturing

BRANDS/DIVISIONS/AFFILIATES:

Paltop Advanced Dental Solutions

CONTACTS: *Note: Officers with more than one job title may be intentionally listed here more than once.*

Russ Bonafede, CEO
Michael Kehoe, Pres.

GROWTH PLANS/SPECIAL FEATURES:

Keystone Dental, Inc. is a developer and manufacturer of dental devices. The company delivers advanced, easy-to-use implants, biomaterials and planning software for dental professionals focused on providing functional and aesthetically-pleasing outcomes for patients. Products and solutions are offered through Keystone Dental and subsidiary Paltop Advanced Dental Solutions. Products fall within five categories: implant solutions, prosthetic solutions, regenerative solutions, surgical units and digital solutions. Implant solutions include the Genesis, TILOBEMAXX, Prima Plus and PrimaConnex implant systems, which mimic the hues and surface topography of biological gum and teeth properties and integrates with the natural bone. Prosthetic solutions include healing abutments, cover screws, impression components, temporary abutments, final abutments and computer aided design/computer aided manufacturing (CAD/CAM) instruments and accessories. Regenerative solutions include bone substitutes, membranes, sutures and related dressings, with brands including Accell Connexus, Dyna, OCS-B, MBCP, Cytoplast and Glycolon. Surgical units include W&H surgical motors and magnetic surgical mallets. Digital solutions include guided surgery software and systems, CAD/CAM, angulation corrective systems, digital libraries and digital learning/instruction. Education and training are offered online, including free classes, with most averaging about an hour in length and range across multiple disciplines, including immediates, esthetics, arches, digital, tissue management and laboratory.

FINANCIAL DATA: *Note: Data for latest year may not have been available at press time.*

In U.S. $	2020	2019	2018	2017	2016	2015
Revenue	32,725,000	42,500,000	42,000,000	40,000,000		
R&D Expense						
Operating Income						
Operating Margin %						
SGA Expense						
Net Income						
Operating Cash Flow						
Capital Expenditure						
EBITDA						
Return on Assets %						
Return on Equity %						
Debt to Equity						

CONTACT INFORMATION:

Phone: 781-328-3300   Fax: 781-328-3400
Toll-Free: 866-902-9272
Address: 154 Middlesex Turnpike, Burlington, MA 01803 United States

STOCK TICKER/OTHER:

Stock Ticker: Private   Exchange:
Employees: Fiscal Year Ends: 12/31
Parent Company: Accelmed Partners

SALARIES/BONUSES:

Top Exec. Salary: $ Bonus: $
Second Exec. Salary: $ Bonus: $

OTHER THOUGHTS:

Estimated Female Officers or Directors: 1
Hot Spot for Advancement for Women/Minorities:

Kindred at Home

www.kindredhealthcare.com/our-services/home-care/about/affiliates/gentiva

NAIC Code: 621610

TYPES OF BUSINESS:

Home Health Care Services
Administrative Services

BRANDS/DIVISIONS/AFFILIATES:

Humana Inc
TPG Capital
Welsh Carson Anderson & Stowe
Asian American Home Health
Emerald Coast Hospice
Gentiva
Girling Community Care
Hospice of Charleston

CONTACTS: *Note: Officers with more than one job title may be intentionally listed here more than once.*

David Causby, CEO
Tom Dolan, CFO
Dean Johnson, Chief Communications Officer
Mark Reid, Chief Human Resources Officer
Craig Klopatek, CIO
John Camperlengo, General Counsel
Charlotte Weaver, Other Executive Officer
Jeff Shaner, President, Divisional
R. Hicks, Vice Chairman of the Board

GROWTH PLANS/SPECIAL FEATURES:

Kindred at Home provides in-home skilled nursing, hospice and rehabilitation therapy services. It is one of the largest home care companies in the U.S. The firm's care focuses on helping patients manage a chronic condition or recover from acute illness, surgery, accident or a change in medical condition. Kindred at Home's services are delivered according to a plan of treatment developed by patients, their family members, physicians and the company's home health staff to maximize independent functioning and reduce re-hospitalizations. In-home care includes disease management, medication management, medication teaching and administration, illness assessment and instruction, post-surgical management, bathing and personal care assistance, assessments at each visit, blood pressure measurement, as well as measurement of pulse, respirations, lung sounds, blood glucose and/or pulse oximetry (as ordered by the patient's doctor). Other types of care include personal home care assistance, community care, cardiac care, dementia and Alzheimer's care, fall prevention, hospice, low vision care, orthopedic care, palliative care, pulmonary care, senior wellness programs and skilled nursing. Through its affiliates, there are nearly 700 office locations in 41 U.S. states, with affiliates including Asian American Home Health, Emerald Coast Hospice, Gentiva, Girling Community Care, Hospice of Charleston, The Home Option, Wake Forest Baptist Health Care and Victorian Home Care. Kindred at Home is 40%-owned by Humana, Inc., with the remaining 60% owned by TPG Capital and Welsh, Carson, Anderson & Stowe. Humana has certain rights to acquire the balance of the shares over the long-term.

FINANCIAL DATA: *Note: Data for latest year may not have been available at press time.*

In U.S. $	2020	2019	2018	2017	2016	2015
Revenue	2,552,100,000	2,715,000,000	2,587,000,000	2,565,800,000	2,499,425,000	2,235,027,000
R&D Expense						
Operating Income						
Operating Margin %						
SGA Expense						
Net Income		28,100,000	27,000,000			
Operating Cash Flow						
Capital Expenditure						
EBITDA						
Return on Assets %						
Return on Equity %						
Debt to Equity						

CONTACT INFORMATION:

Phone: 770-951-6450   Fax:
Toll-Free:
Address: 3350 Riverwood Pkwy., Ste. 1400, Atlanta, GA 30339 United States

STOCK TICKER/OTHER:

Stock Ticker: Subsidiary
Employees: 17,200
Parent Company: Humana Inc

Exchange:
Fiscal Year Ends: 12/31

SALARIES/BONUSES:

Top Exec. Salary: $ Bonus: $
Second Exec. Salary: $ Bonus: $

OTHER THOUGHTS:

Estimated Female Officers or Directors: 1
Hot Spot for Advancement for Women/Minorities:

Sales, profits and employees may be estimates. Financial information, benefits and other data can change quickly and may vary from those stated here.

Kindred Healthcare LLC

www.kindredhealthcare.com

NAIC Code: 623110

TYPES OF BUSINESS:

Nursing Care Facilities
Nursing Centers
Contract Rehabilitation Services

BRANDS/DIVISIONS/AFFILIATES:

Humana Inc
TPG Capital
Welsh Carson Anderson & Stowe
WellBridge Greater Dallas
WellBridge Fort Worth

GROWTH PLANS/SPECIAL FEATURES:

Kindred Healthcare, LLC is a healthcare services company based in Louisville, Kentucky. Through its subsidiaries, the firm provides healthcare services at more than 1,730 locations across 46 U.S. states. These locations include 64 long-term acute-care hospitals, 22 inpatient rehabilitation hospitals, 10 sub-acute units, 94 inpatient rehabilitation units (hospital-based) and contract rehabilitation service businesses that serve more than 1,540 non-affiliated sites of service. Kindred Healthcare is 40%-owned by Humana, Inc., and the remaining 60% is held by TPG Capital and Welsh, Carson, Anderson & Stowe (WCAS). In mid-2020, Kindred Healthcare acquired WellBridge Greater Dallas and WellBridge Fort Worth behavioral health hospitals. That September, Kindred Healthcare and Community Health Network announced a joint venture to build and operate their third inpatient rehabilitation hospital in the Indianapolis, Indiana metro area.

CONTACTS: *Note: Officers with more than one job title may be intentionally listed here more than once.*

Benjamin A. Breier, CEO
Stephen Cunanan, Chief Administrative Officer
Phyllis Yale, Director
William Altman, Executive VP
David Causby, Executive VP
Joseph Landenwich, General Counsel
Pete Kalmey, President, Divisional
Jason Zachariah, President, Divisional
Benjamin Breier, President
John Lucchese, Senior VP
Paul Diaz, Vice Chairman of the Board

FINANCIAL DATA: *Note: Data for latest year may not have been available at press time.*

In U.S. $	2020	2019	2018	2017	2016	2015
Revenue	6,186,936,910	6,652,620,334	6,335,828,890	6,034,122,752	6,292,529,000	6,119,218,000
R&D Expense						
Operating Income						
Operating Margin %						
SGA Expense						
Net Income		-657,079,396	-677,401,440	-698,352,000	-664,230,016	-93,384,000
Operating Cash Flow						
Capital Expenditure						
EBITDA						
Return on Assets %						
Return on Equity %						
Debt to Equity						

CONTACT INFORMATION:

Phone: 502 596-7300   Fax: 502 596-4170
Toll-Free: 800-545-0749
Address: 680 S. Fourth St., Louisville, KY 40202 United States

STOCK TICKER/OTHER:

Stock Ticker: Joint Venture   Exchange:
Employees: 31,800   Fiscal Year Ends: 12/31
Parent Company: Humana Inc

SALARIES/BONUSES:

Top Exec. Salary: $ Bonus: $
Second Exec. Salary: $ Bonus: $

OTHER THOUGHTS:

Estimated Female Officers or Directors: 4
Hot Spot for Advancement for Women/Minorities: Y

KPC Healthcare Inc

kpchealth.com

NAIC Code: 622110

TYPES OF BUSINESS:

General Medical and Surgical Hospitals

BRANDS/DIVISIONS/AFFILIATES:

Anaheim Global Medical Center
Chapman Global Medical Center
Hemet Valley Medical Center
Menifee Valley Medical Center
Orange County Global Medical Center
South Coast Global Medical Center
Victor Valley Global Medical Center

CONTACTS: *Note: Officers with more than one job title may be intentionally listed here more than once.*

Peter Baronoff, CEO
Kenneth K. Westbrook, Pres.
Jeremiah R. Kanaly, Chief Acct. Officer

GROWTH PLANS/SPECIAL FEATURES:

KPC Healthcare, Inc. operates as KPC Health and is engaged in healthcare, pharmaceuticals, education, engineering and real estate, with more than $10 billion in assets. These assets include hospitals, clinics, schools, commercial real estate properties and agricultural research centers. KPC's healthcare division comprises a group of integrated healthcare delivery systems made up of acute care hospitals, independent physicians associations (IPAs), medical groups, urgent care facilities and multi-specialty facilities throughout the western portion of the U.S. California facilities include: Anaheim Global Medical Center, Chapman Global Medical Center, Hemet Valley Medical Center, Menifee Valley Medical Center, Orange County Global Medical Center, South Coast Global Medical Center and Victor Valley Global Medical Center. These facilities collectively serve some of California's most densely populated areas in the southern region, totaling approximately 10 million people.

FINANCIAL DATA: *Note: Data for latest year may not have been available at press time.*

In U.S. $	2020	2019	2018	2017	2016	2015
Revenue	356,107,500	374,850,000	357,000,000	340,000,000		
R&D Expense						
Operating Income						
Operating Margin %						
SGA Expense						
Net Income						
Operating Cash Flow						
Capital Expenditure						
EBITDA						
Return on Assets %						
Return on Equity %						
Debt to Equity						

CONTACT INFORMATION:

Phone: 714 953-3652   Fax:
Toll-Free:
Address: 1301 N. Tustin Ave., Santa Ana, CA 92705 United States

STOCK TICKER/OTHER:

Stock Ticker: Private
Employees: 5,000
Parent Company:

Exchange:
Fiscal Year Ends: 03/31

SALARIES/BONUSES:

Top Exec. Salary: $ Bonus: $
Second Exec. Salary: $ Bonus: $

OTHER THOUGHTS:

Estimated Female Officers or Directors:
Hot Spot for Advancement for Women/Minorities:

Laboratory Corporation of America Holdings   www.labcorp.com

NAIC Code: 621511

TYPES OF BUSINESS:

Clinical Laboratory Testing
Diagnostics
Urinalyses
Blood Cell Counts
Blood Chemistry Analysis
HIV Tests
Genetic Testing
Specialty & Niche Tests

BRANDS/DIVISIONS/AFFILIATES:

LabCorp
LabCorp Diagnositcs
Covance Drug Development

CONTACTS: *Note: Officers with more than one job title may be intentionally listed here more than once.*

John Ratliff, CEO, Divisional
David King, CEO
Glenn Eisenberg, CFO
Peter Wilkinson, Chief Accounting Officer
Sandra van der Vaart, Chief Compliance Officer
Lance Berberian, Chief Information Officer
Brian Caveney, Chief Medical Officer
Lisa Uthgenannt, Other Executive Officer

GROWTH PLANS/SPECIAL FEATURES:

Laboratory Corporation of America Holdings (LabCorp) is a global life sciences company deeply integrated in guiding patient care. LabCorp provides comprehensive clinical laboratory and end-to-end drug development services through LabCorp Diagnostics (LCD) and Covance Drug Development (CDD). The company provides diagnostic, drug development and technology-enabled solutions for more than 120 million patient encounters each year. The firm typically processes tests on more than 2.5 million patient specimens per week and supports clinical trial activity in about 100 countries through its central laboratory and preclinical development businesses. LCD is an independent clinical laboratory business, offering a comprehensive array of testing through an integrated network of primary and specialty laboratories across the U.S. This network is supported by an IT system, with more than 65,000 electronic interfaces to deliver test results, nimble and efficient logistics and local labs offering rapid response testing. LCD's online LabCorp patient portal and mobile app offer access to new and historical test results, information about tests and an option to receive information about clinical trials. CDD provides end-to-end drug development, medical devices and diagnostic development solutions from early-stage research to clinical development and commercial market access. CDD collaborated on 85% of the novel drugs approved by the U.S. Food and Drug Administration (FDA) in 2019, including 100% of the novel oncology drugs and 86% of the rare and orphan disease drugs. In addition, CDD has been involved in the development of all the current top 50 drugs on the market as measured by sales revenue. In March 2020, LabCorp received emergency use authorization from the FDA for a test for COVID-19 to help mitigate the pandemic. That September, LabCorp acquired Franciscan Missionaries of Our Lady Health System's clinical ambulatory business and select assets, and will provide reference testing for all FMOHS facilities and clinics.

FINANCIAL DATA: *Note: Data for latest year may not have been available at press time.*

In U.S. $	2020	2019	2018	2017	2016	2015
Revenue	13,978,500,000	11,554,800,000	11,333,400,000	10,441,400,000	9,641,800,000	8,680,100,000
R&D Expense						
Operating Income	2,948,100,000	1,384,800,000	1,373,800,000	1,435,100,000	1,370,800,000	1,116,800,000
Operating Margin %		.12%	.12%	.14%	.14%	.13%
SGA Expense	1,729,300,000	1,624,500,000	1,570,900,000	1,812,400,000	1,630,200,000	1,622,000,000
Net Income	1,556,100,000	823,800,000	883,700,000	1,268,200,000	732,100,000	436,900,000
Operating Cash Flow	2,135,300,000	1,444,700,000	1,305,400,000	1,459,400,000	1,175,900,000	982,400,000
Capital Expenditure	381,700,000	400,200,000	379,800,000	315,400,000	278,900,000	255,800,000
EBITDA	3,051,200,000	1,922,800,000	2,064,600,000	1,903,200,000	1,823,800,000	1,464,800,000
Return on Assets %		.05%	.05%	.08%	.05%	.04%
Return on Equity %		.11%	.13%	.21%	.14%	.11%
Debt to Equity		0.856	0.867	0.929	0.963	1.212

CONTACT INFORMATION:

Phone: 336 229-1127   Fax: 336 229-7717
Toll-Free:
Address: 358 S. Main St., Burlington, NC 27215 United States

STOCK TICKER/OTHER:

Stock Ticker: LH   Exchange: NYS
Employees: 65,000   Fiscal Year Ends: 12/31
Parent Company:

SALARIES/BONUSES:

Top Exec. Salary: $ Bonus: $
Second Exec. Salary: $ Bonus: $

OTHER THOUGHTS:

Estimated Female Officers or Directors: 3
Hot Spot for Advancement for Women/Minorities: Y

Lakeland Industries Inc

www.lakeland.com

NAIC Code: 339100

TYPES OF BUSINESS:

Safety Clothing
Reusable Industrial & Medical Apparel
Chemical Protection Clothing
Specialty Safety Gloves
Heat Resistant Clothing
Disposable Protective Garments

BRANDS/DIVISIONS/AFFILIATES:

Nomex
Kevlar

CONTACTS: *Note: Officers with more than one job title may be intentionally listed here more than once.*

Christopher Ryan, CEO
Alfred Kreft, Chairman of the Board
Charles Roberson, COO
Daniel Edwards, Senior VP, Divisional

GROWTH PLANS/SPECIAL FEATURES:

Lakeland Industries, Inc. manufactures and sells a comprehensive line of safety garments and accessories for industrial safety and protective clothing industries. The firm's products are sold through a network of over 1,600 global safety and industrial supply distributors, and sold in more than 50 countries internationally. The company's major product areas include disposable and limited-use protective clothing, chemical protective suits, fire-fighting and heat protective apparel, gloves and arm guards for the food service market, reusable woven garments and high visibility clothing for traffic and public safety officials. The firm's disposable and reusable garments protect the wearer from contaminants or irritants, such as chemicals, pesticides, fertilizers, paint, grease and dust; from viruses and bacteria; and from limited exposure to hazardous waste and toxic chemicals, including acids, asbestos, lead and hydro-carbons. Lakeland's products are also used to prevent human contamination of manufacturing processes in clean-room environments. Disposable clothing products include coveralls, lab coats, hoods, aprons, sleeves and smocks. Lakeland's heat protective gear is used by firefighters as well as for maintenance of extreme high-temperature industrial equipment and for crash and rescue operations. The company's high-end chemical protective suits protect wearers from highly concentrated and powerful chemical and biological toxins such as toxic wastes at Super fund sites, accidental toxic chemical spills or biological discharges, the handling of chemical or biological warfare weapons and the cleaning and maintenance of chemical, petrochemical and nuclear facilities. Lakeland buys most of its raw materials for manufacturing from DuPont, including those required for the Nomex and Kevlar brands.

FINANCIAL DATA: *Note: Data for latest year may not have been available at press time.*

In U.S. $	2020	2019	2018	2017	2016	2015
Revenue	107,809,000	99,011,000	95,987,000	86,183,000	99,646,000	
R&D Expense						
Operating Income	5,876,000	3,565,000	8,477,000	6,847,000	11,812,000	
Operating Margin %	.05%	.04%	.09%	.08%	.12%	
SGA Expense						
Net Income	3,281,000	1,459,000	440,000	3,893,000	3,854,000	
Operating Cash Flow	3,590,000	1,785,000	648,000	11,493,000	-518,000	
Capital Expenditure	1,033,000	3,103,000	905,000	413,000	840,000	
EBITDA	7,514,000	4,571,000	9,281,000	8,087,000	12,678,000	
Return on Assets %	.03%	.02%	.00%	.05%	.04%	
Return on Equity %	.04%	.02%	.01%	.06%	.06%	
Debt to Equity	0.017	0.014	0.016	0.01	0.01	

CONTACT INFORMATION:

Phone: 256-350-3873   Fax:
Toll-Free: 800-645-9291
Address: 202 Pride Ln. SW, Decatur, AL 35603 United States

STOCK TICKER/OTHER:

Stock Ticker: LAKE
Employees: 2,000
Parent Company:

Exchange: NAS
Fiscal Year Ends: 01/31

SALARIES/BONUSES:

Top Exec. Salary: $ Bonus: $
Second Exec. Salary: $ Bonus: $

OTHER THOUGHTS:

Estimated Female Officers or Directors:
Hot Spot for Advancement for Women/Minorities:

Sales, profits and employees may be estimates. Financial information, benefits and other data can change quickly and may vary from those stated here.

LCA-Vision Inc

NAIC Code: 621493

www.lasikplus.com

TYPES OF BUSINESS:

Services-Laser Vision Correction Surgery Centers
PRK (photo-refractive keratectomy)
LASIK (Laser-In-Situ Keratomileusis)

BRANDS/DIVISIONS/AFFILIATES:

Vision Acquisitions LLC
LasikPlus

CONTACTS: *Note: Officers with more than one job title may be intentionally listed here more than once.*

Michael J. Celebrezze, CEO
Amy F. Kappen, CFO
Rhonda S. Sebastian, Sr. VP-Human Resources
Bharat Kakar, Sr. VP-Oper. & Mktg.

GROWTH PLANS/SPECIAL FEATURES:

LCA-Vision, Inc. is a provider of fixed-site laser vision correction services at its LasikPlus vision centers. The company's vision centers help correct nearsightedness, farsightedness and astigmatism. Treatments are done by using one of two methods, PRK (photo-refractive keratectomy) and LASIK (laser-in-situ keratomileusis). PRK removes the thin layer of cell covering the outer surface of the cornea (the epithelium) and treats it with excimer laser pulses. LASIK reshapes the cornea with an excimer laser by cutting a flap in the top of the cornea to expose the inner cornea. The corneal flap is then treated with excimer laser pulses according to the patient's prescription. The LASIK procedure now accounts for virtually all of the procedures performed by LCA, as recovery time is significantly shorter and patient discomfort is negligible. The company operates more than 55 LasikPlus vision correction centers in the U.S., including full-service LasikPlus fixed site laser vision correction centers as well as pre- and post-operative LasikPlus satellite centers. LCA-Vision is owned by Vision Acquisitions, LLC.

FINANCIAL DATA: *Note: Data for latest year may not have been available at press time.*

In U.S. $	2020	2019	2018	2017	2016	2015
Revenue	87,269,379	102,069,450	97,209,000	92,580,000	92,500,000	92,000,000
R&D Expense						
Operating Income						
Operating Margin %						
SGA Expense						
Net Income						
Operating Cash Flow						
Capital Expenditure						
EBITDA						
Return on Assets %						
Return on Equity %						
Debt to Equity						

CONTACT INFORMATION:

Phone: 513 792-9292   Fax: 513 792-5620
Toll-Free: 800-688-4550
Address: 7840 Montgomery Rd., Cincinnati, OH 45236 United States

STOCK TICKER/OTHER:

Stock Ticker: Subsidiary   Exchange:
Employees: 380   Fiscal Year Ends: 12/31
Parent Company: Vision Acquisitions LLC

SALARIES/BONUSES:

Top Exec. Salary: $ Bonus: $
Second Exec. Salary: $ Bonus: $

OTHER THOUGHTS:

Estimated Female Officers or Directors: 2
Hot Spot for Advancement for Women/Minorities:

LHC Group Inc

www.lhcgroup.com

NAIC Code: 621610

TYPES OF BUSINESS:

Home Health Care Services
Hospices
Long-Term Acute Care Hospitals

BRANDS/DIVISIONS/AFFILIATES:

Mederi Caretenders
Mederi Private Care

GROWTH PLANS/SPECIAL FEATURES:

LHC Group, Inc. is a national provider of high-quality, affordable in-home healthcare services and innovations. The firm's services cover a wide range of healthcare needs for patients and families dealing with illness, injury or chronic conditions. LHC delivers home health, hospice, home- and community-based services, and facility-based care in 35 U.S. states and the District of Columbia, reaching 60% of the U.S. population aged 65 and older. In August 2020, LHC Group announced a joint venture with Orlando Health System in Orlando, Florida, which will include six locations: three current Orlando Health providers and three current LHC Group providers in Orlando, Clermont, Kissimmee and Altamonte Springs. They home health providers will operate under the name Mederi Caretenders, and the home and community based services location will operate under the name Mederi Private Care.

CONTACTS: *Note: Officers with more than one job title may be intentionally listed here more than once.*

Keith Myers, CEO
Joshua Proffitt, CFO
Collin McQuiddy, Chief Accounting Officer
Bruce Greenstein, Chief Strategy Officer
Donald Stelly, COO
Nicholas Gachassin, Executive VP

FINANCIAL DATA: *Note: Data for latest year may not have been available at press time.*

In U.S. $	2020	2019	2018	2017	2016	2015
Revenue	2,063,204,000	2,080,241,000	1,809,963,000	1,072,086,000	914,823,000	816,366,000
R&D Expense						
Operating Income	179,954,000	159,348,000	115,690,000	76,253,000	71,761,000	67,616,000
Operating Margin %		.08%	.06%	.07%	.08%	.08%
SGA Expense	632,847,000	596,006,000	537,916,000	310,539,000	270,022,000	240,629,000
Net Income	111,596,000	95,726,000	63,574,000	50,112,000	36,583,000	32,335,000
Operating Cash Flow	529,247,000	130,462,000	108,585,000	32,326,000	67,472,000	59,934,000
Capital Expenditure	65,875,000	33,609,000	32,993,000	74,774,000	39,165,000	83,855,000
EBITDA	233,900,000	203,236,000	127,363,000	88,628,000	83,214,000	78,755,000
Return on Assets %		.05%	.05%	.07%	.06%	.06%
Return on Equity %		.07%	.07%	.12%	.10%	.10%
Debt to Equity		0.228	0.179	0.321	0.222	0.278

CONTACT INFORMATION:

Phone: 337 233-1307   Fax: 337 235-8037
Toll-Free:
Address: 901 Hugh Wallis Rd. S., Lafayette, LA 70508 United States

STOCK TICKER/OTHER:

Stock Ticker: LHCG
Employees: 27,959
Parent Company:

Exchange: NAS
Fiscal Year Ends: 12/31

SALARIES/BONUSES:

Top Exec. Salary: $ Bonus: $
Second Exec. Salary: $ Bonus: $

OTHER THOUGHTS:

Estimated Female Officers or Directors: 6
Hot Spot for Advancement for Women/Minorities: Y

Sales, profits and employees may be estimates. Financial information, benefits and other data can change quickly and may vary from those stated here.

Life Healthcare Group Holdings Ltd

www.lifehealthcare.co.za

NAIC Code: 622110

TYPES OF BUSINESS:

Hospitals & Clinics
Higher Education

BRANDS/DIVISIONS/AFFILIATES:

Life Employee Health Solutions
Life Esidimeni
Life College of Learning
Alliance Medical
Scanmed SA
Life Occupantional Health
Careways

CONTACTS: *Note: Officers with more than one job title may be intentionally listed here more than once.*

Peter Wharton-Hood, CEO
Pieter van der Westhuizen, CFO

GROWTH PLANS/SPECIAL FEATURES:

Life Healthcare Group Holdings Ltd. is a leading private health care services provider and hospital operator in South Africa. The company operates in three divisions: hospital, out-of-hospital services and international business. In addition to its 66 hospital facilities, most of which comprise emergency units, the hospital division oversees specialized units for physical rehabilitation, mental health treatment, renal dialysis, maternity, cardiac treatment and radiotherapy. The out-of-hospital services division consists of three units: Life Employee Health Solutions, which provides contracted occupational, primary and other healthcare services to employer groups in commerce, industry, mining and parastatals via Life Occupational Health, and provides outcomes-based employee wellness programs via Careways; Life Esidimeni, a wholly-owned subsidiary with 10 healthcare facilities and 2,942 beds, two of which are non-governmental organizations in partnership with the Department of Social Development; and Life College of Learning, which comprises seven learning centers across South Africa where students are trained in nursing and healthcare sciences. Last, the international business division comprises two units: Alliance Medical, one of Western Europe's leading providers of complex molecular and diagnostic imaging services across the U.K., Italy and Ireland, with participation in 10 European markets; and Scanmed SA, which provides primary care, ambulatory care and acute care services in Poland.

FINANCIAL DATA: *Note: Data for latest year may not have been available at press time.*

In U.S. $	2020	2019	2018	2017	2016	2015
Revenue	1,845,284,000	1,866,073,000	1,707,320,000	1,511,714,000	1,192,391,000	1,064,676,000
R&D Expense						
Operating Income	143,488,200	269,894,400	273,092,800	257,464,600	261,026,400	244,744,000
Operating Margin %		.23%	.25%	.28%	.31%	.31%
SGA Expense	36,271,840	42,305,030	21,225,200			
Net Income	-6,760,082	186,738,200	114,485,300	59,168,880	117,465,500	135,637,800
Operating Cash Flow	293,736,400	338,367,500	322,739,400	270,694,000	222,065,100	213,633,100
Capital Expenditure	142,761,300	149,739,400	163,114,200	120,373,100	73,634,010	85,845,760
EBITDA	254,266,300	466,445,600	396,882,200	337,495,200	294,245,300	298,970,000
Return on Assets %		.07%	.04%	.03%	.10%	.13%
Return on Equity %		.17%	.11%	.08%	.30%	.37%
Debt to Equity		0.581	0.862	0.541	0.997	1.018

CONTACT INFORMATION:

Phone: 27 112199000   Fax: 27 112199001
Toll-Free:
Address: 203 Oxford Road, Johannesburg, GT 2196 South Africa

STOCK TICKER/OTHER:

Stock Ticker: LTGHF   Exchange: GREY
Employees: 15,922   Fiscal Year Ends: 09/30
Parent Company:

SALARIES/BONUSES:

Top Exec. Salary: $ Bonus: $
Second Exec. Salary: $ Bonus: $

OTHER THOUGHTS:

Estimated Female Officers or Directors: 5
Hot Spot for Advancement for Women/Minorities: Y

# LifePoint Health Inc							www.lifepointhealth.net

NAIC Code: 622110

TYPES OF BUSINESS:

General Medical and Surgical Hospitals

BRANDS/DIVISIONS/AFFILIATES:

Apollo Global Management LLC
Health Support Center

CONTACTS: *Note: Officers with more than one job title may be intentionally listed here more than once.*

David M. Dill, CEO
Michael S. Coggin, CFO
Sonny Terrill, Exec. VP-Human Resources
David Dill, COO
Jennifer Peters, General Counsel
Jeffrey Seraphine, Other Executive Officer
Victor Giovanetti, President, Divisional
Melissa Waddey, President, Divisional
Robert Klein, President, Divisional
R. Raplee, President, Divisional

GROWTH PLANS/SPECIAL FEATURES:

LifePoint Health, Inc. is a holding company that operates through its subsidiaries, which own and operate hospitals or other healthcare providers in more than 80 communities throughout the U.S. LifePoint Health's facilities and practices are grouped into four geographic divisions (Eastern, Central, Mountain and Western), which each have their own leadership team. The group's Health Support Center (HSC) in Brentwood, Tennessee has expertise in every area of healthcare operations and provider services. HSC offers resources across the continuum of care, from before a patient accesses healthcare services to after they are sent home. HSC works with the group's local markets to help develop and implement proper strategies that ensure healthcare thrives in those communities. LifePoint Health, Inc. is a subsidiary of Apollo Global Management, LLC.

The company offers its employees medical, dental, vision, life and disability insurance; adoption assistance; flexible spending accounts; a wellness program; a Wells Fargo Employee Home Mortgage Program; and a 401(k) plan.

FINANCIAL DATA: *Note: Data for latest year may not have been available at press time.*

In U.S. $	2020	2019	2018	2017	2016	2015
Revenue	7,153,500,000	7,530,000,000	7,400,000,000	7,263,099,904	7,273,000,000	6,014,400,000
R&D Expense						
Operating Income						
Operating Margin %						
SGA Expense						
Net Income		106,536,960	104,448,000	102,400,000	121,900,000	181,900,000
Operating Cash Flow						
Capital Expenditure						
EBITDA						
Return on Assets %						
Return on Equity %						
Debt to Equity						

CONTACT INFORMATION:

Phone: 615 920-7000   Fax:
Toll-Free:
Address: 330 Seven Springs Way, Brentwood, TN 37027 United States

STOCK TICKER/OTHER:

Stock Ticker: Subsidiary   Exchange:
Employees: 47,000   Fiscal Year Ends: 12/31
Parent Company: Apollo Global Management LLC

SALARIES/BONUSES:

Top Exec. Salary: $ Bonus: $
Second Exec. Salary: $ Bonus: $

OTHER THOUGHTS:

Estimated Female Officers or Directors: 1
Hot Spot for Advancement for Women/Minorities: Y

Sales, profits and employees may be estimates. Financial information, benefits and other data can change quickly and may vary from those stated here.

Lifetime Healthcare Companies (The)

www.lifethc.com

NAIC Code: 524114

TYPES OF BUSINESS:

Insurance-Medical & Health, HMOs & PPOs
Insurance-Group Life
Insurance-Property/Casualty
Insurance-Long-Term Care
Health Care Services
Employee Benefits Services
Medical Centers
Medical Equipment Distribution

BRANDS/DIVISIONS/AFFILIATES:

Excellus BlueCross BlueShield
Univera Healthcare
Lifetime Benefit Solutions Inc
MedAmerica Insurance Company

GROWTH PLANS/SPECIAL FEATURES:

The Lifetime Healthcare Companies is a nonprofit family of companies which provide health coverage and health care services to more than 1.5 million upstate New Yorkers. The family of companies include: Excellus BlueCross BlueShield, a nonprofit independent licensee of the Blue Cross Blue Shield Association, serving upstate New York; Univera Healthcare, which offers managed care, indemnity and dental plans to individuals and groups; Lifetime Benefit Solutions Inc., a provider of flexible benefit programs; and MedAmerica Insurance Company, which offers long-term care insurance to both individuals and employer groups.

CONTACTS: *Note: Officers with more than one job title may be intentionally listed here more than once.*

Christopher C. Booth, CEO
Philip J. Puchalski, Sr. VP-Corp. Comm.
Marie Y. Philippe, Chief Diversity Officer

FINANCIAL DATA: *Note: Data for latest year may not have been available at press time.*

In U.S. $	2020	2019	2018	2017	2016	2015
Revenue	6,000,000,000	7,056,000,000	6,720,000,000	6,400,000,000	6,125,000,000	5,923,166,000
R&D Expense						
Operating Income						
Operating Margin %						
SGA Expense						
Net Income						
Operating Cash Flow						
Capital Expenditure						
EBITDA						
Return on Assets %						
Return on Equity %						
Debt to Equity						

CONTACT INFORMATION:

Phone: 585-454-1700   Fax:
Toll-Free:
Address: 165 Court St., Rochester, NY 14647 United States

STOCK TICKER/OTHER:

Stock Ticker: Nonprofit   Exchange:
Employees: 4,000   Fiscal Year Ends: 12/31
Parent Company:

SALARIES/BONUSES:

Top Exec. Salary: $ Bonus: $
Second Exec. Salary: $ Bonus: $

OTHER THOUGHTS:

Estimated Female Officers or Directors: 1
Hot Spot for Advancement for Women/Minorities: Y

Little Clinic (The)

www.thelittleclinic.com

NAIC Code: 621498

TYPES OF BUSINESS:

Health Clinics
In-Store Clinics

BRANDS/DIVISIONS/AFFILIATES:

Kroger Co (The)

CONTACTS: *Note: Officers with more than one job title may be intentionally listed here more than once.*

Colleen Lindholz, Pres.
Russell Scott, CFO
Tom Shelly, VP-Human Resources
Kenneth Patric, Chief Medical Officer
William D. Wright, Chief Legal Officer
Marc R. Watkins, Chief Medical Officer

GROWTH PLANS/SPECIAL FEATURES:

The Little Clinic, a wholly-owned subsidiary of retail grocer The Kroger Co., manages small, family healthcare facilities primarily within select Kroger locations. Staffed with certified nurse practitioners, physician assistants and dietician nutritionists (who receive contracted consultation from outside collaborating physicians), the clinics offer treatment for minor illnesses for patients 12 months and up (24 months and up in Kentucky), as well as vaccinations, health screenings, physical evaluations and nutrition counseling. In addition to offering telephone consultation to the nursing staff, contracted physicians are expected to provide chart and script reviews, as well as occasional onsite rounds. Each clinic accepts numerous forms of health insurance, including Medicare, Cigna, Aetna, Humana and Blue Cross Blue Shield. The Little Clinic operates more than 215 clinics in select Kroger, Fry's, JayC, Dillons and King Soopers in Ohio, Kansas, Kentucky, Tennessee, Arizona, Georgia, Indiana, Virginia and Colorado.

The Little Clinic offers its employees comprehensive health benefits, 401(k), life and disability insurance, and a variety of employee assistance plans and programs.

FINANCIAL DATA: *Note: Data for latest year may not have been available at press time.*

In U.S. $	2020	2019	2018	2017	2016	2015
Revenue						
R&D Expense						
Operating Income						
Operating Margin %						
SGA Expense						
Net Income						
Operating Cash Flow						
Capital Expenditure						
EBITDA						
Return on Assets %						
Return on Equity %						
Debt to Equity						

CONTACT INFORMATION:

Phone: 877-852-2677   Fax:
Toll-Free:
Address: 2620 Elm Hill Pike, Nashville, TN 37214 United States

STOCK TICKER/OTHER:

Stock Ticker: Subsidiary
Employees:
Parent Company: Kroger Co (The)

Exchange:
Fiscal Year Ends:

SALARIES/BONUSES:

Top Exec. Salary: $ Bonus: $
Second Exec. Salary: $ Bonus: $

OTHER THOUGHTS:

Estimated Female Officers or Directors: 1
Hot Spot for Advancement for Women/Minorities:

Livongo Health Inc

NAIC Code: 325413

www.livongo.com

TYPES OF BUSINESS:

Blood Glucose Test Kits Manufacturing
Computer Software, Healthcare & Biotechnology

BRANDS/DIVISIONS/AFFILIATES:

Livongo for Diabetes
Livongo for Hypertension
Livongo for Prediabetes
Livongo for Weight Management
Livongo for Behavior Health

CONTACTS: *Note: Officers with more than one job title may be intentionally listed here more than once.*

Zane Burke, CEO
Jennifer Schneider, Pres.
Lee Shapiro, CFO
Courtnee Westendorf, CMO
Arnnon Geshuri, Chief People Officer
Anmol Madan, Chief Data Scientist
Glen Tullman, Chmn.

GROWTH PLANS/SPECIAL FEATURES:

Livongo Health, Inc. has created a unified platform that provides smart, connected devices, personalized digital guidance and data-science-enabled insights, facilitating 24/7/365 access to medications across multiple chronic conditions to help users lead better lives. The firm currently offers Livongo for Diabetes, LIvongo for Hypertension, Livongo for Prediabetes, Livongo for Weight Management, and Livongo for Behavioral Health. The diabetes program includes a connected blood glucose meter, test trips, personalized insights, 24/7 support, shareable reports and custom alerts. The hypertension program offers connected blood pressure monitor, personalized insights, shareable reports and expert coaching. The diabetes prevention program includes a connected smart scale, automatic tracking for weight and steps, CDC-approved lesson plan and expert coaching. The weight management program includes a connected smart scale, automatic weight and steps tracking, healthy habits challenges and expert coaching. The behavioral health program includes support for depression, anxiety, stress, sleep and more, as well as interactive programs, tracking tools and coaches. Livongo Health is offered to individuals, employers, health plans and related partners. Headquartered in Mountain View, California, the firm has additional offices in Chicago, Denver and San Francisco. In August 2020, Livongo Health agreed to merge with Teladoc Health, with Teledoc shareholders owning approximately 58% and Livongo shareholders owning the remaining approximately 42% of the combined company.

FINANCIAL DATA: *Note: Data for latest year may not have been available at press time.*

In U.S. $	2020	2019	2018	2017	2016	2015
Revenue		170,198,000	68,431,000	30,850,000		
R&D Expense						
Operating Income						
Operating Margin %						
SGA Expense						
Net Income		-55,270,000	-33,382,000	-16,858,000		
Operating Cash Flow						
Capital Expenditure						
EBITDA						
Return on Assets %						
Return on Equity %						
Debt to Equity						

CONTACT INFORMATION:

Phone: Fax:
Toll-Free: 866-435-5643
Address: 150 W. Evelyn Ave., Ste. 150, Mountain View, CA 94041 United States

STOCK TICKER/OTHER:

Stock Ticker: Subsidiary
Employees: 615
Parent Company: Teladoc Health Inc

Exchange:
Fiscal Year Ends: 12/31

SALARIES/BONUSES:

Top Exec. Salary: $ Bonus: $
Second Exec. Salary: $ Bonus: $

OTHER THOUGHTS:

Estimated Female Officers or Directors:
Hot Spot for Advancement for Women/Minorities:

LogicBio Therapeutics Inc

www.logicbio.com

NAIC Code: 325414

TYPES OF BUSINESS:

Biological Product (except Diagnostic) Manufacturing

BRANDS/DIVISIONS/AFFILIATES:

GeneRide
LB-001

CONTACTS: *Note: Officers with more than one job title may be intentionally listed here more than once.*

Frederic Chereau, CEO
Matthias Jaffe, CFO
Dean Falb, Chief Scientific Officer
Kenneth Huttner, Other Corporate Officer
Tom Wilton, Other Executive Officer

GROWTH PLANS/SPECIAL FEATURES:

LogicBio Therapeutics, Inc. is a genome-editing company focused on developing medicines to treat rare diseases in patients with significant unmet medical need. The firm uses GeneRide, its proprietary technology platform designed to precisely integrate corrective genes into a patient's genome to provide a stable therapeutic effect. LogicBio is initially targeting rare liver disorders in pediatric patients where it is critical to provide treatment early in a patient's life before irreversible disease pathology can occur. The company has demonstrated proof of concept of its therapeutic platform in animal models for a number of diseases and is focusing on its lead product candidate, LB-001, for the treatment of methylmalonic acidemia (MMA), a life-threatening disease present at birth. LB-001 is a recombinant adeno-associated viral vector with human methylmaloynel-COA mutase gene. LogicBio advanced LB-001 to an investigational new drug (IND) filing, and in August 2020 announced a Phase ½ clinical trial in pediatric MMA patients. Achieving clinical proof of concept in an inherited liver disease such as MMA can validate LogicBio's platform technology, including its potential application to other organs and diseases. In addition to MMA, the firm has demonstrated proof of concept of its platform in hemophilia B, alpha-1-antitrypsin deficiency (A1ATD) and Crigler-Najjar syndrome animal disease models.

FINANCIAL DATA: *Note: Data for latest year may not have been available at press time.*

In U.S. $	2020	2019	2018	2017	2016	2015
Revenue	3,454,000					
R&D Expense	22,753,000	30,656,000	11,079,000	3,558,000	2,030,000	
Operating Income	-31,511,000	-41,041,000	-17,943,000	-5,854,000	-3,403,000	
Operating Margin %						
SGA Expense	12,212,000	10,385,000	6,804,000	2,296,000	1,373,000	
Net Income	-32,621,000	-40,128,000	-17,621,000	-5,795,000	-3,428,000	
Operating Cash Flow	-28,925,000	-38,750,000	-15,267,000	-5,782,000	-2,369,000	
Capital Expenditure	476,000	1,415,000	614,000	36,000	232,000	
EBITDA	-30,860,000	-39,271,000	-17,854,000	-5,811,000	-3,387,000	
Return on Assets %		- .58%	- .32%	- .41%	-1.69%	
Return on Equity %		- .66%	- .49%			
Debt to Equity		0.232				

CONTACT INFORMATION:

Phone: 617-245-0399 Fax:
Toll-Free:
Address: 65 Hayden Ave., 2/Fl, Lexington, MA 02421 United States

STOCK TICKER/OTHER:

Stock Ticker: LOGC Exchange: NAS
Employees: 39 Fiscal Year Ends: 12/31
Parent Company:

SALARIES/BONUSES:

Top Exec. Salary: $ Bonus: $
Second Exec. Salary: $ Bonus: $

OTHER THOUGHTS:

Estimated Female Officers or Directors:
Hot Spot for Advancement for Women/Minorities:

Sales, profits and employees may be estimates. Financial information, benefits and other data can change quickly and may vary from those stated here.

Lumenis Ltd
NAIC Code: 339100

www.lumenis.com

TYPES OF BUSINESS:
Laser Surgery Products
Aesthetic Laser Products
Ophthalmic Laser Products

BRANDS/DIVISIONS/AFFILIATES:
Boston Scientific Corporation
Intense Pulsed Light
UltraPulse Encore
LightSheer
VersaPulse
UltraPulse SurgiTouch
SCAAR FX
MOSES

CONTACTS: *Note: Officers with more than one job title may be intentionally listed here more than once.*
Tzipi Ozer-Armon, CEO
Shlomi Cohen, CFO
Amir Lichter, VP-Global R&D
Shlomo Alkalay, VP-Corp. Projects
William Weisel, General Counsel
Eran Cohen, Head-Oper.
Kfir Azoulay, VP
Ido Ben-Tov, VP-Global Service
Rick Gaykowski, VP-Regulatory Affairs & Quality Systems
Kordt Griepenkerl, Pres.
Qiying Zhai, Pres., China & Asia Pacific
Elad Benjamin, VP
Roy Ramati, Sr. VP
Robert Di Silvio, Pres., Americas
Toshio Fukuda, Pres., Lumenis Japan

GROWTH PLANS/SPECIAL FEATURES:
Lumenis, Ltd. is a world leader in laser, light-based and radio frequency technologies for medical and aesthetic applications. The firm holds over 220 registered patents in and outside the U.S., and numerous FDA clearances. Lumenis has more than 80,000 installed systems in medical facilities across 100+ countries. Aesthetic applications include tattoo and hair removal; wrinkle treatment; removal of benign pigmented lesions, including brown spots, age spots, sunspots, scars and stretch marks; reducing the damage from sun, aging or environmental exposure; and removing vascular lesions such as spider veins and other red spots. Products include Intense Pulsed Light (IPL) technology systems that generate high temperature broad band light pulses, including UltraPulse Encore; and various laser systems, including the LightSheer hair removal laser. Surgical systems have a wide variety of applications in urology, neurosurgery, podiatry, gynecology, gastroenterology, otolaryngology (ear, nose and throat), thoracic and pulmonary surgery and general surgery. Its laser systems may be used to resurface skin, ablate (or remove) tissue, vaporize tissue and treat fungal infections. Lasers include VersaPulse and UltraPulse SurgiTouch. The ophthalmic segment develops systems for non-invasive and minimally invasive treatments for conditions such as diabetic retinopathy and retinal detachment; and pioneered the use of selective laser trabeculoplasty (SLT) in the glaucoma market with a demonstrated success rate of 93% as primary therapy and clinical efficacy. The company's SCAAR FX laser treatment solution treats scars up to four millimeters deep. Technology-wise, Leminis' patent-protected MOSES technology is used for holmium laser treatments in both urinary stones and benign prostatic hyperplasia, enabling less stone migration and a more efficient procedure. Lumenis is owned by Boston Scientific Corporation.

FINANCIAL DATA: *Note: Data for latest year may not have been available at press time.*

In U.S. $	2020	2019	2018	2017	2016	2015
Revenue	261,333,843	348,445,125	331,852,500	316,050,000	301,000,000	300,000,000
R&D Expense						
Operating Income						
Operating Margin %						
SGA Expense						
Net Income						
Operating Cash Flow						
Capital Expenditure						
EBITDA						
Return on Assets %						
Return on Equity %						
Debt to Equity						

CONTACT INFORMATION:
Phone: 972-4-959-9000   Fax: 972-4-959-9050
Toll-Free:
Address: Yokneam Industrial Park, Hakidma 6, PO Box 240, Yokneam, 2069204 Israel

STOCK TICKER/OTHER:
Stock Ticker: Subsidiary
Employees: 1,137
Parent Company: Boston Scientific Corporation
Exchange:
Fiscal Year Ends: 12/31

SALARIES/BONUSES:
Top Exec. Salary: $ Bonus: $
Second Exec. Salary: $ Bonus: $

OTHER THOUGHTS:
Estimated Female Officers or Directors: 2
Hot Spot for Advancement for Women/Minorities:

Sales, profits and employees may be estimates. Financial information, benefits and other data can change quickly and may vary from those stated here.

Lumeris Inc

lumeris.com

NAIC Code: 524114

TYPES OF BUSINESS:

Supplementary Health Insurance Coverage
Electronic Medical Record Management
Insurance
Patient Care Accountability Services
Software

BRANDS/DIVISIONS/AFFILIATES:

Essence Group Holdings Corporation
Essence Healthcare

CONTACTS: *Note: Officers with more than one job title may be intentionally listed here more than once.*

W. Michael Long, CEO
Justin Lienemann, CFO
Deborah Zimmerman, Chief Medical Officer
Gail Halterman, General Counsel
Terry Snyder, Sr. VP-Oper.
Lou Anne Gilmore, VP-Dev.
Glenda Holmstrom, VP-Client Svcs.
Jeff Smith, Pres., Mid-Atlantic Initiative
Terry Snyder, Sr. VP-Worldwide Sales

GROWTH PLANS/SPECIAL FEATURES:

Lumeris, Inc. provides strategic advising and cloud-based technology to help providers and payers, via seamless transitions, to deliver improved and more affordable care across populations. The firm works collaboratively with clients to align contracts and engage physicians in programs that drive high-quality, cost-effective care. For health systems and medical groups, Lumeris creates value-based payment arrangements, launches provider-sponsored health plans, optimizes care models, develops population health management strategies, engages physicians and consumers, manages performance and reimbursements, spearheads value-based care transformation and more. For payers, it aligns care delivery models and incentives, deploys population health tools and services, assess provider capabilities, creates empowered networks, retains and optimizes networks, engages physicians and consumers and aims to grow membership. Sister company Essence Healthcare provides comprehensive and affordable health insurance to over 64,000 people with Medicare in Missouri and southern Illinois, with a customer management system rating of 4.5 to 5 stars for the past 10 years (as of mid-2020). Partner organization, Accountable Delivery System Institute, is an educational resource for accountable care, providing solutions and advice to healthcare organizations seeking the benefits of a more connected and aligned healthcare model. Lumeris is privately-held by Essence Group Holdings

FINANCIAL DATA: *Note: Data for latest year may not have been available at press time.*

In U.S. $	2020	2019	2018	2017	2016	2015
Revenue	714,833,437	752,456,250	716,625,000	682,500,000	650,000,000	600,000,000
R&D Expense						
Operating Income						
Operating Margin %						
SGA Expense						
Net Income						
Operating Cash Flow						
Capital Expenditure						
EBITDA						
Return on Assets %						
Return on Equity %						
Debt to Equity						

CONTACT INFORMATION:

Phone: 888-586-3747   Fax:
Toll-Free:
Address: 13900 Riverport Dr., Maryland Heights, MO 63043 United States

STOCK TICKER/OTHER:

Stock Ticker: Private   Exchange:
Employees: 450   Fiscal Year Ends:
Parent Company: Essence Group Holdings Corporation

SALARIES/BONUSES:

Top Exec. Salary: $ Bonus: $
Second Exec. Salary: $ Bonus: $

OTHER THOUGHTS:

Estimated Female Officers or Directors: 6
Hot Spot for Advancement for Women/Minorities: Y

Lupin Limited

NAIC Code: 325412

www.lupin.com

TYPES OF BUSINESS:

Pharmaceutical Preparation Manufacturing
Pharmaceuticals
Active Pharmaceutical Ingredients
Biotechnology

BRANDS/DIVISIONS/AFFILIATES:

Lupifil
Cephalexin
Cefaclor
Ethambutol

CONTACTS: *Note: Officers with more than one job title may be intentionally listed here more than once.*

Manju D. Gupta, Chmn.

GROWTH PLANS/SPECIAL FEATURES:

Lupin Limited is an India-based, innovation-led transnational pharmaceutical company developing and delivering a range of branded and generic formulations, biotechnology products and active pharmaceutical ingredients (APIs). Lupin is a leading player in the cardiovascular, diabetology, asthma, pediatric, central nervous system, gastrointestinal, gynecology, anti-infective and non-steroidal anti-inflammatory drug (NSAID) space. Moreover, the firm holds a global leadership position in the anti-tuberculosis segment. Lupin comprises more than 15 global formulations manufacturing facilities, with its key markets being India, the U.S., Europe, Japan and Commonwealth of Independent States (CIS). Lupin's biotechnology division is based out of Pune, and comprises advanced capabilities such as development, manufacturing and pre-clinical studies to clinical programs in biotech products required for approval in both regulated as well as semi-regulated markets. This division's pipeline includes biosimilars in various stages of development, two of which were commercialized: Lupifil and Lupifil-P. These are biosimilars for molecules Filgrastim and Peg-Filgrastim. A biosimilar for Etanercept is being developed for global markets. Lupin includes a mix of products across indications such as rheumatoid arthritis, oncology, ophthalmology and osteoporosis. Lupin's company name is congruent with a Lupin flower's inherent qualities for nourishing the land and soil it grows in; it is capable of pioneering change even in barren and poor climates. The flower and bean pods are also used as food and sources of nourishment. Lupin's API business serves customers in more than 50 countries, and its flagship products include Cephalexin, Cefaclor and Ethambutol, which are anti-infective and anti-TB treatments. The API division has six manufacturing sites located in Ankleshwar, Tarapur, Vadodara, Mandideep, Indore and Vishakapatnam, India. Lupin's advanced drug delivery division creates and leverages technologies that not only provide clinical advantage but also transforms and facilitates better patient convenience and experience.

FINANCIAL DATA: *Note: Data for latest year may not have been available at press time.*

In U.S. $	2020	2019	2018	2017	2016	2015
Revenue		2,392,128,883	2,278,217,984	2,504,767,232	2,046,302,464	1,839,744,128
R&D Expense						
Operating Income						
Operating Margin %						
SGA Expense						
Net Income		38,049,215	36,237,348	368,843,296	327,484,608	346,601,280
Operating Cash Flow						
Capital Expenditure						
EBITDA						
Return on Assets %						
Return on Equity %						
Debt to Equity						

CONTACT INFORMATION:

Phone: 91 2266402222   Fax: 91 2266402130
Toll-Free:
Address: B/4 Laxmi Towers, Bandra Kurla Complex, Mumbai, Maharashtra 400051 India

STOCK TICKER/OTHER:

Stock Ticker: 500257
Employees: 17,042
Parent Company:

Exchange: Bombay
Fiscal Year Ends: 03/31

SALARIES/BONUSES:

Top Exec. Salary: $ Bonus: $
Second Exec. Salary: $ Bonus: $

OTHER THOUGHTS:

Estimated Female Officers or Directors:
Hot Spot for Advancement for Women/Minorities:

Magee Rehabilitation Hospital

www.mageerehab.org

NAIC Code: 622110

TYPES OF BUSINESS:

General Medical and Surgical Hospital

BRANDS/DIVISIONS/AFFILIATES:

Magee Riverfront
Magee at Oxford Valley
Magee at Watermark
Magee Outpatient Physician Practice
Magee Cherry Hill
Jefferson Health

CONTACTS: *Note: Officers with more than one job title may be intentionally listed here more than once.*

Jack Carroll, Pres.

GROWTH PLANS/SPECIAL FEATURES:

Magee Rehabilitation Hospital is a nonprofit hospital serving the city of Philadelphia. This flagship hospital is a 96-bed specialty medical rehabilitation facility that provides physical and cognitive rehabilitation. This main campus is located in Center City Philadelphia, and offers comprehensive services for spinal cord injury, brain injury, stroke, orthopedic replacement, amputation, pain management, ventilator services, Guillain Barre Syndrome therapy, Multiple Sclerosis therapy and work injury therapy. Magee is a founding member of The Christopher Reeve Foundation NeuroRecovery Network. The firm's objectives include clinical service, education, research and community Involvement. Additional Magee locations include five therapy and/or outpatient services facilities: Magee Riverfront, Magee at Oxford Valley, Magee at Watermark and Magee Outpatient Physician Practice, all of which are in Philadelphia and in close proximity to the hospital; and Magee Cherry Hill, which is located in Cherry Hill, New Jersey. Magee Rehabilitation is a member of the Jefferson Health enterprise, which includes 14 hospitals (including Magee) and over 50 outpatient and urgent care locations across Pennsylvania and New Jersey.

Magee Rehabilitation offers its employees comprehensive benefits, including medical, dental, vision and prescription plans.

FINANCIAL DATA: *Note: Data for latest year may not have been available at press time.*

In U.S. $	2020	2019	2018	2017	2016	2015
Revenue	63,715,771	81,164,616	69,089,211	70,512,682	66,452,011	66,145,518
R&D Expense						
Operating Income						
Operating Margin %						
SGA Expense						
Net Income	-9,591,082	11,866,640	2,838,566	2,689,172	970,510	4,950,375
Operating Cash Flow						
Capital Expenditure						
EBITDA						
Return on Assets %						
Return on Equity %						
Debt to Equity						

CONTACT INFORMATION:

Phone: 215-587-3000   Fax: 215-568-3736
Toll-Free: 800-96-MAGEE
Address: 1513 Race St., Philadelphia, PA 19102 United States

STOCK TICKER/OTHER:

Stock Ticker: Nonprofit
Employees: 838
Parent Company:

Exchange:
Fiscal Year Ends: 06/30

SALARIES/BONUSES:

Top Exec. Salary: $ Bonus: $
Second Exec. Salary: $ Bonus: $

OTHER THOUGHTS:

Estimated Female Officers or Directors:
Hot Spot for Advancement for Women/Minorities:

Magellan Health Inc

www.magellanhealth.com

NAIC Code: 621999

TYPES OF BUSINESS:

Specialty Managed Health Care Services
Psychiatric Hospitals
Residential Treatment Centers

BRANDS/DIVISIONS/AFFILIATES:

Magellan Complete Care

CONTACTS: *Note: Officers with more than one job title may be intentionally listed here more than once.*

Mostafa Kamal, CEO, Subsidiary
Barry Smith, CEO
Jonathan Rubin, CFO
Caskie Lewis-Clapper, Other Executive Officer
Daniel Gregoire, Secretary
Jeffrey West, Senior VP

GROWTH PLANS/SPECIAL FEATURES:

Magellan Health, Inc. is engaged in the healthcare management business. Magellan develops innovative solutions that combine advanced analytics, agile technology and clinical excellence to promote best decision-making capabilities for its clients. The firm serves health plans, managed care organizations, employers, labor unions, various military and governmental agencies and third-party administrators. Magellan operates in two business segments: Magellan healthcare and Magellan pharmacy management. Magellan healthcare includes the firm's management of behavioral healthcare services and employee assistance program services; management of specialty areas such as diagnostic imaging and musculoskeletal management; and the integrated management of physical, behavioral and pharmaceutical health care for special populations delivered via Magellan Complete Care. Special populations include individuals with serious mental illness, dual eligible, long-term services and supports and other populations with unique and often complex health care needs. Magellan pharmacy management comprises products and solutions that provide clinical and financial management of pharmaceuticals paid under medical and pharmacy benefit programs. Its services include pharmacy benefit management, pharmacy benefit administration for state Medicaid and other government-sponsored programs, pharmaceutical dispensing operations, clinical and formulary management programs, medical pharmacy management programs, as well as programs for the integrated management of specialty drugs across both the medical and pharmacy benefit that treat complex conditions.

FINANCIAL DATA: *Note: Data for latest year may not have been available at press time.*

In U.S. $	2020	2019	2018	2017	2016	2015
Revenue	4,577,531,000	7,159,423,000	7,314,151,000	5,838,583,000	4,836,884,000	4,597,400,000
R&D Expense						
Operating Income	20,404,000	97,781,000	64,522,000	155,314,000	152,892,000	75,532,000
Operating Margin %		.01%	.01%	.03%	.03%	.02%
SGA Expense						
Net Income	382,335,000	55,902,000	24,181,000	110,207,000	77,879,000	31,413,000
Operating Cash Flow	450,761,000	115,846,000	164,844,000	162,273,000	66,699,000	239,185,000
Capital Expenditure	75,480,000	60,402,000	68,275,000	57,232,000	60,881,000	71,584,000
EBITDA	109,125,000	248,479,000	211,250,000	276,907,000	261,756,000	180,541,000
Return on Assets %		.02%	.01%	.04%	.03%	.02%
Return on Equity %		.04%	.02%	.09%	.07%	.03%
Debt to Equity		0.486	0.567	0.58	0.195	0.224

CONTACT INFORMATION:

Phone: 602-572-6050   Fax:
Toll-Free: 800-410-8312
Address: 4800 Scottsdale Rd, Ste. 4000, Scottsdale, AZ 85251 United States

STOCK TICKER/OTHER:

Stock Ticker: MGLN
Employees: 9,000
Parent Company:

Exchange: NAS
Fiscal Year Ends: 12/31

SALARIES/BONUSES:

Top Exec. Salary: $ Bonus: $
Second Exec. Salary: $ Bonus: $

OTHER THOUGHTS:

Estimated Female Officers or Directors: 3
Hot Spot for Advancement for Women/Minorities: Y

Sales, profits and employees may be estimates. Financial information, benefits and other data can change quickly and may vary from those stated here.

Main Line Health System

www.mainlinehealth.org

NAIC Code: 622110

TYPES OF BUSINESS:

General Medical and Surgical Hospital

BRANDS/DIVISIONS/AFFILIATES:

Lankenau Medical Center
Bryn Mawr Hospital
Paoli Hospital
Riddle Hospital
Bryn Mawr Rehabilitation Hospital
Bryn Mawr Rehab Concussion Center
Main Line Health King of Prussia

CONTACTS: *Note: Officers with more than one job title may be intentionally listed here more than once.*

John J. Lynch III, Pres.
Mike Buongiorno, Exec. VP
Paul Yakulis, Sr. VP-HR
Luke Olenoski, Sr. VP
Elizabeth (Betsy) Balderston, Chmn.

GROWTH PLANS/SPECIAL FEATURES:

Main Line Health, Inc. is a nonprofit health system serving the Philadelphia area. Main Line Health is comprised of four acute care hospitals: Lankenau Medical Center, Bryn Mawr Hospital, Paoli Hospital and Riddle Hospital. The firm also maintains a leading rehabilitative hospital, Bryn Mawr Rehabilitation Hospital. Other specialties that are offered through Main Line Health include trauma centers, obstetrics/gynecology, maternity, imaging and diagnostic radiology, a heart institute, family medicine, primary care services, the Bryn Mawr Rehab Concussion Center, a stroke recovery program, orthopedic surgery centers, orthopedics, laboratory services, pathology, drug and alcohol treatment and urgent care. Health education programs are available through Main Line Health, including graduate medical education, residency programs, fellowship programs, clerkships, electives and continuing medical education. During 2020, Main Line Health officially opened its 94,000-square-foot Main Line Health King of Prussia location, the firm's first women's specialty center, in collaboration with Axia Women's Health.

The firm offers its employees medical, dental, vision, life, AD&D and disability coverage; a 403(b) retirement savings plan; pension plan; tuition reimbursement; and a nursing student grant program.

FINANCIAL DATA: *Note: Data for latest year may not have been available at press time.*

In U.S. $	2020	2019	2018	2017	2016	2015
Revenue	1,650,000,000	1,680,000,000	1,780,581,600	1,695,792,000	1,660,420,000	1,586,313,000
R&D Expense						
Operating Income						
Operating Margin %						
SGA Expense						
Net Income	-67,600,000	32,100,000		51,550,000	127,040,000	201,155,000
Operating Cash Flow						
Capital Expenditure						
EBITDA						
Return on Assets %						
Return on Equity %						
Debt to Equity						

CONTACT INFORMATION:

Phone: 610-647-2400   Fax: 610-409-6210
Toll-Free:
Address: 130 South Bryn Mawr Ave., Bryn Mawr, PA 19010 United States

STOCK TICKER/OTHER:

Stock Ticker: Nonprofit
Employees: 10,000
Parent Company:

Exchange:
Fiscal Year Ends: 05/30

SALARIES/BONUSES:

Top Exec. Salary: $ Bonus: $
Second Exec. Salary: $ Bonus: $

OTHER THOUGHTS:

Estimated Female Officers or Directors:
Hot Spot for Advancement for Women/Minorities:

Masimo Corporation

www.masimo.com

NAIC Code: 334510

TYPES OF BUSINESS:

Medical Equipment
Patient Monitoring Devices
Circuit Boards
Patient Sensors
Software

BRANDS/DIVISIONS/AFFILIATES:

Masimo Signal Extraction Technology (SET)
MX
NomoLine
O3
Radical
Pronto
Root
Radius

CONTACTS: *Note: Officers with more than one job title may be intentionally listed here more than once.*

Joseph Kiani, CEO
Micah Young, CFO
David Van Ramshorst, Chief Accounting Officer
Yongsam Lee, Chief Information Officer
Anand Sampath, COO
Tao Levy, Executive VP, Divisional
Bilal Muhsin, Executive VP, Divisional
Thomas McClenahan, Executive VP
Jon Coleman, President, Divisional

GROWTH PLANS/SPECIAL FEATURES:

Masimo Corporation is a medical technology company that develops, manufactures and markets noninvasive patient monitoring products. Patient monitoring products are based on its Masimo Signal Extraction Technology (Masimo SET), which provides the capabilities of measure-through motion and low perfusion pulse oximetry to address the primary limitations of conventional pulse oximetry. The firm markets patient monitoring circuit boards, which are incorporated into its proprietary devices or sold to original equipment manufacturer (OEM) customers for incorporation into their monitors; sensors and patient cables; and standalone patient monitoring devices. Circuit boards include Masimo SET pulse oximetry technology as well as circuitry to support rainbow measurements. Measurements include hemoglobin-the oxygen-carrying component of red blood cells, the oxygen content of blood, carbon monoxide, methemoglobin (a reaction to common drugs), changes in the Pi, sound-based respiration rate, pulse and real-time oxygenation status. Circuit board and related modules are marketed under the MX, MS, uSpO2, SedLine, ISA and IRMA brand names. Other noninvasive measurements and technologies based on Masimo's rainbow SET platform include SedLine brain function monitoring, NomoLine capnography and gas monitoring, O3 regional oximetry, patient surveillance and more. Monitors and devices are marketed under the Radical, Rad, Pronto, Root and Radius brand names. Additional products by Masimo span a wide variety of sensors, filters, adapters, alarm solutions, supplemental monitoring solutions, connectivity devices and accessories and consumer monitoring devices. Masimo maintains an approximate 70,700-square-foot manufacturing facility in California, USA and two others in Mexico. In January 2020, Masimo agreed to acquire the Connected Care assets from NantHealth, Inc. for a $47.25 million upfront cash payment. The following March, the firm agreed to acquire TNI medical AG, a German ventilation company.

FINANCIAL DATA: *Note: Data for latest year may not have been available at press time.*

In U.S. $	2020	2019	2018	2017	2016	2015
Revenue	1,143,744,000	937,837,000	858,289,000	798,108,000	694,625,000	630,111,000
R&D Expense	118,659,000	93,295,000	76,967,000	61,953,000	59,362,000	56,617,000
Operating Income	255,349,000	221,216,000	208,469,000	197,361,000	150,770,000	100,641,000
Operating Margin %		.24%	.24%	.25%	.22%	.16%
SGA Expense	369,057,000	314,661,000	289,456,000	275,786,000	253,667,000	252,725,000
Net Income	240,302,000	196,216,000	193,543,000	131,616,000	300,666,000	83,300,000
Operating Cash Flow	210,963,000	221,640,000	239,527,000	56,062,000	416,842,000	114,209,000
Capital Expenditure	79,957,000	72,492,000	22,683,000	46,763,000	24,351,000	54,594,000
EBITDA	293,374,000	257,981,000	229,596,000	217,422,000	167,587,000	116,325,000
Return on Assets %		.15%	.19%	.15%	.42%	.14%
Return on Equity %		.18%	.23%	.21%	.72%	.29%
Debt to Equity		0.014				0.672

CONTACT INFORMATION:

Phone: 949 297-7000   Fax: 949 297-7001
Toll-Free: 800-326-4890
Address: 52 Discovery, Irvine, CA 92618 United States

STOCK TICKER/OTHER:

Stock Ticker: MASI   Exchange: NAS
Employees: 5,300   Fiscal Year Ends: 12/31
Parent Company:

SALARIES/BONUSES:

Top Exec. Salary: $ Bonus: $
Second Exec. Salary: $ Bonus: $

OTHER THOUGHTS:

Estimated Female Officers or Directors:
Hot Spot for Advancement for Women/Minorities:

Mass General Brigham Incorporated   www.massgeneralbrigham.org

NAIC Code: 622110

TYPES OF BUSINESS:

General Medical and Surgical Hospitals
Teaching Hospitals
Mental Health
Radiology
Lab Services
Emergency Care

BRANDS/DIVISIONS/AFFILIATES:

Brigham and Women's Hospital
Massachusetts General Hospital
Brigham and Women's Health Care Center
Brigham and Women's Faulkner Hospital
Brigham and Women's Urgent Care Center
Brigham Health Fast Care
BWH
Cooley Dickinson

CONTACTS: *Note: Officers with more than one job title may be intentionally listed here more than once.*

Anne Klibanski, CEO
Ron M. Walls, COO
Peter K. Markell, CFO
Mark Bohen, CMO
Rosemary R. Sheehan, Chief Human Resources Officer
Elizabeth Mort, Sr. Medical Dir.
Peter K. Markell, Exec. VP-Admin.
Brent L. Henry, General Counsel
Lynne J. Eickholt, Chief Strategy Officer
Sara Andrews, Chief Dev. Officer
Rich Copp, VP-Comm.
Peter K. Markell, Exec. VP-Finance
David E.Storto, VP-Non-Acute Care Svcs.
Peter R. Brown, Chief of Staff
Kathryn E. West, VP-Real Estate & Facility
Tejal K. Gandhi, Chief Quality & Safety Officer
Scott M. Sperling, Chmn.

GROWTH PLANS/SPECIAL FEATURES:

Mass General Brigham Incorporated (formerly Partners HealthCare) is a non-profit hospital and physician network with more than 15 member institutions and several affiliates. Brigham and Women's Hospital is a 793-bed teaching hospital of Harvard Medical School. Massachusetts General Hospital offers diagnostic and therapeutic care in virtually every specialty and subspecialty of medicine and surgery. Brigham and Women's Health Care Center (Westwood) is a state-of-the-art health care center that provides primary and specialty care, as well as on-site diagnostic radiology and lab services. Brigham and Women's Faulkner Hospital is a 171-bed community teaching hospital offering medical, surgical and psychiatric care, as well as emergency, ambulatory and diagnostic services. Brigham and Women's Health Care Center (Chestnut Hill) provides multi-specialty care. Brigham and Women's Health Care Center (Pembroke) offers comprehensive services ranging from annual physical exams to the management of complex medical conditions, on-site diagnostic radiology and lab services and more. Other institutions include Brigham and Women's Urgent Care Center (Foxborough), Brigham Health and Brigham and Women's/Mass General Health Care Center, Brigham Health Fast Care (Pembroke), BWH Brookside Community Health Center, BWH Southern Jamaica Plain Health Center, Cooley Dickinson Hospital, Harbor Medical Associates Urgent Care Center, and many more. In late-2019, Partners HealthCare rebranded as Mass General Brigham to reflect and unify the organization's best-known assets, Massachusetts General Hospital and Brigham and Women's Hospital.

Mass General Brigham offers its employees health, drug, dental and vision coverage; retirement savings and financial counseling; optional life and disability insurance; and flexibla savings accounts.

FINANCIAL DATA: *Note: Data for latest year may not have been available at press time.*

In U.S. $	2020	2019	2018	2017	2016	2015
Revenue	13,020,000,000	14,000,000,000	13,307,269,000	13,371,063,000	12,517,887,000	11,665,645,000
R&D Expense						
Operating Income						
Operating Margin %						
SGA Expense						
Net Income		867,935,250	826,605,000	659,097,000	-249,011,000	-91,989,000
Operating Cash Flow						
Capital Expenditure						
EBITDA						
Return on Assets %						
Return on Equity %						
Debt to Equity						

CONTACT INFORMATION:

Phone: 617-278-1000   Fax:
Toll-Free:
Address: 800 Boylston St., 11/Fl, Boston, MA 02199 United States

STOCK TICKER/OTHER:

Stock Ticker: Nonprofit   Exchange:
Employees: 78,000   Fiscal Year Ends: 09/30
Parent Company:

SALARIES/BONUSES:

Top Exec. Salary: $ Bonus: $
Second Exec. Salary: $ Bonus: $

OTHER THOUGHTS:

Estimated Female Officers or Directors: 11
Hot Spot for Advancement for Women/Minorities: Y

Mayo Clinic

NAIC Code: 622110

www.mayo.edu

TYPES OF BUSINESS:

General Medical and Surgical Hospitals
Physician Practice Management
Medical Research
Health Care Education

BRANDS/DIVISIONS/AFFILIATES:

Mayo Clinic
Mayo Clinic Hospital
Saint Marys Campus
Mayo Clinic Building
Samuel C Johnson Research
Mayo Clinic Collaborative Research
Mayo Clinic Specialty
Civica Rx

CONTACTS: *Note: Officers with more than one job title may be intentionally listed here more than once.*

Gianrico Farrugia, CEO
Dennis E. Dahlen, CFO
Shirley A. Weis, Chief Admin. Officer
Jonathan J. Oviatt, Chief Legal Officer
Harry N. Hoffman, Treas.
William C. Rupp, VP
Wyatt W. Decker, VP
Robert F. Brigham, Assistant Sec.
Sherry L. Hubert, Assistant Sec.
Samuel A. Di Piazza Jr., Chmn.

GROWTH PLANS/SPECIAL FEATURES:

Mayo Clinic is a nonprofit healthcare organization founded in 1864, and part of the Mayo Foundation for Medical Education and Research. Mayo Clinic provides medical treatment, physician management, healthcare education, research and other specialized medical services through a network of clinics and hospitals in Minnesota, Arizona and Florida. The organization's primary clinics are located in Rochester, Minnesota; Jacksonville, Florida; and Scottsdale and Phoenix, Arizona. The Rochester campus has been in business for more than 100 years, and includes the Mayo Clinic, the Mayo Clinic Hospital, Saint Mary's Campus and Mayo Clinic Hospital-Methodist Campus, which together provide comprehensive diagnosis and treatment in virtually every medical and surgical specialty. The Mayo Clinic Hospital, located on the Jacksonville campus, offers over 260 beds and represents more than 40 medical and surgical specialties. In Arizona, Mayo Clinic focuses on adult specialty and surgical disciplines, supported by programs in medical education and research. The original Scottsdale campus opened in 1987, and includes the Mayo Clinic Building, the Samuel C. Johnson Research building and the Mayo Clinic Collaborative Research building. The Phoenix campus includes the Mayo Clinic Specialty building and Mayo Clinic Hospital. Mayo Clinic schools offer more than 400 educational programs across its campuses, which include five schools under the Mayo Clinic name. Mayo Clinic partnered with other health organizations in the 2018 creation of Civica Rx, a not-for-profit generic drug and pharmaceutical company focused on combating life-saving drug shortages and affordability.

Doctors are paid by salary, rather than fee for service. Employees are offered comprehensive benefits, retirement plans and employee assistance programs.

FINANCIAL DATA: *Note: Data for latest year may not have been available at press time.*

In U.S. $	2020	2019	2018	2017	2016	2015
Revenue	13,910,000,000	13,708,000,000	12,603,000,000	11,984,000,000	10,990,000,000	10,315,000,000
R&D Expense						
Operating Income						
Operating Margin %						
SGA Expense						
Net Income	1,971,000,000	1,242,000,000	1,129,000,000	856,000,000	475,000,000	526,000,000
Operating Cash Flow						
Capital Expenditure						
EBITDA						
Return on Assets %						
Return on Equity %						
Debt to Equity						

CONTACT INFORMATION:

Phone: 507-284-2511   Fax: 507-284-0161
Toll-Free: 800-660-4582
Address: 200 First St. SW, Rochester, MN 55905 United States

STOCK TICKER/OTHER:

Stock Ticker: Nonprofit
Employees: 71,350
Parent Company:

Exchange:
Fiscal Year Ends: 12/31

SALARIES/BONUSES:

Top Exec. Salary: $ Bonus: $
Second Exec. Salary: $ Bonus: $

OTHER THOUGHTS:

Estimated Female Officers or Directors: 5
Hot Spot for Advancement for Women/Minorities: Y

Sales, profits and employees may be estimates. Financial information, benefits and other data can change quickly and may vary from those stated here.

McKesson Corporation

www.mckesson.com

NAIC Code: 424210

TYPES OF BUSINESS:

Pharmaceutical Distribution
Medical-Surgical Products Distribution
Health Care Management Software
Consulting
Outsourcing

BRANDS/DIVISIONS/AFFILIATES:

McKesson Canada
McKesson Prescription Technology Solutions

CONTACTS: *Note: Officers with more than one job title may be intentionally listed here more than once.*

Brian Tyler, CEO
Britt Vitalone, CFO
Edward Mueller, Chairman of the Board
Sundeep Reddy, Chief Accounting Officer
Lori Schechter, Chief Compliance Officer
Kathleen McElligott, Chief Information Officer
Bansi Nagji, Executive VP, Divisional
Jorge Figueredo, Executive VP
Michele Lau, Secretary
Paul Smith, Senior VP, Divisional
Brian Moore, Senior VP

GROWTH PLANS/SPECIAL FEATURES:

McKesson Corporation provides healthcare management solutions, retail pharmacy, healthcare technology, community oncology and specialty care. McKesson operates through four business segments: U.S. pharmaceutical and specialty solutions, European pharmaceutical solutions, medical-surgical solutions and other. The U.S. pharmaceutical and specialty solutions segment distributes branded, generic, specialty, biosimilar and over-the-counter (OTC) pharmaceutical drugs and other healthcare-related products. It provides practice management, clinical support and business solutions to community-based oncology and other specialty practices. This division also provides solutions for life sciences companies, including offering multiple distribution channels and clinical trials access to specific patient populations through McKesson's network of oncology physicians. This segment also sells financial, operational and clinical solutions to pharmacies (retail, hospital and alternate sites) and provides consulting, outsourcing and other services. The European pharmaceutical solutions segment provides distribution and related services to wholesale, institutional and retail customers in 13 European countries through McKesson's own pharmacies and participating pharmacies that operate under the brand partnership and franchise arrangements. The medical-surgical solutions segment distributes medical-surgical supplies and provides logistics and other services to healthcare providers in the U.S. The other segment primarily consists of the following: McKesson Canada; a distributor of pharmaceutical and medical products, and an operator of Rexall Health retail pharmacies; and McKesson Prescription Technology Solutions, a provider of innovative technologies that support retail pharmacies. In March 2020, the firm announced the completion of the split-off and subsequent merger of PF2 SpinCo, Inc., which held McKesson's interest in Change Healthcare LLC, into Change Healthcare Inc.

Employee benefits include medical, dental, vision, AD&D and dependent life insurance; an employee assistance program; and flexible spending accounts.

FINANCIAL DATA: *Note: Data for latest year may not have been available at press time.*

In U.S. $	2020	2019	2018	2017	2016	2015
Revenue	231,051,000,000	214,319,000,000	208,357,000,000	198,533,000,000	190,884,000,000	
R&D Expense	96,000,000	71,000,000	125,000,000	341,000,000	392,000,000	
Operating Income	2,759,000,000	3,280,000,000	2,921,000,000	3,464,000,000	3,748,000,000	
Operating Margin %	.01%	.02%	.01%	.02%	.02%	
SGA Expense	9,168,000,000	8,403,000,000	8,138,000,000	7,466,000,000	7,276,000,000	
Net Income	900,000,000	34,000,000	67,000,000	5,070,000,000	2,258,000,000	
Operating Cash Flow	4,374,000,000	4,036,000,000	4,345,000,000	4,744,000,000	3,672,000,000	
Capital Expenditure	506,000,000	557,000,000	580,000,000	562,000,000	677,000,000	
EBITDA	2,315,000,000	1,823,000,000	1,473,000,000	8,109,000,000	4,488,000,000	
Return on Assets %	.01%	.00%	.00%	.09%	.04%	
Return on Equity %	.14%	.00%	.01%	.51%	.27%	
Debt to Equity	1.57	0.898	0.689	0.658	0.732	

CONTACT INFORMATION:

Phone: 972-446-4800   Fax:
Toll-Free: 800-826-9360
Address: 6555 State Hwy. 161, Irving, TX 75039 United States

STOCK TICKER/OTHER:

Stock Ticker: MCK
Employees: 76,000
Parent Company:

Exchange: NYS
Fiscal Year Ends: 03/31

SALARIES/BONUSES:

Top Exec. Salary: $ Bonus: $
Second Exec. Salary: $ Bonus: $

OTHER THOUGHTS:

Estimated Female Officers or Directors: 4
Hot Spot for Advancement for Women/Minorities: Y

MD Anderson Cancer Center

www.mdanderson.org

NAIC Code: 622310

TYPES OF BUSINESS:

Cancer Hospital

BRANDS/DIVISIONS/AFFILIATES:

University of Texas Health Science Centeat Houston
MD Anderson Childrens Cancer Hospital
International Center
MD Anderson Radiation Treatment Center at American
Presbyterian MD Anderson Radiation Treatment Cente

CONTACTS: *Note: Officers with more than one job title may be intentionally listed here more than once.*

Peter WT Pisters, Pres.

GROWTH PLANS/SPECIAL FEATURES:

The University of Texas MD Anderson Cancer Center is both a degree-granting academic institution and a cancer treatment and research center located in Houston, Texas. MD Anderson Cancer Center is affiliated with The University of Texas Health Science Center at Houston. The cancer center aims to eliminate cancer in Texas, the nation and the world through outstanding programs that integrate patient care, research and prevention, as well as through education for undergraduate and graduate students, trainees, professionals, employees and the public. More than 1.5 million patients have been treated since 1944, and the center employs and utilizes approximately 1,780 faculty, 2,100 onsite and offsite volunteers and nearly 7,000 trainees. During 2019, MD Anderson Cancer Center cared for approximately 148,700 patients, more than 47,500 were new; and over 11,600 participants were enrolled in 1,360+ clinical trials exploring innovative treatments. Other group centers include: MD Anderson Children's Cancer Hospital, for children with cancer; and the International Center, which helps patients travel to Houston from all over the world for cancer treatment via patient admissions, travel arrangements and language assistance. Affiliates of the firm include MD Anderson Radiation Treatment Center at American Hospital, in Istanbul; and Presbyterian MD Anderson Radiation Treatment Center, in New Mexico, USA. In September 2020, MD Anderson announced a three-year strategic collaboration with Taiho Pharmaceutical Co. Ltd. to accelerate the development of treatments for significant unmet medical needs in oncology, including patients with brain metastases and those with cancers refractory to available therapies.

MD Anderson Cancer Center offers employees medical, dental and vision coverage; prescriptions; disability, life and accidental death insurances; flexible spending accounts; and long-term care.

FINANCIAL DATA: *Note: Data for latest year may not have been available at press time.*

In U.S. $	2020	2019	2018	2017	2016	2015
Revenue	5,005,869,368	5,155,254,967	4,632,206,543	4,276,505,391	4,480,444,361	4,495,768,037
R&D Expense						
Operating Income						
Operating Margin %						
SGA Expense						
Net Income	1,161,429,710	723,187,056	539,015,009	722,755,482	207,532,713	566,878,526
Operating Cash Flow						
Capital Expenditure						
EBITDA						
Return on Assets %						
Return on Equity %						
Debt to Equity						

CONTACT INFORMATION:

Phone: 713-792-2121	Fax:
Toll-Free: 877-632-6789
Address: 1515 Holcombe Blvd., Houston, TX 77030 United States

STOCK TICKER/OTHER:

Stock Ticker: Nonprofit	Exchange:
Employees: 20,531	Fiscal Year Ends: 08/31
Parent Company:

SALARIES/BONUSES:

Top Exec. Salary: $	Bonus: $
Second Exec. Salary: $	Bonus: $

OTHER THOUGHTS:

Estimated Female Officers or Directors:
Hot Spot for Advancement for Women/Minorities:

Medica Sur SAB de CV   www.medicasur.com.mx

NAIC Code: 621910

TYPES OF BUSINESS:

Ambulance Services

BRANDS/DIVISIONS/AFFILIATES:

Medical-University Complex
Medica Sur Loma Hospital
Holiday Inn & Suites Mexico - Medica Sur

CONTACTS: *Note: Officers with more than one job title may be intentionally listed here more than once.*

Juan Carlos Griera Hernando, CEO

GROWTH PLANS/SPECIAL FEATURES:

Medica Sur SAB de CV is a health care company engaged in medical attention, research, diagnostic, teaching and community service. The group's Medical-University Complex in Mexico City is a high specialty center, and secondary level care is provided at Medica Sur Lomas Hospital, also in Mexico City. Medica Sur medical units include behavioral disorders, blood bank and transfusional medicine, cardiology, check-ups, emergencies, foot/ankle, gastroenterology, imaging, magnetic resonance, weight control, neonatology, neurophysiology, nuclear medicine, obstetrics/gynecology, pediatrics, physical therapy medicine, radiotherapy, short-stay surgery, urology and women's health. Specialized centers include comprehensive diagnostics and treatment, cancer care, radiotherapy, Gamma Knife radiosurgery and laboratory. Holiday Inn & Suites Mexico - Medica Sur comprises hotel facilities strategically located within the company's hospital complex, offering rooms (including luxury suites), a business center and a restaurant. Medica Sur is a hospital member of the Mayo Clinic Care Network, working together with international physicians.

FINANCIAL DATA: *Note: Data for latest year may not have been available at press time.*

In U.S. $	2020	2019	2018	2017	2016	2015
Revenue		158,360,025	150,819,072	143,454,560	138,153,760	119,078,800
R&D Expense						
Operating Income						
Operating Margin %						
SGA Expense						
Net Income		7,431,419	7,077,542	9,690,525	7,607,472	12,594,703
Operating Cash Flow						
Capital Expenditure						
EBITDA						
Return on Assets %						
Return on Equity %						
Debt to Equity						

CONTACT INFORMATION:

Phone: 52 54247200   Fax:
Toll-Free:
Address: Puente de Piedra 150, Toriello Guerra, Mexico DF, 14050 Mexico

STOCK TICKER/OTHER:

Stock Ticker: MEDICA B
Employees: 3,512
Parent Company:

Exchange: MEX
Fiscal Year Ends: 12/31

SALARIES/BONUSES:

Top Exec. Salary: $ Bonus: $
Second Exec. Salary: $ Bonus: $

OTHER THOUGHTS:

Estimated Female Officers or Directors:
Hot Spot for Advancement for Women/Minorities:

Sales, profits and employees may be estimates. Financial information, benefits and other data can change quickly and may vary from those stated here.

Medical Action Industries Inc

www.medical-action.com

NAIC Code: 339100

TYPES OF BUSINESS:

Supplies-Laparoscopy Sponges & Operating Room Towels
Operating Room Disposables
Containment Systems for Medical Waste
Patient Bedside Products
Laboratory Products
Minor Procedure Kits & Trays
Sterilization Products
Dressings and Surgical Sponges

BRANDS/DIVISIONS/AFFILIATES:

Owens & Minor Inc

GROWTH PLANS/SPECIAL FEATURES:

Medical Action Industries, Inc. (MAI) develops, manufactures and distributes disposable medical products primarily to: acute care facilities as well as long-term care facilities; physician, dental and veterinary offices; and out-patient surgery centers. MAI specializes in the provision of medical supplies in six categories: customer procedure trays; minor procedure kits and trays, including infusion therapy, instrument kits and endoscopy kits; operating room supplies; medical products such as wound care; patient apparel such as slippers; and sterilization products such as seal pouches, sterility monitoring products, integrators, bowie dick tests, indicator tape, foam pouches, tray liners, basin separators and foam aligners. MAI is owned by healthcare logistics company Owens & Minor, Inc.

Employee benefits include medical, dental and vision coverage; wellness programs; 401(k); life insurance; flexible spending accounts; short- and long-term disability; and cancer and accident protection.

CONTACTS:
Note: Officers with more than one job title may be intentionally listed here more than once.

Edward A. Pesicka, CEO-Owens & Minor
Paul D. Meringolo, Pres.
John Sheffield, Corp. Sec.
Eric Liu, VP-Oper.

FINANCIAL DATA:
Note: Data for latest year may not have been available at press time.

In U.S. $	2020	2019	2018	2017	2016	2015
Revenue	355,253,250	348,287,500	330,750,000	315,000,000	300,000,000	290,000,000
R&D Expense						
Operating Income						
Operating Margin %						
SGA Expense						
Net Income						
Operating Cash Flow						
Capital Expenditure						
EBITDA						
Return on Assets %						
Return on Equity %						
Debt to Equity						

CONTACT INFORMATION:

Phone: Fax:
Toll-Free: 800-488-8850
Address: 9120 Lockwood Blvd., Mechanicsville, VA 23116 United States

STOCK TICKER/OTHER:

Stock Ticker: Subsidiary   Exchange:
Employees: 525   Fiscal Year Ends: 03/31
Parent Company: Owens & Minor Inc

SALARIES/BONUSES:

Top Exec. Salary: $ Bonus: $
Second Exec. Salary: $ Bonus: $

OTHER THOUGHTS:

Estimated Female Officers or Directors: 1
Hot Spot for Advancement for Women/Minorities: Y

Medical Facilities Corporation

www.medicalfacilitiescorp.ca

NAIC Code: 622310

TYPES OF BUSINESS:

Specialty (except Psychiatric and Substance Abuse) Hospitals

BRANDS/DIVISIONS/AFFILIATES:

Black Hills Surgical Hospital
Oklahoma Spine Hospital
Arkansas Surgical Hospital
Sioux Falls Specialty Hospital
Newport Center Surgical

CONTACTS: Note: Officers with more than one job title may be intentionally listed here more than once.

R. Curd, CEO, Subsidiary
Robert Horrar, CEO
Tyler Murphy, CFO
Marilynne Day-Linton, Chairman of the Board
James Rolfe, Other Executive Officer
Jimmy Porter, Vice President, Divisional

GROWTH PLANS/SPECIAL FEATURES:

Medical Facilities Corporation (MFC) owns controlling interests in four specialty surgical hospitals located in South Dakota, Oklahoma and Arkansas, as well as an ambulatory surgery center in California. In addition, through a partnership with NueHealth, LLC, Medical Facilities owns controlling interests in six ambulatory surgery centers in Michigan, Missouri, Nebraska, Ohio, Oregon and Pennsylvania. The firm's specialty surgical hospitals perform scheduled surgery, imaging and diagnostic procedures. MFC's focus is to be different from regular hospitals by creating a five-star hotel environment and service. Black Hills Surgical Hospital in South Dakota, focuses primarily on orthopedic, neurosurgical and pain management procedures and features 11 operating rooms and 26 overnight rooms. Oklahoma Spine Hospital in Oklahoma, focuses on neurosurgery and pain management procedures and has a total of 7 operating rooms and 25 overnight rooms. Arkansas Surgical Hospital is nationally acclaimed and physician-owned, specializing in orthopedic and spine surgery, with 11 operating rooms and 41 overnight rooms. Sioux Falls Specialty Hospital in South Dakota specializes in orthopedics, ear/nose/throat, pain management, gastroenterology and urology procedures, and comprises 14 operating rooms and 34 overnight rooms. Last, Newport Center Surgical is a licensed ambulatory surgery center in California, with two operating rooms and one procedure room. It specializes in orthopedics, obstetrics/gynecology, pain management, gastroenterology and urology. In 2020, MFC sold its interest in Central Arkansas Surgical Center for an undisclosed amount; the majority of its interest in Unity Medical and Surgical Hospital to a group of local investors, including leading physicians affiliated with South Bend Orthopedics, The South Bend Clinic and Allied Physicians of Michiana; and sold its interest in Two Rivers Surgical Center to two of the managing physicians for an undisclosed amount.

FINANCIAL DATA: Note: Data for latest year may not have been available at press time.

In U.S. $	2020	2019	2018	2017	2016	2015
Revenue	363,854,000	398,103,000	431,602,000	385,329,000	339,472,000	308,778,000
R&D Expense						
Operating Income	67,794,000	66,456,000	73,384,000	66,901,000	68,073,000	74,692,000
Operating Margin %		.17%	.17%	.17%	.20%	.24%
SGA Expense	173,264,000	173,410,000	199,635,000	175,722,000	149,136,000	125,218,000
Net Income	8,813,000	9,824,000	20,927,000	20,637,000	9,754,000	47,127,000
Operating Cash Flow	87,089,000	77,375,000	81,452,000	79,986,000	78,290,000	80,240,000
Capital Expenditure	7,518,000	12,567,000	21,837,000	11,190,000	43,704,000	7,385,000
EBITDA	84,016,000	124,835,000	101,471,000	95,566,000	74,212,000	131,687,000
Return on Assets %		.02%	.04%	.04%	.02%	.12%
Return on Equity %		.07%	.15%	.14%	.06%	.30%
Debt to Equity		1.482	0.868	0.574	0.914	0.351

CONTACT INFORMATION:

Phone: 416 848-7380   Fax:
Toll-Free: 877-42-7162
Address: 4576 Yonge St., Ste. 701, Toronto, ON M2N 6N4 Canada

STOCK TICKER/OTHER:

Stock Ticker: DR   Exchange: TSE
Employees: 1,833   Fiscal Year Ends: 12/31
Parent Company:

SALARIES/BONUSES:

Top Exec. Salary: $ Bonus: $
Second Exec. Salary: $ Bonus: $

OTHER THOUGHTS:

Estimated Female Officers or Directors: 1
Hot Spot for Advancement for Women/Minorities:

Sales, profits and employees may be estimates. Financial information, benefits and other data can change quickly and may vary from those stated here.

Medical Information Technology Inc (MEDITECH)

www.meditech.com

NAIC Code: 511210D

TYPES OF BUSINESS:

Computer Software, Healthcare & Biotechnology

BRANDS/DIVISIONS/AFFILIATES:

Web EHR
Expanse

CONTACTS: *Note: Officers with more than one job title may be intentionally listed here more than once.*

Howard Messing, CEO
Michelle O'Connor, COO
Howard Messing, Pres.
Barbara Manzolillo, CFO
Chris Anschuetz, VP-Tech.
Michelle O'Connor, Exec. VP-Prod. Dev.
Hoda Sayed-Friel, Exec. VP-Strategy & Mktg.
Barbara A. Manzolillo, Treas.
Robert Gale, Sr. VP-Prod. Dev.
Leah Farina, VP-Client Svcs. & Int'l
Scott Radner, VP-Advanced Tech.
A. Neil Pappalardo, Chmn.
Steven Koretz, Sr. VP- Int'l & Client Svcs.

GROWTH PLANS/SPECIAL FEATURES:

Medical Information Technology, Inc. (MEDITECH) develops and markets information system software for the health care industry. MEDITECH's software products automate a variety of hospital functions, and offer various solutions for long-term care facilities, ambulatory care centers, acute-care hospitals, emergency rooms and pharmacies, as well as imaging, therapeutic service and behavioral health facilities. The company specifies aggregate components for each hospital and suggests typical configurations from selected hardware vendors pertaining to software needs. The firm's solutions are accessible via desktop and mobile devices anywhere, any time. MEDITECH'S Web EHR (electronic health record) product offers a cohesive set of software designed to work in conjunction with the overall operation of the hospital. Web EHR facilitates over 300 billion data transactions per year. MEDITECH as a Services (MaaS) is a cloud-based subscription model that powers the firm's Expanse next-generation EHR web platform. The firm's software products will automate clinical laboratory departments, which perform diagnostic tests; and automate hospital billing, accounts receivable and general accounting. MEDITECH's primary international subsidiary locations are based in Canada, Asia Pacific, South Africa, the U.K. and Ireland.

MEDITECH offers its employees health and dental insurance, group life and accidental insurance, short- and long-term disability insurance, as well as a variety of company incentives and perks.

FINANCIAL DATA: *Note: Data for latest year may not have been available at press time.*

In U.S. $	2020	2019	2018	2017	2016	2015
Revenue	502,851,197	493,844,632	488,188,746	480,256,468	462,256,468	475,525,581
R&D Expense						
Operating Income						
Operating Margin %						
SGA Expense						
Net Income	74,542,923	180,157,193	56,205,796	77,428,576	72,890,198	70,066,792
Operating Cash Flow						
Capital Expenditure						
EBITDA						
Return on Assets %						
Return on Equity %						
Debt to Equity						

CONTACT INFORMATION:

Phone: 781-821-3000   Fax: 781-821-2199
Toll-Free:
Address: Meditech Circle, Westwood, MA 02090 United States

STOCK TICKER/OTHER:

Stock Ticker: Private   Exchange:
Employees: 3,700   Fiscal Year Ends: 12/31
Parent Company:

SALARIES/BONUSES:

Top Exec. Salary: $ Bonus: $
Second Exec. Salary: $ Bonus: $

OTHER THOUGHTS:

Estimated Female Officers or Directors: 10
Hot Spot for Advancement for Women/Minorities: Y

Medical Mutual of Ohio

www.medmutual.com

NAIC Code: 524114

TYPES OF BUSINESS:

Insurance-Medical & Health, HMOs & PPOs
Workers' Compensation Insurance
Life Insurance
Dental Insurance
Vision Insurance

BRANDS/DIVISIONS/AFFILIATES:

SuperMed

CONTACTS: *Note: Officers with more than one job title may be intentionally listed here more than once.*

Rick Chiricosta, CEO
Rick Chiricosta, Pres.
Ray Mueller, CFO
Andrea Hogben, CMO
John Kish, CIO
Pat Dugan, Chief Legal Officer
Jared Chaney, Chief Comm. Officer
Sue Tyler, Chief Experience Officer
Steffany Matticola, Chief of Staff
Rick Chiricosta, Chmn.

GROWTH PLANS/SPECIAL FEATURES:

Medical Mutual of Ohio is a nonprofit healthcare company that provides health insurance to individual and group customers through individual and corporate plans. The firm has numerous locations throughout Ohio. As a mutual company, Medical Mutual is owned by its policyholders. Its insurance programs include health maintenance organization (HMO), preferred provider organization (PPO), point of service (POS), indemnity and Medicare supplemental and Advantage plans. Medial Mutual also provides dental, vision, life and workers' compensation insurance. The company sells its insurance under the SuperMed brand. Medical Mutual's website offers information on individual insurance policies as well as healthcare planning, special information on accounts for retirement and general health information. The company also offers a health and wellness section that offers resources for preventative information, smoking cessation, diet/nutrition, mental health, financial health, medications, family/relationships and fitness. During 2020, Medical Mutual agreed to acquire Bravo Wellness LLC, a data-driven provider of wellness solutions to more than 1 million users nationwide. Bravo would operate as a wholly-owned subsidiary of Medica Mutual.

Medical Mutual of Ohio offers its employees a 401(k) program; medical, dental, vision, life and disability insurance; health and wellness programs; professional development and tuition reimbursement programs; and a variety of company perks.

FINANCIAL DATA: *Note: Data for latest year may not have been available at press time.*

In U.S. $	2020	2019	2018	2017	2016	2015
Revenue	3,414,982,173	3,191,572,125	3,039,592,500	2,894,850,000	2,757,000,000	2,402,000,000
R&D Expense						
Operating Income						
Operating Margin %						
SGA Expense						
Net Income						
Operating Cash Flow						
Capital Expenditure						
EBITDA						
Return on Assets %						
Return on Equity %						
Debt to Equity						

CONTACT INFORMATION:

Phone: 216-687-7000   Fax: 216-687-6044
Toll-Free: 800-382-5729
Address: 2060 E. 9th St., Cleveland, OH 44115 United States

STOCK TICKER/OTHER:

Stock Ticker: Nonprofit
Employees: 1,953
Parent Company:

Exchange:
Fiscal Year Ends: 12/31

SALARIES/BONUSES:

Top Exec. Salary: $ Bonus: $
Second Exec. Salary: $ Bonus: $

OTHER THOUGHTS:

Estimated Female Officers or Directors: 3
Hot Spot for Advancement for Women/Minorities: Y

Mediclinic International plc

NAIC Code: 622110

www.mediclinic.com

TYPES OF BUSINESS:

General Medical and Surgical Hospitals

BRANDS/DIVISIONS/AFFILIATES:

Spire Healthcare Group plc
hystrix medical AG

CONTACTS: *Note: Officers with more than one job title may be intentionally listed here more than once.*

Ronnie van der Merwe, CEO
Jurgens Myburgh, CFO
Magnus Oetiker, Chief Human Resources Officer
Dirk le Roux, CIO
Ronnie van der Merwe, Chief Clinical Officer
Gert Hattingh, Exec.-Group Svcs.
Koert Pretorius, CEO-Mediclinic Southern Africa
Ole Wiesinger, CEO-Hirslanden
Inga Beale, Chmn.

GROWTH PLANS/SPECIAL FEATURES:

Mediclinic International plc operates multidisciplinary private hospitals in South Africa, Switzerland and the Middle East. The company's core purpose is to enhance the quality of life of patients by providing cost-effective acute care services. Mediclinic's combined group comprises 76 hospitals and 35 clinics, with approximately 11,600 inpatient beds, as of mid-2020. Within South Africa, Mediclinic Southern Africa operates 52 hospitals, eight sub-acute hospitals and 11 day-case clinics. Within Switzerland, the Hirslanden hospital group operates 17 hospitals and four day-case clinics. Within the Middle East, Mediclinic operates seven hospitals, two day-case clinics and 18 outpatient clinics in the United Arab Emirates. In addition, Mediclinic holds a 29.9% stake in Spire Healthcare Group plc, a U.K.-based private healthcare group. During 2020, Mediclinic announced that it invested in hystrix medical AG, a leading eCommerce marketplace in the Swiss healthcare system for medical goods.

FINANCIAL DATA: *Note: Data for latest year may not have been available at press time.*

In U.S. $	2020	2019	2018	2017	2016	2015
Revenue	4,364,630,000	4,150,858,000	4,063,084,000	3,891,783,000	2,982,898,000	
R&D Expense						
Operating Income	458,689,600	460,105,300	501,160,900	515,318,000	409,139,800	
Operating Margin %						
SGA Expense	1,131,151,000	1,104,253,000	1,051,872,000	975,423,400	784,302,700	
Net Income	-453,026,800	-213,772,000	-696,528,700	324,197,300	250,580,400	
Operating Cash Flow	645,563,200	487,003,800				
Capital Expenditure						
EBITDA	31,145,590	121,751,000	-591,766,300	532,306,500	424,712,600	
Return on Assets %						
Return on Equity %						
Debt to Equity						

CONTACT INFORMATION:

Phone: 44 207954-9548   Fax:
Toll-Free:
Address: 65 Gresham Street, London, EC2V 7NQ United Kingdom

STOCK TICKER/OTHER:

Stock Ticker: ALNRF
Employees: 33,140
Parent Company:

Exchange: PINX
Fiscal Year Ends: 03/31

SALARIES/BONUSES:

Top Exec. Salary: $ Bonus: $
Second Exec. Salary: $ Bonus: $

OTHER THOUGHTS:

Estimated Female Officers or Directors: 1
Hot Spot for Advancement for Women/Minorities:

Medicure Inc

www.medicure.com

NAIC Code: 325412

TYPES OF BUSINESS:

Pharmaceutical Preparation Manufacturing

BRANDS/DIVISIONS/AFFILIATES:

AGGRASTAT
ZYPITAMAGTM
SNP
ReDS PRO
Medicure International Inc
Medicure Pharma Inc
P5P (MC-1, TARDOXAL)
ANDA

CONTACTS: *Note: Officers with more than one job title may be intentionally listed here more than once.*

Albert Friesen, CEO
James Kinley, CFO

GROWTH PLANS/SPECIAL FEATURES:

Medicure, Inc. is a specialty pharmaceutical company involved in research, clinical development and commercialization of human therapeutics. The company's present focus is the sale and marketing of its cardiovascular products, AGGRASTAT, ZYPITAMAGTM and SNP and the sale and marketing of the ReDS PRO medical device. The rights to the products are owned by Medicure's subsidiary, Medicure International, Inc. (Barbados), and the products are distributed in the U.S. by subsidiary Medicure Pharma, Inc. The research and development program of Medicure is ocused on making selective research and development investments in certain additional acute cardiovascular generic and reformulation product opportunities, as well as continuing the development and implementation of its regulatory, brand and life cycle management strategy for AGGRASTAT. The Company is also continuing to explore neurological treatment applications of its legacy product P5P (MC-1, TARDOXAL), a naturally occurring molecule drug to treat neurological conditions such as Tardive Dyskinesia. Medicure's transdermal delivery formulation of AGGRASTAT (tirofiban HCl) has many benefits over intravenous delivery, including being non-invasive, ease of administration and possible reduction of length of hospital stay. The firm's recent AGGRASTAT High-Dose Bolus (HDB) dose regimen achieves greater than 90% inhibition of platelet aggregation within 10 minutes of bolus administration. Zypitamag was launched commercially for the treatment of primary hyperlipidemia or mixed dyslipidemia. ANDA was approved by the U.S. Food and Drug Administration for sodium nitroprusside injection (SNP), which is indicated for the immediate reduction of blood pressure for adult and pediatric patients in hypertensive crisis. Medicure continues to develop two additional generic versions of acute cardiovascular drugs and explore other potential development opportunities.

FINANCIAL DATA: *Note: Data for latest year may not have been available at press time.*

In U.S. $	2020	2019	2018	2017	2016	2015
Revenue	9,619,687	16,714,720	24,119,120	22,481,420	31,302,070	18,297,400
R&D Expense	2,733,449	3,603,447	5,535,681	4,265,667	4,219,484	4,031,200
Operating Income	-6,717,210	-6,829,066	-1,016,010	3,026,165	5,537,688	3,911,583
Operating Margin %		-.41%	-.04%	.13%	.18%	.21%
SGA Expense	8,234,320	13,914,990	16,159,030	12,318,860	13,450,390	8,482,158
Net Income	-5,671,555	-16,394,070	3,252,663	35,977,200	22,916,130	1,382,409
Operating Cash Flow	-1,855,995	-12,131,080	615,024	18,164,830	5,311,800	118,316
Capital Expenditure	1,657	11,472,370	1,224,653	1,095,242	384,628	187,729
EBITDA	-4,419,588	-14,680,590	4,243,682	8,562,384	26,504,050	1,945,174
Return on Assets %		-.27%	.03%	.25%	.23%	.12%
Return on Equity %		-.36%	.05%	.74%	1.34%	6.06%
Debt to Equity		0.032			1.856	0.587

CONTACT INFORMATION:

Phone: 204 487-7412   Fax: 204 488-9823
Toll-Free:
Address: 2-1250 Waverley Street, Winnipeg, MB R3T 6C6 Canada

STOCK TICKER/OTHER:

Stock Ticker: MCUJF   Exchange: PINX
Employees: 45   Fiscal Year Ends: 05/31
Parent Company:

SALARIES/BONUSES:

Top Exec. Salary: $ Bonus: $
Second Exec. Salary: $ Bonus: $

OTHER THOUGHTS:

Estimated Female Officers or Directors:
Hot Spot for Advancement for Women/Minorities:

Sales, profits and employees may be estimates. Financial information, benefits and other data can change quickly and may vary from those stated here.

Medifast Inc

www.medifast1.com

NAIC Code: 812191

TYPES OF BUSINESS:

Weight Management Programs
Diet Products
Online Retail
Direct Marketing

BRANDS/DIVISIONS/AFFILIATES:

Jason Pharmaceuticals Inc
Jason Properties LLC
Jason Enterprises Inc
Seven Crondall Associates LLC
Medifast Nutrition Inc
Optavia LLC
Medifast Franchise Systems Inc
Thrive by Medifast

CONTACTS: *Note: Officers with more than one job title may be intentionally listed here more than once.*

Daniel Chard, CEO
Timothy Robinson, CFO
Michael Macdonald, Chairman of the Board
Anthony Tyree, Chief Marketing Officer
Joseph Kelleman, Controller
William Baker, Executive VP, Divisional
Jason Groves, Executive VP
Frances Lawler, Other Executive Officer
Nicholas Johnson, President, Subsidiary

GROWTH PLANS/SPECIAL FEATURES:

Medifast, Inc. produces, distributes and sells weight loss, weight management and healthy living products. Medifast conducts the majority of its business through wholly-owned subsidiaries: Jason Pharmaceuticals, Inc.; Jason Properties, LLC; Jason Enterprises, Inc.; Seven Crondall Associates, LLC; Medifast Nutrition, Inc.; Optavia, LLC; Corporate Events, Inc.; OPTAVIA (Hong Kong) Limited; OPTAVIA (Singapore) PTE. LTD; OPTAVIA Health Consultation (Shanghai) Co., Ltd.; and Medifast Franchise Systems, Inc. Jason Pharmaceuticals produces approximately 46% of the Medifast products at its facility in Maryland, USA (as of fiscal 2019). Medifast product lines include weight loss, weight management and healthy living meal replacements, snacks, hydration products and vitamins under the Medifast, OPTAVIA, Thrive by Medifast, Optimal Health by OPTAVIA, Flavors of Home and Essential 1 brands. The Thrive by Medifast and Optimal Health by OPTAVIA lines include a variety of specially formulated bars, shakes and smoothies. The company's nutritional products are formulated with high-quality, low-calorie and low-fat ingredients. Its meals are individually portioned, calorie- and carbohydrate-controlled which provide a balance of protein and good carbohydrates, including fiber. The meals replacements are also fortified to contain vitamins and minerals, as well as other nutrients essential for good health. Medifast expanded into the Asia-Pacific markets of Hong Kong and Singapore in 2019 with its integrated Optavia coach model. These independent wellness coaches seek to enrich the lives of its clients through programs that promote healthy living and through the manufacture and distribution of clinically-proven, Medifast proprietary products marketed under the Optavia brand.

FINANCIAL DATA: *Note: Data for latest year may not have been available at press time.*

In U.S. $	2020	2019	2018	2017	2016	2015
Revenue	934,842,000	713,672,000	501,003,000	301,563,000	274,534,000	272,773,000
R&D Expense						
Operating Income	134,159,000	91,039,000	69,063,000	39,632,000	26,859,000	28,684,000
Operating Margin %		.13%	.14%	.13%	.10%	.11%
SGA Expense	563,656,000	445,819,000	310,836,000	188,180,000	178,805,000	172,631,000
Net Income	102,859,000	77,916,000	55,789,000	27,721,000	17,835,000	20,058,000
Operating Cash Flow	145,196,000	84,261,000	60,816,000	43,237,000	25,350,000	29,411,000
Capital Expenditure	5,887,000	10,058,000	4,940,000	3,242,000	2,876,000	2,819,000
EBITDA	141,429,000	95,663,000	73,498,000	43,841,000	32,264,000	35,799,000
Return on Assets %		.43%	.35%	.21%	.15%	.17%
Return on Equity %		.73%	.51%	.27%	.19%	.24%
Debt to Equity		0.10				

CONTACT INFORMATION:

Phone: 410 581-8042   Fax: 410 581-8070
Toll-Free:
Address: 100 International Dr., 18/Fl, Baltimore, MD 21202 United States

STOCK TICKER/OTHER:

Stock Ticker: MED   Exchange: NYS
Employees: 713   Fiscal Year Ends: 12/31
Parent Company:

SALARIES/BONUSES:

Top Exec. Salary: $ Bonus: $
Second Exec. Salary: $ Bonus: $

OTHER THOUGHTS:

Estimated Female Officers or Directors: 3
Hot Spot for Advancement for Women/Minorities: Y

Medipal Holdings Corporation

www.medipal.co.jp

NAIC Code: 424210

TYPES OF BUSINESS:

Drugs and Druggists' Sundries Merchant Wholesalers

BRANDS/DIVISIONS/AFFILIATES:

Mediceo Corporation
MM Corporation
EVERLTH Co Ltd
ATOL Co Ltd
MVC Co Ltd
Paltac Corporation
MP Agro Co Ltd
Medipal Foods Corporation

CONTACTS: *Note: Officers with more than one job title may be intentionally listed here more than once.*

Shuichi Watanabe, CEO
Nobuaki Nozawa, Deputy Gen. Mgr.-Admin. Div.
Kenichi Takase, Mgr.-Corp. Planning Dept.
Toshio Hirasawa, Sr. Managing Exec. Officer-Finance & Acct.
Masanori Kawahara, VP-OrphanPacific, Inc.
Kimio Nakamura, Deputy Gen. Mgr.-Admin. Div.

GROWTH PLANS/SPECIAL FEATURES:

Medipal Holdings Corporation is engaged in the wholesale of pharmaceutical products, cosmetics and daily miscellaneous goods. The company has three business segments: prescription pharmaceutical wholesale; cosmetics, daily necessities and over the counter (OTC) pharmaceutical wholesale; and animal health products and food processing raw materials wholesale. Medipal's subsidiaries include: Mediceo Corporation; MM Corporation; M.I.C. (Medical Information College), Inc.; EVERLTH Co., Ltd.; ASTEC Co., Ltd.; ATOL Co., Ltd.; MVC Co., Ltd.; Trim Co., Ltd.; SPLine Corporation; MEDIE Co., Ltd.; Paltac Corporation; MP Agro Co., Ltd.; and Medipal Foods Corporation. These companies distribute products to the wholesale market, including: prescription pharmaceuticals, medical equipment, medical supplies, clinical diagnostics, cosmetics, daily necessities, over-the-counter pharmaceuticals, animal health products and raw ingredients for food processing. Medipal's joint ventures and affiliates include: Sinopharm Group Beijing Huahong Co. Ltd. (China); Beijing Tianxingpuxin Bio-med Sinopharm Holding Co. Ltd. (China); Shikoku Yakugyo Co., Ltd.; Presuscube Corporation; and Kuraya (USA) Corporation.

FINANCIAL DATA: *Note: Data for latest year may not have been available at press time.*

In U.S. $	2020	2019	2018	2017	2016	2015
Revenue	29,710,780,000	29,060,630,000	28,735,550,000	27,983,900,000	27,656,880,000	
R&D Expense						
Operating Income	485,090,400	455,106,700	404,272,400	362,169,300	386,198,200	
Operating Margin %	.02%	.02%	.01%	.01%	.01%	
SGA Expense	172,887,800	158,430,200	147,534,600	140,319,900	132,757,400	
Net Income	346,761,900	313,800,900	317,645,900	264,957,600	281,031,700	
Operating Cash Flow	519,823,200	581,918,500	580,475,500	437,964,100	200,789,100	
Capital Expenditure	249,806,000	168,878,400	278,556,600	327,299,500	350,661,700	
EBITDA	825,258,200	708,438,000	722,210,600	607,801,500	617,482,400	
Return on Assets %	.02%	.02%	.02%	.02%	.02%	
Return on Equity %	.08%	.07%	.08%	.07%	.08%	
Debt to Equity	0.061	0.069	0.082	0.035	0.029	

CONTACT INFORMATION:

Phone: 81 3 3517 5800   Fax:
Toll-Free:
Address: 2-7-15, Yaesu, Chuo-ku, Tokyo, 1048461 Japan

STOCK TICKER/OTHER:

Stock Ticker: MAHLY   Exchange: PINX
Employees: 21,731   Fiscal Year Ends: 03/31
Parent Company:

SALARIES/BONUSES:

Top Exec. Salary: $ Bonus: $
Second Exec. Salary: $ Bonus: $

OTHER THOUGHTS:

Estimated Female Officers or Directors:
Hot Spot for Advancement for Women/Minorities:

Medline Industries Inc

www.medline.com

NAIC Code: 339100

TYPES OF BUSINESS:

Medical Equipment Manufacturing
Healthcare Product Manufacturing
Healthcare Product Distribution
Healthcare Services
Advanced Wound Care
Furnishings
Medical Equipment
Supplies

BRANDS/DIVISIONS/AFFILIATES:

Blackstone Group Inc
Carlyle Group Inc
Hellman & Friedlman LLC

CONTACTS: *Note: Officers with more than one job title may be intentionally listed here more than once.*

Charlie Mills, CEO
Andy Mills, Pres.
Jimmy Abrams, COO

GROWTH PLANS/SPECIAL FEATURES:

Medline Industries, Inc. manufactures and distributes a wide range of healthcare products, and offers a variety of related services and solutions. Products and solutions address advanced wound care, anesthesia, apparel, beds, mattresses, furnishings, sterilization, diagnostics, medical equipment, environmental services, equipment, foot/ankle, gloves, incontinence, infection prevention, lab supplies, nursing supplies, nutrition, office supplies, surgery, pharmacy, respiratory, skin care, textiles, therapy, rehabilitation, urology, ostomy, vascular access and wound care. Other capabilities offered by Medline include outfitting facilities, laundry services, PPE, scrubs/uniforms, optimizing the supply chain, distribution, kitting (including custom procedure trays), supply chain analytics, logistics and perioperative performance. Medline has more than 20 manufacturing sites across North America, as well as over 45 distribution centers. The firm does business in more than 125 countries. During 2021, Medline Industries was acquired by a consortium of private-equity firms composed of Blackstone Group Inc., Carlyle Group Inc. and Hellman & Friedman LLC in a buyout deal valuing the company, with debt, at approximately $34 billion.

FINANCIAL DATA: *Note: Data for latest year may not have been available at press time.*

In U.S. $	2020	2019	2018	2017	2016	2015
Revenue						
R&D Expense						
Operating Income						
Operating Margin %						
SGA Expense						
Net Income						
Operating Cash Flow						
Capital Expenditure						
EBITDA						
Return on Assets %						
Return on Equity %						
Debt to Equity						

CONTACT INFORMATION:

Phone: Fax:
Toll-Free: 844 249-1979
Address: Three Lakes Dr., Northfield, IL 60093 United States

STOCK TICKER/OTHER:

Stock Ticker: Private   Exchange:
Employees: Fiscal Year Ends:
Parent Company:

SALARIES/BONUSES:

Top Exec. Salary: $ Bonus: $
Second Exec. Salary: $ Bonus: $

OTHER THOUGHTS:

Estimated Female Officers or Directors:
Hot Spot for Advancement for Women/Minorities:

MEDNAX Inc

www.mednax.com

NAIC Code: 621111

TYPES OF BUSINESS:

Hospital-Based Pediatrician Practice Management
Pediatric Intensive Care Unit Management
Neonatal Intensive Care Unit Management
Perinatal Physician Services
Staffing Services
Laboratory Services

BRANDS/DIVISIONS/AFFILIATES:

CONTACTS: *Note: Officers with more than one job title may be intentionally listed here more than once.*

Roger Medel, CEO
Stephen Farber, CFO
Cesar Alvarez, Chairman of the Board
John Pepia, Chief Accounting Officer
David Clark, COO
Dominic Andreano, General Counsel
Joseph Calabro, President

GROWTH PLANS/SPECIAL FEATURES:

MEDNAX, Inc. is a leading provider of physician services including newborn, maternal-fetal, teleradiology, pediatric cardiology and other pediatric subspecialty care. The MEDNAX network comprises over 4,325 affiliated physicians in 50 U.S. states, primarily within hospital-based neonatal intensive care units (NICUs), to babies born prematurely or with medical complications. Approximately 1,300 affiliated physicians provide anesthesia care to patients in connection with surgical and other procedures, as well as pain management. In addition, 400 affiliated physicians provide maternal-fetal and obstetrical medical care to expectant mothers experiencing complicated pregnancies primarily in areas where MEDNAX neonatal physicians practice. Approximately 220 physicians provide pediatric intensive care, 105 physicians provide pediatric cardiology care, 150 physicians provide hospital-based pediatric care, 25 physicians provide pediatric surgical care and 10 physicians provide pediatric ear, nose and throat and pediatric ophthalmology services. MEDNAX also provides radiology services, including diagnostic imaging and interventional radiology through a network of over 810 affiliated radiologists. In May 2020, MEDNAX sold American Anesthesiology to North American Partners in Anesthesia. Later that same year in September, the firm agreed to sell MEDNAX Radiology Solutions to Radiology Partners for $885 million.

MEDNAX offers comprehensive benefits, retirement plans and employee assistance programs.

FINANCIAL DATA: *Note: Data for latest year may not have been available at press time.*

In U.S. $	2020	2019	2018	2017	2016	2015
Revenue	1,733,951,000	3,513,542,000	3,647,123,000	3,458,312,000	3,183,159,000	2,779,996,000
R&D Expense						
Operating Income	171,933,000	408,495,000	445,848,000	480,076,000	571,687,000	557,868,000
Operating Margin %		.12%	.12%	.14%	.18%	.20%
SGA Expense	248,947,000	404,643,000	432,378,000	417,105,000	372,572,000	305,915,000
Net Income	-796,488,000	-1,497,702,000	268,629,000	320,372,000	324,914,000	336,320,000
Operating Cash Flow	204,620,000	346,637,000	289,925,000	511,378,000	443,778,000	368,701,000
Capital Expenditure	28,788,000	31,881,000	48,868,000	49,309,000	39,264,000	27,073,000
EBITDA	146,071,000	-1,043,739,000	568,889,000	587,860,000	666,155,000	627,067,000
Return on Assets %		- .30%	.05%	.06%	.07%	.08%
Return on Equity %		- .65%	.09%	.11%	.13%	.14%
Debt to Equity		1.199	0.639	0.604	0.61	0.518

CONTACT INFORMATION:

Phone: 954 384-0175   Fax:
Toll-Free: 800-243-3839
Address: 1301 Concord Terrace, Sunrise, FL 33323 United States

STOCK TICKER/OTHER:

Stock Ticker: MD
Employees: 7,900
Parent Company:

Exchange: NYS
Fiscal Year Ends: 12/31

SALARIES/BONUSES:

Top Exec. Salary: $ Bonus: $
Second Exec. Salary: $ Bonus: $

OTHER THOUGHTS:

Estimated Female Officers or Directors: 3
Hot Spot for Advancement for Women/Minorities: Y

Sales, profits and employees may be estimates. Financial information, benefits and other data can change quickly and may vary from those stated here.

MedStar Health

NAIC Code: 622110

www.medstarhealth.org

TYPES OF BUSINESS:

General Medical and Surgical Hospitals
Assisted Living Services
Home Health Services
Ambulatory Centers
Rehabilitation Centers
Nursing Homes
Physician Network Management
Research

BRANDS/DIVISIONS/AFFILIATES:

MedStar Franklin Square Medical Center
MedStar Good Samaritan Hospital
MedStar Harbor Hospital
MedStar Montgomery Medical Center
MedStar Southern Maryland Hospital Center
MedStar National Rehabilitation Hospital
MedStar Physician Partners
MedStar Health Research Institute

CONTACTS: *Note: Officers with more than one job title may be intentionally listed here more than once.*

Kenneth A. Samet, CEO
Joy Drass, COO
Susan K. Nelson, CFO
Kevin P. Kowalski, Sr. VP-Mktg. & Strategy
Loretta Young Walker, VP-Chief Human Resources Officer
Stephen R.T. Evans, Chief Medical Officer
Scott T. MacLean, CIO
Michael J. Curran, Chief Admin. Officer
Oliver M. Johnson, II, General Counsel
Eric R. Wagner, Exec. VP-Diversified Oper. & External Affairs
Christine M. Swearingen, Exec. VP-Planning & Community Rel.
Jean Hitchcock, VP-Public Affairs & Mktg.
Susan K. Nelson, VP-Finance & Acct. Oper.
Carl Schindelar, Exec. VP-Oper., Baltimore Region
Jennie P. McConagha, Chief of Staff
Joel N. Bryan, Treas.
Pegeen Townsend, VP-Gov't Affairs
Anthony J. Buzzelli, Chmn.

GROWTH PLANS/SPECIAL FEATURES:

MedStar Health is a nonprofit, community-based health care organization primarily composed of several integrated businesses, including 10 major hospitals, with 30,000 associates and 5,400 affiliated physicians (as of fiscal 2020). The hospitals are located within proximity of the Baltimore/Washington, D.C. area and include the following: MedStar Franklin Square Medical Center, MedStar Good Samaritan Hospital, MedStar Harbor Hospital, MedStar Montgomery Medical Center, MedStar Southern Maryland Hospital Center, MedStar St. Mary's Hospital, MedStar Union Memorial Hospital, MedStar Georgetown University Hospital, MedStar Washington Hospital Center and MedStar National Rehabilitation Hospital. Specialty services include cancer, heart/vascular, neurology, orthopedics, primary care, physical therapy, urgent care, among others. The organization manages MedStar Physician Partners, a comprehensive physician network serving in the region. Its MedStar Health Research Institute conducts research and clinical trials; and MedStar Health has one of the largest graduate medical education programs in the country, training more than 1,100 medical residents annually, and is the medical education and clinical partner of Georgetown University.

MedStar offers its employees wellness benefits, retirement and financial services, employee assistance programs, life and disability insurance and more.

FINANCIAL DATA: *Note: Data for latest year may not have been available at press time.*

In U.S. $	2020	2019	2018	2017	2016	2015
Revenue	5,788,600,000	5,690,400,000	5,604,000,000	5,529,800,000	5,266,000,000	5,027,200,000
R&D Expense						
Operating Income						
Operating Margin %						
SGA Expense						
Net Income	136,400,000	187,900,000	271,900,000	297,100,000	46,100,000	111,300,000
Operating Cash Flow						
Capital Expenditure						
EBITDA						
Return on Assets %						
Return on Equity %						
Debt to Equity						

CONTACT INFORMATION:

Phone: 410-772-6500 Fax: 410-715-3905
Toll-Free: 877-772-6505
Address: 10980 Grantchester Way, Columbia, MD 21044 United States

STOCK TICKER/OTHER:

Stock Ticker: Nonprofit Exchange:
Employees: 32,000 Fiscal Year Ends: 06/30
Parent Company:

SALARIES/BONUSES:

Top Exec. Salary: $ Bonus: $
Second Exec. Salary: $ Bonus: $

OTHER THOUGHTS:

Estimated Female Officers or Directors: 15
Hot Spot for Advancement for Women/Minorities: Y

Medtronic MiniMed Inc

www.medtronicdiabetes.com

NAIC Code: 339100

TYPES OF BUSINESS:

Equipment-Diabetes Management Products
Drug Delivery Microinfusion Systems
External Insulin Pumps & Related Products

BRANDS/DIVISIONS/AFFILIATES:

Medtronic plc
MiniMed 770G
MiniMed 670G
MiniMed 630G
MiniMed 530G
Sugar.IQ

CONTACTS: *Note: Officers with more than one job title may be intentionally listed here more than once.*

Omar Ishrak, Chmn.

GROWTH PLANS/SPECIAL FEATURES:

Medtronic MiniMed, Inc., a subsidiary of Medtronic plc, designs, develops, manufactures and markets advanced micro-infusion systems for the delivery of a variety of drugs, with a primary focus on insulin for the intensive management of diabetes. The company sells external insulin pumps and related disposables designed to deliver small quantities of insulin in a controlled, programmable manner. Medtronic MiniMed operates three global business units: the advanced insulin management business unit serves patients in need of insulin pump therapy; the multiple daily injection solutions business unit delivers innovative solutions that address unmet needs for people with both type 1 and 2 diabetes who rely on multiple daily injections to manage their diabetes; and the non-intensive diabetes therapies business unit addresses the needs of patients with type 2 diabetes who do not use intensive insulin regimens and provides solutions along the diabetes care continuum. The MiniMed family of products include: MiniMed 770G, which automatically adjusts background insulin every five minutes, and glucose readings are offered in real-time and connects directly to the user's smartphone; 670G, which automatically pumps insulin to a diabetic patient's body on sensing its absence or reduction; 630G, which is user-friendly, wireless, waterproof, features airplane mode for traveling and is small and worn on the body, continuously delivering insulin, with required tubing changes every 2-3 days; and 530G, which is worn on the body, delivers tiny drops of rapid-acting insulin which meets individual needs, presents readings every five minutes and requires tubing changes every 2-3 days. Other products include glucose monitoring systems, the Sugar.IQ diabetes assistant, insulin pumps, infusion sets, injection ports and related software and accessories.

Medtronic MiniMed offers employees healthcare coverage, retirement pllans, and a variety of employee assistance programs and perks.

FINANCIAL DATA: *Note: Data for latest year may not have been available at press time.*

In U.S. $	2020	2019	2018	2017	2016	2015
Revenue	2,368,000,000	2,391,000,000	2,140,000,000	1,927,000,000	1,864,000,000	1,762,000,000
R&D Expense						
Operating Income						
Operating Margin %						
SGA Expense						
Net Income						
Operating Cash Flow						
Capital Expenditure						
EBITDA						
Return on Assets %						
Return on Equity %						
Debt to Equity						

CONTACT INFORMATION:

Phone: Fax:
Toll-Free: 866-948-6633
Address: 18000 Devonshire St., Northridge, CA 91325 United States

STOCK TICKER/OTHER:

Stock Ticker: Subsidiary   Exchange:
Employees: Fiscal Year Ends: 04/30
Parent Company: Medtronic plc

SALARIES/BONUSES:

Top Exec. Salary: $ Bonus: $
Second Exec. Salary: $ Bonus: $

OTHER THOUGHTS:

Estimated Female Officers or Directors:
Hot Spot for Advancement for Women/Minorities: Y

Medtronic plc

NAIC Code: 334510

www.medtronic.com

TYPES OF BUSINESS:

Equipment-Defibrillators & Pacing Products
Neurological Devices
Diabetes Management Devices
Ear, Nose & Throat Surgical Equipment
Pain Management Devices
Cardiac Surgery Equipment

BRANDS/DIVISIONS/AFFILIATES:

CONTACTS: *Note: Officers with more than one job title may be intentionally listed here more than once.*

Geoffrey S. Martha, CEO
Greg Smith, Exec. VP-Global Oper. & Supply Chain
Karen L. Parkhill, CFO
Torod Neptune, Sr. VP-Chief Communications Officer
Carol Surface, Sr. VP-Chief Human Resources Officer
Michael Coyle, Executive VP
Hooman Hakami, Executive VP
Robert Hoedt, Executive VP
Bradley Lerman, General Counsel
Richard Kuntz, Other Executive Officer
Carol Surface, Other Executive Officer
Geoffrey Martha, President, Divisional
Bob White, President, Divisional
Chris Lee, President, Geographical
Geoffrey S. Martha, Chmn.

GROWTH PLANS/SPECIAL FEATURES:

Medtronic plc is a global leader in medical device technology, serving physicians, clinicians and patients in more than 150 countries worldwide. Its operations consist of four primary segments: the cardiac and vascular group, which includes the cardiac rhythm and heart failure disease management (CRHF), as well as coronary, structural heart and endovascular therapies; the restorative therapies group, which includes the spinal, brain, specialty and pain therapies; the minimally invasive therapies group, which includes surgical and patient monitoring and recovery solutions; and the diabetes group, which includes intensive insulin management, non-intensive diabetes therapies and diabetes services and solutions. Products in the CRHF division manage cardiac rhythm disorders and include pacemakers, implantable defibrillators, ablation products and products for the treatment of atrial fibrillation (AF). The coronary, structural heart and endovascular therapies makes technology that supports the interventional treatment of coronary artery disease to help improve blood flow, and includes products such as stents, guide wires, and catheters. The spinal division offers medical devices used to treat spinal and cranial conditions. The neuromodulation division develops devices for the treatment of neurological, urological and gastroenterological disorders. The surgical technologies division develops and manufactures minimally invasive products to treat ear, nose and throat and neurological diseases. The patient monitoring and recovery develops and markets sensors, monitors and temperature management products, as well as products and therapies for complication-free recovery. The diabetes unit develops integrated diabetes management systems, insulin pump therapies, continuous glucose monitoring systems and therapy management software.

Medtronic offers its employees healthcare and disability, adoption and elder care assistance, retirement plans and stock options.

FINANCIAL DATA: *Note: Data for latest year may not have been available at press time.*

In U.S. $	2020	2019	2018	2017	2016	2015
Revenue	28,913,000,000	30,557,000,000	29,953,000,000	29,710,000,000	28,833,000,000	
R&D Expense	2,331,000,000	2,330,000,000	2,253,000,000	2,193,000,000	2,224,000,000	
Operating Income	5,222,000,000	6,632,000,000	6,343,000,000	6,313,000,000	5,960,000,000	
Operating Margin %	.18%	.22%	.21%	.21%	.21%	
SGA Expense	10,109,000,000	10,418,000,000	9,974,000,000	9,711,000,000	9,469,000,000	
Net Income	4,789,000,000	4,631,000,000	3,104,000,000	4,028,000,000	3,538,000,000	
Operating Cash Flow	7,234,000,000	7,007,000,000	4,684,000,000	6,880,000,000	5,218,000,000	
Capital Expenditure	1,213,000,000	1,134,000,000	1,068,000,000	1,254,000,000	1,046,000,000	
EBITDA	7,810,000,000	9,300,000,000	9,465,000,000	8,613,000,000	8,542,000,000	
Return on Assets %	.05%	.05%	.03%	.04%	.03%	
Return on Equity %	.09%	.09%	.06%	.08%	.07%	
Debt to Equity	0.434	0.489	0.467	0.515	0.581	

CONTACT INFORMATION:

Phone: 3531-438-1700   Fax:
Toll-Free:
Address: 20 On Hatch, Lower Hatch St., Dublin, 2 Ireland

STOCK TICKER/OTHER:

Stock Ticker: MDT
Employees: 90,000
Parent Company:

Exchange: NYS
Fiscal Year Ends: 04/30

SALARIES/BONUSES:

Top Exec. Salary: $ Bonus: $
Second Exec. Salary: $ Bonus: $

OTHER THOUGHTS:

Estimated Female Officers or Directors: 5
Hot Spot for Advancement for Women/Minorities: Y

Medtronic Vascular Inc

www.medtronic.com/us-en/healthcare-professionals/products/cardiovascular.html

NAIC Code: 339100

TYPES OF BUSINESS:

Medical Instruments-Stents & Catheters
Coronary Products
Perfusion Systems
Peripheral Products
Endovascular Products
Catheters

BRANDS/DIVISIONS/AFFILIATES:

Medtronic plc

CONTACTS: *Note: Officers with more than one job title may be intentionally listed here more than once.*

Omar Isharak, Chmn.

GROWTH PLANS/SPECIAL FEATURES:

Medtronic Vascular, Inc., a subsidiary of Medtronic plc, produces cardiac and vascular products. Cardiac products consist of ablation products, aortic stent grafts, blood management solutions, diagnostics, cannulae, cardiopulmonary products, electrosurgical products, extracorporeal life support solutions, heart valve replacement solutions, pediatric perfusion products, revascularization products (surgical) and transradial experience solutions. Vascular products include chronic total occlusion devices, coronary balloons, catheters, guidewires, stents, directional atherectomy systems, drug-coated balloons, embolic protection devices, infusion therapy products, peripheral and biliary stents, peripheral embolization products, PTA balloons, snares, superficial vein products and more. This division's products, solutions and devices help to treat issues such as abdominal aortic aneurysms, atrial fibrillation, bradycardia, coronary artery disease, atrial fibrillation management, heart palpitations, suspected atrial fibrillation, fainting, stroke, heart failure, heart valve disease, peripheral arterial disease, tachycardia, thoracic aortic aneurysm and vein disease.

FINANCIAL DATA: *Note: Data for latest year may not have been available at press time.*

In U.S. $	2020	2019	2018	2017	2016	2015
Revenue	10,468,000,000	11,505,000,000	11,354,000,000	10,498,000,000	10,196,000,000	9,361,000,000
R&D Expense						
Operating Income						
Operating Margin %						
SGA Expense						
Net Income						
Operating Cash Flow						
Capital Expenditure						
EBITDA						
Return on Assets %						
Return on Equity %						
Debt to Equity						

CONTACT INFORMATION:

Phone: 763-514-4000   Fax:
Toll-Free: 800-633-8766
Address: 3576 Unocal Pl., Fountaingrove A, Santa Rosa, CA 95403 United States

STOCK TICKER/OTHER:

Stock Ticker: Subsidiary
Employees:
Parent Company: Medtronic plc

Exchange:
Fiscal Year Ends: 04/30

SALARIES/BONUSES:

Top Exec. Salary: $ Bonus: $
Second Exec. Salary: $ Bonus: $

OTHER THOUGHTS:

Estimated Female Officers or Directors:
Hot Spot for Advancement for Women/Minorities: Y

Memorial Hermann Healthcare System   www.memorialhermann.org

NAIC Code: 622110

TYPES OF BUSINESS:

General Medical and Surgical Hospitals
Long-Term Care
Retirement & Nursing Homes
Wellness Centers
Rehabilitation Services
Home Health Services
Air Ambulance Services
Sports Medicine

BRANDS/DIVISIONS/AFFILIATES:

Children's Memorial Hermann Pediatrics

CONTACTS: *Note: Officers with more than one job title may be intentionally listed here more than once.*

David L. Callender, CEO
M. Michael Shabot, Chief Medical Officer
Craig Cordola, CEO-Children's Memorial Hermann Hospital
Sean L. Richardson, COO-Memorial Hermann Northeast Hospital

GROWTH PLANS/SPECIAL FEATURES:

Memorial Hermann Healthcare System is a leading provider of healthcare in greater Houston and southeast Texas. Memorial Hermann owns and operates 14 hospitals and has joint ventures with three other hospital facilities, including Memorial Hermann Surgical Hospital First Colony, Memorial Hermann Surgical Hospital Kingwood and Memorial Hermann Rehabilitation Hospital-Katy. Specialties by the healthcare system include neck pain and spine care, cancer, children's health, digestive health, emergency services, heart and vascular care, neurosurgery, neurology, stroke, orthopedics, sports medicine, rehabilitation, physical therapy, sleep medicine, transplant, weight loss, women's health, maternity and more. Services offered by the group include alcohol and drug rehabilitation, diabetes education, durable medical equipment, home care, hospice, Memorial Hermann Medical Group, mental health, pelvic floor health, senior living and specialty pharmacy. Imaging and diagnostic services span breast care centers, imaging, magnetic resonance imaging (MRI), X-ray and lab tests. Care services encompass everyday wellness, convenient care centers, doctor's offices, emergency rooms, urgent care, walk-in clinics and virtual care. The integrated system has 6,700 affiliated physicians. Memorial Hermann Pearland Hospital was designated as a Level IV Trauma Center by the Texas Department State Health Services in 2019 after consistently demonstrating its ability to provide advanced trauma life support, evaluation, stabilization and diagnostic services. During 2020, Memorial Hermann announced a new brand, Children's Memorial Hermann Pediatrics, offering pediatric clinics across the Greater Houston area.

Employees receive comprehensive benefits, retirement plans and employee assistance programs.

FINANCIAL DATA: *Note: Data for latest year may not have been available at press time.*

In U.S. $	2020	2019	2018	2017	2016	2015
Revenue	5,747,742,387	5,580,332,415	5,260,000,000	5,061,526,000	4,894,244,000	4,422,334,000
R&D Expense						
Operating Income						
Operating Margin %						
SGA Expense						
Net Income				315,904,000	106,815,000	249,338,000
Operating Cash Flow						
Capital Expenditure						
EBITDA						
Return on Assets %						
Return on Equity %						
Debt to Equity						

CONTACT INFORMATION:

Phone: 713-448-5555   Fax: 713-448-5665
Toll-Free:
Address: 929 Gessner Dr., Ste 2600, Houston, TX 77024 United States

STOCK TICKER/OTHER:

Stock Ticker: Nonprofit   Exchange:
Employees: 28,000   Fiscal Year Ends: 06/30
Parent Company:

SALARIES/BONUSES:

Top Exec. Salary: $ Bonus: $
Second Exec. Salary: $ Bonus: $

OTHER THOUGHTS:

Estimated Female Officers or Directors:
Hot Spot for Advancement for Women/Minorities:

Memorial Sloan Kettering Cancer Center

www.mskcc.org

NAIC Code: 622310

TYPES OF BUSINESS:

Cancer Hospitals
Cancer Research

BRANDS/DIVISIONS/AFFILIATES:

Sloan-Kettering Institute
Rockefeller Outpatient Pavilion
Sidney Kimmel Center
Evelyn H Lauder Breast Cancer
MSK Bergen

CONTACTS: *Note: Officers with more than one job title may be intentionally listed here more than once.*

Craig B. Thompson, CEO
Kathryn Martin, COO
Michael P. Harrington, CFO
Kerry Bessey, Chief HR Officer
Atefeh Riazi, CIO
Norman C. Selby, Sec.
Clifton S. Robbins, Treas.

GROWTH PLANS/SPECIAL FEATURES:

Memorial Sloan Kettering Cancer Center (MSKCC), a nonprofit organization, provides cancer treatment, research and education. The organization can accurately screen for mutations in more than 400 genes. MSKCC operates one hospital, several outpatient facilities, as well as three research facilities, primarily located in New York, but also in New Jersey. Today, MSKCC is one of 51 National Cancer Institute-designated comprehensive cancer centers, with nearly 500 inpatient beds, a 72,000-square-foot surgical center, as well as a state-of-the-art treatment hub for outpatient procedures. The Sloan-Kettering Institute is the hospital's research arm, with specific focus on cell biology, cancer biology genetics, biochemistry, molecular biology, structural biology, computational and developmental biology, immunology and therapeutics. The institute provides research training in conjunction with Louis V. Gerstner, Jr. Graduate School of Biomedical Sciences, Rockefeller University, Cornell University and Weill Medical College of Cornell University for PhD and MD students. Several of the firm's leading researchers are members of the Institute of Medicine and the National Academy of Science, and some are Howard Hughes Medical Institute investigators. MSKCC also operates the Rockefeller Outpatient Pavilion for the provision of outpatient services, including medical consultation, diagnostic imaging, chemotherapy, pharmacy services, cancer screening and integrative medicine services; and the Sidney Kimmel Center for Prostate and Urologic Cancers, which provides treatment for genitourinary cancers. MSKCC's Evelyn H. Lauder Breast Cancer center provides breast and cervical cancer screening.

Memorial Sloan Kettering offers comprehensive benefits, retirement plans and employee assistance programs.

FINANCIAL DATA: *Note: Data for latest year may not have been available at press time.*

In U.S. $	2020	2019	2018	2017	2016	2015
Revenue	5,407,196,000	5,483,376,000	4,909,854,000	4,409,320,000	3,954,488,000	3,611,291,000
R&D Expense						
Operating Income						
Operating Margin %						
SGA Expense						
Net Income	-417,172,000	194,479,000	219,060,000	239,765,000	189,937,000	169,169,000
Operating Cash Flow						
Capital Expenditure						
EBITDA						
Return on Assets %						
Return on Equity %						
Debt to Equity						

CONTACT INFORMATION:

Phone: 212-639-2000   Fax: 212-639-3576
Toll-Free: 800-525-2225
Address: 1275 York Ave., New York, NY 10065 United States

STOCK TICKER/OTHER:

Stock Ticker: Nonprofit   Exchange:
Employees: 17,301   Fiscal Year Ends: 12/31
Parent Company:

SALARIES/BONUSES:

Top Exec. Salary: $ Bonus: $
Second Exec. Salary: $ Bonus: $

OTHER THOUGHTS:

Estimated Female Officers or Directors: 1
Hot Spot for Advancement for Women/Minorities: Y

Merck & Co Inc

NAIC Code: 325412

www.merck.com

TYPES OF BUSINESS:

Drugs-Diversified
Prescription Medicines
Vaccines
Biologic Therapies
Animal Health Products

BRANDS/DIVISIONS/AFFILIATES:

CONTACTS: *Note: Officers with more than one job title may be intentionally listed here more than once.*

Kenneth Frazier, CEO
Robert Davis, CFO
Rita Karachun, Chief Accounting Officer
Jim Scholefield, Chief Information Officer
Michael Nally, Chief Marketing Officer
Jennifer Zachary, Executive VP
Frank Clyburn, Executive VP
Steven Mizell, Executive VP
Julie Gerberding, Executive VP
Sanat Chattopadhyay, Executive VP
Roger Perlmutter, Executive VP
Richard DeLuca, Executive VP

GROWTH PLANS/SPECIAL FEATURES:

Merck & Co., Inc., known as MSD outside the U.S. and Canada, is a global healthcare company. The firm delivers innovative health solutions through its prescription medicines, vaccines, biologic therapies and animal health products. Merck operates through two business segments: pharmaceutical and animal health. The pharmaceutical segment includes human health pharmaceutical and vaccine products. Human pharmaceutical products consist of therapeutic and preventive agents, generally sold by prescription, for the treatment of human disorders. This division sells its products to drug wholesalers and retailers, hospitals, government agencies and managed healthcare providers. Human health vaccine products consist of preventive pediatric, adolescent and adult vaccines, primarily administered at physician offices. These vaccines are primarily sold to physicians, wholesalers, physician distributors and government entities. The animal health segment discovers, develops, manufactures and markets a wide range of veterinary pharmaceutical and vaccine products, as well as health management solutions and services, for the prevention, treatment and control of disease in all major livestock and companion animal species. This division also offers an extensive suite of digitally-connected identification, traceability and monitoring products. It sells these products to veterinarians, distributors and animal producers. In May 2021, Merck announced the spinoff of Organon & Co. into an independent, publicly-traded company and global healthcare company. The transaction was expected to finalize on June 2, 2021.

FINANCIAL DATA: *Note: Data for latest year may not have been available at press time.*

In U.S. $	2020	2019	2018	2017	2016	2015
Revenue	47,994,000,000	46,840,000,000	42,294,000,000	40,122,000,000	39,807,000,000	39,498,000,000
R&D Expense	13,558,000,000	9,872,000,000	9,752,001,000	10,208,000,000	10,124,000,000	6,704,000,000
Operating Income	8,483,000,000	12,241,000,000	8,931,000,000	7,309,000,000	6,030,000,000	7,547,000,000
Operating Margin %		.26%	.21%	.18%	.15%	.19%
SGA Expense	10,468,000,000	10,615,000,000	10,102,000,000	9,830,000,000	9,762,000,000	10,313,000,000
Net Income	7,067,000,000	9,843,000,000	6,220,000,000	2,394,000,000	3,920,000,000	4,442,000,000
Operating Cash Flow	10,253,000,000	13,440,000,000	10,922,000,000	6,447,000,000	10,376,000,000	12,421,000,000
Capital Expenditure	4,684,000,000	3,473,000,000	2,615,000,000	1,888,000,000	1,614,000,000	1,283,000,000
EBITDA	13,247,000,000	16,009,000,000	13,992,000,000	11,912,000,000	10,793,000,000	12,448,000,000
Return on Assets %		.12%	.07%	.03%	.04%	.04%
Return on Equity %		.37%	.20%	.06%	.09%	.10%
Debt to Equity		0.878	0.742	0.622	0.606	0.536

CONTACT INFORMATION:

Phone: 908 423-1000   Fax: 908 735-1253
Toll-Free:
Address: 2000 Galloping Hill Rd., Kenilworth, NJ 07033 United States

STOCK TICKER/OTHER:

Stock Ticker: MRK   Exchange: NYS
Employees: 71,000   Fiscal Year Ends: 12/31
Parent Company:

SALARIES/BONUSES:

Top Exec. Salary: $ Bonus: $
Second Exec. Salary: $ Bonus: $

OTHER THOUGHTS:

Estimated Female Officers or Directors: 4
Hot Spot for Advancement for Women/Minorities: Y

Merck Serono SA

www.emdserono.com/us-en

NAIC Code: 325412

TYPES OF BUSINESS:

Biopharmaceuticals Development
Biopharmaceuticals
Drug Research
Drug Development
Oncology
Therapeutics
Immunology
Endocrinology

BRANDS/DIVISIONS/AFFILIATES:

Merck KGaA
EMD Serono
MAVENCLAD
Rebig
Serostim
GONAL-f
Ovidrel
BAVENCIO

GROWTH PLANS/SPECIAL FEATURES:

Merck Serono SA is the biopharmaceutical business and subsidiary of Merck KGaA and branded as EMD Serono in the U.S. and Canada. Merck Serono discovers, researches, develops, manufactures and commercializes prescription medicines of chemical and biological origin in specialist indications. The firm has more than 20 projects in development, including potential new oncology and immune-oncology medicines as well as therapeutic options for psoriasis, lupus, multiple sclerosis and other autoimmune diseases. Merck Serono's neurology and immunology products include MAVENCLAD and Rebig. Its endocrinology products include Serostim and Saizen. Its fertility products include GONAL-f, Ovidrel and Cetrotide. Its oncology product includes BAVENCIO. In early-2021, the European commission approved BAVENICO for first-line maintenance treatment of locally advanced or metastatic urothelial carcinoma.

CONTACTS: *Note: Officers with more than one job title may be intentionally listed here more than once.*

Belen Garijo Lopez, Pres.
Thierry Hulot, Head-Global Mfg. & Supply
Thomas Gunning, Head-Legal
Meeta Gulyani, Head-Strategy & Global Franchises
Patrice Grand, Head-Communications
Susan Herbert, Head-Global Bus. Dev. & Strategy
Sascha Becker, Sr. VP
Elchin Ergun, Head-Global Commercial
Annalisa Jenkins, Head-Global Dev. & Medical

FINANCIAL DATA: *Note: Data for latest year may not have been available at press time.*

In U.S. $	2020	2019	2018	2017	2016	2015
Revenue	8,180,550,000	7,717,500,000	7,350,000,000	7,000,000,000	6,900,000,000	6,800,000,000
R&D Expense						
Operating Income						
Operating Margin %						
SGA Expense						
Net Income						
Operating Cash Flow						
Capital Expenditure						
EBITDA						
Return on Assets %						
Return on Equity %						
Debt to Equity						

CONTACT INFORMATION:

Phone: 49-6151-72-0   Fax: 49-6151-72-2000
Toll-Free:
Address: Frankfurter St. 250, Darmstadt, 64293 Germany

STOCK TICKER/OTHER:

Stock Ticker: Subsidiary
Employees: 4,775
Parent Company: Merck KGaA

Exchange:
Fiscal Year Ends: 12/31

SALARIES/BONUSES:

Top Exec. Salary: $ Bonus: $
Second Exec. Salary: $ Bonus: $

OTHER THOUGHTS:

Estimated Female Officers or Directors: 5
Hot Spot for Advancement for Women/Minorities: Y

Sales, profits and employees may be estimates. Financial information, benefits and other data can change quickly and may vary from those stated here.

Mercy

NAIC Code: 622110

www.mercy.net

TYPES OF BUSINESS:

General Medical and Surgical Hospitals
Outpatient Care
Health Classes
Long-Term Care
Community Service & Outreach

BRANDS/DIVISIONS/AFFILIATES:

International Business Machines Corporation (IBM)
IBM Watson Health
Mercy Virtual Care Center
MyMercy
vICU
Mercy Family Center
Mercy Ministries of Laredo
Mercy Cooper-Anthony Child Advocacy Center

CONTACTS: *Note: Officers with more than one job title may be intentionally listed here more than once.*

Lynn Britton, Pres.
Michael McCurry, COO
Shannon Sock, Exec. VP
Joseph Kelly, Sr. VP
Donn Sorensen, Regional Pres., East Communities
Diana Smalley, Regional Pres., West Communities
Shannon Sock, Exec. VP-Organizational Effectiveness
Kim Day, Regional Pres., Central Communities
Donn Sorenson, Exec. VP-Operations

GROWTH PLANS/SPECIAL FEATURES:

Mercy, established in 1986, is one of the largest health systems in the U.S., serving millions of people annually. Mercy comprises more than 40 acute care and specialty hospitals (heart, children's, orthopedic and rehabilitation), 900 physician practices and outpatient facilities, 45,000 co-workers and 2,400 Mercy Clinic physicians in Arkansas, Kansas, Missouri and Oklahoma. It also has outreach ministries in Arkansas, Louisiana, Mississippi and Texas. The Mercy Virtual Care Center monitors patients 24/7/365 using high-speed data and video connections. MyMercy is a free service that allows patients to connect online with their doctors; provides access to their medical information and test results; renew subscriptions; and schedule office appointments as well as schedule e-visits via personal computer, tablet or smartphone. vICU is an electronic intensive care unit (ICU) that provides 24-hour vigilance to critically-ill patients. Mercy Family Center is a behavioral health clinic for adolescents and their families, serving New Orleans, Louisiana. Mercy Ministries of Laredo provides primary health care services, a domestic violence shelter and an education center in Laredo, Texas. Mercy Cooper-Anthony Child Advocacy Center provides essential medical and counseling services to Arkansas' young victims of abuse, ranging from birth to 18 years of age. Mercy's IT division provides technology services, supply chain organization solutions, return on investment solutions and system-wide virtual solutions. Mercy operates as a wholly-owned subsidiary of IBM Watson Health, itself a business unit within International Business Machines Corporation (IBM).

Mercy offers its employees health and wellness benefits and career development opportunities.

FINANCIAL DATA: *Note: Data for latest year may not have been available at press time.*

In U.S. $	2020	2019	2018	2017	2016	2015
Revenue	5,000,000,000	5,540,000,000	5,500,000,000	5,500,000,000	5,250,000,000	5,000,000,000
R&D Expense						
Operating Income						
Operating Margin %						
SGA Expense						
Net Income						
Operating Cash Flow						
Capital Expenditure						
EBITDA						
Return on Assets %						
Return on Equity %						
Debt to Equity						

CONTACT INFORMATION:

Phone: 580-371-2592   Fax:
Toll-Free:
Address: 1000 S. Byrd St., Tishomingo, OK 73460 United States

STOCK TICKER/OTHER:

Stock Ticker: Subsidiary   Exchange:
Employees: 40,000   Fiscal Year Ends: 06/30
Parent Company: International Business Machines Corporation (IBM)

SALARIES/BONUSES:

Top Exec. Salary: $ Bonus: $
Second Exec. Salary: $ Bonus: $

OTHER THOUGHTS:

Estimated Female Officers or Directors: 10
Hot Spot for Advancement for Women/Minorities: Y

Mercy Health

www.mercy.com

NAIC Code: 622110

TYPES OF BUSINESS:

General Medical and Surgical Hospitals
Long-Term Care
Hospice Programs
Home Health Services
Low-Income Housing

BRANDS/DIVISIONS/AFFILIATES:

GROWTH PLANS/SPECIAL FEATURES:

Mercy Health is a non-profit health system serving Ohio and Kentucky, with 23 hospitals and 600 places where patients can receive care. In Ohio, care is provided in the cities of Cincinnati, Lima, Lorain, Springfield, Toledo and Youngstown. In Kentucky, care is provided in Irvine and Paducah. Mercy Health offers more than 30 specialties, which includes medication management, bariatrics, behavioral/mental health, cancer care, breast health, cardiovascular/thoracic surgery, cholesterol, clinical trials/research, diabetes care, dermatology, ear/nose/throat, emergency care, Gamma Knife surgery, heart care, imaging services, laboratory services, liver/pancreas center, orthopedics/sports medicine, pain medicine, palliative care/hospice, rehabilitation, rheumatology and wound care. Mercy Health serves approximately 6 million patients annually. In September 2020, the Kentucky State Board of Trustees approved the sale of 62.88 acres, which Mercy Health intends to acquire for the development of a health care campus.

CONTACTS: Note: Officers with more than one job title may be intentionally listed here more than once.

John M. Starcher, Jr., CEO
Brian Smith, COO
Deborah Bloomfield, CFO
Sandra Mackey, CMO
Joe Gage, Chief Human Resources Officer
Laishy Williams-Carlson, CIO
Michael A. Bezney, General Counsel
Jane Durney Crowley, Exec. VP-Bus. Dev. & Clinical Integration
Doris Gottemoeller, Sr. VP-Mission & Values Integrity
R. Jeffrey Copeland, Sr. VP-Insurance & Physician Svcs.
Stephen R. Grossbart, Chief Quality Officer
Brian Smith, Exec. VP-Networks

FINANCIAL DATA: Note: Data for latest year may not have been available at press time.

In U.S. $	2020	2019	2018	2017	2016	2015
Revenue	6,512,499,304	7,010,225,301	4,557,548,171	4,486,187,127	4,226,007,193	3,876,101,208
R&D Expense						
Operating Income						
Operating Margin %						
SGA Expense						
Net Income		2,102,726,337	32,639,666	190,176,975	73,869,062	67,397,255
Operating Cash Flow						
Capital Expenditure						
EBITDA						
Return on Assets %						
Return on Equity %						
Debt to Equity						

CONTACT INFORMATION:

Phone: 513-952-5000   Fax: 513-639-2700
Toll-Free:
Address: 1701 Mercy Health Place, Cincinnati, OH 45237 United States

STOCK TICKER/OTHER:

Stock Ticker: Nonprofit
Employees: 33,000
Parent Company:

Exchange:
Fiscal Year Ends: 12/31

SALARIES/BONUSES:

Top Exec. Salary: $ Bonus: $
Second Exec. Salary: $ Bonus: $

OTHER THOUGHTS:

Estimated Female Officers or Directors: 15
Hot Spot for Advancement for Women/Minorities: Y

Sales, profits and employees may be estimates. Financial information, benefits and other data can change quickly and may vary from those stated here.

Meridian Bioscience Inc

www.meridianbioscience.com

NAIC Code: 325413

TYPES OF BUSINESS:

Diagnostic Test Kits
Contract Manufacturing
Bulk Antigens, Antibodies & Reagents

BRANDS/DIVISIONS/AFFILIATES:

Isothermal DNA Amplification
Rapid Immunoassay
Enzyme-linke Immunoassay
Curian
BreathTek

CONTACTS: *Note: Officers with more than one job title may be intentionally listed here more than once.*

Jack Kenny, CEO
Eric Rasmussen, CFO
David Phillips, Chairman of the Board
Bryan Baldasare, Chief Accounting Officer
Lourdes Weltzien, Executive VP, Divisional

GROWTH PLANS/SPECIAL FEATURES:

Meridian Bioscience, Inc. is a life science company that develops, manufactures, sells and distributes diagnostic test kits, primarily for respiratory, gastrointestinal, viral and parasitic infectious diseases. The firm also manufactures and distributes bulk antigens, antibodies and reagents; and contract manufactures proteins and other biologicals. The company operates in two segments: diagnostics and life science. The diagnostics segment is Meridian's largest source of revenues and provides clinical diagnostic products that span an array of testing platforms and technologies, including: Isothermal DNA Amplification, a high sensitivity, molecular platform suitable for any moderately-complex laboratory, and provides flexibility to process from 1 to 10 tests per run in under one hour's time, and requires no batching of samples; Rapid Immunoassay, a single-use immunoassay with fast turnaround times (generally under 20 minutes); Enzyme-linked Immunoassay, a batch immunoassay platform that can process up to 96 tests per run, and is highly accurate and economical, and adaptable to automation; and anodic stripping voltammetry, an electrical chemical sensor platform for quantitative determination of lead levels in blood. Meridian's current R&D pipeline for immunoassay products includes an instrumentation that utilizes fluorescent chemistry and has colorimetric capabilities; it is branded under the Curian name. In July 2021, Meridian acquired the North American BreathTek business from Otsuka America Pharmaceutical, Inc. BreathTek is a U.S. Food and Drug Administration approved urea breath test for the detection of H. pylori bacteria.

FINANCIAL DATA: *Note: Data for latest year may not have been available at press time.*

In U.S. $	2020	2019	2018	2017	2016	2015
Revenue	253,667,000	201,014,000	213,571,000	200,771,000	196,082,000	194,830,000
R&D Expense	23,729,000	17,948,000	16,870,000	15,680,000	13,815,000	12,605,000
Operating Income	59,608,000	37,346,000	44,635,000	44,010,000	53,536,000	56,060,000
Operating Margin %		.19%	.21%	.22%	.27%	.29%
SGA Expense	72,911,000	63,031,000	68,956,000	65,143,000	60,436,000	53,217,000
Net Income	46,186,000	24,382,000	23,849,000	21,557,000	32,229,000	35,540,000
Operating Cash Flow	47,976,000	35,831,000	34,783,000	41,355,000	37,223,000	42,809,000
Capital Expenditure	3,299,000	3,797,000	4,201,000	4,467,000	4,004,000	4,764,000
EBITDA	75,492,000	43,466,000	39,824,000	46,189,000	58,168,000	61,278,000
Return on Assets %		.08%	.10%	.09%	.15%	.20%
Return on Equity %		.13%	.14%	.13%	.19%	.22%
Debt to Equity		0.397	0.256	0.296	0.328	

CONTACT INFORMATION:

Phone: 513 271-3700   Fax: 513 271-3762
Toll-Free: 800-543-1980
Address: 3471 River Hills Dr., Cincinnati, OH 45244 United States

STOCK TICKER/OTHER:

Stock Ticker: VIVO   Exchange: NAS
Employees: 560   Fiscal Year Ends: 09/30
Parent Company:

SALARIES/BONUSES:

Top Exec. Salary: $ Bonus: $
Second Exec. Salary: $ Bonus: $

OTHER THOUGHTS:

Estimated Female Officers or Directors: 4
Hot Spot for Advancement for Women/Minorities: Y

Merit Medical Systems Inc

www.merit.com

NAIC Code: 339100

TYPES OF BUSINESS:

Disposable Products-Cardiology & Radiology

BRANDS/DIVISIONS/AFFILIATES:

QuadraSphere
HeRO Graft
ConvertX
ClariVein
CentrosFLO
CorVocet
ReSolve Mini Locking Drainage Catheter

CONTACTS: *Note: Officers with more than one job title may be intentionally listed here more than once.*

Fred Lampropoulos, CEO
Raul Parra, CFO
Brian Lloyd, Chief Legal Officer
Ronald Frost, COO
Justin Lampropoulos, Executive VP, Divisional
Anne-Marie Wright, President, Divisional

GROWTH PLANS/SPECIAL FEATURES:

Merit Medical Systems, Inc. designs, manufactures and markets medical devices used in an array of interventional and diagnostic medical procedures. The company's products offer a high level of quality, value and safety to customers, and are used in the following clinical areas: diagnostic & interventional cardiology, interventional radiology, vascular/general/thoracic surgery, electrophysiology, cardiac rhythm management, interventional pulmonology, interventional nephrology, oncology, pain management, outpatient access centers, computed tomography, ultrasound and interventional gastroenterology. Merit manufactures and sells various products designed to alleviate patient suffering from peripheral vascular and non-vascular disease. Its line of peripheral catheters meet the growing trends of transradial access, a procedure which uses the wrist as the entry point for cardiac catheterization and peripheral procedures rather than the femoral artery approach. Its FDA-approved QuadraSphere microspheres provide another treatment option for patients and physicians with primary liver cancer. HeRO Graft is a fully subcutaneous vascular access system intended for use in maintaining long-term vascular access for chronic hemodialysis in patients who have exhausted peripheral venous access sites suitable for fistulas or grafts. The ConvertX nephroureteral stent system is used for temporary internal drainage in patients with severe ureteral obstructions. ClariVein IC infusion catheter for the minimally-invasive, non-thermal treatment of peripheral vasculature. CentrosFLO catheters anchor the company's chronic dialysis line. And Merit's CorVocet biopsy system is designed to cut full-core of tissue, providing large specimens for pathological examination. The company owns or has a license to more than 1,500 U.S. and international patents and patent applications. In December 2019, the firm announced the commercial launch of the ReSolve Mini Locking Drainage Catheter which allows a catheter to be placed into small fluid pockets.

Merit offers comprehensive benefits, retirement plans and employee assistance programs.

FINANCIAL DATA: *Note: Data for latest year may not have been available at press time.*

In U.S. $	2020	2019	2018	2017	2016	2015
Revenue	963,875,000	994,852,000	882,753,000	727,852,000	603,838,000	542,149,000
R&D Expense	57,537,000	65,615,000	59,532,000	51,403,000	45,229,000	40,810,000
Operating Income	45,916,000	39,477,000	59,220,000	45,716,000	35,398,000	38,623,000
Operating Margin %		.04%	.07%	.05%	.06%	.07%
SGA Expense	297,724,000	327,274,000	276,018,000	229,134,000	184,398,000	156,348,000
Net Income	-9,843,000	5,451,000	42,017,000	27,523,000	20,121,000	23,802,000
Operating Cash Flow	165,270,000	77,813,000	86,533,000	62,727,000	53,599,000	69,458,000
Capital Expenditure	49,276,000	81,497,000	66,336,000	41,200,000	35,054,000	52,915,000
EBITDA	103,579,000	119,253,000	129,425,000	97,199,000	77,939,000	74,854,000
Return on Assets %		.00%	.03%	.03%	.02%	.03%
Return on Equity %		.01%	.05%	.05%	.04%	.05%
Debt to Equity		0.531	0.40	0.383	0.631	0.424

CONTACT INFORMATION:

Phone: 801 253-1600   Fax: 801 253-1652
Toll-Free: 800-356-3748
Address: 1600 W. Merit Pkwy., South Jordan, UT 84095 United States

STOCK TICKER/OTHER:

Stock Ticker: MMSI
Employees: 5,989
Parent Company:

Exchange: NAS
Fiscal Year Ends: 12/31

SALARIES/BONUSES:

Top Exec. Salary: $ Bonus: $
Second Exec. Salary: $ Bonus: $

OTHER THOUGHTS:

Estimated Female Officers or Directors: 2
Hot Spot for Advancement for Women/Minorities:

Sales, profits and employees may be estimates. Financial information, benefits and other data can change quickly and may vary from those stated here.

Mettler-Toledo International Inc

NAIC Code: 334516

www.mt.com

TYPES OF BUSINESS:

Manufacturing-Laboratory Equipment
Product Inspections
Manufacturing-Industrial Weighing Equipment
Manufacturing-Retail Weighing Equipment
Software

BRANDS/DIVISIONS/AFFILIATES:

Rainin
Biotix

CONTACTS: *Note: Officers with more than one job title may be intentionally listed here more than once.*

Olivier Filliol, CEO
Shawn Vadala, CFO
Robert Spoerry, Chairman of the Board
Peter Aggersbjerg, Other Corporate Officer
Marc Gueronniere, Other Corporate Officer
Gerhard Keller, Other Corporate Officer
Christian Magloth, Other Corporate Officer
Michael Heidingsfelder, Other Corporate Officer
Simon Kirk, Other Corporate Officer

GROWTH PLANS/SPECIAL FEATURES:

Mettler-Toledo International, Inc. is a global supplier of precision instruments and services. The firm derived 30% of its 2019 net sales from Europe, 39% from North and South America, and 31% from Asia and other countries. Mettler-Toledo's primary products are laboratory instruments and industrial instruments. Laboratory instruments include laboratory balances that have a range from three-hundred millionths of a gram to 64 kilograms; pipettes, sold under the Rainin and Biotix brand names, which are used in pharmaceutical, biotech and academic settings; and titrators, which measure the chemical composition of samples and are used in research laboratories as well as the pharmaceutical and food and beverage industries. The company also manufactures thermal analysis units, automated lab reactors and other laboratory products such as pH meters. In addition, Mettler-Toledo offers laboratory software to analyze data from its instrumentation. The firm's industrial instruments include vehicle scale systems that can handle weights up to 500 tons, are usable with both trucks and railcars and provide accurate measurements in extreme environmental conditions. It provides product inspections and industrial scales/balances that can handle loads from a few grams to several thousand pounds for applications ranging from chemical production to weighing mail and packages. The company also produces industrial terminals and software to help automatically collect and archive data. In addition to laboratory and industrial instruments, Mettler-Toledo offers retail weighing solutions including stand-alone scales and balances with pricing and printing functions; and networks that integrate backroom, counter, self-service and checkout weighing functions.

FINANCIAL DATA: *Note: Data for latest year may not have been available at press time.*

In U.S. $	2020	2019	2018	2017	2016	2015
Revenue	3,085,177,000	3,008,652,000	2,935,586,000	2,725,053,000	2,508,257,000	2,395,447,000
R&D Expense	140,102,000	143,950,000	141,071,000	129,265,000	119,968,000	119,076,000
Operating Income	784,043,000	728,388,000	682,981,000	613,913,000	546,945,000	501,156,000
Operating Margin %		.24%	.23%	.23%	.22%	.21%
SGA Expense	820,221,000	819,183,000	812,802,000	787,464,000	732,622,000	700,810,000
Net Income	602,739,000	561,109,000	512,611,000	375,972,000	384,370,000	352,820,000
Operating Cash Flow	724,699,000	603,450,000	565,005,000	516,325,000	443,078,000	426,868,000
Capital Expenditure	92,494,000	97,341,000	142,726,000	127,426,000	123,957,000	82,506,000
EBITDA	886,068,000	807,486,000	771,060,000	683,136,000	601,014,000	554,913,000
Return on Assets %		.21%	.20%	.16%	.18%	.18%
Return on Equity %		1.11%	.90%	.77%	.76%	.54%
Debt to Equity		2.936	1.669	1.754	2.012	0.994

CONTACT INFORMATION:

Phone: 614 438-4511　　Fax:
Toll-Free:
Address: 1900 Polaris Pkwy., Columbus, OH 43240-4035 United States

STOCK TICKER/OTHER:

Stock Ticker: MTD　　Exchange: NYS
Employees: 16,500　　Fiscal Year Ends: 12/31
Parent Company:

SALARIES/BONUSES:

Top Exec. Salary: $　　Bonus: $
Second Exec. Salary: $　　Bonus: $

OTHER THOUGHTS:

Estimated Female Officers or Directors:
Hot Spot for Advancement for Women/Minorities:

MiMedx Group Inc

www.mimedx.com

NAIC Code: 325414

TYPES OF BUSINESS:

Implants, Surgical, Manufacturing

BRANDS/DIVISIONS/AFFILIATES:

AmnioFix
EpiFix
EpiBurn
AmnioFill
AmnioCord
EpiCord

CONTACTS: *Note: Officers with more than one job title may be intentionally listed here more than once.*

David Coles, CEO
Edward Borkowski, CFO
Charles Evans, Chairman of the Board
Alexandra Haden, General Counsel

GROWTH PLANS/SPECIAL FEATURES:

MiMedx Group, Inc. is an integrated developer, processor and marketer of patent protected and proprietary regenerative biomaterial products and bioimplants. These bio products are processed from human amniotic membrane and other birth tissues, as well as human skin and bone. Regenerative biomaterials are the framework that provide physician's products and tissues to help the body heal itself. MiMedx's biomaterial platform technologies include AmnioFix, EpiFix, EpiBurn, AmnioFill, AmnioCord and EpiCord. AmnioFix and EpiFix are tissue technologies process from human amniotic membrane derived from donated placentas. Human amniotic membrane is then processed using the company's proprietary PURION process, which produces a safe and effective implant. EpiBurn is a bioactive tissue matrix allograft composed of dehydrated human amnion/chorion membrane that preserves and contains multiple extracellular matrix proteins while promoting normal wound healing and reduced scar formation. AmnioFill is a minimally manipulated, non-viable cellular tissue matrix allograft that contains multiple extracellular matrix proteins, growth factors, cytokines, and other specialty proteins present in placental tissue to help enhance healing. AmnioCord and EpiCord are minimally manipulated, dehydrated, non-viable cellular umbilical cord allografts for homologous use that provide protective environments for the healing process and provide a connective tissue matrix to replace or supplement damaged or inadequate integumental tissue. MiMedx has supplied more than 1.9 million allografts for the application in the wound care, burn, surgical, orthopedic, spine, sports medicine, ophthalmic and dental sectors of healthcare.

FINANCIAL DATA: *Note: Data for latest year may not have been available at press time.*

In U.S. $	2020	2019	2018	2017	2016	2015
Revenue	248,234,000	299,255,000	359,111,000	321,139,000	245,015,000	187,296,000
R&D Expense	11,715,000	11,140,000	15,765,000	17,900,000	12,038,000	8,413,000
Operating Income	-44,371,000	-20,714,000	-3,924,000	46,223,000	18,446,000	24,364,000
Operating Margin %						
SGA Expense	181,022,000	198,205,000	258,528,000	220,119,000	179,997,000	133,384,000
Net Income	-49,284,000	-25,580,000	-29,979,000	64,727,000	11,974,000	29,446,000
Operating Cash Flow	-30,263,000	-39,412,000	35,796,000	62,939,000	25,828,000	18,807,000
Capital Expenditure	4,555,000	2,218,000	10,028,000	5,397,000	7,111,000	6,678,000
EBITDA	-37,516,000	-13,129,000	2,992,000	51,988,000	23,906,000	27,096,000
Return on Assets %						
Return on Equity %						
Debt to Equity						

CONTACT INFORMATION:

Phone: 770-651-9100   Fax:
Toll-Free: 888-543-1917
Address: 1775 West Oak Commons Court, NE, Marietta, GA 30062 United States

STOCK TICKER/OTHER:

Stock Ticker: MDXG
Employees: 696
Parent Company:

Exchange: NAS
Fiscal Year Ends: 12/31

SALARIES/BONUSES:

Top Exec. Salary: $ Bonus: $
Second Exec. Salary: $ Bonus: $

OTHER THOUGHTS:

Estimated Female Officers or Directors:
Hot Spot for Advancement for Women/Minorities:

Mindray Medical International Limited

www.mindray.com

NAIC Code: 339100

TYPES OF BUSINESS:

Medical/Dental/Surgical Equipment & Supplies, Manufacturing

BRANDS/DIVISIONS/AFFILIATES:

Mindray Wuhan Center

CONTACTS: *Note: Officers with more than one job title may be intentionally listed here more than once.*

Li Xiting, Co-CEO
Wayne Quinn, Pres.-North America
Li Xiting, Pres.
Fannie Lin Fan, General Counsel
Cheng Minghe, Chief Strategic Officer
Xu Huang, Chmn.
David Gibson, Pres., Mindray DS USA, Inc.

GROWTH PLANS/SPECIAL FEATURES:

Mindray Medical International Limited is a developer, manufacturer and marketer of medical devices in China, with a significant, growing presence outside of China. Mindray offers products in four categories. Patient monitoring and life support systems includes patient monitoring systems, anesthesia machines, ventilators, electrocardiographs, defibrillators, AEDs, surgical lights operating tables, medical supply units, infusion pumps, endoscope products and accessories. In-Vitro diagnostic products include hematology analyzers and reagents, chemistry analyzers and reagents, chemiluminescence immunoassay, hemoglobin systems, flow cytometry, micro plate readers and washers, urinalysis and microbiology machines. Medical imaging systems include ultrasound machines for cardiology, OB/GYN's, general imaging and POC and mobile and digital radiology machines. Veterinary products include patient monitoring and life support systems, in-vitro diagnostic systems and medical imaging systems. Mindray's products are used in emergency departments, critical care units, step-down units/telemetry, perioperative care and ambulatory surgery centers in over 190 countries. The firm comprises more than 40 subsidiaries with branch offices in over 30 countries throughout North and Latin America, Europe, Africa and Asia-Pacific, as well as 30+ branch offices in China. In June 2020, Mindray began construction on the Mindray Wuhan Center, which will include two major sub-projects: Wuhan Research Institute and Wuhan Manufacturing Center.

FINANCIAL DATA: *Note: Data for latest year may not have been available at press time.*

In U.S. $	2020	2019	2018	2017	2016	2015
Revenue	3,221,260,000	2,369,210,000	1,999,560,000	1,715,700,000	1,365,000,000	1,300,000,000
R&D Expense						
Operating Income						
Operating Margin %						
SGA Expense						
Net Income	1,139,600,000	670,412,000	541,676,000	399,405,000		
Operating Cash Flow						
Capital Expenditure						
EBITDA						
Return on Assets %						
Return on Equity %						
Debt to Equity						

CONTACT INFORMATION:

Phone: 86 75526582888   Fax: 86 75526582500
Toll-Free:
Address: Keji 12th Rd. S., Mindray Bldg., Shenzhen, Guangdong 518057 China

STOCK TICKER/OTHER:

Stock Ticker: 300760
Employees: 11,833
Parent Company:

Exchange: Shenzhen
Fiscal Year Ends: 12/31

SALARIES/BONUSES:

Top Exec. Salary: $ Bonus: $
Second Exec. Salary: $ Bonus: $

OTHER THOUGHTS:

Estimated Female Officers or Directors: 1
Hot Spot for Advancement for Women/Minorities:

MinuteClinic LLC

www.minuteclinic.com

NAIC Code: 621498

TYPES OF BUSINESS:

Health Clinics
In-Store Clinics

BRANDS/DIVISIONS/AFFILIATES:

CVS Health Corporation
CVS Pharmacy
eClinic

CONTACTS: *Note: Officers with more than one job title may be intentionally listed here more than once.*

Nancy Gagliano, Chief Medical Officer
Meredith Dixon, VP-Oper.
Chris Crisafulli, Dir.-Finance
Paulette Thabault, Chief Nurse Practitioner Officer
David W. Dorman, Chmn.-CVS Health

GROWTH PLANS/SPECIAL FEATURES:

MinuteClinic, LLC, a wholly-owned subsidiary of CVS Health Corporation, is a chain of quick service healthcare clinics located in grocery stores, pharmacies and other stores, offering over 125 medical services. The clinics are open seven days a week and are staffed by certified nurse practitioners (CNPs) and physician assistants (PAs) who can diagnose and prescribe medications on-site with an average visit time of approximately 15 minutes. The company staffs clinics with CNPs and PAs able to treat common health problems such as ear infections, allergies and strep throat. The clinics can also administer vaccines, treat a variety of skin conditions, and offers biometric screening services to facilitate early interventions for patients with undiagnosed diabetes, hypertension and high cholesterol. Additional services include ear wax removal, motion sickness prevention, pregnancy testing, suture removal, sprain examination, tuberculosis testing and wound care. Seriously ill patients are referred to a family doctor, area doctors or a larger clinic or hospital. No appointments are needed, and patients can shop in the store while waiting to be seen. Treatments range from $35 to $250, generally less than seeing a doctor, and MinuteClinic accepts most major forms of insurance. More than 1,100 clinics are located within CVS Pharmacy and select Target stores across 33 states nationwide. Telehealth options are also available, offering video consultations with licensed MinuteClinic providers from the patient's home for those with and without insurance. eClinic visits are available from 9am to 5pm in 33 states for those with insurance; and offered 24/7/365 in 46 states for those without insurance for approximately $60 per visit.

FINANCIAL DATA: *Note: Data for latest year may not have been available at press time.*

In U.S. $	2020	2019	2018	2017	2016	2015
Revenue						
R&D Expense						
Operating Income						
Operating Margin %						
SGA Expense						
Net Income						
Operating Cash Flow						
Capital Expenditure						
EBITDA						
Return on Assets %						
Return on Equity %						
Debt to Equity						

CONTACT INFORMATION:

Phone: Fax:
Toll-Free: 866-389-2727
Address: One CVS Dr., Woonsocket, RI 02895 United States

SALARIES/BONUSES:

Top Exec. Salary: $ Bonus: $
Second Exec. Salary: $ Bonus: $

STOCK TICKER/OTHER:

Stock Ticker: Subsidiary   Exchange:
Employees: Fiscal Year Ends:
Parent Company: CVS Health Corporation

OTHER THOUGHTS:

Estimated Female Officers or Directors: 6
Hot Spot for Advancement for Women/Minorities: Y

Sales, profits and employees may be estimates. Financial information, benefits and other data can change quickly and may vary from those stated here.

Misonix Inc
NAIC Code: 339100

www.misonix.com

TYPES OF BUSINESS:
Ultrasonic Medical Devices

BRANDS/DIVISIONS/AFFILIATES:
SonicOne
Bone Scalpel
SonaStar
Nexus
Solsys Medical LLC

CONTACTS: *Note: Officers with more than one job title may be intentionally listed here more than once.*
Stavros Vizirgianakis, Director
Sharon Klugewicz, COO
Joseph Dwyer, CFO
Robert Ludecker, Pres.-Global Sales and Mktg.
Robert Ludecker, Senior VP, Divisional
Joseph Brennan, Vice President, Divisional
John Salerno, Vice President, Divisional
Daniel Voic, Vice President, Divisional

GROWTH PLANS/SPECIAL FEATURES:
Misonix, Inc. designs, manufactures and markets minimally invasive ultrasonic medical devices. These include: the SonicOne wound cleansing and debridement system, used on soft and hard tissue related to ulcers, eschar infections and necrotic bone; the BoneScalpel bone dissection, sculpting and removal tool, used on small bone and spinal tissue; and the SonaStar ultrasonic aspiration device for tumor tissue removal, bone debulking and other sculpting and removal processes in neurosurgery and general surgery applications. Nexus is an integrated ultrasonic surgical platform that combines that combines all the features of Misonix's other products. Clinical specialties served include spine surgery, skull-based surgery (cranio-maxillo-facial), neurosurgery, orthopedic surgery, plastic surgery, as well as wound, burn and vascular surgery. The firm licenses certain manufacturing and distribution rights of SonaStar products to Hunan Xing Rui Kang Biotechnologies. In September 2019, the firm completed its acquisition of Solsys Medical, LLC, a regenerative medical company. In September 2020, Misonix announced that it entered into an exclusive supply and distribution agreement with Gunze Limited for TheraGenesis, an FDA-cleared porcine tendon derived collagen wound matrix with a silicone film layer used to treat trauma, burn and reconstructive wounds.

FINANCIAL DATA: *Note: Data for latest year may not have been available at press time.*

In U.S. $	2020	2019	2018	2017	2016	2015
Revenue	62,483,650	38,848,490	36,679,820	27,269,960	23,113,190	22,204,580
R&D Expense	4,915,943	4,467,969	4,394,149	1,837,497	1,670,347	1,592,923
Operating Income	-19,393,580	-7,409,863	-2,940,741	-6,601,086	-5,829,388	-1,714,939
Operating Margin %		-.19%	-.08%	-.24%	-.25%	-.08%
SGA Expense	58,187,120	30,222,050	25,431,520	23,816,110	19,661,000	15,046,320
Net Income	-17,418,370	-7,386,797	-7,612,435	-1,681,179	-1,172,146	5,571,171
Operating Cash Flow	-26,682,120	-3,683,906	-563,994	-1,272,658	-316,240	2,388,454
Capital Expenditure	446,175	846,675	540,807	714,815	604,560	450,067
EBITDA	-15,770,300	-5,746,092	-1,513,516	-5,534,242	-4,177,416	3,959,396
Return on Assets %		-.25%	-.24%	-.06%	-.04%	.24%
Return on Equity %		-.32%	-.29%	-.06%	-.05%	.28%
Debt to Equity						

CONTACT INFORMATION:
Phone: 631 694-9555   Fax: 631 694-9412
Toll-Free: 800-694-9612
Address: 1938 New Highway, Farmingdale, NY 11735 United States

STOCK TICKER/OTHER:
Stock Ticker: MSON   Exchange: NAS
Employees: 92   Fiscal Year Ends: 06/30
Parent Company:

SALARIES/BONUSES:
Top Exec. Salary: $ Bonus: $
Second Exec. Salary: $ Bonus: $

OTHER THOUGHTS:
Estimated Female Officers or Directors:
Hot Spot for Advancement for Women/Minorities:

ModivCare Solutions, LLC

modivcare.com

NAIC Code: 621910

TYPES OF BUSINESS:

Medical Transportation Management Services
Outsourced Logistics Services

BRANDS/DIVISIONS/AFFILIATES:

ModivCare Inc.
LogistiCAD
EMTrack

CONTACTS: *Note: Officers with more than one job title may be intentionally listed here more than once.*

Daniel E. Greenleaf, CEO
Kenneth W. Wilson, COO
Kevin Dotts, CFO
Laurel Emory, Sr. VP-Human Resources
Walt Meffert, CIO
Albert Cortina, Chief Admin. Officer
Chinta Gaston, General Counsel
Gregg Bryars, Sr. VP-Oper.
Steven D. Linowes, Exec. VP-Corp. Dev.
Chuck DeZearn, Sr. VP-Oper.
Chris Echols, Sr. VP-Oper.
Sandy Reifel, VP-Managed Care Accounts
Bill Walter, VP-Bus. Dev.

GROWTH PLANS/SPECIAL FEATURES:

ModivCare Solutions, LLC, a subsidiary of ModivCare Inc., is an outsourced scheduler of non-emergency patient transport services for insurance companies, managed care organizations and government health agencies. Instead of owning its own vehicles, the firm manages call centers, patient eligibility screening, scheduling, dispatch, billing and quality assurance. It also manages transportation provider networks of local, commercial, nonprofit and public transportation companies. ModivCare recruits and accredits local firms for its network of providers. In summary, the company brokers non-emergency medical transportation (NEMT) services through a network of transportation providers. ModivCare routes transportation requests through one of its call centers. All calls are recorded digitally and archived in the system database. The firm developed its integrated software system, known as LogistiCAD, in order to automatically coordinate all of its data and to and generate scheduling, routing, quality assurance reporting, transportation cost estimates and billing verification. It processes transportation requests and dispatches drivers through its network of carriers using its proprietary EMTrack system, which tracks all of the company's vehicles. ModivCare is able to use its LogistiCAD system in conjunction with sophisticated GPS navigation to gain improved transportation access and service delivery in rural and remote areas. LogistiCare and Lyft have a nationwide partnership to improve solutions for private-, commercial- and government-assisted riders seeking healthcare appointments and social programs. The partnership utilizes ModivCare's proprietary platform and Lyft's application program interface (API) to address riders' needs. Additionally, the firm provides finance and consulting services, including billing management, customer reimbursement, medical services billing, fraud detection and risk management. The company's government clients include state Medicaid agencies, school boards and Americans with Disabilities Act (ADA) paratransit authorities. Healthcare sector clients include hospital systems and many of the nation's largest managed care organizations.

FINANCIAL DATA: *Note: Data for latest year may not have been available at press time.*

In U.S. $	2020	2019	2018	2017	2016	2015
Revenue	1,000,000,000	954,765,000	909,300,000	866,000,000	840,000,000	830,000,000
R&D Expense						
Operating Income						
Operating Margin %						
SGA Expense						
Net Income						
Operating Cash Flow						
Capital Expenditure						
EBITDA						
Return on Assets %						
Return on Equity %						
Debt to Equity						

CONTACT INFORMATION:

Phone: 404-888-5800   Fax: 404-888-5999
Toll-Free:
Address: 1275 Peachtree St NE, 6/Fl, Atlanta, GA 30309 United States

STOCK TICKER/OTHER:

Stock Ticker: Subsidiary   Exchange:
Employees: 2,000   Fiscal Year Ends: 12/31
Parent Company: ModivCare Inc.

SALARIES/BONUSES:

Top Exec. Salary: $ Bonus: $
Second Exec. Salary: $ Bonus: $

OTHER THOUGHTS:

Estimated Female Officers or Directors: 2
Hot Spot for Advancement for Women/Minorities: Y

Molina Healthcare Inc

NAIC Code: 524114

www.molinahealthcare.com

TYPES OF BUSINESS:

HMO-Low Income Patients
Medicaid HMO
SCHIP HMO

BRANDS/DIVISIONS/AFFILIATES:

GROWTH PLANS/SPECIAL FEATURES:

Molina Healthcare, Inc. is a multi-stage, managed care organization participating in government-sponsored health care programs for low-income persons, such as the Medicaid program and Children's Health Insurance Program (CHIP, including Perinatal). The company also focuses on a small number of persons who are dually eligible under the Medicaid and Medicare programs. Molina operates in two segments: health plans and other. Health plans consists of operational health plans in 14 states and Puerto Rico and Molina's direct delivery business. The health plans, serving approximately 3.8 million, are operated by the firm's wholly owned subsidiaries in those states, each of which is licensed as a health maintenance organization (HMO). Molina manages the vast majority of its operations through the health plans segment.

Molina offers employees medical, dental and vision plans; life insurance; disability; employee assistance; flexible spending accounts; 401(k); and an employee stock purchase plan.

CONTACTS:
Note: Officers with more than one job title may be intentionally listed here more than once.

Thomas Tran, CFO
Dale Wolf, Chairman of the Board
Maurice Hebert, Chief Accounting Officer
Jeff Barlow, Chief Legal Officer
Ronna Romney, Director
Mark Keim, Executive VP, Divisional
Pamela Sedmak, Executive VP, Divisional
James Woys, Executive VP, Divisional
Joseph Zubretsky, President

FINANCIAL DATA:
Note: Data for latest year may not have been available at press time.

In U.S. $	2020	2019	2018	2017	2016	2015
Revenue	19,423,000,000	16,829,000,000	18,890,000,000	19,883,000,000	17,782,000,000	14,178,000,000
R&D Expense						
Operating Income	1,078,000,000	1,050,000,000	1,192,000,000	149,000,000	306,000,000	387,000,000
Operating Margin %		.05%	.06%	.00%	.02%	.03%
SGA Expense	1,480,000,000	1,296,000,000	1,333,000,000	1,594,000,000	1,393,000,000	1,146,000,000
Net Income	673,000,000	737,000,000	707,000,000	-512,000,000	52,000,000	143,000,000
Operating Cash Flow	1,890,000,000	427,000,000	-314,000,000	804,000,000	673,000,000	1,125,000,000
Capital Expenditure	74,000,000	57,000,000	30,000,000	86,000,000	176,000,000	132,000,000
EBITDA	1,151,000,000	1,148,000,000	1,241,000,000	-316,000,000	488,000,000	514,000,000
Return on Assets %		.11%	.09%	-.06%	.01%	.03%
Return on Equity %		.41%	.47%	-.34%	.03%	.11%
Debt to Equity		0.749	0.739	1.134	0.711	0.745

CONTACT INFORMATION:

Phone: 562 435-3666   Fax: 562 499-0790
Toll-Free: 888-562-5442
Address: 200 Oceangate, Ste. 100, Long Beach, CA 90802 United States

STOCK TICKER/OTHER:

Stock Ticker: MOH
Employees: 10,000
Parent Company:

Exchange: NYS
Fiscal Year Ends: 12/31

SALARIES/BONUSES:

Top Exec. Salary: $ Bonus: $
Second Exec. Salary: $ Bonus: $

OTHER THOUGHTS:

Estimated Female Officers or Directors: 2
Hot Spot for Advancement for Women/Minorities: Y

Sales, profits and employees may be estimates. Financial information, benefits and other data can change quickly and may vary from those stated here.

Molnlycke Health Care AB

www.molnlycke.com

NAIC Code: 339100

TYPES OF BUSINESS:

Single-Use Surgical & Wound Care Products Manufacturing
Supply Chain & Logistics Management Consulting
Operating Room Staffing

BRANDS/DIVISIONS/AFFILIATES:

Investor AB
Safetac

CONTACTS: *Note: Officers with more than one job title may be intentionally listed here more than once.*

Barry McBride, Interim CEO
Eric De Kesel, Exec. VP-Oper.
Martin Lexa, Exec. VP-Human Resources & Communications
Susanne Larsson, Exec. VP-IT
Rob Bennsion, Exec. VP-Legal, Regulatory & Quality Affairs
Maarten van Beek, Exec. VP-Corp. Comm.
Phil Cooper, Pres., Wound Care Div.
Eric De Kesel, Pres., Surgical Div.
Gunnar Brock, Chmn.
Anders Klinton, Sr. VP-Supply Chain

GROWTH PLANS/SPECIAL FEATURES:

Molnlycke Health Care AB designs and supplies products and solutions for use in wound treatment, pressure ulcer prevention and surgery. Wound management products and solutions cover the continuum of care, from hospital to care in home settings, with foam, film and fiber dressings, as well as negative pressure therapy options. These products are designed to secure ideal wound conditions for effective healing. This division's proprietary Safetac technology is a silicone adhesive layer that enables dressings to be removed with less pain and without damaging the skin. Pressure ulcer prevention products and solutions aim to stop needless patient suffering and unnecessary costs via prophylactic dressings, skin care products and devices that help clinicians turn and re-position patients. This division also provides supporting educational and consultancy services. Surgical solutions include procedure trays that include everything a surgical team needs, as well as the preparation of surgical instruments and related components. For example, laparoscopy specialists perform procedures such as cholecystectomy, appendectomy and hernia repair, and can choose from a full range of trocars, monopolar instruments and essential tray components, all of which Molnlycke provides. Molnlycke Health Care's solutions are used in nearly 100 countries, and the company owns operations in more than 40 of them. The firm is majority-owned (99%) by Swedish investment company, Investor AB.

FINANCIAL DATA: *Note: Data for latest year may not have been available at press time.*

In U.S. $	2020	2019	2018	2017	2016	2015
Revenue	2,202,240,000	1,726,830,000	1,660,790,000	1,730,910,000	1,714,483,842	1,516,865,132
R&D Expense						
Operating Income						
Operating Margin %						
SGA Expense						
Net Income						
Operating Cash Flow						
Capital Expenditure						
EBITDA						
Return on Assets %						
Return on Equity %						
Debt to Equity						

CONTACT INFORMATION:

Phone: 46-31-722-30-00   Fax: 46-31-722-34-00
Toll-Free:
Address: Gamlestadsvaegen 3C, Gothenburg, 415 02 Sweden

STOCK TICKER/OTHER:

Stock Ticker: Private
Employees: 7,895
Parent Company: Investor AB

Exchange:
Fiscal Year Ends: 12/31

SALARIES/BONUSES:

Top Exec. Salary: $ Bonus: $
Second Exec. Salary: $ Bonus: $

OTHER THOUGHTS:

Estimated Female Officers or Directors: 1
Hot Spot for Advancement for Women/Minorities:

Sales, profits and employees may be estimates. Financial information, benefits and other data can change quickly and may vary from those stated here.

Morphic Holding Inc

www.morphictx.com

NAIC Code: 325412

TYPES OF BUSINESS:

Pharmaceutical Preparation Manufacturing

BRANDS/DIVISIONS/AFFILIATES:

MInt

CONTACTS: *Note: Officers with more than one job title may be intentionally listed here more than once.*

Praveen Tipirneni, CEO

GROWTH PLANS/SPECIAL FEATURES:

Morphic Holding, Inc. is a biotechnology company developing oral integrin drugs through its integrin discovery platform, MInT. Integrins are transmembrane receptors that facilitate cell-extracellular matrix adhesion, activating signal transduction pathways that mediate cellular signals. Integrins are the only human receptors known to signal bi-directionally (inside-out and outside-in) to integrate intracellular and extracellular information. This bi-directional signaling ability allows integrins to affect every aspect of cell and organ homeostasis. The combination of the 24 human integrins are all potential targets of Morphic's platform. Therefore, the firm believes oral drugs targeting the integrin protein family can transform the treatment paradigm for patients suffering from serious chronic diseases such as autoimmune, cardiovascular and metabolic, as well as fibrosis and cancer. Morphic's proprietary MInT discovery platform combines integrin dynamics and analytical capabilities with structural biology insights and ongoing input from its integrin research laboratory. The company has a multi-program collaboration with AbbVie focused on fibrotic diseases, with Morphic retaining economic rights in the areas of liver fibrosis. Morphic also has a collaboration with Janssen to develop novel integrin therapeutics.

FINANCIAL DATA: *Note: Data for latest year may not have been available at press time.*

In U.S. $	2020	2019	2018	2017	2016	2015
Revenue	44,945,000	16,977,000	3,358,000			
R&D Expense	73,630,000	53,732,000	22,631,000	14,103,000		
Operating Income	-47,180,000	-46,988,000	-24,628,000	-16,929,000		
Operating Margin %		-2.77%	-7.33%			
SGA Expense	18,495,000	10,233,000	5,355,000	2,826,000		
Net Income	-44,999,000	-43,328,000	-23,831,000	-16,920,000		
Operating Cash Flow	-45,990,000	-41,651,000	76,337,000	-15,415,000		
Capital Expenditure	544,000	2,158,000	659,000	945,000		
EBITDA	-46,054,000	-46,167,000	-24,089,000	-16,495,000		
Return on Assets %		- .20%	- .22%	- .73%		
Return on Equity %		- .98%				
Debt to Equity						

CONTACT INFORMATION:

Phone: 781 996-0955   Fax:
Toll-Free:
Address: 35 Gatehouse Dr., A2, Waltham, MA 02451 United States

SALARIES/BONUSES:

Top Exec. Salary: $ Bonus: $
Second Exec. Salary: $ Bonus: $

STOCK TICKER/OTHER:

Stock Ticker: MORF   Exchange: NAS
Employees: 89   Fiscal Year Ends: 12/31
Parent Company:

OTHER THOUGHTS:

Estimated Female Officers or Directors:
Hot Spot for Advancement for Women/Minorities:

MSA Safety Inc

www.msasafety.com

NAIC Code: 339100

TYPES OF BUSINESS:

Equipment/Supplies-Manufacturer
Safety & Health Equipment
Personal Protective Products
Respiratory Protective Equipment
Combat Helmets
Thermal Imaging Cameras
Security Sensors & Systems

BRANDS/DIVISIONS/AFFILIATES:

CONTACTS: *Note: Officers with more than one job title may be intentionally listed here more than once.*

Nishan Vartanian, CEO
Kenneth Krause, CFO
Douglas McClaine, Chief Legal Officer
William Lambert, Director
Bob Leenen, President, Divisional
Steven Blanco, Vice President

GROWTH PLANS/SPECIAL FEATURES:

MSA Safety, Inc. develops, manufactures and supplies safety and health equipment. The firm divides its product offerings by the geographic areas of its customers: Americas, International and Corporate. The company's safety products are used by workers in fire service, homeland security, the military, construction services and other industries. Customers include industrial and military end-users, distributors and retail consumers. MSA's principle product offerings fall under five categories: respiratory protection; industrial head protection; portable and fixed gas detection instruments; fixed gas and flame detection; and fall protection. The company produces numerous respiratory systems, such as self-contained breathing apparatuses (SCBA); escape hoods, which allow workers to escape from dangerous gases; and air-purifying respirators, such as military full face gas masks, half-mask respirators, respirators and pollen masks. Hand-held thermal imaging cameras are used by firefighters to see victims through dense smoke and to detect a fire's source. Industrial head protection is used in work environments with hazards such as dust, metal fragments, chemicals, extreme glare, optical radiation and items dropped from above. The company produces industrial hard hats; fire helmets; protective eyewear and face shields; and hearing protection products. MSA's portable and fixed gas detection products include single- and multiple-gas hand-held detectors, multi-point permanently installed gas detectors and flame and open-path infrared gas detectors. MSA's fall protection equipment includes confined space equipment, harnesses, fall arrest equipment, and lifelines.

MSA offers its employees life, medical, dental and vision coverage; flexible spending accounts; a disability program; retirement plan; tuition reimbursement; adoption reimbursement; and a bonus system.

FINANCIAL DATA: *Note: Data for latest year may not have been available at press time.*

In U.S. $	2020	2019	2018	2017	2016	2015
Revenue	1,348,223,000	1,401,981,000	1,358,104,000	1,196,809,000	1,149,530,000	1,130,783,000
R&D Expense	58,268,000	57,848,000	52,696,000	50,061,000	46,847,000	48,630,000
Operating Income	241,846,000	248,262,000	189,056,000	66,104,000	170,652,000	137,203,000
Operating Margin %		.16%	.14%	.06%	.15%	.12%
SGA Expense	290,334,000	330,502,000	324,784,000	297,801,000	306,144,000	315,270,000
Net Income	120,101,000	136,440,000	124,150,000	26,027,000	91,936,000	70,807,000
Operating Cash Flow	206,555,000	164,962,000	263,887,000	230,336,000	134,894,000	55,254,000
Capital Expenditure	48,905,000	36,604,000	33,960,000	23,725,000	25,523,000	36,241,000
EBITDA	212,209,000	235,344,000	219,068,000	83,012,000	203,595,000	153,564,000
Return on Assets %		.08%	.08%	.02%	.07%	.05%
Return on Equity %		.20%	.20%	.05%	.17%	.14%
Debt to Equity		0.514	0.541	0.754	0.656	0.897

CONTACT INFORMATION:

Phone: 724 776-8600   Fax:
Toll-Free: 800-672-2222
Address: 1000 Cranberry Woods Dr., Pittsburgh, PA 16066 United States

STOCK TICKER/OTHER:

Stock Ticker: MSA
Employees: 4,800
Parent Company:

Exchange: NYS
Fiscal Year Ends: 12/31

SALARIES/BONUSES:

Top Exec. Salary: $ Bonus: $
Second Exec. Salary: $ Bonus: $

OTHER THOUGHTS:

Estimated Female Officers or Directors: 3
Hot Spot for Advancement for Women/Minorities: Y

MultiPlan Inc

NAIC Code: 524298

www.multiplan.com

TYPES OF BUSINESS:
Medical Cost Evaluation Services

BRANDS/DIVISIONS/AFFILIATES:
Hellman & Friedman LLC

CONTACTS: *Note: Officers with more than one job title may be intentionally listed here more than once.*
Mark Taback, CEO
Derek Reis-Larson, Sr. VP-Claims Pricing Services
David Redmond, CFO
Dale White, Chief Revenue Officer
Michael Kim, CIO

GROWTH PLANS/SPECIAL FEATURES:

MultiPlan, Inc. provides technology-enabled health care cost management solutions. The firm's solutions deliver a single electronic gateway to a comprehensive set of claim cost management solutions that help control the financial risks associated with medical bills, while helping providers more effectively control reimbursements. Electronic claims are compared against cost savings mechanisms in a specific order, consistent with the requirements of contracts and benefit plans. The process also avoids errors and delays that often result when claims are routed from vendor to vendor. MultiPlan has approximately 900,000 healthcare providers under contract, and more than 60 million consumers who access its network products. As a result, 40 million claims are reduced through the firm's network and non-network solutions every year. The company's health care management solutions serve insurers, health plans, third party administrators, self-funded employers, HMOs, PPOs and other entities that pay medical bills in commercial healthcare, government, workers' compensation and auto medical markets. Solutions include primary networks, complementary network, specialty networks, non-networks and network management services, as well as a network of facilities offering contracted savings on various organ and stem cell transplant procedures. MultiPlan is owned by Hellman & Friedman, LLC.

MultiPlan offers its employees medical, dental and vision insurance; 401(k); life insurance plans; short- and long-term disability; paid time off; tuition reimbursement; flexible spending account; and employee assistance programs.

FINANCIAL DATA: *Note: Data for latest year may not have been available at press time.*

In U.S. $	2020	2019	2018	2017	2016	2015
Revenue	937,763,000	982,901,000	1,040,883,000			
R&D Expense						
Operating Income	-131,821,000	368,209,000	427,541,000			
Operating Margin %						
SGA Expense	355,635,000	75,225,000	77,558,000			
Net Income	-520,564,000	9,710,000	36,223,000			
Operating Cash Flow	377,374,000	284,313,000	292,303,000			
Capital Expenditure	70,813,000	66,414,000	63,556,000			
EBITDA	192,410,000	786,309,000	813,913,000			
Return on Assets %						
Return on Equity %						
Debt to Equity						

CONTACT INFORMATION:
Phone: 212-780-2000   Fax: 212-780-0420
Toll-Free: 800-677-1098
Address: 115 Fifth Ave., New York, NY 10003 United States

STOCK TICKER/OTHER:
Stock Ticker: MPLN
Employees: 2,000
Parent Company: Hellman & Friedman LLC
Exchange: NYS
Fiscal Year Ends: 12/31

SALARIES/BONUSES:
Top Exec. Salary: $ Bonus: $
Second Exec. Salary: $ Bonus: $

OTHER THOUGHTS:
Estimated Female Officers or Directors:
Hot Spot for Advancement for Women/Minorities:

Mylan NV

www.mylan.com

NAIC Code: 325412

TYPES OF BUSINESS:

Drugs-Generic
Generic Pharmaceuticals
Active Pharmaceutical Ingredients

BRANDS/DIVISIONS/AFFILIATES:

EipPen
Perforomist
YUPELRI
Cold-EEZE
MidNite
Vivarin

CONTACTS: *Note: Officers with more than one job title may be intentionally listed here more than once.*

Heather Bresch, CEO
Rajiv Malik, Pres.
Ken Parks, CFO
Anthony Mauro, Chief Commercial Officer
C. Todd, Director Emeritus
Rajiv Malik, Director
Rodney Piatt, Director
Anthony Mauro, President, Geographical
Joseph Haggerty, Secretary
Robert J. Coury, Chmn.

GROWTH PLANS/SPECIAL FEATURES:

Mylan NV is a global pharmaceutical company with a portfolio of more than 7,500 products, including prescription generic, branded generic, brand-name drugs and over-the-counter (OTC) remedies. The firm markets its products in more than 165 countries and territories. Mylan reports its results in three segments on a geographic basis as follows: North America (U.S. and Canada), representing 37% of net annual sales; Europe (encompassing 35 countries), 35%; and Rest of World (consisting of more than 120 countries) 28%. A significant portion of the firm's revenue is through the sale of the EpiPen Auto-Injector, which dispenses epinephrine for the treatment of severe allergic reactions. The EpiPen has been sold in the U.S. and internationally since the mid-1980s. Another key product by the company is the Perforomist inhalation solution, a long-acting beta2-adrenergic agonist indicated for long-term, twice-daily administration in the maintenance treatment of bronchoconstriction in chronic obstructive pulmonary disorder patients. Other products by Mylan include: YUPELRI, an inhalation solution for the maintenance treatment of patients with chronic obstructive pulmonary disease; and OTC remedies such as Cold-EEZE, MidNite and Vivarin, among others. Mylan owns 16 manufacturing, distribution and administrative facilities in the U.S., including Puerto Rico. Outside the U.S. and Puerto Rico, the firm owns 37 production, distribution and administrative facilities in 15 countries. In mid-2019, Pfizer, Inc. agreed to merge its off-patent drug business, Upjohn, with Mylan, creating a new company to be named Viatris. The new company will be 57% controlled by Pfizer and 43% by Mylan. The transaction was expected to close by the end of 2020.

FINANCIAL DATA: *Note: Data for latest year may not have been available at press time.*

In U.S. $	2020	2019	2018	2017	2016	2015
Revenue		11,500,499,968	11,433,900,032	11,907,699,712	11,076,899,840	9,429,300,224
R&D Expense						
Operating Income						
Operating Margin %						
SGA Expense						
Net Income		16,800,000	352,500,000	696,000,000	480,000,000	847,600,000
Operating Cash Flow						
Capital Expenditure						
EBITDA						
Return on Assets %						
Return on Equity %						
Debt to Equity						

CONTACT INFORMATION:

Phone: 44 01707853000   Fax: 44 01707261803
Toll-Free:
Address: Bldg. 4, Trident Place, Mosquito Way, Hatfield, Hertfordshire AL10 9UL United Kingdom

STOCK TICKER/OTHER:

Stock Ticker: MYL
Employees: 35,000
Parent Company:

Exchange: NAS
Fiscal Year Ends: 12/31

SALARIES/BONUSES:

Top Exec. Salary: $ Bonus: $
Second Exec. Salary: $ Bonus: $

OTHER THOUGHTS:

Estimated Female Officers or Directors: 3
Hot Spot for Advancement for Women/Minorities: Y

Narayana Hrudayalaya Ltd

NAIC Code: 622110

www.narayanahealth.org

TYPES OF BUSINESS:
General Medical and Surgical Hospitals

BRANDS/DIVISIONS/AFFILIATES:

GROWTH PLANS/SPECIAL FEATURES:
Narayana Hrudayalaya Ltd. is headquartered in Bengaluru, India, and operates a network of hospitals throughout India. The network encompasses 21 hospitals, six heart centers and 19 primary care facilities, as well as an international hospital in the Cayman Islands. The group features nearly 6,000 operational beds and provides advanced levels of care in over 80 specialties. These specialties include cardiology, cancer care, hepato-pancreatico-biliary surgery, liver transplant, neurology, neurosurgery, orthopedics, nephrology, urology and gastroenterology, as well as general surgery, robotic surgery, cranio-maxillo facial surgery, plastic surgery and more.

CONTACTS:
Note: Officers with more than one job title may be intentionally listed here more than once.

Emmanuel Rupert, Group CEO
Viren Shetty, Group COO
Kesavan Venugopalan, Group CFO
Sumanta Ray, CMO
Sirshendu Mookherjee, Group Head-HR
Kumar K V, Group Head-IT
Devi Prasad Shetty, Chmn.

FINANCIAL DATA:
Note: Data for latest year may not have been available at press time.

In U.S. $	2020	2019	2018	2017	2016	2015
Revenue	300,848,000	301,101,000	286,884,000	256,382,000	242,452,000	217,594,000
R&D Expense						
Operating Income						
Operating Margin %						
SGA Expense						
Net Income	9,003,930	7,198,870	8,980,950	14,653,900	6,103,940	945,777
Operating Cash Flow						
Capital Expenditure						
EBITDA						
Return on Assets %						
Return on Equity %						
Debt to Equity						

CONTACT INFORMATION:
Phone: 91-80-71222802   Fax: 91-80-71222611
Toll-Free:
Address: #258/A, Bommasandra Indistrial Area, Anekal Taluk, Bengaluru, Karnataka 562158 India

STOCK TICKER/OTHER:
Stock Ticker: 539551
Employees:
Parent Company:

Exchange: Bombay
Fiscal Year Ends: 03/31

SALARIES/BONUSES:
Top Exec. Salary: $ Bonus: $
Second Exec. Salary: $ Bonus: $

OTHER THOUGHTS:
Estimated Female Officers or Directors:
Hot Spot for Advancement for Women/Minorities:

National HealthCare Corporation

www.nhccare.com

NAIC Code: 623110

TYPES OF BUSINESS:

Nursing Care Facilities
Rehabilitative Services
Medical Specialty Units
Pharmacy Operations
Assisted Living Projects
Managed Care Contracts
Nutritional Support Services
Real Estate

BRANDS/DIVISIONS/AFFILIATES:

Caris Healthcare LP

CONTACTS: *Note: Officers with more than one job title may be intentionally listed here more than once.*

Brian Kidd, Chief Accounting Officer
B. Anderson Flatt, Chief Information Officer
R. Ussery, COO
Stephen Flatt, Director
Robert Adams, Director
Leroy McIntosh, Senior VP, Divisional
Jeffrey Smith, Senior VP

GROWTH PLANS/SPECIAL FEATURES:

National HealthCare Corporation (NHC) operates long-term healthcare centers and home healthcare programs in 10 states. NHC's health services include long-term healthcare centers, rehabilitative services, medical specialty units, pharmacy operations, assisted living projects, managed care contracts, hospice programs and homecare programs. The firm services approximately 75 skilled nursing facilities (9,510 beds) which include 67 centers with 8,598 beds that are leased or owned and eight facilities with 915 beds that are managed for others. NHC also operates or manages 25 assisted living centers that have a total of 1,238 units; five independent living centers that consist of 475 retirement apartments; and 35 homecare programs licensed in four states (Tennessee, South Carolina and Florida). The company's care centers provide in-patient skilled and intermediate nursing care services and in-patient and out-patient rehabilitation services. Its centers also provide rehabilitative care, including physical, occupational and speech therapies. Skilled nursing care consists of 24-hour nursing service by registered or licensed practical nurses and intermediate nursing care by non-licensed personnel. Most of the company's retirement centers are constructed adjacent to NHC's healthcare properties. It operates specialized care units such as Alzheimer's disease care units, sub-acute nursing units and a number of in-house pharmacies. In addition, NHC has a partnership agreement and a 75.1% non-controlling ownership interest in Caris Healthcare, LP, which specializes in hospice care services in NHC-owned healthcare centers and in other settings. Caris provides care to more than 1,000 patients each day in 28 locations within Georgia, Missouri, South Carolina, Tennessee and Virginia. Apart from its healthcare services, NHC is engaged in management, accounting and financial services; nutritional support services; advisory services; and insurance services.

FINANCIAL DATA: *Note: Data for latest year may not have been available at press time.*

In U.S. $	2020	2019	2018	2017	2016	2015
Revenue	980,712,000	996,383,000	980,349,000	966,996,000	926,638,000	906,622,000
R&D Expense						
Operating Income	49,554,000	52,173,000	60,773,000	59,000,000	64,483,000	69,734,000
Operating Margin %		.05%	.06%	.06%	.07%	.08%
SGA Expense	649,800,000	633,349,000	623,644,000	612,410,000	589,299,000	572,702,000
Net Income	41,871,000	68,211,000	58,964,000	56,205,000	50,538,000	53,143,000
Operating Cash Flow	203,259,000	100,103,000	98,435,000	94,466,000	90,882,000	73,963,000
Capital Expenditure	21,873,000	26,400,000	29,772,000	32,347,000	62,601,000	58,416,000
EBITDA	95,840,000	133,569,000	121,475,000	122,091,000	123,171,000	124,996,000
Return on Assets %		.06%	.05%	.05%	.05%	.04%
Return on Equity %		.09%	.08%	.08%	.08%	.08%
Debt to Equity		0.249	0.101	0.175	0.219	0.238

CONTACT INFORMATION:

Phone: 615 890-2020   Fax: 615 890-0123
Toll-Free:
Address: 100 Vine St., Murfreesboro, TN 37130 United States

STOCK TICKER/OTHER:

Stock Ticker: NHC
Employees: 14,881
Parent Company:

Exchange: ASE
Fiscal Year Ends: 12/31

SALARIES/BONUSES:

Top Exec. Salary: $ Bonus: $
Second Exec. Salary: $ Bonus: $

OTHER THOUGHTS:

Estimated Female Officers or Directors: 2
Hot Spot for Advancement for Women/Minorities: Y

Sales, profits and employees may be estimates. Financial information, benefits and other data can change quickly and may vary from those stated here.

National Healthcare Group Pte Ltd

corp.nhg.com.sg

NAIC Code: 622110

TYPES OF BUSINESS:

General Medical and Surgical Hospitals
Psychiatric and Substance Abuse Hospitals
Medical and Diagnostic Laboratories
Medical School
College
Esthetician (i.e., Skin Care) Services
Pharmacies and Drug Stores

BRANDS/DIVISIONS/AFFILIATES:

Tan Tock Seng Hospital
Khoo Teck Puat
Institute of Mental Health
Woodlands Health Campus
National Healthcare Group Polyclinics
NHG College
Primary Care Academy
Admiralty Medical Centre

CONTACTS: *Note: Officers with more than one job title may be intentionally listed here more than once.*

Philip Choo, CEO
Lim Yee Juan, CFO
Olivia Tay, Chief Human Resources Officer
Huan Boon Kean, CIO
Kay Kuok, Chmn.

GROWTH PLANS/SPECIAL FEATURES:

National Healthcare Group Pte. Ltd. (NHG), based in Singapore, is a group of health care institutions composed of multiple divisions. The Tan Tock Seng Hospital is Singapore's second largest acute care general hospital with over 1,500 beds. Khoo Teck Puat Hospital is a 590-bed general and acute care hospital. Yishun Community Hospital is a 428-bed hospital that provides intermediate care for recuperating patients who do not require intensive care services. Yishun Community Hospital is a 428-bed community hospital for intermediate care. The Institute of Mental Health is a 2,000-bed acute tertiary psychiatric hospital that offers a comprehensive range of psychiatric, rehabilitative and counselling services for children, adolescents, adults and the elderly. Woodlands Health Campus is a 1,800-bed campus with an integrated acute and community hospital. The National Healthcare Group Polyclinics, the primary health care arm of the NHG, has nine polyclinics that serve a significant proportion of the population in the central, northern and western parts of Singapore. The National Skin Centre is an outpatient specialist dermatological center that cares for about 1,000 patients daily. NHG College, with programs in the fields of leadership, clinical education, health care and risk management, develops the talent for NHG. NHG Diagnostics provides laboratory and radiography services in primary health care, with an extensive network of tele-radiology and professional service for imaging centers. NHG Pharmacy manages the pharmacy and retail pharmacies of NHG's nine polyclinics. Primary Care Academy provides the training needs and skills upgrading of primary care doctors, nurses, allied health professionals and ancillary staff in Singapore and the region. Johns Hopkins Singapore International Medical Centre, located in Tan Tock Hospital, provides outpatient diagnostic and consultation services, screening programs, expert second opinions and inpatient care focusing on treatment of various cancers. Admiralty Medical Centre provides specialized outpatient consultations, day surgery procedures and endoscopies.

FINANCIAL DATA: *Note: Data for latest year may not have been available at press time.*

In U.S. $	2020	2019	2018	2017	2016	2015
Revenue	1,911,820,995	2,055,721,500	1,957,830,000	1,864,600,000	1,525,000,000	1,498,089,174
R&D Expense						
Operating Income						
Operating Margin %						
SGA Expense						
Net Income						
Operating Cash Flow						
Capital Expenditure						
EBITDA						
Return on Assets %						
Return on Equity %						
Debt to Equity						

CONTACT INFORMATION:

Phone: 65-6496-6000			Fax: 65-6496-6870
Toll-Free:
Address: 3 Fusionopolis Link #03-08, Nexus@one-north, Singapore, 138543 Singapore

STOCK TICKER/OTHER:

Stock Ticker: Government-Owned				Exchange:
Employees: 18,378							Fiscal Year Ends: 03/31
Parent Company:

SALARIES/BONUSES:

Top Exec. Salary: $			Bonus: $
Second Exec. Salary: $			Bonus: $

OTHER THOUGHTS:

Estimated Female Officers or Directors:
Hot Spot for Advancement for Women/Minorities:

National University Health System (NUHS)   www.nuhs.edu.sg

NAIC Code: 622110

TYPES OF BUSINESS:

General Medical and Surgical Hospitals
Medical School
Dental School
Colleges, Universities and Professional Schools

BRANDS/DIVISIONS/AFFILIATES:

National University of Singapore
MOH Holdings Pte Ltd
National University Hospital
Ng Teng Fong General Hospital
Jurong Community Hospital
Alexandra Hospital
National University Cancer Institute
NUS Faculty of Dentistry

CONTACTS: *Note: Officers with more than one job title may be intentionally listed here more than once.*

Hsieh Fu Hua, Chmn.

GROWTH PLANS/SPECIAL FEATURES:

National University Health System (NUHS) is an integrated academic health system and regional health organization in Singapore. The firm was established as a joint venture between the National University of Singapore and MOH Holdings Pte Ltd. Its hospitals include National University Hospital (NUH), Ng Teng Fong General Hospital, Jurong Community Hospital and Alexandra Hospital. NUH is a 1,200-bed tertiary hospital; Ng Teng and Jurong Community are an integrated healthcare development delivering patient-centered services in a seamless manner; and Alexandra offers integrated continuum care via programs, health informatics and technology in collaboration with NUHS and community partners. National specialty centers include: National University Cancer Institute, which offers cancer care and management; National University Heart Centre, which offers cardiology, cardiothoracic and vascular surgery services for patients with heart disease; and National University Centre for Oral Health, which offers oral health services to elderly patients and those with special needs. Other facilities include the National University Polyclinics (clinics), and Jurong Medical Centre (medical center). Last, academic health sciences institutions include NUS Yong Loo Lin School of Medicine, NUS Alice Lee Centre for Nursing Studies, NUS Faculty of Dentistry, and NUS Saw Swee Hock School of Public Health.

FINANCIAL DATA: *Note: Data for latest year may not have been available at press time.*

In U.S. $	2020	2019	2018	2017	2016	2015
Revenue						
R&D Expense						
Operating Income						
Operating Margin %						
SGA Expense						
Net Income						
Operating Cash Flow						
Capital Expenditure						
EBITDA						
Return on Assets %						
Return on Equity %						
Debt to Equity						

CONTACT INFORMATION:

Phone: 65-6779-5555   Fax: 65-6775-0913
Toll-Free:
Address: 1E Kent Ridge Rd., Singapore, 119228 Singapore

STOCK TICKER/OTHER:

Stock Ticker: Joint Venture   Exchange:
Employees: 9,000   Fiscal Year Ends:
Parent Company: National University of Singapore

SALARIES/BONUSES:

Top Exec. Salary: $ Bonus: $
Second Exec. Salary: $ Bonus: $

OTHER THOUGHTS:

Estimated Female Officers or Directors:
Hot Spot for Advancement for Women/Minorities:

Sales, profits and employees may be estimates. Financial information, benefits and other data can change quickly and may vary from those stated here.

Natus Medical Incorporated

NAIC Code: 339100

www.natus.com

TYPES OF BUSINESS:

Medical Diagnostics Manufacturer
Newborn Care Products

BRANDS/DIVISIONS/AFFILIATES:

CONTACTS: Note: Officers with more than one job title may be intentionally listed here more than once.

Jonathan Kennedy, CEO
Drew Davies, CFO
Barbara Paul, Chairman of the Board
Austin Noll, Executive VP
William Hill, General Counsel
Martin Woodrow, Vice President, Divisional
Sean Langan, Vice President, Divisional
Ivan Pandiyan, Vice President, Divisional

GROWTH PLANS/SPECIAL FEATURES:

Natus Medical Incorporated is a provider of health care products used for the screening, detection, treatment, monitoring and tracking of common medical ailments in newborns. These ailments are associated with newborn care, hearing impairment, neurological dysfunction, epilepsy, sleep disorders and balance and mobility disorders. Natus divides its products into three categories: Neuro, Newborn Care and Hearing & Balance. The Neuro segment's includes products and services that provide diagnostic, therapeutic and surgical solutions in neurodiagnostics, neurocritical care and neurosurgery. The segment's comprehensive neurodiagnostic solutions include electroencephalography and long-term monitoring, Intensive Care Unit monitoring, electromyography, sleep analysis or polysomnography and intraoperative monitoring. These solutions enhance the diagnosis of neurological conditions such as epilepsy, sleep disorders and neuromuscular diseases. The newborn care segment offers newborn hearing screening as well as newborn brain injury products to diagnose brain injury, monitor drug therapies and treat the injury. Last, the Hearing & Balance category includes products and services such as computer-based audiological, otoneurologic and vestibular instrumentation and sound rooms for hearing and balance care professionals worldwide. In January 2020, the firm finalized and executed the transition of its Peloton hearing screening services business to Pediatrix Medical Group.

FINANCIAL DATA: Note: Data for latest year may not have been available at press time.

In U.S. $	2020	2019	2018	2017	2016	2015
Revenue	415,684,000	495,175,000	530,891,000	500,970,000	381,892,000	375,865,000
R&D Expense	61,296,000	58,733,000	61,482,000	51,822,000	33,443,000	30,434,000
Operating Income	-16,384,000	29,073,000	12,669,000	9,631,000	56,796,000	55,618,000
Operating Margin %		.06%	.02%	.02%	.15%	.15%
SGA Expense	156,395,000	188,758,000	205,379,000	200,590,000	135,711,000	134,038,000
Net Income	-16,613,000	-15,671,000	-22,935,000	-20,293,000	42,594,000	37,924,000
Operating Cash Flow	34,426,000	60,060,000	33,020,000	19,726,000	72,687,000	36,852,000
Capital Expenditure	8,609,000	5,339,000	8,540,000	4,066,000	3,396,000	5,194,000
EBITDA	9,706,000	14,406,000	8,397,000	40,329,000	72,212,000	68,748,000
Return on Assets %		-.02%	-.03%	-.03%	.08%	.08%
Return on Equity %		-.04%	-.06%	-.05%	.11%	.10%
Debt to Equity		0.078	0.174	0.366	0.335	

CONTACT INFORMATION:

Phone: 608-829-8500   Fax:
Toll-Free: 800-255-3901
Address: 6701 Koll Ctr. Pkwy., Ste. 120, Pleasanton, CA 94566 United States

STOCK TICKER/OTHER:

Stock Ticker: NTUS
Employees: 1,420
Parent Company:

Exchange: NAS
Fiscal Year Ends: 12/31

SALARIES/BONUSES:

Top Exec. Salary: $ Bonus: $
Second Exec. Salary: $ Bonus: $

OTHER THOUGHTS:

Estimated Female Officers or Directors: 1
Hot Spot for Advancement for Women/Minorities:

Netcare Limited

www.netcareinvestor.co.za

NAIC Code: 622110

TYPES OF BUSINESS:

General Medical and Surgical Hospitals

BRANDS/DIVISIONS/AFFILIATES:

Medicross
Netcare 911
Akeso
Tsepong

CONTACTS: *Note: Officers with more than one job title may be intentionally listed here more than once.*

Richard Friedland, CEO
Keith Gibson, CFO
Duncan Empey, Dir.-Medical
Travis Dewing, CIO
Lynelle Bagwandeen, General Counsel
Melanie Da Costa, Dir.-Strategy & Health Policy
Kerishnie Naiker, Dir.-Comm.
Craig Lovelace, CFO-U.K.
Jacques du Plessis, Managing Dir.-Hospitals
Elaine Young, Managing Dir.-Hospitals, U.K.
Tumi Nkosi, Dir.-Bus. Dev. & Corp. Affairs
Charmaine Pailman, Managing Dir.-Primary Care
Thevendrie Brewer, Chmn.
Stephen Collier, CEO-U.K.

GROWTH PLANS/SPECIAL FEATURES:

Netcare Limited is a holding company that operates through subsidiaries to invest in and support healthcare systems throughout South Africa. The firm also invests in innovative and advanced medical technologies and related solutions. Netcare operates the largest private hospital, primary healthcare, emergency medical services and renal care networks in South Africa. Together, the group offers primary health care, sub-acute care, day surgery, occupational health and employee wellness services through Medicross. It offers emergency medical services through Netcare 911; and mental health and psychiatric services through Akeso. Netcare also provides private training for personnel engaged in emergency medical and nursing services. As of September 2020, Netcare's network comprised 54 hospitals, five public private partnership hospitals, 10 cancer care centers, 95 primary healthcare centers, 79 Netcare 911 emergency sites, 12 mental health/psychiatric clinics, 63 renal dialysis units, seven training campuses and more. In Lesotho, majority-owned Tsepong is engaged in a public private partnership (PPP) with the national government. Tsepong provides clinical services in a 425-bed hospital, and provides primary health care services at three filter clinics and a gateway clinic. It also manages these facilities.

FINANCIAL DATA: *Note: Data for latest year may not have been available at press time.*

In U.S. $	2020	2019	2018	2017	2016	2015
Revenue	1,369,680,000	1,569,284,000	1,505,899,000	2,480,514,000	2,747,355,000	2,450,420,000
R&D Expense						
Operating Income	95,876,860	264,588,100	253,394,000	94,277,690	301,514,200	270,984,800
Operating Margin %		.15%	.14%	.02%	.10%	.10%
SGA Expense	563,485,500	562,758,700	536,299,800	893,203,000	929,911,000	838,322,800
Net Income	32,419,320	177,870,100	359,083,900	-35,835,700	124,952,500	178,887,700
Operating Cash Flow	-72,107,540					
Capital Expenditure	72,616,360	103,872,600	110,051,200	177,870,100	205,128,500	192,844,000
EBITDA	211,452,400	291,701,200	166,094,500	-67,382,750	192,989,400	295,699,000
Return on Assets %		.11%	.20%	-.02%	.05%	.08%
Return on Equity %		.25%	.54%	-.06%	.16%	.25%
Debt to Equity		0.531	0.526	0.873	0.603	0.592

CONTACT INFORMATION:

Phone: 27 113010000   Fax: 27 113010499
Toll-Free:
Address: 76 Maude St., Corner West St., Sandown, Sandton 2196 South Africa

STOCK TICKER/OTHER:

Stock Ticker: NWKHY
Employees: 19,214
Parent Company:

Exchange: PINX
Fiscal Year Ends: 09/30

SALARIES/BONUSES:

Top Exec. Salary: $ Bonus: $
Second Exec. Salary: $ Bonus: $

OTHER THOUGHTS:

Estimated Female Officers or Directors: 7
Hot Spot for Advancement for Women/Minorities: Y

New York City Health and Hospitals Corporation

www.nyc.gov/html/hhc

NAIC Code: 622110

TYPES OF BUSINESS:

General Medical and Surgical Hospitals
Community Health Clinics
HMO
Long-Term Care Facilities
Home Health Care
Correctional Facility Health Services

BRANDS/DIVISIONS/AFFILIATES:

MetroPlus
OneCity Health

CONTACTS: *Note: Officers with more than one job title may be intentionally listed here more than once.*

Mitchell Katz, CEO
Machelle Allen, Chief Medical Officer
John Ulberg, CFO
Ana Marengo, Sr. VP-Mktg. & Communications
Yvette Villanueva, VP-Human Resources
Ross Wilson, Sr. VP-Quality
Kim Mendez, CIO
Salvatore J. Russo, Corp. General Counsel
LaRay Brown, Sr. VP-Corp. Planning & Community Health
Ana Marengo, Sr. VP-Corp. Comm.
Marlene Zurack, Sr. VP-Finance
Tamiru Mammo, Chief of Staff
Caroline M. Jacobs, Sr. VP-Safety & Human Dev.
Joanna Omi, Sr. VP-Organizational Innovation & Effectiveness
Lynda D. Curtis, Sr. VP-South Manhattan Health Care Network
Jose A. Pagan, Chmn.

GROWTH PLANS/SPECIAL FEATURES:

New York City Health and Hospitals Corporation (HHC) provides health care to all five boroughs of New York. The company operates 11 acute care hospitals, as well as primary and preventative care facilities. Services offered by the group include child health, adolescent health, alcohol/drug dependency, asthma care, bariatric, behavioral/mental health, burn, cancer, cardiology, colon cancer screening, dental, diabetes, flu vaccination, geriatric, HIV/AIDS, HPV vaccine, language/translation, mammograms, neonatal intensive care, obstetrics/gynecology, palliative care, Parkinson's Disease, pediatrics, quit smoking, rehab, sexual response assault teams, sickle cell disease, sleep disorder labs, stroke prevention/care, telehealth initiatives, trauma centers, vision care, women's health and environmental health. If it is difficult for patients to leave home due to age, chronic condition or other, HHC provides health care services to patients at their homes to residents of Manhattan, Queens, Brooklyn and the Bronx. In addition, MetroPlus is HHC's health plan that offers low to no-cost health insurance to eligible people living in Manhattan, Brooklyn, Queens, Staten Island and the Bronx. OneCity Health is the HHC's sponsored performing provider system (PPS), designed to reduce avoidable and unnecessary hospital stays. OneCity Health comprises hundreds of health care providers and community-based organizations who work together to keep their communities healthy. HHC's long-term care facilities provide 24-hour care for its patients.

FINANCIAL DATA: *Note: Data for latest year may not have been available at press time.*

In U.S. $	2020	2019	2018	2017	2016	2015
Revenue	9,053,438,000	7,896,762,000	7,760,991,000	7,293,634,000	7,682,559,000	6,457,731,000
R&D Expense						
Operating Income						
Operating Margin %						
SGA Expense						
Net Income	423,504,000	176,753,000	39,169,000	-232,945,000	57,368,000	-76,214,000
Operating Cash Flow						
Capital Expenditure						
EBITDA						
Return on Assets %						
Return on Equity %						
Debt to Equity						

CONTACT INFORMATION:

Phone: 212-788-3321   Fax: 212-788-0040
Toll-Free:
Address: 125 Worth St., New York, NY 10013 United States

STOCK TICKER/OTHER:

Stock Ticker: Nonprofit   Exchange:
Employees: 45,031   Fiscal Year Ends: 06/30
Parent Company:

SALARIES/BONUSES:

Top Exec. Salary: $ Bonus: $
Second Exec. Salary: $ Bonus: $

OTHER THOUGHTS:

Estimated Female Officers or Directors: 6
Hot Spot for Advancement for Women/Minorities: Y

New York Health Care Inc

www.nyhc.com

NAIC Code: 621610

TYPES OF BUSINESS:

Home Health Care Services
Home Health Care
Prenatal and Postnatal Care
Dementia and Alzheimer's
Infusion Therapy

BRANDS/DIVISIONS/AFFILIATES:

CONTACTS: Note: Officers with more than one job title may be intentionally listed here more than once.

Murry Englard, CEO
Glen Persaud, Dir.-Human Resources

GROWTH PLANS/SPECIAL FEATURES:

New York Health Care, Inc. (NYHC) is a health care company that delivers home healthcare services to all ages, including the elderly. The firm provides companionship services, pediatric nurses, home health aides, licensed practical nurses, geriatric care and infusion therapy nurses. The company's services include medication reminders, meal preparation, light housekeeping, household organization and tasks, accompaniment to medical appointments/family gatherings/senior centers, socialization, pre- and post-surgery transportation, mental cueing, safety supervision, and more. Baby nurses assist with breastfeeding/lactation support, prenatal/postnatal care, nighttime feedings, promoting healthy feeding habits and sleep environments, bathing and dressing the newborn, sterilization of nursery items and supporting parents with regards to infant care. NYHC uses music to encourage social interaction, brain stimulation, communication and verbal expression for patients with dementia or Alzheimer's. NYHC brings assistance to the client's home, senior residences and assisted living facilities as well as to hospitals. In addition, the firm is approved by the New York State Department of Health to provide consumer directed personal assistance services (CDPAP), a statewide Medicaid program that offers an alternative way of receiving home care services where the consumer has more control over who provides their care and how it is provided. The firm covers Rockland, Orange, Duchess, Westchester, Nassau and Suffolk counties as well as the 5 boroughs of New York.

FINANCIAL DATA: Note: Data for latest year may not have been available at press time.

In U.S. $	2020	2019	2018	2017	2016	2015
Revenue						
R&D Expense						
Operating Income						
Operating Margin %						
SGA Expense						
Net Income						
Operating Cash Flow						
Capital Expenditure						
EBITDA						
Return on Assets %						
Return on Equity %						
Debt to Equity						

CONTACT INFORMATION:

Phone: 718-375-6700   Fax: 718-375-1555
Toll-Free: 888-978-6942
Address: 33 W. Hawthorne Av, Valley Stream, NY 11581 United States

STOCK TICKER/OTHER:

Stock Ticker: Private   Exchange:
Employees: 1,460   Fiscal Year Ends: 12/31
Parent Company:

SALARIES/BONUSES:

Top Exec. Salary: $ Bonus: $
Second Exec. Salary: $ Bonus: $

OTHER THOUGHTS:

Estimated Female Officers or Directors:
Hot Spot for Advancement for Women/Minorities:

Sales, profits and employees may be estimates. Financial information, benefits and other data can change quickly and may vary from those stated here.

NewYork-Presbyterian Healthcare System

www.nyp.org

NAIC Code: 622110

TYPES OF BUSINESS:

General Medical and Surgical Hospitals
Nursing Homes
Rehabilitation Centers

BRANDS/DIVISIONS/AFFILIATES:

NewYork-Presbyterian Hospital
NewYork-Presbyterian/Weill Cornell Medical Center
NewYork-Presbyterian/The Allen Hospital
NewYork-Presbyterian/Lower Manhattan Hospital
NewYork-Presbyterian/Westchester Division
NewYork-Presbyterian/Lawrence Hospital
NewYork-Presbyterian/Hudson Valley Hospital
NewYork-Presbyterian/Queens

CONTACTS: *Note: Officers with more than one job title may be intentionally listed here more than once.*

Steven J. Corwin, CEO
Laura L. Forese, Exec. VP
Michael P. Breslin, Sr. VP
Sarah Lesser Avins, Chief Development Officer
Shaun Smith, Chief Human Resources Officer
Daniel J. Barchi, CIO
Kimlee Roldan-Sanchez, Chief Admin. Officer
Gary J. Zuar, Sr. VP-Finance
Wilhelmina Manzano, Chief Nursing Officer
Eric Vorenkamp, VP-Insurance
Eliot J. Lazar, Chief Quality & Patient Safety Officer
Lori MacDonald, VP-Internal Audit & Corp. Compliance
Jerry I. Speyer, Chmn.

GROWTH PLANS/SPECIAL FEATURES:

NewYork-Presbyterian Healthcare System is a comprehensive, integrated academic health care delivery system. The organization collaborates with two renowned medical schools, Weill Cornell Medicine and Columbia University College of Physicians and Surgeons, to provide medical education, groundbreaking research, as well as patient-centered clinical care. NewYork-Presbyterian is organized into four divisions: hospital, regional hospital network, physician's services and community/population health. The hospital division comprises NewYork-Presbyterian Hospital, an academic center committed to patient care, research, education and community services. The hospital serves more than 2 million visits annually. This division comprises seven campuses: NewYork-Presbyterian/Columbia University Medical Center, NewYork-Presbyterian/Weill Cornell Medical Center, NewYork-Presbyterian/Allen Hospital, NewYork-Presbyterian/Lawrence Hospital, NewYork-Presbyterian/Morgan Stanley Children's Hospital, NewYork-Presbyterian/Lower Manhattan Hospital and NewYork-Presbyterian/Westchester Division. The regional hospital network division comprises regional hospitals in the New York metropolitan region: NewYork-Presbyterian/Brooklyn Methodist Hospital, NewYork-Presbyterian/Hudson Valley Hospital and NewYork-Presbyterian/Queens. The physician's services division connects medical experts with patients in their communities in order to expand coordinated healthcare delivery across the region. This segment includes the NewYork-Presbyterian medical groups in Westchester, Queens and Brooklyn in collaboration with Weill Cornell and ColumbiaDoctors. Last, the community/population health division comprises ambulatory care network sites and community healthcare initiatives.

FINANCIAL DATA: *Note: Data for latest year may not have been available at press time.*

In U.S. $	2020	2019	2018	2017	2016	2015
Revenue	5,490,390,000	5,910,000,000	5,880,000,000	5,600,000,000	5,200,000,000	4,800,000,000
R&D Expense						
Operating Income						
Operating Margin %						
SGA Expense						
Net Income						
Operating Cash Flow						
Capital Expenditure						
EBITDA						
Return on Assets %						
Return on Equity %						
Debt to Equity						

CONTACT INFORMATION:

Phone: 646-962-2357   Fax: 212-746-8235
Toll-Free: 877-697-9355
Address: 520 E. 70th St., New York, NY 10021 United States

STOCK TICKER/OTHER:

Stock Ticker: Nonprofit   Exchange:
Employees: 20,000   Fiscal Year Ends: 12/31
Parent Company:

SALARIES/BONUSES:

Top Exec. Salary: $ Bonus: $
Second Exec. Salary: $ Bonus: $

OTHER THOUGHTS:

Estimated Female Officers or Directors: 5
Hot Spot for Advancement for Women/Minorities: Y

NextCure Inc

www.nextcure.com

NAIC Code: 325412

TYPES OF BUSINESS:

Pharmaceutical Preparation Manufacturing

BRANDS/DIVISIONS/AFFILIATES:

FIND-IO
NC318
NC410

CONTACTS: *Note: Officers with more than one job title may be intentionally listed here more than once.*

Michael Richman, CEO
Steven Cobourn, CFO
David Kabakoff, Chairman of the Board
Kevin Heller, Chief Medical Officer
Sol Langermann, Chief Scientific Officer
James Bingham, Other Executive Officer
Timothy Mayer, Senior VP, Divisional
Linda Liu, Senior VP, Divisional

GROWTH PLANS/SPECIAL FEATURES:

NextCure, Inc. is a clinical-stage biopharmaceutical company that discovers and develops novel, first-in-class immuno-medicines to treat cancer and other immune-related diseases via restoring normal immune function. Through its proprietary Functional Integrated NextCure Discovery in Immuno-Oncology (FIND-IO) platform, the firm studies various immune cells in order to discover and understand targets and structural components of immune cells and their functional impact. From that point, NexCure develops immuno-medicines. The firm's pipeline includes the following product candidates: NC318, a monoclonal antibody, first-in-class immuno-medicine targeting Siglec-15, a novel immunomodulatory protein expressed on highly immunosuppressive cells called M2 macrophages and on tumor cells; and NC410, a novel immuno-medicine that is a fusion protein of LAIR-2 (leukocyte-associated immunoglobulin-like receptor 2), a naturally-occurring soluble version of and decoy protein for LAIR-1, and is designed to block immune suppression mediated by LAIR-1. NC318 is currently in Phase 2 trials. In July 2020, NextCure announced the initiation of a Phase 1/2 clinical trial for NC410.

FINANCIAL DATA: *Note: Data for latest year may not have been available at press time.*

In U.S. $	2020	2019	2018	2017	2016	2015
Revenue	22,378,000	6,347,000				
R&D Expense	46,554,000	34,216,000	19,787,000	12,954,000		
Operating Income	-41,225,000	-37,482,000	-23,196,000	-15,549,000		
Operating Margin %		-5.91%				
SGA Expense	17,049,000	9,613,000	3,409,000	2,595,000		
Net Income	-36,603,000	-33,737,000	-22,799,000	-15,469,000		
Operating Cash Flow	-44,954,000	-35,623,000	7,992,000	-12,514,000		
Capital Expenditure	7,132,000	3,371,000	3,063,000	8,652,000		
EBITDA	-37,812,000	-34,794,000	-21,519,000	-14,967,000		
Return on Assets %		-.13%	-.27%	-.79%		
Return on Equity %		-.25%				
Debt to Equity		0.01				

CONTACT INFORMATION:

Phone: 240 399-4900   Fax:
Toll-Free:
Address: 9000 Virginia Manor Rd., Ste. 200, Beltsville, MD 20705 United States

STOCK TICKER/OTHER:

Stock Ticker: NXTC
Employees: 90
Parent Company:

Exchange: NAS
Fiscal Year Ends: 12/31

SALARIES/BONUSES:

Top Exec. Salary: $ Bonus: $
Second Exec. Salary: $ Bonus: $

OTHER THOUGHTS:

Estimated Female Officers or Directors:
Hot Spot for Advancement for Women/Minorities:

NextGen Healthcare Inc

investor.nextgen.com

NAIC Code: 511210D

TYPES OF BUSINESS:
Computer Software, Healthcare & Biotechnology

BRANDS/DIVISIONS/AFFILIATES:
Quality Systems Inc
Topaz Information LLC
Topaz Information Solutions
Medfusion Inc
OTTO Health

CONTACTS: *Note: Officers with more than one job title may be intentionally listed here more than once.*
John Frantz, CEO
James Arnold, CFO
Sheldon Razin, Chairman Emeritus
David Metcalfe, Chief Technology Officer
Scott Bostick, COO
Jeffrey Margolis, Director
Craig Barbarosh, Director
Jeffrey Linton, Executive VP

GROWTH PLANS/SPECIAL FEATURES:
NextGen Healthcare, Inc. (formerly Quality Systems, Inc.) provides ambulatory-focused healthcare software and services solutions. The company's technology-based solutions are provided to clients that span the ambulatory care market, from small single specialty practices to large multi-specialty organizations. NextGen's fully integrated solutions enable these clients to provide their patients with comprehensive services through a single platform, including complex, heterogeneous healthcare communities where frictionless clinical data exchange is required to coordinate and optimize patient care. NextGen's integrated ambulatory care platform encompasses electronic health records (EHR) and practice management systems that support clinical and financial activities. These can be deployed on-premise or in the cloud. The platform is automated, giving clients control over how platform capabilities are implemented to drive desired outcomes. The workflow layer includes mobile capabilities. The cloud-based population health and analytics engine allows clients to improve results in both fee-for-services and fee-for-value environments. This core offering is surrounded with open, web-based application program interfaces (APIs) to drive the secure exchange of health and patient data with connected health solutions. The technology is also augmented with services as required and is mapped to client imperatives. Solutions within the platform include clinical care, financial management, patient engagement, population health and connected health. All solutions are marketed under the NextGen brand name. NextGen Healthcare provides professional services including training, project management, functional and detailed specification preparation, configuration, testing and installation. Client service and support are offered via telephone, email and the internet. In 2019, the firm acquired Topaz Information, L.L.C, d.b.a. Topaz Information Solutions; Medfusion, Inc.; and OTTO Health. In May 2020, NextGen Healthcare announced the launch of NextGen Advisors, a multidisciplinary team of healthcare and regulatory experts who offer strategic guidance and insights for ambulatory care providers across the U.S.

FINANCIAL DATA: *Note: Data for latest year may not have been available at press time.*

In U.S. $	2020	2019	2018	2017	2016	2015
Revenue	540,239,000	529,173,000				
R&D Expense	83,295,000	80,994,000				
Operating Income	20,188,000	32,259,000				
Operating Margin %	.04%	.06%				
SGA Expense	165,174,000	164,879,000				
Net Income	7,498,000	24,494,000				
Operating Cash Flow	85,601,000	50,475,000				
Capital Expenditure	26,881,000	25,523,000				
EBITDA	54,007,000	75,234,000				
Return on Assets %	.01%	.05%				
Return on Equity %	.02%	.07%				
Debt to Equity	0.419	0.029				

CONTACT INFORMATION:
Phone: 949 255-2600   Fax:
Toll-Free: 800-888-7955
Address: 18111 Von Karman, Ste. 800, Irvine, CA 92612 United States

STOCK TICKER/OTHER:
Stock Ticker: NXGN   Exchange: NAS
Employees: 2,564   Fiscal Year Ends: 02/28
Parent Company:

SALARIES/BONUSES:
Top Exec. Salary: $ Bonus: $
Second Exec. Salary: $ Bonus: $

OTHER THOUGHTS:
Estimated Female Officers or Directors:
Hot Spot for Advancement for Women/Minorities:

Nordion (Canada) Inc

www.nordion.com

NAIC Code: 339100

TYPES OF BUSINESS:

Drug Discovery & Development Services
Medical Isotopes
Imaging Agents
Sterilization Products
Irradiation Systems
Health Care Product Distribution

BRANDS/DIVISIONS/AFFILIATES:

Sotera Health LLC
Nordion GammaFIT Irradiation System
Nordion JS-10000 Hanging Tote Gamma Irradiation
Nordion GammaBeam-127 Gamma Irradiation Sys
Nordion Parallel Row Pallet Gamma Irradiation Sys

CONTACTS: *Note: Officers with more than one job title may be intentionally listed here more than once.*

Kevin Brooks, Pres.
Corby Nicholson, Dir.-Oper.
Don Lim, VP-Finance
Leslee Tape, VP-Human Resources
Leigh Catley, Sr. Dir.-IT, Governance & Security
Grant Gardiner, Corp. Sec.
Tamra Benjamin, VP-Public & Gov't Rel.
Jill Chitra, Sr. VP-Quality & Regulatory Affairs
Christopher Ashwood, Sr. VP-Corp. Svcs.
Tom Burnett, Gen. Mgr.-Medical Isotopes

GROWTH PLANS/SPECIAL FEATURES:

Nordion (Canada), Inc. is a provider of cobalt-60 to customers. The gamma rays emitted by cobalt-60 are used in the sterilization and irradiation processes for the medical device, pharmaceutical, food safety and high-performance materials industries. Nordion combines its capabilities in electro-mechanical design, controls, radiation physics, dosimetry and regulatory affairs with a global reach in sales, installation and service in order to deliver end-to-end gamma processing solutions for its customers. The company's C-188 model is double encapsulated and delivers the industry standard in performance and reliability in gamma processing. Medical-grade cobalt-60 is referred to as high specific activity (HSA) in the healthcare industry, and is double encapsulated and delivers the industry standard in performance and reliability in radiation therapy. Nordion also manufactures irradiation systems, and will custom design gamma irradiators for its customer's applications. Gamma ray solutions include the Nordion GammaFIT Irradiation System, Nordion JS-10000 Hanging Tote Gamma Irradiation System, Nordion GammaBeam-127 Gamma Irradiation System and the Nordion Parallel Row Pallet Gamma Irradiation System. Services by the company include recycling, source transport, source containers, source technical and engineering, irradiator maintenance, upgrades, dosimetry, sterilization, irradiation and training. Nordian is a subsidiary of Sotera Health, LLC.

FINANCIAL DATA: *Note: Data for latest year may not have been available at press time.*

In U.S. $	2020	2019	2018	2017	2016	2015
Revenue	114,745,000	116,165,000	126,787,500	120,750,000	115,000,000	110,000,000
R&D Expense						
Operating Income						
Operating Margin %						
SGA Expense						
Net Income	66,803,000	62,196,000				
Operating Cash Flow						
Capital Expenditure						
EBITDA						
Return on Assets %						
Return on Equity %						
Debt to Equity						

CONTACT INFORMATION:

Phone: 613 592-2790   Fax: 613 592-6937
Toll-Free:
Address: 447 March Rd., Ottawa, ON K2K 1X8 Canada

STOCK TICKER/OTHER:

Stock Ticker: Subsidiary
Employees: 350
Parent Company: Sotera Health LLC

Exchange:
Fiscal Year Ends: 10/31

SALARIES/BONUSES:

Top Exec. Salary: $ Bonus: $
Second Exec. Salary: $ Bonus: $

OTHER THOUGHTS:

Estimated Female Officers or Directors: 4
Hot Spot for Advancement for Women/Minorities: Y

Sales, profits and employees may be estimates. Financial information, benefits and other data can change quickly and may vary from those stated here.

Novanta Inc

www.novanta.com

NAIC Code: 334510

TYPES OF BUSINESS:

Equipment-Laser Systems
Motion Control Components
Lasers-Dermatology & Ophthalmology
Printed Circuit Board Spindles
Encoders
Thermal Printers

BRANDS/DIVISIONS/AFFILIATES:

CONTACTS: Note: Officers with more than one job title may be intentionally listed here more than once.

Matthijs Glastra, CEO
Robert Buckley, CFO
Stephen Bershad, Chairman of the Board
Peter Chang, Chief Accounting Officer
Brian Young, Other Executive Officer

GROWTH PLANS/SPECIAL FEATURES:

Novanta, Inc. designs, develops, manufactures and sells precision photonic and motion control components and subsystems to original equipment manufacturers (OEMs) in the medical and advanced industrial markets. Novanta's business consists of three segments: photonics, vision and precision motion. The photonics segment produces photonics-based solutions such as CO_2 laser sources and laser scanning and laser beam delivery products, to customers worldwide. This division serves highly-demanding applications such as industrial material processing, metrology, medical and life science imaging, and medical laser procedures. Photonics manufacturing facilities are located in Massachusetts, Washington, Arizona, the U.K., Germany and China. The vision segment produces a wide range of medical-grade technologies, including visualization solutions, imaging informatics products, optical data collection and machine vision technologies, radio frequency identification (RFID) technologies, thermal printers, light and color measurement instrumentation and embedded touch screen solutions. Vision manufacturing facilities are in New York, California, Florida and Germany. The precision motion segment produces optical encoders, precision motor and motion control technology, air bearing spindles and precision machined components. Precision motion manufacturing facilities are in Massachusetts, California, the U.K. and China. Many of Novanta's manufacturing facilities are ISO 9001 certified, and the majority of its products manufactured for the medical market are manufactured under the ISO 13485 certification.

FINANCIAL DATA: Note: Data for latest year may not have been available at press time.

In U.S. $	2020	2019	2018	2017	2016	2015
Revenue	590,623,000	626,099,000	614,337,000	521,290,000	384,758,000	373,598,000
R&D Expense	60,996,000	55,965,000	51,024,000	41,673,000	32,002,000	31,043,000
Operating Income	59,698,000	71,856,000	79,054,000	64,737,000	40,508,000	37,187,000
Operating Margin %		.11%	.13%	.12%	.11%	.10%
SGA Expense	109,853,000	118,407,000	115,900,000	102,025,000	81,691,000	82,049,000
Net Income	44,521,000	40,773,000	49,109,000	60,051,000	22,003,000	35,615,000
Operating Cash Flow	140,239,000	63,248,000	89,647,000	63,378,000	47,788,000	33,416,000
Capital Expenditure	13,156,000	10,743,000	14,658,000	9,094,000	12,442,000	5,552,000
EBITDA	97,991,000	110,136,000	116,106,000	95,495,000	60,865,000	56,301,000
Return on Assets %		.05%	.07%	.07%	.05%	.09%
Return on Equity %		.10%	.15%	.14%	.09%	.16%
Debt to Equity		0.634	0.551	0.749	0.304	0.399

CONTACT INFORMATION:

Phone: 781 266-5700   Fax: 613 592-7549
Toll-Free: 800-342-3757
Address: 125 Middlesex Turnpike, Bedford, MA 01730 United States

STOCK TICKER/OTHER:

Stock Ticker: NOVT   Exchange: NAS
Employees: 1,269   Fiscal Year Ends: 12/31
Parent Company:

SALARIES/BONUSES:

Top Exec. Salary: $ Bonus: $
Second Exec. Salary: $ Bonus: $

OTHER THOUGHTS:

Estimated Female Officers or Directors: 1
Hot Spot for Advancement for Women/Minorities:

Novartis AG

www.novartis.com

NAIC Code: 325412

TYPES OF BUSINESS:

Drugs-Diversified
Therapeutic Drug Discovery
Therapeutic Drug Manufacturing
Generic Drugs
Over-the-Counter Drugs
Ophthalmic Products
Nutritional Products
Veterinary Products

BRANDS/DIVISIONS/AFFILIATES:

Sandoz
Novartis Institute for BioMedical Research
Global Drug Development
Novartis Technical Operations
Novartis Business Services
Tasigna
Cosentyx
Gilenya

CONTACTS: *Note: Officers with more than one job title may be intentionally listed here more than once.*

Vasant Narasimhan, CEO
Harry Kirsch, CFO
Steven Baert, Head-Human Resources
Mark C. Fishman, Pres., Novartis Institute for Biomedical Research
Steffen Lang, Global Dir.-Technical Oper.
Peter Kornicker, Chief Compliance Officer
Felix Ehrat, General Counsel
Paul van Arkel, Head-Corp. Strategy & External Affairs
Michele Galen, Head-Comm.
Kevin Buehler, Head-Alcon
David Epstein, Head-Novartis Pharmaceuticals
George Gunn, Head-Novartis Animal Health
Jeffrey George, Head-Sandoz Div.
Joerg Reinhardt, Chmn.

GROWTH PLANS/SPECIAL FEATURES:

Novartis AG specializes in the research, development, manufacturing and marketing of innovative pharmaceuticals and generic medicines. The company comprises two operating divisions, innovative medicines and Sandoz, each of which are supported by the following organization units: Novartis Institute for BioMedical Research, Global Drug Development, Novartis Technical Operations, and Novartis Business Services. The innovated medicines division includes: oncology marketed products such as Tasigna, Promacta/Revolad, Sandostatin, Gleevec/Glivec, Afinitor/Votubia, Everolimus and Kisqali, among others; immunology, hepatology and dermatology products such as Cosentyx, Lucentis, Xiidra and Beovu; neuroscience products such as Gilenya, Zolgensma, Mayzent and Kesimpta; cardiovascular, renal and metabolism products such as Entresto and Leqvio; respiratory product Xolair; and other medicines such as Galvus and Diovan. The innovation medicines division sells its products in approximately 140 countries worldwide, with the majority of sales being derived from the U.S. and Europe, but also in Asia, Africa, Australasia, Canada and Latin America. The Sandoz division is a global leader in generic pharmaceuticals and biosimilars, and sells products in more than 100 countries. Sandoz is organized globally into three franchises: retail generics, anti-infectives and biopharmaceuticals. The retail generics franchise develops, manufactures and markets active ingredients and finished dosage forms of small-molecule pharmaceuticals to third parties across a range of therapeutic areas, as well as finished dosage form anti-infectives sold to third parties. The anti-infectives franchise manufactures and supplies active pharmaceutical ingredients and intermediates, primarily antibiotics, for internal use by retail generics and for sale to third party customers. Last, the biopharmaceuticals franchise develops, manufactures and markets protein- or other biotechnology-based products, including biosimilars, and provides biotechnology manufacturing services to other companies. In early-2021, Novartis agreed to acquire GlaxoSmithKline plc's cephalosporin antibiotics business.

FINANCIAL DATA: *Note: Data for latest year may not have been available at press time.*

In U.S. $	2020	2019	2018	2017	2016	2015
Revenue	49,898,000,000	48,677,000,000	53,166,000,000	50,135,000,000	49,436,000,000	50,387,000,000
R&D Expense	8,980,000,000	9,402,000,000	9,074,000,000	8,972,000,000	9,039,000,000	8,935,000,000
Operating Income	10,152,000,000	9,086,000,000	8,169,000,000	8,629,000,000	8,268,000,000	8,977,000,000
Operating Margin %		.19%	.15%	.17%	.17%	.18%
SGA Expense	14,197,000,000	14,369,000,000	16,471,000,000	14,997,000,000	14,192,000,000	14,247,000,000
Net Income	8,072,000,000	11,732,000,000	12,611,000,000	7,703,000,000	6,712,000,000	17,783,000,000
Operating Cash Flow	13,650,000,000	13,625,000,000	14,272,000,000	12,621,000,000	11,475,000,000	11,897,000,000
Capital Expenditure	2,585,000,000	2,257,000,000	3,355,000,000	2,746,000,000	2,879,000,000	3,505,000,000
EBITDA	17,211,000,000	15,616,000,000	21,684,000,000	15,852,000,000	14,567,000,000	14,260,000,000
Return on Assets %		.09%	.09%	.06%	.05%	.14%
Return on Equity %		.17%	.17%	.10%	.09%	.24%
Debt to Equity		0.398	0.286	0.313	0.239	0.212

CONTACT INFORMATION:

Phone: 41 613241111   Fax: 41 613248001
Toll-Free:
Address: Lichtstrasse 35, Basel, 4056 Switzerland

SALARIES/BONUSES:

Top Exec. Salary: $ Bonus: $
Second Exec. Salary: $ Bonus: $

STOCK TICKER/OTHER:

Stock Ticker: NVS
Employees: 118,393
Parent Company:

Exchange: NYS
Fiscal Year Ends: 12/31

OTHER THOUGHTS:

Estimated Female Officers or Directors: 4
Hot Spot for Advancement for Women/Minorities: Y

Novo Nordisk AS

NAIC Code: 325412

www.novonordisk.com

TYPES OF BUSINESS:

Drugs-Diabetes
Pharmaceuticals
Development
Manufacture
Diabetes
Obesity
Fertility
Hemophilia

BRANDS/DIVISIONS/AFFILIATES:

NovoPen
FlexTouch
NovoFine
Tresiba
Saxenda
NovoSeven
Norditropin
Emisphere Technologies Inc

CONTACTS: *Note: Officers with more than one job title may be intentionally listed here more than once.*

Mads Krogsgaard Thomsen, Chief Science Officer
Helge Lund, Chmn.

GROWTH PLANS/SPECIAL FEATURES:

Novo Nordisk AS is a global healthcare company engaged in the discovery, development, manufacturing and marketing pharmaceutical products. As a leader in diabetes care, the firm has one of the broadest diabetes product portfolios in the industry, including new generation insulins, a full portfolio of modern insulins as well as a human once-daily GLP-1 (glucagon-like peptide) analog. In addition, Novo Nordisk has a leading position within hemophilia care, growth hormone therapy and hormone replacement therapy. Operations are divided into two segments: diabetes and obesity care, and biopharmaceuticals. The diabetes and obesity care segment covers insulin, GLP-1, other protein-related products (such as glucagon, protein-related delivery systems and needles) and oral antidiabetic drugs. The biopharmaceuticals segment covers the therapy areas of hemophilia care, growth hormone therapy and hormone replacement therapy. Novo products include the NovoPen and FlexTouch lines for the treatment of diabetes; the Norditropin and PenMate lines of growth hormone pens; and the NovoFine and NovoTwist lines of injection needles. Diabetes treatment brands include Tresiba, Xultophy, Levemir, Insulatard, Actrapid, Mixtard, Ryzodeg, NovoMix, Rybelsus, Fiasp, NovoRapid and NovoNorm, among many others. Saxenda is Novo Nodisk's obesity drug. NovoSeven, Refixia and Esperoct 1 are the company's hemophilia medicines. Norditropin and Macrilen are growth disorder medications; and Vagifem, Activelle, Kliogest, Trisequens, and Novofem are hormone replacement therapies. Novo Nordisk has operations in 80 countries and markets its products in approximately 170 countries. In December 2020, Novo Nordisk completed its acquisition of Emisphere Technologies, Inc., a drug delivery company that utilizes proprietary technologies to develop new oral formations of therapeutic agents.

FINANCIAL DATA: *Note: Data for latest year may not have been available at press time.*

In U.S. $	2020	2019	2018	2017	2016	2015
Revenue	20,859,890,000	20,050,610,000	18,376,180,000	18,354,000,000	18,367,800,000	17,734,670,000
R&D Expense	2,540,731,000	2,336,645,000	2,432,772,000	2,302,794,000	2,393,007,000	2,236,080,000
Operating Income	8,894,038,000	8,624,058,000	7,763,838,000	8,046,306,000	7,958,394,000	8,124,687,000
Operating Margin %		.43%	.42%	.44%	.43%	.46%
SGA Expense	6,061,144,000	5,887,621,000	5,474,025,000	5,278,647,000	5,313,976,000	5,286,042,000
Net Income	6,924,158,000	6,400,466,000	6,347,391,000	6,265,560,000	6,231,874,000	5,728,229,000
Operating Cash Flow	8,536,640,000	7,687,265,000	7,331,345,000	6,764,766,000	7,939,004,000	6,291,358,000
Capital Expenditure	3,628,372,000	1,845,489,000	2,039,224,000	1,421,048,000	1,358,442,000	1,052,640,000
EBITDA	9,739,798,000	8,944,649,000	8,483,071,000	8,536,804,000	8,389,573,000	7,642,405,000
Return on Assets %		.33%	.36%	.38%	.40%	.41%
Return on Equity %		.71%	.76%	.80%	.82%	.80%
Debt to Equity		0.052				

CONTACT INFORMATION:

Phone: 45 44448888
Fax: 45 44490555
Toll-Free:
Address: Novo Alle 1, BagsvÃ¦rd, 2880 Denmark

STOCK TICKER/OTHER:

Stock Ticker: NVO
Employees: 43,300
Parent Company:

Exchange: NYS
Fiscal Year Ends: 12/31

SALARIES/BONUSES:

Top Exec. Salary: $
Second Exec. Salary: $
Bonus: $
Bonus: $

OTHER THOUGHTS:

Estimated Female Officers or Directors: 3
Hot Spot for Advancement for Women/Minorities: Y

NuVasive Inc

www.nuvasive.com

NAIC Code: 339100

TYPES OF BUSINESS:

Medical Equipment Development
Spinal Surgery Equipment

BRANDS/DIVISIONS/AFFILIATES:

Maximum Access Surgery (MAS)
NVM5
Intra-Operative Monitoring
MaXcess
FormaGraft
AttraX
VuePoint
Armada

CONTACTS: *Note: Officers with more than one job title may be intentionally listed here more than once.*

James Barry, CEO
Gregory Lucier, Chairman of the Board
Jim Garrett, Chief Compliance Officer
Rajesh Asarpota, Executive VP
Nate Sisitsky, General Counsel
Nathaniel Sisitsky, General Counsel
Lucas Vitale, Other Executive Officer
Matthew Link, President
Paul McClintock, President, Divisional

GROWTH PLANS/SPECIAL FEATURES:

NuVasive, Inc. designs, develops and markets minimally invasive products for the surgical treatment of spine disorders. Its principle products include the Maximum Access Surgery (MAS) minimally disruptive surgical platform, which combines three categories of solutions that collectively minimize soft tissue disruption during spine fusion surgery: NVM5, Intra-Operative Monitoring (IOM) and MaXcess. NVM5 is a software-driven intraoperative nerve avoidance system. It allows surgeons to perform fusion surgery through a process called eXtreme Lateral Interbody Fusion (XLIF), meaning the surgeon enters the body from the side rather than front or back. The system is compatible with numerous existing surgical instruments. IOM provides insight into the nervous system which is analyzed in real time by healthcare professionals for the interpretation of intra-operative information. MaXcess is a unique tri-blade system that combines instrumentation and specialized implants that provide maximum surgical spinal access while disrupting soft tissue as little as possible. The firm's line of biologics includes the FormaGraft synthetic collagen product, used to provide a scaffold for bone growth; and AttraX, a synthetic bone graft material delivered in putty and other forms. Specialized implants designed to function with the MAS platform are used for interbody disc height restoration to facilitate fusion and stabilization of the spine and have been developed to be delivered through the MaXcess system, which minimizes the invasiveness of implant procedures. Its products include VuePoint, Armada, Precept and Reline posterior fixation portfolios.

Employee benefits include medical insurance, a stock purchase program and paid holiday/sick leave.

FINANCIAL DATA: *Note: Data for latest year may not have been available at press time.*

In U.S. $	2020	2019	2018	2017	2016	2015
Revenue	1,050,582,000	1,168,070,000	1,101,714,000	1,029,520,000	962,072,000	811,113,000
R&D Expense	79,838,000	72,380,000	61,695,000	50,425,000	47,999,000	35,851,000
Operating Income	50,192,000	121,055,000	102,354,000	122,135,000	98,355,000	103,737,000
Operating Margin %		.10%	.09%	.12%	.10%	.13%
SGA Expense	547,195,000	611,181,000	575,836,000	539,913,000	533,624,000	464,530,000
Net Income	-37,153,000	65,234,000	12,479,000	83,006,000	37,147,000	66,291,000
Operating Cash Flow	185,911,000	235,290,000	219,183,000	178,979,000	156,295,000	88,727,000
Capital Expenditure	109,589,000	130,384,000	109,603,000	112,491,000	94,290,000	107,792,000
EBITDA	163,858,000	254,635,000	176,345,000	233,422,000	207,941,000	207,012,000
Return on Assets %		.04%	.01%	.05%	.03%	.05%
Return on Equity %		.07%	.02%	.11%	.05%	.10%
Debt to Equity		0.761	0.722	0.733	0.812	0.542

CONTACT INFORMATION:

Phone: 858 909-1800   Fax:
Toll-Free: 800-475-9131
Address: 7475 Lusk Blvd., San Diego, CA 92121 United States

STOCK TICKER/OTHER:

Stock Ticker: NUVA
Employees: 2,700
Parent Company:

Exchange: NAS
Fiscal Year Ends: 12/31

SALARIES/BONUSES:

Top Exec. Salary: $ Bonus: $
Second Exec. Salary: $ Bonus: $

OTHER THOUGHTS:

Estimated Female Officers or Directors: 1
Hot Spot for Advancement for Women/Minorities:

Sales, profits and employees may be estimates. Financial information, benefits and other data can change quickly and may vary from those stated here.

Oak Street Health Inc

www.oakstreethealth.com

NAIC Code: 621111

TYPES OF BUSINESS:

Offices of Physicians (except Mental Health Specialists)
Primary Care Center Operation
Medicare Services
Population Health Analytics
Social Support

BRANDS/DIVISIONS/AFFILIATES:

CONTACTS: *Note: Officers with more than one job title may be intentionally listed here more than once.*

Mike Pykosz, CEO
Geoff Price, COO
Tim Cook, CFO
Griffin Myers, Chief Medical Officer
Cynthia Hiskes, Chief Human Resources Officer
Jason Van Den Eeden, CTO

GROWTH PLANS/SPECIAL FEATURES:

Oak Street Health, Inc. operates primary care centers in the U.S., with primary care providers specializing in serving Medicare beneficiaries. The company has a preventative care approach. Through its centers and management services organization, Oak Street engages Medicare eligible patients through a community approach, and once engaged, the firm integrates population health analytics, social support services and primary care into its care model to drive improved outcomes. Oak Street contracts with health plans to generate medical costs savings and realize a return on its investment in primary care. As of October 2021, Oak Street operated more than 130 centers across Alabama, Georgia, Illinois, Indiana, Kentucky, Louisiana, Michigan, Mississippi, Missouri, New Mexico, New York, North Carolina, Ohio, Oklahoma, Pennsylvania, Rhode Island, South Carolina, Tennessee and Texas.

Oak Street offers its employees health benefit options, a health savings account plan, life and AD&D insurance, 401(k), an employee stock purchase plan, an employee assistance program and more.

FINANCIAL DATA: *Note: Data for latest year may not have been available at press time.*

In U.S. $	2020	2019	2018	2017	2016	2015
Revenue	882,765,000	556,604,000	317,938,000			
R&D Expense						
Operating Income	-183,521,000	-103,876,000	-76,037,000			
Operating Margin %		- .19%	- .24%			
SGA Expense	249,706,000	125,781,000	76,269,000			
Net Income	-187,990,000	-107,862,000	-79,544,000			
Operating Cash Flow	-77,219,000	-55,546,000	-75,365,000			
Capital Expenditure	20,883,000	27,705,000	26,046,000			
EBITDA	-172,140,000	-95,944,000	-71,845,000			
Return on Assets %		- .53%	- .54%			
Return on Equity %						
Debt to Equity						

CONTACT INFORMATION:

Phone: 312 773-3374   Fax:
Toll-Free:
Address: 30 W. Monroe St., Ste. 1200, Chicago, IL 60603 United States

STOCK TICKER/OTHER:

Stock Ticker: OSH   Exchange: NYS
Employees: 3,500   Fiscal Year Ends: 12/31
Parent Company:

SALARIES/BONUSES:

Top Exec. Salary: $ Bonus: $
Second Exec. Salary: $ Bonus: $

OTHER THOUGHTS:

Estimated Female Officers or Directors:
Hot Spot for Advancement for Women/Minorities:

OhioHealth Corporation

www.ohiohealth.com

NAIC Code: 622110

TYPES OF BUSINESS:

General Medical and Surgical Hospitals
Health Insurance
Home Health Care
Hospice Services
Long-Term Care
Surgery Centers
Rehabilitation Services

BRANDS/DIVISIONS/AFFILIATES:

WorkHealth
OhioHealth Listens
OhioHealth Physician Group
OhioHealth Research and Innovation Institute
Doctors Hospital
Hardin Memorial Hospital
O'Bleness Hospital
Riverside Methodist Hospital

CONTACTS: *Note: Officers with more than one job title may be intentionally listed here more than once.*

Stephen Markovich, CEO
John McWhorter, COO
Michael Browning, CFO
Sue Jablonski, Chief Mktg. & Communications Officer
Johnni Beckel, Chief Human Resources Officer
Bruce Vanderhoff, Chief Medical Officer
Jim Weeast, Sr. VP
Frank Pandora, II, General Counsel
Michael Bernstein, Chief Strategy Officer
Sue Jablonski, Chief Comm. Officer
Cheryl Herbert, Sr. VP-Clinical Support Services
Hugh Thornhill, Pres., Medical Specialty Foundation
Steve Garlock, Sr. VP-Cancer Services
Karen Morrison, Sr. VP-External Affairs
James Newbrough, Pres., HomeReach
John P. McConnell, Chmn.

GROWTH PLANS/SPECIAL FEATURES:

OhioHealth Corporation, founded in 1891, is a not-for-profit, faith-based health system that serves 47 Ohio counties. The system comprises nearly 35,000 associates, physicians and volunteers, along with a network of 12 hospitals and more than 200 ambulatory sites. OhioHealth provides hospice, home health, medical equipment and other health services. Just a few of OhioHealth's hospitals include Doctors Hospital, Grady Memorial Hospital, Hardin Memorial Hospital, Mansfield Hospital, O'Bleness Hospital, Riverside Methodist Hospital and Shelby Hospital. Health care services and programs of the firm include surgical weight management, cancer, ear/nose/throat, endoscopy, interventional radiology, maternity, palliative care, robotic surgery, sports medicine, blood conservation, eICU, hospice, laboratory services, orthopedics, pastoral care, senior health, breast health, diabetes, emergency and trauma care, heart and vascular, limb reconstruction and preservation, pain management and sleep disorders. In addition to its hospitals, OhioHealth comprises: WorkHealth, a workers' compensation and rehabilitation services provider; OhioHealth Listens, an online community of volunteer patient and their family members focused on providing feedback on strategies, protocols and practices related to the patient experience at OhioHealth; and OhioHealth Physician Group, a group of physicians, advanced practice providers and associates committed to improving the health of those served by OhioHealth, providing convenient access to patient-centered care. The OhioHealth Research and Innovation Institute supports research conducted throughout its hospital system, including clinical studies in various therapeutic areas.

OhioHealth offers employees medical, dental, vision, life, disability and AD&D insurance; flexible spending accounts; adoption assistance; child care centers; concierge services; vendor discounts; a credit union membership; an employee assistance program;

FINANCIAL DATA: *Note: Data for latest year may not have been available at press time.*

In U.S. $	2020	2019	2018	2017	2016	2015
Revenue	5,100,000,000	4,247,970,300	4,045,686,000	3,768,067,800	3,588,636,000	3,284,881,000
R&D Expense						
Operating Income						
Operating Margin %						
SGA Expense						
Net Income		542,948,960	512,216,000	610,616,000	231,665,000	274,875,000
Operating Cash Flow						
Capital Expenditure						
EBITDA						
Return on Assets %						
Return on Equity %						
Debt to Equity						

CONTACT INFORMATION:

Phone: 614-788-8860   Fax:
Toll-Free:
Address: 180 E. Broad St., Columbus, OH 43215 United States

STOCK TICKER/OTHER:

Stock Ticker: Nonprofit   Exchange:
Employees: 30,000   Fiscal Year Ends: 06/30
Parent Company:

SALARIES/BONUSES:

Top Exec. Salary: $ Bonus: $
Second Exec. Salary: $ Bonus: $

OTHER THOUGHTS:

Estimated Female Officers or Directors: 3
Hot Spot for Advancement for Women/Minorities: Y

Sales, profits and employees may be estimates. Financial information, benefits and other data can change quickly and may vary from those stated here.

Olympus Corporation

www.olympus-global.com

NAIC Code: 339100

TYPES OF BUSINESS:

Medical Equipment Manufacturing
Precision Machinery
Precision Instruments
Manufacture
Endoscopic Solutions
Therapeutic Solutions
Scientific Solutions

BRANDS/DIVISIONS/AFFILIATES:

CONTACTS: *Note: Officers with more than one job title may be intentionally listed here more than once.*

Yasuo Takeuchi, CEO
Akihiro Taguchi, Sr. Exec. Managing Officer
Haruo Ogawa, Exec. Managing Officer
Toshiaki Gomi, Exec. Managing Officer
Yasushi Sakai, Exec. Managing Officer

GROWTH PLANS/SPECIAL FEATURES:

Olympus Corporation manufactures and sells precision machinery and instruments, operating through three divisions: endoscopic solutions, therapeutic solutions and scientific solutions. The endoscopic solutions division utilizes Olympus' innovative capabilities in medical technology, therapeutic intervention and precision manufacturing to help healthcare professionals deliver diagnostic, therapeutic and minimally-invasive procedures. Its products include the gastrointestinal endoscopy system, the surgical endoscopy system, the endoscope reprocessor system and operating room systems integration solutions. This division also provides repair services. The therapeutic solutions division offers an array of surgical energy devices and instruments to help prevent, detect and treat disease. These products include endotherapy clips, electrosurgical knives, retrieval baskets, respiratory guided needles and valves, videoscopes and more. The scientific solutions division provides imaging, instrumentation and measurement solutions for the industrial and life sciences sectors. These solutions include industrial microscopes and videoscopes, optical and digital microscope systems, non-destructive testing technology and x-ray analyzers. The firm has 17,000 patents across its product portfolio, as of March 2021. Approximately 60% of the company's research and development expenditures are dedicated to the medical business. During 2021, Olympus transferred its imaging business to Japan Industrial Partners, Inc.; transferred its regenerative medicine developer and manufacturer subsidiary Olympus RMS Corporation to Rohto Pharmaceutical Co. Ltd.; and transferred its IT solutions subsidiary Olympus Systems Corporation to Accenture Japan Ltd.

FINANCIAL DATA: *Note: Data for latest year may not have been available at press time.*

In U.S. $	2020	2019	2018	2017	2016	2015
Revenue	7,282,758,000	7,250,345,000	7,183,081,000	6,831,944,000	7,348,215,000	
R&D Expense						
Operating Income	757,893,200	252,783,300	740,467,500	698,556,100	954,070,200	
Operating Margin %	.10%	.03%	.10%	.10%	.13%	
SGA Expense	3,699,077,000	3,995,781,000	3,896,103,000	3,788,873,000	3,934,252,000	
Net Income	471,902,300	74,406,580	521,165,800	714,118,800	571,671,300	
Operating Cash Flow	1,219,658,000	611,390,700	868,968,800	823,742,200	444,055,800	
Capital Expenditure	602,129,900	561,369,300	579,114,700	431,534,500	515,183,700	
EBITDA	1,403,925,000	814,052,100	1,247,815,000	1,302,330,000	1,173,326,000	
Return on Assets %	.05%	.01%	.06%	.08%	.06%	
Return on Equity %	.13%	.02%	.13%	.19%	.17%	
Debt to Equity	0.539	0.276	0.359	0.507	0.691	

CONTACT INFORMATION:

Phone: 81 333402111   Fax:
Toll-Free:
Address: 3-1 Nishi-Shinjuku 2-chome, Shinjuku Monolith, Tokyo, 163-0914 Japan

STOCK TICKER/OTHER:

Stock Ticker: OCPNY
Employees: 36,520
Parent Company:

Exchange: PINX
Fiscal Year Ends: 03/31

SALARIES/BONUSES:

Top Exec. Salary: $ Bonus: $
Second Exec. Salary: $ Bonus: $

OTHER THOUGHTS:

Estimated Female Officers or Directors:
Hot Spot for Advancement for Women/Minorities:

Omnicare Inc

www.omnicare.com

NAIC Code: 446110

TYPES OF BUSINESS:

Specialty Pharmacies
Infusion Therapy
Consulting Services
Pharmaceutical Research
Medical Records Services
Billing Services
Pharmaceutical Distribution

BRANDS/DIVISIONS/AFFILIATES:

CVS Health Corporation

CONTACTS: *Note: Officers with more than one job title may be intentionally listed here more than once.*

Larry J. Merlo, CEO-CVS Health Corporation
Robert Kraft, CFO
Alexander Kayne, General Counsel
Kirsten Marriner, Other Executive Officer
David Hileman, Senior VP, Divisional
Amit Jain, Senior VP, Divisional

GROWTH PLANS/SPECIAL FEATURES:

Omnicare, Inc. is a leading healthcare services company specializing in the management of complex pharmaceutical care. The company operates in two segments: post-acute care and senior living care. The post-acute care segment delivers more than 70 million prescriptions annually to skilled nursing facility customers nationwide. Its services include 24/7/365 access, cost containment programs, advanced digital tools, daily delivery, medication reviews, specialized packaging and compliance management. The senior living care segment builds consultative partnerships with senior assisted living facilities to provide support to members within those communities. Its services are the same as those listed for post-acute care. For independent living communities, this segment offers a broad range of industry-leading capabilities to serve the healthcare needs of the residents and help businesses and communities manage health in affordable and effective ways. These solutions include pharmacy care team support, hand-delivery of residents' medications and always-on savings for products used daily. Omnicare operates as a wholly owned subsidiary of CVS Health Corporation.

Employees receive medical, dental, vision, prescription, disability, AD&D and life insurance; an employee assistance program; flexible spending accounts; and a wellness plan.

FINANCIAL DATA: *Note: Data for latest year may not have been available at press time.*

In U.S. $	2020	2019	2018	2017	2016	2015
Revenue	8,091,798,750	7,706,475,000	7,339,500,000	6,990,000,000	6,800,000,000	6,630,000,000
R&D Expense						
Operating Income						
Operating Margin %						
SGA Expense						
Net Income						
Operating Cash Flow						
Capital Expenditure						
EBITDA						
Return on Assets %						
Return on Equity %						
Debt to Equity						

CONTACT INFORMATION:

Phone: 513-719-2600   Fax:
Toll-Free: 800-990-6664
Address: 201 E. Fourth St., 900 Omnicare Ctr.,, Cincinnati, OH 45202
United States

STOCK TICKER/OTHER:

Stock Ticker: Subsidiary   Exchange:
Employees: 12,451   Fiscal Year Ends: 12/31
Parent Company: CVS Health Corporation

SALARIES/BONUSES:

Top Exec. Salary: $ Bonus: $
Second Exec. Salary: $ Bonus: $

OTHER THOUGHTS:

Estimated Female Officers or Directors: 3
Hot Spot for Advancement for Women/Minorities: Y

Sales, profits and employees may be estimates. Financial information, benefits and other data can change quickly and may vary from those stated here.

Ontrak Inc

NAIC Code: 623220

www.ontrak-inc.com

TYPES OF BUSINESS:

Substance Abuse Treatment Program
Outpatient Health Care
TeleHealth
Artificial Intelligence
Advanced Data Analytics
Behavioral Health Services
Care Coaching Services

BRANDS/DIVISIONS/AFFILIATES:

OnTrak

CONTACTS: *Note: Officers with more than one job title may be intentionally listed here more than once.*

Terren Peizer, CEO
Curt Medeiros, Pres.
Brandon H. LaVerne, CFO
W. Gregory McLane, CMO
Sandy Gyenes, VP-Human Resources
Jeremiah Stone, CTO
Julie Wright, Chief Medical Officer

GROWTH PLANS/SPECIAL FEATURES:

Ontrak, Inc. is an artificial intelligence (AI) and telehealth-enabled, virtualized outpatient healthcare treatment company. Ontrak applies advanced data analytics and predictive modeling to identify members with untreated behavioral health conditions, whether diagnosed or not, and coexisting medical conditions that may be impacted through treatment in the OnTrak program. The company then engages health plan members who do not typically seek behavioral healthcare by leveraging proprietary enrollment capabilities built on deep insights into the drivers of care avoidance. The OnTrak solution is an integrated suite of services that includes evidence-based psychological and medical interventions delivered either in-person or via telehealth, nurse-led care coaching and local community support. The program helps improve member health and reduces health plan costs for payers. Ontrak has contracts with leading national and regional health plans to make OnTrak available to eligible members in 30 U.S. states and Washington DC.

FINANCIAL DATA: *Note: Data for latest year may not have been available at press time.*

In U.S. $	2020	2019	2018	2017	2016	2015
Revenue	82,837,000	35,095,000	15,177,000	7,717,000	7,075,000	2,705,000
R&D Expense	12,923,000					
Operating Income	-14,923,000	-20,014,000	-13,625,000	-10,731,000	-6,574,000	-8,899,000
Operating Margin %		-.57%	-.90%	-1.39%	-.93%	-3.29%
SGA Expense	41,234,000		17,395,000	11,811,000	8,838,000	9,049,000
Net Income	-22,710,000	-25,659,000	-14,212,000	-13,605,000	-17,936,000	-7,223,000
Operating Cash Flow	-6,282,000	-16,901,000	-8,574,000	-7,368,000	-5,726,000	-5,168,000
Capital Expenditure	1,757,000		9,000	448,000	106,000	107,000
EBITDA	-14,209,000	-21,783,000	-13,353,000	-9,944,000	-12,432,000	-4,502,000
Return on Assets %		-1.70%	-2.20%	-2.80%	-5.99%	-2.76%
Return on Equity %						
Debt to Equity				0.002		

CONTACT INFORMATION:

Phone: 310 444-4300   Fax: 888 975-7712
Toll-Free: 866-517-1414
Address: 2120 Colorado Ave., Ste. 230, Santa Monica, CA 90404 United States

STOCK TICKER/OTHER:

Stock Ticker: OTRK   Exchange: NAS
Employees: 395   Fiscal Year Ends: 12/31
Parent Company:

SALARIES/BONUSES:

Top Exec. Salary: $ Bonus: $
Second Exec. Salary: $ Bonus: $

OTHER THOUGHTS:

Estimated Female Officers or Directors: 2
Hot Spot for Advancement for Women/Minorities:

Opto Circuits (India) Ltd

www.optoindia.com

NAIC Code: 339100

TYPES OF BUSINESS:

Medical Electronics

BRANDS/DIVISIONS/AFFILIATES:

Criticare Systems
Mediaid
Unetixs Vascular
Eurocor
Cardiac Science
Powerheart
Freeway

CONTACTS: *Note: Officers with more than one job title may be intentionally listed here more than once.*

Vinod Ramnani, Managing Dir.
Jayesh Patel, Dir.-Eng.
Thomas Dietker, Dir.-Mergers & Acquisitions
Usha Ramnani, Exec. Dir.

GROWTH PLANS/SPECIAL FEATURES:

Opto Circuits (India) Ltd. (OCI) is a multinational medical device company headquartered in Bengaluru, India. The firm designs, develops, manufactures, markets and distributes medical products used by health care establishments in more than 150 countries. Opto Circuits specializes in vital signs monitoring, emergency cardiac care, vascular treatments and sensing technologies. Its products are U.S. FDA listed and CE marked, with some brands marketed as Criticare Systems, Mediaid, Unetixs Vascular, Eurocor and Cardiac Science. Criticare Systems specializes in monitoring systems and accessories used in anesthesia, critical care, medical transport and outpatient care settings. Mediaid specializes in pulse oximeters, vital signs monitors, oximeter sensors, thermometers, ECG, infusion and syringe pumps, oxygen sensors, oxygen analyzers and monitors, blood pressure cuffs and veterinary products. Unetixs Vascular offers technically advanced, non-invasive vascular diagnostic systems for hospital or mobile services. Eurocor provides interventional physicians with innovative coronary stent technologies and special cardiovascular and endovascular devices, manufactured in Europe. Eurocor's products are indicated for minimally invasive cardiovascular and peripheral surgery and comply with biological and biomechanical principles to offer highly flexible, adaptable solutions. Its Freeway brand of shunt balloon catheters are marketed globally for arteriorvenous (AV) access to help patients with end-stage renal disease. Cardiac Science designs, manufactures and markets Powerheart automated external defibrillators (AEDs) and related services that facilitate successful deployments in order to combat sudden cardiac arrest (SCA). Powerheart G5 is the first FDA-cleared AED to combine fully-automatic shock delivery, dual-language functionality, variable escalating energy and fast shock times to help save a sudden cardiac arrest victim's life.

FINANCIAL DATA: *Note: Data for latest year may not have been available at press time.*

In U.S. $	2020	2019	2018	2017	2016	2015
Revenue	24,716,500	37,315,300	35,318,500	33,832,700	51,994,830	181,709,275
R&D Expense						
Operating Income						
Operating Margin %						
SGA Expense						
Net Income	-183,364,000	7,411,030	5,471,060	-78,316,700	-292,625	-30,213,672
Operating Cash Flow						
Capital Expenditure						
EBITDA						
Return on Assets %						
Return on Equity %						
Debt to Equity						

CONTACT INFORMATION:

Phone: 91-80-2852 1040   Fax: 91-80-2852-1094
Toll-Free:
Address: Plot No. 83 Wipro Ave., 1/Fl, Electronic City, Bengaluru, Kamataka, 560 100 India

STOCK TICKER/OTHER:

Stock Ticker: 532391
Employees: 1,840
Parent Company:

Exchange: Bombay
Fiscal Year Ends: 03/31

SALARIES/BONUSES:

Top Exec. Salary: $ Bonus: $
Second Exec. Salary: $ Bonus: $

OTHER THOUGHTS:

Estimated Female Officers or Directors:
Hot Spot for Advancement for Women/Minorities:

Optos plc

NAIC Code: 334510

www.optos.com

TYPES OF BUSINESS:

Electromedical and Electrotherapeutic Apparatus Manufacturing

BRANDS/DIVISIONS/AFFILIATES:

Nikon Corporation
optomap
Daytona
California
Monaco
Silverstone

CONTACTS: *Note: Officers with more than one job title may be intentionally listed here more than once.*

Robert Kennedy, CEO
Quinn Lyzun, Deputy CEO

GROWTH PLANS/SPECIAL FEATURES:

Optos plc is a retinal imaging company. The firm is primarily engaged in the design, development, manufacture and marketing of medical devices delivering retinal examinations at customer sites. Its proprietary optomap medical devices produce ultra-widefield (UWF), high resolution digital images of approximately 82% of the retina in a single capture. An optomap image provides clinical information that facilitates the early detection, management and effective treatment of disorders and diseases evidenced in the retina such as retinal detachments and tears, glaucoma, diabetic retinopathy and age-related macular degeneration. The firm's Daytona, California, Monaco and Silverstone products represent ultra-widefield retinal imaging technology and have been converted to desktop models. The ergonomic body of these devices is designed to increase patient comfort and to correctly position the eye for image capture. Color, red-free and autofluorescence (AF) are included in all devices. California features fluorescein angiography as well as Optos' UWF imaging modality, indocyanine green angiography used for imaging the choroidal vasculature for the diagnosis, management and treatment of certain eye conditions such as neovascular age-related macular degeneration. Monaco is the only UWF imaging device with integrated Optical Coherence Tomography (OCT) to help eye care professionals enhance their clinical exam and improve practice economics. Silverstone facilitates examination of the retina from vitreous through the choroidal-scleral interface. Optos operates primarily in the U.K. and has additional operations in the Americas, Austria, Australia, France, Germany, Japan, Netherlands, Norway, Spain, Sweden and Switzerland. Optos is a wholly-owned subsidiary of Nikon Corporation.

FINANCIAL DATA: *Note: Data for latest year may not have been available at press time.*

In U.S. $	2020	2019	2018	2017	2016	2015
Revenue	117,700,000	124,400,000	113,900,000	102,900,000	122,900,000	
R&D Expense						
Operating Income						
Operating Margin %						
SGA Expense						
Net Income	21,700,000	37,800,000	30,200,000	25,100,000	5,800,000	
Operating Cash Flow						
Capital Expenditure						
EBITDA						
Return on Assets %						
Return on Equity %						
Debt to Equity						

CONTACT INFORMATION:

Phone: 44 1383843300 Fax:
Toll-Free:
Address: Queensferry House, Enterprise Way, Dunfermline, Scotland KY11 8GR United Kingdom

STOCK TICKER/OTHER:

Stock Ticker: Subsidiary Exchange:
Employees: 391 Fiscal Year Ends: 03/31
Parent Company: Nikon Corporation

SALARIES/BONUSES:

Top Exec. Salary: $ Bonus: $
Second Exec. Salary: $ Bonus: $

OTHER THOUGHTS:

Estimated Female Officers or Directors:
Hot Spot for Advancement for Women/Minorities:

Orchard Therapeutics plc

www.orchard-tx.com

NAIC Code: 325414

TYPES OF BUSINESS:

Biological Product (except Diagnostic) Manufacturing
Biopharmaceuticals

BRANDS/DIVISIONS/AFFILIATES:

Strimvelis
OTL-101
OTL-200
OTL-103

CONTACTS: *Note: Officers with more than one job title may be intentionally listed here more than once.*

Mark Rothera, CEO

GROWTH PLANS/SPECIAL FEATURES:

Orchard Therapeutics plc is a commercial-stage, fully-integrated biopharmaceutical company dedicated to treating patients with serious life-threatening rare diseases via autologous ex vivo gene therapies. Ex vivo means that which takes place outside an organism, such as in or on tissue from an organism. The firm's gene therapy approach seeks to transform a patient's own (autologous) hematopoietic stem cells (HSCs) into a gene-modified drug product to treat the patient's disease through a single administration. This is achieved by utilizing a lentiviral vector to introduce a functional copy of a missing or faulty gene into the patient's autologous HCSs through an ex vivo process, resulting in a drug product that can then be re-introduced into the patient at the bedside. Orchard Therapeutics believes its commercial product and clinical-stage product candidates, in combination with its expertise in the development, manufacturing and commercialization of gene and cell therapies, position it to provide potentially transformative therapies to patients suffering from a broad range of rare diseases. The company is focusing on three therapeutic rare disease franchise areas: primary immune deficiencies, neurometabolic disorders and hemoglobinopathies. Orchard's portfolio includes: Strimvelis, a commercial-stage gammaretroviral-based product for the treatment of adenosine deaminase-severe combined immunodeficiency (ADA-SCID); five lentiviral product candidates in clinical-stage development; and several other product candidates in pre-clinical development. The firm is in ongoing discussions with the applicable regulatory authorities for regulatory submissions for three of its most advanced clinical-stage product candidates: OTL-101, for the treatment of ADA-SCID; OTL-200 for the treatment of metachromatic leukodystrophy (MLD); and OTL-103, for the treatment of Wiskott-Aldrich Syndrome (WAS). During 2020, Orchard Therapeutics announced that the first patient was dosed in an open-label, proof-of-concept investigational study of OTL-201 for Sanfilippo Syndrome.

FINANCIAL DATA: *Note: Data for latest year may not have been available at press time.*

In U.S. $	2020	2019	2018	2017	2016	2015
Revenue	2,595,000	2,513,000	2,076,000			
R&D Expense	93,730,000	117,363,000	205,319,000	32,527,000	16,206,000	
Operating Income	-156,978,000	-172,873,000	-235,031,000	-38,512,000	-19,203,000	
Operating Margin %		-68.79%	-113.21%			
SGA Expense	64,986,000	57,218,000	31,366,000	5,985,000	2,997,000	
Net Income	-151,979,000	-163,422,000	-230,495,000	-39,744,000	-19,085,000	
Operating Cash Flow	-126,274,000	-166,131,000	-97,536,000	-32,487,000	-14,566,000	
Capital Expenditure	12,668,000	4,367,000	4,032,000	1,559,000	190,000	
EBITDA	-148,378,000	-171,198,000	-233,832,000	-38,210,000	-19,197,000	
Return on Assets %		-.43%	-.99%	-.78%	-4.46%	
Return on Equity %		-.54%	-1.75%			
Debt to Equity		0.134				

CONTACT INFORMATION:

Phone: 44 2033846700   Fax:
Toll-Free:
Address: 108 Cannon St., London, EC4N 6EU United Kingdom

STOCK TICKER/OTHER:

Stock Ticker: ORTX
Employees: 224
Parent Company:

Exchange: NAS
Fiscal Year Ends: 12/31

SALARIES/BONUSES:

Top Exec. Salary: $ Bonus: $
Second Exec. Salary: $ Bonus: $

OTHER THOUGHTS:

Estimated Female Officers or Directors:
Hot Spot for Advancement for Women/Minorities:

Organogenesis Inc

www.organogenesis.com

NAIC Code: 325414

TYPES OF BUSINESS:

Tissue Replacement Products
Wound Dressing Products
Regenerative Medicine
Product Design
Product Development
Product Manufacturing
Product Marketing

BRANDS/DIVISIONS/AFFILIATES:

PuraPly
Affinity
NuShield
Apligraf
Dermagraft
FiberOS
Osteoconductive Matrix PLUS
PuraForce

CONTACTS: *Note: Officers with more than one job title may be intentionally listed here more than once.*

Gary S. Gillheeney, Sr., CEO
Patrick Bilbo, COO
David C. Francisco, CFO
Brian Grow, CCO
Thomas L. Pearl, VP-Human Resources
Dolores Baksh, Dir.-Research & Development
Phillip Nolan, VP-Mfg. Oper.
Erik Ostrowski, VP-Finance
Dario Eklund, VP-Bio-Surgery & Oral Regeneration
Zorina Pitkin, VP-Quality Systems
Patrick Bilbo, VP-Regulatory
Milka Bedikian, VP-Global Mktg. & Bioactive Wound Healing
Michael Catarina, Dir.-Enterprise Mgmt.
Zorina Pitkin, VP-Quality Systems

GROWTH PLANS/SPECIAL FEATURES:

Organogenesis, Inc. is a regenerative medicine firm that designs, develops, manufactures and sells products for the advanced wound care, surgical and sports medicine markets. The firm's products are grouped into two categories and divisions: advanced wound care and surgical & sports medicine. The advanced wound care division designs products for the treatment of chronic and acute wounds. It has a comprehensive portfolio of regenerative medicine products capable of supporting patients from early in the wound healing process through to wound closure, regardless of wound type. Organogenesis' advanced wound care products include PuraPly, a purified native collagen matrix with broad-spectrum polyhexamethylene biguanide antimicrobial agent; Affinity, a fresh amniotic membrane containing many types of viable cells, growth factors/cytokines and extracellular matrix (ECM) proteins; NuShield, a dehydrated placental tissue graft preserved to retain all layers of the native tissue; Apligraf , a bioengineered living cell therapy that contains two living cell types, keratinocytes and fibroblasts that produce a broad spectrum of cytokines and growth factors; and Dermagraft, a bio-engineered product with living human fibroblasts, seeded on a bioabsorbable scaffold, that produce human collagen, ECM, protein, cytokines and growth factors. The surgical & sports medicine division produces products that support the healing of musculoskeletal injuries, including degenerative conditions such as osteoarthritis (OA) and tendonitis. This division's products also include PuraPly, Affinity and NuShield, as well as FiberOS cortical fiber blend, Osteoconductive Matrix PLUS cancellous chips and cortical powder blend, and PuraForce tendon reinforcement matrix. Organogenesis operates as a wholly-owned subsidiary of Organogenesis Holdings, Inc. In early-2021, Organogenesis announced that the U.S. Food and Drug Administration granted ReNu regenerative medicine advanced therapy designation. That May, the firm announced that the FDA's enforcement grace period for its ReNu and NuCel product lines expired.

FINANCIAL DATA: *Note: Data for latest year may not have been available at press time.*

In U.S. $	2020	2019	2018	2017	2016	2015
Revenue						
R&D Expense						
Operating Income						
Operating Margin %						
SGA Expense						
Net Income						
Operating Cash Flow						
Capital Expenditure						
EBITDA						
Return on Assets %						
Return on Equity %						
Debt to Equity						

CONTACT INFORMATION:

Phone: 781-575-0775   Fax: 781-575-1570
Toll-Free:
Address: 85 Dan Rd., Canton, MA 02021 United States

STOCK TICKER/OTHER:

Stock Ticker: Subsidiary   Exchange:
Employees: 600   Fiscal Year Ends: 12/31
Parent Company: Organogenesis Holdings Inc

SALARIES/BONUSES:

Top Exec. Salary: $ Bonus: $
Second Exec. Salary: $ Bonus: $

OTHER THOUGHTS:

Estimated Female Officers or Directors: 4
Hot Spot for Advancement for Women/Minorities: Y

ORPEA ACT

www.orpea-group.com

NAIC Code: 623110

TYPES OF BUSINESS:

Nursing Care Facilities (Skilled Nursing Facilities)
Dependency Care

BRANDS/DIVISIONS/AFFILIATES:

CONTACTS: *Note: Officers with more than one job title may be intentionally listed here more than once.*

Yves le Masne, CEO
Jean-Claude Brdenk, COO

GROWTH PLANS/SPECIAL FEATURES:

ORPEA ACT, operating as ORPEA Groupe, is a leading European operator in dependency care. The France-based company specializes in various types of long- and short-term care in relation to physical and mental dependency, including diminished autonomy due to age, rehabilitation and post-acute care, and mental health disorders. Care facilities for those with diminished autonomy primarily take place in nursing homes, but can also include assisted living facilities, retirement homes, post-acute care facilities, rehabilitation facilities and psychiatric care facilities. In addition, ORPEA provides home care services for people with diminished autonomy. The firm's post-acute care and rehabilitation facilities provide medical care and rehabilitation services following surgery or an acute episode of a chronic illness. Psychiatric care facilities care for people with mental health issues, admitted on a voluntary basis, and include those with mood disorders (depression, bipolar disorder), anxiety disorders (obsessive compulsive behavior, panic attacks, anxiety, social phobia), addictions, eating disorders and post-traumatic stress disorder. Home care services include cleaning, ironing, gardening, moral support, supervision, personal hygiene assistance, meal assistance, help in walking or help with car travel. ORPEA has a global dependency care network of 1,028 facilities comprising 105,443 beds (21,137 of which are under construction) across 22 countries (in Europe, and in China and Latam).

FINANCIAL DATA: *Note: Data for latest year may not have been available at press time.*

In U.S. $	2020	2019	2018	2017	2016	2015
Revenue	4,792,288,000	4,569,709,000	4,178,189,000	3,834,222,000	3,471,343,000	2,922,007,000
R&D Expense						
Operating Income	520,995,000	614,374,200	519,745,100	460,000,200	405,731,400	364,098,100
Operating Margin %		.14%	.12%	.11%	.10%	.08%
SGA Expense						
Net Income	195,540,500	285,883,600	269,268,700	109,702,100	313,312,500	154,718,500
Operating Cash Flow	950,212,600	985,311,800	507,174,300	486,150,000	423,601,100	383,563,500
Capital Expenditure						
EBITDA	1,062,356,000	1,089,422,000	716,292,400	484,378,400	571,516,700	425,205,300
Return on Assets %		.02%	.02%	.01%	.03%	.02%
Return on Equity %		.08%	.08%	.04%	.13%	.08%
Debt to Equity		2.694	1.719	1.702	1.831	1.779

CONTACT INFORMATION:

Phone: 33 147757807   Fax:
Toll-Free:
Address: 52, Quai De Dion Bouton, Puteaux Cedex, 92 813 France

STOCK TICKER/OTHER:

Stock Ticker: ORPEF   Exchange: PINX
Employees: 65,511   Fiscal Year Ends:
Parent Company:

SALARIES/BONUSES:

Top Exec. Salary: $ Bonus: $
Second Exec. Salary: $ Bonus: $

OTHER THOUGHTS:

Estimated Female Officers or Directors:
Hot Spot for Advancement for Women/Minorities:

Orthofix International NV

NAIC Code: 339100

www.orthofix.com

TYPES OF BUSINESS:

Medical Equipment-Orthopedic
Bone Reconstruction Equipment
Orthopedic Fixation Devices

BRANDS/DIVISIONS/AFFILIATES:

CervicalStim
SpinalStim
PhysioStim
FIREBIRD SI Fusion System
O-GENESIS

CONTACTS: *Note: Officers with more than one job title may be intentionally listed here more than once.*

Brad Mason, CEO
Mike Finegan, Chief Strategy Officer
Ronald Matricaria, Chairman of the Board
Doug Rice, CFO
Jim Ryaby, Chief Science Officer
Jill Mason, Chief Ethics & Compliance Officer
Tim McGuire, CIO
Kimberley Elting, Other Executive Officer
Michael Finegan, Other Executive Officer
Raymond Fujikawa, President, Divisional
Robert Goodwin, President, Divisional
Bradley Niemann, President, Divisional
Davide Bianchi, President, Divisional
Ronald Matricaria, Chmn.

GROWTH PLANS/SPECIAL FEATURES:

Orthofix International NV designs, manufactures and distributes medical equipment used principally by musculoskeletal medical specialists. The company provides reconstructive and regenerative solutions that aim to restore the quality of life for patients with various spinal and bone-related conditions. Orthofix's innovative solutions incorporate different treatment modalities (mechanical, biological and electromagnetic) to achieve desired clinical outcomes, such as maintaining range of motion or successful spinal fusions. Spine products include: M6 artificial discs for helping preserve motion in patients undergoing cervical or lumbar disc replacement; fixation solutions for repairing spinal alignment, improving disc height and providing nerve decompression; biologic solutions such as structural allografts, bone grafts and amniotic membranes; and bone growth therapy, offering bone growth stimulators such as CervicalStim, SpinalStim and PhysioStim, which provide non-surgical treatment options for promoting spinal fusion and healing nonunion fractures. Extremities products offer comprehensive solutions for pediatric surgery, limb reconstruction, fracture management and foot and ankle repair, whether due to deformities or post-trauma injuries. Headquartered in Italy, Orthofix's products are distributed in more than 70 countries through its sales representatives and distributors. In October 2020, Orthofix announced that the U.S. Food and Drug Administration (FDA) gave 510(k) clearance for its nanotechnology feature of the FIREBIRD SI Fusion System, a 3D-printed titanium bone screw with nanotechnology specifically designed to compress and stabilize the sacroiliac joint during fusion. That same month, Orthofix announced the launch of its new O-GENESIS bone graft delivery system, designed to deliver allograft, autograft or synthetic bone graft to orthopedic surgical sites.

FINANCIAL DATA: *Note: Data for latest year may not have been available at press time.*

In U.S. $	2020	2019	2018	2017	2016	2015
Revenue	406,562,000	459,955,000	453,042,000	433,823,000	409,788,000	396,489,000
R&D Expense	39,056,000	34,637,000	33,218,000	29,700,000	28,803,000	26,389,000
Operating Income	-6,765,000	15,428,000	33,163,000	38,328,000	37,441,000	18,338,000
Operating Margin %		.03%	.07%	.09%	.09%	.05%
SGA Expense	272,382,000	309,283,000	290,033,000	272,758,000	255,691,000	265,237,000
Net Income	2,517,000	-28,462,000	13,811,000	6,223,000	3,056,000	-2,809,000
Operating Cash Flow	74,272,000	32,033,000	49,918,000	53,341,000	44,707,000	43,224,000
Capital Expenditure	17,094,000	20,524,000	15,256,000	16,948,000	18,334,000	27,899,000
EBITDA	36,391,000	40,127,000	51,822,000	58,452,000	58,282,000	39,261,000
Return on Assets %		- .06%	.03%	.02%	.01%	- .01%
Return on Equity %		- .09%	.04%	.02%	.01%	- .01%
Debt to Equity		0.063				

CONTACT INFORMATION:

Phone: 39 045 67 19 000   Fax: 39 045 67 19 380
Toll-Free:
Address: Via delle Nazioni 9, Bussolengo Verona, 37012 Italy

STOCK TICKER/OTHER:

Stock Ticker: OFIX   Exchange: NAS
Employees: 1,036   Fiscal Year Ends: 12/31
Parent Company:

SALARIES/BONUSES:

Top Exec. Salary: $ Bonus: $
Second Exec. Salary: $ Bonus: $

OTHER THOUGHTS:

Estimated Female Officers or Directors: 2
Hot Spot for Advancement for Women/Minorities:

Osmotica Pharmaceuticals plc   www.osmotica.com

NAIC Code: 325412

TYPES OF BUSINESS:

Pharmaceutical Preparation Manufacturing
Biopharmaceuticals

BRANDS/DIVISIONS/AFFILIATES:

Osmolex ER
M-72
Lorzone
ConZip
OB Complete
Divigel
RVL Pharmaceuticals Inc
UPNEEQ

CONTACTS: *Note: Officers with more than one job title may be intentionally listed here more than once.*

Andrew Einhorn, CFO
Brian Markison, Chairman of the Board
James Schaub, COO
Tina deVries, Executive VP, Divisional
Christopher Klein, General Counsel

GROWTH PLANS/SPECIAL FEATURES:

Osmotica Pharmaceuticals plc is a fully-integrated biopharmaceutical company focused on the development and commercialization of specialty products that target markets with underserved patient populations. The company actively promotes six products: Osmolex ER (amantadine extended-release tablets), M-72 (methylphenidate hydrochloride extended-release tables, 72 mg), Lorzone (chlorzoxazone scored tablets) and ConZip (tramadol hydrochloride extended-release capsules) in specialty neurology; and OB Complete, a family of prescription prenatal dietary supplements, and Divigel (estradiol gel, 0.1%) in women's health. Osmodex is the company's proprietary drug delivery system for modulating drug release and achieving pharmacokinetics. Osmotica's current pipeline contains two Phase 3 candidates under clinical development: arbaclofen ER and RVL-1201. Arbaclofen ER is an extended release formulation of arbaclofen, the R isomer of baclofen, that leverages the Osmodex drug delivery system and is being studied for the treatment of spasticity resulting from multiple sclerosis. RVL-1201 is an oxymetazoline ophthalmic solution being studied for the treatment of acquired blepharoptosis, defined as the drooping of the upper eyelid that usually occurs from a partial or complete dysfunction of the muscles that elevate the upper eyelid. Osmotica owns the rights to UPNEEQ (oxymetazoline hydrochloride ophthalmic solution, 0.1%), and is conducting a Phase 3 clinical trial for droopy eyelid/blepharoptosis. In October 2020, Osmotica subsidiary RVL Pharmaceuticals, Inc. announced that its Phase 3 trials showed UPNEEQ was associated with positive outcomes after installation on days 1 and 14 and was well-tolerated, demonstrating its potential for the treatment of acquired ptosis. Ptosis is an abnormal drooping of the upper eyelid margin with the eye in primary gaze, giving the appearance of a sleepy eye.

FINANCIAL DATA: *Note: Data for latest year may not have been available at press time.*

In U.S. $	2020	2019	2018	2017	2016	2015
Revenue	177,884,000	240,031,000	263,701,300	245,749,000	218,459,600	
R&D Expense	19,696,000	32,319,000	48,761,500	42,688,060	29,061,520	
Operating Income	1,747,000	3,052,000	5,683,348	20,918,020	-2,176,004	
Operating Margin %		.01%	.02%	.09%	- .01%	
SGA Expense	81,961,000	93,030,000	74,242,510	56,954,510	65,958,150	
Net Income	-79,589,000	-270,901,000	-109,396,300	-45,154,970	-41,821,240	
Operating Cash Flow	17,590,000	33,567,000	37,558,330	57,837,060	-44,790,640	
Capital Expenditure	3,134,000	4,037,000	4,143,723	6,895,332	15,931,010	
EBITDA	-48,864,000	-222,796,000	-16,300,880	-10,140,030	-8,294,598	
Return on Assets %		- .43%	- .13%	- .04%	- .04%	
Return on Equity %		-1.08%	- .27%	- .09%	- .09%	
Debt to Equity		2.363	0.691	0.749	0.696	

CONTACT INFORMATION:

Phone: 908 809 1300   Fax: 908 809 1301
Toll-Free:
Address: 400 Crossing Blvd., Bridgewater, NJ 8807 United States

STOCK TICKER/OTHER:

Stock Ticker: OSMT   Exchange: NAS
Employees: 84   Fiscal Year Ends: 12/31
Parent Company:

SALARIES/BONUSES:

Top Exec. Salary: $ Bonus: $
Second Exec. Salary: $ Bonus: $

OTHER THOUGHTS:

Estimated Female Officers or Directors:
Hot Spot for Advancement for Women/Minorities:

Owens & Minor Inc

www.owens-minor.com

NAIC Code: 423450

TYPES OF BUSINESS:

Distribution-Medical & Surgical Equipment
Supply Chain Management

BRANDS/DIVISIONS/AFFILIATES:

CONTACTS: *Note: Officers with more than one job title may be intentionally listed here more than once.*

Edward Pesicka, CEO
Robert Snead, CFO
Robert Sledd, Chairman of the Board
Michael Lowry, Chief Accounting Officer
Erika Davis, Chief Administrative Officer
Joseph Pekala, Chief Information Officer
Jeffrey Jochims, Executive VP, Divisional
Nicholas Pace, Executive VP
Shana Neal, Other Executive Officer
Christopher Lowery, President, Divisional
Geoffrey Marlatt, Senior VP, Divisional
Charles Colpo, Senior VP, Divisional
Jonathan Leon, Senior VP

GROWTH PLANS/SPECIAL FEATURES:

Owens & Minor, Inc., founded in 1882, is a leading healthcare logistics company that connects the world of medical products to the point of care. The company provides vital supply chain assistance to the providers of health care services and the manufacturers of health care products, supplies and devices in the U.S. and Europe. Owens & Minor's service portfolio covers procurement, inventory management, delivery and sourcing for the healthcare market. It serves customers ranging from hospitals, integrated healthcare systems, group purchasing organizations and the U.S. federal government to manufacturers of life-science and medical devices and supplies, including pharmaceuticals in Europe. The firm's operations are divided into two segments: Global Solutions and Global Products. The Global Solutions segment offers a comprehensive portfolio of products and services to healthcare providers and manufacturers. The portfolio of medical and surgical supplies includes branded products purchased from manufacturers and its own proprietary products. The segment provides distribution and logistics services to healthcare providers and manufacturers via 48 distribution centers. The Global Products segment manufactures and sources medical surgical products through its production and kitting operations. The segment's manufacturing facilities are located in the U.S., Thailand, Honduras, Mexico and Ireland. The business has recognized brands across its portfolio of product offerings, including sterilization wrap, surgical drapes and gowns, facial protection, protective apparel, medical exam gloves, custom and minor procedure kits and other medical products. In June 2020, Owens & Minor sold its European logistics business, Movianto, to EHDH Holding Group, one of Europe's leading providers of healthcare logistics, for $133 million.

Owens & Minor offers comprehensive benefits and employee assistance programs.

FINANCIAL DATA: *Note: Data for latest year may not have been available at press time.*

In U.S. $	2020	2019	2018	2017	2016	2015
Revenue	8,480,177,000	9,210,939,000	9,838,708,000	9,318,275,000	9,723,431,000	9,772,946,000
R&D Expense						
Operating Income	241,870,000	103,201,000	109,639,000	149,958,000	224,274,000	228,763,000
Operating Margin %		.01%	.01%	.02%	.02%	.02%
SGA Expense	1,041,336,000	1,023,065,000	1,261,748,000	1,016,978,000	970,424,000	933,596,000
Net Income	29,871,000	-62,371,000	-437,012,000	72,793,000	108,787,000	103,409,000
Operating Cash Flow	339,223,000	166,085,000	115,589,000	56,774,000	186,934,000	269,597,000
Capital Expenditure	59,193,000	52,228,000	65,685,000	50,737,000	30,121,000	36,616,000
EBITDA	286,642,000	186,072,000	-290,247,000	148,694,000	254,992,000	266,341,000
Return on Assets %		-.02%	-.12%	.02%	.04%	.04%
Return on Equity %		-.13%	-.57%	.07%	.11%	.10%
Debt to Equity		3.517	3.184	0.887	0.588	0.577

CONTACT INFORMATION:

Phone: 804 723-7000   Fax: 804 270-7281
Toll-Free:
Address: 9120 Lockwood Blvd., Mechanicsville, VA 23116 United States

STOCK TICKER/OTHER:

Stock Ticker: OMI   Exchange: NYS
Employees: 15,400   Fiscal Year Ends: 12/31
Parent Company:

SALARIES/BONUSES:

Top Exec. Salary: $ Bonus: $
Second Exec. Salary: $ Bonus: $

OTHER THOUGHTS:

Estimated Female Officers or Directors: 4
Hot Spot for Advancement for Women/Minorities: Y

Par Pharmaceutical Companies Inc

www.parpharm.com

NAIC Code: 325412

TYPES OF BUSINESS:

Drugs-Generic & Branded
Pharmaceutical Intermediates

BRANDS/DIVISIONS/AFFILIATES:

Endo International plc

CONTACTS: *Note: Officers with more than one job title may be intentionally listed here more than once.*

Thomas Haughey Paul V. Campanelli, Pres.
Suketu Sanghvi, VP-Formulation Dev.
Robert Polke, Sr. VP-Manufacturing
Chad Gassert, VP-Bus. Dev. & Licensing
Allison Wey, VP-Corp. Affairs
Allison Wey, VP-Investor Rel.
Michael Altamuro Michael Altamuro, VP-Mktg. & Bus. Analytics
Joseph Barbarite, Sr. VP-Quality & Compliance
Michelle Bonomi-Huvala, VP-Regulatory Affairs

GROWTH PLANS/SPECIAL FEATURES:

Par Pharmaceutical Companies, Inc. develops, manufactures and markets generic pharmaceutical and branded injectable products that help improve patient quality of life. The company also engages in advancing potential new products through its research and development pipeline program. Generic pharmaceuticals are carefully manufactured formulations of the original patented brand name products in order to make healthcare more affordable. Par Pharmaceutical's products include a range of prescription and over-the-counter products comprised of tablets, capsules, liquids, suspensions, creams and ointments. Therapeutic categories include antihypertensives, analgesics, antibiotics, cough/cold, antidepressants, antipsychotics, among others. The company manufactures and distributes drugs at various dosage strengths, some of which are manufactured by themselves and some by other companies. The company's facilities comprise more than 1 million square feet of manufacturing and packaging space, as well as quality control and R&D labs as well as state-of-the-art distribution facilities with advanced automated shipping systems. U.S. facilities are located in New York, California and Michigan; and international facilities are located in India, including Tamilnadu and Mumbai. Par Pharmaceutical operates as a subsidiary of Endo International plc.

FINANCIAL DATA: *Note: Data for latest year may not have been available at press time.*

In U.S. $	2020	2019	2018	2017	2016	2015
Revenue	4,540,205,250	4,283,212,500	4,079,250,000	3,885,000,000	3,700,000,000	3,660,964,160
R&D Expense						
Operating Income						
Operating Margin %						
SGA Expense						
Net Income						
Operating Cash Flow						
Capital Expenditure						
EBITDA						
Return on Assets %						
Return on Equity %						
Debt to Equity						

CONTACT INFORMATION:

Phone: 845-573-5500   Fax: 845-425-7907
Toll-Free:
Address: Six Ram Ridge Rd., Chestnut Ridge, NY 10977 United States

STOCK TICKER/OTHER:

Stock Ticker: Subsidiary
Employees: 3,700
Parent Company: Endo International plc

Exchange:
Fiscal Year Ends: 12/31

SALARIES/BONUSES:

Top Exec. Salary: $ Bonus: $
Second Exec. Salary: $ Bonus: $

OTHER THOUGHTS:

Estimated Female Officers or Directors: 3
Hot Spot for Advancement for Women/Minorities: Y

Patterson Companies Inc

www.pattersoncompanies.com

NAIC Code: 423450

TYPES OF BUSINESS:

Dental Products & Related Services
Veterinary Products
Non-Wheelchair Assistive Products

BRANDS/DIVISIONS/AFFILIATES:

Patterson Dental Supply Inc
Animal Health International Inc

CONTACTS: *Note: Officers with more than one job title may be intentionally listed here more than once.*

Mark Walchirk, CEO
Donald Zurbay, CFO
John Buck, Chairman of the Board
Dennis Goedken, Controller
Andrea Frohning, Other Executive Officer
Kevin Pohlman, President, Divisional
Les Korsh, Vice President

GROWTH PLANS/SPECIAL FEATURES:

Patterson Companies, Inc. is a value-added specialty distributor serving the U.S. and Canadian dental supply markets and the U.S., Canadian and U.K. animal health supply markets. The company operates through these two market segments: dental supply and animal health. The dental supply segment comprises subsidiary Patterson Dental Supply, Inc., which is one of the largest distributors of dental products in North America, offering full-service, value-added supplies to approximately 200,000 dentists as well as dental laboratories, institutions and other healthcare professionals. The division provides consumable products, including X-ray film, restorative materials, hand instruments and sterilization products; basic and advanced technology dental equipment; practice management and clinical software; patient education systems; and office forms and stationery. Patterson Dental also offers related services including dental equipment installation, maintenance and repair, dental office design and equipment financing. The animal health segment comprises subsidiary Animal Health International, Inc., which distributes biologicals, pharmaceuticals, parasiticides, supplies and equipment to the animal health supply market. This market is engaged in beef and dairy cattle, poultry and swine, and other food-producing animals. It also includes the companion animal supply market, which primarily consists of dogs, cats and horses. This segment offers approximately 100,000 stock-keeping units (SKUs) sources from over 2,000 manufacturers to its customers, including many proprietary branded products, which provide a competitive edge in relation to price as well as to customer loyalty.

Employee benefits include medical, dental and vision coverage; flexible spending accounts; short- and long-term disability; life and accident insurance; a 401(k); employee stock purchase and ownership plans; education and employee assistance; and employee

FINANCIAL DATA: *Note: Data for latest year may not have been available at press time.*

In U.S. $	2020	2019	2018	2017	2016	2015
Revenue	5,490,011,000	5,574,523,000	5,465,683,000	5,593,127,000	5,386,703,000	
R&D Expense						
Operating Income	102,936,000	137,716,000	219,889,000	287,928,000	347,713,000	
Operating Margin %	.02%	.02%	.04%	.05%	.06%	
SGA Expense						
Net Income	-588,446,000	83,628,000	200,974,000	170,893,000	187,184,000	
Operating Cash Flow	-243,544,000	48,158,000	178,895,000	162,719,000	156,329,000	
Capital Expenditure	41,809,000	60,734,000	43,263,000	47,019,000	79,354,000	
EBITDA	-466,438,000	228,667,000	309,822,000	377,759,000	434,141,000	
Return on Assets %	-.20%	.02%	.06%	.05%	.06%	
Return on Equity %	-.51%	.06%	.14%	.12%	.13%	
Debt to Equity	0.764	0.491	0.631	0.716	0.709	

CONTACT INFORMATION:

Phone: 651 686-1600   Fax: 651 686-9331
Toll-Free: 800-328-5536
Address: 1031 Mendota Heights Rd., St. Paul, MN 55120 United States

STOCK TICKER/OTHER:

Stock Ticker: PDCO   Exchange: NAS
Employees: 7,800   Fiscal Year Ends: 04/24
Parent Company:

SALARIES/BONUSES:

Top Exec. Salary: $ Bonus: $
Second Exec. Salary: $ Bonus: $

OTHER THOUGHTS:

Estimated Female Officers or Directors: 4
Hot Spot for Advancement for Women/Minorities: Y

PerkinElmer Inc

www.perkinelmer.com

NAIC Code: 325413

TYPES OF BUSINESS:

Diagnostic Systems
Mechanical Components
Optoelectronics
Pharmaceutical Manufacturing
Life Science Systems
Environmental Safety Equipment

BRANDS/DIVISIONS/AFFILIATES:

Tri-carb
Opera Phenix
EnSight
PerkinElmer
Clarus
NexION
DELFIA
Chitas

CONTACTS: *Note: Officers with more than one job title may be intentionally listed here more than once.*

Robert Friel, CEO
James Mock, CFO
Andrew Okun, Chief Accounting Officer
Prahlad Singh, COO
James Corbett, Executive VP
Joel Goldberg, General Counsel
Deborah Butters, Other Executive Officer
Daniel Tereau, Senior VP, Divisional
Tajinder Vohra, Senior VP, Divisional

GROWTH PLANS/SPECIAL FEATURES:

PerkinElmer, Inc. provides products, services and solutions for the diagnostics, life sciences and applied markets. The company's technologies and solutions address critical issues that help to improve lives. The company operates through two segments: discovery and analytical solutions, and diagnostics. The discovery and analytical solutions segment comprises a portfolio of technologies that help life sciences researchers better understand diseases and develop treatments. This division also serves applied markets such as environmental, food and industrial, offering products and solutions that detect, monitor and manage contaminants and toxic chemicals impacting the environment and food supply. Just a few of the many product, services and application solutions developed by this segment include: gas chromatographs, mass spectrometers, sample-handling equipment, advanced liquid chromatography systems, analyzers, quantitative pathology research solutions, radiometric detection solutions, screening systems and plate readers. The diagnostics segment offers instruments, reagents, assay platforms and software to hospitals, medical labs, clinicians and medical research professionals. This division focuses on reproductive health, emerging market diagnostics and applied genomics. Products, services and application solutions include screening platforms, in vitro diagnostic kits, blood analyzing kits, informatics data management, X-ray detectors, umbilical cord blood banking services, automated liquid handling platforms, next-generation sequencing automation and nucleic acid quantitation and automated small-scale purification. Brand names include Tri-carb, Opera Phenix, EnSight, PerkinElmer, Clarus, NexION, DELFIA, Chitas, JANUS and PG-Seq, among many others. PerkinElmer is headquartered in Waltham, Massachusetts, and markets its products and services in more than 190 countries.

FINANCIAL DATA: *Note: Data for latest year may not have been available at press time.*

In U.S. $	2020	2019	2018	2017	2016	2015
Revenue	3,782,745,000	2,883,673,000	2,777,996,000	2,256,982,000	2,115,517,000	2,262,359,000
R&D Expense	205,389,000	189,336,000	193,998,000	139,404,000	124,278,000	125,928,000
Operating Income	986,594,000	391,401,000	335,028,000	317,460,000	288,190,000	299,724,000
Operating Margin %		.14%	.12%	.14%	.14%	.13%
SGA Expense	917,894,000	815,318,000	811,913,000	616,167,000	600,885,000	598,848,000
Net Income	727,887,000	227,558,000	237,927,000	292,633,000	234,299,000	212,425,000
Operating Cash Flow	892,177,000	363,469,000	311,038,000	288,453,000	350,615,000	287,098,000
Capital Expenditure	77,506,000	81,331,000	93,253,000	39,089,000	31,702,000	29,632,000
EBITDA	1,202,583,000	514,794,000	505,247,000	445,658,000	385,568,000	394,019,000
Return on Assets %		.04%	.04%	.06%	.06%	.05%
Return on Equity %		.08%	.09%	.13%	.11%	.10%
Debt to Equity		0.786	0.726	0.715	0.485	0.479

CONTACT INFORMATION:

Phone: 781 663-6900   Fax:
Toll-Free: 800-762-4000
Address: 940 Winter St., Waltham, MA 02451 United States

STOCK TICKER/OTHER:

Stock Ticker: PKI
Employees: 14,000
Parent Company:

Exchange: NYS
Fiscal Year Ends: 01/31

SALARIES/BONUSES:

Top Exec. Salary: $ Bonus: $
Second Exec. Salary: $ Bonus: $

OTHER THOUGHTS:

Estimated Female Officers or Directors: 1
Hot Spot for Advancement for Women/Minorities: Y

Personalis Inc

NAIC Code: 541711

www.personalis.com

TYPES OF BUSINESS:

Research and Development in Biotechnology
Cancer Genomics
Molecular Data
Liquid Biopsy Assay
Human Gene Analysis

BRANDS/DIVISIONS/AFFILIATES:

ImmunoID NeXT Platform
ACE ImmunoID Platform
NeoantigenID
ImmunogenomicsID
NeXT Liquid Biopsy

CONTACTS: *Note: Officers with more than one job title may be intentionally listed here more than once.*

John West, CEO
Aaron Tachibana, CFO
Jonathan MacQuitty, Chairman of the Board
Richard Chen, Chief Scientific Officer
Clinton Musil, Other Executive Officer

GROWTH PLANS/SPECIAL FEATURES:

Personalis, Inc. is a cancer genomics company. The firm aims to transform the development of next-generation therapies by providing comprehensive molecular data about each patient's cancer and immune response. To accomplish this, Personalis designed the ImmunoID NeXT Platform to adapt to the complex and evolving understanding of cancer, providing biopharmaceutical customers with information on all of the approximately 20,000 human genes, together with the immune system, in contrast to many cancer panels that cover roughly 50 to 500 genes. The company also developed a complementary liquid biopsy assay, NeXT Liquid Biopsy, which analyzes all human genes. By combining technological innovation, operational scale and regulatory differentiation, Personalis' ImmunoID NeXT Platform can help customers obtain new insights into the mechanisms of response and resistance to therapy, as well as new potential therapeutic targets. The company's ACE ImmunoID Platform combines the ACE cancer exome and ACE cancer transcriptome assays to enable broad tumor immunogenomic characterization. The platform can be further customized to unique research and project needs by using NeoantigenID to enable neoantigen identification, and/or ImmunogenomicsID for the assessment of tumor immunogenomics in critical genes, providing information including expression, variant effect impact and DNA/RNA allelic fractions. Personalis' laboratory is both CLIA-certified and CAP-accredited, and is located in California, USA.

FINANCIAL DATA: *Note: Data for latest year may not have been available at press time.*

In U.S. $	2020	2019	2018	2017	2016	2015
Revenue	78,648,000	65,207,000	37,774,000	9,393,000		
R&D Expense	28,568,000	22,418,000	14,304,000	9,919,000		
Operating Income	-42,146,000	-22,418,000	-13,770,000	-22,163,000		
Operating Margin %		- .34%	- .36%	-2.36%		
SGA Expense	33,692,000	22,080,000	11,271,000	9,901,000		
Net Income	-41,280,000	-25,084,000	-19,886,000	-23,598,000		
Operating Cash Flow	-42,653,000	-18,069,000	5,572,000	290,000		
Capital Expenditure	3,246,000	8,382,000	7,852,000	5,158,000		
EBITDA	-35,463,000	-19,194,000	-14,919,000	-21,074,000		
Return on Assets %		- .25%	- .52%	- .70%		
Return on Equity %		-166.12%				
Debt to Equity		0.006				

CONTACT INFORMATION:

Phone: 650 752-1300   Fax:
Toll-Free:
Address: 1330 O'Brien Dr., Menlo Park, CA 94025 United States

STOCK TICKER/OTHER:

Stock Ticker: PSNL   Exchange: NAS
Employees: 235   Fiscal Year Ends: 12/31
Parent Company:

SALARIES/BONUSES:

Top Exec. Salary: $ Bonus: $
Second Exec. Salary: $ Bonus: $

OTHER THOUGHTS:

Estimated Female Officers or Directors:
Hot Spot for Advancement for Women/Minorities:

Pfizer Inc

www.pfizer.com

NAIC Code: 325412

TYPES OF BUSINESS:

Pharmaceuticals
Biopharmaceutical
Therapeutics
Drug Development

BRANDS/DIVISIONS/AFFILIATES:

Viatris Inc

CONTACTS: *Note: Officers with more than one job title may be intentionally listed here more than once.*

Albert Bourla, CEO
Michael Goettler, Pres., Divisional
Frank DAmelio, CFO
Ian Read, Chairman of the Board
Loretta Cangialosi, Chief Accounting Officer
Rady Johnson, Chief Risk Officer
Mikael Dolsten, Chief Scientific Officer
Lidia Fonseca, Chief Technology Officer
Sally Susman, Executive VP, Divisional
Douglas Lankler, Executive VP
Freda Lewis-Hall, Executive VP
Alexander Mackenzie, Executive VP
Dawn Rogers, Executive VP
John Young, Other Executive Officer
Margaret Madden, Other Executive Officer
Angela Hwang, President, Divisional

GROWTH PLANS/SPECIAL FEATURES:

Pfizer, Inc. is a research-based, global biopharmaceutical company. The firm applies science and global resources to bring therapies for extending and improving the lives of people through the discovery, development, manufacture, marketing, sales and distribution of biopharmaceutical products worldwide. Pfizer works across developed and emerging markets to advance wellness, prevention, treatments and cures. The company's therapeutic areas include internal medicine, oncology, hospital, vaccines, inflammation, immunology and rare disease. Pfizer collaborates with healthcare providers, governments and local communities to support and expand access to healthcare around the globe. In November 2020, Pfizer spun off its off-patent branded and generics business, which included a portfolio of 20 globally recognized solid oral dose brands as well as its U.S.-based Greenstone generics platform, and combined it with Mylan to create Viatris, Inc. Viatris trades on the NASDAQ under ticker symbol VTRS. In August 2021, Pfizer received FDA approval for its Coronavirus vaccine which was developed in partnership with BioNTech SE.

FINANCIAL DATA: *Note: Data for latest year may not have been available at press time.*

In U.S. $	2020	2019	2018	2017	2016	2015
Revenue	41,908,000,000	51,750,000,000	53,647,000,000	52,546,000,000	52,824,000,000	48,851,000,000
R&D Expense	9,405,000,000	8,650,000,000	8,006,000,000	7,657,000,000	7,872,000,000	7,690,000,000
Operating Income	8,760,001,000	13,921,000,000	15,045,000,000	14,107,000,000	13,730,000,000	12,976,000,000
Operating Margin %		.27%	.28%	.27%	.26%	.27%
SGA Expense	11,615,000,000	14,350,000,000	14,455,000,000	14,784,000,000	14,837,000,000	14,809,000,000
Net Income	9,616,000,000	16,273,000,000	11,153,000,000	21,308,000,000	7,215,000,000	6,960,000,000
Operating Cash Flow	14,403,000,000	12,588,000,000	15,827,000,000	16,470,000,000	15,901,000,000	14,512,000,000
Capital Expenditure	2,791,000,000	2,594,000,000	2,196,000,000	2,217,000,000	1,999,000,000	1,496,000,000
EBITDA	13,723,000,000	25,266,000,000	19,585,000,000	19,844,000,000	15,294,000,000	15,321,000,000
Return on Assets %		.10%	.07%	.12%	.04%	.04%
Return on Equity %		.26%	.17%	.33%	.12%	.10%
Debt to Equity		0.57	0.519	0.47	0.528	0.445

CONTACT INFORMATION:

Phone: 212 733-2323   Fax: 212 573-7851
Toll-Free:
Address: 235 E. 42nd St., New York, NY 10017 United States

SALARIES/BONUSES:

Top Exec. Salary: $ Bonus: $
Second Exec. Salary: $ Bonus: $

STOCK TICKER/OTHER:

Stock Ticker: PFE   Exchange: NYS
Employees: 93,000   Fiscal Year Ends: 12/31
Parent Company:

OTHER THOUGHTS:

Estimated Female Officers or Directors: 7
Hot Spot for Advancement for Women/Minorities: Y

Sales, profits and employees may be estimates. Financial information, benefits and other data can change quickly and may vary from those stated here.

PharMerica Corporation

www.pharmerica.com

NAIC Code: 446110

TYPES OF BUSINESS:

Specialty Pharmacy Operations
Healthcare Pharmacy Management

BRANDS/DIVISIONS/AFFILIATES:

KKR & Co LP
Walgreens Boots Alliance Inc

CONTACTS: *Note: Officers with more than one job title may be intentionally listed here more than once.*

Bob Dries, Pres.
Jennifer Yowler, CFO
Lisa Bowen, VP-Mktg.
Suresh Vishnubhatla, Executive VP, Divisional
Thomas Caneris, General Counsel
Robert McKay, Senior VP, Divisional

GROWTH PLANS/SPECIAL FEATURES:

PharMerica Corporation provides pharmacy management services for skilled nursing facilities, long-term care facilities, assisted living facilities, hospitals and other institutional care settings. PharMerica collaborates with clients to develop products and services that help them provide quality care, control costs and remain regulatory compliant. The company's solutions include account management and comprehensive reporting and analytics tools. Its services include multiple packaging and dispensing options (from blister packs to multi-dose packs), on-site IV services, online ordering, admission and discharge services, as well as on-site access to emergency, time-sensitive and first dose medications. PharMerica also provides implementation teams that focus exclusively on transitioning new nursing facility customers to its pharmacy service. These teams offer ongoing education and training services. PharMerica itself comprises more than 100 long-term care pharmacies in over 45 U.S. states, including Hawaii. PharMerica is a joint venture between KKR & Co. LP and Walgreens Boots Alliance, Inc.

FINANCIAL DATA: *Note: Data for latest year may not have been available at press time.*

In U.S. $	2020	2019	2018	2017	2016	2015
Revenue	2,500,911,000	2,359,350,000	2,247,000,000	2,140,000,000	2,091,100,032	2,028,499,968
R&D Expense						
Operating Income						
Operating Margin %						
SGA Expense						
Net Income						
Operating Cash Flow						
Capital Expenditure						
EBITDA						
Return on Assets %						
Return on Equity %						
Debt to Equity						

CONTACT INFORMATION:

Phone: 502 627-7000 Fax: 813 318-6459
Toll-Free: 866-209-2178
Address: 805 N. Whittington Pkwy., Louisville, KY 40222 United States

STOCK TICKER/OTHER:

Stock Ticker: Joint Venture Exchange:
Employees: 6,000 Fiscal Year Ends: 12/31
Parent Company:

SALARIES/BONUSES:

Top Exec. Salary: $ Bonus: $
Second Exec. Salary: $ Bonus: $

OTHER THOUGHTS:

Estimated Female Officers or Directors:
Hot Spot for Advancement for Women/Minorities:

Philips Healthcare

www.usa.philips.com/healthcare

NAIC Code: 334510

TYPES OF BUSINESS:

Manufacturing-Medical Equipment
Diagnostic & Treatment Equipment
Imaging Equipment
Equipment Repair & Maintenance
Healthcare Consulting

BRANDS/DIVISIONS/AFFILIATES:

Koninklijke Philips NV

CONTACTS: *Note: Officers with more than one job title may be intentionally listed here more than once.*

Frans van Houten, CEO-Koninklijke Philips
Eric Silfen, Chief Medical Officer
Clement Revetti, Chief Legal Officer
Michael Dreher, Global Head-Oper. & Customer Svcs.
Diego Olego, Chief Strategy & Innovation Officer
Rachel Bloom-Baglin, Media Contact-Global
Frans van Houten, CEO-Royal Philips Electronics NV
Steve Laczynski, Pres., Americas
Desmond Thio, Pres., China
Brent Shafer, CEO-Home Health Care Solutions
Arjen Radder, Pres., Asia Pacific

GROWTH PLANS/SPECIAL FEATURES:

Philips Healthcare, a subsidiary of Koninklijke Philips NV, manufactures medical diagnostic and treatment solutions, distributing its products to more than 100 countries worldwide. The company's many products and services address advanced molecular imaging, breathing/respiratory care, clinical informatics, computed tomography machines/solutions, customer service solutions, diagnostic electrocardiogram (ECG), electroencephalogram (EEG) neuroimaging, emergency care and resuscitation solutions, enterprise telehealth, fluoroscopy, hospital respiratory care, image-guided therapy devices, interventional X-ray systems and solutions, medical parts and related supplies, mother/child care, magnetic resonance imaging (MRI) systems and solutions, pathology, patient monitoring, radiation oncology, radiography, refurbished systems, sleep and ultrasounds. Philips Healthcare provides integrated solutions across the health continuum, from healthy living and prevention to diagnosis, treatment and home care. In August 2020, Philips agreed to acquire Intact Vascular, Inc., a U.S.-based developer of medical devices for minimally-invasive peripheral vascular procedures.

FINANCIAL DATA: *Note: Data for latest year may not have been available at press time.*

In U.S. $	2020	2019	2018	2017	2016	2015
Revenue	24,021,030,000	21,837,300,000	20,726,700,000	21,298,000,000	20,196,679,771	14,406,749,346
R&D Expense						
Operating Income						
Operating Margin %						
SGA Expense						
Net Income		1,343,830,000	1,254,740,000	2,240,000,000	1,570,860,000	697,041,000
Operating Cash Flow						
Capital Expenditure						
EBITDA						
Return on Assets %						
Return on Equity %						
Debt to Equity						

CONTACT INFORMATION:

Phone: 978-659-4278   Fax:
Toll-Free: 800-722-9377
Address: 222 Jacobs St., Cambridge, MA 02141 United States

STOCK TICKER/OTHER:

Stock Ticker: Subsidiary   Exchange:
Employees: 80,495   Fiscal Year Ends: 12/31
Parent Company: Koninklijke Philips NV

SALARIES/BONUSES:

Top Exec. Salary: $ Bonus: $
Second Exec. Salary: $ Bonus: $

OTHER THOUGHTS:

Estimated Female Officers or Directors: 2
Hot Spot for Advancement for Women/Minorities:

Ping An Healthcare and Technology Company Limited

www.pagd.net
NAIC Code: 519130

TYPES OF BUSINESS:
Health Care Internet Portals
Healthcare Consultation

BRANDS/DIVISIONS/AFFILIATES:
Ping An Good Doctor
Health Guard 360

CONTACTS: *Note: Officers with more than one job title may be intentionally listed here more than once.*
Weiho Fang, CEO

GROWTH PLANS/SPECIAL FEATURES:
Ping An Healthcare and Technology Company Limited operates an artificial intelligent (AI)-driven online and mobile healthcare platform called Ping An Good Doctor, which offers related consultations to individuals and corporations in China. The platform offers information about medical and wellness services such as family doctor services, consumer healthcare services, beauty care, medical insurance, pharmacies and health management. It connects consumers and patients with healthcare resources and enables them to retrieve information, obtain advice and book and manage appointments. Moreover, Ping An Good Doctor has provided the employees of over 500 corporate customers across sectors such as real estate, medicine and retail, with services such as one-on-one online consultations with doctors practicing in the private sector and assisting or accompanying the patients throughout the entire process of their visits at physical healthcare organizations, from outpatient registration and payment to diagnosis. The company has worked closely with local governments to promote China's rural healthcare programs. As of June 30, 2020, Ping An Healthcare upgraded over 900 healthcare clinics in outlying and hard-to-reach areas, trained nearly 1 million doctors working in rural districts and provided free healthcare services to thousands living outside of China's urbanized regions. In addition, Health Guard 360 is Ping An's membership-based service for the policy users of Ping An Life Insurance.

FINANCIAL DATA: *Note: Data for latest year may not have been available at press time.*

In U.S. $	2020	2019	2018	2017	2016	2015
Revenue	1,076,055,000	793,867,300	523,116,400	292,761,200	94,267,720	43,677,020
R&D Expense						
Operating Income	-105,981,000	-167,595,200	-203,851,100	-126,650,800	-153,641,500	-50,761,200
Operating Margin %						
SGA Expense	408,060,300	357,637,900	349,986,200	224,774,900	194,671,000	67,395,740
Net Income	-148,648,000	-115,012,500	-142,878,100	-156,980,100	-118,829,400	-50,732,360
Operating Cash Flow	-172,751,000	-79,020,170	-170,074,300	-75,844,660	-41,229,330	-7,040,764
Capital Expenditure	11,467,240	20,847,710	30,977,790	1,891,329	15,381,860	2,260,724
EBITDA	-119,983,400	-90,148,890	-135,936,500	-147,466,900	-114,292,600	-49,858,010
Return on Assets %						
Return on Equity %						
Debt to Equity						

CONTACT INFORMATION:
Phone: Fax: 86 21 3863 3719
Toll-Free:
Address: 166 Kaibin Rd., Block B, Fl. 17-19, Ping Ann Bldg., Shanghai, Shanghai 200032 China

STOCK TICKER/OTHER:
Stock Ticker: PIAHY   Exchange: PINX
Employees: 4,226   Fiscal Year Ends: 12/31
Parent Company:

SALARIES/BONUSES:
Top Exec. Salary: $ Bonus: $
Second Exec. Salary: $ Bonus: $

OTHER THOUGHTS:
Estimated Female Officers or Directors:
Hot Spot for Advancement for Women/Minorities:

PPD Inc

www.ppd.com

NAIC Code: 541711

TYPES OF BUSINESS:

Contract Research
Clinical Development
Laboratory Services
Advanced Testing
Therapeutics

BRANDS/DIVISIONS/AFFILIATES:

GROWTH PLANS/SPECIAL FEATURES:

PPD, Inc. provides a comprehensive suite of clinical development and laboratory services to the pharmaceutical, biotechnology, medical device and government organizations, as well as other industry participants. The company's clinical development division encompasses all phases of development (Phases 1-4), peri- and post-approval and site and patient access services. Laboratory services include a range of high-value, advanced testing services, including bioanalytical, biomarker, vaccine, good manufacturing practice (GMP) and central laboratory services. PPD has developed significant expertise in the design and execution of complex global clinical trials, a result on conducting studies on global, national, regional and local levels across a wide spectrum of therapeutic areas in more than 100 countries. PPD is headquartered in North Carolina, USA, with offices in 46 countries. In April 2021, PPD agreed to be acquired by Thermo Fisher Scientific, Inc.

CONTACTS: *Note: Officers with more than one job title may be intentionally listed here more than once.*

David Simmons, CEO
Christine A. Dingivan, Chief Medical Officer
B. Judd Hartman, General Counsel
William W. Richardson, Sr. VP-Global Bus. Dev.
Randy Buckwalter, Head-Media
Luke Heagle, Head-Investor Rel.
Lee E. Babiss, Chief Science Officer
David Johnston, Exec. VP-Global Lab Svcs.
Paul Colvin, Exec. VP-Global Clinical Dev.

FINANCIAL DATA: *Note: Data for latest year may not have been available at press time.*

In U.S. $	2020	2019	2018	2017	2016	2015
Revenue	4,681,474,000	4,031,017,000	3,748,971,000	3,001,050,000	2,679,565,000	
R&D Expense						
Operating Income	509,431,000	418,489,000	402,237,000	261,328,000	314,264,000	
Operating Margin %		.10%	.11%	.09%	.12%	
SGA Expense	1,010,127,000	938,806,000	813,035,000	809,333,000	718,139,000	
Net Income	153,691,000	47,821,000	104,186,000	296,027,000	183,095,000	
Operating Cash Flow	251,334,000	432,946,000	423,406,000	359,079,000	407,995,000	
Capital Expenditure	163,331,000	125,928,000	116,145,000	105,135,000	90,258,000	
EBITDA	683,596,000	635,849,000	669,222,000	549,426,000	630,674,000	
Return on Assets %		.01%	.02%	.04%		
Return on Equity %						
Debt to Equity						

CONTACT INFORMATION:

Phone: 910-251-0081   Fax: 910-762-5820
Toll-Free:
Address: 929 N. Front St., Wilmington, NC 28401-3331 United States

STOCK TICKER/OTHER:

Stock Ticker: PPD
Employees: 23,000
Parent Company:

Exchange: NAS
Fiscal Year Ends: 12/31

SALARIES/BONUSES:

Top Exec. Salary: $ Bonus: $
Second Exec. Salary: $ Bonus: $

OTHER THOUGHTS:

Estimated Female Officers or Directors: 2
Hot Spot for Advancement for Women/Minorities:

Precision Optics Corporation

www.poci.com

NAIC Code: 334510

TYPES OF BUSINESS:

Endoscopic Equipment, Electromedical (e.g., Bronchoscopes, Colonoscopes, Cystoscopes), Manufacturing Optical Systems

BRANDS/DIVISIONS/AFFILIATES:

Ross Optical Industries Inc
Precise Medical Inc
Woods Precision Optics Corporation Limited
Microprecision

CONTACTS: *Note: Officers with more than one job title may be intentionally listed here more than once.*

Joseph Forkey, CEO
Jack Dreimiller, CFO
Richard Forkey, Director

GROWTH PLANS/SPECIAL FEATURES:

Precision Optics Corporation develops and manufactures advanced optical instruments. The firm's medical instrumentation line includes traditional endoscopes and endocouplers as well as custom imaging and illumination products for use in minimally invasive surgical procedures. Precision Optics' internal research and development programs develop next-generation capabilities for designing and manufacturing 3D endoscopes and very small Microprecision lenses, and its proprietary technology in these areas have allowed the company to commercialize them. Ross Optical Industries, Inc. is a division of Precision Optics that expands its optics components and assemblies business. All products supplied by Ross Optical include a custom or catalog optic, which is sourced through Ross' domestic and global network of optical fabrication companies. Most of Ross Optical systems make use of optical lenses, prisms, mirrors and windows and range from individual optical components to complex mechano-optical assemblies. More than 70% of Ross Optical's revenues are from customers in the U.S., with the rest coming from Europe and Canada. Other wholly-owned subsidiaries of Precision Optics Corporation include Precise Medical, Inc. and Wood's Precision Optics Corporation Limited.

FINANCIAL DATA: *Note: Data for latest year may not have been available at press time.*

In U.S. $	2020	2019	2018	2017	2016	2015
Revenue	9,923,355	6,804,169	4,038,048	3,154,547	3,916,702	3,912,060
R&D Expense	886,129	505,300	456,377	464,162	478,267	492,937
Operating Income	-1,422,983	-484,432	-348,619	-1,003,916	-1,088,141	-1,240,128
Operating Margin %		-.07%	-.09%	-.32%	-.28%	-.32%
SGA Expense	3,899,430	2,101,610	1,374,160	1,313,478	1,551,895	1,545,462
Net Income	-1,426,150	-614,871	-351,390	-1,006,457	-1,034,765	-1,178,793
Operating Cash Flow	-592,492	-1,031,693	100,657	-667,434	-876,298	-773,793
Capital Expenditure	160,292	146,850	21,637	34,931	8,602	73,390
EBITDA	-1,310,764	-573,989	-321,403	-968,741	-1,007,528	-1,218,857
Return on Assets %		-.12%	-.16%	-.51%	-.50%	-.61%
Return on Equity %		-.31%	-.63%	-1.76%	-1.65%	-1.68%
Debt to Equity		0.001	0.026	0.042	0.054	

CONTACT INFORMATION:

Phone: 978 630-1800   Fax: 978 630-1487
Toll-Free:
Address: 22 East Broadway, Gardner, MA 01440 United States

STOCK TICKER/OTHER:

Stock Ticker: PEYE   Exchange: PINX
Employees: 60   Fiscal Year Ends: 06/30
Parent Company:

SALARIES/BONUSES:

Top Exec. Salary: $ Bonus: $
Second Exec. Salary: $ Bonus: $

OTHER THOUGHTS:

Estimated Female Officers or Directors:
Hot Spot for Advancement for Women/Minorities:

Predictive Oncology Inc

www.precisiontherapeutics.com

NAIC Code: 334510

TYPES OF BUSINESS:

Electromedical and Electrotherapeutic Apparatus Manufacturing

BRANDS/DIVISIONS/AFFILIATES:

Helomics
TumorGenesis
Skyline
TruTumor
Oncology Discovery Technology Platform
STREAMWAY
Qualitative Medicine LLC

CONTACTS: *Note: Officers with more than one job title may be intentionally listed here more than once.*

Bob Myers, CFO
Carl Schwartz, Director
Thomas McGoldrick, Director

GROWTH PLANS/SPECIAL FEATURES:

Predictive Oncology, Inc. is a healthcare company that works with the pharmaceutical, diagnostic and biotech industries to develop highly customizable assessment methods for cancer patients. Predictive Oncology operates through four subsidiaries: Helomics, TumorGenesis, Skyline Medical and Skyline Europe. Helomics applies artificial intelligence (AI) to its data gathered from patient tumors to both personalize cancer therapies for patients and drive the development of new targeted therapies in collaborations with pharmaceutical companies. Helomics' CLIA-certified lab provides clinical testing that assists oncologists in individualizing patient treatment decisions, by providing an evidence-based roadmap for therapy. In addition to its proprietary precision oncology platform Helomics offers boutique contact research organization (CRO) services that leverage its TruTumor, patient-derived tumor models coupled to a wide range of multi-omics assays (genomics, proteomics and biochemical), and an AI-powered proprietary bioinformatics platform to provide a tailored solution to clients' specific needs. TumorGenesis is developing a rapid approach to growing tumors in the laboratory, which essentially fools cancer cells into thinking they are still growing inside a patient. Its proprietary Oncology Discovery Technology Platform kits will assist researchers and clinicians to identify which cancer cells bind to specific biomarkers. Once the biomarkers are identified, they can be used in TumorGenesis' oncology capture technology platforms, which isolate and help categorize an individual patient's heterogeneous tumor samples to enable the development of patient-specific treatment options. Helomics and TumorGenesis focus on ovarian cancer. Skyline Medical markets its patented and U.S. Food and Drug Administration (FDA) cleared STREAMWAY system, which automates the collection, measurement and disposal of waste fluid, including blood, irrigation fluid and others. In mid-2020, Predictive Oncology acquired Quantitative Medicine LLC, a biomedical analytics and computational biology company, in an all-stock transaction valued at approximately $1.8 million.

FINANCIAL DATA: *Note: Data for latest year may not have been available at press time.*

In U.S. $	2020	2019	2018	2017	2016	2015
Revenue	1,252,272	1,411,565	1,411,655			
R&D Expense						
Operating Income	-12,483,540	-13,774,490	-7,861,379			
Operating Margin %		-9.76%	-5.57%			
SGA Expense	10,936,910	11,694,120	6,996,149			
Net Income	-25,884,400	-19,390,770	-10,086,480			
Operating Cash Flow	-12,257,730	-8,732,451	-5,287,956			
Capital Expenditure	360,777	26,607	232,003			
EBITDA	-11,458,690	-13,069,610	-7,713,751			
Return on Assets %		-1.51%	-2.75%			
Return on Equity %		-3.50%	-7.37%			
Debt to Equity		0.024				

CONTACT INFORMATION:

Phone: 65389-4800   Fax:
Toll-Free:
Address: 2915 Commers Dr., Ste. 900, Eagan, MN 55121 United States

STOCK TICKER/OTHER:

Stock Ticker: POAI   Exchange: NAS
Employees: 23   Fiscal Year Ends: 12/31
Parent Company:

SALARIES/BONUSES:

Top Exec. Salary: $ Bonus: $
Second Exec. Salary: $ Bonus: $

OTHER THOUGHTS:

Estimated Female Officers or Directors:
Hot Spot for Advancement for Women/Minorities:

Premera Blue Cross

www.premera.com

NAIC Code: 524114

TYPES OF BUSINESS:

Insurance-Medical & Health, HMOs & PPOs
Dental Insurance
Long-Term Care Insurance

BRANDS/DIVISIONS/AFFILIATES:

Blue Cross Blue Shield Association
LifeWise Health Plan
LifeWise Assurance Company
Vivacity Care Center
Calypso Healthcare Solutions
Connexion Insurance Solutions

CONTACTS: Note: Officers with more than one job title may be intentionally listed here more than once.

Jeff Roe, CEO
Jim Messina, COO
Roki Chauhan, Chief Medical Officer
Brajesh Katare, CIO
John Pierce, General Counsel
Kirsten (Kacey) Kemp, Sr. VP-Oper.
Brian Ancell, Exec. VP-Strategic Dev. & Health Care Svcs.
Yoram (Yori) Milo, Chief Legal Public Policy Officer
Richard Maturi, Sr. VP-Health Care Delivery Systems
Jeff Roe, Sr. VP-Employer & Individual Markets

GROWTH PLANS/SPECIAL FEATURES:

Premera Blue Cross is a nonprofit Blue Cross Blue Shield Association licensed health insurance provider for Washington and Alaska. Through a network of thousands of doctors, healthcare providers and hospitals, the firm serves more than 2 million members. Premera health plans include preferred provider organization (PPO) plans, exclusive provider organization (EPO) plans, Medicare supplemental, indemnity coverage, dental and long-term care. Premera also offers a collection of products that allow business customers to tailor health plans with features from health maintenance organizations (HMOs), PPOs or managed indemnity plans. Employers then decide which doctor and hospital network to support along with options for out-of-network coverage, deductibles, co-pays and pharmacy benefits. The company's estimator tool provides patients with an estimate of out-of-pocket costs based on its specific benefits package. Services include programs focused on wellness and prevention, disease management and patient safety. These programs are delivered through health, life, vision, dental, stop-loss, disability, workforce wellness and other related products and services. Premera Blue Cross also works with members of the Premera family of companies, but are not licensees of the Blue Cross Blue Shield Association, and include LifeWise Health Plan of Oregon/Washington, LifeWise Assurance Company, Vivacity Care Center, Calypso Healthcare Solutions, Connexion Insurance Solutions, and Vivacity.

Premera offers its employees medical and dental coverage, life insurance, retirement programs, education and development programs, and an employee assistance program.

FINANCIAL DATA: Note: Data for latest year may not have been available at press time.

In U.S. $	2020	2019	2018	2017	2016	2015
Revenue	4,657,650,165	4,435,857,300	4,224,626,000	4,021,741,000	4,480,796,000	4,286,797,000
R&D Expense						
Operating Income						
Operating Margin %						
SGA Expense						
Net Income		246,020,250	234,305,000	526,808,000	69,873,000	-19,880,000
Operating Cash Flow						
Capital Expenditure						
EBITDA						
Return on Assets %						
Return on Equity %						
Debt to Equity						

CONTACT INFORMATION:

Phone: 425-918-4000   Fax:
Toll-Free: 800-722-1471
Address: 7001 220th SW, Bldg. 1, Mountlake Terrace, WA 98043 United States

STOCK TICKER/OTHER:

Stock Ticker: Nonprofit
Employees: 3,250
Parent Company: Blue Cross Blue Shield Association
Exchange:
Fiscal Year Ends: 12/31

SALARIES/BONUSES:

Top Exec. Salary: $ Bonus: $
Second Exec. Salary: $ Bonus: $

OTHER THOUGHTS:

Estimated Female Officers or Directors: 3
Hot Spot for Advancement for Women/Minorities: Y

Premier Inc

www.premierinc.com

NAIC Code: 531120

TYPES OF BUSINESS:

Management Services
Supply Chain Management
Health Care Consulting
Insurance Services
IT Services
Labor Performance Services

BRANDS/DIVISIONS/AFFILIATES:

PremierConnect
Health Design Plus LLC
Contigo Health LLC
Acurity Inc
Acurity LLC
Nexera Inc
Nexera LLC

CONTACTS: *Note: Officers with more than one job title may be intentionally listed here more than once.*

Susan DeVore, CEO
Craig McKasson, CFO
Richard Statuto, Chairman of the Board
Terry Shaw, Director
David Klatsky, General Counsel
Michael Alkire, President
Leigh Anderson, President, Divisional
David Hargraves, Senior VP, Divisional
Kelli Price, Senior VP, Divisional

GROWTH PLANS/SPECIAL FEATURES:

Premier, Inc. is primarily a medical supply chain management and healthcare consulting company. The firm is a member-owned healthcare alliance of hospitals, health systems and other healthcare organizations located in the U.S., as well as stockholders. Together with its subsidiaries and affiliates, Premier unites more than 4,100 U.S. hospitals and health systems and approximately 200,000 other providers and organizations in order to transform healthcare. It accomplishes this via integrated data and analytics, collaborative services, supply chain solutions and advisory services. Premier delivers a comprehensive technology-enabled platform that offers critical supply chain services, clinical, financial, operational and population health software-as-a-service (SaaS) informatics products, advisory services and performance improvement collaborative programs. The company operates through two business segments: supply chain services, which assists its group purchasing organization (GPO) members in managing their non-labor expense categories through a combination of products, services and technologies, serving acute and alternate sites, and direct sourcing activities; and performance services, which provides information technology analytics and workflow automation and advisory services. The firm's PremierConnect technology platform infrastructure allows members to analyze data through detailed standard and ad-hoc analyses, benchmarking, interactive dashboards, mobile access and custom report services. During 2020, Premier acquired 97% of Health Design Plus, LLC, which was renamed Contigo Health LLC and is part of the performance services segment; and acquired Acurity, Inc. and Nexera, Inc., which were wholly-owned subsidiaries of Greater New York Hospital Association, and were renamed Acurity LLC and Nexera LLC. Acurity is a regional group purchasing organization; and Nexera is a hospital financial improvement consulting firm.

Premier offers its employees medical, dental and vision coverage; business travel insurance; tuition reimbursement; flexible spending accounts; and an employee assistance program.

FINANCIAL DATA: *Note: Data for latest year may not have been available at press time.*

In U.S. $	2020	2019	2018	2017	2016	2015
Revenue	1,299,592,000	1,217,638,000	1,661,256,000	1,454,673,000	1,162,594,000	
R&D Expense	2,376,000	1,224,000	1,423,000	3,107,000	2,925,000	
Operating Income	373,620,000	368,514,000	539,630,000	317,720,000	265,948,000	
Operating Margin %		.30%	.32%	.22%	.23%	
SGA Expense	459,859,000	438,985,000	443,639,000	405,471,000	403,611,000	
Net Income	130,364,000	109,120,000	33,301,000	113,425,000	41,614,000	
Operating Cash Flow	349,524,000	505,339,000	507,706,000	392,247,000	371,470,000	
Capital Expenditure	94,397,000	93,385,000	92,680,000	71,372,000	76,990,000	
EBITDA	526,447,000	508,678,000	666,389,000	424,931,000	350,104,000	
Return on Assets %		.00%	.08%	.03%	.48%	
Return on Equity %						
Debt to Equity						

CONTACT INFORMATION:

Phone: 704-357-0022   Fax: 704-357-6611
Toll-Free: 877-777-1552
Address: 13034 Ballantyne Corporate Pl., Charlotte, NC 28277 United States

STOCK TICKER/OTHER:

Stock Ticker: PINC   Exchange: NAS
Employees: 2,500   Fiscal Year Ends: 06/30
Parent Company:

SALARIES/BONUSES:

Top Exec. Salary: $ Bonus: $
Second Exec. Salary: $ Bonus: $

OTHER THOUGHTS:

Estimated Female Officers or Directors: 5
Hot Spot for Advancement for Women/Minorities: Y

Prevail Therapeutics Inc

www.prevailtherapeutics.com

NAIC Code: 325414

TYPES OF BUSINESS:

Biological Product (except Diagnostic) Manufacturing

GROWTH PLANS/SPECIAL FEATURES:

Prevail Therapeutics, Inc. is a biotechnology company engaged in the research and development of novel gene therapies to treat Parkinson's disease and other neurodegenerative diseases. The firm applies precision medicine to the development of gene therapies to slow or stop disease progression. The U.S. Food and Drug Administration (FDA) declared the Investigational New Drug (IND) application associated with Prevail's lead program, PR001, for the treatment of patients with Parkinson's disease with GBA1 mutations (PD-GBA) and neuronopathic (Type 2 or Type 3) Gaucher disease as open. Prevail's pipeline also includes programs aimed at the treatment of frontotemporal dementia with GRN mutation and synucleinopathies. Other pipeline programs include: PR006, for the treatment of frontotemporal dementia with GRN mutations; and PR004, for the treatment of synucleinopathies.

BRANDS/DIVISIONS/AFFILIATES:

PR001
PR006
PR004

CONTACTS: *Note: Officers with more than one job title may be intentionally listed here more than once.*

Asa Abeliovich, CEO
Brett Kaplan, CFO
Francois Nader, Chairman of the Board
Jeffrey Sevigny, Chief Medical Officer
Yong Dai, Chief Technology Officer
Franz Hefti, Other Executive Officer
Emily Minkow, Other Executive Officer

FINANCIAL DATA: *Note: Data for latest year may not have been available at press time.*

In U.S. $	2020	2019	2018	2017	2016	2015
Revenue						
R&D Expense						
Operating Income						
Operating Margin %						
SGA Expense						
Net Income		-63,188,000	-19,087,540			
Operating Cash Flow						
Capital Expenditure						
EBITDA						
Return on Assets %						
Return on Equity %						
Debt to Equity						

CONTACT INFORMATION:

Phone: 917 336-9310   Fax:
Toll-Free:
Address: 430 East 29th St., Ste. 1520, New York, NY 10016 United States

STOCK TICKER/OTHER:

Stock Ticker: PRVL
Employees: 55
Parent Company:

Exchange: NAS
Fiscal Year Ends: 12/31

SALARIES/BONUSES:

Top Exec. Salary: $ Bonus: $
Second Exec. Salary: $ Bonus: $

OTHER THOUGHTS:

Estimated Female Officers or Directors:
Hot Spot for Advancement for Women/Minorities:

Prime Healthcare Services Inc
www.primehealthcare.com

NAIC Code: 622110

TYPES OF BUSINESS:
General Medical and Surgical Hospitals

BRANDS/DIVISIONS/AFFILIATES:
Prime A Investments LLC
Prime Healthcare Foundation (The)
St Francis Medical Center

CONTACTS: *Note: Officers with more than one job title may be intentionally listed here more than once.*
Prem Reddy, CEO
Luis Leon, COO
Steve Aleman, CFO
Elizabeth Nikels, VP-Mktg. & Communications
Arti Dhuper, VP-Human Resources
Raghu Chennareddy, CTO
Prem Reddy, Chmn.

GROWTH PLANS/SPECIAL FEATURES:
Prime Healthcare Services, Inc. owns and operates 46 acute care hospitals and more than 300 outpatient locations in 14 U.S. states. Of the 45 hospitals, 15 are not-for-profit. The firm's hospitals provide a full range of both inpatient and outpatient services, including general acute care, emergency room, general and specialty surgery, intensive/critical care, obstetrics, behavioral health, rehabilitation and diagnostic services. Prime Healthcare is the largest for-profit operator of hospitals in the state of California, based on the number of facilities, and is one of the Top 5 largest for-profit hospital systems in the nation. The firm is a physician-founded and physician-driven health system with doctors and clinicians leading the organization at every level. The majority of Prime Healthcare's hospitals have contractual agreements with the major managed care providers: Aetna, Blue Cross, Health Net and United Healthcare. The Prime Healthcare Foundation, a 501(c)3 public charity, is dedicated to improving access to health care and increasing educational opportunities in health care. The foundation owns and operates 15 hospitals in California, Texas, Ohio, Pennsylvania, Georgia and Rhode Island. Many of these were acquired in or near bankruptcy and donated to the Foundation debt-free. Prime Healthcare is a subsidiary of Prime A. Investments, LLC., which owns and operates real estate properties. In August 2020, Prime Healthcare acquired St. Francis Medical Center in Lynwood, California, its 46th hospital and 16th in California.

FINANCIAL DATA: *Note: Data for latest year may not have been available at press time.*

In U.S. $	2020	2019	2018	2017	2016	2015
Revenue	3,992,612,912	4,297,753,404	4,089,204,000	4,232,340,000	4,028,093,000	
R&D Expense						
Operating Income						
Operating Margin %						
SGA Expense						
Net Income			114,783,000	-18,236,000	-259,716,000	
Operating Cash Flow						
Capital Expenditure						
EBITDA						
Return on Assets %						
Return on Equity %						
Debt to Equity						

CONTACT INFORMATION:
Phone: 909-235-4400   Fax:
Toll-Free:
Address: 3480 E. Guasti Rd., Ontario, CA 91761 United States

STOCK TICKER/OTHER:
Stock Ticker: Nonprofit   Exchange:
Employees: 40,000   Fiscal Year Ends:
Parent Company: Prime A Investments LLC

SALARIES/BONUSES:
Top Exec. Salary: $ Bonus: $
Second Exec. Salary: $ Bonus: $

OTHER THOUGHTS:
Estimated Female Officers or Directors:
Hot Spot for Advancement for Women/Minorities:

Profarma Distribuidora de Produtos Farmaceuticos SA

www.profarma.com.br

NAIC Code: 424210

TYPES OF BUSINESS:

Wholesale Pharmaceuticals Distribution
Health Care & Cosmetics Distribution

BRANDS/DIVISIONS/AFFILIATES:

Profarma Specialty
Drogasmil
Farmalife
Drogarias Tamoio
Drogaria Rosario

CONTACTS: Note: Officers with more than one job title may be intentionally listed here more than once.

Sammy Birmarcker, CEO
Manoel Birmarcker, VP

GROWTH PLANS/SPECIAL FEATURES:

Profarma Distribuidora de Produtos Farmaceuticos SA is among the largest wholesale distributors of pharmaceutical products in Brazil. The company distributes medicines, personal care products and cosmetics to approximately 40,000 drugstores in 3,800 cities, reaching nearly all of the Brazilian market. Profarma'a delivery network includes 11 distribution centers in Alagoas, Bahia, Espirito Santo, Goias, Minas Gerais, Paraiba, Parana, Pernambuco, Rio de Janeiro, Rio Grande do Sul and Sao Paulo. In many of Brazil's major cities, orders can be delivered in a matter of hours and most shipments arrive within one day. Profarma maintains an electronic ordering system to facilitate transactions and order tracking. The company operates through three segments: pharma distribution, specialties and retail. Pharma distribution derives approximately 70% of sales revenue and comprises the wholesale operations, selling medicines and health and beauty products to pharmaceutical retailers. Specialties derives 15% of sales revenue and comprises Profarma's hospital, dermatological products, vaccines and special medications through joint venture, Profarma Specialty. Retail derives approximately 15% of sales revenue and comprises the Drogasmil, Farmalife, Drogarias Tamoio and Drogaria Rosario retail chains, which together have approximately 300 stores throughout midwestern Brazil.

FINANCIAL DATA: Note: Data for latest year may not have been available at press time.

In U.S. $	2020	2019	2018	2017	2016	2015
Revenue	1,218,160,000	1,333,699,500	1,270,190,000	1,443,000,000	1,302,987,332	1,073,391,133
R&D Expense						
Operating Income						
Operating Margin %						
SGA Expense						
Net Income	146,805,000	182,434,000	-2,498,200	-34,006,400	-15,631,386	-6,762,967
Operating Cash Flow						
Capital Expenditure						
EBITDA						
Return on Assets %						
Return on Equity %						
Debt to Equity						

CONTACT INFORMATION:

Phone: 55-21-4009-0200   Fax: 55-21-2491-4082
Toll-Free:
Address: Av. Ayrton Senna, 2150 Bl. P, 3/Fl, Rio de Janeiro, RJ 22775-900 Brazil

STOCK TICKER/OTHER:

Stock Ticker: PFRM3
Employees: 2,700
Parent Company:

Exchange: Sao Paulo
Fiscal Year Ends: 12/31

SALARIES/BONUSES:

Top Exec. Salary: $ Bonus: $
Second Exec. Salary: $ Bonus: $

OTHER THOUGHTS:

Estimated Female Officers or Directors:
Hot Spot for Advancement for Women/Minorities:

ProMedica Senior Care

promedicaseniorcare.org

NAIC Code: 623110

TYPES OF BUSINESS:

Nursing Care Facilities
Home Health Care
Short-Term Care Facilities
Assisted Living Facilities
Rehabilitation Clinics

BRANDS/DIVISIONS/AFFILIATES:

ProMedica
Welltower Inc
ProMedica Senior Care
HCR ManorCare
Arden Courts
Heartland

GROWTH PLANS/SPECIAL FEATURES:

ProMedica Senior Care is a division of non-profit hospital system ProMedica. ProMedica Senior Care operates in more than 25 states across the U.S., offering skilled nursing, assisted living, home health care and hospice care. Other services include rehabilitation, memory care, independent living, home health care, palliative care and more. ProMedica Senior Care is a joint venture company between ProMedica and Welltower, Inc. Parent ProMedica operates three businesses: providers and acute care, health plan and senior care. In October 2020, ProMedica announced plans to move its HCR ManorCare, Arden Courts and Heartland facilities under the ProMedica Senior Care moniker over the next 18 months.

CONTACTS: *Note: Officers with more than one job title may be intentionally listed here more than once.*

Randy Oostra, CEO-Corporate
Spencer C. Moler, Principal Acct. Officer

FINANCIAL DATA: *Note: Data for latest year may not have been available at press time.*

In U.S. $	2020	2019	2018	2017	2016	2015
Revenue	3,441,850,000	3,623,000,000	3,515,000,000	3,700,000,000	5,250,000,000	5,300,000,000
R&D Expense						
Operating Income						
Operating Margin %						
SGA Expense						
Net Income						
Operating Cash Flow						
Capital Expenditure						
EBITDA						
Return on Assets %						
Return on Equity %						
Debt to Equity						

CONTACT INFORMATION:

Phone: 419-252-5500   Fax: 419-252-6404
Toll-Free:
Address: 333 N. Summit St., Toledo, OH 43604 United States

STOCK TICKER/OTHER:

Stock Ticker: Joint Venture   Exchange:
Employees: 55,000   Fiscal Year Ends: 12/31
Parent Company:

SALARIES/BONUSES:

Top Exec. Salary: $ Bonus: $
Second Exec. Salary: $ Bonus: $

OTHER THOUGHTS:

Estimated Female Officers or Directors:
Hot Spot for Advancement for Women/Minorities:

Protech Home Medical Corp

www.protechhomemedical.com

NAIC Code: 621999

TYPES OF BUSINESS:
In-Home Patient Monitoring

BRANDS/DIVISIONS/AFFILIATES:
Coastal Med Tech
Central Oxygen
Care Medical
Black Bear Medical
Acadia Medical Supply
West Home Healthcare
Riverside Medical
Resource Medical Group

CONTACTS: *Note: Officers with more than one job title may be intentionally listed here more than once.*
Casey Hoyt, CEO
Allan Wallander, CFO
Michael Dalsin, Chairman of the Board
Roger Greene, Director
W. Zehnder, Other Corporate Officer
Brett Stoute, Other Executive Officer
Mike Moore, President

GROWTH PLANS/SPECIAL FEATURES:
Protech Home Medical Corp. is a healthcare services company with operations in the U.S. Protech provides in-home monitoring and disease management services for patients. The firm's in-home monitoring equipment, supplies and services are primarily offered to patients who take prescription blood thinners such as Coumadin (warfarin). Other products and services include oxygen therapy, international normalized ratio (INR) self-testing, daily and ambulatory aids, power mobility options, home ventilation, respiratory equipment rental, oxygen therapy, sleep apnea and PAP (positive airway pressure) treatments. Protech seeks to expand its offerings in regards to the management of several chronic disease states, with a focus on patients with heart or pulmonary disease, sleep disorders, reduced mobility and other chronic health conditions. The company actively works to integrate cutting-edge technology and distribution platforms to streamline its healthcare services with the industry, and utilizes technology to improve its home medical equipment. Brands of Protech include Coastal Med Tech, Central Oxygen, Care Medical, Black Bear Medical, Acadia Medical Supply, West Home Healthcare, Riverside Medical, Resource Medical Group, Patient Aids, Legacy Oxygen, Health Technology Resources, and Cooley Medical. In September 2020, Protech announced that it executed a non-binding letter of intent to acquire an arm's length private respiratory care company in the southeastern U.S., which would enhance Protech's presence in the southeast with five new locations and increase its active patient count by over 15,000.

FINANCIAL DATA: *Note: Data for latest year may not have been available at press time.*

In U.S. $	2020	2019	2018	2017	2016	2015
Revenue		60,829,420	57,746,140	58,177,040	105,635,928	54,733,352
R&D Expense						
Operating Income						
Operating Margin %						
SGA Expense						
Net Income		-5,549,002	14,084,369	-18,099,336	-57,222,620	-18,777,862
Operating Cash Flow						
Capital Expenditure						
EBITDA						
Return on Assets %						
Return on Equity %						
Debt to Equity						

CONTACT INFORMATION:
Phone: 859-300-6455   Fax:
Toll-Free:
Address: 1019 Town Dr., Wilder, KY 41076 United States

STOCK TICKER/OTHER:
Stock Ticker: PTQQF   Exchange: PINX
Employees: 47   Fiscal Year Ends: 09/30
Parent Company:

SALARIES/BONUSES:
Top Exec. Salary: $ Bonus: $
Second Exec. Salary: $ Bonus: $

OTHER THOUGHTS:
Estimated Female Officers or Directors:
Hot Spot for Advancement for Women/Minorities:

Providence

www.providence.org

NAIC Code: 622110

TYPES OF BUSINESS:

General Medical and Surgical Hospitals
Assisted Living Facilities
Low Income Living Facilities
Counseling

BRANDS/DIVISIONS/AFFILIATES:

Providence
St. Joseph Health
Covenant Health
Facey Medical Foundation
Hoag Memorial Presbyterian
Kadlec
Pacific Medical Centers
Civica Rx

CONTACTS: *Note: Officers with more than one job title may be intentionally listed here more than once.*

Rod Hochman, CEO
Jo Ann Escasa-Haigh, CFO
Myron Berdischewsky, Chief Medical & Quality Officer
Cindy Strauss, Sr. VP
David Brown, VP-Strategy & Bus. Dev.
Deborah Burton, VP
Jack Friedman, Sr. VP-Accountable Care & Payor Relations
Joel Gilbertson, VP-Gov't. & Public Affairs
John O. Mudd, Sr. VP-Mission leadership
Dave Hunter, VP-Supply Chain Mgmt.

GROWTH PLANS/SPECIAL FEATURES:

Providence (formerly Providence St. Joseph Health) comprises 51 hospitals, 1,085 clinics, 25,000 physicians, supportive housing facilities and 120,000 caregivers with the goal of improving the health of the communities it serves, especially the poor and the vulnerable. The faith-based firm provides a comprehensive range of services across Alaska, California, Montana, New Mexico, Oregon, Texas and Washington. The Providence family includes: Providence (Alaska, Washington, Montana, Oregon and California), St. Joseph Health (northern California), Covenant Health (west Texas), Facey Medical Group (Los Angeles, California), Hoag Memorial Presbyterian (Orange County, California), Kadlec (southeast Washington), Pacific Medical Centers (Seattle, Washington), as well as Swedish Health Services (Seattle, Washington). The company established integrates mental health care into its primary care clinics to provide effective mental health services for those who struggle with mental health stigmatization, diagnosis and treatment. The funds derived by the foundation support research and startup operations regarding mental health awareness, diagnosis and treatment. Providence partnered with six other health organizations to create Civica Rx, a not-for-profit generic drug and pharmaceutical company founded in 2018 to combat life-saving drug shortages and affordability. In late-2019, Providence St. Joseph Health changed its name to just Providence while retaining the St. Joseph Health cross logo. The name change will span up to three years and begin in southern California.

FINANCIAL DATA: *Note: Data for latest year may not have been available at press time.*

In U.S. $	2020	2019	2018	2017	2016	2015
Revenue	25,675,000,000	25,025,000,000	24,428,000,000	23,163,000,000	18,878,000,000	14,434,000,000
R&D Expense						
Operating Income						
Operating Margin %						
SGA Expense						
Net Income	740,000,000	1,358,000,000	-445,000,000	780,000,000	5,231,000,000	77,000,000
Operating Cash Flow						
Capital Expenditure						
EBITDA						
Return on Assets %						
Return on Equity %						
Debt to Equity						

CONTACT INFORMATION:

Phone: 425-525-3355   Fax:
Toll-Free:
Address: 1801 Lind Avenue SW, Renton, WA 98057 United States

STOCK TICKER/OTHER:

Stock Ticker: Nonprofit   Exchange:
Employees: 120,000   Fiscal Year Ends: 12/31
Parent Company:

SALARIES/BONUSES:

Top Exec. Salary: $ Bonus: $
Second Exec. Salary: $ Bonus: $

OTHER THOUGHTS:

Estimated Female Officers or Directors: 5
Hot Spot for Advancement for Women/Minorities: Y

Quest Diagnostics Incorporated

NAIC Code: 621511

www.questdiagnostics.com

TYPES OF BUSINESS:

Services-Testing & Diagnostics
Clinical Laboratory Testing
Clinical Trials Testing
Esoteric Testing Laboratories

BRANDS/DIVISIONS/AFFILIATES:

Quanum
Mid America Clinical Laboratories

CONTACTS: Note: Officers with more than one job title may be intentionally listed here more than once.

Stephen Rusckowski, CEO
Mark Guinan, CFO
Michael Deppe, Chief Accounting Officer
James Davis, Executive VP, Divisional
Michael Prevoznik, General Counsel
Catherine Doherty, Other Corporate Officer
Everett Cunningham, Senior VP, Divisional
Carrie Eglinton Manner, Senior VP, Divisional

GROWTH PLANS/SPECIAL FEATURES:

Quest Diagnostics Incorporated is a world-leading provider of diagnostic information services. The firm's diagnostic insights reveal new avenues to identify and treat disease, inspire healthy behaviors and improve health care management. Diagnostic testing services range from routine blood tests (such as total cholesterol, Pap testing and white blood cell count) to complex, gene-based and molecular testing. These tests are grouped into two categories: general diagnostics, consisting of routine and non-routine testing; and advanced diagnostics, consisting of genetic and advanced molecular testing. These services enable healthcare partners to deliver health care more efficiently, and help support population health via data analytics and extended care services. Quest Diagnostics is also a global clinical trials laboratory services organization that helps biopharmaceutical, medical device and diagnostics customers improve human health through innovation that transforms science and data into medical insights. Quest Diagnostics offers healthcare information technology (IT) solutions, including its Quanum suite of technology and analytics solutions so that physicians can order lab tests, receive test results, share clinical information quickly and securely, and prescribe drugs. Employer solutions include pre-employment drugs-of-abuse screening, and risk assessment services based on health and wellness laboratory testing. Based in New Jersey, Quest Diagnostics' laboratories, patient service centers, offices and other facilities are located throughout the U.S., as well as select locations outside the U.S. During 2020, Quest Diagnostics wholly-acquired Mid America Clinical Laboratories, a leading independent clinical laboratory provider in Indiana. In June 2021, Quest acquired the outreach laboratory business of Mercy in an all-cash transaction.

FINANCIAL DATA: Note: Data for latest year may not have been available at press time.

In U.S. $	2020	2019	2018	2017	2016	2015
Revenue	9,437,000,000	7,726,000,000	7,531,000,000	7,709,000,000	7,515,000,000	7,493,000,000
R&D Expense						
Operating Income	1,971,000,000	1,231,000,000	1,105,000,000	1,165,000,000	1,159,000,000	1,065,000,000
Operating Margin %		.16%	.15%	.15%	.15%	.14%
SGA Expense	1,550,000,000	1,457,000,000	1,424,000,000	1,750,000,000	1,681,000,000	1,679,000,000
Net Income	1,431,000,000	858,000,000	736,000,000	772,000,000	645,000,000	709,000,000
Operating Cash Flow	2,005,000,000	1,243,000,000	1,200,000,000	1,175,000,000	1,069,000,000	810,000,000
Capital Expenditure	418,000,000	400,000,000	383,000,000	252,000,000	293,000,000	263,000,000
EBITDA	2,411,000,000	1,585,000,000	1,404,000,000	1,453,000,000	1,479,000,000	1,561,000,000
Return on Assets %		.07%	.07%	.07%	.06%	.07%
Return on Equity %		.16%	.14%	.16%	.14%	.16%
Debt to Equity		0.776	0.657	0.762	0.806	0.746

CONTACT INFORMATION:

Phone: 973 520-2700   Fax:
Toll-Free: 800-222-0446
Address: 500 Plaza Dr., Secaucus, NJ 07094 United States

STOCK TICKER/OTHER:

Stock Ticker: DGX
Employees: 47,000
Parent Company:

Exchange: NYS
Fiscal Year Ends: 12/31

SALARIES/BONUSES:

Top Exec. Salary: $ Bonus: $
Second Exec. Salary: $ Bonus: $

OTHER THOUGHTS:

Estimated Female Officers or Directors: 3
Hot Spot for Advancement for Women/Minorities: Y

Sales, profits and employees may be estimates. Financial information, benefits and other data can change quickly and may vary from those stated here.

Quidel Corporation

www.quidel.com

NAIC Code: 325413

TYPES OF BUSINESS:

Rapid Diagnosis Products
Point-of-Care Diagnostic Tests
Research Products

BRANDS/DIVISIONS/AFFILIATES:

Sofia
QuickVue
InflammaDry
Triage
AmpliVue
Solana
Lyra
Savanna

CONTACTS: *Note: Officers with more than one job title may be intentionally listed here more than once.*

Douglas Bryant, CEO
Randall Steward, CFO
Kenneth Buechler, Chairman of the Board
Robert Bujarski, General Counsel
Karen Gibson, Senior VP, Divisional
Werner Kroll, Senior VP, Divisional
Michael Abney, Senior VP, Divisional
Edward Russell, Senior VP, Divisional
Ratan Borkar, Senior VP, Divisional

GROWTH PLANS/SPECIAL FEATURES:

Quidel Corporation develops, manufactures and markets rapid diagnostic testing solutions, which are separated into four product categories: rapid immunoassay, cardiac immunoassay, specialized diagnostic solutions and molecular diagnostic solutions. Rapid immunoassay products include: Sofia and Sofia 2 analyzers, which combine software and fluorescent immunoassay (FIA) tests to yield an automatic, objective result that is readily available on the instrument's screen, in a hard-copy printout and in a transmissible electronic form that can network via lab information system to healthcare databases; QuickVue, which are rapid, visually-read, lateral flow immunoassay products that diagnose a wide variety of infectious diseases and medical conditions; and InflammaDry and AdenoPlus rapid, lateral-flow based point-of-care products for the detection of infectious and inflammatory diseases and conditions of the eye. Cardiac immunoassay products include: Triage MeterPro, a portable testing platform that runs a comprehensive menu of tests concerning diseases, health conditions and the detection of certain drugs of abuse; Triage BNP test for use on Beckman Coulter lab analyzers; and urine-specific screening tests for the detection of drug and/or urinary metabolites for multiple drug classes. Specialized diagnostic solutions include a variety of cell lines, specimen collection devices, media and controls for use in laboratories that culture and test for many human viruses; and specialty biomarker products for bone health. Molecular diagnostic solutions include: AmpliVue, a hand-held molecular diagnostic assay platform; Solana, an amplification and detection system able to run up to 12 assays at once; Lyra, an open system molecular assay; and Savanna, a low-cost, fully integrated system that can run either PCR or HAD assays from multiple sample types. In October 2020, the U.S. Food and Drug Administration issued emergency use authorization (EUA) to Quidel to market its Sofia 2 Flu + SARS Antigen FIA test to detect nucleocapsid protein antigens from SARS-CoV-2, influenza A and B.

FINANCIAL DATA: *Note: Data for latest year may not have been available at press time.*

In U.S. $	2020	2019	2018	2017	2016	2015
Revenue	1,661,668,000	534,890,000	522,285,000	277,743,000	191,603,000	196,129,000
R&D Expense	84,292,000	52,553,000	51,649,000	33,644,000	38,672,000	35,514,000
Operating Income	1,064,020,000	104,383,000	110,126,000	26,058,000	-4,439,000	2,738,000
Operating Margin %		.20%	.21%	.09%	- .02%	.01%
SGA Expense	200,543,000	163,869,000	153,938,000	96,440,000	74,883,000	77,333,000
Net Income	810,287,000	72,921,000	74,183,000	-8,165,000	-13,808,000	-6,079,000
Operating Cash Flow	629,763,000	134,485,000	136,345,000	27,709,000	11,815,000	36,309,000
Capital Expenditure	64,927,000	27,229,000	31,689,000	17,510,000	11,909,000	17,032,000
EBITDA	1,099,031,000	143,759,000	133,933,000	40,314,000	18,357,000	26,124,000
Return on Assets %		.08%	.09%	- .01%	- .03%	- .01%
Return on Equity %		.15%	.23%	- .04%	- .07%	- .03%
Debt to Equity		0.167	0.125	1.661	0.739	0.674

CONTACT INFORMATION:

Phone: 858 552-1100   Fax:
Toll-Free: 800-874-1517
Address: 9975 Summers Ridge Rd., San Diego, CA 92121 United States

STOCK TICKER/OTHER:

Stock Ticker: QDEL   Exchange: NAS
Employees: 1,250   Fiscal Year Ends: 12/31
Parent Company:

SALARIES/BONUSES:

Top Exec. Salary: $ Bonus: $
Second Exec. Salary: $ Bonus: $

OTHER THOUGHTS:

Estimated Female Officers or Directors: 1
Hot Spot for Advancement for Women/Minorities:

RadNet Inc

www.radnet.com

NAIC Code: 621512

TYPES OF BUSINESS:

Diagnostic Imaging Centers
Medical Imaging Centers

BRANDS/DIVISIONS/AFFILIATES:

RadNet Management Inc
Beverly Radiology Medical Group III
Nulogix Inc
Whiterabbit.ai
DeepHealth Inc

CONTACTS: *Note: Officers with more than one job title may be intentionally listed here more than once.*

Howard Berger, CEO
Mark Stolper, CFO
Norman Hames, COO, Divisional
Stephen Forthuber, COO, Divisional
John Crues, Director
Mital Patel, Executive VP, Divisional
Michael Murdock, Executive VP

GROWTH PLANS/SPECIAL FEATURES:

RadNet, Inc. operates a network of more than 330 diagnostic imaging centers in six states. These centers, which are located in California, Maryland, Florida, Delaware, New Jersey and New York, perform millions of procedures annually and specialize in medical imaging services and general diagnostic radiology. The facilities are usually located near RadNet's multi-modality sites to help accommodate overflow in target demographic areas. Some of the firm's most common imaging procedures are X-ray, fluoroscopy, endoscopy and modalities such as CT scans and digital image processing. The centers also offer open MRI, allowing studies with patients not typically compatible with conventional MRI, such as pediatric, claustrophobic or obese patients. Patients are generally referred to the centers by their treating physicians and may be affiliated with an independent physician association (IPA), health maintenance organization (HMO), preferred provider organization (PPO) or similar organization. RadNet Management, Inc. manages the centers. It supplies the equipment as well as non-medical operational, management, financial and administrative services for the centers, with the medical services provided by affiliates such as Beverly Radiology Medical Group III (BRMG). The company derives most of its revenues from commercial insurance payers (56%, as of fiscal 2019-20), 11% from managed care capitated payers, 21% from Medicare and 2% from Medicaid. In addition, RadNet has recently began investing in the field of artificial intelligence (AI), with the acquisition of Nulogix, Inc, Whiterabbit.ai to use AI and other technologies to create new solutions for breast cancer imaging. For example, the company's AI methods are being employed to aid radiologists in scan interpretation by quickly allowing comparison to large imaging databases to enable pinpoint diagnosis within very short time frames. During 2020, RadNet acquired DeepHealth, Inc., which develops solutions in machine learning and artificial intelligence (AI) to assist radiologists in interpreting images and improving patient care.

FINANCIAL DATA: *Note: Data for latest year may not have been available at press time.*

In U.S. $	2020	2019	2018	2017	2016	2015
Revenue	1,071,840,000	1,154,179,000	975,146,000	922,186,000	884,535,000	809,628,000
R&D Expense						
Operating Income	45,407,000	73,880,000	34,700,000	53,013,000	42,124,000	40,728,000
Operating Margin %		.06%	.04%	.06%	.05%	.05%
SGA Expense						
Net Income	-14,840,000	14,756,000	32,243,000	53,000	7,230,000	7,709,000
Operating Cash Flow	233,759,000	104,322,000	116,754,000	142,225,000	91,641,000	67,037,000
Capital Expenditure	125,437,000	101,303,000	145,372,000	88,948,000	65,892,000	133,756,000
EBITDA	199,738,000	225,162,000	154,882,000	133,804,000	122,501,000	116,940,000
Return on Assets %		.01%	.03%	.00%	.01%	.01%
Return on Equity %		.11%	.34%	.00%	.18%	.41%
Debt to Equity		7.10	4.977	9.341	12.626	18.652

CONTACT INFORMATION:

Phone: 310 478-7808   Fax: 310 478-5810
Toll-Free:
Address: 1510 Cotner Ave., Los Angeles, CA 90025 United States

STOCK TICKER/OTHER:

Stock Ticker: RDNT   Exchange: NAS
Employees: 8,327   Fiscal Year Ends: 12/31
Parent Company:

SALARIES/BONUSES:

Top Exec. Salary: $ Bonus: $
Second Exec. Salary: $ Bonus: $

OTHER THOUGHTS:

Estimated Female Officers or Directors:
Hot Spot for Advancement for Women/Minorities:

Ramsay Health Care Limited

www.ramsayhealth.com

NAIC Code: 622110

TYPES OF BUSINESS:

General Medical and Surgical Hospitals

BRANDS/DIVISIONS/AFFILIATES:

Ramsay Australia
Ramsay Generale de Sante
Ramsay UK
Ramsay Sime Darby

CONTACTS: *Note: Officers with more than one job title may be intentionally listed here more than once.*

Craig R. McNally, Managing Dir.
Martyn Roberts, CFO
John D. C. OGrady, General Counsel
Paul Fitzmaurice, Dir.-Oper.
Craig McNally, Dir.-Global Strategy & European Oper.
Bruce Soden, Dir.-Finance
Danny Sims, Dir.-Hospital Oper., Australia & Indonesia
Jill Watts, Dir.-U.K. Oper.
Michael S Siddle, Deputy Chmn.
Michael S. Siddle, Chmn.
Damien Michon, Dir.-French Oper.

GROWTH PLANS/SPECIAL FEATURES:

Ramsay Health Care Limited is a global healthcare company operating 480 facilities across 11 countries. Ramsay Health caters to a broad range of healthcare needs, from day surgery procedures to highly complex surgery as well as psychiatric care and rehabilitation. The company employs over 77,000 staff and treats 8.5 million patients each year in its hospitals and primary care clinics located in Australia, France, the U.K., Sweden, Norway, Denmark, Germany, Italy, Malaysia, Indonesia and Hong Kong. Ramsay Health's businesses consists of four groups: Ramsay Australia, Ramsay Generale de Sante, Ramsay U.K. and Ramsay Sime Darby. Ramsay Australia encompasses 72 hospitals and day surgery units, admitting more than 1.1 million patients each year. This division also includes Ramsay Pharmacy franchises, which are full-service pharmacies that provide the continuum of care for Ramsay Health Care patients. Pharmacy services span medication management and advice programs, home medication reviews, dose administration aids, blood glucose testing and diabetes support programs, cholesterol testing and support programs, chronic pain management and support programs, post discharge services and support, maternal child health nurse consultations and Allied Health consultations and services. Ramsay Generale de Sante is a French subsidiary of Ramsay Health Care, operating hospitals, specialist clinics and primary care units at approximately 300 locations across six European countries. Ramsay U.K. provides independent hospital services in England, with a network of 34 acute hospitals and day procedure centers to private and self-insured patients as well as to patients referred by the National Health System. Last, Ramsay Sime Darby owns and operates eight facilities in Asia through a joint venture arrangement with Malaysian multinational conglomerate Sime Darby Berhad. These facilities include three hospitals in Indonesia, three hospitals and a nursing college in Malaysia, and one day surgery center in Hong Kong.

Ramsay Health offers select benefits subject to location.

FINANCIAL DATA: *Note: Data for latest year may not have been available at press time.*

In U.S. $	2020	2019	2018	2017	2016	2015
Revenue	9,254,960,000	8,929,189,000	7,086,276,000	6,722,178,000	6,707,010,000	5,676,944,000
R&D Expense						
Operating Income	333,271,000	729,309,800	536,069,200	644,840,300	618,355,400	550,167,100
Operating Margin %		.08%	.08%	.10%	.09%	.10%
SGA Expense	5,872,612,000	5,561,939,000	4,390,014,000	4,038,683,000	4,006,317,000	3,363,793,000
Net Income	220,267,600	423,063,400	301,198,800	379,222,400	349,245,900	299,022,500
Operating Cash Flow						
Capital Expenditure	527,866,600	460,539,900	367,506,300	333,856,600	395,755,600	377,070,100
EBITDA	1,198,131,000	1,164,012,000	861,056,900	970,460,100	940,085,700	828,002,000
Return on Assets %		.05%	.04%	.06%	.06%	.06%
Return on Equity %		.22%	.16%	.22%	.23%	.21%
Debt to Equity		2.157	1.634	1.433	1.645	1.465

CONTACT INFORMATION:

Phone: 61-2-9220 1000   Fax: 61-2-9220 1001
Toll-Free:
Address: Level 18, 126 Phillip St., Sydney, NSW 2000 Australia

STOCK TICKER/OTHER:

Stock Ticker: RMSYF
Employees: 80,000
Parent Company:

Exchange: PINX
Fiscal Year Ends: 06/30

SALARIES/BONUSES:

Top Exec. Salary: $ Bonus: $
Second Exec. Salary: $ Bonus: $

OTHER THOUGHTS:

Estimated Female Officers or Directors: 1
Hot Spot for Advancement for Women/Minorities:

Regeneron Pharmaceuticals Inc

www.regeneron.com

NAIC Code: 325412

TYPES OF BUSINESS:

Drugs-Diversified
Protein-Based Drugs
Small-Molecule Drugs
Genetics & Transgenic Mouse Technologies

BRANDS/DIVISIONS/AFFILIATES:

Arcalyst
Praluent
EYLEA
Dupixent
ZALTRAP
VelociGene
VelociMouse
VelocImmune

CONTACTS: Note: Officers with more than one job title may be intentionally listed here more than once.

Leonard Schleifer, CEO
Robert Landry, CFO
P. Vagelos, Chairman of the Board
Christopher Fenimore, Chief Accounting Officer
George Yancopoulos, Chief Scientific Officer
Neil Stahl, Executive VP, Divisional
Joseph Larosa, Executive VP
Daniel Van Plew, Executive VP
Marion McCourt, Senior VP, Divisional

GROWTH PLANS/SPECIAL FEATURES:

Regeneron Pharmaceuticals, Inc. is a biopharmaceutical company that discovers, develops, manufactures and commercializes pharmaceutical drugs. The company's commercialized medicines and product candidates in development are designed to help patients with eye diseases, allergic and inflammatory diseases, cancer, cardiovascular and metabolic diseases, neuromuscular diseases, infectious diseases and rare diseases. Regeneron's marketed-approved products include: Arcalyst (rilonacept), a therapy for cryopyrin-associated periodic syndromes (CAPS), a rare, inherited inflammatory condition; Praluent (alirocumab) injection, an adjunct to diet and maximally-tolerated statin therapy for adults who require additional lowering of LDL cholesterol; EYLEA (aflibercept), an injection treatment for neovascular age-related macular degeneration patients; Dupixent (dupilumab), an injection for the treatment of adult patients with moderate-to-severe atopic dermatitis; Kevzara (sarilumab), a solution for subcutaneous injection for the treatment of rheumatoid arthritis in adults; Inmazeb (atoltivimab, maftivimab and odesivmab-ebgn), an injection for the treatment of infection caused by Zaire ebolavirus; Libtayo (cemiplimab), an injection for the treatment of metastatic or locally-advanced cutaneous squamous cell carcinoma; and ZALTRAP (ziv-aflibercept), an injection, in combination with 5-fluorouracil, leucovorin, irinotecan, for patients with metastatic colorectal cancer. Regeneron's proprietary technologies include VelociGene, VelociMouse and VelocImmune. The VelociGene technology allows precise DNA manipulation and gene staining, helping to identify where a particular gene is active in the body. VelociMouse technology allows for the direct and immediate generation of genetically altered mice from embryonic stem cells, avoiding the lengthy process involved in generating and breeding knock-out mice from chimeras. VelocImmune is a novel mouse technology platform for producing fully human monoclonal antibodies. Additionally, VelociMab technologies allow rapid screenings of therapeutic antibodies; VelociT produces fully-human therapeutic T-cell receptors against tumor and viral antigens; Veloci-Bi allows for the generation of full-length bi-specific antibodies; and VelociHum is used to test human therapeutics against human immune cells.

FINANCIAL DATA: Note: Data for latest year may not have been available at press time.

In U.S. $	2020	2019	2018	2017	2016	2015
Revenue	8,497,100,000	7,863,400,000	6,710,800,000	5,872,227,000	4,860,427,000	4,103,728,000
R&D Expense	2,735,000,000	3,036,600,000	2,186,100,000	2,075,142,000	2,052,295,000	1,620,577,000
Operating Income	3,576,600,000	2,209,800,000	2,534,400,000	2,079,591,000	1,330,741,000	1,251,916,000
Operating Margin %		.28%	.38%	.35%	.27%	.31%
SGA Expense	1,346,000,000	1,834,800,000	1,556,200,000	1,320,433,000	1,177,697,000	838,526,000
Net Income	3,513,200,000	2,115,800,000	2,444,400,000	1,198,511,000	895,522,000	636,056,000
Operating Cash Flow	2,618,100,000	2,430,000,000	2,195,100,000	1,307,112,000	1,473,396,000	1,330,780,000
Capital Expenditure	614,600,000	429,600,000	383,100,000	272,626,000	511,941,000	677,933,000
EBITDA	4,103,200,000	2,669,600,000	2,729,900,000	2,249,097,000	1,441,755,000	1,314,247,000
Return on Assets %		.16%	.24%	.15%	.14%	.13%
Return on Equity %		.21%	.33%	.23%	.22%	.21%
Debt to Equity		0.064	0.081	0.114	0.079	0.099

CONTACT INFORMATION:

Phone: 914 847-7000   Fax:
Toll-Free:
Address: 777 Old Saw Mill River Rd., Tarrytown, NY 10591-6707 United States

STOCK TICKER/OTHER:

Stock Ticker: REGN   Exchange: NAS
Employees: 9,123   Fiscal Year Ends: 12/31
Parent Company:

SALARIES/BONUSES:

Top Exec. Salary: $ Bonus: $
Second Exec. Salary: $ Bonus: $

OTHER THOUGHTS:

Estimated Female Officers or Directors:
Hot Spot for Advancement for Women/Minorities:

Sales, profits and employees may be estimates. Financial information, benefits and other data can change quickly and may vary from those stated here.

Regional Health Properties Inc   www.regionalhealthproperties.com

NAIC Code: 623311

TYPES OF BUSINESS:

Continuing Care Retirement Communities
Assisted Living Facilities for the Elderly

BRANDS/DIVISIONS/AFFILIATES:

GROWTH PLANS/SPECIAL FEATURES:

Regional Health Properties, Inc. is a self-managed healthcare real estate investment company that invests primarily in real estate purposed for long-term care and senior living. As of June 30, 2020, Regional Health owned, leased or managed for third parties 24 facilities, of which: 10 were skilled nursing facilities owned by Regional Health and leased to third-party tenants; nine were skilled nursing facilities leased by Regional Health and subleased to third-party tenants; and two were assisted living facilities owned by Regional Health and leased to third-party tenants. In addition, Regional Health managed two skilled nursing facilities and one independent living facility on behalf of third-party owners.

CONTACTS: *Note: Officers with more than one job title may be intentionally listed here more than once.*

Brent Morrison, CEO
Ben Waites, CFO
David Tenwick, Director

FINANCIAL DATA: *Note: Data for latest year may not have been available at press time.*

In U.S. $	2020	2019	2018	2017	2016	2015
Revenue	17,579,000	20,134,000	22,046,000	25,148,000	27,337,000	18,400,000
R&D Expense						
Operating Income	2,294,000	5,462,000	-792,000	5,138,000	4,255,000	-7,641,000
Operating Margin %		.27%	-.04%	.20%	.16%	-.42%
SGA Expense	9,931,000	9,837,000	12,375,000	13,171,000	16,408,000	16,302,000
Net Income	-688,000	5,500,000	-11,895,000	-985,000	-7,462,000	-23,518,000
Operating Cash Flow	1,295,000	2,396,000	1,348,000	5,145,000	-3,409,000	-17,806,000
Capital Expenditure	450,000	58,000	338,000	846,000	1,500,000	1,799,000
EBITDA	5,067,000	13,577,000	-1,444,000	9,469,000	17,984,000	-1,894,000
Return on Assets %		-.03%	-.19%	-.08%	-.10%	-.15%
Return on Equity %						
Debt to Equity						

CONTACT INFORMATION:

Phone: 678 869-5116   Fax:
Toll-Free:
Address: 454 Satellite Blvd. NW, Ste. 100, Suwanee, GA 30024-7191 United States

STOCK TICKER/OTHER:

Stock Ticker: RHE   Exchange: ASE
Employees: 16   Fiscal Year Ends: 12/31
Parent Company:

SALARIES/BONUSES:

Top Exec. Salary: $ Bonus: $
Second Exec. Salary: $ Bonus: $

OTHER THOUGHTS:

Estimated Female Officers or Directors:
Hot Spot for Advancement for Women/Minorities:

ResMed Inc

www.resmed.com

NAIC Code: 334510

TYPES OF BUSINESS:

Sleep Disordered Breathing Medical Equipment
Diagnosis & Treatment Products

BRANDS/DIVISIONS/AFFILIATES:

AirSense 10
AirCurve 10
AirMini
Stellar
Astral
Lumis
Mobi

CONTACTS: *Note: Officers with more than one job title may be intentionally listed here more than once.*

Michael Farrell, CEO
Brett Sandercock, CFO
Peter Farrell, Chairman of the Board
David Pendarvis, Chief Administrative Officer
Robert Douglas, COO
James Hollingshead, President, Divisional
Rajwant Sodhi, President, Divisional
Richie McHale, President, Divisional

GROWTH PLANS/SPECIAL FEATURES:

ResMed, Inc. is an Australia-founded company that develops, manufactures, distributes and markets medical devices and cloud-based software applications for treating, diagnosing and managing sleep disordered breathing (SDB) and other respiratory disorders. SDB includes obstructive sleep apnea (OSA) and other related respiratory disorders that occur during sleep. Other respiratory disorders include chronic obstructive pulmonary disease (COPD) and neuromuscular disease. ResMed was originally founded to commercialize a continuous positive airway pressure (CPAP) treatment for OSA, which delivers pressurized air, typically through a nasal mask, to prevent collapse of the upper airway during sleep. Since the introduction of nasal CPAP, the firm has developed a number of innovative products, including related mask systems, headgear, airflow generators, diagnostic products and other accessories. The firm's recent CPAP products include AirSense 10 Elite and AirSense 10 CPAP. Its variable positive airway pressure (VPAP) products include the AirCurve 10S, AirCurve 10 V Auto, AirCurve 10 ST, AirCurve 10 ASV and the AirCurve 10 CS. Autoset products include the AirSense 10 Auto and the AirMini. Ventilation products include the Stellar 100 and 150, Astral 100 and 150, Lumis 100 and 150, Lumis ST-A and Mobi. ResMed's business strategy includes expanding into new clinical applications by seeking to identify new uses for its technologies, as well as increasing consumer awareness of little-known conditions. The firm sells products in over 140 countries through wholly-owned subsidiaries and independent distributors. Through various subsidiaries, ResMed owns or has licensed rights to over 6,200 pending patents.

FINANCIAL DATA: *Note: Data for latest year may not have been available at press time.*

In U.S. $	2020	2019	2018	2017	2016	2015
Revenue	2,957,013,000	2,606,572,000	2,340,196,000	2,066,737,000	1,838,713,000	
R&D Expense	201,946,000	180,651,000	155,149,000	144,467,000	118,651,000	
Operating Income	809,059,000	635,986,000	560,263,000	456,732,000	435,866,000	
Operating Margin %		.24%	.24%	.22%	.24%	
SGA Expense	676,689,000	645,010,000	600,369,000	553,968,000	488,057,000	
Net Income	621,674,000	404,592,000	315,588,000	342,284,000	352,409,000	
Operating Cash Flow	802,255,000	459,051,000	505,026,000	414,053,000	547,933,000	
Capital Expenditure	105,938,000	77,342,000	71,457,000	71,476,000	67,829,000	
EBITDA	954,838,000	705,798,000	669,627,000	559,136,000	537,621,000	
Return on Assets %		.11%	.10%	.10%	.13%	
Return on Equity %		.20%	.16%	.19%	.21%	
Debt to Equity		0.608	0.131	0.55	0.516	

CONTACT INFORMATION:

Phone: 858 836-5000   Fax: 858 746-2900
Toll-Free: 800-424-0737
Address: 9001 Spectrum Ctr. Blvd., San Diego, CA 92123 United States

STOCK TICKER/OTHER:

Stock Ticker: RMD   Exchange: NYS
Employees: 7,770   Fiscal Year Ends: 06/30
Parent Company:

SALARIES/BONUSES:

Top Exec. Salary: $ Bonus: $
Second Exec. Salary: $ Bonus: $

OTHER THOUGHTS:

Estimated Female Officers or Directors: 2
Hot Spot for Advancement for Women/Minorities:

Rhon Klinikum AG

en.rhoen-klinikum-ag.com

NAIC Code: 622110

TYPES OF BUSINESS:

General Medical and Surgical Hospitals

BRANDS/DIVISIONS/AFFILIATES:

Rhon-Klinikum Campus Bad Neustadt
Klinikum Frankfurt (Oder)
University Hospital Giessen
University Hospital Marburg
Zentralklinik Bad Berka

CONTACTS: *Note: Officers with more than one job title may be intentionally listed here more than once.*

Esther Walter, Head-Press & Public Relations
Martin L. Hansis, Head-Quality Mgmt.
Franz Mlynek, Head-Major Investments Division
Jan Liersch, Chmn.

GROWTH PLANS/SPECIAL FEATURES:

Rhon-Klinikum AG is a Germany-based company that along with its subsidiaries, builds and acquires acute-care hospitals of all categories. In addition to rehabilitation hospitals, it is focused on outpatient, day clinical and base care facilities. The company owns and operates hospital clinics in four locations. Rhon-Klinikum Campus Bad Neustadt comprises six clinics directly linked at this one location, and includes: the Cardiovascular Clinic, the Frankenklinik for the Rehabilitation of Cardiovascular Patients, the Clinic for Hand Surgery, the Neurological Clinic, the Psychosomatic Clinic and the Saaletalklinik, as well as two additional addiction therapy facilities. Klinikum Frankfurt (Oder) is a hospital with specialized medical services, 773 inpatient beds. Approximately 35,000 inpatients and more than 44,000 outpatients are treated annually from Frankfurt (Oder), which includes 21 clinics, six institutions and psychiatric outpatient institutions, as well as three-day clinics. University Hospital Giessen and Marburg offers medical services, modern diagnostics and comprehensive therapy at the highest international standard. It is a full-service hospital covering the whole range of modern medicine from ophthalmology to trauma surgery to dentistry. This hospital comprises 80 clinics and institutions at the dual locations of Giessen and Marburg, and is Germany's third-largest university hospital. Last, Zentralklinik Bad Berka is an academic teaching hospital, as well as a hospital with a nationwide service mission. Each year, the team of doctors, nurses and medical assistants treat thousands of patients from all over Germany, Europe and several non-European countries in a total of 20 clinics and specialist departments. Services are provided to patients with thoracic, pulmonary and vascular diseases, tumors, neurological conditions, as well as diseases of the spinal column, joints and heart. During 2020, Rhon-Klinikum agreed to be acquired by Asklepios Kliniken GmbH & Co KGaA, which was approved by the German Federal Cartel Office.

FINANCIAL DATA: *Note: Data for latest year may not have been available at press time.*

In U.S. $	2020	2019	2018	2017	2016	2015
Revenue	1,924,830,000	1,460,180,000	1,410,190,000	1,632,700,000	1,411,279,598	1,439,218,866
R&D Expense						
Operating Income						
Operating Margin %						
SGA Expense						
Net Income	3,025,170	44,479,000	58,548,400	44,005,900	70,345,739	97,749,655
Operating Cash Flow						
Capital Expenditure						
EBITDA						
Return on Assets %						
Return on Equity %						
Debt to Equity						

CONTACT INFORMATION:

Phone: 49 9771 65-0   Fax: 49 9771 97 46 7
Toll-Free:
Address: Salzburger Leite 1, Bad Neustadt/Saale, D-97616 Germany

STOCK TICKER/OTHER:

Stock Ticker: RHK   Exchange: Frankfurt
Employees: 18,449   Fiscal Year Ends: 12/31
Parent Company:

SALARIES/BONUSES:

Top Exec. Salary: $ Bonus: $
Second Exec. Salary: $ Bonus: $

OTHER THOUGHTS:

Estimated Female Officers or Directors:
Hot Spot for Advancement for Women/Minorities:

Rite Aid Corporation

www.riteaid.com

NAIC Code: 446110

TYPES OF BUSINESS:

Drug Stores

BRANDS/DIVISIONS/AFFILIATES:

Elixir
Rite Aid
wellness+Rewards
RediClinic
Health Dialog

CONTACTS: *Note: Officers with more than one job title may be intentionally listed here more than once.*

Heyward Donigan, CEO
Bryan Everett, COO
Matthew Schroeder, CFO
Erik Keptner, CMO
Jessica Kazmaier, Chief Human Resources Officer
Bryan Everett, COO
Justin Mennen, CIO
Jocelyn Konrad, Executive VP, Divisional
Bruce Bodaken, Chairman of the Board

GROWTH PLANS/SPECIAL FEATURES:

Rite Aid Corporation is a U.S.-based retail drugstore company which operates over 2,400 drug stores in 18 states. Through Elixir, Rite Aid provides pharmacy benefits and services to approximately 4 million members nationwide. Rite Aid operates two business segments: retail pharmacy and pharmacy services. The retail pharmacy segment consists of Rite Aid retail stores, from which pharmacists dispense prescription medication and educate customers on non-prescription remedies that can supplement traditional options. The stores offer a range of healthcare counseling services, including administering immunizations against the flu and shingles, assist customers with high blood pressure, cholesterol and diabetes, provide guidance on combating obesity and tobacco addiction, and educate on managing medications and potential side effects. The stores also offer a wide assortment of merchandise. The average size of each store is approximately 13,600 square feet. Rite Aid also offers its wellness+Rewards loyalty platform. RediClinic is an operator of retail clinics, where patients can be treated for more than 30 common medical conditions, and RediClinic clinicians are able to write prescriptions for these conditions when appropriate. Health Dialog is a provider of healthcare coaching and disease management services to health plans and employers. The pharmacy services segment provides a fully integrated suite of pharmacy benefit manager (PBM) offerings, including technology solutions, mail delivery services, specialty pharmacy, network and rebate administration, claims adjudication and pharmacy discount programs. This division also provides prescription discount programs and Medicare Part D insurance offerings for individuals and groups. In October 2020, Rite Aid agreed to acquire Bartell Drugs, which fills approximately 5.5 million prescriptions annually across its 67 stores in Seattle and through King, Snohomish and Pierce counties in Washington state.

FINANCIAL DATA: *Note: Data for latest year may not have been available at press time.*

In U.S. $	2020	2019	2018	2017	2016	2015
Revenue	21,928,390,000	21,639,560,000	21,528,970,000	32,845,070,000	30,736,660,000	
R&D Expense						
Operating Income	139,422,000	83,977,000	128,843,000	531,706,000	812,909,000	
Operating Margin %	.01%	.00%	.01%	.02%	.03%	
SGA Expense	4,587,336,000	4,592,375,000	4,651,262,000	7,242,359,000	7,013,346,000	
Net Income	-452,174,000	-422,213,000	943,470,000	4,053,000	165,465,000	
Operating Cash Flow	487,021,000	-228,665,000	266,344,000	225,863,000	997,402,000	
Capital Expenditure	214,386,000	244,689,000	214,764,000	481,111,000	669,995,000	
EBITDA	476,322,000	-3,867,000	545,280,000	1,048,667,000	1,237,190,000	
Return on Assets %	-.05%	-.05%	.09%	.00%	.02%	
Return on Equity %	-.49%	-.30%	.85%	.01%	.52%	
Debt to Equity	8.609	2.931	2.105	11.90	11.983	

CONTACT INFORMATION:

Phone: 717 761-2633   Fax: 717 975-5905
Toll-Free: 800-748-3243
Address: 30 Hunter Lane, Camp Hill, PA 17011 United States

STOCK TICKER/OTHER:

Stock Ticker: RAD
Employees: 50,000
Parent Company:

Exchange: NYS
Fiscal Year Ends: 02/28

SALARIES/BONUSES:

Top Exec. Salary: $ Bonus: $
Second Exec. Salary: $ Bonus: $

OTHER THOUGHTS:

Estimated Female Officers or Directors: 3
Hot Spot for Advancement for Women/Minorities: Y

Roche Holding AG

www.roche.com

NAIC Code: 325412

TYPES OF BUSINESS:

Pharmaceuticals Manufacturing
Antibiotics
Diagnostics
Cancer Drugs
Virology Products
HIV/AIDS Treatments
Transplant Drugs

BRANDS/DIVISIONS/AFFILIATES:

F Hoffmann-La Roche Ltd
Genentech Inc
Chugai Pharmaceutical Co Ltd
GenMark Diagnositcs Inc

CONTACTS: *Note: Officers with more than one job title may be intentionally listed here more than once.*

Severin Schwan, CEO
Alan Hippe, CFO
Cristina A. Wilbur, Head-Human Resources
John C. Reed, Head-Roche Pharmaceutical Research & Early Dev.
Gottlieb Keller, General Counsel
Daniel ODay, COO-Pharmaceuticals
Stephen Feldhaus, Head-Comm.
Richard Scheller, Head-Genentech Research & Early Dev.
Roland Diggelmann, COO-Diagnostics
Sophie Kornowski-Bonnet, Head-Roche Partnering
Christoph Franz, Chmn.
Osamu Nagayama, CEO

GROWTH PLANS/SPECIAL FEATURES:

Roche Holding AG, also referred to as F. Hoffmann-La Roche Ltd. and based in Switzerland, is a world-leading healthcare and biotechnology company. The firm occupies an industry-leading position in the global diagnostics market and ranks as one of the top producers of pharmaceuticals, with recognition in the areas of oncology, autoimmune disease and metabolic disorder treatments, virology and transplantation medicine. The company's operations currently extend to over 100 countries, with additional alliances and research and development agreements with corporate and institutional partners furthering Roche's collective reach. It operates in two divisions: pharmaceuticals, which generates the majority of the firm's annual sales; and diagnostics. The pharmaceuticals division focuses on translating science into breakthrough medicines for patients, with research at Roche and wholly-owned Genentech, Inc. in the U.S., as well as Chugai Pharmaceutical Co., Ltd. in Japan. This segment has more than 150 worldwide partners engaged in clinical development, manufacturing and commercial operations, with a focus on oncology, immunology, ophthalmology, infectious diseases and neuroscience. More than half of the compounds in this division's product pipeline are biopharmaceuticals. The diagnostics division performs blood, tissue and other types of patient samples, as well as in vitro diagnostics for the purpose of obtaining information in relation to improved disease management and patient care. Diagnostic services and solutions provide prevention, screening, diagnosis, prognosis, stratification, treatment and monitoring capabilities in relation to diseases. In April 2021, Roche acquired GenMark Diagnostics, Inc. and announced intention to complete the acquisition through a merger of Geronimo Acquisition Corp with and into GenMark. Following the completion of the merger, GenMark will become a wholly-owned subsidiary of Roche and GenMark's shares will cease to be traded on the NASDAQ stock market.

FINANCIAL DATA: *Note: Data for latest year may not have been available at press time.*

In U.S. $	2020	2019	2018	2017	2016	2015
Revenue	65,021,520,000	68,525,500,000	63,374,880,000	59,420,500,000	56,384,760,000	53,674,550,000
R&D Expense	14,503,110,000	14,241,120,000	13,480,790,000	12,588,910,000	12,856,470,000	10,681,400,000
Operating Income	20,672,700,000	19,563,420,000	16,436,260,000	14,496,420,000	15,684,850,000	15,408,370,000
Operating Margin %		.29%	.26%	.24%	.28%	.29%
SGA Expense	14,062,740,000	16,809,740,000	17,131,930,000	14,796,320,000	12,101,720,000	12,866,510,000
Net Income	15,936,810,000	15,047,160,000	11,705,950,000	9,624,518,000	10,675,820,000	9,880,933,000
Operating Cash Flow	20,698,340,000	24,955,960,000	22,273,630,000	20,094,090,000	16,723,900,000	17,002,610,000
Capital Expenditure	7,458,360,000	5,458,316,000	5,487,302,000	4,696,872,000	5,735,914,000	4,582,042,000
EBITDA	25,726,330,000	24,188,940,000	20,600,240,000	18,841,000,000	19,962,540,000	18,663,740,000
Return on Assets %		.17%	.14%	.11%	.13%	.12%
Return on Equity %		.45%	.39%	.34%	.43%	.44%
Debt to Equity		0.414	0.582	0.599	0.711	0.815

CONTACT INFORMATION:

Phone: 41-61-688-1111   Fax: 41-61-691-9391
Toll-Free:
Address: F. Hoffmann-La Roche Ltd, Basel, CH-4070 Switzerland

STOCK TICKER/OTHER:

Stock Ticker: RHHBF
Employees: 97,735
Parent Company:

Exchange: PINX
Fiscal Year Ends: 12/31

SALARIES/BONUSES:

Top Exec. Salary: $ Bonus: $
Second Exec. Salary: $ Bonus: $

OTHER THOUGHTS:

Estimated Female Officers or Directors: 4
Hot Spot for Advancement for Women/Minorities: Y

Sales, profits and employees may be estimates. Financial information, benefits and other data can change quickly and may vary from those stated here.

SafeGuard Health Enterprises Inc

www.metlife.com/safeguard

NAIC Code: 524114

TYPES OF BUSINESS:

HMO/PPO
Vision Insurance Products
Administrative Services
Dental & Vision Benefit Plans
Employee Assistance Programs

BRANDS/DIVISIONS/AFFILIATES:

MetLife Inc
SafeGuard Health Plans Inc
SafeHealth Life Insurance Company
Metropolitan Life Insurance Company

GROWTH PLANS/SPECIAL FEATURES:

SafeGuard Health Enterprises, Inc., a wholly-owned subsidiary of MetLife, Inc. (Metropolitan Life Insurance Company), provides dental and vision benefit plans (including HMO, PPO and indemnity plans) to government and private sector employers, associations and individuals. The company also offers scheduled benefit plans, administrative services and employee assistance programs. Subsidiaries include SafeGuard Health Plans, Inc. and SafeHealth Life Insurance Company. SafeGuard Health Plans, Inc. provides dental benefits, as well as vision benefits for California-based VHMOs (vision health maintenance organizations). SafeHealth Life Insurance Company provides vision benefits for VPPOs (vision preferred provider organizations). Individual dentist HMO plans are available in California, Florida and Texas only through SafeGuard Health Plans, Inc. Dental managed care plan benefits are provided by Metropolitan Life Insurance Company.

CONTACTS:

Note: Officers with more than one job title may be intentionally listed here more than once.

Michel A. Khalaf, CEO-MetLife
William J. Wheeler, Pres., The Americas-Metlife, Inc.
Ricardo A. Anzaldua, General Counsel-Metlife, Inc.

FINANCIAL DATA:

Note: Data for latest year may not have been available at press time.

In U.S. $	2020	2019	2018	2017	2016	2015
Revenue						
R&D Expense						
Operating Income						
Operating Margin %						
SGA Expense						
Net Income						
Operating Cash Flow						
Capital Expenditure						
EBITDA						
Return on Assets %						
Return on Equity %						
Debt to Equity						

CONTACT INFORMATION:

Phone: 949-425-4300   Fax: 949-425-4586
Toll-Free: 800-880-1800
Address: 95 Enterprise, Ste. 100, Aliso Viejo, CA 92656 United States

STOCK TICKER/OTHER:

Stock Ticker: Subsidiary   Exchange:
Employees: 360   Fiscal Year Ends: 12/31
Parent Company: Metropolitan Life Insurance Company

SALARIES/BONUSES:

Top Exec. Salary: $ Bonus: $
Second Exec. Salary: $ Bonus: $

OTHER THOUGHTS:

Estimated Female Officers or Directors:
Hot Spot for Advancement for Women/Minorities:

Safilo Group SpA

www.safilogroup.com/en

NAIC Code: 339100

TYPES OF BUSINESS:

Ophthalmic Goods Manufacturing

BRANDS/DIVISIONS/AFFILIATES:

Carrera
Polaroid
Safilo
Smith
Blenders Eyewear
Prive Revaux
HAL Holdings NV
Multibrands Italy BV

CONTACTS: *Note: Officers with more than one job title may be intentionally listed here more than once.*

Angelo Trocchia, CEO
Luca Fuso, Head-Licensed Brand Div.
Marco Pessi, General Counsel
Massimo Lisot, Dir.-Bus. Dev.
Ross Brownlee, Head-Americas
Eugenio Razelli, Chmn.
Massimo Renon, Head-EMEA
Maurizio Roman, Global Supply Chain, Logistics & Prod. Officer

GROWTH PLANS/SPECIAL FEATURES:

Safilo Group SpA is an eyewear manufacturer that produces and distributes sunglasses, optical frames and sports eyewear worldwide. The company's in-house brands are: Carrera, Polaroid, Safilo, Smith, Blenders Eyewear and Prive Revaux. Licensed brands include Dior, Fendi, Banana Republic, Bobbi Brown, BOSS, BOSS Orange, Elie Saab, Fossil, Givenchy, Havaianas, Jack Spade, Jimmy Choo, Juicy Couture, kate spade new york, Liz Claiborne, Love Moschino, Marc Jacobs, Max Mara, Max&Co., Moschino, Pierre Cardin, rag&bone, Saks Fifth Avenue, Swatch and Tommy Hilfiger. Safilio's global Havaianas eyewear license agreement with Brazilian company, Alpargatas, runs up to 2021; and its collaboration agreement with Swatch, runs into 2021. The firm's products are divided into three market ranges: high-end, mid-range and lower-end. Sunglasses are responsible for most of the firm's revenue, with prescription frames coming in second and sport and accessory items deriving nearly 10% of sales. Safilo has international design studios, showrooms, global distribution plants and primary distribution centers, reaching approximately 100,000 retail stores worldwide. Multibrands Italy BV holds a 49.8% stake in the share capital of Safilo. Multibrands itself is a subsidiary of HAL Holding NV. In December 2019, Safilo Group acquired Blenders Eyewear, offering prescription eyeglasses, readers, goggles, sunglasses and related accessories. In early-2020, the firm acquired Prive Revaux, a U.S. brand of eyeglasses.

FINANCIAL DATA: *Note: Data for latest year may not have been available at press time.*

In U.S. $	2020	2019	2018	2017	2016	2015
Revenue	953,350,100	1,147,295,000	1,176,401,000	1,279,145,000	1,530,802,000	1,562,604,000
R&D Expense						
Operating Income	-89,013,780	-21,090,310	2,965,253	25,657	51,205,900	74,380,560
Operating Margin %		-.02%	.00%	.00%	.03%	.05%
SGA Expense	239,566,000	273,376,300	281,297,100	307,455,300	375,382,400	383,931,200
Net Income	-84,766,890	-401,060,500	-39,641,780	-307,358,800	-173,615,700	-64,442,620
Operating Cash Flow	1,081,273	32,433,290	3,313,459	-37,966,720	108,817,600	140,258,800
Capital Expenditure	29,642,750	62,861,650	37,475,560	49,109,320	63,911,150	58,372,840
EBITDA	-15,018,080	-237,730,900	44,334,620	-210,631,900	-82,887,790	28,837,600
Return on Assets %		-.33%	-.03%	-.19%	-.09%	-.03%
Return on Equity %		-.66%	-.06%	-.36%	-.15%	-.05%
Debt to Equity		0.322		0.267	0.157	0.133

CONTACT INFORMATION:

Phone: 39 496985111   Fax: 39 496985380
Toll-Free:
Address: Z.I. Settima Strada, 15, Padova, 35129 Italy

STOCK TICKER/OTHER:

Stock Ticker: SAFLF
Employees: 5,754
Parent Company: HAL Holding NV

Exchange: PINX
Fiscal Year Ends: 12/31

SALARIES/BONUSES:

Top Exec. Salary: $ Bonus: $
Second Exec. Salary: $ Bonus: $

OTHER THOUGHTS:

Estimated Female Officers or Directors: 1
Hot Spot for Advancement for Women/Minorities:

Sanford Health

www.sanfordhealth.org

NAIC Code: 622110

TYPES OF BUSINESS:

General Medical and Surgical Hospitals
Medical Research
Health Insurance
Genetic Screening
Nutrition Programs
Fitness Centers
Senior Care

BRANDS/DIVISIONS/AFFILIATES:

Sanford Imagenetics
Sanford Chip
Sanford Research
Center for Biobehavioral Research
Center for Cancer Biology Research CoBRE
Center for Pediatric Research CoBRE
Profile by Sanford
Sanford Wellness Centers

CONTACTS: *Note: Officers with more than one job title may be intentionally listed here more than once.*

Kelby Krabbenhoft, CEO
Kelby Krabbenhoft, Pres.

GROWTH PLANS/SPECIAL FEATURES:

Sanford Health, one of the largest health systems in the United States, is dedicated to the integrated delivery of health care, genomic medicine, senior care and services, global clinics, research and affordable insurance. Headquartered in Sioux Falls, South Dakota, the organization includes 46 hospitals, 1,400 physicians and more than 200 Good Samaritan Society senior care locations in 26 U.S. states and 10 countries. The firm offers Sanford Health Plan individual and family health insurance, and oversees the Sanford Health Foundation, a nonprofit that raises funds to support Sanford health care services and programs. Sanford Imagenetics focuses on genetic medicine an offers the Sanford Chip, a $49 genetic screening test. Sanford Research is comprised of four research centers: Center for Biobehavioral Research, Center for Cancer Biology Research CoBRE, Center for Health Outcomes and Population Research CoBRE and Center for Pediatric Research CoBRE. The firm also offers Profile by Sanford, a nutrition program to promote weight loss. In addition, Sanford Wellness Centers offer fitness classes and personal training in two facilities in Sioux Falls.

FINANCIAL DATA: *Note: Data for latest year may not have been available at press time.*

In U.S. $	2020	2019	2018	2017	2016	2015
Revenue	5,917,528,150	6,228,977,000	4,819,084,000			
R&D Expense						
Operating Income						
Operating Margin %						
SGA Expense						
Net Income		926,114,000	106,118,000			
Operating Cash Flow						
Capital Expenditure						
EBITDA						
Return on Assets %						
Return on Equity %						
Debt to Equity						

CONTACT INFORMATION:

Phone: Fax:
Toll-Free: 800-601-5084
Address: 1305 W. 18th St., Sioux Falls, SD 57117 United States

STOCK TICKER/OTHER:

Stock Ticker: Nonprofit   Exchange:
Employees: 47,757   Fiscal Year Ends: 12/31
Parent Company:

SALARIES/BONUSES:

Top Exec. Salary: $ Bonus: $
Second Exec. Salary: $ Bonus: $

OTHER THOUGHTS:

Estimated Female Officers or Directors:
Hot Spot for Advancement for Women/Minorities:

Sales, profits and employees may be estimates. Financial information, benefits and other data can change quickly and may vary from those stated here.

Sanofi Genzyme

www.sanofi.com/en/your-health/specialty-care

NAIC Code: 325412

TYPES OF BUSINESS:

Pharmaceuticals Discovery & Development
Genetic Disease Treatments
Surgical Products
Diagnostic Products
Genetic Testing Services
Oncology Products
Biomaterials
Medical Devices

BRANDS/DIVISIONS/AFFILIATES:

Sanofi SA

CONTACTS: *Note: Officers with more than one job title may be intentionally listed here more than once.*

David Meeker, Pres.
Richard J. Gregory, Head-R&D
William Aitchison, Head-Global Mfg.
Tracey L. Quarles, General Counsel
Charles Thyne, Head-Global Quality, Industrial Oper.
G. Andre Turenne, Head- Strategy & Bus. Dev.
Caren P. Arnstein, Head-Corp. Comm.
Ron C. Branning, Chief Quality Officer
Nicholas Grund, Sr. VP-Asia Pacific & Canada
Carlo Incerti, Head-Global Medical Affairs
Yoshi Nakamura, Pres., Japan-Asia Pacific
Serge Weinberg, Chmn.
Robin Kenselaar, Head-EMEA

GROWTH PLANS/SPECIAL FEATURES:

Sanofi Genzyme is the specialty care global business unit of Sanofi SA, with a focus on rare diseases, rare blood disorders, neurology, immunology and oncology. The rare diseases segment develops therapeutic products to treat patients suffering from genetic and other chronic debilitating diseases, including lysosomal storage disorders (LSDs) and endocrinology. More than 7,000 different rare disease collectively affect over 350 million people worldwide. The rare blood disorders segment comprises a hemophilia portfolio, an approved treatment for acquired thrombotic thrombocytopenic purpura (aTTP). The neurology segment develops new treatment options for people living with neurological disorders, and is a leader in multiple sclerosis, bringing therapies to patients in more than 80 countries worldwide. The immunology segment researches and develops new therapeutic candidates that may have a significant impact on people affected by immune system disorders, including atopic dermatitis, rheumatoid arthritis, asthma, nasal polyposis and eosinophilic esophagitis. Last, the oncology segment builds on Sanofi Genzyme's established legacy in cancer treatment by researching potential new options to offer in this area of medicine. This division is building a pipeline of future therapies in immune-oncology, in which a patient's immune system is used to fight cancer cells. As of March 2021, Sanofi Genzyme's research and development pipeline contained 80 projects, including 36 new molecular entities in clinical development. More than 35 projects are in phase 3 or have been submitted to the regulatory authorities for approval. In May 2021, Sanofi Genzyme announced that it entered into a three-year research collaboration with Stanford University School of Medicine, which together the organizations and their scientists will work to advance the understanding of immunology and inflammation via open scientific exchange.

Sanofi offers comprehensive employee benefits.

FINANCIAL DATA: *Note: Data for latest year may not have been available at press time.*

In U.S. $	2020	2019	2018	2017	2016	2015
Revenue	13,443,100,000	8,827,062,720	8,265,040,000	6,796,680,000	5,287,820,000	4,097,534,726
R&D Expense						
Operating Income						
Operating Margin %						
SGA Expense						
Net Income						
Operating Cash Flow						
Capital Expenditure						
EBITDA						
Return on Assets %						
Return on Equity %						
Debt to Equity						

CONTACT INFORMATION:

Phone: 617-252-7500   Fax: 617-252-7600
Toll-Free:
Address: 50 Binney St., Cambridge, MA 02142 United States

STOCK TICKER/OTHER:

Stock Ticker: Subsidiary   Exchange:
Employees: 4,700   Fiscal Year Ends: 12/31
Parent Company: Sanofi SA

SALARIES/BONUSES:

Top Exec. Salary: $ Bonus: $
Second Exec. Salary: $ Bonus: $

OTHER THOUGHTS:

Estimated Female Officers or Directors: 4
Hot Spot for Advancement for Women/Minorities: Y

Sales, profits and employees may be estimates. Financial information, benefits and other data can change quickly and may vary from those stated here.

Sanofi SA

NAIC Code: 325412

en.sanofi.com

TYPES OF BUSINESS:

Pharmaceuticals Development & Manufacturing
Pharmaceuticals
Research
Development
Vaccines
Diabetes
Cardiovascular
Specialty Care

BRANDS/DIVISIONS/AFFILIATES:

CONTACTS: *Note: Officers with more than one job title may be intentionally listed here more than once.*

Paul Hudson, CEO
Jean-Baptiste Shasseloup de Chatillon, CFO
Natalie Bickford, Chief People Officer
Elias Zerhouni, Pres., Global R&D
Karen Linehan, General Counsel
David-Alexandre Gros, Chief Strategy Officer
David Meeker, CEO-Genzyme
Olivier Charmeil, Sr. VP-Vaccines
Philippe Luscan, Exec. VP-Global Industrial Affairs
Serge Weinberg, Chmn.
Peter Guenter, Exec. VP-Global Commercial Oper.

GROWTH PLANS/SPECIAL FEATURES:

Sanofi SA is an international pharmaceutical group engaged in the research, development, manufacturing and marketing of healthcare products. The firm has 69 manufacturing sites in 32 countries and provides healthcare solutions in 170 countries worldwide. Sanofi operates through the four core business units of specialty care, vaccines, health and wellbeing, and diabetes and cardiovascular diseases. The specialty care unit focuses on rare diseases, rare blood disorders, neurology, immunology and oncology. The vaccines unit offers a wide range of treatment for infectious diseases, including cholera, dengue, diphtheria, haemophilius influenze Type B, Hepatitis A and B, influenza, Japanese encephalitis, meningococcal meningitis, pertussis, poliomyelitis, respiratory syncytial virus, rabies, tetanus, typhoid fever and yellow fever. The health and wellbeing unit provides innovative self-care solutions for managing personal health, such as coughs and colds, allergies, digestive health, nutritional health and pain care. The diabetes and cardiovascular diseases unit focuses on therapeutic areas for the treatment of diabetes, which is a prime risk factor for cardiovascular disease by having an affect on both systolic and diastolic heart failure. Sanofi SA engages in research and development and clinical trials in all of these focus areas and more, with an R&D pipeline of 80 projects (as of March 2021), including 36 new molecular entities in clinical development. More than 35 projects are in Phase 3 or have been submitted to the regulatory authorities for approval.

FINANCIAL DATA: *Note: Data for latest year may not have been available at press time.*

In U.S. $	2020	2019	2018	2017	2016	2015
Revenue	45,656,580,000	45,976,690,000	43,589,340,000	44,233,210,000	42,405,440,000	42,592,370,000
R&D Expense	6,755,205,000	7,352,654,000	7,201,154,000	6,685,563,000	6,319,030,000	6,209,071,000
Operating Income	9,643,486,000	8,828,560,000	7,642,215,000	8,798,015,000	9,198,759,000	8,714,935,000
Operating Margin %		.19%	.18%	.20%	.22%	.20%
SGA Expense	11,472,490,000	12,074,820,000	12,045,500,000	12,288,630,000	11,589,780,000	11,462,710,000
Net Income	15,044,960,000	3,428,306,000	5,260,972,000	10,304,470,000	5,753,348,000	5,237,758,000
Operating Cash Flow	9,101,016,000	9,461,441,000	6,777,197,000	9,015,492,000	9,576,288,000	10,898,250,000
Capital Expenditure	2,582,836,000	2,218,747,000	2,415,453,000	2,389,796,000	2,544,962,000	3,386,766,000
EBITDA	21,899,130,000	13,095,010,000	11,141,380,000	11,773,040,000	12,099,260,000	12,313,070,000
Return on Assets %		.03%	.04%	.08%	.05%	.04%
Return on Equity %		.05%	.07%	.15%	.08%	.08%
Debt to Equity		0.358	0.374	0.247	0.292	0.226

CONTACT INFORMATION:

Phone: 33-1-53-77-40-00   Fax:
Toll-Free:
Address: 54, rue La Boetie, Paris, 75008 France

STOCK TICKER/OTHER:

Stock Ticker: SNY   Exchange: NAS
Employees: 100,409   Fiscal Year Ends: 12/31
Parent Company:

SALARIES/BONUSES:

Top Exec. Salary: $ Bonus: $
Second Exec. Salary: $ Bonus: $

OTHER THOUGHTS:

Estimated Female Officers or Directors: 6
Hot Spot for Advancement for Women/Minorities: Y

Sartorius Stedim Biotech SA

www.sartorius-stedim.com

NAIC Code: 423450

TYPES OF BUSINESS:

Medical, Dental, and Hospital Equipment and Supplies Merchant Wholesalers

BRANDS/DIVISIONS/AFFILIATES:

Satorius AG

CONTACTS: *Note: Officers with more than one job title may be intentionally listed here more than once.*

Joachin Kreuzburg, CEO
Jorg Pfirrmann, Head-General Admin.
Joachim Kreuzburg, Head-Legal & Compliance
Joachim Kreuzburg, Head-Oper.
Joachim Kreuzburg, Head-Communications
Jorg Pfirrmann, Head-Finance

GROWTH PLANS/SPECIAL FEATURES:

Sartorius Stedim Biotech SA was founded in 1870 and is a provider of equipment and services for the development, quality assurance and production processes of the biopharmaceutical industry. The company's services are divided into two segments: lab products and services and bioprocess solutions. The lab products and services division focuses on high-value laboratory instruments, such as lab balances, pipettes and laboratory water purification systems. It also offers the widest range of consumables, such as laboratory filters and pipette tips. In the bioprocess solutions division, the firm's portfolio of products, technologies and services cover wide areas of the biopharmaceutical process chain ranging from fermentation, cell cultivation, filtration and purification to media storage and transportation. The company's key customers are from the biotech, pharma and food industries as well as from public research institutes and laboratories. Sartorius maintains 60 sites in more than 30 countries, 22 of which are production facilities, and the remainder comprising sales, commercial agencies and R&D sites in Europe, North America and Asia. Sales (for 2019) by region include 40% derived by EMEA (Europe, the Middle East and Africa), 35% by the Americas and 25% by Asia/Pacific. Sartorius Stedim operates as a subsidiary of Satorius AG. In October 2020, Sartorius agreed to acquire purification specialist BIA Separations, which develops and manufactures products for purification and analysis of large biomolecules, such as viruses, plasmids and mRNA, which are used in cell and gene therapies and other advanced therapies.

FINANCIAL DATA: *Note: Data for latest year may not have been available at press time.*

In U.S. $	2020	2019	2018	2017	2016	2015
Revenue	2,333,693,000	1,760,055,000	1,480,979,000	1,320,781,000	1,284,834,000	1,080,455,000
R&D Expense	103,180,300	96,784,280	74,059,230	65,010,750	58,078,390	50,739,180
Operating Income	614,371,800	426,136,300	351,291,400	307,125,400	295,354,800	241,473,200
Operating Margin %		.24%	.24%	.23%	.23%	.22%
SGA Expense	478,375,800	387,071,100	344,800,100	313,906,300	296,979,800	264,029,700
Net Income	437,211,600	286,597,100	254,193,100	196,813,600	187,760,200	144,168,500
Operating Cash Flow	509,333,200	378,908,400	277,696,400	213,431,000	191,402,400	174,456,300
Capital Expenditure	194,497,100	166,128,700	215,692,500	154,953,100	97,391,500	64,735,850
EBITDA	722,963,300	483,148,000	426,957,300	336,856,200	320,204,500	261,129,200
Return on Assets %		.14%	.14%	.12%	.14%	.12%
Return on Equity %		.21%	.22%	.20%	.22%	.20%
Debt to Equity		0.07	0.056	0.071	0.034	0.046

CONTACT INFORMATION:

Phone: 33 442845600   Fax: 33 442845619
Toll-Free:
Address: Otto-Brenner-Str. 20, Goettingen, 37079 Germany

STOCK TICKER/OTHER:

Stock Ticker: SRTOY   Exchange: PINX
Employees: 6,203   Fiscal Year Ends: 12/31
Parent Company: Satorius AG

SALARIES/BONUSES:

Top Exec. Salary: $ Bonus: $
Second Exec. Salary: $ Bonus: $

OTHER THOUGHTS:

Estimated Female Officers or Directors:
Hot Spot for Advancement for Women/Minorities:

SECOM Co Ltd

NAIC Code: 561621

www.secom.co.jp

TYPES OF BUSINESS:

Security Systems Services (except Locksmiths)
Security Services

BRANDS/DIVISIONS/AFFILIATES:

SECOM

CONTACTS: *Note: Officers with more than one job title may be intentionally listed here more than once.*

Ichiro Ozeki, Pres.
Yasuo Nakayama, Chmn.

GROWTH PLANS/SPECIAL FEATURES:

SECOM Co., Ltd. is a provider of security services marketed under the SECOM brand. Personal services include: 24/7/365 home security, global positioning system (GPS) satellites and mobile phone base stations for confirming the location of people and vehicles, insurance (products, home and vehicles), mail-order service for carefully-selected foods, and a feeding support robot that enables those with manual disability to eat by moving just one part of their body. Security services for businesses include: centralized online security systems with on-site sensors and controllers; self-contained (offline) security systems, access-control systems, closed-circuit television systems, automated fire detection systems, fire extinguishing systems, internal/external monitoring systems (online or off), static guard services and armored car services. SECOM serves approximately 2.53 million residential and commercial customers (as of March 31, 2021). International offices are located in 17 countries and territories, including Taiwan, Korea, China, Thailand, Malaysia, Singapore, Indonesia, Vietnam, Myanmar, Philippines, India, Turkey, U.K., Sweden, Australia, New Zealand and the U.S.

FINANCIAL DATA: *Note: Data for latest year may not have been available at press time.*

In U.S. $	2020	2019	2018	2017	2016	2015
Revenue	9,681,624,000	9,259,250,000	8,864,714,000	8,476,323,000	8,046,433,000	
R&D Expense						
Operating Income	1,304,778,000	1,189,300,000	1,237,111,000	1,196,944,000	1,174,422,000	
Operating Margin %	.13%	.13%	.14%	.14%	.15%	
SGA Expense	92,462,540	88,179,160	83,082,940	81,247,210	75,228,560	
Net Income	813,568,000	840,318,600	794,507,500	768,725,000	703,597,600	
Operating Cash Flow	1,603,381,000	1,360,169,000	1,129,068,000	1,562,849,000	1,248,792,000	
Capital Expenditure	637,374,100	592,412,400	527,668,500	484,825,500	544,071,400	
EBITDA	1,952,390,000	1,902,907,000	1,884,532,000	1,852,931,000	1,593,097,000	
Return on Assets %	.05%	.05%	.05%	.05%	.05%	
Return on Equity %	.09%	.09%	.09%	.10%	.09%	
Debt to Equity	0.024	0.027	0.031	0.037	0.048	

CONTACT INFORMATION:

Phone: 81 357758100 Fax:
Toll-Free:
Address: 5-1, Jingumae 1-chome, Tokyo, 150-0001 Japan

STOCK TICKER/OTHER:

Stock Ticker: SOMLY Exchange: PINX
Employees: 65,089 Fiscal Year Ends: 03/31
Parent Company:

SALARIES/BONUSES:

Top Exec. Salary: $ Bonus: $
Second Exec. Salary: $ Bonus: $

OTHER THOUGHTS:

Estimated Female Officers or Directors:
Hot Spot for Advancement for Women/Minorities:

Semler Scientific Inc

www.semlerscientific.com

NAIC Code: 334510

TYPES OF BUSINESS:
Electromedical and Electrotherapeutic Apparatus Manufacturing

BRANDS/DIVISIONS/AFFILIATES:
QuantaFlo

GROWTH PLANS/SPECIAL FEATURES:
Semler Scientific, Inc. provides technology solutions to improve the clinical effectiveness and efficiency of healthcare providers. The firm develops, manufactures and markets innovative proprietary products and services that assist customers in evaluating and treating chronic diseases. Currently, Semler has one U.S. Food and Drug Administration (FDA) patent on the market, QuantaFlo. QuantaFlo is the combination of four proprietary peripheral arterial disease (PAD) tests. QuantaFlo is a four-minute in-office blood flow test that healthcare providers can use to determine blood flow measurements as part of their examinations of a patient's vascular condition, including assessments of patients who have vascular disease. Semler manufactures QuantaFlo in the U.S. through independent contractors.

CONTACTS: *Note: Officers with more than one job title may be intentionally listed here more than once.*
Douglas Murphy-Chutorian, CEO
Andrew Weinstein, CFO
Daniel Conger, Chief Accounting Officer

FINANCIAL DATA: *Note: Data for latest year may not have been available at press time.*

In U.S. $	2020	2019	2018	2017	2016	2015
Revenue	38,603,000	32,767,000	21,491,000	12,452,000	7,434,000	7,001,000
R&D Expense	2,938,000	2,479,000	2,085,000	1,831,000	866,000	1,436,000
Operating Income	15,961,000	10,708,000	5,342,000	-853,000	-2,159,000	-8,419,000
Operating Margin %		.33%	.25%	-.07%	-.29%	-1.20%
SGA Expense	16,348,000	15,919,000	11,361,000	8,921,000	6,854,000	11,137,000
Net Income	14,007,000	15,084,000	5,014,000	-1,510,000	-2,554,000	-8,501,000
Operating Cash Flow	15,417,000	12,728,000	4,697,000	621,000	-1,804,000	-4,135,000
Capital Expenditure	1,061,000	1,698,000	844,000	971,000	814,000	1,104,000
EBITDA	16,537,000	11,340,000	5,841,000	-487,000	-1,711,000	-8,112,000
Return on Assets %		1.16%	.84%	-.41%	-.83%	-1.61%
Return on Equity %		1.75%	6.22%			-7.19%
Debt to Equity						

CONTACT INFORMATION:
Phone: 408-627-4557   Fax:
Toll-Free: 877-774-4211
Address: 911 Bern Court, San Jose, CA 95112 United States

STOCK TICKER/OTHER:
Stock Ticker: SMLR
Employees: 86
Parent Company:

Exchange: PINX
Fiscal Year Ends: 12/31

SALARIES/BONUSES:
Top Exec. Salary: $ Bonus: $
Second Exec. Salary: $ Bonus: $

OTHER THOUGHTS:
Estimated Female Officers or Directors:
Hot Spot for Advancement for Women/Minorities:

Sentara Healthcare

www.sentara.com

NAIC Code: 622110

TYPES OF BUSINESS:

General Medical and Surgical Hospitals
Health Insurance
Primary Care Practices
Home Health Care
Air Medical Transport
Rehabilitation Services
Physical Therapy Services
Organ Transplants

BRANDS/DIVISIONS/AFFILIATES:

Sentara Norfolk General
Sentara Leigh
Sentara Virginia Beach General
Sentara CarePlex
Sentara Obici
Orthopedic Hospital at Sentara Leigh
Sentara Williamsburgh Regional Medical Center
Sentara Brock Cancer Center

CONTACTS:
Note: Officers with more than one job title may be intentionally listed here more than once.

Howard Kern, CEO
Michael Gentry, COO
Robert Broermann, CFO
Phyllis Anderson, CMO
Becky Sawyer, Sr. VP-Human Resources
Vicky G. Gray, VP-System Dev.
Elwood Boone, Pres., Sentara Virginia Beach General Hospital
Michael V. Gentry, VP-Southside
Dian Calderone, Chmn.
Ray Darcey, Pres., Sentara Enterprises

GROWTH PLANS/SPECIAL FEATURES:

Sentara Healthcare is a nonprofit health care provider in Virginia and North Carolina. The firm's system includes advanced imaging centers, nursing and assisted-living centers, outpatient campuses, physical therapy and rehabilitation services, a home health and hospice agency, a 3,800-provider medical staff and four medical groups. Hospitals include Sentara Norfolk General, Sentara Leigh, Sentara Virginia Beach General, Sentara Princess Anne, Sentara CarePlex, Sentara Obici, Sentara Albemarle Medical Center, Orthopaedic Hospital at Sentara CarePlex, Orthopedic Hospital at Sentara Leigh, Sentara Heart, Hospital for Extended Recovery and Sentara Williamsburg Regional Medical Center. The company also extends health insurance to more than 855,000 people through Optima Health and Virginia Premier, Sentara's award-winning health plans. Its air transport system, Nightingale, is an air ambulance service in southeastern Virginia. The firm operates the region's comprehensive solid organ transplant center, which conducts organ transplants, including heart transplants. Long-term life assistance, provided through the Life Care division, includes an adult day care center, the Mobile Meals program and a program for all-inclusive care for the elderly (PACE). Sentara Medical Group, a division of Sentara, provides family and internal medicine to Southeastern Virginia and Northeastern North Carolina. In mid-2020, Sentara announced the opening of its Sentara Brock Cancer Center for patient care and comprehensive cancer treatment.

FINANCIAL DATA:
Note: Data for latest year may not have been available at press time.

In U.S. $	2020	2019	2018	2017	2016	2015
Revenue	5,957,709,587	5,840,891,752	5,562,754,050	5,297,861,000	5,083,409,000	4,833,912,000
R&D Expense						
Operating Income						
Operating Margin %						
SGA Expense						
Net Income	693,174,966	672,985,404	647,101,350	616,287,000	358,984,000	211,520,000
Operating Cash Flow						
Capital Expenditure						
EBITDA						
Return on Assets %						
Return on Equity %						
Debt to Equity						

CONTACT INFORMATION:

Phone: 757-455-7540   Fax: 757-455-7964
Toll-Free: 800-736-8272
Address: 6015 Poplar Hall Dr., Norfolk, VA 23502 United States

STOCK TICKER/OTHER:

Stock Ticker: Nonprofit
Employees: 28,000
Parent Company:

Exchange:
Fiscal Year Ends: 04/30

SALARIES/BONUSES:

Top Exec. Salary: $ Bonus: $
Second Exec. Salary: $ Bonus: $

OTHER THOUGHTS:

Estimated Female Officers or Directors: 6
Hot Spot for Advancement for Women/Minorities: Y

Shandong Weigao Group Medical Polymer Co Ltd

www.weigaogroup.com
NAIC Code: 339100

TYPES OF BUSINESS:

Surgical and Medical Instrument Manufacturing

BRANDS/DIVISIONS/AFFILIATES:

MSG B Sterilizer

CONTACTS: *Note: Officers with more than one job title may be intentionally listed here more than once.*

Long Jing, Managing Dir.
Wu Xue Feng, CFO
Wang Yi, Deputy General Manager
Hua Wei Zhang, Chmn.

GROWTH PLANS/SPECIAL FEATURES:

Shandong Weigao Group Medical Polymer Co., Ltd. is a Chinese firm principally engaged in the research, production and sale of medical supplies, orthopedic materials and heart stents. The company's sales network is made up of customer liaison centers, sales offices and approximately 170 municipal representative offices. Products are sold to thousands of healthcare organizations and distributors, such as hospitals, blood stations and trading companies. Weigao Group's products are organized in eight categories: single use infusion sets, blood collection sets and stations, syringes, trauma and spinal orthopedic products, hemodialysis products, operation room consumables, sterilization supply center products and the MSG B steam sterilizer. These products include pressure extension tubes, catheters, infusion needles, blood transfusion pressure products, blood bags, blood cell separator systems, temperature equipment and supplies, femoral supplies, metal bone screws and plates, blood dialyzers, hemodialysis liquid concentrates, disposable laryngeal masks, medical foam, nasal oxygen cannulas, wound dressings, medical drying cupboards, steam sterilizers and automatic pulse vacuum sterilizers. The MSG B steam sterilizer is a pressure chamber that sterilizes equipment and supplies and comes in various sizes. Products are designed and manufactured according to the standards of International Organization for Standardization and the China Quality Certification Center for Medical Devices. Weigao Group has an international reach with products exported to 30 countries.

FINANCIAL DATA: *Note: Data for latest year may not have been available at press time.*

In U.S. $	2020	2019	2018	2017	2016	2015
Revenue	1,778,058,000	1,624,286,000	1,380,548,000	986,199,200	1,054,796,000	927,630,200
R&D Expense	64,476,310	63,686,280	48,766,280	42,914,570	47,436,650	45,866,130
Operating Income	390,285,900	380,591,800	279,745,300	225,692,300	202,871,800	205,442,500
Operating Margin %		.23%	.19%	.22%	.18%	.21%
SGA Expense	573,186,200	590,441,000	527,811,400	366,995,800	402,876,600	303,777,600
Net Income	318,168,400	289,134,900	230,842,200	271,118,200	173,324,700	174,390,900
Operating Cash Flow	422,619,500	363,751,600	347,798,200	198,568,800	165,050,700	164,992,900
Capital Expenditure	156,037,000	154,386,200	124,669,700	237,064,400	100,162,100	177,198,300
EBITDA	527,474,800	510,137,300	410,955,100	300,349,200	269,606,000	265,860,200
Return on Assets %		.07%	.07%	.11%	.08%	.09%
Return on Equity %		.12%	.11%	.14%	.10%	.11%
Debt to Equity		0.275	0.351	0.06	0.067	0.061

CONTACT INFORMATION:

Phone: 86-631-5621999   Fax: 0631-5621999
Toll-Free:
Address: 18 Xingshan Road, Weihai, 264210 China

STOCK TICKER/OTHER:

Stock Ticker: SHWGF   Exchange: PINX
Employees: 10,433   Fiscal Year Ends: 12/31
Parent Company:

SALARIES/BONUSES:

Top Exec. Salary: $ Bonus: $
Second Exec. Salary: $ Bonus: $

OTHER THOUGHTS:

Estimated Female Officers or Directors:
Hot Spot for Advancement for Women/Minorities:

Shanghai RAAS Blood Products Co Ltd
www.raas-corp.com
NAIC Code: 325414

TYPES OF BUSINESS:
Biological Product (except Diagnostic) Manufacturing
Plasma-derived Production

BRANDS/DIVISIONS/AFFILIATES:
Tonrol Biological & Pharmaceutical Co Ltd

GROWTH PLANS/SPECIAL FEATURES:
Shanghai RAAS Blood Products Co., Ltd. was founded in 1988, and is a leading blood products company throughout China and Asia. The firm's products include human albumin, human immunoglobulin, coagulation factors and more, of which have been registered in nearly 20 countries. Shanghai RAAS is one of the few domestic manufacturers able to export its blood products. The company has more than 25 plasma collection stations (including some under construction), producing up to 11 different kinds of products. Shanghai RAAS' research and development activities primarily focus on plasma-derived products and recombinant protein such as coagulation factors. The firm utilizes advanced biological engineering and processing technologies to increase the yield and quality of its blood products. Subsidiary Tonrol Biological & Pharmaceutical Co., Ltd. specializes in product development, production and marketing.

CONTACTS:
Note: Officers with more than one job title may be intentionally listed here more than once.

Chen Jie, Pres.
Zheng Liu, CFO

FINANCIAL DATA:
Note: Data for latest year may not have been available at press time.

In U.S. $	2020	2019	2018	2017	2016	2015
Revenue	227,170,000	246,955,350	259,953,000	296,000,000	334,747,000	310,182,000
R&D Expense						
Operating Income						
Operating Margin %						
SGA Expense						
Net Income	145,659,000	-216,284,040	-220,698,000	127,744,000	237,494,000	228,082,000
Operating Cash Flow						
Capital Expenditure						
EBITDA						
Return on Assets %						
Return on Equity %						
Debt to Equity						

CONTACT INFORMATION:
Phone: 86-21-22130888   Fax: 86-21-37515875
Toll-Free:
Address: 2009 Wangyuan Rd., Fengxian Dist., Shanghai, Shanghai 201401 China

STOCK TICKER/OTHER:
Stock Ticker: 2252
Employees: 2,967
Parent Company:

Exchange: Shenzhen
Fiscal Year Ends: 12/31

SALARIES/BONUSES:
Top Exec. Salary: $ Bonus: $
Second Exec. Salary: $ Bonus: $

OTHER THOUGHTS:
Estimated Female Officers or Directors:
Hot Spot for Advancement for Women/Minorities:

SHL Telemedicine Ltd

www.shl-telemedicine.com

NAIC Code: 511210D

TYPES OF BUSINESS:

Computer Software, Healthcare & Biotechnology
Personal Telemedicine Systems
Medical Call Center Services
Cardiac Testing Services
Remote Cardiac Monitoring
Ambulance Services
Outpatient Diagnostic Imaging

BRANDS/DIVISIONS/AFFILIATES:

smartheart
CardioSen'C
CardioB
CCM
TeleWeight
TelePress
TeleBreather
TelePulse Oximeter

CONTACTS: *Note: Officers with more than one job title may be intentionally listed here more than once.*

Erez Nachtomy, Acting CEO
Yossi Vadnagra, CFO
Arie Roth, Chief Medical Dir.
Yoni Dagan, CTO
Irit Alroy, CTO
Yoav Rubinstein, Head-Global Bus. Dev.
Yariv Alroy, Co-CEO
Georg F. von Oppen, Managing Dir.-SHL Telemedicine, Germany
Erez Nachtomy, Exec. VP

GROWTH PLANS/SPECIAL FEATURES:

SHL Telemedicine Ltd. develops and markets personal telemedicine systems that transmit medical data from an individual to a medical call and provides medical call center services to patients. The company, headquartered in Tel Aviv, Israel, focuses on providing personal telemedicine services related to heart ailments in markets such as the Netherlands, Germany and Italy. SHL monitors patient's health and wellbeing in order to reduce the need for emergency intervention and hospitalization. The firm's goal is to increase its users' chances of survival if a heart attack strikes, and to generally improve their quality of life following a medical event. SHL has developed a full hospital-grade ECG (electrocardiogram) device to enter the smartphone era, allowing users to travel the world while their smartphones send ECGs from distant business and holiday destinations to their physician, cardiologist or telemedicine center for evaluation. Products include the smartheart mobile ECG device; the CardioSen'C cellular-digital ECG transmitter device; the CardioB for easy handling; the CardioBeeper 12/12 handheld ECG transmitter; the CCM (central communication module), which transmits medical data to the company's telemedicine centers from a variety of medical monitoring devices developed by SHL; the TeleWeight, a trans-telephonic weight monitoring device; the TelePress, a remote blood pressure monitoring device; the TeleBreather, a remote, electronic, hand-held device that tests how well the user's lungs are working; and the TelePulse Oximeter, a small electronic, hand-held diagnostic devices to measure the saturation level of oxygen in the user's blood, and also measures pulse rate.

FINANCIAL DATA: *Note: Data for latest year may not have been available at press time.*

In U.S. $	2020	2019	2018	2017	2016	2015
Revenue	40,164,000	41,884,000	48,863,000	37,378,000	40,548,000	34,581,000
R&D Expense	-360,000	2,511,000	173,000	-981,000	-1,113,000	-1,002,000
Operating Income	945,000	5,715,000	11,840,000	1,283,000	-986,000	-9,546,000
Operating Margin %		.14%	.24%	.03%	- .02%	- .28%
SGA Expense	5,749,000	4,033,000	3,704,000	3,791,000	6,415,000	5,923,000
Net Income	278,000	5,695,000	10,141,000	2,408,000	-11,096,000	-16,635,000
Operating Cash Flow	4,682,000	10,850,000	12,756,000	11,844,000	-429,000	3,980,000
Capital Expenditure	1,772,000	1,974,000	1,247,000	1,602,000	1,814,000	2,750,000
EBITDA	5,410,000	8,983,000	15,775,000	8,650,000	1,144,000	-8,842,000
Return on Assets %		.10%	.17%	.04%	- .16%	- .20%
Return on Equity %		.16%	.30%	.09%	- .33%	- .32%
Debt to Equity		0.315		0.051	0.401	0.222

CONTACT INFORMATION:

Phone: 972 35612212   Fax: 972 36242414
Toll-Free:
Address: Yigal Alon 90, Tel Aviv, 67891 Israel

STOCK TICKER/OTHER:

Stock Ticker: SMDCF   Exchange: GREY
Employees: 800   Fiscal Year Ends: 12/31
Parent Company:

SALARIES/BONUSES:

Top Exec. Salary: $ Bonus: $
Second Exec. Salary: $ Bonus: $

OTHER THOUGHTS:

Estimated Female Officers or Directors: 3
Hot Spot for Advancement for Women/Minorities: Y

ShockWave Medical Inc

www.shockwavemedical.com

NAIC Code: 334510

TYPES OF BUSINESS:

Electromedical and Electrotherapeutic Apparatus Manufacturing

BRANDS/DIVISIONS/AFFILIATES:

ShockWave IVL System
Shockwave M5 IVL
Shockwave C2 IVL
Shockwave S4 IVL

CONTACTS: *Note: Officers with more than one job title may be intentionally listed here more than once.*

Douglas Godshall, CEO
Dan Puckett, CFO
Charles Larkin, Chairman of the Board
Isaac Zacharias, Other Executive Officer

GROWTH PLANS/SPECIAL FEATURES:

ShockWave Medical, Inc. develops and commercializes products intended to transform the way calcified cardiovascular disease is treated. The firm's proprietary local delivery of sonic pressure wave device is used for the treatment of calcified plaque, referred to as intravascular lithotripsy (IVL). ShockWave's IVL System leverages the company's IVL technology and is a minimally invasive, easy-to-use and safe way to significantly improve patient outcomes. The Shockwave M5 IVL catheter is CE-marked and U.S. Food and Drug Administration (FDA) approved for use in its IVL system for the treatment of peripheral artery disease (PAD). Shockwave C2 IVL is currently marketed in Europe is used with the IVL system for the treatment of coronary artery disease (CAD). During 2019, the company received Breakthrough Device Designation from the FDA for its C2 catheters using its IVL system for the treatment of CAD. Shockwave S4 IVL catheter is FDA-approved and approved in several other geographies. ShockWave Medical has ongoing clinical programs across several products and indications, which, if successful, will allow the firm to expand commercialization for its products into new geographies and indications. ShockWave's manufacturing location is in Santa Clara, California. The company's electronics (generators and connector cables) are produced by original equipment manufacturing partners using its design specifications. Its products are marketed to hospitals whose interventional cardiologists, vascular surgeons and interventional radiologists treat patients with PAD and CAD.

FINANCIAL DATA: *Note: Data for latest year may not have been available at press time.*

In U.S. $	2020	2019	2018	2017	2016	2015
Revenue	67,789,000	42,927,000	12,263,000	1,719,000		
R&D Expense	36,926,000	32,853,000	22,698,000	17,963,000		
Operating Income	-65,663,000	-51,839,000	-41,200,000	-30,865,000		
Operating Margin %		-1.21%	-3.36%	-17.96%		
SGA Expense	75,535,000	44,754,000	23,515,000	11,785,000		
Net Income	-65,699,000	-51,109,000	-41,102,000	-30,615,000		
Operating Cash Flow	-71,184,000	-48,107,000	-41,465,000	-30,347,000		
Capital Expenditure	11,520,000	3,817,000	1,981,000	425,000		
EBITDA	-61,061,000	-47,822,000	-39,963,000	-30,063,000		
Return on Assets %		- .36%	- .73%	- .52%		
Return on Equity %		- .46%				
Debt to Equity		0.079	0.438			

CONTACT INFORMATION:

Phone: 510 279-4262   Fax:
Toll-Free:
Address: 5403 Betsy Ross Dr., Santa Clara, CA 95054 United States

STOCK TICKER/OTHER:

Stock Ticker: SWAV   Exchange: NAS
Employees: 449   Fiscal Year Ends: 12/31
Parent Company:

SALARIES/BONUSES:

Top Exec. Salary: $ Bonus: $
Second Exec. Salary: $ Bonus: $

OTHER THOUGHTS:

Estimated Female Officers or Directors:
Hot Spot for Advancement for Women/Minorities:

SI-BONE Inc

si-bone.com

NAIC Code: 339113

TYPES OF BUSINESS:

Surgical Appliance and Supplies Manufacturing

BRANDS/DIVISIONS/AFFILIATES:

iFuse
iFuse 3D
SI-BONE

CONTACTS: *Note: Officers with more than one job title may be intentionally listed here more than once.*

Jeffrey Dunn, CEO
Laura Francis, CFO
Michael Pisetsky, Chief Compliance Officer
W. Carlton Reckling, Chief Medical Officer
Scott Yerby, Chief Technology Officer
Anthony Recupero, Other Executive Officer

GROWTH PLANS/SPECIAL FEATURES:

SI-BONE, Inc. is a medical device company that has developed a proprietary minimally-invasive surgical implant system called iFuse. This implant system is used to fuse the sacroiliac joint to treat sacroiliac joint dysfunction that often causes severe lower back pain. The two sacroiliac joints are the largest joints in the body and connect the sacrum, near the base of the spine, to the iliac bones, the two major bones of the pelvis. The iFuse system includes a series of patented triangular implants, which were developed by SI-BONE to enable the procedure, as well as the diagnostic and surgical techniques it developed to enable physicians to perform the procedure. iFuse 3D is a patented titanium implant that combines the triangular cross-section of the iFuse implant with a proprietary 3D-printed porous surface and fenestrated design. The fenestrations allow the host bone to grow directly into the implant structure, or bony through-growth, and allow the surgeon to fill the implant with ground-up bone before implanting it. SI-BONE received clearance from the U.S. Food and Drug Administration (FDA) to promote the use of its iFuse system with the iFuse Bedrock technique for fusion of the sacroiliac joint in conjunction with multi-level spinal fusion procedures, to provide further stabilization and immobilization of the sacroiliac joint. The company's products are marketed through a direct sales force and through distributors in the U.S., and with a combination of a direct sales force and distributors in other countries. SI-BONE and iFuse Implant System are registered trademarks of SI-BONE, Inc. As of October 2020, the iFuse Implant System had been used in over 45,000 procedures by more than 2,000 surgeons, in the U.S. and 33 other countries.

SI-BONE offers comprehensive health benefits, retirement plans and employee assistance programs.

FINANCIAL DATA: *Note: Data for latest year may not have been available at press time.*

In U.S. $	2020	2019	2018	2017	2016	2015
Revenue	73,387,000	67,301,000	55,380,000	47,983,000	42,101,000	
R&D Expense	9,459,000	7,279,000	5,376,000	5,513,000	6,380,000	
Operating Income	-38,567,000	-36,003,000	-11,965,000	-17,350,000	-17,565,000	
Operating Margin %		-.53%	-.22%	-.36%	-.42%	
SGA Expense	93,593,000	89,235,000	57,136,000	54,708,000	48,121,000	
Net Income	-43,697,000	-38,403,000	-17,453,000	-23,039,000	-20,589,000	
Operating Cash Flow	-30,662,000	-31,627,000	-14,519,000	-17,530,000	-16,753,000	
Capital Expenditure	2,561,000	2,445,000	942,000	478,000	441,000	
EBITDA	-36,466,000	-32,680,000	-11,623,000	-15,822,000	-16,243,000	
Return on Assets %		-.30%	-.20%	-.61%	-.52%	
Return on Equity %		-.50%				
Debt to Equity		0.553	0.432			

CONTACT INFORMATION:

Phone: 408-207-0700 Fax:
Toll-Free:
Address: 471 El Camino Real, Ste. 101, Santa Clara, CA 95050 United States

STOCK TICKER/OTHER:

Stock Ticker: SIBN
Employees: 295
Parent Company:

Exchange: NAS
Fiscal Year Ends: 12/31

SALARIES/BONUSES:

Top Exec. Salary: $ Bonus: $
Second Exec. Salary: $ Bonus: $

OTHER THOUGHTS:

Estimated Female Officers or Directors:
Hot Spot for Advancement for Women/Minorities:

Sidecar Health Inc

sidecarhealth.com

NAIC Code: 524210

TYPES OF BUSINESS:

Health Insurance Brokerage
Online Health Insurance Platform
Insurance Website
Insurance Mobile App
Fixed Indemnity Health Plans

BRANDS/DIVISIONS/AFFILIATES:

Sidecar Health VISA

CONTACTS: *Note: Officers with more than one job title may be intentionally listed here more than once.*

Patrick Quigley, CEO
Veronica Osetinsky, COO
Stuart Battersby, CFO
Jon Ward, VP-Mktg.
Alex Coonce, Chief People Officer
Rodney Barlow, CTO

GROWTH PLANS/SPECIAL FEATURES:

Sidecar Health, Inc. operates a web and mobile app platform for exploring and utilizing fixed indemnity health plans. The company aims to keep premiums low by paying doctors directly, saving up to 40% when compared to traditional insurance. How it works in four steps: 1. Members choose a licensed health care provider of their choice, with the benefit payment and plan displayed before seeing the doctor. This goes for any procedure, test or drug needed by the patient. 2. The patient can either see their preferred plan's doctor or can compare Sidecar prices between doctors to find a better price. 3. Once a doctor has been chosen, the member uses their Sidecar Health VISA benefit card, which provides access to the member's benefits and pays for medical services immediately. 4. Once seen, the patient asks the provider for their itemized bill, and checks the status of claims on the website or app. If a benefit amount is $75 for a particular doctor's visit and the doctor's cash price is $90, the patient would pay $15. If the doctor's cash price is $75, the patient would pay nothing. If the doctor's cash price is $65, the member would gain $10 on their Sidecar Health VISA benefit card. After the member has received care, they upload and submit a picture of the itemized bill onto the Sidecare Health platform. If the itemized bill is not uploaded within 30 days, the member must pay the entire amount of care provided by the physician. Members can sign up and cancel at any time. Sidecar Health also has plans for brokers and employers.

FINANCIAL DATA: *Note: Data for latest year may not have been available at press time.*

In U.S. $	2020	2019	2018	2017	2016	2015
Revenue						
R&D Expense						
Operating Income						
Operating Margin %						
SGA Expense						
Net Income						
Operating Cash Flow						
Capital Expenditure						
EBITDA						
Return on Assets %						
Return on Equity %						
Debt to Equity						

CONTACT INFORMATION:

Phone: 424-286-2971   Fax:
Toll-Free:
Address: 2381 Rosecrans Ave., Ste. 400, El Segundo, CA 90245 United States

STOCK TICKER/OTHER:

Stock Ticker: Private
Employees:
Parent Company:

Exchange:
Fiscal Year Ends:

SALARIES/BONUSES:

Top Exec. Salary: $ Bonus: $
Second Exec. Salary: $ Bonus: $

OTHER THOUGHTS:

Estimated Female Officers or Directors:
Hot Spot for Advancement for Women/Minorities:

Siemens AG

www.siemens.com

NAIC Code: 334513

TYPES OF BUSINESS:

Industrial Control Manufacturing
Digitalization
Smart Infrastructure
Mobility
Advanced Technologies
Artificial Intelligence
Internet of Things
Robotics

BRANDS/DIVISIONS/AFFILIATES:

Siemens Advanta
Siemens Healthineers AG
Siemens Financial Services
Siemens Real Estate
Next47

CONTACTS: *Note: Officers with more than one job title may be intentionally listed here more than once.*

Joe Kaeser, CEO
Ralf P. Thomas, CFO
Peter Y. Solmssen, Head-Corp. Legal & Compliance
Joe Kaeser, Head-Controlling
Roland Busch, CEO-Infrastructure & Cities Sector
Hermann Requardt, CEO-Health Care Sector
Michael Suess, CEO-Energy Sector
Siegfried Russwurm, CEO-Industry Sector
Jim Hagemenn Snabe, Chmn.
Barbara Kux, Chief Sustainability Officer

GROWTH PLANS/SPECIAL FEATURES:

Siemens AG is a technology company engaged in electrification, automation and digitalization. Its businesses are grouped into 10 categories. Digital Industries innovates industry-specific automation and digitalization technologies and solutions. Smart infrastructure intelligently connects energy systems, buildings and industries to respond to industry and customer needs, and for efficiency purposes. Mobility offers transport solutions, including rolling stock rail and road automation and electrification, traffic systems and other related systems. Siemens Advanta offers companies digitalization, specifically designed for their future. This category offers related consulting, design, prototyping, platform solutions, data services, and application development in regards to implementation and operation. The portfolio companies business category consists of six umbrella units engaged in the development and production of large drives applications, the manufacture of mechanical driver systems, wind generation, mechanical systems and related components, systems and solutions for electric commercial vehicles, and products and solutions for mail and parcel logistics and baggage/cargo handling. Siemens Healthineers AG provides innovative medical technologies and services across diagnostic and therapeutic imaging, laboratory diagnostics and molecular medicine, as well as digital health and enterprise services. Siemens Financial Services provides business-to-business financial solutions, supporting customer investments with project and structured financing as well as leasing and equipment financing. Global business services innovates, designs, transforms and operates business services for Siemens' units and external customers. These services include digital end-to-end processing as well as professional services. Siemens Real Estate manages the company's global real estate holdings and supports it with forward-looking strategies for tapping into markets worldwide. Last, Next47 is a global venture firm that invests in entrepreneurs engaged in deep technologies such as artificial intelligence (AI), augmented and virtual reality, cybersecurity, autonomous transportation, Internet of Things (IoT), robotics and more.

FINANCIAL DATA: *Note: Data for latest year may not have been available at press time.*

In U.S. $	2020	2019	2018	2017	2016	2015
Revenue	69,811,110,000	106,110,100,000	101,461,200,000	101,467,300,000	97,307,210,000	92,410,320,000
R&D Expense	5,621,396,000	6,927,476,000	6,790,637,000	6,309,257,000	5,781,449,000	5,477,226,000
Operating Income	5,563,972,000	8,176,131,000	7,223,145,000	8,971,509,000	8,724,709,000	7,000,782,000
Operating Margin %		.08%	.07%	.09%	.09%	.08%
SGA Expense	13,163,420,000	16,304,610,000	15,811,020,000	14,936,220,000	14,256,920,000	13,939,250,000
Net Income	4,923,761,000	6,321,474,000	7,094,859,000	7,386,864,000	6,658,684,000	8,896,980,000
Operating Cash Flow	10,827,390,000	10,331,350,000	10,293,470,000	8,767,472,000	9,298,944,000	8,078,389,000
Capital Expenditure	1,898,641,000	3,188,838,000	3,179,064,000	2,939,596,000	2,608,494,000	2,317,711,000
EBITDA	11,782,820,000	14,833,590,000	15,343,080,000	15,355,290,000	13,631,370,000	12,932,510,000
Return on Assets %		.04%	.04%	.05%	.04%	.06%
Return on Equity %		.11%	.13%	.16%	.16%	.22%
Debt to Equity		0.632	0.596	0.621	0.724	0.774

CONTACT INFORMATION:

Phone: 49 8963633032   Fax: 49 8932825
Toll-Free:
Address: Werner-von-Siemens-Strabe 1, Munich, BY 80333 Germany

STOCK TICKER/OTHER:

Stock Ticker: SMAWF   Exchange: PINX
Employees: 293,000   Fiscal Year Ends: 09/30
Parent Company:

SALARIES/BONUSES:

Top Exec. Salary: $ Bonus: $
Second Exec. Salary: $ Bonus: $

OTHER THOUGHTS:

Estimated Female Officers or Directors: 5
Hot Spot for Advancement for Women/Minorities: Y

Siemens Healthineers AG

www.siemens-healthineers.com

NAIC Code: 334510

TYPES OF BUSINESS:

Electromedical and Electrotherapeutic Apparatus Manufacturing
Medical Technology
Imaging Systems
Diagnostic Tests & Products
Digital Services

BRANDS/DIVISIONS/AFFILIATES:

Siemens AG
Siemens Healthcare GmbH

CONTACTS: *Note: Officers with more than one job title may be intentionally listed here more than once.*

J. Marc Overhage, Chief Medical Informatics Officer
Michael Long, Sr. VP-Exec. & Customer Rel.
Brenna Quinn, Sr. VP-Solutions Dev.
Carlos Arglebe, VP-Quality Mgmt.
Gail Latimer, VP
Ralf P. Thomas, Chmn.
Hartmut Schaper, Sr. VP-Health Svcs., Int'l

GROWTH PLANS/SPECIAL FEATURES:

Siemens Healthineers AG, is a subsidiary of Siemens Healthcare GmbH and a business segment within Siemens AG. The firm is a leading medical technology company and one of the largest suppliers to the healthcare industry in the world. Siemens Healthineers' portfolio provides devices and solutions for clinical decision making across the full healthcare spectrum. The company's diagnostic imaging systems span computed tomography, magnetic resonance imaging, molecular imaging, X-ray products, ultrasound systems and imaging IT. Its clinical and workflow diagnostic products include testing systems, automation and IT. Advanced therapies by Siemens Healthineers include angiography systems, mobile C-arms and hybrid operating rooms for image-guided therapy. The firm's enterprise and digital services help providers to maximize opportunities and minimize risks within the healthcare industry. Siemens Healthineers has 18,500 patents globally, and employees in more than 70 countries. In August 2020, the firm agreed to acquire Varian Medical Systems, Inc., a U.S. based radiation oncology treatments and software maker, for $16.4 billion. The transaction is expected to close in the first half of 2021, and upon completion Varian will continue to operate under the Varian name, as a Siemens Healthineers brand.

FINANCIAL DATA: *Note: Data for latest year may not have been available at press time.*

In U.S. $	2020	2019	2018	2017	2016	2015
Revenue	17,666,900,000	17,737,760,000	16,407,240,000	16,855,630,000	16,551,410,000	15,804,910,000
R&D Expense	1,639,625,000	1,622,520,000	1,565,096,000	1,530,886,000	1,398,935,000	1,288,975,000
Operating Income	2,375,134,000	2,805,200,000	2,395,905,000	2,797,869,000	2,586,502,000	2,398,348,000
Operating Margin %		.16%	.15%	.17%	.16%	.15%
SGA Expense	2,784,430,000	2,705,014,000	2,630,486,000	2,714,789,000	2,695,240,000	2,576,728,000
Net Income	1,723,927,000	1,914,525,000	1,545,548,000	1,743,476,000	1,601,750,000	1,560,209,000
Operating Cash Flow	2,355,586,000	1,975,613,000	1,948,734,000	2,413,010,000	2,259,066,000	2,322,598,000
Capital Expenditure	680,529,800	707,408,800	647,541,800	569,348,100	518,033,400	434,952,600
EBITDA	3,475,955,000	3,587,137,000	3,095,983,000	3,522,383,000	3,329,342,000	3,122,862,000
Return on Assets %		.08%	.06%	.07%	.06%	.07%
Return on Equity %		.17%	.21%	.50%	.43%	.35%
Debt to Equity		0.006	0.002	0.005	0.006	0.004

CONTACT INFORMATION:

Phone: 49-69-797-6602   Fax:
Toll-Free:
Address: Henkestr. 127, Erlangen, D-91052 Germany

STOCK TICKER/OTHER:

Stock Ticker: SMMNY   Exchange: PINX
Employees: 52,000   Fiscal Year Ends: 09/30
Parent Company: Siemens AG

SALARIES/BONUSES:

Top Exec. Salary: $ Bonus: $
Second Exec. Salary: $ Bonus: $

OTHER THOUGHTS:

Estimated Female Officers or Directors: 3
Hot Spot for Advancement for Women/Minorities: Y

Sigma Healthcare Limited

sigmahealthcare.com.au

NAIC Code: 424210

TYPES OF BUSINESS:

Drugs and Druggists' Sundries Merchant Wholesalers

BRANDS/DIVISIONS/AFFILIATES:

Amcal
Guardian
PharmaSave
Chemist King
Discount Drug Stores
WholeLife
Central Healthcare Services (CHS)
InClinic

CONTACTS: *Note: Officers with more than one job title may be intentionally listed here more than once.*

Mark Hooper, CEO
Jackie Pearson, CFO
Scott Jones, Gen. Mgr.-Merch.
Sue Morgan, General Counsel
Vincent Gualtieri, Gen. Mgr.-Wholesale Sales
Michael Robertson, Gen. Mgr.-Retail Oper.
Richard Church, Gen. Mgr.-Logistics
Claire Pallot, Gen. Mgr.-Multi Channel
Alan O Hara, Gen. Mgr.-Supply Chain & Transformation

GROWTH PLANS/SPECIAL FEATURES:

Sigma Healthcare Limited is an Australian wholesaler, manufacturer and retailer of pharmaceuticals. The company's pharmacy network is comprised of more than 1,200 branded and independent stores, including the Amcal, Guardian, PharmaSave, Chemist King, Discount Drug Stores and WholeLife retail brand names. These stores provide pharmaceuticals, health and well-being items, as well as beauty products. WholeLife combines the traditional pharmacy offering and holistic, healthy living nutritional solutions. Sigma maintains long-term alliances with independent pharmacy support groups, enabling the company to offer its solutions to suit any pharmacy, including large format branded pharmacies as well as independent community pharmacies. The firm also distributes to hospital pharmacies and health facilities through wholly-owned Central Healthcare Services, which is branded as CHS. Sigma's supply and logistics division maintains a network of distribution centers, serving more than 4,000 pharmacies nationwide with over 15,500 products lines daily via deliveries by road, sea and air. Sigma Healthcare and its branded pharmacies have a partnership with doctors on-demand, called InClinic. InClinic provides patients with access to professional online consultation from an Australian registered doctor, inside a Sigma pharmacy. This InClinic online service focuses on Australian communities with limited access to general healthcare services.

Sigma Healthcare offers its employees health and wellbeing member programs, corporate private health insurance benefits, professional development activities, an employee assistance program, among other benefits.

FINANCIAL DATA: *Note: Data for latest year may not have been available at press time.*

In U.S. $	2020	2019	2018	2017	2016	2015
Revenue	2,181,480,000	2,864,850,000	3,309,330,000	3,347,451,904	2,661,216,256	2,406,870,016
R&D Expense						
Operating Income						
Operating Margin %						
SGA Expense						
Net Income	-7,710,540	26,684,200	44,765,800	40,270,772	38,239,972	39,959,564
Operating Cash Flow						
Capital Expenditure						
EBITDA						
Return on Assets %						
Return on Equity %						
Debt to Equity						

CONTACT INFORMATION:

Phone: 61-03-92159215   Fax: 61-03-92159188
Toll-Free:
Address: 3 Myer Pl., Rowville, VIC 3178 Australia

STOCK TICKER/OTHER:

Stock Ticker: SHTPY   Exchange: ASX
Employees: 156   Fiscal Year Ends: 01/31
Parent Company:

SALARIES/BONUSES:

Top Exec. Salary: $ Bonus: $
Second Exec. Salary: $ Bonus: $

OTHER THOUGHTS:

Estimated Female Officers or Directors: 4
Hot Spot for Advancement for Women/Minorities: Y

Silk Road Medical Inc

www.silkroadmed.com

NAIC Code: 334510

TYPES OF BUSINESS:

Electromedical and Electrotherapeutic Apparatus Manufacturing

BRANDS/DIVISIONS/AFFILIATES:

ENROUTE
ENHANCE

CONTACTS: *Note: Officers with more than one job title may be intentionally listed here more than once.*

Erica Rogers, CEO
Lucas Buchanan, CFO
Andrew Davis, Executive VP, Divisional

GROWTH PLANS/SPECIAL FEATURES:

Silk Road Medical, Inc. is a medical device company focused on reducing the risk of stroke. The company has developed a technologically-advanced, minimally-invasive solution for patients with carotid artery disease who are at risk for stroke. Silk Road's portfolio of trans-carotid artery revascularization (TCAR) products combine the benefits of endovascular techniques and surgical principles. TCAR relies on two concepts: minimally-invasive direct carotid access in the neck and high-rate blood flow reversal during the procedure to protect the brain. Silk Road manufactures and sells its TCAR products in the U.S., which are designed to provide direct access to the carotid artery to treat blockage and therefore reduce stroke risk throughout the procedure and offer long-term restraint of carotid plaque. The company's TCAR products are marketed under the ENROUTE and ENHANCE brand names, and include the ENROUTE transcarotid neuroprotection system, the ENROUTE transcarotid stent system, the ENHANCE transcarotid peripheral access kit and the ENROUTE 0.014 guidewire.

FINANCIAL DATA: *Note: Data for latest year may not have been available at press time.*

In U.S. $	2020	2019	2018	2017	2016	2015
Revenue	75,227,000	63,354,000	34,557,000	14,258,000		
R&D Expense	21,271,000	12,272,000	10,258,000	7,242,000		
Operating Income	-42,859,000	-28,065,000	-21,395,000	-18,374,000		
Operating Margin %		- .44%	- .62%	-1.29%		
SGA Expense	75,524,000	63,220,000	34,820,000	20,261,000		
Net Income	-47,365,000	-52,415,000	-37,629,000	-19,356,000		
Operating Cash Flow	-42,068,000	-29,610,000	-21,695,000	-25,252,000		
Capital Expenditure	842,000	535,000	2,276,000	443,000		
EBITDA	-41,563,000	-46,169,000	-32,752,000	-15,284,000		
Return on Assets %		- .59%	- .61%	- .45%		
Return on Equity %		-1.79%				
Debt to Equity		0.624				

CONTACT INFORMATION:

Phone: 408 720-9002 Fax: 408 720-9013
Toll-Free:
Address: 1213 Innsbruck Dr., Sunnyvale, CA 94089 United States

STOCK TICKER/OTHER:

Stock Ticker: SILK Exchange: NAS
Employees: 281 Fiscal Year Ends: 12/31
Parent Company:

SALARIES/BONUSES:

Top Exec. Salary: $ Bonus: $
Second Exec. Salary: $ Bonus: $

OTHER THOUGHTS:

Estimated Female Officers or Directors:
Hot Spot for Advancement for Women/Minorities:

Simcere Pharmaceutical Group Ltd

www.simcere.com

NAIC Code: 325412

TYPES OF BUSINESS:

Branded Generic Pharmaceuticals
Drug Research
Pharmaceutical Development

BRANDS/DIVISIONS/AFFILIATES:

CONTACTS: *Note: Officers with more than one job title may be intentionally listed here more than once.*

Jinsheng Ren, CEO
Xiaojin Yin, Sr. VP-R&D
Haibo Qian, VP
Jie Liu DElia, Corp. VP-Bus. Dev.
Jie Liu DElia, Corp. VP-Corp. Communications
Jindong Zhou, Exec. VP
Quanfu Feng, VP
Jialun Tian, VP-Hospital Sales
Jie Liu DElia, Pres., Simcrere of America

GROWTH PLANS/SPECIAL FEATURES:

Simcere Pharmaceutical Group Ltd. is a Chinese innovation and research and development (R&D)-driven pharmaceutical company. The firm has R&D centers in Nanjing and Shanghai, China, as well as in Massachusetts, USA. With the approval of the Ministry of Science and Technology, Simcere has also established a national laboratory of translational medicine and innovative pharmaceuticals. Simcere has nearly 50 innovative product candidates in different stages of development, including small molecule pharmaceuticals, large molecule pharmaceuticals and CAR T-cell therapies, among which over 10 product candidates are at clinical stage, have submitted New Drug Application (NDA) or obtained NDA pending market launch. These products are used for treatment of a wide range of diseases in fields such as oncology, central nervous system, autoimmune, cardiovascular, anti-infection, and others. Simcere's products have included: Bicun, an anti-stroke medication and the first synthetic-free radical scavenger sold in China; Zailin, a generic amoxicillin granule antibiotic; Endostar, a recombinant human endostatin injection to eradicate tumors; Yingtaiqing, a generic diclofenac sodium sustained-release capsule for inflammation and pain relief; Iremod, a disease modifying anti-rheumatic drug; AnQi, an amoxicillin tablet for infections; Sinofuan, an anti-cancer sustained-release fluorouracil implant; and Jiebaili, a nedaplatin injection.

FINANCIAL DATA: *Note: Data for latest year may not have been available at press time.*

In U.S. $	2020	2019	2018	2017	2016	2015
Revenue	706,618,400	789,358,300	707,477,900	606,188,700		
R&D Expense	178,976,600	112,278,000	70,078,210	33,273,620		
Operating Income	89,895,310	177,056,900	130,225,700	107,890,800		
Operating Margin %						
SGA Expense	310,600,600	338,336,400	368,532,800	357,732,200		
Net Income	104,931,100	157,290,600	114,985,300	54,917,020		
Operating Cash Flow	15,159,940	121,115,700	121,588,100	147,174,400		
Capital Expenditure	55,298,160	79,561,490	52,535,930	45,794,350		
EBITDA	181,977,800	213,186,500	171,859,000	103,416,400		
Return on Assets %						
Return on Equity %						
Debt to Equity						

CONTACT INFORMATION:

Phone: 86 2525566666   Fax: 86 2585472579
Toll-Free:
Address: No. 699-18, Xuanwu Road, Nanjing, Jiangsu 210042 China

STOCK TICKER/OTHER:

Stock Ticker: SMHGF
Employees: 14,000
Parent Company:

Exchange: PINX
Fiscal Year Ends: 12/31

SALARIES/BONUSES:

Top Exec. Salary: $ Bonus: $
Second Exec. Salary: $ Bonus: $

OTHER THOUGHTS:

Estimated Female Officers or Directors: 1
Hot Spot for Advancement for Women/Minorities:

Sinopharm Group Co Ltd

www.sinopharmholding.com

NAIC Code: 424210

TYPES OF BUSINESS:

Drugs and Druggists Sundries Merchant Wholesalers

BRANDS/DIVISIONS/AFFILIATES:

China National Pharmaceutical Group Corporation
Shanghai Fosun Pharmaceutical

CONTACTS: *Note: Officers with more than one job title may be intentionally listed here more than once.*

Zhiming Li, Exec. Dir.
Li Zhiming, Chief Legal Officer
Zhang Jian, Head-Auditing
Ma Wanjun, VP
Lu Jun, VP
Shi Jinming, VP
Liu Wei, Joint Sec.

GROWTH PLANS/SPECIAL FEATURES:

Sinopharm Group Co., Ltd. is China's largest pharmaceuticals and healthcare products distributor and a leading provider of supply chain services. The company is jointly-owned by China National Pharmaceutical Group Corporation and Shanghai Fosun Pharmaceutical. Sinopharm has more than 475 subsidiary companies, comprising a business and distribution network covering over 35 provinces, municipalities and autonomous regions. In addition, the group manages retail pharmacy chains. It is a licensed distributor of narcotic drugs in China, and has held a majority of the market share. Operations of the group are divided into pharmaceutical distribution, medicine retail business and medicine and chemical regent production. Its products are supported through research and development centers, manufacturing facilities, traditional Chinese medicine plantations and marketing and distribution networks. Operations are conducted internationally as well, with locations in Africa, France, Germany, Hong Kong, the U.S. and Vietnam.

FINANCIAL DATA: *Note: Data for latest year may not have been available at press time.*

In U.S. $	2020	2019	2018	2017	2016	2015
Revenue	71,530,500,000	66,649,860,000	53,994,990,000	43,416,700,000	40,452,810,000	35,580,590,000
R&D Expense						
Operating Income	3,100,563,000	2,899,887,000	2,469,030,000	1,758,103,000	1,558,333,000	1,430,698,000
Operating Margin %		.04%	.05%	.04%	.04%	.04%
SGA Expense	3,321,196,000	3,051,257,000	2,489,964,000	1,813,344,000	1,681,514,000	1,518,964,000
Net Income	1,126,409,000	979,914,000	914,608,400	827,979,800	728,343,900	589,378,800
Operating Cash Flow	1,748,180,000	2,942,796,000	572,623,600	261,310,700	1,450,932,000	2,125,229,000
Capital Expenditure	327,130,900	399,459,900	533,502,600	296,942,200	213,744,000	202,561,300
EBITDA	3,545,060,000	3,184,038,000	2,783,374,000	2,162,771,000	1,886,325,000	1,645,903,000
Return on Assets %		.02%	.03%	.03%	.03%	.03%
Return on Equity %		.14%	.15%	.16%	.15%	.13%
Debt to Equity		0.242	0.117	0.157	0.35	0.02

CONTACT INFORMATION:

Phone: 86-21-23052666   Fax: 86-21-23052888
Toll-Free:
Address: No. 1001, Zhongshan West Road, Shanghai, 200051 China

STOCK TICKER/OTHER:

Stock Ticker: SHTDY
Employees: 93,764
Parent Company:

Exchange: PINX
Fiscal Year Ends: 12/31

SALARIES/BONUSES:

Top Exec. Salary: $ Bonus: $
Second Exec. Salary: $ Bonus: $

OTHER THOUGHTS:

Estimated Female Officers or Directors:
Hot Spot for Advancement for Women/Minorities:

Smile Brands Inc

www.smilebrands.com

NAIC Code: 621210

TYPES OF BUSINESS:

Dental Practice Management

BRANDS/DIVISIONS/AFFILIATES:

Gryphon Investors
ConsumerHealth Inc
Bright Now! Dental
Monarch Dental
Castle Dental
Johnson Family Dental
AXIOM Implant Specialty Dentistry
Whitney Ranch Dental

CONTACTS: *Note: Officers with more than one job title may be intentionally listed here more than once.*

Steven Bilt, CEO
Brad Schmidt, CFO
Neal Crowley, General Counsel
Dennis R. Fratt, Sr. VP-Oper. Svcs. Group
William P. McCarthy, Sr. VP-Real Estate & Facility Dev.
Stephen R. Ashlock, VP-Specialty Svcs.
Jeff Hamill, VP-West
Steve Laudicino, VP-East
Fred Ward, VP-Central
Brian Stern, Sr. VP-Patient Experience

GROWTH PLANS/SPECIAL FEATURES:

Smile Brands, Inc. provides business support services to more than 440 affiliated dental offices across 18 U.S. states. The group supports the practices of independent dentists by managing the administrative, financial, marketing and information services aspects of their practices. Its brands include, but are not limited to, Bright Now! Dental, Monarch Dental, Castle Dental, Newport Dental, Los Gatos Dental Specialists, OneSmile Dental, A+ Dental Care, Grant Road Dental, Johnson Family Dental, Premier Private Practice Dental Group, AXIOM Implant Specialty Dentistry, Maddison Ave. Dental, Perfect Smile Dental, Summerlin Dental and Whitney Ranch Dental. The firm's affiliated dental offices are located in Arizona, Arkansas, California, Colorado, Florida, Illinois, Indiana, Maryland, Nevada, Ohio, Oregon, Pennsylvania, Tennessee, Texas, Utah, Virginia, Washington and Wisconsin. In addition, wholly-owned subsidiary ConsumerHealth, Inc. (dba Bright Now! Dental) operates as a staff-model dental health service plan licensed by the state of California under the provisions of the California Knox-Keene Health Care Service Plan Act of 1975. ConsumerHealth is a mixed-model plan that provides dental services to enrolled members through its individual, group and Medicaid product lines, as well as through agreements to service group enrollees of other dental plans. The subsidiary owns and operates staff-model dental facilities throughout California, and employs or contracts directly with each of the dentists, specialists and hygienists that work at ConsumerHealth facilities. Smile Brands' primary equity sponsor is Gryphon Investors, a leading middle-market private equity firm based in San Francisco, California. Gryphon focuses on investing in physician-centric healthcare businesses. In October 2020, Smile Brands announced the addition of its newest partner, Reflections Dental, of Seattle, Washington.

Smile Brands offers its employees health, dental, vision, group life, AD&D and short/long-term disability insurance plans, flexible spending accounts, supplemental medical plans, a 401(k) plan and other types of voluntary insurances.

FINANCIAL DATA: *Note: Data for latest year may not have been available at press time.*

In U.S. $	2020	2019	2018	2017	2016	2015
Revenue	403,100,775	523,507,500	507,150,000	483,000,000	460,000,000	459,000,000
R&D Expense						
Operating Income						
Operating Margin %						
SGA Expense						
Net Income						
Operating Cash Flow						
Capital Expenditure						
EBITDA						
Return on Assets %						
Return on Equity %						
Debt to Equity						

CONTACT INFORMATION:

Phone: 714-668-1300 Fax: 714-428-1300
Toll-Free:
Address: 100 Spectrum Center Dr., Ste. 1500, Irvine, CA 92618 United States

STOCK TICKER/OTHER:

Stock Ticker: Private
Employees: 1,300
Parent Company: Gryphon Investors

Exchange:
Fiscal Year Ends: 12/31

SALARIES/BONUSES:

Top Exec. Salary: $ Bonus: $
Second Exec. Salary: $ Bonus: $

OTHER THOUGHTS:

Estimated Female Officers or Directors: 2
Hot Spot for Advancement for Women/Minorities: Y

Sales, profits and employees may be estimates. Financial information, benefits and other data can change quickly and may vary from those stated here.

Smith & Nephew plc

NAIC Code: 339113

www.smith-nephew.com

TYPES OF BUSINESS:

Implants, Surgical, Manufacturing
Reconstructive Joint Implants
Arthroscopic Enabling Technologies
Wound Management Products

BRANDS/DIVISIONS/AFFILIATES:

GROWTH PLANS/SPECIAL FEATURES:

Smith & Nephew plc develops and markets advanced medical technology devices for healthcare professionals, operating in around 100 countries globally. The company organizes its business into three franchise areas: orthopedics & trauma, sports medicine and advanced wound management. The orthopedics & trauma division includes an innovative range of hip and knee implants used to replace diseased, damaged or worn joints, as well as trauma products used to stabilize severe fractures and correct bone deformities. The sports medicine division consists of businesses that offer advanced products and instruments used to repair or remove soft tissue due to injuries and degenerative conditions of the knee, hip and shoulder. Last, the advanced wound management division provides a comprehensive set of products to meet broad and complex clinical needs. These projects help healthcare professionals get closer to zero human and economic consequences of wounds.

CONTACTS:

Note: Officers with more than one job title may be intentionally listed here more than once.

Roland Diggelman, CEO
Mark Gladwell, Pres.
Anne Francoise Nesmes, CFO
Elga Lohler, Chief Human Resources Officer
Jack Campo, Chief Legal Officer
Gordon Howe, Pres., Global Oper.
Cyrille Petit, Chief Corp. Dev. Officer
Phil Cowdy, Head-Corp. Affairs
Phil Cowdy, Head-Corp. Affairs & Strategic Planning
Mike Frazzette, Pres., Advanced Surgical Devices
Arjun Rajaratnam, Chief Compliance Officer
Roberto Quarta, Chmn.
Francisco Canal Vega, Pres., Latin America

FINANCIAL DATA:

Note: Data for latest year may not have been available at press time.

In U.S. $	2020	2019	2018	2017	2016	2015
Revenue	4,560,000,000	5,138,000,000	4,904,000,000	4,765,000,000	4,669,000,000	4,634,000,000
R&D Expense	279,000,000	292,000,000	237,000,000	223,000,000	230,000,000	222,000,000
Operating Income	491,000,000	990,000,000	1,006,000,000	960,000,000	902,000,000	895,000,000
Operating Margin %		.19%	.21%	.20%	.19%	.14%
SGA Expense	2,160,000,000	2,314,000,000	2,187,000,000	2,132,000,000	2,026,000,000	2,104,000,000
Net Income	448,000,000	600,000,000	663,000,000	767,000,000	784,000,000	410,000,000
Operating Cash Flow	935,000,000	1,168,000,000	931,000,000	1,090,000,000	849,000,000	1,030,000,000
Capital Expenditure	443,000,000	408,000,000	347,000,000	376,000,000	392,000,000	358,000,000
EBITDA	883,000,000	1,320,000,000	1,287,000,000	1,393,000,000	1,593,000,000	1,115,000,000
Return on Assets %		.07%	.08%	.10%	.11%	.06%
Return on Equity %		.12%	.14%	.18%	.20%	.10%
Debt to Equity		0.384	0.267	0.306	0.395	0.362

CONTACT INFORMATION:

Phone: 44 2074017646   Fax: 44 2079303353
Toll-Free:
Address: Bldg. 5, Croxley Park, Hatters Ln., Watford, Herfordshire, WD18 8YE United Kingdom

STOCK TICKER/OTHER:

Stock Ticker: SNN   Exchange: NYS
Employees: 17,637   Fiscal Year Ends: 12/31
Parent Company:

SALARIES/BONUSES:

Top Exec. Salary: $ Bonus: $
Second Exec. Salary: $ Bonus: $

OTHER THOUGHTS:

Estimated Female Officers or Directors: 6
Hot Spot for Advancement for Women/Minorities: Y

Smiths Group plc

www.smiths.com

NAIC Code: 339100

TYPES OF BUSINESS:

Machinery, Manufacturing
Medical Devices, Manufacturing
Security Equipment
Electronic Components

BRANDS/DIVISIONS/AFFILIATES:

Smiths Detection
Smiths Medical
Smiths Interconnect
John Crane
Flex-Tek

CONTACTS: *Note: Officers with more than one job title may be intentionally listed here more than once.*

Andy Reynolds Smith, CEO
John Shipsey, CFO
Sheena Mackay, Dir.-Human Resources
George Buckley, Chmn.

GROWTH PLANS/SPECIAL FEATURES:

Smiths Group plc is a global technology company with five main divisions: Smiths Detection, Smiths Medical, Smiths Interconnect, John Crane and Flex-Tek. Smiths Detection provides security equipment for the detection and identification of explosives, chemical and biological agents, weapons, narcotics and contraband. This equipment is used by military forces, airport security, customs officers and emergency services. Smiths Medical is a provider of specialist medical devices and equipment, which include airway management, pain management, needle safety, temperature monitoring, infusion systems, vascular access and in-vitro fertilization. Smiths Interconnect manufactures electronic components and sub-systems such as millimeter wave components and antennas, fiber optic and coaxial cables, industrial surge protectors and wireless technology products. John Crane provides products and services to the oil and gas, power generation, chemicals, pharmaceutical, pulp and paper and mining industries. Flex-Tek provides components such as flexible hose and ducting for heating and conveying gas, liquid and airborne solids to the aerospace, medical, industrial, construction and domestic appliance industries.

FINANCIAL DATA: *Note: Data for latest year may not have been available at press time.*

In U.S. $	2020	2019	2018	2017	2016	2015
Revenue	3,607,226,000	3,536,440,000	4,548,672,000	4,643,525,000	4,174,925,000	4,101,308,000
R&D Expense						
Operating Income	382,241,400	545,047,900	729,090,000	706,438,700	547,879,300	557,789,200
Operating Margin %		.15%	.16%	.15%	.13%	.14%
SGA Expense	937,199,200	908,885,100	1,302,452,000	1,452,517,000	1,384,563,000	1,329,351,000
Net Income	375,162,800	318,534,500	392,151,300	806,954,000	366,668,600	348,264,400
Operating Cash Flow	607,339,100	489,835,200	573,362,000	678,124,500	506,823,700	376,578,500
Capital Expenditure	155,728,000	167,053,600	150,065,100	151,480,800	152,896,500	134,492,300
EBITDA	477,093,900	723,427,200	884,818,000	1,112,747,000	734,752,800	719,180,000
Return on Assets %		.04%	.05%	.12%	.06%	.07%
Return on Equity %		.10%	.13%	.31%	.17%	.19%
Debt to Equity		0.636	0.619	0.765	0.692	0.81

CONTACT INFORMATION:

Phone: 44 2078085500   Fax: 44 2078085544
Toll-Free:
Address: 11-12 St James's Square, London, SW1Y 4LB United Kingdom

STOCK TICKER/OTHER:

Stock Ticker: SMGZY
Employees: 23,100
Parent Company:

Exchange: PINX
Fiscal Year Ends: 07/31

SALARIES/BONUSES:

Top Exec. Salary: $ Bonus: $
Second Exec. Salary: $ Bonus: $

OTHER THOUGHTS:

Estimated Female Officers or Directors:
Hot Spot for Advancement for Women/Minorities: Y

Sonic Healthcare Limited

NAIC Code: 621511

www.sonichealthcare.com.au

TYPES OF BUSINESS:

Medical Laboratories

BRANDS/DIVISIONS/AFFILIATES:

Sonic Clinical Services
IPN Medical Centres
Sonic HealthPlus
Australian Skin Cancer Clinics

CONTACTS: Note: Officers with more than one job title may be intentionally listed here more than once.

Colin Goldschmidt, CEO

GROWTH PLANS/SPECIAL FEATURES:

Sonic Healthcare Limited is an international medical diagnostics company, offering laboratory and diagnostic imaging services to the medical community and their patients. The firm's services are categorized into three groups: laboratory medicine/pathology, diagnostic imaging/radiology and Sonic Clinical Services. The laboratory medicine/pathology group is the largest laboratory medicine company in Australia, Germany, the U.K. and Switzerland. It also has a significant presence in the U.S., and divisions in the U.K., Belgium, Ireland and New Zealand. This group's laboratories are staffed by more than 900 specialist pathologists and thousands of medical scientists and technicians. The diagnostic imaging group comprises more than 100 radiology centers in Australia, performing millions of examinations annually via 200 specialist radiologists and nuclear physicians. Last, Sonic Clinical Services is the primary care division of Sonic Healthcare, and offers general practice services and after hours general practitioner services as well as occupational health services, remote health services, community and home nursing services. Its activities also include primary care research programs, health assessment technologies, hospital avoidance programs, clinical trials and chronic disease management programs. Brands within Sonic Clinical Services include IPN Medical Centres, Sonic HealthPlus and Australian Skin Cancer Clinics. It provides national healthcare services and solutions throughout Australia, including metropolitan, regional and rural locations.

FINANCIAL DATA: Note: Data for latest year may not have been available at press time.

In U.S. $	2020	2019	2018	2017	2016	2015
Revenue	5,260,502,000	4,712,188,000	4,247,267,000	3,919,618,000	3,837,082,000	3,211,791,000
R&D Expense						
Operating Income	591,504,500	542,821,400	488,799,300	446,321,000	434,022,500	358,549,100
Operating Margin %		.12%	.12%	.11%	.11%	.11%
SGA Expense	2,501,377,000	2,481,912,000	2,339,224,000	2,178,029,000	2,131,935,000	1,802,236,000
Net Income	409,316,800	426,361,200	368,875,300	331,776,400	350,081,200	269,671,100
Operating Cash Flow						
Capital Expenditure	258,342,800	299,880,300	254,101,100	317,302,400	305,577,800	204,884,500
EBITDA	1,099,618,000	838,772,700	737,945,200	675,889,500	685,903,900	541,647,200
Return on Assets %		.06%	.06%	.06%	.07%	.06%
Return on Equity %		.11%	.12%	.11%	.13%	.11%
Debt to Equity		0.408	0.668	0.536	0.573	0.679

CONTACT INFORMATION:

Phone: 61 298555444   Fax: 61 298785066
Toll-Free:
Address: Level 22, 225 George St., Sydney, NSW 2000 Australia

STOCK TICKER/OTHER:

Stock Ticker: SKHCF   Exchange: PINX
Employees: 37,000   Fiscal Year Ends: 06/30
Parent Company:

SALARIES/BONUSES:

Top Exec. Salary: $ Bonus: $
Second Exec. Salary: $ Bonus: $

OTHER THOUGHTS:

Estimated Female Officers or Directors: 2
Hot Spot for Advancement for Women/Minorities:

Sonova Holding AG

www.sonova.com

NAIC Code: 334510

TYPES OF BUSINESS:

Auditory Devices & Hearing Aids

BRANDS/DIVISIONS/AFFILIATES:

Phonak
Hansaton
Unitron
Advanced Bionics
AudioNova Group
Audium
Connect Hearing
Vitakustik

CONTACTS: *Note: Officers with more than one job title may be intentionally listed here more than once.*

Arnd Kaldowski, CEO
Ludger Althoff, VP-Operations
Hartwig Grevener, CFO
Hans Mehl, VP-Oper.
Paul Thompson, VP-Corp. Dev.
Ignacio Martinez, VP-Intl Sales
Hansjurg Emch, VP-Medical
Alexander Zschokke, VP-Channel Solutions
Robert F. Spoerry, Chmn.

GROWTH PLANS/SPECIAL FEATURES:

Sonova Holding AG develops and markets medical devices for the hearing-impaired. Based in Switzerland, Sonova is a leading producer of hearing healthcare solutions, wireless communication systems and products for hearing protection. The company, which operates four major subsidiaries in over 90 countries, is divided into two segments: hearing aids and cochlear implants. The hearing aids segment consists of a global brand portfolio: Phonak, Hansaton and Unitron. Phonak has been in business for more than 70 years, and offers innovative, state-of-the-art hearing systems and wireless devices. Hansaton is a unique hearing aid manufacturer with a tradition of creating innovative solutions that focus on giving the joy of life back to people with hearing loss. Unitron partners with hearing care professionals to support in-clinic success via patient experience with products, services and resources. The cochlear implants segment is represented by the Advanced Bionics brand. Advanced Bionics is North America's leading producer of cochlear inner-ear implants, which are neurostimulation devices that offer those suffering from severe hearing loss and deafness the ability to hear. Advanced Bionics develops cutting-edge cochlear implant technology designed to help children and adults enjoy clear, high-resolution sound, optimal speech understanding in noisy settings and quality music experience. In addition, Sonova's AudioNova Group expands its European presence, and is a service network of hearing care providers dedicated to delivering service and technology solutions for people with hearing loss. The firm aims to continually improve information, education, screening, counseling and support for customers. It operates under brands such as Audium, AuditionSante, Boot Hearingcare, Connect Hearing, Lapperre, Schoonenberg, Triton and Vitakustik.

Sonova offers its employees wellness programs, access to health classes and access to childcare.

FINANCIAL DATA: *Note: Data for latest year may not have been available at press time.*

In U.S. $	2020	2019	2018	2017	2016	2015
Revenue	3,251,912,000	3,080,559,000	2,949,816,000	2,670,796,000	2,309,895,000	
R&D Expense	186,180,300	166,558,900	159,311,200	152,884,100	145,215,100	
Operating Income	568,574,500	597,449,200	532,445,500	507,789,500	440,073,300	
Operating Margin %	.17%	.19%	.18%	.19%	.19%	
SGA Expense	1,542,175,000	1,381,971,000	1,337,843,000	1,179,414,000	928,073,100	
Net Income	538,696,500	506,254,300	446,091,300	389,275,100	375,734,100	
Operating Cash Flow	940,154,700	594,439,100	583,487,900	582,388,700	477,650,600	
Capital Expenditure	143,592,900	131,441,100	107,354,700	109,500,800	92,589,580	
EBITDA	790,653,100	735,356,400	685,612,900	631,520,200	543,242,900	
Return on Assets %	.11%	.11%	.10%	.10%	.12%	
Return on Equity %	.22%	.19%	.18%	.17%	.18%	
Debt to Equity	0.381	0.153	0.249	0.36	0.00	

CONTACT INFORMATION:

Phone: 41 589283333   Fax: 41 589283399
Toll-Free:
Address: Laubisrutistrasse 28, Stafa, CH-8712 Switzerland

STOCK TICKER/OTHER:

Stock Ticker: SONVY
Employees: 14,508
Parent Company:

Exchange: PINX
Fiscal Year Ends: 03/31

SALARIES/BONUSES:

Top Exec. Salary: $ Bonus: $
Second Exec. Salary: $ Bonus: $

OTHER THOUGHTS:

Estimated Female Officers or Directors: 2
Hot Spot for Advancement for Women/Minorities:

So-Young International Inc

ir.soyoung.com/investor-relations

NAIC Code: 519130

TYPES OF BUSINESS:

Internet Publishing and Broadcasting and Web Search Portals
Online Reservation Services for Medical Aesthetic Treatment

BRANDS/DIVISIONS/AFFILIATES:

GROWTH PLANS/SPECIAL FEATURES:

So-Young International, Inc. is an online destination for discovering, evaluating and reserving medical aesthetic services in China. The company leverages its media content to reach and attract a vast audience. Users can share their experiences of undergoing medical aesthetic treatments to help others make related decisions. So-Young's services primarily focus on medical aesthetics providers in China, but plans to extend services to health care areas such as dentistry, dermatology, ophthalmology, gynecology and physical examinations.

CONTACTS:
Note: Officers with more than one job title may be intentionally listed here more than once.

Xing Jin, CEO
Min Yu, CFO
Xuejian Li, CTO

FINANCIAL DATA:
Note: Data for latest year may not have been available at press time.

In U.S. $	2020	2019	2018	2017	2016	2015
Revenue	202,953,900	180,487,600	96,733,270	40,638,960	7,693,514	
R&D Expense	35,919,570	27,781,910	14,845,710	5,102,419	2,810,350	
Operating Income	-8,885,232	22,752,210	7,700,566	3,880,766	-11,641,830	
Operating Margin %		.13%	.08%	.10%	-1.51%	
SGA Expense	142,662,100	98,823,640	59,837,010	24,634,760	12,576,830	
Net Income	910,088	27,696,650	8,632,752	2,695,943	-12,700,170	
Operating Cash Flow	28,081,560	60,153,590	31,185,450	14,242,480	-6,387,387	
Capital Expenditure	5,792,782	5,883,994	1,004,279	34,792	139,640	
EBITDA	-6,677,481	23,712,760	7,961,666	3,977,777	-11,553,440	
Return on Assets %		.06%	.06%	-.02%		
Return on Equity %		.07%	.13%			
Debt to Equity		0.046				

CONTACT INFORMATION:

Phone: 86-10-5269 9283   Fax:
Toll-Free:
Address: Block E, Rosin Tech Cntr., No 34 Chuangyuan Rd., Chaoyang Distr., Beijing, 100012 China

STOCK TICKER/OTHER:

Stock Ticker: SY
Employees: 1,564
Parent Company:

Exchange: NAS
Fiscal Year Ends: 12/31

SALARIES/BONUSES:

Top Exec. Salary: $ Bonus: $
Second Exec. Salary: $ Bonus: $

OTHER THOUGHTS:

Estimated Female Officers or Directors:
Hot Spot for Advancement for Women/Minorities:

Span America Medical Systems Inc

www.spanamerica.com

NAIC Code: 339100

TYPES OF BUSINESS:

Supplies-Therapeutic Mattresses
Polyurethane Foam Products
Wound Management Products
Skin Care
Bed Frames

BRANDS/DIVISIONS/AFFILIATES:

Savaria Corporation
MC Healthcare Products
Geo-Matt
PressureGuard
Span-Aids
Isch-Dish
Selan

CONTACTS: *Note: Officers with more than one job title may be intentionally listed here more than once.*

James Ferguson, Pres.
Thomas Henrion, Chairman of the Board
Richard C. Coggins, CFO
Richard Coggins, Director
Clyde Shew, Vice President, Divisional
Erick Herlong, Vice President, Divisional
James Teague, Vice President, Divisional
William Darby, Vice President, Divisional
Mark Sitter, Vice President, Divisional
Robert Ackley, Vice President, Divisional
James OReagan, Vice President, Divisional

GROWTH PLANS/SPECIAL FEATURES:

Span America Medical Systems, Inc. manufactures and distributes polyurethane foam products for the medical and custom products markets. These products include polyurethane foam mattress overlays for powered and non-powered therapeutic replacement mattresses; medical bed frames and patient positioning and seating products all for pressure management; and patient comfort and positioning. Span America markets its products to acute care hospitals, long-term care facilities and home health care providers, primarily in North America. The company produces various foam mattress overlays, including convoluted foam pads and its patented Geo-Matt overlay. The Geo-Matt design includes individual foam cells cut to exacting tolerances on computer-controlled equipment to create a clinically effective mattress surface. These products provide patients with greater comfort and treat patients who have or are susceptible to developing pressure ulcers. Span America's overlay products are mattress pads rather than complete mattresses and are marketed as less expensive alternatives to more complex replacement mattresses. Span America's more complex non-powered replacement mattresses include the PressureGuard line, which combines a polyurethane foam shell and static air cylinders. Through subsidiary M.C. Healthcare Products, the firm manufactures medical bed frames and related products for the long-term care industry. The company's specialty line of positioners is sold primarily under the trademark Span-Aids and consists of items that aid in relieving the basic patient positioning, problems of elevation, immobilization, muscle contracture, foot drop and foot or leg rotation. The company offers Isch-Dish patient seating products that address principal areas of care and wound healing. Span America also markets Selan skin care creams. Span America operates as an indirect, wholly-owned subsidiary of Savaria Corporation.

FINANCIAL DATA: *Note: Data for latest year may not have been available at press time.*

In U.S. $	2020	2019	2018	2017	2016	2015
Revenue	87,781,149	94,388,333	87,803,100	83,622,000	67,627,168	64,314,996
R&D Expense						
Operating Income						
Operating Margin %						
SGA Expense						
Net Income				1,749,000	4,247,331	3,993,398
Operating Cash Flow						
Capital Expenditure						
EBITDA						
Return on Assets %						
Return on Equity %						
Debt to Equity						

CONTACT INFORMATION:

Phone: 864 288-8877   Fax: 864 288-8692
Toll-Free: 800-888-6752
Address: 70 Commerce Ctr., Greenville, SC 29615 United States

STOCK TICKER/OTHER:

Stock Ticker: Subsidiary
Employees: 260
Parent Company: Savaria Corporation

Exchange:
Fiscal Year Ends: 12/31

SALARIES/BONUSES:

Top Exec. Salary: $ Bonus: $
Second Exec. Salary: $ Bonus: $

OTHER THOUGHTS:

Estimated Female Officers or Directors: 2
Hot Spot for Advancement for Women/Minorities:

Spectrum Health

www.spectrumhealth.org

NAIC Code: 622110

TYPES OF BUSINESS:

General Medical and Surgical Hospitals
Trauma Center
Neonatal Center
Burn Center
Poison Center
HMO
Long-Term Care
Children's Hospital

BRANDS/DIVISIONS/AFFILIATES:

CONTACTS: *Note: Officers with more than one job title may be intentionally listed here more than once.*

Tina Freese Decker, CEO
Matthew Cox, CFO
Pamela Ries, Chief Human Resources Officer
Jason Joseph, CIO
Robert W. Roth, Chmn.

GROWTH PLANS/SPECIAL FEATURES:

Spectrum Health is one of the largest health systems in western Michigan. The firm's not-for-profit system of care is dedicated to improving the health of families and individuals. As of fiscal 2020, Spectrum's organization includes 14 hospitals, 150 ambulatory sites (including integrated care campuses, urgent care centers, walk-in clinics and physician offices), 4,600 physicians and advanced practice providers, 111,000 telehealth visits (available 24/7) and 3,300 active volunteers. Spectrum Health provides inpatient and outpatient services throughout Michigan and facilities are located in cities such as Grand Rapids, Holland, Zeeland, Belding, Reed City, Fremont, Kentwood, Rockford, Cutlerville, Greenville, Wyoming, Big Rapids, Canadian Lakes, East Grand Rapids, Allendale, Hastings, Lake Odessa, Grand Blanc, Grand Haven, Coopersville, Stanwood, Evart and many more. Spectrum Health's services include insurance, wellness products, state-of-the-art technology and medical treatments. Major services offered by the firm include cancer, continuing care, diabetes, endocrinology, digestive disease, heart and vascular, neurosciences, orthopedics, pediatrics, rehabilitation, transplant and women's health.

Employees of the company receive benefits including medical, dental, vision, life, disability and AD&D coverage; spending accounts; retirement plans; employee assistance services; and paid time off.

FINANCIAL DATA: *Note: Data for latest year may not have been available at press time.*

In U.S. $	2020	2019	2018	2017	2016	2015
Revenue	8,300,000,000	6,884,000,000	6,103,464,000	5,681,000,000	5,220,515,000	4,625,176,000
R&D Expense						
Operating Income						
Operating Margin %						
SGA Expense						
Net Income	714,100,000	1,147,242,000	278,638,000	282,000,000	212,044,000	367,311,000
Operating Cash Flow						
Capital Expenditure						
EBITDA						
Return on Assets %						
Return on Equity %						
Debt to Equity						

CONTACT INFORMATION:

Phone: 616-391-1774   Fax: 616-391-2780
Toll-Free: 866-989-7999
Address: 100 Michigan St. NE, Grand Rapids, MI 49503 United States

STOCK TICKER/OTHER:

Stock Ticker: Nonprofit   Exchange:
Employees: 31,000   Fiscal Year Ends: 06/30
Parent Company:

SALARIES/BONUSES:

Top Exec. Salary: $ Bonus: $
Second Exec. Salary: $ Bonus: $

OTHER THOUGHTS:

Estimated Female Officers or Directors:
Hot Spot for Advancement for Women/Minorities:

SSM Health

www.ssmhealth.com

NAIC Code: 622110

TYPES OF BUSINESS:

General Medical and Surgical Hospitals
Nursing Homes
HMO
Hospice Services

BRANDS/DIVISIONS/AFFILIATES:

Civica Rx

CONTACTS: *Note: Officers with more than one job title may be intentionally listed here more than once.*

Laura Kaiser, CEO
Maggie Fowler, Chief Nursing Officer
Chris Howard, Pres., Hospital Oper.
Paula J. Friedman, Sr. VP-Strategic Dev.
Dixie L. Platt, Sr. VP-Comm., Public Policy & External Rel.
Gaurov Dayal, Pres., Finance, Integration & Home Care Delivery
Michael Panicola, Sr. VP-Missions & Organizational Ethics
Kris A. Zimmer, Sr. VP-Finance

GROWTH PLANS/SPECIAL FEATURES:

SSM Health is a Catholic not-for-profit health system serving the comprehensive health needs of communities throughout the Midwest. The organization includes 23 hospitals, more than 290 physician offices and other outpatient care sites, 10 post-acute facilities, comprehensive home care and hospice services, a pharmacy benefit company, an insurance company, a technology company and an Accountable Care Organization. Its locations include Illinois, Missouri, Oklahoma and Wisconsin. SSM has been active for more than 125 years. The company has more than 5,370 licensed beds at its owned sites. SSM maintains approximately 11,000 medical staff who provide a range of services from rehabilitation, pediatrics and home health to hospice, residential and skilled nursing care. The company's health-related businesses include information and support services such as materials management and home care. SSM Health has a partnership with six other health organizations which together created Civica Rx, a not-for-profit generic drug company that helps patients by addressing shortages and high prices of lifesaving medications.

SSM Health Care offers comprehensive benefits, retirement plans and employee assistance programs.

FINANCIAL DATA: *Note: Data for latest year may not have been available at press time.*

In U.S. $	2020	2019	2018	2017	2016	2015
Revenue	8,253,201,000	7,934,554,000	7,551,656,000	6,497,006,000	6,109,171,000	5,459,303,000
R&D Expense						
Operating Income						
Operating Margin %						
SGA Expense						
Net Income	286,038,000	415,586,000	513,490,000	242,974,000	98,718,000	209,932,000
Operating Cash Flow						
Capital Expenditure						
EBITDA						
Return on Assets %						
Return on Equity %						
Debt to Equity						

CONTACT INFORMATION:

Phone: 314-994-7800   Fax: 314-994-7900
Toll-Free:
Address: 10101 Woodfield Lane, St. Louis, MO 63132 United States

STOCK TICKER/OTHER:

Stock Ticker: Nonprofit
Employees: 40,000
Parent Company:

Exchange:
Fiscal Year Ends: 12/31

SALARIES/BONUSES:

Top Exec. Salary: $ Bonus: $
Second Exec. Salary: $ Bonus: $

OTHER THOUGHTS:

Estimated Female Officers or Directors: 4
Hot Spot for Advancement for Women/Minorities: Y

Sales, profits and employees may be estimates. Financial information, benefits and other data can change quickly and may vary from those stated here.

St Jude Children's Research Hospital

www.stjude.org

NAIC Code: 622310

TYPES OF BUSINESS:

Children's Hospitals-Specialty
Pediatric Cancer Research & Treatment

BRANDS/DIVISIONS/AFFILIATES:

American Lebanese Syrian Associated Charities
International Outreach Program
Cure4Kids
Pediatric Cancer Genome Project

CONTACTS: *Note: Officers with more than one job title may be intentionally listed here more than once.*

James R. Downing, CEO
James Downing, Scientific Dir.
Robyn Diaz, Interim Chief Legal Officer
Mary Anna Quinn, Sr. VP-Support Oper.
Kimberly Ovitt, Sr. VP
Pam Dotson, Chief Nursing Officer
Richard J. Gilbertson, Exec. VP
Larry E. Kun, Exec. VP
Judy A. Habib, Chmn.

GROWTH PLANS/SPECIAL FEATURES:

St. Jude Children's Research Hospital, founded in 1962, is one of the world's premier centers for research and treatment of pediatric cancers and other catastrophic diseases. St. Jude's fundraising arm, ALSAC (American Lebanese Syrian Associated Charities) covers the cost of treatment not covered by insurance and all costs of treatment for those who have no insurance, including lodging, travel and food. St. Jude has also developed groundbreaking treatments that have dramatically increased survival rates for brain tumors, solid tumors, Hodgkin disease, non-Hodgkin lymphoma and many other catastrophic diseases. The hospital pioneered a treatment for acute lymphoblastic leukemia, the most common form of childhood leukemia, dramatically raising the cure rate from less than 20% in 1962 to over 80% today. Current research at the hospital is focused on work in bone-marrow transplantation, gene therapy, biochemistry of cancerous cells, radiation treatment, blood diseases, hereditary diseases and the psychological effects of catastrophic illnesses. St. Jude operates the International Outreach Program, a program that provides developing countries with the resources and technology to better treat catastrophic childhood diseases. The hospital also maintains Cure4Kids, a medical education and collaboration website for doctors, scientists and healthcare workers who treat children with such diseases. In recent years, St. Jude became the first pediatric cancer center to become a National Cancer Institute (NCI) Comprehensive Cancer Center. Current research efforts include the St. Jude Children's Research Hospital-Washington University Pediatric Cancer Genome Project, a project to sequence and compare the normal and cancer genomes of hundreds of children with cancer. By comparing the complete genomes from cancerous and normal cells for more than 800 patients, the project has successfully pinpointed the genetic factors behind some of the toughest pediatric cancers and is now using multiple approaches to analyze cancer genomes even further.

FINANCIAL DATA: *Note: Data for latest year may not have been available at press time.*

In U.S. $	2020	2019	2018	2017	2016	2015
Revenue	2,210,506,498	2,324,720,240	2,093,475,533	1,971,606,000	1,383,231,000	1,299,851,000
R&D Expense						
Operating Income						
Operating Margin %						
SGA Expense						
Net Income	504,534,171	756,816,944	650,466,460	693,962,000	203,636,000	196,346,000
Operating Cash Flow						
Capital Expenditure						
EBITDA						
Return on Assets %						
Return on Equity %						
Debt to Equity						

CONTACT INFORMATION:

Phone: 901-595-3300   Fax:
Toll-Free: 800-822-6344
Address: 262 Danny Thomas Pl., Memphis, TN 38105 United States

STOCK TICKER/OTHER:

Stock Ticker: Nonprofit   Exchange:
Employees: 4,929   Fiscal Year Ends: 06/30
Parent Company:

SALARIES/BONUSES:

Top Exec. Salary: $ Bonus: $
Second Exec. Salary: $ Bonus: $

OTHER THOUGHTS:

Estimated Female Officers or Directors: 7
Hot Spot for Advancement for Women/Minorities: Y

STAAR Surgical Company   www.staar.com

NAIC Code: 339100

TYPES OF BUSINESS:

Equipment-Ophthalmic Surgery
Intraocular Lenses

BRANDS/DIVISIONS/AFFILIATES:

STAAR Surgical AG
STAAR Japan Inc
Collamer
Visian
CentraFLOW
EVO
EVO+

CONTACTS: *Note: Officers with more than one job title may be intentionally listed here more than once.*

Caren Mason, CEO
Deborah Andrews, CFO
Samuel Gesten, Chief Legal Officer
Keith Holliday, Chief Technology Officer
Hans-Martin Blickensdoerfer, Senior VP, Geographical
Louis Silverman, Chmn.

GROWTH PLANS/SPECIAL FEATURES:

STAAR Surgical Company develops, produces and markets medical devices used to improve or correct vision in patients with refractive conditions, cataracts and glaucoma. STAAR maintains operational and administrative facilities in the U.S., Switzerland and Japan, and sells its products in more than 75 countries. The company's main product line consists of one-piece and three-piece foldable silicone and Collamer intraocular lenses (IOLs) used after cataract extraction. The lens is folded and implanted into the eye behind the iris and in front of the natural lens using minimally invasive techniques. This procedure is performed with topical anesthesia on an outpatient basis, with visual recovery within one to 24 hours. The firm's Monrovia, California manufacturing facility produces the Visian implantable Collamer lens (ICL) product family, the Collamer IOL product family, preloaded silicone IOLs and injector systems. The Aliso Viejo, California manufacturing facility produces the raw material for Collamer lenses (both IOLs and ICLs) and utilizes its proprietary CentraFLOW technology, offering a central port for fluid flow and therefore eliminating the need for an iridotomy or iridectomy. The ICL with CentraFLOW technology is marketed with the brand names EVO and EVO+, to treat a wide range of refractive error. The Lake Forest, California corporate headquarters expects to handle the manufacturing of the EVO Visian ICL with Aspheric Optic Lens (EDOF) to correct or reduce presbyopia after the product's approval and the facility's approval. In Switzerland, STAAR operates administrative offices, manufacturing capabilities, warehouse and distribution facilities in Nidau and Brugg via wholly-owned STAAR Surgical AG. This facility also comprises manufacturing capabilities for the company's ICL products and related devices. In Japan, STAAR operates administrative and distribution facilities in Japan via wholly-owned STAAR Japan, Inc. Final packaging of silicone preloaded IOL injectors and final inspection of its acrylic preloaded IOL injectors are performed at these facilities.

FINANCIAL DATA: *Note: Data for latest year may not have been available at press time.*

In U.S. $	2020	2019	2018	2017	2016	2015
Revenue	163,460,000	150,185,000	123,954,000	90,611,000	82,432,000	77,123,000
R&D Expense	31,918,000	25,298,000	22,028,000	19,116,000	20,294,000	14,761,000
Operating Income	6,769,000	11,852,000	6,595,000	-3,631,000	-12,655,000	-5,337,000
Operating Margin %		.08%	.05%	- .04%	- .15%	- .07%
SGA Expense	79,675,000	74,804,000	62,887,000	48,795,000	50,730,000	43,299,000
Net Income	5,913,000	14,048,000	4,968,000	-2,139,000	-12,129,000	-6,533,000
Operating Cash Flow	20,951,000	25,795,000	12,767,000	2,853,000	1,049,000	-2,162,000
Capital Expenditure	8,404,000	10,178,000	2,245,000	1,046,000	3,205,000	2,045,000
EBITDA	9,864,000	15,551,000	9,059,000	-277,000	-9,437,000	-3,076,000
Return on Assets %		.08%	.04%	- .03%	- .19%	- .11%
Return on Equity %		.10%	.06%	- .05%	- .32%	- .17%
Debt to Equity		0.028	0.003	0.012	0.035	0.005

CONTACT INFORMATION:

Phone: 626 303-7902   Fax: 626 303-2962
Toll-Free: 800-352-7842
Address: 25651 Atlantic Ocean Dr., Lake Forest, CA 92630 United States

STOCK TICKER/OTHER:

Stock Ticker: STAA   Exchange: NAS
Employees: 550   Fiscal Year Ends: 12/31
Parent Company:

SALARIES/BONUSES:

Top Exec. Salary: $ Bonus: $
Second Exec. Salary: $ Bonus: $

OTHER THOUGHTS:

Estimated Female Officers or Directors: 1
Hot Spot for Advancement for Women/Minorities:

Starkey Hearing Technologies

www.starkey.com

NAIC Code: 334510

TYPES OF BUSINESS:

Hearing Aids, Electronic, Manufacturing

BRANDS/DIVISIONS/AFFILIATES:

Thrive Hearing Control
Livio Edge AI
SurfLink
Picasso

CONTACTS: *Note: Officers with more than one job title may be intentionally listed here more than once.*

Brandon Sawalich, CEO
Chris Hillman, COO
Bill Courtney, CFO
Chris McCormick, CMO
Jeffrey Krautkramer, Chief Human Resources Officer
Andy Dulka, CIO
Bill Austin, Chmn.

GROWTH PLANS/SPECIAL FEATURES:

Starkey Hearing Technologies is a manufacturer and distributor of hearing aids and hearing aid accessories. The firm offers many types of hearing aids, including hearing and activity track aids, with sensors and artificial intelligence (AI); smartphone-compatible aids; invisible aids, which rest in the second bend of the ear; receiver-in-canal aids; completely-in-canal aids; behind-the-ear aids; in-the-canal aids, which are custom fit; in-the-ear custom aids; tinnitus aids, which deliver relief from ringing in the ears; and single-sided aids, which improve hearing in the weaker hearing ear by way of the healthy ear. Starkey's aids include a variety of technologies that help the wearer participate in everyday activities without the impediment of hearing loss. Accessories to hearing aids include the Thrive Hearing Control mobile app, which lets the user control listening environments for maximum performance through their smartphone; wireless options that let the user stream sound from the television right to their hearing aids; Livio Edge AI, a vision aid device for people who are visually impaired or have reading difficulties, and takes a pictures of text or object and streams by audio directly into the wearer's hearing aid; and SurfLink, a hands-free cell phone transmitter, assistive listening device, media streamer and hearing aid remote. Other accessories include wireless connectivity solutions, noise protection solutions and custom audio solutions for musicians and professionals. Starkey provides a free online hearing test for adults who believe they may be losing their hearing. Hearing aid brands include Livio Edge AI, Livio AI and Picasso.

FINANCIAL DATA: *Note: Data for latest year may not have been available at press time.*

In U.S. $	2020	2019	2018	2017	2016	2015
Revenue	883,200,000	920,000,000	850,000,000	650,000,000		
R&D Expense						
Operating Income						
Operating Margin %						
SGA Expense						
Net Income						
Operating Cash Flow						
Capital Expenditure						
EBITDA						
Return on Assets %						
Return on Equity %						
Debt to Equity						

CONTACT INFORMATION:

Phone: 952-995-6608 Fax:
Toll-Free: 800-627-5762
Address: 6700 Washington Ave. S., Eden Prairie, MN 55344 United States

STOCK TICKER/OTHER:

Stock Ticker: Private Exchange:
Employees: 5,400 Fiscal Year Ends:
Parent Company:

SALARIES/BONUSES:

Top Exec. Salary: $ Bonus: $
Second Exec. Salary: $ Bonus: $

OTHER THOUGHTS:

Estimated Female Officers or Directors:
Hot Spot for Advancement for Women/Minorities:

STERIS plc

www.steris.com

NAIC Code: 339100

TYPES OF BUSINESS:

Healthcare Products & Related Services
Life Sciences Products
Sterilization Services
Defense-Related Decontamination Systems

BRANDS/DIVISIONS/AFFILIATES:

Key Surgical

CONTACTS: *Note: Officers with more than one job title may be intentionally listed here more than once.*

Walter M. Rosebrough Jr., CEO
John Wareham, Chairman of the Board
J. Zangerle, General Counsel
Kathleen Bardwell, Other Executive Officer
Walter Rosebrough, President
Sudhir Pahwa, Senior VP, Divisinal
Gulam Khan, Senior VP, Divisional
Daniel Carestio, Senior VP, Divisional
Adrian Coward, Senior VP, Divisional
Suzanne Forsythe, Vice President, Divisional
Moshen M. Sohi, Chmn.

GROWTH PLANS/SPECIAL FEATURES:

STERIS plc is a provider of infection prevention and other procedural products and services. The company offers a mix of innovative capital equipment products such as sterilizers and surgical tables, and connectivity solutions such as operating room (OR) integration; consumable products such as detergents and skin care products, gastrointestinal endoscopy accessories and barrier product solutions; and other services such as equipment installation and maintenance, microbial reduction of medical devices, instrument and scope repair, laboratory testing services and off-site reprocessing. STERIS operates in four business segments: healthcare products, healthcare specialty services, life sciences and applied sterilization technologies. The healthcare products segment offers infection prevention and procedural solutions for healthcare providers worldwide. Healthcare specialty services provides a range of specialty services for healthcare providers, including hospital sterilization services and instrumentation/scope repairs. The life sciences segment offers capital equipment and consumable products, as well as equipment maintenance and specialty services for pharmaceutical manufacturers and research facilities. The applied sterilization technologies segment offers contract sterilization and laboratory services for medical device and pharmaceutical customers, among others. In October 2020, STERIS agreed to acquire Key Surgical, a portfolio company of Water Street Healthcare Partners LLC, a global provider of consumable products serving hospitals and surgical facilities.

FINANCIAL DATA: *Note: Data for latest year may not have been available at press time.*

In U.S. $	2020	2019	2018	2017	2016	2015
Revenue	3,030,895,000	2,782,170,000	2,619,996,000	2,612,756,000	2,238,764,000	
R&D Expense	65,546,000	63,038,000	60,782,000	59,397,000	56,664,000	
Operating Income	537,646,000	442,452,000	403,557,000	286,166,000	212,107,000	
Operating Margin %	.18%	.16%	.15%	.11%	.09%	
SGA Expense	716,731,000	669,937,000	629,884,000	680,069,000	626,710,000	
Net Income	407,605,000	304,051,000	290,915,000	109,965,000	110,763,000	
Operating Cash Flow	590,559,000	539,505,000	457,632,000	424,086,000	254,675,000	
Capital Expenditure	214,516,000	189,715,000	165,457,000	172,901,000	126,407,000	
EBITDA	736,195,000	640,406,000	583,943,000	417,308,000	358,332,000	
Return on Assets %	.08%	.06%	.06%	.02%	.03%	
Return on Equity %	.12%	.10%	.10%	.04%	.05%	
Debt to Equity	0.373	0.372	0.41	0.528	0.519	

CONTACT INFORMATION:

Phone: 353 1 232 2000   Fax:
Toll-Free:
Address: 70 Sir John Rogerson's Quay, Dublin, D02 R296 Ireland

STOCK TICKER/OTHER:

Stock Ticker: STE   Exchange: NYS
Employees: 13,000   Fiscal Year Ends: 03/31
Parent Company:

SALARIES/BONUSES:

Top Exec. Salary: $ Bonus: $
Second Exec. Salary: $ Bonus: $

OTHER THOUGHTS:

Estimated Female Officers or Directors: 2
Hot Spot for Advancement for Women/Minorities: Y

Steward Health Care System LLC

www.steward.org

NAIC Code: 622110

TYPES OF BUSINESS:

General Medical and Surgical Hospitals
Primary Care
Specialty Health Care Services

BRANDS/DIVISIONS/AFFILIATES:

Steward Health Care Network
Steward Medical Group

CONTACTS: *Note: Officers with more than one job title may be intentionally listed here more than once.*

Ralph de la Torre, CEO
Mark Rich, Global Oper.
John M. Doyle, CFO
Patrick Lombardo, Exec. VP-Human Resources
Justine Carr, Chief Medical Officer
Julie Berry, CIO
Stuart Grief, Chief Admin. Officer
Joseph Maher, Jr., General Counsel
Michael G. Callum, Pres., Steward Medical Group
Mark Girard, Pres., Steward Health Care Network
Robert Guyon, Exec. VP
Karen Murray, Chief Compliance Officer
Ralph de la Toree, Chmn.

GROWTH PLANS/SPECIAL FEATURES:

Steward Health Care System, LLC is a leading physician-owned health care system in the U.S. The company comprises Steward Health Care Network and Steward Medical Group. Steward Health Care Network is made up of physicians who care for approximately 2.2 million patients annually. The network's primary care doctors and specialists offer preventive care, and work as a collaborative team to manage chronic health issues. Steward Health Care Network is also responsible for the implementation and execution of its managed care contracts, medical management services, quality improvement programs, data analysis and information services. Steward Medical Group is an employed physician group that provides more than 6 million patient encounters each year. The group is a multi-specialty health care practice organization. Steward's health care system consists of 35 community hospitals across nine states and the country of Malta, serving more than 800 communities. It includes more than 25 urgent care centers, 107 preferred skilled nursing facilities and over 7,900 beds under management. In mid-2020, Steward physicians acquired a 90% controlling interest in the company.

FINANCIAL DATA: *Note: Data for latest year may not have been available at press time.*

In U.S. $	2020	2019	2018	2017	2016	2015
Revenue	5,413,904,000	6,727,521,000	1,874,250,000	1,785,000,000	1,700,000,000	1,650,000,000
R&D Expense						
Operating Income						
Operating Margin %						
SGA Expense						
Net Income	-395,670,000	82,157,000	-270,000,000	-322,000,000		
Operating Cash Flow						
Capital Expenditure						
EBITDA						
Return on Assets %						
Return on Equity %						
Debt to Equity						

CONTACT INFORMATION:

Phone: 469-341-8800   Fax:
Toll-Free:
Address: 500 Boylston St., Boston, MA 02116 United States

STOCK TICKER/OTHER:

Stock Ticker: Private   Exchange:
Employees: 42,000   Fiscal Year Ends: 12/31
Parent Company:

SALARIES/BONUSES:

Top Exec. Salary: $ Bonus: $
Second Exec. Salary: $ Bonus: $

OTHER THOUGHTS:

Estimated Female Officers or Directors: 4
Hot Spot for Advancement for Women/Minorities: Y

Straumann Holding AG

www.straumann.com

NAIC Code: 339114

TYPES OF BUSINESS:

Dental Implants
Dental Tissue Regeneration
CAD/CAM Elements & Equipment

BRANDS/DIVISIONS/AFFILIATES:

Straumann Group
Institut Straumann AG
Straumann Villeret SA
Instradent AG
SLActive
Emdogain
BoneCeramic
DrSmile

CONTACTS: *Note: Officers with more than one job title may be intentionally listed here more than once.*

Guillaume Daniellot, CEO
Beat Spalinger, Pres.
Peter Hackel, CFO
Holger Haderer, Head-Mktg. & Education
Alastair Robertson, Chief Human Resources Officer
Gerhard Bauer, Head-Research, Dev. & Oper.
Sandro Matter, Head-Strategic Projects & Alliances
Wolfgang Becker, Head-Sales, Central Europe
Guillaume Daniellot, Head-Sales, Western Europe
Andy Molnar, Head-Sales, North America
Alexander Ochsner, Head-Sales-Asia Pacific
Gilbert Achermann, Chmn.

GROWTH PLANS/SPECIAL FEATURES:

Straumann Holding AG (Straumann) is a world leader in implant and restorative dentistry products and a major provider of dental tissue regeneration products. The firm is the parent company of the Straumann Group which includes the primary subsidiaries Institut Straumann AG, Straumann Villeret SA and Instradent AG. Straumann operates four geographical segments: Europe, North America, Asia/Pacific and the rest of the world. The firm maintains subsidiaries and distributors in more than 70 countries, with its most important markets being Germany and the U.S. Straumann offers three basic products: implants, regenerative systems and computer aided design and manufacturing (CAD/CAM) technology. Implants are designed to mimic natural teeth as closely as possible, being more durable and supporting themselves better than conventional bridges. They include devices inserted at the bone or soft tissue level, surgical tools and 3D modeling software used to plan surgery. Straumann's product, Roxolid, is a high-performance implant material combining high tensile and fatigue strengths with osseointegration. The firm also offers SLActive, an implant surface technology that decreases the healing time after surgery and increases general stability of the dental implants. Regenerative systems include products Emdogain and BoneCeramic that support or repair oral structures. CAD/CAM products are divided into prosthetic elements (crowns, inlays, overlays or bridges) and manufacturing equipment (software, scanners and milling units). Within Straumann's CAD/CAM line are ceramic-based prosthetics, which provides increased durability and aesthetic design. Principal production sites for implant components and instruments are in Switzerland, the U.S., Brazil and Germany; CAD/CAM prosthetics are milled in Germany, the U.S., Japan and Brazil; and biomaterials are manufactured in Sweden. In mid-2020, Straumann acquired a majority stake in DrSmile, a provider of orthodontic treatment solutions in Europe.

FINANCIAL DATA: *Note: Data for latest year may not have been available at press time.*

In U.S. $	2020	2019	2018	2017	2016	2015
Revenue	1,589,613,000	1,779,555,000	1,520,168,000	1,239,829,000	1,022,895,000	890,320,800
R&D Expense						
Operating Income	169,095,200	417,324,800	378,170,100	312,469,600	250,617,600	189,978,600
Operating Margin %		.23%	.25%	.25%	.25%	.21%
SGA Expense	994,449,200	921,028,400	758,137,300	624,523,500	550,435,900	495,586,300
Net Income	101,765,900	341,672,100	304,098,200	304,262,100	255,970,000	78,796,630
Operating Cash Flow	419,846,600	421,947,000	308,924,400	242,246,200	205,961,100	206,914,300
Capital Expenditure	91,494,790	167,071,700	122,336,100	81,834,600	52,059,130	39,217,150
EBITDA	255,301,100	531,325,100	432,027,500	411,786,200	288,606,200	131,125,600
Return on Assets %		.14%	.15%	.20%	.21%	.06%
Return on Equity %		.24%	.24%	.32%	.37%	.11%
Debt to Equity		0.17	0.168	0.188	0.315	0.33

CONTACT INFORMATION:

Phone: 41 619651111   Fax: 41 619651101
Toll-Free:
Address: Peter Merian-Weg 12, Basel, 4002 Switzerland

STOCK TICKER/OTHER:

Stock Ticker: SAUHY
Employees: 7,590
Parent Company:

Exchange: PINX
Fiscal Year Ends: 12/31

SALARIES/BONUSES:

Top Exec. Salary: $ Bonus: $
Second Exec. Salary: $ Bonus: $

OTHER THOUGHTS:

Estimated Female Officers or Directors:
Hot Spot for Advancement for Women/Minorities:

Stryker Corporation

NAIC Code: 339100

www.stryker.com

TYPES OF BUSINESS:

Equipment-Orthopedic Implants
Powered Surgical Instruments
Endoscopic Systems
Patient Care & Handling Equipment
Imaging Software
Small Bone Innovations

BRANDS/DIVISIONS/AFFILIATES:

Wright Medical Group NV

CONTACTS: Note: Officers with more than one job title may be intentionally listed here more than once.

Kevin Lobo, CEO
Glenn Boehnlein, CFO
William Berry, Chief Accounting Officer
Robert Fletcher, Chief Legal Officer
Timothy Scannell, COO
Michael Hutchinson, Other Corporate Officer
Bijoy Sagar, Other Executive Officer
M. Fink, Other Executive Officer
Viju Menon, President, Divisional
Yin Becker, Vice President, Divisional
Katherine Owen, Vice President, Divisional

GROWTH PLANS/SPECIAL FEATURES:

Stryker Corporation develops, manufactures and markets innovative products and services that help improve patient and hospital outcomes. The firm's products are sold in over 80 countries through company-owned subsidiaries and branches, as well as by third-party dealers and distributors. Stryker's products include implants used in joint replacement and trauma surgeries, surgical equipment, surgical navigation systems, endoscopic systems, communications systems, patient handling equipment, emergency medical equipment, intensive care disposable products, neurosurgical devices, spinal devices, neurovascular devices and other products used in a variety of medical specialties. These products are segregated within the three business segments of: MedSurg, deriving 45% of 2020 net sales; orthopedics, 34%; and neurotechnology and spine, 21%. Stryker owns approximately 4,045 U.S. patents and approximately 6,407 international patents. During 2020, Stryker completed its acquisition of Wright Medical Group NV, a global medical device company focused on extremities and biologics. Wright was integrated into Stryker's trauma and extremities business within the orthopedics segment.

Stryker offers employees health insurance, retirement programs, tuition reimbursement and wellness programs.

FINANCIAL DATA: Note: Data for latest year may not have been available at press time.

In U.S. $	2020	2019	2018	2017	2016	2015
Revenue	14,351,000,000	14,884,000,000	13,601,000,000	12,444,000,000	11,325,000,000	9,946,000,000
R&D Expense	984,000,000	971,000,000	862,000,000	787,000,000	715,000,000	625,000,000
Operating Income	2,240,000,000	2,905,000,000	2,560,000,000	2,463,000,000	2,324,000,000	2,157,000,000
Operating Margin %		.20%	.19%	.20%	.21%	.22%
SGA Expense	5,361,000,000	5,356,000,000	5,099,000,000	4,552,000,000	4,137,000,000	3,610,000,000
Net Income	1,599,000,000	2,083,000,000	3,553,000,000	1,020,000,000	1,647,000,000	1,439,000,000
Operating Cash Flow	3,277,000,000	2,191,000,000	2,610,000,000	1,559,000,000	1,812,000,000	899,000,000
Capital Expenditure	487,000,000	649,000,000	572,000,000	598,000,000	490,000,000	270,000,000
EBITDA	3,052,000,000	3,683,000,000	3,283,000,000	3,105,000,000	2,870,000,000	2,554,000,000
Return on Assets %		.07%	.14%	.05%	.09%	.08%
Return on Equity %		.17%	.33%	.10%	.18%	.17%
Debt to Equity		0.799	0.723	0.661	0.70	0.382

CONTACT INFORMATION:

Phone: 269 385-2600   Fax: 269 385-1062
Toll-Free:
Address: 2825 Airview Blvd., Kalamazoo, MI 49002 United States

STOCK TICKER/OTHER:

Stock Ticker: SYK   Exchange: NYS
Employees: 43,000   Fiscal Year Ends: 12/31
Parent Company:

SALARIES/BONUSES:

Top Exec. Salary: $ Bonus: $
Second Exec. Salary: $ Bonus: $

OTHER THOUGHTS:

Estimated Female Officers or Directors: 7
Hot Spot for Advancement for Women/Minorities: Y

Sun Pharmaceutical Industries Ltd

www.sunpharma.com

NAIC Code: 325412

TYPES OF BUSINESS:

Pharmaceuticals, Manufacturing
Pharmaceuticals
Generic Drugs
Specialty Drugs
Over-the-Counter Drugs
Anti-Retrovirals
Active Pharmaceutical Ingredients
Intermediates

BRANDS/DIVISIONS/AFFILIATES:

Alkaloida Chemical Company Zrt
Basics GmbH
Green Eco Development Centre Limited
Office Pharmaceutique Industries et Hospitalier
Ranbaxy UK Limited
SPIL de Mexico SA de CV
Sun Pharma Holdings
SC Terapia SA

CONTACTS: *Note: Officers with more than one job title may be intentionally listed here more than once.*

Dilip Shanghvi, Managing Dir.
Sunil R. Ajmera, Company Sec.
Mira Desai, Contact-Investor Rel.
Dilip S. Shanghvi, Managing Dir.
Israel Makov, Chmn.

GROWTH PLANS/SPECIAL FEATURES:

Sun Pharmaceutical Industries Ltd. (Sun Pharma) is an India-based specialty pharmaceuticals company. Sun Pharma manufactures and markets a portfolio of generics, branded generics, specialty, difficult-to-make technology intensive products, over-the-counter (OTC), anti-retrovirals, and active pharmaceutical ingredients (APIs) and intermediates. The company is present in more than 100 countries. Its generic medications are technology-based and cover the full range of dosage forms, including tablets, capsules, injectables, inhalers, ointments, creams and liquids. The generics division's therapeutic portfolio of over 2,000 molecules span areas such as psychiatry, anti-infectives, neurology, cardiology, orthopedic, diabetology, gastroenterology, ophthalmology, nephrology, urology, dermatology, gynecology, respiratory, oncology, dental and nutritionals. Sun Pharma's specialty medications target dermatology, ophthalmology and oncology, and its initiatives cover the entire value chain, from in-licensing early-to-late-stage clinical candidates to marketing patented products. OTCs include a few flagship brands marketed in several countries globally: Faringosept, for sore throats; Revital, vitamins; and Volini, offering topical analgesics. Other OTC brands include Coldact & Flustat, Brustan, Painamol, Paduden, Aspenter, Aspacardin, Nudrate, Fortifikat, Gestid and Chericof, among others. Anti-retroviral medicines are World Health Organization certified, and supply various national AIDS treatment programs in Africa. This division's portfolio comprises bio-equivalent ARV medicines and APIs manufactured at facilities in India, South Africa and Russia. Last, APIs are a vital input in the manufacturing process of complex formulations. They facilitate vertical integration. Sun Pharma's list of APIs exceed 300, which are used both in-house and marketed to customers in over 60 countries.

FINANCIAL DATA: *Note: Data for latest year may not have been available at press time.*

In U.S. $	2020	2019	2018	2017	2016	2015
Revenue		4,200,000,000	3,809,715,456	4,515,338,240	4,077,128,704	3,956,519,680
R&D Expense						
Operating Income						
Operating Margin %						
SGA Expense						
Net Income		37,321,600	311,744,160	1,004,418,880	680,140,352	654,680,768
Operating Cash Flow						
Capital Expenditure						
EBITDA						
Return on Assets %						
Return on Equity %						
Debt to Equity						

CONTACT INFORMATION:

Phone: 91-22-43244324   Fax: 91-22-43244343
Toll-Free:
Address: Sun House, CTS No. 201 B/1 Western Express Hwy., Mumbai, Mumbai 400 063 India

STOCK TICKER/OTHER:

Stock Ticker: SUNPHARMA   Exchange: PINX
Employees: 30,000   Fiscal Year Ends: 03/31
Parent Company:

SALARIES/BONUSES:

Top Exec. Salary: $ Bonus: $
Second Exec. Salary: $ Bonus: $

OTHER THOUGHTS:

Estimated Female Officers or Directors: 1
Hot Spot for Advancement for Women/Minorities:

Sunrise Medical GmbH

www.sunrisemedical.com

NAIC Code: 339100

TYPES OF BUSINESS:

Medical Supplies-Wheelchairs
Wheelchairs
Wheelchair Accessories
Rollator Walkers
Electric Scooters

BRANDS/DIVISIONS/AFFILIATES:

Nordic Capital
Quickie
Zippie
RGK
Jay
Whitmyer
Gemino
James Leckey Design

CONTACTS: *Note: Officers with more than one job title may be intentionally listed here more than once.*

Thomas Babacan, CEO
Roxane Cromwell, COO
Adrian Platt, CFO
Carol Liu, Sr. VP-Mktg. & Dev.
Bernd Krebs, CTO
Randi Binstock, VP-Bus. Dev.

GROWTH PLANS/SPECIAL FEATURES:

Sunrise Medical GmbH designs, manufactures and markets wheelchairs, electric wheelchairs, electric vehicles and systems for sitting and positioning. Sunrise's range of wheelchairs include: the Quickie line, designed for all purposes, including the playing tennis or basketball; the Zippie Wheelchair line, which is designed for children; and the RGK line, which are custom made to meet specific desires and needs. Sunrise manufactures electronics and alternative drive controls for powered wheelchairs. The firm's Jay line offers cushions for increased comfort and for skin protection. The Whitmyer brand offers wheelchair headrests. The Sterling brand offers electric scooters. The Gemino brand offers rollators (walkers that are pushed, without the need to lift it for movement). Sunrise Medical's education department conducts seminars around the country that provide technical and clinical information for respiratory therapists, nurses, physicians and physical therapists. In addition, the firm customizes its products to meet the needs of the consumer. Sunrise Medical has sales organization and distributors in over 130 countries and is privately-owned by Nordic Capital. During 2020, Sunrise Medical took over Irish specialist manufacturer for therapeutic children's aids, James Leckey Design, including the subsidiaries Firefly Friends and Vida Global.

FINANCIAL DATA: *Note: Data for latest year may not have been available at press time.*

In U.S. $	2020	2019	2018	2017	2016	2015
Revenue	558,851,000	588,480,900	560,458,000	570,465,000	530,000,000	501,461,100
R&D Expense						
Operating Income						
Operating Margin %						
SGA Expense						
Net Income						
Operating Cash Flow						
Capital Expenditure						
EBITDA						
Return on Assets %						
Return on Equity %						
Debt to Equity						

CONTACT INFORMATION:

Phone: 49072539800   Fax: 4.9072539802e+12
Toll-Free: 800-333-4000
Address: Kahlbachring 2-4, Malsch, 69254 Germany

STOCK TICKER/OTHER:

Stock Ticker: Private
Employees: 2,005
Parent Company: Nordic Capital

Exchange:
Fiscal Year Ends: 06/30

SALARIES/BONUSES:

Top Exec. Salary: $ Bonus: $
Second Exec. Salary: $ Bonus: $

OTHER THOUGHTS:

Estimated Female Officers or Directors: 1
Hot Spot for Advancement for Women/Minorities:

Surgery Partners Inc

www.surgerypartners.com

NAIC Code: 621493

TYPES OF BUSINESS:

Freestanding Ambulatory Surgical and Emergency Centers
Eye-Care Services
Laser Vision Correction
Corrective Lenses Labs
Eye-Care Products Distribution
Purchasing and Supply Chain Services
Marketing Services

BRANDS/DIVISIONS/AFFILIATES:

Bain Capital LP
Tampa Pain Relief Center Inc

CONTACTS: *Note: Officers with more than one job title may be intentionally listed here more than once.*

Wayne Deveydt, CEO
Eric Evans, COO
Thomas Cowhey, CFO
Laura Brocklehurst, Chief Human Resources Officer
Matt Petty, Sr. VP
T. Devin O'Reilly, Director
Angela Justice, Executive VP
Brandan Lingle, President, Divisional
George Goodwin, President, Divisional
Anthony Taparo, President, Divisional
Carollee Brinkman, President, Divisional

GROWTH PLANS/SPECIAL FEATURES:

Surgery Partners, Inc. is a health care services company. The firm owns or operates, primarily in partnership with physicians, a portfolio of more than 125 facilities, including ambulatory surgical centers (ASCs), surgical hospitals, a diagnostic laboratory, multi-specialty physician practices and urgent care facilities across 30 U.S. states. Surgery Partners operates three primary segments: surgical facility services, ancillary services and optical services. The surgical facility services segment consists of the company's ASCs and surgical hospitals, which provide non-emergency surgical procedures across many specialties, including gastroenterology, general surgery, ophthalmology, orthopedics and pain management, among many others. The ancillary services segment consists of the firm's diagnostic laboratory ad multi-specialty physician practices. These physician practices included Surgery Partners' owned and operated practices pursuant to long-term management service agreements. The optical services segment consists of an optical laboratory and an optical products group purchasing organization. The optical lab manufactures eyewear, and the optical products purchasing organization negotiates volume-buying discounts with optical product manufacturers. In addition, Surgery Partners' multi-specialty physician practice employs two models in connection with its network of physician practices: in Florida, the firm owns and operates Tampa Pain Relief Center, Inc., which has businesses throughout the state; and in states other than Florida, the firm operates physician practices pursuant to long-term management service agreements with separate professional corporations that are wholly-owned by physicians. The company's urgent care facilities treat injuries or illnesses requiring immediate care, but not serious enough to require an emergency room visit. Bain Capital is the majority shareholder of the firm.

FINANCIAL DATA: *Note: Data for latest year may not have been available at press time.*

In U.S. $	2020	2019	2018	2017	2016	2015
Revenue	1,860,100,000	1,831,400,000	1,771,456,000		1,145,438,000	959,891,000
R&D Expense						
Operating Income	234,100,000	260,100,000	252,795,000		200,586,000	178,736,000
Operating Margin %		.14%	.14%		.18%	.19%
SGA Expense	97,100,000	88,600,000	93,558,000		60,246,000	55,992,000
Net Income	-116,100,000	-74,800,000	-205,706,000		9,453,000	1,429,000
Operating Cash Flow	246,900,000	129,500,000	144,600,000		125,239,000	84,481,000
Capital Expenditure	42,900,000	73,600,000	39,805,000		39,109,000	33,439,000
EBITDA	277,800,000	310,000,000	145,278,000		232,300,000	59,388,000
Return on Assets %		-.02%	-.05%		.00%	.00%
Return on Equity %		-.15%	-.27%		3.35%	
Debt to Equity		4.059	3.169		151.777	

CONTACT INFORMATION:

Phone: 615-234-5900   Fax: 615-234-5998
Toll-Free:
Address: 310 Seven Springs Way, Ste. 500, Brentwood, TN 37027 United States

STOCK TICKER/OTHER:

Stock Ticker: SGRY
Employees: 10,800
Parent Company: Bain Capital LP

Exchange: NAS
Fiscal Year Ends: 12/31

SALARIES/BONUSES:

Top Exec. Salary: $ Bonus: $
Second Exec. Salary: $ Bonus: $

OTHER THOUGHTS:

Estimated Female Officers or Directors: 2
Hot Spot for Advancement for Women/Minorities:

Surgical Care Affiliates Inc

www.scasurgery.com

NAIC Code: 622110

TYPES OF BUSINESS:

Surgery Centers

BRANDS/DIVISIONS/AFFILIATES:

UnitedHealth Group Inc

CONTACTS: *Note: Officers with more than one job title may be intentionally listed here more than once.*

Caitlin Zulla, CEO
Winborne Macphail, COO
Leslie Wachsman, CFO
Tim Buono, Sr. VP-Dev.
Warren Cinnick, VP-Human Resources
Anthony Williams, CIO
Richard Sharff, Executive VP
Joseph Clark, Executive VP
Jason Strauss, Pres.

GROWTH PLANS/SPECIAL FEATURES:

Surgical Care Affiliates, Inc. (SCA) provides inpatient and outpatient surgery throughout the U.S. The company owns than 230 ambulatory surgery centers, surgical hospitals and hospital surgery departments. SCA builds strategic relationships with medical partners in order to acquire, develop and optimize facilities in alignment with customer needs. SCA has partnerships with approximately 8,500 physicians who perform 1 million procedures in SCA facilities each year. SCA also offers management services and solutions such as clinical systems, operating systems and financial systems. Clinical systems include clinical toolkits and checklists, clinical training and detailed clinical variance analysis. Operating systems offer schedule efficiency, supply chain management and benchmarking. Financial systems offer precise case costing and related analytics. Together, the facilities and management solutions offer patients easy scheduling, convenient access, short wait times and billing transparency. On average, patients pay approximately 45% less than they would if they had the identical procedure performed at a hospital. These savings are reflected in patients' co-pays and co-insurance. Physicians are provided advanced clinical systems, health system partnership capabilities, market development, analytics and more. Health plans can improve quality, access and cost by organizing their member surgeons into a new market, and optimize site of service, implant selection and utilization. And health systems can capture additional inpatient and outpatient market share and develop low-cost venue surgical care. The firm is a subsidiary of UnitedHealth Group, Inc.

FINANCIAL DATA: *Note: Data for latest year may not have been available at press time.*

In U.S. $	2020	2019	2018	2017	2016	2015
Revenue	1,923,750,000	2,250,000,000	2,100,000,000	2,000,000,000	1,281,405,056	1,051,489,984
R&D Expense						
Operating Income						
Operating Margin %						
SGA Expense						
Net Income						
Operating Cash Flow						
Capital Expenditure						
EBITDA						
Return on Assets %						
Return on Equity %						
Debt to Equity						

CONTACT INFORMATION:

Phone: 847 236-0921 Fax:
Toll-Free:
Address: 510 Lake Cook Rd., Ste. 400, Deerfield, IL 60015 United States

STOCK TICKER/OTHER:

Stock Ticker: Subsidiary Exchange:
Employees: 18,500 Fiscal Year Ends: 12/31
Parent Company: UnitedHealth Group Inc

SALARIES/BONUSES:

Top Exec. Salary: $ Bonus: $
Second Exec. Salary: $ Bonus: $

OTHER THOUGHTS:

Estimated Female Officers or Directors:
Hot Spot for Advancement for Women/Minorities:

Sutter Health Inc

www.sutterhealth.org

NAIC Code: 622110

TYPES OF BUSINESS:

General Medical and Surgical Hospitals
Neonatal Care
Pregnancy & Birth
Training Programs
Medical Research Facilities
Home Health Services
Hospice Networks
Long-Term Care

BRANDS/DIVISIONS/AFFILIATES:

GROWTH PLANS/SPECIAL FEATURES:

Sutter Health, Inc. is a non-profit healthcare network that delivers personalized care in more than 100 northern California communities. This network includes physician organizations, acute care hospitals, surgery centers, home health and hospice programs, medical research facilities, training programs and specialty services. As a non-profit, Sutter Health invests all of its earnings back into the communities it serves. There are more than 12,000 physicians within the network, 2,000 advanced practice clinicians, 14,500 nurses, 5,000 volunteers, 24 hospitals, 36 ambulatory surgery centers, seven cardiac centers, nine cancer centers, four acute rehabilitation centers, eight behavioral health centers, five trauma centers, 4,188 licensed general acute-care beds and eight neonatal intensive care units.

CONTACTS: Note: Officers with more than one job title may be intentionally listed here more than once.

Sarah Krevans, CEO

FINANCIAL DATA: Note: Data for latest year may not have been available at press time.

In U.S. $	2020	2019	2018	2017	2016	2015
Revenue	13,220,000,000	13,304,000,000	12,700,000,000	12,444,000,000	11,873,000,000	10,998,000,000
R&D Expense						
Operating Income						
Operating Margin %						
SGA Expense						
Net Income	200,000,000	189,000,000	-200,000,000	958,000,000	622,000,000	145,000,000
Operating Cash Flow						
Capital Expenditure						
EBITDA						
Return on Assets %						
Return on Equity %						
Debt to Equity						

CONTACT INFORMATION:

Phone: 916-733-8800   Fax:
Toll-Free:
Address: 2200 River Plaza Dr., Sacramento, CA 95833 United States

STOCK TICKER/OTHER:

Stock Ticker: Nonprofit
Employees: 55,000
Parent Company:

Exchange:
Fiscal Year Ends: 12/31

SALARIES/BONUSES:

Top Exec. Salary: $ Bonus: $
Second Exec. Salary: $ Bonus: $

OTHER THOUGHTS:

Estimated Female Officers or Directors: 3
Hot Spot for Advancement for Women/Minorities: Y

Suven Life Sciences Limited

www.suven.com

NAIC Code: 325412

TYPES OF BUSINESS:

Drug Discovery & Development
Biopharmaceutical
Clinical Studies
Drug Development
Central Nervous System

BRANDS/DIVISIONS/AFFILIATES:

GROWTH PLANS/SPECIAL FEATURES:

Suven Life Sciences Limited is an India-based clinical-stage biopharmaceutical company. The firm's objective is to develop and commercialize novel therapeutics for the treatment of central nervous system disorders. Suven operates through two business segments: drug discovery and development support services, and drug discovery and research/clinical pipeline. The drug discovery and development support services segment is engaged in synthetic and medicinal chemistry, analytical chemistry, in vitro biology, absorption/disruption/metabolism/excretion (ADME), pharmacology, toxicology, bioanalysis and new chemical entity formulations. The drug discovery and research/clinical pipeline segment includes masupirdine (SUVN-502) for the treatment of cognitive deficits in Alzheimer's Disease (AD), and for the treatment of neuropsychiatric symptoms in AD. Other clinical studies are for the treatment of mood disorders, gastrointestinal disorders, narcolepsy, among other purposes. Suven has an international office in New Jersey, USA.

CONTACTS:
Note: Officers with more than one job title may be intentionally listed here more than once.

Venkat Jasti, CEO
K. Hanumantha Rao, Sec.
Kalyani Jasti, Pres., U.S. Oper.

FINANCIAL DATA:
Note: Data for latest year may not have been available at press time.

In U.S. $	2020	2019	2018	2017	2016	2015
Revenue	3,781,510	44,977,100	99,695,400	87,139,900	77,889,165	78,186,338
R&D Expense						
Operating Income						
Operating Margin %						
SGA Expense						
Net Income	-12,522,800	-3,455,660	24,354,300	19,024,100	10,018,370	16,324,759
Operating Cash Flow						
Capital Expenditure						
EBITDA						
Return on Assets %						
Return on Equity %						
Debt to Equity						

CONTACT INFORMATION:

Phone: 91-40-2354-1142   Fax: 91-40-2354-1152
Toll-Free:
Address: 6/Fl. Serene Chambers, Rd. No. 5, Ave. 7, Banjara Hills, Hyderabad, 500 034 India

STOCK TICKER/OTHER:

Stock Ticker: 530239
Employees: 135
Parent Company:

Exchange: Bombay
Fiscal Year Ends: 03/31

SALARIES/BONUSES:

Top Exec. Salary: $ Bonus: $
Second Exec. Salary: $ Bonus: $

OTHER THOUGHTS:

Estimated Female Officers or Directors: 2
Hot Spot for Advancement for Women/Minorities:

Suzuken Co Ltd

www.suzuken.co.jp

NAIC Code: 424210

TYPES OF BUSINESS:

Drugs and Druggists' Sundries Merchant Wholesalers
Pharmaceutical Manufacture
Pharmaceutical Distribution
Healthcare Marketing
Medical Equipment
Nursing Care
Medical Food

BRANDS/DIVISIONS/AFFILIATES:

Sanwa Kagaku Kenkyusho Co Ltd
Kenzemedico Co Ltd
Pfercos Co Ltd
S-mile Inc
Sanki Wellbe Co Ltd
S-Care Mate Co Ltd
Life Medicom Co Ltd

CONTACTS: *Note: Officers with more than one job title may be intentionally listed here more than once.*

Hiromi Miyata, Pres.
Yoshiki Bessho, Chmn.

GROWTH PLANS/SPECIAL FEATURES:

Suzuken Co., Ltd. is engaged in the pharmaceutical business in Japan. The company's businesses include pharmaceutical manufacturing, medical equipment manufacturing, pharmaceutical distribution, dispensing, distribution and logistics, as well as nursing care and other healthcare-related services. Suzuken manufactures proprietary and contract pharmaceuticals at its factories located in Fukushima and Kumamoto. The firm offers comprehensive support in the orphan disease, investigational drug and pharmaceutical manufacturer distribution domains. It also conducts marketing support for pharmaceutical manufacturers. Subsidiary Sanwa Kagaku Kenkyusho Co., Ltd. researches, develops, manufactures and sells pharmaceuticals, diagnostic regents, medical food products, nursing care food products and health care products. The firm also conducts contract manufacturing of pharmaceuticals. Kenzemedico Co., Ltd. manufactures and sells medical equipment and devices such as electrocardiographs and stethoscopes. The company develops related medical materials and health promotion equipment for general consumers. Suzuken is engaged in, and supports, home medical care, in which pharmacists visit the homes of patients or the elderly and give guidance on drug management and drug administration. This involves pharmacies being equipped with a sterile dispensary capable of preparing injections or infusions necessary for home medical care, and which can be used by other pharmacies. Subsidiaries Pfercos Co., Ltd. and S-mile, Inc. are responsible for the company's insurance pharmacy business, with approximately 330 pharmacy clients across 20 prefectures. Subsidiary Sanki Wellbe Co., Ltd. and S-Care Mate Co., Ltd. provide tailored nursing care to elderly in the Chugoku, Kanto and Chubu regions. This nursing care division also provides drug management guidance and support to nursing care facilities. In addition, Life Medicom Co., Ltd. develops publication and public relation activities regarding medical care and health.

FINANCIAL DATA: *Note: Data for latest year may not have been available at press time.*

In U.S. $	2020	2019	2018	2017	2016	2015
Revenue	20,216,200,000	19,474,720,000	19,398,650,000	19,426,590,000	20,350,200,000	
R&D Expense						
Operating Income	297,480,200	248,673,500	180,249,000	170,896,800	257,952,600	
Operating Margin %	.01%	.01%	.01%	.01%	.01%	
SGA Expense						
Net Income	257,669,500	275,853,300	171,883,100	194,606,100	264,491,800	
Operating Cash Flow	-235,786,800	381,312,100	895,637,200	246,709,800	186,833,900	
Capital Expenditure	106,837,900	80,543,970	72,570,860	117,413,900	149,927,400	
EBITDA	480,213,400	514,242,900	364,096,400	402,537,200	520,581,300	
Return on Assets %	.02%	.03%	.02%	.02%	.03%	
Return on Equity %	.07%	.07%	.05%	.05%	.08%	
Debt to Equity			0.00	0.00	0.00	

CONTACT INFORMATION:

Phone: 81 529612331 Fax:
Toll-Free:
Address: 8 Higashi Kataha-machi, Nagoya, 461-8701 Japan

STOCK TICKER/OTHER:

Stock Ticker: SZUKF Exchange: GREY
Employees: 19,122 Fiscal Year Ends:
Parent Company:

SALARIES/BONUSES:

Top Exec. Salary: $ Bonus: $
Second Exec. Salary: $ Bonus: $

OTHER THOUGHTS:

Estimated Female Officers or Directors:
Hot Spot for Advancement for Women/Minorities:

Sales, profits and employees may be estimates. Financial information, benefits and other data can change quickly and may vary from those stated here.

Symmetry Surgical Inc

www.symmetrysurgical.com

NAIC Code: 339100

TYPES OF BUSINESS:

Surgical and Medical Instrument Manufacturing

BRANDS/DIVISIONS/AFFILIATES:

RoundTable Healthcare Partners LP
Bookwalter
Greenberg
Olsen
Symmetry
Flash Pak
Quad-Lock
OR Company (The)

CONTACTS: *Note: Officers with more than one job title may be intentionally listed here more than once.*

Brian J. Straeb, Pres.
Ronda Harris, Chief Accounting Officer
Thomas Sullivan, Director
Craig Reynolds, Director

GROWTH PLANS/SPECIAL FEATURES:

Symmetry Surgical, Inc. is a healthcare company that develops, manufactures and markets surgical instrumentation and solutions. The company's portfolio of brands have a legacy of fine craftsmanship and innovation spanning more than 180 years. The firm's portfolio of single-use, limited-use and reusable surgical instruments and electrosurgery products are sold through a U.S. direct sales force and a global distribution network. They are used in every surgical specialty in hospitals, surgery centers and physician offices worldwide. Symmetry Surgical offers products under the brands Bookwalter, Greenberg, Olsen, Symmetry, Flash Pak, Quad-Lock, RapidClean, MagnaFree, Midas Touch, Riley Medical, Transpak, among many others. Symmetry is privately-held by RoundTable Healthcare Partners LP. In early-2020, Symmetry acquired The O.R. Company, which develops, manufactures and markets innovative surgical devices from niche consumables to proprietary surgical instruments for minimally invasive and open surgery.

FINANCIAL DATA: *Note: Data for latest year may not have been available at press time.*

In U.S. $	2020	2019	2018	2017	2016	2015
Revenue	109,511,325	99,555,750	94,815,000	90,300,000	86,000,000	84,527,000
R&D Expense						
Operating Income						
Operating Margin %						
SGA Expense						
Net Income						
Operating Cash Flow						
Capital Expenditure						
EBITDA						
Return on Assets %						
Return on Equity %						
Debt to Equity						

CONTACT INFORMATION:

Phone: 615 964-5532   Fax: 800 342-3272
Toll-Free: 800 251-3000
Address: 3034 Owen Dr., Antioch, TN 30713 United States

STOCK TICKER/OTHER:

Stock Ticker: Private   Exchange:
Employees: 189   Fiscal Year Ends: 12/31
Parent Company: RoundTable Healthcare Partners LP

SALARIES/BONUSES:

Top Exec. Salary: $ Bonus: $
Second Exec. Salary: $ Bonus: $

OTHER THOUGHTS:

Estimated Female Officers or Directors:
Hot Spot for Advancement for Women/Minorities:

Synthorx Inc

www.synthorx.com

NAIC Code: 325412

TYPES OF BUSINESS:

Pharmaceutical Preparation Manufacturing
Biotechnology
Cancer
Autoimmune Disorders

BRANDS/DIVISIONS/AFFILIATES:

Sanofi SA
Synthorin
THOR-707

GROWTH PLANS/SPECIAL FEATURES:

Synthorx, Inc. is a clinical-stage biotechnology company focused on providing solutions for people with cancer and autoimmune disorders. The company's proprietary Expanded Genetic Alphabet platform technology expands the genetic code by adding a new DNA base pair and designed to create optimized biologics, referred to as Synthorins. A Synthorin in a protein optimized through incorporation of novel amino acids encoded by the new DNA base pair enables site-specific modifications, which enhance the pharmacological properties of the company's therapeutics. THOR-707 is Synthorx's lead product candidate, and is a variant of IL-2, is in development for the treatment of solid tumors as a single agent and in combination with an immune checkpoint inhibitor. In early-2020, Synthorx was acquired by Sanofi SA, becoming its wholly-owned subsidiary.

CONTACTS: *Note: Officers with more than one job title may be intentionally listed here more than once.*

Marcos Milla, Chief Scientific Officer
Tighe Reardon, CFO

FINANCIAL DATA: *Note: Data for latest year may not have been available at press time.*

In U.S. $	2020	2019	2018	2017	2016	2015
Revenue						
R&D Expense						
Operating Income						
Operating Margin %						
SGA Expense						
Net Income		-62,269,900	-56,609,000	-5,850,000	-3,128,000	
Operating Cash Flow						
Capital Expenditure						
EBITDA						
Return on Assets %						
Return on Equity %						
Debt to Equity						

CONTACT INFORMATION:

Phone: 858 750-4700   Fax:
Toll-Free:
Address: 11099 North Torrey Pines Rd., Ste. 190, La Jolla, CA 92037
United States

STOCK TICKER/OTHER:

Stock Ticker: Subsidiary
Employees: 24
Parent Company: Sanofi SA

Exchange:
Fiscal Year Ends: 12/31

SALARIES/BONUSES:

Top Exec. Salary: $ Bonus: $
Second Exec. Salary: $ Bonus: $

OTHER THOUGHTS:

Estimated Female Officers or Directors:
Hot Spot for Advancement for Women/Minorities:

Sales, profits and employees may be estimates. Financial information, benefits and other data can change quickly and may vary from those stated here.

Takeda Oncology

www.takedaoncology.com

NAIC Code: 325412

TYPES OF BUSINESS:

Pharmaceuticals Discovery & Development
Gene-Based Drug Discovery Platform
Small-Molecule Drugs
Oncology

BRANDS/DIVISIONS/AFFILIATES:

Takeda Pharmaceutical Company Limited

CONTACTS: *Note: Officers with more than one job title may be intentionally listed here more than once.*

Teresa Bitetti, Pres.
Karen Ferrante, Head-R&D Site
Laurie Bartlett Keating, General Counsel
Kyle Kuvalanka, VP-Bus. Dev. & Corp. Strategy
Lisa Adler, VP-Corp. Comm.
Todd Shegog, Sr. VP-Finance
Christophe Bianchi, Exec. VP

GROWTH PLANS/SPECIAL FEATURES:

Takeda Oncology is the global oncology business unit of Takeda Pharmaceutical Company Limited. The firm engages in research and development and the discovery, development and delivery of oncology therapies for patients worldwide. The molecules in Takeda Oncology's development pipeline are ordered by phases: Phase 1 trials are conducted to determine proper dosing, and Phase 2 and 3 studies determine the efficacy, side effects and safety of the therapies being researched. Certain molecules may be under study for more than one disease area. As of August 2021, there were 15 drug programs in Phase 1 trials, seven in Phase 2 trials and six in Phase 3 trials. Phase 3 drug candidates include brigatinib, ixazomib, pevonedistat, ponatinib, relugolix and mobocertinib. Takeda Oncology's preclinical drug compound request program supports research studies initiated by researchers worldwide. As part of this program, the company provides investigators with certain research and marketed compounds for eligible preclinical studies. Phase 4 studies encompass the research/investigation of Takeda's treatment patterns to better understand long-term risks and benefits of its medicines. In some cases, Takeda may be able to provide patients access to its investigational drugs outside of a clinical trial if certain conditions are met. Takeda Oncology has hubs in the U.S., Japan, Germany, Spain/Portugal, France, Italy, the U.K./Ireland and Canada.

FINANCIAL DATA: *Note: Data for latest year may not have been available at press time.*

In U.S. $	2020	2019	2018	2017	2016	2015
Revenue	3,904,160,000	3,548,220,000	3,352,450,000	3,184,827,500	3,025,586,125	2,960,000,000
R&D Expense						
Operating Income						
Operating Margin %						
SGA Expense						
Net Income						
Operating Cash Flow						
Capital Expenditure						
EBITDA						
Return on Assets %						
Return on Equity %						
Debt to Equity						

CONTACT INFORMATION:

Phone: 617-679-7000   Fax: 617-374-7788
Toll-Free: 800-390-5663
Address: 40 Landsdowne St., Cambridge, MA 02139 United States

STOCK TICKER/OTHER:

Stock Ticker: Subsidiary   Exchange:
Employees: 1,225   Fiscal Year Ends: 03/31
Parent Company: Takeda Pharmaceutical Company Limited

SALARIES/BONUSES:

Top Exec. Salary: $ Bonus: $
Second Exec. Salary: $ Bonus: $

OTHER THOUGHTS:

Estimated Female Officers or Directors:
Hot Spot for Advancement for Women/Minorities: Y

Takeda Pharmaceutical Company Limited   www.takeda.com

NAIC Code: 325412

TYPES OF BUSINESS:

Pharmaceuticals Discovery & Development
Over-the-Counter Drugs
Vitamins
Research and Development
Biopharmaceuticals
Plasma-based Therapies
Vaccines

BRANDS/DIVISIONS/AFFILIATES:

Adcetris
Cabozantinib
Ninlaro
Takhzyro
Vonvendi
Entyvio
Alofisel
Vonoprazan

CONTACTS: *Note: Officers with more than one job title may be intentionally listed here more than once.*

Christophe Weber, CEO
Costa Saroukos, CFO
Lauren Duprey, Chief Human Resources Officer
Tadataka Yamada, Chief Medical & Scientific Officer
Nancy Joseph-Ridge, Gen. Mgr.-Pharmaceutical Dev. Div.
Toyoji Yoshida, Managing Dir.-Internal Control & Special Missions
Shinji Honda, Sr. VP-Corp. Strategy
Frank Morich, Chief Commercial Officer
Trevor Smith, CEO-Takeda Pharmaceuticals Europe Ltd.
Masato Iwasaki, Sr. VP-Pharmaceutical Mktg. Div.
Haruhiko Hirate, Sr. VP
Anna Protopapas, Exec. VP-Global Bus. Dev.
Frank Morich, CEO-Takeda Pharmaceuticals Intl

GROWTH PLANS/SPECIAL FEATURES:

Takeda Pharmaceutical Company Limited, based in Japan, is an international research-based global biopharmaceutical company. The firm's areas of focus include oncology, rare diseases, neuroscience, gastroenterology, plasma-derived therapies and vaccines. Takeda's team of researchers and scientists collaborate with partners to harness cutting-edge science and develop therapies for patients throughout the world. The company's current (May 2021) pipeline includes clinical stages for each of its target areas, with projected approval dates ranging from 2021 through 2025 and beyond. Programs include: oncology, with Ninlaro, Alunbrig, Inclusig and Cabozantinib in Phase 1-3 trials, as well as Adcetris, Alunbrig, Cabozantinib and Ninlaro having been filed; rare diseases and hematology, with Natpara, Takhzyro, Vonvendi and Adynovate in Phase 1-3 trials, as well as Takhzyro and Vonvendi having been filed; gastroenterology, with Entyvio, Alofisel and Vonoprazan in Phase 1-3 trials, as well as all three having been filed; and plasma-derived therapies, Cuvitru and Hyqvia in Phase 3 trials. Many of these programs received orphan drug designation (ODD). In addition, Takeda Pharmaceutical is engaged in a 10-year joint research program by the Center of iPS Cell Research and Application at Kyoto University, called T-CiRA, which aims to develop innovative drugs and cell treatments in areas such as heart failure, diabetes mellitus, neuro-psychiatric disorders, cancer and intractable muscle diseases.

FINANCIAL DATA: *Note: Data for latest year may not have been available at press time.*

In U.S. $	2020	2019	2018	2017	2016	2015
Revenue	30,058,430,000	19,153,960,000	16,170,270,000	15,818,830,000	16,506,790,000	
R&D Expense	4,496,918,000	3,363,667,000	2,972,254,000	2,852,265,000	3,159,353,000	
Operating Income	2,508,910,000	1,464,614,000	2,208,260,000	1,423,534,000	1,194,853,000	
Operating Margin %	.08%	.07%	.14%	.09%	.07%	
SGA Expense	8,810,948,000	6,553,835,000	5,736,495,000	5,653,887,000	5,943,513,000	
Net Income	404,053,200	996,648,300	1,706,831,000	1,049,748,000	732,156,500	
Operating Cash Flow	6,116,848,000	3,000,000,000	3,450,942,000	2,387,030,000	232,809,400	
Capital Expenditure	1,988,346,000	1,224,864,000	1,171,417,000	1,023,143,000	774,999,400	
EBITDA	6,136,511,000	3,794,764,000	3,938,700,000	3,556,237,000	3,195,191,000	
Return on Assets %	.00%	.01%	.04%	.03%	.02%	
Return on Equity %	.01%	.03%	.10%	.06%	.04%	
Debt to Equity	0.954	0.924	0.493	0.317	0.277	

CONTACT INFORMATION:

Phone: 81 33278-2111   Fax: 81 33278-2000
Toll-Free:
Address: 1-1, Nihonbashi-Honcho 2-Chome, Chuo-ku, Osaka, 103-8668 Japan

STOCK TICKER/OTHER:

Stock Ticker: TAK   Exchange: NYS
Employees: 47,495   Fiscal Year Ends: 03/31
Parent Company:

SALARIES/BONUSES:

Top Exec. Salary: $ Bonus: $
Second Exec. Salary: $ Bonus: $

OTHER THOUGHTS:

Estimated Female Officers or Directors: 3
Hot Spot for Advancement for Women/Minorities: Y

Tandem Diabetes Care Inc

www.tandemdiabetes.com

NAIC Code: 334510

TYPES OF BUSINESS:

Electromedical and Electrotherapeutic Apparatus Manufacturing
Insulin Pumps
Insulin Technology
Software
Diabetes App

BRANDS/DIVISIONS/AFFILIATES:

t:slim X2
Basal-IQ
Control-IQ
Sugarmate

CONTACTS: *Note: Officers with more than one job title may be intentionally listed here more than once.*

John Sheridan, CEO
Leigh Vosseller, CFO
Kim Blickenstaff, Chairman of the Board
Susan Morrison, Chief Administrative Officer
David Berger, Executive VP
Brian Hansen, Executive VP

GROWTH PLANS/SPECIAL FEATURES:

Tandem Diabetes Care, Inc. is a medical device company with an innovative approach to the design, development and commercialization of a family of products for people with insulin-dependent diabetes. The firm's manufacturing and sales activities primarily focus on its flagship product, the t:slim X2 Insulin Delivery System (t:slim X2), based on a proprietary technology platform. The simple-to-use t:slim X2 is the smallest durable insulin pump available, and the only pump currently available that is capable of updating its software from a personal computer. Tandem's Basal-IQ technology is a predictive low glucose suspend feature designed to temporarily suspend insulin delivery to help reduce the frequency and duration of hypoglycemic events. Control-IQ technology is an advanced hybrid-closed loop feature designed to help increase a user's time in targeted glycemic range. It delivers automatic correction boluses in addition to adjusting insulin to help prevent high and low blood sugar. In mid-2020, Tandem and Abbott announced an agreement to develop and commercialize integrated diabetes solutions that combine Abbott's CGM technology with Tandem's insulin delivery systems to provide more options for people to manage their diabetes. Also in 2020, Tandem acquired Sugarmate, a mobile app for people with diabetes who use insulin, allowing them to log glucose data and health and nutrition information, and the app can notifications and alerts to users, their family and caregivers.

FINANCIAL DATA: *Note: Data for latest year may not have been available at press time.*

In U.S. $	2020	2019	2018	2017	2016	2015
Revenue	498,830,000	362,305,000	183,866,000	107,601,000	84,248,000	72,850,000
R&D Expense	63,574,000	45,199,000	29,227,000	20,661,000	18,809,000	16,963,000
Operating Income	-7,957,000	-16,722,000	-44,631,000	-62,944,000	-78,051,000	-69,004,000
Operating Margin %		- .05%	- .24%	- .58%	- .93%	- .95%
SGA Expense	204,903,000	165,735,000	105,226,000	86,377,000	82,834,000	78,621,000
Net Income	-34,382,000	-24,753,000	-122,611,000	-73,033,000	-83,447,000	-72,418,000
Operating Cash Flow	24,669,000	41,905,000	-8,319,000	-66,136,000	-61,173,000	-58,764,000
Capital Expenditure	32,294,000	19,541,000	2,986,000	5,718,000	8,930,000	5,838,000
EBITDA	-13,678,000	-18,454,000	-109,155,000	-54,818,000	-72,266,000	-63,838,000
Return on Assets %		- .09%	- .81%	- .70%	- .70%	- .63%
Return on Equity %		- .15%	-2.40%		-2.90%	-1.23%
Debt to Equity		0.072				0.467

CONTACT INFORMATION:

Phone: 858 366-6900   Fax:
Toll-Free:
Address: 11075 Roselle St., San Diego, CA 92121 United States

STOCK TICKER/OTHER:

Stock Ticker: TNDM
Employees: 1,043
Parent Company:

Exchange: NAS
Fiscal Year Ends: 12/31

SALARIES/BONUSES:

Top Exec. Salary: $ Bonus: $
Second Exec. Salary: $ Bonus: $

OTHER THOUGHTS:

Estimated Female Officers or Directors:
Hot Spot for Advancement for Women/Minorities:

TCR2 Therapeutics Inc

www.tcr2.com

NAIC Code: 325414

TYPES OF BUSINESS:

Biological Product (except Diagnostic) Manufacturing

BRANDS/DIVISIONS/AFFILIATES:

TRuC
TC-210
TC-110

GROWTH PLANS/SPECIAL FEATURES:

TCR2 Therapeutics Inc. is a clinical-stage immunotherapy company that develops next generation T cell (a type of white blood cell) therapies for patients suffering from cancer. The firm's TRuC (TCR Fusion Construct) T cells recognize tumors without the need of human leukocyte antigens (HLAs). TRuC-T cells developed by TRC2 demonstrate superior traits to the current CAR-T cells (another type of T cell therapy). The TRuC-T cell product platform is highlighted by the multiple programs and multiple formats of the product candidates in the firm's pipeline. The clinical pipeline includes programs for solid tumors (TC-210) and hematological malignancies (TC-110). TC-210 is the firm's most advanced program, treating patients with mesothelin-positive solid tumors. TC-110 targets CD19-positive B-cell hematological malignancies and is being developed to improve upon and address the unmet needs of CD19-directed CAR T cell therapies.

CONTACTS:

Note: Officers with more than one job title may be intentionally listed here more than once.

Garry Menzel, CEO
Mayur Somaiya, CFO
Ansbert Gadicke, Chairman of the Board
Alfonso Cardama, Chief Medical Officer
Robert Hofmeister, Chief Scientific Officer

FINANCIAL DATA:

Note: Data for latest year may not have been available at press time.

In U.S. $	2020	2019	2018	2017	2016	2015
Revenue						
R&D Expense	51,980,000	37,488,000	19,673,000	9,569,000	7,670,000	
Operating Income	-68,700,000	-51,382,000	-26,453,000	-13,180,000	-9,930,000	
Operating Margin %						
SGA Expense	16,720,000	13,894,000	6,780,000	3,611,000	2,260,000	
Net Income	-67,124,000	-47,599,000	-24,251,000	-13,070,000	-9,915,000	
Operating Cash Flow	-56,739,000	-41,359,000	-18,778,000	-12,036,000	-9,380,000	
Capital Expenditure	7,164,000	3,879,000	1,019,000	388,000	869,000	
EBITDA	-67,108,000	-50,520,000	-26,034,000	-12,882,000	-9,710,000	
Return on Assets %		- .65%	- .81%	- .74%	- .59%	
Return on Equity %		-2.61%				
Debt to Equity						

CONTACT INFORMATION:

Phone: 617 949-5200 Fax:
Toll-Free:
Address: 100 Binney St., Cambridge, MA 2142 United States

STOCK TICKER/OTHER:

Stock Ticker: TCRR Exchange: NAS
Employees: 118 Fiscal Year Ends: 12/31
Parent Company:

SALARIES/BONUSES:

Top Exec. Salary: $ Bonus: $
Second Exec. Salary: $ Bonus: $

OTHER THOUGHTS:

Estimated Female Officers or Directors:
Hot Spot for Advancement for Women/Minorities:

Team Health Holdings Inc

www.teamhealth.com

NAIC Code: 621111

TYPES OF BUSINESS:

Physicians and Hospital Staff Services
Ambulatory Care
Anesthesiology
Behavioral Health
Emergency Medicine
OB/GYN
Surgery
Post-Acute Care

BRANDS/DIVISIONS/AFFILIATES:

Blackstone Group LP (The)

GROWTH PLANS/SPECIAL FEATURES:

Team Health Holdings, Inc. is a physician-led company offering outsourced integrated care services. This 16,000+ clinician healthcare provider offers outsourced staffing, with practice areas including ambulatory care, anesthesiology, behavioral health, critical care, emergency medicine, hospital medicine, OB/GYN hospital care, orthopedic and general surgery and post-acute care. Team Health's staff include residents, physicians, medical directors and advanced practice clinicians. Team Health is privately-held private The Blackstone Group LP.

CONTACTS: *Note: Officers with more than one job title may be intentionally listed here more than once.*

Leif M. Murphy, CEO
Michael Wiechart, COO
H. Massingale, Chairman of the Board
David Jones, CFO
Oliver Rogers, Executive VP
Steven Clifton, Executive VP
Leif Murphy, President
Lynn Massingale, Chmn.

FINANCIAL DATA: *Note: Data for latest year may not have been available at press time.*

In U.S. $	2020	2019	2018	2017	2016	2015
Revenue	4,222,200,000	4,540,000,000	4,500,000,000	4,200,000,000	3,900,000,000	3,597,246,976
R&D Expense						
Operating Income						
Operating Margin %						
SGA Expense						
Net Income						
Operating Cash Flow						
Capital Expenditure						
EBITDA						
Return on Assets %						
Return on Equity %						
Debt to Equity						

CONTACT INFORMATION:

Phone: 865 693-1000 Fax:
Toll-Free: 800-818-1498
Address: 265 Brookview Ctr. Way, Ste. 400, Knoxville, TN 37919 United States

STOCK TICKER/OTHER:

Stock Ticker: Private Exchange:
Employees: 20,000 Fiscal Year Ends: 12/31
Parent Company: Blackstone Group LP (The)

SALARIES/BONUSES:

Top Exec. Salary: $ Bonus: $
Second Exec. Salary: $ Bonus: $

OTHER THOUGHTS:

Estimated Female Officers or Directors: 3
Hot Spot for Advancement for Women/Minorities: Y

Teladoc Health Inc

teladochealth.com

NAIC Code: 621111

TYPES OF BUSINESS:

Telemedical Clinic
Virtual Health Visits
Medical Records Management

BRANDS/DIVISIONS/AFFILIATES:

InTouch Health

CONTACTS: *Note: Officers with more than one job title may be intentionally listed here more than once.*

Jason Gorevic, CEO
David Sides, COO
Mala Murthy, CFO
Lewis Levy, Chief Medical Officer
Michelle Bucaria, Chief Human Resources Officer
Jeff Nadler, CIO

GROWTH PLANS/SPECIAL FEATURES:

Teladoc Health, Inc. offers a comprehensive virtual care solution capable of serving organizations and people anywhere. The firm's services span the spectrum of healthcare needs, from simple to complex, covering more than 450 medical subspecialties. The Teladoc platform seamlessly and securely connects general medical, mental health and complex care to deliver convenience, health outcomes and value. After a telehealth visit, more than 90% of patients reported resolution, serving members and plan sponsors alike. Medical specialists are matched to the unique needs of each customer's case. They review medical records, pathologies, and test results to confirm the accuracy of diagnoses and treatment plans. With this strategy, insurers and employers gain confidence that members are on the right path for better health outcomes and lower costs. Mental health services range from ongoing visits with a mental healthcare specialist to expert medical opinions for complex cases. More than 33 million sessions have been completed by Teladoc's licensed therapists, psychologists, and counselors. Teladoc's virtual healthcare services enable members to access a wide range of expertise for navigating and solving their healthcare needs, including help with gathering medical records, managing health risks and maintaining wellness. Teladoc provides medical visits across 175 countries, and enables millions of patients and provider touchpoints for hospitals, health systems and physician practices globally. In July 2020, Teledoc acquired InTouch Health, integrating InTouch Health's innovative telehealth capabilities that link providers to one another in complex medical environments. Teladoc planned to connect the care experience across in-patient, outpatient and home care settings. That August, Teladoc agreed to acquire and merge with Livongo, a leading applied health signals company.

Teladoc offers its employees a healthcare program, retirement plans and company incentives and perks.

FINANCIAL DATA: *Note: Data for latest year may not have been available at press time.*

In U.S. $	2020	2019	2018	2017	2016	2015
Revenue	1,093,962,000	553,307,000	417,907,000			
R&D Expense	164,941,000	64,644,000	54,373,000			
Operating Income	-418,185,000	-73,822,000	-65,963,000			
Operating Margin %		- .13%	- .16%			
SGA Expense	886,882,000	339,068,000	263,045,000			
Net Income	-485,136,000	-98,864,000	-97,084,000			
Operating Cash Flow	-53,511,000	29,869,000	-4,860,000			
Capital Expenditure	26,042,000	10,900,000	8,407,000			
EBITDA	-437,411,000	-35,490,000	-35,252,000			
Return on Assets %		- .06%	- .08%			
Return on Equity %		- .10%	- .12%			
Debt to Equity		0.459	0.409			

CONTACT INFORMATION:

Phone: 203 635-2002   Fax:
Toll-Free:
Address: 2 Manhattanville Rd., Ste. 203, Purchase, NY 10577 United States

STOCK TICKER/OTHER:

Stock Ticker: TDOC
Employees: 4,400
Parent Company:

Exchange: NYS
Fiscal Year Ends:

SALARIES/BONUSES:

Top Exec. Salary: $ Bonus: $
Second Exec. Salary: $ Bonus: $

OTHER THOUGHTS:

Estimated Female Officers or Directors:
Hot Spot for Advancement for Women/Minorities:

Teleflex Incorporated

www.teleflex.com

NAIC Code: 339100

TYPES OF BUSINESS:

Medical Equipment & Supplies, Manufacturing
General & Specialized Surgical Products

BRANDS/DIVISIONS/AFFILIATES:

Wattson

CONTACTS: *Note: Officers with more than one job title may be intentionally listed here more than once.*

Thomas Powell, CFO
Benson Smith, Chairman of the Board
Liam Kelly, President
Cameron Hicks, Vice President, Divisional
Karen Boylan, Vice President, Divisional
John Deren, Vice President
James Leyden, Vice President

GROWTH PLANS/SPECIAL FEATURES:

Teleflex Incorporated designs, develops, manufactures and supplies single-use medical devices used by hospitals and healthcare providers for common diagnostic and therapeutic procedures in critical care and surgical applications. Teleflex markets and sells its products worldwide through a combination of direct sellers and distributors. Teleflex has approximately 35 manufacturing sites, with major operations located in the Czech Republic, Germany, Malaysia, Mexico and the U.S. More than 55% of the company's annual revenues are derived from the Americas, 23% from Europe/Middle East/Africa (EMEA), 11% from Asia and 9% from original equipment manufacturers (OEMs). Product categories include vascular access, interventional, anesthesia, surgical, interventional urology, respiratory and urology. In early-2020, Teleflex announced that it received 510(k) clearance from the U.S. Food and Drug Administration for its Wattson temporary pacing guidewire, the first commercially-available bipolar temporary pacing guidewire designed specifically for use during transcatheter aortic valve replacement and balloon aortic valvuloplasty.

Teleflex offers employees comprehensive benefits.

FINANCIAL DATA: *Note: Data for latest year may not have been available at press time.*

In U.S. $	2020	2019	2018	2017	2016	2015
Revenue	2,537,156,000	2,595,362,000	2,448,383,000	2,146,303,000	1,868,027,000	1,809,690,000
R&D Expense	119,747,000	113,857,000	106,208,000	84,770,000	58,579,000	52,119,000
Operating Income	461,559,000	443,382,000	399,546,000	387,069,000	374,313,000	323,302,000
Operating Margin %		.17%	.16%	.18%	.20%	.18%
SGA Expense	743,568,000	934,373,000	878,688,000	699,963,000	563,308,000	568,982,000
Net Income	335,324,000	461,466,000	200,802,000	152,530,000	237,377,000	244,863,000
Operating Cash Flow	436,406,000	439,525,000	437,378,000	419,885,000	408,480,000	300,810,000
Capital Expenditure	90,694,000	102,695,000	80,795,000	70,903,000	53,135,000	61,448,000
EBITDA	651,478,000	634,235,000	532,628,000	522,720,000	418,572,000	414,362,000
Return on Assets %		.07%	.03%	.03%	.06%	.06%
Return on Equity %		.17%	.08%	.07%	.11%	.12%
Debt to Equity		0.658	0.816	0.89	0.397	0.322

CONTACT INFORMATION:

Phone: 610-225-6800   Fax:
Toll-Free:
Address: 550 East Swedesford Rd., Ste 400, Wayne, PA 19087 United States

STOCK TICKER/OTHER:

Stock Ticker: TFX
Employees: 14,000
Parent Company:

Exchange: NYS
Fiscal Year Ends: 12/31

SALARIES/BONUSES:

Top Exec. Salary: $ Bonus: $
Second Exec. Salary: $ Bonus: $

OTHER THOUGHTS:

Estimated Female Officers or Directors: 2
Hot Spot for Advancement for Women/Minorities:

Tenet Healthcare Corporation

www.tenethealth.com

NAIC Code: 622110

TYPES OF BUSINESS:

General Medical and Surgical Hospitals
Specialty Care Facilities
Outpatient Centers
Diagnostic Imaging Centers
Rural Health Care Clinics
HMOs

BRANDS/DIVISIONS/AFFILIATES:

USPI Holding Company Inc
Conifer Holdings Inc

CONTACTS: *Note: Officers with more than one job title may be intentionally listed here more than once.*

Ronald Rittenmeyer, CEO
Daniel Cancelmi, CFO
R. Ramsey, Chief Accounting Officer
Saumya Sutaria, COO
Audrey Andrews, General Counsel
Keith Pitts, Vice Chairman

GROWTH PLANS/SPECIAL FEATURES:

Tenet Healthcare Corporation specializes in the provision of health care services, primarily through the operation of general hospitals. The company operates 65 hospitals and over 510 other healthcare facilities, including surgical hospitals, ambulatory surgery centers, urgent care and imaging centers and other outpatient facilities. Tenet operates through three business segments: hospital operations, ambulatory care and Conifer. The hospital segment operates the 65 hospitals, which primarily serve urban and suburban communities in nine U.S. states. Each general hospital offers acute care services, operating and recovery rooms, radiology services, respiratory therapy services, clinical laboratories and pharmacies. In addition, most have intensive care, critical care and/or coronary care units, as well as cardiovascular, digestive disease, neurosciences, musculoskeletal and obstetrics services, and outpatient services such as physical therapy. The ambulatory care segment is operated through joint venture USPI Holding Company, Inc., which has interests in 260 ambulatory surgery centers, 39 urgent care centers, 23 imaging centers and 24 surgical hospitals in 27 states. USPI is 95%-owned by Tenet and 5%-owned by Baylor University Medical Center. The Conifer segment consists of subsidiary Conifer Holdings, Inc., which provides healthcare business process services in the areas of hospital and physician revenue cycle management and value-based care solutions to healthcare systems, as well as individual hospitals, physician practices, self-insured organizations, health plans and other entities. Revenue cycle management solutions consist of patient services, financial counseling services, clinical revenue integrity solutions and accounts receivable management solutions. Conifer also offers customized communications and engagement solutions to optimize the relationship between providers and patients. Conifer's customer service representatives provide direct, 24-hour multilingual support for physician referral requests, calls regarding maternity services and other patient inquiries, community education, and scheduling appointments.

Tenet offers its employees education/leadership development, comprehensive health benefits, financial benefits and more.

FINANCIAL DATA: *Note: Data for latest year may not have been available at press time.*

In U.S. $	2020	2019	2018	2017	2016	2015
Revenue	17,640,000,000	18,479,000,000	18,313,000,000	19,179,000,000	19,621,000,000	18,634,000,000
R&D Expense						
Operating Income	2,140,000,000	1,679,000,000	1,617,000,000	1,389,000,000	1,432,000,000	1,380,000,000
Operating Margin %		.09%	.09%	.07%	.07%	.07%
SGA Expense	8,418,000,000	8,704,000,000	8,634,000,000	9,274,000,000	9,356,000,000	9,011,000,000
Net Income	399,000,000	-232,000,000	111,000,000	-704,000,000	-192,000,000	-140,000,000
Operating Cash Flow	3,407,000,000	1,233,000,000	1,049,000,000	1,200,000,000	558,000,000	1,026,000,000
Capital Expenditure	540,000,000	670,000,000	617,000,000	707,000,000	875,000,000	842,000,000
EBITDA	2,531,000,000	2,131,000,000	2,445,000,000	1,797,000,000	2,077,000,000	1,853,000,000
Return on Assets %		- .01%	.00%	- .03%	- .01%	- .01%
Return on Equity %				-5.21%	- .35%	- .21%
Debt to Equity					36.125	20.815

CONTACT INFORMATION:

Phone: 469-893-2200   Fax:
Toll-Free:
Address: 14201 Dallas Pkwy., Dallas, TX 75254 United States

STOCK TICKER/OTHER:

Stock Ticker: THC
Employees: 113,600
Parent Company:

Exchange: NYS
Fiscal Year Ends: 12/31

SALARIES/BONUSES:

Top Exec. Salary: $ Bonus: $
Second Exec. Salary: $ Bonus: $

OTHER THOUGHTS:

Estimated Female Officers or Directors: 5
Hot Spot for Advancement for Women/Minorities: Y

Terumo Corporation

NAIC Code: 339100

www.terumo.co.jp

TYPES OF BUSINESS:

Surgical Appliance and Supplies Manufacturing
Medical Device Manufacturer
Medical Device Distributor

BRANDS/DIVISIONS/AFFILIATES:

Cardiac and Vascular Company
General Hospital Company
Blood and Cell Technologies Company
TREO

CONTACTS: *Note: Officers with more than one job title may be intentionally listed here more than once.*

Shinjiro Shato, Pres.
Takahito Mimura, Chmn.

GROWTH PLANS/SPECIAL FEATURES:

Terumo Corporation develops, manufactures and distributes medical devices and services worldwide. The firm operates in three companies and seven divisions. The Cardiac and Vascular Company offers minimally invasive treatments through endovascular interventions for various parts of the body and in cardiovascular surgery. This company's divisions include Terumo interventional systems, neurovascular, cardiovascular and vascular graft. The General Hospital Company offers technology and services for improving the safety and efficiency of medical settings and innovating drug delivery products and solutions. This company's divisions include: hospital systems, offering medical devices and pharmaceuticals used in a variety of medical settings; and alliance, which offers pharmaceutical companies administration devices made from materials tailored to each drug, as well as related manufacturing technology for drug-device combination products. The Blood and Cell Technologies Company and division offers unique technologies in regards to blood and cells, and supplies advanced therapies and products that support patient lives and contribute to healthcare infrastructure. Based in Tokyo, Terumo operates globally, with associates in more than 160 countries and regions. In September 2020, Terumo announced the commercial launch of its TREO abdominal stent graft system in the U.S., for the treatment of patients with abdominal aortic aneurysms.

FINANCIAL DATA: *Note: Data for latest year may not have been available at press time.*

In U.S. $	2020	2019	2018	2017	2016	2015
Revenue	5,743,719,000	5,475,063,000	5,368,152,000	4,695,862,000	4,795,065,000	
R&D Expense						
Operating Income	1,010,211,000	973,916,200	991,424,200	699,396,400	746,193,900	
Operating Margin %	.18%	.18%	.18%	.15%	.16%	
SGA Expense	2,147,571,000	2,067,110,000	1,939,512,000			
Net Income	778,232,400	725,799,900	833,797,600	495,237,200	462,824,100	
Operating Cash Flow	1,072,936,000	854,584,400	1,046,295,000	738,513,000	733,407,600	
Capital Expenditure	762,459,800	496,506,700	377,394,000	333,519,000	300,585,400	
EBITDA	1,499,594,000	1,393,879,000	1,383,257,000	1,110,445,000	1,123,259,000	
Return on Assets %	.07%	.07%	.09%	.06%	.05%	
Return on Equity %	.12%	.13%	.18%	.11%	.09%	
Debt to Equity	0.259	0.323	0.525	0.431	0.312	

CONTACT INFORMATION:

Phone: 81 333748111   Fax:
Toll-Free:
Address: 2-44-1, Hatagaya Shibuya-ku, Tokyo, 151-0072 Japan

STOCK TICKER/OTHER:

Stock Ticker: TRUMY   Exchange: PINX
Employees: 26,438   Fiscal Year Ends: 03/31
Parent Company:

SALARIES/BONUSES:

Top Exec. Salary: $ Bonus: $
Second Exec. Salary: $ Bonus: $

OTHER THOUGHTS:

Estimated Female Officers or Directors:
Hot Spot for Advancement for Women/Minorities:

Teva Pharmaceutical Industries Limited   www.tevapharm.com

NAIC Code: 325412

TYPES OF BUSINESS:

Drugs-Generic
Active Pharmaceutical Ingredients

BRANDS/DIVISIONS/AFFILIATES:

SUDOCREM
NasenDuo
Flegamina
FLUX

CONTACTS: *Note: Officers with more than one job title may be intentionally listed here more than once.*

Kare Schultz, CEO
Eric Drape, Exec. VP-Global Oper.
Eli Kalif, CFO
Eli Shani, Exec. VP-Global Mktg.
Galia Inbar, Exec. VP-Human Resources
Michael Hayden, Chief Scientific Officer
Richard S. Egosi, Chief Legal Officer
Erez Israeli, Chief Bus. Process Officer
Iris Beck-Codner, Chief Comm. Officer
Kevin Mannix, VP-Investor Rel.
Sol J. Barer, Chmn.
Itzhak Krinsky, Chmn.-Teva Japan & South Korea

GROWTH PLANS/SPECIAL FEATURES:

Teva Pharmaceutical Industries Limited, based in Israel, is a pharmaceutical company that produces, distributes and sells pharmaceutical products internationally. The firm operates in three regions: North America, Europe and international markets--each of which manages Teva's entire product portfolio, including generics, specialty medicines and over-the-counter (OTC) medicines. Teva develops, manufactures and sells generic medicines in a variety of dosage forms, including tablets, capsules, injectables, inhalants, liquids, ointments and creams. The generics division also offers a broad range of basic chemical entities, as well as specialized product families such as sterile products, hormones, narcotics, high-potency drugs and cytotoxic substances. The specialty medicines business focuses on delivering innovative solutions to patients and providers via medicines, devices and services in key regions and markets worldwide. These solutions include Teva's core therapeutic areas of central nervous system (CNS) and respiratory medicines. CNS medicines include treatments for multiple sclerosis, neurodegenerative disorders, movement disorders and pain care; and respiratory medicines focus on asthma and chronic obstructive pulmonary disease (COPD). This division also has specialty products in oncology and other areas. Last, the OTC division markets OTC products in more than 1,500 dosage strengths and packaging sizes, including oral solid dosage forms, injectable products, inhaled products, liquids, ointments and creams. OTC brands include SUDOCREM in Europe, NasenDuo in Germany, and Flegamina in Poland.

FINANCIAL DATA: *Note: Data for latest year may not have been available at press time.*

In U.S. $	2020	2019	2018	2017	2016	2015
Revenue	16,658,000,000	16,887,000,000	18,854,000,000	22,385,000,000	21,903,000,000	19,652,000,000
R&D Expense	997,000,000	1,010,000,000	1,213,000,000	1,848,000,000	2,111,000,000	1,525,000,000
Operating Income	3,058,000,000	2,721,000,000	2,869,000,000	3,991,000,000	4,652,000,000	5,114,000,000
Operating Margin %		.16%	.15%	.18%	.21%	.26%
SGA Expense	3,671,000,000	3,806,000,000	4,214,000,000	4,986,000,000	5,096,000,000	4,717,000,000
Net Income	-3,990,000,000	-999,000,000	-2,150,000,000	-16,265,000,000	329,000,000	1,588,000,000
Operating Cash Flow	1,216,000,000	748,000,000	2,446,000,000	3,507,000,000	5,225,000,000	5,542,000,000
Capital Expenditure	578,000,000	525,000,000	651,000,000	874,000,000	901,000,000	772,000,000
EBITDA	-1,886,000,000	1,338,000,000	166,000,000	-15,392,000,000	2,894,000,000	3,930,000,000
Return on Assets %		-.02%	-.04%	-.20%	.00%	.03%
Return on Equity %		-.07%	-.17%	-.76%	.00%	.06%
Debt to Equity		1.789	1.815	2.10	1.094	0.317

CONTACT INFORMATION:

Phone: 972 3 9148213   Fax: 972 392-34050
Toll-Free:
Address: 5 Basel St., Petach Tikva, 4951033 Israel

STOCK TICKER/OTHER:

Stock Ticker: TEVA   Exchange: NYS
Employees: 40,216   Fiscal Year Ends: 12/31
Parent Company:

SALARIES/BONUSES:

Top Exec. Salary: $ Bonus: $
Second Exec. Salary: $ Bonus: $

OTHER THOUGHTS:

Estimated Female Officers or Directors: 4
Hot Spot for Advancement for Women/Minorities: Y

Texas Health Resources

www.texashealth.org

NAIC Code: 622110

TYPES OF BUSINESS:

General Medical and Surgical Hospitals
Hospitals
Health Care
Rehabilitation
Health Plans

BRANDS/DIVISIONS/AFFILIATES:

Southwestern Health Resources

CONTACTS: *Note: Officers with more than one job title may be intentionally listed here more than once.*

Barclay E. Berdan, CEO
Rick McWhorter, CFO
Carla Dawson, Chief People Officer
Winjie Tang Miao, Chief Experience Officer
Jonathan Scholl, Chief Strategy Officer
Oscar L. Amparan, Exec. VP-Southeast Zone Operations Leader
Harold Berenzweig, Exec. VP-Southwest Zone Clinical Leader
Mark C. Lester, Exec. VP-Southeast Zone Clinical Leader
Joan Clark, Chief Nurse Exec.

GROWTH PLANS/SPECIAL FEATURES:

Texas Health Resources (THR) is one of the largest faith-based, non-profit healthcare delivery systems in the U.S. The firm serves more than 7 million people in 16 counties throughout the northern Texas region. THR has 19 acute care stay hospital locations, five short stay hospitals, two rehabilitation hospitals and one transitional care hospital, 27 hospitals in all. They are owned, operated or joint-ventured with THR. In addition, the firm's network includes more than 80 outpatient facilities, surgery centers, behavioral health facilities, fitness centers and imaging centers, as well as over 250 other community access points such as THPG clinics, doctors' offices and Minute Clinics. Southwestern Health Resources in a clinically-integrated 30-facility hospital network that brings together Texas Health Resources and UT Southwestern Medical Center to provide a full spectrum of health care services. Texas Health Resources and Aetna also created a jointly-owned health plan company that combines THR's providers and investment in population health management with Aetna's health plan expertise, care management capabilities and analytical insights to provide affordable quality care.

THR offers its employees health benefits, 401(k), tuition reimbursement and a variety of employee assistance plans and programs.

FINANCIAL DATA: *Note: Data for latest year may not have been available at press time.*

In U.S. $	2020	2019	2018	2017	2016	2015
Revenue	4,900,000,000	5,097,915,900	4,983,300,000	4,746,000,000	4,520,000,000	4,260,792,000
R&D Expense						
Operating Income						
Operating Margin %						
SGA Expense						
Net Income						
Operating Cash Flow						
Capital Expenditure						
EBITDA						
Return on Assets %						
Return on Equity %						
Debt to Equity						

CONTACT INFORMATION:

Phone: 682-236-7900 Fax:
Toll-Free: 877-847-9355
Address: 612 E. Lamar Blvd., Arlington, TX 76011 United States

STOCK TICKER/OTHER:

Stock Ticker: Nonprofit Exchange:
Employees: 26,000 Fiscal Year Ends: 12/31
Parent Company:

SALARIES/BONUSES:

Top Exec. Salary: $ Bonus: $
Second Exec. Salary: $ Bonus: $

OTHER THOUGHTS:

Estimated Female Officers or Directors: 4
Hot Spot for Advancement for Women/Minorities: Y

Thermo Fisher Scientific Inc
www.thermofisher.com
NAIC Code: 423450

TYPES OF BUSINESS:
Laboratory Equipment & Supplies Distribution
Contract Manufacturing
Equipment Calibration & Repair
Clinical Trial Services
Laboratory Workstations
Clinical Consumables
Diagnostic Reagents
Custom Chemical Synthesis

BRANDS/DIVISIONS/AFFILIATES:
Thermo Scientific
Applied Biosystems
Invitrogen
Fisher Scientific
Unity Lab Services
Patheon
TaqPath

CONTACTS: *Note: Officers with more than one job title may be intentionally listed here more than once.*
Marc Casper, CEO
Jim Manzi, Chairman of the Board
Mark Stevenson, COO
Michael Boxer, General Counsel
Gregory Herrema, President, Divisional
Patrick Durbin, President, Divisional
Michel Lagarde, President, Divisional
Stephen Williamson, Senior VP
Peter Hornstra, Vice President

GROWTH PLANS/SPECIAL FEATURES:
Thermo Fisher Scientific, Inc. is a distributor of products and services principally to the scientific-research and clinical laboratory markets. The firm serves over 400,000 customers including biotechnology and pharmaceutical companies; colleges and universities; medical-research institutions; hospitals; reference, quality control, process-control and research and development labs in various industries; as well as government agencies. It operates in four segments: life sciences solutions, analytical instruments, specialty diagnostics and laboratory products and services. Life sciences solutions provides a portfolio of reagents, instruments and consumables used in biological and medical research, discover and production of new drugs and vaccines. This division also provides diagnosis of disease. Analytical instruments provides a broad offering of instruments, consumables, software and services used for a range of applications in the laboratory, on the production line and in the field. These products are used by customers in pharmaceutical, biotechnology, academic, government, environmental, research, industrial markets, as well as clinical laboratories. Specialty diagnostics offers a range of diagnostic test kits, reagents, culture media, instruments and associated products in order to serve customers in healthcare, clinical, pharmaceutical, industrial and food safety laboratories. Laboratory products and services offers everything needed for the laboratory. This segment's products are used primarily for drug discovery and development, as well as for life science research. The company's primary brands include Thermo Scientific, Applied Biosystems, Invitrogen, Fisher Scientific, Unity Lab Services and Patheon. In August 2021, Thermo Fisher Scientific announced that the U.S. Food and Drug Administration granted emergency use authorization for its TaqPath COVID-19 Fast PCR Combo Kit 2.0 and the TaqPath COVID-19 RNase P Combo Kit 2.0, both highly accurate assays designed with increased targe redundancy to compensate for current mutations and emerging SARS-CoV-2 variants.

Employees receive comprehensive benefits.

FINANCIAL DATA: *Note: Data for latest year may not have been available at press time.*

In U.S. $	2020	2019	2018	2017	2016	2015
Revenue	32,218,000,000	25,542,000,000	24,358,000,000	20,918,000,000	18,274,100,000	16,965,400,000
R&D Expense	1,181,000,000	1,003,000,000	967,000,000	888,000,000	754,800,000	692,300,000
Operating Income	7,893,000,000	4,181,000,000	3,833,000,000	3,065,000,000	2,638,400,000	2,451,500,000
Operating Margin %		.16%	.16%	.15%	.14%	.14%
SGA Expense	6,930,000,000	6,144,000,000	6,057,000,000	5,492,000,000	4,975,900,000	4,612,100,000
Net Income	6,375,000,000	3,696,000,000	2,938,000,000	2,225,000,000	2,021,800,000	1,975,400,000
Operating Cash Flow	8,289,000,000	4,973,000,000	4,543,000,000	4,005,000,000	3,156,300,000	2,816,900,000
Capital Expenditure	1,474,000,000	926,000,000	758,000,000	508,000,000	444,400,000	422,900,000
EBITDA	10,103,000,000	7,023,000,000	6,196,000,000	5,054,000,000	4,251,500,000	4,039,500,000
Return on Assets %		.06%	.05%	.04%	.05%	.05%
Return on Equity %		.13%	.11%	.09%	.09%	.09%
Debt to Equity		0.575	0.642	0.743	0.714	0.537

CONTACT INFORMATION:
Phone: 781 622-1000   Fax: 781 933-4476
Toll-Free: 800-678-5599
Address: 168 Third Ave., Waltham, MA 02451 United States

STOCK TICKER/OTHER:
Stock Ticker: TMO
Employees: 80,000
Parent Company:

Exchange: NYS
Fiscal Year Ends: 12/31

SALARIES/BONUSES:
Top Exec. Salary: $ Bonus: $
Second Exec. Salary: $ Bonus: $

OTHER THOUGHTS:
Estimated Female Officers or Directors: 1
Hot Spot for Advancement for Women/Minorities: Y

Sales, profits and employees may be estimates. Financial information, benefits and other data can change quickly and may vary from those stated here.

Thomas Jefferson University Hospitals Inc hospitals.jefferson.edu

NAIC Code: 622110

TYPES OF BUSINESS:

General Medical and Surgical Hospitals

BRANDS/DIVISIONS/AFFILIATES:

Thomas Jefferson University Hospital
Jefferson Hospital for Neuroscience
Jefferson Methodist Hospital
Jefferson at the Navy Yard
Jefferson at Voorhees
Thomas Jefferson University

CONTACTS: *Note: Officers with more than one job title may be intentionally listed here more than once.*

Stephen K. Klasko, CEO
Stephanie Conners, COO
Peter L. DeAngelis, Jr., CFO
Charles G. Lewis, CMO
Clayton Fitzhugh, CHRO
Nassar Nizami, CIO
H. Richard Haverstick, Jr., Chmn.

GROWTH PLANS/SPECIAL FEATURES:

Thomas Jefferson University Hospitals, Inc. is one of the leading healthcare providers in the Philadelphia area. The firm is recognized in 9 different specialty areas: cancer, diabetes and endocrinology, ear/nose/throat, gastroenterology and GI surgery, neurology and neurosurgery, ophthalmology, orthopedics, and pulmonology. Thomas Jefferson University Hospitals have 908 licensed acute care beds via five primary locations, including: Thomas Jefferson University Hospital (the main facility, established in 1825) and Jefferson Hospital for Neuroscience, both in Center City Philadelphia; Jefferson Methodist Hospital and Jefferson at the Navy Yard, both in South Philadelphia; and Jefferson at Voorhees in South Jersey. The hospital partners with Thomas Jefferson University to be a leading innovator in the medical field. In September 2020, the Federal Trade Commission sued to block the Thomas Jefferson University and Einstein Healthcare Network merger, causing the transaction to undergo judicial hearings.

Thomas Jefferson University Hospitals offers its employees comprehensive health benefits, retirement options and a variety of employee assistance plans and programs.

FINANCIAL DATA: *Note: Data for latest year may not have been available at press time.*

In U.S. $	2020	2019	2018	2017	2016	2015
Revenue						
R&D Expense						
Operating Income						
Operating Margin %						
SGA Expense						
Net Income						
Operating Cash Flow						
Capital Expenditure						
EBITDA						
Return on Assets %						
Return on Equity %						
Debt to Equity						

CONTACT INFORMATION:

Phone: 215-955-6000   Fax:
Toll-Free:
Address: 111 South 11th St., Philadelphia, PA 19107 United States

STOCK TICKER/OTHER:

Stock Ticker: Nonprofit   Exchange:
Employees: 9,970   Fiscal Year Ends: 06/30
Parent Company:

SALARIES/BONUSES:

Top Exec. Salary: $ Bonus: $
Second Exec. Salary: $ Bonus: $

OTHER THOUGHTS:

Estimated Female Officers or Directors:
Hot Spot for Advancement for Women/Minorities:

Tivity Health Inc

www.tivityhealth.com

NAIC Code: 524298A

TYPES OF BUSINESS:

Disease Management Programs
Health Care
Fitness
Health Plans
Diet Plans
Nutrition Counseling
Packaged Foods

BRANDS/DIVISIONS/AFFILIATES:

SilverSneakers
Prime Fitness
WholeHealth Living
Nutrisystem
South Beach Diet

CONTACTS: *Note: Officers with more than one job title may be intentionally listed here more than once.*

Donato Tramuto, CEO
Adam Holland, CFO
Kevin Wills, Chairman of the Board
Ryan Wagers, Chief Accounting Officer
Mary Flipse, Chief Legal Officer
Dawn Zier, COO
Steven Janicak, President, Divisional

GROWTH PLANS/SPECIAL FEATURES:

Tivity Health, Inc. provides fitness, nutrition and social connection solutions. The firm operates through two business segments: healthcare and nutrition. The healthcare segment comprises SilverSneakers, Prime Fitness and WholeHealth Living. SilverSneakers is offered to members of Medicare Advantage and Medicare Supplement plans. Prime Fitness is a fitness facility access program through commercial health plans, employers and other sponsoring organizations. Tivity's national network of fitness centers delivers both SilverSneakers and Prime Fitness. These fitness networks encompass approximately 17,000 partner locations and more than 1,000 alternative locations that provide classes outside of traditional fitness centers. The WholeHealth Living program is sold primarily to health plans and offers a continuum of services related to complementary, alternative and physical medicine such as chiropractic care, acupuncture, physical therapy, occupational therapy, massage therapy and more. The WholeHealth Living network includes relationships with approximately 80,000 practitioners. The nutrition segment includes Nutrisystem and South Beach Diet. Customers within this segment typically purchase monthly food packages containing a four-week meal plan consisting of breakfasts, lunches, dinners, snacks and other meals, which they supplement, depending on the program being followed, with items such as fresh fruits, vegetables, lean protein and dairy. In total, plans feature approximately 250 food options, including frozen and unfrozen ready-to-go entrees, snacks and shakes, at different price points. Unlimited counseling from trained weight loss counselors, registered dieticians and certified diabetes educators is offered at no cost. The nutrition segment also offers its products through select retailers and QVC shopping network.

FINANCIAL DATA: *Note: Data for latest year may not have been available at press time.*

In U.S. $	2020	2019	2018	2017	2016	2015
Revenue	437,714,000	1,131,157,000	606,299,000	556,942,000	500,998,000	770,598,000
R&D Expense						
Operating Income	122,234,000	134,281,000	133,805,000	123,619,000	100,315,000	16,692,000
Operating Margin %		.12%	.22%	.22%	.20%	.02%
SGA Expense	55,188,000	268,044,000	35,113,000	34,361,000	39,478,000	68,142,000
Net Income	-223,631,000	-286,821,000	98,803,000	63,715,000	-129,111,000	-30,947,000
Operating Cash Flow	169,447,000	82,305,000	108,739,000	105,276,000	37,902,000	60,960,000
Capital Expenditure	15,525,000	24,713,000	9,053,000	5,910,000	14,474,000	34,730,000
EBITDA	163,763,000	-199,068,000	138,348,000	123,753,000	126,674,000	33,094,000
Return on Assets %		-.27%	.18%	.11%	-.20%	-.04%
Return on Equity %		-.96%	.31%	.28%	-.55%	-.11%
Debt to Equity		4.758	0.083		0.868	0.759

CONTACT INFORMATION:

Phone: 615 614-4929   Fax: 615 665-7697
Toll-Free: 800-869-5311
Address: 701 Cool Springs Blvd., Franklin, TN 37067 United States

STOCK TICKER/OTHER:

Stock Ticker: TVTY   Exchange: NAS
Employees: 350   Fiscal Year Ends: 12/31
Parent Company:

SALARIES/BONUSES:

Top Exec. Salary: $ Bonus: $
Second Exec. Salary: $ Bonus: $

OTHER THOUGHTS:

Estimated Female Officers or Directors: 1
Hot Spot for Advancement for Women/Minorities:

Sales, profits and employees may be estimates. Financial information, benefits and other data can change quickly and may vary from those stated here.

TLC Laser Eye Centers

www.tlcvision.com

NAIC Code: 621493

TYPES OF BUSINESS:

Eye Clinics
Laser Vision Correction Services
Blood Filtration Equipment
Management Software & Systems

BRANDS/DIVISIONS/AFFILIATES:

Vision Group Holdings
Sightpath Medical LLC
TruVision Health LLC

GROWTH PLANS/SPECIAL FEATURES:

TLC Laser Eye Centers provide eye care services, primarily laser refractive surgery. This surgery involves using an excimer laser to treat common refractive vision disorders such as myopia (nearsightedness), hyperopia (farsightedness) and astigmatism by reshaping the cornea of the eye. TLC physicians use excimer lasers to perform refractive, cataract and optometric surgery. The vast majority of procedures performed at the company's TLC Laser Eye Centers are LASIK (laser-assisted-in-situ keratomileusis) treatments. The firm also performs photorefractive keratectomy (PRK) surgery, which helps to reduce or eliminate the need for eyeglasses or contact lenses. Also, through its Sightpath Medical, LLC subsidiary, the company furnishes hospitals and other facilities with mobile or fixed-site access to cataract surgery equipment, supplies and technicians. TruVision Health, LLC is a managed care contractor for elective healthcare services. TLC Laser Eye Centers are owned by Vision Group Holdings.

CONTACTS:

Note: Officers with more than one job title may be intentionally listed here more than once.

George Neal, CEO
Jonathan Compton, Dir.-Taxation
Ellen-Jo E. Plass, Pres

FINANCIAL DATA:

Note: Data for latest year may not have been available at press time.

In U.S. $	2020	2019	2018	2017	2016	2015
Revenue	230,946,187	243,101,250	231,525,000	220,500,000	210,000,000	200,000,000
R&D Expense						
Operating Income						
Operating Margin %						
SGA Expense						
Net Income						
Operating Cash Flow						
Capital Expenditure						
EBITDA						
Return on Assets %						
Return on Equity %						
Debt to Equity						

CONTACT INFORMATION:

Phone: 905-602-2020   Fax: 905-602-2025
Toll-Free: 800-852-1033
Address: 5280 Solar Dr., Ste. 300, Mississauga, ON L4W 5M8 Canada

STOCK TICKER/OTHER:

Stock Ticker: Subsidiary   Exchange:
Employees: 800   Fiscal Year Ends: 12/31
Parent Company: Vision Group Holdings

SALARIES/BONUSES:

Top Exec. Salary: $ Bonus: $
Second Exec. Salary: $ Bonus: $

OTHER THOUGHTS:

Estimated Female Officers or Directors: 2
Hot Spot for Advancement for Women/Minorities:

Toho Holdings Co Ltd

www.tohohd.co.jp

NAIC Code: 424210

TYPES OF BUSINESS:

Drugs and Druggists' Sundries Merchant Wholesalers
Pharmaceuticals

BRANDS/DIVISIONS/AFFILIATES:

Kyoso Mirai Group
Kyosomirai Pharma Co Ltd
Toho Pharmaceutical Co Ltd
PharmaCluster Co Ltd
Tokyo Research Center of Clinical Pharmacology

CONTACTS: *Note: Officers with more than one job title may be intentionally listed here more than once.*

Atsushi Udoh, Pres.
Norio Hamada, Chmn.

GROWTH PLANS/SPECIAL FEATURES:

Toho Holdings Co., Ltd. is a Japan-based company engaged in the manufacture, wholesale, sale and dispensing of pharmaceuticals. Subsidiary Kyosomirai Pharma Co., Ltd. manufactures and sells prescription pharmaceuticals, with a focus on generic drugs. Kyosomirai also manufactures prescription pharmaceuticals for third-parties on a contract basis. Toho Pharmaceutical Co., Ltd. is a pharmaceutical wholesaling company, which distributes the sale of pharmaceutical products to retailers, medical institutions and other related customers. The company offers a fully-automated logistics system and utilizes advanced robot technology for picking and loading, all of which result in a shipment accuracy of 99.99%. PharmaCluster Co., Ltd. is a dispensing pharmacy management company serving home and retail pharmacies engaged in the healthcare sector. In addition, Tokyo Research Center of Clinical Pharmacology Co., Ltd. is a site management organization owned by Toho Holdings that assists certain medical institutions with clinical trials under contract. Toho Holdings is part of the Kyoso Mirai Group of companies.

FINANCIAL DATA: *Note: Data for latest year may not have been available at press time.*

In U.S. $	2020	2019	2018	2017	2016	2015
Revenue	11,542,010,000	11,162,310,000	11,081,280,000	11,244,330,000	11,949,240,000	
R&D Expense						
Operating Income	160,686,100	144,201,000	173,737,100	130,145,300	261,423,100	
Operating Margin %						
SGA Expense	9,827,113	10,649,080	10,119,370	10,018,910	11,087,470	
Net Income	148,228,700	126,610,800	131,369,100	129,917,000	198,834,600	
Operating Cash Flow	98,773,440	122,638,000	474,715,300	146,694,300	21,745,680	
Capital Expenditure	126,674,800	34,696,280	82,251,840	78,187,650	59,455,860	
EBITDA	275,040,400	250,098,200	271,259,400	261,505,300	389,139,100	
Return on Assets %						
Return on Equity %						
Debt to Equity						

CONTACT INFORMATION:

Phone: 81 334197811   Fax: 81 334146042
Toll-Free:
Address: 5-2-1, Daizawa, Tokyo, 155-8655 Japan

STOCK TICKER/OTHER:

Stock Ticker: THPMF   Exchange: PINX
Employees: Fiscal Year Ends: 03/31
Parent Company: Kyoso Mirai Group

SALARIES/BONUSES:

Top Exec. Salary: $ Bonus: $
Second Exec. Salary: $ Bonus: $

OTHER THOUGHTS:

Estimated Female Officers or Directors:
Hot Spot for Advancement for Women/Minorities:

TransEnterix Inc

www.transenterix.com

NAIC Code: 334510

TYPES OF BUSINESS:

Electromedical and Electrotherapeutic Apparatus Manufacturing

BRANDS/DIVISIONS/AFFILIATES:

Senhance Surgical System
Intelligent Surgical Unit

CONTACTS: *Note: Officers with more than one job title may be intentionally listed here more than once.*

Anthony Fernando, CEO
Brett Farabaugh, CFO
Paul Laviolette, Chairman of the Board
Eric Smith, Other Executive Officer

GROWTH PLANS/SPECIAL FEATURES:

TransEnterix, Inc. is a medical device company that is pioneering the use of robotics to improve minimally invasive surgery by addressing the clinical challenges associated with current laparoscopic and robotic options. The firm is focused on the commercialization and further development of the Senhance Surgical System, which digitizes laparoscopic minimally invasive surgery. The Senhance Surgical System is a multi-port robotic surgery system which allows multiple robotic arms to control instruments and a camera. It features advanced technology that gives surgeons haptic feedback and the ability to move the camera via eye movement. The system replicates laparoscopic motion that is familiar to experienced surgeons and integrates three-dimensional high definition (3DHD) vision technology. The Senhance Surgical System also offers responsible economics to hospitals by offering robotic technology with reusable instruments thereby reducing additional costs per surgery when compared to laparoscopy. During 2020, TransEnterix announced that it established a training center in Japan for its Senhance Surgical System; announced that a hospital in New Jersey successfully completed the first surgical procedure using TransEnterix's Intelligent Surgical Unit, for which its technology received FDA clearance and enables machine vision capabilities on the Senhance Surgical System; and announced that surgeons at a medical center in the Netherlands successfully operated on multiple pediatric patients, becoming the first pediatric surgical program in the world to utilize the Senhance Surgical System and integrate digital laparoscopy with instruments as small as 3mm into their standard of surgical care.

FINANCIAL DATA: *Note: Data for latest year may not have been available at press time.*

In U.S. $	2020	2019	2018	2017	2016	2015
Revenue		8,531,000	24,102,000	7,111,000	1,519,000	
R&D Expense						
Operating Income						
Operating Margin %						
SGA Expense						
Net Income		-154,200,992	-61,777,000	-144,796,000	-119,980,000	-46,948,000
Operating Cash Flow						
Capital Expenditure						
EBITDA						
Return on Assets %						
Return on Equity %						
Debt to Equity						

CONTACT INFORMATION:

Phone: 919 765-8400   Fax: 919 765-8459
Toll-Free:
Address: 635 Davis Dr., Ste. 300, Morrisville, NC 27560 United States

STOCK TICKER/OTHER:

Stock Ticker: TRXC
Employees: 163
Parent Company:

Exchange: ASE
Fiscal Year Ends: 12/31

SALARIES/BONUSES:

Top Exec. Salary: $ Bonus: $
Second Exec. Salary: $ Bonus: $

OTHER THOUGHTS:

Estimated Female Officers or Directors:
Hot Spot for Advancement for Women/Minorities:

TransMedics Group Inc

www.transmedics.com

NAIC Code: 334510

TYPES OF BUSINESS:

Electromedical and Electrotherapeutic Apparatus Manufacturing
Organ Transplant Devices

BRANDS/DIVISIONS/AFFILIATES:

Organ Care System (OCS)
OCS Console
OCS Perfusion Set
OCS Solutions

CONTACTS: *Note: Officers with more than one job title may be intentionally listed here more than once.*

Waleed Hassanein, CEO
John Carey, VP-Operations
Stephen Gordon, CFO
Brian Thomson, VP-Human Resources
Tamer Khayal, Other Executive Officer
Miriam Provost, Vice President, Divisional
John Sullivan, Vice President, Divisional
Ike Okonkwo, Vice President, Divisional
Jacqueline Sneve, Vice President, Divisional
Brian Thomson, Vice President, Divisional
John Carey, Vice President, Divisional
James Tobin, Chairman of the Board

GROWTH PLANS/SPECIAL FEATURES:

TransMedics Group, Inc. is a commercial-stage medical technology company focused on organ transplant therapy for end-stage organ failure patients across multi-le disease states. The firm produces and designs the Organ Care System (OCS), a fully portable, multi-organ, normothermic preservation and assessment technology that mirrors human physiology. This allows the organ to mimic its normal function outside the human body during transportation, which makes it possible to monitor organ function and reduce ischemia during organ transport. OCS is designed for three organs: the heart, the lungs and the liver. Each OCS products consists of three primary components customized for each organ: OCS Console, a portable electromechanical medical device that houses and controls the function of the OCS and is designed to fit in the current workflow for organ transplantation; OCS Perfusion Set, a sterile, biocompatible single-use disposable set that stores the organ and circulates blood, and the set includes all accessories needed to place the organ on the system; and OCS Solutions, a set of nutrient-enriched solutions used with blood to replenish depleted nutrients and hormones to optimize the organ's condition outside of the human body. The OCS technology platform is equipped with the following core technologies designed by TransMedics to address the limitations of cold storage and improve transplant outcomes: pulsatile blood pump, software-controlled titanium blood warmer, gas exchanger, hemodynamics sensors, electromechanical system with universal power supply and hot-swappable batteries and a carbon fiber OCS console structure. OCS products for additional organs, including kidneys, are under development. In May 2020, TransMedics announced positive top-line results from its U.S. Pivotal OCS Liver PROTECT Trial.

FINANCIAL DATA: *Note: Data for latest year may not have been available at press time.*

In U.S. $	2020	2019	2018	2017	2016	2015
Revenue	25,639,000	23,604,000	13,017,000	7,685,000	6,209,000	
R&D Expense	18,831,000	19,870,000	13,656,000	14,957,000	15,637,000	
Operating Income	-26,384,000	-29,603,000	-20,237,000	-20,426,000	-22,986,000	
Operating Margin %		-1.25%	-1.55%	-2.66%	-3.70%	
SGA Expense	24,188,000	23,596,000	12,315,000	7,606,000	8,115,000	
Net Income	-28,748,000	-33,547,000	-23,756,000	-20,823,000	-24,065,000	
Operating Cash Flow	-30,265,000	-32,286,000	-25,984,000	-23,098,000	-24,109,000	
Capital Expenditure	455,000	165,000	418,000	263,000	1,478,000	
EBITDA	-23,154,000	-27,932,000	-20,226,000	-19,089,000	-22,660,000	
Return on Assets %		- .46%	- .59%	- .56%		
Return on Equity %		-1.35%				
Debt to Equity		0.625				

CONTACT INFORMATION:

Phone: 978 552-0900   Fax: 978 552-0978
Toll-Free:
Address: 200 Minuteman Road, Andover, MA 1810 United States

SALARIES/BONUSES:

Top Exec. Salary: $ Bonus: $
Second Exec. Salary: $ Bonus: $

STOCK TICKER/OTHER:

Stock Ticker: TMDX
Employees: 110
Parent Company:

Exchange: NAS
Fiscal Year Ends: 12/31

OTHER THOUGHTS:

Estimated Female Officers or Directors:
Hot Spot for Advancement for Women/Minorities:

Trevi Therapeutics Inc

www.trevitherapeutics.com

NAIC Code: 325412

TYPES OF BUSINESS:

Pharmaceutical Preparation Manufacturing
Biopharmaceuticals

BRANDS/DIVISIONS/AFFILIATES:

Haduvio

CONTACTS: *Note: Officers with more than one job title may be intentionally listed here more than once.*

Jennifer Good, CEO
Christopher Seiter, CFO
David Meeker, Chairman of the Board
Thomas Sciascia, Chief Medical Officer
Yann Mazabraud, Other Corporate Officer
Helena Brett-Smith, Other Executive Officer

GROWTH PLANS/SPECIAL FEATURES:

Trevi Therapeutics, Inc. is a clinical-stage biopharmaceutical company that develops and commercializes nalbuphine extended release (ER) to treat serious neurologically-mediated conditions. Currently, the company is developing Haduvio (nalbuphine ER) for the treatment of serious neurologically mediated conditions, including chronic pruritus/chronic cough in patients with idiopathic pulmonary fibrosis (IPF), and levodopa-induced dyskinesia (LID) in patients with Parkinson's disease. Such conditions share a common pathophysiology that is mediated through opioid receptors in the central and peripheral nervous systems. Haduvio is an oral, extended-release formulation of nalbuphine, which has a history of efficacy and safety, having been approved for more than 20 years in the U.S. and Europe as a subcutaneous injection for relief of moderate to severe pain in the hospital setting. Tevi's novel oral formulation has the potential to unlock new market opportunities and improve quality of life for patients who currently have few treatment options. In mid-2020, Trevi announced positive outcome of its pre-specified sample size re-estimation analysis for the ongoing PRISM Phase 2b/3 trial of Haduvio for severe pruritus in patients with prurigo nodularis (PN).

FINANCIAL DATA: *Note: Data for latest year may not have been available at press time.*

In U.S. $	2020	2019	2018	2017	2016	2015
Revenue						
R&D Expense	22,328,000	19,339,000	14,072,000	6,095,000		
Operating Income	-32,489,000	-26,645,000	-18,408,000	-8,237,000		
Operating Margin %						
SGA Expense	10,161,000	7,306,000	4,336,000	2,142,000		
Net Income	-32,758,000	-26,050,000	-20,545,000	-12,860,000		
Operating Cash Flow	-29,000,000	-23,093,000	-18,291,000	-7,975,000		
Capital Expenditure	32,000	9,000	158,000	13,000		
EBITDA	-32,273,000	-26,029,000	-20,472,000	-9,540,000		
Return on Assets %		- .66%	- .86%	- .56%		
Return on Equity %		- .74%				
Debt to Equity		0.005				

CONTACT INFORMATION:

Phone: 203 304-2499   Fax:
Toll-Free:
Address: 195 Church St., 14/Fl, New Haven, CT 6510 United States

STOCK TICKER/OTHER:

Stock Ticker: TRVI   Exchange: NAS
Employees: 22   Fiscal Year Ends: 12/31
Parent Company:

SALARIES/BONUSES:

Top Exec. Salary: $ Bonus: $
Second Exec. Salary: $ Bonus: $

OTHER THOUGHTS:

Estimated Female Officers or Directors:
Hot Spot for Advancement for Women/Minorities:

Trinity Health
www.trinity-health.org

NAIC Code: 622110

TYPES OF BUSINESS:
General Medical and Surgical Hospitals
Assisted Living Facilities
Hospice Programs
Senior Housing Communities
Management & Consulting Services

BRANDS/DIVISIONS/AFFILIATES:
Senior Emergency Departments
Civica Rx

CONTACTS: Note: Officers with more than one job title may be intentionally listed here more than once.
Michael A. Slubowski, CEO
Benjamin R. Carter, COO
Cynthia A. Clemence, Interim CFO
Julie Spencer Washington, CMO
Edmund F. Hodge, CHRO
P. Terrence O'Rourke, Exec. VP-Clinical Transformation
Marcus Shipley, CIO
Benjamin R. Carter, Exec. VP-Finance
James Bosscher, Chief Investment Officer
Paul Conlon, Sr. VP-Clinical Quality & Patient Safety
Rebecca Havlisch, Chief Nursing Officer
Louis Fierens, Sr. VP-Supply Chain & Capital Projects Mgmt.

GROWTH PLANS/SPECIAL FEATURES:

Trinity Health is one of the nation's largest multi-institutional Catholic healthcare delivery systems, serving patients and communities in 22 states. Trinity Health operates 92 hospitals, as well as 100 continuing care locations that include PACE programs, senior living facilities and home care and hospice services. PACE stands for Program of All-inclusive Care for the Elderly. The firm is known for its focus on the country's aging population, and is the innovator of Senior Emergency Departments, the largest non-profit provider of home healthcare services in the nation. Trinity Health's continuing care programs provide nearly 2 million visits annually. The organization returns approximately $1.3 billion to its communities annually in the form of charity care and other community benefits programs. Other services offered by Trinity Health include a military and veteran health program, research activities, population health management and supply chain management solutions. Trinity Health partnered with six other health organizations in 2018 to create Civica Rx, a not-for-profit generic drug and pharmaceutical company focused on combating life-saving drug shortages and offering drug affordability.

Trinity Health offers its employees comprehensive health benefits, retirement plans and a variety of employee assistance programs.

FINANCIAL DATA: Note: Data for latest year may not have been available at press time.

In U.S. $	2020	2019	2018	2017	2016	2015
Revenue	18,833,027,000	19,293,223,000	18,345,405,000	17,627,845,000	16,339,047,000	14,388,150,000
R&D Expense						
Operating Income						
Operating Margin %						
SGA Expense						
Net Income	-34,546,000	834,305,000	949,130,000	1,336,823,000	89,803,000	671,630,000
Operating Cash Flow						
Capital Expenditure						
EBITDA						
Return on Assets %						
Return on Equity %						
Debt to Equity						

CONTACT INFORMATION:
Phone: 734-343-1000   Fax:
Toll-Free:
Address: 20555 Victor Pkwy., Livonia, MI 48152-7018 United States

STOCK TICKER/OTHER:
Stock Ticker: Nonprofit
Employees: 123,000
Parent Company:

Exchange:
Fiscal Year Ends: 06/30

SALARIES/BONUSES:
Top Exec. Salary: $ Bonus: $
Second Exec. Salary: $ Bonus: $

OTHER THOUGHTS:
Estimated Female Officers or Directors: 4
Hot Spot for Advancement for Women/Minorities: Y

Sales, profits and employees may be estimates. Financial information, benefits and other data can change quickly and may vary from those stated here.

Tufts Associated Health Plans Inc

www.tuftshealthplan.com

NAIC Code: 524114

TYPES OF BUSINESS:

Insurance-Medical & Health, HMOs & PPOs
Administrative Services
Health Maintenance Organization
Health Care Coverage
Health Benefits

BRANDS/DIVISIONS/AFFILIATES:

Point32Health Inc
ConnectorCare
CareLink

CONTACTS: Note: Officers with more than one job title may be intentionally listed here more than once.

Cain A. Hayes, CEO
Paul Kasuba, Chief Medical Officer
Patty Blake, Sr. VP-Senior Products
Lois Dehis Cornell, General Counsel
Tricia Trebino, Sr. VP-Oper.
Brian P. Pagliaro, Sr. VP-Client Svcs.
Tracey Carter, Chief Actuary
Marc Spooner, Sr. VP- Health Care Svcs.
Christina Severin, Sr. VP-Tufts Health Plan

GROWTH PLANS/SPECIAL FEATURES:

Tufts Associated Health Plans, Inc. was founded in 1979, and is a not-for-profit health maintenance organization. Tufts offers a broad array of health care coverage options to individuals and employer groups across the life span, regardless of age or circumstance. These products and services include HMO (health maintenance organization) and PPO (preferred provider organization) plans to national, tiered and limited network plans, including commercial, Medicare and Medicaid coverage. For individuals and small groups, Tufts offers two plans: direct, offering low-cost ConnectorCare plans and federal premium tax credits to those who qualify; and premier, offering access to Tuft's standard network. Direct and premier have different networks of doctors, meaning some doctors may be in one network and not the other. Tufts offers employers HMO plans; PPO plans; Advantage HMO and PPO, which offers lower premiums than a traditional HMO and PPO plans in exchange for cost sharing; Advantage Saver HMO and PPO, qualified High-Deductible Health Plans that may be paired with a Health Savings Account; tiered network plans give employers maximum value while encouraging members to choose providers based on cost and quality measures and have lower out-of-pocket costs; CareLink, a plan for large employers with a large portion of employees outside Tufts' coverage area; and Cigna Out-of-Area PPO, a national solution only for members outside the Tufts care area. The firm's online marketplace allows employers to offer a variety of healthcare benefits to its employees. In early-2021, Tufts Associated Health Plan announced that it combined with Harvard Pilgrim Health Care, each of which operate as brands and entities under new parent Point32Health, Inc.

Tufts offers comprehensive benefits, retirement options and employee assistance programs.

FINANCIAL DATA: Note: Data for latest year may not have been available at press time.

In U.S. $	2020	2019	2018	2017	2016	2015
Revenue	8,700,000,000	5,580,000,000	5,350,000,000	4,700,000,000	4,600,000,000	4,300,000,000
R&D Expense						
Operating Income						
Operating Margin %						
SGA Expense						
Net Income	32,800,000	66,800,000	130,400,000	59,400,000	3,000,000	26,100,000
Operating Cash Flow						
Capital Expenditure						
EBITDA						
Return on Assets %						
Return on Equity %						
Debt to Equity						

CONTACT INFORMATION:

Phone: 617-972-9400 Fax:
Toll-Free:
Address: 705 Mount Auburn St., Watertown, MA 02472 United States

STOCK TICKER/OTHER:

Stock Ticker: Private Exchange:
Employees: 3,015 Fiscal Year Ends: 12/31
Parent Company: Point32Health Inc

SALARIES/BONUSES:

Top Exec. Salary: $ Bonus: $
Second Exec. Salary: $ Bonus: $

OTHER THOUGHTS:

Estimated Female Officers or Directors: 5
Hot Spot for Advancement for Women/Minorities: Y

Turning Point Therapeutics Inc

www.tptherapeutics.com

NAIC Code: 325412

TYPES OF BUSINESS:

Pharmaceutical Preparation Manufacturing
Biopharmaceuticals

BRANDS/DIVISIONS/AFFILIATES:

Repotrectinib
TRIDENT-1
TPX-0022
TPX-0046
TPX-0131

CONTACTS: *Note: Officers with more than one job title may be intentionally listed here more than once.*

Athena Countouriotis, CEO
Sheila Gujrathi, Chairman of the Board
Jingrong Jean Cui, Chief Scientific Officer
Annette North, Executive VP
Brian Baker, Vice President, Divisional

GROWTH PLANS/SPECIAL FEATURES:

Turning Point Therapeutics, Inc. is a clinical-stage biopharmaceutical company designing and developing novel small molecule, targeted oncology therapies. The company's internally developed and wholly-owned pipeline of next-generation tyrosine kinas inhibitors (TKIs) targets numerous genetic drivers of cancer in both TKI-native and TKI-pretreated patients. Turning Point's lead drug candidate is repotrectinib, which is being evaluated in an ongoing Phase Â½ trial called TRIDENT-1 for the treatment of patients with ROS1+ advanced non-small-cell lung cancer (NSCLC) and patients with NTRK+ advanced solid tumors. In addition to repotrectinib, the firm's pipeline includes clinical-stage multi-targeted kinase inhibitors TPX-0022 (a novel MET/CSF1R/SRC inhibitor) and TPX-0046 (a novel RET/SRC inhibitor), and a preclinical ALK inhibitor, TPX-0131. During 2020, Turning Point and Zai Lab announced an exclusive license agreement for repotrectinib in Greater China; and Turning Point was granted fast-track designation for repotrectinib in NTRK-positive TKI-pretreated advanced solid tumors.

FINANCIAL DATA: *Note: Data for latest year may not have been available at press time.*

In U.S. $	2020	2019	2018	2017	2016	2015
Revenue	25,000,000					
R&D Expense	113,411,000	57,943,000	21,062,000	15,241,000		
Operating Income	-161,836,000	-77,724,000	-25,640,000	-16,729,000		
Operating Margin %						
SGA Expense	73,425,000	19,781,000	4,578,000	1,488,000		
Net Income	-157,292,000	-72,131,000	-24,785,000	-16,593,000		
Operating Cash Flow	-82,793,000	-57,757,000	-23,533,000	-12,640,000		
Capital Expenditure	1,264,000	1,744,000	302,000	88,000		
EBITDA	-159,443,000	-76,145,000	-25,502,000	-16,666,000		
Return on Assets %		-.27%	-.33%	-.36%		
Return on Equity %		-.29%	-.68%			
Debt to Equity		0.009				

CONTACT INFORMATION:

Phone: 858 926-5251   Fax:
Toll-Free:
Address: 10628 Science Center Dr., Ste. 200, San Diego, CA 92121 United States

STOCK TICKER/OTHER:

Stock Ticker: TPTX
Employees: 142
Parent Company:

Exchange: NAS
Fiscal Year Ends: 12/31

SALARIES/BONUSES:

Top Exec. Salary: $ Bonus: $
Second Exec. Salary: $ Bonus: $

OTHER THOUGHTS:

Estimated Female Officers or Directors:
Hot Spot for Advancement for Women/Minorities:

Twist Bioscience Corporation

www.twistbioscience.com

NAIC Code: 325413

TYPES OF BUSINESS:

In-Vitro Diagnostic Substance Manufacturing
Synthetic Biology

BRANDS/DIVISIONS/AFFILIATES:

CONTACTS: *Note: Officers with more than one job title may be intentionally listed here more than once.*

Emily Leproust, CEO
James Thorburn, CFO
Mark Daniels, Chief Compliance Officer
Bill Peck, Chief Technology Officer
William Banyai, COO
Martin Kunz, Director
Patrick Weiss, General Manager, Divisional
Patrick Finn, Senior VP, Divisional
Paula Green, Vice President, Divisional

GROWTH PLANS/SPECIAL FEATURES:

Twist Bioscience Corporation is a synthetic biology and genomics company that has developed a disruptive DNA synthesis platform to industrialize the engineering of biology. The platform's proprietary technology enables a new method of manufacturing synthetic DNA by writing DNA on a silicon chip. Twist Bioscience has combined this technology with proprietary software, scalable commercial infrastructure and an eCommerce platform to create an integrated technology architecture that enables the firm to achieve high levels of quality, precision, automation and manufacturing cost-effectively. Twist Bioscience's synthetic DNA-based products include synthetic genes, tools for next-generation sample preparation and antibody libraries for drug discovery and development. The company sells its synthetic DNA and synthetic DNA-based products to over 1,900 customers across a broad range of industries. These industries include: healthcare, for the discovery and production of new therapeutics and molecular diagnostics; industrial chemicals, for cost-effective and sustainable production of new and existing chemicals and materials such as spider silk, nylon, rubber, fragrances, food flavors and food additives; agriculture, for effective and sustainable crop production; academic research, for a range of applications; and technology, for potential use as an alternative long-term data storage medium. Twist launched the first application for its platform, synthetic genes and oligo pools in 2016 to disrupt the gene synthesis market and make legacy DNA synthesis methods obsolete. The firm launched its 300 nucleotide length oligo pools in 2019, which are suited for many applications, including drug discovery and development, data storage, CRISPR gene editing and protein engineering. In September 2020, Twist announced data demonstrating the potent neutralizing effects of multiple potential therapeutic antibodies against SARS-CoV-2, the virus that causes COVID-19. The effects were found to be comparable to or better than those seen with antibody candidates derived from patients who had recovered from COVID-19.

FINANCIAL DATA: *Note: Data for latest year may not have been available at press time.*

In U.S. $	2020	2019	2018	2017	2016	2015
Revenue	90,100,000	54,385,000	25,427,000	10,767,000	2,269,000	
R&D Expense	43,006,000	35,683,000	20,347,000	19,169,000	18,230,000	
Operating Income	-117,579,000	-108,850,000	-70,559,000	-58,482,000	-43,656,000	
Operating Margin %		-2.00%	-2.77%	-5.43%	-19.24%	
SGA Expense	103,267,000	80,126,000	43,450,000	26,060,000	18,274,000	
Net Income	-139,931,000	-107,669,000	-71,236,000	-59,310,000	-44,088,000	
Operating Cash Flow	-142,255,000	-87,937,000	-66,164,000	-51,301,000	-38,592,000	
Capital Expenditure	9,868,000	14,757,000	3,688,000	6,594,000	6,229,000	
EBITDA	-132,085,000	-99,972,000	-63,954,000	-53,104,000	-39,113,000	
Return on Assets %		-.71%	-.71%	-.73%	-.58%	
Return on Equity %						
Debt to Equity		0.029				

CONTACT INFORMATION:

Phone: 800 719-0671   Fax:
Toll-Free:
Address: 681 Gateway Blvd., San Francisco, CA 94080 United States

STOCK TICKER/OTHER:

Stock Ticker: TWST   Exchange: NAS
Employees: 525   Fiscal Year Ends: 09/30
Parent Company:

SALARIES/BONUSES:

Top Exec. Salary: $ Bonus: $
Second Exec. Salary: $ Bonus: $

OTHER THOUGHTS:

Estimated Female Officers or Directors:
Hot Spot for Advancement for Women/Minorities:

United Surgical Partners International Inc www.unitedsurgical.com
NAIC Code: 621493

TYPES OF BUSINESS:
Outpatient Surgical Facility Management

BRANDS/DIVISIONS/AFFILIATES:
Tenet Healthcare Corporation
CareSpot
MedPost

GROWTH PLANS/SPECIAL FEATURES:
United Surgical Partners International, Inc. (USPI) is an ambulatory surgery provider in the U.S. and a subsidiary of Tenet Healthcare Corporation. Combined with Tenet, the company's network includes over 400 facilities across the U.S., including ambulatory surgery centers, surgical hospitals, imaging centers and urgent care centers through its CareSpot and MedPost brands. The firm serves more than 3.4 million patients each year via over 50 health systems and 4,000+ physicians. USPI provides the infrastructure and support these healthcare partners need to perform their work and duties.

The company offers employees a comprehensive benefits package, retirement plans and employee assistance programs.

CONTACTS: Note: Officers with more than one job title may be intentionally listed here more than once.
Brett Brodnax, CEO
Mark Garvin, COO
Owen Morris, CFO
Margie Arion, CHRO
David Zarin, Sr. VP-Medical Affairs
John J. Wellik, Sr. VP-Admin
Jason B. Cagle, General Counsel
Jonathan R. Bond, Sr. VP-Oper.
Brett P. Brodnax, Chief Dev. Officer
Kristin Blewett, Sr. VP-Comm.
Philip A. Spencer, Sr. VP-Bus. Dev.
Monica Cintado, Sr. VP-Dev.

FINANCIAL DATA: Note: Data for latest year may not have been available at press time.

In U.S. $	2020	2019	2018	2017	2016	2015
Revenue	2,072,000,000	2,158,000,000	2,085,000,000	1,978,000,000		
R&D Expense						
Operating Income						
Operating Margin %						
SGA Expense						
Net Income						
Operating Cash Flow						
Capital Expenditure						
EBITDA						
Return on Assets %						
Return on Equity %						
Debt to Equity						

CONTACT INFORMATION:
Phone: 972-713-3500   Fax:
Toll-Free:
Address: 14201 Dallas Pkwy., Dallas, TX 75254 United States

STOCK TICKER/OTHER:
Stock Ticker: Subsidiary   Exchange:
Employees: 6,700   Fiscal Year Ends: 12/31
Parent Company: Tenet Healthcare Corporation

SALARIES/BONUSES:
Top Exec. Salary: $ Bonus: $
Second Exec. Salary: $ Bonus: $

OTHER THOUGHTS:
Estimated Female Officers or Directors: 3
Hot Spot for Advancement for Women/Minorities: Y

Sales, profits and employees may be estimates. Financial information, benefits and other data can change quickly and may vary from those stated here.

UnitedHealth Group Inc

NAIC Code: 524114

www.unitedhealthgroup.com

TYPES OF BUSINESS:

Medical Insurance
Wellness Plans
Dental & Vision Insurance
Health Information Technology
Physician Practice Groups
Pharmacy Benefits Management
PBM

BRANDS/DIVISIONS/AFFILIATES:

UnitedHealthcare
Optum
UnitedHealthcare Employer
UnitedHealthcare Medicare & Retirement
UnitedHealthcare Global
OptumHealth
OptumInsight
OptumRx

CONTACTS: *Note: Officers with more than one job title may be intentionally listed here more than once.*

Steven Nelson, CEO, Subsidiary
Andrew Witty, CEO, Subsidiary
David Wichmann, CEO
John Rex, CFO
Stephen Hemsley, Chairman of the Board
Thomas Roos, Chief Accounting Officer
Marianne Short, Executive VP
D. Wilson, Executive VP

GROWTH PLANS/SPECIAL FEATURES:

UnitedHealth Group, Inc. is a diversified health care company. Through its family of businesses, the firm offers core competencies in data and health information, advanced technology and clinical expertise, which are deployed into two platforms: health benefits, operating under UnitedHealthcare; and health services, operating under Optum. UnitedHealthcare provides health care benefits to an array of customers and markets. UnitedHealthcare Employer and Individual serves employers ranging from sole proprietorships to large, multi-site and national employers, public sector employers and individual customers. UnitedHealthcare Medicare & Retirement delivers health and well-being benefits for Medicare beneficiaries and retirees. UnitedHealthcare Community & State manages health care benefit programs on behalf of state Medicaid and community programs and their participants. UnitedHealthcare Global provides health and dental benefits and hospital and clinical services to employer groups and individuals in South America and other diversified global health businesses. Optum is a health services business serving the health care marketplace, including payers, care providers, employers, governments, life sciences companies and consumers, through its OptumHealth, OptumInsight and OptumRx businesses. These businesses have dedicated units that help improve overall health system performance through optimizing care quality, reducing costs and improving consumer experience and care provider performance, leveraging capabilities in data and analytics, pharmacy care services, population health, health care delivery and health care operations.

UnitedHealth Group offers comprehensive benefits, retirement options, tuition reimbursement and a variety of employee assistance programs.

FINANCIAL DATA: *Note: Data for latest year may not have been available at press time.*

In U.S. $	2020	2019	2018	2017	2016	2015
Revenue	255,639,000,000	240,269,000,000	224,871,000,000	200,136,000,000	184,012,000,000	156,397,000,000
R&D Expense						
Operating Income	20,903,000,000	17,799,000,000	15,968,000,000	14,186,000,000	12,102,000,000	10,311,000,000
Operating Margin %		.07%	.07%	.07%	.07%	.07%
SGA Expense						
Net Income	15,403,000,000	13,839,000,000	11,986,000,000	10,558,000,000	7,017,000,000	5,813,000,000
Operating Cash Flow	22,174,000,000	18,463,000,000	15,713,000,000	13,596,000,000	9,795,000,000	9,740,000,000
Capital Expenditure	2,051,000,000	2,071,000,000	2,063,000,000	2,023,000,000	1,705,000,000	1,556,000,000
EBITDA	25,296,000,000	22,405,000,000	19,772,000,000	17,454,000,000	14,985,000,000	12,714,000,000
Return on Assets %		.08%	.08%	.08%	.06%	.06%
Return on Equity %		.25%	.24%	.25%	.19%	.18%
Debt to Equity		0.639	0.669	0.604	0.673	0.753

CONTACT INFORMATION:

Phone: 952 936-1300   Fax: 952 936-0044
Toll-Free: 800-328-5979
Address: 9900 Bren Rd. E., Minnetonka, MN 55343 United States

STOCK TICKER/OTHER:

Stock Ticker: UNH
Employees: 330,000
Parent Company:

Exchange: NYS
Fiscal Year Ends: 12/31

SALARIES/BONUSES:

Top Exec. Salary: $ Bonus: $
Second Exec. Salary: $ Bonus: $

OTHER THOUGHTS:

Estimated Female Officers or Directors: 4
Hot Spot for Advancement for Women/Minorities: Y

UnitedHealthcare Community & State
www.uhccommunityandstate.com
NAIC Code: 524114

TYPES OF BUSINESS:
Insurance-Medical & Health, HMOs & PPOs

BRANDS/DIVISIONS/AFFILIATES:
UnitedHealth Group Inc

GROWTH PLANS/SPECIAL FEATURES:
UnitedHealthcare Community & State (UHCS), a division of UnitedHealth Group, Inc., is a health benefits company. UHCS provides diversified solutions to the economically disadvantaged, the medically underserved and those without the benefit of employer-funded health care coverage. The company helps states and communities serve the impoverished via clinical care, prevention initiatives, food delivery, transportation and educational programs. Products offered include temporary assistance for needy families (TANF), children's health insurance program (CHIP), ABD programs (aged, blind and disabled), long-term services/support, dual special needs plans and more. UHCS participates in programs throughout the U.S., including Washington D.C., and serves millions of beneficiaries.

UnitedHealthcare offers comprehensive benefits, retirement plans and employee assistance programs.

CONTACTS: *Note: Officers with more than one job title may be intentionally listed here more than once.*
Roger Brown, National VP-Bus. Dev.
Kevin Smith, Chief Medical Officer
Bill Hagan, West Region Pres.
Jim Donovan, Sr. VP-Bus. Dev.
John Cosgriff, Chief of Staff
Bror Hultgren, Central Region Pres.
Steve Meeker, Southwest Region Pres.
Heather Cianfrocco, Northeast Region Pres.

FINANCIAL DATA: *Note: Data for latest year may not have been available at press time.*

In U.S. $	2020	2019	2018	2017	2016	2015
Revenue	46,487,000,000	43,790,000,000	43,428,000,000	37,443,000,000	32,945,000,000	28,911,000,000
R&D Expense						
Operating Income						
Operating Margin %						
SGA Expense						
Net Income						
Operating Cash Flow						
Capital Expenditure						
EBITDA						
Return on Assets %						
Return on Equity %						
Debt to Equity						

CONTACT INFORMATION:
Phone: 703-506-3555   Fax: 703-506-3556
Toll-Free:
Address: 8045 Leesburg Pike, 6/Fl, Vienna, VA 22182 United States

STOCK TICKER/OTHER:
Stock Ticker: Subsidiary
Employees: 3,535
Parent Company: UnitedHealth Group Inc

Exchange:
Fiscal Year Ends: 12/31

SALARIES/BONUSES:
Top Exec. Salary: $ Bonus: $
Second Exec. Salary: $ Bonus: $

OTHER THOUGHTS:
Estimated Female Officers or Directors: 3
Hot Spot for Advancement for Women/Minorities: Y

UnitedHealthcare National Accounts www.uhc.com/employer/national-accounts

NAIC Code: 524292

TYPES OF BUSINESS:

Employee Benefits Management
Healthcare Benefits Management
Outsourcing
Retirement Plans

BRANDS/DIVISIONS/AFFILIATES:

UnitedHealth Group Inc
www.uhc.com

CONTACTS: *Note: Officers with more than one job title may be intentionally listed here more than once.*

Thomas C. Choate, CEO
Alison Richards, Sr. VP-Strategic Initiatives
Steve Burdick, Sr. VP-Specialty Client Group
Tom Elliott, Sr. VP-Client Rel.
John Ryan, Sr. VP
John Cravero, Sr. VP-Nat'l Client Oper.
Shawn Mobley, Sr. VP-Client Dev.

GROWTH PLANS/SPECIAL FEATURES:

UnitedHealthcare National Accounts, a subsidiary of UnitedHealth Group, Inc., provides healthcare benefits management, as well as a variety of services such as administration, consulting, technology and outsourcing. The company serves employers, including small businesses and those with more than 5,000 employees in multiple locations. For employers, UnitedHealthcare National provides group benefit plans, group health insurance, medical/dental/vision plans, ancillary/specialty benefits, pharmaceutical subscription plans and group retiree plans. For individuals and families, the firm offers health insurance plans, short-term insurance plans, dental insurance plans and supplemental insurance plans. Medicare services are also provided through UnitedHealthcare, along with related information that can be easily obtained on the www.uhc.com website. Locating doctors can be obtained through the online site or the UnitedHealthcare app.

UnitedHealthcare offers employees medical, vision and dental coverage; various spending accounts; life insurance; tuition reimbursement; and an adoption assistance plan.

FINANCIAL DATA: *Note: Data for latest year may not have been available at press time.*

In U.S. $	2020	2019	2018	2017	2016	2015
Revenue						
R&D Expense						
Operating Income						
Operating Margin %						
SGA Expense						
Net Income						
Operating Cash Flow						
Capital Expenditure						
EBITDA						
Return on Assets %						
Return on Equity %						
Debt to Equity						

CONTACT INFORMATION:

Phone: 860-702-5000   Fax: 860-702-9830
Toll-Free: 800-328-5979
Address: 185 Asylum St., Hartford, CT 06103 United States

SALARIES/BONUSES:

Top Exec. Salary: $ Bonus: $
Second Exec. Salary: $ Bonus: $

STOCK TICKER/OTHER:

Stock Ticker: Subsidiary   Exchange:
Employees: 3,000   Fiscal Year Ends: 12/31
Parent Company: UnitedHealth Group Inc

OTHER THOUGHTS:

Estimated Female Officers or Directors: 3
Hot Spot for Advancement for Women/Minorities: Y

UnityPoint Health

www.unitypoint.org/default.aspx

NAIC Code: 622110

TYPES OF BUSINESS:

General Medical and Surgical Hospitals
Home Care Services
Hospice
Medical Equipment Services

BRANDS/DIVISIONS/AFFILIATES:

Iowa Health System
UnityPoint Health-Des Moines
Methodist Health Services Corporation
Trinity Regional Health System
Meriter Health Services Inc
Allen Health Systems
UnityPoint Clinic
UnityPoint at Home

CONTACTS: Note: Officers with more than one job title may be intentionally listed here more than once.

Susan K. Thompson, CEO
Art Nizza, COO
Dan Carpenter, CFO

GROWTH PLANS/SPECIAL FEATURES:

UnityPoint Health, is a regional health care provider with 15 hospitals in 13 Iowa cities, five hospitals in four Illinois cities and one hospital in Madison, Wisconsin. In addition, UnityPoint offers approximately 2,000 patient service provider full time equivalents in 110 communities. Affiliates include Central Iowa Health System, doing business as UnityPoint Health-Des Moines; Methodist Health Services Corporation (MHSC); Trinity Regional Health System; Meriter Health Services, Inc. (MHS); St. Luke's Healthcare; Allen Health Systems, Inc.; St. Luke's Health System, Inc.; Trinity Health Systems, Inc.; Finley Tri-States Health Group, Inc.; Iowa Physicians Clinic Medical Foundation, doing business as UnityPoint Clinic; and UnityPoint at Home, which provides adult and pediatric home care services, nursing care, rehabilitation therapy, infusion therapy, specialty pharmacy, palliative care, hospice and home medical equipment services in Iowa, Illinois and Wisconsin.

FINANCIAL DATA: Note: Data for latest year may not have been available at press time.

In U.S. $	2020	2019	2018	2017	2016	2015
Revenue	4,612,051,000	4,588,466,000	4,411,461,000	4,157,199,000	3,866,776,000	
R&D Expense						
Operating Income						
Operating Margin %						
SGA Expense						
Net Income	181,665,000	285,522,000	-42,200,000	283,849,000	163,873,000	
Operating Cash Flow						
Capital Expenditure						
EBITDA						
Return on Assets %						
Return on Equity %						
Debt to Equity						

CONTACT INFORMATION:

Phone: 515-241-6161   Fax:
Toll-Free:
Address: 1776 W. Lakes Pkwy., Ste. 400, West Des Moines, IA 50266 United States

STOCK TICKER/OTHER:

Stock Ticker: Nonprofit
Employees: 33,034
Parent Company:

Exchange:
Fiscal Year Ends: 12/31

SALARIES/BONUSES:

Top Exec. Salary: $ Bonus: $
Second Exec. Salary: $ Bonus: $

OTHER THOUGHTS:

Estimated Female Officers or Directors:
Hot Spot for Advancement for Women/Minorities:

Universal Health Services Inc

NAIC Code: 622110

www.uhsinc.com

TYPES OF BUSINESS:

General Medical and Surgical Hospitals
Acute Care Hospitals
Behavioral Health Hospitals
Outpatient Facilities
Ambulatory Care
Real Estate Investment Trust

BRANDS/DIVISIONS/AFFILIATES:

Universal Health Realty Income Trust

GROWTH PLANS/SPECIAL FEATURES:

Universal Health Services, Inc. (UHS), in business for more than 40 years, owns and operates through its subsidiaries acute care hospitals, outpatient facilities and behavioral healthcare facilities. UHS operates 26 acute care hospitals, 330 behavioral health facilities, 41 outpatient facilities and ambulatory care access points, an insurance offering, a physician network and various related services in more than 35 U.S. states, Washington DC, Puerto Rico and the U.K. The firm also acts as the advisor to Universal Health Realty Income Trust, a real estate investment trust.

CONTACTS:

Note: Officers with more than one job title may be intentionally listed here more than once.

Alan Miller, CEO
Steve Filton, CFO
Marc Miller, Director
Marvin Pember, Executive VP

FINANCIAL DATA:

Note: Data for latest year may not have been available at press time.

In U.S. $	2020	2019	2018	2017	2016	2015
Revenue	11,558,900,000	11,378,260,000	10,772,280,000	10,409,870,000	9,766,210,000	9,043,451,000
R&D Expense						
Operating Income	1,358,354,000	1,215,908,000	1,175,262,000	1,280,178,000	1,276,072,000	1,243,580,000
Operating Margin %		.11%	.11%	.12%	.13%	.14%
SGA Expense	5,729,156,000	5,696,702,000	5,360,630,000	5,083,764,000	4,682,854,000	4,307,360,000
Net Income	943,953,000	814,854,000	779,705,000	752,303,000	702,409,000	680,528,000
Operating Cash Flow	2,360,169,000	1,438,469,000	1,340,893,000	1,182,581,000	1,288,474,000	1,020,898,000
Capital Expenditure	786,218,000	663,518,000	811,669,000	609,431,000	1,155,217,000	912,976,000
EBITDA	1,866,727,000	1,718,213,000	1,641,671,000	1,716,807,000	1,681,473,000	1,640,952,000
Return on Assets %		.07%	.07%	.07%	.07%	.07%
Return on Equity %		.15%	.15%	.16%	.16%	.17%
Debt to Equity		0.757	0.73	0.70	0.889	0.797

CONTACT INFORMATION:

Phone: 610 768-3300   Fax: 610 768-3336
Toll-Free:
Address: 367 S. Gulph Rd., King Of Prussia, PA 19406 United States

STOCK TICKER/OTHER:

Stock Ticker: UHS
Employees: 89,000
Parent Company:

Exchange: NYS
Fiscal Year Ends: 12/31

SALARIES/BONUSES:

Top Exec. Salary: $ Bonus: $
Second Exec. Salary: $ Bonus: $

OTHER THOUGHTS:

Estimated Female Officers or Directors: 2
Hot Spot for Advancement for Women/Minorities: Y

UPMC

www.upmc.com

NAIC Code: 622110

TYPES OF BUSINESS:

General Medical and Surgical Hospitals

BRANDS/DIVISIONS/AFFILIATES:

UPMC Cancer Center
UPMC International
UPMC Enterprises

CONTACTS: *Note: Officers with more than one job title may be intentionally listed here more than once.*

Jeffrey Romoff, CEO

GROWTH PLANS/SPECIAL FEATURES:

UPMC (University of Pittsburgh Medical Center) is a non-profit healthcare provider and insurer, and is engaged in inventing new models of cost-effective, patient-centered care. UPMC operates approximately 40 academic, community and specialty hospitals; 700 doctor's offices and outpatient sites; and offers an array of rehabilitation, retirement and long-term care facilities. The firm is organized into four major operating units: provider services, insurance services, UPMC International and UPMC Enterprises. The provider services unit includes regional hospitals; specialty service lines such as transplantation, women's health, behavioral health, pediatrics, UPMC Cancer Centers and rehabilitation; in-home care and retirement living options; and contract services, including pharmacy and clinical laboratories. The insurance services unit offers health insurance to companies and their employees as well as recipients of government programs such as Medicare and Medical Assistance; integrated workers' compensation and disability services; and coverage for behavioral health services to Medical Assistance beneficiaries in most Pennsylvania counties. UPMC International offers advisory services, infrastructure consultation and clinical management in the following countries: China, offering pathology consultation and healthcare collaboration services; Colombia, offering adult and pediatric oncology center consultation; Ireland, offering cancer center consultation; Italy, offering transplantation, radiotherapy, biotechnology and preventative medicine center advisory and consultation; Japan, offering education in primary care and family medicine; Kazakhstan, offering oncology center consultation; Lithuania, offering oncology services; Singapore, offering transplantation and clinical management services; and the U.K., offering IT and cancer care services. Last, UPMC Enterprises utilizes science and technology to solve healthcare challenges, striving to make it more efficient, affordable and personalized. In early 2020, Western Maryland Health System joined the UPMC system, the first Maryland hospital to do so.

FINANCIAL DATA: *Note: Data for latest year may not have been available at press time.*

In U.S. $	2020	2019	2018	2017	2016	2015
Revenue	16,487,763,608	14,874,280,752	13,498,504,493	12,467,253,363	11,695,858,422	10,588,819,964
R&D Expense						
Operating Income						
Operating Margin %						
SGA Expense						
Net Income	87,594,040	-9,009,029	188,506,864	302,839,431	345,735,447	190,880,948
Operating Cash Flow						
Capital Expenditure						
EBITDA						
Return on Assets %						
Return on Equity %						
Debt to Equity						

CONTACT INFORMATION:

Phone: 877-986-9812 Fax:
Toll-Free: 800-533-8762
Address: 200 Lathrop St., Pittsburgh, PA 15213 United States

STOCK TICKER/OTHER:

Stock Ticker: Nonprofit
Employees: 92,000
Parent Company:

Exchange:
Fiscal Year Ends: 12/31

SALARIES/BONUSES:

Top Exec. Salary: $ Bonus: $
Second Exec. Salary: $ Bonus: $

OTHER THOUGHTS:

Estimated Female Officers or Directors:
Hot Spot for Advancement for Women/Minorities:

US NeuroSurgical Holdings Inc

NAIC Code: 621493

www.usneuro.com

TYPES OF BUSINESS:

Neurological Surgery Centers (Gamma Knife)
Radiation Treatment

BRANDS/DIVISIONS/AFFILIATES:

USN Corona Inc
Corona Gamma Knife LLC
NeuroPartners LLC
Medical Oncology Partners LLC
United Oncology Medical Associates of Florida LLC

CONTACTS: Note: Officers with more than one job title may be intentionally listed here more than once.

Alan Gold, CEO
Susan Greenwald, Vice President

GROWTH PLANS/SPECIAL FEATURES:

U.S. NeuroSurgical Holdings, Inc. owns and operates stereotactic radiosurgery centers, utilizing gamma (radiology) knife technology. The company currently owns and operates Gamma Knife centers on the premises of New York University Medical Center (NYU) in New York, New York, as well as San Antonio Regional Hospital (SARH) in Upland, California. U.S. NeuroSurgical's business strategy is to provide cost-effective approaches that allow hospitals, physicians and patients access to gamma knife treatment on a cost-per-treatment basis. U.S. NeuroSurgical's business model is to own, or hold an interest in, the gamma knife units, and charge the medical facility, where the unit is housed and maintained, based on utilization. Its main target market is medical centers in major health care catchment areas that have physicians experienced with and dedicated to the use of the gamma knife. Wholly-owned subsidiary USN Corona, Inc. holds investments in Corona Gamma Knife, LLC and NeuroPartners, LLC, both of which develop and manage the gamma knife center at SARH. USN Corona is a part owner of Medical Oncology Partners, LLC, which wholly-owns United Oncology Medical Associates of Florida, LLC.

FINANCIAL DATA: Note: Data for latest year may not have been available at press time.

In U.S. $	2020	2019	2018	2017	2016	2015
Revenue	3,173,000	3,070,000	3,424,000	3,414,000	3,212,000	2,971,000
R&D Expense						
Operating Income	1,615,000	1,490,000	794,000	688,000	614,000	544,000
Operating Margin %		.49%	.23%	.20%	.19%	.18%
SGA Expense	1,197,000	1,230,000	1,289,000	1,259,000	1,308,000	1,232,000
Net Income	533,000	142,000	-421,000	538,000	536,000	396,000
Operating Cash Flow	1,117,000	1,547,000	2,288,000	2,348,000	1,361,000	1,158,000
Capital Expenditure			570,000	46,000		341,000
EBITDA	915,000	275,000	483,000	1,729,000	2,045,000	1,764,000
Return on Assets %		.03%	-.06%	.07%	.07%	.05%
Return on Equity %		.05%	-.13%	.17%	.20%	.18%
Debt to Equity		0.062	0.328	0.485	0.944	1.249

CONTACT INFORMATION:

Phone: 301 208-8998   Fax: 301 208-3254
Toll-Free:
Address: 2400 Research Blvd., Rockville, MD 20850 United States

STOCK TICKER/OTHER:

Stock Ticker: USNU   Exchange: PINX
Employees: 3   Fiscal Year Ends: 12/31
Parent Company:

SALARIES/BONUSES:

Top Exec. Salary: $ Bonus: $
Second Exec. Salary: $ Bonus: $

OTHER THOUGHTS:

Estimated Female Officers or Directors:
Hot Spot for Advancement for Women/Minorities:

US Oncology Inc

www.usoncology.com

NAIC Code: 621111

TYPES OF BUSINESS:

Oncologists' offices
Oncology Pharmaceutical Services
Outpatient Cancer Center Operations
Research & Development Services

BRANDS/DIVISIONS/AFFILIATES:

McKesson Corporation
US Oncology Network (The)
iKnowMed
Oncology Portal
US Oncology Research Network

CONTACTS: *Note: Officers with more than one job title may be intentionally listed here more than once.*

Claire Crye, Mgr.-Public Rel.
Lucy Langer, Chmn.

GROWTH PLANS/SPECIAL FEATURES:

U.S. Oncology, Inc., operating as The US Oncology Network, is a cancer management company which provides management services under long-term agreements to oncology practices. Part of McKesson Corporation's specialty health segment, the firm provides support services for cancer patients and doctors through more than 470 affiliated sites across the county. Approximately 1 million patients are treated annually through the network. U.S. Oncology has 1,200 affiliated physicians in all aspects of diagnosis and outpatient treatment of cancer, including medical oncology, radiation, gynecologic oncology, stem cell transplantation, diagnostic radiology and clinical research. The company also assists in a number of aspects in the conducting of clinical trials, including protocol development, data coordination, institutional review, board coordination and contract review/negotiation. The firm has two primary technology product offerings: iKnowMed and the Oncology Portal. iKnowMed is an internet-based electronic medical record system designed specifically for oncologists. Oncology Portal is an online community for the discussion of patient care, research discoveries and the latest industry updates. U.S. Oncology also operates U.S. Oncology Research Network (USOR), one of the nation's largest research networks specializing in Phase I-Phase IV oncology clinical trials. In September 2020, U.S. Oncology announced that it had reached a milestone of contributing to the U.S. Food and Drug Administration's approval of over 100 cancer therapies.

FINANCIAL DATA: *Note: Data for latest year may not have been available at press time.*

In U.S. $	2020	2019	2018	2017	2016	2015
Revenue						
R&D Expense						
Operating Income						
Operating Margin %						
SGA Expense						
Net Income						
Operating Cash Flow						
Capital Expenditure						
EBITDA						
Return on Assets %						
Return on Equity %						
Debt to Equity						

CONTACT INFORMATION:

Phone: 281-863-1000   Fax:
Toll-Free: 800-381-2637
Address: 10101 Woodloch Forest, The Woodlands, TX 77380 United States

STOCK TICKER/OTHER:

Stock Ticker: Subsidiary
Employees: 9,600
Parent Company: McKesson Corporation

Exchange:
Fiscal Year Ends: 12/31

SALARIES/BONUSES:

Top Exec. Salary: $ Bonus: $
Second Exec. Salary: $ Bonus: $

OTHER THOUGHTS:

Estimated Female Officers or Directors:
Hot Spot for Advancement for Women/Minorities:

US Physical Therapy Inc

www.usph.com

NAIC Code: 621340

TYPES OF BUSINESS:

Occupational & Physical Therapy Clinics

BRANDS/DIVISIONS/AFFILIATES:

CONTACTS: *Note: Officers with more than one job title may be intentionally listed here more than once.*

Christopher Reading, CEO
Lawrence McAfee, CFO
Jerald Pullins, Chairman of the Board
Graham Reeve, COO, Geographical
Glenn McDowell, COO, Geographical
Jon Bates, Vice President

GROWTH PLANS/SPECIAL FEATURES:

U.S. Physical Therapy, Inc. (UPT) is a holding company engaged in the operation of outpatient physical therapy clinics. These clinics provide pre- and post-operative care/treatment of orthopedic-related disorders, sports-injuries, preventive care, rehabilitation of injured workers and neurological-related injuries. UPT operates through subsidiary clinic partnerships, in which it generally owns a 1% general partnership interest and a 24% through 99% limited partnership interest. The managing therapists of the clinics own the remaining limited partnership interest in the majority of the clinics. UPT also operates some clinics through wholly-owned subsidiaries under profit sharing arrangements with therapists. There are approximately 550 outpatient physical therapy clinics in 39 U.S. Each clinic's staff typically includes one or more licensed physical or occupational therapists along with assistants, aides, exercise physiologists and athletic trainers. The clinics initially perform an evaluation of each patient, which is then followed by a treatment plan specific to the injury as prescribed by the patient's physician. The treatment plan may include procedures such as ultrasound, electrical stimulation, therapeutic exercise, hot packs, iontophoresis, daily life skills management and home exercise programs. A clinic's business primarily comes from referrals by local physicians. UPT also manages approximately 25 physical therapy practices for third parties. In October 2020, UPT acquired a 70% interest in a business that manages six hospital-owned outpatient clinics.

UPT offers its employees medical, dental, vision, life and disability insurance plans; 401(k); continuing education; and other plans and programs.

FINANCIAL DATA: *Note: Data for latest year may not have been available at press time.*

In U.S. $	2020	2019	2018	2017	2016	2015
Revenue	422,969,000	481,969,000	453,911,000	414,051,000	356,546,000	331,302,000
R&D Expense						
Operating Income	65,914,000	67,425,000	60,314,000	54,728,000	49,533,000	47,294,000
Operating Margin %		.14%	.13%	.13%	.14%	.14%
SGA Expense	42,037,000	45,049,000	41,349,000	35,889,000	32,479,000	31,067,000
Net Income	35,194,000	40,039,000	34,873,000	22,256,000	20,551,000	22,279,000
Operating Cash Flow	99,995,000	62,448,000	73,005,000	56,526,000	51,050,000	41,243,000
Capital Expenditure	7,639,000	10,189,000	7,193,000	7,095,000	8,260,000	6,263,000
EBITDA	77,680,000	83,080,000	72,008,000	64,526,000	58,405,000	55,327,000
Return on Assets %		.06%	.04%	.06%	.07%	.08%
Return on Equity %		.14%	.08%	.11%	.12%	.14%
Debt to Equity		0.46	0.178	0.277	0.27	0.297

CONTACT INFORMATION:

Phone: 713 297-7000   Fax: 713 297-7090
Toll-Free: 800-580-6285
Address: 1300 W. Sam Houston Pkwy. S., Ste. 300, Houston, TX 77042
United States

STOCK TICKER/OTHER:

Stock Ticker: USPH   Exchange: NYS
Employees: 4,630   Fiscal Year Ends: 12/31
Parent Company:

SALARIES/BONUSES:

Top Exec. Salary: $ Bonus: $
Second Exec. Salary: $ Bonus: $

OTHER THOUGHTS:

Estimated Female Officers or Directors:
Hot Spot for Advancement for Women/Minorities:

USMD Health System

www.usmd.com

NAIC Code: 622110

TYPES OF BUSINESS:

Hospitals
Primary Care
Specialty Care
Senior Care
Telemedicine
Imaging Services

BRANDS/DIVISIONS/AFFILIATES:

UnitedHealth Group
Optum

GROWTH PLANS/SPECIAL FEATURES:

USMD Health System is a physician-led, integrated health system. Types of care include primary, specialty and senior, as well as telemedicine and imaging services. Primary care is offered for adults and children, and include family medicine, internal medicine and pediatrics. Specialty care includes nearly 20 different specialties, including bariatric surgery, breast disease and surgery, cardiology, general surgery, geriatric medicine, neurology, OB/GYN, podiatry, radiation/oncology, rheumatology, sports medicine, urology, vascular surgery and more. USMD is part of Optum, which delivers outpatient care across the areas of primary care, specialty care and post-acute care. Optum itself is part of the UnitedHealth Group.

CONTACTS: *Note: Officers with more than one job title may be intentionally listed here more than once.*

Richard C. Johnston, CEO
Josh Hardy, CFO
Mary McDonald, CIO
Chris Carr, Executive VP
Richard Johnston, Executive VP

FINANCIAL DATA: *Note: Data for latest year may not have been available at press time.*

In U.S. $	2020	2019	2018	2017	2016	2015
Revenue	360,658,068	387,804,375	369,337,500	351,750,000	335,000,000	325,152,992
R&D Expense						
Operating Income						
Operating Margin %						
SGA Expense						
Net Income						
Operating Cash Flow						
Capital Expenditure						
EBITDA						
Return on Assets %						
Return on Equity %						
Debt to Equity						

CONTACT INFORMATION:

Phone: 214 493-4000   Fax:
Toll-Free:
Address: 6333 N. State Hwy. 161, Ste. 200, Irving, TX 75038 United States

STOCK TICKER/OTHER:

Stock Ticker: Subsidiary   Exchange:
Employees: 1,470   Fiscal Year Ends:
Parent Company: UnitedHealth Group

SALARIES/BONUSES:

Top Exec. Salary: $ Bonus: $
Second Exec. Salary: $ Bonus: $

OTHER THOUGHTS:

Estimated Female Officers or Directors:
Hot Spot for Advancement for Women/Minorities:

Utah Medical Products Inc

www.utahmed.com

NAIC Code: 339100

TYPES OF BUSINESS:

Equipment-Obstetrics & Gynecology
Disposable Products
Electrosurgical Systems
Neonatal Intensive Care Equipment
Blood Pressure Management

BRANDS/DIVISIONS/AFFILIATES:

Utah Medical Products Ltd
Columbia Medical Inc
Abcorp Inc
Femcare Holdings Ltd
Utah Medical Products Canada Ltd
Femcare Canada
INTRAN PLUS
DELTRAN

CONTACTS: *Note: Officers with more than one job title may be intentionally listed here more than once.*

Kevin Cornwell, CEO
Brian Koopman, CFO

GROWTH PLANS/SPECIAL FEATURES:

Utah Medical Products, Inc. (UTMD), produces medical devices that are predominantly proprietary, disposable and for hospital use. Products of the firm are divided into four categories: labor and delivery/obstetrics (LDO), neonatal intensive care (NIC), gynecology/urology/electrosurgery (GUE) and blood pressure monitoring (BPM). LDO products consist of electronic fetal monitoring systems, vacuum-assisted delivery systems and obstetrical tools. Brand names within this category includes INTRAN PLUS intrauterine pressure catheters, AROM-COT pronged finger cover and CORDGUARD clamping system. NIC brands and products include the DISPOSA-HOOD infant respiratory hood that administers oxygen and flushes carbon dioxide while maintaining a neutral thermal environment; DELTRAN blood pressure monitoring system; GESCO and UMBILI-CATH biocompatible silicone catheters; ENFit catheter connectors and oral syringes; URI-CATH pre-assembled, closed urinary drainage system; MYELO-NATE lumbar sampling kit for obtaining cerebral spinal fluid samples; and HEMO-NATE disposable filter that removes microaggregates from stored blood prior to transfusion into a neonate. GUE products include the LETZ loop excision system; EPITOME electrosurgical scalpel; FILSHIE CLIP system; PATHFINDER PLUS endoscopic irrigation device; Add-a-Cath easy suprapubic introduction; LIBERTY device for incontinence in women; EndoCurette endometrial tissue sampling; TVUS/HSG-Cath for assessing persistent abnormal or dysfunctional uterine bleeding and other abnormalities of the uterus; and LUMIN gynecological laparoscopic tool. BPM includes the DELTRAN disposable pressure transducer used to convert physiological pressure into an electrical signal displayed on electronic monitoring equipment. Subsidiaries include Utah Medical Products Ltd.; Columbia Medical, Inc.; Abcorp, Inc.; Femcare Holdings Ltd.; and Utah Medical Products Canada Ltd. (dba Femcare Canada).

UTMD offers full-time employees comprehensive benefits, retirement plans and employee assistance programs.

FINANCIAL DATA: *Note: Data for latest year may not have been available at press time.*

In U.S. $	2020	2019	2018	2017	2016	2015
Revenue	42,178,000	46,904,000	41,998,000	41,414,000	39,298,000	40,157,000
R&D Expense	486,000	483,000	454,000	447,000	475,000	522,000
Operating Income	13,708,000	17,632,000	18,697,000	19,011,000	16,187,000	15,651,000
Operating Margin %		.38%	.45%	.46%	.41%	.39%
SGA Expense	11,354,000	11,351,000	7,155,000	6,937,000	7,028,000	8,012,000
Net Income	10,798,000	14,727,000	18,555,000	8,505,000	12,128,000	11,843,000
Operating Cash Flow	20,137,000	17,056,000	16,834,000	16,908,000	14,528,000	13,801,000
Capital Expenditure	860,000	21,540,000	402,000	1,597,000	3,302,000	246,000
EBITDA	20,917,000	24,514,000	21,653,000	21,855,000	19,255,000	18,757,000
Return on Assets %		.14%	.19%	.10%	.16%	.15%
Return on Equity %		.15%	.22%	.12%	.17%	.18%
Debt to Equity		0.004				

CONTACT INFORMATION:

Phone: 801 566-1200   Fax: 801 566-2062
Toll-Free: 866-754-9789
Address: 7043 S. 300 W., Midvale, UT 84047 United States

STOCK TICKER/OTHER:

Stock Ticker: UTMD   Exchange: NAS
Employees: 224   Fiscal Year Ends: 12/31
Parent Company:

SALARIES/BONUSES:

Top Exec. Salary: $ Bonus: $
Second Exec. Salary: $ Bonus: $

OTHER THOUGHTS:

Estimated Female Officers or Directors: 1
Hot Spot for Advancement for Women/Minorities:

Sales, profits and employees may be estimates. Financial information, benefits and other data can change quickly and may vary from those stated here.

Vapotherm Inc

vapotherm.com

NAIC Code: 334510

TYPES OF BUSINESS:

Electromedical and Electrotherapeutic Apparatus Manufacturing

BRANDS/DIVISIONS/AFFILIATES:

Vapotherm
Hi-VNI
Precision Flow

CONTACTS: *Note: Officers with more than one job title may be intentionally listed here more than once.*

Joseph Army, CEO
John Landry, CFO
James Liken, Chairman of the Board
Jill Dooling, Vice President, Divisional
George Dungan, Vice President, Divisional
Lise Halpern, Vice President, Divisional
Richelle Helman, Vice President, Divisional
Michael McQueen, Vice President, Divisional
Gregoire Ramade, Vice President, Divisional
Lindsay Becker, Vice President, Divisional
John Coolidge, Vice President, Divisional
Marc Davidson, Vice President, Divisional
David Blouin, Vice President, Geographical

GROWTH PLANS/SPECIAL FEATURES:

Vapotherm, Inc. is a global medical technology company that develops and commercializes proprietary Hi-VNI technology products used to treat patients of all ages suffering from respiratory distress. The Hi-VNI technology delivers non-invasive ventilatory support by providing heated, humidified and oxygenated air at a high velocity to patients through a small-bore nasal interface. Hi-VNI technology is mask-free, and is a front-line tool for relieving distresses such as hypercapnia, hypoxemia and dyspnea. Vapotherm's Precision Flow systems, which use Hi-VNI technology, are clinically-validated alternatives to the current standard of care for the treatment of respiratory distress in a hospital setting. The Precision Flow Hi-VNI system is an advanced high-flow nasal cannula system using high velocity to treat the respiratory distress experienced by COVID-19 patients. As of June 30, 2020, more than 2.3 million patients had been treated with Vapotherm's Precision Flow systems. Respiratory distress is caused by a wide range of serious underlying conditions, including pneumonia, chronic obstructive pulmonary disease (COPD), asthma and heart failure. Patients with respiratory distress have severe difficulty breathing and are unable to sustain sufficient oxygen levels or remove retained carbon dioxide in their lungs and airways. These patients require immediate respiratory support. Vapotherm, Hi-VNI and Precision Flow are trademarks within the U.S. and other countries. During 2020, Vapotherm announced that the U.S. Food and Drug Administration granted breakthrough device designation for its oxygen assist module (OAM), which provides clinicians with a solution to more effectively keep their patients with the physician-prescribed target oxygen saturation range with significantly fewer manual adjustments to the equipment. Vapotherm OAM is for use with most versions of its Precision Flow systems.

FINANCIAL DATA: *Note: Data for latest year may not have been available at press time.*

In U.S. $	2020	2019	2018	2017	2016	2015
Revenue	125,733,000	48,104,000	42,377,000	35,597,000	30,122,000	
R&D Expense	16,956,000	13,376,000	8,771,000	7,569,000	6,211,000	
Operating Income	-43,014,000	-48,164,000	-37,112,000	-28,570,000	-22,237,000	
Operating Margin %		-1.00%	-.88%	-.80%	-.74%	
SGA Expense	89,104,000	56,099,000	45,113,000	34,241,000	25,965,000	
Net Income	-51,502,000	-51,059,000	-42,468,000	-31,005,000	-23,072,000	
Operating Cash Flow	-39,468,000	-39,662,000	-39,965,000	-29,246,000	-25,371,000	
Capital Expenditure	9,797,000	4,747,000	5,180,000	5,947,000	4,531,000	
EBITDA	-42,022,000	-43,031,000	-37,237,000	-27,239,000	-21,020,000	
Return on Assets %		-.49%	-.54%	-.68%	-.75%	
Return on Equity %		-.97%				
Debt to Equity		0.778	0.607			

CONTACT INFORMATION:

Phone: 603-658-0411   Fax:
Toll-Free:
Address: 100 Domain Dr., Exeter, NH 03833 United States

STOCK TICKER/OTHER:

Stock Ticker: VAPO
Employees: 284
Parent Company:

Exchange: NYS
Fiscal Year Ends: 12/31

SALARIES/BONUSES:

Top Exec. Salary: $ Bonus: $
Second Exec. Salary: $ Bonus: $

OTHER THOUGHTS:

Estimated Female Officers or Directors:
Hot Spot for Advancement for Women/Minorities:

Sales, profits and employees may be estimates. Financial information, benefits and other data can change quickly and may vary from those stated here.

Varian Medical Systems Inc

www.varian.com

NAIC Code: 334510

TYPES OF BUSINESS:

Radiation Oncology Systems
X-Ray Equipment
Software Systems
Security & Inspection Products

BRANDS/DIVISIONS/AFFILIATES:

CONTACTS: *Note: Officers with more than one job title may be intentionally listed here more than once.*

Dow Wilson, CEO
Gary Bischoping, CFO
R. Eckert, Chairman of the Board
Magnus Momsen, Chief Accounting Officer
Timothy Guertin, Director
John Kuo, General Counsel
Kolleen Kennedy, Other Executive Officer
Christopher Toth, President, Divisional
Chris Toth, President, Divisional

GROWTH PLANS/SPECIAL FEATURES:

Varian Medical Systems, Inc. develops and manufactures medical devices and software for treating cancer and other medical conditions. Varian operates through two segments: oncology systems and proton systems. The oncology systems segment designs, manufactures, sells and services hardware and software products for treating cancer with conventional radiotherapy, and advanced treatments such as fixed field intensity-modulated radiation therapy (IMRT), image-guided radiation therapy (IGRT), volumetric modulated arc therapy (VMAT), stereotactic radiosurgery (SRS), stereotactic body radiotherapy (SBRT) and brachytherapy, as well as associated quality assurance equipment. This segment's software solutions also include informatics software for information management, clinical knowledge exchange, patient care management, practice management and decision-making support for comprehensive cancer clinics, radiotherapy centers and medical oncology practices. Hardware products include linear accelerators, brachytherapy after-loaders, treatment accessories and quality assurance software. The proton solutions segment develops, designs, manufactures, sells and services products and systems for delivering proton therapy, another form of external beam therapy using proton beams, for the treatment of cancer. Varian's current focus is bringing its expertise in X-ray beam radiation therapy to proton therapy to improve its clinical utility and to reduce its cost of treatment per patient. In August 2020, Varian agreed to be acquired by Siemens Healthineers AG, the parent of several European medical technology companies, for $16.4 billion. The transaction is expected to close in the first half of 2021, and upon completion Varian will continue to operate under the Varian name, as a Siemens Healthineers brand.

Varian offers its employees medical, life, AD&D, disability, dental and vision plans; a 401(k); educational reimbursement; an employee assistance program; and a stock purchase plan.

FINANCIAL DATA: *Note: Data for latest year may not have been available at press time.*

In U.S. $	2020	2019	2018	2017	2016	2015
Revenue		3,225,100,032	2,919,099,904	2,668,199,936	3,217,799,936	3,099,110,912
R&D Expense						
Operating Income						
Operating Margin %						
SGA Expense						
Net Income		291,900,000	149,900,000	249,600,000	402,300,000	411,484,992
Operating Cash Flow						
Capital Expenditure						
EBITDA						
Return on Assets %						
Return on Equity %						
Debt to Equity						

CONTACT INFORMATION:

Phone: 650 493-4000 Fax:
Toll-Free: 800-544-4636
Address: 3100 Hansen Way, Palo Alto, CA 94304 United States

STOCK TICKER/OTHER:

Stock Ticker: VAR
Employees: 10,062
Parent Company:

Exchange: NYS
Fiscal Year Ends: 09/30

SALARIES/BONUSES:

Top Exec. Salary: $ Bonus: $
Second Exec. Salary: $ Bonus: $

OTHER THOUGHTS:

Estimated Female Officers or Directors: 6
Hot Spot for Advancement for Women/Minorities: Y

Sales, profits and employees may be estimates. Financial information, benefits and other data can change quickly and may vary from those stated here.

VCA Inc

www.vca.com

NAIC Code: 541940

TYPES OF BUSINESS:

Animal Health Care Services
Veterinary Diagnostic Laboratories
Full-Service Animal Hospitals
Veterinary Equipment
Ultrasound Imaging

BRANDS/DIVISIONS/AFFILIATES:

Mars Incorporated
VCA Animal Hospital
VCA Canada
Companion Animal Practices of North America
Antech Diagnostics
South Technologies Inc
Camp Bow Wow

CONTACTS: *Note: Officers with more than one job title may be intentionally listed here more than once.*

Arthur J. Antin, COO
Josh Drake, President, Subsidiary

GROWTH PLANS/SPECIAL FEATURES:

VCA, Inc. is a leading animal healthcare company operating in the U.S. and Canada. The firm provides services and diagnostic testing to support veterinary care, and sells diagnostic equipment and other medical technology products to the veterinary market. VCA's hospitals offer a full range of general medical and surgical services for companion animals, as well as specialized treatments, including advanced diagnostic services, internal medicine, oncology, ophthalmology, dermatology and cardiology. In addition, the company provides pharmaceutical products and performs a variety of pet wellness programs such as health examinations, diagnostic testing, routine vaccinations, spaying, neutering and dental care. VCA's network of more than 1,000 animal hospitals provides service to over 10 million patients annually, which are located in 46 U.S. states and five Canadian provinces. In addition, VCA provides diagnostic services to more than 17,000 independent hospitals. Dog day care and boarding services are also offered at more than 130 locations. Brands and subsidiaries of VCA include: VCA Animal Hospital; VCA Canada; Companion Animal Practices of North America (CAPNA); Antech Diagnostics; South Technologies, Inc.; and Camp Bow Wow. VCA, Inc. operates as a distinct and separate business unit within Mars Incorporated's pet care segment.

FINANCIAL DATA: *Note: Data for latest year may not have been available at press time.*

In U.S. $	2020	2019	2018	2017	2016	2015
Revenue	3,213,000,000	3,150,000,000	3,000,000,000	2,700,000,000	2,516,863,000	2,133,675,008
R&D Expense						
Operating Income						
Operating Margin %						
SGA Expense						
Net Income						
Operating Cash Flow						
Capital Expenditure						
EBITDA						
Return on Assets %						
Return on Equity %						
Debt to Equity						

CONTACT INFORMATION:

Phone: 310 571-6500 Fax: 310 571-6700
Toll-Free: 800-966-1822
Address: 12401 W. Olympic Blvd., Los Angeles, CA 90064 United States

STOCK TICKER/OTHER:

Stock Ticker: Subsidiary
Employees: 30,000
Parent Company: Mars Incorporated

Exchange:
Fiscal Year Ends: 12/31

SALARIES/BONUSES:

Top Exec. Salary: $ Bonus: $
Second Exec. Salary: $ Bonus: $

OTHER THOUGHTS:

Estimated Female Officers or Directors:
Hot Spot for Advancement for Women/Minorities:

Vision Service Plan

NAIC Code: 524114

www.vsp.com

TYPES OF BUSINESS:

Insurance-Supplemental & Specialty Health
Vision Insurance
Optical Frames
Laboratory Products & Materials, Optometry

BRANDS/DIVISIONS/AFFILIATES:

Marchon Eyewear Inc
Eyefinity Inc
Altair Eyewear Inc
Visionworks of America Inc
VSP Vision Care
VSP Optics Group
VSP Retail
VSP Ventures

CONTACTS: *Note: Officers with more than one job title may be intentionally listed here more than once.*

Michael J. Guyette, Pres.
Earnie Franklin, COO
Alec Mahmood, CFO
Wendy Hauteman, CMO
Kristi Cappelletti-Matthews, CHRO
Matthew Alpert, Sec.
Gordon W. Jennings, Treas.
Claudio Gottardi, Pres.
Jim McGrann, Pres., VSP Vision Care
Steve Baker, Pres., Eyefinity
Gordon W. Jennings, Chmn.

GROWTH PLANS/SPECIAL FEATURES:

Vision Service Plan (VSP) is a vision care health insurance company operating in the U.S., Canada, Australia, Ireland and the U.K. VSP serves its members via private practice doctors in both rural and metropolitan areas. The firm's network consists of more than 40,000 doctor partners as well as nearly 90 million Vision Care members worldwide. VSP brands include VSP Vision Care, Marchon Eyewear, VSP Optics Group, Eyefinity, VSP Retail and VSP Ventures. VSP Vision Care is a national not-for-profit vision benefits and services company. Marchon is one of the largest global designers, manufacturers and distributors of fashionable and technologically-advanced eyewear and sunwear. VSP Optics combines ophthalmic technology and lab services to create custom lens solutions for individual customers. Eyefinity offers integrated products and services to streamline everyday processes for eye care facilities. Its products and solutions include practice management software; electronic health record (EHR) solutions for federal stimulus payments; desktop and cloud-based solutions for single and multi-location practices; website hosting with a customizable eCommerce platform; online transaction services for claim filing, frame and lens purchasing and lab ordering; and business consulting services. VSP Retail focuses on increasing access to eye care and eyewear through multiple channels. Last, VSP Ventures offers care-focused, customized choices for doctors looking to transition their practice. VSP subsidiaries include Marchon Eyewear Inc., Eyefinity Inc., Altair Eyewear Inc. and Visionworks of America Inc. In late-2019, VSP acquired optical retailer Visionworks of America, Inc., with more than 700 stores throughout the U.S. In August 2020, VSP acquired six optometric practices across California, each of which will continue to operate under their existing name, including Optometry at Redwood Shores, Eastgate Optometry Care, Swan Family Optometry, Eagle Vision Eye Care, Stanislaus Optometric Center and Norwalk Family Optometry.

FINANCIAL DATA: *Note: Data for latest year may not have been available at press time.*

In U.S. $	2020	2019	2018	2017	2016	2015
Revenue						
R&D Expense						
Operating Income						
Operating Margin %						
SGA Expense						
Net Income						
Operating Cash Flow						
Capital Expenditure						
EBITDA						
Return on Assets %						
Return on Equity %						
Debt to Equity						

CONTACT INFORMATION:

Phone: 916-851-5000   Fax: 916-851-4858
Toll-Free: 800-852-7600
Address: 3333 Quality Dr., Rancho Cordova, CA 95670 United States

STOCK TICKER/OTHER:

Stock Ticker: Private   Exchange:
Employees: Fiscal Year Ends: 12/31
Parent Company:

SALARIES/BONUSES:

Top Exec. Salary: $ Bonus: $
Second Exec. Salary: $ Bonus: $

OTHER THOUGHTS:

Estimated Female Officers or Directors: 1
Hot Spot for Advancement for Women/Minorities: Y

Sales, profits and employees may be estimates. Financial information, benefits and other data can change quickly and may vary from those stated here.

Vizient Inc

www.vizientinc.com

NAIC Code: 561400

TYPES OF BUSINESS:

Group Buying Programs for Medical Supplies
Consulting to Hospitals and Health Care Services
Supply Chain Management
E-Commerce Services
Health Services Resource Management
Health Care Analytics

BRANDS/DIVISIONS/AFFILIATES:

CONTACTS: *Note: Officers with more than one job title may be intentionally listed here more than once.*

Byron Jobe, CEO
Bharat Sundaram, COO
David Ertel, CFO
Taylor White, Sr. VP-Mktg. & Corp. Dev.
Colleen Risk, Chief People Officer
Jill Witter, General Counsel
Pete Allen, Area Sr. VP-Sourcing Oper.
Larry McComber, Sr. VP-Strategic Svcs.
Kyle Pyron, VP-Corp. Comm.
Mike Woodhouse, VP-Financial Svcs. & Supplier Audit
Cathy Denning, Sr. VP-Sourcing Oper.
David Berry, VP
Mike Clemens, VP-Sourcing Oper., Capital, Construction & Imaging
David P. Blom, Chmn.

GROWTH PLANS/SPECIAL FEATURES:

Vizient, Inc. is one of the largest member-owned health care performance improvement companies in the U.S., backed by network-based insights in clinical, operational and supply chain performance. The firm's solutions leverage analytics and engage consultants in an effort to solve its member's most pressing issues, with focus areas such as COVID-19 preparedness, patient experience, elimination of avoidable practice variation, physician alignment and engagement, service line optimization, quality outcomes, patient safety, care redesign and scale/cost efficiencies. Vizient members are not-for-profit health care organizations of all types and sizes, from academic medical centers to acute and non-acute community providers to pharmacy operations. Membership provides access to the many ways Vizient optimizes each interaction along the continuum of patient care. Within Vizient, more than 10 national groups for senior leaders, numerous performance improvement peer-to-peer networks and a hospital engagement network all provide opportunities to solve common challenges with fellow members. Suppliers are part of the Vizient portfolio as well. Suppliers deliver critical tools and technology for exceptional, cost-effective care, including medications and supplies, as well as cutting-edge medical devices. Headquartered in Irving, Texas, Vizient has offices throughout the U.S.

FINANCIAL DATA: *Note: Data for latest year may not have been available at press time.*

In U.S. $	2020	2019	2018	2017	2016	2015
Revenue						
R&D Expense						
Operating Income						
Operating Margin %						
SGA Expense						
Net Income						
Operating Cash Flow						
Capital Expenditure						
EBITDA						
Return on Assets %						
Return on Equity %						
Debt to Equity						

CONTACT INFORMATION:

Phone: 972-830-0000   Fax:
Toll-Free: 800-842-5146
Address: 290 E. John Carpenter Fwy., Irving, TX 75062 United States

STOCK TICKER/OTHER:

Stock Ticker: Private   Exchange:
Employees: Fiscal Year Ends: 12/31
Parent Company:

SALARIES/BONUSES:

Top Exec. Salary: $ Bonus: $
Second Exec. Salary: $ Bonus: $

OTHER THOUGHTS:

Estimated Female Officers or Directors: 3
Hot Spot for Advancement for Women/Minorities: Y

Walgreens Boots Alliance Inc

NAIC Code: 446110

www.walgreens.com

TYPES OF BUSINESS:

Drug Stores
Mail-Order Pharmacy Services
Pharmacy Benefit Management
Health Care Center Management
Online Pharmacy Services
Photo Printing Services
Specialty Pharmacy Services
Home Infusion Services

BRANDS/DIVISIONS/AFFILIATES:

Boots
Walgreens
Duane Reade
Boots
No7
Botanics
Well Beginnings

CONTACTS: *Note: Officers with more than one job title may be intentionally listed here more than once.*

Stefano Pessina, CEO
James Kehoe, CFO
James Skinner, Chairman of the Board
Heather Dixon, Chief Accounting Officer
Marco Pagni, Chief Administrative Officer
Ornella Barra, Co-COO
Alexander Gourlay, Co-COO
Kathleen Wilson-Thompson, Executive VP
Ken Murphy, Executive VP

GROWTH PLANS/SPECIAL FEATURES:

Walgreens Boots Alliance, Inc. is a global pharmacy-led health and wellbeing enterprise, with more than 18,500 stores worldwide. The company's pharmaceutical wholesale and distribution network is comprised of more than 425 distribution centers delivering to over 250,000 pharmacies, doctors, health centers and hospitals on an annual basis. The firm operates through segments that include retail pharmacy USA and retail pharmacy international. Retail pharmacy USA oversees pharmacy-led health and beauty retail businesses in 50 states, the District of Columbia, Puerto Rico and the U.S. Virgin Islands. It operates more than 9,020 retail stores and fills over 815 million prescriptions (including immunizations) annually. The retail pharmacy international segment oversees pharmacy-led health and beauty retail businesses in eight countries, operating more than 4,425 retail stores across the U.K., Thailand, Norway, Ireland, the Netherlands, Mexico and Chile. Walgreens' portfolio of retail and business global brands include Walgreens, Duane Reade, Boots and Alliance Healthcare, as well as global health and beauty product brands such as No7, NICE!, Botanics, Sleek MakeUP, Liz Earle, Well Beginnings, YourGoodSkin and Soap & Glory. In September 2020, Walgreens launched the Walgreens Test & Program to aid businesses in their COVID-19 work plans and strategies. In early 2021, Walgreens agreed to sell its Allied Healthcare wholesale pharmacy distribution business to AmerisourceBergen.

FINANCIAL DATA: *Note: Data for latest year may not have been available at press time.*

In U.S. $	2020	2019	2018	2017	2016	2015
Revenue	139,537,000,000	136,866,000,000	131,537,000,000	118,214,000,000	117,351,000,000	103,444,000,000
R&D Expense						
Operating Income	972,000,000	4,834,000,000	6,223,000,000	5,422,000,000	5,964,000,000	4,353,000,000
Operating Margin %		.04%	.05%	.05%	.05%	.04%
SGA Expense	27,045,000,000	25,242,000,000	24,569,000,000	23,740,000,000	23,910,000,000	22,571,000,000
Net Income	456,000,000	3,982,000,000	5,024,000,000	4,078,000,000	4,173,000,000	4,220,000,000
Operating Cash Flow	5,484,000,000	5,594,000,000	8,265,000,000	7,251,000,000	7,847,000,000	5,664,000,000
Capital Expenditure	1,374,000,000	1,702,000,000	1,367,000,000	1,351,000,000	1,325,000,000	1,251,000,000
EBITDA	3,309,000,000	7,269,000,000	8,361,000,000	7,200,000,000	7,458,000,000	7,658,000,000
Return on Assets %		.06%	.07%	.06%	.06%	.08%
Return on Equity %		.16%	.19%	.14%	.14%	.16%
Debt to Equity		0.472	0.478	0.462	0.626	0.431

CONTACT INFORMATION:

Phone: 847 315-2500   Fax: 847 914-2804
Toll-Free: 800-925-4733
Address: 108 Wilmot Rd., Deerfield, IL 60015 United States

STOCK TICKER/OTHER:

Stock Ticker: WBA   Exchange: NAS
Employees: 331,000   Fiscal Year Ends: 08/31
Parent Company:

SALARIES/BONUSES:

Top Exec. Salary: $ Bonus: $
Second Exec. Salary: $ Bonus: $

OTHER THOUGHTS:

Estimated Female Officers or Directors: 7
Hot Spot for Advancement for Women/Minorities: Y

WebMD Health Corp

www.webmd.com

NAIC Code: 519130

TYPES OF BUSINESS:

Health Care Internet Portals
Content Licensing

BRANDS/DIVISIONS/AFFILIATES:

KKR & Co Inc
Internet Brands Inc
WebMD Health Network
Medscape
MedicineNet.com
eMedicineHealth.com
RxList.com
StayWell Company (The)

CONTACTS: *Note: Officers with more than one job title may be intentionally listed here more than once.*

Robert Brisco, CEO
Martin Wygod, Chairman of the Board
Blake DeSimone, CFO
Kathleen Tourjee, VP-Human Resources
Michael Glick, Executive VP
Douglas Wamsley, Executive VP
Steven Zatz, President

GROWTH PLANS/SPECIAL FEATURES:

WebMD Health Corp. provides health information services to consumers, physicians, health care professionals, employers and health plan providers via the internet. Additionally, the company provides personalized telephonic, online or onsite health coaching and condition management services. The firm's public online service, WebMD Health Network, offers WebMD Health, its primary public portal; and Medscape from WebMD, a public portal for physicians and healthcare professionals. WebMD Health provides health and wellness articles and features decision-support services to help consumers make informed decisions about healthcare providers, health risks and treatment options. Available information and interactive tools include detailed data on specific diseases or conditions, physician location and individual healthcare data storage. Medscape from WebMD assists physicians and health care professionals in improving clinical knowledge with original content such as daily news, commentary, conference coverage and continuing medical education. Additional websites in the WebMD Health Network include MedicineNet.com, eMedicineHealth.com and RxList.com. The firm generates revenue from its public offerings primarily through advertising sales and sponsorships. Additionally, the company generates revenue through the sale of advertising in its WebMD Magazine consumer publication, distributed free of charge to physicians for use in their office waiting rooms; and is also available online through iOS app. Revenue is also generated from the private side through content and technology licensed to employers and health plans, either directly or through distributors. Private portals offered by WebMD enable employees and health plan members to learn about benefits, providers and treatment decisions, customized to a user's health insurance plan. WebMD is a subsidiary of Internet Brands, Inc., itself a subsidiary of KKR & Co., Inc. During 2020, WebMD acquired The StayWell Company, a subsidiary of Merck, and known as MSD outside the U.S. and Canada. StayWell is a health empowerment company that enables populations to improve health outcomes via behavior change.

FINANCIAL DATA: *Note: Data for latest year may not have been available at press time.*

In U.S. $	2020	2019	2018	2017	2016	2015
Revenue	852,906,949	816,178,899	777,313,237	740,298,321	705,046,016	636,398,976
R&D Expense						
Operating Income						
Operating Margin %						
SGA Expense						
Net Income						
Operating Cash Flow						
Capital Expenditure						
EBITDA						
Return on Assets %						
Return on Equity %						
Debt to Equity						

CONTACT INFORMATION:

Phone: 212-624-3700   Fax:
Toll-Free:
Address: 395 Hudson St., 3/Fl, New York, NY 10011 United States

STOCK TICKER/OTHER:

Stock Ticker: Subsidiary
Employees: 1,815
Parent Company: KKR & Co Inc

Exchange:
Fiscal Year Ends: 12/31

SALARIES/BONUSES:

Top Exec. Salary: $ Bonus: $
Second Exec. Salary: $ Bonus: $

OTHER THOUGHTS:

Estimated Female Officers or Directors: 1
Hot Spot for Advancement for Women/Minorities: Y

Sales, profits and employees may be estimates. Financial information, benefits and other data can change quickly and may vary from those stated here.

WellCare Health Plans Inc

www.wellcare.com

NAIC Code: 524114

TYPES OF BUSINESS:

Insurance-Medical & Health, HMOs & PPOs

BRANDS/DIVISIONS/AFFILIATES:

Centene Corporation

GROWTH PLANS/SPECIAL FEATURES:

WellCare Health Plans, Inc. manages government-sponsored healthcare programs. The company offers plans for beneficiaries of temporary assistance, children's health insurance programs, managed care health plans and other related services. WellCare serves families, children, seniors and individuals in the U.S. In early-2020, WellCare Health Plans was acquired by Centene Corporation, a multi-line healthcare plan firm operating in two segments: managed care and specialty services, for $15.3 billion. WellCare ceased from being publicly traded. Together, WellCare and Centene provides access to affordable healthcare to m ore than 24 million members across all 50 states.

CONTACTS:
Note: Officers with more than one job title may be intentionally listed here more than once.

Andrew Asher, CFO
Mark Leenay, Chief Medical Officer
Christian Michalik, Director
Michael Polen, Executive VP, Divisional
Kelly Munson, Executive VP, Divisional
Michael Radu, Executive VP, Divisional
Anat Hakim, Executive VP
Rhonda Mims, Executive VP
Timothy Trodden, Executive VP
Michael Neidorff, Chmn.

FINANCIAL DATA:
Note: Data for latest year may not have been available at press time.

In U.S. $	2020	2019	2018	2017	2016	2015
Revenue	36,644,650,000	27,901,000,000	20,414,099,456	17,007,200,256	14,237,100,032	13,890,199,552
R&D Expense						
Operating Income						
Operating Margin %						
SGA Expense						
Net Income		583,000,000	439,800,000	373,700,000	242,100,000	118,600,000
Operating Cash Flow						
Capital Expenditure						
EBITDA						
Return on Assets %						
Return on Equity %						
Debt to Equity						

CONTACT INFORMATION:

Phone: 813 290-6200   Fax:
Toll-Free: 800-795-3432
Address: 8725 Henderson Rd., Renaissance 1, Tampa, FL 33634 United States

STOCK TICKER/OTHER:

Stock Ticker: Subsidiary   Exchange:
Employees: 14,700   Fiscal Year Ends: 12/31
Parent Company: Centene Coropration

SALARIES/BONUSES:

Top Exec. Salary: $ Bonus: $
Second Exec. Salary: $ Bonus: $

OTHER THOUGHTS:

Estimated Female Officers or Directors: 3
Hot Spot for Advancement for Women/Minorities: Y

Sales, profits and employees may be estimates. Financial information, benefits and other data can change quickly and may vary from those stated here.

Welltok Inc

welltok.com

NAIC Code: 511210D

TYPES OF BUSINESS:

Computer Software, Healthcare and Biotechnology

BRANDS/DIVISIONS/AFFILIATES:

GROWTH PLANS/SPECIAL FEATURES:

Welltok, Inc. is an enterprise Software-as-a-Service (SaaS) company that designs and develops technology that applies social media and social analytics to the health care industry. Welltok strategies engage members via health-related social networking and fun challenges, and offers an avenue for providers to retrieve the data and perform analytics for business decision-making purposes. The company's solutions include updated COVID-19 communications, customer retention via engagement/communication and more, closing target gaps by locating and strategizing hard-to-reach members, medication adherence by offering reminders and education, various wellbeing programs for employee health engagement, and health system growth strategies for acquiring more patients. Welltok applies artificial intelligence (AI) to its cognitive computing to support the full consumer journey and to help organizations grow and retain initiatives, improve healthcare value and streamline the consumer experience, while upholding security and compliance standards.

CONTACTS: Note: Officers with more than one job title may be intentionally listed here more than once.

Bob Fabbio, CEO
James Sullivan, Chief Administration Officer
Linda Fenton, CFO
Erica Morgenstern, CCO
Chaz Hinkle, Chief People Officer
David MacLeod, CIO

FINANCIAL DATA: Note: Data for latest year may not have been available at press time.

In U.S. $	2020	2019	2018	2017	2016	2015
Revenue	88,021,500	87,150,000	83,000,000	68,800,000	625,000,000	
R&D Expense						
Operating Income						
Operating Margin %						
SGA Expense						
Net Income						
Operating Cash Flow						
Capital Expenditure						
EBITDA						
Return on Assets %						
Return on Equity %						
Debt to Equity						

CONTACT INFORMATION:

Phone: 720-222-9490   Fax:
Toll-Free: 888-935-5865
Address: 1515 Arapahoe St., Tower 3, Ste. 700, Denver, CO 80202 United States

STOCK TICKER/OTHER:

Stock Ticker: Private
Employees: 443
Parent Company:

Exchange:
Fiscal Year Ends:

SALARIES/BONUSES:

Top Exec. Salary: $ Bonus: $
Second Exec. Salary: $ Bonus: $

OTHER THOUGHTS:

Estimated Female Officers or Directors:
Hot Spot for Advancement for Women/Minorities:

Wright Medical Group NV

www.wright.com

NAIC Code: 339100

TYPES OF BUSINESS:

Orthopedic Implants
Reconstructive Joint Devices
Biologics Materials

BRANDS/DIVISIONS/AFFILIATES:

CHARLOTTE
DARCO
INBONE
PRO-TOE
SALVATION
EVOLVE
GRAFTJACKET
FUSIONFLEX

CONTACTS: *Note: Officers with more than one job title may be intentionally listed here more than once.*

Robert J. Palmisano, CEO
Lance A. Berry, CFO
Kevin OBoyle, Director
James Lightman, General Counsel
William Griffin, General Manager, Divisional
Julie Tracy, Other Executive Officer
Jonathan Porter, Other Executive Officer
Kevin Cordell, President, Divisional
Peter Cooke, President, Divisional
Robert Palmisano, President
Robert Burrows, Senior VP, Divisional
Jennifer Walker, Senior VP, Divisional
Gregory Morrison, Senior VP, Divisional
Lance Berry, Senior VP

GROWTH PLANS/SPECIAL FEATURES:

Wright Medical Group NV is a global medical device company focused on extremities and biologics products. The firm is a recognized leader of surgical solutions for the upper extremities (shoulder, elbow, wrist and hand), lower extremities (foot and ankle) and biologics markets, three of the fastest growing segments in orthopedics. Wright Medical markets its products in over 50 countries worldwide. Foot and ankle hardware include the CHARLOTTE system, which comprises the CLAW compression plate designed for corrective foot surgeries; the DARCO plating system designed as implants to incorporate fixed angle, locking screw technology into a fixation set for foot surgery; INBONE ankle systems; trauma devices such as plates, pins, nails and screws to help stabilize fractures; PRO-TOE hammertoe fixation systems; TENFUSE nail allograft; BIOFOAM wedge system for corrective osteotomies of the foot; VALOR fusion nail systems; SALVATION limb salvage products; and BIOARCH subtalar arthroereisis implant; and the Swanson line of toe joint replacement products. Upper extremity hardware includes EVOLVE radial head replacement prosthesis for the elbow; MICRONAIL intramedullary fracture repair systems; and RAYHACK precision cutting guides and plates for shortening procedures. Biologics include the GRAFTJACKET soft tissue graft for augmentation of tendon and ligament repairs; PRO-DENSE injectable graft of calcium sulfate and calcium phosphate; OSTEOSET synthetic bone graft substitute; MIIG injectable graft; FUSIONFLEX demineralized moldable scaffold; AUGMENT bone graft; ALLOPURE allograft bone wedges; and ALLOMATRIX injectable putty. In November 2019, Stryker Corporation agreed to acquire Wright Medical Group in an all-cash tender offer; but, as of October 13, 2020, the offer was scheduled to expire at 5pm Eastern Time on October 28, 2020, unless the offer was further extended or earlier terminated.

FINANCIAL DATA: *Note: Data for latest year may not have been available at press time.*

In U.S. $	2020	2019	2018	2017	2016	2015
Revenue		920,899,968	836,190,016	744,988,992	690,361,984	415,460,992
R&D Expense						
Operating Income						
Operating Margin %						
SGA Expense						
Net Income		-114,225,000	-169,504,992	-202,598,000	-432,372,992	-298,700,992
Operating Cash Flow						
Capital Expenditure						
EBITDA						
Return on Assets %						
Return on Equity %						
Debt to Equity						

CONTACT INFORMATION:

Phone: 3120-521-4777   Fax:
Toll-Free:
Address: Prins Bernhardplein 200, Amsterdam, 1097 Netherlands

STOCK TICKER/OTHER:

Stock Ticker: WMGI   Exchange: NAS
Employees: 3,030   Fiscal Year Ends: 12/31
Parent Company:

SALARIES/BONUSES:

Top Exec. Salary: $ Bonus: $
Second Exec. Salary: $ Bonus: $

OTHER THOUGHTS:

Estimated Female Officers or Directors: 4
Hot Spot for Advancement for Women/Minorities: Y

WW International Inc

www.weightwatchers.com

NAIC Code: 812191

TYPES OF BUSINESS:

Weight Management Programs
Franchising
Branded Diet Products

BRANDS/DIVISIONS/AFFILIATES:

myWW
SmartPoints
ZeroPoints
Green
Purple
Blue

CONTACTS: *Note: Officers with more than one job title may be intentionally listed here more than once.*

Mindy Grossman, CEO
Nicholas Hotchkin, CFO
Raymond Debbane, Chairman of the Board
Amy Kossover, Chief Accounting Officer
Michael Colosi, General Counsel
Corinne Pollier-Bousquet, President, Geographical

GROWTH PLANS/SPECIAL FEATURES:

WW International, Inc. (WWI) is a global wellness company and a leading commercial weight management program. Its WW brand represents a focus on overall health and wellness. WWI operates four segments based on an integrated geographical structure: North America, which includes U.S. and Canada company-owned operations; Continental Europe, which includes Germany, Switzerland, France, Belgium, Netherlands and Sweden company-owned operations; United Kingdom, including U.K. company-owned operations; and other, consisting of Australia, New Zealand and Brazil company-owned operations, as well as revenues and costs from franchises in the U.S. and certain other countries. Each of these segments provide similar services and products. In these markets, WWI offers services and products based on its myWW program, which is comprised of a range of nutritional, activity, behavioral and lifestyle tools and approaches that can be personalized. There are three comprehensive ways to follow myWW: the Green, Purple or Blue food plan, each of which encompass WWI's SmartPoints system. With the SmartPoints system, each food has a SmartPoints value determined by the food's calorie, saturated fat, sugar and protein content. Customers can eat any food as long as the SmartPoints value of their total food consumption stays within their personalized daily and weekly budget, which is based on age, weight, height and sex. Each of myWW's Green, Purple and Blue food plans has a unique balance of SmartPoints and ZeroPoint foods. ZeroPoint foods do not need to be weighed, measured or tracked and form the foundation of a healthy eating pattern. In addition to healthy eating, the program addresses healthy mindset, activity and community. Customers can participate in the WW program digitally and through in-person group workshops.

FINANCIAL DATA: *Note: Data for latest year may not have been available at press time.*

In U.S. $	2020	2019	2018	2017	2016	2015
Revenue	1,378,124,000	1,413,337,000	1,514,121,000	1,306,911,000	1,164,902,000	1,164,419,000
R&D Expense						
Operating Income	219,827,000	287,985,000	388,985,000	280,628,000	200,811,000	168,058,000
Operating Margin %		.20%	.26%	.21%	.17%	.14%
SGA Expense	558,014,000	498,697,000	477,425,000	412,021,000	384,690,000	406,029,000
Net Income	75,079,000	119,616,000	223,749,000	163,514,000	67,699,000	32,945,000
Operating Cash Flow	135,940,000	182,383,000	295,592,000	222,274,000	119,044,000	54,815,000
Capital Expenditure	50,431,000	47,983,000	46,813,000	40,648,000	34,341,000	36,259,000
EBITDA	266,490,000	331,244,000	430,468,000	308,744,000	251,920,000	230,628,000
Return on Assets %		.08%	.17%	.13%	.05%	.02%
Return on Equity %						
Debt to Equity						

CONTACT INFORMATION:

Phone: 212 589-2700   Fax:
Toll-Free:
Address: 675 Avenue of the Americas, 6/Fl, New York, NY 10010 United States

STOCK TICKER/OTHER:

Stock Ticker: WW
Employees: 10,000
Parent Company:

Exchange: NAS
Fiscal Year Ends: 12/31

SALARIES/BONUSES:

Top Exec. Salary: $ Bonus: $
Second Exec. Salary: $ Bonus: $

OTHER THOUGHTS:

Estimated Female Officers or Directors: 1
Hot Spot for Advancement for Women/Minorities: Y

Sales, profits and employees may be estimates. Financial information, benefits and other data can change quickly and may vary from those stated here.

Yuhan Corporation

eng.yuhan.co.kr/main

NAIC Code: 325412

TYPES OF BUSINESS:

Pharmaceuticals
Traditional Foods
Cleaning Products
Fine Chemicals

BRANDS/DIVISIONS/AFFILIATES:

Yuhan Chemical Inc
Yuhan Medica Corporation
Yuhan-Clorox Co Ltd
Gujarat Themis Biosyn Ltd
Yuhan Research Institute

CONTACTS: Note: Officers with more than one job title may be intentionally listed here more than once.

Jung Hee Lee, CEO
Chris C.K. Sa, Dir.-New Prod. Dev.
Chris C.K. Sa, Dir.-Bus. Dev.
Yoon-Saerb Kim, Co-CEO
Do Hwan Oh, Managing Dir.

GROWTH PLANS/SPECIAL FEATURES:

Yuhan Corporation is a pharmaceuticals company that develops drugs for diabetes, viral and fungus infection, osteoporosis, arthritis, cancer and hepatitis C. Yuhan's first fully-developed drug, Revanex, an anti-ulcer agent for gastrointestinal diseases, is one of the first new drugs ever developed in Korea. The firm conducts its research through the Yuhan Research Institute. Yuhan's drug discovery laboratory engages in new drug development including combinatorial chemistry, molecular design, high-throughput screening and joint development programs. Its biotech laboratory research ranges from genetically-engineered pharmaceuticals to home test kits and hospital diagnosis kits. The lab has developed new veterinary medicines, home pregnancy test kits and prostate cancer diagnosis kits. The pharmaceuticals development lab mainly researches novel drug delivery systems, including nano-particle and nano-emulsion production techniques, and seeks to improve existing drugs. The process development lab researches active pharmaceutical ingredient production methods and conducts contract manufacturing of custom pharmaceutical materials. The drug evaluation lab conducts pre-clinical trials and studies new drug candidates. The pharmaceuticals analysis lab develops analysis systems and equipment, analyzing areas such as drug stability, protein structure and clinical samples. It also studies the physical and chemical properties of drugs and verifies the viability of proposed analysis techniques. Subsidiary Yuhan Chemical, Inc. has designed plants that produce pharmaceutical ingredients meeting cGMP (current good manufacturing practice) standards, while subsidiary Yuhan Medica Corporation produces third-party owned pharmaceutical products and is expanding its traditional food business. Joint venture (with Clorox) Yuhan-Clorox Co. Ltd. produces hygienic, disinfectant and plumbing relief products. Joint venture Gujarat Themis Biosyn Ltd., based in India, produces and markets finished products such as Rifampicin and Rifa-S antibiotics, which are used to treat various bacterial infections.

FINANCIAL DATA: Note: Data for latest year may not have been available at press time.

In U.S. $	2020	2019	2018	2017	2016	2015
Revenue	1,488,210,000	1,278,420,000	1,359,620,000	1,056,920,000	1,094,810,000	1,011,809,783
R&D Expense						
Operating Income						
Operating Margin %						
SGA Expense						
Net Income	174,927,000	31,618,000	52,220,300	117,988,000	133,619,000	112,980,182
Operating Cash Flow						
Capital Expenditure						
EBITDA						
Return on Assets %						
Return on Equity %						
Debt to Equity						

CONTACT INFORMATION:

Phone: 82-2-828-0181　　　Fax: 82-2-828-0050
Toll-Free:
Address: 74, Noryangjin-ro, dongjak-gu, Seoul,　South Korea

STOCK TICKER/OTHER:

Stock Ticker: 100　　　　　　　Exchange: Seoul
Employees: 1,700　　　　　　　Fiscal Year Ends: 12/31
Parent Company:

SALARIES/BONUSES:

Top Exec. Salary: $　　　　Bonus: $
Second Exec. Salary: $　　　Bonus: $

OTHER THOUGHTS:

Estimated Female Officers or Directors:
Hot Spot for Advancement for Women/Minorities:

Zimmer Biomet Holdings Inc

www.zimmerbiomet.com

NAIC Code: 339100

TYPES OF BUSINESS:

Orthopedic Supplies
Human Bone Joint Replacement Systems
Orthopedic Support Devices
Operating Room Supplies
Powered Surgical Instruments
Dental Implants

BRANDS/DIVISIONS/AFFILIATES:

Persona
Zimmer
Taperloc
JuggerKnot
Gel-One
ALPS
3i T3
ROSA

CONTACTS: Note: Officers with more than one job title may be intentionally listed here more than once.

Bryan Hanson, CEO
Daniel Florin, CFO
Larry Glasscock, Director
Aure Bruneau, President, Divisional
Ivan Tornos, President, Divisional
Didier Deltort, President, Geographical
Sang Yi, President, Geographical
Chad Phipps, Senior VP

GROWTH PLANS/SPECIAL FEATURES:

Zimmer Biomet Holdings, Inc. designs, manufactures and markets musculoskeletal products for the healthcare industry. These include orthopedic reconstructive products; sports medicine, biologics, extremities and trauma products; spine, bone healing, craniomaxillofacial and thoracic products; dental implants; and related surgical products. Zimmer Biomet collaborates with healthcare professionals worldwide to advance the pace of innovation. The company's products and solutions help treat patients suffering from disorders of, or injuries to bones, joints or supporting soft tissues. Knee products include the Persona, NexGen, Vanguard and Oxford branded systems. Hip products include the Zimmer, Taperloc, Arcos, Avenir Complete, Continuum and G7 branded systems. Surgical, sports medicine, biologics, foot and ankle, extremities and trauma products include A.T.S. automatic tourniquet systems, JuggerKnot soft anchor system, Gel-One cross-linked hyaluronate, Zimmer trabecular metal reverse shoulder system, Comprehensive shoulder system, Zimmer Natural Nail system and A.L.P.S. plating system. Dental products include the Tapered Screw-Vent and 3i T3 implant systems. Spine and craniomaxillofacial and thoracic products include the Polaris spinal system, Mobi-C cervical disc and SternaLock closure and fixation systems brand lines. During 2021, Zimmer Biomet announced that it received U.S. Food and Drug Administration clearance for its ROSA partial knee system for robotically-assisted partial knee arthroplasty, and for its ROSA hip system for robotically-assisted direct anterior total hip arthroplasty.

FINANCIAL DATA: Note: Data for latest year may not have been available at press time.

In U.S. $	2020	2019	2018	2017	2016	2015
Revenue	7,024,500,000	7,982,200,000	7,932,900,000	7,824,100,000	7,683,900,000	5,997,800,000
R&D Expense	372,000,000	449,300,000	391,700,000	369,900,000	365,600,000	268,800,000
Operating Income	697,900,000	1,269,800,000	1,147,200,000	1,347,700,000	1,087,200,000	929,000,000
Operating Margin %		.16%	.14%	.17%	.14%	.15%
SGA Expense	3,177,800,000	3,343,800,000	3,379,300,000	3,369,700,000	3,283,400,000	2,660,500,000
Net Income	-138,900,000	1,131,600,000	-379,200,000	1,813,800,000	305,900,000	147,000,000
Operating Cash Flow	1,204,500,000	1,585,800,000	1,747,400,000	1,582,300,000	1,632,200,000	816,700,000
Capital Expenditure	117,900,000	404,700,000	162,700,000	156,000,000	184,700,000	167,700,000
EBITDA	970,300,000	2,138,800,000	1,058,700,000	1,854,800,000	1,796,800,000	1,152,200,000
Return on Assets %		.05%	- .02%	.07%	.01%	.01%
Return on Equity %		.10%	- .03%	.17%	.03%	.02%
Debt to Equity		0.543	0.746	0.76	1.103	1.169

CONTACT INFORMATION:

Phone: 574-267-6639   Fax: 574-267-8137
Toll-Free: 800-613-6131
Address: 345 E. Main St., Warsaw, IN 46580 United States

STOCK TICKER/OTHER:

Stock Ticker: ZBH
Employees: 19,900
Parent Company:

Exchange: NYS
Fiscal Year Ends: 05/31

SALARIES/BONUSES:

Top Exec. Salary: $ Bonus: $
Second Exec. Salary: $ Bonus: $

OTHER THOUGHTS:

Estimated Female Officers or Directors: 3
Hot Spot for Advancement for Women/Minorities: Y

Zoll Medical Corporation

www.zoll.com

NAIC Code: 339100

TYPES OF BUSINESS:

Cardiac Resuscitation Devices
Disposable Electrodes
Intravascular Temperature Management
Information Management

BRANDS/DIVISIONS/AFFILIATES:

Asahi Kasei Corporation
Zoll
731
RescueNet
ZOLL LifeVest
ZOLL TherOx System

CONTACTS: *Note: Officers with more than one job title may be intentionally listed here more than once.*

Jonathan A. Rennert, CEO
Jonathan A. Rennert, Pres.
E. Jane Wilson, VP-R&D
A. Ernest Whiton, VP-Admin.
Aaron M. Grossman, General Counsel
John P. Bergeron, Treas.
Steven K. Flora, Sr. VP-North American Sales
Ward M. Hamilton, Sr.VP
Richard A. Packer, Chmn.
Alex N. Moghadam, VP-Int'l Oper.

GROWTH PLANS/SPECIAL FEATURES:

Zoll Medical Corporation, an Asahi Kasei Corporation company, develops and markets medical devices and software solutions that assist in emergency care. Its products include defibrillation, monitoring, circulation, CPR feedback, data management, fluid resuscitation and therapeutic temperature management devices. Market sectors that use Zoll products and technologies include emergency medical services (EMS), fire departments, hospitals, public safety, alternate care, military, government and homeland security and remote patient management. Products and technologies include: automated external defibrillators (AEDs), providing treatment for sudden cardiac arrest (SCA), and include real-time cardiopulmonary resuscitation feedback on the depth and rate of chest compressions; the 730+ family of portable ventilators, for environments ranging from emergency departments to military operations, and provide therapies to ventilate and support infants through adults. Additional products include temperature management systems, which provide power and control to manage the core body temperature of critically-ill or surgical patients; intrathoracic pressure regulation (IPR) therapy, which creates a vacuum inside the chest cavity that enhances circulation, increases blood pressure and lowers intracranial pressure; and the RescueNet suite of patient data management, which helps medical professionals manage information such as vital signs, end-tidal CO2 trends and CPR performance. ZOLL LifeVest is a wearable defibrillator worn by patients at risk for SCA. During 2020, Zoll Medical announced plans to build 10,000 ventilators per month in response to the COVID-19 pandemic; and announced that the U.S. Food and Drug Administration approved its next-general ZOLL TherOx System, which provides supersaturated oxygen therapy and reduces heart muscle damage in widowmaker heart attack patients.

FINANCIAL DATA: *Note: Data for latest year may not have been available at press time.*

In U.S. $	2020	2019	2018	2017	2016	2015
Revenue	1,484,654,062	1,099,743,750	1,047,375,000	997,500,000	950,000,000	900,000,000
R&D Expense						
Operating Income						
Operating Margin %						
SGA Expense						
Net Income						
Operating Cash Flow						
Capital Expenditure						
EBITDA						
Return on Assets %						
Return on Equity %						
Debt to Equity						

CONTACT INFORMATION:

Phone: 978-421-9655   Fax: 978-421-0025
Toll-Free: 800-348-9011
Address: 269 Mill Rd., Chelmsford, MA 01824 United States

STOCK TICKER/OTHER:

Stock Ticker: Subsidiary   Exchange:
Employees: 4,000   Fiscal Year Ends: 09/30
Parent Company: Asahi Kasei Corporation

SALARIES/BONUSES:

Top Exec. Salary: $ Bonus: $
Second Exec. Salary: $ Bonus: $

OTHER THOUGHTS:

Estimated Female Officers or Directors:
Hot Spot for Advancement for Women/Minorities:

ADDITIONAL INDEXES

CONTENTS:

INDEX OF FIRMS NOTED AS HOT SPOTS FOR ADVANCEMENT FOR WOMEN & MINORITIES

Organogenesis Inc
Owens & Minor Inc
Par Pharmaceutical Companies Inc
Patterson Companies Inc
PerkinElmer Inc
Pfizer Inc
Premera Blue Cross
Premier Inc
Providence
Quest Diagnostics Incorporated
Rite Aid Corporation
Roche Holding AG
Sanofi Genzyme
Sanofi SA
Sentara Healthcare
SHL Telemedicine Ltd
Siemens AG
Siemens Healthineers AG
Sigma Healthcare Limited
Smile Brands Inc
Smith & Nephew plc
Smiths Group plc
SSM Health
St Jude Children's Research Hospital
STERIS plc
Steward Health Care System LLC
Stryker Corporation
Sutter Health Inc
Takeda Oncology
Takeda Pharmaceutical Company Limited
Team Health Holdings Inc
Tenet Healthcare Corporation
Teva Pharmaceutical Industries Limited
Texas Health Resources
Thermo Fisher Scientific Inc
Trinity Health
Tufts Associated Health Plans Inc
United Surgical Partners International Inc
UnitedHealth Group Inc
UnitedHealthcare Community & State
UnitedHealthcare National Accounts
Universal Health Services Inc
Varian Medical Systems Inc
Vision Service Plan
Vizient Inc
Walgreens Boots Alliance Inc
WebMD Health Corp
WellCare Health Plans Inc
Wright Medical Group NV
WW International Inc
Zimmer Biomet Holdings Inc

INDEX OF SUBSIDIARIES, BRAND NAMES AND AFFILIATIONS

INDEX OF SUBSIDIARIES, BRAND NAMES AND AFFILIATIONS, CONT.

INDEX OF SUBSIDIARIES, BRAND NAMES AND AFFILIATIONS, CONT.

INDEX OF SUBSIDIARIES, BRAND NAMES AND AFFILIATIONS, CONT.

INDEX OF SUBSIDIARIES, BRAND NAMES AND AFFILIATIONS, CONT.

INDEX OF SUBSIDIARIES, BRAND NAMES AND AFFILIATIONS, CONT.

INDEX OF SUBSIDIARIES, BRAND NAMES AND AFFILIATIONS, CONT.

Health Care Service Corporation; **Blue Cross and Blue Shield of Texas**
Health Design Plus LLC; **Premier Inc**
Health Dialog; **Rite Aid Corporation**
Health Guard 360; **Ping An Healthcare and Technology Company Limited**
Health Industry Technology Trust; **Intalere Inc**
Health Net Community Solutions Inc; **Health Net Inc**
Health Net Life Insurance Company; **Health Net Inc**
Health Net LLC; **Health Net Inc**
Health Net of California Inc; **Health Net Inc**
Health Options Inc; **Blue Cross and Blue Shield of Florida Inc**
Health Plans Inc; **Harvard Pilgrim Health Care Inc**
Health Support Center; **LifePoint Health Inc**
Healthcare Management Administrators; **Cambia Health Solutions Inc**
HealtheIntent; **Cerner Corporation**
HealthiNation Inc; **GoodRx Holdings Inc**
HealthNow Systems Inc; **HealthNow New York Inc**
HealthSource Global Staffing; **AMN Healthcare Services Inc**
HealthSun; **Anthem Inc**
Healthy Blue Living; **Blue Care Network of Michigan**
Heartland; **ProMedica Senior Care**
HearUSA Hearing Care Network; **HearUSA Inc**
Hellman & Friedlman LLC; **Medline Industries Inc**
Hellman & Friedman LLC; **Cordis Corporation**
Hellman & Friedman LLC; **MultiPlan Inc**
Helomics; **Predictive Oncology Inc**
Hemasphere; **Haemonetics Corporation**
Hemet Valley Medical Center; **KPC Healthcare Inc**
Henry Ford Hospital; **Henry Ford Health System**
Henry Ford Macomb Hospital in Clinton Township; **Henry Ford Health System**
Henry Ford West Bloomfield Hospital; **Henry Ford Health System**
Henry Ford Wyandotte Hospital; **Henry Ford Health System**
Henry Schein; **Henry Schein Inc**
Henty Ford Allegiance Health; **Henry Ford Health System**
Hepcludex; **Gilead Sciences Inc**
HeRO Graft; **Merit Medical Systems Inc**
HIG Capital; **Jenny Craig Inc**
Highmark Blue Cross Blue Shield of Western New Yor; **HealthNow New York Inc**

Highmark Blue Shield of Northeastern New York; **HealthNow New York Inc**
Highmark Inc; **Highmark Health**
Highmark Inc; **HealthNow New York Inc**
Hilcrest Healthcare System; **Ardent Health Services LLC**
Hillrom; **Hill-Rom Holdings Inc**
HiRes 3D; **Advanced Bionics LLC**
HiResolution Bionic Ear System; **Advanced Bionics LLC**
Hitachi Healthcare Americas Corporation; **Fujifilm Healthcare Americas Corporation**
Hi-VNI; **Vapotherm Inc**
HM Health Solutions; **Highmark Health**
HM Insurance Group LLC; **Highmark Health**
HMO Louisiana Inc; **Blue Cross and Blue Shield of Louisiana**
HMS Holdings Corp; **HMS**
Hoag Memorial Presbyterian; **Providence**
Holiday Inn & Suites Mexico - Medica Sur; **Medica Sur SAB de CV**
Horizon BCBSNJ Dental; **Horizon Healthcare Services Inc**
Horizon Blue Cross Blue Shield of New Jersey; **Horizon Healthcare Services Inc**
Horizon Casualty Services; **Horizon Healthcare Services Inc**
Horizon NJ Health; **Horizon Healthcare Services Inc**
Hospice of Charleston; **Kindred at Home**
Houston Methodist Academic Institute; **Houston Methodist**
Houston Methodist Breast Care; **Houston Methodist**
Houston Methodist Emergency Care; **Houston Methodist**
Houston Methodist Hospital; **Houston Methodist**
Houston Methodist Hospital Foundation; **Houston Methodist**
Houston Methodist Imaging; **Houston Methodist**
Houston Methodist Institute for Technology; **Houston Methodist**
Houston Methodist Outpatient Center; **Houston Methodist**
HPN217; **Harpoon Therapeutics Inc**
HPN328; **Harpoon Therapeutics Inc**
HPN424; **Harpoon Therapeutics Inc**
HPN536; **Harpoon Therapeutics Inc**
hStream; **HealthStream Inc**
HT Intermediate Company LLC; **HealthTronics Inc**
Humalog; **Eli Lilly and Company**
Humana Inc; **Conviva Care Centers**
Humana Inc; **Kindred at Home**
Humana Inc; **Kindred Healthcare LLC**
HVHC Inc; **Highmark Health**
Hydrofiber; **ConvaTec Inc**

HyFlex; **Ansell Limited**
hystrix medical AG; **Mediclinic International plc**
IBM iConnect; **IBM Watson Health**
IBM Micromedex; **IBM Watson Health**
IBM Phytel; **IBM Watson Health**
IBM Watson Health; **Mercy**
ICLUSIG; **Incyte Corporation**
Icon; **Cynosure Inc**
ICU Medical MedNet; **ICU Medical Inc**
IDEXX VetLab; **IDEXX Laboratories Inc**
IFC LLC; **InfuSystem Holdings Inc**
Ifetroban; **Cumberland Pharmaceuticals Inc**
iFuse; **SI-BONE Inc**
iFuse 3D; **SI-BONE Inc**
iKnowMed; **US Oncology Inc**
ImmunogenomicsID; **Personalis Inc**
ImmunoID NeXT Platform; **Personalis Inc**
immunoSEQ; **Adaptive Biotechnologies Corporation**
Impella; **Abiomed Inc**
INBONE; **Wright Medical Group NV**
InClinic; **Sigma Healthcare Limited**
INFINITI; **Cordis Corporation**
Infinity; **Draegerwerk AG & Co KGaA**
InflammaDry; **Quidel Corporation**
InfuSystem Holdings USA Inc; **InfuSystem Holdings Inc**
InfuSystem Inc; **InfuSystem Holdings Inc**
IngenioRx; **Anthem Inc**
Innovian; **Draegerwerk AG & Co KGaA**
INSPIRIS RESILIA; **Edwards Lifesciences Corporation**
InstaCare; **Intermountain Healthcare**
Institut Straumann AG; **Straumann Holding AG**
Institute of Mental Health; **National Healthcare Group Pte Ltd**
Instradent AG; **Straumann Holding AG**
Intalere Choice; **Intalere Inc**
Intalere Insurance Services; **Intalere Inc**
Integra; **Integra LifeSciences Holdings Corporation**
Intelligent Surgical Unit; **TransEnterix Inc**
Intense Pulsed Light; **Lumenis Ltd**
Interacoustics; **Demant AS**
Intermountain Home Care; **Intermountain Healthcare**
Intermountain Medical Center Campus; **Intermountain Healthcare**
Intermountain Medical Group; **Intermountain Healthcare**
International Business Machines Corporation; **IBM Watson Health**
International Business Machines Corporation (IBM); **Mercy**
International Center; **MD Anderson Cancer Center**

INDEX OF SUBSIDIARIES, BRAND NAMES AND AFFILIATIONS, CONT.

INDEX OF SUBSIDIARIES, BRAND NAMES AND AFFILIATIONS, CONT.

INDEX OF SUBSIDIARIES, BRAND NAMES AND AFFILIATIONS, CONT.

INDEX OF SUBSIDIARIES, BRAND NAMES AND AFFILIATIONS, CONT.

INDEX OF SUBSIDIARIES, BRAND NAMES AND AFFILIATIONS, CONT.

INDEX OF SUBSIDIARIES, BRAND NAMES AND AFFILIATIONS, CONT.

INDEX OF SUBSIDIARIES, BRAND NAMES AND AFFILIATIONS, CONT.

INDEX OF SUBSIDIARIES, BRAND NAMES AND AFFILIATIONS, CONT.

A Short HealthCare Industry Glossary

3DCRT: Three-dimensional conformal radiotherapy (3DCRT) is a method of radiation therapy whereby PET CAT and other imaging technologies are used to more precisely map tumors or tissues to be treated with radiation. The intent is to better focus the radiation and limit damage to surrounding tissues. (Also, see "Image Guided Radiation Therapy (IGRT).")

510(k): An application filed with the FDA for a new medical device to show that the apparatus is "substantially equivalent" to one that is already marketed.

Abbreviated New Drug Application (ANDA): An application filed with the FDA showing that a substance is the same as an existing, previously approved drug (i.e., a generic version).

Absorption, Distribution, Metabolism and Excretion (ADME): In clinical trials, the bodily processes studied to determine the extent and duration of systemic exposure to a drug.

ACA: See "Affordable Care Act (ACA)."

Accountable Care Organization (ACO): A network of health care providers, including hospitals and primary and specialty care physicians, that provides care and services. The intent is to create large health systems featuring virtually all possible types of specialties and care. The intent is to modernize health care delivery, foster care via teams of doctors, improve communications and efficiency, and make better use of resources such as digital patient records.

Accountable Health Plan: See "Accountable Care Organization (ACO)."

ACO: See "Accountable Care Organization (ACO)."

Adaptive Trial Design: A process in which drug trials are altered or improved in response to trial progression. Recent discoveries may be introduced, and trials may proceed despite the fact that the drugs involved may be successful in only a small number of patients that share specific variables such as DNA defects.

ADME: See "Absorption, Distribution, Metabolism and Excretion (ADME)."

Adverse Event (AE): In clinical trials, a condition not observed at baseline or worsened if present at baseline. Sometimes called Treatment Emergent Signs and Symptoms (TESS).

AE: See "Adverse Event (AE)."

Affordable Care Act (ACA): Short for Patient Protection and Affordable Care Act. Sometimes called Obamacare. Federal Regulations established in March 2010 that greatly expand government oversight of the availability of health care insurance, including Medicaid, Medicare and private insurance. The act also expands regulation of medical practices and pricing.

Alternate Site Care: Health care that was previously provided in general hospitals, but is now offered in less costly, alternate sites. Examples of alternate care include home IV therapy, outpatient surgery centers, rehabilitation units within nursing homes and free-standing centers providing dialysis, radiation therapy and imaging.

Analytics: Generally refers to the deep examination of massive amounts of data, often on a continual or real-time basis. The goal is to discover deeper insights, make recommendations or generate predictions. Advanced analytics includes such techniques as big data, predictive analytics, text analytics, data mining, forecasting, optimization and simulation.

ANDA: See "Abbreviated New Drug Application (ANDA)."

Angiogenesis: Blood vessel formation, typically in the growth of malignant tissue.

Angioplasty: The re-opening of a blood vessel by non-surgical techniques such as balloon dilation or laser, or through surgery.

Antibody: A protein produced by white blood cells in response to a foreign substance. Each antibody can bind only to one specific antigen. See "Antigen."

Antigen: A foreign substance that causes the immune system to create an antibody. See "Antibody."

APAC: Asia Pacific Advisory Committee. A multi-country committee representing the Asia and Pacific region.

Apoptosis: A normal cellular process leading to the termination of a cell's life.

Applied Research: The application of compounds, processes, materials or other items discovered during basic research to practical uses. The goal is to move discoveries along to the final development phase.

Arthroscopy: The examination of the interior of a joint using a type of endoscope that is inserted into the joint through a small incision. See "Endoscope."

Assay: A laboratory test to identify and/or measure the amount of a particular substance in a sample. Types of assays include endpoint assays, in which a single measurement is made at a fixed time: kinetic assays, in which increasing amounts of a product are formed with time and are monitored at multiple points: microbiological assays, which measure the concentration of antimicrobials in biological material: and immunological assays, in which analysis or measurement is based on antigen-antibody reactions.

Baby Boomer: Generally refers to people born from 1946 to 1964. In the U.S., the initial number of Baby Boomers totaled about 78 million. The term evolved to describe the children of soldiers and war industry workers who were involved in World War II and who began forming families after the war's end. In 2011, the oldest Baby Boomers began reaching the traditional retirement age of 65.

Baseline: A set of data used in clinical studies, or other types of research, for control or comparison.

Basic Research: Attempts to discover compounds, materials, processes or other items that may be largely or entirely new and/or unique. Basic research may start with a theoretical concept that has yet to be proven. The goal is to create discoveries that can be moved along to applied research. Basic research is sometimes referred to as "blue sky" research.

Behavioral Health: The assessment and treatment of mental health and/or substance abuse disorders. Substance abuse includes alcohol and other drugs.

Big Pharma: The top tier of pharmaceutical companies in terms of sales and profits (e.g., Pfizer, Merck, Johnson & Johnson).

Bioavailability: In pharmaceuticals, the rate and extent to which a drug is absorbed or is otherwise available to the treatment site in the body.

Bioequivalence: In pharmaceuticals, the demonstration that a drug's rate and extent of absorption are not significantly different from those of an existing drug that is already approved by the FDA. This is the basis upon which generic and brand name drugs are compared.

Biogenerics: Genetic versions of drugs that have been created via biotechnology. Also, see "Follow-on Biologics."

Bioinformatics: Research, development or application of computational tools and approaches for expanding the use of biological, medical, behavioral or health data, including those to acquire, store, organize, archive, analyze or visualize such data. Bioinformatics is often applied to the study of genetic data. It applies principles of information sciences and technologies to make vast, diverse and complex life sciences data more understandable and useful.

Biologics: Drugs that are synthesized from living organisms. That is, drugs created using biotechnology, sometimes referred to as biopharmaceuticals. Specifically, biologics may be any virus, therapeutic serum, toxin, antitoxin, vaccine, blood, blood component or derivative, allergenic or analogous product, or arsphenamine or one of its derivatives used for the prevention, treatment or cure of disease. Also, see "Biologics License Application (BLA)," "Follow-on Biologics," and "Biopharmaceuticals."

Biologics License Application (BLA): An application to be submitted to the FDA when a firm wants to obtain permission to market a novel, new biological drug product. Specifically, these are drugs created through the use of biotechnology. It was formerly known as Product License Application (PLA). Also see "Biologics."

Biopharmaceuticals: That portion of the pharmaceutical industry focused on the use of biotechnology to create new drugs. A biopharmaceutical can be any biological compound that is intended to be used as a therapeutic drug, including recombinant proteins, monoclonal and polyclonal antibodies, antisense oligonucleotides, therapeutic genes, and recombinant and DNA vaccines. Also, see "Biologics."

Biosimilar: See "Follow-on Biologics."

Biotechnology: A set of powerful tools that employ living organisms (or parts of organisms) to make or modify products, improve plants or animals (including

humans) or develop microorganisms for specific uses. Biotechnology is most commonly thought of to include the development of human medical therapies and processes using recombinant DNA, cell fusion, other genetic techniques and bioremediation.

BLA: See "Biologics License Application (BLA)."

BPO: See "Business Process Outsourcing (BPO)."

Brachytherapy: A method of internal radiation therapy whereby tiny containers of radioactive material, sometimes referred to as "seeds," are implanted directly in contact with tissue that is afflicted with cancerous tumors. It is a common method of treating prostate cancer and is sometimes used for the treatment of breast cancer. These seeds are never removed from the body. They typically have a radioactive half-life of six months. Eventually, they emit virtually no radiation at all.

Brand: A marketing strategy that places a focus on the brand name of a product, service or firm in order to increase the brand's market share, increase sales, establish credibility, improve satisfaction, raise the profile of the firm and increase profits. Also, see "Brand."

Branding: A marketing strategy that places a focus on the brand name of a product, service or firm in order to increase the brand's market share, increase sales, establish credibility, improve satisfaction, raise the profile of the firm and increase profits. Also, see "Brand."

B-to-B, or B2B: See "Business-to-Business."

B-to-C, or B2C: See "Business-to-Consumer."

B-to-E, or B2E: See "Business-to-Employee."

B-to-G, or B2G: See "Business-to-Government."

Business Process Outsourcing (BPO): The process of hiring another company to handle business activities. BPO is one of the fastest-growing segments in the offshoring sector. Services include human resources management, billing and purchasing and call centers, as well as many types of customer service or marketing activities, depending on the industry involved. Also, see "Knowledge

Process Outsourcing (KPO)" and Business Transformation Outsourcing (BTO)."

Business Transformation Outsourcing (BTO): A segment within outsourcing in which the client company revamps its business processes with the goal of transforming its business by following a collaborative approach with its outsourced services provider.

Business-to-Business: An organization focused on selling products, services or data to commercial customers rather than individual consumers. Also known as B2B.

Business-to-Consumer: An organization focused on selling products, services or data to individual consumers rather than commercial customers. Also known as B2C.

Business-to-Employee: A corporate communications system, such as an intranet, aimed at conveying information from a company to its employees. Also known as B2E.

Business-to-Government: An organization focused on selling products, services or data to government units rather than commercial businesses or consumers. Also known as B2G.

CANDA: See "Computer-Assisted New Drug Application (CANDA)."

Capex: Capital expenditures.

Capitation: A method of contracting for health services in which care providers, such as physicians, receive a fixed, per-patient fee each year, rather than a payment for each office visit and each procedure. Also see "Fee-For-Service" and "Value-Based Reimbursement."

Captive Offshoring: Used to describe a company-owned offshore operation. For example, Microsoft owns and operates significant captive offshore research and development centers in China and elsewhere that are offshore from Microsoft's U.S. home base. Also see "Offshoring."

Carcinogen: A substance capable of causing cancer. A suspected carcinogen is a substance that may cause cancer in humans or animals but for which the evidence is not conclusive.

Cardiac Catheterization Laboratory: Facilities offering special diagnostic procedures for cardiac patients, including the introduction of a catheter into the interior of the heart by way of a vein or artery or by direct needle puncture. Procedures must be performed in a laboratory or a special procedure room.

Cardiac Intensive Care Services: Services provided in a unit staffed with specially trained nursing personnel and containing monitoring and specialized support or treatment equipment for patients who (because of heart seizure, open-heart surgery or other life-threatening conditions) require intensified, comprehensive observation and care. May include myocardial infarction care, pulmonary care, and heart transplant units.

Case Report Form (CRF): In clinical trials, a standard document used by clinicians to record and report subject data pertinent to the study protocol.

CAT Scan: See "Computed Tomography (CT)."

Catheter: A tubular instrument used to add or withdraw fluids. Heart or cardiac catheterization involves the passage of flexible catheters into the great vessels and chambers of the heart. IV catheters add intravenous fluids to the veins. Foley catheters withdraw fluid from the bladder. Significant recent advances in technology allow administration of powerful drug and diagnostic therapies via catheters.

CBER: See "Center for Biologics Evaluation and Research (CBER)."

CDC: See "Centers for Disease Control and Prevention (CDC)."

CDER: See "Center for Drug Evaluation and Research (CDER)."

CDRH: See "Center for Devices and Radiological Health (CDRH)."

Center for Biologics Evaluation and Research (CBER): The branch of the FDA responsible for the regulation of biological products, including blood, vaccines, therapeutics and related drugs and devices, to ensure purity, potency, safety, availability and effectiveness. www.fda.gov/cber

Center for Devices and Radiological Health (CDRH): The branch of the FDA responsible for the regulation of medical devices. www.fda.gov/cdrh

Center for Drug Evaluation and Research (CDER): The branch of the FDA responsible for the regulation of drug products. www.fda.gov/cder

Centers for Disease Control and Prevention (CDC): The federal agency charged with protecting the public health of the nation by providing leadership and direction in the prevention and control of diseases and other preventable conditions and responding to public health emergencies. Headquartered in Atlanta, it was established as an operating health agency within the U.S. Public Health Service on July 1, 1973. See www.cdc.gov.

Centers for Medicare and Medicaid Services (CMS): A federal agency responsible for administering Medicare and monitoring the states' operations of Medicaid. See www.cms.hhs.gov.

Chemotherapy: The treatment of cancer using anticancer drugs, often conducted in association with radiation therapy. See "Radiation Therapy."

Chromosome: A structure in the nucleus of a cell that contains genes. Chromosomes are found in pairs.

Class I Device: An FDA classification of medical devices for which general controls are sufficient to ensure safety and efficacy.

Class II Device: An FDA classification of medical devices for which performance standards and special controls are sufficient to ensure safety and efficacy.

Class III Device: An FDA classification of medical devices for which pre-market approval is required to ensure safety and efficacy, unless the device is substantially equivalent to a currently marketed device. See "510 K."

Clinical Research Associate (CRA): An individual responsible for monitoring clinical trial data to ensure compliance with study protocol and FDA GCP regulations.

Clinical Trial: See "Phase I Clinical Trials," along with definitions for Phase II, Phase III and Phase IV.

Clone: A group of identical genes, cells or organisms derived from one ancestor. A clone is an identical copy. "Dolly" the sheep is a famous case of a clone of an animal. Also see "Cloning (Reproductive)" and "Cloning (Therapeutic)."

Cloning (Reproductive): A method of reproducing an exact copy of an animal or, potentially, an exact copy of a human being. A scientist removes the nucleus from a donor's unfertilized egg, inserts a nucleus from the animal to be copied and then stimulates the nucleus to begin dividing to form an embryo. In the case of a mammal, such as a human, the embryo would then be implanted in the uterus of a host female. Also see "Cloning (Therapeutic)."

Cloning (Therapeutic): A method of reproducing exact copies of cells needed for research or for the development of replacement tissue or organs. A scientist removes the nucleus from a donor's unfertilized egg, inserts a nucleus from the animal whose cells are to be copied and then stimulates the nucleus to begin dividing to form an embryo. However, the embryo is never allowed to grow to any significant stage of development. Instead, it is allowed to grow for a few hours or days, and stem cells are then removed from it for use in regenerating tissue. Also see "Cloning (Reproductive)."

CMS: See "Centers for Medicare and Medicaid Services (CMS)."

COBRA: See "Consolidated Omnibus Budget Reconciliation Act (COBRA)."

Code of Federal Regulations (CFR): A codification of the general and permanent rules published in the Federal Register by the executive departments and agencies of the Federal Government. The code is divided into 50 titles that represent broad areas subject to federal regulation. Title 21 of the CFR covers FDA regulations.

Coinsurance (Co-insurance): A practice in some medical coverage plans, homeowners insurance, Medicare and other types of insurance coverage whereby the beneficiary is required to pay a set percentage of costs in certain circumstances. For example, the covered party may be required to pay 20% of costs.

Committee for Veterinary Medicinal Products (CVMP): A committee that is a veterinary equivalent of the CPMP (see "Committee on Proprietary Medicinal Products (CPMP)") in the EU. See "European Union (EU)."

Committee on Proprietary Medicinal Products (CPMP): A committee, composed of two people from each EU Member State (see "European Union (EU)"), that is responsible for the scientific evaluation and assessment of marketing applications for medicinal products in the EU. The CPMP is the major body involved in the harmonization of pharmaceutical regulations within the EU and receives administrative support from the European Medicines Evaluation Agency. See "European Medicines Evaluation Agency (EMEA)."

Compounding Pharmacy: Compounding pharmacies are those that combine or alter drugs in order to meet a physician's prescription requirements. Examples include altering the contents of a pill so that it becomes a drinkable formula, modifying chemotherapy drugs to meet a specific patient'sneeds or adding flavoring to a medicine to make it more acceptable to a child.

Computed Tomography (CT): An imaging method that uses x-rays to create cross-sectional pictures of the body. The technique is frequently referred to as a "CAT Scan." A patient lies on a narrow platform while the machine's x-ray beam rotates around him or her. Small detectors inside the scanner measure the amount of x-rays that make it through the part of the body being studied. A computer takes this information and uses it to create several individual images, called slices. These images can be stored, viewed on a monitor, or printed on film. Three-dimensional models of organs can be created by stacking the individual slices together. The newest machines are capable of operating at 256 slice levels, creating very high resolution images in a short period of time.

Computer-Assisted New Drug Application (CANDA): An electronic submission of a new drug application (NDA) to the FDA.

Concierge Care: A medical practice in which patients typically receive enhanced access to physicians by paying a monthly or annual retainer fee. Services may include same-day or next-day appointments and after-hours access to physicians via pagers, cellphone or email.

Consolidated Omnibus Budget Reconciliation Act (COBRA): A federal law that requires employers to offer uninterrupted health care coverage to certain employees and their beneficiaries whose group coverage has been terminated.

Continuing Care Retirement Communities (CCRCs): Communities that provide coordinated housing and health-related services to older individuals under an agreement which may last as little as one year or as long as the life of the individual.

Continuity of Care: A systematic approach to a patient's care through the patient's continuous relationship with a team of health care providers, led by the primary care physician. In order to facilitate this approach, all of the patient's care providers must have real time access to the patient's health records, which is one of the goals of Electronic Health Records (EHRs) and Electronic Health Interchanges (EMIs). See "Electronic Health Record (EHR)."

Contract Research Organization (CRO): An independent organization that contracts with a client to conduct part of the work on a study or research project. For example, drug and medical device makers frequently outsource clinical trials and other research work to CROs.

Coordinator: In clinical trials, the person at an investigative site who handles the administrative responsibilities of the trial, acts as a liaison between the investigative site and the sponsor, and reviews data and records during a monitoring visit.

Copayment (Co-payment): An amount that is commonly required to be paid by the patient under health care plans including Medicare. For example, the patient may be required to pay $20 toward the cost of a doctor's office visit, or $15 toward the cost of a prescription drug.

COSTART: In medical and drug product development, a dictionary of adverse events and body systems used for coding and classifying adverse events.

CPMP: See "Committee on Proprietary Medicinal Products (CPMP)."

CRA: See "Clinical Research Associate (CRA)."

CRF: See "Case Report Form (CRF)."

CRM: See "Customer Relationship Management (CRM)."

CRT: Conformal radiotherapy. See "3DCRT."

Cryoablation: A technology based on the use of extremely cold temperatures delivered via a catheter or other device to treat tissues. It is an accepted method of treating cancer of the prostate. It also has applications in the prevention of heart arrhythmia.

Cryosurgery: See "Cryoablation."

CT: See "Computed Tomography (CT)."

Current Procedural Terminology (CPT): The most widely accepted medical nomenclature used to report medical procedures and services under public and private health insurance programs. CPT is also used for administrative management purposes, such as claims processing and developing guidelines for medical care review.

Customer Relationship Management (CRM): Refers to the automation, via sophisticated software, of business processes involving existing and prospective customers. CRM may cover aspects such as sales (contact management and contact history), marketing (campaign management and telemarketing) and customer service (call center history and field service history). Well known providers of CRM software include Salesforce, which delivers via a Software as a Service model (see "Software as a Service (Saas)"), Microsoft and Oracle.

CVMP: See "Committee for Veterinary Medicinal Products (CVMP)."

Data and Safety Monitoring Board (DSMB): See "Data Monitoring Board (DMB)."

Data Monitoring Board (DMB): A committee that monitors the progress of a clinical trial and carefully observes the safety data.

Deductible (Insurance Deductible): The initial amount of a loss that must be paid by the insurance policy holder. For example, a typical automobile policy deductible is $500, which means that the first $500 of any loss must be paid by the policy holder before the insurance company will pay for a portion above $500.

Defibrillator: In medicine, an instrument used externally (as electrodes on the chest) or implanted (as a small device similar in size to a pacemaker) that delivers an electric shock to return the heart to its normal rhythm.

Demand Chain: A similar concept to a supply chain, but with an emphasis on the end user.

Demographics: The breakdown of the population into statistical categories such as age, income, education and sex.

Deoxyribonucleic Acid (DNA): The carrier of the genetic information that cells need to replicate and to produce proteins.

Development: The phase of research and development (R&D) in which researchers attempt to create new products from the results of discoveries and applications created during basic and applied research.

Device: In medical products, an instrument, apparatus, implement, machine, contrivance, implant, in vitro reagent or other similar or related article, including any component, part or accessory, that 1) is recognized in the official National Formulary or United States Pharmacopoeia or any supplement to them, 2) is intended for use in the diagnosis of disease or other conditions, or in the cure, mitigation, treatment or prevention of disease, in man or animals or 3) is intended to affect the structure of the body of man or animals and does not achieve any of its principal intended purposes through chemical action within or on the body of man or animals and is not dependent upon being metabolized for the achievement of any of its principal intended purposes.

Diagnostic Radioisotope Facility: A medical facility in which radioactive isotopes (radiopharmaceuticals) are used as tracers or indicators to detect an abnormal condition or disease in the body.

Dialysis: An artificial blood-filtering process used to clean the blood of patients with malfunctioning kidneys.

Dietary Supplements Sold as Food: Legal diet aids that do not require licensing under medical regulations. Typically, dietary supplements sold as food are offered in powder, tablet, pill or capsule form.

Direct Primary Care: A physicians' business model whereby patients pay a monthly fee for unlimited access to their doctors. Additional enhanced services, such as preventative care and email access to doctors, are often added in a comprehensive package. An important reason enabling direct primary care firms to offer reasonable rates is the fact that the patient pays directly, so there is no overhead involved in dealing with insurance companies.

Disease Management: The use of programs that closely monitor the condition of a patient on a regular basis while educating and motivating that person about lifestyle and treatment alternatives that will reduce the impacts of certain conditions.

Distributor: An individual or business involved in marketing, warehousing and/or shipping of products manufactured by others to a specific group of end users. Distributors do not sell to the general public. In order to develop a competitive advantage, distributors often focus on serving one industry or one set of niche clients. For example, within the medical industry, there are major distributors that focus on providing pharmaceuticals, surgical supplies or dental supplies to clinics and hospitals.

DMB: See "Data Monitoring Board (DMB)."

DNA: See "Deoxyribonucleic Acid (DNA)."

DNA Chip: A revolutionary tool used to identify mutations in genes like BRCA1 and BRCA2. The chip, which consists of a small glass plate encased in plastic, is manufactured using a process similar to the one used to make computer microchips. On the surface, each chip contains synthetic single-stranded DNA sequences identical to a normal gene.

Doctor of Nursing Practice (DNP): A designation for a nurse who has completed rigorous educational, clinical and testing requirements in order to achieve doctoral-level nurse status, with an emphasis on clinical competence. This is a step beyond a Nurse Practitioner. A Doctor of Nursing Practice may use the DrNP designation after their names, or begin their names with "Dr." as a title, but they do not have the same status as MDs. In many states in the U.S., DNPs will be able to write prescriptions and operate independent health clinics, but regulations may vary from state to state, and they will not have all of the authority enjoyed by MDs. Many top schools of nursing also offer Ph.D. programs for nurses, typically with an emphasis on preparing them to be professors of nursing and educational leaders. Also, see "Nurse Practitioner."

Dosimetry: The accurate measurement of doses of radiation as used in medical treatment and imaging. The sources of such radiation may be x-ray, radiation therapy used for cancer treatment or other types of radiation.

Drug Utilization Review: A quantitative assessment of patient drug use and physicians' patterns of prescribing drugs in an effort to determine the usefulness of drug therapy.

DSMB: See "Data and Safety Monitoring Board (DSMB)."

EBRT: See "External Beam Radiation Therapy (EBRT)."

Echo Boomers: See "Generation Y."

Ecology: The study of relationships among all living organisms and the environment, especially the totality or pattern of interactions: a view that includes all plant and animal species and their unique contributions to a particular habitat.

EDI: See "Electronic Data Interchange (EDI)."

EEG: See "Electroencephalography (EEG)."

Efficacy: A drug or medical product's ability to effectively produce beneficial results within a patient.

EFGCP: See "European Forum for Good Clinical Practices (EFGCP)."

EHR: See "Electronic Health Record (EHR)."

ELA: See "Establishment License Application (ELA)."

Electroencephalography (EEG): Measures electrical activity in the brain.

Electronic Data Interchange (EDI): An accepted standard format for the exchange of data between various companies' networks. EDI allows for the transfer of e-mail as well as orders, invoices and other files from one company to another.

Electronic Health Record (EHR): An electronic record of patient health care information which can be updated by all of a patient's care providers from any location. Information may include patient demographics, details regarding progress and care, medications, vital signs, past medical history, immunizations, laboratory data and radiology reports. The EHR automates and streamlines workflow throughout the care spectrum.

Electroporation: A health care technology that uses short pulses of electric current (DC) to create openings (pores) in the membranes of cancerous cells, thus leading to death of the cells. It has potential as a treatment for prostate cancer. In the laboratory, it is a means of introducing foreign proteins or DNA into living cells.

EMEA: The region comprised of Europe, the Middle East and Africa.

Employee Assistance Program (EAP): A program designed to help employees, employers and family members find solutions to workplace and personal problems.

EMR: Electronic Medical Record. See "Electronic Health Record (EHR)."

Endoscope: A tiny, flexible tube-shaped instrument with a fiber optic light and a video camera lens at the end. It is inserted into the body through a natural body opening or a small incision, and has both diagnostic and therapeutic capabilities. Laparoscopic surgery is conducted in a minimally invasive manner using the endoscope to enable the surgeon to see the tissue being operated on. Such surgery is often conducted through an incision as small as one or two centimeters in length. Consequently, patients tend to heal very quickly after such surgery.

Enterprise Resource Planning (ERP): An integrated information system that helps manage all aspects of a business, including accounting, ordering and human resources, typically across all locations of a major corporation or organization. ERP is considered to be a critical tool for management of large organizations. Suppliers of ERP tools include SAP and Oracle.

Enzyme: A protein that acts as a catalyst, affecting the chemical reactions in cells.

ERP: See "Enterprise Resource Planning (ERP)."

Establishment License Application (ELA): Required for the approval of a biologic (see "Biologics"). It permits a specific facility to manufacture a biological product for commercial purposes. Compare to "Product License Agreement (PLA)."

ESWL: See "Extracorporeal Shock Wave Lithotripter (ESWL)."

Etiology: The study of the causes or origins of diseases.

EU: See "European Union (EU)."

EU Competence: The jurisdiction in which the European Union (EU) can take legal action.

European Community (EC): See "European Union (EU)."

European Forum for Good Clinical Practices (EFGCP): The organization dedicated to finding common ground in Europe on the implementation of Good Clinical Practices. See "Good Clinical Practices (GCP)." www.efgcp.org

European Medicines Evaluation Agency (EMEA): The European agency responsible for supervising and coordinating applications for marketing medicinal products in the European Union (see "European Union (EU)" and "Committee on Proprietary Medicinal Products (CPMP)"). The EMEA is headquartered in the U.K. www.eudraportal.eudra.org

European Union (EU): A consolidation of European countries (member states) functioning as one body to facilitate trade. Previously known as the European Community (EC). The EU has a unified currency, the Euro. See europa.eu.int.

Exclusive Provider Organization: Technically the same as an HMO, with the exception that the organization provides coverage only for services from contracted providers. See "Health Maintenance Organization (HMO)."

External Beam Radiation Therapy (EBRT): The application of radiation to a patient via external sources, such as X-ray, gamma ray or proton beam, in order to kill cancerous cells and shrink tumors.

Extracorporeal Shock Wave Lithotripter (ESWL): A medical device used for treating stones in the kidney or urethra. The device disintegrates kidney stones noninvasively through the transmission of acoustic shock waves directed at the stones.

FASB: See "Financial Accounting Standards Board (FASB)."

FD&C Act: See "Federal Food Drug and Cosmetic Act (FD&C Act)."

FDA: See "Food and Drug Administration (FDA)."

Federal Food, Drug and Cosmetic Act (FD&C Act): A set of laws passed by the U.S. Congress, which controls, among other things, residues in food and feed.

Fee-For-Service: Payment to health care providers, such as physicians, calculated for each service provided, such as an office visit, MRI, blood test or other procedure. The more services that a patient receives, the higher the bill. Also, see "Capitation" and "Value-Based Reimbursement" for discussions of alternatives to Fee-For-Service.

Fee-For-Service Equivalency: The amount of reimbursement for treatment of patients via a capitation payment schedule compared to a fee-for-service reimbursement. See "Capitation" and "Fee-For-Service."

Financial Accounting Standards Board (FASB): An independent organization that establishes the Generally Accepted Accounting Principles (GAAP).

Fissure: A long narrow crack or opening.

Follow-on Biologics: A term used to describe generic versions of drugs that have been created using biotechnology. Because biotech drugs ("biologics") are made from living cells, a generic version of a drug probably won't be biochemically identical to the original branded version of the drug. Consequently, they are described as "follow-on" biologics to set them apart. Since these drugs won't be exactly the same as the originals, there are concerns that they may not be as safe or effective unless they go through clinical trials for proof of quality. In Europe, these drugs are referred to as "biosimilars." See "Biologics."

Food and Drug Administration (FDA): The U.S. government agency responsible for the enforcement of the Federal Food, Drug and Cosmetic Act, ensuring industry compliance with laws regulating products in commerce. The FDA's mission is to protect the public from harm and encourage technological advances that hold the promise of benefiting society. www.fda.gov

Formulary: A preferred list of drug products that typically limits the number of drugs available within a therapeutic class for purposes of drug purchasing, dispensing and/or reimbursement. A government body, third-party insurer or health plan, or an institution may compile a formulary. Some institutions or health plans develop closed (i.e. restricted) formularies where only those drug products listed can be dispensed in that institution or reimbursed by the health plan. Other formularies may have no restrictions (open formulary) or may have certain restrictions such as higher patient cost-sharing requirements for off-formulary drugs.

Functional Imaging: The uses of PET scan, MRI and other advanced imaging technology to see how an area of the body is functioning and responding. For example, brain activity can be viewed, and the reaction of cancer tumors to therapies can be judged using functional imaging.

GAAP: See "Generally Accepted Accounting Principles (GAAP)."

Gamma Knife: A unique type of radiation therapy with tissue-sparing properties. It involves focusing low-dose gamma radiation on a tumor, while exposing only a small amount of healthy, nearby tissue to radiation. It is often used to treat certain brain cancers.

Gated Benefit Plans: Health insurance plans that require holders to pass general health tests such as screenings for diabetes, thyroid problems and the presence of nicotine to qualify for higher levels of coverage. To keep coverage, holders must have annual physicals and procedures such as mammograms and colonoscopies if over age 50.

GCP: See "Good Clinical Practices (GCP)."

GDP: See "Gross Domestic Product (GDP)."

Gene: A working subunit of DNA: the carrier of inheritable traits.

Gene Chip: See "DNA Chip."

Gene Therapy: A type of treatment based on first identifying the fact that a patient has a specific gene mutation related to a specific disease, followed by the introduction of healthy genes into the patient's body with the goal of altering or replacing the defective genes. This is the Holy Grail of the biotechnology industry, as it offers the potential to cure otherwise incurable diseases. It has also proven to be extremely difficult to carry out without significant side effects. A major commercial hurdle was passed in late 2012, when the European Medicines Agency (EMA) approved a gene therapy to treat a rare lipoprotein lipase (LPL) deficiency. The therapy, called Glybera and developed by Dutch biotech company uniQure, was the first approved gene therapy drug in the Western world.

Generally Accepted Accounting Principles (GAAP): A set of accounting standards administered by the Financial Accounting Standards Board (FASB) and enforced by the U.S. Security and Exchange Commission (SEC). GAAP is primarily used in the U.S.

Generation M: A very loosely defined term that is sometimes used to refer to young people who have grown up in the digital age. "M" may refer to any or all of media-saturated, mobile or multi-tasking. The term was most notably used in a Kaiser Family Foundation report published in 2005, "Generation M: Media in the Lives of 8-18 year olds." Also, see "Generation Y" and "Generation Z."

Generation X: A loosely-defined and variously-used term that describes people born between approximately 1965 and 1980, but other time frames are recited. Generation X is often referred to as a group influential in defining tastes in consumer goods, entertainment and/or political and social matters.

Generation Y: Refers to people born between approximately 1982 and 2002. In the U.S., they number more than 90 million, making them the largest generation segment in the nation's history. They are also known as Echo Boomers, Millennials or the Millennial Generation. These are children of the Baby Boom generation who will be filling the work force as Baby Boomers retire.

Generation Z: Some people refer to Generation Z as people born after 1991. Others use the beginning date of 2001, or refer to the era of 1994 to 2004. Members of Generation Z are considered to be natural and rapid adopters of the latest technologies.

Genetic Code: The sequence of nucleotides, determining the sequence of amino acids in protein synthesis.

Genetically Modified (GM) Foods: Food crops that are bioengineered to resist herbicides, diseases or insects: have higher nutritional value than non-engineered plants: produce a higher yield per acre: and/or last longer on the shelf. Additional traits may include resistance to temperature and moisture extremes. Agricultural animals also may be genetically modified organisms.

Genetically Modified Organism (GMO): An organism that has undergone genome modification by the insertion of a foreign gene. The genetic material of a GMO is not found through mating or natural recombination.

Genetics: The study of the process of heredity.

Genome: A genome is an organism's complete set of DNA, including all of its genes. Each genome contains all of the information needed to build and maintain that organism. In humans, a copy of the entire genome—more than 3 billion DNA base pairs—is contained in all cells that have a nucleus.

Genomics: The study of genes, their role in diseases and our ability to manipulate them.

GI Generation: Generally considered to be Americans who were born between 1901 and 1924. They made up the bulk of people who entered the U.S. Armed Forces during World War II. "GI" stands for Government Issue, a reference to the equipment issued to members of the military.

Globalization: The increased mobility of goods, services, labor, technology and capital throughout the world. Although globalization is not a new development, its pace has increased with the advent of new technologies.

GLP: See "Good Laboratory Practices (GLP)."

GM: See "Genetically-Modified (GM) Foods."

GMO: See "Genetically Modified Organism (GMO)"

GMP: See "Good Manufacturing Practices (GMP)."

Good Clinical Practices (GCP): FDA regulations and guidelines that define the responsibilities of the key figures involved in a clinical trial, including the sponsor, the investigator, the monitor and the Institutional Review Board. See "Institutional Review Board (IRB)."

Good Laboratory Practices (GLP): A collection of regulations and guidelines to be used in laboratories where research is conducted on drugs, biologics or devices that are intended for submission to the FDA.

Good Manufacturing Practices (GMP): A collection of regulations and guidelines to be used in manufacturing drugs, biologics and medical devices.

Gross Domestic Product (GDP): The total value of a nation's output, income and expenditures produced with a nation's physical borders.

Gross National Product (GNP): A country's total output of goods and services from all forms of economic activity measured at market prices for one calendar year. It differs from Gross Domestic Product (GDP) in that GNP includes income from investments made in foreign nations.

Group Practice Without Walls: A "quasi" group formed when a hospital sponsors or provides capital to physicians for the establishment of a practice to share administrative expenses while remaining independent practitioners.

Health Indemnity Insurance: Provides traditional insurance coverage, after a deductible, for specified health care needs. Typically, the patient can go to any physician or any hospital, and there is no aspect of managed care involved.

Health Information Exchange (HIE): An electronic network for health care providers that enables easy access to patients' health care records.

Health Maintenance Organization (HMO): An insurance entity that provides managed health care services. An HMO functions as a form of health care insurance which is sold on a group basis. The HMO contracts with doctors, hospitals, labs and other medical facilities for low rates in exchange for high volume. For the patient, only visits to professionals within the HMO network are covered in the highest possible amount by the HMO. The patient selects a primary care physician who is approved by the HMO. For care, the patient first visits the primary care physician who may refer the patient to a specialist on an as-needed basis. Also see "Managed Care" and "Preferred Provider Organization (PPO)."

Health Reimbursement Account (HRA): A form of health care coverage plan provided to employees by their employer. Under an HRA, the employer places a given amount of money into a special account each year for the employee to spend on health care. The employer also provides a high-deductible health coverage plan. The employee elects when and how to spend the money in the account on health care. Because of the high deductible, the employee's share of the monthly premium tends to be much lower than under an HMO or PPO, but the employee faces the burden of paying the high deductible when necessary. Unspent funds in the account can roll over from year to year so that the account grows, but the employee loses the fund balance when leaving the employer.

Health Savings Account (HSA): A plan that combines a tax-free savings and investment account (somewhat similar to a 401k) with a high-deductible health coverage plan. The intent is to give the consumer more incentive to control health care costs by reducing unnecessary care while shopping for the best prices. The consumer contributes pre-tax dollars annually to a savings account (up to $2,850 for an individual or $5,650 for a family, as of 2007). The employer may or may not match part of that contribution. The account may be invested in stocks, bonds or mutual funds. It grows tax-free, but the money may be spent only on health care. Unspent money stays in the account at the end of each year. The consumer must purchase an insurance policy or health care plan with an annual deductible of at least $1,000 for individuals or $2,000 for families.

HESC: See "Human Embryonic Stem Cell (HESC)."

HHS: See "U.S. Department of Health and Human Services (HHS)."

HIE: See "Health Information Exchange (HIE)."

HIFU: See "High Intensity Focused Ultrasound (HIFU)."

High Intensity Focused Ultrasound (HIFU): A method of using sound waves to produce a focused amount of high heat in tumors or tissues in order to destroy them through thermoablation. Target temperature is about 70 to 90 degrees Centigrade (158 to 194 degrees Fahrenheit). This is a noninvasive treatment that is already in wide use in Europe, Asia and Canada for treatment of particular conditions, particularly cancer of the prostate. Late stage clinical trials were being conducted in the U.S. as of 2007. Several additional uses are being studied, including treatment of cancer of the kidney.

HIPAA: The Health Insurance Portability and Accountability Act of 1996, which demands that all billing and patient data must be exchanged electronically between care givers and insurance payers. A major focus of HIPAA requirements is the protection of patient data privacy.

HMO: See "Health Maintenance Organization (HMO)."

Home Care Agencies: Home health agencies, home care aid organizations and hospices.

Human Embryonic Stem Cell (HESC): See "Stem Cells."

Human Resources Outsourcing (HRO): Refers to the practice of hiring an outsourced services provider to manage an organization's day-to-day human resources needs.

ICD9: International Classification of Diseases - Version 9. A government coding system used for classifying diseases and diagnoses.

IFRS: See "International Financials Reporting Standards (IFRS)."

IGRT: See "Image Guided Radiation Therapy (IGRT)."

Image Guided Radiation Therapy (IGRT): A radiation technique that takes advantage of sophisticated imaging technologies in order to best target radiation therapy. Prostate cancer is often treated with IGRT. To treat that disease, tiny metal markers are implanted in the prostate using an outpatient procedure. The IGRT equipment is then able to locate the position of the prostate exactly by determining the location of the markers in real time. Varian is a leading manufacturer of IGRT equipment. The technology is similar to IMRT, but better enables radiation technicians to use ultrasound, CT or X-ray images to line up the radiation beam with the intended target. Also, see "Intensity Modulated Radiation Therapy (IMRT)."

Imaging: In medicine, the viewing of the body's organs through external, high-tech means. This reduces the need for broad exploratory surgery. These advances, along with new types of surgical instruments, have made minimally invasive surgery possible. Imaging includes MRI (magnetic resonance imaging), CT (computed tomography or CAT scan), MEG (magnetoencephalography), improved x-ray technology, mammography, ultrasound and angiography.

Imaging Contrast Agent: A molecule or molecular complex that increases the intensity of the signal detected by an imaging technique, including MRI and ultrasound. An MRI contrast agent, for example, might contain gadolinium attached to a targeting antibody. The antibody would bind to a specific target, a metastatic melanoma cell for example, while the gadolinium would increase the magnetic signal detected by the MRI scanner.

Immunoassay: An immunological assay. Types include agglutination, complement-fixation, precipitation, immunodiffusion and electrophoretic assays. Each type of assay utilizes either a particular type of antibody or a specific support medium (such as a gel) to determine the amount of antigen present.

Immunotherapy: A biotech related therapy that based on a strategy to stimulate and/or suppress the immune system in order to help the body fight cancer, infection, and other diseases. Some types of immunotherapy only target certain cells of the immune system. Others affect the immune system in a general way. Types of immunotherapy include cytokines, vaccines and certain monoclonal antibodies. Advancements in genetic sequencing and analysis are aiding significant advances in immunotherapy.

IMRT: See "Intensity Modulated Radiation Therapy (IMRT)."

In Vitro: Laboratory experiments conducted in the test tube, or otherwise, without using live animals and/or humans.

In Vivo: Laboratory experiments conducted with live animals and/or humans.

IND: See "Investigational New Drug Application (IND)."

Independent Practice Organization (IPO): A legal entity that holds managed care contracts. The IPO then contracts with physicians, often in solo practice, to provide care either on a fee-for-services or capitated basis. The purpose of an IPO is to assist solo physicians in obtaining managed care contracts, while allowing them to maintain their own private practices. (Sometimes referred to as Independent Practice Association.)

Indication: Refers to a specific disease, illness or condition for which a drug is approved as a treatment. Typically, a new drug is first approved for one indication. Then, an application to the FDA is later made for approval of additional indications.

Induced Pluripotent State Cell (IPSC): A human stem cell produced without human cloning or the use of human embryos or eggs. Adult cells are drawn from a skin biopsy and treated with four reprogramming factors, rendering cells that can produce all human cell types and grow indefinitely.

Industry Code: A descriptive code assigned to any company in order to group it with firms that operate in similar businesses. Common industry codes include the NAICS (North American Industrial Classification System) and the SIC (Standard Industrial Classification), both of which are standards widely used in America, as well as the International Standard Industrial Classification of all Economic Activities (ISIC), the Standard International Trade Classification established by the United Nations (SITC) and the General Industrial Classification of Economic Activities within the European Communities (NACE).

Information Technology (IT): The systems, including hardware and software, that move and store voice, video and data via computers and telecommunications.

Informed Consent: Must be obtained in writing from people who agree to be clinical trial subjects prior to their enrollment in the study. The document must explain the risks associated with the study and treatment and describe alternative therapy available to the patient. A copy of the document must also be provided to the patient.

Infusion Therapy: The introduction of fluid other than blood into a vein. See "Intravenous Therapy."

Initial Public Offering (IPO): A company's first effort to sell its stock to investors (the public). Investors in an up-trending market eagerly seek stocks offered in many IPOs because the stocks of newly public companies that seem to have great promise may appreciate very rapidly in price, reaping great profits for those who were able to get the stock at the first offering. In the United States, IPOs are regulated by the SEC (U.S. Securities Exchange Commission) and by the state-level regulatory agencies of the states in which the IPO shares are offered.

Institutional Review Board (IRB): A group of individuals usually found in medical institutions that is responsible for reviewing protocols for ethical consideration (to ensure the rights of the patients). An IRB also evaluates the benefit-to-risk ratio of a new drug to see that the risk is acceptable for patient exposure. Responsibilities of an IRB are defined in FDA regulations.

Intellectual Property (IP): The exclusive ownership of original concepts, ideas, designs, engineering plans or other assets that are protected by law. Examples include items covered by trademarks, copyrights and patents. Items such as software, engineering plans, fashion designs and architectural designs, as well as games, books, songs and other entertainment items are among the many things that may be considered to be intellectual property. (Also, see "Patent.")

Intensity Modulated Radiation Therapy (IMRT): A radiation technology that enables the technician to apply narrowly focused radiation directly toward cancerous tumors. IMRT helps to limit the amount of damage to surrounding tissues. The process includes using multiple beams (typically from seven to 12) aimed at the tumor from various directions. The beams meet at the tumor to administer the desired dosage. Breaking the dose down into multiple beams lessens the level of radiation that healthy tissues are exposed to. The point at which the beams join can be shaped to conform to the exact size, shape and location of the tumor, thus further sparing healthy tissue. Advanced imaging, such as CT, is used to provide precise guidance to the tumor's location. Also see "Image Guided Radiation Therapy (IMRT)."

International Financials Reporting Standards (IFRS): A set of accounting standards established by the International Accounting Standards Board (IASB) for the preparation of public financial statements. IFRS has been adopted by much of the world, including the European Union, Russia and Singapore.

Intravenous Therapy: The introduction of fluid other than blood into a vein. See "Infusion Therapy."

Investigational New Device Exemption (IDE): A document that must be filed with the FDA prior to initiating clinical trials of medical devices considered to pose a significant risk to human subjects.

Investigational New Drug Application (IND): A document that must be filed with the FDA prior to initiating clinical trials of drugs or biologics.

Investigator: In clinical trials, a clinician who agrees to supervise the use of an investigational drug, device or biologic in humans. Responsibilities of the investigator, as defined in FDA regulations, include administering the drug, observing and testing the patient, collecting data and monitoring the care and welfare of the patient.

Iontophoresis: The transfer of ions of medicine through the skin using a local electric current.

IP: See "Intellectual Property (IP)."

IPO: In health care, see "Independent Practice Organization (IPO)."

IRB: See "Institutional Review Board (IRB)."

IRE: Irreversible Electroporation. See "Electroporation."

ISO 9000, 9001, 9002, 9003: Standards set by the International Organization for Standardization. ISO 9000, 9001, 9002 and 9003 are the highest quality certifications awarded to organizations that meet exacting standards in their operating practices and procedures.

IT: See "Information Technology (IT)."

IT-Enabled Services (ITES): The portion of the Information Technology industry focused on providing business services, such as call centers, insurance claims processing and medical records transcription, by utilizing the power of IT, especially the Internet. Most ITES functions are considered to be back-office procedures. Also, see "Business Process Outsourcing (BPO)."

ITES: See "IT-Enabled Services (ITES)."

Just-in-Time (JIT) Delivery: Refers to a supply chain practice whereby manufacturers receive components on or just before the time that they are needed on the assembly line, rather than bearing the cost of maintaining several days' or weeks' supply in a warehouse. This adds greatly to the cost-effectiveness of a manufacturing plant and puts the burden of warehousing and timely delivery on the supplier of the components.

Knowledge Process Outsourcing (KPO): The use of outsourced and/or offshore workers to perform business tasks that require judgment and analysis. Examples include such professional tasks as patent research, legal research, architecture, design, engineering, market research, scientific research, accounting and tax return preparation. Also, see "Business Process Outsourcing (BPO)."

LAC: An acronym for Latin America and the Caribbean.

Laparoscope: See "Endoscope."

Laparoscopic Surgery: See "Endoscope."

LDCs: See "Least Developed Countries (LDCs)."

Least Developed Countries (LDCs): Nations determined by the U.N. Economic and Social Council to be the poorest and weakest members of the international community. There are currently 50 LDCs, of which 34 are in Africa, 15 are in Asia Pacific and the remaining one (Haiti) is in Latin America. The top 10 on the LDC list, in descending order from top to 10th, are Afghanistan, Angola, Bangladesh, Benin, Bhutan, Burkina Faso, Burundi, Cambodia, Cape Verde and the Central African Republic. Sixteen of the LDCs are also Landlocked Least Developed Countries (LLDCs) which present them with additional difficulties often due to the high cost of transporting trade goods. Eleven of the LDCs are Small Island Developing States (SIDS), which are often at risk of extreme weather phenomenon (hurricanes, typhoons, Tsunami): have fragile ecosystems: are often dependent on foreign energy sources: can have high disease rates for HIV/AIDS and malaria: and can have poor market access and trade terms.

Licensed Practical Nurse (LPN): A nurse who has completed a practical nursing program and is licensed to provide basic patient care under the supervision of a registered nurse or physician. Also known as a Licensed Vocational Nurse (LVN).

Ligand: Any atom or molecule attached to a central atom in a complex compound.

Lithotripsy: See "Extracorporeal Shock Wave Lithotripter (ESWL)."

LOHAS: Lifestyles of Health and Sustainability. A marketing term that refers to consumers who choose to purchase and/or live with items that are natural, organic, less polluting, etc. Such consumers may also prefer products powered by alternative energy, such as hybrid cars.

Low-Calorie: Refers to foods with 40 or fewer calories per serving.

Low-Cholesterol: Refers to foods with 20 or fewer milligrams of cholesterol and two or fewer grams of saturated fat per serving.

Low-Fat: Refers to foods with three or fewer grams of fat per serving.

Low-Sodium: Refers to foods with 140 or fewer milligrams of sodium per serving.

Magnetic Resonance Imaging (MRI): The use of a uniform magnetic field and radio frequencies to study tissues and structures of the body. This procedure enables the visualization of biochemical activity of the cell in vivo without the use of ionizing radiation, radioisotopic substances or high-frequency sound.

Magnetoencephalography (MEG): A newer technology derived from both MRI and electroencephalography (EEG). Like EEG, MEG registers brain patterns, but whereas EEG measures electrical activity in the brain, MEG measures magnetic waves, primarily in the cerebral cortex of the brain.

Managed Care: A system of prepaid medical plans providing comprehensive coverage to voluntarily enrolled members. Managed health care typically covers professional fees, hospital services, diagnostic services, emergency services, limited mental services, medical treatment for drug or alcohol abuse, home health services and preventive health care. The most common systems in managed care are HMOs (Health Maintenance Organizations) and PPOs (Preferred Provider Organizations), but there are other variations on these models. The word "managed" is used to describe this type of coverage because the total cost and extent of a patient's care is carefully managed and controlled by the group's administrators. Part of this management includes limiting the patient's choice to physicians, hospitals and labs that have agreed to provide reduced fees in exchange for high volume. Patients who receive care outside of this network will receive lesser reimbursement from the managed care provider. Also see "Health Maintenance Organization (HMO)," "Preferred Provider Organization (PPO)" and "Utilization Management."

Management Services Organization (MSO): A corporation, owned by a hospital or a physician/hospital joint venture, that provides management services to one or more medical group practices. The MSO purchases the tangible assets of the practices and leases them back as part of a full-service management agreement, under which the MSO employs all non-physician staff and provides all supplies and administrative systems for a fee.

Manufacturing Resource Planning (MRP II): A methodology that supports effective planning with regard to all resources of a manufacturing company, linking MRP with sales and operations planning, production planning and master production scheduling.

Market Segmentation: The division of a consumer market into specific groups of buyers based on demographic factors.

Medicaid: A federally supported and state-administered assistance program providing medical care for certain low-income individuals and other citizens. Medicaid was initially envisioned as a safety net for the poor. Today, in addition to meeting many of the health needs of low income households, the majority of Medicaid funds go to seniors and the seriously disabled to pay for nursing home care.

Medical Device: See "Device."

Medical Home: A physician practice model that is designed to be something of a collaborative partnership between patient, family and primary care physician. The medical home calls on outside specialists when they are needed as part of this team. The medical home is intended to foster communication and understanding, while maintaining a continuous record of all of a patient's medical history.

Medical Savings Account (MSA): See "Health Savings Account (HSA)."

Medical Tourism: The practice of patients in countries such as the U.S., Canada and the U.K. seeking inexpensive medical care in foreign countries.

Medicare: A U.S. government program that pays hospitals, physicians and other medical providers for serving patients aged 65 years and older, certain disabled people and most people with end-stage renal disease (ESRD). Medicare consists of two basic programs: Part A covers hospice care, home health care, skilled nursing care and inpatient hospital stays. Part B covers doctors' fees, outpatient care, X-rays, medical equipment and other fees not covered by Part A. Medicare Part C is designed to expand the types of private plans that beneficiaries may choose from, such as PPOs, and allows for the use of medical savings accounts. Prescription coverage was recently added as Medicare Part D.

MEG: See "Magnetoencephalography (MEG)."

Millenials: See "Generation Y."

Minimally Invasive Surgery: The use of very small incisions and advanced instruments that may be viewed through microscopes or video. Includes laparoscopy, endoscopy, electrosurgery and cryosurgery. This practice promotes rapid healing.

Minimally-Invasive Surgery: See "Endoscope."

Molecular Imaging: An emerging field in which advanced biology on the molecular level is combined with noninvasive imaging to determine the presence of certain proteins and other important genetic material.

Monoclonal Antibodies (mAb, Human Monoclonal Antibody): Antibodies that have been cloned from a single antibody and massed produced as a therapy or diagnostic test. An example is an antibody specific to a certain protein found in cancer cells.

NAICS: North American Industrial Classification System. See "Industry Code."

Nanotechnology: The science of designing, building or utilizing unique structures that are smaller than 100 nanometers (a nanometer is one billionth of a meter). This involves microscopic structures that are no larger than the width of some cell membranes.

National Drug Code (NDC): An identifying drug number maintained by the FDA.

National Institutes of Health (NIH): A branch of the U.S. Public Health Service that conducts biomedical research. www.nih.gov

NCE: See "New Chemical Entity (NCE)."

NDA: See "New Drug Application (NDA)."

Neonatal Intensive Care Services (NICU): A unit that must be separate from the newborn nursery. It provides intensive care to all sick infants, including those with very low birth weights (less than 1500 grams). The NICU can provide mechanical ventilation, neonatal surgery and special care for the sickest infants.

New Chemical Entity (NCE): See "New Molecular Entity (NME)."

New Drug Application (NDA): An application requesting FDA approval, after completion of the all-important Phase III Clinical Trials, to market a new drug for human use in the U.S. The drug may contain chemical compounds that were previously approved by the FDA as distinct molecular entities suitable for use in drug trials (NMEs). See "New Molecular Entity (NME)."

New Molecular Entity (NME): Defined by the FDA as a medication containing chemical compound that has never before been approved for marketing in any form in the U.S. An NME is sometimes referred to as a New Chemical Entity (NCE). Also, see "New Drug Application (NDA)."

NIH: See "National Institutes of Health (NIH)."

Nonclinical Studies: In vitro (laboratory) or in vivo (animal) pharmacology, toxicology and pharmacokinetic studies that support the testing of a product in humans. Usually at least two species are evaluated prior to Phase I clinical trials. Nonclinical studies continue throughout all phases of research to evaluate long-term safety issues.

Nurse Practitioner: A registered nurse (RN) who has completed advanced training and licensing. Nurse practitioners may work independent of a physician, or sometimes with a physician's light supervision. They provide direct examination, diagnosis and treatment of patients, and in many states they may write prescriptions and operate clinics. Also, see "Doctor of Nursing Practice (DNP)."

ODM: See "Original Design Manufacturer (ODM)."

OECD: See "Organisation for Economic Co-operation and Development (OECD)."

OEM: See "Original Equipment Manufacturer (OEM)."

Offshoring: The rapidly growing tendency among U.S., Japanese and Western European firms to send knowledge-based and manufacturing work overseas. The intent is to take advantage of lower wages and operating costs in such nations as China, India, Hungary and Russia. The choice of a nation for offshore work may be influenced by such factors as language and education of the local workforce, transportation systems or natural resources. For example, China and India are graduating high numbers of skilled engineers and scientists from their universities. Also, some nations are noted for large numbers of workers skilled in the

English language, such as the Philippines and India. Also see "Captive Offshoring" and "Outsourcing."

Oncology: The diagnosis, study and treatment of cancer.

Onshoring: The opposite of "offshoring." Providing or maintaining manufacturing or services within or nearby a company's domestic location. Sometimes referred to as reshoring.

Open Access: Typically found in an IPA HMO, this arrangement allows members to consult specialists without obtaining a referral from another doctor.

Organisation for Economic Co-operation and Development (OECD): A group of more than 30 nations that are strongly committed to the market economy and democracy. Some of the OECD members include Japan, the U.S., Spain, Germany, Australia, Korea, the U.K., Canada and Mexico. Although not members, Estonia, Israel and Russia are invited to member talks: and Brazil, China, India, Indonesia and South Africa have enhanced engagement policies with the OECD. The Organisation provides statistics, as well as social and economic data: and researches social changes, including patterns in evolving fiscal policy, agriculture, technology, trade, the environment and other areas. It publishes over 250 titles annually: publishes a corporate magazine, the OECD Observer: has radio and TV studios: and has centers in Tokyo, Washington, D.C., Berlin and Mexico City that distributed the Organisation's work and organizes events.

Original Design Manufacturer (ODM): A contract manufacturer that offers complete, end-to-end design, engineering and manufacturing services. ODMs design and build products, such as consumer electronics, that client companies can then brand and sell as their own. For example, a large percentage of laptop computers, cell phones and PDAs are made by ODMs. Also see "Original Equipment Manufacturer (OEM)" and "Contract Manufacturing."

Original Equipment Manufacturer (OEM): 1) A company that manufactures a component (or a completed product) for sale to a customer that will integrate the component into a final product. The OEM's customer will put its own brand name on the end product and distribute or resell it to end users. 2) A firm that buys a component and then incorporates it into a final product,

or buys a completed product and then resells it under the firm's own brand name. This usage is most often found in the computer industry, where OEM is sometimes used as a verb. Also see "Original Design Manufacturer (ODM)" and "Contract Manufacturing."

Orphan Drug: A drug or biologic designated by the FDA as providing therapeutic benefit for a rare disease affecting less than 200,000 people in the U.S. Companies that market orphan drugs are granted a period of market exclusivity in return for the limited commercial potential of the drug.

Orthodontics: A specialized branch of dentistry that restores the teeth to proper alignment and function. There are several different types of appliances used in orthodontics, braces being one of the most common.

OTC: See "Over-the-Counter Drugs (OTC)."

Outsourcing: The hiring of an outside company to perform a task otherwise performed internally by the company, generally with the goal of lowering costs and/or streamlining work flow. Outsourcing contracts are generally several years in length. Companies that hire outsourced services providers often prefer to focus on their core strengths while sending more routine tasks outside for others to perform. Typical outsourced services include the running of human resources departments, telephone call centers and computer departments. When outsourcing is performed overseas, it may be referred to as offshoring. Also see "Offshoring."

Over-the-Counter Drugs (OTC): FDA-regulated products that do not require a physician's prescription. Some examples are aspirin, sunscreen, nasal spray and sunglasses.

Panomics: The individual combination of factors including genes, proteins and molecular pathways, that fuel the growth of malignant cells.

Paramedical: A person trained to assist medical professionals and supplement physicians and nurses in their activities in order to give emergency medical treatment.

Patent: An intellectual property right granted by a national government to an inventor to exclude others from making, using, offering for sale, or selling the

invention throughout that nation or importing the invention into the nation for a limited time in exchange for public disclosure of the invention when the patent is granted. In addition to national patenting agencies, such as the United States Patent and Trademark Office, and regional organizations such as the European Patent Office, there is a cooperative international patent organization, the World Intellectual Property Organization, or WIPO, established by the United Nations.

Pathogen: Any microorganism (e.g., fungus, virus, bacteria or parasite) that causes a disease.

Patient Protection and Affordable Care Act (PPACA): See "Affordable Care Act."

PCMH: Patient Centered Medical Home. See "Medical Home."

PCR: See "Polymerase Chain Reaction (PCR)."

Peer Review: The process used by the scientific community, whereby review of a paper, project or report is obtained through comments of independent colleagues in the same field.

PET (Imaging): See "Positron Emission Tomography (PET)."

Pharmacodynamics (PD): The study of reactions between drugs and living systems. It can be thought of as the study of what a drug does to the body.

Pharmacoeconomics: The study of the costs and benefits associated with various drug treatments.

Pharmacogenetics: The investigation of the different reactions of human beings to drugs and the underlying genetic predispositions. The differences in reaction are mainly caused by mutations in certain enzymes responsible for drug metabolization. As a result, the degradation of the active substance can lead to harmful by-products, or the drug might have no effect at all.

Pharmacokinetics (PK): The study of the processes of bodily absorption, distribution, metabolism and excretion of compounds and medicines. It can be thought of as the study of what the body does to a drug. See "Absorption, Distribution, Metabolism and Excretion (ADME)."

Pharmacology: The science of drugs, their characteristics and their interactions with living organisms.

Pharmacy Benefit Manager (PBM): An organization that provides administrative services in processing and analyzing prescription claims for pharmacy benefit and coverage programs. Many PBMs also operate mail order pharmacies or have arrangements to include prescription availability through mail order pharmacies.

Phase I Clinical Trials: Studies in this phase include initial introduction of an investigational drug into humans. These studies are closely monitored and are usually conducted in healthy volunteers. Phase I trials are conducted after the completion of extensive nonclinical or pre-clinical trials not involving humans. Phase I studies include the determination of clinical pharmacology, bioavailability, drug interactions and side effects associated with increasing doses of the drug.

Phase II Clinical Trials: Include randomized, masked, controlled clinical studies conducted to evaluate the effectiveness of a drug for a particular indication(s). During Phase II trials, the minimum effective dose and dosing intervals should be determined.

Phase III Clinical Trials: Consist of controlled and uncontrolled trials that are performed after preliminary evidence of effectiveness of a drug has been established. They are conducted to document the safety and efficacy of the drug, as well as to determine adequate directions (labeling) for use by the physician. A specific patient population needs to be clearly identified from the results of these studies. Trials during Phase III are conducted using a large number of patients to determine the frequency of adverse events and to obtain data regarding intolerance.

Phase IV Clinical Trials: Conducted after approval of a drug has been obtained to gather data supporting new or revised labeling, marketing or advertising claims.

Physician-Hospital Organization (PHO), Closed: A PHO that restricts physician membership to those practitioners who meet criteria for cost effectiveness and/or high quality.

Physician-Hospital Organization (PHO), Open: A joint venture between the hospital and all members of the medical staff who wish to participate. The PHO can act as a unified agent in managed care contracting, own a managed care plan, own and operate ambulatory care centers or ancillary services projects, or provide administrative services to physician members.

Pivotal Studies: In clinical trials, a Phase III trial that is designed specifically to support approval of a product. These studies are well-controlled (usually by placebo) and are generally designed with input from the FDA so that they will provide data that is adequate to support approval of the product. Two pivotal studies are required for drug product approval, but usually only one study is required for biologics.

PMA: See "Pre-Market Approval (PMA)."

Point-of-Service Plan (POS): A managed care plan in which member patients may go outside of the network to be attended by their preferred physicians, but pay a higher deductible if they so choose. Routine care is provided by a primary care physician who also provides referrals to in-network specialists.

Polymerase Chain Reaction (PCR): In molecular biology, PCR is a technique used to reproduce or amplify small, selected sections of DNA or RNA for analysis. It enables researchers to create multiple copies of a given sequence.

Positron Emission Tomography (PET): Positron Emission Tomography (often referred to as a PET scan) is a nuclear medicine imaging technology that uses computers and radioactive (positron emitting) isotopes, which are created in a cyclotron or generator, to produce composite pictures of the brain and heart at work. PET scanning produces sectional images depicting metabolic activity or blood flow rather than anatomy.

Post-Marketing Surveillance: The FDA's ongoing safety monitoring of marketed drugs.

PPACA: Patient Protection and Affordable Care Act. See: "Affordable Care Act."

Pre-Boomer: A term occasionally used to describe people who were born between 1935 and 1945. They are somewhat older than Baby Boomers (born between 1946 and 1962). Also see "Baby Boomer."

Precision Medicine: The use of genomic, epigenomic, and other data to define individual patterns of disease within a patient, potentially leading to better individual treatment, particularly through drugs targeted at specific gene mutations.

Preclinical Studies: See "Nonclinical Studies."

Predictive Analytics: See "Analytics."

Preferred Provider Organization (PPO): Insurance entities that provide "managed health care" services. A PPO is a modified version of the HMO model. Generally, patients who are members of PPOs have more flexibility in the personal choice of physicians than do members of HMOs. Patients pay higher premiums than HMOs because of this flexibility. Patients are encouraged to visit physicians who are part of the PPO's system, but may also receive very good reimbursement for visiting physicians who are "out-of-network." Also see "Health Maintenance Organization (HMO)" and "Managed Care."

Pre-Market Approval (PMA): Required for the approval of a new medical device or a device that is to be used for life-sustaining or life-supporting purposes, is implanted in the human body or presents potential risk of illness or injury.

Premium (Insurance Premium): An insurance premium is the monthly or yearly fee charged for coverage by the insurance underwriter.

Primary Care Network: A group of primary care physicians who pool their resources to share the financial risk of providing care to their patients who are covered by a particular health plan.

Private Fee For Service (PFFS): Insurance provided under Medicare, in which private companies offer Centers for Medicare and Medicaid Services approved plans that allow patients to choose their own doctors and hospitals. PFFS plans provide beneficiaries with all of their Medicare benefits plus any additional benefits the company chooses to provide. Services generally require a co-payment plus, in certain cases, up to 35% of a Medicare-approved amount.

Product License Agreement (PLA): See "Biologics License Application (BLA)."

Proton Beam Radiation Therapy (PBRT): The use of a highly advanced technology to deliver external beam radiation therapy (EBRT) to a patient in order to kill cancerous cells and shrink tumors. While traditional radiation therapies rely on photons delivered by X-rays or gamma rays, Proton Beam Radiation Therapy relies on a particle accelerator to create and deliver protons. Protons are high-energy particles that carry a charge. By varying the velocity of the particles at the time that they enter the body, physicists are able to control the exact spot within the body where the radiation is released. The higher the velocity, the deeper within the body the radiation begins to take effect. With traditional radiation (based on photons rather than protons), there is a significant entry dose of radiation that can be harmful to healthy tissues. Proton beam therapy has the ability to better focus the radiation on the exact place of the tumor, significantly cutting down on side effects and damage to surrounding tissues. There are only a handful of proton beam centers in the world.

Provider Service Network (PSN): An insurance entity, owned by hospitals and physicians, that provides managed health care services.

PSN: See "Provider Service Network (PSN)."

Psychiatry: A branch of medicine concerned with the study, treatment and prevention of mental, emotional and behavioral disorders. Psychiatrists are doctors and can treat patients using drugs and other physical methods.

Psychology: The scientific study of human behavior and mental processes. Psychologists treat patients using therapeutic methods, including counseling or group work.

Public Health Service (PHS): May stand for the Public Health Service Act, a law passed by the U.S. Congress in 1944. PHS also may stand for the Public Health Service itself, a U.S. government agency established by an act of Congress in July 1798, originally authorizing hospitals for the care of American merchant seamen. Today, the Public Health Service sets national health policy: conducts medical and biomedical research: sponsors programs for disease control and mental health: and enforces laws to assure the safety and efficacy of drugs, foods, cosmetics and medical devices. The FDA (Food and Drug Administration) is part of the Public Health Service, as are the Centers for Disease Control and Prevention (CDC).

Public-Private Partnership (PPP, or P3): Partnerships that involve government agencies with private companies in the construction, operation and/or funding of publicly-needed buildings and infrastructure, such as toll roads, airports, waterworks, sewage plants or power plants.

QOL: See "Quality of Life (QOL)."

Quality of Life (QOL): In medicine, an endpoint of therapeutic assessment used to adjust measures of effectiveness for clinical decision-making. Typically, QOL endpoints measure the improvement of a patient's day-to-day living as a result of specific therapy.

Quantified Self: An evolving concept that refers to the use of electronic devices and electronic communications to gather, record and transmit personal information. An extreme practice of quantified self would be a person who uses a wearable, digital camera to record his surroundings 24/7, and who blogs, tweets or posts to social media his daily activities on a continuous basis. The most practical application of quantified self will most likely be in mobile health, (the personal health Internet). Examples include the wearing of wireless heart monitors, sleep monitors or pedometers that record daily health and exercise data in order to manage health problems or improve fitness.

R&D: Research and development. Also see "Applied Research" and "Basic Research."

Radiation Therapy: Radiation therapy is frequently used to destroy cancerous cells. This branch of medicine is concerned with radioactive substances and the usage of various techniques of imaging, for the diagnosis and treatment of disease. Services can include megavoltage radiation therapy, radioactive implants, stereotactic radiosurgery, therapeutic radioisotope services, or the use of x-rays, gamma rays and other radiation sources.

Radio Frequency Ablation (RFA): The use of focused radiowaves to produce high levels of heat within tumors in order to kill cancer. It is typically applied via needles that have been placed in the tumor, using ultrasound or other imaging techniques to insure correct placement. It is often used in the treatment of cancer of the kidney.

Radio Frequency Identification (RFID): A technology that applies a special microchip-enabled tag to an individual item or piece of merchandise or inventory. RFID technology enables wireless, computerized tracking of that inventory item as it moves through the supply chain from factory to transport to warehouse to retail store or end user. Also known as radio tags.

Radioisotope: An object that has varying properties that allows it to penetrate other objects at different rates. For example, a sheet of paper can stop an alpha particle, a beta particle can penetrate tissues in the body and a gamma ray can penetrate concrete. The varying penetration capabilities allow radioisotopes to be used in different ways. (Also called radioactive isotope or radionuclide.)

Radiotherapy: The use of doses of high-energy radiation to kill cancer cells and shrink tumors. Radiation may be applied externally, through external beam radiation therapy, or internally through small radioactive implants. Sources of radiation may include X-ray, gamma ray or proton beams.

Radiowave Therapy: See "Radio Frequency Ablation (RFA)."

Registered Nurse (RN): A graduate of an accredited school of nursing who has been registered and licensed to practice by a state authority. A registered nurse (RN) typically has received more formal education than an LPN (licensed practical nurse) or LVN (licensed vocational nurse). An RN often has received a 4-year college degree leading to the bachelors in science-nursing (BSN).

RFID: See "Radio Frequency Identification (RFID)."

Ribonucleic Acid (RNA): A macromolecule found in the nucleus and cytoplasm of cells: vital in protein synthesis.

RNA: See "Ribonucleic Acid (RNA)."

Safe Medical Devices Act (SMDA): An act that amends the Food, Drug and Cosmetic Act to impose additional regulations on medical devices. The act became law in 1990.

SIC: Standard Industrial Classification. See "Industry Code."

Silent Generation: Generally considered to be people born between 1925 and 1945, although the dates vary. Most of the Silent Generation were born during the Great Depression, through the end of World War II.

Single Nucleotide Polymorphisms (SNPs): Stable mutations consisting of a change at a single base in a DNA molecule. SNPs can be detected by HTP analyses, such as gene chips, and they are then mapped by DNA sequencing. They are the most common type of genetic variation.

SMDA: See "Safe Medical Devices Act (SMDA)."

SNP: See "Single-Nucleotide Polymorphisms (SNPs)."

SPECT: Single Photon Emission Computerized Tomography. A nuclear medicine imaging technology that combines existing technology of gamma camera imaging with computed tomographic (CT) imaging technology to provide a more precise and clear image.

Sponsor: The individual or company that assumes responsibility for the investigation of a new drug, including compliance with the FD&C Act and regulations. The sponsor may be an individual, partnership, corporation or governmental agency and may be a manufacturer, scientific institution or investigator regularly and lawfully engaged in the investigation of new drugs. The sponsor assumes most of the legal and financial responsibility of the clinical trial.

Stem Cells: Cells found in human bone marrow, the blood stream and the umbilical cord that can be replicated indefinitely and can turn into any type of mature blood cell, including platelets, white blood cells or red blood cells. Also referred to as pluripotent cells.

Stereotactic Body Radiation Therapy (SBRT): See "Stereotactic Radiotherapy."

Stereotactic Radiotherapy: The use of precise three dimensional positioning while delivering a high dose of radiation to a tumor. It is often used to treat brain tumors. The procedure involves the bolting of a metallic frame, like a halo, to the patient's head to prevent any movement and to enhance delivery of radiation.

Study Coordinator: See "Coordinator."

Subsidiary, Wholly-Owned: A company that is wholly controlled by another company through stock ownership.

Summary Plan Description: A description of an employee's entire benefit package as required by self-funded plans.

Supply Chain: The complete set of suppliers of goods and services required for a company to operate its business. For example, a manufacturer's supply chain may include providers of raw materials, components, custom-made parts and packaging materials.

Taste Masking: The creation of a barrier between a drug molecule and taste receptors so the drug is easier to take. It masks bitter or unpleasant tastes.

TESS: See "Adverse Event (AE)."

Third-Party Administrator: An independent person or organization that administers the group plan's benefits and claims and administration for self-insured companies.

Tomotherapy: A relatively new method of radiation treatment that combines the use of very sophisticated computer-controlled radiation beam collimation with an on-board computed tomography (CT) scanner to image the treatment site. The intent is to create an enhanced level of accuracy in beam delivery.

Trial Coordinator: See "Coordinator."

U.S. Department of Health and Human Services (HHS): This agency has more than 300 major programs related to human health and welfare, the largest of which is Medicare. See www.hhs.gov

Ultrashort Pulse Laser (USP): A technology that utilizes ultrafast lasers that pulse on and off at almost immeasurable speed. Scientists estimate that USP flashes once every femtosecond, which is a billionth of a millionth of a second. USP destroys atoms by knocking out electrons, which causes no rise in temperature in surrounding atoms as is associated with traditional lasers. Potential applications include vastly improved laser surgery, scanning for explosives, gemstone verification and processing donated human tissue for transplantation.

Ultrasound: The use of acoustic waves above the range of 20,000 cycles per second to visualize internal body structures. Frequently used to observe a fetus.

Unitized Pricing: Pricing for insurance coverage in which employees pay per person as opposed to choosing between individual and family coverage.

Utility Patent: A utility patent may be granted by the U.S. Patent and Trademark Office to anyone who invents or discovers any new, useful, and non-obvious process, machine, article of manufacture, or composition of matter, or any new and useful improvement thereof.

Utilization Management: A system in which utilization case managers (frequently registered nurses with several years of hospital experience) are assigned to each patient who receives hospitalization or extended treatment. These case managers constantly review the amount of care being provided to the patient in question, frequently resulting in significant cost savings. Also see "Managed Care."

Validation of Data: The procedure carried out to ensure that the data contained in a final clinical trial report match the original observations.

Value Added Tax (VAT): A tax that imposes a levy on businesses at every stage of manufacturing based on the value it adds to a product. Each business in the supply chain pays its own VAT and is subsequently repaid by the next link down the chain: hence, a VAT is ultimately paid by the consumer, being the last link in the supply chain, making it comparable to a sales tax. Generally, VAT only applies to goods bought for consumption within a given country: export goods are exempt from VAT, and purchasers from other countries taking goods back home may apply for a VAT refund.

Value-Based Reimbursement: A method of payment from health care insurers to care providers. In value-based reimbursement, as opposed to fee-for-service, physicians and hospitals may be paid recurring fees for improving patients' health, reducing trips to the emergency room and other wellness-enhancing measures, with the goal of reducing the overall cost of care. Also see "Fee-For-Service."

Vegan: A person whose diet includes only plant products and excludes all forms of animal products, including meat, fish, poultry, eggs, dairy, gelatin and honey.

Vegetarian: A person whose diet includes only plant products, but may also eat dairy products, eggs and/or honey.

Vendor: Any firm, such as a manufacturer or distributor, from which a retailer obtains merchandise.

Videolaseroscopy: A procedure using an endoscope equipped with a laser that is being used in minimally-invasive surgery to excise and or cauterize damaged tissue in the abdomen and lungs.

World Health Organization (WHO): A United Nations agency that assists governments in strengthening health services, furnishing technical assistance and aid in emergencies, working on the prevention and control of epidemics and promoting cooperation among different countries to improve nutrition, housing, sanitation, recreation and other aspects of environmental hygiene. Any country that is a member of the United Nations may become a member of the WHO by accepting its constitution. The WHO currently has 191 member states.

World Trade Organization (WTO): One of the only globally active international organizations dealing with the trade rules between nations. Its goal is to assist the free flow of trade goods, ensuring a smooth, predictable supply of goods to help raise the quality of life of member citizens. Members form consensus decisions that are then ratified by their respective parliaments. The WTO's conflict resolution process generally emphasizes interpreting existing commitments and agreements, and discovers how to ensure trade policies to conform to those agreements, with the ultimate aim of avoiding military or political conflict.

WTO: See "World Trade Organization (WTO)."

Xenotransplantation: The science of transplanting organs such as kidneys, hearts or livers into humans from other mammals, such as pigs or other agricultural animals grown with specific traits for this purpose.

Zoonosis: An animal disease that can be transferred to man.

Zootechnical Feed Additives: Medicines, such as growth promoters and antibiotics, which are incorporated as additives into feed.